T0397460

THE GLOBAL COMMUNITY

Yearbook of International Law and Jurisprudence

2022

Edited by

Giuliana Ziccardi Capaldo

OXFORD
UNIVERSITY PRESS

Oxford University Press is a department of the University of Oxford. It furthers the University's objective of excellence in research, scholarship, and education by publishing worldwide. Oxford is a registered trade mark of Oxford University Press in the UK and certain other countries.

Published in the United States of America by Oxford University Press
198 Madison Avenue, New York, NY 10016, United States of America.

© Oxford University Press 2023

CIP data is on file at the Library of Congress
ISBN 978–0–19–775226–5

DOI: 10.1093/oso/9780197752265.001.0001

Printed by Integrated Books International, United States of America

Note to Readers
This publication is designed to provide accurate and authoritative information in regard to the subject matter covered. It is based upon sources believed to be accurate and reliable and is intended to be current as of the time it was written. It is sold with the understanding that the publisher is not engaged in rendering legal, accounting, or other professional services. If legal advice or other expert assistance is required, the services of a competent professional person should be sought. Also, to confirm that the information has not been affected or changed by recent developments, traditional legal research techniques should be used, including checking primary sources where appropriate.

(Based on the Declaration of Principles jointly adopted by a Committee of the American Bar Association and a Committee of Publishers and Associations.)

You may order this or any other Oxford University Press publication
by visiting the Oxford University Press website at www.oup.com.

Contents

PART 6: RECENT LINES OF INTERNATIONALIST THOUGHT

PART II: RECENT LINES OF INTERNATIONALIST THOUGHT

The Temping Ethical Evolution: The Evolute of Connection Between
the Environmental Crisis, Philosophical Considerations of Public International
Law, and the International Criminal Court's Twentieth Anniversary..... 720
Anjaskamalma d Benuda Jangohur

AIMS & SCOPE

The *Global Community Yearbook of International Law and Jurisprudence* (*Yearbook*) is a peer-reviewed journal, covered in Scopus, and first published in 2001 (with twenty-two editions, that is, annual publications so far). Over the years it has become an authoritative reference on the most significant transformations in the world constitutive process. While providing researchers and practitioners with access to a uniquely rich resource for the study of international jurisprudence, the *Yearbook* promotes discussion on current issues that impact substantive and procedural aspects of global law. In this way, the *Yearbook* makes it possible to monitor—from year to year and from several perspectives—the development of the international order towards a legal system for a global community.

The *Yearbook* provides scientific and practice-oriented articles on recent developments in global law, as well as new insights on the contribution of judicial pronouncements to the constitutional global order.

The theoretical parts of the *Yearbook* (Articles, Notes and Comments, In Focus, Forum) contain analyses by leading scholars and judges from all over the world focusing on the global challenges for law, policy, and justice.

Furthermore, the *Yearbook* constitutes the only thorough annual survey of major developments in international jurisprudence. The decisions of international courts and tribunals are covered extensively, to reflect their recognized importance for the development of international/global law. A comprehensive survey by eminent international law scholars who explore, document, and evaluate this process provides an innovative approach to the interactions between courts with the objective of reducing conflicts and paving the path towards harmonization of legal principles governing the global community. The relevant part ("Global Justice—Decisions of International Courts and Tribunals"), which is divided into sections and which is primarily devoted to the highest judicial bodies, reports annually on significant international case law, as systematically ordered by legal maxims. International courts and tribunals covered include: International Court of Justice (ICJ), International Tribunal for the Law of the Sea (ITLOS), WTO Dispute Settlement System (WTO DSS), International Criminal Court (ICC), International Residual Mechanism for Criminal Tribunals (MICT), General Court and Court of Justice of the European Union (ECJ), European Court of Human Rights (ECtHR), Inter-American Court of Human Rights (IACtHR), African Court on Human and Peoples' Rights (ACtHPR), International

Centre for Settlement of Investment Disputes (ICSID), Permanent Court of Arbitration (PCA), and International Administrative Tribunals (IATs).

In this manner, the *Yearbook* fills in the gaps left by other journals that provide partial coverage of international judicial decisions; and international law scholars can rely on it to better understand the wealth of case law emanating from international jurisdictions. The originality and utility of this *Yearbook* lies precisely in its "intermediation" role between case law and international scholars, practitioners, and students.

Finally, an updated overview of the current international law literature in the part entitled "Recent Lines of Internationalist Thought" provides readers with an opportunity to study and interpret global legal issues from different perspectives, examine different methodologies, and explore ideas from different cultures. The 2017 edition introduced a change to this part. The novelty concerns the subject behind the original authorship— meaning that the Scholar/Judge who contributes thoughts and ideas is also talking about his own work.

The *Yearbook* is a one-stop resource for all researchers of international/global law, various related disciplines, and the jurisprudence of international courts and tribunals. It is aimed at academics, legal practitioners, and law students in the fields of international/ global law, national law, legal philosophy and ethics, political science, and economics.

Giuliana Ziccardi Capaldo

General Editor

OUTLINE OF THE PARTS

The *Yearbook* is structured into the following parts:

ARTICLES

This part is devoted to significant doctrinal contributions to international legal theory and gives priority to works dealing with changes in the rules and structure of the international community. The aim is to follow the development of the international legal order and the building of the global community heralded at the end of the second millennium. This part is at all times open to report on fresh developments and to debate new, and other contradictory, trends.

NOTES AND COMMENTS

This part contains short articles on current issues in international/global law. In line with the *Yearbook*'s orientation, comments addressing international case law are given precedence.

IN FOCUS

Beginning with the 2008 issue, the *Yearbook* includes a part entitled "In Focus—Global Policies and Law," exploring the globalization of politics, communication, economics, culture, and the environment, while identifying objectives, programmes, models, public policy choices, and emerging global policies, and considering some of the major issues and challenges facing the world as a whole, in an attempt to enhance the coordination and harmonization of norms and procedures and the implementation of global law.

FORUM—JURISPRUDENTIAL CROSS-FERTILIZATION: AN ANNUAL OVERVIEW

Beginning with the 2010 issue, the *Yearbook* includes a new part, aiming to compare and analyse the interconnections between the decisions of international courts and tribunals, as a way of exploring and examining judicial dialogue and the development of common legal principles and concepts in all branches of international law.

To this end we have chosen to focus on the areas of international law in which different international courts operate; therefore, this part consists of eight modules corresponding to the areas listed below (in addition, an introductory module has been added to illustrate key concepts):

Introductory Module—MISSION AND CONCEPTS
Module—CRIMINAL LAW—The Relationship Between International Criminal Tribunals and Their Relationship with the ICJ or Another International Court or Arbitral Tribunal
Module—EUROPEAN LAW—The Relationship Between the European Courts and Their Relationship with the ICJ or Another International Court or Arbitral Tribunal
Module—HUMAN RIGHTS LAW—The Relationship Between Courts of Human Rights and Their Relationship with the ICJ or Another International Court or Arbitral Tribunal
Module—ECONOMIC AND FINANCIAL LAW—The Relationship Between International Judicial Bodies in Economic Matters and Their Relationship with the ICJ or Another International Court or Arbitral Tribunal
Module—INVESTMENT LAW—The Relationship Between the ICSID Tribunals and the ICJ or Another International Court or Arbitral Tribunal
Module—ENVIRONMENTAL LAW, LAW OF THE SEA, GLOBAL COMMONS LAW—The Relationship Between the ITLOS and the ICJ or Another International Court or Arbitral Tribunal
Module—INTERNATIONAL AND DOMESTIC LAW—The Relationship Between International Courts and Domestic Courts

The aim is to identify the emergence of common rules (substantial and procedural) in the various contexts. In each area eminent international law scholars will carry out an analysis of the points of convergence and divergence not just between the decisions handed down by courts operating in the same area but also between the decisions of tribunals and international courts operating in other areas, dealing with different matters, examining the coherence (or lack thereof) of their jurisprudence when they apply the same international norms, also of a customary law nature. In comparing the decisions of the various tribunals, a constant element will be the reference to the International Court of Justice and the way the decisions of other international tribunals relate to its jurisdiction. However, not all the modules will be offered annually but only whenever there are developments in each of them that will be interesting to note.

The *Yearbook* is the first academic journal to present an annual overview of the process of cross-fertilization between courts, based on the drafting and systematic classification of legal maxims (i.e., points of law decided by various international courts) in the part entitled "Global Justice—Decisions of International Courts and Tribunals." A comprehensive and complete survey by eminent international law scholars exploring, evaluating, and documenting this process has the potential to enhance our contribution and thus further guide our understanding of how to reduce conflicts and create an effective exchange of legal reasoning between different courts. The aim is to promote a favourable environment for the courts to advance the process of judicial cooperation with a view to the possible harmonization of legal principles governing the global community.

GLOBAL JUSTICE—DECISIONS OF INTERNATIONAL COURTS AND TRIBUNALS

The decisions of international courts and tribunals receive ample coverage in the *Yearbook*, reflecting their recognized importance for the development of international law.

International courts and tribunals covered include: International Court of Justice (ICJ), International Tribunal for the Law of the Sea (ITLOS), WTO Dispute Settlement System (WTO DSS), International Criminal Court (ICC), International Residual Mechanism for Criminal Tribunals (MICT), General Court and Court of Justice of the European Union (ECJ), European Court of Human Rights (ECtHR), Inter-American Court of Human Rights (IACtHR), African Court on Human and Peoples' Rights (ACtHPR), International Centre for Settlement of Investment Disputes (ICSID), Permanent Court of Arbitration (PCA), and International Administrative Tribunals (IATs). Moreover, if there were no decisions issued by these tribunals for the year under consideration, we would omit the relating section.

Each major international court or tribunal has its own section, which includes an Introductory Note on the activity of that judicial body over the course of the year under consideration. The activities of the court and tribunals are presented in the form of "legal maxims," i.e., brief and easily understood extracts of statements on international law announced in a judicial decision, focusing on points of law decided by various international courts, systematically arranged.

Normally, the maxims consist of integral citations from the text of the judgment. However, divergences from the original text (i.e., omissions or additions) are marked by the use of square brackets (round brackets with dots are used to indicate that the quotation which follows is situated in the original text before the previous quotation). Maxims usually reproduce the text of several extracts drawn from different paragraphs of the decision to which reference is made. Further, to give the reader an immediate idea of the constituent parts of the maxim, the paragraph number corresponding to each extract is given below each legal maxim in the order in which they have been used.

The maxims are collected according to the "Systematic Classification Scheme," which can be found at the beginning of this part. This scheme has two parts, dealing respectively with substantive and procedural international law. Each of these parts is further divided into headings and sub-headings.

The maxims are systematically presented and also logically arranged in such a manner as to permit the reading of the overall context of each decision, serving as a forerunner to the full reading of the text of each judgment.

The chosen working-method has been adapted from the one successfully employed in the "Repertory of Decisions of the International Court of Justice/Répertoire de la Jurisprudence de la Cour Internationale de Justice" (1947–1992), by Giuliana Ziccardi Capaldo, 1995.

The following information is also given for each decision covered: (a) the full title of the case and the parties to it, where these exist; (b) the type of decision, the date, and the original language; and (c) reference to the collection of Reports in which the original text of the decision is to be found and/or specialized websites for internet access.

RECENT LINES OF INTERNATIONALIST THOUGHT

This part, included in the *Yearbook* since 2006, focuses on the thought of leading international law scholars "innovative" in their responses to challenges that have faced contemporary world society. The 2017 edition introduced a change to this part. The novelty concerns the subject behind the original authorship—meaning that the Scholar/Judge who contributes thoughts and ideas is also talking about his *own work*. The purpose is to give an overview of the current international law literature providing readers with an opportunity to view arguments from different perspectives, to examine different methodologies, and to explore ideas reflecting cultural diversity. This would certainly allow an understanding of the relevance of internationalist thought on the changes in international law and contemporary politics in the context of globalization.

GENERAL INFORMATION

This issue may be cited as 22 *Global Community YILJ* 2022, G. Ziccardi Capaldo General ed. (2023).

All views expressed in the articles, notes and comments, editorial comments, and other contributions to the *Yearbook* represent the opinions of the individual authors and should not be interpreted as an expression of the views of the Editors.

Submission of Manuscripts

Manuscripts should be submitted by email to globalcommunityyearbook@gmail.com preferably in English, although a small percentage of papers may be accepted in other languages (French, German, and Spanish) at the discretion of the General Editor. Abstracts should be submitted in English only.

The *Yearbook* is committed to ensuring ethics in publication and quality of articles. Manuscripts submitted for publication are blindly peer-reviewed. The *Yearbook* will not consider submissions whose content has been, or will be, published before it appears in this *Yearbook*. It is therefore important to agree upon ethical guidelines for *Yearbook* publication—see *Publication Ethics & Malpractice Statement* available on the journal's website at http://www.globalcommunityyearbook.org/forauthor-publication.php where you can find other useful information.

Manuscripts should meet the editorial standards specified in the *Yearbook's* stylesheet which may be obtained from the journal's website. The latter also provides other helpful information about the *Yearbook*, including the content of previous volumes.

Orders

The *Global Community Yearbook of International Law and Jurisprudence* is published annually (in two volumes from 2002 to 2014 edition; in one volume from 2015 edition on) in English. For more information and to order a volume, please see: https://global.oup.com/academic/content/series/g/global-community-yearbook-of-international-law-and-jurisprudence-glocom/?lang=en&cc=us

The *Yearbook* is also available in nonprint form on Oxford Scholarship Online (OSO), one of the leading academic research resources in the world accessed by students, academics, and researchers across the globe at https://www.universitypressscholarship.com/search?isQuickSearch=true&pageSize=10&q=global+community+yearbook+of+international+law+and+jurisprudence&sort=datedescending

It is also available as an ebook.

Indexing Services

The *Global Community Yearbook of International Law and Jurisprudence* is included in:

- Google Scholar
- IBR—International Bibliography of Book Reviews
- IBZ—Internationale Bibliographie der Zeitschriftenliteratur
- LexisNexis
- Library of Congress
- Max Planck Institute for Comparative Public Law and International Law–Library
- Peace Palace Library
- PhilPapers—Philosophical Research Online
- ProQuest
- Scopus
- SwetsWise Catalog
- The Dag Hammarskjöld Library–UN Libraries (New York, Geneva Bangkok)

EDITORIAL

Monitoring the Construction of the Global Community: Key Changes in Global Law and Governance

BY GIULIANA ZICCARDI CAPALDO*

Abstract

This Editorial contains the General Editor's own Note for the current edition of the *Global Community Yearbook of International Law and Jurisprudence* (*Global Community YILJ* or *Yearbook*). Apart from connecting an outline of the general contents with the *Global Community YILJ*'s aim and scope, Professor Emeritus Giuliana Ziccardi Capaldo provides a description and, in some cases, a succinct commentary for a particular section and/or contribution. The General Editor has allowed for an exception as regards the standard format— on account of the War in Ukraine. More precisely, a special "Overview" is accommodated. Furthermore, the General Editor captures the main ideas as well as their special significance on behalf of all the authors of individual or joint research essays and articles that, together, make up a thematic collection that spans several branches of public international law. The General Editor introduces the readership to the collection in a way that also accentuates the *Yearbook*'s overarching interest in global law and governance.

In keeping with the mission statement of the *Global Community Yearbook of International Law and Jurisprudence* (*Yearbook*), the 2022 edition takes stock of key changes in global governance and global law, both substantive and procedural. Continuous monitoring of the dynamically but only gradually developing legal world order, together with a focus on possible remedies for improvement is a distinctive trait of this *Yearbook*. In the present edition, this activity is emphasized by a change in the otherwise usual arrangement of the *Yearbook*, thereby diverging from the standard format.

---

* Professor Emeritus of International Law, University of Salerno, Italy; General Editor.

Giuliana Ziccardi Capaldo, *Monitoring the Construction of the Global Community: Key Changes in Global Law and Governance* In: *The Global Community Yearbook of International Law and Jurisprudence 2022*. Edited by: Giuliana Ziccardi Capaldo, Oxford University Press.

Since this edition coincides with the escalation of the War in Ukraine, the volume opens with an overview entitled: "Nuclear Weapons Threat." It contains two wide-ranging essays that address an important field of study in global law—that of the terrible nuclear threat and its current reawakening in the Russian aggression of Ukraine—answering pressing questions like "What has already been done?," "What should be done?," and "Which structural remedies and strategies are available?" The overarching goal is to define some tools of resistance, tools with which to withstand and/or counter the serious effects to help humanity during a period of time characterized by legal deficits to tackle the challenge effectively—if possible. For that is another question: What can be done?

The first feature essay, by *Louis René Beres*, explains how the decentralized system of international law has never actually "worked" and how its next very serious and troubling failures could become fatal. Then the author addresses the implications of globalization for Westphalian international law, warning that, in a nuclear age, a new or post-Westphalian system of international law would have to deal with the problem of decisional irrationality as a generic rather than leader-specific problem. Starting from the theory that identifies the "verticalization" of the international legal community and the primacy of the individual as the "pillars of global law" (G. Ziccardi Capaldo, The Pillars of Global Law, 2008), Beres argues that further and continuous "verticalization" of the international legal community is absolutely necessary to avoid nuclear war, but still not sufficient to ensure long-term planetary survival. It follows from this that a suitably adjusted system of international law requires a comprehensive multi-national effort to provide legal remediation directed simultaneously to ensure needed structural remedies (the macrocosm) and appropriate individual human transformations (the microcosm). The latter is a fundamental element of world order reform. *Richard Falk* undertakes the complex and arduous task of analysing the future role of nuclear weapons. He takes a deconstructivist approach to reexamining the most prominent views of mitigating nuclear dangers. By examining the leading perspectives of arms control and disarmament, he deconstructs classical themes of arms control and nonproliferation of nuclear weaponry policy considered as the pillars of global stability in the nuclear age. Challenging the canonical view of the moral, political and humanitarian values underlying this policy, he argues that, despite all of the obstacles, "radical disarmament" and "total denuclearization" are the only safe and humane path to take. Falk's article—passionate, illuminating and erudite—attempts the enterprise of averting the terrible spectre of nuclear war. There is, underlying a series of propositions he makes in the final part, connecting the arms control/disarmament interface, the ongoing Ukraine War that creates risks of nuclear disaster with the broader conflict between Russia and the United States understood as a "geopolitical war" which will affect the future world models. His article will remain an essential conceptual reference point for a long time to come.

In the "ARTICLES" part, some aspects relating to the principles of law concerning both their emergence and the ascertainment of their existence are examined. In the first article *Shane Darcy* discusses the contribution of the UN treaty bodies to business and human rights, examines their influence on the development of the UN Guiding Principles, explores recent developments and argues for a deeper engagement by the treaty bodies in this sphere, one of the most challenging areas of human rights. *Luis A. López Zamora* concludes this part with a critical analysis of the International Law Commission (ILC)'s study on the general principles of law, the most controversial source of international law. Critically assessing the methodology formulated by the Special Rapporteur in 2018, López Zamora seeks to identify the appropriate methodology for ascertaining the existence of the general principles in the field of international law, as well as the ways the general principles of domestic law are to be incorporated into international law.

"NOTES AND COMMENTS," in Part 2, deals with many subjects that are at present preoccupying the world. *Paul Schiff Berman* addresses the processes of international law-making while taking a broad and multi-faceted view of the proliferation of a multitude of sources of legality that tend to interact with and sometimes compete against each other. In doing so, he argues that the interaction between international and domestic law brings to light the "vernacularization" of international law in local settings, as well as the creation of international law in domestic courts and tribunals. Moving from three recent cases, he analyses the ways in which domestic courts are vernacularizing the Paris Climate Agreement, creating legal duties under domestic law for greenhouse gas emissions as an example of "global legal pluralism in action." Taking the US Federal Court of Appeals (Ninth Circuit) in the child rights climate change case *Juliana v. United States* as a starting point, *Sonja C. Grover* examines the denial of the child's right to truth, involving current and future generations, and the larger societal implications of that denial. Highlighting that the existential threat of the climate change crisis to humanity is difficult for most to comprehend due to disinformation and climate change denial, she points to the fallacies inherent in the court's approach, warning the courts of the risk of becoming "enablers of truth deniers." Shifting the focus to the Russian war of aggression against Ukraine, *Lando Kirchmair* takes on yet another central aspect of disinformation and its negative repercussions on the affirmation of fundamental rights. He highlights an unprecedented rise in manipulation through disinformation in the twenty-first century, emphasizing that the case of Ukraine is no exception to this trend. Arguing that actively fighting manipulative disinformation across national boundaries with international information campaigns is important for a resilient global legal order in the (digital) information age, he suggests (hoping for it) that the United Nations, in the long run, would put itself in a position to communicate on all available channels to the people concerned in their mother tongue in order to inform them objectively on behalf of the international community. Still in the context of the protection of fundamental human rights, *Geert-Jan Alexander Knoops* and *Sara Pedroso* focus on the ascertainment of procedural truth within international criminal proceedings. The authors shed light on a subject matter which has not yet been dealt with in detail within the academic literature, namely, the evidentiary value of reports drafted by non-governmental organizations and other international organizations (such as reports of the UN commissions about certain international or internal armed conflicts) within international criminal proceedings. Through an analysis based on ICC jurisprudence, on this subject, Knoops and Pedroso distinguish between hearsay where the source is known and anonymous hearsay, arguing that the latter should be excluded in principle by the chamber in its determination of guilt or innocence. *Juan-Pablo Pérez-León-Acevedo* concludes Part 2 by ascertaining how diverse UN legal sources have continuously and increasingly recognized the need for reparation modalities that go well beyond a single reparation modality (traditionally compensation) in contexts of atrocities and how this practice, in turn, should advance the process of increasing comprehensive and coordinated reparation awards and programmes that combine compensation with non-compensatory reparation measures. The author suggests that such a provision in reparation awards and programmes should be incorporated when reparations are granted and implemented in ongoing scenarios of mass atrocities in *inter alia* Syria, Yemen, Myanmar (affecting the Rohingya people), and Ukraine to redress harm inflicted on victims of gross abuses in an effective, prompt, and proportional manner.

In Part 3, "GLOBAL POLICIES AND LAW," *Thomas G. Weiss* focuses on the protection of cultural heritage while weighing politics and law. His contribution creates an approach that embodies the very purpose and spirit of Part 3. Contrary to the view that the protection of vulnerable populations and the tangible cultural heritage that sustains them are separate, the author shows that the two are inseparable. At the same time, he argues for the value of inserting politics into what has been largely a legal conversation for over a century, cleverly highlighting the main features of this mutually constructive relationship. The efforts to protect immovable cultural heritage amidst mass atrocities is the beginning of a comparable normative and political journey—although the law is more advanced, today's better-informed politics may be propitious for normative and policy advances.

The article "The Emerging Ethics Evolution: The Evasive Connection Between Environmental Crimes, Philosophical Considerations of Public International Law, and the International Criminal Court's Twentieth Anniversary" by *Anja Matwijkiw* and *Bronik Matwijkiw* is included in Part 6 on "RECENT LINES OF INTERNATIONALIST THOUGHT." This part provides readers with a unique opportunity to study and interpret global legal issues from different perspectives, cultures and methodologies, so as to enhance an understanding of changes in international law and contemporary affairs, including international relations in the context of globalization. Both leading scholars and judges from all over the world have contributed their internationalist thought in the past. In this edition, *Matwijkiw* and *Matwijkiw* capture some of the global justice trends that introduce doctrinal tensions in the debate and dispute over ecocide. The twentieth anniversary of the International Criminal Court (ICC) coincides with the reality of controversy. In the future, the ICC's norm-expansion may come to integrate ecocide, but it may realistically only amount to what the two authors describe as a "narrow" crime category. Politics and ethics, so it appears, pull in different directions. Apart from the absence of general rights theory, which poses a problem for interpretation, the study is innovative by virtue of demonstrating that the project of building a new world order is faced with obstructions that are related to human rights perceptions, such as a one-dimensional value-prescriptive strategy for international criminal law.

The primary attention to international jurisprudence of this *Yearbook* has represented a characteristic feature since the time of the drafting of its Project.[1] It is a founding philosophy. Its aim and scope, the very identity of this *Yearbook*, revolves around jurisprudential practice, in the belief that the jurisdiction of international courts and tribunals is fundamental to the strengthening of global law and governance.

In turn, this is why Part 4, dedicated to "JURISPRUDENTIAL CROSS-FERTILIZATION," is central and important. The *Yearbook* deals with the formation and development of principles of global law through dialogue between international judges and between international and national judges. In this edition, the relevant part includes two articles. The first article, by *Ravindra Pratap*, conducts a thorough and extensive survey of the views expressed by the judges at the International Court of Justice (ICJ) regarding *erga omnes* obligations, to show that the differences of geography and legal culture of ICJ judges are not without discernible convergence in their consideration of these international obligations. He then goes on to suggest some explanations for this trend and assesses its merits, attributable in some measure to a combination of an essentially unifying nature of *erga omnes* obligations and a cross-fertilization between legal cultures in that there's a sense of universality in the very concept of legal culture. The second article, by *Yoshifumi Tanaka*, examines key issues of the ICJ *Nicaragua v. Colombia* judgment of 21 April 2022, in which the Court made some important statements with regard to the customary law nature of relevant provisions of the UN Convention on the Law of the Sea while referring to the jurisprudence of ITLOS. Drawing on a detailed analysis of the rich content of the judgment, the article identifies its main innovative features, while emphasizing the fact that the judicial

---

[1] *See* Giuliana Ziccardi Capaldo, *Facing the Crisis of Global Governance—GCYILJ's Twentieth Anniversary at the Intersection of Continuity and Dynamic Progress*, Editorial, 20 GLOBAL COMMUNITY YILJ 2020 (Giuliana Ziccardi Capaldo General ed.) 5–14 (2021), at 5.

decision provides a crucial precedent on the matter concerning the criteria for constructing straight baselines.

The next part, Part 5 of the *Yearbook*, "GLOBAL JUSTICE—DECISIONS OF INTERNATIONAL COURTS AND TRIBUNALS," offers a detailed analysis of international jurisprudence. It contains eleven sections dedicated to major international courts/tribunals. In this edition leading experts, scholars and international judges analyze and comment on the jurisdictional activity of these judicial bodies in 2021: *Momchil Milanov* and *Robert Kolb* (International Court of Justice (ICJ)), *Yoshifumi Tanaka* (International Tribunal for the Law of the Sea (ITLOS)), *Joanna Gomula* (WTO Dispute Settlement System (WTO DSS)), *Geert-Jan Alexander Knoops* and *Sara Pedroso* (International Criminal Court (ICC)), *Rafael Nieto-Navia* (International Residual Mechanism for Criminal Tribunals (MICT)), *Koen Lenaerts* (Court of the European Union (ECJ)), *Robert Spano* (European Court of Human Rights (ECtHR)), *Ricardo C. Pérez Manrique* (Inter-American Court of Human Rights (IACtHR)), *August Reinisch* and *Johannes Tropper* (International Centre for Settlement of Investment Disputes (ICSID)), *Patrícia Galvão Teles* and *João Gil Antunes* (Permanent Court of Arbitration (PCA)), and *Francesco Seatzu* (International Administrative Tribunals (IATs)). Their comment essays are complemented by legal maxims extracted from the most relevant judgments and advisory opinions rendered by these courts/tribunals over the course of the year under consideration.

I will end by expressing my warmest thanks to the members of the Editorial and Advisory Boards, to the authors and to the reviewers for their dedicated professional service and unwavering expert contributions to the ongoing success of the *Yearbook*. I extend my thanks to the Oxford University Press team, especially the current editor, Dennis Gargano, who, in addition to taking care of the production of the *Yearbook* with great skill and dedication, has been heavily involved in the process of growth and change.

The *Yearbook* is available on Oxford Scholarship Online at https://oxford.universityp ressscholarship.com/, as well as on Oxford Academic at https://global.oup.com/acade mic/?lang=en&cc=us.

OVERVIEW ESSAYS

GRAND CHALLENGES OF OUR TIME—NUCLEAR WEAPONS THREAT

Endgame

Obligations to Transform "Westphalian" International Law

BY LOUIS RENÉ BERES*

Abstract

Our decentralized system of international law has never actually "worked," and its next conspicuous failures could become existential and irremediable. Here, recalling the seminal work of Professor Giuliana Ziccardi Capaldo, this chapter argues that further and continuous "verticalization" of the international legal community will prove indispensable to nuclear war avoidance and genocide prevention, but still not be sufficient for long-term planetary survival. In the final analysis, an informed case is made to augment plainly needed structural remedies with certain apt transformations of the individual person. Only when jurisprudential remediation is directed simultaneously to the *macrocosm* (world legal institutions) and *microcosm* (individual human beings) could international law ever meaningfully "work."

I. INTRODUCTION: THE PROBLEM AND ITS "WESTPHALIAN" ORIGINS

Since the seventeenth-century Peace of Westphalia,[1] international law has been based upon varying combinations of belligerent nationalism,[2] threats of interstate violence, and war.

---

* Louis René Beres (PhD, Princeton, 1971), Emeritus Professor of International Law, Purdue University; member of Advisory Board, lberes@purdue.edu.

[1] *See* Treaty of Peace of Munster, Oct. 1648, 1 Consol. T.S. 271; and Treaty of Peace of Osnabruck, Oct. 1648, 1., Consol. T.S. 119. Together, these two treaties comprise the *Peace of Westphalia*.

[2] This belligerent nationalism stands in marked contrast to authoritative legal assumptions concerning solidarity between nation-states. These jurisprudential assumptions concern a presumptively common legal struggle against aggression, terrorism and genocide. Such a "peremptory" expectation, known formally in law as a *jus cogens* assumption, was already mentioned in Justinian, *Corpus Juris Civilis* (533 CE); in Hugo Grotius, 2 *De Jure Belli ac Pacis Libri Tres*, ch. 20 (Francis W. Kesey, tr., 1925) (1690); and in Emmerich de

Louis René Beres, *Endgame* In: *The Global Community Yearbook of International Law and Jurisprudence 2022.* Edited by: Giuliana Ziccardi Capaldo, Oxford University Press. © Oxford University Press 2023. DOI: 10.1093/oso/9780197752265.003.0002

Though it should be obvious to capable social scientists and historians that this threat-oriented system of law has never succeeded—in fact, it has consistently failed with increasingly catastrophic outcomes—almost two hundred separate states now still insist upon passing from one untenable position to another. (remove quote marks). Understandably, corresponding searches for justification on this same plane have been ill-fated.[3]

Though the time for believing in *realpolitik*[4] is already over,[5] Westphalian power politics[6] remains essentially unchecked. What remains uncertain is (1) whether a catastrophic world-system ending would manifest itself suddenly or incrementally, and (2) whether it would augur new beginnings or just the same as usual (remove quote marks),

There is more for legal scholars to consider.[7] As is true for the questions, certain correct answers could be interrelated or synergistic. If the latter, a "whole" expected ending would actually be greater than the sum of its "parts." That worrisome calculation would be true by definition.

What then?

In such unstable matters, global policy imperatives would become clear and unambiguous. Going forward, world leaders would be well advised to recognize the inherent limitations of always seeking national security within a global threat system.[8] It follows, for these

---

Vattel, 1 *Le Droit des Gens*, ch. 19 (1758). The Founding Fathers of the United States were most likely made aware of these expectations by Blackstone's *Commentaries on the Law of England* (1765), a comprehensive classic work which quickly became the conceptual basis of subsequent United States law.

[3] "The state," warned Jose Ortega y Gasset in *The Revolt of the Masses* (1930), "after sucking out the very marrow of society, will be left bloodless, a 'skeleton,' dead with that rusty death of machinery, more gruesome even than the death of a living organism."

[4] A previous book by this author deals with these issues from an expressly American point of view. *See* LOUIS RENÉ BERES, REASON AND REALPOLITIK: US FOREIGN POLICY AND WORLD ORDER (1984). Professor Beres is also the author of three earlier books dealing with alternative world futures: REORDERING THE PLANET: CONSTRUCTING ALTERNATIVE WORLD FUTURES (1974); PLANNING ALTERNATIVE WORLD FUTURES: VALUES, METHODS AND MODELS (1975); and PEOPLE, STATES AND WORLD ORDER (1981).

[5] Ironically, the core argument for *realpolitik* has always been its alleged "realism."

[6] For political philosophy origins of such assumptions, *see especially* the terse comment of Thrasymachus in bk. 1, sec. 338 of Plato, *The Republic*: "Right is the interest of the stronger."

[7] In this connection, the present author is indebted to the pioneering intellectual work of Professor Giuliana Ziccardi Capaldo. Long devoted to complex issues of transforming Westphalian world legal order, especially in her major book *The Pillars of Global Law* (2008), Professor Ziccardi Capaldo's core thesis has been that the verticalization of the international community, due to globalization, has determined the shift in the distribution of international power, namely the transfer of powers from states to international organizations, above all to the UN, and also to other centers of power, such as international courts, religious groups, large international companies, mass media, etc., and other actors of the global community (non-state actors). (See Giuliana Ziccardi Capaldo, *The Law of the Global Community: An Integrated System to Enforce "Public" International Law*, 1 GLOBAL COMMUNITY YILJ 2001 (Giuliana Ziccardi Capaldo General ed.) 71, 114, 116 (2001) and Id., THE PILLARS OF GLOBAL LAW 10–11, 39–41, 102 (2008). In the final analysis, Professor Ziccardi Capaldo recognizes the primacy of the individual, the microcosm, as both the ultimate object of world legal reform and the ultimate creator of now-indispensable legal norms and procedures (THE PILLARS, at 8, 155–156).

[8] In his seventeenth-century classic of political philosophy, *Leviathan*, Thomas Hobbes points out interestingly that while the anarchic "state of nature" has likely never actually existed between individual human beings, it nonetheless defines the legal structures of world politics, patterns within which nations must co-exist in "the state and posture of gladiators. . . . " This uneasy "posture," explains Hobbes famously, is a condition of "war."

leaders, that now is the optimal time to identify more durable configurations of international relations and international law.[9]

This time represents planet earth's "eleventh hour."

And there could be no more urgent kinds of identification.

Any such identifications will have to be systematic. This means, above all, a process informed by creative intellectual imaginations and by variously plausible hypotheses. These imaginations and hypotheses should always proceed *together*, in tangibly judicious "tandem."[10]

There is more. In science, which includes jurisprudence, every inquiry must begin with a hypothesis. The appropriate rules for conducting this process should include useful descriptions of relevant analytic models and an exploration of these models by verifiable methods of empirical-scientific inquiry.[11]

What might first have seemed promising in the historic "state of nature" (the global condition of anarchy dating back to the Peace of Westphalia in 1648) is apt to prove injurious or even lethal for humankind's longer-term survival prospects. Pertinent national and international harms could be experienced not merely as tangible debits in any one country's national security calculus, but also as an irremediable set of intolerable costs.

II. OBLIGATIONS OF SUPPLANTING *REALPOLITIK*

Ultimately, on national security matters, each major state's most important task must be a far-reaching rejection of *realpolitik* thinking. Substantially more will need to be accomplished on such increasingly urgent matters. To the main point, it is high time for world leaders to think meaningfully beyond *realpolitik*, beyond global power-politics.

On such time-related and history-related subjects, it's best to begin at the beginning. Accordingly, each state is a part of a much larger and interdependent world system. This more comprehensive system has steadily diminishing chances for any sustainable success within the recalcitrant pattern of competitive sovereignties. What is the rationale, our decision makers should finally inquire, of seeking a "qualitative military edge"[12] in a system that is inherently inclined to "self-destruct"?[13]

---

[9] In the words of Mr. Justice Gray, delivering the judgment of the US Supreme Court in *Paquete Habana* (1900): "International law is part of our law, and must be ascertained and administered by the courts of justice of appropriate jurisdiction. . . . " (175 U.S. 677(1900)). *See also* Opinion in *Tel-Oren v. Libyan Arab Republic* (726 F. 2d 774 (1984)). The specific incorporation of treaty law into US municipal law is expressly codified at Article 6 of the *US Constitution*, the so-called "Supremacy Clause."

[10] Among other things, this means a Nietzsche-like "overcoming" of "Mass Man." Says Jose Ortega y Gasset in *The Revolt of the Masses* (1930): "The mass-man has no attention to spare for reasoning; he learns only in his own flesh."

[11] Among the earliest books laying out such rules, <u>see</u>, by this author, LOUIS RENÉ BERES, REORDERING THE PLANET: CONSTRUCTING ALTERNATIVE WORLD FUTURES (1974); LOUIS RENÉ BERES, THE MANAGEMENT OF WORLD POWER: A THEORETICAL ANALYSIS (1973); LOUIS RENÉ BERES, TRANSFORMING WORLD POLITICS: THE NATIONAL ROOTS OF WORLD PEACE (1975); LOUIS RENÉ BERES, PLANNING ALTERNATIVE WORLD FUTURES: VALUES, METHODS AND MODELS (1975); and LOUIS RENÉ BERES, PEOPLE, STATES AND WORLD ORDER (1981).

[12] This is an especially reasonable question to ask of Israeli leaders in Jerusalem (political) and Tel Aviv (military), where the only palpable issues are seemingly still drawn from immutable core assumptions of perpetual regional conflict.

[13] We may recall here the pertinent parable from Marcus Aurelius's *Meditations*: "What does not benefit the entire hive is no benefit to the bee." Unless we take meaningful steps to implement an organic and

Basic issues here are not just narrowly scientific. They are also broadly philosophic. For scholars of world politics and world law,[14] the "bottom line" must always be the primacy of intellect or "mind" as the basic font of a particular nation-state's variable power.[15] World legal reform is always dependent upon apt considerations of "mind."

There is more. Truth is always exculpatory. Pain, worldwide, is always "deep."[16] It can never be overridden by the visceral chanting of political nonsense or by cynical substitution of empty witticism for historical fact.

Prima facie, realpolitik or balance of power world politics has never succeeded for longer than variously brief intervals.[17] In the future, this unsteady foundation could be further undermined by multiple systemic failures, failures that could be mutually reinforcing or "synergistic."[18] These failures could sometime involve weapons of mass destruction.

Most portentous, in this regard, would be nuclear weapons. By definition, any failure of nuclear *realpolitik* could prove not "only" catastrophic, but also *sui generis*. This troubling assessment would surely obtain if any such failure were judged in the full or cumulative scope of its unprecedented declensions.

For proper remediation, certain specific steps would need to be taken. Immediately, all states that depend upon some form of nuclear deterrence should begin to think more self-consciously about fashioning alternative systems of world politics; that is, about creating prospectively viable configurations that are reliably war-averse and simultaneously cooperation-centered. While any hint of interest in such speculative patterns of

---

cooperative planetary civilization—one based on the irremediably central truth of human "oneness"—there will be no civilization at all.

[14] According to William Blackstone's *Commentaries* (Book IV, "Of Pubic Wrongs," Chapter V): "All law results from those principles of natural justice in which all the learned of every nation agree. . . ." In legal philosophy, the classic definition of Natural Law is given by Cicero in *The Republic*: "True law is right reason, harmonious with nature, diffused among all, constant, eternal. . . ."

[15] Consider here the observation of French poet Guillaume Apollinaire: "It must not be forgotten that it is perhaps more dangerous for a nation to allow itself to be conquered intellectually than by arms." *See* "The New Spirit and the Poets" (1917).

[16] In "The drunkard's song," a passage in *Zarathustra*, Nietzsche sums up such pain with unparalleled simplicity: "*Tief ist ihr Weh*" ("Deep is its pain") says the philosopher about the world. This "lied" was put to music by Gustav Mahler in his Third Symphony, 4th Movement: https://www.youtube.com/watch?v=6aM9hezKudY&list=RDuPQSokfeQN8&index=2.

[17] The concept of a *balance of power*—an idea of which the nuclear-age *balance of terror* is a more fearful variant—has never been more than a facile metaphor. Further, it has never had anything to do with any calculable *equilibrium*. As such a balance is always a matter of individual and more or less subjective perceptions, adversary states may never be sufficiently confident that strategic circumstances are "balanced" in their favor. In consequence, as each side must perpetually fear that it will be "left behind," the search for balance continually produces only widening insecurity and perpetual disequilibrium.

[18] Such synergies could shed light upon the entire world system's state of disorder—a view that would reflect what the physicists call "entropic" conditions—and could become more or less dependent upon each pertinent decision-maker's subjective *metaphysics of time*. For an early article by this author dealing with linkages obtaining between such a metaphysics and national decision-making, *see* Louis René Beres, *Time, Consciousness and Decision-Making in Theories of International Relations*, VIII(3) THE JOURNAL OF VALUE INQUIRY 175–186 (Fall 1974).

global integration will sound utopian or fanciful to "realists,"[19] an opposite interpretation could actually prove more plausible.

At this tipping point in human evolution, it is more realistic to acknowledge that any traditional "every man for himself" ethos in world politics would be infinitely degrading. Accordingly, this rancor-based ethos is incapable of offering any serious survival reassurances. "The visionary," reminds Italian film director Federico Fellini, "is the only realist."

Again and again—and at some point, perhaps irretrievably—"Westphalian" world systemic failures could become tangibly dire and potentially irreversible. In the final analysis, it will not be enough to tinker tentatively at the ragged edges of our current world legal order. At that decisive turning point, simply continuing to forge assorted ad hoc agreements between stubborn states or (as "hybridized" actors) between these states and various surrogate or sub-state organizations would prove conclusively wrongheaded.

III. OBLIGATIONS OF HUMAN "ONENESS" OR "COSMOPOLIS"

In the longer term, the only sort of realism that can make any sense for America and other leading states in world politics is a posture that points toward some "higher" awareness of global "oneness"[20] and (however incrementally) greater world system interdependence.

In its fully optimized expression, such a now-indispensable awareness would resemble what the ancients had called "cosmopolitan." For the moment, let us be candid, the insightful prophets of a more collaborative "world city" civilization must remain few and far between,[21] but this consequential absence would not be due to an intrinsic lack of need or witting forfeiture. Rather, it would reflect a progressively imperiled species' retrograde

---

[19] "Whenever the new Muses present themselves," warned twentieth-century Spanish existentialist philosopher, José Ortega y Gasset, "the masses bristle." *See* Ortega y Gasset, The Dehumanization of Art 7 (1925) (1948, 1968).

[20] In medieval Western civilization, the world was conceived as a hierarchical order, extending from lowest to highest, and the earthly divisions of authority (always artificial or contrived) were reunited at the level of God. Below this divine stratum, the realm of humanity was to be considered as "one," especially because the world had been created as backdrop for human salvation. Only in its relation to the universe itself was the world to be considered as a part rather than whole. Accordingly, as conceptualized here, the medieval universe was tidy, ordered, and neatly arranged. Imagined in metaphoric fashion as an immense cathedral, this universe was so simply conceived that it was often represented in art by great painted clocks. At its center lay the earth, a mere part of God's larger creation but still a single unified whole unto itself. For this pertinent history, literary as well as philosophic, *see* Anatole France, The Garden of Epicurus (1923).

[21] The best studies of such modern world order "prophets" are still W. Warren Wagar, The City of Man (1963), and W. Warren Wagar, Building the City of Man (1971). The history of Western philosophy and jurisprudence includes variously illustrious advocates of global unity or "oneness." Notable among them are Voltaire and Goethe. We need only recall Voltaire's biting satire in the early chapters of *Candide* and Goethe's oft-repeated comment linking belligerent nationalism to the declining stages of any civilization. One may also note Samuel Johnson's expressed conviction that patriotism "is the last refuge of a scoundrel"; William Lloyd Garrison's observation that "[w]e cannot acknowledge allegiance to any human government . . . Our country is the world, our countryman is all mankind"; and Thorsten Veblen's comment that "[t]he patriotic spirit is at cross-purposes with modern life." Similar sentiments are discoverable in Friedrich Nietzsche's *Human, all too Human*. Let scholars also recall Santayana's coalescing remark in *Reason and Society*: "A man's feet must be planted in his country, but his eyes should survey the world." The unifying point of all such cosmopolitan remarks is that narrow-minded patriotism is not "merely"

unwillingness to take itself seriously—that is, to recognize that the only sort of loyalty that can ultimately rescue all states must first embrace a redirected commitment (both individual and national) to *humankind*.[22]

At its heart, this is not a bewilderingly complicated idea. To wit, it is hardly a medical or biological secret that the core factors and behaviors common to all human beings greatly outnumber those that unnaturally differentiate one from another. Unless the leaders of all major states on Planet Earth can finally understand that the survival of any one state must inevitably be contingent upon the survival of all, true national security will continue to elude every nation. This includes even the purportedly "most powerful" states, and especially those that fitfully declare themselves "first."

The bottom line? The most immediate security task in the global state of nature must be to become more *collaboratively self-centered*. Simultaneously, the leaders of all pertinent countries must learn to understand that our planet always represents a recognizably organic *whole*, a fragile but variously intersecting "unity."

Incontestably, Westphalian anarchy now exhibits rapidly diminishing options for managing world power[23] or providing law-based mechanisms of successful war avoidance.[24]

More precisely, to seize upon the disappearing opportunities for longer-term survival, our leaders must build sensibly upon certain foundational insights of Francis Bacon, Galileo, Isaac Newton,[25] and on the more contemporary observations of philosopher Lewis

---

injurious, it is also *de facto* "unpatriotic." Though always proclaimed with robotic fanfare, such alleged patriotism never actually serves the tangible interests of a state's citizens or subjects.

[22] Here we may learn from Epictetus: "You are a citizen of the universe." A similarly broad idea of human "oneness" followed the death of Alexander in 322 BCE; and with it came a coinciding doctrine of "universality" or interconnectedness. By the Middle Ages, this political and social doctrine had fused with the notion of a *Respublica Christiana*, a worldwide Christian commonwealth, and Thomas, John of Salisbury and Dante were looking upon Europe as a single and unified Christian community. Below the level of God and his heavenly host, all the realm of humanity was to be considered as one. This is because all the world had been created for the same single and incontestable purpose; that is, to provide secular background for the necessary drama of human salvation. Here, only in its relationship to the universe itself, was the world considered as a part rather than a whole. Says Dante in *De Monarchia*: "The whole human race is a whole with reference to certain parts, and, with reference to another whole, it is a part. For it is a whole with reference to particular kingdoms and nations, as we have shown; and it is a part with reference to the whole universe, which is evident without argument." Today, the idea of human "oneness" should be fully justified/explained in more expressly historical/philosophic terms.

[23] *See* LOUIS RENÉ BERES, THE MANAGEMENT OF WORLD POWER (1973), *op cit.*

[24] Because war and genocide are not mutually exclusive, either strategically or jurisprudentially, taking proper systemic steps toward war avoidance would plausibly also reduce the likelihood of always-egregious "crimes against humanity." Under international law, *crimes against humanity* are defined as "murder, extermination, enslavement, deportation, and other inhumane acts committed against any civilian population before or during a war; or persecutions on political, racial or religious grounds in execution of or in connection with any crime within the jurisdiction of the Tribunal, whether or not in violation of the domestic law of the country where perpetrated. . . ." *See* Charter of the International Military Tribunal, Aug. 8, 1945, art. 6(c), 59 stat. 1544, 1547, 82 UNTS 279, 288

[25] Regarding science in such matters, Niccolo Machiavelli joined Aristotle's plan for a more scientific study of politics generally with various core assumptions about geopolitics or *realpolitik*. His best known conclusion, in this particular suggestion, focuses on the eternally stark dilemma of practicing goodness in a world that is generally evil. "A man who wishes to make a profession of goodness in everything, must necessarily come to grief among so many who are not good." *See* THE PRINCE, ch. XV. Although this argument is largely unassailable, there exists a corresponding need to disavow "naive realism," and to

Mumford: "Civilization is the never ending process of creating one world and one humanity."[26] These earlier names will mean little or nothing to the world's present-day policy planners, but there will still likely exist capable advisors who can draw properly upon the dignities of serious study and dialectical thought.[27]

Everywhere, erudition deserves some conspicuous pride of place.

IV. PERTINENT PARTICULARS OF JURISPRUDENCE

Jurisprudentially, no particular national leadership has any special or primary obligations in this regard. Nor could it reasonably afford to build a nation's most immediate security policies upon vaguely distant hopes. Nonetheless, the United States remains a key part of the interrelated community of nations and must do whatever it can to detach a steadily wavering state of nations from a time-dishonored "state of nature."

Any such willful detachment should be expressed as part of a much wider vision for a durable and law-centered world politics.[28] Over the longer term, Washington will have to do its primary part to preserve the global system as a whole. However naive or impractical this imperative may sound at first, nothing could be more fanciful than continuing indefinitely on a discredited course.

For the moment, there is no further need for detailing analytic or intellectual particulars. There are bound to be many, but at least for now, only a more evident and dedicated awareness of this civilizational obligation need be expected.[29]

In *The Plague*, Albert Camus instructs: "At the beginning of the pestilence and when it ends, there's always a propensity for rhetoric . . . It is in the thick of a calamity that one

---

recognize that in the longer term, the only outcome of "eye for an eye" conceptions in world politics will be universal "blindness."

[26] We may think also of the corresponding Talmudic observation: "The earth from which the first man was made was gathered in all the four corners of the world."

[27] Dialectic formally originated in the fifth century BCE, as Zeno, author of the *Paradoxes*, had been acknowledged by Aristotle as its inventor. In the middle dialogues of Plato, dialectic, with its conceptual root in the Greek verb meaning "to converse," emerges as the supreme form of philosophical/analytic method. Plato describes the dialectician as one who knows best how to ask and answer questions. This particular knowledge—how to ask, and to answer questions, sequentially—should now be usefully transposed to the improved study of American national security issues.

[28] Because US law is founded upon "the law of nature" (*see* US Declaration of Independence and US Constitution), Trump-era opposition to human rights and freedom was *ipso facto* in opposition to Natural Law. Natural Law is based upon the acceptance of certain principles of right and justice that prevail because of their own intrinsic merit. Eternal and immutable, they are external to all acts of human will and interpenetrate all human reason. It is a dynamic idea, and, together with its attendant tradition of human civility runs continuously from Mosaic Law and the ancient Greeks and Romans to the present day. For a comprehensive and far-reaching assessment of the Natural Law origins of international law, *see* Louis René Beres, *Justice and Realpolitik: International Law and the Prevention of Genocide*, 33 THE AMERICAN JOURNAL OF JURISPRUDENCE 123–159 (1988). This article was adapted from Professor Beres' earlier presentation at the International Conference on the Holocaust and Genocide, Tel-Aviv, Israel, June 1982.

[29] International law, which is an integral part of the legal system of all states in world politics, assumes a reciprocally common general obligation of states to supply benefits to one another, and to avoid war at all costs. This core assumption of jurisprudential solidarity is known formally as a "peremptory" or *jus cogens* expectation, that is, one that is never subject to question. It can be found in JUSTINIAN, CORPUS JURIS CIVILIS; HUGO GROTIUS, THE LAW OF WAR AND PEACE (1625); and EMMERICH DE VATTEL, THE LAW OF NATIONS OR PRINCIPLES OF NATURAL LAW (1758).

gets hardened to the truth—in other words—to silence." As long as the states in world politics continue to operate in narrowly zero-sum terms of engagement—that is, as grim archeologists of ruins endlessly-in-the-making—they will be unable to stop the next wave of terror attacks,[30] genocides,[31] and/or catastrophic wars.[32]

Until now, for various unsound reasons, the traditional expectations of *realpolitik* have managed to appear fundamentally sensible. Accordingly, there are no good reasons for expressing any still-lingering or retrospective regrets. Nevertheless, from the overriding standpoint of improving our longer-term security prospects, both national and global, the American president must substantially expand his visionary imagination.

By ignoring the complex interrelatedness of all peoples and all states, former US President Donald J. Trump's "America First" represented the literal opposite of what was urgently needed. Even more starkly egregious have been the overtly barbarous Russian aggressions of Vladimir Putin toward Ukraine.[33] More than ever, affirming the extremity of "everyone for himself" in world politics is a prescription not for realism, but for recurrent conflict and crimes against humanity. Should this prescription be allowed to stay in place, the costs could sometime be nuclear.[34]

---

[30] Under international law, terrorist movements are always *Hostes humani generis*, or "Common enemies of mankind." *See Research in International Law: Draft Convention on Jurisdiction with Respect to Crime*, 29 AM J. INT'L L. 435, 566 (Supp. 1935) (*quoting* King V. Marsh (1615), 3 BULSTR. 27, 81 ENG. REP. 23 (1615) (*"a pirate est Hostes humani generis"*)).

[31] Neither international law nor US law specifically advises any particular penalties or sanctions for states that choose not to prevent or punish genocide committed by others. Nonetheless, all states, most notably the "major powers" belonging to the UN Security Council are bound, among other things, by the peremptory obligation (defined at Article 26 of the Vienna Convention on the Law of Treaties) known as *pacta sunt servanda* to act in continuous "good faith." In turn, this *pacta sunt servanda* obligation is itself derived from an even more basic norm of world law. Commonly known as "mutual assistance," this civilizing norm was most famously identified within the classical interstices of international jurisprudence, most notably by the eighteenth-century legal scholar, Emmerich de Vattel in *The Law of Nations* (1758).

[32] In broad legal terms, stopping such "wars" could be properly described as a "peremptory" obligation of states. According to Article 53 of the *Vienna Convention on the Law of Treaties*: ". . . a peremptory norm of general international law is a norm accepted and recognized by the international community of states as a whole as a norm from which no derogation is permitted and which can be modified only by a subsequent norm of general international law having the same character." *See* Vienna Convention on the Law of Treaties, Done at Vienna, May 23, 1969. Entered into force, Jan. 27, 1980. UN Doc. A/CONF. 39/27 at 289 (1969), 1155 U.N.T.S. 331, *reprinted in* 8 I.L.M. 679 (1969).

[33] Responsibility of leaders for pertinent crimes is not limited by official position *or* by requirement of direct personal actions. On the principle of command responsibility, or *respondeat superior, see In re* Yamashita, 327 U.S. 1 (1945); The High Command Case (The Trial of Wilhelm von Leeb) 12 LAW REPORTS OF TRIALS OF WAR CRIMINALS 1, 71 (United Nations War Crimes Commission Comp. 1949); *see* William H. Parks, *Command Responsibility for War Crimes*, 62 MILITARY LAW REVIEW 1 (1973); William V. O'Brien, *The Law of War, Command Responsibility and Vietnam*, 60 GEORGE TOWN LAW JOURNAL 605 (1972); U.S. DEPT. OF THE ARMY, ARMY SUBJECT SCHEDULE No. 27-1 (Geneva Conventions of 1949 and Hague Convention No. IV of 1907) 10 (1970). The direct individual responsibility of leaders for genocide and genocide-like crimes is unambiguous in view of the London Agreement, which denies defendants the protection of the Act of State defense. *See* Agreement for the Prosecution and Punishment of the Major War Criminals of the European Axis, Aug. 8, 1945, 59 Strat. 1544, E.A.S. No. 472, 82 U.N.T.S. 279, art. 7. Under traditional international law, violations were the responsibility of the state, as a corporate actor, and not of the individual human decision makers in government and in the military.

[34] The cumulative costs could also be overwhelming and more or less unbearable. This references security costs, economic costs and even broadly "human costs."

V. ANARCHY VERSUS CHAOS

Before Americans or any other state's citizens can hope to survive as a nation, all will have to survive as a species; that is, as a planet-wide civilization. In matters of world politics, this means, among other things, understanding vital differences between the traditional anarchy of "Westphalian" international relations and the more disruptive dynamics associated with "chaos." When compared to "Westphalian" anarchy, an impending chaos could be more expressly primal, more starkly primordial, even self-propelled or palpably "lascivious." For further elucidation, we should think here of the "state of nature" described in William Golding's prophetic novel, *Lord of the Flies*. Long before Golding, the seventeenth-century English philosopher Thomas Hobbes (see chapter XIII of *Leviathan*) warned that in any such rabidly dissembling conditions, the "life of man" must be "solitary, poor, nasty, brutish and short."

Looking ahead, such fearsome warnings could become manifestly more plausible in circumstances where expanding threats of a nuclear war would coincide with expanding levels of pandemic. One potential source of optimism, however, is the paradoxical prospect of a beneficent or peace-guided chaos. Whether described in the Old Testament or in certain other sources of Western philosophy, chaos can represent as much a source of large-scale human improvement as one of decline. It is this prospectively positive side of chaos that is intended by Friedrich Nietzsche's seemingly indecipherable remark in *Thus Spoke Zarathustra* (1883): "I tell you, ye have still chaos in you."

When expressed in more aptly neutral tones, chaos is that condition which prepares the world *for all things*, whether sacred or profane. More exactly, it represents that yawning gulf of "emptiness" where nothing is as yet, but where some still-remaining civilizational opportunity can originate. As eighteenth-century German poet Friedrich Hölderlin observes: "There is a desert sacred and chaotic, which stands at the roots of the things, and which prepares all things."

In the ancient pagan world, Greek philosophers thought of this "desert" as *logos*, as a primal concept which indicates that chaos is anything but starkly random or intrinsically without merit. Getting meaningfully beyond the former American president's retrograde impulse and its generic template—that is, beyond *realpolitik*—will first require "fixing the microcosm."[35] Before anyone can conceptualize a system of world politics that rejects the refractory mantra of "everyone for himself," a far-reaching and prior re-conceptualization will have to take place at an *individual human level*.[36]

There is nothing to suggest that American leadership will expect anything more ambitious than transient national improvements in the short term, and little more for the long term. The "prize" should not be just another few years of planetary political life, but rather a more lastingly durable pattern of global survival.

Always, worldwide security and renewal must be brought back to the *individual human being*. Building upon Dante's *De Monarchia* (1310)[37] and the later cosmopolitanism of

---

[35] This idea of "man as microcosm" was already developed in Francis Bacon's *Advancement of Learning* as a model that took individual man as an accurate representation of the entire world—that is, ". . . as if there were to be found in man's body certain correspondences and parallels which should have respect to all varieties of things . . . which are extant in the greater world."

[36] A properly antecedent question was raised earlier by Jose Ortega y Gasset in 1925: "Where," the Spanish philosopher queried, "shall we find the material to reconstruct the world?" *See* Ortega's THE DEHUMANIZATION OF ART 129 (1925) (1968).

[37] Says Dante: ". . . the whole human race is a whole with reference to certain parts, and, with reference to another whole, it is a part. For it is a whole with reference to particular kingdoms and nations, as we have shown and it is a part with reference to the whole universe, as is manifest without argument."

H.G. Wells, Lewis Mumford, and J.W. von Goethe, twentieth-century French philosopher Pierre Teilhard de Chardin concludes helpfully in *The Phenomenon of Man*: "Each element of the cosmos is positively woven from all the others. . . ." Before an American leader can meaningfully oppose the traditional and crippling dominance of power politics in world affairs, an opposition that would inevitably outlast his own presidential tenure, he would first have to understand what Chardin calls "the idea of a worldwide totalization of human consciousness."

This is the incomparably key idea of the world as a single, organic, legal unity.

Whatever its apparent differences and divergences, the world displays an ineradicable and eventually irrepressible "oneness." All human beings are cemented to each other not by the nefarious aggregations of belligerent nationalism, but instead by their immutably basic likeness and by their inevitable interdependence. When Siddhartha listened attentively to the river, says Herman Hesse in his novel of the same name, ". . . he did not bind his soul to any one particular voice and absorb it is his Self, but heard them all, the Whole, the unity. . . ."

VI. THE STATE AS DIVINE MANIFESTATION

There is one last but indispensable observation, one that concerns various presumed connections between individual nation states and the divine. Here, the German philosopher Georg F. Hegel had commented famously: "The State is the Divine Idea as it exists on earth. . . . We must therefore worship the State as the manifestation of the Divine on earth, and consider that, if it is a difficult to comprehend Nature, it is harder to grasp the Essence of the State. . . . The State is the march of God through the world. . . ."[38] To date, this is an idea that is responsible for literally uncountable numbers of individual human deaths and collective disasters.

This brings us all back to the connected phenomena of individual human death fears and belligerent nationalism. In the nineteenth century, as part of his posthumously published lecture on *Politics* (1896), Heinrich von Treitschke looked insightfully beyond the daily news. Citing to Johan Gottlieb Fichte, the German historian had opined prophetically: "Individual man sees in his own country the realization of his earthly immortality."[39] Here, Fichte understood something of utterly uncommon and incomparable importance. It is that there can be no greater power on earth than *power over death*.[40] We may also be

---

[38] *See* Wilhelm Friedrich Hegel, as quoted by KARL R. POPPER, THE OPEN SOCIETY AND ITS ENEMIES, 4th ed., 2 vols. (1963), vol. 2, at 31.

[39] One must consider the *contra* view of Spanish philosopher Jose Ortega y Gasset in *The Revolt of the Masses* (1932). Here, Ortega identifies the state not as a convenient source of immortality, but instead as the very opposite. For him, the state is "the greatest danger," mustering its immense and irresistible resources "to crush beneath it any creative minority that disturbs it. . . ." Earlier, in his chapter "On the New Idol" in *Thus Spoke Zarathustra*, Friedrich Nietzsche wrote similarly: "State is the name of the coldest of all cold monsters. . . . All-too-many are born—for the superfluous the state was invented." Later, in the same chapter: "A hellish artifice was invented there (the state), a horse of death. . . . Indeed, a dying for many was invented there; verily, a great service to all preachers of death!" "The State," says Nietzsche, "lies in all the tongues of good and evil; and whatever it says it lies—and whatever it has it has stolen. Everything about it is false. . . . All-too-many are born: for the superfluous, the State was invented." (*See* Friedrich Nietzsche, *Thus Spoke Zarathustra: On the New Idol*, in THE PORTABLE NIETZSCHE 161 (Walter A. Kaufman tr., 1954)).

[40] How does killing in world politics hold out a promise of immortality for the perpetrator? According to Eugene Ionesco, "I must kill my visible enemy, the one who is determined to take my life, to prevent him from killing me. Killing gives me a feeling of relief, because I am dimly aware that in killing him, I have

reminded by philosopher Emmanuel Levinas that "[a]n immortal person is a contradiction in terms."[41]

For too long, a starkly illogical search for immortality has lain at the heart of human wrongdoing, wrongs including war, terrorism, and genocide. This is because so many diverse civilizations have regarded death-avoidance as a necessarily zero-sum commodity, a goal that can be met only at the correlative expense of certain designated "others." In such "traditional" calculations, the presumed prospects for success have typically been linked to the *de facto* degree of hatred expressed for despised "others."

The greater the hatred, the greater the justifications for killing, the greater the personal chances of living forever.

Though absurd and perverse, this operational calculus was captured correctly by psychologist Ernest Becker's paraphrase of author Elias Canetti: "Each organism raises it head over a field of corpses, smiles into the sun, and declares life good."[42] Additionally, we may consider the explanatory reasoning of psychologist Otto Rank: "The death fear of the ego is lessened by the killing, the sacrifice, of the other; through the death of the other, one buys oneself free from the penalty of dying, of being killed."[43]

What next? Looking ahead, the United States must act together with other states on more firmly logical foundations than those supplied by variously recurrent myths of "sacrifice" and irrationality.[44] By discarding the toxic gibberish of *realpolitik* or belligerent nationalism, cooperating states could finally affirm what ought to have been obvious from the beginnings of world legal order. This is the obligatory replacement of "everyone for himself" calculations with affirmations of human *oneness*. The only alternative, as we may extrapolate from Russia's ongoing aggressions[45] against Ukraine, is a sordid global future of war crimes, crimes against peace, and crimes against humanity.[46]

---

killed death. Killing is a way of relieving one's feelings, of warding off one's own death." This comment from Ionesco's *Journal* appeared in the British magazine, *Encounter*, May 1966. *See also* EUGENE IONESCO, FRAGMENTS OF A JOURNAL (1968).

[41] *See God, Death and Time*; originally *Dieu, la mort et le temps* (1993). *See also*, by Professor Louis René Beres, at *Horasis* (Switzerland): https://horasis.org/soaring-above-politics-death-time-and-immortality/.

[42] *See* ERNEST BECKER, ESCAPE FROM EVIL 2 (1975).

[43] *See* OTTO RANK, WILL THERAPY AND REALITY 130 (1936; 1945).

[44] This is the key message of twentieth-century German philosopher Karl Jaspers' *Reason and Anti-Reason in Our Time* (1952). Jaspers writes, *inter alia*, of the overriding human obligation to rise above "the fog of the irrational."

[45] For the crime of *aggression* under international law, *see* Resolution on the Definition of Aggression, adopted by the UN General Assembly, Dec. 14, 1974. UNGA Res. 3314 (XXIX), 29 UN GAOR, Supp. (No. 31), 142, UN Doc. A/9631 (1975), *reprinted in* 13 I.L.M., 710 (1974).

[46] *Crimes against humanity* are defined as "murder, extermination, enslavement, deportation, and other inhumane acts committed against any civilian population before or during a war; or persecutions on political, racial or religious grounds in execution of or in connection with any crime within the jurisdiction of the Tribunal, whether or not in violation of the domestic law of the country where perpetrated. . . ." Charter of the International Military Tribunal, Aug. 8, 1945, art. 6(c), 59 stat. 1544, 1547, 82 UNTS 279, 288. In law, states must judge every use of force twice: once with regard to the underlying right to wage war (*jus ad bellum*) and once with regard to the means used in actually conducting war (*jus in bello*). Following the Kellogg-Briand Pact of 1928 and the UN Charter, there can be absolutely no right to aggressive war. However, the long-standing customary right of post-attack self-defense remains codified at Article 51 of the UN Charter. Similarly, subject to conformance, *inter alia*, with *jus in bello* criteria, certain instances of humanitarian intervention and collective security operations may also be consistent with *jus ad bellum*. The law of war, the rules of *jus in bello*, comprise: (1) laws on weapons; (2) laws on warfare; and

Realpolitik should end, but not without the simultaneous establishment of promisingly new global beginnings. Such establishment, in turn, should begin with the individual human being, with the microcosm,[47] and build incrementally upon certain extraordinary acts of "will."[48] Reciprocally, species solidarity or "oneness" must represent the *sine qua non* for all new human beginnings.

What increasingly draws near represents both an end and a beginning. This is because termination and commencement are never discrete states of human development; more correctly, they represent complementary parts of a single civilizational process. This indispensable process must be ubiquitous and universal. To narrow or particularize it in any way would only cheapen both its attractions and its benefits.

VII. CONCLUSION: WHY PASS FROM ONE UNTENABLE POSITION TO ANOTHER?

In Samuel Becket's *Fin de Partie*, first performed at London's Royal Court Theater on April 3, 1957, Nell queries Nagg: "Why this farce, day after day?" The same question now needs to be asked about *realpolitik* and Westphalian international law. In essence, we must finally inquire: "Why should humankind continue to abide a system of world law that has never succeeded[49] and can never meet this vulnerable planet's most minimal survival expectations?"

This question should bring us back to the Natural Law origins of contemporary international law. The Stoics, whose legal philosophies arose on the threshold of the Greek and Roman worlds, regarded Nature as humankind's supreme legislator. Applying Platonic and Aristotelian thought to a then-emerging *cosmopolis*, they defined this nascent order as one

---

(3) humanitarian rules. Codified primarily at The Hague and Geneva Conventions, these rules attempt to bring *discrimination, proportionality*, and *military necessity* into all belligerent calculations.

[47] The American Founding Fathers expressed little faith in "The American People." Nurtured by the philosophy of Thomas Hobbes and the religion of John Calvin, they began their constitutional deliberations with the notion that every citizen must potentially be an unregenerate being, one who has to be continually and strictly controlled. Fearing popular participation as much as leadership tyranny, Elbridge Gerry spoke openly of democracy as "the worst of all political evils," while William Livingston opined: "The people have been and ever will be unfit to retain the exercise of power in their own hands." George Washington, as presiding officer at the Constitutional Convention, sternly urged delegates not to produce a document to "please the people," while Alexander Hamilton—made newly famous by the popular Broadway musical— expressly charged America's government "to check the imprudence of any democracy."

[48] Modern philosophic origins of "will" are best discovered in the writings of Arthur Schopenhauer, especially *The World as Will and Idea* (1818). For his own inspiration, Schopenhauer drew freely upon Johann Wolfgang von Goethe. Later, Nietzsche drew just as freely and perhaps more importantly upon Schopenhauer. Goethe was also a core intellectual source for Spanish existentialist Jose Ortega y Gasset, author of the singularly prophetic twentieth-century work, *The Revolt of the Masses* (*Le Rebelion de las Masas*; 1930). See, accordingly, Ortega's very grand essay, "In Search of Goethe from Within" (1932), written for *Die Neue Rundschau* of Berlin on the centenary of Goethe's death. It is reprinted in Ortega's anthology, *The Dehumanization of Art* (1948) and is available from Princeton University Press (1968).

[49] Plato's theory, offered in the fourth century BCE, explains politics as an unstable realm formed by lies, half-truths, and distorted reflections. In contrast to the stable realm of immaterial *Forms*, a realm from which all knowledge must be derived, the political realm is dominated by always multiplying uncertainties of the sensible world. At the basis of Plato's political theory is a physical-mental analogy that establishes correlations between head, heart, and abdomen, and the human virtues of intelligence, courage, and moderation

wherein humankind, by means of its seemingly well-established capacity to *reason*, could commune directly with "the gods."

This definition required further expansion of Plato's and Aristotle's developing notions of universalism. Accordingly, the Stoics articulated a further division between *lex aeterna, ius natural* and *ius humanum*. Though certainly not yet understood by the world's principal national leaders, this ancient division can help to clarify and elucidate the intellectual background of these leaders' rapidly expanding legal responsibilities. A key element of this background must be the underlying question of human *rationality*. In the end, any productive transformations of Westphalian international law will require much deeper understanding of this core question. Though not expressly jurisprudential, it is a question that remains indispensable to any tangible hopes for world legal reform.

We are back to the beginning. International law scholars continue to build their assorted replacement systems of world legal order on more centralized or "verticalized" institutions and procedures, but never really challenge the assumption that the individual human being, the *microcosm*, must already understand the reasonableness of their proposals. But because this assumption ignores what the jurists ought already to have learned from Nietzsche, Freud, Dostoyevsky, Kierkegaard, Kafka, Jaspers, and many others, these well intentioned and gifted legal scholars continue in a condition of protracted bewilderment, wondering incessantly why the world is deaf to such an utterly clear voice of *reason*.[50]

Though it would be easier for us to proceed with our work by continuing to accept traditional assumptions of rationality, such assumptions are too often (and potentially) incorrect. It follows (among many other things) that serious hopes for transforming Westphalian international law must coincide with a new willingness to accept decisional irrationality or anti-reason as potentially determinative. Although not what we would welcome in the best of all possible worlds, such a new willingness must still be regarded as necessary for long-term planetary survival. This is not meant to suggest that anti-reason would be a valid assumption in many or all cases, but that it could still become urgently important from time to time.

Even just a single case of decisional irrationality involving nuclear weapons could have world-transforming effects. Presently, the most obvious and potentially catastrophic subject of such behavior would be Russia's Vladimir Putin. Nonetheless, there could also be other worrisome subjects—most plainly, North Korea's Kim Jung Un—and such seemingly separate cases could intersect or combine in various foreseeable and unforeseeable ways.

In conceivably worst-case intersections, the pertinent relationships would be synergistic. Here, by definition, the cumulative injurious effects would exceed the sum of constituent parts. Understood in terms of military nuclear exchanges, such effects could plausibly be *sui generis* and intolerable.

A new or post-Westphalian system of international law would have to deal with the problem of decisional irrationality as a generic rather than leader-specific problem. What will be required are not visceral or ad hoc reactions to Putin, Kim, or any other present-day national leaders, but a standing jurisprudential mechanism applicable to any prospective resorts to decisional irrationality. To best identify such a durable and sustainable mechanism, scholars and policy planners will have to bear in mind the absolute primacy of good theory. In the end, to deal satisfactorily with decisional irrationality in a nuclear age, the dedicated creators of a post-Westphalian world legal order will need to remember that their

---

[50] *See* by this writer, at *US News & World Report*, Louis René Beres, https://www.usnews.com/opinion/op-ed/articles/2017-07-13/donald-trump-and-the-triumph-of-anti-reason-in-america.

herculean task is preeminently an intellectual one. This task ought never be taken as a narrowly political or nationalistic obligation.

There remains one last world law design observation. It is that any improved world legal order will have to account for egregious leadership miscalculations as well as for decisional irrationality. Even if the leaders of pertinent nuclear weapon states could somehow avoid making irrational national security decisions, they would still remain subject to assorted liabilities of imperfect information, incorrect reasoning, and/or calculation error. It follows from all this that a suitably reformed system of international law could never be created by simple happenstance or hope. What will be required is a comprehensive multi-national effort to manage circumstances of staggering jurisprudential complexity. Though daunting and unprecedented, such an effort is literally a *sine qua non* for global survival.

This is now an authentic "endgame." Accordingly, there could be no good argument to still seek justifications on a time-dishonored seventeenth-century plane. Neither the nuclear weapons threat nor the often coinciding threat of genocide can ever be suitably diminished within the long-failed structures of Westphalian international law.

Deconstructing the Struggle Against Nuclearism

BY RICHARD FALK*

Abstract

The prolonged, ongoing Ukraine War has raised dormant concerns in the global public about the clear and present danger of a nuclear war than at any time since the Cuban Missile Crisis of 1962. The damaged Ukrainian nuclear reactor complex at Zaporizhzhia additionally suggests that nuclear energy facilities should be treated dangerous alongside the weaponry. The broader conflict between Russia and the United States can be best understood as a "geopolitical war" the outcome of which will influence whether future world order will be shaped by the logic of unipolarity, bipolarity, or multipolarity. This article argues that "arms control" and "disarmament" as approaches to mitigating nuclear dangers are radically different, with the former aiming at stability and emphasizing commitments to non-proliferation and the latter seeking transformative results by eliminating nuclear weaponry altogether. The disarmament approach has a juridical appeal due to its rejection of present hegemonic and hierarchical structures controlling nuclear weaponry, anchored in the US managed non-proliferation regime.

I. INTRODUCTION

Not since the Cuban Missile Crisis of 1962 have the dangers associated with nuclear weapons and nuclear energy facilities been as existentially frightening as during the Ukraine War. Even if the war ends without anything catastrophic actually taking place, the Ukraine experience should change the way we think about security in the contemporary world, and specifically about the organic connections between nuclear weaponry and nuclear

---

* Professor Emeritus of International Law, Princeton University and Visiting Distinguished Professor in Global and International Studies, University of California, Santa Barbara. Member of the Advisory Board.

Richard Falk, *Deconstructing the Struggle Against Nuclearism* In: *The Global Community Yearbook of International Law and Jurisprudence 2022*. Edited by: Giuliana Ziccardi Capaldo, Oxford University Press. © Oxford University Press 2023. DOI: 10.1093/oso/9780197752265.003.0003

energy facilities. No longer is it reasonable, if it ever was, to treat the weaponry and energy capabilities in separate silos of concern.

Given such complexity and unavoidable coexistence with catastrophic risk levels, it may give some relief to think like a Hindu, accepting contradiction as woven into the fabric social and political reality rather than remain tied to the Enlightenment model of search for the single right answer to difficult policy puzzles. What is almost impossible for those trained within Western scientific and rationalist frames of reference to grasp is the fact that there are diverse yet overlapping perspectives of existential understanding that will result in contradictory policy recommendations despite shared values and goals associated with national and global security. Civilizational, nationalist, regional, and geopolitical perspectives as well as personal and local experience inevitably color what we feel, think, and do, and so being likeminded when it comes to overcoming or mitigating nuclear dangers is often coupled with sharply divergent views on what to advocate when it comes to tactics, priorities, and policy orientations. If this approach to nuclear danger is accepted, it becomes a mistake to presuppose a consensus exists as to the desirability of prudent military and energy denuclearization even among those who would like to minimize the security and energy roles of nuclearism. There are those who sincerely believe that retaining nuclear weaponry is the safest hedge against catastrophic occurrences.[1] In essence, there are those who see maximum stability as the best path to living with nuclear weaponry, and those who believe only by adopting a disarmament approach can nuclear dangers be minimized.

Animated by such a spirit, this article sets forth a set of reasons why the goal of nuclear disarmament can never be reached so long as arms control and non-proliferation of nuclear weaponry are seen as the pillars of global stability in the nuclear age.[2] By this focus on points of fundamental disagreement I do not deny the significance of overlapping beliefs between managers and transformers. At the same time, transformers, a category that includes most anti-nuclear activists, are in general agreement with respect to the following tenets: the desirability and attainability of a world without *any* nuclear weapons is an attainable goal to be pursued with a sense of urgency by way of an intergovernmental treaty negotiated among the existing nuclear weapons states that achieves nuclear zero by stages of reliably monitored and verified implementation, a process formally endorsed by non-nuclear states; such a treaty would unconditionally prohibit acquisition, possession, and further development of the weaponry, reinforce existing prohibitions on threat or use of nuclear weapons, and reduce existing nuclear arsenals to an eventual zero by a phased, monitored, verified, and implemented procedures with levels of confidence and ample mechanisms for complaint and dispute-settlement; there are many confidence-building steps that could be taken along the way, either unilaterally or by agreement with other nuclear weapons states, including de-alerting of existing weapons, redefining strategic deterrence doctrine in minimalist and purely defensive terms, and adapting doctrine and deployments in compliance with a formally declared adoption of a No First Use Policy, and adherence to the UN Treaty of Prohibition of Nuclear Weapons (TPNW), which entered into force on January 21, 2021.[3]

---

[1] *E.g.*, JOSEPH S. NYE JR., NUCLEAR ETHICS (1986).

[2] For a comprehensive presentation of my approach, *see* RICHARD FALK, ON NUCLEAR WEAPONS: DENUCLEARIZATION, DEMILITARIZATION, DISARMAMENT (Stefan Andersson & Curt Dahlgren eds., 2019)

[3] At present, none of the nine nuclear weapons state is a party to the TPNW. The three NATO states possessing nuclear weapons issuing a statement explaining their opposition. Each of the nine nuclear weapons states had its own reasons for acquiring the weaponry arising from its perception of security threats and extraterritorial

Another area of convergence is with respect to the status of nuclear weapons from the perspective of international law. Most advocates of total disarmament, even if arms control friendly, agree that any use of nuclear weaponry, other than for the defensive survival of a sovereign state under attack is inherently unlawful under existing international law, that is, without the desirable clarification and reinforcement provided by the TPNW. In keeping with this view, any threat or use of a nuclear weapon would be an international crime for which individual accountability should attach. Such a consensus affirms the influential dissenting opinion of Judge Christopher Weeramantry in the Advisory Opinion addressing comprehensively and critically the legality of nuclear weapons in the International Court of Justice.[4]

It is also crucial not to neglect the relevance of nuclear energy capabilities when addressing the security environment. Earlier events such as the 1986 accident at Chernobyl nuclear plant complex or the 2011 tsunami resulting from a large underwater earthquake off the Pacific coast of Japan caused the serious disruption of the Fukushima facilities, releasing radioactivity over a large area. If the wind from Fukushima was blowing, as it often does, in a Tokyo direction 30 million people would have been at risk of exposure to the deadly radioactive discharges. These past events were illustrative of the dangers arising from accidents and extreme natural events associated with the production of electricity by way of nuclear reactors, but it took the Ukraine War to underscore their close connections to international conflictual behavior due to their vulnerability to accidental or deliberate damage in the course of warfare.

The Ukraine War (2022) dramatized this dangerous vulnerability of nuclear facilities in combat areas. Russian shelling near the huge Zaporizhzhia nuclear energy complex that supplies Ukraine with 1/5th of its electricity supply was the most alarming event to date. The complex was damaged by artillery fire, whether negligently or deliberately caused by Russian military operations. Among other concerns are those stemming from false flag operations intended to escalate tensions and induce outside actors to intervene. This evidently happened in the Syrian War when a chemical weapons attack on Douma in 2018 was misleadingly attributed to the Damascus government, and used by the United States to justify 'retaliatory' missile strikes against Syrian targets.[5]

A quite different concern with respect to 'peaceful' national nuclear programs is a consequence of sophisticated nuclear technology being susceptible to dual use. Such a characteristic of reliance on nuclear power for electricity could feed suspicions, whether genuine or manipulated, that might easily cause countries dismantling their weapons arsenals to withdraw from a disarming process, or pause their participation until confidence is restored. Any serious disenchantment with the trustworthy nature of a comprehensive nuclear disarmament process underway, would inevitably give rise to international tensions, and might even generate war-threatening crises. Indeed, such anxieties about the weapons potential of

---

ambitions. North Atlantic Council Statement as the Treaty on the Prohibition of Nuclear Weapons Enters into Force, Dec. 15, 2020.

[4] *See The Legality of the Threat or Use of Nuclear Weapons*, Advisory Opinion, International Court of Justice (1996); *see also Shimoda* case decided in 1963 by the Tokyo District Court as interpreted, Richard Falk, *The Shimoda Case*, 51 AMERICAN JOURNAL OF INTERNATIONAL LAW 759–793 (1965).

[5] *See* various critiques of official version of Douma attacks. Jonathan Steele, *The OPCW and Douma: Chemical Weapons Watchdog Accused of Evidence-Tampering by Its Own Inspectors*, COUNTERPUNCH, Nov. 15, 2019; *Chemical Weapons Expert at the UN: Douma Attack Didn't Happen*, MIDDLE EAST MONITOR, June 29, 2020; Errik von de Beek, *Rising Tensions Within OPCW*," DIPLOMAT MAGAZINE, Nov. 15, 2019. Nick Waters, *Berlin Group 21, Ivan's Emails and Chemical Weapons Conspiracy Theories*," BELLINGCAT, May 14, 2021.

nuclear energy technology and production has been relied upon as one of the justifications relied upon to sustain the nuclear status quo.

The allegations, denials, contradictory intelligence reports, and conflict potential surrounding Iran's nuclear program during the last 20 years is indicative of the problems that would face a world monitoring and verifying disarmament commitments in which adversaries maintained nuclear facilities. The breakdown of such an agreement would likely cause dangerous nuclear rearmament races in an atmosphere of geopolitical panic. After Ukraine, the world order benefits of maximum investments in the development of solar and wind energy sources of electricity become obvious, as does the phasing out of existing nuclear power programs. For climate change reasons, it is dangerously unwise to respond, as some countries already have, by renewed and expanded reliance on fossil fuels rather than accelerate the development of renewable energy capabilities.

It is against this background of historical context and increased skepticism about separating military and non-military forms of nuclearism that the broader issues of how to proceed is investigated.

The position adopted here is that the search for *stability* with respect to nuclear dangers is a fool's errand, and that despite all of the obstacles, nuclear disarmament, and total denuclearization is the only safe and humane path to take. This can be best consided by examining the leading perspectives of arms control and disarmament, putting to one side strategic use of nuclear threat diplomacy as a hierarchical and hegemonic dimension of current world order.[6]

II. THE INCOMPATIBILITY OF ARMS CONTROL AND DISARMAMENT

In imagining how to respond to nuclear dangers, it is sensible to draw a sharp distinction between arms control as *managerial* and *geopolitical* in its nature and disarmament as *transformative* and *juridical* in character.[7] By managerial, I mean that the primary purpose of a given measure is to reduce risks posed by and costs associated with the nuclear status quo. Typical arms control proposals involve de-alerting weapons systems, agreeing to forgo certain modernizing technologies, abandoning, or at least mitigating, provocative doctrines and deployments, and reducing numbers of warheads and missile launchers.

By geopolitical, I reference the fact that the intended and actual goal of most managerial initiatives is to add stability to the nuclear status quo, including not challenging the possession, control, and legitimacy of the weaponry as currently exercised by the main nuclear weapons states. An arms control approach also helps explain the priorities accorded to non-proliferation and counter-proliferation policies as in the dealing by the nuclear weapons states alleged to be a supposed nuclear aspirant as Iran or such a pariah state as North Korea. Indeed, in mainstream media and political discourse, the challenge of nuclear weaponry is reduced to strengthening, stabilizing, and enforcing the non-proliferation regime, and nuclear disarmament is clearly struck from the existential policy agenda of the nuclear weapons states, while deceptively retained rhetorically as an 'ultimate' goal.[8]

---

[6] *See* strategic literature that views nuclear weapons as usable in contexts other than non-proliferation. *E.g.,* BERNARD BRODIE, STRATEGY IN THE NUCLEAR AGE (1995); HERMAN KAHN, ON THERMONUCLEAR WAR (2007); THOMAS C. SCHELLING, THE STRATEGY OF CONFLICT (1960).

[7] *See* Falk, *supra* note 2, for more extended arguments along these lines.

[8] This interpretation of the acceptance of 'stability' was underscored in the decade of the 1990s when the Cold War was over and the Soviet Union imploded, which established a temporary global setting without

My view is that the endorsement of arms control approaches subtly, perhaps unconsciously, and indirectly substitutes the management of nuclear dangers for their attempted elimination. Such an orientation leaves the world facing unacceptable risks of intended and unintended uses of nuclear weapons for the indefinite future, as well as 'the nuclear apartheid' structure of allowing possession, development, deployment, use and threat doctrine to be placed under the internationally unregulated control of existing nuclear weapons states and prohibiting such prerogatives to all others. Beyond this, it overlooks the cultural and collective legal/ethical/spiritual (normative) costs associated with deterrence strategies that regard retaliatory uses of nuclear weapons as a legal and ethical security policy despite their indiscriminate, toxic, genocidal, catastrophic, and possibly omnicidal impacts on tens of millions of innocent people, with harmful effects lingering long after the event.[9] For reasons noted above, it understates the scope of nuclear dangers to focus only on its military dimensions, which means overlooking the risks associated with nuclear facilities devoted to the production of electricity.

Geopolitical factors are not generally considered in discussions of these issues, but given world order and global security aspects of nuclearism, such an exclusion is misleading. It is notable that geopolitics with respect to nuclearism have the effect of subverting the major legal premise of state-centric world order, namely, the juridical equality of sovereign states.[10] Of course, this formulation in the UN Charter is mendacious language that cannot be reconciled with the P-5 permanent membership and right of veto in the Security Council. A prime ingredient of Westphalian national sovereignty is the unconditional authority of states to determine their own security policy when it comes to self-defense, especially in response to external threats. The irony of the managerial approach is that the two states with the most plausible security justifications for recourse to nuclear deterrence, Iran and North Korea, are the only states under pressure to forgo or renounce all intentions of retaining or acquiring such weaponry.[11] Even worse, this policy of denial is not a collective decision reached through reliance on available procedures at the United Nations. It is a self-serving geopolitical policy articulated by the nuclear weapons states, especially the NATO members of the nuclear club, United States, the United Kingdom, and France, which have assumed for themselves the role of nuclear gatekeepers while keeping their own nuclear use options discretionary and secret. Instead of juridical equality, nuclear weapons policy as a global reality is geopolitically hierarchical and hegemonic.

Admittedly, drawing such a sharp line between arms control and disarmament has several drawbacks. Perhaps, the most important of these is to make the goals of anti-nuclear activism seem unattainable and utopian because of the weak political will present to challenge the nuclear status quo, a political reality that has persisted since 1945 without any further weapons use, this avoidance being widely perceived as the best that can be done. It can be argued in favor of arms control, that some of its measures are inherently valuable from a

---

serious geopolitical and ideological rivalry or balance, and yet US global leadership was silent with respect to exploring denuclearizing options.

[9] Vividly underscored more than forty years ago by E.P. Thompson, *Notes on Exterminism: The Last Stage of Civilization*, NEW LEFT REVIEW, May/June, 1980.

[10] *See* UN Charter, Article 2(1): "The Organization is based on the principle of the sovereign equality of all of its members."

[11] A further observation is the irony that the two states that in different circumstances abandoned nuclear weapons, Ukraine and Libya, were subsequently victimized by foreign military interventions, which arguably would not have occurred if Ukraine had retained its nuclear weapons capability and Libya proceeded to produce such weaponry.

risk reduction perspective, and raise anti-nuclear credibility by demonstrating that concrete steps can be taken to reduce overall risks and costs of nuclearism, that something positive is happening in response to these concerns. Further, the claim of most arms control advocates persists that when and if a more peace-oriented political atmosphere emerges, it would be a simple matter to shift the emphasis of arms control in the direction of a diplomatic process that is dedicated to achieving total nuclear disarmament. On this basis, it would be prudent and feasible to mobilize a political mood that encourages political leaders to seize the moment as the time had arrived to pursue transformative initiatives. In effect, as matters now stand, arms control seems better than nothing, and in this period, it is prudent to obtain what is possible, while maintaining the expectation that at some time under conditions impossible to anticipate, nuclear disarmament would rise to the top of the political agenda.

These expectations, and the supportive reasoning, are persuasive, yet only to a limited extent. I continue to hope that a transformative agenda will at some point (other than in a post-catastrophe context) be supported by an insistent public opinion and acted upon by responsive political leaders of the dominant nuclear weapons states. The experience of the 1990s induces a certain amount of pessimism about waiting for the appropriate moment. After the collapse of the Soviet Union, the conditions seemed right, yet no surge of populist and governmental enthusiasm for nuclear disarmament materialized. This was both disappointing and revealing as to the embeddedness of nuclearism. Despite political developments having undermined the main deterrence rationale for retaining and developing the weaponry had made it seemingly irresponsible to retain such potentially catastrophic weaponry, and yet the Cold War nuclear status quo persisted. My expectation that both leaders and citizens would respond to this historic opportunity to work toward a nuclear-free world was disappointed. Relevant elites of the nuclear weapons states were satisfied with present arrangements, while the public and the Global South was apathetic and complacent. Denuclearization didn't happen, and was not even seriously considered. There was no push from below, and no interest from above. We should all be asking ourselves why such a mood of nuclear complacency prevailed when there seemed so much to gain, including the savings of billions, by working toward an attainable and historic agreement to rid future generations of the fear that somewhere, somehow this infernal weaponry would again produce a catastrophe as it had in Japan in 1945, and to a different degree in Chernobyl and Fukushima subsequently. One part of an explanation is that the nuclear dimension of the militarized bureaucracy, government weapons labs, and private sector in the United States, and elsewhere, is sufficiently influential to inhibit or subvert any concerted political moves to rid the world of nuclear weaponry.

I want to stress the perception that the driving force behind arms control is enhancing the stability of the nuclear environment and saving money on wasteful or excessive weapons innovations or fanciful conflict scenarios. In my view, forgoing certain nuclear innovations and deployments makes nuclear disarmament seem less necessary rather than more attainable. In this regard, arms control falls within the domain of political liberalism, which is itself under attack from neoconservative militarists who regard any international arrangements that purports to reduce risks associated with nuclear weaponry as a snare and delusion. As so understood, most arms control measures are believed not to be in the national security interests of the United States, which must include retaining a *superior* nuclear weapons arsenal as well as a flexible array of nuclear weapons designed for possible threat or use in certain confrontational and combat situations. Other nuclear weapons states may also have strategic uses of these weapons of mass destruction other than security from attack such as regional hegemony, intimidating or destroying regional rivals, maintenance of Great Power status, and achieving greater political space for aggressive policies. In short, arms control is connected in many ways with strategic ambitions other than overall systemic stability, which is one of the reasons to distrust views that posit arms control as the best and safest adjustment to nuclearism. In the setting of nuclear power programs, arguments recently gathering strength beneath the various shadows cast by the Ukraine War and in light of global warming trends is the need for an increased reliance on electricity produced by nuclear reactors. In short, the quest for stability in relation to nuclearism is far from the whole story.

Such a mainstream debate on the pros and cons of arms control needs to be understood as most essentially about the managerial form. Geopolitical hawks consistently favor the *national* management of nuclearism without engendered regulation that would interfere with the pursuit of strategic national interests. Most liberals, in comparison, favor negotiated *international* management arrangements that limit geopolitical options, including the avoidance of expensive nuclear arms races. Arms control liberals also seek to minimize risks of the nuclear status quo, exhibiting their approval for efforts to implementing the non-proliferation regime by force as necessary even if lacking UN authorization. The more idealistic arms controllers feel that success with partial measures would over time build confidence of governments needed to take more ambitious denuclearizing steps in the future.[12] Each of these perspectives is further complicated by nuanced differences in perception and belief.

As suggested, my divergence of views from arms control advocates can to some extent be regarded as complementary rather than posing an either/or choice. I regard it as useful to understand that arms control generally tends to work, at least for the foreseeable future, against rather than in support of nuclear disarmament. I respect the view of some nuclear zero advocates who suggest that while abolition is the primary goal, during the foreseeable it is desirable to do whatever becomes politically feasible by way of reducing risks and costs associated with the existing nuclear arms environment. This outlook may help explain why some of those dedicated to nuclear disarmament are nevertheless reluctant to make the point that while a given arms control measure may be a constructive contribution in some respects, it has the unacknowledged effect of moving the world further from nuclear disarmament rather than closer to it.

Nevertheless, there is considerable room for convergence as between arms control supporters and advocates of the abolition of nuclear weaponry. David Krieger, founder and longtime former President of the Nuclear Age Peace Foundation, basically denies tensions between arms control and disarmament.[13] Krieger's position does not oblige him to regard every arms control measure under consideration as beneficial, nor am I committed to rejecting automatically every arms control measure that comes along. For instance, we would both favor a declaratory No First Use policy either unilaterally undertaken or through a formal agreement among nuclear weapons states, and both favor dealerting measures adopted in relation to deployed weaponry. Contrariwise, we would likely both oppose an international agreement that permitted the development of defense systems that would have the effect of making First Strike Options appear to be a plausible

---

[12] It is a mistake to merge in analysis the NPT, as treaty framework, with the non-proliferation enforcement regime administered under the leadership of the United States. The treaty monitors and verifies adherence, permits withdrawal, and has no provisions for enforcement in the event of non-compliance. The non-proliferation enforcement is a geopolitical tool selectively applied (e.g., Iran and Israel), entails threats and uses of force that are not compatible with international law or the UN Charter.

[13] For comparison of the two positions on the relations between arms control and disarmament, as well as relationship to the NPT, *see* RICHARD FALK & DAVID KRIEGER, PATH TO ZERO: DIALOGUES ON NUCLEAR DANGERS (2016).

preemptive or even preventive option while at the same time claiming to make a rogue surprise attack less likely.

My position insists that those who seek permanent nuclear peace need to understand that the denuclearizing struggle must confront the bipartisan national consensus on these issues in the United States, which has survived without controversy despite the end of the Cold War. The consensus holds that the existing nuclear weapons regime needs to be managed, if possible, in concert by the three NATO nuclear states and never disassembled. The consensus is somewhat split as to who should do the managing, and what should be the role of geopolitics and grand strategy in the overall scheme. It regressively excludes from political imagination any endorsement on principle of nuclear disarmament. The Statement of the United States, the United Kingdom, and France expressing their reasons of these governments for rejection of TPNW makes this clear. The main contention of this Statement is that even after the Cold War, nuclear weapons by way of deterrence continue to enhance national security rather than erode it. By such reasoning, all sovereign states should have a legal entitlement to acquire the weaponry, and hence it even becomes reckless for a government not to become a nuclear weapons state, and thereby withdrawing from the Non-Proliferation Treaty in accord with Article X specifying such a right.

III. THE NORMATIVE AMBIGUITY OF NON-PROLIFERATION AND COUNTER-PROLIFERATION POLICIES

As earlier indicated, the geopolitical essence of the managerial approach is shaped by the nuclear governmental oligarchs rather than by global institutional authority as problematically represented by the United Nations. In other settings, the weakness of community at the global level makes it unrealistic to expect the United Nations to be effective or even influential whenever a policy issue clashes with serious geopolitical interests. This difficulty is compounded by vesting veto power in the governments that happened to be the first five states to acquire nuclear weapons. In other words, when it comes to matters of peace and security, geopolitics was written into the constitutional framework of the UN System, with juridical considerations based on sovereign equality put aside at least so far as the Security Council is concerned.

To achieve a world order bargain, a deal of sort was struck, and incorporated into the text of the NPT. Non-nuclear states would receive the technology needed for what was put forward as a good faith pledge and, as well, Article VI of the treaty obliging the governments of the nuclear weapons states to seek nuclear disarmament through international negotiations, and even more ambitiously, general and complete disarmament.[14] This tradeoff was flawed in conception and even more so in execution. It was flawed because it was based on vague and unmonitored commitments that were almost impossible to interpret, much less implement. It was flawed in practice by selective application of the non-proliferation pledge between states, discriminating in favor of Israel by facilitating its covert acquisition of nuclear weapons, while undertaking an aggressive war in Iraq that was partly justified on counter-proliferation grounds and subsequently relying on irresponsible coercive diplomacy to threaten Iran and North Korea with potentially grave repercussions of military attack if they dared to cross the nuclear threshold.

---

[14] *See* text of Treaty on the Non-Proliferation of Nuclear Weapons, entered into force on March 5, 1970. SUPPLEMENT OF BASIC DOCUMENTS TO INTERNATIONAL LAW AND WORLD ORDER (Burns H. Weston et al. eds., 4th ed. 1990).

The fundamental flaw of the approach taken in the NPT became increasingly evident over time. The nuclear weapons states without exception, yet for diverse reasons, were not interested in pursuing nuclear disarmament as policy objectives. Occasionally, politicians would put forward a genuine belief in nuclear disarmament as did Barack Obama shortly after becoming president in 2009.[15] But it was at best an empty wish that lacked political traction, and at worst a public relations stunt used to gain a propaganda or partisan advantage.

A. Should the NPT Be Repudiated in View of the Flagrant Breach of Article VI by the Nuclear Weapons States?

The issue of non-proliferation is central to my understanding of the challenge of nuclearism.[16] It is central because the establishment of a non-proliferation regime is what has linked geopolitical interests to the retention of nuclear weapons by a small number of countries, above all the five permanent members of the UN Security Council.[17] These weapons states are reluctant to fulfill their part of the treaty bargain that lent an aura of equality to the NPT as negotiated: a pledged obligation not to seek nuclear weaponry in exchange for assistance in developing the non-military potential of nuclear energy and the firm legal commitment to seek nuclear disarmament, and beyond this, to set general and complete disarmament as a goal, that is, coupling the process of denuclearization to demilitarization.

Another important consideration is the distinction between the non-proliferation treaty regime (NPT) and the implementation of the treaty by the de facto geopolitical establishment of a *non-proliferation regime* (NPR) devised by and under the control of the United States, and not the United Nations. Note that the NPT purports, at least, to be based on the formal equality of states, and supposedly relied on a logic of reciprocity and mutual interests with respect to obligations. The non-proliferation regime, in contrast, proceeds from assumptions of inequality, claiming for nuclear weapons states a responsibility for preventing or even reversing proliferation, while imposing no denuclearizing responsibilities on any nuclear weapons state, except possibly North Korea.

In this sense, due to geopolitics, non-proliferation rather than denuclearization becomes the operative manner of partially integrating or normalizing the weaponry with respect to world order. With this background, it seems indicative that the NPT is formally titled

---

[15] *See* Barack Obama speech in Prague containing passage important: "... as a nuclear power, as the only nuclear power to have used a nuclear weapon, the United States has a moral responsibility to act. We cannot succeed in this endeavor alone, but we can lead it, we can start it. So today, I state clearly and with conviction America's commitment to seek the peace and security of a world without nuclear weapons." *See Remarks by President Barack Obama*, THE WHITE HOUSE (Apr. 5, 2009). The contrast with the bland approach of President Joe Biden is striking. *See* his Cover Letter to National Security Strategy document, Oct. 12, 2022, where the treatment of nuclear weapons is limited to reducing risks of nuclear war by arms control measures consistent with deterrent strategy and strengthening 'the global non-proliferation regime.'

[16] *See* ROBERT J. LIFTON & RICHARD FALK, INDEFENSIBLE WEAPONS: THE LEGAL AND POLITICAL CASE AGAINST NUCLEARISM (1982)

[17] This assessment is confirmed by the only notable instance where security specialists associated with the US foreign policy elite seriously considered the pursuit of strategic interests in response to their view that the world was becoming too dangerous as a result of proliferation and that these interests could be better uphold by sustaining military superiority in conventional weaponry. *See* George P. Shultz et al., *A World Free of Nuclear Weapons*, WALL STREET JOURNAL, January 4, 2007; *see* by same authors, *Deterrence in the Age of Nuclear Proliferation*, WALL STREET JOURNAL, Mar. 7, 2011. In effect, removing nuclear weapons from international relations was thought to allow greater freedom to project globally US military superiority.

'Non-proliferation Treaty' rather than the 'Non-proliferation and Disarmament Treaty.' This weighting of the treaty toward non-acquisition alone signaled that geopolitics would be given precedence over international law and global justice, when it came to issues of interpretation and implementation. Until recently, few seem to notice, and even fewer appear to care. By treating non-proliferation as independent from the broader issues of peace and justice, the nuclear policy question is reduced to whether if country X acquires the bomb will the world or region be safer or more dangerous. This kind of reasoning has provided the justification for insisting that Iran demonstrate to the world that it does not possess nuclear weapons, and is not seeking to produce the weaponry despite its technological capacity and the infrastructure of its nuclear program that confers the potentiality. Geopolitical prerogatives authorize the nuclear weapons states to overlook the unlawfulness of threats to the security of these potential proliferators that might justify their temptations to develop a nuclear weapons capability.

Further concerns relate to ignoring the operational deficiencies of the non-proliferation regime in the United States beneath the banner of national nuclear bipartisanship. For one thing, the counter-proliferation regime tacitly authorizes threats and uses of force to carry out its non-proliferation prerogatives. This sets these five states, as well as Israel due to its special relationship with the United States, apart even in relation to remaining three nuclear weapons states for whom the weaponry is more closely connected with specific national policy priorities relating only to their own security, status, and regional influence (India, Pakistan, and North Korea). I believe it is important to clarify these varied unacceptable geopolitical links between nuclear weaponry, non-proliferation, strategic ambitions, world peace, international law, and security. Liberal anti-nuclearists tend not to take notice of these geopolitical dimensions of nuclear policy, and support the non-proliferation regime based on their reasonable assumption that the world becomes that more dangerous whenever a new political actor acquires nuclear weapons. Arguably, in certain situations the acquisition of nuclear weapons may be balancing, as when one state in a configuration possesses the weaponry and the other doesn't, raising risks of use or preemptive efforts to prevent use. The India/Pakistan standoff is illustrative of a pro-nuclearist logic.[18]

As with arms control more generally, the policy issue raised by non-proliferation is complicated, defies any dogmatic view, and cannot be resolved by rational analysis or even by recourse to moral and legal considerations. Other things being equal, any sane person would like to live in a world with as few governments having access to nuclear weapons as possible, but there are a variety of considerations that qualify such a conclusion. How desirable is non-proliferation policy if these other considerations are taken into consideration? Aside from destabilizing conflict patterns, an important limitation of focusing on non-proliferation is a resulting tendency to diminish incentives to seek nuclear disarmament. If the nuclear club can be kept small, it allows the major nuclear weapons states to retain their security options and geopolitical status associated with the possession of the weaponry, as well as strengthens hegemonic control. Non-proliferation imposes on non-nuclear states the prospect of annihilation without any credible means of retaliation, which giving the leading nuclear weapons states a terrifying military option. It is not surprising that the nuclear missions are themselves in violation of international law. Such threats and uses of force have been relied upon to justify attacking and occupying Iraq since 2003 despite the refusal of the UN Security Council to accept the US/UK argument or authorize the undertaking.

---

[18] For an overview of a realist approach to international relations that believes that geopolitics has absorbed the development and possession of nuclear weapons, *see* JOHN J. MEARSHEIMER, THE TRAGEDY OF THE GREAT POWERS (2001).

Since this undertaking could not be validated by reference to self-defense as defined in the UN Charter, Article 51, it must be considered a violation of Article 2 (4) prohibiting recourse to non-defensive force by states.

Enforcement of the NPT regime, if not justifiable as a defensive response to a war of aggression, is a violation of international law, and as such, is itself an act of aggression. After World War II aggressive war was treated as the prime Crime against Peace, and viewed as the most encompassing and severe of international war crimes at the Nuremberg trials. It was also a damaging show of disdain for the authority of the United Nations and the global leadership claimed by the United States, given that authorization was urgently requested yet denied.[19] The same dynamic is at play with regard to Iran at the present time. Threats and sanctions, without any UN authorization, have been directed at Iran, a state that seems at the mercy of geopolitical and regional instability, further accentuated by Donald Trump's irresponsible repudiation of the Joint Comprehensive Plan of Action (JCPOA) agreed upon in 2015 during Obama's presidency. The main conclusion to be reached is that implementing non-proliferation has been achieved at the expense of international law and even the UN Charter. By relying on a one-sided interpretation of the NPT that grants impunity to the nuclear weapons states while selectively imposing punitive measures against non-nuclear states that are alleged to be seeking nuclear weapons, the NPT has reinforced the hegemonic structures of global governance. My impression is that advocates of continuing validity of the NPT arrangement are insensitive to or ignorant of double standards relating to compliance with the NPT. Double standards vitiate the rule of law by treating equals (sovereign states) unequally (geopolitical actors, selective application). The most vivid instances of double standards are flagrant treaty violations over a half century with the material obligation contained in Article VI[20] while insisting on compliance with the pledge of non-nuclear states to forgo the nuclear option unconditionally. A second instance is the absence of any adverse consequences for violating Article VI while selectively implementing by force violations of Article IV.

Geopolitical manipulation is also expressed by way of the selective and discriminatory implementation of the extra-legal NPT regime, concretely in relation to Israel. It seems evident that Israel was actually helped to gain entry to the nuclear club despite its covert means of acquiring the capability, even receiving secret technological assistance from NATO nuclear weapons states.[21] Whether by agreement or choice, Israel has maintained a formal posture of neither admitting nor denying the existence of its weapons arsenal, although it is widely accepted that it possesses a substantial arsenal of nuclear weapons and continues with further development activities.

Geopolitical manipulation is also experienced by countries outside the P-5 in the manner by which they are treated when it comes to nuclear weaponry. What is clear is that the NPR discriminates among states based on their international alignments and size, allowing Israel and India in, while keeping Iraq and Iran out. This discriminatory practice illustrates the tendency of geopolitical rivals to divide the world into friends and enemies

---

[19] *See* RICHARD FALK, THE COSTS OF WAR: INTERNATIONAL LAW, THE UN, AND WORLD ORDER AFTER THE IRAQ WAR (2008).

[20] The text of Article VI: "Each of the Parties to the Treaty undertakes to pursue negotiations in good faith on effective measures relating to cessation of the nuclear arms race at an early date and to nuclear disarmament, and on a treaty on general and complete disarmament under strict and effective international control." For full text of treaty, *see supra* note 14.

[21] SEYMOUR HERSH, THE SAMSON OPTION: ISRAEL'S NUCLEAR ARSENAL & AMERICAN FOREIGN POLICY (1991).

when allocating rights and duties among sovereign states. A secondary explanation of treating differently countries that approach or cross the nuclear threshold is a matter of size as it affects the practicality of implementing the NPR. In other words, geopolitical rather than legal criteria are relied upon to establish and maintain the policy interface between nuclear haves and have-nots, as well as to give ground (as with India, Pakistan, and earlier the Soviet Union and China).

Allowing the NPR selectively to override the treaty text without any attempt at reconciling these two sources of normative order, or even to alter the NPT so that it conforms to the practices of the NPR, is itself expressive of the hegemonic character attaching to counter-proliferation threats and uses of force. As previously suggested, the NPT imposes a clear legal obligation on nuclear weapons states to pursue nuclear disarmament in good faith with an intention to conclude an agreement.[22] The language used by the 14–0 vote, which included the American judge, is suggestive: "There exists an obligation to pursue in good faith and bring to a conclusion negotiations leading to nuclear disarmament in all its aspects under strict and effective international control." The finding in the Advisory Opinion follows closely the wording and spirit of Article VI of the NPT.

These states are parties to the NPT, and yet they have passively accepted the virtual negation of this most fundamental feature of the treaty text. The reciprocal obligation of nuclear weapons states to pursue disarmament undoubtedly explains the initial willingness of most non-nuclear states to become parties to the treaty. We can only speculate as to whether the NPT would have ever come into force without having this reciprocal feature that bound together nuclear and non-nuclear states in an encompassing agreement. The NPT seemed to have the intrinsic merit of seeking to rid the world of nuclear weapons by negotiation while freezing nuclear membership as of 1962. The treaty has been reasonably successful in inhibiting further acquisition of this highly dangerous and legally dubious category of weaponry, while being an under acknowledged failure so far as the pursuit of its reciprocal goal of denuclearization.

In the end, this double standard raises the question as to whether the NPT should be repudiated, or at the very least subjected to sharp criticism by non-nuclear parties. From a legal point of view, the nuclear weapons states appear to have violated material provisions of the treaty, giving non-nuclear parties an option to void the agreement. As matters now stand, the NPT provides a tacit legal rationale for the extra-legal claims put forward by the NPR. Yet the repudiation of the NPT could be interpreted as a green light to acquisition of the weaponry as an insurance policy. In view of such a dilemma, the best response might be a heightened effort to apply the treaty as drafted, especially insisting on compliance with Article VI, and further construed by seeking a second Advisory Opinion from the World Court. Perhaps, the failure of the last two periodic NPT review conferences can be viewed as a partial sign of wakefulness on the part of non-nuclear states, especially in the Global South, that they are no longer apathetic with respect to the hegemonic dimensions of nuclearism.

The 2021 TPNW can be regarded another sort of overdue pushback by the Global South against both the NPT and the NPR as well. It obviously challenges the legality and legitimacy of the geopolitical nuclear apartheid as pertaining to the control of nuclear weaponry by putting forward a treaty seeking a wide-ranging normative prohibition of nuclear weaponry that is intended to become eventually applicable to all states.

---

[22] *See* unanimous finding in 1996 of the International Court of Justice on this point in the Nuclear Weapons Advisory Opinion, *supra* note 4.

Alongside concerns about proliferation is the absence of overt negative response to the maneuvers of geopolitics as these bear on the sovereign right of states to uphold their security and to exercise their inherent right of self-defense. Actually, Iran and North Korea have far more reasonable security arguments for acquiring nuclear weapons than do any of the other members of the nuclear weapons club. This recognition does not justify acquiring the weaponry, but it helps explain the reasonableness of their behavior as compared to the examples being set by leading states. Such vulnerable states are faced with defending their territorial sovereignty against coercive diplomacy and possible interventions and encroachments on their security carried out and promoted by political actors with vastly superior military forces at their disposal, and in some of these instances allied with nuclear weapons states. If ever a good argument for a posture of nuclear deterrence existed, it is in relation to a state under attack by more powerful, hostile adversaries.

By this pronounced unwillingness of the NPR to allow certain states to determine their own security needs if it undermines efforts to prevent further proliferation, unaccountable and often irresponsible geopolitical managers of the NPR are effectively given the authority to override national security policy of these weaker states. For instance, Iran is threatened with military attack if it crosses certain technological thresholds. As significant, geopolitical forces have made no effort to reassure Iran with respect to its future security or to replace a non-proliferation approach by pushing for the establishment of a Middle East Nuclear Free Zone. There was no response by the West to Iran's moderate president, Hassan Rouhani, who presented a peace plan for the Persian Gulf in 2019 at the UN General Assembly, given the name Hormuz Peace Endeavor with a fitting acronym: HOPE.

The example of Libya, and more recently Ukraine, haunts this topic of forgoing the nuclear weapons option, as many believe that if Muammar Qaddafi had not abandoned plans to acquire nuclear weapons, he would be alive today. Similarly, if Saddam Hussein had really possessed a stockpile of weapons of mass destruction, many believe that Iraq would never have been attacked in 2003. In other words, nuclear deterrence is possibly a more effective approach to national security if invoked by relatively weaker nuclear states. The NPR offers no compensatory steps to offset security concerns of such obviously vulnerable states as Iran beyond their rather tenuous conditional willingness to remove sanctions, and thus it is not surprising that non-proliferation is tied to militarism.

It is also notable that the most prominent instance in which hawkish foreign policy establishment figures advocated nuclear disarmament was in reaction to their skepticism about the viability of the NPR in containing future proliferation.[23] In effect, these geopolitically oriented political figures, influential former holders of high-profile security positions, favored nuclear disarmament not because of any moral scruples or fear of an impending apocalypse, but because of their worries that the NPR was breaking down and this would imperil the hegemonic edge enjoyed by US foreign policy. In effect, it was their belief that further proliferation would likely occur, and make it so much more difficult to achieve geopolitical political goals that led them to uncharacteristically cast themselves as advocates of phased denuclearization as an altered grand strategy for the United States. They did this in the belief that the West would enjoy conventional military dominance in a denuclearizing world through their retention of far superior non-nuclear capabilities, which were in any event more usable in the course of foreign policy if there seemed to be no risk of an unwanted escalation above the nuclear threshold. I believe these complexities need to be discussed, while disarmament proponents tend to believe that such issues are often

---

[23] *See* Shultz et al., *supra* note 17.

'academic' distractions that fail to keep the proper focus on what is wrong about the weaponry and how to get rid of the weapons before they get rid of humanity.

B. Can We Have Stage III Nuclear Disarmament Without Non-Nuclear Demilitarization?

A final issue touched upon is whether a credible posture toward a disarmament process for nuclear weapons must at some stage also address issues relating to non-nuclear demilitarization, and indeed war itself. Arms control oriented thinkers stress the distinctive policy priorities arising from the acute dangers posed by nuclear war, excluding other considerations. Those that favor nuclear disarmament stress the need to remove the obstacles to nuclear disarmament created by existing levels of militarism as well as by the role of war in international relations and as embedded in the political realist mentality that continues to regulate the behavior of national leaders.

There is a practical argument about inducing the weaker nuclear states to enter into a treaty framework that leaves them more vulnerable after giving up their arsenal of nuclear weapons. The governments of such states might fear nuclear disarmament to the extent that their leaders believe that exposure to hostile states wielding superior conventional weaponry would embolden their enemies. Such beliefs discourage efforts to tamper with the nuclear status quo. Such security-minded states likely include Pakistan, Israel, North Korea, and possibly India (in relation to China as well as Pakistan), especially in light of the Libyan and Ukrainian experience in ending their nuclear weapons programs.

As a nuclear disarmament process deepened, there would be more attention given to a denuclearizing security environment. To achieve the goal of total abolition, the only acceptable outcome of a denuclearizing process, parallel steps would need to be taken to reduce non-defensive armaments, which has become more difficult as a result of the emergence, rapid spread, and widespread use of attack drones and accurate long-range missile technology.

IV. CONCLUDING NOTE

Some anti-nuclear moderates believe that the most promising way to reach a world without nuclear weapons is to convince society that fears of a nuclear war are well-founded, that the results of a war fought with nuclear weapons would be unimaginably horrible in its devastation and aftermath, and that phased, verified nuclear disarmament offers a safer and more humane alternative that would give permanent nuclear peace its best chance.[24]

I do not agree. In contrast, I am convinced that to move forward toward total nuclear disarmament we need to take full account of the obstacles, frictions, and nuances, explaining why the anti-nuclear movement has so far failed to challenge effectively the nuclear weapons establishment. This position is open to criticism as being overly concerned with obstacles, and less focused on issues of morality, prudence, political action, and war prevention (relating to the implicit arms control claim that nuclear deterrence has prevented all major wars for more than 75 years, including those that might have acted aggressively had nuclear weapons not existed).

In the end, I think we need to continue to have dialogues between those anti-nuclearists who are uncritical about the friction between pursuing arms control and disarmament and

---

[24] *See* DANIEL ELLSBERG, THE DOOMSDAY MACHINE: CONFESSIONS OF A NUCLEAR WAR PLANNER (2017).

those who believe that their antagonisms must be addressed. It remains crucial to keep mobilizing moral outrage as the foundation for political action. By contrast, I believe that anti-nuclearism will not get far until it clarifies the tensions between seeking arms control and favoring nuclear disarmament. It seems a serious confusion to suppose that arms control is a halfway house and a serious moral and political failure not to critique the non-proliferation regime that sustains nuclear apartheid, which is self-servingly asserted to be the only path to global security.[25]

My assessment of the arms control/disarmament interface can be summarized in a series of propositions:

-- that it is morally, legally, politically, and prudentially imperative to rid the world of nuclear weaponry through a verified nuclear disarmament treaty and accompanying implementation regime, and this should be regarded as the paramount goal of anti-nuclearism, taking precedence over other goals;

-- that arms control approaches must be explicitly understood as *managing* nuclear weapons, which is generally not consistent with achieving the paramount goal, and may actually make the goal of total nuclear disarmament less attainable;

-- that the two top priorities of the managerial approach to nuclear weaponry are to prevent a major war and to prevent further proliferation of nuclear weaponry to additional sovereign states, and especially to those potential nuclear weapons states that have adversary relationship to regional and global geopolitical regimes;

-- that despite the NPT, avoiding further proliferation of nuclear weaponry requires reliance on implementation by geopolitical regimes, by threats, and if necessary, by military action;

-- that the coercive maintenance of non-proliferation has produced a structure of nuclear apartheid, which is inconsistent with the world order premise of the equality of sovereign states and will be resisted from time to time by states whose security is under threat or who harbor hegemonic ambitions;

-- that the final stages in any disarmament process must also address global militarism in general and reduce non-nuclear military capabilities;

-- that overcoming current high levels of complacency about the risks and effects of a nuclear war will depend on civil society activism and a more peace literate public opinion, and will not be achieved by normal diplomacy until anti-nuclear pressures mount well beyond what exists today.

---

[25] *See* George W. Bush, *National Security Strategy of the United States of America*, THE WHITE HOUSE (2002), an important interpretation of global security that neglects even to acknowledge nuclear disarmament as a desirable goal.

PART

1

ARTICLES

The Contribution of the UN Treaty Bodies to Business and Human Rights

BY SHANE DARCY*

Abstract

The relationship between business and human rights has been the subject of considerable attention within the UN human rights system. The treaty monitoring bodies have played an important but insufficiently explored role in this context. This article discusses the contribution of the treaty bodies to business and human rights and argues for a deeper engagement by the treaty bodies in this sphere. It examines their influence on the development of the UN Guiding Principles and explores recent developments, including the adoption of specialised general comments. It addresses divergences between the treaty bodies' understanding of state obligations and private sector responsibilities compared with those articulated in the UN Guiding Principles. The article reflects on the potential future contribution of the treaty bodies against the backdrop of continued but faltering efforts to implement the Guiding Principles at the national level and to develop a new treaty on business and human rights.

I. INTRODUCTION

Business and human rights has become a key concern within the human rights machinery of the United Nations. The endorsement of the UN Guiding Principles on Business and Human Rights by the Human Rights Council in 2011 has without question served to give greater prominence to the human rights issues raised by business activities within the international human rights system.[1] Since that time, business and human rights has become

---

* Deputy Director, Irish Centre for Human Rights, School of Law, University of Galway (shane.darcy@ universityofgalway.ie).

[1] Human Rights Council, *Guiding Principles on Business and Human Rights: Implementing the United Nations "Protect, Respect and Remedy" Framework*, A/HRC/17/31 (Mar. 21, 2011).

Shane Darcy, *The Contribution of the UN Treaty Bodies to Business and Human Rights* In: *The Global Community Yearbook of International Law and Jurisprudence 2022*. Edited by: Giuliana Ziccardi Capaldo, Oxford University Press. © Oxford University Press 2023.
DOI: 10.1093/oso/9780197752265.003.0004

established as a field of scholarly research, a prominent theme of human rights advocacy and activism, an area of national and transnational litigation, and a growing aspect of the work of various international and regional intergovernmental organisations. While the UN Guiding Principles, and the work of their chief architect, the late John Ruggie, as UN Special Representative to the Secretary General on the issue of human rights and transnational corporations and other business enterprises, undoubtedly generated the impetus for this surge of interest and activity, the need to address the relationship between business and human rights has long been recognised and been the subject of considerable attention within the United Nations.[2] The treaty monitoring bodies of the UN human rights system have played an important but insufficiently explored role in this context primarily through their articulation of states' human rights obligations regarding the private sector. The treaty bodies have addressed core issues at the heart of business and human rights prior to the adoption of the UN Guiding Principles and have continued to do so to an even greater degree since. To describe the Guiding Principles as "the end of the beginning," as Ruggie did,[3] downplays in a sense the work of the treaty bodies and other initiatives that went beforehand.

This article explores the contribution of the UN human rights treaty monitoring bodies to business and human rights and argues for a deeper engagement by the treaty bodies in this sphere. Section II examines their initial engagement with human rights concerns regarding harmful corporate activity, before tracking their influence on the work of the UN Special Representative. As will be discussed, Ruggie was able to draw on the treaty bodies' general comments and concluding observations in designing the pillars of the Guiding Principles. General comments and recommendations in particular provide an important distillation of the interpretative views of the treaty bodies on thematic issues and the substance of particular rights.[4] While not formally of a binding legal nature, they can be considered authoritative and are not to be lightly dismissed.[5] General comments and recommendations guide the work of the treaty bodies themselves, are applied by courts and civil society organisations, and can influence the application of relevant treaties by states parties, notwithstanding that some states have taken issue with the understandings of the treaty bodies,[6] including in the realm of business and human rights.

The occasionally narrow approach adopted by Ruggie in the Guiding Principles was at times at odds with the views of the treaty bodies. As explored in section III, the treaty bodies have either consciously or by default embraced a differing understanding of the scope and content of obligations of states under relevant treaties regarding business and human rights compared with the Guiding Principles. This is particularly the case with regard to extraterritorial human rights obligations. In analysing the treaty body developments

---

[2] *See* NADIA BERNAZ, BUSINESS AND HUMAN RIGHTS: HISTORY, LAW AND POLICY—BRIDGING THE ACCOUNTABILITY GAP 163–208 (2017); Florian Wettstein, *The History of 'Business and Human Rights' and Its Relationship with Corporate Social Responsibility*, *in* RESEARCH HANDBOOK ON HUMAN RIGHTS AND BUSINESS 23 (Surya Deva & David Birchall eds., 2020).

[3] UN Guiding Principles on Business and Human Rights, *supra* note 1, at 5.

[4] *See, e.g.,* Helen Keller & Leena Grover, *General Comments of the Human Rights Committee and Their Legitimacy*, *in* UN HUMAN RIGHTS TREATY BODIES: LAW AND LEGITIMACY 116 (Helen Keller & Geir Ulfstein eds., 2012).

[5] *Id.*, at 128–133.

[6] *See* Birgit Schlütter, *Aspects of Human Rights Treaty Interpretation by the UN Treaty Bodies*, *in* Keller & Ulfstein, *supra* note 4, at 261, 289–292; Kirsten Mechlem, *Treaty Bodies and the Interpretation of Human Rights*, 42(3) VANDERBILT JOURNAL OF TRANSNATIONAL LAW 950 (2009) 926–930.

since the endorsement of the Guiding Principles by the Human Rights Council in 2011, section III also explores these potential divergences. It is evident that the treaty bodies have been able to go beyond the generality of the UN Guiding Principles and examine specific forms of corporate human rights abuse in particular countries, as well as elaborating upon human rights obligations of relevance to the treaties they monitor. As will be discussed, the *acquis* of rights, particularly as they relate to certain persons or groups protected across the nine core treaties and additional protocols goes beyond the International Bill of Rights which is drawn on in the Guiding Principles.[7]

The potential future contribution of the treaty bodies is explored in section IV, against the backdrop of continued efforts to implement the UN Guiding Principles at the national level and to develop a new treaty on business and human rights at the international level. It is argued that with the treaty process in a seeming state of stasis, the existing treaty monitoring system could be better harnessed to meet some of the objectives of those advocating for a binding business and human rights instrument. Treaty bodies can also contribute to furthering implementation of the Guiding Principles, and perhaps even contribute to addressing their limitations where possible. The treaty bodies provide a well-established mechanism for regular expert oversight of and engagement with states regarding their human rights obligations and they invariably contribute to the progressive development of international human rights law in their activities.[8] In limited instances, they may even provide access to remedies for victims of corporate human rights harms insufficiently addressed by states.

Deepening the engagement with business and human rights by the treaty bodies in a coherent, consistent, and progressive manner may yield valuable benefits. Efforts aimed at the domestic implementation of the UN Guiding Principles and the development of a new international treaty on business and human rights could be supplemented by greater attention to the treaty bodies as a means for further elaboration of relevant standards and for potential remediation of human rights violations arising from the activities of business enterprises. In a world of limited enforcement options at the international level, such bodies should be engaged and strengthened where possible.

The contribution of all nine of the UN treaty monitoring bodies is considered in this article, notwithstanding their differing ages and standing amongst states.[9] The level of engagement with business and human rights has varied amongst them, with the Committee

---

[7] UN Guiding Principles on Business and Human Rights, *supra* note 1, at 13–14.

[8] *See generally* THE UNITED NATIONS AND HUMAN RIGHTS: A CRITICAL APPRAISAL 309–664 (Philip Alston & Frederic Megrét eds., 2d ed. 2020).

[9] The nine treaty bodies are the Committee on the Elimination of Racial Discrimination (CERD), the Human Rights Committee (HRC), the Committee on Economic, Social and Cultural Rights (CESCR), the Committee on Migrant Workers (CMW), the Committee on the Elimination of Discrimination Against Women (CEDAW), the Committee on the Rights of the Child (CRC), the Committee Against Torture (CAT), the Committee on the Rights of Persons with Disabilities (CRPD) and the Committee on Enforced Disappearances (CED). At the time of writing, the number of States which are parties to the core human rights treaties is as follows: Convention on the Elimination of All Forms of Racial Discrimination (182); International Covenant on Civil and Political Rights (173), International Covenant on Economic, Social and Cultural Rights (171), Convention on the Elimination of All Forms of Discrimination Against Women (189); Convention Against Torture and Other Cruel, Inhuman or Degrading Treatment or Punishment (173); Convention on the Rights of the Child (196); International Convention on the Protection of the Rights of All Migrant Workers and Members of Their Families (58); International Convention on the Rights of Persons with Disabilities (186); International Convention for the Protection of All Persons from Enforced Disappearance (71). *See* https://treaties.un.org/.

on Economic, Social and Cultural Rights and the Committee on the Rights of the Child having been particularly active in this realm. Most of the treaty bodies have contributed to business and human rights in some way, and those that may seem less relevant because of their narrower foci, such as on torture or enforced disappearances, are not to be discounted, given that "business enterprises can have an impact on virtually the entire spectrum of internationally recognised human rights."[10] While reference will also be made to a number of UN Charter–based bodies, the article will concentrate in the main on the contribution to business and human rights of the UN treaty monitoring bodies. The former, as well as certain regional human rights bodies, have also played significant roles in developing and advancing business and human rights,[11] but the treaty bodies occupy a unique and influential position and have yet to be exploited to their full potential in the context of business and human rights.

II. THE PATH TO THE UN GUIDING PRINCIPLES ON BUSINESS AND HUMAN RIGHTS

The concern of both the treaty and Charter-based human rights bodies of the United Nations with the impact of business activities on human rights, particularly around the turn of the millennium at a time of marked growth in privatisation, market liberalisation, and growing corporate power, prompted various pioneering efforts on their part. Drawing on the substance of relevant human rights treaties, the treaty bodies elaborated on the duty to protect human rights from private actors, including business enterprises, while within the Charter bodies, there were initiatives to develop human rights standards applicable to corporations, as well as the institutional structure which led to the UN Guiding Principles. Previous and parallel efforts within the United Nations, such as the work of the UN Centre for Transnational Corporations and the Global Compact, as well as the promulgation of soft law instruments by the Organisation for Economic Cooperation and Development and the International Labour Organisation, emphasised the widespread acceptance of the potentially harmful nature of business activities, albeit with differing approaches as to how to address the matter.[12]

A. Laying the Foundations

The treaty bodies have long emphasised that while international human rights law is primarily addressed to states, it recognises that harm to human rights emanate not only from public authorities, but also from private bodies, and that states have a duty to protect people from such harm. Some treaties are explicit on this. The International Convention for the Elimination of All Forms of Racial Discrimination (ICERD), for example, obliges states

---

[10] UN Guiding Principles on Business and Human Rights, *supra* note 1, at 13.

[11] *See, e.g.,* Inter-American Commission on Human Rights, *Business and Human Rights: Inter-American Standards,* OEA/Ser.L/V/II, CIDH/REDESCA/INF.1/19 (2019).

[12] *See* Surya Deva, *The UN Guiding Principles on Business and Human Rights and Its Predecessors; Progress at a Snail's Pace?, in* ILIAS BANTEKAS & MICHAEL ASHLEY STEIN, THE CAMBRIDGE COMPANION TO BUSINESS & HUMAN RIGHTS LAW 145 (2021); Andreas Rasche, *The UN Global Compact and the OECD Guidelines for Multinational Enterprises and their Enforcement Mechanism, in* BANTEKAS & STEIN 191; Khalil Hamdani & Lorraine Ruffing, *Lessons from the UN Centre on Transnational Corporations for the Current Treaty Initiative, in* SURYA DEVA & DAVID BILCHITZ, HUMAN RIGHTS OBLIGATIONS OF BUSINESS: BEYOND THE CORPORATE RESPONSIBILITY TO RESPECT? 27 (2017); BERNAZ, *supra* note 2, at 164–176, 196–203.

parties to prohibit and bring to an end racial discrimination "by any persons, group or organization."[13] The Convention on the Elimination of All Forms of Discrimination Against Women requires parties to eliminate discrimination against women "by any person, organization or enterprise."[14] In the first communication under Article 14 of ICERD, the Committee on the Elimination of Racial Discrimination (CERD) found a violation arising from discrimination against the complainant by a private company.[15] As the Committee observed in General Recommendation 20, "[t]o the extent that private institutions influence the exercise of rights or the availability of opportunities, the state party must ensure that the result has neither the purpose nor the effect of creating or perpetuating racial discrimination."[16] The Committee on the Elimination of Discrimination Against Women (CEDAW) has elaborated that "[u]nder general international law and specific human rights covenants, states may also be responsible for private acts if they fail to act with due diligence to prevent violations of rights or to investigate and punish acts of violence, and for providing compensation."[17]

Notwithstanding the absence of such explicit references to the private sector in their treaties, the Human Rights Committee (HRC) and the Committee on Economic, Social and Cultural Rights (CESCR) have also elaborated on the state duty to protect human rights in relation to the private sector. This duty forms the basis of the first pillar of the subsequently adopted UN Guiding Principles. Prior to then, the treaty bodies had referred specifically to business enterprises in this context and touched on a range of issues, some of which, such as the scope of extraterritorial obligations and the question of direct obligations for companies, would go on to feature centrally in debates during and subsequent to the development of the Guiding Principles.

In General Comment 16, the Human Rights Committee explained that the protection of the right to privacy must be guaranteed against interferences and attacks "whether they emanate from state authorities or from natural or legal persons."[18] The gathering and holding of personal information must be regulated by law, whether done by "public authorities or private individuals or bodies."[19] The Human Rights Committee also found that the obligation of states parties to uphold the prohibition of torture and cruel, inhuman or degrading treatment or punishment was relevant in the private sphere, while the requirement of humane treatment of those deprived of their liberty was applicable in the context of private institutions.[20] In General Comment 28 concerning equality under Article 3 of the

---

[13] International Convention for the Elimination of All Forms of Racial Discrimination (1966), 660 UNTS 195, entered into force 4 January 1969, Article 2(1)(d).

[14] Convention on the Elimination of All Forms of Discrimination Against Women (1979), 1249 UNTS 13, entered into force Sept. 3, 1981, Article 2(e).

[15] *Yilmaz-Dogan v. Netherlands*, Communication No. 1/1984, CERD/C/36/D/1/1984 (Aug. 10, 1988). *See also Ziad Ben Ahmed Habassi v. Denmark*, Communication No. 10/1997, Denmark, CERD/C/54/D/10/1997 (Apr. 6, 1999).

[16] CERD, *General Recommendation No. 20 on article 5 of the Convention*, Forty-Eighth session, reprinted in A/51/18, 124 (1996), para. 5.

[17] CEDAW, *General Recommendation No. 19: Violence Against Women*, Eleventh Session, reprinted in A/47/38, 1 (1992), para. 9.

[18] HRC, *General Comment No. 16: Article 17 (Right to privacy)*, Thirty-second session (1988), para. 1.

[19] *Id.*, at para. 10.

[20] HRC, *General Comment 20: Article 7 (Prohibition of torture, or other cruel, inhuman or degrading treatment or punishment)*, Forty-fourth session (1992), para. 2; HRC, *General Comment 21: Article 10 (Humane treatment of persons deprived of their liberty)*, Forty-fourth session (1992), para. 2.

Covenant, the Committee again noted its relevance "in the public and the private sector," giving the example of how employers requesting a pregnancy test before hiring would be violating women's privacy.[21] States parties were requested to implement and report on measures to eliminate discrimination, such as those "prohibiting discrimination by private actors in areas such as employment, education, political activities and the provision of accommodation, goods and services."[22]

The Committee on Economic, Social and Cultural Rights paid particular attention to the obligations of states parties towards businesses in its general comments concerning the rights to food and water. "As part of their obligations to protect people's resource base for food," the Committee stated in General Comment 12, "States parties should take appropriate steps to ensure that activities of the private business sector and civil society are in conformity with the right to food."[23] Conscious of the legal nature of human rights obligations, the Committee also elaborated that:

> While only States are parties to the Covenant and are thus ultimately accountable for compliance with it, all members of society individuals, families, local communities, non-governmental organizations, civil society organizations, as well as the private business sector have responsibilities in the realization of the right to adequate food. The State should provide an environment that facilitates implementation of these responsibilities. The private business sector—national and transnational—should pursue its activities within the framework of a code of conduct conducive to respect of the right to adequate food, agreed upon jointly with the Government and civil society.[24]

The Committee not only emphasised how the state duty to protect human rights required measures by states vis-à-vis private actors to ensure protection of the right to food, but also spoke of the responsibilities of such actors themselves. And in the case of the business sector, it referred explicitly to both its national and transnational iterations, reflecting the increasing attention of the time to the harmful impacts of certain activities of multinational corporations in the context of globalization.[25]

In General Comment 14 on the right to health, CESCR repeated almost verbatim its position regarding the ultimate duties of states parties and the responsibilities of private actors.[26] States parties should "take appropriate steps to ensure that the private business sector and civil society are aware of, and consider the importance of, the right to health in pursuing their activities."[27] The Committee on the Rights of the Child (CRC)

---

[21] HRC, *General Comment No. 28: Article 3 (The equality of rights between men and women)*, Sixty-eighth session, HRI/GEN/1/Rev.9 (Vol. I) (2000), paras. 4, 20.

[22] *Id.*, at paras. 20, 31.

[23] CESCR, *General Comment No, 12: the right to adequate food (art. 11)*, E/C.12/1999/5 (May 12, 1999), para. 27.

[24] *Id.*, at para. 20.

[25] *See* Statement by the Committee on Economic, Social and Cultural Rights, *Globalization and Economic Social and Cultural Rights* (May 1999); NAOMI KLEIN, NO LOGO (1999); HUMAN RIGHTS WATCH, THE OGONI CRISIS: A CASE-STUDY OF MILITARY REPRESSION IN SOUTHEASTERN NIGERIA (July 1, 1995).

[26] CESCR, *General Comment No. 14: the right to the highest attainable standard of health (article 12)*, E/C.12/2000/4 (Aug. 11, 2000), para. 42.

[27] *Id.*, at para. 55. *See also* CESCR, *General Comment No. 15: The right to water*, E/C.12/2002.11 (2002), para. 49.

in turn expressed its agreement with the view put forward by CESCR concerning states' duties and non-state actors' responsibilities.[28] It considered that the Convention on the Rights of the Child created "indirect obligations" for non-state service providers.[29] The CRC went so far as to issue specific recommendations to such entities, calling on them to "respect the principles and provisions" of the Convention.[30] The CESCR also broke new ground in General Comment 15 on the right to water by articulating extraterritorial obligations for states parties, albeit in somewhat guarded language:

> Steps should be taken by States parties to prevent their own citizens and companies from violating the right to water of individuals and communities in other countries. Where States parties can take steps to influence other third parties to respect the right, through legal or political means, such steps should be taken in accordance with the Charter of the United Nations and applicable international law.[31]

As will be discussed in the next section, this issue proved contentious during the elaboration of the Guiding Principles, and continues to be so.[32]

The picture which emerges from this brief survey of the work of the treaty bodies prior to the establishment of Ruggie's mandate is of a clear recognition of the impact on human rights of business activities and a pioneering articulation of the obligations of states in this respect. Regarding the latter, the CESCR had stated in relation to the right to water that "[t]he obligation to *protect* requires State parties to prevent third parties from interfering in any way with the enjoyment of the right to water."[33] Third parties, the Committee expressly put it, include corporations.[34] In the year preceding the appointment of Ruggie as Special Representative to the Secretary-General on the issue of human rights and transnational corporations and other business enterprises, the Human Rights Committee explained what the obligation of state parties might require in relation to private actors:

> There may be circumstances in which a failure to ensure Covenant rights as required by article 2 would give rise to violations by States Parties of those rights, as a result of States Parties' permitting or failing to take appropriate measures or to exercise due diligence to prevent, punish, investigate or redress the harm caused by such acts by private persons or entities.[35]

---

[28] CRC, *General Comment No. 5: General measures of implementation of the Convention on the Rights of the Child (arts. 4, 42 and 44, para. 6)*, CRC/GC/2003/5 (2003), para. 56.

[29] *Id.,* at para. 43.

[30] CRC, *Day of General Discussion: "The private sector as service provider and its role in implementing child rights,"* Report on the Thirty-First Session, CRC/C/121 (Dec. 11, 2002), para. 653.

[31] CESCR, *General Comment 15, supra* note 27, para. 33.

[32] *See, e.g.,* Robert McCorquodale & Penelope Simons, *Responsibility Beyond Borders: State Responsibility for Extraterritorial Violations by Corporations of International Human Rights Law,* 70(4) Modern Law Review 598 (2007); Claire Methven O'Brien, *The Home State Duty to Regulate the Human Rights Impacts of TNCs Abroad: A Rebuttal,* 3(1) Business and Human Rights Journal 47 (2018).

[33] CESCR, *General Comment 15, supra* note 27, para. 23 (original emphasis).

[34] *Id.*

[35] HRC, *General Comment No. 31: The nature of the general legal obligation imposed on state parties to the Covenant,* CCPR/C/21/Rev.1/Add.13 (May 26, 2004), para. 8.

Treaty bodies also referred to specific business sectors, such as hospitality and the media, as being particularly relevant in relation to certain human rights concerns.[36] During this period, as Andrew Clapham has summarised, the treaty bodies "managed to develop simultaneously the primary obligations of states to protect individuals from infringements by non-state actors, and to give some guidance as to what is expected from non-state actors in the context of these different treaties."[37] These achievements laid the foundation for subsequent efforts concerning business and human rights at the United Nations.

B. Influencing the Ruggie Mandate

The Charter-based human rights bodies were similarly engaged with business and human rights prior to the establishment of the mandate of the Special Representative to the Secretary General on the issue of human rights and transnational corporations and other business enterprises in 2005. The Sub-Commission on the Protection and Promotion of Human Rights was particularly active, establishing a sessional working group on the "working methods and activities of transnational corporations" in 1998 and adopting the "Norms on the responsibilities of transnational corporations and other business enterprises with regard to human rights" in 2003.[38] David Weissbrodt, who was a member of the Working Group, had put forward "principles relating to human rights conduct of companies" in 2000 and was invited by the working group to elaborate further on their content, while Asbjørn Eide was requested to prepare a working paper examining procedures for implementing human rights standards for companies.[39] Both were asked to consult with relevant organs in doing so, including the treaty bodies.[40] Eide, as Special Rapporteur on the right to food, had devised the respect, protect, and fulfil schema in 1987.[41] In relation to business and human rights, he observed the differing obligations of home and host states in this context, and how for the latter, "the capacity and sometimes the will to control the activities of [transnational corporations] properly was lacking."[42]

Weissbrodt's efforts concentrated on the development of "legally binding standards,"[43] culminating in the Sub-Commission's adopting of the draft Norms in 2003. The

---

[36] CERD, *General Recommendation 30: discrimination against non-citizens*, CERD/C/64/Misc.11/rev.3 (2004), paras. 12 and 38.

[37] ANDREW CLAPHAM, HUMAN RIGHTS OBLIGATIONS OF NON-STATE ACTORS 319 (2006).

[38] Sub-Commission on Prevention of Discrimination and Protection of Minorities, Resolution 1998/8 (Aug. 20, 1998); *Report of the Sub-Commission on the Protection and Promotion of Human Rights on its Fifty-second Session*, E/CN.4/2001/2, E/CN.4/Sub.2/2000/46 (Nov. 23, 2000), 76; Sub-Commission on the Protection and Promotion of Human Rights, *Norms on the responsibilities of transnational corporations and other business enterprises with regard to human rights*, E/CN.4/Sub.2/2003/12/Rev.2 (Aug. 26, 2003).

[39] *Report of the sessional working group on the "working methods and activities of transnational corporations"*, E/CN.4/Sub.2/2000/12 (Aug. 28, 2000), paras. 10, 61.

[40] *Id.*, at para. 61.

[41] *Report on the right to adequate food as a human right submitted by Mr. Asbjørn Eide, Special Rapporteur*, E/CN.4/Sub.2/1987/23 (July 7, 1987), paras. 66–69. See also CESCR, *General Comment 12, supra* note 23, at para. 15; CESCR, *General Comment No. 13: the right to education*, E/C.12/1999/10 (Dec. 8, 1999), para. 46; CESCR, *General Comment 14, supra* note 26, at para. 33.

[42] *Report of the sessional working group on the working methods and activities of transnational corporations on its third session*, E/CN/4/Sub.2/2001/9 (Aug. 14, 2001), para. 21. See also Asbjørn Eide, "Corporations, States and Human Rights: A Note on Responsibilities and Procedures for Implementation and Compliance," E/CN.4/Sub.2/WG.2/WP.2 (2001).

[43] *Sessional working group on the working methods and activities of transnational corporations, supra* note 42, at para. 24.

Sub-Commission transmitted the norms to the Commission on Human Rights, although the latter Commission set the proposed instrument aside and proceeded instead with the establishment of Ruggie's mandate. It bears noting for present purposes, however, that the influence of the treaty bodies on the preparation of the Norms is evident. The published commentary on Norms on the human rights responsibilities of transnational corporations and other business enterprises referred not only to specific treaty articles, but also to several CESCR and HRC general comments.[44] A role for the treaty bodies in monitoring implementation was also envisaged, as well as the further elaboration of standards through "the adoption of general comments and recommendations interpreting treaty obligations."[45] Treaty bodies could draw on the Norms "to receive communications about governments that have failed to take effective action in response to business abuses under the respective treaties."[46]

The response of the Commission on Human Rights to the draft Norms was hostile. While expressing its appreciation to the Sub-Commission for its work on elaborating the draft Norms, it did not undertake any action for their advancement and instead asked the High Commissioner for Human Rights to compile a report on the scope and legal status of existing standards and initiatives on business and human rights.[47] Moreover, the Commission said that the Sub-Commission's proposed instrument "has not been requested by the Commission and, as a draft proposal, has no legal standing, and that the Sub-Commission should not perform any monitoring function in this regard."[48] The High Commissioner's report noted the divided opinion on the draft Norms, but recommended their further consideration. It also asked whether a UN statement might be adopted to, *inter alia*, "assist treaty bodies in the process of constructive dialogue with States parties to human rights treaties by identifying with clarity the requirements on States to protect human rights from the actions of third parties."[49]

The Commission on Human Rights chose a different route, requesting in 2005 that the Secretary-General of the United Nations appoint a special representative on the issue of human rights and transnational corporations and other business enterprises.[50] The Special Representative was tasked with identifying and clarifying "standards of corporate responsibility and accountability for transnational corporations and other business enterprises with regard to human rights," as well as elaborating on the role of states "in effectively regulating and adjudicating the role of transnational corporations and other business enterprises with regard to human rights."[51] The resolution also instructed the office holder to consult closely with "all stakeholders."[52] Although there was no explicit reference to the treaty bodies,

---

[44] Sub-Commission on the Protection and Promotion of Human Rights, *supra* note 38, at 14.

[45] *Id.*, at 18.

[46] David Weissbrodt & Muria Kruger, *Norms on the Responsibilities of Transnational Corporations and Other Business Enterprises with regard to Human Rights*, 97 AMERICAN JOURNAL OF INTERNATIONAL LAW 901, 917 (2003).

[47] Commission on Human Rights, *Responsibilities of transnational corporations and related business enterprises with regard to human rights*, Decision 2004/116 (Apr. 20, 2004).

[48] *Id. See further* David Kinley & Rachel Chamber, *The UN Human Rights Norms for Corporations: The Private Implications of Public International Law* 6(3) HUMAN RIGHTS LAW REVIEW 447 (2006).

[49] *Report of the United Nations High Commissioner on Human Rights on the responsibilities of transnational corporations and related business enterprises with regard to human rights*, E/CN.4/2005/91 (Feb. 15, 2005) 16–18.

[50] Commission on Human Rights, *Resolution 2005/69* (Apr. 20, 2005).

[51] *Id.*, at para. 1.

[52] *Id.*, at para. 3.

Ruggie took account of their work and engaged with them during his mandate. His general approach was one that encompassed significant consultation with a view to building consensus amongst various actors,[53] albeit with the result that human rights were often treated "too lightly."[54]

Special Representative Ruggie undertook extensive research at the outset of his mandate, drawing upon a variety of sources, including the "commentaries of United Nations treaty bodies on State obligations concerning business-related human rights abuses."[55] A thorough review of those commentaries as part of a mapping exercise of state obligations enabled Ruggie to conclude in one of his first substantive reports on the scope of the state duty to protect:

> The duty to protect exists under the core United Nations human rights treaties as elaborated by the treaty bodies, and is also generally agreed to exist under customary international law. Moreover, the treaty bodies unanimously affirm that this duty requires steps by States to regulate and adjudicate abuses by all social actors including businesses.[56]

While the duty to protect may have been addressed by the treaty bodies in the context of specific rights, it "applies to all substantive rights."[57] Ruggie found that the various treaty bodies "tend not to specify the precise content of required State action, but generally recommend regulation through legislation and adjudication through judicial remedies, including compensation where appropriate."[58] The increasing attention of the treaty bodies to the protection from corporate human rights harms indicated "growing concern that States either do not fully understand or are not always able or willing to fulfil this duty."[59]

Ruggie found less guidance from the treaty bodies regarding the human rights responsibilities of companies, even though the various committees had "exhibited growing interest in the role of business itself with regard to human rights."[60] It was not clear whether such responsibility could be considered "legal in nature," he concluded.[61] In sum:

> [T]he treaties do not address direct corporate legal responsibilities explicitly, while the commentaries of the treaty bodies on the subject are ambiguous. However, the increased attention the Committees are devoting to the need to prevent corporate

---

[53] *See generally* JOHN GERARD RUGGIE, JUST BUSINESS: MULTINATIONAL CORPORATIONS AND HUMAN RIGHTS (2013).

[54] Surya Deva, *Treating Human Rights Lightly: A Critique of the Consensus Rhetoric and the Language Employed by the Guiding Principles, in* DEVA & BILCHITZ, *supra* note 12, at 78, 80.

[55] UN Guiding Principles on Business and Human Rights, *supra* note 1, at 3.

[56] *Report of the Special Representative of the Secretary-General on the issue of human rights and transnational corporations: and other business enterprises, John Ruggie: Business and human rights: mapping international standards of responsibility and accountability for corporate acts,* A/HRC/4/35 (Feb. 19, 2007), para. 10 (footnotes omitted). *See also Report of the Special Representative of the Secretary-General on the issue of human rights and transnational corporations and other business enterprises, Addendum: State responsibilities to regulate and adjudicate corporate activities under the United Nations core human rights treaties: an overview of treaty body commentaries,* A/HRC/4/35/Add.1 (Feb. 13, 2007).

[57] *Id.,* at para. 14.

[58] *Id.,* at para. 14.

[59] *Id.,* at para. 16.

[60] *Id.,* at para. 39.

[61] *Id.,* at para. 40.

abuse acknowledges that businesses are capable of both breaching human rights and contributing to their protection.[62]

The Human Rights Committee, for example, had not "mentioned business responsibilities" in its work to date, even though it had focused on corporate activities in the context of the state duty to protect.[63]

The contribution of the treaty bodies provided a valuable foundation for Ruggie's work, but he felt that they could do more in this sphere:

> [T]he treaty-based human rights machinery has been paying increasing attention to the regulation of States and adjudication of corporate activities and already plays an important role in elaborating the duties of States. However, even more guidance from the treaty bodies on the scope and content of State obligations arising from the treaties regarding such activities could further support States in the fulfilment of these duties and bring additional clarity to rights-holders and business enterprises. To this end, it would seem beneficial if the treaty bodies were to engage in discussions amongst themselves on this issue, as well as to address more specifically these duties.[64]

When he met with the treaty bodies at their sixth Inter-Committee meeting in June 2007, he reiterated his view that they should develop guidance for states concerning the scope of the state duty to protect human rights.[65]

The influence of the treaty bodies is evident in the Protect, Respect and Remedy Framework put forward by Ruggie in 2008 as a "conceptual and policy framework to anchor the business and human rights debate, and to help guide all relevant actors."[66] He drew on the treaty bodies to explain the state duty to protect and to highlight the debate regarding extraterritorial obligations of states concerning corporate activities abroad.[67] In terms of access to remedies, the report noted that:

> Expectations for States to take concrete steps to adjudicate corporate-related human rights harm are expanding. Treaty bodies increasingly recommend that States investigate and punish human rights abuse by corporations and provide access to redress for such abuse when it affects persons with their jurisdiction.[68]

Ruggie considered that the treaty bodies could "play an important role in making recommendations to States on implementing their obligations to protect rights

---

[62] *Id.,* at para. 41.

[63] *Meeting between the SRSG on Human Rights and Business and Treaty Bodies, June 19, 2007, Background Paper, Mapping States parties' responsibilities to regulate and adjudicate corporate activities under seven of the United Nations' Core Human Rights Treaties: Main trends and issues for further consideration,* paras. 21–24.

[64] SRSG, *Overview of treaty body commentaries, supra* note 56, at 3.

[65] *Report of the Special Representative of the Secretary-General on the issue of human rights and transnational corporations: and other business enterprises, Addendum: Summary of five multi-stakeholder consultations,* A/HRC/8/5/Add.1 (Apr. 23, 2008), para. 21.

[66] *Protect, Respect and Remedy: a Framework for Business and Human Rights, Report of the Special Representative of the Secretary-General on the issue of human rights and transnational corporations: and other business enterprises, John Ruggie,* A/HRC/8/5 (Apr. 7, 2008), 1.

[67] *Id.,* at paras. 18–19.

[68] *Id.,* at para. 83.

vis-à-vis corporate activities."[69] The Human Rights Council adopted a resolution in June 2008 welcoming the framework, recognising the need for its operationalisation and extending the Special Representative's mandate.[70]

As he worked towards developing the Guiding Principles, Ruggie briefed various international entities on the Framework, including the treaty monitoring bodies.[71] He continued to draw on their work, in particular the "useful guidance" they had provided regarding remedies.[72] He found there to be "common strands" in the approaches of the treaty bodies to elaborating state obligations concerning provision of access to remedy, "whether committed by public or private actors":

- Conducting prompt, thorough and fair investigations
- Providing access to prompt, effective and independent remedial mechanisms, established through judicial, administrative, legislative and other appropriate means
- Imposing appropriate sanctions, including criminalizing conduct and pursuing prosecutions where abuses amount to international crimes
- Providing a range of forms of appropriate reparation, such as compensation, restitution, rehabilitation and changes in relevant laws.[73]

He also noted the emphasis by several treaty bodies on the need for special attention to be paid to "at-risk" groups, such as women, children, and Indigenous peoples.[74]

While Ruggie was fulfilling his mandate, the treaty bodies continued to address business and human rights.[75] After the Special Representative had put forward the Guiding Principles in March 2011 but before they were endorsed by the Human Rights Council in June 2011, the Committee on Economic, Social and Cultural Rights adopted a statement at their 46th Session in May 2011 on state obligations regarding the corporate sector in the context of the rights protected by the Covenant.[76] While the statement took note of the Respect, Protect and Remedy Framework, it made no mention of the Guiding Principles, yet squarely addressed a number issues also touched upon by the Ruggie in the Guiding Principles.[77] What is particularly notable is that the language deployed by the Committee in relation to issues such as human rights due diligence and extraterritorial obligations

---

[69] *Id.*, at para. 43.

[70] Human Rights Council, Resolution 8/7, 28th Meeting (June 18, 2008), paras. 2–4.

[71] *Report of the Special Representative of the Secretary-General on the issue of human rights and transnational corporations: and other business enterprises,* A/65/310 (Aug. 19, 2010), para. 51.

[72] *Report of the Special Representative of the Secretary-General on the issue of human rights and transnational corporations: and other business enterprises, Addendum, State obligations to provide access to remedy for human rights abuses by third parties, including business: an overview of international and regional provisions, commentary and decisions,* A/HRC/11/13/Add.1 (May 15, 2009), 25.

[73] *Id.*

[74] *Id.*

[75] *See, e.g.,* CESCR, *General Comment No. 18: Article 6 on the right to work,* E/C.12/GC/18 (Feb. 6, 2006), paras. 43, 53; CRC, *General Comment No. 11: Indigenous children and their rights under the Convention,* CRC/C/GC/11 (Feb. 12, 2009), para. 23; CEDAW, *General Recommendation No. 28 on the core obligations of States parties under Article 2 of the Convention on Elimination of All Forms of Discrimination against Women,* CEDAW/C/GC/28 (Dec. 16, 2010), para. 28.

[76] CESCR, *Statement on the obligations of States parties regarding the corporate sector and economic, social and cultural rights,* E/C.12/2011/1 (July 12, 2011).

[77] *Id.*, at 2.

was stronger than that used in the Guiding Principles.[78] It can be read as evidence that despite the rhetoric of consensus, and the extensive consideration given by the Special Representative to the work of the treaty bodies on business and human rights, there was no doubt tension between their understanding of state obligations on certain issues and those enunciated by Ruggie in the Guiding Principles. The endorsement by states of the Guiding Principles would serve to generate an evident impetus, notwithstanding some divergence on key issues.

III. DEVELOPMENTS AND DIVERGENCES

The engagement by the treaty bodies with business and human rights since the Guiding Principles has expanded considerably. It reveals some divergence by those bodies with key aspects of the Guiding Principles. In the past decade or so, business and human rights has become an increasingly prominent thematic concern of the UN human rights treaty monitoring bodies, as evidenced, for example, by dedicated general comments concerning state obligations in the context of business activities and frequent references to business and human rights matters in concluding observations issued. As will be discussed in this section, both the Committee on the Rights of the Child and the Committee on Economic, Social and Cultural Rights have issued general comments specifically addressed to business and human rights, while discussion of the obligations of states towards business enterprises has also featured more prominently in the general comments and recommendations of other treaty bodies since 2011.[79] In relation to concluding observations, dedicated sections on business and human rights are increasingly common, as are direct references to the UN Guiding Principles alongside the obligations arising under relevant treaties.[80] An increased engagement with business and human rights prompted by the Guiding Principles is also evident in the work of the Charter bodies, as well as beyond the UN human rights machinery.[81] The Working Group on the issue of human rights and transnational corporations and other business enterprises, established in 2011, has been tasked with promoting dissemination and implementation of the Guiding Principles.[82] Its mandate requires it to work in cooperation and coordination with relevant UN human rights institutions, including the treaty bodies.[83]

In his final report as Special Representative, Ruggie acknowledged both the contribution of the treaty bodies to his work on elaborating the Protect, Respect and Remedy Framework and the Guiding Principles, and the potential for divergence between the two.[84]

---

[78] *Id.*

[79] CRC, *General comment No. 16 on State obligations regarding the impact of the business sector on children's rights*, CRC/C/GC/16 (Apr. 17, 2013); CESCR, *General comment No. 24 on State obligations under the International Covenant on Economic, Social and Cultural Rights in the context of business activities*, E/C.12/GC/24 (Aug. 10, 2017); HRC, *General Comment No. 36 on article 6 of the International Covenant on Civil and Political Rights, on the right to life*, CCPR/C/GC/36 (Oct. 30, 2018).

[80] For an overview, *see* Mirbek Sydygaliev, "UN Guiding Principles Business and Human Rights in UN treaty bodies' concluding observations," Informal reference paper (Sept. 2020), available at https://www.ohchr.org/Documents/Issues/Business/UNGPsBHRnext10/treaty_bodies_uptake.pdf.

[81] For a more general overview of the uptake of the Guiding Principles, *see* Report of the Working Group on the issue of human rights and transnational corporations and other business enterprises, *Guiding Principles on Business and Human Rights at 10: taking stock of first decade*, A/HRC/47/39 (Apr. 22, 2021).

[82] Human Rights Council, Resolution 17/4, A/HRC/Res/17/4 (July 6, 2011), para. 6(a).

[83] *Id.*, at para. 6(f). The Working Group has met with UN treaty bodies—*see, e.g.*, CESCR, *Report on the sixtieth, sixty-first and sixty-second sessions*, E/2018/22 (2018), para. 97.

[84] UN Guiding Principles on Business and Human Rights, *supra* note 1, at 3, 7.

With Guiding Principle 2 setting out that states "should set out clearly the expectation that all business enterprises domiciled in their territory and/or jurisdiction respect human rights throughout their operations," the Commentary to the Guiding Principles notes in somewhat diplomatic terms the differing opinion on this matter of certain treaty bodies:

> At present States are not generally required under international human rights law to regulate the extraterritorial activities of businesses domiciled in their territory and/or jurisdiction. Nor are they generally prohibited from doing so, provided there is a recognized jurisdictional basis. Within these parameters some human rights treaty bodies recommend that home States take steps to prevent abuse abroad by business enterprises within their jurisdiction.[85]

Before addressing this issue in more detail, this section first addresses how the endorsement of the Guiding Principles by the Human Rights Council in June 2011 led to increased engagement and activity on business and human rights in various quarters, including on the part of the treaty bodies. In many respects, the treaty bodies have followed the advice offered by Special Representative Ruggie in 2007.

A. Specialised General Comments

The Committee on the Rights of the Child was the first of the treaty bodies to elaborate a general comment specifically addressed to state party obligations in the context of business activities. General Comment 16, one of four general comments published by the Committee in 2013, "aims to clarify these obligations and outline the measures that should be undertaken by States to meet them."[86] It does not seek to address every relevant article of the Convention and protocols, but seeks to provide an overall framework for their implementation, as well as offering a focus on specific contexts "where the impact of business activities can be most significant."[87]

General Comment 16 discusses the general principles of the Convention, specifically non-discrimination, the best interests of the child, the right to life, survival and development, and the right to be heard, as they relate to business activities, as well as state obligations to respect, protect, fulfil, and provide remedies and reparation.[88] In addition to examining certain contexts of concern, including the informal economy, emergencies, and conflict situations, General Comment 16 offers specific examples of business activity that can harm the rights of children:

> [E]nvironmental degradation and contamination arising from business activities can compromise children's rights to health, food security and access to safe drinking water and sanitation. Selling or leasing land to investors can deprive local populations of access to natural resources linked to their subsistence and cultural heritage; the rights of indigenous children may be particularly at risk in this context. The marketing to children of products such as cigarettes and alcohol as well as foods and drinks high in saturated fats, trans-fatty acids, sugar, salt or additives can have a long-term impact on their health. When business employment practices require adults to work long hours, older children,

---

[85] *Id.*, at 7.
[86] CRC, *General Comment 16*, *supra* note 79, at para. 2.
[87] *Id.*, at para. 5.
[88] *Id.*, at paras. 12–31.

particularly girls, may take on their parent's domestic and childcare obligations, which can negatively impact their right to education and to play; additionally, leaving children alone or in the care of older siblings can have implications for the quality of care and the health of younger children.[89]

The pharmaceutical sector, the media, advertising and marketing industries, and the information and communication technology industry are amongst some of the sectors highlighted in General Comment 16.[90] Unlike the Guiding Principles, which the CRC refers to,[91] general comments provide a vehicle for identifying particular business practices that may harm human rights and addressing state and business responsibilities in such contexts, and how they can be fulfilled. In the case of General Comment 16, the CRC elaborates its "[f]ramework for implementation" of obligations under the Convention.[92] It also calls on states parties to address business and human rights in their periodic reports.[93] Over sixty concluding observations adopted since 2013 have included a section entitled "Children's rights and the business sector" and made reference to General Comment 16.[94]

With the considerable emphasis in the International Covenant on Economic, Social and Cultural Rights on the rights of workers, it is unsurprising that the CESCR also produced a specialized general comment on business and human rights. This had been suggested even prior to Ruggie's mandate.[95] No doubt prompted by the Guiding Principles, and perhaps the adoption of General Comment 16 by the CRC, CESCR began the task of developing a new general comment in 2016 by preparing a draft general comment, asking for and receiving submissions from interested parties, including states, civil society, and industry organisations,[96] and holding a general day of discussion of the draft in February 2017.[97] The process, according to the Committee, served to highlight "the importance of the general comment to bridge protection gaps in the existing international norms and principles and to provide States with guidance."[98] That the Committee views General Comment 24 as providing a gap-filling role indicates both the underdeveloped nature of human rights law relating to harmful business activities and the high regard for the role of general comments in addressing this deficit.

General Comment 24 itself does not refer to this claimed gap-filling role, but rather states that it is aimed at clarifying state party duties under ICESCR, while taking into consideration other developments, including the Guiding Principles.[99] With regard to the second pillar of the latter, the Committee states that General Comment 24 "seeks to assist the corporate sector in discharging their human rights obligations and assuming their responsibilities," but by only addressing their conduct "indirectly."[100] It focuses in the main, however, on state obligations, following to some extent the schema of General Comment

---

[89] *Id.,* at para. 19.

[90] *Id.,* at paras. 57–60.

[91] *Id.,* at para. 7.

[92] *Id.,* at paras. 53–84.

[93] *Id.,* at para. 86.

[94] Sydygaliev, *supra* note 80, at 3.

[95] *See, e.g.,* Weissbrodt & Kruger, *supra* note 46, at 917.

[96] *See* https://www.ohchr.org/EN/HRBodies/CESCR/Pages/Submissions2017.aspx.

[97] CESCR, *Report on the sixtieth, sixty-first and sixty-second sessions, supra* note 83, paras. 54–56.

[98] *Id.,* at para. 56.

[99] CESCR, *General comment 24, supra* note 79, at 1–2.

[100] *Id.,* at 4.

16 of the CRC by addressing non-discrimination and the obligations to respect, protect, and fulfil human rights. A considerable section of the general comment is devoted to extraterritorial obligations to respect, protect, and fulfil, which are discussed further in the following, while the Committee also gives consideration to remedies and implementation.

General Comment 24 provides an adroit discussion of how protected persons and specific rights are at risk from a broad range of business practices by different types of companies, and of the role of various laws, including international law on state responsibility, trade and investment, and domestic criminal, civil and administrative laws. It firmly eschews market solutions, stating plainly that the obligation to protect "sometimes necessitates direct regulation and intervention."[101] For example:

> States parties should consider measures such as restricting marketing and advertising of certain goods and services in order to protect public health, such as of tobacco products, . . . and of breast-milk substitutes, . . . combating gender role stereotyping and discrimination; exercising rent control in the private housing market as required for the protection of everyone's right to adequate housing; establishing a minimum wage consistent with a living wage and a fair remuneration; regulating other business activities concerning the Covenant rights to education, employment and reproductive health, in order to combat gender discrimination effectively; and gradually eliminating informal or "non-standard" (i.e. precarious) forms of employment, which often result in denying the workers concerned the protection of labour laws and social security.[102]

General Comment 24 provides an assertive assessment of state obligations under the Covenant, reflecting the Committee's clear expertise in this domain and its undiluted concern regarding the negative impact of business activities on the rights protected under the treaty.[103]

Other treaty bodies have yet to adopted specialized general comments or recommendations on business and human rights, but have addressed this subject matter in their general comments. The Human Rights Committee, for example, makes its most forthright assertions on the obligations of states parties in the context of business activities in General Comment 36 on the right to life.[104] It reiterates the obligation of parties to the Covenant to exercise due diligence in order to protect the lives of individuals from non-state actors, referring specifically to private companies operating in areas such as security, health, transport, and detention.[105] Where private companies have been given previously public functions:

> [A] State party must rigorously limit the powers afforded to private actors, and ensure that strict and effective measures of monitoring and control, and adequate training, are in place, in order to guarantee, inter alia, that the powers granted are not misused, and do not lead to arbitrary deprivation of life.[106]

---

[101] *Id.*, at 6.

[102] *Id.* (footnotes omitted).

[103] *See also* CESCR, *General comment No. 25 on science and economic, social and cultural rights (article 15 (1) (b), (2), (3) and (4) of the International Covenant on Economic, Social and Cultural Rights)*, E/C.12/GC/25 (Apr. 30, 2020).

[104] HRC, *General Comment 36, supra* note 79.

[105] *See id.*, at paras. 7, 15, 18, 20, 25.

[106] *Id.*, at para. 15.

There is a "heightened duty of care" on the part of states parties towards persons held in "private incarceration facilities operating pursuant to an authorization by the State."[107] The Committee also adopts a more expansive view towards extraterritorial obligations, as discussed in the following. General Comment 36 refers specifically to the UN Guiding Principles,[108] as does General Comment 37, on the right to peaceful assembly, adopted in 2020. In the case of the latter, the HRC does so for the purposes of addressing business responsibilities:

States parties hold the primary responsibility for the realization of the right of peaceful assembly. However, business enterprises have a responsibility to respect human rights, including the right of peaceful assembly of, for example, communities affected by their activities and of their employees. Private entities and broader society may be expected to accept some level of disruption as a result of the exercise of the right.[109]

These general comments, together with a number of concluding observations over the past decade,[110] reveal an important coming to terms by the Human Rights Committee with the pervasiveness of corporate activity and its propensity for harming rights protected by the International Covenant on Civil and Political Rights.

Since 2011, business and human rights concerns have become increasingly embedded in the work of the treaty bodies. Beyond the examples discussed previously, numerous other instances can be found of various treaty bodies addressing such issues in their general comments and concluding observations, as well as individual complaints.[111] The preceding discussion has shown how the treaty bodies have gone beyond the at times generic language of the UN Guiding Principles to refer to specific industries or business practices that give rise to particular human rights concerns. They have also been more demanding at times regarding the obligations of states in certain respects. With regard to human rights due diligence, for example, treaty bodies have gone beyond the relatively weak language regarding human rights due diligence in the Guiding Principles, wherein states might require this "where appropriate," to make more direct calls. The view of CESCR is that "[s]tates should adopt measures such as imposing due diligence requirements to prevent abuses of Covenant rights in a business entity's supply chain and by subcontractors, suppliers, franchisees, or other business partners."[112] This is particularly the case in the context of mining and oil projects.[113] Clear divergence between the Guiding Principles and the treaty bodies can be

---

[107] *Id.*, at para. 25.

[108] *Id.*, footnote 71.

[109] HRC, *General Comment No. 37 on the right of peaceful assembly (article 21)*, CCPR/C/GC/37 (Sept. 17, 2020), para. 31 (footnote omitted). *See also* paras. 57, 61, 93.

[110] *See, e.g.*, HRC, *Concluding Observations on the sixth periodic report of Germany*, CCPR/C/DEU/CO/6 (Nov. 12, 2012), para. 16; HRC, *Concluding observations on the sixth report of Canada*, CCPR/C/CAN/CO/6 (Aug. 13, 2015), para. 6; HRC, *Concluding observations on the fourth periodic report of Republic of Korea*, CCPR/C/KOR/CO/4 (Nov. 5, 2015), para. 11.

[111] *See, e.g., Basem Ahmad Issa Yassin et al. v. Canada*, Human Rights Committee, Decision adopted by the Committee under Article 5(4) of the Optional Protocol, concerning communication No. 2285/2013 CCPR/C/120/D/2285/2013 (Dec. 7, 2017); CESCR, Communication No. 2/2014, *I.D.G. v. Spain*, Views adopted on June 17, 2015.

[112] CESCR, *General Comment 24, supra* note 79, at 5. *See also* CRC, *General Comment 16, supra* note 79, paras. 62–65. *See, however, Submission of the United Kingdom to the Committee on Economic, Social and Cultural Rights on the Draft General Comment on State Obligations under the ICESCR in the Context of Business Activities* (Jan. 31, 2017), 1–2.

[113] CESCR, *General Comment 24, supra* note 79, para. 32.

found on the subject of extraterritorial human rights obligations and the scope of the corporate responsibility to respect human rights.

B. Human Rights Obligations Beyond Borders

The debate of the existence and scope of extraterritorial obligations of states parties to human rights treaties arose early in Ruggie's mandate as Special Representative. As noted at the beginning of this section, the Guiding Principles and accompanying Commentary take the view that international human rights law does not require states to regulate the extraterritorial activities of business enterprises, but they are not prohibited from doing so where an accepted jurisdictional basis exists. In a nod to the views of the treaty bodies, the Commentary adds that "some human rights treaty bodies recommend that home States take steps to prevent abuse abroad by business enterprises within their jurisdiction."[114] This stance was telegraphed in the 2007 *Mapping Report* of the Special Representative:

> Current guidance from the Committees suggests that the treaties do not require States to exercise extraterritorial jurisdiction over business abuse. But nor are they prohibited from doing so. International law permits a State to exercise such jurisdiction provided there is a recognized basis: where the actor or victim is a national, where the acts have substantial adverse effects on the State, or where specific international crimes are involved. Extraterritorial jurisdiction must also meet an overall "reasonableness" test, which includes non-intervention in the internal affairs of other States. Debate continues over precisely when the protection of human rights justifies extraterritorial jurisdiction.[115]

The report acknowledged that "[s]ome treaty bodies seem to be encouraging states to pay greater attention to preventing corporate violations abroad," specifically referring to CESCR General Comment 15 in a footnote.[116]

Ruggie did not seek to emulate the efforts of treaty bodies on the question of extraterritoriality and push a progressive interpretation of state obligations in this context. While in 2009 he referred to relevant CESCR general comments and concluding observations from CERD which aim to do so, he preferred to highlight that international human rights law is "unsettled" on the question of extraterritorial state duties.[117] A subsequent report noted the use of extraterritorial jurisdiction in the context of anti-corruption and other domains, but how "this is typically not the case in business and human rights."[118] The debates have been "heated," and extraterritorial jurisdiction itself "broad and highly politicized."[119] In order to take the issue forward, Ruggie put it that "[d]istinguishing what is truly problematic from measures that are entirely permissible under international law would be in the best interests of all concerned."[120] He returned to the issue some months later, differentiating between domestic measures that may have extraterritorial implications, like non-financial

---

[114] UN Guiding Principles on Business and Human Rights, *supra* note 1, at 7.

[115] SRSG, *Mapping* report, *supra* note 56, para. 15 (footnotes omitted).

[116] *Id.*, footnote 9.

[117] SRSG, *An overview of international and regional provisions, commentary and decisions, supra* note 72, at 3.

[118] SRSG Report, *Business and human rights: further steps towards the operationalization of the "Protect, Respect and Remedy" Framework*, A/HRC/14/27 (Apr. 9, 2010), para. 46.

[119] *Id.*, at paras. 48, 50.

[120] *Id.*, at para. 50.

reporting, and the exercise of extraterritorial jurisdiction, such as under criminal law, over activities outside of a state's territory.[121] The Special Representative also painted a picture of human rights advocacy groups on one side demanding greater exercise of extraterritorial jurisdiction, but business and "many States" on the other remaining "opposed to this practice."[122] For victims of human rights abuse related to corporate activities "[t]he status quo," he rightly observed, "does [them] no favours."[123]

The language in the draft Guiding Principles put forward for consultation in November 2010 differed a little on the topic of extraterritoriality but the essence of the stance remained the same: extra-jurisdictional regulation is not required by international human rights law, but nor is it prohibited, where there is a jurisdictional basis and it is reasonable to exercise jurisdiction.[124] Treaty bodies have taken a different view. In General Recommendation 28, issued by CEDAW in 2010, for example, the Committee put it that certain state party obligations under the Convention "extend to acts of national corporations operating extraterritorially."[125] Various human rights organisations took issue with the draft Guiding Principles, asserting that the document was not an accurate statement of the law and that it took "a more regressive approach towards the human rights obligations of States and the responsibilities of non-State actors than authoritative interpretations of international human rights law and current practices."[126]

The draft Guiding Principles regarding the state duty to protect, according to Amnesty International, Human Rights Watch, and a number of other civil society organisations, "at times depart from existing interpretations of international law provided by UN human rights treaty bodies."[127] Draft Principle 2, calling on states to encourage business enterprises to respect human rights throughout their operations, did not "reflect increasing international recognition, including by UN treaty bodies, of the legal obligation for States to take action to prevent abuses by their companies overseas."[128] The organisations called for the Guiding Principles to state clearly that states should "adopt and implement regulatory measures to prevent, put an end to and punish business abuses of human rights at home and in other countries, and to ensure the provision of effective remedies."[129] Such an approach would "be more consistent with the interpretation by UN treaty bodies of States' duties to prevent human rights abuses in other countries."[130]

After the *Financial Times* reported on the civil society statement,[131] Special Representative Ruggie wrote a strongly worded letter to the newspaper criticising as "bizarre" the position taken by Amnesty International and "some other pressure groups."[132]

---

[121] SRSG Report, *supra* note 71, para. 22.

[122] *Id.*

[123] *Id.*, at para. 30.

[124] SRSG Report, *Guiding Principles for the Implementation of the United Nations "Protect, Respect and Remedy" Framework* (Nov. 22, 2010), 2.

[125] CEDAW, *General Recommendation 28, supra* note 75, at para. 36. *See also* CEDAW, *General Recommendation No. 38 on trafficking in women and girls in the context of global migration*, CEDAW/C/GC/38 (Nov. 20, 2020), paras. 17 and 63.

[126] Amnesty International et al., Joint Civil Society Statement on the draft Guiding Principles on Business and Human Rights 1 (Jan. 2011).

[127] *Id.*

[128] *Id.*

[129] *Id.*, at 2.

[130] *Id.*

[131] Hugh Williamson, *Human Rights Guide in Question*, Financial Times, Jan. 18, 2011, at 7.

[132] John Ruggie, *Bizarre Response by Human Rights Groups to UN Framework Plan*, Letter to the Editor, Financial Times, Jan. 19, 2011, at 10.

The organisations "would have a lot to answer for if they actually were to oppose Human Rights Council endorsement of this hard-won initiative."[133] There followed a number of other letters to the *Financial Times*, both by representatives of these organisations and by others in support of Ruggie.[134] The issue of extraterritorial jurisdiction featured in this fraught exchange, with Amnesty International putting it that the approach of the draft Guiding Principles entailed a "much weaker formulation" compared with the CESCR interpretation of state party obligations under Article 12 of the Covenant.[135] The final version of the Guiding Principles did not involve any greater change of approach by Ruggie, although the explicit reference to the views of the treaty bodies on extraterritoriality in the Commentary may have been an outcome of this episode. That being said, in his subsequently published book *Just Business*, Ruggie wrote pointedly that "most countries do not accept treaty bodies' views as a source of law," including specifically on the subject of extraterritorial jurisdiction.[136]

The International Court of Justice has cited treaty bodies as authoritative sources on the question of the extraterritorial human rights obligations of states.[137] Their interpretation of obligations under the relevant treaties are without doubt influential. Regarding extraterritorial obligations in the context of business and human rights, treaty bodies have both drawn on the contested language of the Guiding Principles,[138] but also gone further. The Human Rights Committee held in 2015 that Canada should "ensure that all Canadian corporations under its jurisdiction, in particular mining corporations, respect human rights standards when operating abroad."[139] In General Comment 36 on the right to life, the Committee elaborated a more expansive understanding of the jurisdictional scope of the Covenant. Reflecting the mainstreaming of business and human rights, the Committee focused not only on the use of force overseas by states and situations of armed conflict, but also on business activities:

> States parties . . . must also take appropriate legislative and other measures to ensure that all activities taking place in whole or in part within their territory and in other places subject to their jurisdiction, but having a direct and reasonably foreseeable impact on the right to life of individuals outside their territory, including activities taken by corporate entities based in their territory or subject to their jurisdiction, are consistent with article 6, taking due account of related international standards of corporate responsibility, and of the right of victims to obtain an effective remedy.[140]

---

[133] *Id.*

[134] *See* Mark Moody-Smith, *Business Groups Spurred to Improve Complaints System*, Letter to the Editor, FINANCIAL TIMES, Jan. 20, 2011, at 10; Widney Brown, *Stronger UN Draft on Human Rights Abuses Needed*, Letter to the Editor, FINANCIAL TIMES, Jan. 20, 2011, at 10; Arvind Ganesan, *Proper Powers Needed to Uphold Human Rights*, Letter to the Editor, FINANCIAL TIMES, Jan. 28, 2011, at 10.

[135] James Melik, *Can Human Rights Guide for Businesses Work?*, BBC NEWS, Jan. 25, 2011.

[136] RUGGIE, *supra note* 53, at xxxi, 45.

[137] *See, e.g.*, ICJ, *Legal Consequences of the Construction of a Wall in the Occupied Palestinian Territory*, Advisory Opinion (July 9, 2004), paras. 109–112.

[138] *See, e.g.*, HRC, *Concluding Observations on the sixth periodic report of Germany*, *supra* note 109, para. 16; HRC, *Concluding Observations on the fourth periodic report of the Republic of Korea* (Dec. 3, 2015), paras. 10–11.

[139] HRC, *Concluding observations on the sixth report of Canada*, CCPR/C/CAN/CO/6 (Aug. 15, 2015), para. 6.

[140] HRC, *General Comment 36*, *supra* note 36, at para. 22 (references omitted).

The language goes further than the Guiding Principles on Business and Human Rights, which are cited as relevant international standards, and reflects the more assertive approach of other treaty bodies on this matter.

The Committee on the Rights of the Child situated its discussion of extraterritorial obligations in General Comment 16 in the context of the global nature of business operations.[141] It noted the challenges this presents for states parties, but avowed any interpretation of jurisdiction that would be limited to a state's own territory. For home states, there are obligations under the Convention and Optional Protocols "to respect, protect and fulfil children's rights in the context of businesses' extraterritorial activities and operations, provided that there is a reasonable link between the State and the conduct concerned."[142] Such a link exists, in the view of the Committee, "when a business enterprise has its centre of activity, is registered or domiciled or has its main place of business or substantial business activities in the State concerned."[143] The Maastricht Principles on Extraterritorial Obligations of States in the area of Economic, Social and Cultural Rights (2012) are cited as the authority supporting this approach. Where a "reasonable link" exists, states should provide access to remedial mechanisms, whether judicial or non-judicial.[144] The Committee sets out a number of measures that states parties can take utilising public finance and other forms of support to prevent infringement of children's rights by business enterprises operating abroad.[145]

The Maastricht Principles were also drawn upon by the Committee on Economic, Social and Cultural Rights in its extensive discussion of extraterritorial obligations in General Comment 24. This emphasis is owed in no small part to the part played by Olivier de Schutter. He served as a "lead author" of the Maastricht Principles and the Committee's co-rapporteur in the drafting of General Comment 24.[146] Extraterritorial obligations in the context of business and human rights had been previously articulated by the Committee, as summarised in its 2011 statement on the corporate sector,[147] but the issue remained controversial during the drafting of General Comment 24. The United Kingdom, for example, stated plainly that "the obligations under the Covenant are primarily territorial and do not have extra-territorial effect."[148] For the International Organisation of Employers, the draft general comment focused "too much on extraterritorial jurisdiction instead of supporting States to improve access to remedy at local level."[149] The Committee was accused of ignoring the "shortcomings" around extraterritorial jurisdiction, such as higher costs and evidentiary challenges, notwithstanding its repeated references to the need for effective remedies.[150]

---

[141] CRC, *General Comment 16, supra* note 79, at para. 39.

[142] *Id.,* at para. 39.

[143] *Id.,* at para. 43.

[144] *Id.,* at para. 44.

[145] *Id.,* at para. 45.

[146] *See* https://www.srpoverty.org/about/the-mandate/; Olivier De Schutter et al., *Commentary to the Maastricht Principles on Extraterritorial Obligations of States in the Area of Economic, Social and Cultural Rights,* 34 HUMAN RIGHTS QUARTERLY 1084 (2012); CESCR, *General Comment on State Obligations under the International Covenant on Economic, Social and Cultural Rights in the Context of Business Activities, Draft prepared by Olivier De Schutter and Zdzislaw Kedzia, Rapporteurs,* E/C.12/60/R.1 (Oct. 17, 2016).

[147] CESCR, *Statement on the obligations of States parties, supra* note 76, at 2.

[148] *Submission of the United Kingdom, supra* note 112, at 3.

[149] International Organisation of Employers, *Preliminary Comments on the draft General Comment 24 on State Obligations under the International Covenant on Economic, Social and Cultural Rights in the Context of Business Activities* (Nov. 15, 2016), 2.

[150] *Id. See* CESCR, *Draft General Comment, supra* note 112, at paras. 41–51.

Civil society organisations were more supportive of the Committee's proposed text on extraterritorial obligations. One submission put it that the position adopted in the draft general comment on the extraterritorial dimensions of the state duty to protect "is consistent with a number of UN Treaty Bodies and the Maastricht Principles."[151] FIAN International welcomed the engagement with extraterritorial obligations and viewed the general comment as "an opportunity for the Committee to clearly spell out and specify these obligations, and broaden its work in this regards when monitoring States' compliance."[152] It recommended drawing on the Committee's own prior general comments which addressed this issue, as well as those of other treaty bodies. The submission of Lorand Bartels and Claire Methven O'Brien, however, was more critical of the draft general comment, arguing that it did not "accurately reflect the status quo in international human rights law concerning the scope and content of States' extraterritorial obligations."[153] The authors were dismissive of the Committee's reliance on previous general comments, which "are not in themselves authoritative, nor do they qualify as subsequent practice," as well as the Maastricht Principles, which have "no legal status, being no more than an academic commentary."[154] The approach of the Committee was "apt to cause confusion, and to undermine the authority of human rights law and institutions."[155]

The Committee on Economic, Social and Cultural remained steadfast in its views on extraterritorial obligations. In support, the Committee made reference in General Comment 24 to its own previous general comments, as well as those of other treaty bodies, including General Comment 16 of the Committee on the Rights of the Child, although a reference to the Maastricht Principles in the text was relegated to the footnotes.[156] General Comment 24 notes the absence of any jurisdictional restriction in the Covenant, as well as the obligation of international assistance and cooperation of states parties. It would be "contradictory," in the Committee's view, if a state could "remain passive where an actor domiciled in its territory and/or under its jurisdiction, and thus under its control or authority, harmed the rights of others in other States, or where conduct by such an actor may lead to foreseeable harm being caused."[157] The UN Charter, the International Court of Justice, and the Human Rights Council were deployed to support the Committee's stance, as was customary international law, which "prohibits a State from allowing its territory to be used to cause damage on the territory of another State."[158] Measures taken by states parties must remain "consistent with the limits imposed by international law."[159]

---

[151] International Corporate Accountability Roundtable, Interfaith Center on Corporate Responsibility and Due Process of Law Foundation, *Submission on the draft General Comment No. 24 on State Obligations under the International Covenant on Economic, Social and Cultural Rights in the Context of Business Activities* (Jan. 20, 2017), 3–4.

[152] *Written Contribution by FIAN International to the the draft General Comment No. 24 on State Obligations under the International Covenant on Economic, Social and Cultural Rights in the Context of Business Activities* (Jan. 2017), 1.

[153] Lorand Bartels & Claire Methven O'Brien, *Submission to UN Committee on Economic, Social and Cultural Rights on its draft General Comment No. 24 on State Obligations under the International Covenant on Economic, Social and Cultural Rights in the Context of Business Activities* (Jan. 20, 2016), 1.

[154] *Id.,* at 4.

[155] *Id.,* at 5.

[156] CESCR, *Draft General Comment, supra* note 112, paras. 31–33; CESCR, *General Comment 24, supra* note 79, paras. 26–28.

[157] CESCR, *General Comment 24, supra* note 79, at para. 27.

[158] *Id.,* at para. 27.

[159] *Id.,* at para. 28.

General Comment 24 addresses extraterritorial obligations with regard to states parties' obligations to respect, protect, and fulfil Covenant rights using language that at times goes further than that used in the draft and the UN Guiding Principles. Concerning the extraterritorial obligation to respect, for example, states parties are required to "refrain from interfering directly or indirectly with the enjoyment of the Covenant rights by persons outside their territories."[160] While the draft general comment had stated that this entails that states "should" ensure that they do not obstruct other states in meeting their Covenant obligations, General Comment 24 uses the more forceful "must."[161] Similarly, the tentative opening line of the draft general comment on the extraterritorial obligation to protect, that states parties "pay close attention to the adverse impacts outside their territories of the activities and operations of business entities that are domiciled under their jurisdiction," was replaced with the punchier:

> The extraterritorial obligation to protect requires States parties to take steps to prevent and redress infringements of Covenant rights that occur outside their territories due to the activities of business entities over which they can exercise control, especially in cases where the remedies available to victims before the domestic courts of the State where the harm occurs are unavailable or ineffective.[162]

General Comment 24 moderated the draft language which had extended the obligation to companies over which the state party "may exercise influence," to those over which it may "exercise control."[163]

The draft general comment featured the concept of a "reasonable link" in relation to the exercise of extraterritorial jurisdiction, albeit in a somewhat more expansive way than the Committee on the Rights of the Child had in General Comment 16.[164] General Comment 24, however, was more circumspect:

> States may seek to regulate corporations that are domiciled in their territory and/or jurisdiction: this includes corporations incorporated under their laws, or which have their statutory seat, central administration or principal place of business on their national territory.[165]

While parties to the Covenant might not be directly responsible for violations arising from business activities abroad, except in limited circumstances, the Committee put it that:

> [A] State party would be in breach of its obligations under the Covenant where the violation reveals a failure by the State to take reasonable measures that could have prevented the occurrence of the event. The responsibility of the State can be engaged in such circumstances even if other causes have also contributed to the occurrence of the

---

[160] *Id.*, at para. 29.
[161] CESCR, *Draft General Comment, supra* note 112, at para. 34; CESCR, *General Comment 24, supra* note 79, at para. 29.
[162] CESCR, *General Comment 24, supra* note 79, at para. 30.
[163] CESCR, *Draft General Comment, supra* note 112, at para. 36; CESCR, *General Comment 24, supra* note 79, at para. 31.
[164] CESCR, *Draft General Comment, supra* note 112, at para. 36.
[165] CESCR, *General Comment 24, supra* note 79, at para. 31.

violation, and even if the State had not foreseen that a violation would occur, provided such a violation was reasonably foreseeable.[166]

Human rights due diligence on the part of business enterprises was emphasised as a means of meeting the extraterritorial obligation to protect and the Committee did so in a way that goes further than the UN Guiding Principles, wherein the application of the concept to companies was first mooted.

General Comment 24 rounds off its discussion of extraterritoriality by addressing the obligation to fulfil, which it situates within the general expectation of international cooperation and assistance. Here the Committee calls on states parties to encourage those business actors who they may be in a position to influence "to ensure that they do not undermine the efforts of the States in which they operate to fully realize the Covenant rights."[167] It highlights abusive tax practices by transnational corporations in this context given that they significantly hinder states' abilities to marshal sufficient resources to meet their human rights obligations.[168] This marks a departure from the approach of the UN Guiding Principles, which made no reference to tax matters, such as corporate tax avoidance.[169] In all, the Committee's approach to extraterritorial obligations aligns with Tara van Ho's observation that General Comment 24 is "more forceful in its foundational legal claims and more explicit and demanding in the steps states should take."[170]

The Concluding Observations of various treaty bodies often contain recommendations to states parties on their obligations towards overseas business activities.[171] CEDAW, for example, called upon Switzerland to "strengthen its legislation governing the conduct of corporations registered or domiciled in the State party in relation to their activities abroad."[172] The impact of transnational corporations on Indigenous peoples outside the territories of state parties has consistently been highlighted by CERD, even prior to the adoption of the Guiding Principles.[173] It issued the following straightforward recommendation to Canada:

> The Committee recommends that the State party take appropriate legislative measures to prevent transnational corporations registered in Canada from carrying out activities that negatively impact on the enjoyment of rights of indigenous peoples in territories outside Canada, and hold them accountable.[174]

---

[166] *Id.*, at para. 32 (footnotes omitted).

[167] *Id.*, at para. 37.

[168] CESCR, *General Comment 24, supra* note 79, at para. 37. *See also* CESCR, *Concluding Observations on the sixth periodic report of the United Kingdom of Great Britain and Northern Ireland* (July 14, 2016) E/C.12/GBR/CO/6, paras. 16 and 17.

[169] *See generally* Shane Darcy, *"The Elephant in the Room": Corporate Tax Avoidance & Business and Human Rights*, 2(1) BUSINESS AND HUMAN RIGHTS JOURNAL 1 (2017).

[170] Tara van Ho, *Introductory Note to General Comment No. 24 (2017) on State obligations under the International Covenant on Economic, Social and Cultural Rights in the Context of Business Activities (CESCR)*, 58 INTERNATIONAL LEGAL MATERIALS 872, 872 (2019).

[171] *See, e.g.,* CRC, *Concluding observations on the combined second and third periodic reports of Monaco*, CRC/C/MCO/CO/2-3 (Oct. 29, 2013), paras. 20–21; CRC, *Concluding observations: Italy*, CRC/C/ITA/CO/3-4 (Oct. 31, 2011), paras. 20–21; CRC, *Concluding observations: Australia*, CRC/C/AUS/CO/4 (Aug. 28, 2012), paras. 27–28.

[172] CEDAW, *Concluding observations on the combined fourth and fifth periodic reports of Switzerland*, CEDAW/C/CHE/CO/4-5 (Nov. 25, 2016), para. 41.

[173] *See, e.g.,* CERD, *Concluding Observations: Norway*, CERD/C/NOR/CO/19-20, (Apr. 8, 2011), para. 17.

[174] CERD, *Concluding observations: Canada*, CERD/C/CAN/CO/19-20 (Apr. 4, 2012), para. 14.

States parties "should ensure that no obstacles are introduced in the law that prevent the holding of such transnational corporations accountable in the State party's courts when such violations are committed outside the State party."[175] The tone adopted is emblematic of an approach that is more assertive and progressive by the treaty bodies than that of the UN Guiding Principles on what is a core business and human rights issue.

C. Protected Persons and Groups

The UN Guiding Principles take a bifurcated approach to the scope of human rights responsibilities, making a distinction between the rights covered under the state duty to protect human rights and those falling under the corporate responsibility to respect. States must protect "the human rights of individuals [...] [from] abuse by third parties, including business enterprises" without any differentiation.[176] While businesses "should respect human rights," the Guiding Principles take a seemingly narrower view as to the scope of such responsibility:

> The responsibility of business enterprises to respect human rights refers to internationally recognized human rights—understood, at a minimum, as those expressed in the International Bill of Human Rights and the principles concerning fundamental rights set out in the International labour Organization's Declaration on Fundamental Principles and Rights at Work.[177]

This minimalist statement seems at odds with the accompanying Commentary, which acknowledges that "business enterprises can have an impact on virtually the entire spectrum of internationally recognised human rights." The responsibility to respect is said to apply "to all such rights."[178] The Commentary, adds, however, that companies may need "to consider additional standards" in certain circumstances, such as during armed conflict, where international humanitarian law applies.[179] It also states that business enterprises should respect the rights of persons "belonging to specific groups or populations that require particular attention, where they may have adverse human rights impacts on them."[180] The Commentary notes how international instruments variously address the rights of Indigenous peoples, minorities, women, children, persons with disabilities, and migrant workers and their families, but without explicitly incorporating them within the relevant "foundational principles" of the second pillar.[181]

The Guiding Principles thus offer an incoherent statement of the scope of companies' responsibility to respect human rights, one which is a "global standard of expected conduct," but not a legal standard.[182] Ruggie may have been motivated to establish an

---

[175] CERD, *Concluding Observations: United Kingdom of Great Britain and Northern Ireland*, CERD/C/GBR/CO/18-20 (Sept. 14, 2011), para. 29.

[176] UN Guiding Principles on Business and Human Rights, *supra* note 1, at 6–7.

[177] *Id.*, at 13.

[178] *Id.*

[179] *Id.*, at 14. *See further* United Nations Working Group on Business and Human Rights, *Business, Human Rights and Conflict-Affected Regions*, A/75/212 (July 21, 2020).

[180] *Id.*

[181] *Id.*

[182] *Id.*, at 13. *See* Justine Nolan, *The Corporate Responsibility to Respect Human Rights: Soft Law or Not Law?*, in DEVA & BILCHITZ, *supra* note 12, at 107–137.

identifiable minimum in order to generate broad acceptance and consensus, while at the same time having to acknowledge the relevance of the full range of human rights for business enterprises. In his 2008 report, he criticised the Draft Norms for identifying a "limited list of rights":

> [A]ny attempt to limit internationally recognized rights is inherently problematic. [...] there are few if any internationally recognized rights business cannot impact - or be perceived to impact—in some manner. Therefore, companies should consider all such rights.[183]

The Special Representative looked at such rights, however, in a particularly individualistic sense and without any reference at that time to the groups protected by international human rights law. When the Human Rights Council renewed his mandate in 2008, it specifically requested that he "integrate a gender perspective throughout his work and to give special attention to persons belonging to vulnerable groups, in particular children."[184]

The Special Representative cannot have been unaware of the narrowness of his approach and the attendant criticism. After he put forward the draft Guiding Principles towards the end of 2010, civil society organisations called for greater guidance therein on respecting the rights of particular individuals and groups, including women, children, and Indigenous peoples. It was suggested that Ruggie could draw upon the existing recommendations of various international bodies, including the human rights treaty bodies in this respect.[185] The organisations also advocated for more direct reference to instruments beyond the two covenants and the ILO Declaration, but without success. The Guiding Principles as finalised address gender and the rights of members of vulnerable groups in a rudimentary fashion. For Surya Deva, it was "neither clear nor defensible why other core international conventions such as CERD, CRC, and CRPD or other instruments in the area of environmental rights and indigenous rights, were not included in the moral minimum" of the corporate responsibility to respect human rights.[186] He considered it "highly problematic" that the Guiding Principles adopted an "unprincipled (or pragmatically principled) 'pick and choose' approach" which served to "under-define" internationally recognised human rights.[187] This defect, he suggested, could be remedied in future international instruments in this field.[188] Given the challenges of adopting a business and human rights treaty, more of which follows in the next section, it is submitted that the treaty bodies have and could play an important role here, particularly those focusing on the rights of specific individuals and groups.

The private sector has loomed large in the work of certain treaty bodies, particularly those concerned with discrimination. The International Convention on the Elimination of All Forms of Racial Discrimination, the oldest of the core treaties, explicitly establishes obligations for states parties to address racial discrimination by private actors.[189] The

---

[183] SRSG Report, *supra* note 66, at 15.
[184] Human Rights Council, Resolution 8/7, 28th Meeting (June 18, 2008), para. 4(d).
[185] Amnesty International et al., *supra* note 126, at 1.
[186] Surya Deva, *Business and Human Rights: Time to Move Beyond the "Present"?, in* César Rodriguez-Garavito, Business and Human Rights 62, 70 (2017).
[187] *Id.*
[188] *Id.*
[189] Convention on the Elimination of Racial Discrimination (entered into force 4 January 1969) 660 UNTS 195, Articles 2, 4.

Declaration which preceded the Declaration had highlighted discrimination in access to citizenship, education, religion, employment, occupation, and housing.[190] The Committee on the Elimination of Racial Discrimination has repeatedly raised its concerns with states parties concerning harmful business activities. For example, during Ruggie's mandate, CERD highlighted the "adverse effects of economic activities connected with the exploitation of natural resources . . . on the right to land, health, living environment and the way of life of indigenous peoples."[191] While the recommendations were aimed at the state in question, rather than the companies themselves, the Committee's comments were addressed to rights protections going beyond those protected in the International Bill of Rights and which recognised the unique situation of Indigenous peoples and the risks presented by harmful business activities.

The Committee on the Rights of the Child, as noted previously, has taken the view that the Convention creates "indirect obligations" for non-state service providers.[192] It issued specific recommendations in 2002, calling on such entities to "respect the principles and provisions" of the Convention.[193] In General Comment 16, the Committee presented an even more robust view on the application of the instrument to business enterprises:

> [T]he Committee recognizes that duties and responsibilities to respect the rights of children extend in practice beyond the State and State-controlled services and institutions and apply to private actors and business enterprises. Therefore, all businesses must meet their responsibilities regarding children's rights and States must ensure they do so. In addition, business enterprises should not undermine the States' ability to meet their obligations towards children under the Convention and the Optional Protocols thereto.[194]

The "best interests of the child" principle is, in the view of the Committee, "directly applicable to business enterprises that function as private or public social welfare bodies by providing any form of direct services for children, including care, foster care, health, education and the administration of detention facilities."[195]

While the Covenant on Economic, Social and Cultural Rights is integral to the International Bill of Rights and thus included within the scope of the corporate responsibility to respect human rights of the Guiding Principles, the Committee has identified in greater detail the particular groups that are disproportionately affected by harmful business activities:

> [W]omen, children, indigenous peoples, [. . .] peasants, fisherfolk and other people working in rural areas, and ethnic or religious minorities where these minorities are politically disempowered. Persons with disabilities [. . .] asylum seekers and undocumented migrants [. . .] migrant workers are particularly vulnerable to exploitation, long working hours, unfair wages and dangerous and unhealthy working environments.[196]

---

[190] United Nations Declaration on the Elimination of All Forms of Racial Discrimination, General Assembly Resolution 1904 (XVIII) (Nov. 20, 1963), Article 3.

[191] CERD, *Concluding observations: Canada*, CERD/C/CAN/CO/18 (May 25, 2007), para. 17.

[192] CRC, *General Comment 5, supra* note 28, para. 43.

[193] CRC, *Day of General Discussion, supra* note 30, para. 653.

[194] CRC, *General Comment 16, supra* note 79, at para. 8.

[195] *Id.*, at para. 16.

[196] CESCR, *General Comment 24, supra* note 79, at para. 8.

Some are at risk of facing intersectional and multiple types of discrimination, particularly Indigenous women and girls.[197] The Committee's rich discussion of what it is needed to "guarantee the enjoyment of Covenant rights to all without discrimination" stands in contrast to the weaker approach of the UN Guiding Principles.

States and indeed companies can draw on the work of the treaty bodies for a fuller understanding of the "additional standards" which the Guiding Principles refer to. Treaty bodies of a more recent vintage are equally as relevant as those mentioned previously, in particular the Committee on Migrant Workers and the Committee on the Rights of Persons with Disabilities. The Committee on Migrant Workers, for example, has emphasised the need for states to regulate private entities, in particular those operating prisons or immigration detention facilities, given the risks posed to the human rights of migrant workers, their families, and asylum seekers.[198] The Convention on the Rights of Persons with Disabilities obliges states parties "[t]o take all appropriate measures to eliminate discrimination on the basis of disability by any person, organization or private enterprise."[199] The Convention has enjoyed extensive ratification, with 185 states parties at the time of writing, while 100 states have ratified the Optional Protocol permitting individual communications to the Committee.[200] The Convention makes extensive references to states parties' obligations as they relate to the private sector, including business enterprises,[201] while the Committee itself has turned to such matters in its general comments.

In General Comment 2 (2014) on accessibility under Article 9 of the Convention, the Committee on the Rights of Persons with Disabilities directly addresses harms to human rights by the private sector and seeks to collapse to some extent the distinction between public and private actors in the context of accessibility:

> The focus is no longer on legal personality and the public or private nature of those who own buildings, transport infrastructure, vehicles, information and communication, and services. As long as goods, products and services are open or provided to the public, they must be accessible to all, regardless of whether they are owned and/or provided by a public authority or a private enterprise. Persons with disabilities should have equal access to all goods, products and services that are open or provided to the public in a manner that ensures their effective and equal access and respects their dignity. This approach stems from the prohibition against discrimination; denial of access should be considered to constitute a discriminatory act, regardless of whether the perpetrator is a public or private entity.[202]

---

[197] *Id.*, at para. 8.

[198] CMW, *General Comment No. 2 on the rights of migrant workers in an irregular situation and members of their families*, CMW/C/GC/2 (Aug. 28, 2013), paras. 21, 39; CMW, *General Comment No. 5 (2021) on migrants' rights to liberty and freedom from arbitrary detention*, CMW/C/GC/5 (Sept. 23, 2021), paras. 5, 30, 31.

[199] Convention on the Rights of Persons with Disabilities, entered into force 3 May 2008, 2515 UNTS 3, Article 4(1)(e).

[200] *See* https://treaties.un.org.

[201] *See, e.g.*, Article 4(1)(f)–(g), Article 8(2)(c), Article 8(2)(c), Article 12(5), Article 21(c), Article 27.

[202] CRPD, *General Comment No. 2, Article 9: Accessibility*, CRPD/C/GC/2 (May 22, 2014), para. 13. *See also Nyusti and Takács v. Hungary*, Communication No. 1/2010, CRPD/C/9/D/1/2010 (June 21, 2013).

Demonstrating the influence of the work of the treaty bodies on each other, the Committee has drawn on CESCR General Comment 24 on business and human rights in the preparation of its forthcoming general comment on Article 27 concerning the right to work.[203]

This combined output of the treaty bodies concerning protected persons and groups serves to both illustrate the more limited approach of the UN Guiding Principles concerning human rights protections which should be of concern to business enterprises and to elaborate a more inclusive way forward. As with the matter of extraterritorial human rights obligations, the treaty bodies' general comments have served as an important vehicle for informing states of the various Committees' interpretation of existing standards. Such understanding will guide the treaty bodies' engagement with states parties via periodic reporting or individual complaints on such matter. They also provide a means by which the treaty bodies can play an important role in advancing the future business and human rights agenda at the United Nations.

IV. LOOKING AHEAD

Despite over two decades of initiatives at the United Nations to address business practices which harm human rights in a context of continued growth in size and power of transnational corporations, such entities remain the subject of only "fragile international regulation."[204] That business enterprises should be regulated to prevent or punish their violation of human rights has long been a clarion call of certain UN treaty monitoring bodies.[205] The development of the Guiding Principles contributed significantly to the mainstreaming of business and human rights within the UN human rights machinery, and beyond, but did not, nor was it intended to, provide an international regulatory regime concerning business and human rights. Since the endorsement of the Guiding Principles in 2011, efforts at the United Nations to progress the business and human rights agenda have focused mainly on two initiatives: the development of national action plans to implement the Guiding Principles domestically and the adoption of a new treaty on business and human rights.

Such efforts have been endorsed by the treaty bodies, with the Committee on Economic, Social and Cultural Rights describing the adoption of national plans on business and human rights as a "welcome development," particularly where they "set specific and concrete targets, allocate responsibilities across actors, and define the time frame and necessary means for their adoption."[206] The Committee also expressed its indirect support for a new treaty in this area, by supporting "any efforts at the adoption of international instruments that could strengthen the duty of States to cooperate in order to improve accountability and access to remedies for victims of violations of Covenant rights in transnational cases."[207]

Progress in the development of national action plans and a binding instrument on business and human rights has been limited. National action plans have been adopted by only a

---

[203] CRPD, *Draft General Comment on article 27 on the rights of persons with disabilities to work and employment*, 2021, para. 19.

[204] Fernando Frizzo Bragato & Alex Sandro de Silveira Filho, *The Colonial Limits of Transnational Corporations' Accountability for Human Rights Violations*, 2 TWAIL REVIEW 34, 34 (2021).

[205] *See, e.g.,* CRC, *Concluding observations: Bahrain* CRC/C/BHR/CO/2-3 (Aug. 3, 2011), para. 21; CRC, *Concluding observations: Republic of Korea*, CRC/C/KOR/CO/3-4 (Oct. 6, 2011), para. 27; CRC, *Concluding observations: Turkey* CRC/C/TUR/CO/2-3 (July 20, 2012), paras. 22–23; CRC, *Concluding Observations: Lao People's Democratic Republic*, CRC/C/LAO/CI/3-6 (Nov. 1, 2018), para. 13.

[206] CESCR, *General Comment 24, supra* note 79, at para. 59.

[207] *Id.,* at para. 35.

handful of states and are often lacking in substance, limited in ambition and neglectful of effective implementation.[208] They offer a mere illusion of progress. According to the Working Group on Business and Human Rights:

> [T]he relatively low number of national action plans so far demonstrates that most States have still to prioritize implementation of the Guiding Principles. Moreover, the relative lack of quality in the content of many national action plans and in several processes highlights the shortcomings of these initiatives if they are not backed by concrete State action and inclusive stakeholder engagement.[209]

As to a new treaty, several drafts of a "binding legal instrument" on business and human rights have been published by the Open-Ended Intergovernmental Working Group on transnational corporations and other business enterprises with respect to human rights,[210] but the majority of states remain largely unconvinced of the merits of such an approach at present.[211] Michelle Bachelet, the UN High Commissioner for Human Rights sounded a word of warning in her opening statement at the seventh session of the Intergovernmental Working Group in October 2021: "Do not let this opportunity go by; if progress is too slow, we risk disillusionment and disengagement from this process."[212]

As these initiatives have advanced slowly and with halting progress, the treaty bodies have persevered in their efforts to address business and human rights in the main through the elaboration of general comments and recommendations, and when taking states to task on their periodic reports. Regardless of the outcome of the treaty process, which could indeed peter out, and irrespective of how efforts to develop national action plans unfold, the work of the treaty monitoring bodies on business and human rights will endure. Even taking into consideration current financial difficulties,[213] the treaty bodies will continue to engage states on their responsibilities in this sphere. In some respects, continuing and indeed expanding their activities in relation to business and human rights could serve to address current gaps in human rights law, including those highlighted by advocates of a new binding instrument. An invigorated business and human rights focus on the part of the treaty bodies could mitigate the likely absence of new institutional machinery, would

---

[208] *See generally* Humberto Cantú Rivera, *National Action Plans on Business and Human Rights: Progress or Mirage?*, 4(2) BUSINESS AND HUMAN RIGHTS JOURNAL 213 (2019).

[209] Report of the Working Group, *Guiding Principles on Business and Human Rights at 10, supra* note 81, para. 44.

[210] For the most recent version, *see* United Nations Open-Ended Intergovernmental Working Group on a binding treaty on business and human rights, *Third Revised Draft,* 2021, available at https://www.ohchr.org/Documents/HRBodies/HRCouncil/WGTransCorp/Session6/LBI3rdDRAFT.pdf.

[211] Claire Methven O'Brien, *Transcending the Binary: Linking Hard and Soft Law Through a UNGPs-Based Framework Convention,* 114 AJIL UNBOUND 186 (2020). *See also* Nadia Bernaz, *Conceptualizing Corporate Accountability in International Law: Models for a Business and Human Rights Treaty,* 22 HUMAN RIGHTS REVIEW 45 (2021).

[212] *Opening Statement of the UN High Commissioner for Human Rights at the 7th session of the Intergovernmental Working Group on transnational corporations and other business enterprises with respect to human rights,* 25 October 2021, available at https://www.ohchr.org/EN/NewsEvents/Pages/DisplayNews.aspx?NewsID=27711&LangID=E.

[213] Office of the High Commissioner for Human Rights, *UN budget shortfalls seriously undermine the work of the Human Rights Treaty bodies,* Press Release (May 17, 2019). *See also* UN Secretary General, *Status of the human rights treaty body system* A/77/279 (Aug. 8, 2022), paras. 79–81.

further socialise states as to their human rights obligations vis-à-vis the private sector, and may provide some victims with an avenue for remedy for corporate human rights abuses.

A. Institutional and Substantive Issues

Civil society, intergovernmental organisations and a small number of states invested considerable resources in the implementation of the UN Guiding Principles via national plans and in the development of a new business and human rights treaty. While the return on such investment may not have matched expectations, such efforts have doubtlessly sharpened understandings of the relationship between business and human rights and served to highlight areas of weakness in the international human rights system. The development of the UN Guiding Principles and these subsequent efforts at their implementation have increased awareness of business and human rights concerns amongst the various relevant actors and a firm commitment to their resolution in some quarters. A further investment of such expertise and energy into the treaty body system may prove beneficial for advancing the business and human rights agenda.

How can the treaty bodies deepen their engagement with business and human rights? The development of specialized general comments or recommendations on business and rights comprises an important step in elaborating upon state obligations under the relevant instrument with regards to private sector activities. Specialised general comments on business and human rights should no longer remain "unusual" for the treaty bodies.[214] For those treaty bodies that have not yet adopted such general comments, those of the Committee on the Rights of the Child and the Committee on Economic, Social and Cultural Rights provide a valuable template. Consideration might also be given to joint general comments on business and human rights issues of common concern to the treaty bodies. Patrick Thornberry, a former member of the Committee on the Elimination of Racial Discrimination, has suggested a joint general comment on "the operations of business enterprises in indigenous territories."[215] At the very least, it will be important to ensure a consistent approach to business and human rights in the adoption of non-specialised general comments. In this vein, the Convention on the Rights of Persons with Disabilities tasks the Committee with consulting with the other treaty bodies "with a view to ensuring the consistency of their respective reporting guidelines, suggestions and general recommendations."[216]

General comments and recommendations remain the foremost vehicle for articulating the understanding of the treaty bodies of state's obligations under applicable treaties. They serve to "provide clarification, development and persuasive interpretations of the obligations imposed in the covenants," and accordingly, David Bilchitz has argued that there is "a need for a similar mechanism for the release of authoritative guidance on the application of international human rights to companies."[217] In the absence of a new treaty body, given the failure to adopt a business and human rights instrument to date, it is submitted that the existing treaty bodes could bridge the gap, in part by continuing to deploy general comments and recommendations, specialised or otherwise, which address business and human rights.

---

[214] van Ho, *supra* note 170, at 872.

[215] Patrick Thornberry, *The Committee on the Elimination of Racial Discrimination*, in Alston & Megrét, *supra* note 8, 309, at 335–336.

[216] Convention on the Rights of Persons with Disabilities, Article 38(b).

[217] David Bilchitz, *The Necessity for a Business and Human Rights Treaty*, 1(2) Business and Human Rights Journal 203, 212 (2016).

It remains the case that the treaty bodies must remain faithful to their respective treaties and may have a somewhat narrow focus on specific rights or protected persons groups within their mandate. General Comment 24 of the Committee on Economic, Social and Cultural Rights, for example, refers pointedly to "Covenant rights."[218] In addition, the treaty bodies focus in the main on state obligations. Nonetheless, a concerted and coordinated engagement by all treaty bodies with business and human rights could ensure that the relevant obligations of states regarding the full range of rights, protected persons and groups are clearly set out, perhaps even going further than the Guiding Principles in some respects. As discussed in the previous section, it is also the case that the treaty bodies have spoken to the human rights responsibilities of companies, thus eschewing an overly strict state-centric approach.[219] For Elena Pribytkova, some treaty bodies "go beyond the *U.N. Guiding Principles* and stipulate that [transnational corporations] also have obligations to protect human rights."[220] In the context of business and human rights, treaty bodies can continue to contribute to the progressive development of international human rights law,[221] and can use their influential position to shape developments in this domain even where a consensus on the part of states has yet to emerge.

The concluding observations of treaty bodies on the periodic reports of states parties can also be harnessed to reinforce state obligations concerning business and human rights. State reporting allows for monitoring of compliance with treaty obligations and for regular engagement between states parties and the treaty bodies. Recommendations on areas of concern necessarily entail elaboration on the content of the obligations of states. Treaty bodies should follow the example set by the Committee on the Rights of the Child and include a dedicated section on business and human rights in their concluding observations. Such an approach not only prompts states to address business and human rights issues in their reports, but also encourages civil society and national human rights institutions to highlight such issues in their submissions to the Committee. The Committee on the Rights of the Child then maintains a continuous dialogue with states parties with a view to improving compliance and rights protection.

The most critical point of engagement between the treaty bodies and victims of violations of human rights is in the individual complaints procedures. Where states parties have agreed to be subject to such complaints, whether through ratification of an optional protocol or making a declaration under a relevant treaty article, individuals can petition the relevant treaty body and seek a remedy.[222] In the business and human right context, the absence of effective remedies renders the state duty to protect human rights "weak or even meaningless."[223] The treaty bodies have begun to address the right to remedy in the business

---

[218] *See, e.g.,* CESCR, *General Comment 24, supra* note 79, at para. 33.

[219] *See, e.g.,* CRC, *Day of General Discussion, supra* note 30, para. 653; CESCR, *General Comment 24, supra* note 79, paras. 4, 5, 11; CRC, *General Comment 16, supra* note 79, paras. 8, 16. *See also* John Gerard Ruggie, *Business and Human Rights: The Evolving International Agenda,* 101 AMERICAN JOURNAL OF INTERNATIONAL LAW 819, 833 (2007); *Nevsun Resources Ltd. v. Araya,* 2020 SCC 5.

[220] Elena Pribytkova, *Extraterritorial Obligations in the United Nations System: U.N. Treaty Bodies, in* THE ROUTLEDGE HANDBOOK ON EXTRATERRITORIAL HUMAN RIGHTS OBLIGATIONS 95, 100 (Mark Gibney et al. eds., 2021).

[221] *See, e.g.,* Scott Jerbi, *Business and Human Rights at the UN: What Might Happen Next?,* 31 HUMAN RIGHTS QUARTERLY 299, 314 (2009); César Rodriguez-Garavito, *Business and Human Rights: Beyond the End of the Beginning. in* RODRIGUEZ-GARAVITO, *supra* note 186, at 38.

[222] On the acceptance of the nine individual complaints procedures, *see* https://www.ohchr.org/sites/defa ult/files/Documents/Issues/HRIndicators/IndividualCommunications_map.pdf.

[223] UN Guiding Principles on Business and Human Rights, *supra* note 1, at 22.

and human right context, albeit without placing sufficient emphasis on their own potential role as an avenue of accountability. The Committee on Economic, Social and Cultural Rights, for example, has highlighted the importance of "effective monitoring, investigation and accountability mechanisms must be put in place to ensure accountability and access to remedies, preferably judicial remedies, for those whose Covenant rights have been violated in the context of business activities."[224] It does not mention individual communications under the Optional Protocol, although admittedly only twenty-six states have ratified the instrument.[225]

Communications to the treaty bodies have begun to draw on relevant business and human rights terminology. The Human Rights Committee was recently confronted by a petition involving the extent of Canada's extraterritorial human rights obligations in relation to the activities of business enterprises overseas.[226] It deemed the complaint inadmissible as insufficient information had been provided regarding how Canada "could be considered responsible as a result of a failure to exercise reasonable due diligence over the relevant extraterritorial activities of the two corporations."[227] Demonstrating the challenges of seeking extraterritorial remedies, the Committee outlined how information was needed concerning relevant domestic regulations in Canada, the states party capacity to regulate the activities in question, the nature of the companies' role in the violations and impact on the rights of the authors, and the information available to the state regarding the activities in question, including whether their consequences were foreseeable. The Human Rights Committee held that the nexus between Canada's covenant obligations, the actions of the relevant enterprises and the alleged rights violation "is not sufficiently substantiated to render the case admissible."[228] For the individual complaints procedures of the treaty bodies to provide a means of accountability in the context of business and human rights, it is essential that clear guidance is available to would-be complainants on the necessary ingredients of any complaint. The views of the Human Rights Committee in this particular complaint have been described as entailing "denial of justice."[229] Two Committee members saw the decision as a missed opportunity and sought to elaborate on what would be required to sufficiently substantiate a communication.[230]

In addition to the foregoing, various other tools at the disposal of the treaty bodies could be deployed in the business and human rights realm. Inter-state procedures, which have become more prominent in recent years,[231] could play a role in ensuring the maintenance of rights protections in the trade and investment agreements made between home and host

---

[224] CESCR, *General Comment 24, supra* note 79, at para. 38.

[225] *See* https://indicators.ohchr.org.

[226] *Basem Ahmad Issa Yassin et al. v. Canada*, Human Rights Committee, Decision adopted by the Committee under Article 5(4) of the Optional Protocol, concerning communication No. 2285/2013, CCPR/C/120/D/2285/2013 (Dec. 7, 2017).

[227] *Id.*, at para. 6.7.

[228] *Id.*

[229] *See* Marco Fasciglione, *An International Mechanism of Accountability for Adjudicating Corporate Violations of Human Rights? Problems and Perspectives, in* JUDICIAL POWER IN A GLOBALIZED WORLD: LIBER AMICORUM VINCENT DE GAETANO 179, 187–188 (Paulo Pinto de Albuquerque & Krzysztof Wojtyczek eds., 2019).

[230] *Basem Ahmad Issa Yassin et al. v. Canada*, Annex, Concurring opinion of Committee members Olivier de Frouville & Yadh Ben Achour, para. 2.

[231] *See, e.g.*, David Keane, *Inter-State Cases Under the International Convention for the Elimination of All Forms of Racial Discrimination, in* HUMAN RIGHTS AND HUMANITARIAN LAW: CHALLENGES AHEAD 199 (Andreas Zimmermann & Norm Weiß eds., 2022).

states of multinational business enterprises. The issuance of statements, the conducting of country inquiries, and the use of early warning and urgent appeals processes in cases of acute concern would signal further advancement of the mainstreaming of business and human rights in the activities and outputs of the treaty bodies.[232] In their joint statement on human rights and climate change, five treaty bodies reminded states of their duty to "regulate private actors, including by holding them accountable for the harm they generate both domestically and extraterritorially."[233] With the operations of the treaty bodies the subject of proposals for strengthening and reform,[234] there is scope to further embed how they engage with business and rights.

From a substantive perspective, the treaty bodies are in a position to go beyond the general and at times abstract approach of the UN Guiding Principles on business and human rights. The Guiding Principles avoid singling out particularly harmful industries or business practices as meriting particular attention. Only the context of conflict is addressed separately, albeit without referring to the evidently problematic private military and arms industries. The challenges of climate change and protection of the environment are conspicuously absent from the Guiding Principles, despite the considerable contribution of fossil fuel companies to the climate emergency.[235] The treaty bodies have not adopted such a constrained approach, can address business and human rights in a more holistic manner, and are better placed to respond to emerging and pressing human rights concerns implicating the private sector. In General Comment 36, for example, the Human Rights Committee highlights that the implementation of the obligations concerning this right to life depends "on measures taken by States parties to preserve the environment and protect it against harm, pollution and climate change caused by public and private actors."[236] The treaty bodies are increasingly addressing issues such as tax avoidance and the protection of rights in the digital environment, both of which implicate the business enterprises.[237] Statements issued by the treaty bodies concerning COVID-19 touched upon concerns related to the private sector.[238] As discussed previously, the treaty bodies have played a formative role in advancing extraterritorial human rights obligations, including in relation to business activities.

---

[232] For an overview of treaty body activities, *see* Office of the High Commissioner for Human Rights, *The United Nations Human Rights Treaty System*, Fact Sheet No. 30/Rev.1 (2012), 19–39.

[233] CEDAW, CESCR, CMW, CRC and CRPD, *Statement on human rights and climate change*, HRI/2019/1 (May 14, 2020), para. 12.

[234] *See, e.g., Report on the process of the consideration of the state of the United Nations human rights treaty body system*, A/75/601 (Nov. 17, 2020); Suzanne Egan, *Strengthening the United Nations Human Rights Treaty Body System*, 13(2) HUMAN RIGHTS LAW REVIEW 209 (2013); Basak Çali & Alexandre Skander Galand, *Towards A Common Institutional Trajectory? Individual Complaints before UN Treaty Bodies During Their "Booming" Years*, 24(8) INTERNATIONAL JOURNAL OF HUMAN RIGHTS 1103 (2020).

[235] *See, e.g.*, CLIMATE ACCOUNTABILITY INSTITUTE, THE CARBON MAJORS, DATABASE; CDP CARBON MAJORS REPORT 2017 (2017).

[236] HRC, *General Comment 36, supra* note 79, at para. 62.

[237] *See* CRC, *General Comment No. 25 on children's rights in relation to the digital environment*, CRC/C/GC/25 (Mar. 2, 2021), paras. 35–39; CRC, *General Comment 16, supra* note 79, at para. 55; CRC, *Concluding observations on the combined fifth and sixth period reports of the Kingdom of the Netherlands*, CRC/C/NLD/CO/5-6 (Mar. 9, 2022), para. 9(c); CEDAW, *Concluding observations on the combined fourth and fifth periodic reports of Switzerland*, CEDAW/C/CHE/CO/4-5 (Nov. 25, 2016), paras. 40–41.

[238] *See* CESCR, *Statement on universal and equitable access to vaccines for the coronavirus disease (COVID-19)*, E/C.12/2020/2 (Dec. 15, 2000); Office of the High Commissioner on Human Rights, *Compilation of statements by human rights treaty bodies in the context of Covid-19* (Sept. 2020), 5, 30, 40, 48.

The Guiding Principles refrain from considering whether the size, form, and power of business enterprises are in of themselves inimical to human rights. Consumerism and the relentless pursuit of resources, growth, and profit as central elements of capitalism were not under consideration during the Ruggie mandate. The treaty bodies could consider broader structural issues in this context that lead to rights violations. Privatisation, for example, has clear implications for human rights yet the treaty bodies have been somewhat tentative in addressing it. The UN Special Rapporteur on extreme poverty and human rights, Philip Alston, wrote in 2018 that "most human rights bodies have either ignored the phenomenon or assumed that tweaking existing procedures provides an adequate response."[239] The UN Guiding Principles on business and human rights can be said to have taken the same "path of agnosticism"[240] by reiterating the view of the treaty bodies that human rights obligations continue even where states "contract with, or legislate for, business enterprises to provide services that may impact upon the enjoyment of human rights" even if privatisation itself is not contrary to human rights law.[241] Given that "large swathes of public life are increasingly devoid of human rights protections,"[242] Alston found a pressing need for finding "new ways in which treaty bodies . . . can meaningfully hold States and private actors accountable in privatization contexts."[243] Privatisation has certainly been addressed by the treaty bodies for a number of years,[244] and quite forcefully more recently, particularly by the Committee on Migrant Workers.[245] With the almost inevitable human rights challenges posted by privatisation, the treaty bodies may need be even more assertive and creative in this context.

V. CONCLUSION

The UN treaty monitoring bodies have played a pioneering if at times underappreciated part in the elaboration of the role of international human rights law in managing the relationship between states, the private sector, communities, and individuals. The treaty bodies' articulation of the scope and content of a state's obligation to protect human rights from being harmed by business enterprises forms the foundation of the UN Guiding Principles. The influence of the treaty bodies on the Guiding Principles is also evident on other areas, such as access to remedy under the third pillar. Demonstrating how the treaty bodies have ploughed their own furrow on aspects of business and human rights, they have on occasion taken a different stance on certain matters, such as extraterritorial human rights obligations, and in doing so have highlighted limitations of the Guiding Principles.

The UN Guiding Principles loom large in the field of business and human rights, for ample reason, but as Surya Deva has written, they should be seen "as part of a continuing process to develop standards at the UN level, rather than as a complete new start."[246]

---

[239] *Report of the Special Rapporteur on extreme poverty and human rights*, A/73/396 (Sept. 26, 2018), 2. *See generally* Manfred Nowak, Human Rights or Global Capitalism: The Limits of Privatization (2016); Aoife Nolan, *Privatization and Economic and Social Rights*, 40(4) Human Rights Quarterly 815 (2018); Antenor Hallo de Wolf, Reconciling Privatization with Human Rights (2012).

[240] *Id.*, at 5.

[241] UN Guiding Principles on Business and Human Rights, *supra* note 1, at 10.

[242] *Report of the Special Rapporteur on extreme poverty and human rights*, *supra* note 239, para. 76.

[243] *Id.*, at paras. 39–41, 87.

[244] CRC, *General Comment 5*, *supra* note 28, at paras. 4–44; CESCR, *General Comment 24*, *supra* note 79, at paras. 21–22.

[245] CMW, *General Comment No 2*, *supra* note 198, at paras. 21, 39. *See also* CMW, *General Comment 5*, *supra* note 198, at paras. 5, 29–31, 84, 91.

[246] Deva, *supra* note 12, at 147.

The treaty bodies efforts on business in human rights preceded the mandate of John Ruggie, impacted his work in various respects and will continue to shape the business and human rights agenda as other initiatives unfold. While efforts to implement the Guiding Principles at the national level via national action plans and to develop a new business and human rights treaty progress have faltered, the treaty bodies persevere in advancing business and human rights via specialised general comments or recommendations, in their concluding observations on state party periodic reports, and in their various other outputs. Communications to the treaty bodies by victims of corporate human rights abuses may yield a remedy where other avenues have been obstructed.

The UN treaty bodies are well placed to continue their positive engagement with business and human rights. A number have a considerable pedigree within the international human rights system, while all strive to be representative in their composition and count various experts with relevant specialization within their ranks. The regular engagement with states offers a privileged platform, while their encounters with victims provide a reminder of the need to ensure access to remedies and the effectiveness of international human rights standards in addressing violations irrespective of the actor in question. The work of the treaty bodies in this realm may be less susceptible to political interference when compared with the Charter bodies, as was the case with the stymying of the *Draft Norms* by the Human Rights Commission. Unsympathetic states have not been able to block the elaboration by the treaty bodies of obligations and responsibilities in the sphere of business and human rights. Yet states play a preeminent role in the realisation of rights at the national level, and it is prudent to not overstate the contribution of the treaty bodies to business and human rights, as with any other rights issues.[247] Nevertheless, by a process of accretion spanning a number of decades, they have brought to bear their considerable influence in one of the most challenging areas of human rights and will likely continue to shape the evolution of human rights standards in this context.

---

[247] Philip Alston, *The Committee on Economic, Social and Cultural Rights*, *in* Alston & Megrét, *supra* note 8, at 439, 469.

Algunos Comentarios Al Estudio De La Comisión De Derecho Internacional, Sobre Los Principios Generales Del Derecho

BY LUIS A. LÓPEZ ZAMORA*

Resumen

La Comisión de Derecho Internacional (CDI) inició en 2018 un estudio sobre los principios generales del derecho. Esta contribución tiene como propósito analizar los dos primeros informes del Relator Especial, en particular, la forma como los principios generales del derecho de origen doméstico habrían de incorporarse en el Derecho Internacional. Después, pasaremos a cuestionar el método construido por el Relator e indicaremos si puede considerarse el más adecuado. Tomar en cuenta el estudio del Relator Especial es importante, pues su análisis—hasta el momento—implica: (a) el establecimiento de un proceso intrincado para la identificación de los principios generales del derecho, haciendo más difícil su aplicación; y, debido (b) al efecto restrictivo que tendría en el rol que los tribunales y cortes internacionales (y la comunidad internacional) podrían desempeñar en aquella tarea. Además, analizaremos el método y la identificación de los principios generales del derecho formados directamente en el Derecho Internacional.

Abstract

In 2018, the International Law Commission (ILC) started a study on the general principles of law. This contribution will analyze the provisional conclusions reached by the Special Rapporteur in the matter, specifically regarding the ways the general principles of domestic

* Research Fellow en el Max Planck Institute Luxembourg for International, European and Regulatory Procedural Law. El borrador inicial de este ensayo, fue presentado en el Departamento de Derecho Internacional y Resolución de Disputas del Max Planck Institute Luxembourg y se benefició de los amables comentarios de los presentes ahí. Agradezco a mis colegas y a la di-rectora, la Prof. Hélène Ruiz-Fabri. Especial agradecimiento a Arpita Goswami y Carlos Bichet por sus comentarios a lo largo de la elaboración del presente ensayo. Como es usual, cualquier imprecisión es responsabilidad única del autor.

Luis A. López Zamora, *Algunos Comentarios Al Estudio De La Comisión De Derecho Internacional, Sobre Los Principios Generales Del Derecho* In: *The Global Community Yearbook of International Law and Jurisprudence 2022*. Edited by: Giuliana Ziccardi Capaldo, Oxford University Press © Oxford University Press 2023. DOI: 10.1093/oso/9780197752265.003.0005

law are to be incorporated in International Law and—thereon—questions the appropriateness of the methodology offered by him. The Special Rapporteur's study in the matter is relevant, insofar as it has implied: (a) the establishment of an intricate process, which makes the applicability of the general principles of law more stringent; and (b) the reduction of the role of international tribunals and courts in that endeavour. At the same time, the article will tackle the method formulated by the Special Rapporteur with regards to the identification of the general principles of law formed within International Law.

I. INTRODUCCION

La doctrina del Derecho Internacional aún centra muchos de sus esfuerzos en esclarecer nociones que –desde la perspectiva de otras ramas jurídicas– son consideradas precondiciones necesarias para hablar de un sistema normativo funcional; por ejemplo, haber construido una teoría sobre el origen de su normatividad (teoría de las fuentes). La falta de una teoría general relativa a la formación del Derecho Internacional no ha pasado desapercibida en la doctrina especializada, ni tampoco ha sido ignorada por la comunidad internacional. Por ello, en los últimos años, la Comisión de Derecho Internacional (CDI o la Comisión) ha intentado esclarecer el funcionamiento de las fuentes de nuestra disciplina. Ejemplo de ello, fue el estudio de más de 25 años sobre el derecho de los tratados; o el trabajo efectuado recientemente sobre la costumbre del Derecho Internacional,[1] así, como el estudio recientemente culminado sobre las normas de *ius cogens*.[2] Esto muestra un esclarecimiento en el funcionamiento de las fuentes del Derecho Internacional y fenómenos conexos. Sin embargo, en aquella tarea aún faltaba cubrir la fuente faltante del Derecho Internacional: los principios generales del derecho.

La falta de consideración de esta última fuente fue resuelta durante la Septuagésima Sesión de la CDI, ocasión en que se decidió que los principios generales del derecho debían incluirse en el programa de trabajo de la Comisión, eligiéndose a Marcelo Vázquez-Bermúdez como relator especial. Desde entonces, en el seno de la CDI se han elaborado dos reportes, en donde:[3] (a) Se ha analizado el significado de los principios generales del derecho a la luz del Artículo 38, párrafo 1 (c) del Estatuto de la Corte Internacional de Justicia (CIJ o Corte); (b) Se ha determinado la presencia de dos tipos de principios bajo la rúbrica 'principios generales del derecho' en el artículo 38 (los de origen doméstico y los de origen propiamente internacional); (c) Se ha llegado al convencimiento de que el 'reconocimiento' de los principios generales del derecho (de origen doméstico o internacional) constituye un paso esencial para que ellos

---

[1] Por ejemplo, véase: Anuario de la Comisión de Derecho Internacional. Vol. II (Part 2), 2011. Report of the Commission to the General Assembly on the work of its Sixty-Third Session. A/CN.4/SER.A/2011/Add.1 (Part 2).

[2] Véase: Comisión de Derecho Internacional. Primer Informe sobre la Formación y Evidencia del Derecho Internacional Consuetudinario, por Sir Michael Wood, Special Rapporteur. A/CN.4/663. 17 de mayo de 2013; ILC. Sixty-Ninth Session. Second Report on Jus Cogens. 16 de marzo de 2017. A/CN.4/706 y Comisión de Derecho Internacional. Seventieth Session. Tercer Informe sobre las Normas del Derecho Internacional General (*jus cogens*) por Dire Tladi, Relator Especial. A/CN.4/714. 12 de febrero de 2018.

[3] Véase: Comisión de Derecho Internacional. Primer Informe sobre los Principios General del Derecho. Seventy-First Session. A/CN.4/732. 5 de abril de 2019, y Segundo Informe sobre los Principios Generales del Derecho. Marcelo Vázquez-Bermúdez. Seventy-Second Session. 27 de abril–5 de junio y 6 de julio–7 de agosto de 2020. A/CN.4/741. Los Informes emitidos por el Relator Especial son pasos importantes para descifrar la naturaleza y funcionalidad de los principios generales del derecho; sin embargo, algunos puntos necesitan de mayor consideración por parte del Relator. Aquellos puntos, de ser tomados en cuenta, permitirán observar que el estudio tiene la potencialidad de llevar a sus límites la coherencia misma del Derecho Internacional.

puedan ser reputados aplicables en el Derecho Internacional; (d) Se ha efectuado un análisis sobre las formas en que el 'reconocimiento' de un principio general puede verificarse; (e) Se ha establecido que la 'transposición' constituye un requisito para que los principios generales del derecho de origen doméstico puedan aplicarse en el Derecho Internacional; y (f) Se ha realizado un análisis sobre la posible interacción entre la identificación de los principios generales del derecho y la identificación de las normas consuetudinarias del Derecho Internacional.

En este ensayo, nos centraremos en revisar –específicamente– los elementos que el Relator Especial consideró necesarios para que un principio general del derecho pueda ser parte del Derecho Internacional: los requisitos de 'reconocimiento' y 'transposición'. Después de ello, explicaremos los efectos que las consideraciones del Relator Especial (dados en sus primeros dos informes) podrían tener en la teoría general del Derecho Internacional. Argumentaremos, que el método del Relator requiere de escrutinio pues –tal y como actualmente se encuentra planteado– implica: (a) El establecimiento de un proceso intrincado, que haría la aplicación de los principios general del derecho más difícil en el plano internacional; y (b) La reducción del rol que los tribunales y cortes internacionales podrían desempeñar en aquel ejercicio. El origen de esto pareciera encontrarse en la preferencia del Relator, como de los otros miembros de la CDI –quienes hasta el momento han concordado con sus posturas– en concebir la identificación y funcionalidad de aquellos productos normativos desde un enfoque eminentemente positivista voluntarista.[4]

Para desentrañar dicha preferencia, debe recordarse que las conclusiones a las que el Relator Especial llegó en sus informes, solo pueden entenderse teniendo presente la base legal que él utilizó en su estudio: el artículo 38, párrafo 1 (c) del Estatuto de la CIJ. Dicha disposición tiene su propia historia, y una estructura tal, que ha permitido –hasta cierto punto– darle prevalencia a la participación de los Estados en la formación, surgimiento o identificación de los principios generales del derecho. Por ello, y con la finalidad de examinar el método ofrecido por el Relator Especial para la identificación de los principios generales del derecho, en la Sección B de este ensayo, haremos una breve revisión de su base legal (artículo 38), y consideraremos los elementos que la componen, como los problemas que surgen alrededor de ellos. En la Sección C, consideraremos propiamente el estudio del Relator Especial, teniendo presente: (i) el contenido particular que éste le diera al artículo 38, párrafo 1 (c) del Estatuto de la CIJ y luego, pasaremos a comentar (ii) las posibles falencias de su método.[5]

En relación a esto último, sostendremos que hasta el momento, el método del Relator presentaría: (i) problemas respecto al lenguaje empleado; (ii) problemas en el contenido dado a los dos componentes básicos del método de identificación de los principio general

---

[4] Si bien hemos señalado que el Relator Especial habría incorporado una aproximación positivista al momento de estructurar el método de identificación de los Principios Generales del Derecho, debe tenerse en cuenta que esto se debería –hasta cierto punto– a las características que su trabajo entraña, pues éste debe reflejar las posturas generalmente aceptadas en la CDI. Sobre esto último, debe recordarse que, en el trabajo de la CDI, las visiones más tradicionales sobre el Derecho Internacional aún son preponderantes. Esto último se debe a ciertos factores, como –por ejemplo– el hecho de que una parte importante de la labor de esta organización involucra la codificación del Derecho Internacional, lo cual se ve plasmado en borradores de instrumentos convencionales, que deben ser aceptado por los Estados. Por consiguiente, la CDI debe expresar posturas en consonancia con el hecho de que la voluntad de los Estados es clave para la formación del Derecho Internacional. Dado ello, las posturas individuales de los Relatores Especiales – muchas veces– deben de ceder frente a la posición que la mayoría podría tener en la CDI.

[5] Debe indicarse que, si bien haremos referencia a las 'posibles falencias' del método ofrecido por el Relator Especial, esto se dirige a ambos de sus primeros reportes, los cuales son provisionales. En ese sentido, es entendible que el método ofrecido por el Relator no se encuentre completamente acabado y que ante una revisión minuciosa, presente ciertas contradicciones. Esas contradicciones son parte de los comentarios que los otros miembros de la CDI han resaltado y que la doctrina especializada debe efectuar con el fin de poder hacer más clara una temática, que por naturaleza es difícil de discernir.

del derecho ('reconocimiento' y 'transposición'), (iii) un problema relativo al hecho de que la técnica podría no ser aplicable uniformemente a todos los principios generales del derecho que son utilizados en el Derecho Internacional, y que –además– se superpone al método utilizado para la identificación de las normas consuetudinarias; (iv) un problema relativo a que la técnica del Relator Especial no se encuentra lo suficiente respaldado por la práctica internacional, y (v) que todo ello conduciría a la reducción del rol de los tribunales y cortes internacionales en la identificación de los principios generales del derecho.

En la sección que sigue, revisaremos el marco legal que le sirvió de punto de partida al Relator Especial para efectuar el estudio de los principios generales del derecho.

II. LOS PRINCIPIOS GENERALES DEL DERECHO Y SU ESTATUS ACTUAL EN EL DERECHO INTERNACIONAL—SUS COMPONENTES, Y ALGUNOS PROBLEMAS ALREDEDOR DE SU TEORIZACION

El Relator Especial inició su análisis en base al artículo 38, párrafo 1 (c) del Estatuto de la CIJ. Por consiguiente, debemos de partir teniendo en cuenta lo indicado en aquella disposición.

Lo primero que debe indicarse es que la referencia hecha ahí no involucra sólo la referencia de los principios generales del derecho como categorías legales; aquella provisión añade –además– los elementos escenciales que deben de presentarse para considerar que un producto normativo ha surgido (o puede surgir) desde aquella fuente. Para ello, aquella disposición indica que los principios generales del derecho son 'reconocidos' por las 'naciones civilizadas'.[6]

Con esta técnica se mencionan los requisitos necesarios para que las reglas formadas a través de dicha fuente puedan operar y puedan ser utilizadas por la CIJ. Este método no es exclusivo de los principios generales del derecho. El artículo 38, párrafo 1, también hace alusión a las otras dos fuentes del Derecho Internacional: la costumbre y los tratados. Respecto a la costumbre internacional, la referencia hecha en el Estatuto de la CIJ viene acompañada de su calificación como "(...) prueba de una práctica generalmente aceptada como derecho"[7], mientras que la referencia realizada al derecho convencional, se complementa al indicarse que dicha fuente involucra el establecimiento de "(...) reglas expresamente reconocidas por los Estados litigantes."[8] De esa forma, en ambos casos la mención de las fuentes se complementa con los requerimientos necesarios para que una norma que se forma a través de éstas sea considerada válida por la CIJ (opinio juris –practica estatal, consentimiento).

En segundo lugar, el artículo 38, párrafo 1 es parte del Estatuto de la CIJ –por ende– cualquier indagación sobre la aplicabilidad de una regla en una disputa (frente a aquel tribunal) inicia teniéndose presente las definiciones incluidas en la base normativa de aquel órgano. Por esto mismo, la CIJ en su práctica, verifica previamente la presencia de los elementos referidos en el artículo 38, párrafo 1, antes de considerar que una regla es en efecto aplicable. En relación a los tratados, dado el convencimiento de que los Estados constituyen sujetos del derecho y que su manifestación de voluntad es necesaria para la formulación de toda regla internacional,[9] hasta cierto punto, el derecho convencional ha sido teorizado en proximidad a la teoría de los contratos del derecho doméstico.[10] Esto

---

[6] Estatuto de la Corte Internacional de Justicia. Artículo 38, 1 (c).

[7] *Id.*, Artículo 38, 1 (b).

[8] *Id.*, Artículo 38, 1 (a).

[9] Véase: E. DeWitt Dickinson, *The Analogy between Natural Persons and International Persons in the Law of Nations*, 26 YALE LAW JOURNAL 564, 591 (1917).

[10] *Id.*, at 578. Véase, igualmente: A. Nussbaum, *Significance of Roman Law in the History of International Law*, 100 UNIVERSITY OF PENNSYLVANIA LAW REVIEW 681 y sgtes (1952).

ha permitido utilizar ciertas nociones del derecho contractual, facilitando la teorización del derecho convencional internacional. En contraste con ello, para el caso del derecho consuetudinario, un proceso diferente se produjo, pues las vías de incorporación de la costumbre, que existen en el derecho doméstico, no existen en el Derecho Internacional.[11]

Como consecuencia de aquello, y dada la premisa de que los Estados deben de manifestar su voluntad para estar sujetos a una regla internacional, se hizo necesario el ajuste de la teoría de la costumbre concebida desde la Teoría del Derecho. Con ello, se buscaba que aquella fuente del derecho encajara con las características de nuestra disciplina.[12] Es así que emergieron los requisitos de la *opinio iuris* y la práctica estatal con las características a las que hace alusión el artículo 38, párrafo 1 del Estatuto de la CIJ.

En lo que respecta a los principios generales del derecho, cuando se revisa la referencia efectuada en el artículo 38, párrafo 1 (c) del Estatuto de la CIJ, queda claro que los elementos claves para determinar si algún producto normativo puede reputarse como

---

[11] En la teoría del derecho civil, el derecho consuetudinario debe de considerarse con la idea de que los ordenamientos jurídicos son sistemas coherentes y predecibles. En consecuencia, en los sistemas del derecho civil, para que la costumbre sea considerada como un producto normativo válido y aplicable es necesario que aquel pase por una examinación, la cual incluye la identificación de un elemento materia (conducta repetitiva) y un elemento subjetivo (*opinio juris seu necessitates*), y –finalmente–, requiere de la intervención de un poder público, el cual –implícita o expresamente– reconoce la exigibilidad de aquellas normas (por ejemplo, mediante su inclusión en el sistema legal, al ser recepcionada en la legislación, o por medio de su integración en el orden legal). Véase, A. Montoro Ballesteros, *La Costumbre en el Ordenamiento Jurídico. La Integración de las Lagunas Legales*, 20 ANALES DE DERECHO (Universidad de Murcia) 99, 110 (2000). Véase en general: H. KELSEN, TEORÍA PURA DEL DERECHO 238 y sgtes (1982). Con aquellos pasos, los Estados de tradición civilista evitan la fragmentación de sus ordenamientos legales y previenen el surgimiento de derecho particular en conflicto con el derecho general nacional. Una aproximación similar fue adoptada en los ordenamientos de *common law*. Por ejemplo, Austin recuerda que, *'[e]n su origen, la costumbre es una regla de conducta que los gobernados observaban espontáneamente, o no, al dar seguimiento a una ley establecida por un superior político. La costumbre es transmutada en derecho positivo cuando es adoptado, como tal, por las cortes de justicia, y luego cuando las decisiones judiciales formadas, en base a ellas, son ejecutadas por los poderes del Estado. Sin embargo, antes de ser adoptada por las cortes y revestida con sanción legal (la costumbre) es solo una regla de mera positividad moral.'* (traducción del autor). Véase: J. AUSTIN, LECTURES ON JURISPRUDENCE OR THE PHILOSOPHY OF POSITIVE LAW, 101, 102 (2006). Respecto a la costumbre, y cómo ésta ha sido entendida en diferentes momentos históricos, en los sistemas del *civil* y *common law*, véase: M. Smith, *Customary Law. I.*, 18 POLITICAL SCIENCE QUARTERLY 256, 281 (1903).

[12] Por ejemplo, los elementos que hacen posible el surgimiento de la costumbre en el derecho doméstico (practica y *opinión juris*) son entendidos –de una forma tal– que de ser aplicados en el Derecho Internacional produciría efectos incompatibles. Esto se debe a que en el Derecho Internacional, no existe una judicatura centralizada y al hecho de que la obligatoriedad de toda norma internacional requiere del consentimiento de los Estados. Como resultado, es difícil de imaginar la costumbre en el Derecho Internacional como un producto normativo que primero debiera aparecer como un hecho y después incorporado al sistema internacional por medio de una institución o procedimiento fuera del control de los Estados. Véase, D. Canale, *Paradojas de la Costumbre Jurídica*, 32 DOXA 223 (2009). Corbett explica este punto, al indicar que *'[e]l significado de 'costumbre' puede –sin duda– estirarse para cubrir, no solo el mero hábito de una acción, sino una regla de conducta, sostenida en una aprobación general. Aquel es –sin duda– el significado del término, cuando el litigante inglés es llamado a 'probar la costumbre'. Existen dos objeciones para extender esto a la ciencia del Derecho Internacional, y al mismo tiempo hacerla la fuente maestra o una de las fuentes maestras del Derecho Internacional. En primer lugar, confunde la fuente con el derecho en sí y, en segundo lugar, le asigna un rol legislativo antes que de evidencia a la costumbre. La costumbre es importante para el litigante internacional, solo en tanto demuestre el asentimiento general de los Estados; es aquel asentimiento lo que forma el derecho.'* (traducción del autor) Véase: P.E. Corbett, *The Consent of States and the Sources of The Law of Nations*, 6 BRITISH YEARBOOK OF INTERNATIONAL LAW 26 (1925).

principio general, son los términos: 'reconocidos' por las 'naciones civilizadas'. La forma en la que dicha disposición fue formulada podría dar la impresión de que el ajuste teórico sufrido por la costumbre también se habría producido en este caso. Sin embargo, en el caso de los principios generales, existen diferencias importantes. Los elementos que ayudan a identificar un producto consuetudinario, y que fueron recogidos en el articulo 38 del Estatuto de la CIJ, contaban con teoría y práctica que las avalaba,[13] y la misma se continuó desarrollando en los años posteriores (aun cuando los debates alrededor de aquel concepto durante la redacción del artículo 38 fueron limitados).[14] En contraste con esto, los principios generales del derecho (si bien acapararon atención en los debates de la redacción del artículo 38) difícilmente presentaban una teorización previa que sustentara la redacción final relativa a sus elementos esenciales tal y como fueran incluidos en el artículo 38, párrafo 1 (c).[15] Más aún, los elementos de aquella disposición: 'reconocidos' ('reconocimiento') y 'naciones civilizadas', apuntan a los elementos necesarios para la identificación de los principios generales de origen doméstico y que serian eventualmente utilizados en el Derecho Internacional, y no apuntaban necesariamente a requisitos de identificación de los principios generales del derecho formados directamente en el Derecho Internacional.

Esto último abría las puertas a complicaciones. Por ejemplo: ¿Cuáles son los elementos constitutivos de los principios generales del derecho formados directamente en el Derecho Internacional?

Por otro lado, debido a la redacción del artículo 38, párrafo 1 (c), el requisito de 'reconocimiento' es incluido, sin explicarse lo que ello involucra, y dada la escasa práctica adjudicativa que la interpretara, ello condujo a que el término se volviese presa del positivismo voluntarista de conectarla con el consentimiento de los Estados. Por esto mismo, existe cierta tendencia doctrinal de sostener que, para la utilización de los principios generales del derecho, se hace necesario la participación de los Estados, ya sea en su identificación o formación.[16] Sin embargo, debemos indicar que, para que esa conexión sea aceptada, por lo

---

[13] Véase: Permanent Court of International Justice. Advisory Committee of Jurists. Proceedings of the Committee (June 16th–July 24th 1920). The Hague—Van Langenhuysen Brothers, 1929. p. 306.

[14] Véase: Jean D'Aspremont, *The Decay of Modern Customary International Law in Spite of Scholarly Heroism*, GLOBAL COMMUNITY YILJ (GIULIANA ZICCARDI CAPALDO General ed.) 13 y sgtes (2015).

[15] Como recordara Cançado Trindade, la redacción final fue el resultado de un compromiso al que llegó el Comité Asesor de Juristas, entre las posiciones del iusnaturalismo y del positivismo respecto a los principios generales del derecho. Al respecto, véase: Opinión Individual del Juez Cançado Trindade. Corte Internacional de Justicia. Pulp Mills on the River Uruguay (Argentina v. Uruguay). Sentencia del 20 de abril de 2010. p. 130.

[16] Aun así, existe cierta doctrina que problematiza esta fuente del derecho, de forma más minuciosa. Por ejemplo, la Profesora Ziccardi Capaldo recuerda que, conjuntamente con los principios generales del derecho originados según lo dispuesto por el articulo 38 1(c) del Estatuto de la CIJ (en el cual la aceptación de los Estados forma un elemento fundamental de la identificación de las reglas que emergen de aquella fuente), también existen otros principios, los cuales pueden denominarse 'nuevos principios del Derecho Internacional'. Estos últimos, no emergerían de la aceptación prestada por los Estados sino de la voluntad de las fuerzas dominantes de la comunidad global. Estos principios se trasforman en Derecho, no porque sean impuestos, sino porque existe un consenso general sobre su aplicabilidad. Aquella aproximación describe el proceso dinámico detrás de la formación de los principios constitucionales globales como proceso integrado. La intersección entre la 'propuesta' de las fuerzas sociales prevalecientes y el 'consenso' proveniente de los actores gubernamentales y de la sociedad civil, las instituciones globales y cortes, al tiempo que facilitan la integración de voluntades dan surgimiento a la formación de los principios constitucionales antes indicados. Al respecto, véase: GIULIANA ZICCARDI CAPALDO, THE PILLARS OF GLOBAL LAW, 36, 38 (2008). También cabe resaltar la posibilidad de que existan principios históricos o intrínsecos dentro de un orden

menos se requeriría: (a) Justificar la utilización del voluntarismo positivista para entender la incorporación de los principios generales del derecho en el plano Internacional, lo cual no es una tarea simple, (b) Dar una explicación de cómo debería entenderse la conexión entre el 'reconocimiento' y el consentimiento estatal; y (c) Cómo ello podría ser aplicable a los principios generales del derecho formados directamente en el Derecho Internacional.

En el caso de los principios generales de origen doméstico, cuando el requisito de 'reconocimiento' es entendido desde un enfoque voluntarista aparecen ciertas dudas. Por ejemplo: ¿Por qué tendría que reducirse el 'reconocimiento' de los principios generales domésticos en el Derecho Internacional (actividad que implica la aplicación analógica del Derecho en el plano internacional) al reconocimiento dado por los Estados? El 'reconocimiento' de tipo 'voluntarista' solo ganaría razonabilidad si se entendiese que la mediación de la voluntad de los Estados o la comunidad internacional, se vuelve necesaria al brindar un servicio concreto y razonable al buen funcionamiento del sistema legal. En el segundo caso, para los principios generales del derecho formados directamente en el Derecho Internacional, el requisito de 'reconocimiento' se vuelve aun más controversial.

Para entender lo indicado, debe considerarse que el requisito de 'reconocimiento' podría tener un rol razonable en el proceso de identificación y/o formación de los principios generales si ello ayudara a restringir –razonablemente– el ingreso de productos foráneos en nuestra disciplina.[17] Después de todo, cuando un principio general del derecho (de origen doméstico) busca utilizarse en el Derecho Internacional es razonable que ciertos criterios deban de cumplirse. Uno de aquellos requisitos involucra el criterio de 'reconocimiento'. Aquel ejercicio, que Hersch Lauterpacht desde 1927 calificara como un tipo de aplicación analógica del Derecho doméstico en el Derecho Internacional, debe cumplir con ciertos criterios para su aplicación, como son: (i) Que se determine que no existen reglas convencionales o consuetudinarias que puedan ser aplicadas por un tribunal en un caso concreto (lo cual resalta la naturaleza complementaria y residual de los principios generales del derecho[18]); (ii) Que serán utilizados cuando un tribunal o corte internacional se vea en el peligro de declarar un *non-liquet*; y (iii) (para el caso de los principios generales del derecho de origen domestico) cuando se torne claro que algunos de aquellos principios han sido reputados de utilidad para resolver una disputa a nivel internacional.

El último criterio antes mencionado, es el que más se acerca al requisito de 'reconocimiento' referido por el artículo 38, párrafo 1 (c) del Estatuto de la CIJ. Es decir, 'reconocimiento' implica un ejercicio en el que se constata que un principio general del derecho de origen doméstico se encuentra reconocido en diferentes órdenes municipales de la comunidad internacional y que –dada la generalidad de su uso– podría ser útil y no controversial en el Derecho Internacional. Los principios generales del derecho que no cumpliesen con aquel requisito (o los otros indicados antes) no deberían ser incorporados.

---

social. Aquellos principios no pasarían por el filtro positivista al que haría referencia el articulo 38 1(c) del Estatuto de la CIJ, sino que serían principios que estarían reconocidos implícitamente en el ordenamiento desde su gestación. Serian principios originarios, sin los cuales el ordenamiento posteriormente formado no podría funcionar. Al respecto, véase: Luis A. López Zamora, *La Constitución del Derecho Internacional, su Extinción y Reconstrucción*, Vol. XXXIV Anuario de Filosofía del Derecho 333, 374 (2018).

[17] Aquella noción (reconocimiento), para operar de forma coherente y efectiva en el Derecho Internacional, no debe ser entendida puramente desde el prisma del consentimiento de los Estados (tendremos oportunidad de ahondar en ello más adelante).

[18] Alfred Verdross, Völkerrecht 126 (Spanish translation, 1957), referido en: Rafael Nieto-Navia, *Are Those Norms Truly Peremptory? With Special Reference to Human Rights Law and International Humanitarian Law*, 14 Global Community YILJ 2015 (Giuliana Ziccardi Capaldo General ed.) 54 (2015).

De no existir filtro alguno en la aplicación de los principios generales de origen doméstico, un sinnúmero de principios podrían aplicarse directamente en el Derecho Internacional, siendo que ello podría implicar la inclusión de máximas en colisión con las reglas más fundamentales del Derecho Internacional. Además, sin filtro alguno, podría darse la incorporación de principios que –en buena medida– no tendrían utilidad práctica en nuestra disciplina.

Sin embargo, aquí es importante matizar lo antes indicado. La relevancia del criterio de 'reconocimiento' mencionado antes (al que alude el artículo 38, párrafo 1 (c) del Estatuto de la CIJ) solo cobra importancia cuando hacemos frente al posible uso de principios generales del derecho de origen doméstico pues son estos los que necesitan ser transferidos desde los ordenamientos municipales a la realidad internacional. El escenario de problemas de coherencia con el Derecho Internacional no aparece (al menos no en el mismo sentido) con los principios general del derecho formados directamente en nuestra disciplina. Por consiguiente, el uso del requisito del 'reconocimiento' para este último grupo de principios debería llamar a cuestionamientos.

Sea como fuese, teniendo en cuenta el balance que debe de lograrse –por un lado– de ofrecer a los tribunales internacionales la posibilidad de acceder a una fuente del derecho para resolver potenciales lagunas en el ordenamiento internacional y –por otro lado– la necesidad de evitar los problemas que generaría aceptar la inclusión indiscriminada de principios generales foráneos (afectando así la integridad del Derecho Internacional); es que el Relator Especial construyó su interpretación particular del artículo 38, párrafo 1 (c) del Estatuto de la CIJ.

A continuación, daremos cuenta de la forma en que el Relator Especial ha entendido los elementos constitutivos del artículo 38, párrafo 1 (c) del Estatuto de la CIJ.

Si bien podríamos analizar detalladamente los dos informes del Relator Especial, hemos optado por dar cuenta breve de lo que sus estudios han incluido, para después mencionar las posibles críticas a su enfoque. La razón de esto, se debe a que su teorización, varía según se revise el primero o el segundo de sus informes. Será en las críticas que daremos a su enfoque general que mayores detalles podrán observarse respecto a la forma en que el Relator construyó su conceptualización sobre la formación o identificación de los principios generales de derecho.

III. EL ESTUDIO EFECTUADO POR EL RELATOR ESPECIAL RESPECTO A LOS PRINCIPIOS GENERALES DEL DERECHO Y *ALGUNOS PROBLEMAS ESTRUCTURALES*

A. El Contenido dado por el Relator Especial, al Artículo 38, párrafo 1 (c) del Estatuto de la Corte Internacional de Justicia

Lo primero que debe resaltarse respecto a la interpretación hecha por el Relator Especial al artículo 38, párrafo 1 (c) del Estatuto de la CIJ, es que su enfoque se encuentra influenciado por los potenciales problemas que se producirían, si se aceptase la inclusión indiscriminada de principios generales en el Derecho Internacional. La necesidad de restringir la incorporación de principios extra-sistemáticos empujó al Relator, a crear una técnica capaz de ofrecer certidumbre, respecto a la incorporación de construcciones legales foráneas en nuestra disciplina. Aquello resultó en la creación del denominado proceso de dos pasos (*two-step process* o *two-step analysis*) en el que se sostiene que, para la utilización de un principio general del derecho en el Derecho Internacional, es necesario: (i) Que se dé su 'reconocimiento' por parte de la 'comunidad de las naciones' y (ii) Que se produzca la 'transposición' de estos en el Derecho Internacional.

Según el Relator Especial, el primer paso ('reconocimiento') depende de si un principio general del derecho ha sido 'reconocido' en diferentes sistemas jurídicos domésticos, por ejemplo, en las legislaciones estatales, o en las decisiones de tribunales o cortes nacionales. El 'reconocimiento' de un principio general del derecho –según él– se verificará por la inclusión de aquel principio en fuentes estatales. Cuando aquel 'reconocimiento' es generalizado en diferentes Estados y diferentes familias legales, será posible considerar que el 'reconocimiento' ha sido efectuado por la 'comunidad de naciones'. Este último término remplaza el término referido en el artículo 38, párrafo 1 (c) de 'naciones civilizadas'.

El segundo paso referido por el Relator Especial –'transposición'– exige que el principio pueda ser aplicado harmoniosamente dentro del sistema legal internacional. Es importante subrayar que el requerimiento de 'transposición' no es parte de los elementos dispuestos en el artículo 38, párrafo 1 (c) del Estatuto de la CIJ, sino que es una innovación del Relator Especial y –por eso mismo– necesita un escrutinio más estricto.

Para el caso de los principios generales formados directamente en el Derecho Internacional, el método formulado por el Relator Especial exige que aquellos sean –por lo menos– 'reconocidos' por la 'comunidad de naciones'.

Como indicamos antes, es posible analizar detalladamente la posición del Relator Especial sobre a la formación de los principios generales del derecho. Sin embargo, su método cambia según revisemos su primer o segundo informe, por lo que será preferible realizar una crítica general a su aproximación, siendo que –en aquella critica– será posible ver los detalles de su método.[19]

En las siguientes secciones discutiremos seis deficiencias que hemos encontrado en el método empleado por el Relator Especial.

B. Las Deficiencias del Método Provisional Ofrecido por el Relator Especial

1. *Problema con la Claridad del Lenguaje Utilizado*

El 'proceso de dos pasos' propuesto por el Relator Especial es nuevo en el Derecho Internacional. Su método muestra la preocupación por ofrecer una forma estricta de incorporación de los principios generales del derecho de origen doméstico en el Derecho Internacional.[20] A pesar de ello, la técnica presenta ciertos problemas; por ejemplo, relacionado con la claridad terminológica. Sobre esto, debe tenerse presente que el Relator Especial utilizó diferentes términos para describir el proceso aplicable para la utilización de los principios generales. Por ejemplo, junto al término 'reconocimiento' (que es el utilizado por el Estatuto de la CIJ), el Relator Especial hace uso del término 'identificación'. El problema con esto es que aquél término es utilizado –a su vez– en el estudio del Derecho Internacional consuetudinario, lo que podría llevar a confusiones.[21] El Relator Especial,

---

[19] Para una revisión general del trabajo del Relator Especial en la material, véase: Marcelo Vázquez-Bermúdez & Alfredo Crosato, *General Principles of Law: The First Debate within the International Law Commission and the Sixth Committee*, 19 Chinese Journal of International Law 157, 172 (2020).

[20] Según el Relator Especial, *'[e]l análisis de dos pasos, es un examen riguroso; la existencia de principios generales del derecho no puede ni debe asumirse fácilmente.'* Comisión de Derecho Internacional. Segundo Informe sobre los Principios Generales del Derecho. Marcelo Vázquez-Bermúdez . . . Para. 20. (nota: 3).

[21] El Relator Especial reconoció la proximidad de ambos términos, por lo que señaló que, *'[a]l igual que en el tema 'Identificación del derecho internacional consuetudinario', la Comisión puede proporcionar orientaciones prácticas sobre cómo identificar los principios generales del derecho. Esta cuestión está estrechamente relacionada con el significado de la expresión 'reconocidos por las naciones civilizadas [. . .] en la medida en que, para poder identificar los principios generales del derecho, quizá sea necesario examinar la manera en que son reconocidos.'*

también utilizó otras referencias terminológicas, como 'formulación' y 'demostración', lo que genera la duda de si el elemento clave para que un principio general del derecho pueda ser utilizado, es su 'identificación', 'reconocimiento', 'formulación' o 'demostración'.[22]

2. *El Problema Alrededor del 'Reconocimiento' de los Principios Generales del Derecho*

Como indicáramos antes, el requisito de 'reconocimiento' cobra sentido para los principios generales originados extra-sistemáticamente. Un ejemplo del uso razonable de dicho requisito se da con los principios generales de origen doméstico, ya que su inclusión debe producirse solo si es absolutamente necesario. En esos casos, el 'reconocimiento' de un principio, funciona como un filtro que ayuda a excluir construcciones normativas foráneas que no funcionarían apropiadamente en el Derecho Internacional, o que podrían ser esgrimidos por los Estados sin que existan razones para que ellos sean útiles en la resolución de una disputa internacional. Sin embargo –como adelantáramos– es cuestionable que este paso deba exigirse para la utilización de los principios generales del derecho formados directamente en el Derecho Internacional, pues ellos emergen directamente en este sistema normativo. Por consiguiente, para esta última categoría de principios, sería necesaria una aproximación diferente. A pesar de ello, el Relator prefirió hacer extensivo a todos los principios generales del derecho la aplicación del 'reconocimiento'. Esa decisión podría llamar a cuestionamientos, pues, los principios generales del derecho formados directamente en el Derecho Internacional no constituyen normatividad externa, y –por ende– predicar su existencia en base al 'reconocimiento' efectuado por la 'comunidad internacional' podría ser tildado de injustificado al llevar a que estos fuesen entendidos como reglas creadas en base a otras fuentes del Derecho Internacional, como podría ser la costumbre internacional. Esto es aún más cierto, cuando en la doctrina internacionalista, aún no está resuelta la cuestión de si los principios generales del derecho formados directamente en el Derecho Internacional requieren de alguna expresión de voluntad o reconocimiento proveniente de los Estados. Es por ello que la decisión del Relator de conectar todos los principios generales del derecho a dicho requisito podría verse como controversial.

Por ejemplo, la artificialidad de expandir el requisito de 'reconocimiento' se torna más evidente al recordar que los principios generales del derecho utilizados en el Derecho Internacional comprenden, además de los mencionados por el Relator Especial, aquellos cuya presencia se produce independientemente de la participación, acción, voluntad o 'reconocimiento' de los actores del orden internacional. Por ejemplo: (i) Los principios generales intrínsecos al Derecho, como son, los principios de la lógica legal; y (ii) Los principios generales que son estructurales al Derecho, y que presentan su origen en las bases sociales e históricas del sistema internacional,[23] antes que en una manifestación o

---

En esta sección, el Relator Especial pareciera entender que existen dos ejercicios involucrados para la utilización de los principios generales del derecho (cuando aquellos provienen del derecho doméstico); por un lado, el reconocimiento de aquellos y, por el otro, su identificación. Como veremos más adelante esto es dejado de lado, cuando el Relator especifica los pasos necesarios para la utilización de los principios generales del derecho formados en el derecho domésticos.

[22] Comisión de Derecho Internacional. Segundo Informe sobre los Principios Generales del Derecho. Marcelo Vázquez-Bermúdez . . . Para. 10. (note: 3).

[23] En la teoría del derecho (doméstico) (por ejemplo, desde la filosofía del derecho), se encuentra bien establecido que ciertos principios tienen su origen fuera del sistema normativo (sistema legal); por ejemplo, los originados en otras disciplinas y que –sin embargo– son adoptadas y eventualmente incluidos en un orden legal particular. Aquellos principios son denominados principios extra-sistemáticos. Por ende, la forma por las que estos principios son incluidos en la realidad legal, no pueden reducirse a un solo

'reconocimiento' ficticio proviniente de los sujetos del orden legal. Algunos casos históricos servirán de ejemplo. Por ejemplo, en relación al principio de prescripción, el tribunal arbitral en el caso Loretta G. Barberie v. Venezuela, sostuvo que:

> Es cierto que esta Comisión constituye un tribunal internacional y que –en cierto sentido– no está limitado por las reglas restrictivas y los procesos estrictos que le son aplicables a los tribunales domésticos; [. . .] sin embargo, existen ciertos principios que tienen su origen en el orden público [y que están] fundados en la naturaleza y necesidad de las cosas, las cuales, son obligatorias para todo tribunal que busca administrar justicia. Un gran lapso de tiempo es conocido por producir ciertos resultados inevitables [. . .]. El tiempo –en sí mismo– constituye una regla de finalización. Los tribunales de equidad actúan constantemente en línea con este principio constituyente, el cual no pertenece a ningún código o sistema judicial doméstico, sino que, es tan amplio y universal en su utilización como lo son las controversias humanas. Un reclamo estatal no es menos reclamo por que implique uno de tipo internacional y –este tribunal– al hace frente a esto, no puede escapar de la obligatoriedad de un principio universalmente reconocido solo por el hecho de que no exista un código positivo de reglas por el cual sus acciones deban de regirse.[24] (énfasis agregado)

El tribunal en cuestión, consideró aplicable el principio de prescripción pues lo consideró necesario para la resolución de la disputa, no porque el principio hubiese sido 'reconocido' por la 'comunidad de naciones'. Si el 'reconocimiento' indicado por el Relator hubiese sido necesario, se hubiese creado un nexo entre aquel principio y alguna forma de participación estatal. Eso tendría poco sentido para los principios que son parte esencial de la racionalidad del Derecho y que no son de origen doméstico ni internacional, y que se encuentran más allá de cualquier reconocimiento al estar sostenidos en la necesidad de la adjudicación. Lo mismo seria cierto respecto a los principios generales del derecho que forman parte del origen histórico de nuestra disciplina y que no pueden ser explicados en base a la participación de los sujetos del orden legal internacional vía su reconocimiento.

Esta preocupación no fue considerada en profundidad por el Relator Especial en su primer informe, y solo fue –indirectamente– analizado en su segundo informe. A decir verdad, en ambos informes, el Relator entiende la aplicación de los principios generales de origen doméstico y los propiamente internacionales cercana a la teoría del consentimiento. Esto, aun cuando el Relator trató de enmarcar el término 'reconocido por', como uno diferente al término 'aceptado por' (este último perteneciente al proceso de identificación de las normas consuetudinarias). Sin embargo, y a pesar de aquel esfuerzo, el Relator no logró convencer en el seno de la CDI que el requisito de 'reconocimiento' –en la práctica– no pudiese eventualmente constituir una manifestación indirecta de voluntad de los Estados.[25]

---

método. En relación a la existencia de principios extra-sistemáticos del derecho y las complejidades que proyectan en la ciencia legal, véase: Antonio Enrique Pérez Luño, *Los Principios Generales del Derecho: ¿Un Mito Jurídico?*, 98 Revista de Estudios Políticos 9, 24 (1997).

[24] Loretta G. Barberie v. Venezuela, N. 47. Véase: J. Bassett Moore, History and Digest of the International Arbitrations to Which the United States Has Been a Party. Vol. IV 4203 (1898). (traducción del autor).

[25] En ese sentido, algunos miembros de la Comisión de Derecho Internacional insistieron en la imposibilidad de identificar principios generales del Derecho Internacional de forma independiente al Derecho Internacional consuetudinario. Por ejemplo, véase, Argüello Gómez. Comisión de Derecho Internacional. Seventy-First Session (Second Part). A/CN.4/SR.3492. 2 de octubre de 2019. p. 4. Otros miembros de

Si el requisito de 'reconocimiento' en el sentido dado por el Relator Especial (hasta el momento) fuese correcto, la única diferencia con la identificación de la costumbre internacional sería que la constatación del reconocimiento de un principio general, se produciría sólo en base a circunstancias producidas a nivel del derecho domestico estatal (y no en el plano internacional como sucede con la costumbre internacional). Además, la verificación de la participación del Estado en el 'reconocimiento' no se verificaría Estado por Estado, sino mediante el 'reconocimiento' que la 'comunidad de naciones' habría prestado en su conjunto para tal efecto. Con ello, la posibilidad del objetor persistente –propio de la costumbre– desaparecería.

Lo que es claro es que el significado dado al requisito del 'reconocimiento' en los informes del Relator Especial, han sido convenientes para el positivismo, pues –con dicho enfoque– la admisión del uso de un principio general termina dependiendo de la acción de los sujetos del orden legal internacional (los Estados). Sea que no se le denomine a aquella acción 'manifestación de voluntad' sino 'reconocimiento', si se sigue el sentido del término tal y como el Relator Especial lo entiende hasta el momento, queda incólume el principio positivista de que los Estados no pueden estar sujetos a regla alguna a menos que la hayan aceptado. De esa forma, el método del Relator Especial termina defendiendo (directa o indirectamente) la inclusión de los principios generales mediante mecanismos que exigen la participación estatal en su identificación y formación. Debe recordarse que – en su momento– el Relator Especial indicó que, '(. . .) *el requisito de reconocimiento se ve cumplido cuando un principio exista dentro de un numero suficientemente amplio de ordenes legales domésticos.*'[26] En otras palabras, los Estados –por medio del reconocimiento y aplicación de principios legales en sus órdenes internos– pueden dar nacimiento a un principio que –eventualmente– podría ser incluido en el Derecho Internacional. Con ello, el surgimiento de los principios generales en el Derecho Internacional evita colisionar con el principio del consentimiento de los Estados, pues la formación de aquellos productos normativos proviene –al final de cuentas– de la práctica desarrollada por éstos.

Entonces, la pregunta final es: ¿Cuál es la diferencia entre el requisito de 'reconocimiento' y cualquier otra forma de manifestación de voluntad o participación de los Estados, como sería la 'aceptación' vinculada con la identificación de la costumbre internacional? ¿Son el 'reconocimiento' y la 'aceptación' diferentes, o son lo mismo, solo que una producida en el plano doméstico mientras que la otra a nivel internacional?[27]

---

la Comisión de Derecho Internacional como Nilüfer Oral (Comisión de Derecho Internacional. Seventy-First Session (Second Part). A/CN.4/SR.3492. 2 de October 2019. p. 8) y Ruda Santolaria (Comisión de Derecho Internacional. Seventy-First Session (Second Part). A/CN.4/SR.3492. 2 de octubre de 2019. p. 12) concordarían –en diferentes grados– con la necesidad de hacer más clara la distinción entre el 'reconocimiento' como requisito de la identificación de los principios generales del derecho y el 'reconocimiento' que constituye el Derecho Internacional consuetudinario.

[26] Comisión de Derecho Internacional. Primer Informe sobre los Principios Generales del Derecho . . . Para. 167 (nota: 3).

[27] Comisión de Derecho Internacional. Seventy-First Session (Second Part). A/CN.4/SR.3492. 2 de octubre de 2019. p. 9. Las palabras de Gómez-Robledo, comentando el Primer Informe del Relator Especial, resumen las complejidades de diferenciar apropiadamente los principios generales del derecho (tal y como lo entiende el Relator Especial) y el Derecho Internacional consuetudinario. Él sostendría que: *'[s]ería fundamental clarificar la distinción entre la 'identificación' del Derecho International consuetudinario y el 'reconocimiento' de los principios generales del derecho, para así evitar cualquier confusión que pudiese surgir de un uso excesivo de la analogía entre ambas nociones. [. . .] el Relator Especial recordó, que ha sido sugerido que 'el elemento básico debería ser la actitud de los Estados de considerarse obligados'. Aquel uso de palabras era*

3. *El Problema Alrededor de la Transposición de los Principios Generales del Derecho*

Cuando se considera el siguiente paso para la utilización de los principios generales del derecho las cosas se tornan más complicadas. Este último paso, llamado test de aplicabilidad de los principios generales del derecho, constituye una acción adicional que debe verificarse respecto a un principio general que ya ha sido 'reconocido'.

Según el Relator Especial,[28] el requisito de 'transposición' encuentra sustento en la doctrina y en la jurisprudencia, por lo que, en su entender *'[l]a razón de ello es "que las condiciones en el ámbito internacional son a veces muy diferentes de las que se dan en el ámbito nacional, y ciertas normas que están plenamente justificadas en este último pueden ser más difíciles de defender, si se aplican estrictamente, cuando se transponen al plano internacional"'.*[29]

El Relator Especial consideró que la práctica estatal en la materia y la jurisprudencia demostraban que un proceso adicional, de 'transposición', debía de constatarse para que un principio general del derecho (de origen doméstico) pudiese aplicarse en el Derecho Internacional. Aun cuando el Relator Especial ilustró aquello con una serie de sentencias y decisiones donde dicho requisito habría sido formulado, al final, ni aquella nomenclatura ('transposición') ni su contenido puede extraerse fácilmente de los casos citados por él.[30] Por esa razón, algunos miembros de la CDI –en su momento–, indicaron que, aun cuando en ciertas sentencias de la CIJ podía observarse el proceso enunciado por el Relator Especial, era –no obstante– difícil identificar concretamente el método que la CIJ siguió para hacer uso de ciertos principios generales. Es así que los miembros de la CDI consideraron que, *'(. . .) la jurisprudencia de la Corte, podría no ser de tanta ayuda, y que la Comisión debía aproximarse a ella con precaución.'*[31]

Por esta razón, el Relator en su Segundo Informe, reconoció respecto a la 'transposición', que *'(. . .) aquella parte de la metodología es usualmente referida en la literatura aunque en términos generales y usualmente, sin entrar en los detalles de lo que de forma precisa implica.'*[32] Como resultado de ello, muchos de los hallazgos del Relator Especial –en este punto– fueron más una creación de él[33] que una codificación de la práctica internacional sobre la

---

similar a la conclusión provisional 9(1) de las conclusiones referidas a la identificación del Derecho Internacional consuetudinario adoptado por la Comisión'. (traducción del autor).

[28] Ciertos principios generales del derecho en estricto no han pasado por una 'transposición' antes de ser incluidos en el Derecho Internacional. Como ha sido mencionado antes –en ciertas oportunidades–, la inclusión de los principios generales domésticos, es efectuado por razones prácticas o como último recurso. En aquellos casos, el núcleo esencial de un principio general es incluido, sin que el mismo se vea ajustado adecuadamente, con la esperanza de que aquel principio ofrezca solución a un conflicto donde ninguna regla internacional ha sido identificada como aplicable; mientras que el significado accesorio del principio general, es dejado para su desarrollo posterior.

[29] Comisión de Derecho Internacional. Primer Informe sobre los Principios Generales del Derecho . . . Para. 169 (nota: 3).

[30] Esta posición fue reconocida por otros miembros de la Comisión de Derecho Internacional. Ellos consideraron que las decisiones de la Corte Internacional de Justicia en la que se consideró la aplicación de los principios generales del derecho eran de ayuda limitada para desentrañar la forma en que estos debían aplicarse en el Derecho Internacional. Véase, por ejemplo: Comments of Michael Wood (International Law Commission. Seventy-First Session (Second Part). A/CN.4/SR.3490. 30 September 2019. p. 3–4).

[31] Comentarios de Jalloh (Véase: Comisión de Derecho Internacional. Seventy-First Session (Second Part)). A/CN.4/SR.3491. 2 October 2019. p. 6.

[32] Comisión de Derecho Internacional. Segundo Informe sobre los Principios Generales del Derecho. Marcelo Vazquez-Bermudez . . . Para. 20. (nota: 3).

[33] La 'jurisprudencia' al que hace referencia el Relator Especial para sostener aquel paso raramente es producto de un método concreto para la identificación de los principios generales del derecho utilizados

materia. Un ejemplo es el hecho de que el Relator Especial no fue capaz de dar respuesta concreta a las dudas expuestas por el Sr. Hassouna, en el sentido de que '(. . .) *mientras el primer paso parecía relativamente claro, el segundo generaba diversos cuestionamientos. ¿Cómo es que el acto de transposición, adaptación o transferencia, sería administrado? ¿Cómo es que la trasposición de un principio general del derecho doméstico, podría cambiar su valor normativo o su sustancia? ¿Qué factores deben tenerse en cuenta para asimilar un principio general dentro del sistema legal internacional?*'[34]

Teniendo en cuenta ello, puede decirse respecto al requisito de 'transposición' que diversos aspectos no lograron ser explicados con claridad.

Por lo demás, la forma en que el Relator Especial explicó el contenido de este requisito dejaba aún más patente la cercanía de su método con la teoría del consentimiento estatal. Esto, ya que si bien este último paso 'transposición' involucra determinar la compatibilidad de los principios generales del derecho de origen doméstico con la realidad internacional (ejercicio que lógicamente se vincula con el ejercicio adjudicativo), su constatación sería efectuado, nuevamente, por la 'comunidad internacional', excluyéndose de este ejercicio a los tribunales o cortes internacionales. Para ello, el Relator Especial entendió que, para que la 'transposición' fuese constatada, sería necesario identificar evidencias que dicha 'transposición' se produjo. Ello implica que no solo es necesario que un principio sea 'transpuesto', sino que –además– debía encontrarse evidencias que aquella 'transposición' fue 'reconocida' por los Estados. Esto lleva a que sea necesario un segundo 'reconocimiento' proveniente de la 'comunidad internacional'. Al respecto, el Relator Especial indicó que '(. . .) *(l)a segunda etapa del análisis tiene por objeto demostrar que esos principios también son reconocidos por la comunidad de naciones como parte del derecho internacional si son compatibles con los principios fundamentales del derecho internacional, por una parte, y si se dan las condiciones para su aplicación adecuada en el sistema jurídico internacional, por otra.*'[35] Con esto, el 'método de dos pasos' elaborado por el Relator Especial se transforma en un proceso sumamente complejo, casi imposible de cumplir.

Por lo demás, la necesidad de exigir un segundo 'reconocimiento' –esta vez dentro del proceso de 'transposición'– no encuentra sustento en la teoría (doctrina) ni tampoco en la práctica internacional. Las críticas que hemos realizado al requisito del 'reconocimiento' como parte del primer paso del método del Relator Especial, son aplicables a este segundo 'reconocimiento'.

Lo único por añadir es que, la decisión de incluir un 'reconocimiento' dentro de la fase de 'transposición' (ésta última creación del Relator Especial) apuntaría a reducir el

---

o para entender su relación con las otras fuentes del Derecho Internacional. Aún más, algunas veces la 'jurisprudencia' referida por el Relator no sustenta concretamente ciertas de sus afirmaciones. Véase sobre esto, la opinión de Murphy: Comisión de Derecho Internacional. Seventy-First Session. 30 September 2019. A/CN.4/SR.3490. pp. 10–12. En algunos otros casos, aun cuando los tribunales han utilizado el término 'principios generales del derecho' aquello ha sido realizado con la intención de hacer referencia al Derecho Internacional consuetudinario. Por consiguiente, no todos los casos citados en los primeros dos Informes del Relator Especial, realmente sirven para defender su posición. Al respecto, véase: las opiniones de Reinisch. Véase: International Law Commission. Seventy-First Session (Second Part). 2 October 2019. A/CN.4/SR.3491. pp. 18–19.

[34] Comisión de Derecho Internacional. Seventy-First Session (Second Part). A/CN.4/SR.3490. 30 September 2019. p. 24.

[35] Comisión de Derecho Internacional. Segundo Informe sobre los Principios Generales del Derecho. Marcelo Vázquez-Bermúdez. Seventy-Second Session. 27 April–5 June and 6 July–7 August 2020. A/CN.4/741. Para. 22.

rol que tendrían los tribunales y corte internacionales en la formulación o identificación de los principios generales del derecho (véase: Sección III(B)6 de este ensayo). Es importante recordar esto –en tanto– los efectos de este requisito podrían ser profundos, si la aproximación del Relator es finalmente aceptada, pues implicaría un requisito casi imposible de cumplir y –en ese sentido– podría conllevar al bloqueo del uso de los principios generales del derecho en el Derecho Internacional.

Ahora, ese no es el único problema que se genera respecto al requisito de 'transposición'. El enfoque del Relator no solo añadió un 'reconocimiento' dentro de la etapa de la 'transposición' sino que también sostuvo la existencia de una categoría de principios llamados 'principios fundamentales del Derecho Internacional'. Estos jugarían un rol al momento de llevar a cabo la fase de 'transposición'. Debe recordarse que –según el Relator Especial– la 'transposición' involucra un examen de compatibilidad entre los principios generales a incluirse en el sistema internacional y el Derecho Internacional. Esto implica, constatar la compatibilidad que existiría entre los principios generales de origen doméstico con los principios fundamentales del Derecho Internacional. Si lo indicado por el Relator Especial es correcto, entonces surge la pregunta: ¿Son aquellos principios generales (denominados fundamentales) ellos mismos incorporados en aplicación del artículo 38, párrafo 1 (c) del Estatuto de la CIJ, o es que los principios fundamentales provienen de otra fuente del derecho?

Si estos fuesen principios en el sentido dado por aquella disposición, entonces ellos tendrían que haber sido incorporados en el orden internacional por medio del 'proceso de dos pasos' construido por el Relator Especial. Sin embargo, algunos de los principios identificados por el Relator como fundamentales, como son, el principio de soberanía o la noción de soberanía territorial, o los principios incluidos en la Declaración sobre los Principios de Derecho Internacional Referentes a las Relaciones de Amistad y a la Cooperación Entre los Estados,[36] son tan básicos y conectados con las bases históricas del Derecho Internacional, que ninguna examinación (aplicando las etapas y evidencias del Relator Especial) sería exitoso. Por tanto, si los denominados principios fundamentales del Derecho Internacional no logran ser explicados a la luz del artículo 38, párrafo 1 (c) del Estatuto de la CIJ, una conclusión válida sería que el método propuesto por el Relator Especial no es una herramienta adecuada para identificar todos los principios del derecho aplicables en nuestra disciplina. Entonces, la falta de predictibilidad alrededor de la identificación de los principios generales del derecho pasaría hacia la nueva categoría de los principios fundamentales del Derecho Internacional, los cuales, necesitarían de una teoría que explicase cómo emergen en el sistema internacional. Esto es vital, dado que aquella categoría podría bloquear la inclusión de otros principios generales del derecho. Debe recordarse, que los otros principios generales del derecho solo se considerarán 'transpuestos' si es que los Estados han 'reconocido' que son compatibles con el orden internacional, lo cual implica que sean compatibles con los principios fundamentales del Derecho Internacional. Por esto mismo, dicha categoría podría ser esgrimida por los actores en procesos de adjudicación para limitar la utilización de los principios 'comunes'.

Sin embargo, esta no es la única paradoja que podría producirse si aceptáramos que los 'principios fundamentales' del Derecho Internacional –en efecto– constituyen una categoría especial de principios generales. Si esto fuese así, –entonces– ello no solo implicaría la existencia de un conjunto de reglas con una fuente de derecho potencialmente diferente, sino que –además– podrían ser la manifestación de una segunda forma de jerarquización en

---

[36] Comisión de Derecho Internacional. Segundo Informe sobre los Principios Generales del Derecho. Marcelo Vázquez-Bermúdez. . . . Para. 83. (nota: 3).

el Derecho Internacional. Para entender esto, es necesario recordar que, el entendimiento general alrededor de las fuentes del Derecho Internacional, es que ellas al igual que sus productos legales, no están establecidas jerárquicamente unas respeto a las otras (con la sola excepción de las normas de *ius cogens*).

Por ejemplo, si un Estado celebra un acuerdo con otro, nada debería prevenir para que una norma consuetudinaria posterior aplicables a ambos Estados[37] (o a toda la comunidad internacional)[38] pudiese derogar una o más de las estipulaciones convencionales,[39] exceptuándose –bajo ciertas condiciones– el principio de especialidad de la norma. Aquello sucede igualmente y –de forma más clara–, cuando un Estado celebra un tratado con otro Estado, dejando de lado el contenido de una norma consuetudinaria del Derecho Internacional. Esta última situación se produce debido a que el derecho consuetudinario en el Derecho Internacional, aunque de aplicación general, es pasible de derogación por el Derecho Internacional particular (provisiones de tratados). Ello implica que, en términos generales, con la excepción de las normas de *ius cogens*, el Derecho Internacional es dispositivo.[40]

Aquella falta de prevalencia entre normas consuetudinarias y normas convencionales se produce –también– entre los principios generales del derecho y las reglas emanadas de las demás fuentes del Derecho Internacional, así como entre principios generales del derecho entre sí. Sin embargo, las características normativas particulares de los principios generales permiten evitar situaciones en donde estos tendrían que prevalecer frente a reglas provenientes de otras fuentes del derecho. A decir verdad, una de las tareas principales de los principios generales (tanto en el Derecho Internacional, como en los ordenamientos domésticos) es cubrir las lagunas presentes en un sistema jurídico. Por tanto, su rol, se encuentra enfatizado ahí en donde no existen reglas o normas aplicables. Esto significa que una potencial colisión entre principios generales del derecho con otras reglas o normas (o con otros principios generales del derecho), no es el problema que

---

[37] Sobre el debate respecto a esto, véase: Rebecca Crootof, *Change without Consent: How Customary International Law Modifies Treaties*, 41 YALE JOURNAL OF INTERNATIONAL LAW 237, 299 (2016).

[38] Si se acepta que las normas de *jus cogens* pueden emerger a través del Derecho Internacional consuetudinario, entonces es claro que una regla consuetudinaria (de carácter perentorio) puede derogar estipulaciones convencionales (o un tratado en su totalidad) si el tratado en cuestión se opone al contenido de una norma perentoria. Véase: Vienna Convention on the Law of Treaties of 1969. United Nations, Treaty Series, vol. 1155. Article 64.

[39] Aceptando esta posibilidad, véase MARK VILLIGER, CUSTOMARY INTERNATIONAL LAW AND TREATIES (2d ed. 1997) y Maarten Bos, *The Hierarchy Among the Recognized Manifestations ('Sources') of International Law*, 25 NETHERLANDS INTERNATIONAL LAW REVIEW 334, 344 (1978).

[40] Véase: Alfred Verdross, *Jus Dispositivum and Jus Cogens in International Law*, 60 AMERICAN JOURNAL OF INTERNATIONAL LAW 55, 63 (1966). Véase, de igual forma, la Conclusión Provisional 2, del estudio efectuado por el Relator Especial en material de normas de *ius cogens*. '1. *Rules of international law may be modified, derogated from or abrogated by agreement of States to which the rule is applicable unless such modification, derogation or abrogation is prohibited by the rule in question (jus dispositivum). [...] 2. An exception to the rule set forth [...] is peremptory norms of general international law'.* (Comisión de Derecho Internacional. Primer Informe sobre las Normas de Ius Cogens de Dire Tladi. Sixty-Eighth Session. 8 de marzo de 2016. A/CN.4/693. Para. 74). Explicando el significado de aquella conclusion provisional, el Relator Especial (de las normas de *ius cogens*), añadiría que el, *'Draft conclusion 2 stated that jus cogens is an exception to the general rule that international law rules are jus dispositivum.'* Comisión de Derecho Internacional. Segundo Informe sobre las Normas de Ius Cogens de Dire Tladi. Sixty-Ninth Session. 16 March 2017. A/CN.4/706. Para. 4.

normalmente se presenta.[41] Por lo demás, gracias a la forma en que éstas se encuentran formuladas (términos generales y abstractos), de producirse una potencial colisión con otras normas, los principios generales no tienden a derogarlas, sino que –en lugar de ello– sirven como mecanismos de interpretación que esculpen el significado concreto que normas consuetudinarias o convencionales (o el significado de otro principio general del derecho) deberían de tener para que así los diferentes productos normativos convivan armónicamente en un sistema legal.

Por ello, cuando el Relator Especial mencionó que los 'principios fundamentales del Derecho Internacional' podrían prevenir el surgimiento o –incluso– que podrían invalidar un principio general del derecho en el Derecho Internacional, el Relator Especial –consciente o no de ello– estaría describiendo un rol que los principios generales desempeñan solo excepcionalmente y –en ese sentido– el Relator estaría describiendo un rol que solo podría llevar a cabo normatividad internacional con efectos jerárquicos.

Aun si se aceptara que los 'principios fundamentales' del Derecho Internacional son incorporados en aplicación del artículo 38, párrafo (c) del Estatuto de la CIJ, y que –por ello– la limitación que producirían solo se efectuaría dentro de la categoría de los 'principios generales del derecho' (no implicando una jerarquización general en el Derecho Internacional), aquello no invalidaría la conclusión a la que hemos llegado. Por ejemplo, las normas de *ius cogens* emergen –entre otras formas– a través de normas consuetudinarias del Derecho Internacional, teniendo la habilidad de limitar la formación de lo que podría denominarse normas consuetudinarias 'ordinarias' y, por ese solo hecho (que no excluye otros escenarios), aquellas proyectan efectos normativos jerárquicos en el Derecho Internacional.[42] La misma racionalidad es aplicable a los denominados principios fundamentales del Derecho Internacional si el Relator Especial mantiene su postura en este punto.[43]

4. *Una Técnica que No Puede ser Aplicada Uniformemente a Todos los Principios Utilizados en el Derecho Internacional, y que se Superpone con la Identificación de las Normas Consuetudinarias del Derecho Internacional*

La técnica propuesta por el Relator Especial fue formulada inicialmente para explicar el proceso de incorporación de los principios generales del derecho de origen doméstico en el Derecho Internacional. Por ello, la aplicación de algunas etapas de esta técnica a los

---

[41] Es por esta razón que Thirlway dio comentarios en el sentido de que los principios generales del derecho son, '(. . .) *esencialmente* (. . .) *llamados a operar solo cuando las reglas derivadas de un tratado o costumbre no logran resolver un problema legal. En las disputas que son presentadas para su resolución frente un tercero, esto se ha producido raramente y en ningún caso aquellos principios han estado en contradicción con otras reglas aplicables.'* Véase: HUGH THIRLWAY, THE SOURCES OF INTERNATIONAL LAW 160 (2d ed. 2019).

[42] Véase: Luis Angel López Zamora, *El Unificador Fragmentado. La fenomenología de las normas de ius cogens en un contexto de cambio*, 30 ANUARIO ESPAÑOL DE DERECHO INTERNACIONAL 203, 250 (2014).

[43] Como parte de los comentarios realizados al Primer Informe del Relator Especial, George Nolte recordaría que el término 'principios fundamentales' *'no hacían referencia necesariamente a una jerarquía mayor o a una cualidad sustantiva en particular de algún principio, como era el caso de las normas perentorias del Derecho Internacional general. En el contexto de los 'principios generales del derecho' el término 'fundamental', apunta más bien a un carácter subyacente o estructural de cualquier principio.'* (traducción del autor). Sin embargo, la decisión del Relator Especial de darle a aquella categoría la misión de prevenir el surgimiento de normatividad internacional, catapultaría aquellos principios a una construcción jerárquicamente superior. Resolución de la Asamblea General 2625 (XXV). Declaration on Principles of International Law Friendly Relations and Co-operation among States in Accordance with the Charter of the United Nations. A/RES/2625 (XXV). 24 October 1970.

principios generales del derecho formados directamente en el Derecho Internacional produce consecuencias cuestionables. En relación a esto, debe de resaltarse –una vez más– que
el alcance del requisito de 'reconocimiento' aun no es claro en la doctrina y bien podría
entenderse que involucra alguna forma de participación o consentimiento de los Estados
o no. Este es un problema especialmente claro para el caso de los principios generales del
Derecho que surgen directamente en el Derecho Internacional, pues la participación de los
Estados en su identificación formulación o aplicabilidad es dudosa.

Esta posición fue compartida por algunos miembros de la CDI, quienes consideraron
que los principios generales formados dentro del sistema internacional podrían tener una
fuente diferente al artículo 38, párrafo 1 (c) del Estatuto de la CIJ.[44] Nuestra posición es que
el requisito de 'reconocimiento' debió haber sido descartado para los principios generales
del derecho formados directamente en el Derecho Internacional, pues estos principios no
emergen fuera del Derecho Internacional y –por ello mismo– no hay razones para que deban
ser 'reconocidas' por las 'comunidad de naciones' por medio de sus tribunales domésticos
o la legislación municipal, que es la forma como se constata aquel 'reconocimiento' según
el Relator Especial.

A pesar de ello, el Relator entendió esto de forma diferente y sostuvo que los principios
generales del derecho formados directamente en el Derecho Internacional, aunque no
requerirían ser 'transpuestos', si requerirían ser 'reconocidos' por la 'comunidad de naciones'.
En palabras del Relator Especial:

> Si, por otra parte, la Comisión llega a la conclusión de que los principios generales del
> derecho comprenden principios formados en el sistema jurídico internacional que
> no se basan en principios comunes a los sistemas jurídicos nacionales, el método de
> identificación podría ser diferente. Puede que el análisis en dos etapas mencionado
> anteriormente no sea necesario, pero en cualquier caso habría que constatar el
> "reconocimiento" en el sentido del Artículo 38, párrafo 1 (c), del Estatuto.[45]

La forma en la que el Relator Especial arribó a dicha conclusión no fue explicada y tampoco
encontramos razones en su argumentación. Al final, el Relator Especial, al insistir en la
aplicabilidad del requisito de 'reconocimiento' en el caso de los principios generales del
derecho formados directamente en el Derecho Internacional, lleva a una confusión entre
la formación e identificación de aquellos principios con la identificación y formación
de las normas consuetudinarias del Derecho Internacional; especialmente, cuando el

---

[44] Comisión de Derecho Internacional. Report of the ILC on the Work of its Seventy-First Session (2019).
27 April–5 June and 6 July–August 2020. A/CN.4/734. Para. 34. Es más, la dificultad de entender
los principios generales del derecho en términos de 'reconocimiento' surgió –una vez más– cuando
otros tipos de principios generales tuvieron que ser considerados, como los principios de la lógica
legal. Véase: Comisión de Derecho Internacional. Primer Informe sobre los Principios Generales del
Derecho . . . Para. 23 (nota: 3). El Relator Especial tomó nota de las referencias hechas a aquellos principios
generales, por parte de internacionalistas como Mosler o Schachter; sin embargo, no los consideró en sus
Informes (solo se hace referencia a aquello en un párrafo). Por esta razón, algunos de los miembros de
la Comisión subrayaron el hecho de que la clasificación realizada por el Relator Especial a los principios
generales del derecho no fue comprensiva y consideraron que otros principios debían de ser tomados
en cuenta para así establecer la relación existente entre aquellas sub-categorías. Véase el comentario de
Aurescu, Comisión de Derecho Internacional. Seventy-First Session (Second Part). A/CN.4/SR.3491. 2
October 2019. p. 9. (traducción del autor).

[45] Comisión de Derecho Internacional. Primer Informe sobre los Principios Generales del Derecho . . . Para.
31 (note: 3).

'reconocimiento' final de aquellos principios se produce a nivel internacional y no a nivel del orden municipal de los "Estados," como es en el caso del 'reconocimiento' de los principios generales del derecho de origen doméstico.

Es por esta potencial confusión entre fuentes del Derecho Internacional, que el Relator vio necesario tratar en su Segundo Informe las diferencias entre las formas de identificación de las normas consuetudinarias del Derecho Internacional y los principios generales. El Relator recibió numerosos comentarios sobre la evidente dificultad de separar los métodos de identificación de ambas categorías; por ello, en su Segundo Informe, añadió una sección tratando el tema. Aun así, aquella sección es breve (va del Párrafo 107 al 112 de aquel Informe). El Relator Especial indicó que, *"(. . .) la distinción es a la luz de los capítulos previos, clara y ninguna confusión debería existir entre ambas fuentes."*[46] Sin embargo, añadió que, *'(e)stas <u>formas de práctica y prueba de la opinio iuris, coinciden con los materiales que son pertinentes a los efectos de la identificación de principios generales del derecho derivados de sistemas jurídicos nacionales,</u> que, como se explica más arriba, son esencialmente fuentes jurídicas internas como la legislación nacional y las decisiones de las cortes y tribunales nacionales'*[47]

Nuestra conclusión en este punto es que la explicación del Relator Especial fue insuficiente al no dar respuesta a los comentarios formulados por los miembros de la CDI. Aun así, el Relator trató de subrayar las diferencias metodológicas en la identificación de ambas fuentes del Derecho Internacional, lo cual veremos a continuación.

(A) DIFERENCIANDO LA INCORPORACIÓN DE LOS PRINCIPIOS GENERALES DEL DERECHO DOMÉSTICO DE LA IDENTIFICACIÓN DE LAS NORMAS CONSUETUDINARIAS

En tanto la costumbre debe ser 'aceptada' por los Estados para ser oponible, y los principios generales del derecho de origen doméstico requieren ser 'reconocidos', el Relator enfocó sus esfuerzos en esclarecer el significado del término 'reconocimiento' en contraposición al término 'aceptación'. Tal y como él indicó, la principal característica del término 'reconocimiento' (en contraposición al de 'aceptación' de una norma consuetudinaria) es que para que aquel se cumpla y –por tanto– para que un principio general esté más cercano a ser aplicado en el plano internacional, no todo Estado al que aquel principio le será oponible necesita haber efectuado su 'reconocimiento'. Siguiendo la posición del Relator Especial, ello significa que basta el reconocimiento general de los Estados dentro de sus órdenes legales (y no por cada uno de ellos) para iniciar el proceso de incorporación de un principio general en el Derecho Internacional.

Si el método del Relator Especial hubiese finalizado en aquella fase, o si aquel no hubiese sido extendido a los principios generales del derecho formados directamente en el Derecho

---

[46] Véase: Segundo Informe sobre los Principios Generales del Derecho. Marcelo Vázquez-Bermúdez . . . Para. 107. (nota: 3).

[47] *Id.*, Para. 110. Sin embargo, el Relator Especial añadiría que: *'No obstante, es preciso matizar esta coincidencia. En primer lugar, para que la legislación nacional y las decisiones de las cortes y tribunales nacionales sean pertinentes a los efectos de la identificación del derecho internacional consuetudinario, deben ir acompañadas de la opinio iuris, o la convicción de que el Estado actúa en virtud de un derecho o una obligación de derecho internacional. Sin embargo, esto no es necesario para que surja un principio general del derecho: lo pertinente es la forma en que las legislaciones y las cortes y tribunales nacionales regulan y resuelven los asuntos esencialmente internos. Además, la segunda etapa del análisis para la identificación de principios generales del derecho derivados de sistemas jurídicos nacionales (es decir, la constatación de la transposición) es exclusiva de esta fuente del derecho internacional. No se requiere dicho análisis para identificar una norma de derecho internacional consuetudinario.'* *Id.*, Para. 109–111.

Internacional, la distinción entre la identificación de los principios generales y la costumbre se podría haber logrado. Después de todo, mientras que el 'reconocimiento' de los principios generales del derecho se produce a nivel doméstico, la 'aceptación' de la costumbre se produce –en buena parte– a nivel internacional. Esta posible diferenciación –sin embargo– se pierde con la segunda fase del método propuesto por el Relator Especial ('transposición'), el cual ocurre en el plano internacional, necesitando de un nuevo 'reconocimiento' que confirme que la 'transposición' de un principio se ha producido.

En nuestra perspectiva, la segunda fase del método del Relator Especial es controversial, pues, el segundo 'reconocimiento' (en la fase de transposición) –finalmente– se entremezcla con alguna forma indirecta de manifestación de voluntad de los Estados, haciendo –casi imposible– diferenciar la incorporación de un principio general de origen doméstico con la identificación de la costumbre internacional. El hecho de que el Relator Especial pareciera haber dado preferencia a una visión positivista en este punto se observa en el hecho de que aquel entendió que el segundo 'reconocimiento' de su método necesitaría ser verificado por ciertas evidencias, como es por la inclusión de los principios generales en tratados, en tanto ello confirma que un principio común a los principales sistemas legales del mundo, ha sido transpuesto al sistema internacional.[48] Si dicho criterio es seguido, entonces el segundo 'reconocimiento' de un principio general del derecho se producirá en el plano internacional por medio de evidencias como la recepción del mismo en el derecho de los tratados. Con ello, la diferencia entre aquella etapa y las formas por las que se demuestra la existencia de una norma consuetudinaria se borran del todo.[49]

Ahora, es preciso añadir que, aunque ello origina una falta de delimitación entre la noción de 'reconocimiento' y 'aceptación', aun en aquel caso hubiese sido posible diferenciar la identificación los principios generales del derecho, de la identificación de las normas consuetudinarias. Para ello, la fase de 'transposición' de los principios generales de origen doméstico pudo: (a) Haberse dejado en manos de los tribunales o cortes internacionales, quienes habrían de constatar que los principios a incorporarse fueran coherentes con el Derecho Internacional o, (ii) El 'reconocimiento' de la 'transposición' debió haberse dejado en manos de la 'comunidad internacional', en el sentido de una comunidad que incluyera no solo a los Estados, sino a organizaciones y otros actores internacionales. De esa forma, la fase de 'transposición' podría haberse diferenciado de la formación e identificación de las normas consuetudinarias, pues esas últimas requieren ser aceptadas individualmente por cada Estado para ser oponibles, y no necesitan de la 'aceptación' proveniente de otros actores internacionales.

Sin embargo, al final, diferentes aspectos juegan en contra de esa salida. Uno de ellos es el sentido dado por el Relator Especial al término 'naciones civilizadas'. El artículo 38, párrafo 1 (c) del Estatuto de la CIJ, si bien establece como elemento clave para el reconocimiento

---

[48] *Id.*, Para. 97.

[49] Un ejemplo de aquella confusión, puede observarse en las dudas formuladas por Michael Wood: *'[. . .] la relación entre aquellas dos fuentes no solo requiere atención especial; sino que también requiere de cuidado. Se esperaba que dentro de aquel tema la Comisión, no solo explicara los límites de los principios generales del derecho, como fuente del derecho internacional, sino también que estableciera claramente la diferencia entre aquella fuente del derecho y la costumbre del Derecho Internacional. Existen diferentes fuentes del derecho internacional, con diferentes 'reglas de reconocimiento'. Cuando no es posible identificar una regla aplicable del derecho internacional consuetudinaria, por la ausencia de uno o dos de sus elementos constitutivos no puede aceptarse el recurrir ligeramente a los principios generales del derecho para encontrar la regla deseada.'* Comisión de Derecho Internacional. Seventy-First Session (Second Part). 30 de septiembre de 2019. A/CN.4/SR.3490. p. 5. (traducción del autor).

de los principios generales el que aquellos sean 'reconocidos', añade que ello lo realizan las 'naciones civilizadas'. El Relator Especial reemplazaría el término por 'comunidad de naciones', el cual no obstante fue referido en su Primer Informe como 'comunidad de Estados', lo cual termina complicando el asunto al restringir los actores que comprenderían aquella 'comunidad' a básicamente entidades soberanas.

(B) DIFERENCIANDO LA IDENTIFICACIÓN DE LOS PRINCIPIOS GENERALES DEL DERECHO INTERNACIONAL, DE LA IDENTIFICACIÓN DE LAS NORMAS CONSUETUDINARIAS DEL DERECHO INTERNACIONAL

La diferenciación en la identificación de los principios generales del derecho formados directamente en el Derecho Internacional, de las normas consuetudinarias es aún más complicado. Por ello, el Relator Especial, en una sección de su Segundo Informe, trató la diferencia entre ambos procesos. Sin embargo, resultó difícil esclarecer el punto. Él sostendría que '(...) en el caso de los principios generales del derecho que caen dentro de la segunda categoría, no es necesario buscar una práctica general y su aceptación como derecho (opinio iuris)'[50], sin embargo, reconocería que '(...) respecto a los principios que son reconocidos ampliamente en tratados y otros instrumentos internacionales, cierta superposición pareciera existir, en tanto el materia por medio del cual el requisito del reconocimiento puede ser evidenciado también sirve (...) como evidencia para determinar la existencia de una regla del Derecho Internacional consuetudinario.'[51]

Al final, la aproximación ofrecida por el Relator Especial genera un acercamiento peligroso entre la identificación de los principios generales del derecho y la identificación de la costumbre internacional. La razón, como antes se ha indicado, es que el Relator sostuvo que los principios generales formados directamente en el Derecho Internacional, requerirán del 'reconocimiento' de la 'comunidad de naciones', y dado que aquel 'reconocimiento' –en este caso– se produce a nivel internacional (al tratarse de principios generales formados originalmente en el Derecho Internacional) las dificultades de separar el requisito de 'reconocimiento' del elemento de 'aceptación' (de la costumbre) también aparece en esta categoría especifica de principios generales.[52]

---

[50] Segundo Informe sobre los Principios Generales del Derecho. Marcelo Vázquez-Bermúdez . . . Para. 165. (note: 3).

[51] *Id.,* . . . Para. 161. (note: 3).

[52] Los comentarios efectuados por Marja Lehto al Primer Informe del Relator Especial, resumen el problema en cuestión. Ella indicaría que: '*los principios generales del derecho, que no tienen una contraparte en los sistemas legales domésticos generan una serie de interrogantes, en especial relacionados al requisito de reconocimiento, en tanto también le son aplicables a estos, aquel requisito. Una de las interrogantes está relacionada con distinguir aquellos principios de los principios de derecho consuetudinario. Palabras de precaución se han escuchado en los debates respecto al rol de los principios generales del derecho como una suerte de 'costumbre light' o como 'costumbre sin practica' o 'costumbre sin opinio juris.'* [Comisión de Derecho Internacional. Seventy-First Session (Second Part). A/CN.4/SR.3492. 2 de octubre de 2019. p. 15] (traducción del autor). Argüello Gómez subrayaría las dificultades al respecto. Él *'dudaba, que incluso fuera del contexto del Estatuto, algún principio general del derecho formado dentro del sistema legal internacional, no fuese o no se tornase –ipso facto– en una regla del derecho internacional consuetudinario. Era inconcebible pensar en principios generales del derecho que no fuesen evidencia de práctica –en otras palabras– de costumbre internacional. [. . .]. En su sentir, debía concluirse que, tan pronto como aquellos principios fuesen declarados como generalmente aceptados por la comunidad internacional, ellos dejaban de ser simples principios generales del derecho y se convertían en parte de la costumbre internacional.'* [*Id.*, p. 4]. (traducción del autor). Aun cuando es difícil concordar con la afirmación implícita, de que los principios generales del derecho formados dentro del Derecho Internacional no existirían –como tales–, concordamos con que, el intento efectuado por el Relator, de diferenciar la identificación de ambas fuentes del Derecho no fue exitoso. Adicionalmente, los comentarios

5. Una Técnica que no Encuentra Soporte en la Práctica Internacional

El sentido dado a los requisitos del artículo 38, párrafo 1 (c) del Estatuto de la CIJ (y que fueron la base para la elaboración del 'proceso de dos pasos' del Relator Especial) no encuentra soporte en la práctica de los tribunales o cortes internacional y –aún menos evidencia– existe de que el 'proceso de dos pasos' haya sido –alguna vez– seguido de forma integral en la adjudicación internacional. Esto queda claro, cuando se indaga si existe respaldo a nivel adjudicativo para las etapas que componen la técnica del Relator Especial: el 'reconocimiento' y la 'transposición' de los principios.

Por ejemplo, la Corte Interamericana de Derechos Humanos (Corte Interamericana), en unas de sus primeras decisiones, sostuvo que:

> La Comisión [Interamericana] no señaló de manera expresa la violación del artículo 1.1 de la Convención, pero ello no impide que sea aplicado por esta Corte, debido a que dicho precepto constituye el fundamento genérico de la protección de los derechos reconocidos por la Convención y porque sería aplicable, de todos modos, en virtud de un principio general de Derecho, **iura novit curia**, del cual se ha valido reiteradamente la jurisprudencia internacional en el sentido de que el juzgador posee la facultad e inclusive el deber de aplicar las disposiciones jurídicas pertinentes en una causa, aun cuando las partes no las invoquen expresamente [. . .].[53]

Como puede observarse, la Corte Interamericana decidió aplicar el principio de *iura novit curia* no porque aquel principio hubiese sido 'reconocido' por la comunidad de naciones, ni tampoco por que aquella corte hubiese concluido que la 'transposición' de dicho principio

---

de otros miembros de la Comisión no fueron considerados comprensivamente, dejando al lector de los informes, la duda sobre el método que debería aplicarse para diferenciar la identificación de los principios generales del derecho de la identificación del Derecho Internacional consuetudinario. Ahora, el problema antes mencionado, no es el único que surgiría alrededor del trabajo efectuado por el Relator Especial. Por ejemplo, en su Primer Informe, el Relator Especial consideraría importante tomar en cuenta la posibilidad no solo del 'reconocimiento' o 'identificación' de los principios generales del derecho, sino también su 'formación'. El relator Especial sostendría que existen '(. . .) *opiniones según las cuales las decisiones de las cortes y tribunales internacionales no solo son una ayuda para identificar los principios generales del derecho, sino que también desempeñan un papel sustantivo en la formación de esta fuente del derecho internacional.*' [Comisión de Derecho Internacional. Primer Informe sobre los Principios Generales del Derecho . . . Para. 32 (note: 3).] Aun cuando el Relator Especial hizo aquella referencia, para considerarla en profundidad en un futuro, ello demostró una falta de limitación del trabajo aun por realizar. Por ejemplo, este punto no fue vuelto a tratar en el Segundo Informe, y pareciera haberse puesto de lado en el trabajo del Relator Especial.

[53] Corte Interamericana de Derechos Humanos. Caso Velásquez-Rodríguez v. Honduras. Sentencia (Méritos). 29 de julio de 1988. Para. 163. Otro ejemplo de un principio reconocido por la Corte Interamericana, en donde no se siguió el 'método de dos pasos' se observa en el caso Genie Lacayo. En aquella ocasión, la Corte Interamericana, con el fin de justificar su poder de revisar sus propias decisiones sostuvo que, '*(d) e acuerdo con lo establecido por el Estatuto de la Corte Internacional de Justicia y los Reglamentos del citado Tribunal Europeo, en aplicación de los principios generales del derecho procesal, tanto interno como internacional y, siguiendo el criterio de la doctrina generalmente aceptada, el carácter definitivo o inapelable de una sentencia no es incompatible con la existencia de un recurso de revisión en algunos casos especiales.*' (Corte Interamericana de Derechos Humanos. Caso Genie Lacayo v. Nicaragua. (Solicitud de Revisión de la Sentencia de Fondo, Reparaciones y Costas) (Resolución de la Corte de 13 de septiembre de 1997). Para. 9). En esta sección la Corte Interamericana se limitó a sostener su poder de revisión en base a algunos principios generales del derecho procesal y en el derecho doméstico, ejercicio que –sin duda– no siguió el 'método de dos pasos' sugerido por el Relator Especial.

se hubiese producido en el orden internacional. Por el contrario, la Corte sostuvo que el principio de *iura novit curia* era aplicable en aplicación de dos antecedentes en donde aquel principio habría sido identificado y aplicado: la sentencia del Tribunal Permanente de Justicia Internacional (TPJI) en el caso Lotus y la sentencia del Tribunal Europeo de Derechos Humanos (TEDH) en el caso *Handyside*. Sin embargo, debe señalarse que en el caso Lotus, ningún principio procesal fue desarrollado por el TPJI (ello se deduce de los argumentos dados por aquel Tribunal) y –por lo demás– los pasos del Relator para la identificación de los principios generales del derecho no fueron mencionados ni seguidos por el TPJI. Por su parte, en el caso *Handyside*, aun cuando el TEDH habría hecho referencia al principio *iura novit curia*, los pasos del Relator no fueron mencionados ni seguidos. Por el contrario, el TEDH, se limitó a aplicar aquel principio sobre la base de la práctica desarrollada por ella misma. Si se observa más en detalle los casos que le sirvieron de sustento a aquel tribunal, se vuelve claro que el TEDH no ofreció una explicación de porqué el principio de *iura novit curia* debía ser aplicado en aquel caso en particular.[54]

Otro ejemplo, lo encontramos en la decisión adoptada por la Organización Mundial de Comercio (OMC), en el caso Prohibición de Importar Ciertos Camarones y sus Productos, en donde el Órgano de Apelación, sostuvo que:

El preámbulo del artículo XX en realidad no es sino una expresión del principio de buena fe. <u>Este principio, que es a la vez un principio general del derecho y un principio general del derecho internacional, regula el ejercicio de los derechos por los Estados. Una aplicación de este principio general, aplicación que se conoce corrientemente como la doctrina del abuso de derecho, prohíbe el ejercicio abusivo de los derechos</u> [...]. (énfasis añadido)[55]

El Órgano de Apelación sostuvo aquello en base a tres casos resueltos por la CIJ. Más allá de ello, ninguna otra acción fue seguida por dicho órgano para demostrar la existencia del principio de buena fe y –aparte de los casos mencionados– ninguna argumentación fue efectuada que reflejara o hiciera eco del método propuesto por el Relator Especial.

En relación a ello, podría argumentarse que algunos principios del derecho están tan claramente reconocidos en el Derecho Internacional, que el 'proceso de dos pasos' sería innecesario. Sin embargo, de aceptarse ello, el problema sería determinar qué principios están tan claramente establecidos que ningún test sería necesario. Esto, además, debe hacernos reflexionar sobre el rol asignado a la jurisprudencia o decisiones de los tribunales internacionales, donde se identifican principios generales del derecho[56]; especialmente,

---

[54] Véase: Tribunal Europeo de Derechos Humanos. Casos de De Wilde, Ooms y Versyp ('Vagrancy') v. Belgium (Merits). Sentencia del 18 de Junio de 1971. Para. 49 y Caso 'Relating to Certain Aspects of the Law on the Use of Languages in Education in Belgium' v. Belgium (Merits). Sentencia del 23 de Julio de 1968. p. 27. Para. 1.

[55] Organización Mundial de Comercio. United States—Import Prohibition of Certain Shrimp and Shrimp Products. AB-1998-4. WT/DS58/AB/R. 12 de octubre de 1998. para. 158.

[56] *Id.*, Esto –por lo demás– apunta a un elemento más complejo. La indagación de si el método ofrecido por el Relator Especial tiene verdadero sustento en la práctica adjudicativa internacional es importante, pero lo es igualmente, determinar si las referencias hechas a los principios generales del derecho por los tribunales o cortes internacionales, han tenido la verdadera intención de hacer referencia a la fuente acuñada en el artículo 38, 1(c) del Estatuto de la CIJ. Por ello, es importante revisar las referencias hechas a las decisiones adoptadas en la práctica adjudicativa internacional que han servido de sustento para la interpretación del artículo 38, 1(c) de Estatuto de la CIJ. Desde la doctrina, esto ya ha sido resaltado. Para las decisiones provenientes del TPJI, véase: A. Cassese, International Law 157 (2001). Haciendo una referencia

cuando ellos son utilizados por otros tribunales o cortes, como fundamento para su aplicación. La pregunta es: ¿Puede un tribunal internacional verse exento de llevar a cabo la identificación de un principio general del derecho, si otro tribunal o corte internacional ha identificado –previamente– aquel, como aplicable en el Derecho Internacional? Si la respuesta es afirmativa: ¿Puede un tribunal internacional concluir que la examinación hecha por otro tribunal internacional ha sido realizada incorrectamente y declarar que el principio ha sido proclamado erróneamente y –por ende– que no podrá ser alegado por una de las partes en una disputa en particular?

Este tipo de problemas demuestran la dificultad de sostener que el 'proceso de dos pasos' efectivamente constituye una condición para que un principio general del derecho sea aplicable en la litigación internacional. Una solución posible sería argumentar que el estudio del Relator Especial (y su método) se encuentra limitado al artículo 38, párrafo 1 (c) del Estatuto de la CIJ y que sus conclusiones, son aplicables a la identificación de principios generales que la CIJ habría de realizar, y que –por tanto– otros tribunales o cuerpos adjudicativos se encontrarían en libertad de establecer métodos propios para reconocer principios generales. Sin embargo, en el trabajo del Relator Especial, sentencias y decisiones de diferentes tribunales y cortes fueron utilizadas para defender la aplicabilidad del 'proceso de dos pasos'. Parece una conclusión válida que el método referido por el Relator Especial no ha sido seguido consistentemente por los tribunales internacionales o cuerpos de adjudicación internacional.

Lo indicado sobre la falta de respaldo práctico al método del Relator con respecto al requisito de 'reconocimiento', se vuelve aún más claro para el requisito de 'transposición'. En este caso, aun cuando el Relator Especial mencionó casos donde ciertos ajustes fueron realizados a principios generales del derecho de origen doméstico antes de su aplicación en el Derecho Internacional, el requisito de 'transposición' –en el sentido dado por el Relator Especial– no ha sido considerado ni verificado consistentemente por los primeros tribunales arbitrales, el TPJI o por tribunales regionales. El uso de los principios generales –en muchos casos– ha sido efectuado sin un ejercicio de 'transposición' (es decir, sin realizar formalmente su ajuste al Derecho Internacional). "En aquellos casos," la incorporación de los principios generales ha sido llevado a cabo sin que se ofrezca una justificación legal concreta. Lo que sucede ahí es que la incorporación de los principios generales se efectúa sin una justificación legal precisa,[57] empujado por la necesidad de resolver un caso concreto, para lo cual, el tribunal o

---

similar, pero respecto a la actividad adjudicativa en general, véase: I. SAUNDERS, GENERAL PRINCIPLES AS A SOURCE OF INTERNATIONAL LAW. ART 38(1)(C) OF THE STATUTE OF THE INTERNATIONAL COURT OF JUSTICE, 53 (2021).

[57] El establecimiento explícito de fases o pasos para que un principio general del derecho sea incorporado en los órdenes legales domésticos no constituye una práctica común. La forma como normalmente los principios generales del derecho son reconocidos en esas realidades, es mediante el uso de diferentes métodos que, en distintas oportunidades, están condicionados a diferentes propósitos y necesidades de la adjudicación doméstica. Por esto mismo, el establecimiento de un método legal estricto para el reconocimiento de aquellos productos normativos genera el riesgo de –potencialmente– limitar su uso y –en ese sentido– de hacer su acceso por parte de los jueces, uno más complicado. Por esto, creemos que el trabajo llevado a cabo por el Relator Especial debe ser conducido, de forma tal, de no reducir aquella fuente del derecho a una sola de sus facetas, en detrimento de su compleja fenomenología. Dworkin ha ofrecido una buena explicación de cómo formas de explicar el surgimiento de los principios generales, podrían no ser convincentes ni útiles.

Véase: R. DWORKIN, LOS DERECHOS EN SERIO 95 (1989).

corte internacional aplica el núcleo básico del principio dejando sus contornos a ser formulados posteriormente.[58,59]

Por todo ello, puede decirse que la 'transposición' no siempre ha sido seguida en la práctica adjudicatoria internacional.

6. *La Reducción del Rol de los Tribunales y Cortes Internacionales en la Identificación de los Principios Generales del Derecho*

Uno de los efectos que el método propuesto por el Relator Especial podría producir (si se continuase con el contenido que tiene hoy en día) podría ser la reducción del rol de los tribunales internacionales en el proceso de identificación de los principios generales del derecho. Por ejemplo, en el Primer Informe del Relator, 'transposición' significaba el ajuste de un principio general de origen doméstico al orden legal internacional; sin embargo, quién exactamente debía efectuar la 'transposición' y declararla efectuada era una pregunta por responder. En su Segundo Informe, el Relator sostuvo que un subsiguiente 'reconocimiento' de la 'transposición' tendría que producirse. Como ya hemos indicado, aquel segundo 'reconocimiento' lo tendría que efectuar la 'comunidad de naciones' mediante la incorporación del principio en tratados.

Ese segundo 'reconocimiento' hace de la fase de 'transposición' uno orientado totalmente a los Estados. Esto no pasó desapercibido en la CDI. Algunos de sus miembros cuestionaron cómo el 'reconocimiento' de la 'transposición' de un principio general podría darse en la práctica. Al respecto, Michael Wood se preguntaba,

¿[si] el reconocimiento era relevante al momento de determinar, si un principio común a los sistemas legales nacionales había sido transpuesto a nivel internacional? En otros términos, si un proceso de transposición era definitivamente requerido: ¿Cuál era el rol (si acaso alguno) del reconocimiento de los Estados en aquel proceso? ¿Si el reconocimiento no jugaba un rol, cuáles eran los criterios necesarios para determinar que un principio legal, que existe dentro de la generalidad de sistemas legales domésticos, era adecuado para su transposición dentro del sistema legal internacional?[60]

---

[58] Como se ha explicado antes, la inclusión de los principios generales del derecho –en aquellos casos– se efectúa por medio del uso de analogía. Como Kamm indica, '*[t]he relevance of an analogous case can be clear, even if one does not have a theory that links the analogous case and the original case, and even if one is initially uncertain about what one may permissibly do in the analogous case. While we may need a theory to explain why case A is really more like case B than case C, we may still, without deep theoretical justification, see that case A is more like B than C and use that conclusion to help us find a solution to case A. Indeed, sometimes one reaches a conclusion about a case by way of an analogous case and still cannot provide an adequate theoretical justification of one's position in either case.*' F.M. Kamm, *Theory and Analogy in Law*, 29 Arizona State Law Journal 413, 414 (1997).

[59] Este tipo de incorporación normativa es lo que Weil denomina 'proceso de deshidratación', es decir un proceso que implica, '*(. . .) un juicio de valor, sobre cuáles son los elementos esenciales de una regla, y cuáles serían las características especiales vinculadas con su origen en el derecho doméstico; y el proceso de 'rehidratación' podría tener que hacer frente al problema de la compatibilidad de la regla con los requerimientos del orden legal internacional.*' Hugh Thirlway, *Concepts, Principles, Rules and Analogies: International and Municipal Legal Reasoning*, 294 Recueil des Cours 294, 288 (2002).

[60] Comisión de Derecho Internacional. Seventy-First Session (Second Part). 30 de septiembre de 2019. A/CN.4/SR.3490. p. 7 (traducción del autor). Un comentario similar fue efectuado por Murphy, lo cual, pareciera haber influenciado en las conclusiones a la que arribaría el Relator Especial. Murphy indicaría en sus comentarios del Primer Informe que: '*another area of study that should be considered concerned whether recognition arose at different stages, in which case there might be differing standards of recognition at each stage.*'

Creemos que pudo evitarse esta incorporación artificial del segundo 'reconocimiento'. Para ello, hubiese sido necesario dejar la determinación de la compatibilidad de un principio general del derecho doméstico a los tribunales y cortes internacionales. Después de todo, son aquellos los que se encuentran en la mejor posición para determinar si un principio general en concreto, funcionaría adecuadamente en el plano internacional y si podría ser útil para la resolución de un caso en particular. Sin embargo, el Relator adoptó la posición opuesta y decidió que el proceso de 'transposición' requería de un subsecuente 'reconocimiento' el cual implica 'reconocer' que la transposición se ha efectuado. Aquel 'reconocimiento' debe provenir de la 'comunidad de naciones'. Como resultado, la 'transposición' no podría ser declarada por tribunales o cortes, aun si un principio general de origen doméstico hubiese sido 'reconocido' por los Estados en diferentes sistemas legales municipales, y aun si fuese evidente que no contradice nociones fundamentales del Derecho Internacional. La posición del Relator Especial –en este punto– es que el 'reconocimiento' de aquel proceso (de transposición) era necesario y que ello se constata –como indicáramos antes– por la incorporación del principio en cuestión en tratados. En ese sentido, el Relator Especial señaló que:

> La segunda etapa del análisis tiene por objeto demostrar que esos principios <u>también son reconocidos por la comunidad de naciones como parte del derecho internacional</u> *si son compatibles con los principios fundamentales del derecho internacional, por una parte, y si se dan las condiciones para su aplicación adecuada en el sistema jurídico internacional, por otra.* (énfasis agregado)[61]

En términos más claros, el Relator Especial añadiría en su Segundo Informe que:

> cabe concluir que, el hecho de que un principio común a los principales sistemas jurídicos del mundo esté reflejado a nivel internacional, <u>ya sea en tratados u otros instrumentos internacionales, puede ser la prueba que confirma que el principio se ha transpuesto al sistema jurídico internacional</u>. Esto parece deberse a que, <u>si la comunidad de naciones expresa de esta manera su reconocimiento de la aplicabilidad de ese principio a nivel internacional</u>, ello implica que el principio se considera compatible con los principios fundamentales del derecho internacional y que en el sistema jurídico internacional se dan las condiciones para la aplicación adecuada del principio. (énfasis agregado)[62]

Esta aproximación hace difícil la incorporación de los principios generales del derecho doméstico al Derecho Internacional. Por un lado, exige un doble 'reconocimiento' a ser efectuado por la 'comunidad de naciones' y –por el otro lado– reduce el rol de los tribunales y cortes internacionales a meros identificadores de los múltiples requisitos señalados, y cuyos pasos solo se ven completados, de mediar la participación y reconocimiento de los Estados. Con esto, se reduce –a su mínima expresión– la participación de la justicia

---

For example, there might be two stages relating to general principles of law derived from national legal systems, in the sense that in the first instance a principle of law had to be operating in some sense across legal systems. If only some of those general legal principles were transposed to the international domain, a second stage of recognition might then occur in the course of that transposition.' International Law Commission. Seventy-First Session (Second Part). 30 de septiembre de 2019. A/CN.4/SR.3490. p. 13.

[61] Segundo Informe sobre los Principios Generales del Derecho. Marcelo Vázquez-Bermúdez . . . Para. 22. (nota: 3).

[62] Véase: *Id.*, . . . Para. 106. (nota: 3).

internacional en la formación de los principios generales del derecho. Debe tenerse en cuenta que la preocupación de que la identificación de los principios generales del derecho pudiera involucrar la creación de reglas internacionales en sede judicial fue puesto de relieve por miembros de la CDI durante los debates del Primer Informe del Relator Especial,[63] lo cual habría influenciado en la decisión del Relator de adoptar una aproximación que –al fin de cuentas– limita la participación de aquellos en la utilización de los principios generales.

IV. CONCLUSIONES

En base al análisis efectuado, podemos concluimos que el trabajo realizado por el Relator Especial es prometedor. Sin embargo, ciertos aspectos en su estudio requieren de mayor claridad. Tal vez, el tema más importante por resolver –más allá de lograr una mayor coherencia teórica– es la dimensión política involucrada en aquel estudio, lo cual implica tener presente las razones detrás de entender los principios generales del derecho como productos positivistas.

La tendencia del Relator de entender esta fuente del derecho como una manifestación positivista cobra sentido al recordar que éste debe de ofrecer (en el seno de la CDI), un estudio que pueda eventualmente influenciar a los destinatarios finales de aquel órgano como son los Estados. Sin embargo, ello crea complicaciones teóricas e inconsistencias, llegando a restringir el rol de los tribunales y cortes internacionales en la identificación/ formación de los principios generales del derecho, transformando potencialmente aquella fuente del derecho en una con poca aplicabilidad práctica. Más aun, la decisión del Relator Especial de limitar el rol de los tribunales y cortes internacionales podría resultar en que aquellas entidades dejen de lado el método ofrecido –eventualmente– por la CDI; pues, complica de sobremanera el uso de una fuente de derecho primordial para el buen funcionamiento de la adjudicación internacional.

Esperamos que en los siguientes informes del Relator Especial algunas de las dudas formuladas en este espacio sean clarificadas.

---

[63] Véase: Comments of some of the ILC members, such as Rajput (International Law Commission. Seventy-First Session (Second Part). A/CN.4/SR.3490. 30 de septiembre de 2019. p. 17).

PART

2

NOTES AND COMMENTS

Global Legal Pluralism and the Making of International Climate Change Law

BY PAUL SCHIFF BERMAN*

Abstract

Where and how is international law made? For decades, the conventional narrative was that international law is located only in the treaties and institutions that nation-states construct in coordination with each other. However, global legal pluralism scholars have advanced a different account, observing that in any given social field there are many sources of legality that tend to interact with and sometimes compete against each other. In addition, pluralists studied both the "vernacularization" of international law in local settings, as well as the creation of international law in domestic courts and tribunals. The rise of climate change litigation in domestic courts provides a new setting to see these dynamics at play. Focusing on three recent cases, this essay explores the ways in which domestic courts are vernacularizing the Paris Climate Agreement, creating legal duties under domestic law for greenhouse gas emissions.

I.

Where and how is international law made? For decades, the conventional narrative was that international law is located only in the treaties and institutions that nation-states construct in coordination with each other. Thus, if we wanted to find international law, we would look only to multilateral treaties, the United Nations and related bodies, and other formal agreements signed by governmental bodies.

---

* Walter S. Cox Professor of Law, The George Washington University Law School. Some background material in this essay is derived from Paul Schiff Berman, *Seeing Beyond the Limits of International Law* (reviewing JACK L. GOLDSMITH & ERIC A. POSNER, THE LIMITS OF INTERNATIONAL LAW), 84 TEXAS LAW REVIEW 1265 (2006).

Paul Schiff Berman, *Global Legal Pluralism and the Making of International Climate Change Law* In: *The Global Community Yearbook of International Law and Jurisprudence 2022*. Edited by: Giuliana Ziccardi Capaldo, Oxford University Press. © Oxford University Press 2023.
DOI: 10.1093/oso/9780197752265.003.0006

In addition, so-called international relations realists have tended to dismiss the power of international law generally. They have argued that because international law has minimal enforcement power, states only obey international law when it is in their interest to do so and ignore it otherwise. On this reading, international law has no independent compliance pull and is only an epiphenomenon of state interests.[1]

During the post–Cold War era of the 1990s and early 2000s, global legal pluralism scholars advanced a significantly different account. Building on anthropological analyses of colonial and other societies, legal pluralists observed that in any given social field there are many sources of legality that tend to interact with, and sometimes compete against, each other.[2] With that move, the potential field of international law expanded.[3] Freed from formalist categories, scholars could study the ways in which jurisdictional assertions in one legal arena could impact actors in a different arena. And these impacts can occur regardless of formal enforcement mechanisms. In addition, global legal pluralists, building on the work of constructivist scholars,[4] observed that international law actually helps shape state interests in the first place and therefore it is incoherent to argue that states only follow international law when it is in their interest to do so, as if the interests of states exist separate from the legal context.[5] Finally, pluralists studied both the "vernacularization" of international law in local settings,[6] as well as the creation of international law in domestic courts and tribunals,[7] and in other sub-state entities, such as cross-border networks of cities.[8]

Global legal pluralism therefore provided a more capacious way of understanding how international and transnational law actually operate on the ground. For example, although the celebrated efforts of Spanish Judge Baltasar Garzón to try former Chilean leader Augusto Pinochet[9] were in a sense not literally "successful" because Pinochet was never extradited to Spain,[10] those efforts had real impact because they strengthened the hands

---

[1] See generally, e.g., JACK L. GOLDSMITH & ERIC A. POSNER, THE LIMITS OF INTERNATIONAL LAW (2005).

[2] For a discussion of this move from legal pluralism to global legal pluralism, see Paul Schiff Berman, The New Legal Pluralism, 5 ANNUAL REVIEW OF LAW AND SOCIAL SCIENCE 225 (2009).

[3] See, e.g., Paul Schiff Berman, A Pluralist Approach to International Law, 32 YALE JOURNAL OF INTERNATIONAL LAW 301 (2007), reprinted in THEORY AND PHILOSOPHY OF INTERNATIONAL LAW (Andrea Bianchi ed., 2016).

[4] See, e.g., MARTHA FINNEMORE, NATIONAL INTERESTS IN INTERNATIONAL SOCIETY 3 (1996).

[5] See, e.g., Paul Schiff Berman, Seeing Beyond the Limits of International Law (reviewing JACK L. GOLDSMITH & ERIC A. POSNER, THE LIMITS OF INTERNATIONAL LAW), 84 TEXAS LAW REVIEW 1265 (2006).

[6] See, e.g., SALLY ENGLE MERRY, HUMAN RIGHTS & GENDER VIOLENCE: TRANSLATING INTERNATIONAL LAW INTO LOCAL JUSTICE (2006); Sally Engle Merry & Peggy Levitt, The Vernacularization of Women's Human Rights, in HUMAN RIGHTS FUTURES 213 (Hopgood et al. eds., 2017).

[7] See, e.g., PLURALISM IN INTERNATIONAL CRIMINAL LAW (Elies van Sliedregt & Sergey Vasilev eds., 2014).

[8] See, e.g., GLOBAL URBAN JUSTICE: THE RISE OF HUMAN RIGHTS CITIES (Oomen et al. eds., 2016).

[9] Judge Garzón issued an arrest order based on allegations of kidnappings, torture, and planned disappearances of Chilean citizens and citizens of other countries. Spanish Request to Arrest General Pinochet, Oct. 16, 1998, reprinted in THE PINOCHET PAPERS: THE CASE OF AUGUSTO PINOCHET IN SPAIN AND BRITAIN 57–59 (Reed Brody & Michael Ratner eds., 2000) [hereinafter THE PINOCHET PAPERS].

[10] Pinochet was physically in Great Britain. The British House of Lords ultimately ruled that Pinochet was not entitled to head-of-state immunity for acts of torture and could be extradited to Spain. Regina v. Bow St. Metro. Stipendiary Magistrate, Ex parte Pinochet (No. 3), [2000] 1 A.C. 147, 204–05 (H.L. 1999) (appeal taken from Q.B. Div'l Ct.) (holding that the International Convention Against Torture, incorporated into United Kingdom law in 1988, prevented Pinochet from claiming head-of-state immunity after 1988, because the universal jurisdiction contemplated by the Convention is inconsistent with immunity for former heads of state). Nevertheless, the British government refused to extradite, citing Pinochet's

of human rights advocates within Chile itself and provided the impetus for a movement that ultimately led to a Chilean Supreme Court decision stripping Pinochet of his lifetime immunity.[11] Likewise, Spanish efforts to prosecute members of the Argentine military bolstered reformers within the Argentine government, most notably then-President Nestor Kirschner. In August 2003, Judge Garzón sought extradition from Argentina of dozens of Argentines for human rights abuses committed under the Argentine military government in the 1970s.[12] In addition, Garzón successfully sought extradition from Mexico of one former Argentine Navy lieutenant who was accused of murdering hundreds of people.[13] In the wake of Garzón's actions, realist observers complained that such transnational prosecutions were illegitimate because Argentina had previously conferred amnesty on those who had been involved in the period of military rule and therefore any prosecution would infringe on Argentina's sovereign "choice" to grant amnesty.[14]

But the amnesty decision was not simply a unitary choice made by some unified "state" of Argentina; it was a politically contested act that remained controversial within the country.[15] And the Spanish extradition request itself gave President Kirschner more leverage in his tug-of-war with the legal establishment over the amnesty laws. Just a month after Garzón's request, both houses of the Argentine Congress voted by large majorities to annul the laws.[16] Meanwhile the Spanish government decided that it would not make the formal extradition request to Argentina that Garzón sought, but it did so based primarily on the fact that Argentina had begun to scrap its amnesty laws and the accused would therefore be subject to domestic human rights prosecution.[17] President Kirshner therefore could use

---

failing health. *See* Jack Straw, Sec'y of State Statement in the House of Commons (Mar. 2, 2000), *in* THE PINOCHET PAPERS, *supra* note 9, at 481, 482 ("[I]n the light of th[e] medical evidence . . . I . . . conclude[d] that no purpose would be served by continuing the Spanish extradition request."). Pinochet was eventually returned to Chile.

[11] *See Chile's Top Court Strips Pinochet of Immunity*, NEW YORK TIMES, Aug. 27, 2004, at A3 ("Chile's Supreme Court stripped the former dictator Augusto Pinochet of immunity from prosecution in a notorious human rights case on Thursday, raising hopes of victims that he may finally face trial for abuses during his 17-year rule.").

[12] *See* Larry Rohter, *Argentine Congress Likely to Void "Dirty War" Amnesties*, NEW YORK TIMES, Aug. 21, 2003, at A3 (recounting Garzón's extradition request).

[13] Emma Daly, *Spanish Judge Sends Argentine to Prison on Genocide Charge*, NEW YORK TIMES, June 30, 2003, at A3 ("In an unusual act of international judicial cooperation, and a victory for the Spanish judge Baltasar Garzón, Mexico's Supreme Court ruled this month that the former officer, Ricardo Miguel Cavallo, could be extradited to Spain for crimes reportedly committed in a third country, Argentina.").

[14] *See* David B. Rivkin Jr. & Lee A. Casey, *Crimes Outside the World's Jurisdiction*, NEW YORK TIMES, July 22, 2003, at A19 (noting that Argentina had granted amnesty to Cavallo and arguing that "Judge Garzón is essentially ignoring Argentina's own history and desires").

[15] The Argentine army, for example, made known its desire for amnesty for human rights abuses through several revolts in the late 1980s. The Argentine Congress granted amnesty after one such uprising in 1987. *See* Joseph B. Treaster, *Argentine President Orders Troops to End Revolt*, NEW YORK TIMES, Dec. 4, 1988, sec. 1, at 13 (describing an army revolt in Buenos Aires).

[16] *Argentina's Day of Reckoning*, CHICAGO TRIBUNE, Apr. 24, 2004, at C26.

[17] Elizabeth Nash, *Garzón Blocked Over "Dirty War" Extraditions*, THE INDEPENDENT, Aug. 30, 2003, at 14; *see also* Al Goodman, *Spain Blocks Trials of Argentines*, CNN.COM, Aug. 29, 2003, http://www.cnn.com/2003/WORLD/europe/08/29/spanish.argentina/index.html (quoting the Spanish attorney for the victims saying that the Spanish government's decision sends a "powerful message" to Argentina's Supreme Court to overturn the amnesty laws).

Spain's announcement to increase pressure on the Argentine Supreme Court to officially overturn the amnesty laws.[18]

Finally, on June 14, 2005, the Argentine Supreme Court did in fact strike down the amnesty laws, thus clearing the way for domestic human rights prosecutions.[19] Not only was the pressure exerted by Spain instrumental in these efforts, but it is significant that the Argentine Court cited as legal precedent a 2001 decision of the Inter-American Court of Human Rights striking down a similar amnesty provision in Peru as incompatible with the American Convention on Human Rights and hence without legal effect.[20] So, in the end, the "sovereign" state of Argentina made political and legal choices to repeal the amnesty laws just as it had previously made choices to create them. But in this change of heart we can see the degree to which international and transnational legal pronouncements, even if they are without any literal constraining effect, may significantly alter the domestic political terrain.

Likewise, local actors, operating outside of official government bureaucracies or judicial institutions, can at times leverage international legal norms to press causes within their countries.[21] For example, as late as 1994, women in Hong Kong were unable to inherit land.[22] That year a group of rural Indigenous women joined forces with urban women's groups to demand legal change. As detailed by Sally Engle Merry and Rachel E. Stern, "[t]he indigenous women slowly shifted from seeing their stories as individual kinship violations to broader examples of discrimination."[23] Ultimately, the women learned to protest these unjust customary laws in the language of international human rights and gender equality.[24] Having done so, they were successful at getting the inheritance rules overturned.[25] While we might regret the fact that these women were forced to "translate" their grievances into an internationally recognized language in order to be heard, the success of the movement in accessing political power surely attests to the strength and importance of the international law discourse.

---

[18] See Héctor Tobar, *Judge Orders Officers Freed: The Argentine Military Men Accused of Rights Abuses in the '70s and '80s May Still Face Trials*, Los Angeles Times, Sept. 2, 2003, at A3 ("President Nestor Kirchner used Spain's announcement to increase pressure on the Argentine Supreme Court to overturn the amnesty laws that prohibit trying the men here.").

[19] Corte Suprema de Justicia [CSJN], 14/6/2005, "Simón, Julio Héctor y otros s/ privación ilegítima de la libertad," causa No. 17.768, S.1767.XXXVIII (Arg.). *See also* Press Release, Human Rights Watch, Argentina: Amnesty Laws Struck Down (June 14, 2005), available at https://perma.cc/V6PT-GTFN.

[20] Corte Suprema de Justicia [CSJN], 14/6/2005, "Simón, Julio Héctor y otros s/ privación ilegítima de la libertad," causa No. 17.768, S.1767.XXXVIII (Arg.). *See also* Press Release, *supra* note19.

[21] Of course, such local actors do not only "use" international law as "given" to them, but also, through their social movements, shape the international legal norms themselves. For an argument that human rights discourse has been fundamentally shaped by Third World resistance to development, *see generally* BALAKRISHNAN RAJAGOPAL, INTERNATIONAL LAW FROM BELOW: DEVELOPMENT, SOCIAL MOVEMENTS, AND THIRD WORLD RESISTANCE (2003).

[22] Sally Engle Merry & Rachel E. Stern, *The Female Inheritance Movement in Hong Kong: Theorizing the Local/Global Interface*, 46 CURRENT ANTHROPOLOGY 387, 387 (2005).

[23] *Id.* at 399.

[24] *See id.* at 390 (explaining the evolution of the Anti-Discrimination Female Indigenous Residents Committee from a group that perceived the prohibition of female inheritance as a personal wrong perpetrated by relatives to a group arguing that the male-only inheritance laws failed to comply with international agreements, such as the Convention on the Elimination of Discrimination Against Women and the International Covenant on Civil and Political Rights).

[25] *Id.*, at 394.

Finally, nation-states themselves can enforce international norms in domestic courts. Most famously, Belgium and Germany have at times invoked principles of universal jurisdiction to prosecute those accused of massive human rights abuses.[26] Likewise, local laws against torture can be invoked even in the absence of international tribunals.[27]

Regardless of whether or not one thinks the proliferation and deployment of international norms in domestic political and legal forums is a good thing, it is difficult to deny that such interaction occurs. Thus, the relationship between the international and the local cannot simply be viewed as a state pursuing a single set of interests either completely constrained or completely unconstrained by international norms. Rather, as part of the multivalent, messy process by which various state constituencies vie to have their preferred policies adopted, international legal norms are a powerful tool. These norms provide a set of moral, rhetorical, and strategic arguments that may empower constituencies that might not otherwise have a voice, or they may be used by already powerful forces to protect their own interests. In any event, only by going beyond the simplistic model of the unitary state pursuing a single set of interests can we see the power of international law coursing below the surface.

II.

So far, I have focused on the impact of international legal norms on local polities and decision makers, as well as the way in which such norms seep into legal consciousness more generally.[28] But an additional aspect of legal pluralism is that localities can sometimes be *leaders* rather than *followers*, deploying local law to instantiate international legal norms even when the adoption of those norms is stalled at the nation-state level.

For example, states within a federalist system might recognize greater rights protections under their state constitutions than the national constitution does.[29] In the wake of the US Supreme Court's 2021 ruling that the federal constitution affords no protection to abortion rights,[30] some states have located such rights within their state constitutions.[31] In addition, localities can use their own economic power to impose standards on commercial entities that wish to sell products in that locality. In 2020, California entered into agreements with automakers to improve the fuel efficiency of their vehicles beyond what the Trump administration required.[32]

Even outside of federalist systems, cities have in recent years often led the way in enacting migration-friendly policies over and above what their nation-states were

---

[26] *See, e.g., Universal Jurisdiction Law and Practice in Belgium* (2022), available at https://perma.cc/JBJ9-D9QQ; UNIVERSAL JURISDICTION LAW AND PRACTICE IN GERMANY (2019), available at https://perma.cc/PU75-8LBB.

[27] *See, e.g.,* Torture Victim Protection Act of 1991 (TVPA), Pub. L. No. 102–256, 106 Stat. 73 (1992) (codified as amended at 28 U.S.C. § 1350 (2012)).

[28] For a discussion of how international law can shape legal consciousness, *see* Berman, *supra* note 5, at 1280–1295.

[29] *See, e.g.,* Amanda Powers, *Voters Amend State Constitutions to Enshrine New Rights,* Nov. 16, 2022, available at https://perma.cc/5MBW-EBW4.

[30] Dobbs v. Jackson Women's Health Organization, No. 19-1392, 597 U.S. ___ (2022).

[31] *See Abortion Policy in the Absence of Roe,* available at https://perma.cc/4MBL-LW2R.

[32] Rebecca Beitsch & Rachel Frazin, *California Finalizes Fuel Efficiency Deal with Five Automakers, Undermining Trump,* THE HILL, Aug. 17, 2020, available at https://thehill.com/policy/energy-environment/512414-california-finalizes-fuel-efficiency-deal-with-five-automakers/.

providing. These cities have tried to assert a kind of urban citizenship regime independent from national citizenship.[33] They have also engaged in regional and global political and legal debates,[34] created their own foreign affairs departments, and established massive regional and transnational city networks that resemble international organizations,[35] while drafting normative documents using the language of international law.[36] And, over the past decade, "in reaction to the Syrian Civil War and Russia's invasion of Ukraine, many local governments have taken proactive stances welcoming refugees, at times in open defiance of their national governments, even seeking to open their ports to ships rescuing people in the Mediterranean Sea."[37]

III.

This same kind of pluralist interplay between international and domestic law can be seen in the context of efforts to respond to climate change. Here again, the world's attention often focuses on the obvious sites of international law: the large gatherings, the official communiques, the treaties, protocols, and group statements, and so on. But as global legal pluralism would predict, much of the real legal action can be found in the strategic litigation pursued by local actors deploying a combination of local and international norms in an attempt to hold governments and polluters responsible for the grave externalities that greenhouse gas emissions have caused over many years.

Indeed, the 2020s may well come to be seen as an important turning point in greenhouse gas litigation, just as the 1990s were for human rights litigation in domestic courts. Increasingly, litigation is being brought in local courts by a transnational network of NGOs and activists, with the number of cases filed having nearly doubled, from 884 to 1,550 between 2017 and 2020.[38]

The three highest profile cases to date have been brought in the Netherlands and in Germany. And each use run-of-the mill assertions of jurisdiction because they are suits brought against defendants who are within the forum country. But what is most striking about these cases—aside from the sheer willingness of the courts to entertain these suits at all—is that in all three cases the decisions of the courts appear to be based neither fully on international law nor fully on domestic law. Instead, we see a creative hybrid being fashioned by local courts using a mixture of international and domestic law norms, thus reflecting the legal pluralism at the heart of even this most global of societal problems.

---

[33] *See, e.g.,* Barbara Oomen, *Cities of Refuge: Rights, Culture and the Creation of Cosmopolitan Citizenship,* in CULTURE, CITIZENSHIP AND HUMAN RIGHTS (Rosemarie Buikema et al. eds., 2019). For the observations in this paragraph, I draw from ELIF DURMUS, BREAKING FREE: LOCAL GOVERNMENTS' BOUNDARY-DEFYING ENGAGEMENT WITH HUMAN RIGHTS AND MIGRATION (2022, unpublished manuscript on file with author).

[34] *See, e.g.,* Barbara Oomen & Moritz Baumgärtel, *Frontier Cities: The Rise of Local Authorities as an Opportunity for International Human Rights Law,* 29 EUROPEAN JOURNAL OF INTERNATIONAL LAW 607 (2018).

[35] *See, e.g.,* Thomas Lacroix, *Migration-Related City Networks: A Global Overview,* LOCAL GOVERNMENT STUDIES (2021).

[36] *See, e.g.,* Barbara Oomen & Moritz Baumgärtel, *Human Rights Cities,* in THE SAGE HANDBOOK OF HUMAN RIGHTS 709 (Anja Mihr & Mark Gibney eds., 2014).

[37] Durmus, *supra* note 33, at 5.

[38] *See Global Climate Change Litigation Report: 2020 Status Review,* a Report of the United Nations Environment Program (2021), available at https://perma.cc/F274-43LJ.

First, is the 2021 case of *Neubauer et al. v. Germany*.[39] As is clear from the case caption, this suit was brought against the federal government itself. A group of German youth filed a legal challenge to Germany's Federal Climate Protection Act (Bundesklimaschutzgesetz or KSG) in the Federal Constitutional Court. The claimants argued that the KSG's target for reducing greenhouse gases was insufficient. And significantly, this challenge to the federal law was based on a set of arguments that effectively combined domestic and international legal norms.

To begin, the KSG was alleged to violate Articles 1(1), 2(2), and 20a of the German Basic Law. Article 1(1) guarantees that the state will protect human dignity,[40] and the claimants argued that climate change is depriving them of a future with human dignity. Article 2(2) guarantees the right to life and physical integrity,[41] both of which were allegedly threatened by climate change. Meanwhile Article 20a invokes the state's "responsibility towards future generations" and requires the state to "protect the natural foundations of life and animals by legislation and . . . executive and judicial action."[42] Thus, the claimants argued that an insufficient set of federal targets would violate their basic rights.

So far, this seems like only a domestic lawsuit. But note how the claimants attempted to show that the KSG was inadequate. They alleged that the KSG's 2030 target did not take sufficient account of Germany's obligations under the Paris Climate Agreement to limit global temperature rise to "well below 2 degrees Celsius."[43] According to the complainants, the KSG would not reduce the country's greenhouse gas emissions sufficiently to meet the Paris Agreement obligations. The complaint therefore deftly vernacularizes the international agreement. By making compliance with the Paris Agreement part of the government's obligation to protect fundamental rights, the complainants essentially imported the Paris Agreement targets into the German Basic Law.

In a decision issued on April 29, 2021, the German Federal Constitutional Court accepted the complainants' arguments and struck down parts of the KSG as incompatible with fundamental rights.[44] Significantly, the court ruled that Article 20a of the Basic Law not only requires the legislature to protect the climate in general, but it specifically requires the legislature to pay attention to inter-generational equity and therefore prevents greenhouse gas reduction burdens from "being unilaterally offloaded onto the future."[45] Using the Paris climate targets as the appropriate standard, the court determined that the national legislature had not proportionally allocated the costs of reducing emissions as between current and future generations. The court therefore ordered the legislature to set improved reduction targets, and in August 2021 federal lawmakers passed a bill approving an adapted KSG that requires larger reductions in greenhouse gas emissions.[46]

Thus, the court ultimately issued an opinion that was not a fully international law decision nor a fully domestic law decision, but rather an amalgam of both. The court first accepted that the international law standards adopted in the Paris Climate Agreement were in fact the relevant standards to be applied. Then, the court effectively imported those standards into the framework of the German Basic Law by ruling that Article 20a requires

---

[39] For case documents, *see* https://perma.cc/48TX-Y2M5.

[40] For the text of the German Basic Law, *see* https://perma.cc/4S3V-6CFE.

[41] *See id.*

[42] *Id.*

[43] *See supra* note 39.

[44] *See id.*

[45] *See id.*

[46] *See id.*

the legislature to implement those international standards and to do so in an aggressive way so as to preserve inter-generational equity. Therefore, going forward the Paris Climate Agreement targets are now a part of German Basic Law, and the legislature is required to take action to meet those targets as a matter of the legislature's core national constitutional obligations.

The 2021 Dutch decision in *Milieudefensie et al. v. Royal Dutch Shell* reflects a similar vernacularization of the international climate standards, but here the court arguably went even farther by imposing those standards not against the government but against a private corporation.[47] And again the mechanism for applying the Paris Climate Agreement was local law. However, unlike in the German case, here the plaintiffs did not rely on national constitutional principles, but simply on ordinary tort law. In that sense, the vernacularization of international law in this case is possibly even more radical and significant than in the German case.

The *Milieudefensie* court noted that the core tort principles laid out in Book 6 Section 162 of the Dutch Civil Code prevent an entity such as Royal Dutch Shell from acting "in violation of a duty imposed by law or of what according to unwritten law has to be regarded as proper social conduct."[48] According to the court, this requirement includes the obligation of companies to take action to meet the Paris Climate targets, especially "where these emissions form the majority of a company's CO2 emissions, as is the case for companies that produce and sell fossil fuels."[49] Accordingly, the court concluded that Royal Dutch Shell must reduce its emissions 45 percent by 2030.[50]

Royal Dutch Shell has appealed this ruling,[51] but if it stands, it is difficult to overstate how important the decision is, both for climate change litigation specifically and for the pluralism of international law more generally. For if other courts around the world pick up the logic of the Dutch court it will mean that international legal norms—whether embodied in treaties, declarations, executive agreements, or customary international law—can potentially form the basis for tort duties that are then enforceable in national courts through ordinary civil tort suits. The result would be a true hybrid: national law stitched from international norms, and international norms explicated and enforced in domestic courts.

Most recently, a German appellate court has picked up the climate change litigation baton and reinstated a lawsuit brought by a Peruvian farmer against a German energy company, even though the suit had previously been dismissed in the lower court.[52] Unlike the two cases discussed previously, this case, *Luciano Lliuya v. RWE AG*, is inherently transnational because the plaintiff is not from the forum country, and the environmental harm at issue is located abroad. Yet, despite the transnational context, the German court has so far used local principles of nuisance law under the German Civil Code. Section 1004 of the Code provides that a property owner can sue if their ownership of property "is interfered with by means other than removal or retention of possession."[53] Using this idea, the plaintiff claimed that the German company, by contributing to global greenhouse gas emissions, had helped cause a glacial lake sitting 4,650 meters above his hometown of Huaraz to grow

[47] For case documents, *see* https://perma.cc/WM7T-WDZG.
[48] *See id.*
[49] *See id.*
[50] *See id.*
[51] *See id.*
[52] For case documents, *see* https://perma.cc/NA93-8Y9B.
[53] German Civil Code, § 1004.

in volume due to ice-melt from receding glaciers, such that the lake poses an ongoing threat to flood the town.[54]

This is clearly a transnational expansion of nuisance law, which is usually used to regulate neighboring property uses. But in an era when climate change is a truly global problem, the court rightly recognized that entities can create the sorts of externalities regulated by nuisance law even if they are not physically proximate. Of course, since RWE is only one of many contributors to greenhouse gas emissions, it cannot be held solely responsible. But the plaintiff argued that, according to a reliable source, the Carbon Majors Database,[55] RWE has caused 0.47 percent of global post–Industrial Revolution carbon emissions. Thus, he is suing for that proportion of the costs of flood prevention in his town.[56]

It is, of course, not at all clear whether this claim will ultimately be successful. For now, the litigation has been allowed to proceed, but there are many remaining issues that might still block the plaintiff from recovering. The same is true of the *Milieudefensie* decision, which is currently on appeal.[57]

Yet, the key point is that there is now a path for climate change litigation to proceed, both against governments and against polluters. And this path is based neither fully in international law, nor fully in domestic law. Instead, courts are fashioning a hybrid approach, either by blending domestic law norms with international law standards, or by translating domestic law litigation into the transnational context.

Thus, the future success of climate change litigation does not rely on the creation of new treaties or new international enforcement bodies. Instead, domestic courts applying domestic law can be a potent force in enforcing international standards.

But on the other hand, international law is not at all irrelevant to this flurry of domestic activity. Nor is this international environmental law emerging as only an epiphenomenon of state interests. To the contrary, we can see that the Paris Climate Agreement has become a key *shaper* of state interests. It has galvanized a transnational network of climate activists, it has helped mobilize legal action within domestic polities, it has articulated standards that can be deployed by those domestic polities in litigation, and it has provided consensus facts for domestic judges to draw upon in their rulings.

Thus, instead of maintaining a rigid differentiation between international and domestic law, a global legal pluralist lens allows us to see how this hybrid process of vernacularization creates cascades of norms and incubates new generations of litigants who will draw on international norms even while using domestic law. And then those domestic cases will in turn create and shape international legal norms (including customary international law) in the future. This is global legal pluralism in action.

---

[54] *See supra* note 52.

[55] https://perma.cc/BAQ5-EY9E.

[56] *See supra* note 52.

[57] *See supra* note 51.

The Court's Role in Upholding Inter-Generational Obligations Respecting the Child's Right to Truth: *Juliana v. United States* as a Case in Point

BY SONJA C. GROVER*

Abstract

The UN Commission on Human Rights has long recognized that the right to truth regarding grievous human rights violations constituting international crimes is inalienable and non-derogable. Yet children's right to truth is often not respected especially if they are not the contemporary proximate victims of the atrocities perpetrated. This ignores inter-generational obligations regarding the right to truth. The neglect of the right to truth belonging to *children qua children* may be related to a general failure to acknowledge the persecutory targeting of children as a particular identifiable collective defined by age intersecting with other characteristics. This commentary examines the denial of the child's right to truth involving current and future child generations and the larger societal implications of that denial. The issue is discussed using the specific holding of the US Federal Court of Appeals (Ninth Circuit) in the child rights climate change case *Juliana v. United States*.

I. INTRODUCTION

The UN 2006 Commission on Human Rights study[1] on the right to truth concluded that:

---

* PhD; Full Professor, Faculty of Education, Lakehead University, Ontario, Canada; sgrover@lakeheadu.ca.
[1] Office of the UN High Commissioner for Human Rights (UNOHCHR), *Promotion and Protection of Human Rights Study on the Right to Truth*, E/CN.4 2006/91 (Feb. 8, 2006), at <https://www.refworld.org/docid/46822b6c2.html> (accessed Oct. 3, 2022).

Sonja C. Grover, *The Court's Role in Upholding Inter-Generational Obligations Respecting the Child's Right to Truth: Juliana v. United States as a Case in Point* In: *The Global Community Yearbook of International Law and Jurisprudence 2022*. Edited by: Giuliana Ziccardi Capaldo, Oxford University Press. © Oxford University Press 2023. DOI: 10.1093/oso/9780197752265.003.0007

... the right to truth about gross human rights violations and serious violations of human rights law is an inalienable and autonomous right linked to the duty and obligation of the State to protect and guarantee human rights, to conduct effective investigations, and to guarantee effective remedy and reparations. This right is closely linked with other rights and has both an individual and a societal dimension and should be considered as a non-derogable right and not be subject to limitations.[2]

Traditionally the scope of the legal concept of the right to truth has been interpreted to concern the right of surviving victims and their families to know the fate of missing loved ones who have, for instance, been forcibly disappeared and the whole truth of the circumstances that led to and involved the human rights violations they and their relatives suffered. It is here suggested, however, that knowing the truth regarding grievous human rights violations is also an essential educational right. The right to truth then, on the view here, implicates the educational rights in particular (but not exclusively) for generations to come of all children of that jurisdiction where the atrocities occurred and of any jurisdiction that was complicit in some way in the perpetrating of those atrocities. Arguably there is then an educational right to know the truth of gross human rights violations that is held collectively by all children regardless of the state which exercises jurisdiction over those children. This in that such information is part of the historical truth of humanity globally and is instructive as to what measure of accountability if any was realized and regarding necessary potential preventive and mitigation measures that might be implemented to avoid such human rights atrocities in future. The right to education as articulated in the Convention on the Rights of the Child (CRC) in fact includes being educated on respect for human rights, peace and democratic values. The right to truth about the current state and the history of gross human rights violations (amounting in many cases to international crimes) would hence appear to be part and parcel of the fundamental right to education as articulated at Article 29 of the CRC:

CRC ARTICLE 29

1. States Parties agree that the education of the child shall be directed to:
   ... (b) *The development of respect for human rights and fundamental freedoms*, and for the principles enshrined in the Charter of the United Nations ... (d) The preparation of the child for responsible life in a free society, in the spirit of understanding, peace, tolerance, equality of sexes, and friendship among all peoples, ethnic, national and religious groups and persons of indigenous origin ... (emphasis added).[3]

These aforementioned educational objectives can only be achieved where children have access also to painful historical truths framed in a manner that takes into consideration the child's developmental level and always with regard to the best interests of the individual child and the children collectively to whom the information is conveyed. A remarkable example of appreciation of the child's right to truth is that of an eighth-grade

---

[2] Office of the UN High Commissioner for Human Rights (UNOHCHR), *Promotion and Protection of Human Rights Study on the Right to Truth*, E/CN.4 2006/91, at 2 (Feb. 8, 2006), at <https://www.refworld.org/docid/46822b6c2.html> (accessed Oct. 3, 2022).

[3] UN Convention on the Rights of the Child (entry into force Sept. 2, 1990), at <https://www.ohchr.org/en/instruments-mechanisms/instruments/convention-rights-child> (accessed Oct. 3, 2022).

US civics teacher Carrie LaPierre of North Handover, Massachusetts, located forty minutes from Salem, Massachusetts. As a project for her civics class, she and her students petitioned the Massachusetts legislature to clear the name of Elizabeth Johnson Jr. whose name had for some reason been omitted from a 1711 Massachusetts statute exonerating persons accused and convicted of witchcraft in 1692 in Salem, Massachusetts. Being persecuted for alleged witchcraft and suffering imprisonment, torture and, in many cases, execution based on conviction for this concocted offence is arguably a crime against humanity that disproportionately but not exclusively targets and targeted females. Elizabeth Johnson Jr. had been convicted of witchcraft at age twenty-two and sentenced to death but was later spared and suffered a long imprisonment and the indignity of never having had her name officially cleared. After three hundred years, the Massachusetts legislature in 2022 added Elizabeth Johnson Jr.'s name to a resolution exonerating of purported witchcraft all those listed in the resolution. The teacher Carrie LaPierre commented that this effort had taught her students about the importance of the enduring struggle for justice and that though they were young people they too had a critical role to play in that struggle.[4]

It has been commented by others that child activism around human rights identifies the individual activist child or child collective with all those persons recognized as human rights defenders.[5] This then elevates the child activists' status as political actors despite their young age but, at the same time, exposes child activists to potential "manipulation or co-option."[6] To the foregoing point, in a later section of this commentary we will consider how US child activism-specifically regarding climate change was, on the analysis here, manipulated and/or thwarted in the legal and political arena. This is the case we explore here (the *Juliana* case) through the legal characterization assigned the child activist initiative in *Juliana*[7] by the government and largely adopted by the federal appeals court.

The right to truth across generations of young people is also relevant given the phenomenon of inter-generational trauma. Coming to terms with such trauma requires as a first step access to and acknowledgement of truths relating to historical gross human rights violations. Yet there is a contemporary effort, for instance, in many American states where Republicans hold the majority in the legislature, to impede by means of statutory restrictions US schoolchildren's access to, for instance, information regarding historical truths about colonization and racial inequities and persistent institutional structures that perpetuate systemic racism.[8]

---

[4] Scottie Andrew, *The Last Salem Witch Has Been Exonerated, Thanks to an Eighth-Grade Teacher and Her Students*, CNN (Aug. 6, 2022), at <https://www.cnn.com/2022/08/06/us/salem-witch-trials-exonerated-elizabeth-johnson-cec/index.html> (accessed Oct. 3, 2022).

[5] E. Kaye, M. Tisdall & P. Cuevas-Parra, *Beyond the Familiar Challenges for Children and Young People's Participation Rights: The Potential of Activism* 26 (5) INTERNATIONAL JOURNAL OF HUMAN RIGHTS 792, at 801 (2022).

[6] Kaye, Tisdall & Cuevas-Parra, *supra* note 5, at 802.

[7] Juliana v. United States, at <http://climatecasechart.com/case/juliana-v-united-states/> (accessed Oct. 4, 2022).

[8] *Florida Moves to Restrict What Schools Can Teach About Systemic Racism*, PBS NEWS HOUR (July 8, 2022) (Florida's Stop Woke Act prohibits school instruction on critical race theory from K–12 Those who violate the law could face lawsuits where the defendant could be fined up to USD 10,000), at <https://www.pbs.org/newshour/show/florida-moves-to-restrict-what-schools-can-teach-about-systemic-racism> (accessed Oct. 3, 2022).

Not only is the right to truth linked to the fundamental right to a remedy and potential reparations but also to freedom of expression and freedom to access information.[9] The latter civil and political rights are also articulated in the CRC:

CRC ARTICLE 13

1. The child shall have the right to freedom of expression; this right shall include freedom to seek, receive and impart information and ideas of all kinds, 2. The exercise of this right may be subject to certain restrictions, but these shall only be such as are provided by law and are necessary: (a) For respect of the rights or reputations of others; or (b) For the protection of national security or of public order . . . or of public health or morals.[10]

The argument will be made here in the context of the *Juliana v. United States* child rights climate case[11] that the US federal government (on the view here and arguably on the factual record in *Juliana*) misled the general public—including children—as to its level of devotion to upholding its public trust obligation to adequately protect the land, sea, and air of the Republic for posterity. This then denied its constituents access to informational critical truths about climate change and its potential devastating *irrevocable* consequences if not, at least in part, remedied effectively. Those consequences include significant violations of children's basic rights to good health and long-term survival:

[T]alking about children, of course, a healthy environment is crucial for children to grow, with good nutrition and free of disease. The climate crisis threatens children's wellbeing in other ways too, for example with poverty driving up child marriage.[12]

In the next section we consider what this author respectfully characterizes as the denial by the federal US government of children's right to truth associated with its negligent creation of conditions that threaten the health, well-being and potentially the very survival of vast numbers of the generations of U.S. children current and yet to come due to non-mitigated climate change effects. We will examine this issue in the context of a climate change legal case *Juliana v. United States*.[13] It is argued that since children as a distinct collective are amongst those most at risk of the severe adverse consequence to health due to climate change,[14] the severity of the situation is tantamount to persecution of children at

---

[9] International Centre for Transitional Justice, Truth Seeking: Elements Creating a Effective Truth Commission, Chapter 1: *The Right to the Truth*, at 3 (2013), at <https://www.ictj.org/publication/truth-seeking-elements-creating-effective-truth-commission> (accessed Oct. 3, 2022).

[10] UN Convention on the Rights of the Child (entry into force Sept. 2, 1990), at <https://www.ohchr.org/en/instruments-mechanisms/instruments/convention-rights-child> (accessed Oct. 3, 2022).

[11] Juliana v. United States, at <http://climatecasechart.com/case/juliana-v-united-states/> (accessed Oct. 4, 2022).

[12] Children's Rights International Network, interview with Fithriyyah Iskandar, an environmental youth activist and doctor from Indonesia, *Planetary Health as A Prerequisite to Children's Health* (Aug. 3, 2022), at <https://home.crin.org/readlistenwatch/stories/planetary-health> (accessed Oct. 5, 2022).

[13] Juliana v. United States at <http://climatecasechart.com/case/juliana-v-united-states/> (accessed Oct. 5, 2022).

[14] SONJA C. GROVER, THE PERSECUTION OF CHILDREN AS A CRIME AGAINST HUMANITY (1st ed. 2021).

imminent such risk as a crime against humanity.[15] This climate situation knowingly and intentionally not sufficiently addressed may constitute a continuing international crime should the issue not be adequately resolved in the brief time left to do so before ongoing widespread climate catastrophe. The destruction of children's health and/or even their lives due to climate change can, on the analysis here, be considered a crime against humanity under Rome Statute Article 7(k): "Other inhumane acts of a similar character intentionally causing great suffering, or serious injury to body or to mental or physical health."[16] Further the child's right to survival, good health and development is covered in the CRC at Article 6:

> 1. States Parties recognize that every child has the inherent right to life. 2. States Parties shall ensure to the maximum extent possible the survival and development of the child.[17]

Note also that the UN General Assembly has recognized in a 2022 resolution the right to a clean, healthy and sustainable environment as a universal human right.[18] At the same time there has been an effort to mobilize support for including an international crime of ecocide (mass environmental destruction) in the Rome Statute by further amendment, though such an amendment has not yet materialized.[19]

Let us consider then the case of *Juliana v. United States*[20] and in what way it highlights the inter-generational obligation to honor the child's right to truth and the devastating consequences that are possible in some contexts when that obligation is sidestepped.

II. *JULIANA V. UNITED STATES* AND INTER-GENERATIONAL OBLIGATIONS RELATING TO THE CHILD'S RIGHT TO TRUTH

In the *Juliana* case, the twenty-one child plaintiffs and a legal representative of future generations[21] argued that their constitutional rights under the US Constitution pertaining to due process, equal protection and "public trust principles" were violated by the United States in its support for the corporate defendants to continue to create unmanageable levels of CO_2

---

[15] ICC Rome Statute, in force on July 1, 2002 (Article 7(h) Persecution against *any* identifiable group or collectivity on political, racial, national, ethnic, cultural, religious, gender as defined in Paragraph 3, *or other grounds that are universally recognized as impermissible under international law*, in connection with any act referred to in this paragraph or any crime within the jurisdiction of the Court), at <https://www.icc-cpi.int/sites/default/files/RS-Eng.pdf≥ (accessed Aug. 19, 2022).

[16] ICC Rome Statute in force on July 1, 2002, Article 7(k), at <https://www.icc-cpi.int/sites/default/files/RS-Eng.pdf≥ (accessed Aug. 19, 2022).

[17] UN Convention on the Rights of the Child (entry into force Sept. 2, 1990), at <https://www.ohchr.org/en/instruments-mechanisms/instruments/convention-rights-child> (accessed Oct. 3, 2022).

[18] *Climate and Environment: UN General Assembly Declares Access to Clean and Healthy Environment a Universal Human Right*, UN NEWS (July 28, 2022), at < https://news.un.org/en/story/2022/07/1123482> (accessed Oct. 3, 2022).

[19] *UN Environmental Program: Observations on the Scope and Application of Universal Jurisdiction to Environmental Protection*, at <https://www.un.org/en/ga/sixth/75/universal_jurisdiction/unep_e.pdf> (accessed Oct. 3, 2022).

[20] Juliana v. United States, at <https://casetext.com/case/juliana-v-united-states-4> (accessed Aug. 19, 2022).

[21] USCA (9th Circuit) Juliana v. United States, 947 F.3d 1159 (9th Cir. 2020) No. 18-36082 United States Court of Appeals for the Ninth Circuit (Decided Jan. 17, 2020), at 2.

emissions.[22] The plaintiffs referenced the US constitutional guarantee to life, liberty and property and the government's obligation to protect these rights "which belong to present generations as well as to Posterity (or future generations)."[23] The children maintained that they had been discriminated against (a violation of the equality constitutional guarantee embedded in the due process clause) in that "the harm caused by Defendants has denied Plaintiffs the same protection of fundamental rights afforded to prior and present generations of adult citizens."[24] They further argued that:

> The reason why a stable climate system is inherent in our fundamental rights to life, liberty, and property becomes more clear and compelling because of the grave and continuing harm to children that results from discriminatory laws and actions that prevent a stable climate system.[25]
>
> Plaintiffs are separate suspect classes in need of extraordinary protection from the political process pursuant to the principles of Equal Protection. As evidenced by their affirmative aggregate acts, *Defendants have a long history of deliberately discriminating against children and future generations in exerting their sovereign authority over our nation's air space and federal fossil fuel resources for the economic benefit of present generations of adults.* Plaintiffs are an insular minority with no voting rights and little, if any, political power or influence over Defendants and their actions concerning fossil fuels. Plaintiffs have immutable age characteristics that they cannot change. *Future generations do not have present political power or influence, have immutable characteristics, and are also an insular minority* (emphasis added).[26]

The District Court in *Juliana*, however, rejected age as a suspect class but "allowed the Juliana equal protection claim to proceed on a fundamental rights theory."[27] Note further that "both the [US] Supreme Court and the Ninth Circuit have held that age is not a suspect class" upon which one can claim a discriminatory violation of the US equality guarantee.[28]

---

[22] USDC, Juliana v. United States (United States District Court of Oregon—Eugene Division Opinion) Case No. 6:15-cv-01517-AA10-15-2018, at <https://casetext.com/case/juliana-v-united-states-4> (accessed Aug. 19, 2022).

[23] USDC, Kelsey Cascadia Rose Juliana et al. v. United States et al. (United States District Court of Oregon—Eugene Division). First Amended Complaint for Declaratory and Injunctive Relief at 84. Filed 09/10/15, at <http://climatecasechart.com/wp-content/uploads/sites/16/case-documents/2015/20150910_docket-615-cv-1517_complaint-2.pdf (accessed Oct. 4, 2022).

[24] USDC, Kelsey Cascadia Rose Juliana et al. v. United States et al. (United States District Court of Oregon—Eugene Division). First Amended Complaint for Declaratory and Injunctive Relief at 88. Filed 09/10/15, at <http://climatecasechart.com/wp-content/uploads/sites/16/case-documents/2015/20150910_docket-615-cv-1517_complaint-2.pdf> (accessed Oct. 4, 2022).

[25] USDC, Kelsey Cascadia Rose Juliana et al. v. United States et al. (United States District Court of Oregon—Eugene Division). First Amended Complaint for Declaratory and Injunctive Relief at 89. Filed 09/10/15, at <http://climatecasechart.com/wp-content/uploads/sites/16/case-documents/2015/20150910_docket-615-cv-1517_complaint-2.pdf> (accessed Oct. 4, 2022).

[26] USDC, Kelsey Cascadia Rose Juliana et al. v. United States et al. (United States District Court of Oregon—Eugene Division). First Amended Complaint for Declaratory and Injunctive Relief at 89. Filed 09/10/15, at <http://climatecasechart.com/wp-content/uploads/sites/16/case-documents/2015/20150910_docket-615-cv-1517_complaint-2.pdf> (accessed Oct. 4, 2022).

[27] USCA (9th Circuit) Juliana v. United States, 947 F.3d 1159 (9th Cir. 2020) No. 18-36082 United States Court of Appeals for the Ninth Circuit (Decided Jan. 17, 2020).

[28] USDC, Juliana v. United States, 339 F. Supp. 3d 1062 (D. Or. 2018). Decided Oct 15, 2018 (Case No. 6:15-cv-01517-AA) United States District Court for the District of Oregon—Eugene Division at 34.

Arguably this US federal court legal precedent disqualifying age as a suspect class, at a minimum, undercut the *Juliana* child plaintiffs' request *as a child class* (pertaining to current and future generations of children) for remedial action by US federal authorities regarding climate change. Further, the US Federal Courts have either *not* affirmed future generations as a suspect class or declined to address the matter.[29]

The *Juliana* child plaintiffs public trust argument rests ultimately on the federal government's sovereign responsibility to protect the country's natural resources, land, sea and air, water and wildlife.[30] The child plaintiffs noted that:

> In 1968, Congress declared that the Federal Government has "continuing responsibility" to "use all practicable means" so as to *"fulfill the responsibilities of each generation as trustee of the environment for succeeding generations* (emphasis added)." 42 U.S.C. § 4331(b)(1).[31]

The U.S. State Department and various other US federal government agencies in effect acknowledged "*'an obligation to current and future generations to take action' on climate change* (emphasis added)."[32]

The child plaintiffs in *Juliana* argued that the defendants were knowingly over a long period and currently creating the conditions for climate catastrophes:

> For over fifty years, the United States of America has known that carbon dioxide ("CO2") pollution from burning fossil fuels was causing global warming and dangerous climate change, and that continuing to burn fossil fuels would destabilize the climate system on which present and future generations of our nation depend for their wellbeing and survival.[33]

In essence, the child plaintiffs were alleging that the United States was complicit in contributing to what likely would meet the criteria for "ecocide." The proposed legal definition of "ecocide" as an international crime (not as yet recognized under international law

---

[29] USDC, Juliana v. United States, 339 F. Supp. 3d 1062 (D. Or. 2018). Decided Oct 15, 2018 (Case No. 6:15-cv-01517-AA) United States District Court for the District of Oregon—Eugene Division at 34.

[30] USDC, Kelsey Cascadia Rose Juliana et al. v. United States et al. (United States District Court of Oregon—Eugene Division). First Amended Complaint for Declaratory and Injunctive Relief at 81. Filed 09/10/15, at <http://climatecasechart.com/wp-content/uploads/sites/16/case-documents/2015/20150910_docket-615-cv-1517_complaint-2.pdf> (accessed Oct. 4, 2022).

[31] USDC, Kelsey Cascadia Rose Juliana et. al. v. United States (United States District Court of Oregon—Eugene Division). First Amended Complaint for Declaratory and Injunctive Relief at -81. Filed 09/10/15, at <http://climatecasechart.com/wp-content/uploads/sites/16/case-documents/2015/20150910_docket-615-cv-1517_complaint-2.pdf> (accessed Oct. 4, 2022).

[32] USDC, Kelsey Cascadia Rose Juliana et al. v. United States et al. (United States District Court of Oregon—Eugene Division). First Amended Complaint for Declaratory and Injunctive Relief at 83 Filed 09/10/15, at <http://climatecasechart.com/wp-content/uploads/sites/16/case-documents/2015/20150910_docket-615-cv-1517_complaint-2.pdf> (accessed Oct. 4, 2022).

[33] USDC, Kelsey Cascadia Rose Juliana et al. v. United States et al. (United States District Court of Oregon—Eugene Division). First Amended Complaint for Declaratory and Injunctive Relief at 1. Filed 09/10/15, at <http://climatecasechart.com/wp-content/uploads/sites/16/case-documents/2015/20150910_docket-615-cv-1517_complaint-2.pdf> (accessed Oct. 4, 2022).

but recommended by various nongovernmental organizations and others to be added to the Rome Statute) is as follows:

> For the purpose of this Statute, "ecocide" means unlawful or wanton acts committed with knowledge that there is a substantial likelihood of severe and either widespread or long-term damage to the environment being caused by those acts.[34]

The *Juliana* child plaintiffs outlined among the harms allegedly knowingly and intentionally created by the US defendants—through their unabated willingness to continue to exploit fossil fuels despite the severe climate change risks—the concrete particularized injuries they and their families had already suffered and would continue to suffer for the foreseeable years to come. Plaintiffs alleged that:

> Through its policies and practices, the Federal Government bears a higher degree of responsibility than any other individual, entity, or country for exposing Plaintiffs to the present dangerous atmospheric CO2 concentration. In fact, the United States is responsible for more than a quarter of global historic cumulative CO2 emissions.[35]

The *Juliana* plaintiffs further argued that the US federal government knew for decades that (i) massive CO_2 emissions due to exploitation of fossil fuels by US corporations was causing major climate destabilization for the United States and creating significant harms that violated the child plaintiffs' constitutional rights and that (ii) if not curbed through a nation-wide transition to other energy sources those harms would impact also children of future generations.[36]

The *Juliana* child plaintiffs over the course of their filings evinced evidence that as children they were particularly vulnerable to the harmful effects of climate change and highlighted the fact that the courts were their perceived best and factually only option for a remedy given that the ballot box was and is inaccessible to all US children in federal elections (persons under age eighteen years) in the United States.[37] Furthermore, the children argued based on scientific evidence that "[t]here is an extremely limited amount of time to preserve a habitable climate system for our country" [the United States].[38]

---

[34] Evan Van Trigt, *A Legal Definition of Ecocide* (July 15, 2021), at <https://peacepalacelibrary.nl/blog/2021/legal-definition-ecocide#:~:text='For%20the%20purpose%20of%20this,being%20caused%20by%20those%20acts≥ (accessed Aug. 19, 2022).

[35] USDC, Kelsey Cascadia Rose Juliana et al. v. United States et al. (United States District Court of Oregon—Eugene Division). First Amended Complaint for Declaratory and Injunctive Relief at 3. Filed 09/10/15, at <http://climatecasechart.com/wp-content/uploads/sites/16/case-documents/2015/20150910_docket-615-cv-1517_complaint-2.pdf> (accessed Oct. 4, 2022).

[36] USDC, Kelsey Cascadia Rose Juliana et al. v. United States et al. (United States District Court of Oregon—Eugene Division). First Amended Complaint for Declaratory and Injunctive Relief at 51. Filed 09/10/15, at <http://climatecasechart.com/wp-content/uploads/sites/16/case-documents/2015/20150910_docket-615-cv-1517_complaint-2.pdf> (accessed Oct. 4, 2022).

[37] USDC, Kelsey Cascadia Rose Juliana et al. v. United State et al. (United States District Court of Oregon—Eugene Division). First Amended Complaint for Declaratory and Injunctive Relief at 4. Filed 09/10/15, at <http://climatecasechart.com/wp-content/uploads/sites/16/case-documents/2015/20150910_docket-615-cv-1517_complaint-2.pdf> (accessed Oct. 4, 2022).

[38] USDC, Kelsey Cascadia Rose Juliana et al. v. United States et al. (United States District Court of Oregon—Eugene Division). First Amended Complaint for Declaratory and Injunctive Relief at 4. Filed 09/10/15, at <http://climatecasechart.com/wp-content/uploads/sites/16/case-documents/2015/20150910_docket-615-cv-1517_complaint-2.pdf> (accessed Oct. 4, 2022).

The children held that they had standing as the matter was one reliant on the laws of equity under the US Constitution and as such the child plaintiffs thus in essence pleaded that this was a novel case requiring a creative judicial remedy.[39] The requested remedy was:

> an injunction requiring the government not only to cease permitting, authorizing, and subsidizing fossil fuel use, but also to prepare a plan subject to judicial approval to draw down harmful emissions.[40]

The *Juliana* defendants in part argued in rebuttal that though US regulations governing CO_2 emissions arising from burning fossil fuels were arguably inadequate and hence facilitating the adverse effects of climate change; this issue is strictly the purview of the US Congress and executive and not a matter in which the court should intervene. The defendants argued hence that the "separation of powers" principle stripped the child plaintiffs of legal standing to pursue their alleged constitutional claims.[41]

> [P]laintiffs have no due process right to a climate system capable of sustaining human life; and the federal government has no obligations under the public trust doctrine[42]

At the same time the defendants did not dispute the facts advanced by the child plaintiffs including that the defendants had persisted in endangering the stability and sustainability of the climate system in the manner the plaintiffs alleged and did so knowingly.[43]

We turn next to the redressability issue upon which the *Juliana* Court of Appeals focused as the key point in making its decision to dismiss the children's appeal.

III. REDRESSIBILITY CANNOT BE LEGITIMATELY VOIDED BY THE COURTS GROUNDED ON THE IMMENSITY OF THE HARMS CREATED WHERE THE CAUSES FOR THOSE HARMS WERE HELD CLANDESTINE BY THE OFFENDERS' PERSISTENT VIOLATION OF THE RIGHT TO TRUTH: THE *JULIANA* CLIMATE CHANGE CASE AS AN EXAMPLE

The *Juliana* case has a long and very complicated procedural history and at the time of writing the potential for settlement talks between the parties continuing is, to say the least, itself "unsettled." We will for the purposes of this commentary focus on the *Juliana* child plaintiffs' loss of their case at the Federal Court of Appeals (Ninth Circuit) based

[39] USDC, Kelsey Cascadia Rose Juliana et al. v. United States (United States District Court of Oregon—Eugene Division F). First Amended Complaint for Declaratory and Injunctive Relief at 5. Filed 09/10/15, at <http://climatecasechart.com/wp-content/uploads/sites/16/case-documents/2015/20150910_docket-615-cv-1517_complaint-2.pdf> (accessed Oct. 4, 2022).
[40] USCA (9th Circuit), Juliana v. United States, 947 F.3d 1159 (9th Cir. 2020) No. 18-36082 United States Court of Appeals for the Ninth Circuit (Decided Jan. 17, 2020) at 7.
[41] USCA (9th Circuit), Juliana v. United States, 947 F.3d 1159 (9th Cir. 2020) No. 18-36082 United States Court of Appeals for the Ninth Circuit (Decided Jan. 17, 2020) at 11.
[42] USDC, Juliana v. United States, 339 F. Supp. 3d 1062 (D. Or. 2018) Decided Oct 15, 2018 (Case No. 6:15-cv-01517-AA United States District Court for the District of Oregon—Eugene Division) at 5.
[43] USDC, Juliana v. United States, 339 F. Supp. 3d 1062 (D. Or. 2018) Decided Oct 15, 2018 (Case No. 6:15-cv-01517-AA United States District Court for the District of Oregon—Eugene Division) at 3.

on the issue of redressability. The Court of Appeals noted that there was for the most part no factual dispute between the parties.[44] The Appeals Court held that the child plaintiffs had established their own concrete particularized injury and the causation (linked to the exploitation of fossil fuels) as required for legal standing and that it did not matter then how many people were affected by climate change.[45] The *Juliana* Federal Appeals Court then expressed the view that "[t]he more difficult question is whether the plaintiffs' claimed injuries are redressable by an Article III court."[46] The Court of Appeals maintained that the child plaintiffs' sole claim was that "the government has deprived them of a substantive constitutional right to a 'climate system capable of sustaining human life.'"[47] The experts agreed that without immediate remedial action the catastrophic effects of climate could not be meaningfully mitigated to some extent and would be irreversible.[48] The majority of the *Juliana* Court of Appeals rejected the child plaintiff's suit based on the view that:

> it was beyond the power of an Article III court to order, design, supervise, or implement the plaintiffs' requested remedial plan where any effective plan would necessarily require a host of complex policy decisions entrusted to the wisdom and discretion of the executive and legislative branches.[49]

In effect, the *Juliana* Court of Appeals majority were holding the child plaintiffs' case to be non-judiciable specifically on the question of redressability. Rather the Appeals Court majority chose in the *Juliana* case to relegate the climate change emergency matter to the very branches that had been largely remiss in telling the public the truth about the potential devastating and irreversible climate change effects of inaction on greatly reducing the reliance on fossil fuels:

> The panel reluctantly concluded that the plaintiffs' case must be made to the political branches or to the electorate at large.[50]

On the view here, in essence the majority of the Appeals Court panel in *Juliana* ruled such that the named defendants: certain members of the US executive and US agencies responsible for the environment of the United States and the then US President (Donald J. Trump) along with the unnamed defendants[51] should benefit legally in *Juliana* from the magnitude and complexity of the climate change redressability quandary *they themselves*

---

[44] USCA (9th Circuit), Juliana v. United States, 947 F.3d 1159 (9th Cir. 2020) No. 18-36082 United States Court of Appeals for the Ninth Circuit (Decided Jan. 17, 2020) at 4.

[45] USCA (9th Circuit), Juliana v. United States, 947 F.3d 1159 (9th Cir. 2020) No. 18-36082 United States Court of Appeals for the Ninth Circuit (Decided Jan. 17, 2020) at 4.

[46] USCA (9th Circuit), Juliana v. United States, 947 F.3d 1159 (9th Cir. 2020) No. 18-36082 United States Court of Appeals for the Ninth Circuit (Decided Jan. 17, 2020) at 6.

[47] USCA (9th Circuit), Juliana v. United States, 947 F.3d 1159 (9th Cir. 2020) No. 18-36082 United States Court of Appeals for the Ninth Circuit (Decided Jan. 17, 2020) at 6.

[48] USCA (9th Circuit), Juliana v. United States, 947 F.3d 1159 (9th Cir. 2020) No. 18-36082 United States Court of Appeals for the Ninth Circuit (Decided Jan. 17, 2020) at 34.

[49] USCA (9th Circuit) Juliana v. United States, 947 F.3d 1159 (9th Cir. 2020) No. 18-36082 United States Court of Appeals for the Ninth Circuit (Decided Jan. 17, 2020) at 5.

[50] USCA (9th Circuit), Juliana v. United States, 947 F.3d 1159 (9th Cir. 2020) No. 18-36082 United States Court of Appeals for the Ninth Circuit (Decided Jan. 17, 2020) at 5.

[51] Referring to those US corporations exploiting fossil fuels to such an extent as to seriously damage the US environment and contribute to the severity of the US and global climate crisis

had significantly contributed to through (i) inaction on any remediation efforts and (ii) *denial of the truth of climate change and its current and future severity*. Such an approach arguably violates a principle of fundamental justice that perpetrators should not benefit from fundamental human rights violations—here violation of the constitutional right of children and future generations of children (among others) to survive and thrive in part through living in a healthy, stable and sustainable climate environment.

Since (i) ecocide is likely to become an international human rights crime in the not too distant future given the severity of the climate change crisis and the urgent need for remediation and (ii) based on a proper sensibility to the basic needs of humanity for a hospitable climate capable of sustaining life and a basic good quality of life, one can reasonably argue that the *Juliana* defendants should *not* have been permitted by the court to violate the following basic international human rights law principles of victim rights:

3. The obligation to respect, ensure respect for and implement international human rights law ... [which] includes, inter alia, the duty to:
    (c) Provide those who claim to be victims of a human rights ... violation with equal and effective access to justice ... irrespective of who may ultimately be the bearer of responsibility for the violation; and
    (d) Provide effective remedies to victims, including reparation
        ...

The application and interpretation of these Basic Principles and Guidelines must be consistent with international human rights law and international humanitarian law and be *without any discrimination of any kind or on any ground, without exception.*[52]

The US Federal Court of Appeals *Juliana* ruling in denying the children's claim based on *redressability* is thus inconsistent with the aforementioned principles of international human rights law that set out the victim's right to a remedy and reparations for gross human rights violations.

The *Juliana* Court of Appeals further departs from adherence to the victims' rights principles under international human rights law in holding that children are not a suspect class[53] under the US Constitution's equality guarantee. The *Juliana* Appeals Court maintained then that children are purportedly *not* protected by an equality guarantee regarding non-discrimination in the availability of a judicial remedy for gross violations of basic human rights (here the child plaintiffs' right to live and develop in a life-affirming US climate eco system). Though the United States is a signatory to but has not ratified the CRC,[54] it should

---

[52] Office of the High Commissioner of Human Rights (OHCHR), *Basic Principles and Guidelines on the Rights to a Remedy and Reparation for Victims of Gross Violations of International Human Rights Law and Serious Violations of International Humanitarian Law*, at <https://www.ohchr.org/en/instruments-mechanisms/instruments/basic-principles-and-guidelines-right-remedy-and-reparation> (accessed Aug. 24, 2022).

[53] Leaving aside here the issue of whether future generations of children can be considered a victim class under the *Basic Principles and Guidelines on the Rights to a Remedy and Reparation for Victims of Gross Violations of International Human Rights Law and Serious Violations of International Humanitarian Law*, at <https://www.ohchr.org/en/instruments-mechanisms/instruments/basic-principles-and-guidelines-right-remedy-and-reparation> (accessed Aug. 24, 2022).

[54] UN Convention on the Rights of the Child Adopted and opened for signature, ratification and accession by General Assembly Resolution 44/25 of Nov. 20, 1989, Article 29 (entry into force Sept. 2, 1990), at <https://www.ohchr.org/en/instruments-mechanisms/instruments/convention-rights-child> (accessed Oct. 3, 2022).

be noted that there is (setting aside the issue of judicial punishments) universal agreement amongst the 196 UN member states that have ratified the CRC[55] regarding the child's non-derogable right to life and good development.[56]

It is essential to note in regard to the *Juliana* child plaintiffs' right to the truth that "[d]espite countless studies over the last half century warning of the catastrophic consequences of anthropogenic greenhouse gas emissions, many of which the government conducted, the *government not only failed to act but also affirmatively promoted fossil fuel use in a host of ways.*"[57] In so doing, it is here contended that the corporations enabled by the US government violated the children plaintiffs' fundamental right to the truth and hence blocked the possibility of a much more timely, effective and simple remedy. It is here argued that the courts which can enforce constitutional human rights guarantees, many of which mirror international human rights provisions, should not provide a shield for such corporate and/or government gross human rights violations as are implicated in the decisions which facilitated severe climate change effects.

The Court of Appeals in *Juliana* held that there was no judiciable administrable standard to assess whether any proposed remedial plan for climate change effects in America were adequate and being implemented properly and effectively.[58] This author, however, maintains that such an analysis sidesteps the Court's *parens patriae* obligation to the child plaintiffs to safeguard their health and well-being. By declining to recognize the children as a vulnerable protected class, the Court of Appeals in *Juliana* essentially (improperly on the view here) removed the court's *parens patriae* inherent jurisdiction consideration from the *Juliana* case. This though realistically the children had no *independent power* given their ineligibility for the vote to substantively affect the political solution the court envisioned. Note further that the dissenting judge on the *Juliana* Court of Appeals held that the children's stated climate change plan as a remedy to be enforced through the courts "is neither novel nor judicially incognizable. Rather, consistent with our historical [US federal court] practices, their request is a recognition that decades of institutionalized violations may take some time."[59]

To deny the *Juliana* child plaintiffs the right to a remedy for climate change sufficient to afford them a reasonably healthy stable climate environment is in effect to destroy the nation. This in that *the children are an essential component to perpetuity of the state and its culture.* That component of an effective climate change remedy—remedial climate action that allows children to survive and not to suffer the adverse *significant* health effects of climate change—could be considered one aspect of what would constitute a *judicial standard of effective climate remedial action that can be realistically administered by the courts.* Such a standard could be administered by the courts in the same way that the courts administer standards for child well-being in other complex situations (e.g., see the Flores settlement

[55] CRC ratifications as of August 23, 2022, at <https://treaties.un.org/pages/ViewDetails.aspx?src=IND&mtdsg_no=IV-11&chapter=4&clang=_en> (accessed Oct. 5, 2022).

[56] UN Convention on the Rights of the Child Adopted and opened for signature, ratification and accession by General Assembly Resolution 44/25 of Nov. 20, 1989, Article 29 (entry into force Sept. 2, 1990), at <https://www.ohchr.org/en/instruments-mechanisms/instruments/convention-rights-child> (accessed Oct. 3, 2022).

[57] USCA (9th Circuit), Juliana v. United States, 947 F.3d 1159 (9th Cir. 2020) No. 18-36082 United States Court of Appeals for the Ninth Circuit (Decided Jan. 17, 2020) at 35.

[58] USCA (9th Circuit), Juliana v. United States, 947 F.3d 1159 (9th Cir. 2020) No. 18-36082 United States Court of Appeals for the Ninth Circuit (Decided Jan. 17, 2020) at 36.

[59] USCA (9th Circuit), Juliana v. United States, 947 F.3d 1159 (9th Cir. 2020) No. 18-36082 United States Court of Appeals for the Ninth Circuit (Decided Jan. 17, 2020) at 60.

regarding a class-action suit brought by unaccompanied migrant children against the then US Immigration and Naturalization Service).[60]

Furthermore, it was clear in the filings that the *Juliana* child plaintiffs were *not* pleading for a remedy that would free them *entirely* of the harmful effects of climate change but rather were asking the court to order a remedy that would free them from "irreversible and catastrophic climate change" effects.[61] The dissenting judge on the Federal Court of Appeals in *Juliana* noted that:

> The majority portrays any relief we [the Ninth Circuit US Federal Court of Appeals] can offer as just a drop in the bucket. But we are perilously close to an overflowing bucket. The final drops matter. *A lot.*[62]

The dissenting judge in the Federal Court of Appeals in *Juliana* in addition makes the point that the Appeals Court majority in rejecting the child plaintiffs right to a remedy were, in effect, denying the state's responsibility not to *willfully* destroy the nation (in this instance by the state's lack of action on the urgent climate crisis).[63]

On the view here, the *Juliana* Court of Appeals in referring the children back to a political process rather than offering a judicially enforceable remedy risks contributing itself to the denial of the truth of urgent catastrophic climate change amongst a large segment of the US public. This given the largely weak and inept US government response to climate change to date.[64] This then is the case notwithstanding that the Courts in *Juliana* acknowledged the scientific evidence that dire harmful *irreversible* climate effects are almost upon the United States and will occur globally if serious mitigation efforts are not made now.

IV. CONCLUSION

It is evident that young people have clearly shown their need for and openness to learning the truth of catastrophic climate change effects as they have more and more come to see those consequences and some, not unexpectedly or unrealistically, even suffer what has been termed "eco anxiety."[65] The *Juliana* case, on this author's view, is instructive as

---

[60] Justice for Immigrants, *The Flores Settlement* ("*Flores* sets forth foundational principles and critical protections regarding the care, custody, and release of immigrant children who are in federal custody"), at 1, at <https://justiceforimmigrants.org/what-we-are-working-on/unaccompanied-children/what-is-the-flores-settlement-agreement-and-what-does-it-mean-for-family-separation-and-family-detention/> (accessed Aug. 24, 2022).

[61] USCA (9th Circuit), Juliana v. United States, 947 F.3d 1159 (9th Cir. 2020) No. 18-36082 United States Court of Appeals for the Ninth Circuit (Decided Jan. 17, 2020) at 45.

[62] USCA (9th Circuit), Juliana v. United States, 947 F.3d 1159 (9th Cir. 2020) No. 18-36082 United States Court of Appeals for the Ninth Circuit (Decided Jan. 17, 2020) at 45–46.

[63] USCA (9th Circuit), Juliana v. United States, 947 F.3d 1159 (9th Cir. 2020) No. 18-36082 United States Court of Appeals for the Ninth Circuit (Decided Jan. 17, 2020) at 5–6.

[64] President' Biden's Inflation Reduction Act contains provisions regarding climate change that are intended to cut greenhouse gases to 40% below what they were in 2005 by 2030. *See* Ben Lefebvre, Kelsey Tamborrino & Josh Siegel *Historic Climate Bill to Supercharge Clean Energy Industry*, POLITICO (Aug. 7, 2022), at <https://www.politico.com/news/2022/08/07/inflation-reduction-act-climate-biden-00050 230> (accessed Aug. 24, 2022).

[65] A. Bryan, *Pedagogy of the Implicated: Advancing a Social Ecology of Responsibility Framework to Promote Deeper Understanding of the Climate Crisis*, 30(3) PEDAGOGY, CULTURE & SOCIETY 329, 331 (2021), DOI: 10.1080/14681366.2021.1977979.

to (i) children's fundamental autonomous right to important truths that implicate gross human rights violations as does climate change (those harms of massive climate change disproportionately more greatly affecting vulnerable populations and groups, i.e., Indigenous communities, children and the poor) and as to their right to truths regarding (ii) the barriers children encounter in accessing a remedy when the courts become, in effect, and for whatever reason, enablers of truth deniers.

Various scholars have noted that the enormity of the climate change crisis and its existential threat to humanity is difficult for most to comprehend and that difficulty is compounded by disinformation and climate change denial.[66] It is nevertheless essential that children be educated about the truth of the climate change matter so that they can act responsibly, encourage others to do so and learn to empathize with those most affected by climate change disasters.[67] This chapter has hopefully served to highlight the court's role in also honoring the child's right to truth in particular when the judicial system is requested to resolve child-led climate change complaints and for that matter any complex social injustice.

---

[66] L. ZIMMERMAN, TRAUMA AND THE DISCOURSE OF CLIMATE CHANGE: LITERATURE, PSYCHOANALYSIS AND DENIAL (2020).

[67] *See* Bryan, *supra* note 65.

Information Interventions in the Twenty-First Century

Fighting Disinformation Across National Boundaries with International Information Campaigns

BY LANDO KIRCHMAIR*

Abstract

The twenty-first century has seen an unprecedented rise in manipulation by disinformation, the Russian war of aggression against Ukraine being no exception to this trend. Shocked by the blatant violation of fundamental international norms, the international legal community is not as defenseless as might have seemed at first glance. Creative solutions are needed, however. This note argues that information interventions, advocated here in the form of international information campaigns, have been given little thought so far and are an underrated but important tool which might provide relief. Actively fighting manipulative disinformation across national boundaries is important for a resilient international legal order in the (digital) information age. This insight might come too late in the case of Ukraine: still, it is a lesson to be learned for future conflicts lurking behind the veil of authoritarian regimes and totalitarian states.

* Prof. Dr. *iur. habil.*, Deputy Professor for National and International Public Law with a Focus on the Protection of Cultural Heritage, Department of Social Sciences and Public Affairs, Bundeswehr University Munich (Werner-Heisenberg-Weg 39, 8557 Neubiberg, Germany), Co-PI of the EMERGENCY-VRD project at dtec.bw. I am grateful to Björnstjern Baade, Philipp Janig, Benedikt Pirker, Monika Polzin, Cornelia Schäffer, and Stephan Stetter for very helpful comments. Contact: lando.kirchmair@unibw.de.

Lando Kirchmair, *Information Interventions in the Twenty-First Century* In: *The Global Community Yearbook of International Law and Jurisprudence 2022*. Edited by: Giuliana Ziccardi Capaldo, Oxford University Press. © Oxford University Press 2023. DOI: 10.1093/oso/9780197752265.003.0008

I. INTRODUCTION

The twenty-first century has seen an unprecedented rise in manipulation by disinformation. While lies have always been part of the political game, the shamelessness of asserting whatever is deemed convenient or expedient, the extent to which facts are disregarded, and, in particular, the technologies available nowadays pose enormous challenges. The dawn of disinformation has been facilitated by modern technological possibilities for spreading fake news almost instantaneously on a global scale. Russian disinformation is a particularly extreme example of manipulating people, both at home and abroad. While the international debate on classifying and combating manipulation by disinformation is already in full swing, this note argues that the Russian war of aggression against Ukraine demonstrates that international law and its institutions need to step up the fight against manipulation by disinformation across national boundaries. This note contends that it is legally permissible to combat disinformation at home *as well as* abroad, especially when that disinformation is used to support an illegal war. The international community can and, indeed, should engage in information interventions by launching international information campaigns—either through the United Nations, within the framework of collective self-defense, or by explaining sanctions—to clear the heads of apparently disinformed (or even brainwashed) Russian citizens in order to cut off social support for the war of aggression in Ukraine. As the technological capacities to create and spread disinformation are likely to grow, it is further argued that this war shows that international institutions need to adapt by developing information campaigns based on a broad international consensus which are meant to correct war lies as an important tool for restoring and maintaining international peace and security. In the long run, it might be obligatory for UN member states to broadcast UN information campaigns on national TV channels when, for instance, the Security Council or the General Assembly has passed a resolution deeming it necessary to do so.

A. Lies and War Go Hand in Hand

The history of consciously and artificially created reasons for military interventions is long. An outrageous example in this regard is Adolf Hitler. In a declaration on 22 September 1938, he repeatedly assured the British prime minister Neville Chamberlain that if the problem of the Sudetenland were solved, Germany would not make any more territorial claims in Europe. On 29 September 1938, the Sudetenland was handed over to Hitler in the Munich agreement and yet right at the beginning of October, Hitler instructed General Keitel to draw up plans to destroy the rest of Czechoslovakia. In fact, as early as 22 April 1938, Hitler had already agreed to a proposal by General Jodl which said that the "initiative green" (against Czechoslovakia) would be triggered by an incident in Czechoslovakia which would allow Germany to intervene militarily.[1] In a speech on 22 August 1939, before the Blitzkrieg against Poland, Hitler said:

> I will find a propagandistic reason for starting a war, no matter whether this is credible or not. The victor will not be asked whether he told the truth. When starting

---

[1] Gustav Radbruch, *Entwurf Eines Nachworts Zur "Rechtsphilosophie" (Um 1947)*, *in* Rechtsphilosophie: Studienausgabe (Ralf Dreier & Stanley L. Paulson eds., 2003). "Studie Grün" is available at https://www.ns-archiv.de/krieg/1938/tschechoslowakei/fall-gruen-22-04-1938.php (accessed 12 September 2022) Note that *Radbruch* talked about 30 August 1938 in this passage of the afterword.

and waging war, it is not right that matters but victory. [...] The strongest man is right![2]

Lies in times of war are not rare events. More recently, the dictum that the first casualty of war is the truth was painfully proven true by the war in former Yugoslavia.[3] Lies also played a central role in deliberately misleading the general public before and during the Iraq War launched in 2003.[4] Vladimir Putin was no different when he asserted that Russia had no plans to invade Ukraine, and he continues to claim that he is protecting ethnic Russians from an alleged genocide in the Donbas region, a blatant lie rebutted by the International Court of Justice.[5]

B. Why the Truth Matters

Gustav Radbruch provided an important insight into why truth matters for the rule of law and democracy. While Radbruch's famous justice formula (denouncing "flawed law") was directed at dealing with National Socialist injustice in the post–World War II era in Germany,[6] he also offered a largely neglected diagnosis as to why the creation of his justice formula had become necessary in the first place:

> The most conspicuous characteristic of Hitler's personality, which became through his influence the pervading spirit of the whole of National Socialist "law" as well, was a complete lack of any sense of truth or any sense of right and wrong. Because he had no sense of truth, he could shamelessly, unscrupulously lend the ring of truth to whatever was rhetorically effective at the moment. And because he had no sense of right and wrong, he could without hesitation elevate to a statute the crudest expression of despotic caprice.[7]

This diagnosis is not only relevant for the past. It is also—as this note claims—of utmost relevance for understanding lessons to be learned from the war of aggression against Ukraine for the future of international law and its institutions because, again, in Radbruch's words, "Truthfulness is the sister of justice."[8]

---

[2] Quoted after *id.*, 199 (Footnotes have been omitted.) English translations—if not indicated otherwise—are those of the author.

[3] PETER HÄBERLE, WAHRHEITSPROBLEME IM VERFASSUNGSSTAAT, 32, n. 33 (1995).

[4] *See, e.g.,* TELL ME LIES: PROPAGANDA AND MEDIA DISTORTION IN THE ATTACK ON IRAQ (DAVID MILLER ed., 2003).

[5] ICJ, Allegations of Genocide under the Convention on the Prevention and Punishment of the Crime of Genocide (Ukraine v. Russian Federation), Order, 16 March 2022, paras. 37 ff., 59, at https://www.icj-cij.org/public/files/case-related/182/182-20220316-ORD-01-00-EN.pdf. *Cf. also* PETER POMERANTSEV, THIS IS NOT PROPAGANDA: ADVENTURES IN THE WAR AGAINST REALITY (2019) on propaganda in Russia.

[6] Gustav Radbruch, *Statutory Lawlessness and Supra-Statutory Law (1946)*, 26 OXFORD JOURNAL OF LEGAL STUDIES 1–11, 7 (2006); Brian H. Bix, *Radbruch's Formula and Conceptual Analysis*, 56 THE AMERICAN JOURNAL OF JURISPRUDENCE 45–57 (2011). *See also* Lando Kirchmair, *On the Importance of a Sense of Truth for a Democratic Legal Culture and the International Order, in* DEMOCRACY AND SOVEREIGNTY: RETHINKING THE LEGITIMACY OF INTERNATIONAL LAW 95–118 (Daniel-Erasmus Khan et al. eds., 2023).

[7] Radbruch, *supra* note 6, at 7.

[8] Radbruch, *supra* note 1, at 199.

C. (International) Responses to Disinformation at Home

International law is not completely defenseless and does, indeed, respond to disinformation and propaganda.[9] For instance, the prohibition of intervention guaranteed by customary international law provides for some relief as it includes false reporting, at least when directed towards revolution.[10] Article 20(1) of the International Covenant on Civil and Political Rights furthermore holds that "[a]ny propaganda for war shall be prohibited by law."[11] In the fight against disinformation at home, for instance, the European Union has banned the broadcasting of *Russia Today* and *Sputnik*, and social media platforms have taken some action in order to combat disinformation by Russia.[12] However, the extent to which Russia operates its disinformation campaigns abroad and at home necessitates a pro-active stance which confronts disinformation across national boundaries.

---

[9] For an overview, *see* Henning Lahmann, *Information Operations and the Question of Illegitimate Interference Under International Law*, 53 ISRAEL LAW REVIEW 189–224 (2020), who also points out (at 191) the difference between disinformation (which is "deliberately false or misleading") and misinformation (which is "factually wrong information yet not intentionally so"); *cf. also* Björnstjern Baade, *Fake News and International Law*, 29 EUROPEAN JOURNAL OF INTERNATIONAL LAW 1357–1376 (2018); and COMPUTATIONAL PROPAGANDA: POLITICAL PARTIES, POLITICIANS, AND POLITICAL MANIPULATION ON SOCIAL MEDIA (SAMUEL C. WOOLLEY & PHILIP N. HOWARD eds., 2019), arguing for a distinctively new mechanism labelled "computational propaganda" and providing case studies from a wide range of countries.

[10] *See, e.g.*, Eric de Brabandere, *Propaganda*, in MAX PLANCK ENCYCLOPEDIA OF PUBLIC INTERNATIONAL LAW, para. 11 (2012), arguing that states must refrain from subversive propaganda aiming at civil disobedience; *cf. also* Michael G. Kearney, *Propaganda for War, Prohibition*, MAX PLANCK ENCYCLOPEDIA OF PUBLIC INTERNATIONAL LAW (2009); Baade, *supra* note 9, at 1363, quoting Maziar Jamnejad & Michael Wood, *The Principle of Non-Intervention*, 22 LEIDEN JOURNAL OF INTERNATIONAL LAW 345–381, 374 (2009).

[11] *Cf.* MICHAEL G. KEARNEY, THE PROHIBITION OF PROPAGANDA FOR WAR IN INTERNATIONAL LAW at 133ff. (2007).

[12] The ban was implemented by the insertion of Article 2f into Regulation No. 833/2014, as amended on 1 March 2022 by Council Regulation 2022/350 (OJ EU L 65/1, at 1, 2 March 2022); the grand chamber of the General Court, RT France v. Council, Case T-125/22, Judgment (GC) (July 27, 2022) dismissed the action for annulment of this decision. The case is currently pending at the ECJ, RT France v. Council, Case C-620/22 P. *Cf.* Björnstjern Baade, *The EU's "Ban" of RT and Sputnik*, VERFASSUNGSBLOG (8 March 2022), at https://verfassungsblog.de/the-eus-ban-of-rt-and-sputnik, making the argument that the ban is lawful to counter war propaganda (but should not be done to counter mere propaganda); *see furthermore* Kata Balint et al., *Effectiveness of the Sanctions on Russian State-Affiliated Media in the EU—An Investigation into Website Traffic & Possible Circumvention Methods*, ISD REPORT (6 October 2022), at https://www.isdglobal.org/wp-content/uploads/2022/10/Effectiveness-of-the-sanctions-on-Russian-state-media-1.pdf; on social media platforms, *see* Sophie Bushwick, *Russia's Information War Is Being Waged on Social Media Platforms: But Tech Companies and Governments Are Fighting Back*, SCIENTIFIC AMERICAN (8 March 2022), at https://www.scientifica merican.com/article/russia-is-having-less-success-at-spreading-social-media-disinformation/. For an empirical investigation on the question as to whether censorship of social media is effective in fighting propaganda, *see* Yevgeniy Golovchenko, *Fighting Propaganda with Censorship: A Study of the Ukrainian Ban on Russian Social Media*, 84 THE JOURNAL OF POLITICS 639–654 (2022)(finding—simplified—that censorship works).

II. MAKING THE CASE FOR INTERNATIONAL INFORMATION CAMPAIGNS

A. The Necessity of Expanding Combating Disinformation at Home to Fighting Disinformation Abroad

While combating disinformation at home is common practice and clearly protected by (international) law, disinformation abroad has not been considered a central issue so far. Currently we are experiencing how disinformation abroad (in our case now in Russia) is nurturing the war of aggression against Ukraine. Assuming that the Russian people had access to information which is not manipulated, the possibility is arguably high that this current war—or special military operation in the terminology of the Russian regime—would have much less support within Russia. Hence, the "democratic peace argument,"[13] suggesting that democracies rarely fight each other, is considered to contain a grain of truth which is worth exploring further in terms of informing people living under authoritarian regimes and in totalitarian states. This note argues that one lesson to be learned from the current war of aggression by Russia is that international law and international institutions should stop not blindly at inter-state international relations. To put it bluntly, instead of fighting the Russian military directly (although this would be legally permissible under Article 51 UN Charter), it would be much less invasive to address the Russian people by correcting the Russian disinformation campaign in Russia(n).[14]

B. International Information Campaigns

There is a long history of propaganda in war, and many types of propaganda have been applied.[15] As an example of international information campaigns, albeit negative, airborne leaflets, a form of psychological warfare, were used as propaganda in both world wars.[16] Likewise, there are instances when—at least in retrospect—so-called information

---

[13] For a general overview, *see, e.g.,* Steve Chan, *In Search of Democratic Peace: Problems and Promise,* 41 MERSHON INTERNATIONAL STUDIES REVIEW 59–91 (1997); for the argument that democracies are also more prone to peace towards non-liberal states, *see* John MacMillan, *Beyond the Separate Democratic Peace,* 40 JOURNAL OF PEACE RESEARCH 233–243 (2003); *cf.* Michael R. Tomz & Jessica L. Weeks, *Public Opinion and the Democratic Peace,* 107 AMERICAN POLITICAL SCIENCE REVIEW 849–865 (2013) for an interesting empirical analysis finding that individuals are more prone to peace towards other democracies (in contrast to autocracies) presumably because they feel less threatened; *see* Anna Geis, Harald Müller & Niklas Schörnig, *Liberale Demokratien Und Krieg: Warum Manche Kämpfen Und Andere Nicht. Ergebnisse Einer Vergleichenden Inhaltsanalyse Von Parlamentsdebatten,* 17 ZEITSCHRIFT FÜR INTERNATIONALE BEZIEHUNGEN 171–202 (2010), for an analysis of the reasoning of democracies which go to war.

[14] *See,* in this vein, Bruce Russett, *Bushwhacking the Democratic Peace,* 6 INTERNATIONAL STUDIES PERSPECTIVES 395–408 (2005), holding that democratic regime change by military force is difficult to achieve, but UN peacekeeping operations among other things have a better track record of success in democratization.

[15] For an overview of various frames in "the apogee of a propaganda war," *see* Seong C. Hong, *Propaganda Leaflets and Cold War Frames During the Korean War,* 11 MEDIA, WAR & CONFLICT 244–264 (2018).

[16] *See, e.g.,* HAROLD D. LASSWELL, PROPAGANDA TECHNIQUE IN WORLD WAR I, at 184 (1971), speaking of the Allies distributing 100,000 leaflets a day in August 1918 increasing to 4 to 5 million leaflets a month 150 miles deep behind German lines. *Cf.* Lyneyve Finch, *Psychological Propaganda: The War of Ideas on Ideas During the First Half of the Twentieth Century,* 26 ARMED FORCES & SOCIETY 367–86 (2000), highlighting a shift towards so-called total warfare in the late nineteenth century, making propaganda an important element of modern warfare.

interventions should have been implemented. For instance, radio jamming was discussed in the case of Rwanda but did not happen, inter alia due to its implications for the enjoyment of freedom of speech under international human rights law.[17]

International information campaigns in the current context might involve campaigns directed at informing recipients about the role of the United Nations under the UN Charter for the maintenance of international peace and security in general and about important issues in recent and pertinent UN resolutions and potential peacekeeping measures in particular.[18] This would include communications to counter the spread of disinformation in Russia as an essential component of restoring and maintaining peace, which also depends on the easy availability of somehow objective information.[19] If the information level of the average person is poor, or individuals' knowledge is manipulated by disinformation (e.g., Russian propaganda concerning its actual war of aggression in Ukraine), this presents a significant obstacle to maintaining or restoring international peace and security. While propaganda, in the past through leaflets and nowadays via technologically more advanced means, is omnipresent in times of war, UN practices in this field are rather rare and generally unknown.[20] This is an important failing, which must arguably be ended in order to render international law and its institutions fit for the (digital) information age.[21]

Without going into details of how specific information campaigns should be designed and who should be responsible for them, this note argues in favor of such campaigns, which might well have different designs and content, for instance, depending on the UN organ which advances them. While a potential source of inspiration might be transitional justice, which is familiar with public outreach as actively providing the public with information has become an important instrument in this field,[22] the envisaged campaigns are likely to

---

[17] See Jamie F. Metzl, *Rwandan Genocide and the International Law of Radio Jamming*, 91 AMERICAN JOURNAL OF INTERNATIONAL LAW 628–651 (1997). Consider in this vein, too, the dark sides of the freedom of the internet (which is not only used in support of liberal democracy), expressed by EVGENY MOROZOV, THE NET DELUSION: HOW NOT TO LIBERATE THE WORLD 225ff. (2012).

[18] See Eytan Gilboa, *Mass Communication and Diplomacy: A Theoretical Framework*, 10 COMMUNICATION THEORY 275–309 (2000); as well as Eytan Gilboa, *Diplomacy in the Media Age: Three Models of Uses and Effects*, 12 DIPLOMACY & STATECRAFT 1–28 (2001), for an overview of conceptual models using the media as an instrument of diplomacy; see also Martin F. Herz, *Some Psychological Lessons from Leaflet Propaganda in World War II*, 13 PUBLIC OPINION QUARTERLY 471–486 (1949), giving some insights, like not trying to export domestic propaganda, which still seem accurate and helpful today.

[19] See generally, on media promoting peace across the world, providing insights into potentials for improvement, Vladimir Bratic, *Examining Peace-Oriented Media in Areas of Violent Conflict*, 70 INTERNATIONAL COMMUNICATION GAZETTE 487–503 (2008).

[20] See, however, Jamie F. Metzl, *Information Intervention: When Switching Channels Isn't Enough*, 76 FOREIGN AFFAIRS 15–20, 16 (1997), reporting an "increasing number of successful 'information interventions' in recent years" by the UN, e.g., through "U.N. radio stations and programs in peace missions in Namibia, Cambodia, and eastern Slavonie [which] have disseminated impartial, reliable news and information in conflicts rife with propaganda."

[21] See already Lando Kirchmair, *It's Not Propaganda If It's True. Why the International Community Should Start Information Campaigns in Russian* VERFASSUNGSBLOG (2 March 2022), at https://verfassungsblog.de/its-not-propaganda-if-its-true/. In support of such campaigns, see also Metzl, *supra* note 20; cf. ROLAND PARIS, AT WAR'S END: BUILDING PEACE AFTER CIVIL CONFLICT 198 (2004).

[22] See, e.g., Patrick Vinck & Phuong N. Pham, *Outreach Evaluation: The International Criminal Court in the Central African Republic*, 4 INTERNATIONAL JOURNAL OF TRANSITIONAL JUSTICE 421–442 (2010); for an overview of outreach programmes of international criminal courts, see Janine N. Clark, *International War Crimes Tribunals and the Challenge of Outreach*, 9 INTERNATIONAL CRIMINAL LAW REVIEW 99–116 (2009).

be confronted with skepticism, based on legal questions as well as questions of practical implementation.

III. REPLYING TO POTENTIAL SKEPTICISM

A. There Is No Objective Truth

Skeptical voices might hold that there is no objective truth. Indeed, to Hannah Arendt, "truthfulness has never been counted among the political virtues, and lies have always been regarded as justifiable tools in political dealings."[23] This is quite astonishing, however, as she is nevertheless convinced that a liar cannot succeed against reality, for which there is no replacement.[24] She continues that this is a lesson to be learned from totalitarian experiments and the alarming trust totalitarian rulers place in lies.[25] And, thus, to Arendt, organized lies are an eminent problem as they destroy the capacity of human beings to differentiate between the truth and the untruth.[26]

In her work, Arendt followed the German philosopher Gottfried Wilhelm Leibniz in differentiating between a "rational truth," which includes mathematical, scientific, and philosophical truths, and a "factual truth."[27] Precisely the latter is important to politics because it can endanger the whole process in a way that the "rational truth" cannot.[28] If historical facts, such as the fact that a majority of Germans supported Hitler, become mere opinions, our factual reality is eroded. This is a political problem of great importance. It is precisely this problem that might force us to reconsider the contradiction between truth and opinion. Yet this does not mean that factual truths and opinions are antagonisms. Factual truths are also political in nature. Facts are subject to opinion, and opinions can serve various interests and passions, can differ widely, and, yet, still be legitimate. However, integrity must always be guaranteed. For if this is not the case, in Arendt's words, "freedom of opinion is a farce unless factual information is guaranteed and the facts themselves are not in dispute."[29] As a direct consequence thereof, we lose the basis for exchanging opinions (which must be related to factual truths in order to be legitimate according to Arendt) and, thus, the basis for politics.[30] The antagonist of rational truth is error, illusion, or mere opinion. The opposite of factual truth is outright lies.

Because liars can invent facts as they wish, they can adjust their lies to whatever their audience would like to hear. This seems to be a pertinent issue of what is referred to as

---

[23] Hannah Arendt, *Lying in Politics: Reflections on The Pentagon Papers*, THE NEW YORK REVIEW OF BOOKS (18 November 1971), reprinted as Hannah Arendt, *Lying in Politics: Reflections on the Pentagon Papers*, in CRISES OF THE REPUBLIC 4 (Hannah Arendt ed., 1972). Similarly, Hannah Arendt, *Truth and Politics*, THE NEW YORKER (25 February 1967), reprinted as Hannah Arendt, *Truth and Politics*, in TRUTH: ENGAGEMENTS ACROSS PHILOSOPHICAL TRADITIONS 295 (José Medina & David Wood eds., 2005). *Cf.* Kirchmair, *supra* note 6.

[24] Arendt, *Lying in Politics, supra* note 23, at 7.

[25] *Id.*, 7.

[26] *Id.*, 7.

[27] Arendt, *Truth and Politics, supra* note 23, at 297 explicitly emphasizing that she uses "this distinction for the sake of convenience without discussing its intrinsic legitimacy."

[28] *Id.*, 297.

[29] *Id.*

[30] *See also* Judith Zinsmaier, *Hannah Arendt und das "postfaktische Zeitalter,"* PRAEFAKTISCH (16 August 2016), at https://www.praefaktisch.de/postfaktisch/hannah-arendt-und-das-postfaktische-zeitalter/#_ft n11 (accessed 12 September 2022), with the assessment that precisely this is an important problem.

"alternative facts" nowadays and brings us back to the importance of truth for international law, which also holds against the apparent skepticism of Hannah Arendt.

B. The Principle of Non-Intervention

The principle of non-intervention is considered to be an important pillar of the international legal order, and skeptics might claim that international information campaigns would violate this principle. According to this principle, certain interferences with the domestic affairs of another nation are prohibited. The general principle of non-intervention—derived from Articles 2(1) and (4) UN Charter and also based on customary international law—forbids any state to violate this prohibition.[31] Article 2(7) UN Charter, the *lex specialis*, applies to the United Nations. Neither principle is, however, absolute, and arguably they both allow for international information campaigns. Concerning the United Nations, the enforcement of measures under Chapter VII of the Charter are expressly excluded from the prohibition of intervention in Article 2(7) UN Charter. In relation to the general prohibition, Article 51 UN Charter provides the legal exemption.

1. International Information Campaigns Under the Auspices of the United Nations
If the Security Council were to set up an international information campaign under Chapter VII, the principle of non-intervention would not be an obstacle.[32] In our specific case, however, a Security Council resolution is unlikely due to Russia's veto power. Along the lines of the UN Uniting for Peace Resolution, which allowed the General Assembly to exercise the powers of the blocked Council, the power to establish international information campaigns could be considered as covered too.[33] If such proceedings were considered implausible, however, the question as to whether international information campaigns would actually violate the non-intervention principle remains; or rather more specifically, the question as to how international information campaigns would have to be designed in order to be in line with this principle.

Therefore, it is important to take a closer look at the wording of Article 2(7) UN Charter, which states that the United Nations is not authorized "to intervene in matters which are essentially within the domestic jurisdiction of any State." The term "to intervene" can be understood broadly, including any discussion or recommendation related to internal affairs, or narrowly, focusing merely on interventions bordering on the use of force.[34] The Friendly Relations Declaration and the ICJ in the *Nicaragua* case have generally conceptualized "intervention" as comprising direct as well as indirect intervention, including the act as well as

---

[31] See Georg Nolte, *Article 2(7)*, in THE CHARTER OF THE UNITED NATIONS: A COMMENTARY, para. 7 (Bruno Simma et al. eds., 2013), with further references.

[32] Considering such an option for a special unit focusing on information intervention, *see* Metzl, *supra* note 20, at 19, holding that a standing authority (with the possibility of a veto by the Council) would be better suited to perform the intended function.

[33] Uniting for Peace, UN Doc. A/RES/377(V) (3 November 1950). *Cf.* Andrew J. Carswell, *Unblocking the UN Security Council: The Uniting for Peace Resolution*, 18 JOURNAL OF CONFLICT AND SECURITY LAW 453–480 (2013). The "Veto Resolution" by the Assembly could be interpreted as a certain readiness to take innovative steps to this end: Standing Mandate for a General Assembly Debate when a Veto is Cast in the Security Council, UN Doc. A/76/L.52 (20 April 2022).

[34] For a discussion, *see* Nolte, *supra* note 31, para. 10ff. providing a historical analysis, examples, and further references, but concluding (para. 18) that these are early debates and that modern developments have put the term "domestic jurisdiction" at the forefront.

its effect.[35] Bearing this in mind when considering the interpretation of the notion "to intervene" in Article 2(7) UN Charter, international information campaigns would have to be understood as "information interventions" and be justified as such if they include coercive elements. Another term in need of interpretation in Article 2(7) UN Charter is "domestic jurisdiction," which has to be analysed in the context of the measure concerned.[36] In relation to matters concerning the maintenance of international peace and security, the earlier view, namely, that such matters fall within domestic jurisdiction, has been rejected by practice.[37] It could thus be questioned whether it is within the remit of domestic jurisdiction to manipulate a country's own people by disinformation in order to encourage support for a war of aggression. Nevertheless, information policy, without a proper mandate, "can constitute an intervention into the domestic jurisdiction of a State if it goes beyond the spreading of information about the mission and turns into an effort to influence the domestic political process beyond the terms of the mandate."[38]

2. International Information Campaigns by a UN Member State Collective

With regard to UN member states (both individually and collectively), an *argumentum a maiore ad minus* could be made in order to make the case for an exception to the general prohibition of intervention in relation to international information campaigns. According to Article 51 UN Charter, any state would be allowed to exercise military force against Russia within the framework of collective self-defense on behalf of Ukraine. It could, thus, be argued that international information campaigns must be legal, too, as they are much less invasive, given an invitation from Ukraine and a formal note to this respect provided to the United Nations.[39] In the event of economic sanctions having been put in place, an information campaign aimed at explaining the reasons and conditions for sanctions could also be justified.[40]

IV. CONCLUSION: FUTURE INTERNATIONAL LAW AND ITS INSTITUTIONS ASK FOR INTERNATIONAL INFORMATION CAMPAIGNS

While a large majority of 140 UN member states voted for a resolution condemning the Russian aggression,[41] and 143 UN member states demanded in another resolution a reverse

---

[35] Declaration on Principles of International Law Friendly Relations and Co-Operation among States in accordance with the Charter of the United Nations, UN Doc. A/RES/2625(XXV) (24 October 1970); ICJ, Military and Paramilitary Activities in and against Nicaragua (Nicaragua v. US), Merits, Judgment, 1986 ICJ REPORTS 14, para. 205 (27 June 1986), however pointing to the element of coercion as "the very essence of" prohibited intervention.

[36] For an insightful discussion, *see again* Nolte, *supra* note 31, paras. 23ff., espec. 35ff.

[37] *Id.*, para. 50 with further references.

[38] *Id.*, para. 60 with reference to Monroe E. Price, *Information Intervention: Bosnia, the Dayton Accords, and the Seizure of Broadcasting Transmitters*, 33 CORNELL INTERNATIONAL LAW JOURNAL 67–112, 80, and 108 (2000).

[39] For details on Article 51 UN Charter, *see* Georg Nolte & Albrecht Randelzhofer, *Article 51*, *in* THE CHARTER OF THE UNITED NATIONS: A COMMENTARY (Bruno Simma et al. eds., 2013).

[40] *Cf.* Nolte, *supra* note 31, para. 61.

[41] During its 11th Emergency Special Session (9th GA Plenary meeting on Mar. 24, 2022) (UN Doc. A/RES/ES-11/2), 193 member states adopted a resolution—drafted by Ukraine and 90 co-sponsors entitled the Humanitarian consequences of the aggression against Ukraine—with 140 votes in favor, 5 against— Belarus, the Democratic People's Republic of Korea, Eritrea, Russia, and Syria—and 38 others abstaining.

course on the "attempted illegal annexation" of four Ukrainian territories by Russia,[42] only a minority of mainly so-called Western states actively engages in sanctioning Russia. Working towards objective information countering manipulative disinformation from aggressor states might be a middle ground between acknowledging the illegality of as well as condemning this war and actively sanctioning Russia. Information campaigns could, arguably, find enough supporters, be minimally invasive, and bring about the chance to emancipate the Russian people somewhat, who are not directly but nevertheless indirectly responsible for the war of aggression and war crimes allegedly committed by their government and the military.[43]

Clearly, "[p]ermitting limited radio and television jamming in defense of human rights is no magic bullet,"[44] and handing out flyers in Moscow might not be a realistic option. The high tide of disinformation in the twenty-first century and the likelihood of lies in war as well as lies which lead to war, however, force the United Nations to actively engage in countering disinformation, especially in order to restore and maintain peace. The actions of Anonymous, hacking Russian TV channels in order to counter disinformation by providing information—banned in Russia—on the war in Ukraine to Russians, are a blunt but possibly helpful inspiration for international information campaigns. If worldwide disinformation campaigns like that of Russia are not actively countered in the future, it will become all the more difficult to obtain a broad condemnation of such acts at the United Nations. In the long run, the United Nations could be in a position to communicate on all available channels to the people concerned in their mother tongue in order to inform them objectively on behalf of the international community.

The trauma of information intervention associated with the legally excessive NATO bombings of the Radio Television of Serbia (RTS) headquarters in the Yugoslav wars needs to be left behind in order to render international law and its institutions fit for the (digital) information age by engaging in international information campaigns.[45]

---

[42] During its 11th Emergency Special Session (12th GA Plenary meeting on Oct. 12, 2022) (UN Doc. A/RES/ES-11/4), 183 member states adopted a resolution—entitled Territorial integrity of Ukraine: Defending the principles of the Charter of the United Nations—with 143 votes in favor, 5 against—Belarus, the Democratic People's Republic of Korea, Nicaragua, Russia, and Syria—and 35 others abstaining.

[43] In relation to information intervention, precisely on this middle ground, see Metzl, supra note 20, at 15, as well as (at 17) worrying about the danger that in a world "less willing to respond forcefully to international crises, the baby of information intervention will be thrown out with the bath water of armed humanitarian intervention."

[44] Showing no illusions to this end, id., 20.

[45] See Bruno Simma, NATO, the UN and the Use of Force: Legal Aspects, 10 EUROPEAN JOURNAL OF INTERNATIONAL LAW 1–22 (1999). Cf. for the essay by Price, supra note 38, which was, in a certain way, also a reaction to the proposal by Metzl, supra note 20. Although critical of the events in Bosnia, Price, too, is not against "information intervention." However, he (at 96) calls, in the year 2000, for paying greater attention to "the legal framework, the circumstances in which it is justified, the extent to which it is multilateral as opposed to unilateral, the structure of standards and remedies, the relationship of the military to civilian authorizations, and the role existing international norms should pay." This plea is still pertinent and is renewed here in the wake of the question as to how future international law and its institutions have to grow after the Russian war of aggression on Ukraine. Unfortunately, Price's finding (at 107) that the "literature of 'information intervention' is thinner than its practice" still applies today.

The Evidentiary Value of NGO and IO Reports in International Criminal Proceedings

BY GEERT-JAN ALEXANDER KNOOPS* & SARA PEDROSO**

Abstract

This article examines a subject matter which has so far yielded little attention in academic literature, namely, the evidentiary value within international criminal proceedings of reports drafted by non-governmental and international organisations, for instance, about a conflict situation. Most often these reports do not disclose the identity nor information about the sources upon which the information is based, which amounts to anonymous hearsay. The question arises whether non-governmental organisation or international organisation reports are admissible in international criminal trials in light of the unverifiability of sources by both the parties and the judges. This article reviews the existing case law of the various international criminal tribunals on this subject, with a focus on the International Criminal Court.

---

* Professor of Politics of International Law at the University of Amsterdam and visiting Professor of International Criminal Law at Shandong University (Jinan, China). He practices as a lawyer at Knoops' International Lawyers in Amsterdam, The Netherlands, and currently acts as lead counsel at the International Criminal Court in two cases. Member of the Editorial Board.

** Lawyer (member of the Ontario Bar, Canada) and Graduate of the Advanced Master's Degree in Public International Law at Leiden University. Currently working as Assistant to Counsel at the International Criminal Court.

Geert-Jan Alexander Knoops and Sara Pedroso, *The Evidentiary Value of NGO and IO Reports in International Criminal Proceedings* In: *The Global Community Yearbook of International Law and Jurisprudence 2022*. Edited by: Giuliana Ziccardi Capaldo, Oxford University Press. © Oxford University Press 2023. DOI: 10.1093/oso/9780197752265.003.0009

I. INTRODUCTION

The use of reports issued by non-governmental organisations (NGOs) and international organisations (IOs) on conflict situations is prevalent in international criminal trials, including before the International Criminal Court (ICC). Yet such reports, which are at times drafted on the basis of short-term fact-finding missions, should be received with considerable circumspection in the context of international criminal proceedings. Given the identity of sources are most often not provided in such reports, information contained therein often amounts to anonymous hearsay. The use of NGO/IO reports has significant repercussions on a suspect's or accused's basic fair trial rights, given that the anonymous hearsay information is effectively subtracted from testimonial scrutiny by the defence. Moreover, reliance on such evidence impacts on a chamber's assessment of the evidence in its ultimate determination of guilt or innocence, given the opaqueness of such reports.

In its decision adjourning the hearings on the confirmation of charges pursuant to Article 61(7)(c)(i) of the Rome Statute, Pre-Trial Chamber I in the case of *Prosecutor v. Laurent Gbagbo* of 3 June 2013 aptly summarised the evidentiary challenges arising from a party's reliance on NGO/IO reports for both the chamber and for the defence:

> 29. Heavy reliance upon anonymous hearsay, as is often the basis of information contained in reports of non-governmental organizations ("NGO reports") and press articles, is problematic for the following reasons. Proving allegations solely through anonymous hearsay puts the Defence in a difficult position because it is not able to investigate and challenge the trustworthiness of the source(s) of the information, thereby unduly limiting the right of the Defence under article 61(6)(b) of the Statute to challenge the Prosecutor's evidence, a right to which the Appeals Chamber attached "considerable significance". Further, it is highly problematic when the Chamber itself does not know the source of the information and is deprived of vital information about the source of the evidence. In such cases, the Chamber is unable to assess the trustworthiness of the source, making it all but impossible to determine what probative value to attribute to the information.
> [...]
> 35. In light of the above considerations, the Chamber notes with serious concern that in this case the Prosecutor relied heavily on NGO reports and press articles with regard to key elements of the case, including the contextual elements of crimes against humanity. Such pieces of evidence cannot in any way be presented as the fruits of a full and proper investigation by the Prosecutor in accordance with article 54(1)(a) of the Statute. Even though NGO reports and press articles may be a useful introduction to the historical context of a conflict situation, they do not usually constitute a valid substitute for the type of evidence that is required to meet the evidentiary threshold for the confirmation of charges.[1]

The Office of the Prosecutor's (Prosecution) excessive reliance on NGO reports and press articles to prove key elements of its case in the *Gbagbo* case was deemed so egregious that Pre-Trial Chamber I adjourned the hearing on the confirmation of charges against Mr Gbagbo and enjoined the Prosecution to consider conducting further investigations with

---

[1] Prosecutor v. Laurent Gbagbo, No. ICC-02/11-01/11-432, Decision adjourning the hearing on the confirmation of charges pursuant to article 61(7)(c)(i) of the Rome Statute (3 June 2013), paras. 29 and 35.

respect to all charges. This decision is exemplary of the caution which should be exercised upon considering NGO/IO reports in the context of international criminal proceedings.

II. THE PROBLEMATIC NATURE OF NGO/IO REPORTS USED AS EVIDENCE

The capacity of a chamber to assess the reliability of a piece of evidence is essential for performing its overall assessment of the weight to be attached to that evidence. In the ICC regime, the admissibility of an item of evidence depends not only on its reliability, but also on its probative value and the weighing of any prejudicial effect the admission may have on the defence. As held by ICC Trial Chamber II in *Katanga and Ndgudjolo*, NGO reports "can be considered *prima facie* reliable if they provide sufficient guarantees of non-partisanship and impartiality," but they should include sufficient information on their sources and methodology used to compile and analyse the evidence used to make factual assertions.[2] However, the Chamber held that if such particulars are not available, it cannot assess the reliability of the content of the reports and is therefore unable to qualify those documents as sufficiently reliable to be admitted into evidence. The Chamber further cautioned that where such reports are based for the most part on hearsay information, especially when that information was twice or further removed from its source, the "reliability of their content was seriously impugned."[3] In this particular case, for these reasons, the Chamber rejected the admission of a Human Rights Watch report from a prosecution bar table motion given it lacked probative value.[4]

Hearsay and anonymous evidence contained in NGO/IO reports typically cannot be fully scrutinised or tested in the courtroom, for instance, through examination and cross-examination, in order to determine its reliability and probative value given the anonymity of the underlying sources. In other words, this type of evidence remains outside the ambit of judicial scrutiny. As held by the Appeals Chamber in the *Milošević* case, with respect to summarised statements amounting to hearsay evidence, the opportunity to examine the persons who summarised statements "does not overcome the absence of the opportunity to cross-examine the person who made them."[5] The Trial Chamber in *Milošević* considered *inter alia* the importance of verifying whether the hearsay evidence is "firsthand" hearsay.[6] Similarly, the Trial Chamber in the ICTY *Milutinović* case denied the admission of Human Rights Watch reports on the basis that it was not "in a position to assess the reliability of the factual contentions contained therein."[7] The Trial Chamber further added that "neither the

---

[2] ICC, Prosecutor v. Katanga and Ngudjolo, No. ICC-01/04-01/07-2635, Decision on the Prosecutor's Bar Table Motions (17 December 2010), para. 30.

[3] *Id.*

[4] *Id.*, para. 36. *See also* ICC, Prosecutor v. Katanga, No. ICC-01/04-01/07-3217-Red, Version publique expurgée de "Décision relative à trois requêtes tendant à la production d'éléments de preuve supplémentaires et à un accord en matière de preuve" (ICC-01/04-01/07-3217-Conf) (4 January 2012), para. 13, where the Chamber rejected the LRV's request for the admission of a Human Rights Watch report titled "En quête de justice: Poursuivre les auteurs de violences sexuelles commises pendant la guerre au Congo."

[5] ICTY, Prosecutor v. Milošević, IT-02-54-AR73.2, "Decision on Admissibility of Prosecution Investigator's Evidence" (30 September 2002), para. 22.

[6] ICTY, Prosecutor v. Milošević, IT-02-54-AR73.2, "Decision on Admissibility of Prosecution Investigator's Evidence" (30 September 2002), para. 22.

[7] ICTY, Milutinović et al., No. IT-05-87-T, Decision on evidence tendered through Sandra Mitchell and Frederick Abrahams (1 September 2006), para.21.

report's acknowledgement of these problems, nor the opportunity to cross-examine one of the authors and editors of the report, can adequately replace the opportunity to test the reliability of any of the person's making the statements."[8] In the case of anonymous hearsay evidence, the verification of whether information is first-, second-, or third-hand information cannot be effectuated.

This problem stems partly from the fact that given several NGOs and IOs implement a policy of confidentiality with regard to the protection of sources of information. As indicated in a 2011 Manual on Human Rights Reporting published by the Office of the UN High Commissioner for Human Rights:

> As a general rule, the identities and other personally identifiable data (PID) of victims, witnesses, alleged individual perpetrators and other sources of information (e.g., date of birth, address, phone number) must be kept confidential at all times. This means that HROs [human rights officers] must conceal (e.g., using code names) or omit any information from reports that could lead to such a person being identified. Such information should be included only in the corresponding case file, which should be securely stored in the field presence's information management system.[9]

The Manual on Human Rights Reporting further indicates that a person's identity may be disclosed in a report only under "exceptional circumstances," where informed consent is obtained and following a careful security assessment by the organisation.[10] Such is the policy of several NGOs such as Human Rights Watch, which ensures the anonymity and confidentiality of persons interviewed.[11]

The fact that Human Rights Watch workers could not divulge the organisation's sources of information was also confirmed during the testimony of a Human Rights Watch staff member who testified before the ICC.[12] In the case of *Gbagbo and Blé Goudé*, the defence for Mr Blé Goudé had requested the Chamber to exclude the anticipated testimony of a Human Rights Watch investigator or, alternatively, to restrict the scope of his testimony.[13] While ultimately finding that the request was premature, Trial Chamber I held that Witness P-369 should not be asked to pronounce himself on the conclusions he drew from his research in Ivory Coast and he should not be asked to give his personal views as to the trustworthiness of any individuals he spoke to as part of his inquiry. The Chamber observed that it could not "simply rely on the impressions of NGO representatives or other third persons"

---

[8] ICTY, Milutinović et al., No. IT-05-87-T, Decision on evidence tendered through Sandra Mitchell and Frederick Abrahams (1 September 2006), para. 22. In the Krajišnik Trial Judgment at the ICTY, the Trial Chamber indicated that although hearsay evidence is not inadmissible per se, "in those cases where a witness did not specify the source of the hearsay, the Chamber has generally not relied on the hearsay," Prosecutor v. Krajišnik, No. IT-00-39-T, Judgement (27 September 2006), para. 1190.

[9] Manual on Human Rights Monitoring, Chapter 13: Human Rights Reporting, available at https://www.ohchr.org/sites/default/files/Documents/Publications/Chapter13-MHRM.pdf, at 8.

[10] Manual on Human Rights Monitoring, Chapter 13: Human Rights Reporting, available at https://www.ohchr.org/sites/default/files/Documents/Publications/Chapter13-MHRM.pdf, at 9.

[11] Human Rights Watch, "About Our Research," available at https://www.hrw.org/about/about-us/about-our-research#5.

[12] ICC, Prosecutor v. Gbagbo and Blé Goudé, Transcript No. ICC-02/11-01/15-T-42-ENG ET (19 May 2016), at 35.

[13] ICC, Prosecutor v. Gbagbo and Blé Goudé, No. ICC-02/11-01/15-509, Defence's Motion to Preclude and Exclude the prospected Evidence of Witnesses P-369, or, in the alternative, to restrict the Scope of Witness P-0369's intended Evidence (10 May 2016).

in relation to the trustworthiness of any relevant evidence.[14] Significantly, the Chamber noted that "this restriction applies with even greater force when the identity of the sources of the Witness is not disclosed to the parties and the Chamber," in other words, where a witness is anonymous.[15] As result of this reasoning, Trial Chamber I concluded:

> Finally, since the Chamber has decided that Witness P-369 is not permitted to keep his sources anonymous; it will not allow the Prosecutor to question Witness P-369 on facts which he learned from anonymous sources, regardless of whether the Witness had a single or multiple sources for a particular fact. The reason for this is clear: when the sources remain anonymous, the Chamber has no independent means to ascertain the trustworthiness of those sources or to determine whether different sources genuinely corroborate each other.[16]

Trial Chamber I's finding that whether a witness relied on a single source or multiple sources is irrelevant is based on the acknowledgment that the reliability of those sources remained beyond the reach of judicial checks and balances. Another principle which is at the core of this reasoning is the fundamental principle that an accused is entitled to be apprised of the evidence used against him or her, as further developed in the following. In his reasons to the judgment acquitting Laurent Gbagbo and Charles Blé Goudé at the no case to answer stage, Judge Henderson presented further guidance as to the use of NGO/ IO reports containing anonymous hearsay:[17]

> 44. It is important to emphasise that simply knowing the identity of the source is not sufficient. Just as in the case of in-court testimony, in order to determine what weight should be given, it is necessary to have reliable information about how the source of the information came to know it, if there are any concerns about his or her memory and whether or not there may be reasons to think that the source may have deliberately given information which he or she did not believe to be correct.
> 45. Accordingly, when the only evidence in relation to a particular proposition is based primarily on anonymous hearsay without adequate information about the reliability and credibility of the source, the Chamber must conclude that such a proposition is unsupported.

At the European Court of Human Rights (ECtHR), a distinction was made between absent witnesses and anonymous witnesses, in the 2012 *Ellis and Simms and Martin v. the United Kingdom* case. In that case, the ECtHR held that unlike absent witnesses, anonymous witnesses were confronted in person by defence counsel, who was able to

---

[14] ICC, Prosecutor v. Gbagbo and Blé Goudé, No. ICC-02/11-01/15-509, Decision on "Defence's Motion to Preclude and Exclude the prospected Evidence of Witness P-369, or, in the alternative, to restrict the Scope of Witness P-0369's intended Evidence" (13 May 2016), para. 7.

[15] ICC, Prosecutor v. Gbagbo and Blé Goudé, No. ICC-02/11-01/15-509, Decision on "Defence's Motion to Preclude and Exclude the prospected Evidence of Witness P-369, or, in the alternative, to restrict the Scope of Witness P-0369's intended Evidence" (13 May 2016), para. 7.

[16] ICC, Prosecutor v. Gbagbo and Blé Goudé, No. ICC-02/11-01/15-509, Decision on "Defence's Motion to Preclude and Exclude the prospected Evidence of Witness P-369, or, in the alternative, to restrict the Scope of Witness P-0369's intended Evidence" (13 May 2016), para. 8.

[17] ICC, Prosecutor v. Gbagbo and Blé Goudé, No. ICC-02/11-01/15-1263-AnxB-Red, Public Redacted Version of Reasons of Judge Geoffrey Henderson (16 July 2019).

cross-examine them and question inconsistencies in their account. The witness's presence, albeit anonymously, allowed that the judge, jury, and counsel could observe the witness's demeanor and for a view as to the reliability of the witness testimony. The ECtHR drew from the ECHR *Al-Khawaja and Tahery v. United Kingdom* case to recall that Article 6(3)(d) ECHR[18] imposed three requirements concerning reliance on anonymous witnesses: (i) there had to be a good reason to keep secret the identity of the witness; (ii) the Court had to consider whether the evidence of the anonymous witness was the sole or decisive basis of the conviction; and (iii) where a conviction was based solely or decisively on the evidence of anonymous witnesses, the Court had to satisfy itself that there were sufficient counterbalancing factors, including strong procedural safeguards, to permit a fair and proper assessment of the reliability of that evidence to take place.[19] In other words, the ECHR jurisprudence has established that an applicant should not be prevented from testing an anonymous witness's reliability, and safeguards must be implemented to ensure that an accused's fair trial rights are guaranteed in such exceptional circumstances.

In the case of NGO/IO reports, the sources of information which are kept confidential are akin to "absent" witnesses, whose accounts cannot be questioned or verified by either defence counsel or by a chamber. In such cases, the defence and the Chamber are simply not in a position to make their own assessment of the reliability of anonymous hearsay evidence contained in such reports. In contrast to the *Ellis* case, in most cases where the Prosecution relies on NGO reports, there is no "substantial disclosure about the anonymous witness which had provided extensive material for cross-examination."[20] Moreover, most often there is no other evidence which could attest to the reliability and credibility of the sources contained in the NGO/IO statements. It cannot be said that such evidence may be therefore corroborative.

In addition, NGO/IO reports covering conflict and post-conflict situations are often drafted on the basis of fact-finding missions. As explained by Stephen Wilkinson, a specialist in international humanitarian law and human rights in armed conflict, fact-finding missions have, by nature, "a limited and restricted mandate, work under strict time constraints, have no powers of enforcement, [and therefore] are not in a position to apply the same levels of scrutiny to their findings that would be expected of formal judicial processes."[21] These factors should be taken into consideration in the context of international criminal proceedings, when assessing the evidentiary value of NGO/IO reports, and in particular, the reliability of such evidence.

---

[18] Providing that a person charged with a criminal offence has the right to "examine or have examined witnesses against him and to obtain the attendance and examination of witnesses on his behalf under the same conditions as witnesses against him." In the United States, the opportunity for a defendant to challenge her or his accusers is protected under the sixth amendment. *See also* Article 14(3) of the ICCPR.

[19] Ellis and Simms and Martin v. United Kingdom, Application Nos. 46099/06 and 46699/06 (10 April 2012), paras. 73–74, relying on the Al-Khawaja and Tahery v. United Kingdom, Nos. 26766/05 and 22228/06 (15 December 2011), paras. 119, 147.

[20] Ellis and Simms and Martin v. United Kingdom, Application Nos. 46099/06 and 46699/06 (10 April 2012), paras. 87.

[21] S. Wilkinson, Standards of Proof in International Humanitarian and Human Rights Fact-Finding and Inquiry, Missions, Geneva Academy of International Humanitarian Law, at 49, available at https://www.geneva-academy.ch/joomlatools-files/docman-files/Standards%20of%20Proof%20in%20Fact-Finding.pdf.

III. THE USE OF NGO/IO REPORTS AT DIFFERENT STAGES OF ICC PROCEEDINGS

At the ICC, hearsay evidence is not inadmissible *ab initio*, although it is typically given a lower probative value and approached with caution.[22] Judges at the ICC have typically approached hearsay evidence as a matter of probative value rather than admissibility, reflecting a rather inclusionary (albeit *sui generis*) approach to evidence.[23] ICC Chambers have taken a "cautious approach" to anonymous hearsay and have found that due consideration must be given to the "impossibility of cross-examining the information source" with this type of evidence.[24]

Article 69(4) of the Rome Statute provides that the criteria for assessing the relevance and admissibility of a piece of evidence at the ICC are (i) probative value and (ii) any prejudice that such evidence may cause to a fair trial or to a fair evaluation of the testimony of a witness. Rule 63(2) of the ICC Rules of Procedure and Evidence provides for the judges' discretionary power "to assess freely all evidence submitted in order to determine its relevance or admissibility in accordance with article 69."

Article 61(6) of the Rome Statute provides the right of a suspect before the Court to "challenge the evidence presented by the Prosecutor." Article 67(1)(e) of the Rome Statute expressly provide for the right of an accused to "examine, or have examined, the witnesses against him or her and to obtain the attendance and examination of witnesses on his or her behalf under the same conditions as witnesses against him or her." These are fundamental fair trial guarantees matching several legal systems worldwide, including the framework provided by the ECHR, as indicated previously.

At the pre-trial level, where the evidentiary threshold is that of "reasonable grounds to believe," ICC Chambers have indicated that "there is nothing in the Statute or the Rules which expressly provides that the evidence which can be considered hearsay from anonymous sources is inadmissible *per se*."[25] However, they have warned that this type of evidence "may cause difficulties for the defence because it is deprived of the opportunity to challenge its probative value."[26] In *Bemba*, the Pre-Trial Chamber found that the use of anonymous witness statements was permitted at the pre-trial stage because of the lower evidentiary threshold (compared with the trial stage), but that this evidence must be given low probative value because of the disadvantage caused to the defence:

> With regard to direct evidence emanating from an anonymous source, the Chamber shares the view, adopted in other pre-trial decisions, that it may cause difficulties to the

---

[22] ICC, Prosecutor v. Ngudjolo, No. ICC-01/04-02/12-3-tENG, Judgment pursuant to article 74 of the Statute (18 December 2012), para. 55; Prosecutor v. Katanga and Ngudjolo, No. ICC-01/04-01/07-717, Decision on the confirmation of charges (30 September 2008), para. 137.

[23] *See* ICC, Prosecutor v. Lubanga, No. ICC-01/04-01/06-803-tEN (29 January 2007), paras. 101–103.

[24] ICC, Prosecutor v. Ngudjolo, No. ICC-01/04-02/12-3-tENG, Judgment pursuant to article 74 of the Statute (18 December 2012), para. 56.

[25] ICC, Prosecutor v. Lubanga, No. ICC-01/04-01/06-803-tEN, Decision on the confirmation of charges (29 January 2007), paras. 101–103; Prosecutor v. Bemba, No. ICC-01/05-01/08-424, Decision Pursuant to Article 61(7)(a) and (b) of the Rome Statute on the Charges of the Prosecutor Against Jean-Pierre Bemba Gombo (15 June 2009), para. 50.

[26] ICC, Prosecutor v. Bemba, No. ICC-01/05-01/08-424, Decision Pursuant to Article 61(7)(a) and (b) of the Rome Statute on the Charges of the Prosecutor Against Jean-Pierre Bemba Gombo (15 June 2009), para. 50, citing Prosecutor v. Lubanga, No. ICC-01/04-01/06-803-tEN, Decision on the confirmation of charges (29 January 2007), para. 106; Prosecutor v. Katanga, No. ICC-01/04-01/07-717, Decision on the confirmation of charges (1 October 2008), para. 11.

Defence because it is deprived of the opportunity to challenge its probative value. This also holds true for summaries of witness statements. The Chamber is fully aware that the use of anonymous witness statements and summaries is permitted at the pre-trial stage, particularly because the evidentiary threshold is lower than the threshold applicable at the trial stage. However, to counterbalance the disadvantage that it might cause to the Defence, such evidence is considered as having a rather low probative value. More specifically, the probative value of anonymous witness statements and summaries is lower than the probative value attached to the statements of witnesses whose identity is known to the Defence.[27]

Similarly, in *Lubanga*, the Pre-Trial Chamber held that as a general rule, it will only rely on anonymous hearsay evidence—such as NGO reports and press articles—to corroborate other evidence, "mindful of the difficulties that such evidence may present to the Defence in relation to the possibility of ascertaining its truthfulness and authenticity."[28] The Pre-Trial Chamber also held, relying on ECtHR jurisprudence, that the use of anonymous statements as sufficient evidence to found a conviction may be irreconcilable with Article 6 of the ECHR:

> 102. Furthermore, ECHR jurisprudence evinces that the European Convention does not preclude reliance at the investigation stage of criminal proceedings on sources such as anonymous informants. Nevertheless, the ECHR specifies that the subsequent use of anonymous statements as sufficient evidence to found a conviction is a different matter in that it can be irreconcilable with article 6 of the European Convention, particularly if the conviction is based to a decisive extent on anonymous statements.
> 103. Accordingly, the Chamber considers that objections pertaining to the use of anonymous hearsay evidence do not go to the admissibility of the evidence, but only to its probative value.[29]

---

[27] ICC, Prosecutor v. Bemba, No. ICC-01/05-01/08-424, Decision Pursuant to Article 61(7)(a) and (b) of the Rome Statute on the Charges of the Prosecutor Against Jean-Pierre Bemba Gombo (15 June 2009), para. 50.

[28] ICC, Prosecutor v. Lubanga, No. ICC-01/04-01/06-803-tEN, Decision on the confirmation of charges (29 January 2007), para. 106; Prosecutor v. Katanga, No. ICC-01/04-01/07-717, Decision on the confirmation of charges (30 September 2008), paras. 159–160, also cited *inter alia* by the Pre-Trial Chamber in Prosecutor v. Banda and Jerbo, No. ICC-02/05-03/09-121-Corr-Red, Corrigendum of the "Decision on the Confirmation of Charges" (8 March 2011), para. 41; Prosecutor v. Mbarushimana, No. ICC-01/04-01/10-465-Red, Decision on the confirmation of charges (16 December 2011), para. 49; Prosecutor v. Ruto and Sang, No. ICC-01/09-01/11-373, Decision on the Confirmation of Charges Pursuant to Article 61(7)(a) and (b) of the Rome Statute (23 January 2012), para. 78; Prosecutor v. Kenyatta et al., ICC PT. Ch. II, 23 January 2012, para. 90; the Trial Chamber in Mladic at the ICTY similarly held that "the Chamber considers that it is most appropriate to allow the parties to clarify any unclear, vague, or hearsay portions of a statement during the testimony of the witnesses. In the absence of any clarification, the Chamber may attach less weight, if any, to such portions," *see* Prosecutor v. Mladic, Trial Chamber II, Transcript of 30 August 2012.

[29] ICC, Prosecutor v. Lubanga, No. ICC-01/04-01/06-803-tEN, Decision on the confirmation of charges (29 January 2007), paras. 102–103, citing ECtHR jurisprudence Kostovski v. The Netherlands, No. 11454/85, Judgment of 20 November 1989, para. 44; *see also* Prosecutor v. Mbarushimana, No. ICC-01/04-01/10-465-Red, Decision on the confirmation of charges (16 December 2011), para. 49.

In the ICC Decision on the confirmation of charges in the case against Mr Abu Garda, the Pre-Trial Chamber recognised that the Rome Statute and ICC Rules of Procedure and Evidence expressly permitted the Office of the Prosecutor to rely on anonymous witness summaries at the confirmation stage. The Pre-Trial Chamber noted, however, that the Office of the Prosecutor's right to rely on such summary evidence must be balanced with the right of the Defence, in accordance with Article 61(6) of the Statute, to challenge the evidence presented by the Prosecution. It concluded that therefore, statements of anonymous witnesses will be given a lower probative value and will be evaluated on a case-by-case basis, according to whether the information contained therein is corroborated or supported by other evidence tendered into the case file.[30]

At the trial stage, the assessment of NGO/IO report at trial does not differ significantly than at the pre-trial stage. In assessing the admissibility of an NGO report,[31] the Trial Chamber in *Lubanga* rejected the admission of the document both on the basis of its low probative value and of it causing material prejudice to the parties:

> [. . .] the authors of the report are not to be called, and counsel will be unable, through questioning, to investigate the significant criticisms that have been made of its contents [. . .] it follows that, if admitted, this document is likely to cause material prejudice to the parties.[32]

In her partially dissenting opinion from the majority decision admitting NGO reports into the *Ntaganda* case, Judge Ozaki explained:

> The Majority holds that these reports "contain sufficient details of their sources of information and methodology" and therefore bear sufficient indicia of authenticity and reliability. The reports contain information relevant to the crimes with which the accused is charged. However, the identities of the authors and the sources of the information relied on in the reports are not revealed with sufficient detail, and as a result it is not possible to fully investigate their reliability. The three FIDH reports and the AI report admitted into evidence by the Majority are based almost entirely on information obtained from other NGOs, journalists, or unidentified eyewitnesses,

---

[30] ICC, Prosecutor v. Abu Garda, No. ICC-02/05-02/09-243-Red, Decision on the Confirmation of Charges (8 February 2010), para. 42. For this finding, it relied on the Pre-Trial Chamber's finding in the *Katanga* case, which stated that while "there is no requirement per se that summaries of the statements of anonymous witnesses are corroborated in order for them to be admissible, the Chamber is of the view that lack of support or corroboration from other evidence in the record of the proceedings could affect the probative value of those summaries or statements," Prosecutor v. Katanga and Ngudjolo, No. ICC-01/04-01/07-717, Decision on the confirmation of charges (30 September 2008), para. 160.

[31] "Report of the Panel of Experts on the illegal exploitation of natural resources and other forms of wealth of the Democratic Republic of the Congo."

[32] See ICC, Prosecutor v. Lubanga, No. ICC-01/04-01/06-2135, Decision on the request by the legal representative of victims a/0001/06, a/0002/06, a/0003/06, a/0049/06, a/0007/08, a/0149/08, a/0155/07, a/0156/07, a/0404/08, a/0405/08, a/0406/08, a/0407/08, a/0409/08, a0149/07 and a/0162/07 for admission of the final report of the Panel of Experts on the illegal exploitation of natural resources and other forms of wealth of the Democratic Republic of the Congo as evidence (22 September 2009), paras. 33–34.

thus rendering it very difficult to adequately assess the reliability of the accounts contained therein.[33]

Judge Ozaki concluded that the lack of guarantees concerning the reliability of the NGO reports' sources, in the absence of witness testimony of the authors of the reports render their probative value very low, while at the same time posing a high potential prejudice for the defence.[34] Significantly, Judge Ozaki held that the Majority's reasoning that the NGO reports could be admitted "for the limited purpose that the information contained therein may serve to corroborate other pieces of evidence" did not justify their admission into evidence.

In *Bemba*, in the context of an abuse of process motion, Trial Chamber V held that NGO reports had little, if any, evidential weight, given that their provenance and reliability were entirely uninvestigated and untested.[35] Interestingly here, the motion was determined on the standard of balance of probabilities; as a logical extension, if NGO reports are found to be unreliable on this lower standard, they would surely not meet the more rigorous standard of beyond reasonable doubt, as applied in the course of trial.[36]

The Majority to the Appeals Judgment in *Bemba* further held that the Trial Chamber had "failed to properly analyse [anonymous hearsay] evidence and address its potentially extremely low probative value."[37] As held by Judges Van den Wyngaert and Morrison in their separate opinion to the Appeals Judgment, "[w]hereas hearsay is not per se inadmissible before the Court, this does not mean that it is permissible to make findings beyond a reasonable doubt on this basis, especially when the Trial Chamber does not seem to have tried to establish the reliability of the source of the information." The judges reasoned that although the Trial Chamber accepted the need to be cautious when relying on hearsay evidence, "it appears that in practice it often threw its own caution to the wind." Thus, it is insufficient for a Trial Chamber to simply express caution; such caution must be applied in practice in order to pass muster. Further, Judges Van den Wyngaert and Morrison also referred to the inherent unreliability of hearsay evidence, emphasising the distinction between hearsay and anonymous hearsay evidence, concluding that in the latter case, reliability could simply not be established:

> One of the central findings of the Conviction Decision is contained in paragraph 563, where the Trial Chamber found that there was "consistent and corroborated evidence that MLC soldiers committed many acts of rape and murder against civilians throughout

---

[33] ICC, Prosecutor v. Bemba, No. ICC-01/05-01/08-2300, Partly Dissenting Opinion of Judge Ozaki on the Prosecution's Application for Admission of Materials into Evidence Pursuant to Article 69(4) of the Rome Statute (6 September 2012), para. 11.

[34] ICC, Prosecutor v. Bemba, No. ICC-01/05-01/08-2300, Partly Dissenting Opinion of Judge Ozaki on the Prosecution's Application for Admission of Materials into Evidence Pursuant to Article 69(4) of the Rome Statute (6 September 2012), para. 12.

[35] ICC, Prosecutor v. Bemba, No. ICC-01/05-01/08-802, Decision on the Admissibility and Abuse of Process Challenges (24 June 2010), paras. 235, 254–255.

[36] This was argued by the Sang Defence in ICC, Prosecutor v. Ruto and Sang, No. ICC-01/09-01/11-1130, Sang Defence Response to the Prosecution's Application for Admission of Documents from the Bar Table Pursuant to Article 64(9) (24 December 2013), para. 34.

[37] ICC, Prosecutor v. Bemba, No. ICC-01/05-01/08-3636-Red, Judgment on the appeal of Mr Jean-Pierre Bemba Gombo against Trial Chamber III's "Judgment pursuant to Article 74 of the Statute" (8 June 2018), para. 183.

the 2002-2003 CAR operation". However, closer inspection of the relevant footnote reveals that the evidence in question consists mainly of documentary and testimonial hearsay evidence. As set out above, we have grave concerns about excessive reliance on hearsay evidence, especially if the reliability of the source of the information cannot be established. We also reject the Trial Chamber's apparent conclusion that weak testimonial evidence can somehow be corroborated by weak documentary evidence, especially if one or both are based on (anonymous) hearsay.[38]

Significantly, the judges found that "holistic fact-finding should not be an excuse or a reason for making findings beyond a reasonable doubt on the basis of a collection of weak evidence." In their view, this "creates the risk that the Chamber may consider evidence that is not relevant or has no evidentiary weight to speak of and make findings under the illusion of corroboration."[39]

> There is indeed a difference between claiming that one has 'twenty' coins and that one has 'many' such coins. However, in the end one can only legally prove that one has 'many' coins by defining how much 'many' is and then presenting evidence to prove the existence of each individual coin. It is thus certainly not true that a 'piecemeal' approach would lead the Chamber to exclude potentially relevant evidence. On the contrary, the Prosecutor's proposed 'cumulative' approach creates the risk that the Chamber may consider evidence that is not relevant or has no evidentiary weight to speak of and make findings under the illusion of corroboration. As indicated above, the dangers of the Prosecution's suggested approach are illustrated by the impugned Conviction Decision. We refer to our concerns expressed above about the opacity of the reasoning, the reliance on (anonymous) hearsay evidence and the findings beyond a reasonable doubt based on dubious circumstantial evidence.[40]

The debate around the use of NGO/IO reports also arose in the context of a defence request for interim release. Judges Ušacka and Van den Wyngaert held, in their dissenting opinions, that the Pre-Trial Chamber II "erred in its sole reliance on anonymous hearsay evidence contained in press releases, blog articles and two UN group of expert reports." In her dissenting opinion, Judge Van den Wyngaert held that such evidence "must be treated with utmost caution in the context of a criminal trial and without considerably more, independently verified, information cannot, [be] safely relied upon to justify the continued detention of Mr Bosco Ntaganda."[41]

It appears there is a jurisprudential foundation at the ICC to reject the admission of NGO/IO reports in the context of pre-trial and especially trial proceedings, particularly when containing anonymous hearsay. Anonymous hearsay evidence, which often forms the basis of such reports, is inherently unreliable and should not used by a chamber to found a conviction.

---

[38] ICC, Prosecutor v. Bemba, No. ICC-01/05-01/08-3636-Anx2, Separate opinion Judge Christine Van den Wyngaert and Judge Howard Morrison (8 June 2018), footnote 5.

[39] ICC, Prosecutor v. Bemba, No. ICC-01/05-01/08-3636-Anx2, Separate opinion Judge Christine Van den Wyngaert and Judge Howard Morrison (8 June 2018), para. 67.

[40] ICC, Prosecutor v. Bemba, No. ICC-01/05-01/08-3636-Anx2, Separate opinion Judge Christine Van den Wyngaert and Judge Howard Morrison (8 June 2018), para. 67.

[41] ICC, Prosecutor v. Ntaganda, Dissenting Opinion of Judge Christine Van den Wyngaert, ICC-01/04-02/06-271-Anx2 (5 March 2014), para. 2.

IV. CONCLUSION

In conclusion, there seems to be a consensus among international criminal tribunals, such as the ICC, that caution must be exercised in assessing NGO/IO reports. Such reports, used as evidence, most often stand at odds with an accused's right to confront the evidence presented against him or her, which is an essential requirement of a fair trial.[42] The evidentiary value of such reports should be assessed with extreme caution due to the absence of any opportunity for the participants in these proceedings to know the source of the information, the identity of which may be vital for the truth. Moreover, as the ICC jurisprudence has shown, caution must also be exercised and demonstrated by the judges with respect to reliance on NGO/IO reports for corroborative purposes. In addition, hearsay where the source is known should be distinguished from anonymous hearsay, given the latter, as opposed to the former, cannot be verified, by either the parties to a trial or by the judges.

In addition, the potential use of anonymous hearsay at the pre-trial and trial stages at the ICC may be distinguished. If anonymous hearsay evidence may at times, be used, as an "introduction to the historical context of a conflict situation," or to corroborate other evidence at the pre-trial stage, this cannot be true at the trial stage, where the evidentiary threshold is much higher. At the trial phase, anonymous hearsay evidence should be excluded altogether, or given extremely little to no weight by the Chamber in its determination of guilt or innocence. Reliance on NGO/IO reports in international criminal proceedings may contaminate the truth-finding mandate of international courts and tribunals.

---

[42] ICC Prosecutor v. Gbagbo and Blé Goudé, No. ICC-02/11-01/15-466-Conf-Anx, Separate Opinion of Judge Henderson annexed to "Decision on the Prosecutor's Application to protect the confidentiality of the sources of P-0369" (21 March 2016), para. 8.

Non-compensatory Reparation Modalities in UN Legal Sources

Focus on Gross Violations of Human Rights

BY JUAN-PABLO PÉREZ-LEÓN-ACEVEDO*

Abstract

Compensation has been traditionally the most common reparation modality to redress harm inflicted. However, UN legal sources have increasingly evidenced that compensation is only one among other reparation modalities, especially regarding victims of gross violations of human rights. The main research question of this piece is: How have key UN legal sources addressed non-compensatory that states are obliged to provide to victims of gross violations of human rights? Non-compensatory reparation modalities are identified, systematized, and examined under four internationally recognized categories: restitution, rehabilitation, satisfaction, and guarantees of non-repetition. The selected UN legal sources are primarily treaties, resolutions, draft instruments, case law, general comments, general observations, and reports adopted by diverse UN organs. These organs are specifically: the UN General Assembly, UN human rights treaty bodies, the International Law Commission, the International Court of Justice, and the Special Rapporteur on truth, justice, reparation, and guarantees of non-recurrence.

* Post-doctoral researcher and lecturer, Faculty of Humanities and Social Sciences (Department of Language and Communication Studies), University of Jyväskylä, Finland; visiting/affiliated researcher, PluriCourts, Faculty of Law, University of Oslo; visiting professor, Universidad Tecnológica del Perú. Funding for this piece came from the Academy of Finland (grant 325535) and, previously, the Research Council of Norway (PluriCourts, project 223274).

Juan-Pablo Pérez-León-Acevedo, *Non-compensatory Reparation Modalities in UN Legal Sources* In: *The Global Community Yearbook of International Law and Jurisprudence 2022*. Edited by: Giuliana Ziccardi Capaldo, Oxford University Press.

I. INTRODUCTION

Compensation, namely, monetary payment of damages,[1] has been traditionally the most common reparation modality to redress harm inflicted.[2] Yet UN legal sources especially regarding gross violations of human rights, which may also constitute international crimes,[3] have evidenced that compensation is only one among other reparation modalities. The present piece pursues this main research question: How have key UN legal sources addressed non-compensatory reparation modalities that states are obliged to provide to victims of gross violations of human rights? Within the nature and limits of a piece like this, non-compensatory reparation modalities are identified, systematized, and examined under four internationally recognized categories: restitution, rehabilitation, satisfaction, and guarantees of non-repetition. Scholars have also identified these modalities.[4]

Under Article 34 of the International Law Commission (ILC)'s Draft Articles on Responsibility of States for Internationally Wrongful Acts (ARSIWA), reparation "shall take the form of restitution, compensation and satisfaction."[5] Nevertheless, other UN legal sources additionally include rehabilitation and guarantees of non-repetition. Although the International Covenant on Civil and Political Rights (ICCPR) lists no specific reparation modalities, the Human Rights Committee (HRC) has referred to them and fleshed out their contents, including non-compensatory reparations. Regarding the right to an effective remedy (ICCPR, Article 2(3)), the HRC found that "reparation can involve restitution, rehabilitation, [...] satisfaction [and] guarantees of non-repetition."[6] The Convention against Torture and Other Cruel, Inhuman or Degrading Treatment or Punishment only mentions compensation and rehabilitation (Article

---

[1] On compensation, *see generally*, *e.g.*, Stephan Wittich, *Compensation*, in MAX PLANCK ENCYCLOPEDIA OF PUBLIC INTERNATIONAL LAW (Anne Peters & Rüdiger Wolfrum eds., 2008) [electronic version]; Martins Paparinskis, *A Case Against Crippling Compensation in International Law of State Responsibility*, 83 MODERN LAW REVIEW 1246–1286 (2020); VICTOR STOICA, REMEDIES BEFORE THE INTERNATIONAL COURT OF JUSTICE 108–144 (2021).

[2] CONOR MCCARTHY, REPARATIONS AND VICTIM SUPPORT IN THE INTERNATIONAL CRIMINAL COURT 162 (2012).

[3] *See*, *e.g.*, Lyal Sunga, INDIVIDUAL RESPONSIBILITY IN INTERNATIONAL LAW FOR SERIOUS HUMAN RIGHTS VIOLATIONS (1992); Theodor Meron, *International Law in the Age of Human Rights*, 301 RECUEIL DES COURS DE L'ACADÉMIE DE DROIT INTERNATIONAL DE LA HAYE 9, 165 (2003); Heidy Rombouts et al., *The Right to Reparations for Victims of Gross and Systematic Violations of Human Rights*, in OUT OF THE ASHES: REPARATION FOR VICTIMS OF GROSS AND SYSTEMATIC HUMAN RIGHTS VIOLATIONS 309, 349–352 (Koen de Feyter et al. eds., 2005); William Schabas, *Atrocity Crimes*, in THE CAMBRIDGE COMPANION TO INTERNATIONAL CRIMINAL LAW 199, 199–205 (William Schabas ed., 2016); UN Office on Genocide Prevention and the Responsibility to Protect, Framework of Analysis for Atrocity Crimes (2014); anonymised reference.

[4] Cherif Bassiouni, *International Recognition of Victims' Rights*, 6 HUMAN RIGHTS LAW REVIEW 203, 267–274 (2006); Pablo de Greiff, *Justice and Reparations*, in THE HANDBOOK OF REPARATIONS 452, 452 (Pablo de Greiff ed., 2006); DINAH SHELTON, REMEDIES IN INTERNATIONAL HUMAN RIGHTS LAW 377–401 (3d ed. 2015); Theo van Boven, *Victims' Rights to a Remedy and Reparation*, in REPARATIONS FOR VICTIMS OF GENOCIDE, WAR CRIMES AND CRIMES AGAINST HUMANITY 1, 36–37 (Carla Ferstman et al. eds., ed. 2020); STOICA, *supra* note 1, 61–107, 145–156.

[5] ILC, *Draft Articles on Responsibility of States for Internationally Wrongful Acts with Commentaries* (2001), UN Doc. A/56/10.

[6] HRC, *General Comment 31. The Nature of the General Legal Obligation Imposed on States Parties to the Covenant*, UN Doc. CCPR/C/21/Rev.1/Add.13 (Mar. 29, 2004), para. 16.

14(1)); however, the Committee against Torture (CAT) has considered other non-compensatory reparations in its practice.

Pivotal and diverse UN sources adopted in this century indeed recognize that the victims' right to full and effective reparations includes the said non-compensatory reparation modalities. These sources are primarily: (i) Principles to Combat Impunity adopted by the former Commission on Human Rights (2005); (ii) Basic Principles and Guidelines on the Right to a Remedy and Reparation for Victims of Gross Violations of International Human Rights Law and Serious Violations of International Humanitarian Law (UN Reparation Principles) adopted by the UN General Assembly (2005);[7] (iii) the 2006 International Convention for the Protection of All Persons from Enforced Disappearance (Article 24); and (iv) the ILC's 2019 Draft Articles on Prevention and Punishment of Crimes Against Humanity (Article 12(3)).[8] Indeed, the ILC remarked that the right to reparation involves a "comprehensive reparative concept."[9] It is also significant that the Human Rights Council established, in 2011, the Special Rapporteur on the promotion of truth, justice, reparation and guarantees of non-recurrence (TJR Special Rapporteur).[10]

The International Court of Justice (ICJ)'s jurisprudence on gross violations of human rights has progressively considered most of the aforementioned non-compensatory reparation modalities in *Wall Opinion*[11] and the *Genocide Convention Case (Bosnia and Herzegovina v. Serbia and Montenegro)*.[12] The ICJ in *Diallo*, which involved the unlawful detention and expulsion of a Guinean national, however, only discussed and granted compensation.[13] In *Armed Activities on the Territory of the Congo*, which concerned gross and large-scale violations of human rights and international humanitarian law, the ICJ ordered Uganda to pay US$325,000,000 in favour of the Democratic Republic of Congo as a global compensatory amount.[14] Nevertheless, the ICJ rejected the Democratic Republic of Congo's request for satisfaction measures.[15]

Against this background and to unpack the main research question, the present piece has five sections. Section II contains general considerations about the diverse UN legal sources examined. The following four sections discuss primarily the aforementioned UN sources. This means one section per non-compensatory reparation modality, namely, restitution (section III), satisfaction (section IV), rehabilitation (section V), and guarantees of non-repetition (section VI). Comprehensive conclusions (section VII) complete this piece.

---

[7] UN General Assembly, UN Doc. A/RES/60/147 (Dec. 15, 2005).

[8] ILC, *Draft Articles on Prevention and Punishment of Crimes Against Humanity with Commentaries* (2019), UN Doc. A/74/10.

[9] *Id.*, at 108.

[10] *See* HRC, *Special Rapporteur on the Promotion of Truth, Justice, Reparation and Guarantees of Non-recurrence*, UN Doc. A/HRC/RES/18/7 (Oct. 13, 2011).

[11] ICJ, Legal Consequences of the Construction of a Wall in the Occupied Palestinian Territory, Advisory Opinion, 2004 ICJ REPORTS 136 (July 9, 2004), paras. 149–153.

[12] ICJ, Application of the Convention on the Prevention and Punishment of the Crime of Genocide (Bosnia and Herzegovina v. Serbia and Montenegro), Merits, Judgment, 2007 ICJ REPORTS 43 (Feb. 26, 2007), paras. 462–470.

[13] ICJ, Ahmadou Sadio Diallo (Guinea v. Democratic Republic of Congo), Compensation, Judgment, 2012 ICJ REPORTS 324 (June 19, 2012).

[14] ICJ, Armed Activities on the Territory of the Congo (Democratic Republic of the Congo v. Uganda), Judgment (Feb. 9, 2022), paras. 405, 409.

[15] *Id.*, paras. 385–392.

II. GENERAL CONSIDERATIONS ABOUT THE DIVERSE UN LEGAL SOURCES EXAMINED

Concerning the UN legal sources considered herein, the following points must be noted. First, the UN sources referred to in this note are of diverse nature. Such a diversity is given by *inter alia*: (i) the different level of binding effects that they have; (ii) the state-centric or victim-centred approach followed by the source; (iii) the kind of organ that renders them, namely, judicial, quasi-judicial, and non-judicial bodies; and (iv) the scope of the respective source, namely, general or specialized. Yet in terms of the specific object of study of the present note, namely, *non-compensatory reparation modalities* in UN legal sources with a focus on gross violations of human rights, it is arguably possible to identify to a greater or lesser extent the increasing presence of a common grammar or vocabulary across the sources considered herein.[16]

Second, while some of the legal sources examined herein correspond to binding international treaties, other sources such as resolutions of UN organs are not per se legally binding. Nevertheless, for example, the UN Reparation Principles have been regarded by scholars to reflect or be consistent with general principles of law or (emerging) customary international law.[17] Importantly, the UN Reparation Principles have been invoked by diverse international,[18] regional,[19] and hybrid courts[20] dealing with reparations in cases of gross violations of human rights and/or international crimes. With regard to the ARSIWA, they have been recognized as (totally or partially) reflecting or "codifying" the (customary) international law of state responsibility, including reparation modalities.[21] The ARSIWA have also been continuously invoked by the ICJ.[22] In turn, although the decisions and

---

[16] *See similar analyses, e.g.*: Shelton, *supra* note 4, at 285–440; anonymized reference.

[17] *E.g.*, Bassiouni, *supra* note 4, at 265–275; Van Boven, *supra* note 4, at 20–24; JEAN-MARIE HENCKAERTS & LOUISE DOSWALD-BECK, CUSTOMARY INTERNATIONAL HUMANITARIAN LAW. VOLUME I: RULES 547–549 (2005), (*see* jointly with ICRC, *IHL Database Customary IHL, Practice Relating to Rule 150. Reparation,* <https://ihl-databases.icrc.org/customary-ihl/eng/docindex/v2_rul_rule150> (last visited May 26, 2022)).

[18] *See, e.g.*, ICC, Prosecutor v. Lubanga, Case No. ICC-01/04-01/06-3129-AnxA, Appeals Chamber, Order for Reparations (Mar. 3, 2015), paras. 13–16, 35–42; ICJ, Diallo Case, *supra* note 13, Separate Opinion of Judge Cançado Trindade, paras. 53–56; ICJ, Armed Activities on the Territory of the Congo, *supra* note 14, Separate Opinion of Judge Yusuf, para. 39.

[19] *E.g.*, African Court of Human and Peoples' Rights, Beneficiaries of Late Norbert Zongo and Burkinabè Movement on Human and Peoples' Rights v. Burkina Faso, Judgment on Reparations, Application No. 013/2011 (June 5, 2015), para. 47.

[20] *E.g.*, Extraordinary Chambers in the Courts of Cambodia, Case 001, Appeal Judgment (Feb. 3, 2012), paras. 413, 649, 661, 675; Extraordinary African Chambers in the Senegalese Courts, Prosecutor v. Habré, Arrêt (Apr. 27, 2017), para. 611.

[21] *See, e.g.*, James Crawford, *The ILC's Articles on Responsibility of States for Internationally Wrongful Acts: A Retrospect*, 96 AMERICAN JOURNAL OF INTERNATIONAL LAW 874–890 (2002); THE LAW OF INTERNATIONAL RESPONSIBILITY (James Crawford et al., eds. 2010); Dinah Shelton, *Remedies and Reparations, in* GLOBAL JUSTICE, STATE DUTIES: THE EXTRATERRITORIAL SCOPE OF ECONOMIC, SOCIAL, AND CULTURAL RIGHTS IN INTERNATIONAL LAW 367–390 (Malcolm Langford et al. eds., 2013); HENCKAERTS & DOSWALD-BECK, *supra* note 17, at 530–550; Cedric Ryngaert, *Attributing Conduct in the Law of State Responsibility: Lessons from Dutch Courts Applying the Control Standard in the Context of International Military Operations*, 36 UTRECHT JOURNAL OF INTERNATIONAL AND EUROPEAN LAW 170, 171 (2021).

[22] *E.g.*, ICJ, Genocide Convention Case (Bosnia and Herzegovina v. Serbia and Montenegro), *supra* note 12, paras. 170, 173, 385, 398, 407, 414, 420, 431, 460.

findings of UN treaty human rights committees are not judgments, they are issued based on the mandate and powers of these bodies under UN human rights treaties that bind the respective states parties to the said treaties.[23]

Third, while the ARSIWA or the ICJ judgments primarily or originally correspond to or are related to inter-state relationships, the other legal sources considered herein concern state reparations for individual victims. Nonetheless, scholars have recognized that the reparation modalities and other general principles or elements contained in the ARSIWA are *mutatis mutandis* and to a greater or lesser extent applicable to reparations owned by states to individual victims.[24] In turn, there is increasing recognition that individual victims are or should be indeed the final or primary beneficiaries of reparations for (serious) violations of human rights in the inter-state proceedings at the ICJ although states are formally the beneficiaries of the said reparations.[25]

Finally, fragmentation and divergence trends are expected as a result of the diversification of international law; however, there are fundamental elements that underlie reparations (including non-compensatory reparations) such as the violation of an international law rule, the existence of harm, as well as the need for a causal link between the said violation and the harm inflicted.[26] Supranational bodies, including UN organs, arguably to varying degrees have followed convergent trends when dealing with reparations in contexts or cases of atrocities.[27] In contrast, (excessively) compartmentalized developments are not fully coherent with the effective realization of the right to claim and receive reparations held by victims of gross violations of human rights.[28] Reparations are post-violence or post-conflict justice mechanisms,[29] and holistic approaches to reparations (including non-compensatory reparations) are indeed advisable.[30] The construction of a general international law of reparations, including non-compensatory reparations, for victims of gross

---

[23] *See for further discussion, e.g.,* Helen Keller & Geir Ulfstein, UN Human Rights Treaty Bodies Law and Legitimacy (2012); Navanethem Pillay, Strengthening the United Nations Human Rights Treaty Body System, A Report by the United Nations High Commissioner for Human Rights (June 2012).

[24] *See, e.g.,* Julio Rojas-Baez, *La Jurisprudencia de la Corte Interamericana de Derechos Humanos en Materia de Reparaciones y los Criterios del Proyecto de Artículos sobre Responsabilidad del Estado por Hecho Internacionalmente Ilícitos*, 23 American University International Law Review, 91–126 (2007); Brigitte Stern, *The Obligation to Make Reparation, in* Crawford et al., *supra* note 21, at 567; Crawford et al., *supra* note 21, at 725–788; Shelton, *supra* note 21, at 367–390; Henckaerts & Doswald-Beck, *supra* note 17, at 537–549; Shelton, *supra* note 4, at 37; Van Boven, *supra* note 4, at 20–24.

[25] *See, e.g.,* Separate Opinion of Judge Cançado Trindade, *supra* note 18, paras. 41–101; Separate Opinion of Judge Yusuf, *supra* note 18, paras. 37–46.

[26] *See, e.g.,* Shelton, *supra* note 4, at 22–103; Shuichi Furuya, *The Right to Reparation for Victims of Armed Conflict: The Intertwined Development of Substantive and Procedural Aspects, in* Reparation for Victims of Armed Conflict 1, 55–59 (Cristian Correa et al., 2020).

[27] *See* Bassiouni, *supra* note 4, at 640–650.

[28] *See id.,* at 577.

[29] *See* Giuliana Ziccardi Capaldo, *Challenges and Prospects for Global Law: Reconsidering the World's Conflicts and Post-Conflict Justice. The Legal Thought of Cherif Bassiouni and Other Scholars,* 10 Global Community YILJ (Giuliana Ziccardi Capaldo General ed.) 929, 934, 936–937 (2012).

[30] *See id.,* at 937; Cherif Bassiouni, *Assessing Conflict Outcomes, in* The Pursuit of International Criminal Justice: A World Study on Conflicts, Victimization, and Post-Conflict Justice 1, 5–6 (Cherif Bassiouni ed., 2010).

violations of human rights involves and includes "cross-judging,"[31] "cross-citation,"[32] "cross-pollination,"[33] or "cross-fertilization"[34] among UN bodies. As Higgins soundly remarks, coherence should be pursued in the international legal order to protect "core predictability that is essential if law is to perform its functions in society."[35] States, individuals, and even international organizations can thus adopt informed choices, take courses of action, and have disputes settled with respect for the rule of law.[36]

All of this arguably suggests and requires increasing efforts towards the development of a coherent international law of non-compensatory reparations across UN bodies. Certainly, careful attention needs to be drawn to the specific and different nature and mandate of each UN body that deals with reparations for victims of gross human rights violations within a concrete legal and institutional context and framework. Mechanical or automatic legal transplants should hence be avoided. Indeed, authors have highlighted that it is important to take into account institutional differences or better justify cross-fertilization in the context of reparations for victims of atrocities.[37]

III. RESTITUTION

Restitution conceptually consists of "measures that seek to re-establish the victim's *status quo ante*,"[38] and "take from the wrongdoer that to which the victim is entitled and restore it to the victim."[39] Restitution includes restoration of rights such as liberty and citizenship, restitution of property, and reinstatement of job.[40] Restitution may be the preferred reparatory remedy in international law.[41] Nevertheless, restitution may be unfeasible for a number of human rights violations and, in these cases, other reparation modalities are granted as a substitute.[42]

Under the ARSIWA (Article 35), restitution seeks to re-establish the situation as it existed before the wrongful act if this is materially possible and proportional to benefits deriving from restitution rather than compensation. The ILC's Commentaries on its Draft Articles on Crimes against Humanity illustratively list the return of property, the return of victims to their homes, and the reconstruction of public or private buildings such as

---

[31] Ruti Teitel & Robert Howse, *Cross-Judging: Tribunalization in a Fragmented but Interconnected Global Order*, 41 NEW YORK UNIVERSITY JOURNAL OF INTERNATIONAL LAW AND POLICY 959–990 (2009).

[32] Mads Andenas & Johan Leiss, *The Systemic Relevance of "Judicial Decisions" in Article 38 of the ICJ Statute*, 77 HEIDELBERG JOURNAL OF INTERNATIONAL LAW 907, 913 (2017).

[33] Philip Moremen, *National Court Decisions As State Practice: A Transnational Judicial Dialogue?*, 32 NORTH CAROLINA JOURNAL OF INTERNATIONAL LAW AND COMMERCIAL REGULATION 259, 261 (2006).

[34] JEAN D'ASPREMONT, FORMALISM AND THE SOURCES OF INTERNATIONAL LAW 205 (2011).

[35] ROSALYN HIGGINS, PROBLEMS AND PROCESS: INTERNATIONAL LAW AND HOW WE USE IT 50 (1994).

[36] PHILIPPA WEBB, INTERNATIONAL JUDICIAL INTEGRATION AND FRAGMENTATION 5 (2013).

[37] *E.g.*, DIANA ODIER CONTRERAS-GARDUNO, COLLECTIVE REPARATIONS: TENSIONS AND DILEMMAS BETWEEN COLLECTIVE REPARATIONS WITH THE INDIVIDUAL RIGHT TO RECEIVE REPARATIONS 317–318 (2018); Annika Jones, *Insights into an Emerging Relationship: Use of Human Rights Jurisprudence at the International Criminal Court*, 16 HUMAN RIGHTS LAW REVIEW 701, 728–729 (2016).

[38] De Greiff, *supra* note 4, at 452. *See also* Lucas Grossman, *Principle 34: Scope of the Right to Reparation, in* THE UNITED NATIONS PRINCIPLES TO COMBAT IMPUNITY: A COMMENTARY 369, 371 (Frank Haldemann & Thomas Unger eds., 2018).

[39] Shelton, *supra* note 4, at 298.

[40] De Greiff, *supra* note 4, at 452.

[41] Shelton, *supra* note 4, at 298.

[42] *Id.*; Grossman, *supra* note 38, at 371.

schools, hospitals, and religious sites.[43] Such measures are *mutatis mutandis* partially similar to examples from the ARSIWA Commentaries.[44] This arguably shows the applicability of the ARSIWA as *lex generalis* on reparations but subject to some necessary adaptations to the specific field of reparations for victims of gross violations of human rights.

In turn, UN Reparation Principle 19 establishes that restitution "should, whenever possible, restore the victim to the original situation before the gross violations." Illustratively, Principle 19 mentions: "restoration of liberty, enjoyment of human rights, identity, family life and citizenship, return to one's place of residence, restoration of employment and return of property." This evidences that, to redress harm resulting from gross atrocities properly, restitution cannot be limited only to property restitution but also should include more comprehensive measures. The TJR Special Rapporteur has recognized that reparations go beyond compensation, including restitution if possible.[45] Such an approach once again shows that the concept of reparations is (much) broader than compensation and may include restitution provided that it is feasible.

Regarding UN human rights treaties, the wording of Article 14 of the Convention against Torture and Other Cruel, Inhuman or Degrading Treatment or Punishment is narrow because it refers to "compensation" and "rehabilitation" rather than the broader concept of reparations. However, the CAT has correctly approached reparation modalities comprehensively. Under its practice, reparation modalities to redress damages suffered by victims also include other non-compensatory reparations such as restitution.[46] More recent UN legal sources have adopted the wording and reparation modalities included in the UN Reparation Principles. Thus, the International Convention for the Protection of All Persons from Enforced Disappearance explicitly lists restitution (Article 24(5)(a)).

Concerning the ICJ's jurisprudence, the ICJ in *Wall Opinion* found that Israel is obliged "to return the land, orchards, olive groves and other immovable property seized from any natural or legal person for purposes of construction of the wall in the Occupied Palestinian Territory."[47] The ICJ added that, should restitution be materially impossible, Israel shall compensate those individuals affected for damages suffered.[48] By following up on the ICJ's *Wall Opinion*, the UN General Assembly adopted the resolution "Establishment of the United Nations Register of Damage Caused by the Construction of the Wall in the Occupied Palestinian Territory," recognizing the need for accurate documentation of damages caused by the construction of the wall to fulfil "the obligation to make the abovementioned reparations, including restitution and compensation."[49] This shows avenues to make reparative processes move forward via coordination between UN judicial and UN non-judicial organs. The follow-up to *Wall Opinion* also demonstrates that the UN General Assembly may mobilize resources for reparation implementation albeit the non-binding nature of its recommendations.[50]

---

[43] ILC, *supra* note 8, at 108.

[44] ILC, *supra* note 5, at 97.

[45] TJR Special Rapporteur, *Report: Apologies for Gross Human Rights Violations and Serious Violations of International Humanitarian Law*, UN Doc. A/74/147 (July 12, 2019), para. 29.

[46] CAT, Guridi v. Spain, Views, UN Doc. CAT/C/34/D/212/2002 (May 24, 2005), para. 6.8.

[47] ICJ, Wall Opinion, *supra* note 11, para. 153.

[48] *Id.*

[49] UNGA, UN Doc. A/RES/ES-10/17 (Jan. 24, 2007), Preamble.

[50] Conor McCarthy, *Reparation for Gross Violations of Human Rights Law and International Humanitarian Law at the International Court of Justice*, in Ferstman et al., *supra* note 4, at 374.

Moreover, *Wall Opinion* is arguably an important example of the increasing practice that recognizes that individuals (and not only states) are beneficiaries of reparations to redress harm stemming from serious abuses committed during occupation or armed conflicts. Unlike international human rights law, international humanitarian law traditionally did not recognize individuals as (primary) holders of the right to reparations.[51] Nevertheless, both practice[52] and scholars[53] have increasingly recognized that victims of grave violations of international humanitarian law can also claim and benefit from reparations, including restitution.

IV. REHABILITATION

Rehabilitation conceptually "refers to measures that provide social, medical, and psychological care, as well as legal services."[54] Rehabilitation addresses abuse and trauma, "dealing with grief and anger, as well as rehabilitation of physical injury."[55] Rehabilitation is a process of restoring health and reputation after an "'on physical or mental integrity"[56] and empowers victims to "move past their pain."[57] Reinserting victims as full members of society is a clear goal of rehabilitation.[58] Rehabilitation may have restorative effects and prevent further deterioration.[59] Occupational therapy, surgery, and physiotherapy exemplify rehabilitation.[60]

The ARSIWA contain no explicit reference to rehabilitation as a reparation modality. The state-centric approach followed in the ARSIWA may explain this gap. However, the ILC's Commentaries on its Draft Articles on Crimes Against Humanity have soundly

---

[51] *See* Hague Convention IV of 1907 respecting the Laws and Customs of War on Land, art. 3; and Protocol Additional to the Geneva Conventions of 1949 and relating to the Protection of Victims of International Armed Conflicts of 1977, art. 91. *See also, e.g.,* HENCKAERTS & DOSWALD-BECK, *supra* note 17, at 537–549; CORREA ET AL., *supra* note 26; anonymized reference.

[52] For example, at the ICC, victims of *inter alia* war crimes, i.e., serious violations of international humanitarian law, have claimed reparations. *See* ICC, Prosecutor v. Lubanga, Case No. ICC-01/04-01/06-3129-AnxA, Appeals Chamber, Order for Reparations (Mar. 3, 2015); ICC, Prosecutor v. Katanga, Case No. ICC-01/04-01/07-3728-tENG, Trial Chamber II, Order for Reparations (Mar. 24, 2017); ICC, Prosecutor v. Al Mahdi, Case No. ICC-01/12-01/15-236, Trial Chamber VIII, Reparations Order (Aug. 17, 2017); ICC, Prosecutor v. Ntaganda, Case No. ICC-01/04-02/06-2659, Trial Chamber VI, Reparations Order (Mar. 8, 2021). *See also* ICRC, *supra* note 17, Practice Relating to Rule 150; HENCKAERTS & DOSWALD-BECK, *supra* note 17, at 537–550.

[53] *See generally, e.g.,* Furuya, *supra* note 26, at 16–91; CHRISTINE EVANS, THE RIGHT TO REPARATION IN INTERNATIONAL LAW FOR VICTIMS OF ARMED CONFLICT (2012); Paola Gaeta, *Are Victims of Serious Violations of International Humanitarian Law Entitled to Compensation?, in* INTERNATIONAL HUMANITARIAN LAW AND INTERNATIONAL HUMAN RIGHTS LAW 305–327 (Orna Ben-Naftali ed., 2011); Clara Sandoval, *International Human Rights Adjudication, Subsidiarity, and Reparation for Victims of Armed Conflicts, in* Correa et al., *supra* note 26, at 179–264; MARCO SASSÒLI, INTERNATIONAL HUMANITARIAN LAW 91–98 (2019); EMILY CRAWFORD & ALISON PERT, INTERNATIONAL HUMANITARIAN LAW 289–290 (2d ed. 2020); anonymized reference.

[54] De Greiff, *supra* note 4, at 452. *See also* Bassiouni, *supra* note 4, at 270; Van Boven, *supra* note 4, at 36.

[55] SHELTON, *supra* note 4, at 394.

[56] *Id.*

[57] Bassiouni, *supra* note 4, at 270.

[58] Grossman, *supra* note 38, at 373.

[59] SHELTON, *supra* note 4, at 394.

[60] *Id.*

established that rehabilitation programmes may be required, including medical treatment, prosthetic limbs, and trauma-focused therapy.[61]

Furthermore, UN General Assembly Resolutions on gross violations of human rights have listed and fleshed out rehabilitation. Under UN Reparation Principle 21, "[r]ehabilitation should include medical and psychological care as well as legal and social services." Indeed, the UN General Assembly stressed that victims of torture and other mistreatments should receive appropriate social and medical rehabilitation and urged states to develop rehabilitation centres.[62] Concerning the elimination of rape and other forms of sexual violence, the UN General Assembly has also urged states to provide "victims with access to appropriate healthcare, including sexual and reproductive health care, psychological care and trauma counselling, as well as to rehabilitation, social reintegration."[63] As the TJR Special Rapporteur actually determined, gender perspectives are necessary concerning reparations.[64]

As for UN human rights treaties, there is no explicit reference to rehabilitation (or other reparation modalities) in the ICCPR. Nevertheless, the HRC has continuously determined that the right to a remedy (ICCPR, Article 2(3)(a)) includes rehabilitation.[65] Importantly, under Article 14 of the CAT, victims' right to redress includes "as full rehabilitation as possible." Former CAT member Sørensen often referred to moral, monetary, and medical rehabilitation, namely, the obligation to redress under Article 14 is not confined to compensation but it must include mental, physical, and social rehabilitation.[66] Indeed, the CAT has defined rehabilitation comprehensively:

> [...] rehabilitation [...] should be holistic and include medical and psychological care as well as legal and social services. Rehabilitation [...] refers to the restoration of function or the acquisition of new skills required as a result of the changed circumstances of a victim [...] Rehabilitation for victims should aim to restore [...] their independence, physical, mental, social and vocational ability; and full inclusion and participation in society.[67]

The CAT has continuously confirmed that compensation is insufficient regarding atrocities such as torture[68] and that redress must include rehabilitation.[69] Furthermore, it

---

[61] ILC, *supra* note 8, at 108.

[62] UNGA, *Torture and other Cruel, Inhuman or Degrading Treatment or Punishment*, UN Doc. A/RES/60/148 (Feb. 21, 2006), para. 9.

[63] UNGA, *Eliminating Rape and other Forms of Sexual Violence in all Their Manifestations, Including in Conflict and Related Situations*, UN Doc. A/RES/62/134 (Feb. 7, 2008), para. 1(c).

[64] TJR Special Rapporteur, *Report. The Gender Perspective in Transitional Justice Processes*, UN Doc. A/75/174 (July 17, 2020).

[65] *E.g.*, HRC, Kazantis v. Cyprus, Decision, UN Doc. CCPR/C/78/D/972/2001 (Sept. 19, 2003), para. 6.6; HRC, *supra* note 6, para. 16.

[66] *See* CAT, *3rd Session (13 November 1989–24 November 1989)*, UN Doc. CAT/C/SR.36 (Nov. 21, 1989), para. 21. *See also* Elizabeth McArthur & Manfred Nowak, The United Nations Convention Against Torture: A Commentary 464 (2008).

[67] CAT, *General Comment 3: Convention against Torture and other Cruel, Inhuman or Degrading Treatment or Punishment*, UN Doc. CAT/C/GC/3 (Nov. 19, 2012), para. 11.

[68] *E.g.*, CAT, Guridi v. Spain, *supra* note 46, para. 8; CAT, Ndagijimana v. Burundi, Views, UN Doc. CAT/C/62/D/496/2012 (Nov. 30, 2017), para. 8.7.

[69] *E.g.*, CAT, Aarrass v. Morocco, Decision, UN Doc. CAT/C/68/D/817/2017 (Nov. 25, 2019), para. 8.6.

has pointed out the right of victims of torture, including sexual violence, to rehabilitation.[70] It has also requested states to set up all-round care and support programmes, including treatment of trauma and other rehabilitation measures, for victims and to provide adequate resources to guarantee their functioning.[71] State programmes should grant full physical, psychological, and social rehabilitation and the Committee asks states to give information on these programmes.[72] The UN Voluntary Fund for Victims of Torture, established via the UN General Assembly's resolution, seeks to heal the physical and psychological consequences of torture on victims through projects implemented by civil society organizations.[73] Precisely, the CAT has welcomed both contributions to this fund and support of existing national rehabilitation centres.[74]

Under Article 24(5)(b) of the Convention against Enforced Disappearances, whose wording follows the UN Reparation Principles, rehabilitation is a reparation modality. This is a good example of how binding international treaty provisions can codify contents already contained in resolutions and, thus, arguably rehabilitation (and other reparation modalities) can be enhanced in practice. Actually, the UN Committee against Enforced Disappearances (CED) has applied this article in individual cases, urging states to provide rehabilitation for victims of the said heinous abuse.[75]

As for the ICJ, it has yet to order rehabilitation. Nevertheless, Judge Cançado Trindade in his Separate Opinions to the *Diallo* compensation judgment and a reparation-related order in *Armed Activities on the Territory of the Congo* powerfully invoked the need for awarding rehabilitation and other non-compensatory reparations (alongside compensation) because individuals are properly speaking the ultimate subjects and beneficiaries of reparations in cases concerning human rights violations although reparations are formally due to states at the ICJ.[76] In another order related to the reparations stage in *Armed Activities on the Territory of the Congo*, Judge Cançado Trindade explicitly stated that the virtual impossibility of providing *restitutio in integrum* in cases of mass atrocities requires the use of "not only compensation and satisfaction, but also rehabilitation of the victims (medical and social services), apologies (as satisfaction), guarantees of non-repetition of the grave breaches."[77] Judge Yusuf in the reparation judgment in *Armed Activities on the Territory of the Congo* indeed criticized the ICJ's narrow approach in this case by stating *inter alia* that the judgment lacks consideration of "the communities, collectivities and individuals who have directly suffered as a result of the wrongful acts of Uganda" and that the Court could have ordered "a wide range of forms of reparation [. . .] without necessarily altering the

---

[70] E.g., CAT, *Conclusions and recommendations. Bosnia and Herzegovina*, UN Doc. CAT/C/BIH/CO/1 (Dec. 15, 2005), paras. 10(d) and (e).

[71] E.g., CAT, *Conclusions and recommendations. Sri Lanka*, UN Doc. CAT/C/LKA/CO/2 (Dec. 15, 2005), para. 16.

[72] E.g., CAT, *Conclusions and recommendations. Venezuela*, UN Doc. CAT/C/CR/29/2 (Dec. 23, 2002), para. 11(c); CAT, *Conclusions and recommendations. Hungary*, UN Doc. CAT/C/HUN/CO/4 (Feb. 6, 2007), para. 17. *See also* MCARTHUR AND NOWAK, *supra* note 66, at 468.

[73] Board of Trustees of the UN Voluntary Fund for Victims of Torture, *Mission Statement* (Mar. 2014).

[74] MCARTHUR & NOWAK, *supra* note 66, at 468–469.

[75] E.g., CED, Estela Deolinda Yrusta and Alejandra del Valle Yrusta v. Argentina, Views, UN Doc. CED/C/10/D/1/2013 (Apr. 12, 2016), para. 12(d).

[76] ICJ, Separate Opinion of Judge Cançado Trindade, *supra* note 18, paras. 41–101; ICJ, Armed Activities on the Territory of the Congo (Democratic Republic of the Congo v. Uganda), Order, 2020 ICJ REPORTS 272, Separate Opinion of Judge Cançado Trindade (Sept. 8, 2020), paras. 7 and 9.

[77] ICJ, Armed Activities on the Territory of the Congo (Democratic Republic of the Congo v. Uganda), Order, 2016 ICJ REPORTS 1137, Separate Opinion of Judge Cançado Trindade (Dec. 6, 2016), para. 9.

interstate nature of the proceedings. They include individual and collective reparations, compensation, rehabilitation and non-pecuniary satisfaction."[78] Therefore, human beings rather than states should primarily benefit from reparations (including rehabilitation) in ICJ inter-state litigation cases concerning atrocities.

V. SATISFACTION

Satisfaction and guarantees of non-repetition may be considered to be "symbolic" reparations.[79] Scholars recognize that satisfaction and guarantees of non-repetition are especially broad categories and that drawing a line between the two is not easy.[80] For example, a judicial decision punishing the offenders constitutes a satisfaction measure *but also* aims that the perpetrator will not commit the same violation.[81] These overlaps and/or close relationship are indeed present in the TJR Special Rapporteur's mandate. Despite some intersection, authors have generally accepted that these reparation modalities can be conceptually approached as autonomous categories.[82] Overall, satisfaction includes a wide variety of measures that range from "aiming at cessation of violations to truth seeking, the search for the disappeared, the recovery and the reburial of remains, public apologies, judicial and administrative sanctions, commemoration, human rights training."[83] Satisfaction measures such as apologies correspond to "moral" reparations.[84]

Article 37(1) of the ARSIWA establishes that states are obligated to "give satisfaction for the injury caused by that act insofar as it cannot be made good by restitution or compensation." Such wording suggests that satisfaction would be merely a subsidiary or secondary reparation modality. Under Article 37(2)/(3), satisfaction may include "an acknowledgement of the breach, an expression of regret, a formal apology," and satisfaction should not be disproportional to the injury.

Unlike the ARSIWA,[85] later UN legal sources have not considered satisfaction merely as an exceptional or subsidiary reparation modality, particularly concerning gross violations of human rights. This is an important development considering that victims of atrocities (may) regard satisfaction measures as important as the other reparation modalities. Thus, the UN Reparation Principles appropriately contain no "hierarchy" of reparation modalities in which satisfaction is merely subsidiary. Principle 22 illustratively lists these measures: (i) cease violations; (ii) verify facts and disclose the truth; (iii) search for the disappeared and recover bodies; (iv) issue decisions restoring victims' rights; (v) give public apologies, including factual acknowledgement and acceptance of responsibility; (vi) sanction perpetrators; and (vii) organize commemorations and tributes to victims. Whether some of these measures are exclusively satisfaction or may also correspond to guarantees of non-repetition can be discussed. Thus, while the TJR Special Rapporteur has examined

---

[78] ICJ, Separate opinion of Judge Yusuf, *supra* note 18, para. 43.

[79] EVA DWERTMANN, THE REPARATION SYSTEM OF THE INTERNATIONAL CRIMINAL COURT: ITS IMPLEMENTATION, POSSIBILITIES AND LIMITATIONS 150–159 (2010); SHELTON, *supra* note 4, at 382.

[80] De Greiff, *supra* note 4, at 452; SHELTON, *supra* note 4, at 397.

[81] SHELTON, *supra* note 4, at 397.

[82] Bassiouni, *supra* note 4, at 270–274; De Greiff, *supra* note 4, at 452; SHELTON, *supra* note 4, at 397; Van Boven, *supra* note 4, at 36–37.

[83] Van Boven, *supra* note 4, at 36.

[84] Christian Tomuschat, *Reparation for Victims of Grave Human Rights Violations*, 10 TULANE JOURNAL OF INTERNATIONAL & COMPARATIVE LAW 157, 174 (2002); SHELTON, *supra* note 4, at 399.

[85] ILC, *supra* note 5, at 105, para. 1.

memorialization as both satisfaction and guarantees of non-recurrence,[86] the Rapporteur has approached apologies as satisfaction.[87]

Importantly, the ILC's Commentaries on its Draft Articles on Crimes against Humanity clearly determined that satisfaction may be a desirable reparation form, including apology or regret statements.[88] Such an approach arguably updates the ILC's more traditional or state-centric perspective adopted in the ARSIWA where satisfaction was partially relegated.

In turn, the HRC has under the ICCPR (Article 2(3)) found that states are obligated to provide victims with an appropriate and effective remedy, including: information on the burial place of a person's child or return of victim's remains to his/her family;[89] investigation of victim's claims of ill-treatment;[90] as well as independent investigations and appropriate actions against those guilty.[91] Furthermore, it found that reparations may include "satisfaction, such as public apologies, public memorials" and that "[c]essation of an ongoing violation is an essential element of the right to an effective remedy."[92] These measures are consistent with other UN legal sources.

Although the CAT contains no explicit reference to satisfaction, the CAT has considered satisfaction measures. Thus, the CAT has urged states to ensure that perpetrators "are appropriately punished" and that victims receive full redress as well as to inform victims "of all steps taken in response to the views expressed."[93] Moreover, it has referred to several examples of satisfaction measures,[94] which follow those listed in the UN Reparation Principles.

UN Principle on Impunity 34 refers to satisfaction as a reparation modality and it is worth noting that this principle provides specific contents related to forced disappearances, namely, the direct victim's family is entitled to "be informed of the fate and/or whereabouts of the disappeared person and, in the event of decease, that person's body must be returned to the family." Moreover, Article 24(5)(c) of the Convention against Enforced Disappearance lists: "Satisfaction, including restoration of dignity and reputation." By closely following the wording of the UN Reparation Principles, this is indeed the first UN human rights treaty that explicitly includes satisfaction as a reparation modality.

As for the ICJ's jurisprudence, the ICJ in *Wall Opinion* emphasized that Israel must guarantee the Palestinian people their freedom of access to the Holy Places that came under its control after the 1967 Arab-Israeli War[95] and remarked that Israel is obligated to end "the violation of its international obligations flowing from the construction of the wall in the Occupied Palestinian Territory."[96] By following its previous jurisprudence,[97] the ICJ added

---

[86] TJR Special Rapporteur, *Report. Memorialisation processes*, UN Doc. A/HRC/45/45 (July 9, 2020).

[87] TJR Special Rapporteur, *Report. Apologies for Gross Human Rights Violations and Serious Violations of International Humanitarian Law*, UN Doc. A/74/147 (July 12, 2019).

[88] ILC, *supra* note 8, at 108.

[89] *E.g.*, HRC, Khalilov v. Tajikistan, Views, UN Doc. CCPR/C/83/D/973/2001 (Mar. 30, 2005), para. 9; HRC, Braih v. Algeria, Views, UN Doc. CCPR/C/128/D/2924/2016 (Mar. 27, 2020), para. 8.

[90] *E.g.*, HRC, Kouidis v. Greece, Views, UN Doc. CCPR/C/86/D/1070/2002 (Mar. 28, 2006), para. 9.

[91] *E.g.*, HRC, Benitez Gamarra v. Paraguay, Views, UN Doc. CCPR/C/104/D/1829/2008 (May 30, 2012), para. 7.5; HRC, Braih v. Algeria, *supra* note 89, para. 8.

[92] HRC, *supra* note 6, para. 16.

[93] CAT, Guridi v. Spain, *supra* note 46, para. 8.

[94] CAT, *supra* note 67, para. 16.

[95] ICJ, Wall Opinion, *supra* note 11, para. 149.

[96] *Id.*, para. 150.

[97] *E.g.*, ICJ, Military and Paramilitary Activities in and against Nicaragua (Nicaragua v. United States of America), Merits, Judgment, 1986 ICJ Reports 14 (June 27, 1986), at 145.

that "the obligation of a State responsible for an internationally wrongful act to put an end to that act is well established in general international law."[98] To cease these violations, it concluded that Israel has to, among other measures, cease forthwith the construction of the wall in the Occupied Palestinian Territory, and dismantle forthwith those parts of the structure located within the Occupied Palestinian Territory.[99] Overall, these findings are *mutatis mutandis* similar to some measures listed as "satisfaction" in UN Principle Reparation 22 as adapted to the specific factual and legal circumstances surrounding *Wall Opinion*. However, their implementation is severely limited by the fact that, *inter alia*, this is an ICJ's advisory opinion rather than an ICJ's binding judgment.

Conversely, the ICJ rendered a binding judgment in the *Genocide Convention Case (Bosnia and Herzegovina v. Serbia and Montenegro)* in which it provided some satisfaction as a reparation modality. Although the ICJ rejected compensation claims, it granted satisfaction,[100] particularly, when it established that the respondent state "failed to comply with the obligation imposed by the Convention to prevent [. . .] genocide."[101] By quoting its jurisprudence,[102] the ICJ correctly found that a declaration of this type is "in itself appropriate satisfaction,"[103] and it introduced such declaration in the operative clause of its judgment.[104] The ICJ determined that the respondent state has to meet its obligation to punish under the Genocide Convention, namely, transfer individuals accused of genocide to the International Criminal Tribunal for the former Yugoslavia (ICTY), especially concerning General Ratko Mladic.[105] He was later transferred to and convicted at the ICTY.

Nevertheless, the ICJ's denial of ordering compensation in the *Genocide Convention Case* can overall be criticized from victim-centred perspectives, especially the victims' right to comprehensive reparations and not only symbolic reparations, particularly in cases of genocide. Other authors have similarly criticized the ICJ for not having ordered broader reparations against Serbia and Montenegro in favour of Bosnia and Herzegovina.[106] Yet the *Genocide Convention Case* shows that the process of effectively granting and implementing non-compensatory reparations may require and be achieved via synergetic actions by more than one UN organ (e.g., the ICJ and the ICTY). Having said so, not all satisfaction requests have been successful. The ICJ in the *Genocide Convention Case (Croatia v. Serbia)* found no Serbia's internationally wrongful act concerning the Genocide Convention and, hence, rejected Croatia's reparation requests, including measures that would constitute satisfaction such as ordering Serbia to punish perpetrators of genocide committed in Croatia.[107]

In *Armed Activities on the Territory of the Congo*, the ICJ however missed an extremely important opportunity to construe jurisprudence on non-compensatory reparations,

---

[98] ICJ, Wall Opinion, *supra* note 11, para. 150.

[99] *Id.*, para. 151.

[100] ICJ, Genocide Convention Case (Bosnia and Herzegovina v. Serbia and Montenegro), *supra* note 12, paras. 462–463.

[101] *Id.*, para. 463.

[102] ICJ, Corfu Channel Case (United Kingdom v. Albania), Merits, Judgment, 1949 ICJ Reports 4 (Apr. 9, 1949), at 35–36.

[103] ICJ, Genocide Convention Case (Bosnia and Herzegovina v. Serbia and Montenegro), *supra* note 12, para. 463.

[104] *Id.*, para. 470.

[105] *Id.*, para. 465.

[106] McCarthy, *supra* note 50, at 364.

[107] ICJ, Application of the Convention on the Prevention and Punishment of the Crime of Genocide (Croatia v. Serbia), Judgment, 2015 ICJ Reports 3 (Feb. 3, 2015), paras. 520–521.

including satisfaction measures. Certain compensation-related aspects of the ICJ's reparation judgment in the said case have been criticized by commentators.[108] Nevertheless, there has been no similar level of critical remarks about the ICJ's (almost) exclusive focus on compensation at the expense of the Democratic Republic of Congo's satisfaction requests that included criminal investigation and prosecution of officers and soldiers of the Uganda People's Defence Force and the payment of US$25 million to establish a fund to promote reconciliation.[109] The ICJ found that it does not need to order any additional specific satisfaction measure relating to criminal investigations or prosecutions since Uganda is already required to investigate and prosecute under its treaty international humanitarian law obligations (Geneva Conventions and Additional Protocol I to the Geneva Conventions).[110] The ICJ also rejected the request about the payment of US$25 million to establish a reconciliation fund since, in the Court's understanding, "the material damage caused by the ethnic conflicts in Ituri is already covered by the compensation awarded for damage to persons and to property."[111] In agreement with the Separate Opinion of Judge Yusuf[112] and in the light of the previously examined UN legal sources, the ICJ's narrow approach to reparations that excluded all requests for satisfaction measures request is criticized herein.

VI. GUARANTEES OF NON-REPETITION

Guarantees of non-repetition correspond to broad structural measures of a policy nature, including institutional reforms.[113] These aim "at civilian control over military and security forces, strengthening judicial independence, the protection of human rights defenders, the promotion of human rights standards in public service, law enforcement, the media, industry, and psychological and social services."[114] States must undertake guarantees of non-repetition "to prevent human rights violations from recurring."[115] According to the TJR Special Rapporteur, these guarantees can be "satisfied by a broad variety of measures," including reparations, and they are preventive in nature.[116] The TJR Special Rapporteur's mandate soundly does not confine these guarantees to reparations only. However, guarantees of non-repetition are approached herein as a reparations modality as done by other authors,[117] and most UN practice examined in the following paragraphs.

Under the ARSIWA (Article 30(b)), a state responsible for an internationally wrongful act has "to offer appropriate assurances and guarantees of non-repetition." As the ILC

---

[108] *See* Diane Desierto, *The International Court of Justice's 2022 Reparations Judgment in DRC v. Uganda: "Global Sums" as the New Device for Human Rights-Based Inter-State Disputes*, EJIL TALK! (Feb. 14, 2022), <https://www.ejiltalk.org/the-international-court-of-justices-2022-reparations-judgment-in-drc-v-uganda-a-new-methodology-for-human-rights-in-inter-state-disputes/> (last visited May 26, 2021); Ori Pomson, *The ICJ's Armed Activities Reparations Judgment: A Brave New World?*, ARTICLES OF WAR (Feb. 16, 2022), <https://lieber.westpoint.edu/icj-armed-activities-reparations-judgment/> (last visited May 26, 2021).

[109] ICJ, Armed Activities on the Territory of the Congo, *supra* note 14, para. 385.

[110] *Id.*, para. 390.

[111] *Id.*, para. 391.

[112] Separate Opinion of Judge Yusuf, *supra* note 18, para. 43.

[113] Van Boven, *supra* note 4, at 36.

[114] *Id.*

[115] Alexander Mayer-Rieckh & Roger Duthie, *Principle 35: General Principles*, *in* Haldemann & Unger, *supra* note 38, at 386.

[116] TJR Rapporteur, *Report. Guarantees on Non-recurrence*, UN Doc. A/HRC/30/42 (Sept. 7, 2015), paras. 23–24.

[117] De Greiff, *supra* note 4, at 452; Bassiouni *supra* note 4, at 270; Van Boven, *supra* note 4, at 36–37.

recognized, although there may be some overlap between satisfaction and guarantees of non-repetition in practice, these two non-compensatory reparation modalities are better treated independently.[118] The ILC has actually been consistent in this approach for decades. Thus, the ILC's Commentaries on its Draft Articles on Crimes against Humanity refer to assurances or guarantees of non-repetition as an autonomous reparation modality.[119]

Similar to satisfaction, UN Reparation Principles 23 illustratively lists guarantees of non-repetition measures, "which will also contribute to prevention," including: (i) civilian control of military and security forces; (ii) fair and impartial civilian and military proceedings; (iii) independent judiciary; (iv) protection of rights defenders, lawyers, healthcare professionals, and journalists; (v) human rights and humanitarian law education; (vi) adoption of ethical and conduct international standards; (vii) prevention, monitoring, and resolution of social conflicts; and (viii) revision and reformulation of laws contributing to or allowing atrocities. Hence, this list of guarantees of non-repetition is arguably the broadest and lengthiest among similar catalogues in the UN sources examined.

In turn, the HRC has stated that the fight against corruption is necessary to properly implement Article 2 of the ICCPR, including the right to an effective remedy (Article 2(3)).[120] Such finding arguably illustrates the broad scope of guarantees of non-repetition, which goes beyond reparative dimensions, by connecting two pressing issues: corruption and reparation implementation. The HRC has found that, to combat impunity, states should disqualify perpetrators of serious human rights violations from public office and conduct justice and truth inquiry processes.[121] Moreover, it emphasized that the failure to investigate and bring to justice offenders may importantly contribute to "the recurrence of the violations."[122] Under Article 2(3) of the ICCPR, the HRC in individual cases has determined that states parties to the ICCPR have "to prevent similar violations in the future,"[123] which speaks volumes about the potential preventive aspect of reparations.

Under Article 2(1) of the CAT, which establishes that states parties shall take effective measures to prevent torture, the CAT has found that "the absence of appropriate punishment," including pardons granted to civil guards, which in practice allowed "torture to go unpunished [...] encouraging its repetition," is incompatible with the obligation to prevent torture.[124] In turn, the CED has ordered states to adopt "all necessary measures to enforce the guarantees of non-repetition stipulated in article 24(5)(d) of the Convention."[125] As the CED further clarified, this includes "compiling and maintaining registers that meet the requirements of the Convention and to ensure that the relevant information is accessible to all persons with a legitimate interest therein."[126]

---

[118] ILC, *supra* note 5, p. 90, para. 11.

[119] ILC, *supra* note 8, at 108.

[120] *E.g.*, HRC, *Concluding Observations. Macedonia*, UN Doc. CCPR/C/MKD/CO/2 (Apr. 17, 2008), para. 8; HRC, *Concluding Observations. Chad*, UN Doc. CCPR/C/TCD/CO/1 (Aug. 11, 2009), para. 11; HRC, *Concluding Observations. Turkmenistan*, UN Doc. CCPR/C/TKM/CO/1/Add.1 (Apr. 19, 2012), para. 13. *See also* SARAH JOSEPH & MELISSA CASTAN, THE INTERNATIONAL COVENANT ON CIVIL AND POLITICAL RIGHTS. CASES, MATERIALS, AND COMMENTARY 868 (2013).

[121] *E.g.*, HRC, *Concluding Observations. Brazil*, UN Doc. CCPR/C/BRA/CO/2 (Dec. 1, 2005), para. 18; HRC, *Concluding Observations. Spain*, UN Doc. CCPR/C/ESP/CO/5 (Jan. 5, 2009), para. 9.

[122] HRC, *supra* note 6, para. 18.

[123] HRC, Khalilov v. Tajikistan, *supra* note 89, para. 9.

[124] CAT, Guridi v. Spain, *supra* note 46, para. 6.6.

[125] CED, Yrusta and del Valle Yrusta v. Argentina, *supra* note 75, para. 12.

[126] *Id.*

According to Principle 35 of the UN Principles on Impunity, "[s]tates shall ensure that victims do not again have to endure violations of their rights" and states must adopt institutional reforms and other measures to respect the rule of law and human rights, as well as restore public trust in government institutions. Furthermore, Principle 35 establishes that institutional reforms to prevent the recurrence of violations should be conducted via public consultation, including victim participation. Principles 35–38 list examples of guarantees of non-recurrence, including legislative and administrative reform of state institutions, disbandment of parastatal armed forces, demobilization and social reintegration of children, as well as legal or institutional reform. These measures are largely similar to guarantees of non-repetition under the UN Reparation Principles. This is important to keep consistency across UN legal sources, which should *inter alia* help adopt more convergent approaches to guarantees of non-repetition as well as certainty when victims claim reparations at different fora and later during reparation implementation.

Concerning the ICJ's jurisprudence, the ICJ found in *Wall Opinion* that "legislative and regulatory acts adopted with a view to its construction [wall construction], and to the establishment of its associated regime, must forthwith be repealed or rendered ineffective."[127] Such finding fits into the measures listed as guarantees of non-repetition in the UN Reparation Principles.

In turn, Bosnia and Herzegovina (applicant) in the *Genocide Convention Case* requested the ICJ to decide that "Serbia and Montenegro shall provide specific guarantees and assurances that it will not repeat the wrongful acts complained of."[128] However, the ICJ rejected this. First, regarding Bosnia and Herzegovina's allegations of (back then) recent events that allegedly caused concern about whether pro-genocide movements in Serbia and Montenegro have disappeared, the ICJ found that such "indications do not constitute sufficient grounds for requiring guarantees of non-repetition."[129] Second, the ICJ also dismissed non-compliance with provisional measures by Serbia and Montenegro because it was part of state responsibility rather than reparations.[130] The Court found that it was sufficient the declaration concerning Serbia and Montenegro's obligation to transfer persons accused of genocide to the ICTY to comply with the state's Genocide Convention obligations.[131] Thus, the ICJ did "not consider that this is a case in which a direction for guarantees of non-repetition would be appropriate."[132] From a victim-centred approach, the ICJ should have deepened its discussion of the guarantees of non-repetition requested, especially considering the seriousness of the international crime in question (genocide).

Interestingly enough, guarantees of non-repetition as a reparation measure were not as such or explicitly requested by the Democratic Republic of Congo in *Armed Activities on the Territory of the Congo*, which determined that the ICJ could not directly adjudicate over them. Nevertheless, the ICJ could and should have *obiter dicta* referred to them due to the large-scale and cyclical context of mass atrocities in the region. Indeed, ICJ Judges Cançado Trindade[133] and Yusuf[134] in respectively their separate opinions in a reparation-related order

---

[127] ICJ, Wall Opinion, *supra* note 11, para. 151.

[128] ICJ, Genocide Convention Case (Bosnia and Herzegovina v. Serbia and Montenegro), *supra* note 12, para. 466.

[129] *Id.*

[130] *Id.*

[131] *Id.*

[132] *Id.*

[133] *See* Separate Opinion of Judge Cançado Trindade, *supra* note 77, para. 9.

[134] *See* Separate Opinion of Judge Yusuf, *supra* note 18, para. 43.

and the reparation judgment in the same case have referred to the need for granting not only compensation but also, *inter alia*, guarantees of non-repetition in order to (more) appropriately, effectively, and proportionally redress the harm in cases of gross violations of human rights and international humanitarian law.

VII. CONCLUSION

Non-compensatory reparation modalities, namely, restitution, rehabilitation, satisfaction, and guarantees of non-repetition, have been to a greater or lesser extent invoked, developed, and/or granted in UN legal sources, particularly concerning gross violations of human rights. While some earlier UN legal sources did not explicitly include or only partially included non-compensatory reparations, more recent UN instruments and practice of UN bodies have increasingly recognized non-compensatory remedies and fleshed out the contents thereof.

Thus, this piece has shown that diverse UN legal sources have continuously and increasingly recognized the need for reparation modalities that go well beyond compensation in contexts of atrocities. Reparation awards and reparation programmes for victims of gross violations of human rights should not rely exclusively or mainly on a single reparation modality (traditionally compensation) and/or exclude one or more reparation modalities. The ICJ's future reparation awards should increasingly, where applicable, render all reparation modalities, particularly in cases of gross violations of human rights. Thus, the ICJ's reparation award in *Armed Activities on the Territory of the Congo* should be criticized as the ICJ only focused on compensation, dismissed the Democratic Republic of Congo's explicit satisfaction requests, and did not discuss (at least *obiter dicta*) the other reparation modalities. Due to the nature and scale of violations in this case and similar cases of mass atrocities, reparations indeed should have been or should be (more) substantial,[135] importantly including non-compensatory reparations.

There may be some overlaps between non-compensatory reparations, particularly, between satisfaction and guarantees of non-repetition. However, these conceptually and in practice arguably constitute independent reparation modalities. Alongside compensation, non-compensatory reparations "are not mutually exclusive."[136] Especially in cases of gross abuses, reparation awards and programmes should ideally combine material, rehabilitative, and symbolic or moral elements to fully redress the harm inflicted on victims of atrocities. In turn, victims themselves generally request reparations that include non-compensatory remedies to address different dimensions and types of harm arising from serious abuses.

Non-compensatory reparation modalities alongside compensation are interdependent and, where applicable, their combined provision in reparation awards and programmes would result in comprehensive, adequate, and effective redress as UN Reparation Principle 15 indicates and authors have remarked.[137] Thus, UN instruments and the practice of UN organs should continue and increase their combined use of or approach to these reparatory remedies in contexts of gross violations of human rights. This certainly requires that states fulfil their obligations to deal with *inter alia* challenges and limitations present during reparation implementation. Moreover, for instance, the Security Council can make recommendations or even order compliance of ICJ's reparation awards in cases of atrocities under a reasonable interpretation of Article 94(2) of the UN Charter (concerning the

---

[135] McCarthy, *supra* note 50, at 369.

[136] Van Boven, *supra* note 4, at 37.

[137] *E.g.*, Grossman, *supra* note 38, at 377.

compliance of ICJ's judgments), and the UN General Assembly can mobilize resources for award implementation.[138] Last but not least, gender and intersectionality approaches should be incorporated when reparations are granted and implemented.[139]

Therefore, the UN legal sources examined herein to varying degrees provide an important normative framework to be adapted and applied if and when reparation awards or reparation programmes are designed, rendered, and/or implemented by national and/or international judicial, quasi-judicial, and non-judicial bodies and policymakers in ongoing scenarios of mass atrocities in *inter alia* Syria, Yemen, Myanmar (affecting the Rohingya people), and Ukraine. For instance, the fact that the scale of damages stemming from international crimes/serious violations of human rights and international humanitarian law committed by Russian armed forces against Ukrainians (and Ukraine) is staggering (totalling over US$100 billion as of May 2022 according to some estimations)[140] requires comprehensive and coordinated reparation awards and programmes that combine compensation with non-compensatory reparation measures to redress harm inflicted on victims of gross abuses in an effective, prompt, and proportional manner.

---

[138] *See* McCarthy, *supra* note 50, at 369–370, 374.

[139] TJR Special Rapporteur, *supra* note 64, para. 40.

[140] *See, e.g.*, Ashish Valentine, *Here's How Much It Could Cost to Rebuild Ukraine—And Who Would Pay for It*, NATIONAL PUBLIC RADIO (May 26, 2022), at <https://www.npr.org/2022/05/26/1100501433/heres-how-much-it-could-cost-to-rebuild-ukraine-and-who-would-pay-for-it> (last visited May 26, 2022).

IN FOCUS—GLOBAL POLICIES AND LAW

Protecting Heritage

Weighing Politics and Law

BY THOMAS G. WEISS*

Abstract

Some observers claim that it is necessary to prioritize either the protection of vulnerable populations or the tangible cultural heritage that sustains them; but there is no need because the two are inseparable. The moment is propitious because the international political disputes about when and where to intervene in specific crises to protect tangible heritage are less fraught than those to protect people. Moreover, protecting heritage is visible on the international public policy agenda; it is no longer a "niche topic," the exclusive domain of cultural specialists. This chapter begins with the relevance of responsibility to protect (R2P) for the protection of cultural heritage. It continues with the value of inserting politics into what has been largely a legal conversation for over a century. The third section explores the possible "force multiplier" resulting from the use of heritage protection as a routine part of the peaceful resolution of disputes and of the mandates for outside military forces.

I. INTRODUCTION

Shortly after the Islamic State of Iraq and the Levant (ISIL, or sometimes ISIS or Da'esh) captured the city of Palmyra in summer 2015, they exploded the two-thousand-year-old Temple of Baalshamin. For international audiences, the destruction was logically and visibly linked to the group's ongoing murder, human trafficking, slavery, and terror in Syria and

---

* Presidential Professor of Political Science at the CUNY Graduate Center; Distinguished Fellow, Global Governance, at the Chicago Council on Global Affairs; and Eminent Scholar, Kyung Hee University, Korea. He was Co-chair of the Cultural Heritage at Risk Project of the J. Paul Getty Trust, Past Andrew Carnegie Fellow and president of the International Studies Association and recipient of its "Distinguished IO Scholar Award," chair of the Academic Council on the UN System, editor of *Global Governance*, and Research Director of the International Commission on Intervention and State Sovereignty.

Thomas G. Weiss, *Protecting Heritage* In: *The Global Community Yearbook of International Law and Jurisprudence 2022*. Edited by: Giuliana Ziccardi Capaldo, Oxford University Press. © Oxford University Press 2023. DOI: 10.1093/oso/9780197752265.003.0011

Iraq. That same link was clear earlier when mass atrocities also accompanied the destruction of cultural heritage when insurgents deliberately shelled the Mostar Bridge in 1993, destroyed the fabled mosques, mausoleums, and libraries of Timbuktu in 2012, as well as when the Taliban dynamited the sixth-century Bamiyan Buddhas in 2001.

Russia's illegal war of choice in Ukraine is the most recent illustration. It has produced thousands of deaths and an unprecedented crisis of forced displacement of a quarter of its prewar population (some 7 million refugees and perhaps twice that number of internally displaced). Along with indiscriminate attacks on civilians, schools, and hospitals, there is ample evidence to justify an investigation by the International Criminal Court of Vladimir Putin's war crimes. Following requests from some 40 member states, the ICC's Chief Prosecutor Karim Khan announced in March 2022 that he would investigate possible war crimes committed in Ukraine. The evidence has increased dramatically since then.

Can anything be done? An affirmative response is suggested by the history of the International Commission on Intervention and State Sovereignty (ICISS), a remarkable human rights achievement despite its contested application and nonapplication—e.g., in Libya but not in Syria, Myanmar, and Ukraine.[1] The resulting responsibility to protect (R2P) doctrine rests on ethical, political, legal, and operational foundations. Heightened attention in academic and public discourse to the demands of coming to the rescue of people now also characterizes the challenge of protecting cultural heritage as it intersects with mass atrocities.[2]

In fact, the intimate link between attacking bricks and blood provides a means to unite the dual tasks of protecting heritage and humans because the international political disputes about when and where to intervene in specific crises to protect people do not characterize the protection of cultural heritage, or at least are considerably less fraught.[3] Rogue attackers—such nonstate thugs as ISIS, pariah states as Taliban Afghanistan, and major powers as China—are immediate targets for widespread external opprobrium. Ubiquitous if not quite universal international condemnation erupts rather than endless debates about whether interested outsiders are neo-colonialists or cosmopolitan saviors.

Could reframing intervention to protect heritage make it easier to reach consensus about robust international action that also would protect the people whose culture is under siege? That question animated a J. Paul Getty Trust research project and a 2022 edited volume, *Cultural Heritage and Mass Atrocities*.[4] The destruction of cultural heritage

---

[1] ICISS, THE RESPONSIBILITY TO PROTECT: REPORT OF THE INTERNATIONAL COMMISSION ON INTERVENTION AND STATE SOVEREIGNTY (2001); and THE RESPONSIBILITY TO PROTECT: RESEARCH, BIBLIOGRAPHY, BACKGROUND (Thomas G. Weiss & Don Hubert eds., 2001). Truth in packaging: the author was the ICISS research director; *see* THOMAS G. WEISS, HUMANITARIAN INTERVENTION: IDEAS IN ACTION (3d ed. 2016).

[2] Thomas G. Weiss & Nina Connelly, *Cultural Cleansing and Mass Atrocities: Protecting Heritage in Armed Conflicts*, 1 J. PAUL GETTY TRUST OCCASIONAL PAPERS IN CULTURAL HERITAGE POLICY (2017); and James Cuno & Thomas G. Weiss eds., *Cultural Heritage under Siege: Laying the Foundation for a Legal and Political Framework to Protect Cultural Heritage at Risk in Zones of Armed Conflict*, 4 J. PAUL GETTY TRUST OCCASIONAL PAPERS IN CULTURAL HERITAGE POLICY (2020).

[3] Parts of this argument appeared in abbreviated form in: Thomas G. Weiss, *Moving beyond R2P: Protecting Heritage and Humans, Items: Insights from the Social Sciences* (from the Social Sciences Research Council) (Feb. 2022), available at https://items.ssrc.org/where-heritage-meets-violence/moving-beyond-r2p/; and *Finessing R2P with an International Peace Force to Protect Heritage and Humans*, in GLOBAL GOVERNANCE AND INTERNATIONAL COOPERATION: MANAGING GLOBAL CATASTROPHIC RISKS IN THE 21ST CENTURY (Augusto Claro-Lopez ed., 2023).

[4] CULTURAL HERITAGE AND MASS ATROCITIES (James Cuno & Thomas G. Weiss eds., 2022).

amidst violence and atrocities is a continuing plague—Hitler's Germany, Mao's Cultural Revolution, Soviet pogroms, and Pol Pot's killing fields provided some of the twentieth century's worst images until the post–Cold War era's manifestations of death, displacement, and cultural wastelands.

Despite the current political doldrums, there is a bit of good news. Because of the public's awareness and shock about the destruction of such visible sites as the Bamiyan Buddhas, Mostar Bridge, Palmyra, Sana'a, and Timbuktu, nearly universal international revulsion and outrage erupted in January 2020 when Donald Trump mindlessly threatened to target fifty-two Iranian cultural sites when Tehran menaced retaliation for the assassination of Maj. Gen. Qassim Suleimani. While he later retracted the menace—following pressure from, among others, the Department of Defense—Trump's initial statement drew attention to the role of cultural heritage in times of political and military turmoil.

Protecting heritage thus has become visible on the international public policy agenda. It is no longer a "niche topic," the exclusive domain of cultural specialists. It is linked to the rescue of individuals caught in the crosshairs of violence, invariably menaced by mass atrocities. Indeed, for those of us who analyze politics and design responses, including military ones, it is noteworthy that insiders at the North Atlantic Treaty Organization (NATO) speak of the "security-heritage nexus."[5]

It is essential that analyses consider not only visible World Heritage sites recognized by the UN Educational, Cultural and Scientific Organization (UNESCO) but also less well-known, everyday structures—Uyghur mud-brick temples in China, Christian village cemeteries in Iraq, or local Rohingya mosques in Myanmar, and Russia's campaign since 2014 to eliminate Tatar traces in occupied Crimea. It has compiled a seemingly ever-growing list that as 2023 dawned counted over 230 sites that had been damaged or destroyed since Moscow's invasion began on 24 February 2022. These commonplace sites have become a daily bill-of-fare of destruction, which reflects the accompanying onslaught against the people whose heritage is demolished, as part of efforts to murder histories along with human beings.

This chapter begins with the relevance of the R2P norm for the protection of cultural heritage. It continues with the value of inserting politics into what, for over a century, has been largely a legal conversation. The third section explores the possible "force multiplier" resulting from the use of heritage protection as a routine part of the peaceful resolution of disputes and of the mandates for outside military forces—the logic being not only ethical but strategic and tactical as well.

II. MOVING BEYOND R2P, THE POLITICS OF NORMATIVE ADVANCE

Can anything be done to counter the immoral, illegal, wanton attacks on heritage? Progress is possible on the normative and policy fronts to attenuate the deliberate destruction of sites—what former UNESCO director-general Irina Bokova aptly called "cultural cleansing."[6]

---

[5] Claire Finkelstein, Derek Gilman, & Frederik Rosén, *Introduction*, *in* THE PRESERVATION OF HERITAGE IN TIMES OF WAR (Claire Finkelstein, Derek Gilman & Frederik Rosén eds., 2022).

[6] She first used the term in December 2014 in UNESCO, HERITAGE AND CULTURAL DIVERSITY AT RISK IN IRAQ AND SYRIA (2014).

While some observers see competition between bricks and blood,[7] the two are intertwined—indeed, inseparable. While academics struggle to parse atrocities versus heritage, most publics view the images of heritage destruction accompanied by mass murder, forced displacement, rape, ethnic cleaning, sterilization, human trafficking, slavery, and terrorism. They almost always occur in tandem. This is not a new reality. Drawing upon the nineteenth-century German poet Heinrich Heine, the drafter of the 1948 Convention on the Prevention and Punishment of the Crime of Genocide Raphael Lemkin noted, "Burning books is not the same as burning bodies . . . but when one intervenes . . . against mass destruction of churches and books one arrives just in time to prevent the burning of bodies."[8]

While governments and citizens loudly deplore such devastation, they do too little to protect it; indeed, not only do they have other domestic and foreign policy priorities, but also they see little that they can do. Yet modest collective steps could constitute a plausible contribution to a "shift from defending and preserving multilateralism to strengthening and renewing it."[9]

We should recall that a similar reaction—resignation and throwing up diplomatic hands in despair along with the weeping and gnashing of humanitarian teeth—also initially characterized fledgling efforts to conceptualize action against those who murdered and abused civilians in the civil wars of the 1990s. That is, until humanitarian interventions were followed by the ICISS's 2001 report, *The Responsibility to Protect.* The commission's Cochair Gareth Evans correctly calculated the norm's progress to date as "a blink of the eye in the history of ideas."[10] R2P has advanced from the passionate prose of an eminent group toward being a mainstay of international public policy debates, even if follow-up actions remain inconsistent. Edward Luck, the first special advisor to the UN Secretary-General on R2P, reminded us that the lifespan of successful norms is "measured in centuries, not decades."[11] R2P is embedded in the values of international society and, occasionally, also in specific policies and responses to mass atrocities.

Linking the protection of people and their heritage, a journalist working at the interface, Hugh Eakin, noted: "While the United Nations has adopted the 'responsibility to protect' [R2P] doctrine, to allow for international intervention to stop imminent crimes of war or genocide, no such parallel principle has been introduced for cultural heritage."[12] Yet the argument here is that we do not need another principle because of the intimate link between protecting heritage as well as vulnerable populations. Attacks on culture invariably accompany genocide, war crimes, crimes against humanity, and ethnic cleansing—the mass atrocities that the United Nations' 2005 World Summit already agreed should trigger an R2P response.[13]

---

[7] Helen Frowe & Derek Matravers, *Conflict and Cultural Heritage: A Moral Analysis of the Challenges of Heritage Protection,* 3 J. PAUL GETTY TRUST OCCASIONAL PAPERS IN CULTURAL HERITAGE POLICY (2019).

[8] Quoted in ROBERT BEVAN, THE DESTRUCTION OF MEMORY: ARCHITECTURE AT WAR 15 (2d ed. 2016).

[9] RICHARD PONZIO ET AL., BEYOND UN75: A ROADMAP FOR INCLUSIVE, NETWORKED & EFFECTIVE GLOBAL GOVERNANCE 9 (2021).

[10] GARETH EVANS, THE RESPONSIBILITY TO PROTECT: ENDING MASS ATROCITY CRIMES ONCE AND FOR ALL 28 (2009).

[11] Edward C. Luck, *The Responsibility to Protect: The First Decade,* 3(4) GLOBAL RESPONSIBILITY TO PROTECT 387 (2011).

[12] Hugh Eakin, *Use Force to Stop ISIS' Destruction of Art and History,* NEW YORK TIMES, Apr. 3, 2015.

[13] UN, 2005 World Summit Outcome, General Assembly Resolution 60/1, Oct. 24, 2005, paras. 138–140.

The most obvious costs associated with the attacks on cultural heritage and the people sustained by it are borne directly by vulnerable populations. Costs can be measured in lost lives and livelihoods, reduced longevity, infant stunting. In terms of cultural heritage, the destruction of tangible and intangible heritage sounds an alarm bell for a forthcoming genocide or ethnic cleansing—*Kristallnacht* in 1938 is perhaps the best known example of a pattern. Curators and archivists are custodians of cultural heritage who recognize the warning signals; indeed, many have died while attempting to save it in the face of violent attacks.

There are two reasons behind R2P's analytical, ethical, and operational pertinence for cultural heritage. The first is the logic of ICISS's original three-part framework. While it differs from the one now more widely applied in UN circles, namely, former Secretary-General Ban Ki-moon's three pillars,[14] the original concept is more appropriate for this arena. Cultural specialists apply the same three concepts—to prevent, to react, and to rebuild—for tangible cultural heritage. There is an imperative to prevent destruction but when that fails, it is necessary to react; when both of those fail, as is too often the case, it is essential to rebuild. The second reason is that the major constraint facing international preparedness and reactions to protect heritage often is the same as vulnerable civilians: sacrosanct state sovereignty.

While normative advances do not guarantee action, they are an essential prerequisite for moving beyond ad hoc, inconsistent, local, and short-term responses toward more systematic, global, rules-based, predictable, and coordinated ones. R2P's normative journey is pertinent because it reflected an altered political reality: Suddenly, it was no longer taboo to discuss how best to halt mass atrocities. State sovereignty was no longer absolute but rather conditional on a modicum of respect for life.

Although when and where to invoke R2P remains contested, few commentators suggest that it is completely flawed for organizing global conversations and responses to mass atrocities. Instead, discourse now revolves is less about whether and more about how. Robust action does not necessarily follow, but the language and logic have changed. R2P occupies a prominent spot in mainstream policy debates. For instance, the UN Security Council has invoked it in eighty-six resolutions (along with four presidential statements) and the Human Rights Council in sixty-six resolutions. The UN General Assembly's consideration of the norm in May 2021 was indicative: 115 for and 15 against (28 abstentions).[15]

Efforts to protect immovable cultural heritage amidst mass atrocities is at the beginning of a comparable normative and political journey—although the law is more advanced as seen later in this chapter. In the best case, the protection of tangible cultural heritage could elicit enhanced international attention, growing consensus, and more vigorous policies in a changing political landscape; perhaps action could occasionally follow as well. Similarities exist between today's political environment for protecting cultural heritage and the 1990s, when states were searching for a rationale after doing too little too late in Rwanda and, some but not I argued, too much too soon in Kosovo. In short, destruction of immovable cultural heritage accompanied by state and nonstate atrocities is not new, but today's better-informed politics may be propitious for normative and policy advances.

It is useful to recall that the responsibility to react includes sanctions, international criminal pursuit, and military intervention; this trio of options is pertinent because the first two have been applied in reaction to the Russian invasion of Ukraine, even if outside

---

[14] For more on the three pillars, *see* Ban Ki-moon, *Implementing the Responsibility to Protect, Report of the Secretary-General*, UN Doc. A/63/677, Jan. 12, 2009.

[15] For up-to-date tallies, *see* the Global Centre for the Responsibility to Protect.

military intervention, although not massive military assistance, is off the table. Less intrusive should always be pursued before more intrusive options. Hence, military force should be deployed in rare cases of profound humanitarian distress and, by extension, significant attacks on immovable cultural heritage—for itself and as a precursor for the mass atrocities that often follow. As indicated, in 2005 UN member states enumerated four triggers: "genocide, war crimes, ethnic cleansing and crimes against humanity." As with just war theory, precautionary R2P principles (right intention, last resort, proportional means, and reasonable prospects) should also govern international reactions to the destruction of cultural heritage.

The link between protecting people and their cultures is intimate, whether one stresses the intrinsic or extrinsic value of immovable heritage. Cosmopolitans emphasize the former as humanity benefits from all specific manifestations of culture and suffers from their disappearance. Humanitarians emphasize the extrinsic value because those who commit mass atrocities understand that the annihilation of heritage is a prelude to or an integral part of targeting people. For military tacticians and strategists too, protecting people and culture are inseparable although not always part of standard operating procedures (SOPs). Moreover, there is no need for any hierarchy; the choice between bricks and blood is false, as is a choice between people and their environment. Air, water, and culture are essential for life.

III. POLITICS, NOT LAW, IS THE PROBLEM

Politics provides a clearer lens than the law through which to examine cultural heritage even though public international law is very developed in this arena. Bokova's "cultural cleansing" resonates because, like "ethnic cleansing," it is not a legal construct; but both have political traction. Like former US Supreme Court Justice Potter Stewart's definition of pornography, we know cultural and ethnic cleansing when we see them.

That said, it is helpful to keep in mind the legal conventions deposited at UNESCO, which have garnered a large number of state signatories: the 1954 Hague Convention for the Protection of Cultural Property in the Event of Armed Conflict; the 1970 Convention on the Means of Prohibiting and Preventing the Illicit Import, Export and Transfer of Ownership of Cultural Property; and the 1972 Convention Concerning the Protection of the World Cultural and Natural Heritage.[16] Their common feature is the "value" or "importance" of heritage as the criterion to determine the status as cultural "property" or "heritage." A growing preference, certainly mine, is to use the latter label because "heritage" stresses stewardship and trusteeship for tangible heritage with a universal value rather than the accidents of current deeds or contemporary national borders. The 1972 definition outlines the "outstanding universal value" of an artifact or site that elevates it to protected status; the 1954 definition implies the same by pointing to "the cultural heritage of every people." The shared human value of immovable and movable tangible cultural heritage in these two conventions is not limited to those who have inherited it directly or indirectly, those living within the contemporary boundaries of states. The 1954 and 1972 conventions thus both stand in stark contrast with the state-centric 1970 one that makes "cultural property" contingent upon that designation by a state, which stresses self-interested judgments by current owners not more objective evaluations by stewards for humanity.

---

[16] http://whc.unesco.org/en/conventiontext/.

This body of heritage law is to be viewed side-by-side with substantial body of international humanitarian law (IHL) and international human rights law. All remain essential elements of international society, of course; but a broader, deeper, and more adequate policy agenda must encompass other disciplines, perspectives, and orientations in addition to legal tenets.

Although they are sometimes dismissed as academic toys,[17] counterfactuals focus the mind—here, to explore an especially intriguing "what if?" Thus, it is worth parsing the politics behind the decision *not* to include the protection of heritage in arguably the strictest of international laws, the 1948 Genocide Convention. What if the Polish lawyer Raphael Lemkin's inclusion of vandalism had not been omitted from the 1948 Genocide Convention that he had helped to draft? Would cultural heritage have fared better in the ongoing tragedies in Syria, Yemen, Myanmar, Xinjiang, and Ukraine as well as earlier in Afghanistan, Iraq, Sri Lanka, the Balkans, and Mali?

Scholars have paid only fleeting attention to this emphasis in Lemkin's work—the relevance not only of biological *but also* of cultural genocide.[18] The negotiators of the 1948 Convention eliminated the latter. The politics of that time were a converse of today's: the reluctance about R2P in parts of the Global South versus the enthusiasm of the Global North.[19] At that time, the opposition to "vandalism" in the convention came from colonial powers (Belgium, Denmark, France, Netherlands, and United Kingdom) and settler countries (the United States, Canada, Brazil, Australia, and New Zealand) fearing condemnation for their crimes against Indigenous populations. Ironically, enthusiasm for the inclusion of cultural genocide came from independent developing countries and colonies about to become independent, some of which now label R2P as a Trojan Horse for Western imperialism.

Public international law, here as elsewhere, is not standing in the way of action. Rather, it is the absence of political will to enforce the provisions of the law. Gary Bass, in his history of humanitarian intervention, provides an appropriate summary: "We are all atrocitarians now—but so far only in words, and not yet in deeds."[20] The lack of enforcement is the largest deficit in global governance;[21] its absence renders immovable heritage especially vulnerable.

It is worth noting that none of the ten distinguished international lawyers who contributed to the Getty's 2022 comprehensive collection suggested spending time and energy refining cultural heritage law.[22] A topic that has been dominated for over a century by the pursuit of better public international law should make room for the more pragmatic and strategic tasks of strengthening the emerging R2P norm as well as supporting

---

[17] COUNTERFACTUAL THOUGHT EXPERIMENTS IN WORLD POLITICS: LOGICAL, METHODOLOGICAL, AND PSYCHOLOGICAL PERSPECTIVES (Philip E. Tetlock & Aaron Belkin eds., 1996).

[18] RAPHAEL LEMKIN, ACTS CONSTITUTING A GENERAL (TRANSNATIONAL) DANGER CONSIDERED AS OFFENCES AGAINST THE LAW OF NATIONS (1933); and AXIS RULE IN OCCUPIED EUROPE: LAWS OF OCCUPATION, ANALYSIS OF GOVERNMENT, AND PROPOSALS FOR REDRESS xiii (1944).

[19] Edward C. Luck, *Cultural Genocide and the Protection of Cultural Heritage*, 2 J. PAUL GETTY TRUST OCCASIONAL PAPERS IN CULTURAL HERITAGE POLICY 23–27 (2018).

[20] GARY BASS, FREEDOM'S BATTLE: THE ORIGINS OF HUMANITARIAN INTERVENTION 382 (2008).

[21] THOMAS G. WEISS & RAMESH THAKUR, GLOBAL GOVERNANCE AND THE UN: AN UNFINISHED JOURNEY (2010).

[22] Patty Gerstenblith, Benjamin Charlier, Tural Mustafayev, Marc-André Renold, Allesandro Chechi, Francesco Francioni, Joseph Powderly, Sabine von Schormerler, Philippe Sands, and Ashrutha Rai in CULTURAL HERITAGE AND MASS ATROCITIES, *supra* note 4, at 367–478.

policies and actions for its implementation. They would include protecting cultural heritage and mobilizing the political will to enforce existing laws and enhance compliance with their tenets.

There are political mobilization tasks, of course, which are linked to the law—particularly, to increase the number of signatures and ratifications. An immediate priority is to encourage the 60 reticent or hostile member states—there are currently 133 states party—to ratify the 1954 Hague Convention for the Protection of Cultural Property in the Event of Armed Conflict and its First Protocol. In addition, the absence of three permanent members of the Security Council (China, Russia, and the United States) is an especial weakness for the Second Protocol, which has only 84 states party and is especially crucial for so many contemporary armed conflicts. This protocol strives to limit the broad interpretation of "imperative military necessity" and expands the convention's scope to cover civil wars and non-state parties, which have been the source of so much recent destruction.

Space does not permit the elaboration of political support for the law and building on recent precedents, but they are worth mentioning briefly. For instance, would it be worth pursuing Vladimir Putin's war crimes based on the International Criminal Court's first sentence for the war crime of attacking cultural heritage in the case of the *Prosecutor v. Ahmad Al Faqi Al Mahdi* and the wanton heritage destruction in Timbuktu? What exactly could be used from the Commission of Inquiry established by the UN Human Rights Council?

In moving away from the strict provisions of the law, could we build on the recent experience with transitional justice, a related but not strictly judicial action that has been pioneered in peacebuilding following atrocities and mass violations of human rights? Of pertinence here is France's decision to organize a Commission "Mémoires et Verité" (Memories and Truth Commission) regarding the country's role in the Algerian Civil War, as well as similar German and Belgian government efforts to document colonial atrocities.

So, human rights and R2P advocates should elevate not downgrade the destruction of tangible cultural heritage because it reliably foreshadows mass atrocities and, almost invariably, accompanies them. In brief, there are adequate international legal tools to protect such heritage should UN member states decide to do so. There also is evidence—most dramatically, the West's solidarity in the face of Russia's illegal war in Ukraine—that political will can be mobilized. That, of course, is not easy but requires addressing, among others, military issues that also are hard to finesse.

We need to understand better the range of conscience-shocking perpetrators, crimes, and incentives characterizing the interconnections between attacks on cultural heritage and on people, from bombings by nonstate actors to military strikes by internationally recognized governments. This task requires far better inter-disciplinary analyses and conversations than those of the past, which have been too narrowly legal.

IV. PROTECTING TANGIBLE HERITAGE CAN BE A FORCE MULTIPLIER FOR OUTSIDE MILITARY FORCES

While peacekeeping was not in the UN Charter, this "invention" of the world organization has long been viewed as a legitimate deployment of outside military forces under UN command and control. Continual adaptations have characterized the evolution of peace operations including, most pertinently for our purposes, the evolution of more robust operations (including, on occasion, Chapter VII enforcement) and more recently still the inclusion of the protection of Mali's cultural heritage as part of the mandate of the UN Multidimensional Integrated Stabilization Mission in Mali (MINUSMA). Thus far, this is the only such UN experiment, and that part of its mandate was eliminated after an initial two years. However, from the outset, NATO's Kosovo Force (KFOR) had, and continues to have, pertinent heritage-protection activities.[23]

Rather than being an after-thought, could heritage protection become a more essential component for peace operations and their SOPs—by the United Nations, by regional organizations, by hybrid forces? Rather than being a peripheral and occasional task, could such protection become central and routine?

With numerous competing claims for limited resources, commanders in the field and decision makers in political and military headquarters too often view such tasks as distractions. The argument here is different: they should be reframed as integral to protecting people and fostering peace processes. The value of heritage protection by international peace forces—including an independent one, a possibility that I discuss elsewhere[24]—could be justified by attenuating the most obvious direct human costs of attacks on cultural heritage. Vulnerable populations directly bear the direct burden: lost lives and livelihoods, forced displacement, reduced longevity, and misery. In terms of cultural heritage, protection by such a peace force could have a valuable preventive dimension. The destruction of tangible cultural heritage sounds an alarm about forthcoming mass atrocities—targeted destruction of people almost always comes next.

The brutal human costs are apparent; but conversations about heritage loss should incorporate a full range of consequences in considering why it is worth protecting, and how protection could be justified to politicians and publics in three ways. First, destruction is ruinous for cultural identity and social cohesion. The buildings, museums, cemeteries, libraries, and infrastructure around which societies organize themselves help define a culture and people. Second, destruction of high-profile tangible heritage impedes post-crisis recovery; the negative impact on the economics of post-conflict financing is essential but often downplayed.[25] With the loss of tourist attractions comes the concomitant loss of investment opportunities as well as the loss of employment related to care and upkeep, and revenue derived from tourism. Third, the destruction of heritage deepens a society's wounds and intensifies lingering animosities and the accounts eventually to be settled among belligerents after any negotiated end to armed conflict. Destroying cultural heritage complicates reconciliation and unravels the safety net of resilience supporting violence-torn communities. With this reality in mind, for instance, the 1995 Dayton Accords addressed specifically the reconstruction of lost heritage as an essential component of peace in the Balkans, a necessary prelude to and prerequisite for peacebuilding in the former Yugoslavia. That insight was crucial; the impact was significant. The inclusion of cultural heritage protection in NATO's follow-on to the subsequent Kosovo War suggests the importance of that lesson.

The protection of cultural heritage as a routine task in mandates for military peace operations should routinely include three tasks: removing hazards, suppressing looting, and deterring politically motivated attacks.[26] The first is the technical task of removing such immediate hazards as land mines and unexploded ordnance near heritage sites. After initial

---

[23] Frederik Rosén, NATO and Cultural Property: Embracing New Challenges in the Era of Identity Wars (2017).

[24] Thomas G. Weiss, *Finessing R2P with an International Peace Force to Protect Humans and Heritage, in* Global Governance and International Cooperation: Managing Global Catastrophic Risks in the 21st Century (Augusto Claro-Lopez ed., 2023)

[25] Graciana del Castillo, Obstacles to Peacebuilding (2017).

[26] This discussion uses the framework of Richard Gowan, *Peace Operations and the Protection of Cultural Heritage, in* Cultural Heritage and Mass Atrocities, *supra* note 4, at 534–547.

dismal performances in Iraq and Afghanistan, NATO forces in Afghanistan helped secure the area around the Bamiyan Buddhas as did MINUSMA in northern Mali. The latter also attempted to rectify some damage by launching short-term projects (QIPs, quick impact projects) to repair libraries and religious sites around Timbuktu. MINUSMA also provided logistical support to experts from UNESCO, who were surveying damage and planning reconstruction.

The second broad task for peace forces helping to protect tangible heritage would be the suppression of looting, a task that the Italian Carabinieri pioneered in 2003 in their area of operations while serving in the US-led occupation force in Iraq.[27] Through a mix of ground and helicopter patrols, the Italians disrupted looting at archaeological sites, an example not followed by other coalition forces.

The third task for military peace operations draws on the NATO efforts in Kosovo, which seek to deter and counter politically motivated attacks on cultural sites. In pursuing this protective task, KFOR initially set up static defense posts at prominent monasteries, then shifting towards mobile patrols as a less militarily intensive approach when security conditions permitted. Eventually, Kosovo police assumed these responsibilities. Following some two decades of deployment, Frederik Rosén argues that both tactically and strategically "destabilising issues related to CP [cultural property] remain one of the top three reasons for NATO to sustain the mission."[28]

Military intervention as an option for "blue helmets" within UN forces was a component of James Cuno's five-point proposal to protect cultural heritage in Syria and Iraq as well as to police borders to discourage the illegal export or import of movable artifacts.[29] UN peacekeepers face problems everywhere: intelligence; resources; doctrines and rules of engagement that shape and circumscribe activities; and the difficulty of sustaining complex operations for lengthy periods.[30] Most important for UN or other peacekeepers would be the requirement to contribute to longer-term efforts to protect heritage sites; tasks would include training the local military and police to assume direct protection as well as to support preservation and reconstruction and help improve the skills of heritage personnel. Training and technical projects are unlikely to succeed unless local political actors and populations buy into the overall need to protect heritage and own the effort.

How can heritage protection activities be considered a diversion for external military personnel? Often cavalierly dismissed as a "Christmas tree ornament," they improve relations with the local community, presumably an essential and central objective. Is this not valuable and sensible "mission creep"? If cultural heritage can be part of a "hybrid threat," can it not also constitute a "hybrid benefit"? Thus, rather than a bauble, a better question is, could heritage protection produce a "virtuous circle" and be a possible "force multiplier"? The key to protecting cultural heritage during and after armed conflicts and civil strife is political—indeed, it is impossible to disentangle heritage protection from the broader reasons that justify the deployment of outside military personnel as peacekeepers or peace-enforcers.

---

[27] John M. Russell, *Efforts to Protect Archaeological Sites and Monuments in Iraq, 2003–2004, in* CATASTROPHE! THE LOOTING AND DESTRUCTION OF IRAQ'S 36 (Geoff Emberling & Katharyn Hanson eds., 2008).

[28] FREDERIK ROSÉN, NATO AND CULTURAL PROPERTY: A HYBRID THREAT PERSPECTIVE 3 (2022).

[29] James Cuno, *The Responsibility to Protect the World's Cultural Heritage*, 23(1) BROWN JOURNAL OF WORLD AFFAIRS 106 (2016).

[30] Mathilde Leloup, *Heritage Protection as Stabilisation, the Emergence of a New "Mandated Task" for UN Peace Operations*," 26(4) INTERNATIONAL PEACEKEEPING : 408–430 (2019).

Beginning with the High-Level Independent Panel on Peace Operations (HIPPO), numerous UN documents looking to the future and gleaning lessons from the past prioritize that "politics must drive the design and implementation of peace operations."[31] Shortly before launching the 2018 "Action for Peacekeeping" (A4P) initiative, for example, Secretary-General António Guterres noted that "peace operations are deployed in support of active diplomatic efforts, not as a substitute."[32] As part of the need to ensure collective coherence in "political solutions," negotiators should provide incentives and prioritize the essential need for tangible heritage protection because arguably the most decisive factor in success is local buy-in. As such, it would make operational and ethical sense for future international military peace forces to incorporate the protection of tangible heritage as a routine component in SOPs—indeed, as part of a relatively low-cost sales-pitch for outside assistance when parliaments are facing budget requests. The logic is ethical, strategic, and tactical. The protection of tangible heritage helps win battles and wars as well as occupations. However, such protection matters even it were not helpful. As Scott Sagan argues: "We should follow the law because it reflects who we are, or at least who we aspire to be."[33]

V. CONCLUSION

The core R2P ethical framework is to halt mass murder and mass forced displacement; its emergence reflected an altered political reality. Although specific decisions about when and where to invoke R2P remain controversial, few observers question whether global responses to mass atrocities are justified. Instead, the debate centers on precisely how best to achieve R2P's lofty aims.

Because of the intersection between violent attacks on humans and their tangible cultural heritage, the protection of such heritage is not a distraction for proponents of the robust protection of people. There is no need to add another crime to the four mass atrocities agreed by the 2005 World Summit. Rather, protecting cultural heritage is a fundamental aspect of protecting people from genocide, war crimes, crimes against humanity, and ethnic cleansing. In addition, emphasizing such protection within the R2P framework has the potential to widen support for the evolving norm and its evolution in customary law as well as contribute to ongoing conversations about the attributes of legitimate sovereigns. Responsible states view mass atrocities as an international concern and not merely one of domestic jurisdiction; the destruction of tangible cultural heritage, whether movable or immovable, should be viewed similarly because of its universal value and the intimate links between attacks on cultural objects, structures, and monuments and attacks on vulnerable populations. Damage to Ukraine's cultural heritage, for instance, became a feature of the extraordinarily wide condemnation of Moscow's onslaught against Ukrainians.

While destroying cultural heritage is not new, neither is the impulse to protect and preserve it. There is a substantial body of law, but its implementation is feeble. Yet the contemporary convergence of two factors has altered the politics of protection and the feasibility of international action. First, the destruction of cultural heritage has riveted the attention not

---

[31] HIPPO, *Uniting Our Strengths for Peace—Politics, Partnership and People*, UN Doc. (June 16, 2015), available at https://peaceoperationsreview.org/wp-content/uploads/2015/08/HIPPO_Report_1_June_2 015.pdf.

[32] United Nations, *UN News* (Sept. 20, 2017), available at https://news.un.org/en/story/2017/09/565672-peace-operations-not-substitute-diplomatic-efforts-security-council-told.

[33] Scott D. Sagan, *From Kyoto to Baghdad to Tehran: Leadership, Law, and the Protection of Cultural Heritage, in* Cultural Heritage and Mass Atrocities, *supra* note 4, at 496.

only of curators, archaeologists, historians, and activists but also of major media outlets and popular audiences. Second, these new consumers find themselves in the company of a cottage industry of social scientists and military officers who have joined international lawyers in exploring R2P's application; indeed, in 2022 specially trained experts have become part of the US Army Reserve to save artifacts in war zones, a version 2.0 of Monuments Men and Women.[34]

It is worth repeating that there is no need to split hairs between safeguarding people and the cultural heritage that sustains them. The staffs from the Middle East Institute, the Asia Society, and the Antiquities Coalition evaluated the region's devastation and concluded: "The fight to protect the peoples of the region and their heritage cannot be separated."[35]

---

[34] Matt Stevens, *Officers Train to Protect Art Amid Wars*, NEW YORK TIMES, Aug. 12, 2022.

[35] Middle East Institute, Asia Society, and the Antiquities Coalition, *Culture under Threat: Recommendations for the U.S. Government* (Apr. 2016), available at http://www.academia.edu/30873427/Culture_Under_Threat_Recommendations_for_the_U.S_Governmet.

Appendix of the Part—Topics Covered in the Previous Issues (2008-2021)

*B*eginning with the 2008 issue, the Yearbook includes this part that aims to explore the emerging global policies (and the norms implementing them) in various sectors of public activity and their increasing importance in building a global law.

Our goal is to cover the majority of areas of public activity most affected by global policies and to group under various headings homogeneous contributions to give an overall picture of the development of global law.

Here are listed the topics covered in the issues 2008–2021, which we have attempted to group according to general subject matter.

- **Editor's Introduction:** Global Law and Policies. A Legal Approach to Political Changes, *Giuliana Ziccardi Capaldo*, 8 GLOBAL COMMUNITY YILJ 2008 (2009), at 3.

- **Global arbitration policies**
  Public and Private Authority in Transnational Dispute Resolution: International Trade and Investment Arbitration, *A. Claire Cutler*, 12 GLOBAL COMMUNITY YILJ 2012 (2013), at 31.

  PRIME Finance Arbitration—A Role Model for the Settlement of International Financial Disputes?, *Francesco Seatzu*, 13 GLOBAL COMMUNITY YILJ 2013 (2014), at 27.

- **Global corporate cultures**
  Managing Across Cultures in a Globalized World. Findings from a Systematic Literature Review, *Antonio Capaldo, Bice Della Piana & Alessandra Vecchi*, 11 GLOBAL COMMUNITY YILJ 2011 (2012), at 7.

- **Global criminal policy and justice systems**
  "I Think, Therefore I Am Guilty": Suppressing Speech and Hijacking History—The Case Against Criminalizing Hate Speech and Revisionism as Global Policy, *Steven W. Becker*, 9 GLOBAL COMMUNITY YILJ 2009 (2010), at 7.

Crímenes Internacionales, Jueces Estatales: De la Universalidad, las Inmunidades y Otras Soledades, *Antonio Remiro Brotóns*, 9 GLOBAL COMMUNITY YILJ 2009 (2010), at 43.

The Legal-Political Connotation of Material Support to Terrorism, *Geert-Jan Alexander Knoops*, 10 GLOBAL COMMUNITY YILJ 2010 (2011), at 53.

Crimes contre l'humanité, *Robert* Kolb, 14 GLOBAL COMMUNITY YILJ 2014 (2015), at 153.

Balancing Competing Interests and Values: Drone Strikes as National Policy but International Crime?, *Ramesh Thakur*, 15 GLOBAL COMMUNITY YILJ 2015 (2016), at 171.

- **Global environmental and energy policies**
Climate Law: Gap Between Normative Rhetoric and Politics, *Joyeeta Gupta*, 9 GLOBAL COMMUNITY YILJ 2009 (2010), at 127.

Towards the 2012 Rio Earth Summit and the Evolution of International Environmental Law in a Multi-Polar World, *Kishan Khoday*, 9 GLOBAL COMMUNITY YILJ 2009 (2010), at 143.

Sustainable Development as Freedom: On the Nature of International Law and Human Development, *Kishan Khoday & Usha Natarajan*, 10 GLOBAL COMMUNITY YILJ 2010 (2011), at 35.

The Global Governance of Energy and Development, *Gilles Carbonnier & Sijbren de Jong*, 11 GLOBAL COMMUNITY YILJ 2011 (2012), at 41.

Defending Nature: The Evolution of the International Legal Restriction of Military Ecocide, *Peter Hough*, 14 GLOBAL COMMUNITY YILJ 2014 (2015), at 137.

- **Global health policies**
Global Health Takes a Normative Turn: The Expanding Purview of International Health Law and Global Health Policy to Meet the Public Health Challenges of the 21st Century, *Benjamin Mason Meier*, 11 GLOBAL COMMUNITY YILJ 2011 (2012), at 69.

Globalization and Post–COVID-19 Public Health Order, *Guiguo Wang*, 20 GLOBAL COMMUNITY YILJ 2020 (2021), at 297.

- **Global intellectual property policy**
Global Intellectual Property Law and Policy, *Graham Dutfield & Uma Suthersanen*, 10 GLOBAL COMMUNITY YILJ 2010 (2011), at 7.

Responding to the Global Food Fraud Crisis: What Is the Role of Intellectual Property and Trade Law?, *Graham Dutfield & Uma Suthersanen*, 20 GLOBAL COMMUNITY YILJ 2020 (2021), at 271.

- **Global justice policies**
The Role of ICJ Procedure in the Emergence and Evolution of *Erga Omnes* Obligations, *Ravindra Pratap*, 19 GLOBAL COMMUNITY YILJ 2019 (2020), at 211.

- **Global maritime policy**
Le Règlement Obligatoire des Différends Relatifs au Droit de la Mer et la Pratique des Etats, *Philippe Gautier*, 9 GLOBAL COMMUNITY YILJ 2009 (2010), at 107.

- **Global migration politics**
Global Migration Governance: Beyond Coordination and Crises, *Nicholas R. Micinski & Thomas G. Weiss*, 17 GLOBAL COMMUNITY YILJ 2017 (2018), at 175.

 Illiberal *versus* Liberal State Branding and Public International Law: Denmark and the Approximation to Human(itarian) Rightlessness, *Anja Matwijkiw & Bronik Matwijkiw*, 18 GLOBAL COMMUNITY YILJ 2018 (2019), at 207.

 The UN Global Compact for Safe, Orderly and Regular Migration: What Does It Mean in International Law?, *Elspeth Guild & Raoul Wieland*, 19 GLOBAL COMMUNITY YILJ 2019 (2020), at 191.

- **Global nuclear policies**
From Pandemic to Apocalypse—Nuclear War as Terminal Disease, *Louis René Beres*, 20 GLOBAL COMMUNITY YILJ 2020 (2021), at 183.

 The Disruptor-in-Chief Wrecks the Nuclear Arms Control Architecture, *Ramesh Thakur*, 20 GLOBAL COMMUNITY YILJ 2020 (2021), at 235.

- **Global policies on human rights**
Global Importance of Human Rights for Environmental Protection, *Malgosia Fitzmaurice*, 9 GLOBAL COMMUNITY YILJ 2009 (2010), at 73.

 The Legal Status of Decisions by Human Rights Treaty Bodies: Authoritative Interpretations or *mission éducatrice*?,

 Leonardo Borlini & Luigi Crema, 19 GLOBAL COMMUNITY YILJ 2019 (2020), at 129.

- **Global politics and governance**
From Leadership to Organization: The Evolution of Global Politics, *George Modelski*, 8 GLOBAL COMMUNITY YILJ 2008 (2009), at 43.

 Framing Global Governance, Five Gaps, *Ramesh Thakur & Thomas G. Weiss*, 8 GLOBAL COMMUNITY YILJ 2008 (2009), at 77.

 Win-Win Formula for Reforming the UN Security Council, *Vesselin Popowski*, 15 GLOBAL COMMUNITY YILJ 2015 (2016), at 153.

 Globalising Security Law for a Globalised Arms Trade, *Shavana Musa*, 16 GLOBAL COMMUNITY YILJ 2016 (2017), at 191.

- **Global politics and religion**
Religion, Democratisation and the Arab Spring, *Jeffrey Haynes*, 12 GLOBAL COMMUNITY YILJ 2012 (2013), at 3.

 Human Rights and the Politics of Religious Freedom in Europe, *Jeffrey Haynes*, 15 GLOBAL COMMUNITY YILJ 2015 (2016), at 139.

- **Global power politics**
The Politics of Global Powers, *Hans Köchler*, 9 GLOBAL COMMUNITY YILJ 2009 (2010), at 173.

Normative Inconsistencies in the State System with Special Emphasis on International Law, *Hans Köchler*, 16 GLOBAL COMMUNITY YILJ 2016 (2017), at 175.

Demilitarizing Palestine. A Flawed Legal Approach to Middle East Peace, *Louis René Beres*, 18 GLOBAL COMMUNITY YILJ 2018 (2019), at 191.

America's Foreign Policy under Donald Trump, *Richard W. Mansbach*, 20 GLOBAL COMMUNITY YILJ 2020 (2021), at 201.

- **Globalization and policies**
The Great Globalization Debate, *Richard W. Mansbach*, 8 GLOBAL COMMUNITY YILJ 2008 (2009), at 21.

- **Military global policies**
Enhancing Civilian Risk Mitigation by Expanding the Commander's Information Aperture, *Geoffrey S. Corn & Michael W. Meier*, 19 GLOBAL COMMUNITY YILJ 2019 (2020), at 159.

- **Pandemics/Epidemics and global policies**
Migratory Flows Between Colombia and Venezuela Since 1950: The Impact of the Covid-19 Pandemic, *Héctor Olasolo, Mario Urueña-Sánchez & María Paula López Velásquez*, 21 GLOBAL COMMUNITY YILJ 2021 (2022), at 177.

Covid-19, the Belt and Road Initiative, *Tianxia*/the Chinese Universe, and Universal Human Rights, *Xiaoqing Diana Lin*, 21 GLOBAL COMMUNITY YILJ 2021 (2022), at 197.

- **Policies established by the global Internet community**
International Regulation by International Regulatory Organisations—A Model for ICANN?, *Robert Uerpmann-Wittzack*, 8 GLOBAL COMMUNITY YILJ 2008 (2009), at 113.

Global Media and Communication Policy: Turbulence and Reform, *Robin Mansell*, 13 GLOBAL COMMUNITY YILJ 2013 (2014), at 3.

A Constitutional-Driven Change of Heart ISP Liability, AI and the Digital Single Market, *Oreste Pollicino & Giovanni De Gregorio*, 18 GLOBAL COMMUNITY YILJ 2018 (2019), at 237.

- **Policies on fundamental rights**
The Protection of Fundamental Rights: The ECJ Key Contribution to EU Constitutional Developments, *Antonio Tizzano*, 8 GLOBAL COMMUNITY YILJ 2008 (2009), at 99.

Addressing Member State Deviations from EU Foundational Values and the Rule of Law, *Vivian Grosswald Curran*, 21 GLOBAL COMMUNITY YILJ 2021 (2022), at 145.

- **Principles for global policies**
Rise and Shine: The No Harm Principle's Increasing Relevance for the Global Community, *Jelena Bäumler*, 17 GLOBAL COMMUNITY YILJ 2017 (2018), at 149.

- **Regional and global economic integration policies**
Economic Integration in the Caribbean Region: Re-Discussing the Capacity of the CARICOM, *Francesco Seatzu*, 14 GLOBAL COMMUNITY YILJ 2014 (2015), at 171.

Subsidies Regulation Beyond the WTO: Substance, Procedure and Policy Space in the "New Generation" EU Trade Agreements, *Leonardo Borlini*, 16 GLOBAL COMMUNITY YILJ 2016 (2017), at 145.

China's "Belt and Road Initiative": A Research Study of a Multifaceted Policy, *Xiaoqing Diana Lin, Anja Matwijkiw, Bronik Matwijkiw & Su Yun Woo*, 20 GLOBAL COMMUNITY YILJ 2020 (2021), at 325.

FORUM

Jurisprudential Cross-Fertilization:
An Annual Overview

I

Introductory Module—MISSION AND CONCEPTS

Geography and Legal Culture of ICJ Judges and Their Consideration of *Erga Omnes* Obligations

BY RAVINDRA PRATAP*

Abstract

The emergence and evolution of *erga omnes* obligations seem to afford an interesting basis for exploring the influence of geography and legal culture on International Court of Justice (ICJ) judges as they tend to offer a somewhat unifying contrast to rather divisive, but not necessarily decisive, geography and legal culture. If it is judges' significant background that in some measure is represented by their geography and legal culture, it is nothing but a critical past of the international community which has been no less noticeably represented by *erga omnes* obligations. This article seeks to examine the overall argument that the differences of geography and legal culture of ICJ judges are not without discernible convergence in their consideration of *erga omnes* obligations.

I. INTRODUCTION

International Court of Justice (ICJ) judges represent geography by representing "the main forms of civilizations"[1] and perform a human activity which is relatable to earth and atmosphere. Conceptions of legal culture may include "legal systems,"[2] "a common prior

---

* Professor and Dean, Faculty of Legal Studies, South Asian University (A University of SAARC countries), New Delhi, India. Email: ravindrapratap@sau.int. The author would like to thank Professor Giuliana Ziccardi Capaldo and all anonymous reviewers for their helpful suggestions on an earlier draft of this article. All errors are mine.

[1] Article 9 of the Statute of the International Court of Justice. Further, *see generally* GIULIANA ZICCARDI CAPALDO, THE PILLARS OF GLOBAL LAW (2008), sec. III.

[2] *Id.*

Ravindra Pratap, *Geography and Legal Culture of ICJ Judges and Their Consideration of Erga Omnes Obligations* In: *The Global Community Yearbook of International Law and Jurisprudence 2022*. Edited by: Giuliana Ziccardi Capaldo, Oxford University Press.
© Oxford University Press 2023. DOI: 10.1093/oso/9780197752265.003.0012

understanding concerning law,"[3] "legally-oriented social behaviour and attitudes,"[4] "a heuristic device" probative of "individual decision-making,"[5] conditioning of and conditioned by legal profession,[6] and "can mean various things in its different uses."[7] The international contextualization of legal culture may encompass a rights-embedded international recognition of legal culture,[8] "commitment to the principles of normative universality and normative equality,"[9] internationality underlying the Cultural Diversity Convention, 2005,[10] and a plurality of legal cultures inherent in the transcivilizational perspective of international law.[11] *Erga omnes* obligations, i.e., obligations against all,[12] have been conceived in terms of "all obligations of customary international law,"[13] "between is and ought,"[14] "horizontal and vertical,"[15] the "international community"[16] and "multilateral by procedure,"[17] and inspiring "cosmopolitan thinking in international law"[18] to communicate claims and contestations of universality and contents, forms and relativity of normativity and internationality.[19]

This article argues that the differences of geography and legal culture of ICJ judges are not without discernible convergence in their consideration of *erga omnes* obligations. This is because *erga omnes* obligations seem to offer a somewhat unifying contrast to apparently

---

[3] Franz Wieacker & Edgar Bodenheimer, *Foundations of the European Legal Culture*, 38 AMERICAN JOURNAL OF COMPARATIVE LAW 1, 3 (1990).

[4] David Nelken, *Using the Concept of Legal Culture*, 29 AUSTRALIAN JOURNAL OF LEGAL PHILOSOPHY 1, 1 (2004).

[5] Jeremy Weber, *Culture, Legal Culture, and Reasoning: A Comment on Nelken*, 29 AUSTRALIAN JOURNAL OF LEGAL PHILOSOPHY 27, 32 (2004).

[6] Lawrence M. Friedman & Harry N. Scheiber, *Legal Cultures and the Legal Profession*, 48 BULLETIN OF THE AMERICAN ACADEMY OF ARTS AND SCIENCES 6 (1995).

[7] Roger Cotterrell, *Comparative Law and Legal Culture*, in OXFORD HANDBOOK OF COMPARATIVE LAW 710, 721 (2006).

[8] International Covenant on Civil and Political Rights, 1966, art. 27.

[9] Thomas M. Franck, *The Legal Culture and the Culture Culture*, 93 PROCEEDINGS OF THE ANNUAL MEETING OF THE AMERICAN SOCIETY OF INTERNATIONAL LAW 271, 271 (1999).

[10] Convention on the Protection and Promotion of the Diversity of Cultural Expressions, Recital four.

[11] ONUMA YASUAKI, INTERNATIONAL LAW IN A TRANSCIVILIZATIONAL WORLD, 19 (2017).

[12] *See generally* Bruno Simma, *Does the UN Charter Provide an Adequate Legal Basis for Individual or Collective Responses to Violations of Obligations Erga Omnes?*, in THE FUTURE OF INTERNATIONAL LAW ENFORCEMENT: NEW SCENARIOS—NEW LAW? 115 PROCEEDINGS OF AN INTERNATIONAL SYMPOSIUM OF THE KIEL INSTITUTE OF INTERNATIONAL LAW, MARCH 25 TO 27 1992, at 125 ff. (Jost Delbrück ed., 1993).

[13] R. Ago, *Obligations Erga Omnes and the International Community*, in INTERNATIONAL CRIMES OF STATES. A CRITICAL ANALYSIS OF THE ILC's DRAFT ARTICLE 19 ON STATE RESPONSIBILITY 237, 237 (J.H.H. Weiler, A. Cassese & M. Spinedi eds., 1989).

[14] B. Simma, *From Bilateralism to Community Interest*, 250 RECUEIL DES COURS 229, 297–301 (1997).

[15] A.A. Cançado Trindade, *International Law for Humankind: Towards a New Jus Gentium—General Course on Public International Law*, 316 RECUEIL DES COURS 9, 353–354 (2005).

[16] C. TAMS, ENFORCING OBLIGATIONS ERGA OMNES IN INTERNATIONAL LAW 3 (2005).

[17] G.I. Hernández, *A Reluctant Guardian: The International Court of Justice and the Concept of "International Community,"* 83 BRITISH YEARBOOK OF INTERNATIONAL LAW 13 (2013).

[18] David Armstrong, *Evolving Conceptions of Justice in International Law*, 37 REVIEW OF INTERNATIONAL STUDIES 2121, 2128 (2011).

[19] Further, *see generally* M. RAGAZZI, THE CONCEPT OF INTERNATIONAL OBLIGATIONS ERGA OMNES (1997).

divisive, but not necessarily decisive, geography and legal culture.[20] With this introduction of the argument, section II of the article seeks to examine the argument that the differences of geography and legal culture of ICJ judges are not without significant convergence in their consideration of *erga omnes* obligations. The surveyed literature extends beyond ICJ judgments, orders and advisory opinions for a fuller account of the views of ICJ judges and relative and complementary to their consideration of *erga omnes* obligations on the bench. This also enables their geography and legal culture to be viewed beyond the composition of the Court as contemplated in its Statute and in the setting of their international law view broadly. We follow the timeline of cases as far as posisble and do not purposively distinguish between members of the Court and judges ad hoc. Section III summarizes the discussion and concludes.

II. GEOGRAPHY AND LEGAL CULTURE OF ICJ JUDGES AND *ERGA OMNES* OBLIGATIONS

ICJ judges have variously considered *erga omnes* obligations. It is this treatment of *erga omnes* obligations that we take up herein for discussion to see convergence of the differences of geography and legal culture of ICJ judges in their consideration of *erga omnes* obligations. The discussion also surveys their views expressed outside of the bench for their fuller understanding relative and complementary to their consideration of these obligations. This also allows their geography and legal culture to be reflected beyond the compositional structure of the Court envisaged by its Statute and in the context of their international law views generally. Our discussion possibly follows the temporal trajectory of consideration of these obligations and without objectively maintaining the distinction between members of the Court and judges ad hoc.

A. Judge ad hoc Riphagen of the Netherlands

In his dissenting opinion in the *Barcelona Traction Case*,[21] Judge Riphagen found it "difficult to hold that this distinction [between *erga omnes* obligations and other obligations] would necessarily correspond to an a priori classification in accordance with the nature of the interests protected by such obligations, a classification which is already in itself a fairly doubtful one."[22] He however seems to have added that a "state's obligation to keep within the limits of its jurisdiction on the international plane is, without any doubt, an obligation *erga omnes*."[23]

Judge ad hoc Riphagen was a Dutch national nominated by Belgium as its judge ad hoc. He viewed sovereignty functionally[24] and without admissibility of norms not subject to sovereignty.[25] He held the view that "law purports to regulate human

---

[20] Cooperation under international law in inherent in the concept of *erga omnes* obligations. *See, in particular,* UN Friendly Relations Declaration, GA Res. 2625 of 24 October 1970 casts on states a duty to cooperate.

[21] ICJ, Barcelona Traction, Light and Power Company, Limited, Merits, Judgment, ICJ Reports 1970, 3 (Feb. 5, 1970) [hereinafter Barcelona Traction Case].

[22] *Id.,* Dissenting Opinion of Judge *ad hoc* Riphagen 334, 354, para. 28.

[23] *Id.*

[24] W. Riphagen, *Some Reflections on "Functional Sovereignty,"* 6 NETHERLANDS YEARBOOK OF INTERNATIONAL LAW 121 (1975).

[25] W. Riphagen, *From Soft Law to Ius Cogens and Back,* 17 VICTORIA UNIVERSITY OF WELLINGTON LAW REVIEW 81 (1987).

relations,"[26] that "there is an analogy between the physical and the legal universe"[27] and that state measures are "bound to affect"[28] "the interests of the international community as a whole,"[29] including in the field of international economic law.[30] It is hardly surprising that he defended the Belgian claim,[31] but not apparently without employing the framework of *erga omnes* obligations for underscoring the Spanish state's obligation to keep within its jurisdiction and seemingly for guarding against the rights of the Belgian state or its shareholders from any encroachment by Spain by any exercise of its jurisdiction.[32] The geographical propinquity between the Netherlands and Belgium and a measure of similarity of their legal culture thus seems to have come in for the defence of the Belgian interest in the hands of the judge ad hoc, but apparently not by way of a conceptual understanding of *erga omnes* obligations entirely shared with the Court.

B. Judge Fitzmaurice of the United Kingdom

In his dissent in the *Namibia Advisory Opinion*,[33] Judge Fitzmaurice believed that the basic issue in this case was the survival of the mandate in the form of an obligation owed to the United Nations. In other words, he seems to be saying whether there remained for South Afrcia an *erga omnes* obligation upon dissolution of the League of Nations.[34] Judge Fitzmaurice seems to be denying the existence of any such obligation on the ground that the mandated territory was never placed under the UN trusteeship system[35] and that there was no obligation to do so.[36] According to him, "the so called organized world community is not a separate juridical entity . . ."[37] He however recognized that "the Mandate survived the dissolution of the League,—that it has an international character . . ."[38]

Fitzmaurice held the view that "the law is in the last analysis binding simply because it is the law; and if this is true even in that field, it is a fortiori true on the international plane,"[39] that "[c]onsent to the content of the rule therefore involves, internationally, an automatic obligation to conform to it,"[40] that "treaties only (directly) impose obligations on the parties

---

[26] W. Riphagen, *The Relationship Between Public and Private Law and the Rules of Conflict of Laws*, 102 RECUEIL DES COURS 215, 220 (1961).

[27] W. Riphagen, *Techniques of International Law*, 246 RECUEIL DES COURS 235, 248 (1994).

[28] W. Riphagen, *National and International Regulation of International Movement and the Legal Position of the Private Individual Techniques of International Law*, 131 RECUEIL DES COURS 489, 496 (1970).

[29] *Id.*

[30] Riphagen, *supra* note 25, at 81, 98.

[31] Further, *see* Karen J. Alter, *Delegating to International Courts: Self-Binding vs. Other-Binding Delegation*, 71 LAW AND CONTEMPORARY PROBLEMS 37, 42 (2008).

[32] *Barcelona Traction Case*, Dissenting Opinion of Judge *ad hoc* Riphagen, *supra* note 21, at 354, para. 28.

[33] ICJ, Legal Consequences for States of the Continued Presence of South Africa in Namibia (South West Africa) notwithstanding Security Council Resolution 276, Advisory Opinion, ICJ Reports 1971, 16 (June 21, 1971) [hereinafter Namibia Advisory Opinion].

[34] *Id.*, Dissenting Opinion of Judge Sir Gerald Fitzmaurice 220, 220, para. 1.

[35] Id., 224, para. 10.

[36] *Id.*, 234, para. 21.

[37] *Id.*, 241, para. 33.

[38] *Id.*, 295, para. 118.

[39] Gerald Fitzmaurice, *The General Principles of International Law Considered from the Standpoint of the Rule of Law*, 92 RECUEIL DES COURS 1, 46 (1957).

[40] *Id.*, 44.

to them,"[41] and that "[a]n obligation to ratify is juridically meaningless, and a contradiction in terms, since the whole point of ratification is that the State concerned thereby confirms its signature, which it may or may not do, as it pleases."[42] He saw older and younger generations of international lawyers relative to the "values they respectively attach to general principles of law and to customary international law, on the one hand, and to treaties on the other, as sources of rights and obligations."[43] He believed that the definition of *jus cogens* in the Vienna Convention on the Law of Treaties, 1969, "does give the adjudicator something to go by, at all events as to the *nature* of the notion involved."[44] Fitzmaurice "as a legal technician . . . was able to perceive those necessary qualifications and distinctions."[45] He lamented the neglect of the "methods and Procedures"[46] of obtaining legal advice by international law teachers and practitioners.

Needless to say, Fitzmaurice's approaching of the issue is not without links to his national state's historical ties with South Africa and to the nature of his legal thinking and legal culture. His consistent underscoring of the requirement of state consent in any legal relationship between state and international organizations seems to underscore a somewhat restrictive nature of the role of the positivist legal thinking[47] in the emergence or evolution of *erga omnes* obligations underlying the idea of the existence of an international community.[48] And if geography may also be understood historically, it would be instructing to recall that none other than the United Kingdom had been given the mandate of South West Africa administered by South Africa.

C. Judge Gros of France

Judge Gros in the *Namibia Advisory Opinion*[49] believed that even those states who voted for the adoption of the UNGA Resolution 2145 (XXI), which had terminated the mandate of South Africa over Southwest Africa, "are under no legal obligation to act in conformity with its provisions, and remain free to determine their own course of action."[50] This view seems to have been informed more by some form of legal thinking that apparently accords little or doubtful juridical recognition to the idea of an international community and the ensuing *erga omnes* obligations.[51] While distinguishable from the category of these

---

[41] *Id.,* 9.

[42] Gerald Fitzmaurice, *The Juridical Clauses of the Peace Treaties,* 73 RECUEIL DES COURS 255, 352 (1948).

[43] Gerald Fitzmaurice, *The Older Generation of International Lawyer and the Question of Human Rights,* 21 REVISTA ESPAÑOLA DE DERECHO INTERNATIONAL 471, 471 (1968).

[44] Gerald Fitzmaurice, *Vae Victis or Woe to the Negotiators! Your Treaty or Our "Interpretation" of It,* 65 AMERICAN JOURNAL OF INTERNATIONAL LAW 358, 371 (1971).

[45] Robert Jennings, *Gerald Gray Fitzmaurice,* 55 BRITISH YEARBOOK OF INTERNATIONAL LAW 1, 49 (1985).

[46] Gerald Fitzmaurice, *Legal Advisers and Foreign Affairs,* 59 AMERICAN JOURNAL OF INTERNATIONAL LAW 72, 72 (1965).

[47] *See, in particular,* ICJ, Case concerning the Northern Cameroons (Cameroons v. United Kingdom), Preliminary Objections, Judgment, ICJ Reports 1963, 15 (Dec. 2, 1963) Separate Opinion of Judge Fitzmaurice 97, 129.

[48] Further, *see* J.G. MERRILLS, JUDGE SIR GERALD FITZMAURICE AND THE DISCIPLINE OF INTERNATIONAL LAW, 54–55 (1998).

[49] *Supra* note 33.

[50] *Id.,* Dissenting Opinion of Judge Gros 323, 328, para. 33.

[51] *Cf.* Goler Teal Butcher, *Legal Consequences for States of the Illegality of Apartheid,* 8 HUMAN RIGHTS QUARTERLY 404, 405, 409, 421 (1986).

obligations,[52] it is neither without critical parallels bordering on and oscillating between legal and political theories, including those of pragmatism, positivism and "subjectivism,"[53] nor devoid of a consciousness of the proper role of a judge in the proceedings of the Court.[54] Although France, the national state of Judge Gros, did not have any significant geographical or legal culture ties with South Africa, it was no less a colonial power in Africa than the United Kingdom and that might itself be suggested as a geography and thus not wholly without a semblance of some irreducibly common legal culture embedded in the use of law and legal methods in the institution, advocacy, expansion and/or defense of colonialism.[55]

D. Judge de Castro of Spain

Judge de Castro in the *Nuclear Tests Case*[56] expressed "numerous doubts"[57] in the claim that the Court should declare that atmospheric nuclear tests are unlawful as a general rule of international law and that all states have the right to enjoin France from performing these tests.[58] He seemed to contest any judicial pronouncement of the existence of any *erga omnes* obligation of the prohibition of atmospheric nuclear tests on the ground of the lack of the Court's jurisdiction.

Judge de Castro "sum[med] up a century of Spanish learning."[59] He did not believe that the evolution of law can "modify the meaning which the words had for the authors of the declaration."[60] To him, "[dissenting and separate] opinions are evidence of the life and of the evolution of legal doctrine."[61] His work has been described as an "attempt to overcome legal positivism."[62] He drew on a common civil law legal culture of France and Spain for acknowledging Australia's right to protect it from any external interference (and for that reason dissented from the judgment in that it did not require adjudication on merits)[63] but doubtfully on that legal culture for his view that Australia could not legally invoke against France any *erga omnes* obligation to prohibit any atmospheric nuclear tests.[64]

---

[52] *See, for instance,* André Gros, *The Convention on Fishing and Conservation of the Living Resources of the High Seas,* 97 RECUEIL DES COURS 1, 55 (1959).

[53] ICJ, Fisheries Jurisdiction (United Kingdom v. Iceland), Merits, Judgment, ICJ Reports 1974, 3 (July 25, 1974), Dissenting Opinion of Judge André Gros 234, 236, 238, paras. 4 and 8 [hereinafter Fisheries Jurisdiction Case (UK)].

[54] ICJ, Aegean Sea Continental Shelf, Judgment, ICJ Reports 1978, 3 (Dec. 19, 1978), Declaration of Judge André Gros 49, 49 [hereinafter Aegean Sea Continental Shelf Case].

[55] Further, *see* JOHN BELL, FRENCH LEGAL CULTURES (2001).

[56] In 1973, Australia instituted proceedings against France in respect of a dispute concerning the holding of atmospheric tests of nuclear weapons by France in the Pacific Ocean. ICJ, Nuclear Tests (Australia v. France) Judgment, ICJ Reports 1974, 253 (Dec. 20, 1974) [hereinafter Nuclear Tests Case].

[57] *Id.,* Dissenting Opinion of Judge De Castro 372, 387, para. 3.

[58] He did not find it necessary for the Court to take action when the claim was "not properly made." *Fisheries Jurisdiction Case,* Separate Opinion of Judge De Castro, *supra* note 53, at 225, 225.

[59] UNIDROIT, *In Memorium* (1984-I) UNIFORM LAW REVIEW, Biannual, vi, xix [In Memorium].

[60] *Aegean Sea Continental Shelf Case,* Dissenting Opinion of Judge De Castro, *supra* note 54, at 62, 68, para. 12.

[61] ICJ, Appeal Relating to the Jurisdiction of the ICAO Council, Judgment, ICJ Reports 1972, 46 (Aug. 18, 1972), Separate Opinion of Judge De Castro 116, 116 [hereinafter ICAO Council Case].

[62] *In Memorium, supra* note 59, at xxi.

[63] *Nuclear Tests Case,* Dissenting Opinion of Judge De Castro, *supra* note 56, at 372, 389–390, para. 4.

[64] *Id.,* 390, para. 5.

E. Judges Onyeama of Nigeria, Dillard of the United States, Jiménez de Aréchaga of Uruguay and Waldock of the United Kingdom

In his joint dissenting opinion in the *Nuclear Tests Case*,[65] Judge Onyeama endorsed Australia's invoking of *erga omnes* obligations underlying its argument that a state possesses a legal interest "in the protection of its territory from any form of external harmful action . . ."[66] He "displayed an almost scientific like art of deduction and reasoning in the way he came to his conclusion on a judgment."[67] It was perhaps his reasoning that did not jointly favour the "genuine connection principle."[68] He could see "reason" also as an attribute of "principle"[69] and believed that "each nation has a cluster of interests centering on 'security', 'stability' and 'the economic well-being of its people', . . ."[70]

Judge Dillard was "by temperament inclined to worry about the meaning of his own activities."[71] He distinguished between substantive and procedural jurisdictional issues in that only the "former engages the fundamental rights of the parties and is usually non-waivable; the latter do not."[72] He did not support the necessity of the assessment of damages for an apposite finding of unlawful act that would engage international responsibility.[73] He remains perhaps best known for his dictum that "[i]t is for the people to determine the destiny of the territory and not the territory the destiny of the people."[74] Needless to say, territory and people bear an enduring relation to self-determination creating *erga omnes* obligations.

Judge Jiménez de Aréchaga supported the view that there is "no lawmaking organ" in "the international community."[75] He seemed to accord no less importance to "the substance of the grievances" than to their form for deciding on the admissibility of a procedure for redressal.[76] He believed that rules of procedure are "important, their function is limited."[77] He subscribed to the view of the necessity of distinguishing between substantive and incidental jurisdiction of the Court.[78] He did not dissent necessarily for "differences and

---

[65] *Supra* note 56.

[66] *Id.*, Joint Dissenting Opinion of Judges Onyeama, Dillard, Jiménez de Aréchaga, and Sir Humphrey Waldock 312, 362, para. 103.

[67] Joliba, BOOK REVIEW: DADI: THE MAN, THE LEGEND. HIS EXCELLENCY JUDGE CHARLES DADI ONYEAMA OF THE INTERNATIONAL COURT OF JUSTICE BY DILLIBE ONYEAMA, https://joliba-africa.com/2019/07/16/book-review-dadi-the-man-the-legend-his-excellency-judge-charles-dadi-onyeama-of-the-international-court-of-justice-the-hague-by-dillibe-onyeama/ (visited Apr. 13, 2020).

[68] *Barcelona Traction Case*, Joint Declaration of Judges Petrén and Onyeama, *supra* note 21, at 52, 52.

[69] *ICAO Council Case*, Separate Opinion of Judge Onyeama, *supra* note 61, at 86, 89.

[70] Hardy Cross Dillard, *Some Aspects of Law and Diplomacy*, 91 RECUEIL DES COURS 447, 459 (1957).

[71] André Gros, *Hardy Cross Dillard: Judge of the International Court of Justice*, 23 VIRGINIA JOURNAL OF INTERNATIONAL LAW 369, 370–371 (1983).

[72] *ICAO Council Case*, Separate Opinion of Judge Dillard, *supra* note 61, at 92, 92–93.

[73] ICJ Fisheries Jurisdiction (Federal Republic of Germany v. Iceland), Merits, Judgment, ICJ Reports 1974, 175 (July 25, 1974), Declaration of Judge Dillard 207, 207 [hereinafter Fisheries Jurisdiction Case (FRG)].

[74] ICJ Western Sahara, Advisory Opinion, ICJ Reports 1975, 12 (Oct. 16, 1975), Separate Opinion of Judge Dillard 116, 122.

[75] Eduardo Jiménez de Aréchaga, *Treaty Stipulations in Favor of Third States*, 50 AMERICAN JOURNAL OF INTERNATIONAL LAW 338, 355 (1956).

[76] *ICAO Council Case*, Separate Opinion of Judge Jiménez de Aréchaga, *supra* note 61, at 140, 142, para. 6.

[77] Eduardo Jiménez de Aréchaga, *The Amendment to the Rules of Procedure of the International Court of Justice*, 67 AMERICAN JOURNAL OF INTERNATIONAL LAW 1, 22 (1973).

[78] ICJ Continental Shelf (Libyan Arab Jamahiriya/Malta), Application to Intervene, Judgment, ICJ Reports 1984, 3 (Mar. 21, 1984), Separate Opinion of Judge Jiménez de Aréchaga 55, 60, para. 5.

doubts"[79] and thus seemed to suggest a conclusion of dissent to be more or other than the extent of such differences and doubts.

Judge Waldock noted the existence of international community in terms of the "intransigent nature of the problem of power"[80] in it, "duty"[81] demanded by it, its "common policy"[82] its "judgment and control,"[83] its "authority"[84] and its "constitutional framework."[85] He was equally cognizant of the legal rights of the international community.[86] He believed that "a State can never be brought before the Court except on the conditions on which it has consented to jurisdiction."[87]

It therefore seems possible to discern a significant influence of legal culture in the judges' thinking as Nigeria, the United Kingdom and the United States share a strong similarity or influence of the common law legal system. There also appears a clear influence of geography in their legal thinking in the strong political geographical ties between the United Kingdom and Australia. It seems therefore clear that both geography and legal culture were not without discernible role or influence in the elucidation of *erga omnes* obligations by these jointly dissenting ICJ Judges.

F. Judge ad hoc Barwick of Australia

Judge ad hoc Barwick in the *Nuclear Tests Case*[88] seems to find a procedural fault with the Court in that it took "cognizance of information as to events said to have occurred since the close of the oral proceedings and treated it as evidence in the proceedings."[89] He countenanced the view that the Court did not accept that the "obligation to observe the prohibition is *erga omnes*"[90] as the Court did not believe Australia to have the requisite legal interest. In other words, he would have the Court to accept that the obligation to observe prohibition of nuclear test is *erga omnes*.

Barwick was a former member of "the central seat of the Court"[91] in Australia. His judgments "seemed to blend the certainty concerning legal principles."[92] He is said to have "persuaded a number of judges of the justice of Australia's case."[93] In specifically finding

---

[79] ICJ Continental Shelf (Tunisia/Libyan Arab Jamahiriya), Judgment, ICJ Reports 1982, 18 (Feb. 24, 1982), Separate Opinion of Judge Jiménez de Aréchaga 100, 139–140, para. 124.

[80] C.H.M. Waldock, *The Regulation of the Use of Force by Individual States in International Law*, 81 RECUEIL DES COURS 455, 455 (1952).

[81] *Id.*, 481.

[82] *Id.*, 482.

[83] *Id.*, 495.

[84] *Id.*, 506.

[85] C.H.M. Waldock, *General Course on Public International Law*, 106 RECUEIL DES COURS 1, 7 (1962).

[86] C.H.M. Waldock, *The Plea of Domestic Jurisdiction before International Legal Tribunals*, 31 BRITISH YEARBOOK OF INTERNATIONAL 99, 127 (1954).

[87] C.H.M. Waldock, *Decline of the Optional Clause*, 32 BRITISH YEARBOOK OF INTERNATIONAL LAW 244, 259 (1955–1956).

[88] *Supra* note 56.

[89] *Id.*, Dissenting Opinion of Judge *ad hoc* Barwick 391, 391.

[90] *Id.*, 437.

[91] James A. Thomson, *Sir John Did His Duty, by Sir Garfield Barwick, Book Review*, 6 UNSW LAW JOURNAL 257, 258 (1983).

[92] John Dowsett, *Barwick—His Place in the Legal Pantheon* (Oct. 25, 2018), https://archive.sclqld.org.au/judgepub/2018/dowsett20181025.pdf (visited May 26, 2021).

[93] R.J. Ellicott, *The Life and Career of Garfield Barwick*, BAR NEWS: JOURNAL OF THE NSW BAR ASSOCIATION, 62, 68 (2011–2012).

the right of Australia to have the matter adjudicated on merits,[94] the argument of the judge ad hoc does not appear to be solely motivated by the reasoning underlying *erga omnes* obligations. However, the intended final objective of that argument is undeniably not without contribution to the evolution of those obligations.

G. Judge ad hoc Tarazi of Syria

In his dissenting opinion in the *Tehran Hostage Case*,[95] while not raising the issue of any more recognizable *erga omnes* obligations, Judge ad hoc Tarazi upheld the Court's finding of the violation by Iran of its obligations under the two Vienna Conventions concerning diplomatic and consular relations.[96] However, the underlying claim of some measure of universality in the nature of *erga omnes* obligations and discernible in another conventional form was more expressly noticed by Tarazi in the UN Charter.[97]

Tarazi was of the view that the "philosophy of law has made considerable progress since the end of the Second World War."[98] Noting that "Christianity asserts itself by opposing an international community,"[99] Tarazi expressed the view that "Islam did not approach 'collaboration' and that it contented itself with confrontation."[100] Geography of the region of nationality seems to have informed no one particular judicial consideration. It seems that the judge ad hoc was influenced more by the inviolability of diplomatic personnel in the Islamic legal culture than by the geography of the region of his nationality.[101]

H. Judge Morozov of the Former USSR

In dissenting from the Court in the *Tehran Hostage Case*,[102] Judge Morozov held the view that "freely accepted international obligations may be followed by a duty to make compensation"[103] and concluded that "the Applicant [the U.S.] has forfeited the legal right as well as the moral right to expect the Court to uphold any claim for reparation."[104]

---

[94] *Id.*

[95] In 1980, the Court found that Iran had also violated "obligations" under international conventions and "long-established rules of general international law." ICJ United States Diplomatic and Consular Staff in Tehran (United States v. Iran), ICJ Reports 1980, 3 (May 24, 1980), 44, para. 94 [hereinafter Tehran Hostage Case]. The Court observed that "the obligations of the Iranian Government . . . are not merely contractual obligations" (*Id.* para. 62).

[96] *Id.*, Dissenting Opinion of Judge *ad hoc* S Tarazi 58, 65.

[97] Salah Ed Dine Tarazi, *The Risk of Revision: Appraisal of United Nations Preparations for Charter Review*, THE ANNALS OF THE AMERICAN ACADEMY OF POLITICAL AND SOCIAL SCIENCE (Jan. 1, 1954), at 6, https://doi.org/10.1177/000271625429600120; https://journals.sagepub.com/doi/abs/10.1177/000 271625429600120 (visited June 3, 2021).

[98] *Aegean Sea Continental Shelf Case*, Separate Opinion of Judge S Tarazi, *supra* note 54, at 55, 57.

[99] Georges Scelle, MANUAL OF PUBLIC INTERNATIONAL LAW, mimeographed edition, Paris, 1948, at 31 (cited in Salah Ed Dine Tarazi, *The Solution of Personal Status Problem in the Law of Arab and African Countries*, 159 RECUEIL DES COURS 345, 380 (1978).

[100] Tarazi, *id.*, 345, 380–381.

[101] *Tehran Hostage Case*, Dissenting Opinion, *supra* note 95, at 54, 59.

[102] *Supra* note 95.

[103] *Id.*, Dissenting Opinion of Judge Morozov 51, 53, para. 4.

[104] *Id.*

Morozov advanced the view of equal opportunity in matters of a country's treatment of other countries.[105] As a judge, he wrote noticeably short,[106] but seemed to mince no words when expressing his dissents.[107] The particular characterizations of obligations and rights by Judge Morozov are not noticeably without some influence of the continental legal culture inasmuch his own legal system is not significantly different from that legal culture.[108] However, the inference he seems to draw from those obligations expressly corresponds also as a moral right, and a right expressed as a moral right is not without elements that correspond to obligations resembling *erga omnes*.

I. Judge Weeramantry of Sri Lanka

In his dissent in the *East Timor Case*,[109] Judge Weeramantry agreed with the Court as regards "the *erga omnes* nature"[110] of the right to self-determination which raised "important juristic question of the nature of international duties correlative to rights *erga omnes*."[111] He argued that if "self-determination is a right assertible *erga omnes*, . . . Australia's individual action, . . . would not appear to be in conformity with the duties it owes to East Timor under international law."[112] He believed that, "[a]gainst the background of the Security Council reaffirming a right admittedly of fundamental importance, and admittedly enjoyed *erga omnes*, it seems academic to examine its obligatory nature.. . . ."[113] He argued that, "[i]f the people of East Timor have a right *erga omnes* to self-determination, there is a duty lying upon all Member States to recognize that right."[114] He expressed the view that "[i]f, therefore, Australia has an obligation *erga omnes* towards all States to respect the right of self-determination, Portugal (as the administering Power of East Timor) and East Timor would have a legal interest in the observance of that duty."[115] He however regretted that "the *erga omnes* principle has . . . not yet drawn a definitive decision from the Court . . ."[116] The practical consequences of Weeramantry's *erga omnes* obligations argument would be to overcome the necessary party argument of Indonesia which had not accepted the jurisdiction of the Court.

---

[105] Paul G. Dembling & Daniel M. Arons, *The Evolution of the Outer Space Treaty*, 33 JOURNAL OF AIR LAW AND COMMERCE 419, 442 (1976).

[106] *Aegean Sea Continental Shelf Case*, Declaration by Judge Platon Morozov, *supra* note 54, at 54.

[107] *ICAO Council Case*, Dissenting Opinion of Judge Platon Morozov, *supra* note 61, at 157.

[108] It has been argued that "the victory of Leninist-Marxism in the October Revolution did not signify a turning away from the continental European relationships." Wieacker & Bodenheimer, *supra* note 3, at 1, 8.

[109] In 1991, Portugal filed an application against Australia and stated that it had "failed to observe . . . the obligation to respect the duties and powers of [Portugal as] the administering Power [of East Timor] . . . and . . . the right of the people of East Timor to self-determination," ICJ, East Timor (Portugal v. Australia), ICJ Reports 1995, 90 (June 30, 1995), 99, para. 20 [hereinafter East Timor Case].

[110] *Id.*, Dissenting Opinion of Judge Weeramantry 139, 142.

[111] *Id.*, 143.

[112] *Id.*, 202.

[113] *Id.*, 208.

[114] *Id.*, 209.

[115] *Id.*, 214.

[116] *East Timor Case*, Dissenting Opinion of Judge Weeramantry, *supra* note 109, at 139, 214.

In his dissent in the *Nuclear Weapons Advisory Opinion 1996 (GA Request),*[117] Judge Weeramantry emphasised *"other sources of international law"*[118] "whose principles are universally accepted."[119] He also reiterated the duty of all states not to allow knowingly their territory to be used for acts contrary to the rights of other states[120] and the prohibition of the use of force.[121] These seem to testify and crystallize *erga omnes* obligations in which he saw a consequential role of the Court by way of building public opinion.[122] Weeramantry would seem to stand here for a common geography, as it were, of the non-nuclear weapons states whom he defended by the persuasiveness of his arguments underlying some of *erga omnes* obligations.

Judge Weeramantry was trained and practiced in the common law legal cultures. His judicial work was at once academic.[123] His understanding and contribution to the clarification and elaboration of *erga omnes* obligations seem to have drawings from the common law legal culture. He noted that the Preamble to the UN Charter contemplates the maintenance of justice also from "other sources of international law."[124] He believed that the foundations of global community were narrowly constructed,[125] spoke of the "special interest" of the international community and with reference to the treaties envisaging *erga omnes* obligations[126] and viewed the ICJ's optional clause to the "international community's answer . . . to the hitherto intractable problem of carving out an area for the judicial settlement of international disputes."[127] He recalled that "international community has expressed concern for many years regarding the protection of environmental resources . . ."[128] He saw "a congruence of cultures . . . on all the basic principles of international law,"[129] believed that

---

[117] In 1994, the UNGA requested the ICJ of an advisory opinion on the following question: "Is the threat or use of nuclear weapons in any circumstance permitted under international law?" ICJ Legality of the Threat or Use of Nuclear Weapons, Advisory Opinion [1996] ICJ Reports 1996, 226 (July 8, 1996), 228, para. 1) [hereinafter Nuclear Weapons Advisory Opinion 1996 (GA Request)].

[118] *Id.,* Dissenting Opinion of Judge Weeramantry 429, 442 (italics in the original).

[119] *Id.,* 442.

[120] *Id.,* 506.

[121] *Id.,* 542.

[122] *Id.,* 550.

[123] ICJ Arbitral Award of 31 July 1989, Judgment, ICJ Reports 1991, 53 (Nov. 12, 1991), Dissenting Opinion of Judge Weeramantry 130 [hereinafter Arbitral Award of 1989 Case].

[124] ICJ Maritime Delimitation in the Area between Greenland and Jan Mayen, Judgment, ICJ Reports 1993, 38 (June 14, 1993), Separate Opinion of Judge Weeramantry 211, 241, para. 100.

[125] ICJ Request for an Examination of the Situation in Accordance with Paragraph 63 of the Court's Judgment of 20 December 1974 in the Nuclear Tests (New Zealand v. France) Case [1995] ICJ Reports 288 (Sept. 22, 1995), Dissenting Opinion of Judge Weeramantry 317, 319 [hereinafter Request for an Examination (New Zealand v. France Case)].

[126] Application of the Convention on the Prevention and Punishment of the Crime of Genocide, Preliminary Objections, Judgment [1996] ICJ Reports 1996, 595 (July 11, 1996), Separate Opinion of Judge Weeramantry 640, 645. For a background, *see* GIULIANA ZICCARDI CAPALDO, REPERTORY OF DECISIONS OF THE INTERNATIONAL COURT OF JUSTICE (1947–1992) 69, 71 (1995)[hereinafter Genocide Convention 1996 Case].

[127] ICJ, Fisheries Jurisdiction (Spain v. Canada), Jurisdiction of the Court, Judgment [1998] ICJ Reports 1998, 432 (Dec. 4, 1998) [hereinafter Fisheries Jurisdiction (Spain v. Canada) Case], Dissenting Opinion of Judge Weeramantry 496, 510, para. 56.

[128] ICJ Kasikili/Sedudu Island (Botswana/Namibia), Judgment, ICJ Reports 1999, 1045 (Dec. 13, 1999), Dissenting Opinion of Vice-President Weeramantry 1153, 1193–1194, para. 112.

[129] Christopher G. Weeramantry, *The Dialogue of Cultures, Religions and Legal Cultures: An Imperative Need of Our Times,* 19 GLOBAL CHANGE, PEACE & SECURITY 149, 156 (2007).

"no culture is an island unto itself"[130] and saw trade and enterprise properly within "a moral framework."[131] He did not agree with the view that the Court's function is "merely to decide the case,"[132] believed that "judges must always be cautious"[133] and opined that "[l]egal philosophy and theories of justice . . . constitute essential parts of the basic equipment of the judge."[134] He subscribed to the view that "peace depends on justice"[135] and considered the Court "as custodians of justice for the entire international community."[136] He underscored caution in accepting that the lapse of time would lessen the binding force of the resolution containing an *erga omnes* obligation. Clearly, Weeramantry made a most significant contribution to the understanding of *erga omnes* obligations across geography and legal cultures represented on the international bench.

J. Judge ad hoc Skubiszewski of Poland

In his dissenting opinion in the *East Timor Case*,[137] Judge ad hoc Skubiszewski underscored the inapplicability of the necessary party rule in the matters of adjudication of *erga omnes* obligations.[138] He was alert to acknowledge the creation of "an estoppel situation,"[139] a concept no less known to the civil law than to common law legal culture.[140] For him, the "content"[141] of a right was no less important than the extent of a right. He foresaw in the decisions of international bodies the possibility of "improving and strengthening the structure of the international community."[142] His civil law legal culture background seems to have made discernibly no different impact on his understanding of *erga omnes* obligations than those of the judges of the common law legal culture. If so, it is attributable in some measure to an essentially unifying nature of *erga omnes* obligations and a somewhat universalizing character of legal culture.

[130] Christopher G. Weeramantry, *Challenges Facing Developing Countries*, 16 COLORADO JOURNAL OF INTERNATIONAL ENVIRONMENTAL LAW AND POLICY 1, 7 (2004).

[131] Christopher G. Weeramantry, *Human Rights and the Global Marketplace*, 25 BROOKLYN JOURNAL OF INTERNATIONAL LAW 27, 29 (1999).

[132] C.G. Weeramantry, *Some Practical Problems of International Adjudication*, 17 AUSTRALIAN YEARBOOK OF INTERNATIONAL LAW 1, 6 (1996).

[133] Christopher G. Weeramantry, *The Function of the International Court of Justice in the Development of International Law*, 10 LEIDEN JOURNAL OF INTERNATIONAL LAW 309, 340 (1997).

[134] C.G. Weeramantry, *The Importance of Philosophical Perspectives to the Judicial Process*, 6 CONNECTICUT JOURNAL OF INTERNATIONAL LAW 599, 608 (1991).

[135] C.G. Weeramantry, *Insights for International Law from Religious Reflections on Peace*, 29 MONASH UNIVERSITY LAW REVIEW 213, 223 (2003).

[136] ICJ, Sovereignty over Pulau Ligatan and Pulau Sipadan (Indonesia/Malaysia), Application for Permission to Intervene, Judgment, ICJ Reports 2002, 575 (Dec. 17, 2002), Separate Opinion of Judge Weeramantry 630, 639–640, para. 21 [hereinafter Sovereignty over Pulau Ligatan Case].

[137] *Supra* note 109.

[138] *Id.*, Dissenting Opinion of Judge Skubiszewski 224, 248, para. 79.

[139] ICJ, Gabčíkovo-Nagymaros Project (Hungary/Slovakia), Judgment, ICJ Reports 1997, 7 (Sept. 25, 1997), Dissenting Opinion of Judge Skubiszewski 232, 233–234, para. 6.

[140] *Id.*, 240, paras. 23 and 24.

[141] Krzysztof Skubiszewski, *Administration of Territory and Sovereignty: A Comment on the Postdam Agreement*, 23 ARCHIV DES VÖLKERRECHTS 31, 33 (1985).

[142] Krzysztof Skubiszewski, *Forms of Participation of International Organizations in the Lawmaking Processes*, 18 INTERNATIONAL ORGANIZATIONS 790, 805 (1964).

K. Judge Shahabuddeen of Guyana

In his dissent in the *Nuclear Weapons Advisory Opinion 1996 (GA Request)*,[143] Judge Shahabuddeen touched upon *erga omnes* obligations. He subscribed to the obligation of all countries "to make every effort to achieve the goal of eliminating nuclear weapons, the terror which they hold for humankind and the threat which they pose to life on earth."[144] He underscored the absence of the subject matter of the right on the basis of which states exist and the presence of a corresponding obligation of all states within the international community.[145] Later, he spoke of the considerations of humanity in giving rise to obligations in *"themselves."*[146] Not so much the influence of legal culture as perhaps of the geographical consideration of Guyana being a non-nuclear weapons state that seems to further underlie the perspective of an *erga omnes* obligation of nuclear disarmament.

Judge Shahabuddeen held the view that "[c]ontemporary international law has been developing responsively."[147] He believed that the "international community rightly values" the process of arbitration[148] and found in international community evidence of the essential distinction between "recognizing and undertaking to recognize" the optional clause jurisdiction of the Court.[149] He believed that Australia could have been sued alone as its obligation under the Trusteeship Agreement was joint and several[150] and that judicial propriety and judicial restraint "intrinsically influence the exercise of this Court's judicial function."[151] He felt that a "select community" called itself "international community"[152] despite the fact that the "important principles of contemporary international law . . . , have changed" its shape.[153] Clearly, Judge Shahabuddeen's contribution to the treatment of *erga omnes* obligation is not without a critical perspective not only of the idea of international community but also of the role of various international law actors.

L. Judge Koroma of Sierra Leone

In his dissent in the *Nuclear Weapons Advisory Opinion 1996 (GA Request)*,[154] Judge Koroma saw "a proper sense of restraint within the international community"[155] in *erga omnes* obligations. He represented a common geography of the non-nuclear weapons states

---

[143] *Supra* note 117.

[144] *Id.*, Dissenting Opinion of Judge Shahabuddeen 375, at 385, referring to Protocol 2 of the 1985 South Pacific Nuclear Free Zone Treaty.

[145] *Id.*, 393.

[146] *Id.*, 407 (italics in the original).

[147] *Request for an Examination (New Zealand v. France) Case*, Separate Opinion of Judge Shahabuddeen, *supra* note 125, at 312, 312.

[148] *Arbitral Award of 1989 Case*, Separate Opinion of Judge Shahabuddeen, *supra* note 123, at 106, 119.

[149] ICJ, Border and Transborder Armed Actions (Nicaragua v. Honduras), Jurisdiction and Admissibility, Judgment, ICJ Reports 1988, 69 (Dec. 20, 1988), Separate Opinion of Judge Shahabuddeen 133, 136.

[150] ICJ, Certain Phosphate Lands in Nauru (Nauru v. Australia), Preliminary Objections, Judgment, ICJ Reports 1992, 240 (June 26, 1992), Separate Opinion of Judge Shahabuddeen 270, 300.

[151] ICJ, Maritime Delimitation in the Area between Greenland and Jan Mayen, Judgment, ICJ Reports 1993, 38 (June 14, 1993), Separate Opinion of Judge Shahabuddeen 130, 205.

[152] ICJ, Territorial Dispute (Libyan Arab Jamahiriya/Chad), Judgment, ICJ Reports 1994, 6 (Feb. 3, 1994), Separate Opinion of Judge Shahabuddeen 44, 44.

[153] *East Timor Case*, Separate Opinion of Judge Shahabuddeen, *supra* note 109, at 119, 119.

[154] *Supra* note 117.

[155] *Id.*, Dissenting Opinion of Judge Koroma 556, 573.

for whom the force of law seems to be the only available option in a world of deterrence by nuclear weapons.

The expressions of Judge Koroma's views had many sides and shades. He spoke of "fundamental principles of human rights"[156] with reference to the UN Charter provision which obligates members to comply with ICJ decisions. To him, "reciprocity is one of the precepts underlying a bilateral treaty"[157] and reliance on the "principle of effectiveness"[158] in treaty interpretation was important to effectuate the "intention of the parties."[159] He considered as "general principles of international law" "the principle that the exception to a rule should not negate the principal rule."[160] He favoured the "rules of international law as well as equitable Principles"[161] for determining "the relevance and weight of the geographical features"[162] and believed that "control by a riparian State of its own fluvial territory is matched by that of free navigation."[163] He subscribed to the position that "everyone is entitled to benefit from judicial guarantees."[164] To Judge Koroma, "there is probably a duty not to cause gross or serious damage which can reasonably be avoided."[165]

With specific reference to the Court, he believed that "clear and indubitable consent remains the basis for the assumption of jurisdiction"[166] and that the Court's "function to decide on its jurisdiction is both primary and imperative."[167] He was of the view that Article 38 of the Statute establishes "a hierarchy as to the application of the law"[168] and supported the Court in that "the application of general international law on the question [of the use of

---

[156] ICJ, Request for Interpretation of the Judgment of 31 March 2004 in the Case Concerning Avena and Other Mexican Nationals (Mexico v. United States of America) (Mexico v. United States of America), Judgment, ICJ Reports 2009, 3 (Jan. 19, 2009), Separate Opinion of Judge Koroma 23, 26, para. 11.

[157] ICJ, Certain Questions of Mutual Assistance in Criminal Matters (Djibouti v. France), Judgment, ICJ Reports 2008, 117 (June 4, 2008), Separate Opinion of Judge Koroma 252, 254–255, para. 10 [hereinafter Certain Questions of Mutual Assistance Case].

[158] ICJ, Application of the International Convention on the Elimination of All Forms of Racial Discrimination (Georgia v. Russian Federation), Preliminary Objections, Judgment, ICJ Reports 2011, 70 (Apr. 1, 2011), Separate Opinion of Judge Koroma 183, 185, para. 8 [hereinafter Racial Discrimination Case].

[159] Id., 186, para. 8.

[160] Fisheries Jurisdiction (Spain v. Canada) Case, Separate Opinion of Judge Koroma, supra note 127, at 486, 487–488, para. 6.

[161] ICJ, Territorial and Maritime Dispute between Nicaragua and Honduras in the Caribbean Sea (Nicaragua v. Honduras), Judgment, ICJ Reports 2007, 659 (Oct. 8, 2007), Separate Opinion of Judge Koroma 774, 775, para. 6.

[162] Id., Separate Opinion of Judge Koroma 774, 775, para. 6.

[163] ICJ, Kasikili/Sedudu Island (Botswana/Namibia), Judgment, ICJ Reports 1999, 1045 (Dec. 13, 1999), Declaration of Judge Koroma 1111, 1112.

[164] ICJ, LaGrand (Germany v. United States of America), Judgment, ICJ Reports 2001, 466 (June 27, 2001), Separate Opinion of Judge Koroma 541, 543, para. 6.

[165] Request for an Examination (New Zealand v. France), Dissenting Opinion of Judge Koroma, supra note 125, at 363, 378.

[166] ICJ, Maritime Delimitation and Territorial Questions between Qatar and Bahrain, Jurisdiction and Admissibility, Judgment, ICJ Reports 1995, 6 (Feb. 15, 1995), Dissenting Opinion of Judge Koroma 67, 71.

[167] ICJ, Legality of Use of Force (Serbia and Montenegro v. United Kingdom), Preliminary Objections, Judgment, ICJ Reports 2004, 1307 (Dec. 15, 2004), Declaration of Judge Koroma 1358, 1358.

[168] ICJ, Land and Maritime Boundary between Cameroon and Nigeria, Preliminary Objections, Judgment, ICJ Reports 275 (June 11, 1998), Dissenting Opinion of Judge Koroma 377, 380.

force] forms part of the interpretation process."[169] He believed that the Court cannot take "a neutral position on the issue of heinous crimes"[170] and was of the view that the mission of the Court was "not to act as a universal supreme court of criminal appeal."[171] He held the view that "it is the function of the Court to declare the law in a specific dispute before it"[172] and that an application for revision "is not to be regarded as impugning the Court's earlier legal decision."[173] He underscored for the Court the importance of the "principle of good faith"[174] and cautioned that the "[j]udgment should not be read as a license for States to commit acts of torture, crimes against humanity . . ."[175] He held the view that it is "the prerogative of a party to present the elements of fact and law of its case rather than for the Court to authorize such elements,"[176] but considered the Court to be "entitled to contribute to the peaceful settlement of disputes"[177] and "under a positive obligation to contribute to the maintenance of international peace and security."[178] In his view, "it is not the function of the Court to recognize or consecrate political reality but rather to apply the law."[179] The judicial outlook of Judge Koroma was thus not without influence of the common law legal culture that viewed the role of the Court in relation to a restrained international community with respect to nuclear weapons.

---

[169] ICJ, Oil Platforms (Islamic Republic of Iran v. United States of America), Judgment, ICJ Reports 161 (Nov. 6, 2003), Declaration of Judge Koroma 223, 223 [hereinafter Oil Platforms Case].

[170] ICJ, Arrest Warrant of 11 April 2000 (Democratic Republic of the Congo v. Belgium), Judgment, ICJ Reports 2002, 3 (Feb. 14, 2002), Separate Opinion of Judge Koroma 59, 63 [hereinafter Arrest Warrant Case].

[171] ICJ, Vienna Convention of Consular Relations (Paraguay v. United States of America), Provisional Measures, Order of 9 April 1998, ICJ Reports 1998, 248 (Apr. 9, 1998), Declaration of Judge Koroma 263, 263.

[172] *Sovereignty over Pulau Ligitan Case*, Separate Opinion of Judge Koroma, *supra* note at 136, 622, 622–623, para. 4.

[173] *Application for Revision of the Judgment of 11 July 1996 in the Case concerning* Application of the Convention on the Prevention and Punishment of the Crime of Genocide (Bosnia and Herzegovina v. Yugoslavia), Preliminary Objections *(Yugoslavia v. Bosnia and Herzegovina), Judgment,* ICJ Reports 2003, 7 (Feb. 3, 2003), Separate Opinion of Judge Koroma 34, 38, para. 11 [hereinafter Application for Revision of the Judgment of 11 July 1996 Case]. For a background, *see* ZICCARDI CAPALDO, *supra* note 126, at 69, 71.

[174] ICJ, Armed Activities in the Territory of the Congo (New Application: 2002) (Democratic Republic of the Congo v. Rwanda), Jurisdiction and Admissibility, Judgment, ICJ Reports 2006, 6 (Feb. 3, 2006), Dissenting Opinion of Judge Koroma 55, 59–60, para. 17 [hereinafter Armed Activities in Congo (New Application) Case].

[175] ICJ, Jurisdictional Immunities of the State (Germany v. Italy: Greece Intervening), Judgment [2012] ICJ Reports 2012, 99 (Feb. 3, 2012), Separate Opinion of Judge Koroma 157, 157, para. 2 [hereinafter Jurisdictional Immunities Case].

[176] ICJ, Request for Interpretation of the Judgment of 11 June 1998 in the Case concerning the Land and Maritime Boundary between Cameroon and Nigeria (Cameroon v. Nigeria), Preliminary Objections (Nigeria v. Cameroon), Judgment, ICJ Reports 1999, 31 (Mar. 25, 1999), Dissenting Opinion of Judge Koroma 49, 51–52, para. 11.

[177] ICJ, Aerial Incident of 10 August 1999 (Pakistan v. India), Jurisdiction of the Court, Judgment, ICJ Reports 2000, 12 (June 21, 2000), Separate Opinion of Judge Koroma 45, 46 [hereinafter Aerial Incident Case].

[178] ICJ, Legality of Use of Force (Yugoslavia v. United States of America), Provisional Measures, Order of 2 June 1999, ICJ Reports 1999, 916 (June 2, 1999), Declaration of Judge Koroma 929, 930.

[179] ICJ, Land and Maritime Boundary between Cameroon and Nigeria (Cameroon v. Nigeria: Equatorial Guinea intervening), Judgment, ICJ Reports 2002, 303 (Oct. 10, 2002), Dissenting Opinion of Judge Koroma 474, 474, para. 3 [hereinafter Cameroon v. Nigeria: Equatorial Guinea intervening Case].

M. Judge Al-Khasawneh of Jordan

While dissenting from the judgment of the Court in the *Oil Platforms Case*,[180] Judge Al-Khasawneh did not discernibly touch upon *erga omnes* obligations although he was critical of the "formalistic" approach of the Court.[181] Consequently, his voting in favour of Iran is not without some measure of influence of both geography and legal culture that Jordan irreducibly shares with Iran.

Judge Al-Khasawneh believed that "the legislator should leave room to the judge."[182] To him, "implicit in the very notion of an optional system is a presumption of temporariness."[183] He was of the view that "the requirement of prior negotiations . . . is ultimately a matter of form."[184] He argued that "the move towards greater personal accountability represents a higher norm than the rules on immunity."[185] He opined that "the Court could have found genocide and Federal Republic of Yugoslavia (FRY) responsibility"[186] as it was "bound by the Genocide Convention."[187] To him, "the concept of the intertemporal law is an irretrievably elusive one."[188] He believed that the "aim of any judicial settlement is to put to rest, on the basis of law, an existing dispute before a judicial body."[189] He considered that "international trade law concepts are ill-suited to be used as a yardstick against which a treaty-protected freedom of commerce can be measured."[190] In his view, "[g]eographic proximity cannot displace a clearly established title."[191] He firmly subscribed to the view that "[t]he discharge of international obligations including *erga omnes* obligations cannot be made

---

[180] The case came up before the Court in 1992 by way of an Application filed by Iran against the United States mainly in respect of a dispute arising out of the attack on and destruction of three offshore oil production complexes, owned and operated for commercial purposes by the National Iranian Oil Company, by several warships of the US Navy in 1987 and 1988. *Oil Platforms Case, supra* note 169, at 166, para. 1.

[181] *Id.,* Dissenting Opinion of Judge Al-Khasawneh 266, 268, para. 6.

[182] ICJ, Maritime Delimitation in the Caribbean Sea and the Pacific Ocean (Costa Rica v. Nicaragua), Judgment, ICJ Reports 2018, 139 (Feb. 2, 2018) [hereinafter Maritime Delimitation in the Caribbean Sea Case], Declaration of Judge *Ad hoc* Al-Khasawneh 278, 278.

[183] *Aerial Incident Case,* Dissenting Opinion of Judge Al-Khasawneh, *supra* note 177, at 48, 52, para. 15.

[184] *Armed Activities in Congo (New Application) Case,* Separate Opinion of Judge Al-Khasawneh, *supra* note 174, at 77, 81, para. 13.

[185] *Arrest Warrant Case,* Dissenting Opinion of Judge Al-Khasawneh, *supra* note 170, at 95, 99, para. 8.

[186] ICJ, Application of the Convention on the Prevention and Punishment of the Crime of Genocide (Bosnia and Herzegovina v. Serbia and Montenegro), Judgment, ICJ Reports 2007, 43 (Feb. 26, 2007), Dissenting Opinion of Vice-President Al Khasawneh 241, 254, para. 34 [hereinafter Genocide Convention 2007 Case]. For a background, *see* ZICCARDI CAPALDO, *supra* note 126, at 69, 71.

[187] ICJ, Application of the Convention on the Prevention and Punishment of the Crime of Genocide (Croatia v. Serbia), Preliminary Objections, Judgment, ICJ Reports 2008, 412 (Nov. 18, 2008), Separate Opinion of Vice-President Al-Khasawneh 468, 471 [hereinafter Genocide Convention 2008 Case].

[188] *Cameroon v. Nigeria: Equatorial Guinea intervening Case,* Separate Opinion of Judge Al Khasawneh, *supra* note 179, at 492, 500, para. 11.

[189] *Maritime Delimitation in the Caribbean Sea Case,* Dissenting Opinion of Judge *Ad hoc* Al-Khasawneh, *supra* note 182, at 271, 271.

[190] *Oil Platforms Case,* Dissenting Opinion of Vice-President Al-Khasawneh, *supra* note 169, at 266, 267, para. 4.

[191] ICJ, Maritime Delimitation and Territorial Questions between Qatar and Bahrain, Merits, Judgment, ICJ Reports 2001, 40 (Mar. 16, 2001), Separate Opinion of Vice-President Al-Khasawneh 248, 255, para. 20.

conditional upon negotiations"[192] and accordingly underscored that those obligations are not merely a matter of voluntariness.

N. Judge Elaraby of Egypt

In his dissenting opinion in the *Oil Platforms Case*,[193] Judge Elaraby underscored the duty of non-use of force, a norm of *jus cogens*,[194] generating *erga omnes* obligations. His emphasis could be attributable in some measure to his shared geography and legal culture of Iran.

Judge Elaraby believed that "[d]eclining jurisdiction while a dispute persists does not represent a positive contribution to the settlement of international disputes, which is the central function of the Court."[195] He believed that "[d]ecisions with far-reaching consequences were taken on the basis of political expediency, without due regard for the legal requirements"[196] and that "[s]tates, in general, should not be permitted to evade international judicial scrutiny regarding a crime as grave as genocide."[197] Judge Elaraby therefore underscored an international law concern that ought to address certain concerns of the international community, particularly those that generate *erga omnes* obligations.

O. Judge Skotnikov of Russian Federation

In the *Genocide Convention 2007 Case*,[198] Judge Skotnikov objected to the idea of an unstated obligation of states to not commit genocide.[199] However, he objected to it qua the Genocide Convention, which seems to imply the obligation of states to not commit genocide under non-treaty sources of international law, i.e., general international law.[200] He did not appear to dilute or doubt the *erga omnes* character of the obligation underlying the international law prohibition of genocide. Judge Skotnikov thus undescored a sense of universality in the very concept of legal culture, including of his own, and the geography of the European legal culture which may include that of his country.

In his dissenting opinion in the *Kosovo Advisory Opinion*,[201] Judge Skotnikov seems to underscore the *erga omnes* nature of obligations arising from the Security Council Resolution 1244 and against the propriety of the Court to give this advisory opinion.[202]

---

[192] ICJ, Legal Consequences of the Construction of a Wall in the Occupied Palestinian Territory, Advisory Opinion, ICJ Reports 2004, 136 (July 9, 2004), Separate Opinion of Judge Al-Khasawneh 235, 238–239, para. 13 [hereinafter Wall Advisory Opinion].

[193] *Supra* note 169.

[194] ICJ, Military and Paramilitary Activities in and Against Nicaragua (Nicaragua. v. United States) [1986] ICJ Reports 1986, 14 (June 27, 1986) 101, para. 190.

[195] ICJ, Certain Property (Liechtenstein v. Germany), Preliminary Objections, Judgment, ICJ Reports 2005, 6 (Feb. 10, 2005), Dissenting Opinion of Judge Elaraby 40, 45, para. 17.

[196] *Wall Advisory* Opinion, Separate Opinion of Judge Elaraby, *supra* note 192, at 246, 247.

[197] *Armed Activities in Congo (New Application: 2002) Case*, Declaration of Judge Elaraby, *supra* note 174, at 82, 82, para. 1

[198] The Court significantly stated that "the rights and obligations enshrined by the [Genocide] Convention are rights and obligations *erga omnes*." *Genocide Convention 1996 Case, supra* note 126, at 616, para. 31.

[199] *Genocide Convention 2007 Case*, Dissenting Opinion of Judge Skotnikov, *supra* note 186, at 366, 370.

[200] *Id.*, 371

[201] ICJ, Accordance with International Law of the Unilateral Declaration of Independence in Respect of Kosovo, Advisory Opinion [2010], ICJ Reports 2010, 403 (July 22, 2010) 453, para. 123 [hereinafter Kosovo Advisory Opinion].

[202] *Id.*, 515, paras. 1–3.

Judge Skotnikov too shared the civil law legal culture of, and the geographical proximity to, Kosovo.

In his separate opinion in *Obligation to Prosecute*,[203] Judge Skotnikov diagreed with the Court on its grounds for the admissibility of Belgium's claims.[204] He would have the Court to appreciate the special interest of Belgium undelying its legislation, request for extradition and diplomatic negotiaitons with Senegal rather than relying on Senegal's failure to comply with its *erga omnes partes* obligations.[205] He did not believe that a common interest and the right to invoke a state's responsibility are not one and the same thing.[206] He believed that if it were otherwise, treaties containing a common interest would not admit of reservations to the said right,[207] or would not make optional the scrutiny of states' accountability from the Committee Against Torture as in Article 21.[208] He thus seems to favour a more formal or positivist approach to the consideration of *erga omnes* obligations.[209]

In his separate opinion in the *Genocide Convention 2015 Case*,[210] Judge Skotnikov pointed out the peculiaritites of this case that required the Court to determine whether FRY was bound by the Genocide Convention before it became a state.[211] He considered the doctrine of succession to responsibility decisive for it, but found it impossible to locate it either in general international law or in state practice.[212] It seems to imply, in his view, the absence of *erga omnes* obligations of FRY arising out of the prevention of the crime of genocide.[213] Judge Skotnikov's reasoning thus contributes to the understanding of the nature of *erga omnes* obligation and for which the geogrpahical proximity and the civil law legal culture ingrained in a socialist background of the state of his nationality and that of FRY appear to have taken the form of positivism.

Judge Skotnikov further expressed his views on a wide variety of subjects, including on Genocide. He was of the view that "a State fails its duty to prevent under the Genocide Convention if genocide is committed within the territory where it exercises its jurisdiction or which is under its control"[214] and believed that "responsibility under the general rules of State responsibility, even if established, cannot mutate into the jurisdiction of the Court, which, unlike State responsibility, is based on consent."[215] He considered that the

---

[203] ICJ, Questions Relating to the Obligation to Prosecute or Extradite (Belgium v. Senegal), Judgment, ICJ Reports 2012, 422 (July 20, 2012) 450, para. 69 [hereinafter Obligation to Prosecute Case].

[204] *Id.*, Separate Opinion of Judge Skotnikov 481, 481, para. 1.

[205] *Id.*, 481, paras. 2–3.

[206] *Id.*, 483, para. 12.

[207] *Id.*, 483, para. 14.

[208] *Id.*, 483–484, paras. 15–16.

[209] Further, *see* Diego Germán Mejía-Lemos, *On Obligations Erga Omnes Partes' in Public International Law: "Erga Omnes" or "Erga Partes"?*, 10 Ars Boni Et Aequi 177 (2014).

[210] For the background, *see Genocide Convention 1996 Case, supra* note 198, at 616, para. 31. In his Declaration, Judge Oda also underlined that the obligations contained in the Convention "are borne in a general manner *erga omnes* by the Contracting Parties in their relations . . . with the international community as a whole . . ." *Id.*, Declaration of Judge Oda 625, 626, para. 4.

[211] Application of Genocide Convention on the Prevention and Punishment of the Crime of Genocide (Croatia v. Serbia), Judgment, ICJ Reports 2015, 3 (Feb. 3, 2015) [hereinafter Genocide Convention 2015 Case], 198, para. 8; for a background, *see* Ziccardi Capaldo, *supra* note 126, at 69, 71.

[212] *Id.*, 196, para. 4.

[213] *Id.*, 199–200, para. 12.

[214] *Genocide Convention 2007 Case*, Declaration of Judge Skotnikov, *supra* note 186, at 366, 379.

[215] *Genocide Convention 2008 Case*, Dissenting Opinion of Judge Skotnikov, *supra* note 187, at 546, 547–548, para. 4.

"exchange of accusations by the Parties . . . cannot be sufficient in determining the existence of a legal dispute."[216] He opined that "[a] media campaign directed against a foreign Head of State . . . cannot in itself be seen as a constraining act of authority."[217] In his view, the Court may not conclude contrary to "the principle that limitations on sovereignty are not to be presumed."[218] He "fail[ed] to see how the extent of an all-purpose maritime boundary can be determined by the Parties' 'extractive and enforcement capacity.'"[219] He underscored the importance of provision of an instrument and its object and purpose for its interpretation.[220]

P. Judge ad hoc Kreća of Serbia and Montenegro

In his dissent in the *Genocide Convention 2007 Case*,[221] Judge ad hoc Kreća underscored the UN General Assembly Resolution 55/12 as a manifestation of the *erga omnes* obligation.[222] He considered that "the question of jurisdiction need not necessarily be raised by the parties themselves but the Court can and should examine it ex officio."[223] He considered it "binding *erga omnes* not as a judicial act in the formal sense, but as a result of its intrinsic persuasive force, in parallel with the mandatory force of the judgment in the technical sense, based on the presumption of truthfulness—*pro veritate accipitur*—which must, in questions of status, as absolute law, have universal effect."[224] The influence or persuasiveness of the civil law legal culture seems clear that regards decisions on status to act *erga omnes*.[225]

Later, in his detailed dissenting opinion in the *Genocide Convention 2015 Case*,[226] he underscored the *erga omnes* nature of the obligations stemming from the Genocide Convention.[227] But he expressed the view against the existence of the Court's jurisdiction to adjudicate the obligation under customary law in the absence of an intention to the contrary in the treaty.[228] He also seems to favour a rather well-known and somewhat consistent view of the Court that the *erga omnes* character of an obligation and the rule of consent to jurisdiction are two different things.[229] It seems hardly doubtful that the *erga omnes* character of an obligation is not sufficient to overcome the consensual nature of adjudication by the Court.

---

[216] *Racial Discrimination Case*, Declaration of Judge Skotnikov, *supra* note 157, at 235, 238, 12.

[217] *Certain Questions of Mutual Assistance*, Declaration of Judge Skotnikov, *supra* note 157, at 284, 297, para. 21.

[218] ICJ, Dispute regarding Navigational and Other Rights (Costa Rica v. Nicaragua), Judgment, ICJ Reports 2009, 213 (July 13, 2009), Separate Opinion of Judge Skotnikov 283, 284, para. 6.

[219] ICJ, Maritime Dispute (Peru v. Chile), Judgment, ICJ Reports 2014, 3 (Jan. 27, 2014), Declaration of Judge Skotnikov 98, 99, para. 5 [hereinafter Peru v. Chile Case].

[220] ICJ, Pulp Mills on the River Uruguay (Argentina v. Uruguay), Judgment, ICJ Reports 2010, 14 (Apr. 20, 2010), Declaration of Judge Skotnikov 132, 132, para. 2 [hereinafter Pulp Mills Case].

[221] *Supra* note 186.

[222] *Id.*, Separate Opinion of Judge *ad hoc* Kreća 457, 493–494, para. 51.

[223] *Genocide Convention 2008 Case*, Dissenting Opinion of Judge *ad hoc* Kreća, *supra* note 187, at 556, 577 para. 54.

[224] *Genocide Convention 2007 Case*, Separate Opinion of Judge *ad hoc* Kreća, *supra* note 186, at 457, 497, para. 58.

[225] *Id.*, footnote 34, at 497.

[226] *Supra* note 211.

[227] *Id.*, Separate Opinion of Judge *ad hoc* Kreća, 450, 471, para. 35.

[228] *Id.*, 522, para. 105.

[229] *East Timor Case*, *supra* note 109.

Q. Judge ad hoc Mahiou of Algeria

In his Declaration in the *Ahmadou Sadio Diallo 2010 Case*,[230] Judge ad hoc Mahiou of Algeria seemed to clarify the nature of *erga omnes* obligations.[231] He clearly shared a common African geography and the civil law legal culture of his nominating state applicant Congo to the proceedings before the ICJ.

Judge ad hoc Mahiou's further views on the bench covered many other areas of international law. He did not accept "a very rigid interpretation and overly formalistic application of the Court's jurisprudence."[232] He believed that, "in the more precise context of human rights violations, the relevant texts and practice require the culpable State to compensate the injured person in full."[233] He considered that "*travaux préparatoires* traditionally form part of the elements that may at least support evidence."[234] He believed that in this case "all possible and conceivable means have been called upon and exploited . . ."[235] He considered that "the fault is one attributable to the State concerned, notwithstanding that there has been a change of régime . . ."[236] He thus represented on the ICJ a diverse geography and legal culture that is not uncommon with that which was shared by his predecessors and its members.

R. Judge Bennouna of Morocco

In his dissenting opinion in the *Kosovo Advisory Opinion*,[237] Judge Bennouna first spoke of the duty of the Court to preserve its role for the benefit of the international community,[238] which seemed to have been premised not necessarily on the absence of *erga omnes* obligations.[239] He then underscored the *erga omnes* nature of the obligations flowing from the Security Council Resolution 1244.[240]

Judge Bennouna shared his civil law legal culture with that of Kosovo and its demographical geography. He believed "that the unlawful and arbitrary character of Mr. Diallo's

---

[230] In 2010, the Court found that Congo had violated its certain human rights obligations under the 1966 Human Rights Covenants and the 1964 Consular Convention. ICJ, Ahmadou Sadio Diallo (Republic of Guinea v. Democratic Republic of the Congo), Merits, Judgment, ICJ Reports 2010, 639 (Nov. 30, 2010) [hereinafter Ahmadou Sadio Diallo 2010 Case].

[231] ICJ, Ahmadou Sadio Diallo (Republic of Guinea v. Democratic Republic of the Congo), Preliminary Objections, Judgment, ICJ Reports 2007, 582 (May 24, 2007), Declaration of Judge *Ad hoc* Mahiou 619, 620–621, paras. 3–4 [hereinafter Ahmadou Sadio Diallo 2007 Case].

[232] *Ahmadou Sadio Diallo 2010 Case*, Dissenting Opinion of Judge *Ad hoc* Mahiou, *supra* note 230, at 812, 812.

[233] ICJ, Ahmadou Sadio Diallo (Republic of Guinea v. Democratic Republic of the Congo), Compensation, Judgment, ICJ Reports 2012, 324 (June 19, 2012), Separate Opinion of Judge *Ad hoc* Mahiou 396, 397, para. 5 [Ahmadou Sadio Diallo 2012 Case].

[234] ICJ, Frontier Dispute (Burkina Faso/Niger), Judgment, ICJ Reports 2013, 44 (Apr. 16, 2013), Separate Opinion of Judge *Ad hoc* Mahiou 149, 149–151, para. 3 [Burkina Faso/Niger Case].

[235] *Genocide Convention 2007 Case*, Dissenting Opinion of Judge *Ad hoc* Mahiou, *supra* note 186, at 381, 383, para. 1.

[236] *Application for the Revision of the Judgment of 11 July 1996 Case*, Separate Opinion of Judge *Ad hoc* Mahiou, *supra* note 173, at 70, 75, para. 14.

[237] *Supra* note 201.

[238] *Id.*, Dissenting Opinion of Judge Bennouna 500, 505, para. 25.

[239] Further, *see* Ignacio de la Rasilla del Moral, *Nihil Novum Sub Sole Since the South West Africa Cases? On Ius Standi, the ICJ and Community Interests*, 10 INTERNATIONAL COMMUNITY LAW REVIEW 171 (2008).

[240] *Kosovo Advisory Opinion*, Dissenting Opinion of Judge Bennouna, *supra* note 201, at 500, 512, para. 56.

arrest, detention and expulsion . . . resulted in the violation of his direct rights as *associé* in the two companies."[241] He considered that "the search for peace among States also entails ensuring human security, namely respect for the fundamental human rights of the persons concerned and their protection, including by international justice."[242] He found it "difficult to understand why the Court avoided any pronouncement on the definition of complicity . . ."[243] and believed that the "principal judicial organ of the United Nations is expected to work to clarify complex legal situations."[244] He expressed his "regret that the Court's reasoning was not founded on the characteristics of contemporary international law, where immunity, . . . could not be justified if it would ultimately pose an obstacle to the requirements of the justice owed to victims."[245] He questioned "how can [the Court] shelter behind purely formalistic considerations . . ."[246] and considered that "the Court should have shown some hesitation about venturing into the realm of colonial law . . ."[247] He considered that "[i]n a fragmented community, . . . the judge owes it to himself to engage in a dynamic analysis of international law . . ."[248] Clearly, Judge Bennouna's conception of the international community would seem to require a less formal treatment and, consequently, a more meaningful consideration of *erga omnes* obligations.

S. Judge Tomka of Slovakia

In his Declaration in the *Kosovo Advisory Opinion,*[249] Judge Tomka stated that the declaration of independence was adopted by the Provisional Institutions of Self-Government[250] but did not seem to believe that it created *erga omnes* obligations.[251] The judicial restraint[252] that he would have the Court to exercise in this case may in some measure be attributable to the influence of geography that the country of his nationality shared with Kosovo.

In the *Genocide Convention 2015 Case,*[253] Judge Tomka argued for a strict interpretation of the jurisdcition of the Court[254] under Article IX of the Genocide Convention, a treaty that creates *erga omnes* obligations. He seems to favour a rather well-known and somewhat consistent view of the Court that the *erga omnes* character of an obligation and the rule of consent to jurisdcition are two different things.[255] The legal formalism in this view seems

---

[241] *Ahmadou Sadio Diallo 2010 Case*, Dissenting Opinion of Judge Bennouna, *supra* note 230, at 724, 724, 1.

[242] *Burkina Faso/Niger*, Declaration of Judge Bennouna, *supra* note 234, at 94, 95.

[243] *Genocide Convention 2007 Case*, Declaration of Judge Bennouna, *supra* note 186, at 359, 362.

[244] *Genocide Convention 2008 Case*, Declaration of Judge Bennouna, *supra* note 187, at 543, 545.

[245] *Jurisdictional Immunities Case,* Separate Opinion of Judge Bennouna, *supra* note 175, at 172, 177, para. 31.

[246] ICJ, Obligations Concerning Negotiations Relating to Cessation of the Nuclear Arms Race and to Nuclear Disarmament (Marshall Islands v. India), Jurisdiction and Admissibility, Judgment, ICJ Reports 2016, 255 (Oct. 5, 2016), Dissenting Opinion of Judge Bennouna 314, 316 [Marshall Islands Case].

[247] ICJ, Sovereignty over Pedra Branca/Pulau Batu Puteh, Middle Rocks and South Ledge (Malaysia/Singapore), Judgment, ICJ Reports 2008, 12 (May 23, 2008), Declaration of Judge Bennouna 128, 128, para. 3.

[248] ICJ, Application of the Interim Accord of 13 September 1995 (the former Yugoslav Republic of Macedonia v. Greece), Judgment, ICJ Reports 2011, 644 (Dec. 5, 2011), Declaration of Judge Bennouna 709, 711.

[249] *Supra* note 201.

[250] *Id.*, Declaration of Judge Tomka 454, 464, para. 32.

[251] *Id.*, 465, para. 33.

[252] *Id.*, 466, para. 35.

[253] *Supra* note 211.

[254] *Id.*, Separate Opinion of Judge Tomka 155, 167, para. 35.

[255] *East Timor Case, supra* note 109.

somewhat at variance with the universality shared by both *erga omnes* obligations and the geography of the European legal culture.

In giving expression to his views expressed on the bench on international law generally, Judge Tomka considered that "the majority has further lowered the standard."[256] He opined that the compromissory clause is "usually not the source of substantive obligations,"[257] that "it is not the emergence of a dispute which establishes the Court's jurisdiction or perfects it"[258] and that the "Applicant should not benefit from any ambiguity on its part."[259] He believed that "[w]hat is "equitable"[260] is a matter of their [states'] perception"[261] and considered "intention of the Parties" as a relevant consideration in the interpretation of an agreement. He stated that "[s]tates remain responsible for acts attributable to them which are contrary to international law,"[262] such as those that derogate from their *erga omnes* obligations.

T. Judge Donoghue of the United States

In her declaration in the *Obligation to Prosecute Case*,[263] Judge Donoghue underscored the *erga omnes* nature of the obligation under Article 7(1) of the Convention against Torture and clarified that otherwise the territorial state of the offender would be "free to accord impunity to the alleged offender"[264] on its territory. Further, she termed as substantive law the primary rules specified in the Convention and distinguished it with the dispute resolution mechanisms which do not "detract from the *erga omnes partes* character of particular obligations."[265] Judge Donoghue thus contributed to the clarificaion of an avoidable confusion about the nature of *erga omnes* obligations and that of the provisions consented for their adjudication.

Judge Donoghue believed that "the ICJ is accountable not only to disputing States but also the entire membership of the United Nations."[266] She believed that the Court can influence the behaviour of non-disputants[267] and that the existence of the Court also has "influence on national decision-making."[268] She identified "the development of international law in a manner that reflects the views of Judges coming from diverse backgrounds."[269]

---

[256] *Racial Discrimination Case*, Declaration of Vice-President Tomka, *supra* note 157, at 181, 182.
[257] *Genocide Convention 2007 Case*, Separate Opinion of Judge Tomka, *supra* note 186, at 310, 333, para. 41.
[258] *Marshall Islands Case*, Separate Opinion of Judge Tomka, *supra* note 246, at 300, 303, para. 13.
[259] *Certain Questions of Mutual Assistance*, Separate Opinion of Judge Tomka, *supra* note 157, at 269, 275, para. 25.
[260] *Peru v. Chile*, Declaration of the President Tomka, *supra* note 219, at 74, 75, para. 4.
[261] *Maritime Delimitation in the Caribbean Sea Case*, Declaration of Judge Tomka, *supra* note 182, at 228, 228, para. 3.
[262] *Genocide Convention 2008 Case*, Separate Opinion of Judge Tomka, *supra* note 187, at 521, 522, para. 19.
[263] *Supra* note 203.
[264] *Id.*, Declaration of Judge Donoughe 584, 587, para. 11.
[265] *Id.*, 588, para. 16.
[266] Joan E. Donoghue, *Expert Scientific Evidence in a Broader Context*, 9 JOURNAL OF INTERNATIONAL DISPUTE SETTLEMENT 379, 381 (2018).
[267] Joan E. Donoghue, *International Adjudication: Peaks, Valleys, and Rolling Hills*, 34 AMERICAN UNIVERSITY INTERNATIONAL LAW REVIEW 265, 273 (2018).
[268] Joan E. Donoghue, *The Role of the World Court Today*, 47 GEORGIA LAW REVIEW 181, 198 (2012).
[269] Joan E. Donoghue, *The Effectiveness of the International Court of Justice*, 108 AMERICAN SOCIETY OF INTERNATIONAL LAW PROCEEDINGS 114, 116 (2014).

Judge Donoghue's wider appreciation of international law, particularly her views on the ICJ, are not without underscoring unifying elements in the diversity of the background of members composing it and, consequently, of its significance in their consideration of *erga omnes* obligations as a discenible manifestation of that unity.

U. Judge Owada of Japan

In his declaration in the *Obligation to Prosecute Case*,[270] Judge Owada pointed out that the Court focussed "exclusively on the claim that Belgium is a state party to a convention which allegedly creates obligations *erga omnes partes*."[271] He believed that the Court's ruling on Belgium's standng to invoke the responsibility of Senegal had a "controversial basis."[272] It would seem in Judge Owada's view that the standing of a state party in respect of *erga omnes* obligations may not be assimilated to the claims of a state party having special interest.[273]

Judge Owada believed that the "international community is increasingly becoming a single global society"[274] and that its geographical scope has expanded beyond Europe.[275] He shared the view that international community regards "fundamental justice and human rights" as "universal values."[276] He contemplated the future emergence of a "new paradigm for international law . . . which will focus more on the dignity of the individual rather than on states' rights"[277] and perceived a "transformation of international society from a community of nations to a community of mankind."[278] He believed that "solidarity of the international community has grown"[279] as a result of the opening of the sphere of criminal justice.[280] He did not entirely reject the view of differences in the international community, but hoped that the situation would stabilize in the long run.[281] Judge Owada's views thus underscored an international community whose geography has expanded, together with a measure of assimilation of legal cultures represented by judges of the international court.

---

[270] *Supra* note 203.

[271] *Id.,,* Declaration of Judge Owada 464, 469, para. 19.

[272] *Id.,* 469–470, para. 21.

[273] Further, *see* Fernando Lusa Bordin, *Procedural Developments at the International Court of Justice*, 12 Law and Practice of International Courts and Tribunals 81, 86–87 (2013).

[274] Hisashi Owada, *Problems of Interaction Between the International and Domestic Orders*, 5 Asian Journal of International Law 246, 254 (2015).

[275] Hisashi Owada & Theodor Meron, *Some Reflections on Justice in a Globalized World*, 97 Proceedings of the Annual Meeting (American Society of International Law) 181, 183 (2003).

[276] Hisashi Owada, *The Rule of Law in a Globalized World—An Asian Perspective*, 8 Washington University Global Studies Law Review 187, 196 (2009).

[277] Hisashi Owada, *Remarks*, 101 American Society of International Law Proceedings 231, 233 (2007).

[278] Hisashi Owada, *Asia and International Law*, 1 Asian Journal of International Law 3, 10 (2011).

[279] Hisashi Owada, *The Changing Docket of the International Court of Justice the Significance of the Change Going Forward*, 103 Proceedings of the American Society of International Law 399, 399 (2009).

[280] Further, *see* Josh Bowers & Paul H. Robinson, *Perceptions of Fairness and Justice: The Shared Aims and Occasional Conflicts of Legitimacy and Moral Credibility*, 47 Wake Forest Law Review 211 (2012).

[281] Hisashi Owada, *What Future for the International Court of Justice*, 65 American Journal of International Law 268, 271 (1971).

V. Judge Xue Hanqin of China

In her dissenting opinion in the *Obligation to Prosecute Case*,[282] Judge Xue did not agree with the Court that Belgium had standing before the Court by "virtue of the nature of . . . *erga omnes partes* obligations."[283] She believed that the Court "referred to substantive law rather than procedural rules",[284] required the existence of "injury," as contemplated under Article 42 of ILC Articles on State Responsibility, for bringing a claim[285] and denied that the state parties to the Convention against Torture intended to create *erga omnes partes* obligations in Articles 6(2) and 7(1).[286] Thus, the views of Judge Xue seem to accord with the earlier and formal nature of the Court's jurisprudence.[287]

Judge Xue recognized the existence of "a common and indivisible world,"[288] believed that "international law has become part of the public discourse of the international community,"[289] noticed "the continuous efforts of international commnuty"[290] in the development of international criminal law and underscored the difficulty of the normative claim of the international community.[291] In her view, "[l]egal discourse has not yet become a signifi-cant part of international dialogue within Asia,"[292] "[j]ustice should be placed at the centre of international law development"[293] and "[d]iversity for the Court is not something ab-stract, but tangible."[294] The variety of areas covered by the expressions of Judge Xue is not without reflective of a diversity of backgrounds of the international bench, together with its consequences for a judicial fruition of the recognition of *erga omnes* obligations.

W. Judge ad hoc Sur of France

In his dissenting opinion in the *Obligation to Prosecute Case*,[295] Judge ad hoc Sur did not agree with the Court that the Convention against Torture establishes an "*erga omnes partes* obliga-tion to submit the case to the competent authorities for the purpose of prosecution"[296] and

---

282 *Supra* note 203.

283 *Id.,* Dissenting Opinion of Judge Xue 571, 574, para. 14.

284 *Id.,* 574–575, para. 15.

285 *Id.,* 575, para. 17.

286 *Id.,* 576, para. 20.

287 *See, in particular,* the *East Timor* and *Jurisdictional Immunities* cases, *supra* notes 109 and 175, respectively.

288 Xue Hanqin, *Relativity in International Water Law,* 3 COLORADO JOURNAL OF INTERNATIONAL ENVIRONMENTAL LAW AND POLICY 45, 52 (1992).

289 Xue Hanqin, *Closing Plenary: Global Governance, State Sovereignty, and the Future of International Law,* 107 AMERICAN SOCIETY OF INTERNATIONAL LAW PROCEEDINGS 489, 494 (2013).

290 Xue Hanqin, *Chinese Observations on International Law,* 6 CHINESE JOURNAL OF INTERNATIONAL LAW 83, 91 (2007).

291 Xue Hanqin, *Chinese Contemporary Perspectives in International Law: History, Culture and International Law,* 355 RECUEIL DES COURS 47, 111 (2012). Further, *see Marshall Islands Case,* Declaration of Judge Xue, *supra* note 246, at 441, 443–444, para. 8.

292 Xue Hanqin, *Meaningful Dialogue Through a Common Discourse: Law and Values in a Multi-Polar World,* 1 ASIAN JOURNAL OF INTERNATIONAL LAW 13, 18 (2011).

293 Xue Hanqin, *A Point to Meet: Justice and International Criminal Law,* 4 ASIAN JOURNAL OF INTERNATIONAL LAW 35, 39 (2014).

294 Xue Hanqin, *The Effectiveness of International Law: Plenary Discussion: A Conversation with International Court of Justice Judges,* 108 PROCEEDINGS OF THE ANNUAL MEETING (AMERICAN SOCIETY OF INTERNATIONAL LAW) 385, 385 (2014).

295 *Supra* note 203.

296 *Id.,* Dissenting Opinion of Judge *ad hoc* Sur 605, 608, para. 13.

believed that the Court failed to justify the *erga omnes* obligation basis of admissibility of the Belgium's Application.[297] To him, the "*erga omnes* partes jurisdiction takes effect immediately and is not dependent on individual complaints"[298] and that the "*erga omnes character* of a treaty as a whole cannot be presumed or inferred from the presence of an erga omnes obligation therein."[299] Somewhat like Judge Xue, he seems to favour a more formal role of the Court in matters of *erga omnes* obligations.

Judge ad hoc Sur inherited a European geography and was trained in the civil law legal culture of France. He acknowledged a discernibly embedded positivism that nuclear "proliferation is no longer the privilege of rich and developed countries . . ."[300] He believed the "international community" to be "dear to development law and globalistic aspirations."[301] But on that account alone, he could hardly be fully seen to accord it a place before the Court which is not discernible from international law expressly recognized by contesting states.

X. Judge Cançado Trindade of Brazil

In his separate opinion in the *Obligation to Prosecute Case*,[302] Judge Cançado Trindade expressed the view that obligations *erga omnes* ensue from the Convention against Torture and which are "necessarily of conduct"[303] for being in "the domain of peremptory norms of international law, *jus cogens* . . ."[304] Next, in his dissenting opinion in the *Marshall Islands Case*,[305] he endorsed the International Law Association view of nuclear disarmament as "evolving customary international obligation with an *erga omnes* character . . ."[306] His universalist-naturalist conception of international law underlying his advocacy of such an obligation seems informed also by the geography of a non-nuclear weapons state of his nationality and a measure of universality of legal culture. Later, in the *Jadhav Case*,[307] he believed that "an unlawful condemnation to death is clearly discarded . . ."[308] as the rights of the individual are "constructed on the basis of evolving concepts of . . . obligations *erga omnes* of protection."[309]

Judge Cançado Trindade considered that the evolving law on the conservation and sustainable use of living marine resources has contributed to "the gradual formation of an *opinio juris communis*."[310] He believed that "[o]urs are the times of a new *jus gentium*, focused

---

[297] *Id.*, 611, para. 20.

[298] *Id.*, 612, para. 24.

[299] *Id.*, 614, para. 29.

[300] Serge Sur, *Non-Proliferation and the NPT Review*, 40 INTERNATIONAL SPECTATOR 7, 17 (2005).

[301] Serge Sur, *The State between Fragmentation and Globalization*, 3 EUROPEAN JOURNAL OF INTERNATIONAL LAW 421, 429.

[302] *Supra* note 207.

[303] *Id.*, Separate Opinion of Judge Cançado Trindade 487, 555–556, para. 175.

[304] *Id.*, 556, para. 176.

[305] By its judgment of October 5, 2016, the Court upheld India's objection to jurisdiction based on the absence of a dispute between the parties. *Supra*, note 246.

[306] *Marshall Islands Case*, Dissenting Opinion of Judge Cançado Trindade, *supra* note 246, at 321, 379–380, para. 155.

[307] By its judgment of July 17, 2019, the Court found violations of the Vienna Convention by Pakistan. ICJ, Jadhav (India v. Pakistan), Judgment, ICJ Reports 2019, 418 (July 17, 2019) [hereinafter Jadhav Case].

[308] *Id.*, Separate Opinion of Judge Cançado Trindade 462, 476, para. 44.

[309] *Id.*, 466 and 491, paras. 14 and 96.

[310] ICJ, Whaling in the Antarctic (Australia v. Japan: New Zealand intervening), Judgment, ICJ Reports 2014, 226 (Mar. 31, 2014), Separate Opinion of Judge Cançado Trindade 348, 381, para. 89 (italics in the original).

on the rights of the human person,"[311] that the "theory of the 'act of State' cannot at all be relied upon, in face of grave breaches of human rights"[312] and that the "international judicial function" ultimately seeks "the goal of the *realization of justice* . . ."[313] Thus, what irreducibly underlies successively the views of Judge Cançado Trindade is a humanist conception of international law that regards it beyond voluntarism and sustains the international legal thinking in affirmation of *erga omnes* obligations.

III. CONCLUSIONS

Differences of geography and legal culture have not been without discernible convergence in the treatment of *erga omnes* obligations by ICJ judges. Geographical propinquity between the Netherlands and Belgium and the similarity of their legal culture came in for the defence of the Belgian interest in the hands of Judge ad hoc Riphagen, but apparently not by way of an identical conceptual understanding or manifestation of *erga omnes* obligations in the *Barcelona Traction Case*. Judge Al-Khasawneh's voting in favour of Iran in the *Oil Platforms Case* is not without some influence of both geography and legal culture that Jordan shares with Iran. Judge Elaraby's emphasis on the principle of non-use of force is attributable in some measure to his shared geography and legal culture of Iran. Judge ad hoc Mahiou clearly shared a common African geography and civil law legal culture with his nominating state applicant Congo to the proceedings before the ICJ in *Ahmadou Sadio Diallo*. In appreciating the significance of the international community in the *Kosovo Advisory Opinion*, Judge Bennouna underscored his civil law legal culture with that of Kosovo and the latter's demographical geography. Later, in underscoring the *erga omnes* nature of obligations arising from the Security Council Resolution 1244 in the *Kosovo Advisory Opinion*, Judge Skotnikov also testified to his shared civil law legal culture of, and geographical proximity to, Kosovo. The judicial restraint in giving the character of *erga omnes* obligation to the declaration of independence in preference to the Security Council Resolution 1244 that Judge Tomka would have the Court to exercise in the *Kosovo Advisory Opinion* was in some measure attributable to the influence of geography that his country shared with Kosovo. The legal formalism embedded in the view of strict interpretation of the Court's jurisdiction taken by Judge Tomka in the *Genocide Convention 2015 Case* seems at variance with the universality shared by both *erga omnes* obligations and legal culture and geography of the European legal culture. Judge ad hoc Kreća's essential reiteration of the consensual nature of the Court's jurisdiction in the *Genocide Convention 2015 Case* seems to draw not so much on legal culture than on the geography of the state of his nationality and respondent in the case. Judge Donoghue's wider appreciation of international law, particularly her views on the ICJ, are not without underscoring unifying elements in the diversity of the background of members composing it and, consequently, of its significance in their consideration of *erga omnes* obligations as a discenible manifestation of that unity. The variety of areas covered by the expressions of Judge Xue is not without reflective of a diversity of backgrounds of

---

[311] *Ahmadou Sadio Diallo 2010 Case*, Separate Opinion of Judge Cançado Trindade, *supra* note 241, at 729, 735, para. 22.

[312] *Jurisdictional Immunities Case*, Dissenting Opinion of Judge Cançado Trindade, *supra* note 175, at 179, 205–206, para. 69.

[313] ICJ, Certain Activities Carried Out by Nicaragua in the Border Area (Costa Rica v. Nicaragua), Compensation, Judgment, ICJ Reports 2018, 15 (Dec. 16, 2015), Separate Opinion of Judge Cançado Trindade 61, 62, para. 4 (italics in the original).

the international bench, together with its consequences for a judicial fruition of the recognition of *erga omnes* obligations.

Legal reasoning and precepts employed by judges from across geography and legal culture have shown some discernible commonality. Judge Fitzmaurice's underscoring of the requirement of state consent in any legal relationship between state and international organizations in the *Namibia Advisory Opinion* seems to underscore a restrictive nature of the role of positivist legal thinking in the emergence and/or evolution of *erga omnes* obligations significantly underlying the idea of the existence of an international community. Judge Morozov of Russia spoke in the *Tehran Hostage Case* also of a moral right which is neither without elements that correspond to obligations resembling *erga omnes* obligations nor devoid of the influence on him of the civil law legal culture. Judge Weeramantry's legal reasoning seems to have been deeply ingrained in the common law legal culture the practical consequences of which were intended to overcome the necessary party argument of Indonesia in the *East Timor Case* and to underscore caution in accepting that the lapse of time would lessen the binding force of the resolution containing an *erga omnes* obligation. Judge Xue in her disenting opinion in the *Obligation to Prosecute Case* underscored the Court's reliance on the substantive law of Convention Against Torture and diagreed with the accordance of standing to each state for vindication of *erga omnes* obligations. In his declaration in the *Obligation to Prosecute Case*, Judge Owada seems to be saying that the standing of a state party in respect of *erga omnes* obligations may not be assimilated to the claims of a state party having special interest. Judge Skotnikov's reasoning in the *Genocide Convention 2015 Case* contributes to the understanding of the nature of *erga omnes* obligation and for which the geographical proximity and the civil law legal culture ingrained in a socialist background of the state of his nationality and that of FRY appears to have taken the form of positivism that does not seem to allow the Court any discernible room for the development of *erga omnes* obligations underlying the Convention. Somewhat like Judge Xue, Judge ad hoc Sur seems to favour a more formal role of the Court in matters of *erga omnes* obligations.

The influence of legal culture is not without a certain measure of universality in and universalization of its conception. Judge ad hoc Skubiszewski's civil law legal culture background seems to have had discernibly no different impact in the *East Timor Case* on his understanding of *erga omnes* obligations than those of the judges of the common law legal culture and thereby underscores in no small measure to essentially universalizing character of legal culture and unifying character of *erga omnes* obligations. Judge Skotnikov of Russian Federation in the *Genocide Convention 2007 Case* underscored a sense of universality in the very concept of legal culture inasmuch as he had no objection to the obligation of states not to commit genocide under non-treaty sources of international law, i.e., general international law. The persuasiveness of the civil law legal culture was clear on Judge ad hoc Kreća in the *Genocide Convention 2007 Case* that regards that decisions on status act *erga omnes*. In her declaration in the *Obligation to Prosecute Case*, Judge Donoghue distinguished the substantive law of CAT with the dispute resolution mechanisms which are not inconsistent with the *erga omnes partes* character of certain obligations. Judge Owada's views underscored an international community whose geography has expanded, together with a measure of assimilation of legal cultures represented by judges of the international court.

There seems to have emerged what may be termed as geographies of non-nuclear weapons states and the colonial past probative in some measure of the evolution of *erga omnes* obligations, such as an evolving *erga omnes* obligation of nuclear disarmament and protection of the individual. Although France, the national state of Judge Gros, did not have any significant geographical or legal culture ties with South Africa, it was no less a colonial power in Africa than the United Kingdom. Not so much the influence of legal culture as of the geographical consideration of Guyana being a non-nuclear weapons state that seems to underlie the perspective of *erga omnes* obligation of nuclear disarmament in the dissent of Judge Shahabuddeen of Guyana in the *Nuclear Weapons Advisory Opinion (GA Request)*. Like Judge Weeramantry, Judge Koroma represented the common geography of the non-nuclear weapons states; for them the force of law is the only available option in a world of deterrence by nuclear weapons. Judge Weeramantry stood in the *Nuclear Weapons Advisory Opinion (GA Request)* for the common geography of the non-nuclear weapons states whom he defended by the persuasiveness of his arguments underlying some of *erga omnes* obligations. Judge Cançado Trindade endorsed the ILA view of nuclear disarmament in the *Marshall Islands Case* as "evolving customary international obligation with an *erga omnes* character, affecting 'the international community as a whole'"[314] and likened in the *Jadhav Case* the rights of the individual corresponding to obligations *erga omnes*. His universalist-naturalist conception of international law underlying his advocacy of such an obligation seems also informed by the geography of a non-nuclear weapons state of his nationality and a certain measure of the universality of legal culture.

Geographical considerations in the form of nationality have not necessarily resulted in only an identical or predictable judicial behaviour. It seems that Judge ad hoc Tarazi in the *Tehran Hostage Case* was influenced more by the inviolability of diplomatic personnel in the Islamic legal culture than by the geography of his nationality. The argument of Judge ad hoc Barwick in the *Nuclear Tests Case* does not appear to be solely motivated by the reasoning underlying *erga omnes* obligations. However, the intended final objective of that argument was undeniably to also advance the evolution of *erga omnes* obligations.

---

[314] *Marshall Islands Case*, Dissenting Opinion of Judge Cançado Trindade, *supra* note 246, at 321, 379, para. 154.

II

Module—
ENVIRONMENTAL
LAW, LAW OF THE SEA,
GLOBAL COMMONS LAW

The Relationship Between the ITLOS and the ICJ or Another International Court or Arbitral Tribunal

II.I

Alleged Violations of Sovereign Rights and Maritime Spaces in the Caribbean Sea (*Nicaragua v. Colombia*)

Reflections on the ICJ Judgment of 21 April 2022

BY YOSHIFUMI TANAKA*

Abstract

The *Nicaragua v. Colombia* judgment of 21 April 2022 is rich in its content, examining both jurisdictional and substantive issues of international law. In the *Nicaragua v. Colombia* case, the International Court of Justice (ICJ), for the first time, examined the question of whether the Court's jurisdiction *ratione temporis* covers facts or events that allegedly occurred after the lapse of the title of jurisdiction. Furthermore, the Court made some important statements with regard to the customary law nature of relevant provisions of the UN Convention on the Law of the Sea. In this regard, the Court declared that Nicaragua's straight baselines are contrary to customary international law as reflected in Article 7(1) of the Convention. The *Nicaragua v. Colombia* judgment provides a crucial precedent on this matter. In light of its importance, this article examines key issues of the judgment, inter alia: (1) jurisdiction *ratione temporis* of the ICJ, (2) Colombia's contested activities in Nicaragua's maritime zones, (3) the legality of Colombia's "integrated contiguous zone," (4) the artisanal fishing rights of the inhabitants of the San Andrés Archipelago, in particular the Raizales, and (5) the legality of Nicaragua's straight baselines.

* Professor of International Law, Faculty of Law, University of Copenhagen; Member of the Editorial Board.

Yoshifumi Tanaka, *Alleged Violations of Sovereign Rights and Maritime Spaces in the Caribbean Sea (*Nicaragua v. Colombia*)* In: *The Global Community Yearbook of International Law and Jurisprudence 2022*. Edited by: Giuliana Ziccardi Capaldo, Oxford University Press.
© Oxford University Press 2023. DOI: 10.1093/oso/9780197752265.003.0013

I. INTRODUCTION

On 19 November 2012, the International Court of Justice (ICJ) delivered its judgment concerning territorial and maritime dispute between Nicaragua and Colombia.[1] However, the judgment could not end the dispute because Colombia refused to implement the judgment.[2] In reality, Colombia has continued certain activities in marine spaces which now fall within Nicaragua's exclusive economic zone (EEZ). In response, on 26 November 2013, Nicaragua instituted proceedings against Colombia before the ICJ on the basis of Article XXXI of the American Treaty on Pacific Settlement (Pact of Bogotá).[3] In its application, Nicaragua requested that the Court adjudge and declare, inter alia that "(a) By its conduct, the Republic of Colombia has breached its international obligation to respect Nicaragua's maritime zones as delimited in paragraph 251 of the Court Judgment of 19 November 2012, as well as Nicaragua's sovereign rights and jurisdiction in these zones."[4]

In response, Colombia raised five preliminary objections to the jurisdiction of the Court on 19 December 2014.[5] In its judgment of 17 March 2016, however, the ICJ found that it had jurisdiction to entertain the dispute concerning the alleged violations by Colombia of Nicaragua's right in the maritime zones concerned.[6] Subsequently, Colombia, in its Counter-Memorial, submitted four counter-claims.[7] The counter-claims related to: (1) Nicaragua's alleged breach of its obligation to protect and pre-serve the marine environment of the south-western Caribbean Sea, (2) Nicaragua's alleged breach of rights of Colombia and the Raizal community as an Indigenous group, (3) Nicaragua's alleged breach of the traditional fishing rights of the Raizal community and Colombia in the same maritime area, and (4) Nicaragua's straight baselines.[8] The ICJ, in its Order of 15 November 2017, found that only Colombia's third and fourth

---

[1] *Territorial and Maritime Dispute (Nicaragua v. Colombia)*, Judgment, ICJ Reports 2012, 624 (19 November 2012).

[2] In this regard, the Colombian President stated that the Court had committed serious mistakes. Statement of Colombian President, Mr. Juan Manuel Santos. Application of Instituting Proceedings by Nicaragua, 26 November 2013, para. 4, at 6–7, available at < https://www.icj-cij.org/public/files/case-related/155/17978.pdf>. *See also* <http://wsp.presidencia.gov.co/Prensa/2012/Noviembre/Paginas/20121119_02.aspx>. For a reaction of Colombia to the 2021 judgment, *see also* presentation by Carlos José Argüello Gómez, Verbatim Record, CR 2021/13, at 19–21 (20 September 2021), available at <https://www.icj-cij.org/public/files/case-related/155/155-20210920-ORA-01-00-BI.pdf>.

[3] Application of Instituting Proceedings by Nicaragua, *supra* note 1, para. 16, at 20.

[4] Verbatim Record, CR 2021/17, at 50 (27 September 2021), available at <https://www.icj-cij.org/public/files/case-related/155/155-20210927-ORA-01-00-BI.pdf>.

[5] Preliminary Objections of Colombia, 19 December 2014, available at <https://www.icj-cij.org/public/files/case-related/155/18788.pdf>.

[6] The ICJ upheld the second preliminary objection raised by Colombia in so far as it concerns the existence of a dispute regarding alleged violations by Colombia of its obligation not to use force or threaten to use force. Apart from this, the Court rejected all other preliminary objections. *Alleged Violations of Sovereign Rights and Maritime Spaces in the Caribbean Sea (Nicaragua v. Colombia)*, Preliminary Objections, ICJ Reports 2016, para. 111, at 42–43 (17 March 2016).

[7] Counter-Memorial of Colombia, Vol. I, 17 November 2016, available at <https://www.icj-cij.org/public/files/case-related/155/155-20161117-WRI-01-00-EN.pdf>.

[8] *Id.*, para. 1.27, at 14–15.

counter-claims were admissible as such and formed part of the current proceedings.[9] Subsequently, on 21 April 2022, the Court delivered its judgment (merits).[10]

The *Nicaragua v. Colombia* judgment contains some crucial issues concerning jurisdiction of the ICJ and the interpretation or application of the UN Convention on the Law of the Sea (hereinafter UNCLOS or the Convention).[11] In light of its importance, this article examines the judgment focusing on: (1) jurisdiction *ratione temporis* of the ICJ, (2) Colombia's contested activities in Nicaragua's maritime zones, (3) the legality of Colombia's "integrated contiguous zone," (4) the artisanal fishing rights of the inhabitants of the San Andrés Archipelago, in particular the Raizales, and (5) the legality of Nicaragua's straight baselines.

Following the introduction in section I, section II considers the scope of jurisdiction *ratione temporis* of the ICJ. Section III examines Colombia's contested activities in Nicaragua's maritime zones and the legality of Colombia's "integrated contiguous zone," respectively. Section IV turns to address Nicaragua's alleged infringement of the artisanal fishing rights of the inhabitants of the San Andrés Archipelago and the legality of Nicaragua's straight baselines. Finally, section V concludes.

II. SCOPE OF THE JURISDITION *RATIONE TEMPORIS* OF THE COURT

A. The ICJ's View

This section examines the scope of jurisdiction *ratione temporis* of the ICJ. On 27 November 2012, Colombia noticed its denunciation of the Pact of Bogotá. As a consequence, the Pact ceased to be in force for Colombia as of 27 November 2013, the day after Nicaragua's Application was filed. "Given that Colombia's consent to the Court's jurisdiction lapsed as of that date," Colombia claimed, "the Court has no jurisdiction *ratione temporis* to consider any alleged violations that occurred afterwards."[12] The question is whether the Court's jurisdiction covers facts or events that allegedly occurred after the lapse of the title of jurisdiction under the Pact of Bogotá.[13] Under Article XXXI of the Pact:

> In conformity with Article 36, paragraph 2, of the Statute of the International Court of Justice, the High Contracting Parties declare that they recognize in relation to any other American State, the jurisdiction of the Court as compulsory *ipso facto*, without the necessity of any special agreement so long as the present Treaty is in force, in all disputes of a juridical nature that arise among them concerning: *a)* The interpretation of a treaty; *b)* Any question of international law; *c)* The existence of any fact which, if established, would constitute the breach of an international obligation; *d)* The nature or extent of the reparation to be made for the breach of an international obligation.

---

[9] *Alleged Violations of Sovereign Rights and Maritime Spaces in the Caribbean Sea (Nicaragua v. Colombia),* Counter-Claims, ICJ Reports 2017, para. 82, at 314–315 (15 November 2017).

[10] *Alleged Violations of Sovereign Rights and Maritime Spaces in the Caribbean Sea (Nicaragua v. Colombia),* Judgment, ICJ Reports 2022 (not yet reported), available at <https://www.icj-cij.org/public/files/case-related/155/155-20220421-JUD-01-00-EN.pdf>.

[11] Adopted 10 December 1982, entered into force 16 November 1994. Text in: 1833 UNTS 3.

[12] Counter-Memorial of Colombia, *supra* note 7, para. 4.21, at 166. *See also* Rejoinder of Colombia, Vol. 1, paras. 3.8–3.19, at 88–94 (15 November 2018), available at <https://www.icj-cij.org/public/files/case-related/155/155-20181115-WRI-01-00-EN.pdf>; the 2022 *Nicaragua v. Colombia* case, *supra* note 10, para. 34.

[13] The 2022 *Nicaragua v. Colombia* case, *supra* note 10, para. 40.

In light of the phrase "so long as the present Treaty in force" under the provision, Colombia submitted that "the Court has no jurisdiction to rule on the legality of any alleged wrongful acts said to be attributed to Colombia after 27 November 2013 when the Pact was no longer in force for Colombia."[14]

However, the Colombia's claim was declined by the Court, stating that "the 2016 Judgment does not preclude the Court from entertaining those incidents that allegedly occurred after the filing of the application."[15] In the view of the Court, "its Judgment [of 2016] implies that the Court has jurisdiction to examine every aspect of the dispute that the Court found to have existed at the time of the filing of the Application."[16] In this regard, the Court specified two criteria. The first is whether the incidents alleged to have occurred after the lapse of the jurisdiction are connected that the alleged incidents that have already been found to fall within the Court's jurisdiction. For the purposes of this article, this criterion can be called the "connexity" test. The second criterion is whether consideration of those alleged incidents does not transform the nature of the dispute between the parties in dispute.[17] This criterion can be called "continuity test." By applying the two criteria, the Court held that those alleged incidents did not transform the nature of the dispute between the parties. It accordingly concluded that it "has jurisdiction *ratione temporis* over Nicaragua's claims relating to those alleged incidents."[18]

B. Discussion

As regards the Court's view, four points merit discussion. The first concerns a legal basis for the Court's interpretation. As the Court stated, it may be true that "[t]here is nothing in the Court's jurisprudence to suggest that the lapse of the jurisdictional title after the institution of proceedings has the effect of limiting the Court's jurisdiction *ratione temporis* to facts which allegedly occurred before that lapse."[19] However, the Court did not refer to any authority or legal basis for supporting the Court's interpretation.[20] In this regard, the majority referred to the dictum stated in *Certain Questions of Mutual Assistance in Criminal Matters*.[21] Yet this case, which relied on *forum prorogatum*, concerned the Court's

---

[14] Rejoinder of Colombia, *supra* note 12, para. 3.9, at 88–89; presentation by Bundy, CR 2021/15, paras. 33–46, at 14–18 (22 September 2021), available at <https://www.icj-cij.org/public/files/case-related/155/155-20210922-ORA-02-00-BI.pdf>; presentation by Bundy, CR 2021/18, paras. 18–33, at 32–35 (29 September 2021), available at <https://www.icj-cij.org/public/files/case-related/155/155-20210929-ORA-01-00-BI.pdf>; the 2022 *Nicaragua v. Colombia* case, *supra* note 10, para. 39.

[15] The 2022 *Nicaragua v. Colombia* case, *supra* note 10, para. 41.

[16] *Id.*, para. 45.

[17] *Id.*, paras. 45–47.

[18] *Id.*, para. 47.

[19] *Id.*

[20] In fact, the Court itself admitted that "the question posed by Colombia has not previously been presented to the Court." *Id.*, para. 43. Judge ad hoc McRae stated that "there is nothing in the Court's jurisprudence to say that the Court can take jurisdiction over events that have occurred after the lapse of jurisdiction title." Dissenting Opinion of Judge ad hoc McRae, para. 10, available at <https://www.icj-cij.org/public/files/case-related/155/155-20220421-JUD-01-10-EN.pdf>. *See also* Dissenting Opinion of Judge Abraham, para. 4, available at <https://www.icj-cij.org/public/files/case-related/155/155-20220421-JUD-01-03-FR.pdf>; Separate Opinion of Judge Yusuf, para. 6, available at <https://www.icj-cij.org/public/files/case-related/155/155-20220421-JUD-01-05-EN.pdf>.

[21] The 2022 *Nicaragua v. Colombia* case, *supra* note 10, para. 44; *Certain Questions of Mutual Assistance in Criminal Matters (Djibouti v. France)*, Judgment, ICJ Reports 2008, para. 87, at 211–212 (4 June 2008).

jurisdiction *ratione materiae*, not jurisdiction *ratione temporis*.[22] In the end, the Court, in the *Nicaragua v. Colombia* judgment, seemingly failed to refer to the precedents that support its interpretation in the jurisprudence.[23]

The second point relates to the validity of the criteria adopted by the Court. As regards the connexity test, it is less clear to what extent facts or events subsequent to the lapse of the Court's jurisdiction must be connected to the alleged incidents that have already been found to fall within the Court's jurisdiction. Concerning the continuity test, the Court offered no guidance with regard to the standard for deciding the same nature of the dispute. In light of this, the practical application of the criteria is not free from challenges.[24]

The third point pertains to the distinction between the jurisdictional title and the temporal scope of the jurisdiction. According to its established jurisprudence, the termination of the Pact of Bogotá after the filling of the Application cannot affect the jurisdiction of the Court.[25] However, this does not directly mean that the termination of the Pact of Bogotá after the filling of the Application does not affect the scope of the Court's jurisdiction *ratione temporis*.[26] The legal effect of the cease of a treaty that provides a jurisdictional basis on the Court's jurisdiction *ratione temporis* must be distinguished from the effect on the jurisdictional title.

Fourth, an issue arises whether the parties to the Pact of Bogotá intended to allow the Court to extend its jurisdiction to facts or events which occurred after the treaty ceases to be in force for a state party or, conversely, whether the parties to the Pact intended to limit the temporal scope of the Court's jurisdiction by excluding facts or events which occur after the Pact ceases to be in force for a state party.[27] This issue needs to be considered in light of Article 31 of the Vienna Convention on the Law of Treaties[28] and, if necessary, by referring to supplementary means of interpretation, including the *travaux préparatoires*. However, the Court did not take a trouble to do so. To say the least, the Court did not positively prove that the parties presumably have intended to allow the Court to extend the jurisdiction of the Court to facts or events which occurred after the expiration of the Court's jurisdictional basis. Given that the Court's jurisdiction must rest on the clear consent of the parties, one cannot easily presume that the parties to the Pact of Bogotá intended to extend the jurisdiction of the Court to facts or events which occurred after the treaty ceases to be in force

---

[22] Dissenting Opinion of Judge Nolte, para. 6, available at <https://www.icj-cij.org/public/files/case-related/155/155-20220421-JUD-01-09-EN.pdf>. The ICJ itself recognised this point. The 2022 *Nicaragua v. Colombia* case, *supra* note 10, para. 44.

[23] Dissenting Opinion of Judge ad hoc McRae, *supra* note 20, para. 6.

[24] In fact, opinions of the members of the Court can be divided on this matter. Contrary to the majority of the Court, Judge Yusuf, in the 2022 *Nicaragua v. Colombia* case, considered that "the incidents that have allegedly occurred before and after 27 November 2013 are neither uniform in character nor do they always relate to identical facts or common legal bases." Separate Opinion of Judge Yusuf, *supra* note 20, para. 13. Judge Abraham opined that "[l]es faits allégués par le Nicaragua et qui se seraient produits après le 27 novembre 2013 sont parfaitement dissociables des faits antérieurs (car il ne suffit pas selon moi qu'ils soient plus ou moins de même nature), et chacun d'entre eux appelle un examen séparé, auquel procède l'arrêt." Dissenting Opinion of Judge Abraham, *supra* note 20, para. 10.

[25] The 2022 *Nicaragua v. Colombia* case, *supra* note 10, para. 42.

[26] In this regard, Judge Bennouna considered that "jurisdiction cannot extend to facts and events which occurred after the critical date of 27 November 2013." Declaration of Judge Bennouna, para. 5, available at <https://www.icj-cij.org/public/files/case-related/155/155-20220421-JUD-01-04-EN.pdf>.

[27] Dissenting Opinion of Judge Nolte, *supra* note 22, para. 9.

[28] Adopted 22 May 1969. Entered into force 27 January 1980. Text in: 1155 UNTS 331.

for a state party. In light of this, it appears that the validity of the Court's interpretation on jurisdiction *ratione temporis* needs further consideration.[29]

III. ALLEGED VIOLATION BY COLOMBIA OF NICARAGUA'S RIGHTS IN ITS MARITIME ZONES

This section examines the ICJ's view with regard to Colombia's contested activities in Nicaragua's maritime zones and the legality of Colombia's "integral contiguous zone," respectively.

A. Colombia's Contested Activities in Nicaragua's Maritime Zones

1. The ICJ's View

The first issue concerns the legality of Colombia's activities in Nicaragua's maritime zones. Since Colombia is not a state party to UNCLOS, customary international law applied to the present case.[30] In this regard, the ICJ made clear that "[c]ustomary rules on the rights and duties in the exclusive economic zone of coastal States and other States are reflected in several articles of UNCLOS, including Articles 56, 58, 61, 62 and 73."[31] Specifically, the Court examined three issues under customary international law: (1) Colombia's jurisdiction with regard to the preservation of the marine environment of the south-western Caribbean Sea, (2) Colombia's alleged authorisation of fishing activities and marine scientific research, and (3) Colombia's alleged oil exploring licensing. As regards the third issue, the Court dismissed Nicaragua's claim because Nicaragua had failed to prove that Colombia continues to offer petroleum blocks situated in Nicaragua's EEZ.[32] Therefore, only the first two issues merit discussion.

First, the legality of Colombia's actions in the south-western Caribbean Sea must be examined. After an examination of some ten incidents claimed by Nicaragua, the ICJ held that the Colombian naval vessels purported to exercise enforcement jurisdiction in Nicaragua's EEZ.[33] An issue that arose here was the legality of Colombia's actions relating to the protection of the environment of the south-western Caribbean Sea. In this regard, Colombia relied on three types of rights and duties recognised by international law: (1) the right and duty to protect and preserve the environment of the south-western Caribbean Sea, (2) the due diligence duty within the relevant maritime area, and (3) the right and duty to protect the habitat of the Raizales and other local communities inhabiting the Archipelago.[34]

Colombia has become a party to bilateral and regional agreements to protect and preserve the area, in particular, the 1983 Convention for the Protection and Development of the Marine Environment of the Wider Caribbean Region (hereinafter the Cartagena Convention)[35] and the 1990 Protocol Concerning Specially Protected Areas and Wildlife to the Convention for the Protection and Development of the Marine Environment of

---

[29] *See* Dissenting Opinion of Judge Nolte, *supra* note 22, para. 12; Separate Opinion of Judge Yusuf, *supra* note 20, paras. 7 and 10.

[30] The 2022 *Nicaragua v. Colombia* case, *supra* note 10, para. 48.

[31] *Id.*, para. 57.

[32] *Id.*, para. 143.

[33] *Id.*, para. 92.

[34] *Id.*, para. 54.

[35] Both Colombia and Nicaragua are parties to the Cartagena Convention.

the Wider Caribbean Region (hereinafter the SPAW Protocol).[36] The ICJ called the two treaties the "Cartagena regime."[37] Later on, Colombia established the Seaflower Biosphere Reserve and the Seaflower Marine Protected Area in 2000 and 2005, respectively, with a view to protecting the marine environment in the south-western Caribbean Sea and the habitat of the Raizales community.[38]

A key issue is to what extent Colombia may exercise its rights and discharge its obligation under the Cartagena regime in an area that presently falls within the Nicaragua's EEZ.[39] As the 2015 Advisory Opinion of the International Tribunal for the Law of the Sea (ITLOS) stated, a third state has "an obligation to ensure compliance by vessels flying its flag with relevant conservation measures concerning living resources enacted by the coastal State for its exclusive economic zone."[40] According to the ICJ, however, "[a] third State has no jurisdiction to enforce conservation standards on fishing vessels of other States in the exclusive economic zone."[41] Colombia is under an international obligation to respect Nicaragua's sovereign rights and jurisdiction in its EEZ on the basis of the Cartagena Convention and the SPAW Protocol. In this regard, Article 10 of the Cartagena Convention provides that "[t]he establishment of such areas shall not affect the rights of other Contracting Parties and third States." It follows that Colombia may not enforce conservation standards and protection measures in Nicaragua's EEZ.[42] Similarly, under Article 3(2) of the SPAW Protocol, each party must "endeavour to co-operate in the enforcement of these [protective] measures without prejudice to the sovereignty, or sovereign rights of jurisdiction of other States." Accordingly, the power of the states parties to adopt an enforce conservation measures is limited to the marine areas in which they exercise sovereignty, or sovereign rights, or jurisdiction.[43] In light of the preceding considerations, the Court found that Colombia had violated its international obligation to respect Nicaragua's sovereign rights and jurisdiction in the latter's EEZ.[44]

Second, the legality of Colombia's fishing activities and marine scientific research in Nicaragua's EEZ must be considered. After an examination of the evidence presented by the parties, the Court accepted, inter alia, that the fishing vessels allegedly authorised by Colombia did engage in fishing activities in Nicaragua's EEZ during the relevant time.[45] The fact was confirmed by the conduct of Colombian naval frigates.[46] The Court accordingly found, by 9 votes to 6 that by authorising fishing activities in Nicaragua's EEZ, Colombia has violated Nicaragua's sovereign rights and jurisdiction in this maritime zone.[47] However, the Court found that it cannot conclude that Colombia also authorised marine scientific research in Nicaragua's EEZ.[48]

---

[36] Both Colombia and Nicaragua are parties to the SPAW Protocol.

[37] The 2022 *Nicaragua v. Colombia* case, *supra* note 10, para. 95.

[38] Counter-Memorial of Colombia, *supra* note 7, para. 3.51, at 122; para. 11.3, at 344. The Seaflower Biosphere Reserve and the Seaflower Marine Protected Area largely overlap Nicaragua's EEZ. *Id.*, Figure 2.3, at 51.

[39] The 2022 *Nicaragua v. Colombia* case, *supra* note 10, para. 97.

[40] *Request for Advisory Opinion submitted by the Sub-Regional Fisheries Commission*, Advisory Opinion, ITLOS Reports 2015, para. 120, at 37 (2 April 2015).

[41] The 2022 *Nicaragua v. Colombia* case, *supra* note 10, para. 95.

[42] *Id.*, para. 98.

[43] *Id.*, para. 99.

[44] *Id.*, para. 101.

[45] *Id.*, para. 131.

[46] *Id.*, para. 261(3); para. 132.

[47] *Id.*, para. 134.

[48] *Id.*, para. 133.

2. Discussion

An essential issue that arises here concerns the question of whether Colombia can exercise its enforcement jurisdiction with regard to the protection of the marine environment in Nicaragua's EEZ. Under Article 192 of UNCLOS, "States have the obligation to protect and preserve the marine environment." The obligation extends both to "protection" of the marine environment from *future* damage and "preservation" in the sense of maintaining or improving its *present* condition. Article 192 thus entails both the positive obligation to take active measures to protect and preserve the marine environment as a whole, and the negative obligation not to degrade the marine environment at the same time.[49] As ITLOS stated, "the conservation of the living resources of the sea is an element in the protection and preservation of the marine environment."[50] Furthermore, the Annex VII Arbitral Tribunal, in the 2016 *South China Sea* Arbitration Award, considered that the general obligation to protect and preserve the marine environment in Article 192 includes a due diligence obligation to prevent the harvesting of species that are recognised internationally as being at risk of extinction and requiring international protection.[51] Hence, it can be considered that the protection of marine biological diversity also constitutes part of the obligation to protect and preserve the marine environment. It would be fair to say that this obligation reflects a rule of customary international law.[52] Furthermore, as discussed elsewhere, the obligation can be considered as an obligation *erga omnes*.[53] Thus some consideration must be given to the legal consequences of a breach of an obligation *erga omnes* in a particular context of the protection of the marine environment.[54]

---

[49] The *South China Sea* Arbitration (*The Philippines v. The People's Republic of China*) (Merits), 33 *RIAA*, para. 941, at 519 (12 July 2016).

[50] *Southern Bluefin Tuna Cases (New Zealand v. Japan; Australia v. Japan)*, Provisional Measures, ITLOS Reports 1999, para. 70, at 295 (27 August 1999). *See also Request for an Advisory Opinion Submitted by the Sub-Regional Fisheries Commission (SRFC)*, Advisory Opinion, ITLOS Reports 2015, at 37, para. 120, at 37 (2 April 2015).

[51] The *South China Sea* arbitral award (Merits), *supra* note 49, para. 956, at 526; *see also* para. 959, at 527.

[52] *See* UNGA, *Protection and Preservation of the Marine Environment: Report of the Secretary-General* UN Doc. A/44/461, para. 29, at 10 (18 September 1989). In addition, the OSPAR Convention, in its Preamble, recalled "the relevant provisions of customary international law reflected in Part XII of the United Nations Law of the Sea Convention." Convention for the Protection of the Marine Environment of the North-East Atlantic. Opened for signature 22 September 1992, entered into force 25 March 1998. Text in: 2354 UNTS 67. This view is supported by commentators, including: ALAN BOYLE & CATHERINE REDGWELL, BIRNIE, BOYLE AND REDGWELL'S INTERNATIONAL LAW AND THE ENVIRONMENT 511 (4th ed. 2021); PHILIPPE SANDS & JACQUELINE PEEL, WITH ADRIANA FABRA & RUTH MACKENZIE, PRINCIPLES OF INTERNATIONAL ENVIRONMENTAL LAW 462 (3d ed. 2018); Detlef Czybulka, *Article 192, in* UNITED NATIONS CONVENTION ON THE LAW OF THE SEA: A COMMENTARY 1284–1285 (Alexander Proelss ed., 2017); JAMES HARRISON, SAVING THE OCEANS THROUGH LAW: THE INTERNATIONAL LEAL FRAMEWORK FOR THE PROTECTION OF THE MARINE ENVIRONMENT 24–25 (2017).

[53] Yoshifumi Tanaka, *Changing Paradigms in the Law of the Sea and the Marine Arctic*, 35(3) INTERNATIONAL JOURNAL OF MARINE AND COASTAL LAW 441–443 (2020). *See also* HARRISON, *supra* note 52, at 24–25. For a definition of the obligation *erga omnes*, *see* Institut de Droit International, *Resolution: Obligations* Erga Omnes *in International Law* (Krakow Session 2005), Article 1, <https://www.idi-iil.org/app/uploads/2017/06/2005_kra_01_en.pdf>.

[54] Generally on this issue, *see* Yoshifumi Tanaka, *Legal Consequences of Obligations* Erga Omnes *in International Law*, 68(1) NETHERLANDS INTERNATIONAL LAW REVIEW 1 (2021).

A breach of obligations *erga omnes* creates an obligation not to recognise unlawful situations.[55] This point is confirmed by Article 5(b) of the 2005 Resolution of the Institut de droit international:

> Should a widely acknowledged grave breach of an *erga omnes* obligation occur, all the States to which the obligation is owed:
> [...]
> (b) shall not recognize as lawful a situation created by the breach.[56]

It follows that if a coastal state continuously breaches an obligation to protect and preserve the marine environment, including marine ecosystems, other states are under the obligation not to recognise the illegal situations.[57] However, this does not mean that instead of a responsible state, a third state can exercise its jurisdiction to protect and preserve the marine environment in the EEZ of the responsible state. In this regard, Colombia asserted that "where a fragile ecosystem is at stake, international law requires both Parties to take proactive action and not adopt a 'wait-and-see' attitude."[58] Nonetheless, the Colombia's claim was dismissed by the ICJ, stating that "[t]he fragility of the ecological environment of a protected area established by a State party does not provide a legal basis for it to take measures in areas that are subject to the sovereignty, sovereign rights or jurisdiction of another State party."[59]

On the other hand, it may be possible for third states to ask an international court or tribunal to declare the breach by the coastal state of an obligation to protect and preserve the marine environment. As noted by the Institut de Droit International:

> In the event of there being a jurisdictional link between a State alleged to have committed a breach of an obligation *erga omnes* and a State to which the obligation is owed, the latter State has standing to bring a claim to the International Court of Justice or other international judicial institution in relation to a dispute concerning compliance with that obligation.[60]

Chandrasekhara Rao, former Judge of ITLOS, and Philippe Gautier, former Registrar of ITLOS, also took the view that "any State Party to the Convention is entitled to institute proceedings with respect to a violation of provision of the Convention relating to the preservation of the marine environment, committed outside marine areas under its

---

[55] *Id.*, at 12–16.

[56] Institut de droit international, *supra* note 53. *See also* Article 41(2) of the ILC's Draft Articles on State Responsibility for Internationally Wrongful Acts. Reproduced in JAMES CRAWFORD, THE INTERNATIONAL LAW COMMISSIONS' ARTICLES ON STATE RESPONSIBILITY: INTRODUCTION, TEXT AND COMMENTARIES (2002).

[57] However, the obligation of non-recognition will have little effect in a factual action that has already been accomplished since those acts do not create situations that are capable of being denied by States.

[58] Counter-Memorial of Colombia, *supra* note 7, para. 3.47, at 121. *See also* presentation by Boisson de Chazournes, CR 2021/14, paras. 33–44, at 43–46 (22 September 2021), available at <https://www.icj-cij.org/public/files/case-related/155/155-20210922-ORA-01-00-BI.pdf>.

[59] The 2022 *Nicaragua v. Colombia* case, *supra* note 10, para. 99.

[60] Institut de droit international, *supra* note 53, Article 3. Further, *see* Tanaka, *supra* note 54, at 20–28.

jurisdiction."[61] This view was supported by the *South China Sea* arbitral award (merits). The Annex VII arbitral tribunal, in the *South China Sea* arbitral award, accepted the *locus standi* of the Philippines with regard to an alleged breach of environmental obligations by China in areas beyond 200 nautical miles from the coasts of the Philippines, even though no material damage occurred to the Philippines.[62] As discussed elsewhere,[63] the jurisprudence seems to hint in the direction that there may be room for the view that all states, including states that are not directly injured, can have *locus standi* to invoke responsibility for a breach of the obligation to protect and preserve the marine environment, including marine ecosystems, before an international court or tribunal, if that court or tribunal can establish its jurisdiction. Thus, for a third state, the better approach may be to invoke the state responsibility for an alleged breach of an obligation *erga omnes* to protect and preserve the marine environment, not to exercise enforcement jurisdiction in the EEZ of the responsible state.

B. Colombia's "Integral Contiguous Zone"

1. *The ICJ's View*

The second issue concerns the legality of Colombia's "integral contiguous zone" which was established by Colombia's Presidential Decree 1946.[64] Some parts of the Colombia's "integral contiguous zone" extend more than 24 nautical miles from Colombia's baselines and overlap with Nicaragua's EEZ.[65] In the contiguous zone, Colombia was empowered to exercise the faculties of enforcement and control necessary to prevent and control the infractions of the laws and regulations related with the integral security of the state.[66] In response, Nicaragua maintained that the geographical extent and the material scope of the Colombia's powers within the zone was contrary to customary international law.[67] The ICJ, in its judgment of 2022, made some important statements concerning rules governing the contiguous zone. Here, four points merit being highlighted.

First, contrary to Colombia's claim,[68] the Court explicitly accepted the customary law character of the contiguous zone, stating:

> Article 33 of UNCLOS reflects contemporary customary international law on the contiguous zone, both in respect of the powers that a coastal State may exercise there and the limitation of the breadth of the contiguous zone to 24 nautical miles.[69]

---

[61] CHANDRASEKHARA RAO & PHILIPPE GAUTIER, THE INTERNATIONAL TRIBUNAL FOR THE LAW OF THE SEA: LAW, PRACTICE AND PROCEDURE 327 (2018).

[62] The *South China Sea* arbitral award (Merits), *supra* note 49, paras. 925–931, at 515–516.

[63] YOSHIFUMI TANAKA, THE SOUTH CHINA SEA ARBITRATION: TOWARD AN INTERNATIONAL LEGAL ORDER IN THE OCEANS 205 (2019).

[64] Counter-Memorial of Colombia, *supra* note 7, para. 5.1, at 189.

[65] Reply of Nicaragua, para. 3., at 39 *et seq.* (15 May 2018), available at <https://www.icj-cij.org/public/files/case-related/155/155-20180515-WRI-01-00-EN.pdf>; presentation by Paul Reichler, CR 2021/13, para. 14, at 45 (20 September 2021); the 2022 *Nicaragua v. Colombia* case, *supra* note 10, para. 171.

[66] *Id.*, para. 170. *See also* Counter-Memorial of Colombia, *supra* note 7, para. 5.35, at 209.

[67] The 2022 *Nicaragua v. Colombia* case, *supra* note 10, para. 145.

[68] Colombia submitted that Article 33 of UNCLOS does not reflect customary international law. Counter-Memorial of Colombia, *supra* note 7, para. 5.39, at 211.

[69] The 2022 *Nicaragua v. Colombia* case, *supra* note 10, para. 155.

The Court accordingly held that "Colombia is under an international obligation to observe the 24-nautical-mile rule" and that "[t]he geographical extent of the 'integrated contiguous zone' is not conformity with customary international law, as reflected in Article 33, paragraph 2, of UNCLOS."[70]

Second, the Court held that "Colombia has the right to establish a contiguous zone around the San Andrés Archipelago in accordance with customary international law."[71] According to the Court, while the contiguous zone and EEZ may overlap, but "the powers that may be exercised therein and the geographical extent are not the same" in the two zones.[72]

Third, the Court dismissed Colombia's argument that coastal state's powers in its contiguous zone includes control over security and marine pollution. In the words of the Court:

> [S]ecurity was not a matter that States agreed to include in the list of matters over which a coastal State may exercise control in the contiguous zone; nor has there been any evolution of customary international law in this regard since the adoption of UNCLOS.[73]

Furthermore, the Court was not convinced that "the meaning of that word, as used in Article 33, paragraph 1, of UNCLOS, has evolved to extend to the protection of the marine environment, a matter that is separately governed by customary international law on the environment."[74] Thus the Court adopted a cautious stance with regard to expansion of the coastal state's power in its contiguous zone.

Fourth, in light of a growing number of states that have extended the application of their cultural heritage legislation over the contiguous zone and multilateral treaties on this subject, the Court took the view that Article 303(2) of the UNCLOS reflects customary international law.[75]

In light of the preceding considerations, the ICJ concluded:

> [T]he "integral contiguous zone" established by Colombia's Presidential Decree 1946 is not in conformity with customary international law in two respects. First, the geographical extent of the "integral contiguous zone" contravenes the 24-nautical-mile rule for the establishment of the contiguous zone. Secondly, Article 5 (3) of Presidential Decree 1946 confers certain powers on Colombia to exercise control over infringements of its laws and regulations in the "integral contiguous zone" that extend to matters that are not permitted by customary rules as reflected in Article 33, paragraph 1, of UNCLOS.[76]

It followed that Colombia must, by means of its own choosing, bring into conformity with customary international law the provisions of Presidential Decree 1946 of 9 September 2013, as amended by Decree 1119 of 17 June 2014.[77]

---

[70] *Id.*, para. 175.

[71] *Id.*, para. 163.

[72] *Id.*, para. 161.

[73] *Id.*, para. 177. *See also* para. 180.

[74] *Id.*, para. 180.

[75] *Id.*, paras. 185–186.

[76] *Id.*, para. 187. *See also* operative paragraph 261(5).

[77] *Id.*, para. 261(6).

2. Discussion

Two points merit being highlighted. First, as explained earlier, the ICJ accepted Colombia's entitlement to the contiguous zone in the Nicaragua's EEZ. Following the Court's view, a coastal state's contiguous zone can overlap an EEZ of another state. According to a majority view, the coastal state has only enforcement jurisdiction in its contiguous zone and, consequently, action of the coastal state may only be taken concerning offences committed within the territory or territorial sea of the coastal state, not in respect of anything done within the contiguous zone itself. It appears that the interpretation of the ICJ is linked to a restrictive interpretation of the scope of powers of a coastal state in its contiguous zone.[78]

Second, the Court refuted to apply evolutionary interpretation "of Article 33(1) of the UNCLOS. However, Judge ad hoc McRae opined that "this was an appropriate case for the Court to interpret Article 33 of UNCLOS in an evolutionary manner."[79] According to Judge ad hoc McRae:

> An assessment of the security needs of States today might well include the suppression of the drug trade and the protection of the marine environment. Indeed, at a time of heightened concern about the impact of climate change, the protection of the marine environment might be seen for some States as their primary security concern. Moreover, the last twenty years have shown that piracy, which might have been dealt with adequately under international law in 1956, has been posing an increasing problem for States in certain regions, including in their territorial seas. It is not surprising then that a State might wish to act in its contiguous zone to prevent piracy within its territorial sea or to punish when piracy has occurred within its territorial sea.[80]

As a matter of policy, this view seems to have some merits. However, the question is whether the expansion of the coastal state's power in the contiguous zone has been supported by subsequent state practice.[81] As the Annex VII arbitral tribunal rightly stated in the *South China Sea* arbitral award (Merits), the threshold the ICJ establishes for accepting an agreement on the interpretation by state practice is quite high.[82] In this regard, the ICJ observed that "[a]lthough there are a few States that maintain in their national laws the power to exercise control with respect to security in the contiguous zone, their practice has been opposed by other States."[83] The Court also dismissed Colombia's argument that the word "sanitary" can include marine environmental protection because "[t]here is no basis, either in law or in State practice, to give this term the expansive interpretation proposed by Colombia."[84] In light of the high threshold for accepting an agreement on the interpretation

---

[78] According to Sir Gerald Fitzmaurice, the power over the contiguous zone is "essentially supervisory and preventative." Gerald Fitzmaurice, *Some Results of the Geneva Conference on the Law of the Sea*, 8 INTERNATIONAL AND COMPARATIVE LAW QUARTERLY 114 (1959). However, Oda argued that in the contiguous zone, the coastal state should be entitled to exercise its authority as exercisable in the territorial sea only for some limited purposes of customs or sanitary control. Shigeru Oda, *The Concept of the Contiguous Zone*, 11 INTERNATIONAL AND COMPARATIVE LAW QUARTERLY 153 (1962); *see also* D.P. O'CONNELL, THE INTERNATIONAL LAW OF THE SEA, vol. 2, at 1060 (I.A. Shearer ed., 1984).

[79] Dissenting Opinion of Judge ad hoc McRae, *supra* note 20, para. 49.

[80] *Id.*, para. 43.

[81] Article 31(3) of the Vienna Convention on the Law of Treaties.

[82] The *South China Sea* arbitral award (Merits), *supra* note 49, para. 552, at 391.

[83] The 2022 *Nicaragua v. Colombia* case, *supra* note 10, para. 154.

[84] *Id.*, para. 180.

by state practice, it seems difficult to support the expansion of coastal state's power in the contiguous zone through subsequent state practice.

IV. COUNTER-CLAIMS MADE BY COLOMBIA

This section addresses Colombia's third and fourth counter-claims: the artisanal fishing rights and the legality of Nicaragua's straight baselines.

A. The Artisanal Fishing Rights

1. The ICJ's View·

The Colombia's third counter-claim concerns Nicaragua's alleged infringement of the artisanal fishing rights of the inhabitants of the San Andrés Archipelago to access and exploit the traditional banks.[85] In this regard, Colombia asserted that "[t]he artisanal fishermen of the Archipelago have been fishing in their traditional fishing grounds since time immemorial, regardless of past and present disputes."[86] Here, two issues arose. The first was whether the inhabitants of the San Andrés Archipelago, in particular the Raizales, have historically enjoyed "artisanal fishing rights" in areas that now fall within Nicaragua's EEZ and the second was whether those "rights" have survived the establishment of Nicaragua's EEZ.[87] The ICJ, in its judgment, focused on the first issue.

The Colombia's counter-claim regarding the traditional fishing rights relied on two main contentions: the alleged long-standing practices and statements of President Ortega, the Head of State of Nicaragua. However, the ICJ dismissed both contentions.

When considering the alleged long-standing practices, historical evidence is of critical importance to prove the existence of the rights since the artisanal fishing rights can be considered as a sort of historic rights.[88] In this regard, Colombia relied on eleven affidavits annexed to its Counter-Memorial to prove the existence of a long-standing practice of artisanal fishing by the inhabitants of the San Andrés Archipelago, in particular the Raizales.[89] However, the ICJ was cautious in giving weight to affidavit evidence.[90]

In this context, the Court noted three points. First, "[s]ome affiants refer to fishing expeditions beyond the Colombian islands being limited to 'a few times a year', while others

---

[85] Generally on artisanal fishing rights, *see* Stephen Allen, *The Jurisprudence of Artisanal Fishing Rights Revisited*, *in* THE RIGHTS OF INDIGENOUS PEOPLES IN MARINE AREAS 97 (Stephen Allen, Nigel Bankes & Øyvind Ravna eds., 2019).

[86] Counter-Memorial of Colombia, *supra* note 7, para. 3.102, at 149. According to Colombia, "[a]rtisanal fishing generally comprises traditional, small-scale fishing practices undertaken by local inhabitants for subsistence or the local community." *Id.*, para. 2.69, at 60.

[87] The 2022 *Nicaragua v. Colombia* case, *supra* note 10, para. 218. According to Colombia, Raizales have inhabited and derived economic sustenance from the Archipelago of San Andrés and the associated maritime areas for almost 400 years. Presentation by Kent Francis James, CR 2021/14, para. 4, at 19 (22 September 2021).

[88] In fact, Colombia, in its Counter-Memorial, often referred to the "historical fishing rights." *See, for instance*, Counter-Memorial of Colombia, *supra* note 7, para. 3.3, at 96; paras. 3.95–3.97, at 145–146; para. 3.109, at 152; para. 9.1, at 287; para. 9.13–9.14, at 293–294. For a monograph of historic rights, *see* CLIVE R. SYMMONS, HISTORIC WATERS AND HISTORIC RIGHTS IN THE LAW OF THE SEA: A MODERN REAPPRAISAL (2d ed. 2019).

[89] The 2022 *Nicaragua v. Colombia* case, *supra* note 10, para. 218.

[90] *Territorial and Maritime Dispute between Nicaragua and Honduras in the Caribbean Sea (Nicaragua v. Honduras)*, Judgment, ICJ Reports 2007 (II), para. 244 at 731 (8 October 2007).

claim to have carried out fishing in those areas since the 1980s and 1990s."[91] According to the Court, a time span was not "long enough to qualify such fishing as 'a long-standing practice' or to support Colombia's claim concerning the existence of a local custom or of 'a local customary right to artisanal fishing.' "[92] Second, most of the artisanal fishing has been conducted in waters surrounding the Colombian features or in fishing grounds located within Colombia's territorial sea. Third, certain affidavits did not address the alleged historical nature of the fishing conducted in waters now falling in Nicaragua's EEZ.[93] In light of this, the ICJ considered that "the 11 affidavits submitted by Colombia do not sufficiently establish its claim that the inhabitants of the San Andrés Archipelago, in particular the Raizales, have been engaged in a long-standing practice of artisanal fishing in 'traditional fishing banks' located in waters now falling within Nicaragua's exclusive economic zone."[94]

In summary, it may be said that affidavits submitted by Colombia contained deficiencies in both space (location of fishing) and time (a short time span). There is no established standard for the length of time necessary for a historic right to emerge.[95] In accordance with the dictum of the ICJ in the *Nicaragua v. Colombia* judgment, however, it can be reasonably considered that only decades would be inadequate to generate historic fishing rights.

As regards statements of President Ortega, the Court took the view that "the statements by President Ortega do not establish that Nicaragua has recognized that the inhabitants of the San Andrés Archipelago, in particular the Raizales, have the right to fish in Nicaragua's maritime zones without having to request prior authorization."[96] Related to this, the Court paid attention to the factual circumstances in which the unilateral statement was made. According to the Court, the statements of Nicaragua's head of state merely indicated that the Nicaraguan authorities were aware of the issues regarding the fishing activities of the inhabitants of the Archipelago. Furthermore, both parties agreed that the statements were made in the context of political protests in the aftermath of the 2012 judgment of the Court. In light of the context and a need for adopting a restrictive interpretation, the Court declined the Colombia's argument on the basis of the statements of President Ortega.[97]

In conclusion, the Court held that Colombia has failed to establish the artisanal fishing rights of the inhabitants of the San Andrés Archipelago.[98] Consequently, the Court did not address the second issue regarding the legal status of the traditional fishing right of a particular community in the EEZ of another state.[99]

2. Discussion

The ICJ's approach in the *Nicaragua v. Colombia* judgment contrasted with the Annex VII arbitral tribunal's approach in the *South China Sea* arbitration (Merits). In the *Nicaragua*

---

[91] The 2022 *Nicaragua v. Colombia* case, *supra* note 10, para. 220.

[92] *Id.*

[93] *Id.*

[94] *Id.*, para. 221.

[95] *Juridical Regime of Historic Waters including Historic Bays: Study Prepared by the Secretariat*, A/CN.4/143, (1962) 2 *Yearbook of the International Law Commission*, para. 123, at 18.

[96] The 2022 *Nicaragua v. Colombia* case, *supra* note 10, para. 227.

[97] *Id.*, para. 230. However, Judge ad hoc McRae disagreed with the majority opinion. Judge ad hoc McRae argued that the artisanal fishing rights of Raizal should be considered as analogous to claims to the rights of Indigenous peoples. Dissenting Opinion of Judge ad hoc McRae, *supra* note 20, paras. 51–71.

[98] The 2022 *Nicaragua v. Colombia* case, *supra* note 10, para. 231.

[99] *Id.*

v. Colombia judgment, the ICJ focused on historical evidence regarding the alleged artisanal fishing rights claimed by Colombia, without examining the relationship between
the historic rights and UNCLOS. By contrast, the arbitral tribunal, in the *South China
Sea* arbitration (Merits), gave much weight to the relationship between the historic rights
and UNCLOS. An essential feature of the arbitral tribunal's approach was that the tribunal minimized the role of the historical elements. In the *South China Sea* arbitral award
(Merits), the arbitral tribunal examined the validity of China's claimed historic rights at
the three phases:

> Phase I – China's historic rights prior to the entry into force of the Convention
> in1996.
> Phase II – China's historic rights when the Convention entered into force in relation
> to China in 1996.
> Phase III – China's historic rights after the entry into force of the Convention in 1996.

At all phases, the tribunal dismissed China's historic rights.[100]

Of particular note concerns the Annex VII arbitral tribunal's approach in phase II.
There, the arbitral tribunal examined the question regarding whether the UNCLOS intended the continued operation of historic rights that are at variance with it.[101] The arbitral
tribunal's view was clear:

> The Convention does not include any express provisions preserving or protecting his-
> toric rights that are at variance with the Convention. On the contrary, the Convention
> supersedes earlier rights and agreements to the extent of any incompatibility. The
> Convention is comprehensive in setting out the nature of the exclusive economic zone
> and continental shelf and the rights of other States within those zones. China's claim to
> historic rights is not compatible with these provisions.[102]

For the tribunal:

> The Tribunal considers the text and context of the Convention to be clear in superseding
> any historic rights that a State may once have had in the areas that now form part of the
> exclusive economic zone and continental shelf of another State. There is no ambiguity
> here that would call for the Tribunal to have recourse to the supplementary means of
> interpretation set out in Article 32 of the Vienna Convention.[103]

---

[100] Further, *see* Yoshifumi Tanaka, *Reflections on Historic Rights in the South China Sea Arbitration (Merits)*, 32
THE INTERNATIONAL JOURNAL OF MARINE AND COSTAL LAW 458 (2017); TANAKA, *supra* note 63, 59
et seq.

[101] The *South China Sea* arbitral award, *supra* note 49, para. 239, at 275.

[102] *Id.*, para. 246, at 279.

[103] *Id.*, para. 247, at 279. Symmons, in his authoritative study on historic waters and historic rights, opined
that the arbitral tribunal's view could be supported by the supposed comprehensive coverage of
UNCLOS and the provisions relating to a coastal state's rights under the Convention in its EEZ or on its
continental shelf. SYMMONS, *supra* note 88, at 50. Symmons further argued that the clear aim of Article
62(3) of the Convention "was to eliminate all historically-claimed rights per se in what is now another
State's EEZ." *Id.*, 55.

Following the arbitral tribunal's view, artisanal fishing rights in the EEZ are not safeguarded by UNCLOS.[104] Accordingly, to protect artisanal fishing rights, there will be a need to negotiate on a bilateral basis.[105]

Furthermore, some consideration must be given to the legal effect of unilateral declaration of Nicaragua's head of state concerning the artisanal fishing rights of the inhabitants of the San Andrés Archipelago. In the *Nuclear Tests* case, the ICJ recognised that in appropriate circumstances, unilateral declarations can create legal obligations, stating:

> It is well recognized that declarations made by way of unilateral acts, concerning legal or factual situations, may have the effect of creating legal obligations . . . When it is the intention of the State making the declaration that it should become bound according to its terms, that intention confers on the declaration the character of a legal undertaking, the State being thenceforth legally required to follow a course of conduct consistent with the declaration.[106]

Inspired by the *dictum* of the *Nuclear Tests* judgment, Guiding Principles Applicable to Unilateral Declarations of States Capable of Creating Legal Obligations adopted by the ILC (hereinafter the ILC's Guiding Principles) states:

> Declarations publicly made and manifesting the will to be bound may have the effect of creating legal obligations. When the conditions for this are met, the binding character of such declarations is based on good faith; States concerned may then take them into consideration and rely on them; such States are entitled to require that such obligations be respected.[107]

In practice, however, the ICJ has been cautious when accepting the binding nature of unilateral declarations. In this regard, the Chamber of the ICJ, in the 1986 *Frontier Dispute* case, stated that it had a duty to show even greater caution when it is a question of a unilateral declaration not directed to any particular recipient.[108] In the view of the Court, "it all depends on the intention of the State in question."[109] Furthermore, the Court, in the *Nicaragua v. Colombia* judgment, stressed "the need to consider the factual circumstances in which the unilateral statement was made and the need to consider carefully whether the State issuing the declaration intended to be bound by it."[110] The Court's view is echoed by the ILC's Guiding Principles, which states:

> 3. To determine the legal effects of such declarations, it is necessary to take account of their content, of all the factual circumstances in which they were made, and of the reactions to which they gave rise.[111]

---

[104] Judge Xue, in her Declaration, argued that "[t]he advent of the régime of the exclusive economic zone, as set forth in UNCLOS, does not by itself extinguish traditional fishing rights that may be found to exist under customary international law." Declaration of Judge Xue, para. 9, available at <https://www.icj-cij.org/public/files/case-related/155/155-20220421-JUD-01-06-EN.pdf>. However, the learned judge omitted reference to the *South China Sea* arbitral award.

[105] The *South China Sea* arbitral award, *supra* note 49, para. 804(b), at 469; Allen, *supra* note 85, at 115.

[106] *Nuclear Tests (Australia v. France)*, Judgment, ICJ Reports 1974, para. 43, at 267 (20 December 1974).

[107] ILC, Guiding Principles applicable to unilateral declarations of states capable of creating legal obligations, available at < https://legal.un.org/ilc/texts/instruments/english/draft_articles/9_9_2006.pdf>.

[108] *Frontier Dispute (Burkina Faso v. Republic of Mali)*, ICJ Reports 1986, para. 39, at 574 (22 December 1986).

[109] *Id.*, at 573, para. 39.

[110] The 2022 *Nicaragua v. Colombia* case, *supra* note 10, para. 229.

[111] ILC, *supra* note 107, Principle 3.

The Court, in the *Nuclear Tests* case, took the view that "[w]hen States make statements by which their freedom of action is to be limited, a restrictive interpretation is called for."[112] Following the precedent, the Court applied a restrictive interpretation to the statements of Nicaragua's head of state in the *Nicaragua v. Colombia* judgment.[113] It appears that the restrictive interpretation is also supported by the ILC's Guidelines, which states:

> A unilateral declaration entails obligations for the formulating State only if it is stated in clear and specific terms. In the case of doubt as to the scope of the obligations resulting from such a declaration, such obligations must be interpreted in a restrictive manner.[114]

Overall it can be said that the *Nicaragua v. Colombia* judgment confirmed a restrictive interpretation of unilateral statements in the jurisprudence.

B. Nicaragua's Straight Baselines

Finally, the legality of Nicaragua's straight baselines must be considered.[115] Nicaragua established straight baselines in the Caribbean Sea by Degree 33 of 27 August 2013.[116] According to Nicaragua, two base points are located on its mainland coast and the seven basepoints are located on the low-water line along the "island" fringing Nicaragua's mainland coast.[117] The conditions for drawing straight baselines are set out in Article 7 of UNCLOS. There, the ICJ considered that Article 7(1) reflects customary international law.[118] However, the practical application of this provision encounters formidable challenges. An issue at point was whether or not Nicaragua's straight baselines are conformity with Article 7(1).

1. "Deeply Indented and Cut Into"

In order to draw straight baselines, the coast must be "deeply indented and cut into" under Article 7(1). It is clear that this condition derives from the *Norwegian Fisheries* judgment.[119] The Court admitted that "[a]n examination of the relevant maps reveals that Nicaragua's southernmost coast does, in fact, curve inward."[120] According to the Court, however, "it is not sufficient for the coast to have slight indentations and concavities" under Article 7(1).[121] For the Court:

> The indentations along the relevant portion of Nicaragua's coast do not penetrate sufficiently inland or present characteristics sufficient for the Court to consider the said

---

[112] *Nuclear Tests (Australia v. France)*, Judgment, ICJ Reports 1974, para. 44, at 267.

[113] The 2022 *Nicaragua v. Colombia* case, *supra* note 10, para. 231.

[114] ILC, *supra* note 107, Principle 7.

[115] For Colombia's claims, *see* presentation by Jean-Marc Thouvenin, CR 2021/15, paras. 8–62, at 52–64 (22 September 2021).

[116] Reply of Nicaragua, *supra* note 65, para. 7.3, at 151. Nicaragua's Degree No. 33-2013 was adopted in the wake of the 2002 *Nicaragua v. Colombia* judgment of the ICJ. *Id.*, para. 7.9, at 153. The text of the Degree was reproduced in: 83 LAW OF THE SEA BULLETIN 35 (2014). *See also* a figure at the end of this article.

[117] Reply of Nicaragua, *supra* note 65, para. 7.15, at 156. According to Nicaragua, "[t]he individual segments of Nicaragua's straight baseline system measure between 44 and 83 nautical miles." Presentation by Oude Elferink, CR 2021/16, para. 13, at 40 (24 September 2021), available at <https://www.icj-cij.org/public/files/case-related/155/155-20210924-ORA-01-00-BI.pdf>.

[118] The 2022 *Nicaragua v. Colombia* case, *supra* note 10, para. 244.

[119] *Fisheries (United Kingdom v. Norway)*, Judgment, ICJ Reports 1951, at 128–129 (18 December 1951).

[120] The 2022 *Nicaragua v. Colombia* case, *supra* note 10, para. 245.

[121] *Id.*

portion as "deeply indented and cut into". The relevant portion is not "of a very distinctive configuration", nor "broken along its whole length" or "constantly open[ing] out into indentations often penetrating for great distances inland" (*Fisheries (United Kingdom v. Norway), Judgment, I.C.J. Reports 1951*, p. 127).[122]

It thus concluded that "the straight baseline segment between base points 8 and 9 defined by Decree 33, as amended, does not conform with customary international law on the drawing of straight baselines as reflected in Article 7, paragraph 1, of UNCLOS."[123]

2. A "Fringe of Islands"

Another criterion set out in Article 7(1) concerns "a fringe of islands along the coast in its immediate vicinity." Here two issues arise: the insular nature of maritime features and the existence of a fringe of islands.

The first concerns the insular nature of maritime features. Under Article 7(4), in principle, base points used to construct straight baselines may not be placed on low-tide elevations.[124] Some base points of Nicaragua's straight baselines are located on features such as Edinburgh Cay, the Miskitos Cays, Ned Thomas Cay, the Man of War Cays, and the Corn Islands. The opinions of the parties were divided with regard to the insular nature of Edinburgh Cay.[125] The ICJ, in its judgment of 2012, placed a base point on this feature for the construction of the provisional equidistance line.[126] However, it "did not at that time consider the appropriateness of this feature for the purpose of drawing straight baselines, nor did the Court qualify it as an 'island' within the meaning of Article 7, paragraph 1, of UNCLOS."[127] In this regard, the Court recalled its dictum in the *Romania v. Ukraine* case:

> [T]he issue of determining the baseline for the purpose of measuring the breadth of the continental shelf and the exclusive economic zone and the issue of identifying base points for drawing an equidistance/median line for the purpose of delimiting the continental shelf and the exclusive economic zone between adjacent/opposite States are two different issues.[128]

According to the Court, the data put forward by Nicaragua concerning the nature of Edinburgh Cay is contradictory. In fact, Nautical Chart NGA 28139, annexed to the

---

[122] *Id.*

[123] *Id.*

[124] The 2022 *Nicaragua v. Colombia* case, *supra* note 10, para. 246.

[125] *See in particular* presentation by Jean-Marc Thouvenin, CR 2021/15, paras. 32–33, at 57–58 (22 September 2021); presentation by Oude Elferink, CR 2021/16, para. 17, at 41 (24 September 2021); presentation by Jean-Marc Thouvenin, CR 2021/18, paras. 29–41, at 67–70 (29 September 2021), available at < https://www.icj-cij.org/public/files/case-related/155/155-20210929-ORA-01-00-BI.pdf>; presentation by Oude Elferink, CR 2021/19, paras. 19–21, at 24 (1 October 2021), available at < https://www.icj-cij.org/public/files/case-related/155/155-20211001-ORA-01-00-BI.pdf>.

[126] *Territorial and Maritime Dispute (Nicaragua v. Colombia), supra* note 1, ICJ Reports 2012 (II), para. 21, at 638.

[127] The 2022 *Nicaragua v. Colombia* case, *supra* note 10, para. 250.

[128] *Maritime Delimitation in the Black Sea (Romania v. Ukraine)*, Judgment, ICJ Reports 2009, para. 137, at 108 (3 February 2009). The validity of baselines or base points for the purposes of maritime delimitation has been discussed by international courts and tribunals. Generally on this issue, *see* YOSHIFUMI TANAKA, PREDICTABILITY AND FLEXIBILITY IN THE LAW OF MARITIME DELIMITATION 276–286 (2d ed. 2019).

Nicaragua's written pleadings, indicates that Edinburg Cay is not an island. In light of the uncertainty, the Court questioned the nature of Edinburgh Cay as an island for the purpose of Article 7(1). Thus the Court opined that "significant questions arise as to its appropriateness as the location for a base point for the drawing of straight baselines under the same provision."[129] It is particular interest to note that the ICJ required Nicaragua to demonstrate the insular nature of a maritime feature. This is not a new obligation, but is already provided in Article 7(4) of UNCLOS. When drawing straight baselines across a fringe of islands, the Baseline Committee of the International Law Association (ILA) clearly stated that "[e]ach island must meet the criteria set by Article 121" of UNCLOS.[130] For the purpose of straight baselines, it is not necessary that maritime features must be fully entitled islands. Given that rocks under Article 121(3) have a minimum entitlement to a territorial sea, it can be considered that straight baselines may be drawn from either a fully entitled island or a rock.[131]

The second issue relates to the existence of a fringe of islands. Nicaragua asserted that there are ninety-five "islands" that fringe Nicaragua's Caribbean coast.[132] The question was whether those islands amount to a fringe of islands. In this regard, the Court noted that "there are no specific rules regarding the minimum number of islands, although the phrase 'fringe of islands' implies that there should not be too small a number of such islands relative to the length of the coast."[133] Here, the Court attempted to specify, in particular, two criteria for identifying a fringe of islands: continuity and integrity.

As regards continuity, the Court stated that "a certain continuity must be observed in respect of the islands in question for them to form a 'fringe of islands' within the meaning of Article 7, paragraph 1, of UNCLOS" and that "a 'fringe' must enclose a set, or a cluster of islands which present an interconnected system with some consistency or continuity."[134]

Concerning the integrity, the Court opined that "a 'fringe of islands' must be sufficiently close to the mainland so as to warrant its consideration as the outer edge or extremity of that coast."[135] This condition is set out in Article 7(3). Related to this, following the *Eritrea/ Yemen* arbitral award (Maritime Delimitation),[136] the Court referred to the "masking effect." In the words of the Court:

> In certain instances, a fringe of islands "guard[ing] [a] part of the coast" may have a masking effect on a large proportion of the coast from the sea, a criterion

---

[129] The 2022 *Nicaragua v. Colombia* case, *supra* note 10, para. 251.

[130] ILA, Sydney Conference: Final Report, para. 105 (2018), available at <https://www.ila-hq.org/index.php/committees>.

[131] *Id.*, para. 85.

[132] Reply of Nicaragua, *supra* note 65, para. 7.26, at 163.

[133] The 2022 *Nicaragua v. Colombia* case, *supra* note 10, para. 252. *See also Maritime Delimitation and Territorial Questions between Qatar and Bahrain (Qatar v. Bahrain)*, Merits, Judgment, ICJ Reports 2001, para. 214, at 103 (16 March 2001). This view was shared by the UN Office for Ocean Affairs and the Law of the Sea (DOALOS). DOALOS, The Law of the Sea: Baselines: An Examination of the Relevant Provision of the United Nations Convention on the Law of the Sea (1989), para. 43, at 21.

[134] The 2022 *Nicaragua v. Colombia* case, *supra* note 10, para. 254.

[135] *Id.*, para. 255; *Fisheries (United Kingdom v. Norway)*, Judgment, ICJ Reports 1951, at 128 (18 December 1951).

[136] The arbitral tribunal referred to "[a] tightly knit group of islands and islets, or 'carpet' of islands and islets' or to 'an intricate system of islands, islets and reefs which guard this part of the coast.'" *Second stage of the proceedings between Eritrea and Yemen (Maritime Delimitation)*, Award, 22 RIAA (2001), para. 151, at 369 (17 December 1999).

which has been used and discussed by the Parties in the present proceedings to demonstrate or refute the existence of a fringe of islands along the Nicaraguan coastline.[137]

In light of the preceding considerations, the Court held that "the Nicaraguan 'islands' are not sufficiently close to each other to form a coherent 'cluster' or a 'chapelet' along the coast and are not sufficiently linked to the land domain to be considered as the outer edge of the coast";[138] and that "Nicaragua's straight baselines enclose large maritime areas where no maritime feature entitled to a territorial sea has been shown to exist."[139] The Court accordingly held that "Nicaragua's straight baselines do not meet the requirements of customary international law reflected in Article 7, paragraph 1, of UNCLOS."[140]

In conclusion, the Court held:

> [B]y converting certain areas of its exclusive economic zone into internal waters or into territorial sea, Nicaragua's straight baselines deny to Colombia the rights to which it is entitled in the exclusive economic zone, including the freedoms of navigation and overflight and of the laying of submarine cables and pipelines, as provided under customary international law as reflected in Article 58, paragraph 1, of UNCLOS.[141]

Unlike the Colombia's "integral contiguous zone," the Court did not oblige Nicaragua to bring its straight baselines into conformity with customary international law. As Judge Tomka rightly stated, however, it is clear that Nicaragua is obliged to bring its straight baselines in the Caribbean Sea into conformity with the provisions of UNCLOS that reflect customary international law.[142]

3. Discussion

Given that many states established straight baselines in an imaginary manner, the impact of the Court's judgment would be significant. The question that merits discussion is whether and to what extent the ICJ, in its judgment of 2022, could clarify the criteria for constructing straight baselines. The answer seems to be subtle. Among other things, three elements needs further consideration: (1) "deeply indented and cut into," (2) "a fringe of islands," and (3) a maximum length of straight baselines.

As regards the first element, the Court noted that "there appears to be no single test for identifying a coastline that is 'deeply indented and cut into.'"[143] In fact, unlike judicial

---

[137] The 2022 *Nicaragua v. Colombia* case, *supra* note 10, para. 254.

[138] *Id.*, para. 256.

[139] *Id.* According to the Court, "These areas are between Ned Thomas Cay and the Man of War Cays, between East of Great Tyra Cay and the Corn Islands, and from Corn Islands to the land." *Id.*

[140] *Id.*, para. 258. *See also* para. 260.

[141] *Id.*, para. 259.

[142] Separate Opinion of Judge Tomka, para. 32, available at <https://www.icj-cij.org/public/files/case-related/155/155-20220421-JUD-01-02-EN.pdf>.

[143] The 2022 *Nicaragua v. Colombia* case, *supra* note 10, para. 245.

bay,[144] there is no objective criteria for deciding whether a coast is "deeply indented and cut into."[145] In this regard, DOALOS stated:

> It is generally agreed, however, that there must be several indentations which individually would satisfy the conditions establishing a juridical bay (see article 10), though there may be other less marked indentations associated with them.[146]

However, the origin and contents of rules governing straight baselines differ from rules governing a judicial bay. Thus rules governing straight baselines must be distinguished from those governing a judicial bay. If an indentation of the coast must always fulfil the conditions for a judicial bay, this would deprive the meaning of Article 7(1). In fact, DOALOS did seem to accept that the coastal state can draw a straight baseline across "less marked indentations" that cannot fulfil the conditions of a judicial bay. Another issue that arises here concerns the scale of maps. The degree of indentation may vary according to the scale of maps. It might have been helpful if the Court had been able to specify the relevant scale of maps.

Furthermore, referring to the *Norwegian Fisheries* judgment, the Court identified some key elements, that is, "a very distinctive configuration," "broken long its whole length," or "constantly open[ing] out into indentations often penetrating for great distances inland." Here, one can identify three conditions: "the distinctiveness" test, "constantly broken nature" test, and "great distance" test, respectively. Still the tests are less objective.[147] For instance, there is no objective standard for identifying a "distinctive" configuration. Nor is there any objective standard for deciding the "great distance." In this sense, it seems difficult to avoid the criticism that the Court's decision relies on its subjective appreciation.[148]

Second, when considering the existence of a "fringe of islands," the Court held:

> It is not sufficient that the concerned maritime features be part, in general terms, of the overall geographical configuration of the State. They need to be an integral part of its coastal configuration.[149]

An issue that arises here concerns the criterion for identifying the integrity between a "fringe of islands" and costal configuration. In approaching this issue, a "masking effect" merits discussion. The "masking effect" has horizontal and vertical dimensions.

As regards the horizontal dimension, the Court seemingly considered that a fringe of islands must form a coherent "cluster" or a "chapelet" along the coast. In the *Qatar v. Bahrain*

---

[144] *See* Article 10 of UNCLOS.

[145] This view was supported by the UN Office for Ocean Affairs and the Law of the Sea (DOALOS). DOALOS, The Law of the Sea: Baselines: An Examination of the Relevant Provision of the United Nations Convention on the Law of the Sea, para. 36, at 18 (1989).

[146] *Id.* Trümpler also argued that "in a specific locality a straight baseline system should only be applied if it encloses several indentations of which at least some meet the requirements of Art.10(2)." Kai Trümpler, *Article 7, in* United Nations Convention on the Law of the Sea: A Commentary 72 (Alexander Proelss ed., 2017).

[147] *See also* Dissenting Opinion of Judge ad hoc McRae, *supra* note 20, para. 76.

[148] *Id.*, para. 76.

[149] The 2022 *Nicaragua v. Colombia* case, *supra* note 10, para. 255.

case, the ICJ has equated the term "fringe of islands" to a "cluster of islands."[150] Yet the Court did not furnish any guidance with regard to geographical conditions to form a coherent "cluster," such as distance between islands.

The vertical dimension concerns the relationship between a "fringe of islands" and coasts. In this regard, Nicaragua asserted that "25 percent of the Nicaraguan mainland coast is masked by islands."[151] However, the ICJ considered:

> [E]ven if it were to accept Nicaragua's approach, the masking effect of the maritime features that the Applicant identifies as "islands" is not significant enough for them to be considered as masking a large proportion of the coast from the sea.[152]

The statement seems to suggest that the Court focused on a portion of the mainland coast that may be influenced by a "fringe of islands."[153] Here, an issue immediately arises to what extent the mainland coast must have masking effect. Yet the Court remained mute on this matter.

A related issue that arises here concerns the distance between a "fringe of islands" and the coasts.[154] On this issue, DOALOS stated that "[i]t is generally agreed that with a 12-mile territorial sea, a distance of 24 miles would satisfy the condition."[155] Furthermore, the United States has taken the position that a fringe of islands must meet all of the following characteristics:

- the most landward point of each island lies no more than 24 miles from the mainland coastline;
- each island to which a straight baseline is to be drawn is not more than 24 miles apart from the island from which the straight baseline is drawn; and
- the islands, as a whole, mask at least 50 percent of the mainland coastline in any given locality.[156]

However, adjudicative bodies have been wary about presenting objective criteria that display in numbers. Even though a context differed, the arbitral tribunal in the *Eritrea/Yemen* arbitral award (Maritime Delimitation) held that the Dahlaks "is a typical example of a group of islands that forms an integral part of the general coastal configuration."[157] Yet the external fringe of the Dahlaks lie some 40 miles off the coast.[158] There, the arbitral tribunal's criterion for identifying "a group of islands that forms an integral part of the general coastal configuration" remains obscure.

---

[150] *Maritime Delimitation and Territorial Questions between Qatar and Bahrain (Qatar v. Bahrain), supra* note 133, ICJ Reports 2001, para. 214, at 103.

[151] Reply of Nicaragua, *supra* note 65, para. 7.34, at 167.

[152] The 2022 *Nicaragua v. Colombia* case, *supra* note 10, para. 257.

[153] *Id.*, para. 257.

[154] In this regard, *see also* VICTOR PRESCOTT & CLIVE SCHOFIELD, THE MARITIME POLITICAL BOUNDARIES OF THE WORLD, at 147 *et seq.* (2d ed. 2005); Trümpler, *supra* note 146, at 74–75.

[155] DOALOS, *supra* note 145, para. 46, at 22.

[156] ASHLEY ROACH, EXCESSIVE MARITIME CLAIMS 83–84 (4th ed. 2021).

[157] *Second stage of the proceedings between Eritrea and Yemen (Maritime Delimitation), supra* note 136, 22 RIAA (2001), para. 139, at 367.

[158] TANAKA, *supra* note 128, at 262.

Third, a length limit of straight baselines must be considered. Despites various length limits proposed by commentators, to date, there is no consensus on this matter.[159] According to the survey of the ILA Baseline Committee, forty-nine out of the ninety states (including their dependencies) that have drawn straight baseline segments, have one or more straight baseline segments longer than 40 nautical miles. In this regard, the Committee concluded that "the state practice is variable and concludes that it is not possible to assert that state practice has crystallized around the permissible length of a straight baseline."[160] The ICJ, in the *Nicaragua v. Colombia* judgment, remained mute with regard to a length limit of straight baselines. However, as the ILA Baseline Committee rightly stated, "Article 7 straight baselines cannot be of unlimited length."[161] Thus it is hard to disagree with the Committee's view that "the longer the length of a straight baseline the more difficult it will be for that baseline to comply with Article 7."[162]

All in all, despite the ICJ's examination of criteria for constructing straight baselines in the *Nicaragua v. Colombia* judgment, still it seems difficult to objectivize the criteria.[163] In any event the *Nicaragua v. Colombia* judgment did seem to demonstrate that the ICJ applied a rigid approach to straight baselines. This is hardly surprising because, in the *Qatar v. Bahrain* case (Merits), the Court already stressed:

> [T]he method of straight baselines, which is an exception to the normal rules for the determination of baselines, may only be applied if a number of conditions are met. This method must be applied restrictively.[164]

Thus the *Nicaragua v. Colombia* judgment will call on states to reflect on the manner of drawing straight baselines.

V. CONCLUSION

The preceding considerations revealed that the *Nicaragua v. Colombia* judgment of 21 April 2022 is rich in its content, examining both jurisdictional and substantive issues of international law. The key points of the above considerations can be summarised as follows.

First, as regards its jurisdiction *ratione temporis*, the ICJ took the view that the Court's jurisdiction covers facts or events that allegedly occurred after the lapse of the title of jurisdiction. In this regard, the Court applied two tests: the "connexity" test and "continuity test." However, the Court offered no further precision with regard to the standard for deciding the connectivity between facts or events subsequent to the lapse of the Court's jurisdiction and the alleged incidents that have already been found to fall within the Court's jurisdiction. Nor is there any guidance with regard to the standard for deciding the same nature of the dispute. Thus the practical application of the two tests is less easy. More fundamentally, the legal effect of the cease of a treaty that provides a jurisdictional basis on the Court's jurisdiction *ratione temporis* must be distinguished from the effect on the jurisdictional title.

---

[159] ILA, *supra* note 130, para. 108.

[160] *Id.*, para. 108.

[161] *Id.*, para. 109.

[162] *Id.*

[163] Dissenting Opinion of Judge ad hoc McRae, *supra* note 20, para. 81.

[164] *Maritime Delimitation and Territorial Questions between Qatar and Bahrain (Qatar v. Bahrain)*, *supra* note 133, ICJ Reports 2001, para. 212, at 103.

Thus the validity of the ICJ's view in the *Nicaragua v. Colombia* judgment needs careful consideration.

Second, the ICJ held that a third state cannot exercise its jurisdiction to protect and preserve the marine environment in the EEZ of another state. In the Court's view, it is only the coastal state that has jurisdiction to discharge the obligation to protect and preserve the marine environment in its EEZ. It is argued that the *erga omnes* nature of that obligation does not change the conclusion of the Court. If a coastal state fails to fulfil the obligation to protect and preserve the marine environment in its EEZ, an available option for a third state may be to invoke the responsibility of the coastal state.

Third, the Court explicitly accepted the customary law character of the contiguous zone as reflected in Article 33 of UNCLOS. It also accepted that the coastal state is entitled to establish a contiguous zone in the EEZ of another state. However, the Court did not support Colombia's argument that coastal state's powers in its contiguous zone includes control over security and marine pollution. It can be said that the Court adopted a cautious stance regarding expansion of the coastal state's power in its contiguous zone.

Fourth, the ICJ did not accept the artisanal fishing rights claimed by Colombia, by examining historical evidence and unilateral declaration made by Nicaragua's head of state. Concerning evidence of the artisanal fishing rights, the Court considered that affidavits submitted by Colombia contained deficiencies in both space (location of fishing) and time (a short time span). Regarding time span, one can say that only decades would be inadequate to generate historic fishing rights in light of the *Nicaragua v. Colombia* judgment. Furthermore, the ICJ applied a restrictive interpretation to the statements of Nicaragua's head of state. The restrictive interpretation is in line with the jurisprudence of the Court.

Fifth, the ICJ, in the *Nicaragua v. Colombia* judgment, decided the legality of the coastal state's straight baselines. In this regard, the Court attempted to elaborate criteria for drawing straight baselines. Some doubts can be expressed whether the Court adequately clarified the rules of customary international law regarding straight baselines as reflected in Article 7(1) of UNCLOS. Even so, the *Nicaragua v. Colombia* judgment itself may be a point of departure to develop a standard for judging the legality of straight baselines. Thus the *Nicaragua v. Colombia* judgment would provide an important precedent when considering the legality of straight baselines.[165]

---

[165] *See also* Declaration of Judge Bennouna, *supra* note 26, para. 17.

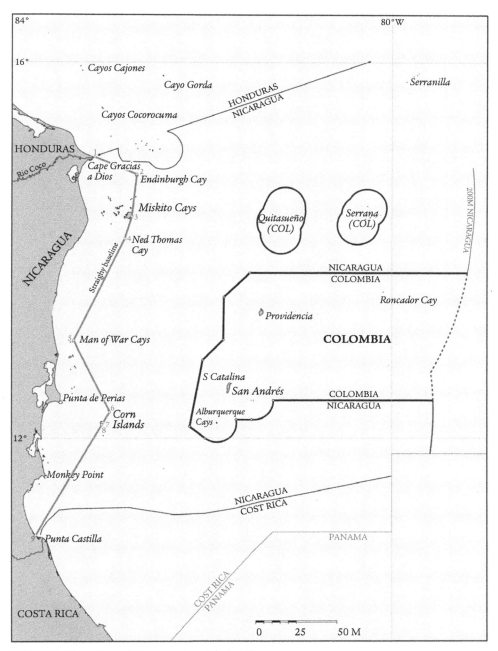

FIGURE 13.1 *Figure: Nicaragua's straight baselines*

Source: Reproduced from "Dispute Concerning Alleged Violations of Sovereign Rights and Maritime Spaces in the Caribbean Sea (Nicaragua vs. Colombia) Reply of the Republic of Nicaragua," at 159, Figure 7.1 © International Court of Justice 2018.

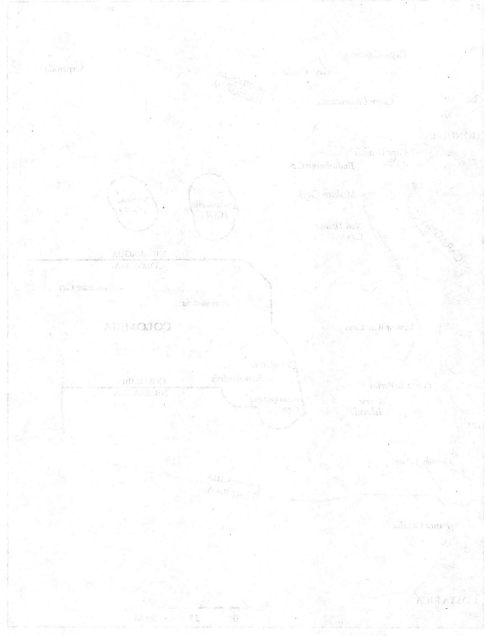

PART

5

GLOBAL JUSTICE— DECISIONS OF INTERNATIONAL COURTS AND TRIBUNALS IN 2021

EDITED BY
GIULIANA ZICCARDI CAPALDO*

* Professor Emeritus of International Law, University of Salerno, Italy; General Editor.

PART

5

GLOBAL JUSTICE:
DECISIONS OF
INTERNATIONAL
COURTS AND TRIBUNALS
IN 2021

EDITED BY
GIULIANA ZICCARDI CAPALDO

Systematic Classification Scheme**

** A classification scheme has been devised to collect the legal maxims excerpted from the jurisprudence examined (*see* "Outline of the Parts," *supra* at xv). This scheme is set out on the following pages. At the end of the sections dedicated to each court or tribunal a list of the headings will be found under which the jurisprudence has been classified.

Systematic Classification Scheme In: *The Global Community Yearbook of International Law and Jurisprudence 2022.* Edited by: Giuliana Ziccardi Capaldo, Oxford University Press. © Oxford University Press 2023. DOI: 10.1093/oso/9780197752265.003.0014

I.13.02	2. War of liberation
I.13.03	3. Non-international armed conflict
I.13.04	4. Other armed conflicts
I.13.1	B. Use of force
I.13.11	1. Armed attack
I.13.12	2. Aggression
I.13.13	3. Self-defence
I.13.14	4. Humanitarian intervention
I.13.15	5. Other forms of use of force
I.13.16	6. Armed forces
I.13.2	C. Neutrality, non-belligerency
I.13.3	D. Weapons
I.13.31	1. Conventional weapons
I.13.32	2. Nuclear weapons
I.13.321	2.1 Non-Proliferation of Nuclear Weapons Treaty
I.13.33	3. Chemical weapons
I.13.4	E. Ceasefire
I.13.5	F. Demilitarized zone
I.13.6	G. Disarmament

I.14	XV. PEACEFUL SETTLEMENT OF DISPUTES
I.14.0	A. Concept of international dispute
I.14.1	B. Diplomatic settlement of disputes
I.14.11	1. Negotiation
I.14.111	1.1 Obligation to negotiate
I.14.112	1.2 Rule of prior diplomatic negotiation
I.14.12	2. Enquiry of facts
I.14.13	3. Good offices
I.14.14	4. Mediation
I.14.15	5. Conciliation
I.14.16	6. Other means of settlement
I.14.2	C. Arbitration
I.14.21	1. General questions
I.14.211	1.1 Request for arbitration
I.14.212	1.2 Procedure of arbitration
I.14.213	1.3 Rules used in arbitral proceedings
I.14.214	1.4 Arbitral tribunal's jurisdiction
I.14.2141	1.4.1 Objection to arbitral tribunal's jurisdiction
I.14.22	2. Permanent Court of Arbitration
I.14.221	2.1 PCA jurisdiction
I.14.222	2.2 Law applied by PCA
I.14.23	3. Arbitration agreement
I.14.24	4. Arbitral tribunal
I.14.25	5. Arbitral award
I.14.3	D. Judicial settlement of disputes by international courts (see Part Two: Procedural Law)

I

International Court
of Justice

INTRODUCTORY NOTE

The International Court of Justice in 2021

BY MOMCHIL MILANOV* AND ROBERT KOLB**

Abstract

During the second year of the pandemic the International Court of Justice celebrated its seventy-fifth year. Just like the previous year, the Court dealt with three very diverse cases concerning economic sanctions and treaty of amity, violations of the International Convention on the Elimination of All Forms of Racial Discrimination (CERD) and maritime delimitation. Unsurprisingly, two out of three cases dealt with preliminary objections and only one was decided on the merits. A couple of newly instituted proceedings show clearly that states intend to keep the Court busy in the years to come.

I. INTRODUCTION AND GENERAL OVERVIEW

The seventy-fifth year of the Court was, like the past several years, a very dynamic one. The jubilee of the Court was marked by the second year of the COVID-19 pandemic and the everyday functioning of the Court was inevitably affected by it. Hybrid hearings in the presence of a limited number of judges and delegations reduced to the absolute minimum characterised the more visible part of the activity of the Court. It continued to function at full speed, rendering judgments in three cases in three very different fields of international law. The first one concerned the preliminary objections judgment in the case concerning the compatibility of economic sanctions with the treaty of amity between Iran and the

---

* PhD researcher and teaching assistant, University of Geneva; former Judicial Fellow at the International Court of Justice (2018–2019). The views expressed are those of the author and do not necessarily reflect the views of the abovementioned institutions.

** Professor at the University of Geneva; member of the Editorial Board.

Momchil Milanov and Robert Kolb, *Introductory Note* In: *The Global Community Yearbook of International Law and Jurisprudence 2022*. Edited by: Giuliana Ziccardi Capaldo, Oxford University Press. © Oxford University Press 2023.
DOI: 10.1093/oso/9780197752265.003.0015

United States. The second concerned the preliminary objections judgment in the case opposing Qatar and the United Arab Emirates on the alleged violations of the International Convention on the Elimination of All Forms of Racial Discrimination (CERD). The third one was the merits judgment in the maritime delimitation case between Somalia and Kenya.

In February, Judge Joan Donoghue was elected as president and Judge Kirill Gevorgian as vice-president. The terms of Judges Iwasawa, Sebutinde, Tomka and Xue were renewed. Judge Georg Nolte was elected in November 2020 and his term also started on February 8th. The year was marked by the death of Judge James Crawford who passed away on May 31. The Court and the entire community of international lawyers lost one of its most distinguished members who contributed immensely to the development of international law in both his capacity of a scholar and as a practitioner. He was replaced by Judge Hilary Charlesworth who was elected by a simultaneous vote at the General Assembly and the Security Council in November 2021. Her term expires in February 2024.

On April 19th, the Court commemorated the seventy-fifth anniversary of its inaugural sitting, which took place on 18 April 1946 in the Great Hall of Justice of the Peace Palace in The Hague. President Donoghue noted that since the establishment of the ICJ, "States have submitted over 140 disputes to it," adding that the Court has also received "over 25 requests for advisory opinions . . . referred to [it] by United Nations organs and specialized agencies."[1]

New applications were filed in three cases. In March, Gabon and Equatorial Guinea brought a case concerning the delimitation of their land and maritime boundaries before the Court by a special agreement.[2] This is a rare sight in the docket dominated by cases instituted under compromissory clauses.[3] In September, with a difference of only a week, first Armenia filed an application against Azerbaijan alleging violations of CERD and then Azerbaijan did the same. There are currently fifteen pending cases in total.

Another important development was the amendment of the Practice Direction III in the beginning of 2021 which imposed a page limit of the annexes attached by a party to its written pleadings. Henceforth, the number of pages of annexes shall not exceed 750 unless the Court decides, upon request of a party, that in the particular circumstances of the case the excess of that limit is warranted. It is entirely understandable that the Court wants to curb the tendency of some parties to submit excessive amounts of material in the annexes. On the other hand, the annexes often contain the evidence for the allegations made in the written pieces. In order not to fear a rejection of some plea for lack of proper substantiation, the tendency of the parties will then be, if the pieces to be submitted span over more than 750 pages (which in a complex case may quickly occur), to provide extracts in the annexes and to deposit full documents with the registry. The parties might also refer the Court to publicly available documents by putting some links into the annexes. Finally, the parties might ask in more cases than the Court would like for an exception. In short terms, the Court has tendered its rule on the limitation of annex material; and the concerned states will find answers to that limitation in order to protect their interests.

---

[1] Press release No. 2021/15.

[2] ICJ, Press release No. 2021/10, available at < https://www.icj-cij.org/public/files/case-related/179/179-20210305-PRE-01-00-EN.pdf >.

[3] Currently the only cases in which the jurisdiction of the Court is based on a special agreement are Guatemala/Belize, Gabon/Equatorial Guinea and to a certain extent the *Arbitral Award of 3 October 1899 (Guyana v. Venezuela)* case.

II. JUDICIAL ACTIVITY OF THE COURT IN 2021

A. Alleged Violations of the 1955 Treaty of Amity, Economic Relations, and Consular Rights (*Islamic Republic of Iran v. United States of America*)

1. *Summary*

In July 2018, the Islamic Republic of Iran in the Registry of the Court an Application instituting proceedings against the United States with regard to alleged violations of the Treaty of Amity, Economic Relations, and Consular Rights of 1955. The jurisdiction of the Court was based on the compromissory clause of Article XXI, Paragraph 2, of the 1955 Treaty.

Iran claimed that the sanctions adopted by the United States were in breach of several provisions of the 1955 Treaty and that therefore the United States must terminate the sanctions without delay and as well as its threats with respect to the announced further sanctions. Furthermore, the United States must ensure that no steps shall be taken to circumvent the decision to be given by the Court and provide a guarantee of non-repetition of its violations of the Treaty. Iran asks for compensation for the violation of its international legal obligations. The United States requested the Court to dismiss the claims in their entirety for both lack of jurisdiction and inadmissibility.

It seems appropriate to recall briefly the factual background of the case. At the date of the filing of the application, the 1955 Treaty was in force. The United States denounced the treaty in October 2018. As a part of the verification of the fulfilment of Iran's obligations under the Treaty on the Non-Proliferation of Nuclear Weapons of 1968, the International Atomic Energy Agency has noted the failure of Iran to comply with its obligations. The matter was referred to the Security Council which adopted a number of resolutions, among which Resolution 1737 (2006) in which it decided *inter alia* that all states must take the necessary measures to prevent the supply, sale or transfer of all items, materials, equipment, goods and technology which could contribute to Iran's nuclear-related activities. Subsequently, several resolutions were adopted on the Iranian nuclear issue. The European Union and the United States adopted sanctions which have led to the conclusion of the Joint Comprehensive Plan of Action (JCPOA) in 2015. The agreement was endorsed by the Security Council and some of the restrictive measures were lifted. In 2018, President Donald Trump announced the end of the participation of the United States in the JCPOA and directed the reimposition of "sanctions lifted or waived in connection with the JCPOA."

The United States has raised five preliminary objections in the present case. The respondent argued that the claims of Iran fell outside the scope of the compromissory clause for two separate reasons. According to the first preliminary objection *ratione materiae* (§§42ff), the true subject matter of the dispute concerns the application of the JCPOA and not the Treaty of Amity. At the time when Iran complained for the first time of the measures in question, the 1955 Treaty was not even mentioned.

The Court considered that the determination of the subject-matter of the dispute is ultimately a task for the Court, part of its judicial function (§52). Particular attention is attributed to the formulation of the dispute by the applicant and to the facts identified by the latter as the basis for its claim. The Court recalled that while the dispute arose in the particular context of the withdrawal of the United States from the JCPOA, this circumstance in no way precluded the dispute from relating to the interpretation or application of the Treaty of Amity. The same acts may fall within the scope of more than one instrument and the measures in question were susceptible to constitute breaches of the 1955 Treaty. Accepting the respondent's argument would be tantamount to a misrepresentation of the claims of Iran. Thus, the first preliminary objection is rejected.

According to the second objection (§§61ff), the vast majority of the measures in question principally concern trade and transactions between Iran and third countries and not between Iran and the United States. These so called "third country measures" fall outside the scope of the Treaty. The objection concerns not all the measures, but only part of them, and in any case some of them would relate to the merits. What is decisive for the Court is whether the measures of the United States are susceptible to impair the rights of Iran under the Treaty. That third states are targeted does not suffice to automatically exclude them from the scope of the Treaty. The only way to determine whether the measures could constitute a breach of the Treaty is to conduct a detailed examination of each of the measures in question. The proper place of this analysis, however, is the merits phase. The second preliminary objection is rejected as well.

The third objection concerns the admissibility of the case (§§85ff). The United States argued that all claims brought by Iran are inadmissible because they would amount to an abuse of process and would raise questions of judicial propriety. The United States argued that through this case Iran is seeking to obtain "an illegitimate advantage" in respect of its nuclear activities because Iran could be granted relief from United States' nuclear-related sanctions without being bound to uphold its own commitments under the JCPOA. It would be "reasonable, necessary and appropriate" for that purpose for the Court to declare the present case inadmissible. In its view, by hearing a case that is intrinsically bound to the JCPOA, the Court could compromise its judicial integrity. The Court swiftly rejected this objection recalling its established case law that it would uphold a claim based on abuse of process only in exceptional circumstances and that the evidence has to be clear. Any finding on the merits of the present case would not constitute an "illegitimate advantage," for such a finding would be confined to the treaty in question. In the present case there were no exceptional circumstances. The fact that Iran's claims are related to measures that had been lifted in conjunction with the JCPOA and then reinstated in May 2018, without discussing other measures affecting Iran and its nationals or companies, is irrelevant and does not constitute an abuse of process. The third preliminary objection was rejected.

The fourth and the fifth objection (§§97ff) were based on Article XX(1)(b) and (d) of the treaty, which is commonly described as a "security exception." The United States argued that the measures at issue are "nuclear-related," "relating to fissionable materials" and they are necessary to protect a state's "essential security interests." Therefore, they are all covered by Article XX(1)(b) and (d) of the Treaty. The United States contends that "wide discretion" and "substantial deference" must be granted to the state invoking Subparagraph (d) in determining whether national security is at stake and what measures are necessary. In its view, the Court can pronounce itself on these issues at this stage without prejudging the merits.

In its treatment of these preliminary objections, the Court once again relied on its established case law and concluded that the decision on the matters related to Article XX(1) (b) and (d) requires an analysis of issues of law and fact, that these issues do not have a preliminary character and that consequently they should be left to the stage of the merits. In particular, in regard to the objection based on the "essential security interests," the analysis may require an assessment of the reasonableness and necessity of the measures in so far as they affect the obligations under the Treaty of Amity. The two preliminary objections are rejected.

The Court unanimously rejected the objections *ratione materiae* and the one based on Article XX(1)(d). In the other two cases, Judge ad hoc Brower voted against. He also appended a separate (partially dissenting) opinion. Judge Tomka appended a Declaration.

2. Commentary

Some observations are warranted. First of all, and on a general level, the judgment confirmed once again the importance of the jurisdictional phase. The case is the latest in a long and rich series of case law and reveals some continuities and disruptions. In the present case, the Court explicitly expressed a preference for the line of its case law in which the dispute is determined "while giving particular attention to the formulation of the dispute chosen by the Applicant" (§53). The importance of this formulation resides in the implicit acceptance of the applicant's claims as sufficiently plausible, unlike previous decisions in *Oil Platforms* and *Certain Iranian Assets* where the Court conducted its own analysis already at the preliminary objections stage and rejected some claims. Certainly, the Court's approach is contingent on the manner in which the objections are formulated. The lack of success of the United States in this particular case is arguably due to at least two separate reasons: the preliminary objections *ratione materiae* might have been felt by the Court as a challenge to its judicial function; and second, there was a dangerous proximity to facts bound up with the merits. When confronted with objections intrinsically related to facts, the Court is extremely cautious and prefers to reject them since the respondent is free to raise them as defence on the merits.

The main novelty of the present case resides in the attempt by the respondent to frame its objections based on Article XX as a *tertium genus*, not belonging to jurisdiction or admissibility. The approach does not constitute a radical departure from *Oil Platforms* and *Certain Iranian Assets*; it is rather a variation in form of non-justiciability, but the objective remains the same: to force the Court to make an early pronouncement with the sweeping effect of preventing the Iranian claims from reaching the merits. No matter how some objections are formulated or categorised, they have no chance to persuade the Court either because they require an in-depth analysis of the facts or simply because they purport to substitute the final appreciation of the Court with the subjective views of the respondent.

B. Application of the International Convention on the Elimination of All Forms of Racial Discrimination (*Qatar v. United Arab Emirates*), Preliminary Objections, Judgment of 4 February 2021

1. Summary

On 11 June 2018, the State of Qatar (Qatar) filed in the Registry of the Court an Application instituting proceedings against the United Arab Emirates (UAE) with regard to alleged violations of Articles 2, 4, 5, 6, and 7 of the International Convention on the Elimination of All Forms of Racial Discrimination (CERD). The jurisdictional basis relied on by the applicant was the compromissory clause of Article 22 of the Convention. The actions complained of by Qatar included collective expulsions, violations of fundamental rights (rights to marriage, freedom of opinion and expression, public health and medical care, education and training, property, work, participation in cultural activities, and equal treatment before tribunals), failure to condemn and instead encouragement of racial hatred against Qatar and Qataris and failure to take measures that aim to combat prejudices, failure to provide effective protection and remedies to Qataris to seek redress against acts of racial discrimination through UAE courts and institutions. Qatar requested the immediate revocation of all the measures, compliance with the CERD, reparation and assurances of non-repetition. The UAE filed three preliminary objections.

The factual background of the following: in 2017, the UAE issued a statement accusing Qatar of undermining the security and the stability of the region. The abovementioned measures were undertaken in response to these concerns. Later on the UAE took additional measures. In 2018, Qatar deposited a communication with the CERD Committee, a treaty body created by the Convention. The Committee rejected the preliminary objections raised by the UAE.

Qatar contended that the dispute concerned the interpretation and application of the Convention as required by the compromissory clause. The UAE argued that the Court lacked jurisdiction *ratione materiae* over the dispute because the alleged acts did not fall within the scope of CERD. Second, the UAE asserted that Qatar failed to satisfy the procedural preconditions of Article 22 of the Convention. The third objection concerned the admissibility and according to the UAE Qatar's claims constituted an abuse of process.

Before addressing the objections, the Court determined the subject-matter of the dispute. Once again, as in the case discussed previously and almost routinely, the Court insisted that it has to determine on an objective basis the real issue in the case, while giving particular attention to the formulation of the dispute chosen by the applicant. For Qatar, the subject-matter of the dispute concerns the violations of the CERD, in particular the collective expulsions, the ban on entering the UAE by Qataris, anti-Qatari hate propaganda and prejudice, and suppressing Qatari media and speech deemed to support Qatar. All these measures discriminate against Qataris on the basis of their current nationality, which in the view of Qatar is covered by the definition of "racial discrimination" in Article 1 of the Convention. In addition, the measures concern Qatari media corporations which are also protected by the Convention. As a separate claim, Qatar also argued that the CERD applied to measures that would result in indirect discrimination.

The Court found (§70) that the subject-matter of the dispute is formed by the disagreements of Qatar and the UAE in respect of the three claims of Qatar. The first was related to the "travel bans" and "expulsion order," which made express reference to Qatari nationals, the second arose from the restrictions on Qatari media corporations and the third concerned the question of "indirect discrimination."

In its analysis of the first preliminary objection, which focused on the lack of subject-matter jurisdiction, the Court had to decide whether the dispute was one related to the interpretation or application of CERD. Three key points of contention are emphasised in this regard. The first is whether the term "national origin" encompasses current nationality in the definition of "racial discrimination" in Article 1(1) CERD. The UAE contends that "national origin" does not include current nationality and that the Convention does not prohibit differentiation based on the current nationality. The Court relied on the rules of treaty interpretation as codified by the Vienna Convention on the Law of Treaties which reflect customary international law (the Convention was not in force between the parties).

In order to determine the meaning and the scope of the term "national origin," the Court explicitly acknowledges that the analysis requires it to take into account the practice of the CERD Committee and of regional human rights courts. The references to "origin" in Article 1(1) denote, respectively, a person's bond to a national or ethnic group at birth, whereas nationality is a legal attribute which is within the discretionary power of the state and can change during a person's lifetime. The other elements of the definition of racial discrimination, as set out in Article 1, Paragraph 1, of the Convention, namely, race, colour and descent, are also characteristics that are inherent at birth. Paragraphs 2 and 3 of Article 1 also support the interpretation of the ordinary meaning of the term "national origin" as not encompassing current nationality (§83). The object and the purpose of the Convention, as exemplified by the Preamble, demonstrate that the Convention was drafted in the context of the 1960s decolonization movement. Therefore, the aim of the Convention is to eliminate all forms and manifestations of racial discrimination against human beings on the basis of real or perceived characteristics as of their origin, namely, at birth. At the same time, it was not aimed to cover every instance of differentiation between persons based on nationality, which is reflected in the legislation of many states. The Court accordingly concluded that the term "national origin" does not encompass current nationality. The detailed analysis of the preparatory work of the Convention (§§89ff). The Court took the view that the drafters of the Convention did have in mind the differences between national origin and nationality. The practice of the CERD Committee was taken into account, but it did not change the conclusion to which the Court has arrived earlier (§101). The jurisprudence of regional human rights courts is equally of little help for the interpretation of the term "national origin" in CERD (§104). The Court accordingly concluded that the term "national origin" in Article 1, Paragraph 1, of the Convention does not encompass current nationality.

The second claim by Qatar concerned the measures imposed on certain Qatari media corporations in the UAE which in the view of the applicant infringed their right to freedom of opinion and expression. The Court swiftly reached the conclusions that the Convention applies only to individuals.

The third question was whether the measures characterized by Qatar as "indirect discrimination" fell within the scope of the Convention. Qatar argued that a measure may fall into the scope of Article 1 if, by its effect, it concerns a protected group. While the Court acknowledges that discrimination "by effect" is included in Article 1, it does not consider that the measures in question give rise to racial discrimination against Qataris as a distinct social group on the basis of their national origin. Declarations criticizing a state or its policies cannot be characterized as racial discrimination within the meaning of CERD. The Court concluded that it had no jurisdiction *ratione materiae* to entertain the claims. It was, therefore, unnecessary to examine the second preliminary objection.

The Court upheld the first preliminary objection and by 11 votes to 6 decided that it had no jurisdiction to entertain the application. President Yusuf and Judges Cançado Trindade, Sebutinde, Bhandari, Robinson and Iwasawa voted against. President Yusuf and Judge ad hoc Daudet appended a declaration to the judgment. Judges Sebutinde, Bhandari and Robinson appended dissenting opinions. Judge Iwasawa appended a separate opinion.

2. Commentary

In the last years, the compromissory clause of CERD became among the most favourite provisions of counsel pleading before the Court. Several cases were filed, mostly relying exclusively on the Convention. The increasing reliance on the Convention comes with the risk that the Court will attempt to limit the access provided by the compromissory clause before the CERD opens the floodgates of international litigation.[4] This is precisely what the Court did in the present case. It applied a restrictive interpretation and concluded that current nationality is excluded from the scope of Article 1. It bears noting that: (1) the Court went through all the elements of the general rule of interpretation and (2) it apparently considered necessary to support this conclusion by having recourse to the *travaux* as a supplementary means of interpretation. Justice must be seen to be done, as the old saying goes. The Court had to be persuasive in order to compensate for the lapidary tone of its judgments. Current nationality was excluded by the Court in what constituted a rare departure from the practice of the CERD Committee. It was justified by two separate considerations. First, the ICJ is not an international court of human rights and even though it has acknowledged the importance of human rights treaty bodies, it is not absolutely bound by their pronouncements. Second, as already mentioned, there is a non-negligible aspect related to the judicial policy of the Court, and the latter is by no means under an obligation to follow the very expansive interpretation of the treaty body.

---

[4] In 2021, two more cases brought under Article 22 CERD were filed, opposing Armenia and Azerbaijan. See *infra* Section III. B and C.

Once again, the formulation of the preliminary objections is of paramount importance. Having framed them in a manner that put the emphasis on the legal aspects, the Court was greatly facilitated in its task and could disregard the factual side, which would be a matter for the merits. The only aspect which required a careful treatment of facts was the one on "indirect discrimination." Here the reasoning of the Court leaves much to be desired. There is merely a sweeping pronouncement that "even if the measures of which Qatar complains in support of its 'indirect discrimination' claim were to be proven on the facts, they are not capable of constituting racial discrimination within the meaning of the Convention" (§112).

The reasoning and the conclusion of the Court were criticized by Judge Iwasawa who has an extensive experience at the Human Rights Committee. In his view, Qatar's claim required a detailed analysis at the merits and the Court should have declared that the first preliminary objection of the UAE does not possess an exclusively preliminary character (§46ff, in particular §66). Judge Iwasawa points out that the majority has in effect determined the dispute on the merits at the preliminary objections stage. In *Ukraine v. Russia*, the Court, however, pointed out that, at the preliminary objections stage, it only needed to ascertain whether the challenged measures were capable of affecting the rights protected by CERD, and that it was not necessary to satisfy itself that the measures actually constituted racial discrimination within the meaning of Article 1(1) CERD, or to what extent certain acts may be covered by Article 1(2) and (3) CERD.[5] Judge Robinson disagreed with the majority on the exclusion of current nationality because "the place where one was born can give rise to both one's nationality as well as one's national origin" (§8). He also criticized the treatment of the third Qatari claim (§20ff, in particular §§26–27), view, which was shared by Judge Sebutinde. The declaration by President Yusuf requires particular attention. He criticized the majority for its treatment of "indirect discrimination" claim and considered that it had misrepresented the applicant's claims thus mischaracterizing the subject-matter of the dispute. The criticism of these judges is not unfounded. One may indeed have the impression that the threshold of preliminary objections phase was unduly high and that it was used to get rid of a complex and perhaps politically undesirable case.

C. Maritime Delimitation in the Indian Ocean (*Somalia v. Kenya*), Merits, 21 October 2021

1. Summary

On 28 August 2014, Somalia filed an Application instituting proceedings against Kenya "concerning a dispute in relation to the maritime delimitation of the territorial sea, exclusive economic zone and continental shelf, including the continental shelf beyond 200 nautical miles." The jurisdiction of the Court was based on the declarations made, pursuant to Article 36, Paragraph 2, of its Statute. Somalia also claimed that by its conduct in the disputed area, Kenya has violated its international obligations to respect the sovereignty, and sovereign rights and jurisdiction of Somalia, and is responsible under international law to make full reparation to Somalia. Kenya did not participate in the oral proceedings.

Somalia and Kenya are adjacent states on the coast of East Africa. In 1924, Italy and the United Kingdom concluded a treaty regulating certain questions concerning the boundaries of their respective territories in East Africa. A year later, by an Exchange of Notes, the boundary between the colonial territories was redefined in its southernmost section. After

---

[5] *See, in particular*, ICJ, *Application of the International Convention for the Suppression of the Financing of Terrorism and of the International Convention on the Elimination of All Forms of Racial Discrimination (Ukraine v. Russian Federation)*, Preliminary Objections, Judgment, 2019 ICJ Reports 595, para. 94.

the boundary has been demarcated, an agreement was concluded in 1927, formally confirmed by an Exchange of Notes in 1933. Somalia and Kenya ratified UNCLOS in 1989 and it entered into force for them in November 1994.

The parties have adopted fundamentally different approaches to the delimitation of the maritime areas (§35). Somalia argues that no maritime boundary exists between the two states and asks the Court to plot a boundary line using the equidistance/special circumstances method. Kenya contends that there is already an agreed maritime boundary between the parties, because Somalia has acquiesced to a boundary which follows the parallel of latitude. Kenya submits that, even if the Court were to conclude that there is no maritime boundary in place, it should delimit the maritime areas following the parallel of latitude, and that, even if the Court were to employ the delimitation methodology suggested by Somalia, the outcome, following adjustment to reach an equitable result, would be a delimitation that follows the parallel of latitude.

Kenya maintains that there is an agreed boundary because Somalia has acquiesced to its claim that the maritime boundary between the parties follows the parallel of latitude. Kenya contends that the absence of protest to the proclamations by the President of Kenya and to Kenya's Submission on the Continental Shelf beyond 200 nautical miles deposited with the Commission on the Limits of the Continental Shelf (CLCS) constitutes acquiescence under international law. Kenya also asserts that the conduct of the parties between 1979 and 2014 "confirms" Somalia's acceptance of the parallel of latitude as the maritime boundary (§43). Somalia argues that lack of protest against a notification of a claim cannot automatically amount to an acceptance of that claim. A maritime boundary cannot be established by unilateral acts. Moreover, Kenya's own public statements and positions directly contradict its contention that the parties have already delimited their maritime boundary. Moreover, for Somalia, its claim to an equidistance line during the Third United Nations Conference on the Law of the Sea which was also embodied in its Maritime Law of 1988 equalled an implicit protest. It insisted on several occasions that the maritime boundary had not yet been delimited. In Somalia's view, Kenya's purported displays of authority in the disputed area were in any event sporadic, infrequent and recent, and were undertaken at a time when, on account of civil war, there was no functioning Somali government able to monitor such activities or exercise effective control over them.

The Court recalled that that maritime delimitation between states with opposite or adjacent coasts must be effected by means of an agreement between them, and that, where such an agreement has not been achieved, delimitation should be effected by recourse to a third party possessing the necessary competence (§§48–49). The essential question is whether there is a "shared understanding" between the states concerned regarding their maritime boundaries. As for the question of acquiescence (§51), the Court observed that if the circumstances are such that the conduct of the other state calls for a response, within a reasonable period, the absence of a reaction may amount to acquiescence. In determining whether a state's conduct calls for a response from another state, it is important to consider whether the state has consistently maintained that conduct. In evaluating the absence of a reaction, duration may be a significant factor. The Court has set a high threshold for proof that a maritime boundary has been established by acquiescence or tacit agreement (§52). Evidence of a tacit legal agreement must be compelling and acquiescence presupposes clear and consistent acceptance of another state's position. The Court has recognized the existence of a tacit agreement delimiting a maritime boundary in only one case (*Peru v. Chile,* ICJ Reports 2014, at 38, para. 90).

The Court thus observes that Kenya was not consistently claiming a maritime boundary with Somalia at a parallel of latitude in all maritime areas (§57). Kenya's position is at odds with the text of the 1989 Maritime Zones Act, which refers neither to the 1979 Proclamation nor to a boundary at the parallel of latitude, for either the territorial sea or the exclusive economic zone (§60). Kenya considered in 1989 that there was no agreement with Somalia on their maritime boundary and it was reasonable for Somalia to understand Kenya's position to be that an agreement was to be negotiated and concluded at a later date. In 2007 and 2008, Kenya has sent two *notes verbales* to the Transitional Federal Government of Somalia concerning the maritime boundaries, but the Court observed that they did not characterize the maritime boundary claimed by Kenya as an agreed boundary. Rather, they invited Somalia to confirm its agreement. It has not been shown that Somalia provided such confirmation (§§63–64). The 2009 Submission to the CLCS by Kenya also reveals that the maritime boundary dispute has not been resolved (including the Exclusive Economic Zone (EEZ)) and that consequently, the delimitation of the maritime boundary remains to be determined by agreement between the two coastal states. During the negotiations which took place in 2014, the parties could not reach an agreement on the method. The Court concluded that Kenya has not consistently maintained its claim that the parallel of latitude constituted the single maritime boundary with Somalia. There was no compelling evidence that Kenya's claim and related conduct were consistently maintained and, consequently, called for a response from Somalia (§71).

The Court reached the conclusion that the conduct of Somalia between 1979 and 2014 in relation to its maritime boundary with Kenya, in particular its alleged absence of protest against Kenya's claim, did not establish Somalia's clear and consistent acceptance of a maritime boundary at the parallel of latitude (§80).

Kenya also argued that the conduct of the parties between 1979 and 2014 (naval patrols, fisheries, marine scientific research and oil concessions) confirmed Somalia's acceptance of a maritime boundary at the parallel of latitude (§§81ff). The Court recalled the importance of establishing the critical date in the context of both territorial and maritime delimitation dispute. Acts occurring after such date are in principle irrelevant to the determination of a maritime boundary and cannot be taken into consideration (§82). In the present case, the Court took the view that the critical date on which the dispute crystallised was 2009. The argument raised by Kenya on the existence of a *de facto* maritime boundary along the parallel of latitude was not accepted. The Court considered that "proof of the existence of a maritime boundary requires more than the demonstration of longstanding oil practice or adjoining oil concession limits." There was no compelling evidence that Somalia has acquiesced to the maritime boundary claimed by Kenya and that, consequently, there was no agreed maritime boundary between the parties at the parallel of latitude (§89).

The Court proceeded to the delimitation of the maritime areas (§90). Since both states were parties to UNCLOS, it was the applicable law to the case. Both parties agreed that the appropriate starting-point is the Primary Beacon 29 (PB 29). The Court connected PB 29 to a point on the low-water line by a straight line in accordance with the terms of the 1927/1933 treaty arrangement. The Court determined the exact coordinates for the starting-point of the boundary (§98).

The parties had differing views on the delimitation of the territorial sea (§99). Neither party asked the Court to confirm the existence of any segment of a maritime boundary or to delimit the boundary in the territorial sea on the basis of the 1927/1933 treaty arrangement. The median or equidistance line is therefore constructed by using the usual base points. The Court is not bound by the points proposed by the parties. It has the power to decide itself on the base points to be used in the process. The Court considered it appropriate to eliminate the effects of some maritime features and to place base points for the construction of the median line solely on the mainland coasts of the parties. It thus departed from the base points proposed by the parties and selected its own points. The Court noted that the course of the median line corresponded closely to the course of the line in the 1927/1933 treaty agreement (§118).

The Court then proceeded to the delimitation of the EEZ and the continental shelf within 200 nautical miles from the coasts of the parties (§§119ff). According to the relevant rules of UNCLOS (Articles 74(1) and 83(1)), the objective of the delimitation is to achieve an equitable solution. Since the adoption of the Convention, the Court has gradually developed a maritime delimitation methodology to assist it in carrying out its task. In determining the maritime delimitation line, the Court proceeds in three stages, which it described in the case concerning *Maritime Delimitation in the Black Sea* (*Romania v. Ukraine*).[6]

The Court starts by establishing the provisional equidistance line. Then it considers whether there are factors calling for the adjustment or shifting of the provisional equidistance line in order to achieve an equitable result. In the third stage, the Court applies a disproportionality test in order to ensure that there is no marked disproportion between the ratio of the lengths of the relevant coasts and the ratio of the respective shares of the parties in the relevant area to be delimited. The Court observes that the three-stage methodology is not prescribed by UNCLOS and therefore is not mandatory; but it is based on objective criteria, it has brought predictability to the process of maritime delimitation and has been applied by the Court in a number of past cases. There are no factors which make the application of the equidistance method inappropriate. The use of the parallel of latitude, relied on by Kenya, is not the appropriate method to achieve an equitable solution because it would produce a severe cut-off effect on the maritime projections of the southernmost coast of Somalia. There is no reason to depart from its usual practice of using the three-stage method to establish the maritime boundary between Somalia and Kenya.

The Court identified the relevant coasts namely those coasts whose projections overlap (§132). The Court, using radial projections which overlap within 200 nautical miles, has identified that the relevant coast of Somalia extends over approximately 733 kilometres and that of Kenya over approximately 511 kilometres. Concerning the relevant area, the Court considers it appropriate to use the overlap of the 200-nautical-mile radial projections from the land boundary terminus. The relevant area, as identified by the Court for the purpose of delimiting the exclusive economic zone and the continental shelf up to 200 nautical miles from the coasts, measures approximately 212,844 square kilometres. The Court next identified the base points and constructed the provisional equidistance line.

Kenya invoked five circumstances which required the adjustment of the provisional equidistance line. This would eventually result in a boundary following the parallel of latitude. The Court once again rejected the relevance of the parallel of latitude, because it would represent a radical adjustment while clearly not achieving an equitable solution. It then began examining each of the factors relied on by Kenya. The Court acknowledged the security interests of Kenya (§158); but the current security situation did not justify the adjustment of the provisional equidistance line. Legitimate security considerations may be a relevant circumstance if a maritime delimitation was effected particularly near to the coast of a state, which is not the case here. The provisional equidistance line does not pass near the coast of Kenya. Second, in some exceptional cases, access for Kenya's fisherfolk to natural resources might be a relevant factor. However, in the present case the Court did not accept Kenya's argument that the provisional equidistance line would deny equitable access to fisheries resources vital to its population. Third, the Court rejected the argument that the

---

[6] ICJ, *Maritime Delimitation in the Black Sea* (*Romania v. Ukraine*), Merits, Judgment, 2009 ICJ Reports 101–103, paras. 115–122.

conduct of the parties has created a *de facto* boundary. The final two arguments put forth by Kenya concern the risk of producing a cut-off effect of with respect to its maritime areas, including from the outer limit of the continental shelf. The Court has acknowledged this risk in the past, particularly where the coastline is characterized by concavity. The Court considered that any cut-off effect as a result of the Kenya-Tanzania maritime boundary is not a relevant circumstance. The agreements between Kenya and Tanzania are *res inter alios acta* which cannot per se affect the maritime boundary between Kenya and Somalia. The issue is whether the use of an equidistance line produces a cut-off effect for Kenya as a result of the configuration of the coastline. At the same time, examining only the coastlines of the two states concerned to assess the extent of any cut-off effect resulting from the geographical configuration of the coastline may be an overly narrow approach. In the present case, the potential cut-off of Kenya's maritime entitlements should be assessed in a broader geographical configuration which meant taking into account the coast of Tanzania. The provisional equidistance line between Somalia and Kenya progressively narrows the coastal projection of Kenya, substantially reducing its maritime entitlements within 200 nautical miles. The adjustment of the provisional equidistance line is warranted if the cut-off effect is "serious" or "significant." The Court found that the cut-off in the present case is sufficiently serious to warrant some adjustment. The Court believes that it is necessary to shift the line to the north in order to attenuate in a reasonable and mutually balanced way the cut-off effect produced by the unadjusted equidistance line due to the geographical configuration of the relevant coasts. Then thus Court conducts the disproportionality test. Thus, the ratio of the relevant coasts is 1:1.43 in favour of Somalia. The ratio between the maritime zones that would belong respectively to Kenya and Somalia is 1:1.30 in favour of Kenya. A comparison of these two ratios does not reveal any significant or marked disproportionality.

The Court then turns to the delimitation of the continental shelf beyond 200 nautical miles (§§178ff). Any claim to continental shelf rights beyond 200 miles (by a state party to UNCLOS) must be in accordance with Article 76 of UNCLOS and reviewed by the Commission on the Limits of the Continental Shelf established thereunder. The Commission on the Limits of the Continental Shelf has not pronounced itself on the question. However, in the view of the Court, this was not an impediment to the delimitation. According to the provisions of UNCLOS, the entitlement of a state to the continental shelf beyond 200 nautical miles thus depends on geological and geomorphological criteria. The Court concluded that the maritime boundary beyond 200 nautical miles continued along the same geodetic line as the adjusted line within 200 nautical miles until it reached the outer limits of the parties' continental shelves which were to be delineated on the basis of the recommendations to be made by the Commission or until it reached the area where the rights of third states may be affected. Depending on the extent of Kenya's entitlement to a continental shelf beyond 200 nautical miles as it may be established in the future on the basis of the Commission's recommendation, the delimitation line might give rise to an area of limited size located beyond 200 nautical miles from the coast of Kenya and within 200 nautical miles from the coast of Somalia, but on the Kenyan side of the delimitation line ("grey area"). Since the existence of this "grey area" is only a possibility, the Court did not consider it necessary to pronounce itself on the legal regime that would be applicable in that area.

Finally, the Court turned to the alleged violations of Kenya of its international obligations and its responsibility under international law to make full reparation to Somalia (§§198ff). Concerning the claim by Somalia according to which by its unilateral actions in the disputed area Kenya has violated Somalia's sovereignty over the territorial sea and its sovereign rights and jurisdiction in the exclusive economic zone and on the continental shelf, the Court observed that when maritime claims of states overlap, maritime activities undertaken by a state in an area which is subsequently attributed to another state by a judgment cannot be considered to be in violation of the sovereign rights of the latter if those activities were carried out before the judgment was delivered and if the area concerned was the subject of claims made in good faith by both states. As for the surveying and drilling activities conducted or authorized by Kenya, there was no evidence that Kenya's claims over the area concerned were not made in good faith. Consequently, it has not been established that Kenya's maritime activities, including those that may have been conducted in parts of the disputed area that have now been attributed to Somalia, were in violation of Somalia's sovereignty or its sovereign rights and jurisdiction. The Court could not conclude that the activities carried out by Kenya in the disputed area jeopardized or hampered the reaching of a final agreement on the delimitation of the maritime boundary, in violation of Article 74, Paragraph 3, or Article 83, Paragraph 3, of UNCLOS. Kenya has not violated its international obligations through its maritime activities in the disputed area and its international responsibility is not engaged.

The Court decided (§214) unanimously that there was no agreed maritime boundary between Somalia and Kenya that follows the parallel of latitude; and it determined the starting-point of the single maritime boundary of the territorial sea and its course, which followed the median line. Then, by 10 votes to 4 (against: Judges Abraham, Yusuf, Bhandari, Salam), the Court delimited the EEZ and the continental shelf. By 9 votes to 5 (Judges Abraham, Yusuf, Bhandari, Robinson, Salam), it delimited the continental shelf beyond the 200-mile limit. It unanimously rejected the claim of Somalia on the alleged violations by Kenya. President Donoghue and Judges Abraham, Yusuf and Judge ad hoc Guillaume appended separate opinions to the judgment. Judge Xue appended a declaration. Judge Robinson appended an individual, partly concurring and partly dissenting, opinion to the judgment of the Court.

2. *Commentary*

As a general observation, the merits judgment in the present case brings another confirmation of the solidity of the three-step approach elaborated by the Court, which has by now become part of its established case law of maritime delimitation. While this approach is not prescribed by law, it is a "judicial legislation" and it is difficult to imagine a situation in which the Court would depart from it. It is also worth mentioning that *Somalia v. Kenya* is another example of the unwelcome trend of non-appearance, which renders the task of the Court more difficult and may have some nefarious effects on the judgment.

Some salient points require particular attention. The first one is the extensive analysis of acquiescence operated by the Court. It acknowledged that acquiescence and tacit agreement may be of assistance when examining whether there exists an agreement that is not in written form regarding the maritime boundary between two states (§51). In particular, acquiescence is equivalent to tacit recognition manifested by unilateral conduct which the other party may interpret as consent. The threshold for proof that a maritime boundary has been established by acquiescence or tacit agreement is high. Acquiescence "presupposes clear and consistent acceptance" and its "evidence . . . must be compelling." Thus, on the one hand it is clear that proving acquiescence will be an arduous task, but the Court is ready to approach each situation in its own terms and decide on a case-by-case basis. The rejection of acquiescence should be seen both in terms of the broader judicial policy of the Court against unilateral determinations (crucially important in the context of maritime delimitation) but equally in terms of legal security. Moreover, the Court seems here to depart from the general law on acquiescence and establish a stricter standard in the context of action/silence in the context of delimitation lines. Overall, this case sheds light on this important issue which seasoned counsel will not fail to notice in the preparation of future cases. The Court also refused to attribute decisive importance to the internal conflict in Somalia, since third states are affected in their rights and duties by such a situation. It is plausible to believe that in future cases, this approach will be further refined in order to try to establish a careful balance between the position of a state affected by an internal conflict and the interests of thirds.

Second, the selection of the base points is once again confirmed as one of the most important elements in the process of delimitation. They were progressively elevated to an indispensable precondition for the equitable delimitation. It bears noting the trend for the Court to select base points which are placed on the mainland and to avoid placing them on islets. Such a choice would have a disproportionate impact on the course of the median line in comparison to the size of these features.

Third, the role of the factors militating for the adjustment of the provisional equidistance line become more and more limited. From "relevant circumstances," they are progressively relegated to the rank of "special circumstances." In order for the Court to adjust the provisional line, these factors must be serious and objective in nature. The only factor which was accepted by the Court in the present case and which remains of lasting importance is the cut-off effect. It is a factor of geographic, i.e., objective nature.

One final point concerns the finding of the Court that unilateral actions taken in disputed maritime areas do not engage the international responsibility of the state before the end of the judicial proceedings. The conduct in question may be exonerated on the basis of good faith, functioning as some sort of a circumstance precluding wrongfulness. The approach taken by the Court is marked by pragmatism and it is based on considerations of reasonableness: it would be hard to sanction a state for certain actions if that state has acted in good faith—and it is well known that good faith is presumed. At the same time the approach opens the door wide for the possibility for unilateral actions, whilst knowing that it would be hard to prove that they were not taken in good faith. And it bears also noting that in the general law of state responsibility good faith is not a circumstance precluding wrongfulness. Here also, the Court may have indulged into some *lex specialis* for maritime delimitation issues—and *lex specialis* is explicitly allowed by Article 55 of the Articles on Responsibility of States for Internationally Wrongful Acts (ARSIWA) (2001).

III. NEW CASES INSTITUTED IN 2021 AND REQUESTS FOR PROVISIONAL MEASURES

A. Land and Maritime Delimitation and Sovereignty over Islands (Gabon/Equatorial Guinea)

The Court was seized of a dispute on 5 March 2020 between Gabon and Equatorial Guinea by way of special agreement, which was signed in 2016 and entered into force in March 2020. Pursuant to the agreement, the Court is requested to determine whether the legal titles, treaties and international conventions invoked by the parties have the force of law in the relations between Gabon and Equatorial Guinea in so far as they concern the delimitation of their common maritime and land boundaries and sovereignty over the islands of Mbanié/Mbañe, Cocotiers/Cocoteros and Conga.

B. Application of the International Convention on the Elimination of All Forms of Racial Discrimination (*Armenia v. Azerbaijan*)

On 16 September, the Republic of Armenia instituted proceedings against the Republic of Azerbaijan with regard to alleged violations of the International Convention on the

Elimination of All Forms of Racial Discrimination (CERD). Armenia contends that "[f]or decades, Azerbaijan has subjected Armenians to racial discrimination" and that, "[a]s a result of this State-sponsored policy of Armenian hatred, Armenians have been subjected to systemic discrimination, mass killings, torture and other abuse." According to Armenia, these violations are directed at individuals of Armenian ethnic or national origin regardless of their actual nationality. Armenia claims that "[t]hese practices once again came to the fore in September 2020, after Azerbaijan's aggression against the Republic of Artsakh and Armenia" and that "[d]uring that armed conflict, Azerbaijan committed grave violations of the CERD." The applicant alleges that "[e]ven after the end of hostilities," following a cease-fire which entered into effect on 10 November 2020, "Azerbaijan has continued to engage in the murder, torture and other abuse of Armenian prisoners of war, hostages and other detained persons." Armenia claimed that Azerbaijan breached several provisions of the CERD. It based the jurisdiction of the Court on Article 22 of the Convention and argued that the procedural requirements under Article 22 of the Convention are fulfilled. Armenia also requested the indication of provisional measures which will be discussed on the next section.

Armenia requested the indication of provisional measures related to the treatment and the release of prisoners of war, the right to access to Armenian historic, cultural and religious heritage, the prevention of the destruction and preservation of evidence related to allegations under the CERD, the non-aggravation of the dispute. Lastly, it requested that Azerbaijan shall provide a report on the implementation of the provisional measures indicated by the Court. The Court indicated provisional measures concerning prisoners of war, the prevention of the incitement and promotion of racial hatred, the protection of cultural heritage and the non-aggravation of the dispute.

C. Application of the International Convention on the Elimination of All Forms of Racial Discrimination (*Azerbaijan v. Armenia*)

Only a week after Armenia seized the Court, on 23 September Azerbaijan instituted proceedings under the same instrument. Azerbaijan claimed that "Armenia has engaged and is continuing to engage in a series of discriminatory acts against Azerbaijanis on the basis of their 'national or ethnic' origin within the meaning of CERD." The applicant claims that "through both direct and indirect means, Armenia continues its policy of ethnic cleansing," and that it "incites hatred and ethnic violence against Azerbaijanis by engaging in hate speech and disseminating racist propaganda, including at the highest levels of its government."

Azerbaijan also requested the indication of provisional measures related to the demining of landmines on its territory, the prevention of racial hatred and hate speech, the preservation of evidence related to allegations of ethnically motivated crimes, non-aggravation of the dispute and the reporting of the measures taken to give effect to the provisional measures. The Court indicated provisional measures in respect of the prevention of racial hatred and non-aggravation of the dispute.

LEGAL MAXIMS: SUMMARIES AND EXTRACTS FROM SELECTED CASE LAW*

Alleged Violations of the 1955 Treaty of Amity, Economic Relations, and Consular Rights (Islamic Republic of Iran v. United States of America), Preliminary Objections, Judgment, 3 February 2021

---

* The working method chosen for the formulation of legal maxims is explained *supra*, Outline of the Parts, at page xv.

Legal Maxims: Summaries and Extracts from Selected Case Law In: *The Global Community Yearbook of International Law and Jurisprudence 2022*. Edited by: Giuliana Ziccardi Capaldo, Oxford University Press. © Oxford University Press 2023.
DOI: 10.1093/oso/9780197752265.003.0016

I.2.1

Alleged Violations of the 1955 Treaty of Amity, Economic Relations, and Consular Rights (Islamic Republic of Iran v. United States of America), **Preliminary Objections, Judgment, 3 February 2021***

Contents**

I. BACKGROUND

II. PRELIMINARY OBJECTIONS TO ICJ JURISDICTION *RATIONE MATERIAE* UNDER ARTICLE XXI OF THE TREATY OF AMITY, ECONOMIC RELATIONS, AND CONSULAR RIGHTS (1955)

    A. FIRST PRELIMINARY OBJECTION: SUBJECT-MATTER OF DISPUTE — QUESTION WHETHER DISPUTE CONCERNS INTERPRETATION AND APPLICATION OF THE 1955 TREATY OR EXCLUSIVELY JCPOA

    B. SECOND PRELIMINARY OBJECTION: QUESTION WHETHER "THIRD COUNTRY MEASURES" FALL OUTSIDE THE SCOPE OF THE 1955 TREATY

III. PRELIMINARY OBJECTION TO ADMISSIBILITY OF IRAN'S APPLICATION

IV. OBJECTIONS ON THE BASIS OF ARTICLE XX, PARAGRAPH 1 *(B)* AND *(D)*, OF THE 1955 TREATY

V. DECISION

I.

II.2.1   PRELIMINARY STAGE OF THE PROCEEDINGS

        See also: I.1.143; II.2.02; II.7.09

"[1] On 16 July 2018, the Islamic Republic of Iran (hereinafter "Iran") filed in the Registry of the Court an Application instituting proceedings against the United States of America (hereinafter the "United States") with regard to alleged violations of the Treaty of Amity, Economic Relations, and Consular Rights, which was signed by the two States in Tehran on 15 August 1955 and entered into force on 16 June 1957 (hereinafter the "Treaty of Amity" or the "1955 Treaty"). [2] In its Application, Iran seeks to found the Court's jurisdiction on Article 36, paragraph 1, of the Statute of the Court and on Article XXI, paragraph 2, of the 1955 Treaty. [3] On 16 July 2018, Iran also submitted a Request for the indication of provisional measures, referring to Article 41 of the Statute and to Articles 73, 74 and 75 of the Rules of Court. [10] By an Order of 3 October 2018, the Court, having heard the Parties, indicated [...] provisional measures [...]."

[**Paras. 1, 2, 3, 10**]

---

* Summaries prepared by Giuliana Ziccardi Capaldo, Professor Emeritus of International Law, University of Salerno, Italy. General Editor. Text of judgment available online at the Court's Web site <http://www.icj-cij.org>. Original: English (authoritative) and French.

** This is not a faithful reproduction of the Table of Contents of the Judgment.

I.1.143   VIOLATION OF TREATY OBLIGATIONS
           See also: I.2.0641; I.2.2141; I.2.22771; I.11.0341; I.12.47; I.13.32; I.13.321

"[**24**] In the present proceedings, Iran alleges violations by the United States of the Treaty of Amity, which was signed by the Parties on 15 August 1955 and entered into force on 16 June 1957 [...]. It is not disputed by the Parties that on the date of the filing of the Application, namely, on 16 July 2018, the Treaty of Amity was in force. In accordance with Article XXIII, paragraph 3, of the Treaty of Amity, "[e]ither High Contracting Party may, by giving one year's written notice to the other High Contracting Party, terminate the present Treaty [...]" [...] [**25**] [...] Iran is a party to the Treaty on the Non-Proliferation of Nuclear Weapons of 1 July 1968. According to Article III of this Treaty, each non-nuclear-weapon State party undertakes to accept safeguards, as set forth in an agreement to be negotiated and concluded with the International Atomic Energy Agency (hereinafter the "IAEA" or "Agency"), for the exclusive purpose of verification of the fulfilment of its obligations assumed under the Treaty "with a view to preventing diversion of nuclear energy from peaceful uses to nuclear weapons or other nuclear explosive devices". The Agreement between Iran and the Agency for the Application of Safeguards in Connection with the Treaty on the Non-Proliferation of Nuclear Weapons has been in force since 15 May 1974. In a report dated 6 June 2003, the IAEA Director General stated that Iran had "failed to meet its obligations under its Safeguards Agreement [...]. In its resolution GOV/2006/14 of 4 February 2006, the Agency's Board of Governors [...] requested the Director General to report the matter to the Security Council of the United Nations. [**27**] On 31 July 2006, the Security Council, acting under Article 40 of Chapter VII of the Charter of the United Nations, adopted resolution 1696 (2006), in which it noted, with serious concern, Iran's decision "to resume enrichment-related activities" and demanded "in this context, that Iran shall suspend all enrichment-related and reprocessing activities, including research and development, to be verified by the IAEA". [...] [**28**] On 23 December 2006, the Security Council, acting under Article 41 of Chapter VII of the Charter of the United Nations, adopted resolution 1737 (2006), in which it [...] decided that Iran must suspend "all enrichment-related and reprocessing activities [...]" [...]. It further decided that all States must take the necessary measures to prevent the supply, sale or transfer of all items, materials, equipment, goods and technology which could contribute to Iran's nuclear-related activities. Subsequently, the Security Council adopted further resolutions on the Iranian nuclear issue, namely, resolutions 1747 (2007), 1803 (2008), 1835 (2008), 1929 (2010) and 2224 (2015). [**29**] On 26 July 2010, the Council of the European Union adopted Decision 2010/413/CFSP and, on 23 March 2012, Regulation No. 267/2012 concerning nuclear-related "restrictive measures against Iran", banning arms exports, restricting financial transactions, imposing the freezing of assets and restricting travel for certain individuals. [**30**] The United States, by Executive Orders 13574 of 23 May 2011, 13590 of 21 November 2011, 13622 of 30 July 2012, 13628 of 9 October 2012 (Sections 5 to 7, and 15) and 13645 of 3 June 2013, imposed a number of nuclear-related "additional sanctions" with regard to various sectors of Iran's economy. [**31**] On 14 July 2015, China, France, Germany, the Russian Federation, the United Kingdom and the United States, with the High Representative of the European Union for Foreign Affairs and Security Policy, and Iran concluded the Joint Comprehensive Plan of Action (hereinafter the "JCPOA") concerning the nuclear programme of Iran. The declared purpose of that instrument was to ensure the exclusively peaceful nature of Iran's nuclear programme and to produce "the comprehensive lifting of all UN Security Council sanctions as well as multilateral and national sanctions related to Iran's nuclear programme". [**32**] On 20 July 2015, the Security Council adopted resolution 2231 (2015), whereby it endorsed the JCPOA and urged its "full implementation on the timetable established [therein]". [...] [**33**] The

JCPOA describes, in particular, the steps to be taken by Iran within a set time frame, regarding agreed limitations on all uranium enrichment and uranium enrichment-related activities and addresses the co-operation of Iran with the IAEA. It provides for the termination of all sanctions adopted by the Security Council and the European Union, respectively, as well as the cessation of the implementation of certain United States sanctions (as described in Annex II to the JCPOA) [. . .]. [34] On 16 January 2016, the President of the United States issued Executive Order 13716 revoking or amending a certain number of earlier Executive Orders on "nuclear-related sanctions" imposed on Iran or Iranian nationals. [35] On 8 May 2018, the President of the United States issued a National Security Presidential Memorandum announcing the end of the participation of the United States in the JCPOA and directing the reimposition of "sanctions lifted or waived in connection with the JCPOA". In the Memorandum, the President of the United States indicated that Iranian or Iran-backed forces were engaging in military activities in the surrounding region and that Iran remained a State sponsor of terrorism. [. . .] [37] On 6 August 2018, the President of the United States issued Executive Order 13846 reimposing "certain sanctions" on Iran, its nationals and companies. Earlier Executive Orders implementing the commitments of the United States under the JCPOA were revoked."

[**Paras. 24, 25, 27, 28, 29, 30, 31, 32, 33, 34, 35, 37**]

II.2.11 PRELIMINARY OBJECTIONS

"[**38**] The United States has raised five preliminary objections. The first two relate to the jurisdiction of the Court *ratione materiae* to entertain the case on the basis of Article XXI, paragraph 2, of the Treaty of Amity. The third contests the admissibility of Iran's Application by reason of an alleged abuse of process and on grounds of judicial propriety. The last two are based on subparagraphs *(b)* and *(d)* of Article XX, paragraph 1, of the Treaty of Amity. [. . .]"

[**Para. 38**]

II.

II.2.111 OBJECTIONS TO JURISDICTION
See also: II.7.022; II.7.032

"[**39**] The United States contests the Court's jurisdiction to entertain the Application of Iran. It submits that the dispute before the Court falls outside the scope *ratione materiae* of Article XXI, paragraph 2, of the Treaty of Amity, the basis of jurisdiction invoked by Iran, which provides that: "Any dispute between the High Contracting Parties as to the interpretation or application of the present Treaty, not satisfactorily adjusted by diplomacy, shall be submitted to the International Court of Justice, unless the High Contracting Parties agree to settlement by some other pacific means.""

[**Para. 39**]

A.

II.7.032 COMPROMISSORY CLAUSE
See also: I.1.15; I.1.16; II.7.04; II.7.042

"[**40**] [. . .] First, the United States contends that "the true subject matter of this case is a dispute as to the application of the JCPOA, an instrument entirely distinct from the Treaty of Amity, with no relationship thereto". [. . .] [46] [. . .] According to the United States, the JCPOA is a multilateral political arrangement which does not create legally binding obligations. Moreover, it does not contain any clause giving the Court jurisdiction to entertain a dispute arising between two or more JCPOA participants. [51] The Court notes that the Parties do not contest that there is a dispute between them, but they disagree as to whether this dispute concerns the interpretation and application of the Treaty of Amity, as Iran claims, or exclusively the JCPOA, as the United States contends. In the latter case, the dispute would fall outside the scope *ratione materiae* of the compromissory clause of the Treaty of Amity."

[Paras. 40, 46, 51]

II.7.042   SUBJECT OF THE DISPUTE
           See also: I.1.143; I.13.32; II.7.04; II.7.0411

"[52] As the Court has consistently recalled, [. . .] it is for the Court to determine, taking account of the parties' submissions, the subject-matter of the dispute of which it is seised (see *Fisheries Jurisdiction (Spain v. Canada), Jurisdiction of the Court, Judgment, I.C.J. Reports 1998*, pp. 447-449, paras. 29-32). [. . .] (*Nuclear Tests (Australia v. France), Judgment, I.C.J. Reports 1974*, p. 262, para. 29; *Nuclear Tests (New Zealand v. France), Judgment, I.C.J. Reports 1974*, p. 466, para. 30.) [53] The Court's determination of the subject-matter of the dispute is made "on an objective basis" (*Obligation to Negotiate Access to the Pacific Ocean (Bolivia v. Chile), Preliminary Objection, Judgment, I.C.J. Reports 2015 (II)*, p. 602, para. 26), "while giving particular attention to the formulation of the dispute chosen by the Applicant" (*Fisheries Jurisdiction (Spain v. Canada), Jurisdiction of the Court, Judgment, I.C.J. Reports 1998*, p. 448, para. 30). To identify the subject-matter of the dispute, the Court bases itself on the application, as well as on the written and oral pleadings of the parties. In particular, it takes account of the facts that the applicant identifies as the basis for its claim (*Obligation to Negotiate Access to the Pacific Ocean (Bolivia v. Chile), Preliminary Objection, Judgment, I.C.J. Reports 2015 (II)*, pp. 602-603, para. 26). [54] In the present case, according to the submissions presented in its Application and its Memorial, Iran essentially seeks to have the Court declare that the measures reimposed pursuant to the United States' decision expressed in the Presidential Memorandum of 8 May 2018 are in breach of various obligations of the United States under the Treaty of Amity, and consequently to have the situation prior to that decision restored. The United States contests that the impugned measures constitute violations of the Treaty of Amity. Hence there exists an opposition of views which amounts to a dispute relating to the Treaty of Amity."

[Paras. 52, 53, 54]

II.7.0411   DETERMINATION OF THE EXISTENCE OF A DISPUTE
            See also: I.1.15; I.1.16; II.7.042

"[56] The fact that the dispute between the Parties has arisen in connection with and in the context of the decision of the United States to withdraw from the JCPOA does not in itself preclude the dispute from relating to the interpretation or application of the Treaty of Amity (cf. *Oil Platforms (Islamic Republic of Iran v. United States of America), Preliminary Objection, Judgment, I.C.J. Reports 1996 (II)*, pp. 811-812, para. 21). Certain acts may fall within the ambit of more than one instrument and a dispute relating to those acts may relate to the "interpretation or application" of more than one treaty or other instrument. To the extent that the measures adopted by the United States following its decision to withdraw from the JCPOA might constitute breaches of certain obligations under the Treaty of Amity, those measures relate to the interpretation or application of that Treaty. [**58**] [...] [T]he dispute is part of a broader context that includes the JCPOA. [**59**] [...] The Court's "duty to isolate the real issue in the case and to identify the object of the claim" [...] does not permit it to modify the object of the submissions, especially when they have been clearly and precisely formulated. In particular, the Court cannot infer the subject-matter of a dispute from the political context in which the proceedings have been instituted, rather than basing itself on what the applicant has requested of it. [**60**] For the reasons set out above, the Court cannot uphold the first preliminary objection to jurisdiction raised by the United States."

[**Paras. 56, 58, 59, 60**]

B.

I.1.16   TREATY INTERPRETATION
         See also: I.1.161; II.7.022

"[**75**] The Court recalls that, according to its well-established jurisprudence, in order to de-termine its jurisdiction *ratione materiae* under a compromissory clause concerning disputes relating to the interpretation or application of a treaty, it cannot limit itself to noting that one of the parties maintains that such a dispute exists, and the other denies it. It must ascertain whether the acts of which the applicant complains fall within the provisions of the treaty containing the compromissory clause. This may require the interpretation of the provisions that define the scope of the treaty (see *Immunities and Criminal Proceedings (Equatorial Guinea v. France), Preliminary Objections, Judgment, I.C.J. Reports 2018 (I)*, p. 308, para. 46; *Oil Platforms (Islamic Republic of Iran v. United States of America), Preliminary Objection, Judgment, I.C.J. Reports 1996 (II)*, p. 810, para. 16)."

[**Para. 75**]

I.1.161   OBJECT AND PURPOSE OF A TREATY
          See also: I.1.16; I.2.0641

"[**61**] [...] According to the Respondent [to the United States], the Treaty of Amity is applicable only to trade between the two States parties, or their nationals and companies, and not to trade between one of them and a third country, or their nationals and companies. [**62**] According to the United States, the vast majority of the measures implemented or reinstated under the Memorandum of 8 May 2018 concern the trade or transactions of Iran (or its companies and nationals) with third countries (or their companies and nationals). [...] [S]uch measures, which it [the Respondent] characterizes as "third country meas-ures", fall outside the scope of the Treaty of Amity. [**70**] Iran challenges the concept of "third country measures" which underlies the United States' second preliminary objection to jurisdiction. [...]"

[**Paras. 61, 62, 70**]

I.2.0641   MEASURES OF CONSTRAINT AGAINST A FOREIGN STATE

"[**78**] The Court observes that the Parties are in disagreement about the relevance of the concept of "third country measures" and about the effects that should follow from the ap-plication of such a concept in this case. While, according to the United States, the Court should find that it lacks jurisdiction to entertain most of Iran's claims, since the vast ma-jority of the measures complained of by the Applicant are directed against "non-U.S." per-sons, companies or entities, Iran, on the other hand, contends that the concept of "third country measures" is irrelevant. It is only necessary, according to the Applicant, to examine each category of measures at issue in order to determine whether they fall within the scope of the various provisions of the Treaty of Amity which it claims to have been violated."

[Para. 78]

I.1.143   VIOLATION OF TREATY OBLIGATIONS
            See also: I.1.16

"[79] Moreover, the Parties disagree on the interpretation of the provisions of the Treaty which Iran claims to have been breached by the United States, as regards their territorial scope and their ambit. [...] [81] Conversely, the fact that some of the measures challenged — whether or not they are "the vast majority", as the United States maintains— directly target third States or the nationals or companies of third States does not suffice for them to be automatically excluded from the ambit of the Treaty of Amity. Only through a detailed examination of each of the measures in question, of their reach and actual effects, can the Court determine whether they affect the performance of the United States' obligations arising out of the provisions of the Treaty of Amity invoked by Iran, taking account of the meaning and scope of those various provisions."

[Paras. 79, 81]

II.2.23   QUESTIONS OF MERITS

"[82] In sum, the Court considers that the second preliminary objection of the United States relates to the scope of certain obligations relied upon by the Applicant in the present case and raises legal and factual questions which are properly a matter for the merits (cf. *Application of the International Convention for the Suppression of the Financing of Terrorism and of the International Convention on the Elimination of All Forms of Racial Discrimination (Ukraine v. Russian Federation), Preliminary Objections, Judgment, I.C.J. Reports 2019 (II),* p. 586, para. 63). If the case were to proceed to the merits, such matters would be decided by the Court at that stage, on the basis of the arguments advanced by the Parties. [83] In light of the above, the Court finds that the second preliminary objection to jurisdiction raised by the United States cannot be upheld. [84] For all the reasons set out above, the Court finds that it has jurisdiction *ratione materiae* to entertain the Application of Iran on the basis of Article XXI, paragraph 2, of the 1955 Treaty of Amity."

[Paras. 82, 83, 84]

III.

II.2.112   OBJECTIONS TO ADMISSIBILITY
            See also: II.0.81

"[92] The objection to admissibility raised by the United States is based on the contention that "Iran's claims amount to an abuse of process and would work an injustice that would raise serious questions of judicial propriety". This is because "Iran has invoked the Treaty [of Amity] in a case involving a dispute that solely concerns the application of the JCPOA". The Court notes that the United States did not address its objection to the admissibility of Iran's Application during the oral hearings, but expressly maintained that objection."

[Para. 92]

II.0.81   ABUSE OF PROCESS
            See also: I.1.143; II.7.071

"[**93**] As the Court observed in *Immunities and Criminal Proceedings (Equatorial Guinea v. France)*, "[i]t is only in exceptional circumstances that the Court should reject a claim based on a valid title of jurisdiction on the ground of abuse of process" (*Preliminary Objections, Judgment, I.C.J. Reports 2018 (I)*, p. 336, para. 150). The Court has specified that there has to be "clear evidence" that the Applicant's conduct amounts to an abuse of process (for analogous statements, see *Certain Iranian Assets (Islamic Republic of Iran v. United States of America), Preliminary Objections, Judgment, I.C.J. Reports 2019 (I)*, pp. 42-43, para. 113; *Jadhav (India v. Pakistan), Judgment, I.C.J. Reports 2019 (II)*, p. 433, para. 49). [**94**] In the present case, the Court has already ascertained that the dispute submitted by the Applicant concerns alleged breaches of obligations under the Treaty of Amity and not the application of the JCPOA [. . .]. The Court has also found that the compromissory clause included in the Treaty of Amity provides a valid basis for its jurisdiction with regard to the Applicant's claims [. . .]. [**95**] In the view of the Court, there are no exceptional circumstances that would justify considering Iran's Application inadmissible on the ground of abuse of process. In particular, the fact that Iran only challenged the consistency with the Treaty of Amity of the measures that had been lifted in conjunction with the JCPOA and then reinstated in May 2018, without discussing other measures affecting Iran and its nationals or companies, may reflect a policy decision. However, as was noted in *Border and Transborder Armed Actions (Nicaragua v. Honduras)*, the Court's judgment "cannot concern itself with the political motivation which may lead a State at a particular time, or in particular circumstances, to choose judicial settlement" (*Jurisdiction and Admissibility, Judgment, I.C.J. Reports 1988*, p. 91, para. 52). In any event, the fact that most of Iran's claims concern measures that had been lifted in conjunction with the JCPOA and were later reinstated does not indicate that the submission of these claims constitutes an abuse of process. [**96**] In light of the foregoing, the Court finds that the objection to the admissibility of the Application raised by the United States must be rejected."

[**Paras. 93, 94, 95, 96**]

IV.

II.2.13   OTHER PRELIMINARY QUESTIONS
            See also: II.2.11; II.7.024

"[**97**] The United States maintains that Article 79 (now Article 79*bis*) of the Rules of Court sets out three types of preliminary objections, namely objections to the jurisdiction of the Court, objections to the admissibility of the Application, and any "other objection the decision upon which is requested before any further proceedings on the merits". [. . .] [**108**] Article XX, paragraph 1, of the Treaty of Amity reads as follows:

"1. The present Treaty shall not preclude the application of measures:
. . . .
(b) relating to fissionable materials, the radio-active
by-products thereof, or the sources thereof;
. . . .

(*d*) necessary to fulfill the obligations of a High Contracting
Party for the maintenance or restoration of international peace
and security, or necessary to protect its essential security interests.'"

[Paras. 97, 108]

II.2.23   QUESTIONS OF MERITS
            See also: I.1.143; II.2.11; II.2.2

"[**109**] The Court recalls that in the *Oil Platforms* case (*Islamic Republic of Iran* v. *United States of America*), it found that "Article XX, paragraph 1 (*d*), [of the Treaty of Amity] does not restrict its jurisdiction in the present case, but is confined to affording the Parties a possible defence on the merits" (*Preliminary Objection, Judgment, I.C.J. Reports 1996 (II)*, p. 811, para. 20). A similar view was expressed in the case concerning *Certain Iranian Assets* (*Islamic Republic of Iran* v. *United States of America*) (*Preliminary Objections, Judgment, I.C.J. Reports 2019 (I)*, p. 25, para. 45), where the Court noted that the interpretation given to Article XX, paragraph 1, with regard to subparagraph (*d*) also applies to subparagraph (*c*) [. . .]" (*ibid.*, p. 25, para. 46). The Court finds that there are equally no relevant grounds for a distinction with regard to subparagraph (*b*), which may only afford a possible defence on the merits. [**110**] [. . .] [T]he Respondent argues that objections formulated on the basis of Article XX, paragraph 1 (*b*) and (*d*), may be presented as preliminary according to Article 79 of the Rules of Court as "other objection[s] the decision upon which is requested before any further proceedings on the merits". For the following reasons, the two objections raised by the United States on the basis of Article XX, paragraph 1 (*b*) and (*d*), cannot be considered as preliminary. A decision concerning these matters requires an analysis of issues of law and fact that should be left to the stage of the examination of the merits. [**111**] [. . .] The question of the meaning to be given to subparagraph (*b*) and that of its implications for the present case do not have a preliminary character and will have to be examined as part of the merits. [**112**] The same applies to measures taken by the United States allegedly because they are deemed "necessary to protect its essential security interests" and are therefore argued to be comprised in the category of measures that are outlined in subparagraph (*d*). The analysis of this objection would raise the question of the existence of such essential security interests and may require an assessment of the reasonableness and necessity of the measures in so far as they affect the obligations under the Treaty of Amity (see *Military and Paramilitary Activities in and against Nicaragua* (*Nicaragua* v. *United States of America*), *Merits, Judgment, I.C.J. Reports 1986*, p. 117, para. 224). Such an assessment can be conducted only at the stage of the examination of the merits. [**113**] [. . .] Therefore, the preliminary objections raised by the United States based on these provisions [Article XX, paragraph 1 (*b*) and (*d*), of the Treaty of Amity] must be rejected."

[Paras. 109, 110, 111, 112, 113]

V.

II.2.113   DECISION ON PRELIMINARY OBJECTIONS
            See also: I.2.0641; II.2.111; II.2.112; II.2.13

"[**114**] For these reasons,
THE COURT,
(1) Unanimously, *Rejects* the preliminary objection to its jurisdiction raised by the United States of America according to which the subject-matter of the dispute does not relate to

the interpretation or application of the Treaty of Amity, Economic Relations, and Consular Rights of 1955; (2) Unanimously, *Rejects* the preliminary objection to its jurisdiction raised by the United States of America relating to the measures concerning trade or transactions between the Islamic Republic of Iran (or Iranian nationals and companies) and third countries (or their nationals and companies); (3) By fifteen votes to one, *Rejects* the preliminary objection to the admissibility of the Application raised by the United States of America [...]; AGAINST: *Judge* ad hoc Brower; (4) By fifteen votes to one, *Rejects* the preliminary objection raised by the United States of America on the basis of Article XX, paragraph 1 *(b)*, of the Treaty of Amity, Economic Relations, and Consular Rights of 1955 [...]; AGAINST: *Judge* ad hoc Brower; (5) Unanimously, *Rejects* the preliminary objection raised by the United States of America on the basis of Article XX, paragraph 1 *(d)*, of the Treaty of Amity, Economic Relations, and Consular Rights of 1955; (6) By fifteen votes to one, *Finds*, consequently, that it has jurisdiction, on the basis of Article XXI, paragraph 2, of the Treaty of Amity, Economic Relations, and Consular Rights of 1955, to entertain the Application filed by the Islamic Republic of Iran on 16 July 2018, and that the said Application is admissible. [...]; AGAINST: *Judge* ad hoc Brower. [...] [Judge Tomka appends a declaration to the Judgment of the Court; Judge *ad hoc* Brower appends a separate, partly concurring and partly dissenting, opinion to the Judgment of the Court]."

[**Para. 114**]

Systematic Key Items of the Section*

I.1.143	VIOLATION OF TREATY OBLIGATIONS
I.1.16	TREATY INTERPRETATION
I.1.161	OBJECT AND PURPOSE OF A TREATY
I.2.0641	MEASURES OF CONSTRAINT AGAINST A FOREIGN STATE
II.0.81	ABUSE OF PROCESS
II.2.1	PRELIMINARY STAGE OF THE PROCEEDINGS
II.2.11	PRELIMINARY OBJECTIONS
II.2.111	OBJECTIONS TO JURISDICTION
II.2.112	OBJECTIONS TO ADMISSIBILITY
II.2.113	DECISION ON PRELIMINARY OBJECTIONS
II.2.13	OTHER PRELIMINARY QUESTIONS
II.2.23	QUESTIONS OF MERITS
II.7.032	COMPROMISSORY CLAUSE
II.7.0411	DETERMINATION OF THE EXISTENCE OF A DISPUTE
II.7.042	SUBJECT OF THE DISPUTE

---

* *See* Systematic Classification Scheme, *supra* at page 255.

II

International Tribunal for the Law of the Sea

INTRODUCTORY NOTE

The International Tribunal for the Law of the Sea in 2021

BY YOSHIFUMI TANAKA*

Abstract

This introductory note examines cases before the International Tribunal for the Law of the Sea for the year 2021. Specifically, it reviews *Dispute Concerning Delimitation of the Maritime Boundary between Mauritius and Maldives in the Indian Ocean (Mauritius/Maldives)* (preliminary objections) and discontinuance of the proceedings of the *M/T "San Padre Pio" (No. 2) Case (Switzerland/Nigeria)*. The special chamber of ITLOS dismissed all preliminary objections raised by Maldives. The chamber's judgment contains some issues that merit discussion with regard to, inter alia, legal effects of an advisory opinion of the International Court of Justice and the UN General Assembly resolution. The *M/T "San Padre Pio" (No. 2)* provides a third case of discontinuance in the ITLOS jurisprudence. This note also refers to the amendments of the Rules of the Tribunal and the activity of the Tribunal concerning capacity-building.

I. INTRODUCTION

On 28 January 2021, the special chamber of the International Tribunal for the Law of the Sea (ITLOS or the Tribunal) rendered the judgment with regard to the *Mauritius/Maldives* case (Preliminary Objection).[1] This case raised some interesting issues concerning the legal

---

* Professor of International Law, Faculty of Law, University of Copenhagen; Member of the Editorial Board.

[1] Dispute Concerning Delimitation of the Maritime Boundary between Mauritius and Maldives in the Indian Ocean (Mauritius/Maldives), Preliminary Objections, Judgment, available at https://www.itlos.org/fileadmin/itlos/documents/cases/28/preliminary_objections/C28_Judgment_prelimobj_28.01.2021_orig.pdf. For a summary of this judgment, *see* Graig D. Gaver, *Dispute Concerning Delimitation of the Maritime Boundary between Mauritius and Maldives in the Indian Ocean (Mauritius/Maldives)*, 115 AMERICAN JOURNAL OF INTERNATIONAL LAW 519–526 (2021); *Annual Report of the International Tribunal for the Law of the Sea for 2021*, 18 April 2022, SPLOS/32/2, 7–10, paras. 25–44.

Yoshifumi Tanaka, *Introductory Note* In: *The Global Community Yearbook of International Law and Jurisprudence 2022*. Edited by: Giuliana Ziccardi Capaldo, Oxford University Press. © Oxford University Press 2023. DOI: 10.1093/oso/9780197752265.003.0017

effects of an advisory opinion of the International Court of Justice (ICJ) in the ITLOS juris-prudence. Furthermore, the Tribunal, in its Order of 29 December 2021, removed the *M/T "San Padre Pio" (No. 2)* case from the list of cases on the basis of the agreement between the parties.[2] This case provides a precedent concerning the discontinuance of the proceedings of ITLOS and an out-of-court settlement. As regards other activity, the Tribunal amended the Rules of the Tribunal on 15 March and 25 March 2021, respectively.

Following the introduction, the introductory note succinctly reviews the two cases (section II). It then discuss the amendments of the Rules of the Tribunal (section III.A). It also refers to the activity of the Tribunal with regard to capacity-building (section III.B), before offering conclusion (section IV).

II. CASES

A. Dispute Concerning Delimitation of the Maritime Boundary between Mauritius and Maldives in the Indian Ocean

1. Judgment of 28 January 2021
On 18 June 2019, Mauritius instituted arbitral proceedings against the Maldives under Annex VII of the UN Convention on the Law of the Sea (UNCLOS)[3] "in the dispute concerning the maritime boundary between Mauritius and Maldives."[4] Subsequently, on 24 September 2019, Mauritius and Maldives concluded a Special Agreement, thereby transferred the dispute to a special chamber of ITLOS.[5] Nonetheless, Maldives raised five preliminary objections to the jurisdiction of the special chamber: (i) indispensable third party, (ii) disputed issue of sovereignty, (iii) the obligation to negotiate under Articles 74 and 83, (iv) existence of a dispute, and (v) abuse of process. Mauritius countered these preliminary objections.[6]

The first preliminary objection raised by the Maldives concerned the existence of indispensable third party, that is, the United Kingdom. There, Maldives submitted that there is a territorial dispute over the Chagos Archipelago between Mauritius and the United Kingdom and that a decision on Mauritius' maritime claims would necessarily require the special chamber to rule on the United Kingdom's legal interests. Maldives thus claimed that since the United Kingdom is absent from the present proceedings, the special chamber should decline jurisdiction in accordance with the Monetary Gold principle.[7]

---

[2] The *M/T "San Padre Pio" (No. 2)* case (Switzerland/Nigeria). Order 2021/6 of 29 December 2021, para. 8, available at https://www.itlos.org/fileadmin/itlos/documents/cases/29/C29_Order_20211229.pdf. All Orders of the *M/T "San Padre Pio" (No. 2)* case are available at https://www.itlos.org/en/main/cases/list-of-cases/the-m/t-san-padre-pio-no-2-case-switzerland/nigeria/. For a summary of the case, *see Annual Report, supra* note 1, at 11–12, paras. 45–51.

[3] Adopted 10 December 1982. Entered into force 16 November 1994. Text in: 1833 UNTS 3.

[4] The *Mauritius/Maldives* case, *supra* note 1, para. 1.

[5] *Id.*, para. 2.

[6] Written Observation of the Republic of Mauritius on the Preliminary Objections Raised by the Republic of Maldives of 17 February 2020, available at https://www.itlos.org/fileadmin/itlos/documents/cases/28/preliminary_objections/C28_PO_Written_Observations_Mauritius.pdf.

[7] The *Mauritius/Maldives* case, *supra* note 1, paras. 81–89; preliminary objections of the Republic of Maldives of 18 December 2019, paras. 45–58, at 15–19, available at https://www.itlos.org/fileadmin/itlos/docume nts/cases/28/preliminary_objections/C28_PO_Preliminary_Objections_Maldives.pdf.

The Maldives' second preliminary objection related to the existence of disputed issue of sovereignty over the Chagos Archipelago. According to Maldives, determining whether Mauritius is currently the state with the "opposite or adjacent coast" to the Maldives would inevitably require the special chamber to determine the territorial dispute between Mauritius and the United Kingdom over the Chagos Archipelago, but the special chamber has no jurisdiction to determine a disputed issue of sovereignty.[8]

The special chamber examined the two objections together. The chamber's view can be summarised as follows:

- While the Arbitral Tribunal in the *Chagos* arbitral award recognized the existence of a sovereignty dispute between the United Kingdom and Mauritius over the Chagos Archipelago, it found that it lacked jurisdiction to address said dispute. On the other hand, the Arbitral Tribunal recognized, without prejudice to the question of sovereignty, that Mauritius had certain rights in respect of the Chagos Archipelago, including fishing rights, the right to its return when no longer needed for defence purposes and the right to the benefit of minerals or oil discovered. This demonstrates that, aside from the question of sovereignty, the Chagos Archipelago has been subject to a special regime, according to which Mauritius is entitled to certain maritime rights;
- The determinations made by the ICJ with respect to the issues of the decolonization of Mauritius in the *Chagos* advisory opinion have legal effect and clear implications for the legal status of the Chagos Archipelago. The United Kingdom's continued claim to sovereignty over the Chagos Archipelago is contrary to those determinations. While the process of decolonization has yet to be completed, Mauritius' sovereignty over the Chagos Archipelago can be inferred from the ICJ's determinations;
- Resolution 73/295 of the General Assembly, within the remit of which the modalities necessary for ensuring the completion of the decolonization of Mauritius fall, demanded that the United Kingdom withdraw its administration over the Chagos Archipelago within six months from its adoption. The fact that the time-limit set by the General Assembly has passed without the United Kingdom complying with this demand further strengthens the special chamber's finding that its claim to sovereignty over the Chagos Archipelago is contrary to the authoritative determinations made in the advisory opinion.[9]

In light of the preceding findings, the special chamber ruled that the United Kingdom is not an indispensable party to the present proceedings. It then held that Mauritius can be regarded as the coastal state in respect of the Chagos Archipelago for the purpose of the delimitation of a maritime boundary. In conclusion, the special chamber unanimously rejected the first preliminary objection and also rejected, by 8 votes to 1, second preliminary objections.[10]

The Maldives' third preliminary objection related to the obligation to negotiate under Articles 74 and 83 of the UNCLOS.[11] There, two issues arose with regard to the interpretation and application of Articles 74 and 83, respectively. As regards the interpretation of the obligation to negotiate under the provisions, the special chamber held:

[A]rticle 74, paragraph 1, and article 83, paragraph 1, of the Convention entail an obligation to negotiate in good faith with a view to reaching an agreement on

---

[8] *Id.*, paras. 59–62, at 19–21; the *Mauritius/Maldives* case, *supra* note 1, paras. 104–105.

[9] *Id.*, para. 246.

[10] *Id.*, paras. 247–251; para. 354(1) and (2).

[11] Preliminary objections of the Republic of Maldives, *supra* note 7, paras. 63–72, at 22–24.

delimitation. However, this obligation does not require the States concerned to reach such agreement.[12]

Concerning the application of Articles 74 and 83, the special chamber noted that "the Maldives, for most of the time, refused to negotiate with Mauritius".[13] It then opined that "in situations in which "no agreement can be reached," to resort to the procedures of Part XV of the Convention, as set out in Paragraph 2 of each of Articles 74 and 83, is not only justified but also an obligation of the States concerned."[14] In conclusion, the special chamber rejected, by 8 votes to 1, the third preliminary objection of the Maldives, stating that the obligations under Articles 74(1) and 83(1) of the UNCLOS have been fulfilled.[15]

The Maldives's fourth preliminary objection concerned the existence of a dispute. In this regard, the Maldives made two arguments. First, for the Maldives, there can be no dispute between the Maldives and Mauritius over maritime delimitation until such time as Mauritius becomes the undisputed opposite coastal state within the meaning of Articles 74(1) and 83(1) of the UNCLOS.[16] However, the special chamber dismissed this argument because Mauritius can be regarded as the state with an opposite or adjacent coast to the Maldives within the meaning of Articles 74(1) and 83(1) of the Convention.[17] Second, the Maldives argued that there was no maritime boundary dispute between Mauritius and the Maldives at the time that proceedings under Part XV of the UNCLOS were initiated.[18] However, the special chamber considered that "a disagreement existed between the Parties regarding maritime delimitation long before the *Chagos* advisory opinion was rendered."[19] Accordingly, the special chamber unanimously rejected the fourth preliminary objection of the Maldives.[20]

Finally, the Maldives, in its fifth preliminary objection, argued that "[u]sing UNCLOS compulsory procedures to obtain a ruling on a territorial dispute with a third State is the very definition of an abuse of process."[21] However, the special chamber considered that Mauritius' claim are confined to Articles 74 and 83 of the Convention and that it does not constitute an abuse of process. Thus it unanimously rejected the fifth preliminary objection of the Maldives.[22]

On the basis of the preceding considerations, the special chamber concluded, 8 votes to 1, that "it has jurisdiction to adjudicate upon the dispute concerning the delimitation of the maritime boundary between the Parties in the Indian Ocean and that the claim submitted by Mauritius in this regard is admissible."[23] At the same time, it deferred to the proceedings on the merits questions regarding the extent to which the special chamber may exercise its

---

[12] The *Mauritius/Maldives* case, *supra* note 1, para. 273.

[13] *Id.*, para. 289.

[14] *Id.*, para. 292.

[15] *Id.*, para. 293; para. 354(3).

[16] Preliminary objections of the Republic of Maldives, *supra* note 7, paras. 77–79, at 25.

[17] The *Mauritius/Maldives* case, *supra* note 1, para. 321.

[18] Preliminary objections of the Republic of Maldives, *supra* note 7, paras. 80–92, at 25–28.

[19] The *Mauritius/Maldives* case, *supra* note 1, para. 334.

[20] *Id.*, para. 335; para. 354(4).

[21] Presentation by Mr Akhavan, Verbatim Record, ITLOS/PV.20/C28/2/Rev.1, 35. *See also* preliminary objections of the Republic of Maldives, *supra* note 7, paras. 103–106, at 31.

[22] The *Mauritius/Maldives* case, *supra* note 1, paras. 348–350; para. 354(5).

[23] *Id.*, para. 98; para. 354(6).

jurisdiction, including questions arising under Article 76 of the Convention.[24] It also unani-mously reserved for consideration and decision in the proceedings on the merits the question of jurisdiction and admissibility with respect to Mauritius' claim stated in Paragraph 28 of its Notification concerning the obligations under Articles 74 (3) and 83(3) of the Convention.[25]

2. *Commentary*

The *Mauritius/Maldives* case (Preliminary Objections) contrasted with *Dispute Concerning Coastal State Rights in the Black Sea, Sea of Azov, and Kerch Strait* (Preliminary Objection) in some respects.[26] Although no comprehensive examination can be made here, in particular, two points that are closely intertwined merit being highlighted.

The first concerns the existence of territorial disputes. In the *Ukraine v. Russia* arbitra-tion, the existence of territorial dispute over Crimea was key. In this regard, the Russian Federation submitted that "the great majority of the claims advanced by Ukraine depend on a prior determination by, or assumption on the part of, the Arbitral Tribunal as to which State is the coastal State in Crimea."[27] According to Russia, "[a] dispute over territorial sov-ereignty is not a dispute concerning the 'interpretation or application of the Convention' pursuant to Article 288(1) of UNCLOS, the sole jurisdictional basis invoked by Ukraine."[28] Unlike the *Maldives/Mauritius* case, the Annex VII arbitral tribunal, in its award of 2015, accepted the existence of a sovereignty dispute between the parties.[29] In the view of the tri-bunal, "the question as to which State is sovereign over Crimea, and thus the 'coastal State' within the meaning of several provisions of the Convention invoked by Ukraine, is a prereq-uisite to the decision of the Arbitral Tribunal on a significant part of the claims of Ukraine."[30] In this connection, the arbitral tribunal applied the "ancillary" test. In accordance with the test, "where a dispute concerns the interpretation or application of the Convention, the ju-risdiction of a court or tribunal pursuant to Article 288(1) extends to making such findings of fact or ancillary determinations of law as are necessary to resolve the dispute presented to it."[31] Furthermore, a minor issue of territorial sovereignty that could be ancillary to a dispute concerning the interpretation or application of the UNCLOS is not categorically excluded from the jurisdiction of a court or tribunal pursuant to Article 288(1).[32] In light of the ancillary test, the arbitral tribunal, in the *Ukraine v. Russia* arbitration, held:

> [T]he Parties' dispute regarding sovereignty over Crimea is not a minor issue ancillary to the dispute concerning the interpretation or application of the Convention. On the

---

[24] *Id.*

[25] *Id.*, para. 354(7). Judges ad hoc Oxman and Schrijver added joint declaration, available at https://www. itlos.org/fileadmin/itlos/documents/cases/28/preliminary_objections/C28_Judgment_28.01.2021_ Decl_Oxman-Schrijver_orig.pdf. Judge ad hoc Oxman made separate and dissenting opinion, available at https://www.itlos.org/fileadmin/itlos/documents/cases/28/preliminary_objections/C28_Judgment _28.01.20210_Sep-DissOp_Oxman_corr.pdf.

[26] PCA Case No. 2017-06, *Dispute Concerning Coastal State Rights in the Black Sea, Sea of Azov, and Kerch Strait*, Award Concerning the Preliminary Objections of the Russian Federation, 21 February 2020 [here-inafter the *Ukraine v. Russia* arbitration], available at https://pcacases.com/web/sendAttach/9272.

[27] *Id.*, para. 146.

[28] *Id.*, para. 65.

[29] *Id.*, para. 166.

[30] *Id.*, para. 154.

[31] *Chagos Marine Protected Area Arbitration (Mauritius v. United Kingdom)*, Award of 18 March 2015, 31 *Reports of International Arbitral Awards*, para. 220, at 460.

[32] *Id.*, para. 221.

contrary, the question of sovereignty is a prerequisite to the Arbitral Tribunal's decision on a number of claims submitted by Ukraine under the Convention.[33]

It thus concluded that "it lacks jurisdiction over the dispute as submitted by Ukraine to the extent that a ruling of the Arbitral Tribunal on the merits of Ukraine's claims necessarily requires it to decide, expressly or implicitly, on the sovereignty of either Party over Crimea."[34] The finding shows a sharp contrast with the finding of the special chamber of ITLOS in the *Maldives/Mauritius* case. Since the special chamber, in the *Maldives/Mauritius* case, denied the existence of a sovereignty dispute over the Chagos Archipelago,[35] there was no room to apply the ancillary test.

The second point relates to the legal effect of the UN General Assembly resolution. In this regard, Ukraine submitted that "the UNGA resolutions, all of which passed with 'overwhelming support,' codify a 'powerful consensus of the international community' regarding Ukraine's sovereignty in Crimea."[36] Ukraine thus argued that "the Arbitral Tribunal should not 'contravene a determination made five times by the [UNGA],' given the unique role that the UNGA plays in 'coordinating the international law obligation of non-recognition.' "[37] However, the arbitral tribunal dismissed the Ukraine's claim, stating:

> [I]f the Arbitral Tribunal were to accept Ukraine's interpretation of those UNGA resolutions as correct, it would *ipso facto* imply that the Arbitral Tribunal finds that Crimea is part of Ukraine's territory. However, it has no jurisdiction to do so.[38]

By contrast, the ITLOS special chamber, in the *Maldives/Mauritius* case, accepted the relevance of the UN General Assembly Resolution 73/295 for the legal status of the Chagos Archipelago. In the words of the chamber:

> The General Assembly has thus been entrusted to take necessary steps toward the completion of the decolonization of Mauritius. In light of the general functions of the General Assembly on decolonization and the specific task of the decolonization of Mauritius with which it was entrusted, the Special Chamber considers that resolution 73/295 is relevant to assessing the legal status of the Chagos Archipelago.[39]

The difference between the *Ukraine v. Russia* arbitration and the *Maldives/Mauritius* case derives from the existence of ICJ's advisory opinion. As regards the Chagos Archipelago, the ICJ has already given an advisory opinion, stating:

> [T]he obligations arising under international law and reflected in the resolutions adopted by the General Assembly during the process of decolonization of Mauritius

---

[33] The *Ukraine v. Russia* arbitration, *supra* note 26, para. 195.

[34] *Id.*, para. 197.

[35] The *Mauritius/Maldives* case, *supra* note 1, para. 245.

[36] The *Ukraine v. Russia* arbitration, *supra* note 26, para. 101; Ukraine's Written Observations and Submissions of Ukraine on Jurisdiction, 27 November 2018, para. 28, at 12–13; Rejoinder of Ukraine on Jurisdiction, 28 March 2019, para. 16, at 6–7.

[37] The *Ukraine v. Russia* arbitration, *supra* note 26, para. 104; Rejoinder of Ukraine on Jurisdiction, para. 19, at 8–9.

[38] The *Ukraine v. Russia* arbitration, *supra* note 26, para. 176.

[39] The *Mauritius/Maldives* case, *supra* note 1, para. 227.

require the United Kingdom, as the administering Power, to respect the territorial integrity of that country, including the Chagos Archipelago.[40]

According to the special chamber, the dictum "can be interpreted as suggesting Mauritius' sovereignty over the Chagos Archipelago."[41] In light of this, the special chamber considered that "the continued claim of the United Kingdom to sovereignty over the Chagos Archipelago cannot be considered anything more than 'a mere assertion'" which does not prove the existence of a dispute.[42] It thus dismissed the Maldives' second preliminary objection related to the existence of disputed issue of sovereignty over the Chagos Archipelago.[43] There, the special chamber made a sensitive distinction between the binding character and the authoritative nature of an advisory opinion of the ICJ[44] and it did give legal effect to the ICJ's advisory opinion.[45] However, the distinction is not free from controversy.[46] Indeed, following the dictum of the special chamber, the difference between binding judgments and non-binding advisory opinion would be thin.

B. Removal of the *M/T "San Padre Pio" (No. 2)* Case (Switzerland/Nigeria) from the List of Cases

1. *Course of the Litigation*
On 17 December 2019, Switzerland and Nigeria concluded a special agreement to submit to the Tribunal their dispute concerning the arrest and detention of the M/T "San Padre Pio" its crew and cargo.[47] Pursuant to the Order dated 18 June 2021, the President of ITLOS fixed 9 September 2021 as the date for the opening of the oral proceedings.[48] Subsequently, however, the Agent of Switzerland requested that the oral proceedings be postponed in view of the ongoing implementation of a Memorandum of Understanding (MoU) between Switzerland and Nigeria of 20 May 2021. Although Nigeria was invited to indicate its view regarding Switzerland's request, no response was received from Nigeria. In light of the special circumstances of the case, the President of the Tribunal postponed the opening of the oral proceedings.[49]

By letter dated 13 August 2021, the Agent of Nigeria requested that the case be formally terminated by the Tribunal.[50] By letter dated 18 August 2021, however, the Agent

---

[40] *Legal Consequences of the Separation of the Chagos Archipelago from Mauritius in 1965*, Advisory Opinion, ICJ Reports 2019, para. 173, at 137.

[41] The *Mauritius/Maldives* case, *supra* note 1, para. 174.

[42] *Id.*, para. 243.

[43] *Id.*, para. 251.

[44] *Id.*, para. 203.

[45] *Id.*, para. 205.

[46] Separate and Dissenting Opinion of Judge ad hoc Oxman, *supra* note 25, para. 29. *See also* Sara Thin, *The Curious Case of the "Legal Effect" of ICJ Advisory Opinions in the Mauritius/Maldives Maritime Boundary Disputes*, EJIL TALK, https://www.ejiltalk.org/the-curious-case-of-the-legal-effect-of-icj-advisory-opinions-in-the-mauritius-maldives-maritime-boundary-dispute/.

[47] The text of the Special Agreement is available at https://www.itlos.org/fileadmin/itlos/documents/cases/29/C29_Sp_Agr_Mins_17.12.2019_en.pdf.

[48] The *M/T "San Padre Pio" (No. 2)* case, *supra* note 2, Order 2021/3 of 18 June 2021.

[49] Order 2021/4 of 10 August 2021.

[50] Order 2021/6 of 29 December 2021, para. 8.

of Switzerland opposed Nigeria's request to terminate the proceedings.[51] In this connection, by letter dated 10 December 2021, the Agent of Switzerland informed the Tribunal as follows:

> According to the MoU, "the proceedings of the M/T 'San Padre Pio (No. 2) case (Switzerland/Nigeria) (Case No 29) before the International Tribunal for the Law of the Sea shall be discontinued from the moment that the M/T 'San Padre Pio enters the high seas, or the territorial sea or Exclusive Economic Zone of another State."[52]

According to the Switzerland, as of 10 December 2021, the M/T "San Padre Pio" exited the exclusive economic zone (EEZ) of Nigeria, and entered the EEZ of Bénin.[53] Switzerland accordingly requested the Tribunal to record the discontinuance of the M/T "San Padre Pio" (No. 2) case in accordance with Article 105 of the ITLOS Rules and to remove the case from Tribunal's List of cases.[54] Nigeria did not object to the discontinuance of the case by the Tribunal.[55] Accordingly, the President of ITLOS placed on record "the discontinuance, by agreement of the Parties, of the proceedings initiated on 17 December 2019 by Switzerland and Nigeria" and ordered that "the case be removed from the List of cases."[56]

2. Commentary

Discontinuance of the case is provided in Article 105 of the Rules of the Tribunal. Under Article 105(1) of the Rules, the parties, either jointly or separately, notify the Tribunal in writing that they have agreed to discontinue the proceedings at any time before the final judgment on the merits has been delivered. In this case, ITLOS is to make an order recording the discontinuance and directing the Registrar to remove the case from the List of cases. Under Article 105(2) of the Rules, "[i]f the parties have agreed to discontinue the proceedings in consequence of having reached a settlement of the dispute and if they so desire, the Tribunal shall record this fact in the order for the removal of the case from the List, or indicate in, or annex to, the order the terms of the settlement."

The M/T "San Padre Pio"(No. 2) case was not the first case of out-of-court settlement. Before the M/T "San Padre Pio" case, there were two discontinuance cases in the jurisprudence of ITLOS.

The first was Case concerning the Conservation and Sustainable Exploitation of Swordfish Stocks in the South-Eastern Pacific Ocean (Chile/European Union, 2009).[57] The European Community and Chile submitted the Swordfish Stocks dispute to a special chamber of ITLOS in December 2000.[58] At the request of Chile and the European Community, ITLOS, by an Order dated 20 December 2000, formed a special chamber which was composed

---

[51] Id., para. 10.

[52] Id., para. 11.

[53] The fact was confirmed by Nigeria by letter dated 24 December 2021. Id., para. 14.

[54] Id., para. 12.

[55] Id., para. 14.

[56] Id., para. 15.

[57] For a commentary of this case, see Marcos A. Orellana, The Swordfish Dispute between the EU and Chile at the ITLOS and the WTO, 71 NORDIC JOURNAL OF INTERNATIONAL LAW 55–81 (2002); Peter-Tobias Stoll & Silja Vöneky, The Swordfish Case: Law of the Sea v. Trade, 62 ZAöRV/HJIL 21–35 (2002).

[58] The European Community on 19 April 2000 requested consultations with Chile regarding the prohibition on unloading of swordfish in Chilean ports at the WTO (WT/DS193/1, 2000).

of five members.[59] Subsequently, however, the parties informed the special chamber that they had concluded a new Understanding agreed between negotiators for both parties on 16 October 2008.[60] In light of this, the parties requested the special chamber to issue an Order for discontinuance of the case. Accordingly, the special chamber, in its Order of 16 December 2009, placed on record, pursuant to Article 105(2) of the Rules, "the discontinuance, by agreement of the Parties, of the proceedings initiated on 20 December 2000 by Chile and the European Community."[61] The chamber thus ordered that "the case be removed from the List of cases on 16 December 2009."[62]

The second case was the *"Chaisiri Reefer 2" Case (Panama v. Yemen*, 2001). On 3 July 2001, Panama instituted proceedings against Yemen under Article 292 of UNCLOS for the prompt release of a vessel flying the flag of Panama, *Chaisiri Reefer 2*, and its crew.[63] Subsequently, Yemen released the vessel and its cargo and crew on 12 July 2001. As a consequence, the parties had reached a settlement of the dispute concerning the arrest of the *Chaisiri Reefer 2* and agreed to discontinue the proceedings in accordance with Article 105(2) of the Rules of the Tribunal. Accordingly, the President of ITLOS, by Order of 13 July 2001, placed on record "the discontinuance, by agreement of the Parties, of the proceedings initiated on 3 July 2001 on behalf of Panama against Yemen" and ordered that "the case be removed from the List of cases."[64]

To date, discontinuance of proceedings of ITLOS relied on explicit agreement between the parties in dispute. All discontinuance cases were settled outside of the Tribunal. Unlike the *Swordfish Stocks* and *"Chaisiri Reefer 2"* cases, ITLOS, in the *M/T "San Padre Pio"* case, prescribed provisional measures before discontinuance of the case. On this point, the *M/T "San Padre Pio"* case differed from the *Swordfish Stocks* and *"Chaisiri Reefer 2"* cases.

ITLOS ordered, in its provisional measures of 6 July 2019, that upon the posting of the bond or other financial security, Nigeria must "immediately release the M/T 'San Padre Pio', its cargo and the Master and the three officers and shall ensure that the M/T 'San Padre Pio', its cargo and the Master and the three officers are allowed to leave the territory and maritime areas under the jurisdiction of Nigeria."[65] Subsequently, Switzerland informed that "[a]ll crew members were able to leave Nigeria following criminal charges against 12 crew members being dropped on 19 March 2018 and the acquittal of the four officers on 28 November 2019."[66] Here, the provisional measures prescribed by ITLOS seemingly affected the release of crew members. At the same time, however, Switzerland also stated that "[t]here remains no legal basis under Nigerian domestic law for the continued detention of the vessel and its cargo" and that "Nigeria has repeatedly failed to engage in negotiations with Switzerland in relation to the financial guarantee."[67] It seemed that in the *M/T "San Padre Pio"* case, the provisional measures prescribed by ITLOS were not properly implemented.

---

[59] *Conservation and Sustainable Exploitation of Swordfish Stocks (Chile/European Community)*, Order of 20 December 2000, ITLOS Reports 2000, at 153.

[60] Order of 16 December 2009, ITLOS Reports 2008–2010, para. 8, at 15.

[61] *Id.*, at 18.

[62] *Id.*

[63] Application submitted on behalf of Panama, available at https://www.itlos.org/fileadmin/itlos/documents/cases/case_no_9/published/C9_Application_Panama_20010702.pdf.

[64] Order of 13 July 2001, ITLOS Reports 2001, 84.

[65] *Id.*, para. 146(1).

[66] Additional Report of the Swiss Confederation of 5 November 2020, at 3, available at https://www.itlos.org/fileadmin/itlos/documents/cases/27/C27_Switzerland_20201105_Report.pdf.

[67] Ibid.

It is not suggested that provisional measures prescribed by ITLOS are of modest utility in the settlement of international disputes. In some cases, provisional measures prescribed by ITLOS contributed to facilitating an out-of-court settlement.[68] In the *Southern Bluefin Tuna Cases (New Zealand v. Japan; Australia v. Japan*, 1999), ITLOS, in its Order of 27 August 1999, prescribed provisional measures which required the parties, that is, Australia, Japan, and New Zealand, to refrain from conducting an experimental fishing programme involving the taking of a catch of southern bluefin tuna and to resume negotiations without delay with a view to reaching agreement on measures for the conservation and management of southern bluefin tuna.[69] Following the Order, the parties reached an agreement in 2001. The Order seemingly provided an impetus to resume negotiations between the parties to reach an ex post out-of-court settlement. Likewise, ITLOS, in *Case concerning Land Reclamation by Singapore in and around the Straits of Johor*, prescribed provisional measures that ordered the establishment of an expert group to study the effects of Singapore's land reclamation.[70] These measures seemingly contributed to reaching an out-of-court settlement. In the *"ARA Libertad"* case, the ITLOS prescribed provisional measures that ordered Ghana to release the Argentinian frigate *ARA Libertad*.[71] The measures also seemed to serve for an out-of-court settlement.

C. The Tribunal's Docket

As explained earlier, at the end of 2021, only one case remains on the Tribunal's docket:

- Dispute Concerning Delimitation of the Maritime Boundary between Mauritius and Maldives in the Indian Ocean (Mauritius/Maldives)[72]

III. OTHER ACTIVITIES AND DEVELOPMENTS

A. Amendments to the Rules of the Tribunal

In 2021, the Rules of the Tribunal were amended twice.

On 15 March 2021, acting pursuant to Article 16 of the Statute of ITLOS, Annex VI to the UNCLOS, ITLOS adopted the following amendments to the Rules of the Tribunal:

(i) in article 111, paragraph 4, for the words and the figure "no later than 24 hours", the words and the figure "as soon as possible but not later than 96 hours" shall be substituted;

(ii) in article 112, paragraph 3, for the words "but not exceeding ten days from the date of receipt of the application", the words and the figure "within a period of 15 days

---

[68] Further, *see* Yoshifumi Tanaka, *Out-of-Court Settlement*, in Max Planck Encyclopedia of International Procedural Law (Hélène Ruiz Fabri ed., online edition, July 2020).

[69] *Southern Bluefin Tuna Cases (New Zealand v. Japan; Australia v. Japan)*, Order of 27 August 1999, ITLOS Reports 1999, para. 90, at 299.

[70] *Case concerning Land Reclamation by Singapore in and around the Straits of Johor (Malaysia v. Singapore)*, Order of 8 October 2003, ITLOS Reports 2003, para. 106, at 27.

[71] The *"ARA Libertad"* case (Argentina v. Chile), Order of 15 December 2012, ITLOS Reports 2012, para. 108(1), at 350.

[72] The special chamber delivered its judgment on 28 April 2023. Furthermore, on 12 December 2022, the Commission of Small Island States on Climate Change and International Law requested ITLOS to render an advisory opinion addressing climate change under the UNCLOS. In addition, the Republic of the Marshall Islands and the Republic of Equatorial Guinea agreed to submit the M/T "Heroic Idun" dispute to a special chamber of ITLOS by the Special Agreement dated 18 April 2023.

commencing with the first working day following the date on which the application is received" shall be substituted;

(iii) in article 112, paragraph 4, for the word "ten", the figure "14" shall be substituted.[73]

Furthermore, President of ITLOS, Judge Hoffman, in the Annual Report of the Tribunal for 2020, stated:

> The use of gender-inclusive language, or language which does not employ any gender stereotypes, is a widespread preoccupation of organizations within the United Nations system. Sharing this concern, the Tribunal decided, on 25 March 2021, to amend its Rules with a view to rendering them gender inclusive.[74]

Accordingly, on 25 March 2021, acting pursuant to Article 16 of the Statute of ITLOS, Annex VI to the UNCLOS, ITLOS adopted the amendments to the Rules of the Tribunal.[75]

B. Capacity-Building

Capacity-building constitutes part of activities of ITLOS. In this regard, at the administrative session of the judges in September 2021, ITLOS decided to establish a Junior Professional Officer programme for young professionals.[76] The programme is governed by Guidelines concerning the Junior Professional Officer Programme of the International Tribunal for the Law of the Sea adopted on 30 September 2021.[77] The aims of the programme are: (a) to enhance the development and capacity of the Tribunal by recruiting young professionals who are qualified for entry-level positions; (b) to provide young professionals with an opportunity to gain hands-on experience in the field of the law of the sea, dispute settlement and procedures before the Tribunal; (c) to enable states sponsoring Junior Professional Officers ("participating States") to provide on-the-job training and multilateral capacity-building for young graduates and at the same time contribute to enhancing the Tribunal's capacities.[78] Junior Professional Officers are to be recruited under memoranda of understanding concluded between the Tribunal and participating states.[79]

---

[73] Amendments to the Rules of the International Tribunal for the Law of the Sea as adopted by the Tribunal on 15 March 2001, available at https://www.itlos.org/fileadmin/itlos/documents/basic_texts/Rules.amend.15.03.01.E_01.pdf.

[74] Statement given on the occasion of the presentation of the Report of the Tribunal at the thirty-first Meeting of States Parties, 21 June 2021, para. 20, available at https://www.itlos.org/fileadmin/itlos/documents/statements_of_president/hoffmann/Statement_Hoffmann_31st_MOSP_2021.pdf.

[75] For amended provisions, *see* Amendments to the Rules of the International Tribunal for the Law of the Sea as adopted by the Tribunal on 25 March 2021, available at https://www.itlos.org/fileadmin/itlos/documents/basic_texts/Rules_amend_EN_25032021.pdf. *See also Annual Report, supra* note 1, at 12, para. 54.

[76] News Letter 2021/4, available at https://www.itlos.org/en/main/press-media/itlos-newsletters/newsletter-2021/4/. *See also Annual Reports, supra* note 1, at 17, para. 91.

[77] The Guidelines are available at https://www.itlos.org/fileadmin/itlos/documents/registry/JPO/Guidelines_JPO_Eng.pdf.

[78] *Id.*, para. 1.2.

[79] *Id.*, para. 2.1.

IV. CONCLUSION

By way of conclusion, three points can be made.

First, in light of its authoritative nature, the special chamber gave legal effect to the *Chagos* advisory opinion in assessing the legal status of the Chagos Archipelago. The *Mauritius/ Maldives* judgment provides an insight into the legal effect of an advisory opinion of the ICJ in the jurisprudence of another court or tribunal.

Second, the *M/T "San Padre Pio"* case is the third case of discontinuance of proceedings of ITLOS on the basis of an agreement between the parties in dispute. To this day, all discontinuance cases—the *Swordfish Stocks,* *"Chaisiri Reefer 2,"* and *M/T "San Padre Pio"* cases—were settled outside of the Tribunal by agreement.

Third, unlike the *Swordfish Stocks* and *"Chaisiri Reefer 2"* cases, ITLOS, in the *M/T "San Padre Pio"* case, prescribed provisional measures before discontinuance of the case. The *M/T "San Padre Pio" (No. 2)* case provides a unique precedent that a dispute was settled outside the ITLOS after the prescription of provisional measures by the Tribunal.

II.2

LEGAL MAXIMS: SUMMARIES AND EXTRACTS FROM SELECTED CASE LAW*

Dispute Concerning Delimitation of the Maritime Boundary Between Mauritius and Maldives in the Indian Ocean (Mauritius v. Maldives), Preliminary Objections, Case No. 28, Special Chamber, Judgment, 28 January 2021

---

* The working method chosen for the formulation of legal maxims is explained *supra* 'Outline of the Parts', at page xv.

Legal Maxims: Summaries and Extracts from Selected Case Law In: *The Global Community Yearbook of International Law and Jurisprudence 2022*. Edited by: Giuliana Ziccardi Capaldo, Oxford University Press. © Oxford University Press 2023.
DOI: 10.1093/oso/9780197752265.003.0018

LEGAL MAXIMS SUMMARIES AND EXTRACTS FROM SELECTED CASE LAW *

II.2.1

Dispute Concerning Delimitation of the Maritime Boundary Between Mauritius and Maldives in the Indian Ocean (Mauritius v. Maldives), Preliminary Objections, Case No. 28, Special Chamber, Judgment, 28 January 2021*

Contents**

---

* Summaries prepared by Emilio Sessa, Ph.D. in International Law, Department of Legal Sciences (School of Law), University of Salerno, Italy. Text of judgment available online at the Tribunal's Web site <http://www.itlos.org>. Original: English and French.

** This is not a faithful reproduction of the Table of Contents of the Judgment.

XI. JURISDICTION RATIONE MATERIAE AND EXISTENCE OF
A DISPUTE ON MARITIME BOUNDARY DELIMITATION

XII. ABUSE OF PROCESS

XIII. CONCLUSIONS ON JURISDICTION AND ADMISSIBILITY

I.

II.2.0   INSTITUTION AND COURSE OF PROCEEDINGS
See also: I.1.16; I.5.0; I.5.01; II.2.022; II.7.12

"[1] By letter dated 23 August 2019, [. . .] Mauritius [. . .] informed the [. . .]
International Tribunal for the Law of the Sea (hereinafter "the Tribunal") of the institution of arbitral proceedings by Mauritius against the Republic of the Maldives (hereinafter "the Maldives") on 18 June 2019, pursuant to Annex VII to the United Nations
Convention on the Law of the Sea (hereinafter "the Convention").[. . .] [2] Following
consultations held by the President of the Tribunal with representatives of Mauritius and
the Maldives in Hamburg on 17 September 2019, a Special Agreement was concluded between the two States on 24 September 2019 to submit the dispute concerning the delimitation of the maritime boundary between them in the Indian Ocean to a special chamber
of the Tribunal to be formed pursuant to article 15, paragraph 2, of the Statute of the
Tribunal (hereinafter "the Statute"). [15] By communication addressed to the Registrar
[. . .] within the time-limit set by article 97, paragraph 1, of the Rules, the Maldives
filed with the Special Chamber written preliminary objections "under article 294 of the
Convention and article 97 of the Rules" to the jurisdiction of the Special Chamber and
the admissibility of Mauritius' claims [. . .]. The Preliminary Objections were notified to
Mauritius on the same date."

[**Paras. 1, 2, 15**]

II.

I.2.032   SOVEREIGNTY DISPUTE
See also: I.2.031; I.2.0331; I.5.0; I.5.01; I.5.011; I.5.12; II.7.12

"[56] Mauritius and the Maldives are States situated in the Indian Ocean. Both States
consist of several islands. According to Mauritius, "[t]he territory of Mauritius includes,
in addition to the main Island, *inter alia*, the Chagos Archipelago, which is located approximately 2,200 kilometres north-east of the main Island of Mauritius." Mauritius states that
the Chagos Archipelago "is about 517 kilometres from Maldives". [57] In 1814, France,
by the Treaty of Paris, ceded Mauritius and its dependencies to the United Kingdom.
According to Mauritius, between 1814 and 1965, the United Kingdom administered the
Chagos Archipelago as "a dependency of the colony of Mauritius." [59] On 8 November
1965, the United Kingdom adopted *The British Indian Ocean Territory Order*, which provided that the Chagos Archipelago, with certain other islands, "shall together form a separate colony which shall be known as the British Indian Ocean Territory." On 12 March
1968, Mauritius became an independent State. The United Kingdom continues to administer the Chagos Archipelago. [61] According to the Maldives, since 1814 and following the
establishment of the British Indian Ocean Territory (hereinafter "the BIOT") in 1965, "the
United Kingdom has consistently claimed sovereignty over the Chagos Archipelago." The

Maldives states that, "since at least 1980, Mauritius has claimed that it is sovereign over the Chagos Archipelago"."

[**Paras. 56, 57, 59, 61**]

A.

I.14.2   ARBITRATION
            See also: I.1.143; I.5.12; I.14.23; II.2.51

"[**64**] On 1 April 2010, the United Kingdom announced the creation of a marine protected area (hereinafter "the MPA") in and around the Chagos Archipelago. On 20 December 2010, Mauritius instituted arbitral proceedings against the United Kingdom pursuant to Annex VII of the Convention [...]. [**69**] On 18 March 2015, the Arbitral Tribunal [...] rendered its award in the *Arbitration regarding the Chagos Marine Protected Area* (hereinafter "the *Chagos* arbitral award").[...] In relation to the merits, the Arbitral Tribunal found that, in establishing the MPA surrounding the Chagos Archipelago, the United Kingdom breached its obligations under article 2, paragraph 3, article 56, paragraph 2, and article 194, paragraph 4, of the Convention."

[**Paras. 64, 69**]

B.

II.4.3   ADVISORY OPINION
            See also: I.1.143; I.2.032; I.5.12; I.10; II.4.01

"[**70**] In resolution 71/292 of 22 June 2017, the UNGA decided to request the ICJ, pursuant to Article 65 of its Statute, to give an advisory opinion on the [legal consequences of the separation of the Chagos Archipelago from Mauritius in 1965][...]. [**71**] On 25 February 2019, the ICJ delivered its advisory opinion [...] [providing] as follows: The Court [...] *Is of the opinion that,* having regard to international law, the process of decolonization of Mauritius was not lawfully completed when that country acceded to independence in 1968, following the separation of the Chagos Archipelago; [...] is of the opinion that the United Kingdom is under an obligation to bring to an end its administration of the Chagos Archipelago as rapidly as possible;[...] *Is of the opinion that* all Member States are under an obligation to cooperate with the United Nations in order to complete the decolonization of Mauritius.[...] [**74**] On 22 May 2019, the UNGA adopted resolution 73/295 [...], [demanding] *inter alia*, 3. [...] that the United Kingdom [...] withdraw its colonial administration from the Chagos Archipelago unconditionally within a period of no more than six months from the adoption of the present resolution, thereby enabling Mauritius to complete the decolonization of its territory as rapidly as possible [...]. [**77**] The United Kingdom did not take any action on the demand of the UNGA within the period indicated in paragraph 3 of the above-mentioned resolution."

[**Paras. 70, 71, 74, 77**]

III.

II.2.11   PRELIMINARY OBJECTIONS
             See also: I.1.15; I.5.12; II.0; II.2.013; II.2.014; II.2.111; II.7.12

"[**79**] The Maldives raises five preliminary objections to the jurisdiction of the Special Chamber and the admissibility of Mauritius' claims. According to the Maldives' first preliminary objection, the United Kingdom is an indispensable third party to the present proceedings, and, as the United Kingdom is not a party to these proceedings, the Special Chamber does not have jurisdiction over the alleged dispute. In its second preliminary objection, the Maldives submits that the Special Chamber has no jurisdiction to determine the disputed issue of sovereignty over the Chagos Archipelago, which it would necessarily have to do if it were to determine Mauritius' claims in these proceedings. The Maldives contends in its third preliminary objection that, as Mauritius and the Maldives have not engaged, and cannot meaningfully engage, in the negotiations required by articles 74 and 83 of the Convention, the Special Chamber lacks jurisdiction. According to the Maldives' fourth preliminary objection, there is not, and cannot be, a dispute between Mauritius and the Maldives concerning its maritime boundary. Without such a dispute, the Special Chamber has no jurisdiction. Finally, the Maldives submits that Mauritius' claims constitute an abuse of process and should therefore be rejected as inadmissible at the preliminary objections phase."

[**Para. 79**]

IV.

II.2.014   CAPACITY TO BE A PARTY TO PROCEEDINGS
            See also: I.2.03; I.2.031; I.2.032; I.2.213; I.5.01; I.5.011; II.0; II.2.111;
            II.2.112; II.7.12

"[**98**] [. . .][T]he Parties disagree as to whether the United Kingdom is an indispensable party to the present proceedings. While the Maldives argues that the United Kingdom is an indispensable party [according to the Monetary Gold Principle] as there is an extant sovereignty dispute between the United Kingdom and Mauritius over the Chagos Archipelago, Mauritius contends that the United Kingdom is not such a party because the ICJ has already determined that it has no sovereignty, or sovereign rights, in respect of any part of the Chagos Archipelago.[. . .] [**97**] [T]he Tribunal stated in the *M/V "Norstar"* Case that the Monetary Gold principle is "a well-established procedural rule in international judicial proceedings" [. . .]. The Parties further agree that Mauritius' claims can be entertained only if the Special Chamber accepts that Mauritius, not the United Kingdom, has sovereignty over the Chagos Archipelago. [**99**] Accordingly, if a sovereignty dispute over the Chagos Archipelago exists, the United Kingdom may be regarded as an indispensable party and the Monetary Gold principle would prevent the Special Chamber from exercising its jurisdiction. On the other hand, if such sovereignty dispute has been resolved in favour of Mauritius, the United Kingdom may not be regarded as an indispensable party and the Monetary Gold principle would not apply."

[**Paras. 98, 97, 99**]

A.

"[**247**] [. . .][T]he Special Chamber considers that, whatever interests the United Kingdom may still have with respect to the Chagos Archipelago, they would not render the United Kingdom a State with sufficient legal interests, let alone an indispensable third party, that would be affected by the delimitation of the maritime boundary around the Chagos Archipelago. In the Special Chamber's view, it is inconceivable that the United Kingdom, whose administration over the Chagos Archipelago constitutes a wrongful act of a continuing character and thus must be brought to an end as rapidly as possible, and yet who has failed to do so, can have any legal interests in permanently disposing of maritime zones around the Chagos Archipelago by delimitation. [**248**] For these reasons, [. . .] the United

Kingdom is not an indispensable party to the present proceedings. Accordingly, the first preliminary objection of the Maldives is rejected."

[**Paras. 247, 248**]

V.

I.2.032   SOVEREIGNTY DISPUTE

        See also: I.1.43; I.2.031; I.2.0331; I.2.213; I.5.01; I.5.12; I.14.2; II.7.08; II.7.12

"[**114**] [...][T]he Parties disagree on the validity of the premise that Mauritius has sovereignty over the Chagos Archipelago. The Maldives argues that such premise is untenable in light of the longstanding, unresolved sovereignty dispute between Mauritius and the United Kingdom. For its part, Mauritius contends that such premise must be accepted by the Special Chamber as the advisory opinion of the ICJ has already determined that the United Kingdom has no rights as a sovereign over the Chagos Archipelago and has confirmed that, as a matter of international law, the Chagos Archipelago is an integral part of Mauritius, and Mauritius only. Mauritius adds that the Special Chamber is called upon simply to recognize and respect the ICJ's authoritative determination of this issue and proceed to delimit the maritime boundary between the Parties. [**128**] The Special Chamber is aware that, before the present dispute was submitted to it, the questions relating to the legal status of the Chagos Archipelago had been considered first by the Annex VII Arbitral Tribunal in relation to the dispute between Mauritius and the United Kingdom concerning the MPA established by the United Kingdom around the Chagos Archipelago [*Chagos Arbitral award*], and then by the ICJ in relation to the request made by the UNGA for an advisory opinion regarding the decolonization of Mauritius [*Chagos Advisory Opinion*]."

[**Paras. 114, 128**]

A.

II.2.21   PRELIMINARY QUESTIONS RAISED OR EXAMINED IN THE PHASE DEVOTED TO THE MERITS

        See also: I.1.14; I.5.11; I.5.111; I.5.12; II.7.12

"[**139**] [The] *Chagos* arbitral award is of some relevance to the legal status of the Chagos Archipelago. While the Arbitral Tribunal recognized the existence of the sovereignty dispute over the Chagos Archipelago, it was unable to address it owing to its jurisdictional limitation as an Annex VII tribunal. On the other hand, [...] the Arbitral Tribunal's findings on the rights of Mauritius in respect of the Chagos Archipelago pursuant to the legally binding undertakings of the United Kingdom, such as fishing rights in the waters of the Archipelago, the right to the return of the Archipelago when no longer needed for defence purposes, and the right to the benefit of any minerals or oil discovered in or near the Archipelago, may play a role in the assessment of whether Mauritius can be regarded as the State with an opposite or adjacent coast to the Maldives for the purpose of maritime boundary delimitation.[...]"

[**Para. 139**]

B.

II.0.0   CONSENSUAL JURISDICTION

        See also: I.1.02; I.1.14; I.2.032; I.5.01; I.5.11; I.5.12; II.7; II.7.14

"[**168**] [...][T]he Special Chamber notes that the principle of consent by a State to the judicial settlement of its dispute with another State is fundamental to international judicial proceedings. It would be contrary to the principle of consent to accept the proposition that international courts or tribunals, through contentious or advisory proceedings, can resolve a bilateral dispute without the consent of a party to the dispute. However, this does not mean that the advisory opinion could not entail implications for the disputed issue of sovereignty."

[Para. 168]

C.

I.2.031   SOVEREIGNTY TITLE

See also: I.1.02; I.2.0331; I.2.036; I.2.213; I.5.01; I.5.1; I.11.012; I.14.11; II.2.511; II.4.3; II.7.02; II.7.08; II.7.12

"[163] The Special Chamber notes that the questions posed by the General Assembly are concerned with the lawfulness of the process of decolonization of Mauritius and the consequences under international law arising from the United Kingdom's continued administration of the Chagos Archipelago. [171] [...][T]he ICJ determined that the detachment of the Chagos Archipelago, which was clearly an integral part of Mauritius in 1965, was not based on the free and genuine expression of the will of the people concerned and consequently the process of decolonization of Mauritius was not lawfully completed. [...] [173] The ICJ thus determined that the United Kingdom's continued administration of the Chagos Archipelago is an unlawful act of a continuing character, entailing its international responsibility, and must be brought to an end as rapidly as possible. The Special Chamber considers that these determinations, together with those previously mentioned, have unmistakable implications for the United Kingdom's claim to sovereignty over the Chagos Archipelago. [...], such claim is contrary to the determinations made by the ICJ that the detachment of the Chagos Archipelago was unlawful and that the United Kingdom's continued administration of the Chagos Archipelago constitutes an unlawful act of a continuing character."

[Paras. 163, 171, 173]

VI.

I.2.031   SOVEREIGNTY TITLE

See also: I.1.16; I.2.032; I.2.0331; I.2.213; I.5.01; I.5.12; I.14.11; I.14.2; II.2.511; II.4.3; II.7.02; II.7.081

"[188] The Special Chamber considers that decolonization of a territory entails considerable consequences regarding the question of sovereignty over the territory, as decolonization and territorial sovereignty are closely interrelated. To what extent decolonization may implicate territorial sovereignty depends on the particular circumstances of each case. [189] In the Special Chamber's view, the decolonization and sovereignty of Mauritius, including the Chagos Archipelago, are inseparably related. This was recognized by the Arbitral Tribunal in the *Chagos* arbitral award when it stated that the validity or otherwise of the "1965 Agreement" was "a central element of the Parties' submissions on Mauritius' [...] sovereignty, and the identity of the coastal State"[...]. This was also implied when the ICJ stated in the *Chagos* advisory opinion that "[t]he issues raised by the request are located in the broader frame of reference of decolonization, including the General Assembly's role therein, from which those issues are inseparable"[...]."

[Paras. 188, 189]

VII.

II.7.08   ICJ ADVISORY FUNCTION

See also: I.1.15; I.1.16; I.2.0223; I.2.21; I.5.01; I.5.12; I.14.11; I.14.2; II.4.3; II.7.02; II.7.081

"[**202**] [. . .] [I]t is generally recognized that advisory opinions of the ICJ cannot be considered legally binding.[. . .] However, it is equally recognized that an advisory opinion entails an authoritative statement of international law on the questions with which it deals. [**203**] In this regard, [. . .] it necessary to draw a distinction between the binding character and the authoritative nature of an advisory opinion of the ICJ. An advisory opinion is not binding because even the requesting entity is not obligated to comply with it in the same way as parties to contentious proceedings are obligated to comply with a judgment. However, judicial determinations made in advisory opinions carry no less weight and authority than those in judgments because they are made with the same rigour and scrutiny by the "principal judicial organ" of the United Nations with competence in matters of international law. [**205**] [. . .] [D]eterminations made by the ICJ in an advisory opinion cannot be disregarded simply because the advisory opinion is not binding. This is true of the ICJ's determinations in the *Chagos* advisory opinion, *inter alia*, that the process of decolonization of Mauritius was not lawfully completed when that country acceded to independence in 1968, following the separation of the Chagos Archipelago, and that the United Kingdom is under an obligation to bring to an end its administration of the Chagos Archipelago as rapidly as possible. The Special Chamber considers that those determinations do have legal effect."

[**Paras. 202, 203, 205**]

VIII.

I.2.213   UN GENERAL ASSEMBLY

See also: I.2.02; I.2.21; I.2.0223; I.5.01; I.5.12; I.14.11; I.14.2; II.4.3; II.7.08

"[**226**] [. . .] It should be noted [. . .] that, in the advisory opinion, the ICJ emphasized the functions of the General Assembly with regard to decolonization, in particular the "crucial role" which it has played in the work of the United Nations on decolonization [. . .]. [**227**] The General Assembly has thus been entrusted to take necessary steps toward the completion of the decolonization of Mauritius. In light of the general functions of the General Assembly on decolonization and the specific task of the decolonization of Mauritius with which it was entrusted, the Special Chamber considers that resolution 73/295 is relevant to assessing the legal status of the Chagos Archipelago. [**228**] In resolution 73/295, the General Assembly affirmed, "in accordance with the advisory opinion of the Court", that: "[t]he Chagos Archipelago forms an integral part of the territory of Mauritius". The Special Chamber considers that this affirmation is the General Assembly's view of the advisory opinion."

[**Paras. 226, 227, 228**]

IX.

I.5.0   MARITIME DELIMITATION

See also: I.1.02; I.1.15; I.1.16; I.2.213; I.5.01; I.5.12; I.14.3; I.14.11; II.2.11; II.2.113; II.2.511; II.7.12

"[**250**] The Special Chamber considers that [. . .] Mauritius can be regarded as the coastal State in respect of the Chagos Archipelago for the purpose of the delimitation of a maritime boundary even before the process of the decolonization of Mauritius is completed. In the Special Chamber's view, to treat Mauritius as such State is consistent with the determinations made in the *Chagos* arbitral award, and, in particular, the determinations made in the *Chagos* advisory opinion which were acted upon by UNGA resolution 73/295. [**251**] [. . .][I]in the circumstances of the present case, the Special Chamber is satisfied that Mauritius can be regarded as the State with an opposite or adjacent coast to the Maldives within the meaning of article 74, paragraph 1, and article 83, paragraph 1, of the Convention and the concerned State within the meaning of paragraph 3 of the same articles. Accordingly, the second preliminary objection of the Maldives is rejected."

[**Paras. 250, 251**]

X.

I.1.022   GOOD FAITH
See also: I.1.02; I.1.14; I.1.1425; I.1.16; I.5.01; I.5.3; I.5.4; I.5.12; I.14.3; I.14.11; II.7.12

"[**271**] The Special Chamber wishes to state that the main purpose of article 74, paragraphs 1 and 2, and article 83, paragraphs 1 and 2, of the Convention is to ensure that, where States with opposite or adjacent coasts are confronted with overlapping claims regarding the exclusive economic zone and the continental shelf, no State shall settle its maritime limits unilaterally and such limits shall rather be effected by agreement between the States concerned or by resorting to the procedures provided for in Part XV, if no agreement can be reached within a reasonable period of time. [**273**] [A]rticle 74, paragraph 1, and article 83, paragraph 1, of the Convention entail an obligation to negotiate in good faith with a view to reaching an agreement on delimitation. However, this obligation does not require the States concerned to reach such agreement.[. . .] [**275**] [. . .][A]rticle 74, paragraphs 1 and 2, and article 83, paragraphs 1 and 2, of the Convention, in a mutually reinforcing way, establish substantive obligations for the States concerned not to delimit their exclusive economic zones and continental shelves unilaterally but to do so by way of agreement or, failing such agreement, by resorting to the dispute settlement procedures under Part XV of the Convention."

[**Paras. 271, 273, 275**]

A.

"[**288**] [. . .][O]n the basis of the records before it, Mauritius, on several occasions, attempted to engage the Maldives in negotiations concerning the delimitation of their claimed overlapping exclusive economic zones and continental shelves. [**290**] By persisting in its position that, "in circumstances where the sovereignty dispute between Mauritius and the United Kingdom remains unresolved, Mauritius and the Maldives . . . cannot meaningfully engage . . . in the negotiations mandated by Articles 74 and 83 UNCLOS", the Maldives demonstrates that "no agreement can be reached within a reasonable period of time", whatever time could have been reserved for that negotiation. [**293**] On the basis of the foregoing, the Special Chamber concludes that the obligation under article 74, paragraph 1, and article 83, paragraph 1, of the Convention has been fulfilled. Accordingly, the third preliminary objection of the Maldives is rejected."

[**Paras. 288, 290, 293**]

XI.

II.7.13   ITLOS JURISDICTION
            See also: I.1.15; I.1.16; I.1.441; I.2.032; I.5.01; I.5.11; I.5.12; II.2.113; II.7.12

"[**322**] [...][T]he Special Chamber recalls the jurisprudence of the Tribunal to the effect that, for it to have jurisdiction *ratione materiae* to entertain a case, "a dispute concerning the interpretation or application of the Convention between the Parties must have existed at the time of the filing of the Application [...]. [**327**] [I]t is clear from the national legislation adopted by the Parties that their respective claims to an exclusive economic zone in the relevant area overlap. This is further illustrated by the graphic representations made by Mauritius in these proceedings. [**332**] [...][I]t is clear from the above that there is an overlap between the claim of the Maldives to a continental shelf beyond 200 nautical miles and the claim of Mauritius to an exclusive economic zone in the relevant area.[...] [**333**] The Special Chamber cannot accept the Maldives' argument that "[a] dispute requires disagreement on where the actual maritime boundary should lie".[...] [M]aritime delimitation disputes are not limited to disagreement concerning the location of the actual maritime boundary and may arise in various other forms and situations. [**335**] [...][I]n the present case a dispute existed between the Parties concerning the delimitation of their maritime boundary at the time of the filing of the Notification. [**336**] Accordingly, the fourth preliminary objection of the Maldives is rejected."

[**Paras. 322, 327, 332, 333, 335, 336**]

XII.

II.0.81   ABUSE OF PROCESS
            See also: I.1.14; I.2.032; I.5.01; I.5.12; II.7.12

"[**345**] The Special Chamber concluded [...] that the obligation under article 74, paragraph 1, and article 83, paragraph 1, of the Convention has been fulfilled. It concluded further [...] that a dispute existed between the Parties concerning the delimitation of their maritime boundary at the time of the filing of the Notification. [**349**] The Special Chamber, therefore, does not consider that Mauritius' claims constitute an abuse of process. [**350**] Accordingly, the fifth preliminary objection of the Maldives is rejected."

[**Paras. 345, 349, 350**]

XIII.

II.2.013   TITLE OF JURISDICTION
             See also: I.1.14; I.2.032; I.5.01; I.5.12; II.2.021; II.2.23; II.7.12

"[**351**] For the above reasons, the Special Chamber concludes that it has jurisdiction to adjudicate upon the dispute concerning the delimitation of the maritime boundary between the Parties in the Indian Ocean and that the claim submitted by Mauritius in this regard is admissible. [**352**] The Special Chamber finds it appropriate to defer to the proceedings on the merits questions concerning the extent to which it may exercise its jurisdiction over the above dispute, including questions arising under article 76 of the Convention."

[**Paras. 351, 352**]

Systematic Key Items of the Section*

---

* *See* Systematic Classification Scheme, *supra* at page 255.

III

WTO Dispute Settlement System

INTRODUCTORY NOTE

The WTO Dispute Settlement System in 2021

BY JOANNA GOMULA*

Abstract

The year 2021 was the first year in which no WTO Appellate Body report was issued. Although in this year seven panel reports were issued, notices of appeal were filed in five of these disputes, thus blocking their timely finalization. Only one panel report was adopted. The parties to the seventh dispute in which a panel report was circulated agreed to appellate review in accordance with the multi-party interim appeal arbitration arrangement pursuant to Article 25 Dispute Settlement Understanding (award issued in 2022). There was a mutually agreed solution notified with respect to another dispute. By 31 December 2021, there were twenty-three disputes pending in which a panel report had been circulated and a notice of appeal filed.

I. INTRODUCTION

In 2021, the crisis regarding the WTO Appellate Body remained unresolved and the deadlock in appointing new judges resulted in appellate review being suspended for an indefinite period. However, the dispute settlement system, as such, continued to be available to WTO members, with new disputes being notified to the Dispute Settlement Body (DSB) and panels, once established, carrying out their work "as usual," in accordance with the principles of the Dispute Settlement Understanding (DSU). In 2021 panel reports were issued in seven cases. Of these, the report in one dispute, initiated by the European Union against the United States (concerning anti-dumping and countervailing duties imposed on imports

* LLM, University of Warsaw, Poland; LLM, University of Michigan, US; PhD, Polish Academy of Sciences; Fellow, Lauterpacht Research Centre for International Law, University of Cambridge, UK; member of the Editorial Board.

Joanna Gomula, *Introductory Note* In: *The Global Community Yearbook of International Law and Jurisprudence 2022.* Edited by: Giuliana Ziccardi Capaldo, Oxford University Press. © Oxford University Press 2023. DOI: 10.1093/oso/9780197752265.003.0019

of olives from Spain),[1] was adopted by the DSB at the end of the year, on 20 December 2021. In another case, concerning Turkey's allegedly discriminatory measures on pharmaceutical products,[2] rather than filing a notice of appeal from the Panel's findings to the Appellate Body, Turkey made a "notification of appeal under Article 25 DSU" (in 2022). To this effect, Turkey signed an ad hoc arbitration agreement with the European Union that subjected the dispute to the WTO Multi-Party Interim Appeal Arbitration Arrangement (MPIA), an alternative appeals mechanism notified to the WTO by a group of forty-seven members on 30 April 2020.[3]

In five of the remaining cases, notices of appeal were filed and the disputes joined the now long queue of cases waiting for appellate review. In 2021, a notice of appeal was also filed from a panel report circulated in 2020, bringing the total number of notices of appeal filed in 2021 to six.

In a dispute between Canada and Australia (concerning measures affecting the sale of imported wine), in which the panel report was expected to be released in 2021, the parties reached a mutually agreed solution prior to the issuance of the interim report.[4]

There were no arbitration decisions issued in 2021. However, the WTO dispute settlement system displayed some signs of life, particularly due to the still modest but interesting activity occurring within the scope of the above-mentioned MPIA (see following section IV).

II. LONELY: OLIVES FROM SPAIN

The sole dispute in which a report was adopted in 2021 was initiated in 2019 by the European Union. It concerned countervailing and anti-dumping duties imposed by the United States on imports of ripe olives from Spain. The European Union alleged that the duties—ranging from 30 percent to 44 percent—and certain actions of the US investigating authorities were contrary to various provisions of the Agreement on Subsidies and Countervailing Measures (SCM Agreement) and the Anti-Dumping Agreement. The United States imposed the duties in 2018, to counteract alleged subsidies received by Spanish olives producers, resulting from the reform of the EU Common Agricultural Policy.

This Panel operated in adverse circumstances not only because of the paralysis of the Appellate Body (its work shrouded with the gloom of indefinite notices of appeal), but also because of the outbreak of the COVID-19 pandemic, which affected the conduct of the proceedings, as they started in 2020. Despite some opposition voiced by the United States, the Panel decided to hold the proceedings mainly in a virtual format and adopted

---

[1] United States—Anti-Dumping and Countervailing Duties on Ripe Olives from Spain (WT/DS577), report of the Panel adopted on 20 December 2021 (*US—Ripe Olives from Spain*).

[2] Turkey—Certain Measures Concerning the Production, Importation and Marketing of Pharmaceutical Products (WT/DS583) (*Turkey—Pharmaceutical Products*), arbitration award issued under Article 25 DSU on 25 July 2022. The findings in this award will be covered in the next volume of this *Global Community Yearbook*.

[3] *See* Statement on a Mechanism for Developing, Documenting and Sharing Practices and Procedures in the Conduct of WTO disputes (containing the Multi-Party Interim Appeal Arbitration Arrangement Pursuant to Article 25 of the DSU), 30 April 2020 (JOB/DSB/1/Add.12). Turkey was not a party to the MPIA; hence, it signed a separate ad hoc arbitration agreement with the European Union.

[4] Canada—Measures Governing the Sale of Wine (WT/DS557) (*Canada—Sale of Wine*), mutually agreed solution notified on 12 May 2021; final report of the Panel (reporting the mutually agreed solution) circulated on 25 May 2021.

additional working procedures to that effect. The Panel's meetings were open (online) to the public.

On substance, the Panel report gives the impression of a well-balanced award, with some EU claims acknowledged, but a bulk of other claims rejected on reasonable grounds. The Panel found in favour of the complainant, among others, with respect to the claim that the US authorities had not determined whether the subsidies were targeted at olive producers, in violation of the specificity requirements of Article 2 of the SCM Agreement. The European Union's also raised an "as such" claim with respect to Section 771B of the US 1930 Tariff Act, attacking its provisions on "pass-through" benefits (the presumption that the entire benefit of a subsidy for a raw agricultural input product passes through to the downstream processed agricultural product). The Panel agreed that the "pass-through" benefit was "as such" inconsistent with VI:3 of the GATT 1994 and Article 10 of the SCM Agreement because its consideration was based only on two factors, to the exclusion of other relevant factors. Consequently, the application by the US authorities of the presumption that the entire subsidies provided to raw olive producers were transferred to ripe olive processors was also deemed inconsistent with the preceding provisions. The Panel also found violations of Article 12 of the SCM Agreement for the US authorities' failure to notify and inform the parties about certain matters.

However, as mentioned, the Panel rejected many other EU claims. In particular, it disagreed with the European Union about alleged violations of WTO law in the final injury determinations in the relevant countervailing and anti-dumping duty investigations.

Worth noting are the Panel's conclusions with respect to the standard of review. The dispute concerned matters under the SCM Agreement and the Anti-Dumping Agreement, which meant that Article 11 of the DSU (the general standard of review) applied to the former, while Article 17.6 of the Anti-Dumping Agreement (a "special" standard of review for anti-dumping matters) applied to the latter agreement. The Panel, however, neutralized the distinction between these two standards. It stated that there was no conflict between those standards (a view shared by the parties) and agreed with the parties that "disputes arising from anti-dumping and countervailing duty measures should be resolved in a consistent manner."[5] The practical aspects of applying a standard of review to trade remedy matters prevailed, this being the right path, in particular, considering that the standard of review in "general" matters has been inscribed by WTO jurisprudence in Article 11 DSU rather artificially, with the elements of the standard in Article 17.6 of the Anti-Dumping Agreement being incorporated into a provision that is not even described as one denoting a standard of review. The only query that may arise in this context is that in 1994 the standard of review in anti-dumping matters was intended by the negotiators to be "special"; however, thirty years later, it appears to have lost its distinctiveness—thus, where are we standing today?

The United States did not appeal the Panel's findings and the report was adopted on 20 December 2021. This case may serve as an example of co-operation between two WTO members, usually known as unyielding trade adversaries, to overcome the ailments of the WTO dispute settlement system. Among others, the parties agreed to postpone the release of the report for several months while other issues were being negotiated, in this way supporting the rule-based fundaments of the WTO dispute settlement system with a system of negotiations. In the current situation (and considering the provisions of the DSU itself) this may not be a detrimental strategy at all, and it offers another remedy to the Appellate Body paralysis.

---

[5] *US—Ripe Olives from Spain*, Panel Report, para. 7.6.

III. WTO CRISIS: "HOARDING" HOUSE FOR PANEL REPORTS

As mentioned previously, *US—Ripe Olives from Spain* was a notable example where two WTO members succeeded in finalizing the main part of the WTO dispute settlement process, without resorting to the mechanism of a mutually agreed solution or yielding to the temptation to block the dispute through a notice of appeal. With respect to most other cases, the WTO dispute settlement system is experiencing a continuing increase of unresolved matters. The situation resembles a hoarder's home, with a bulk of panel reports continuing to flow into an already overburdened WTO disputes' abode.

As of 31 December 2021, there were twenty-three pending WTO disputes where panel reports had been circulated, with notices of appeal filed with respect to the following: five panel reports issued in 2018 and six panel reports issued in each year in 2019, 2020, and 2021. The cases pending on 31 December 2021 included claims based on the provisions of the GATT 1994, the SCM Agreement, the Anti-Dumping Agreement, the Agreement on Safeguards, the Customs Valuation Agreement, the Agreement on Agriculture, the SPS Agreement, and the TRIPS Agreement (two disputes). It may be noted that both disputes concerning the TRIPS Agreement were resolved in the first part of 2022. In the first case, after having filed a notice of appeal in 2020, Qatar withdrew its complaint in 2022, terminating the dispute.[6] The second dispute was the above-mentioned *Turkey—Pharmaceutical Products* (see previous section II).

IV. NASCENT OF THE MULTI-PARTY INTERIM ARBITRATION ARRANGEMENT (MPIA)

The MPIA has been slowly gaining in momentum, as a viable alternative to review by the Appellate Body. The first notifications referring to the MPIA procedures were both made on 3 June 2020: by Australia and Canada in *Canada—Sale of Wine*, and by Brazil and Canada in a dispute concerning aircraft subsidies.[7] As mentioned previously, in the first case the parties reached a mutually agreed solution in 2021. With respect to the second dispute, Brazil withdrew its WTO complaint in 2021.

In 2021 acceptance of the procedure was notified in two disputes brought by Australia against China. In both cases China was the respondent and both concerned anti-dumping and countervailing duties imposed, respectively, on Australian barley[8] and on Australian wine[9] (in mid-2022 both disputes were ongoing). Notifications were also made: by Costa Rica and Mexico in a dispute concerning measures on imported avocados (the panel report was subsequently adopted in 2022, no appeal was filed);[10] by Colombia and the European Union in an anti-dumping dispute concerning frozen fries (panel review not completed by

---

[6] Saudi Arabia—Measures Concerning the Protection of Intellectual Property Rights (WT/DS567), report of Panel circulated on 16 June 2020; agreement to terminate the dispute communicated on 25 April 2022. The findings in this award will be covered in the next volume of this *Global Community Yearbook*.

[7] Canada—Measures Concerning Trade in Commercial Aircraft (WT/DS522).

[8] China—Anti-dumping and Countervailing Duty Measures on Barley from Australia (WT/598).

[9] China—Anti-dumping and Countervailing Duty Measures on Wine from Australia (WT/602).

[10] Costa Rica—Measures Concerning the Importation of Fresh Avocados from Mexico (WT/DS524), report of the Panel adopted on 31 May 2022. The findings in this report will be covered in the next volume of this *Global Community Yearbook*.

mid-2022);[11] and by China and Canada in a dispute concerning the importation of canola seed (panel review not completed by mid-2022).[12]

As mentioned previously, in 2022 the first decision was issued under the Article 25 procedure, in *Turkey—Pharmaceutical Products*.

The interim appeal procedure under Article 25 of the DSU thus appears to have been accepted by the parties as a true alternative mechanism to appellate review by the standing Appellate Body. Although by 31 December 2021 no decision had been issued and three of the cases subjected to the MPIA were concluded through different procedural means (the adoption of a panel report, a mutually agreed solution, and a withdrawal of the complaint), what matters is that the procedure appears to serve as an additional incentive for the parties to finalize their disputes, in one way or another, but in accordance with the DSU. Efforts of WTO members to finalize their disputes enhance the spirit of co-operation, which, hopefully, will result in the re-establishment of the standing Appellate Body, in its traditional form or based on a modified *modus operandi*.

---

[11] Colombia—Anti-Dumping Duties on Frozen Fries from Belgium, Germany, and the Netherlands (WT/DS591).

[12] China—Measures Concerning the Importation of Canola Seed from Canada (WT/DS589).

LEGAL MAXIMS: SUMMARIES AND EXTRACTS FROM SELECTED CASE LAW*

United States – Anti-Dumping and Countervailing Duties on Ripe Olives from Spain (WT/DS577/R), Panel Report circulated on 19 November 2021, adopted on 20 December 2021

---

* The working method chosen for the formulation of legal maxims is explained *supra* 'Outline of the Parts', at page xv.

Legal Maxims: Summaries and Extracts from Selected Case Law In: *The Global Community Yearbook of International Law and Jurisprudence 2022*. Edited by: Giuliana Ziccardi Capaldo, Oxford University Press. © Oxford University Press 2023.
DOI: 10.1093/oso/9780197752265.003.0020

III.2.1

United States—Anti-Dumping and Countervailing Duties on Ripe Olives from Spain (WT/DS577/R), **Panel Report circulated on 19 November 2021, adopted on 20 December 2021***

Contents**

---

* Summary prepared by Joanna Gomula, Fellow, Lauterpacht Centre for International Law, University of Cambridge. Text of report available online at the WTO Web site <https://www.wto.org/english/tratop_e/dispu_e/577r_e.pdf>. Original: English. Footnotes appearing in the original text have been omitted.

** This is not a faithful reproduction of the Table of Contents of the Judgment.

ANTI-DUMPING AGREEMENT AND ARTICLE 15.1 OF THE SCM
AGREEMENT)

XIII. EXAMINATION OF CHANGE IN VOLUME SUFFICIENT TO
CONSIDER 'SIGNIFICANT INCREASE' IN VOLUME (ARTICLE 3.2
OF THE ANTI-DUMPING AGREEMENT AND ARTICLE 15.2 OF THE
SCM AGREEMENT)

XIV. EXAMINATION OF EFFECT ON PRICES IN THE DOMESTIC
MARKET (ARTICLE 3.2 OF THE ANTI-DUMPING AGREEMENT
AND ARTICLE 15.2 OF THE SCM AGREEMENT)

XV. FINDINGS AND CONCLUSIONS

I.

II.2.0   INSTITUTION AND COURSE OF PROCEEDINGS
           See also: I.16.5

"[**2.1.**] The measures at issue in the present dispute concern countervailing and anti-dumping duties that the United States imposed in connection with its investigations concerning imports of ripe olives from Spain. In particular, the European Union's panel request refers to the following: a. Ripe Olives from Spain: Amended Final Affirmative Countervailing Duty Determination and Countervailing Duty Order, 83 FR 37469, 1 August 2018; b. Ripe Olives from Spain: Antidumping Duty Order, 83 FR 37467, 1 August 2018; c. Ripe Olives from Spain: Final Affirmative Countervailing Duty Determination, C-469-818, DOC, 11 June 2018, 83 FR 28186, 18 June 2018; d. Ripe Olives from Spain: Final Affirmative Determination of Sales at Less Than Fair Value, A-469-817, DOC, 11 June 2018, 83 FR 28193, 18 June 2018; and e. Ripe Olives from Spain, Investigation Nos. 701-TA-582 and 731-TA-1377 (Final), United States International Trade Commission (USITC), Publication 4805, July 2018. [**2.2.**] The Panel also accepted the European Union's request to address certain aspects of the USDOC's Remand Redetermination of 29 May 2020, reflected in the following document: a. USDOC, Final Results of Remand Redetermination, Asociación de Exportadores e Industriales de Aceitunas de Mesa, Aceitunas Guadalquivir, S.L.U., Agro Sevilla Aceitunas S. Coop. And., and Ángel Camacho Alimentación, S.L. v. United States (29 May 2020). [**2.3.**] The European Union also challenges "as such" Section 771B of the Tariff Act of 1930, relating to the calculation of countervailable subsidies on certain processed agricultural products. [**3.1.**] The European Union requests the Panel to find that the USDOC and the USITC acted inconsistently with the United States' obligations under the Anti-Dumping Agreement, the SCM Agreement, and the GATT 1994."

[**Paras. 2.1., 2.2., 2.3., 3.1.**]

II.

II.7.235   STANDARD OF REVIEW
           See also: I.16.5

"[**7.3.**] [...] Article 11 of the DSU sets out a general standard of review for panels [...].
[**7.5.**] In addition to the obligation to conduct an objective assessment under Article 11

of the DSU, in disputes concerning anti-dumping measures, Article 17.6(i) of the Anti-Dumping Agreement [applies] [...]. [**7.6.**] Although the SCM Agreement does not contain a similar provision, Members have declared that disputes arising from anti-dumping and countervailing duty measures should be resolved in a consistent manner. Likewise, the parties have argued that the Panel should apply a consistent approach in resolving the claims at issue in this dispute, arguing, furthermore, that there is no conflict between Article 17.6(i) of the Anti-Dumping Agreement and Article 11 of the DSU. We share the parties' views about the absence of conflict between Article 11 of the DSU and Article 17.6(i) of the Anti-Dumping Agreement, and we will conduct our review of the merits of the European Union's claims accordingly."

[**Paras. 7.3., 7.5., 7.6.**]

III.

II.7.231   PANEL'S TERMS OF REFERENCE
            See also: II.7.232

"[**7.12.**] We agree with previous panel and Appellate Body reports that Article 6.2 of the DSU does not categorically preclude the inclusion within a panel's terms of reference of measures that come into existence after the panel establishment is requested. Rather, there may be circumstances in which it is necessary for a Panel to review measures enacted after its establishment so that it can make the findings and recommendations necessary to resolve the matter in dispute. This may include, for example, a measure that amends a measure that is explicitly identified in a panel request, without changing the essence of that original measure."

[**Para. 7.12.**]

IV.

II.7.231   PANEL'S TERMS OF REFERENCE
            See also: II.7.232

"[**7.182.**] In its first written submission the United States requested the Panel to preliminarily rule that the European Union's claims under Article 15.4 of the SCM Agreement and Article 3.4 of the Anti-Dumping Agreement are outside the Panel's terms of reference, arguing that neither claim was identified in the European Union's consultations request or panel request. [...] [**7.186.**] The European Union acknowledges that its panel request does not specify either Article 15.4 or Article 3.4, and that normally, compliance with Article 6.2 of the DSU requires that only the specific provisions mentioned in the panel request may fall within the panel's terms of reference. [...]As its main contention, the European Union argues that the narrative language of its panel request clearly states that the European Union takes issue with the fact that the USITC did not carry out an objective examination of the "consequent impact" on the domestic producers. According to the European Union, the reference to the examination of impact logically cannot constitute a stand-alone claim under Article 15.1 or Article 3.1, but necessarily presupposes a claim under Article 15.4 and Article 3.4 because those provisions speak to the examination of impact. [...] [**7.195.**] [...][I]n citing Article 15.1 of the SCM Agreement and Article 3.1 of the Anti-Dumping Agreement, and in referring to certain language contained in Article 15.1 and Article 3.1 to make an "objective examination of . . . *the consequent impact of [subsidized/dumped] imports on domestic producers of such products*", the European Union has provided a brief summary of the legal basis of the complaint sufficient to meet the minimum requirements of Article 6.2 of the DSU with respect to claims under Article 15.4 of the SCM Agreement and Article 3.4 of the Anti-Dumping Agreement."

[Paras. 7.182., 7.186., 7.195.]

V.

II.7.233   COMPLAINTS AGAINST LEGISLATION
             See also: II.7.231

"[**7.146.**] We agree with past panel and Appellate Body reports that in order for an "as such" challenge against a provision of domestic legislation to succeed, the complaining Member must establish that the relevant provision of domestic law requires the responding Member to violate its obligations under the relevant covered agreement or otherwise restricts, in a material way, the responding Member's discretion to act in a manner that is consistent with those obligations. [. . .]"

[Para. 7.146.]

VI.

II.7.233   COMPLAINTS AGAINST LEGISLATION
             See also: I.16.7

"[**7.167.**] Section 771B *does not leave open the possibility* for the USDOC to consider factors that may be affecting the market for the investigated product other than those Section 771B lists explicitly. [. . .] Likewise, Section 771B does not envisage that the USDOC should consider the market power of the different producers and processors, or the extent to which national or international competition could potentially affect the reliability of input product pricing. [. . .] Section 771B, therefore, shuts out any consideration of the circumstances of any specific case other than the two circumstances that are mandated. Circumstances that are non-mandatory from the perspective of Section 771B are not able to be considered by the investigating authority, meaning that Section 771B limits the investigating authority's analysis of the factual extent of any pass-through. [. . .] [**7.169.**] [U]nder the terms of Article VI:3 of the GATT 1994 and Article 10 of the SCM Agreement, an investigating authority is required to establish the existence and extent of indirect subsidization (i.e. pass-through of a benefit) taking into account *facts and circumstances* that are relevant to that exercise. An investigating authority is not entitled to exclude from its determination of pass-through factors that are potentially relevant to its determination and to proceed on the basis of a *presumption* of indirect subsidization. Accordingly, for these reasons, we find that Section 771B is inconsistent with Article VI:3 of the GATT and Article 10 of the SCM Agreement because it *does not leave open the possibility* for the USDOC to consider other factors affecting the market for the investigated product."

[Paras. 7.167., 7.169.]

VII.

II.7.236   EVIDENCE IN WTO PROCEEDINGS
See also: II.1.3

"[**7.200.**] Article 13.1 of the DSU thus allows a Panel to request information "from any individual or body which it deems appropriate" and indicates that a "Member should respond promptly and fully to any request by a panel". [. . .] Article 13.1 grants discretionary authority to panels to seek information from relevant sources. [. . .] [A]s part of its objective assessment of the facts under Article 11 of the DSU a panel is entitled to draw adverse inferences from a party's refusal to provide information. [**7.201.**] [. . .][W]e decline to draw adverse inferences from the United States' failure to provide the requested redacted information in full. First, we note that the United States clarified a number of factual issues in response to questions from the Panel following the second substantive meeting. The accuracy of these factual statements has not been challenged by the European Union, and the United States' clarifications are of assistance to us in resolving certain issues in dispute between the parties. Second, the European Union has explained that additional factual information is not necessary, in its view, to make out its claims in relation to the Injury Determination. For these reasons, we decline the European Union's request to draw adverse inferences from the United States' failure to provide the Panel with the requested information."

[**Paras. 7.200., 7.201.**]

VIII.

I.16.73   ACTIONABLE SUBSIDIES
See also: II.7.232

"[**7.17.**] [. . .] According to the European Union, the USDOC's finding of *de jure* specificity in relation to the BPS and GP programmes is inconsistent with Articles 2.1, 2.1(a), and 2.4 of the SCM Agreement because, in its view, the key determinant of whether "access" to a subsidy is explicitly limited to certain enterprises, within the meaning of Article 2.1(a), is a programme's *eligibility criteria* [. . .]. [**7.22.**] The United States maintains that the text of Article 2.1(a) does not prescribe a particular form that a limit on "access" must take. While the United States accepts that such a limit may be found in the criteria determining *eligibility* for a subsidy, it also considers that the criteria determining the *eligibility for certain amounts* of a subsidy could be an explicit limitation on access to a subsidy. [. . .] [**7.25.**] [. . .] Article 2.1(a) does not [. . .] prescribe that any particular feature of the legislation pursuant to which the granting authority operates must be examined or be the source of an explicit limitation on access to a subsidy. On the contrary, the analysis that is called for under Article 2.1(a) simply focuses on the granting authority, or the legislation pursuant to which the granting authority operates, *without further precision or qualification*. In our view, this suggests that in principle any one or more aspects of the legislation pursuant to which the granting authority operates may potentially – and depending upon the facts – serve to demonstrate the existence of an explicit limitation on "access" to a subsidy. What matters under Article 2.1(a) is that the granting authority, or the *legislation* pursuant to which the granting authority operates, is shown to limit explicitly access to a subsidy. To this extent, we do not understand Article 2.1(a) to preclude the possibility of a finding of *de jure* specificity based on the rules governing the calculation of subsidy amounts available under a programme. [. . .] [**7.33.**] [. . .][W]e find that Article 2.1(a) of the SCM Agreement does not preclude reliance on criteria or conditions governing the amount of a subsidy to establish that access to a subsidy is explicitly limited to certain enterprises, within the meaning of that provision. We emphasize, however, that because the rules governing the calculation of the amount of a subsidy may not be the only feature of a subsidy programme bearing upon "the right or opportunity to benefit from or use" a subsidy, a finding of *de jure* specificity that ignores other relevant features of the subsidy programme would not be well-founded. Thus, although Article 2.1(a) does not exclude the possibility of grounding a finding of *de jure* specificity on the criteria or conditions governing the amount of a subsidy, any such reliance must not be selective in the light of other relevant *de jure* features of the subsidy programme. [...]"

[**Paras. 7.17., 7.22., 7.25., 7.33.**]

IX.

I.16.73   ACTIONABLE SUBSIDIES

"[**7.147.**] [W]here a producer of the upstream input product operates at arm's length from the producer of the downstream product produced using the upstream input, an investigating authority is required, under Article VI:3 of the GATT 1994 and Article 10 of the SCM Agreement, to establish that the benefit of the subsidy provided directly in respect of the upstream product has been passed-through to the downstream product in order to levy countervailing duties on imports of the downstream product. [T]here is no prescribed methodology in either of these provisions for assessing pass-through. Thus, [...] investigating authorities retain a degree of discretion with respect to how to determine the existence and extent of the pass-through of indirect subsidies. [...]"

[**Para. 7.147.**]

X.

I.16.73   ACTIONABLE SUBSIDIES
See also: I.16.74; II.7.236

"[**7.150.**] The first sentence of Article VI:3 [of GATT 1994] establishes that no countervailing duty shall be levied on any imported product *in excess* of an amount equal to the subsidy *determined* to have been granted, *directly or indirectly*, on the manufacture, production, or export of that product. The second sentence of Article VI:3 as well as footnote 36 to Article 10 define a countervailing duty as a special duty levied *for the purpose of offsetting* any subsidy bestowed, directly or indirectly, upon the manufacture, production, or export of *any merchandise*. [...] [I]t follows from a combined reading of these two provisions that Members are entitled to offset "indirect" subsidization by imposing duties on imported products that benefit from subsidies conferred on "upstream" companies and products. In our view, it also follows from the terms of Article VI:3 and, in particular, the requirement not to apply a countervailing duty *in excess of* the *estimated amount of subsidy* determined to have been granted on the imported product, that an importing Member is not entitled to simply presume that a subsidy bestowed on an input product passes through, in total or in part, to the processed imported product. Rather, an investigating authority must work out, as accurately as possible, how much of the subsidy has flowed indirectly from an input product to the downstream product, to ensure that any countervailing duty imposed on the downstream product is not in excess of the total amount of subsidies bestowed on the investigated product. To this end, an investigating authority must take into account all relevant facts and circumstances to ensure that a countervailing duty is not imposed in excess of the estimated subsidy. Thus, [

...] countervailing duties may not be applied on any amount of a subsidy that has not been found to have passed-through to the imported product. [...]"

[**Para. 7.150.**]

XI.

I.16.73   ACTIONABLE SUBSIDIES
          See also: I.16.74; II.7.236

"[**7.151.**] [W]e note that neither Article VI:3 nor Article 10 of the SCM Agreement prescribe that a particular methodology must be followed to perform a pass-through analysis where one is required. To this extent, investigating authorities have a certain amount of discretion in evaluating whether and to what extent the benefit of a subsidy provided directly to a producer of an upstream product has passed-through to the downstream product produced by an unrelated enterprise (an indirect subsidy). [...] [**7.154.**] In our view, the discretion afforded to an investigating authority under Article VI:3 for the purpose of establishing the pass-through of subsidies is not unfettered. As already noted, pursuant to Article VI:3 an investigating authority is required to analyse to what extent direct subsidies on inputs may have indirectly flowed to the processed investigated product where the respective producers operate at arm's length and which therefore may be included in the determination of the estimated total amount of subsidies bestowed on the investigated product. In our assessment, this means that an investigating authority must provide an *analytical basis* for its findings of the existence and extent of pass-through that takes into account *facts and circumstances* that are *relevant* to the exercise and that are directed to ensuring that any countervailing duty imposed on the downstream product is not in excess of the total amount of subsidies bestowed on the investigated product. Thus, we do not understand an investigating authority's discretion in evaluating the pass-through of subsidies under Article VI:3 to be so wide as to permit it to exclude any consideration of facts and circumstances that may be relevant to the very analysis that it must perform. [**7.162.**] [...] [W]hatever methodology is chosen, an investigating authority must analyse to what extent subsidies on inputs may be included in the determination of the total amount of subsidies bestowed upon processed products. This must be done to ensure that countervailing duties are not applied in an amount that is in excess of the estimated subsidy determined to have been granted to the investigated product. Therefore, to ensure compliance with the requirements of Article VI:3 of the GATT 1994 and Article 10 of the SCM Agreement, an investigating authority must take into account facts and circumstances that may be relevant to that determination and is not entitled to exclude from its determination factors that are potentially relevant."

[**Paras. 7.151., 7.154., 7.162.**]

XII.

I.16.751   DETERMINATION OF INJURY AND CAUSATION
            See also: II.7.236

"[**7.209.**] [...] In our view "positive evidence" [in Article 3.1 of the Anti-Dumping Agreement and Article 15.1 of the SCM Agreement] must be evidence that is affirmative, objective, and capable of credibly supporting the injury determination. To be "objective", an investigating authority's examination must be impartial and supported by reasoning that is coherent and internally consistent. We consider the obligation to conduct an objective examination based on positive evidence in Article 3.1 and Article 15.1 to be an overarching requirement that applies to every aspect of an injury determination. [**7.210.**] [...] We observe that Article 3 [of the Anti-Dumping Agreement] and Article 15 [of the SCM Agreement] do not direct investigating authorities to address parts, sections, or segments of a market in a particular way when undertaking an injury investigation. In our view, the absence of guidance in this respect indicates that an investigating authority has discretion to examine parts, sections, or segments of a market as the investigating authority deems appropriate. An analysis of parts, sections, or segments of a market must, nonetheless, be based on an objective examination of positive evidence. [**7.211.**] We note, further, that the term "segmented analysis" is not contained in Articles 3.1 and 3.2, or Articles 15.1 and 15.2, or any other provision of the Anti-Dumping Agreement or the SCM Agreement. In our view the rights and obligations contained in Articles 3.1 and 3.2, and Articles 15.1 and 15.2, thus apply equally to a determination of injury that is labelled as involving a "segmented analysis", as to one that is not so characterized. [...]"

[**Paras. 7.209., 7.210., 7.211.**]

XIII.

I.16.751   DETERMINATION OF INJURY AND CAUSATION
             See also: II.7.236

"[**7.227.**] [...] The European Union maintains that [...] the "text of [Article 3.2 and] Article 15.2 unequivocally stipulate[s] that a volume effect requires an increase of [dumped or] subsidized imports", and that "the authority must show a growth in [dumped or] subsidized imports". [...][**7.229.**] [...] In our view the European Union's argument that an investigating authority "must show a growth in [dumped or] subsidized imports" to "consider whether" there has been a significant increase in volume is based on an erroneous construction of the term "consider whether" in Article 3.2 and Article 15.2. [...] [T]he language of the first sentence of Article 3.2 and Article 15.2 makes clear that an investigating authority's consideration of whether there has been a "significant increase" in volume may be evidenced by an examination of the change in volume, regardless of whether volumes in fact increased, decreased, or remained stable. [**7.230.**] [...] [C]ompliance with Article 3.2 and Article 15.2 is unaffected by whether the volume of dumped or subsidized imports in fact increased, decreased, or remained stable."

[**Paras. 7.227., 7.229., 7.230.**]

XIV.

I.16.751   DETERMINATION OF INJURY AND CAUSATION
             See also: II.7.236

"[**7.257.**] We first observe that Article 3.1 and Article 15.1 direct an investigating authority to examine the "effect of the [dumped or subsidized] imports on prices in the domestic market for like products". [...] The second sentence of Article 3.2 and Article 15.2 [...] describes what an investigating authority should examine "[w]ith regard to the effect of the [dumped or subsidized] imports on prices". While the second sentence in Article 3.2 and Article 15.2 does not specify which "prices" are the object of the enquiry, we understand this to be a reference to "prices in the domestic market for like products". We consider this to be correct based on the clear cross-reference to Article 3.1 and Article 15.1. [...] We are thus of the view that the second sentence in Article 3.2 and Article 15.2 is intended to detail what actions by an investigating authority constitutes an examination of the effect on domestic prices as required by Article 3.1 and Article 15.1. [**7.258.**] Article 3.2 and Article 15.2 instruct an investigating authority to consider whether the dumped or subsidized imports result in any of three phenomena, i.e. significant price undercutting, significant price depression, or significant price suppression. The use of the disjunctive "or" between these three phenomena indicates that they are independent lines of inquiry. A view that only price depression and price suppression constitute price effects would read out of the text the option to consider price undercutting as an independent channel of inquiry. This would be inconsistent with the requirement that effect be given to all terms of a treaty. We thus interpret Article 3.2 and Article 15.2 to mean that a consideration of any of the three price effects can independently satisfy the requirement in Article 3.1 and Article 15.1 to examine the "effect ... on prices in the domestic market for like products". [**7.259.**] [...] We [...] reject the European Union's argument that price undercutting is not a "'true' stand-alone" price effect [...]."

[**Paras. 7.257., 7.258., 7.259.**]

XV.

II.2.5   JUDGMENT/DECISION/ORDER
         See also: I.16.5; I.16.7

"[**8.1.**] For the reasons set forth in this Report, the Panel concludes as follows: a. With respect to the European Union's claims regarding the USDOC's *de jure* specificity determination: i. the European Union has demonstrated that the USDOC's 29 May 2020 Remand Redetermination as it relates to the USDOC's original findings of *de jure* specificity is a measure or is part of the measure that is before the Panel in this dispute; ii. the European Union has not demonstrated that the USDOC acted inconsistently with Articles 2.1 and 2.1(a) of the SCM Agreement merely because the USDOC based its findings of *de jure* specificity in the ripe olives countervailing duty investigation on the rules in the relevant subsidy programmes governing the calculation of the amounts of subsidies available to eligible enterprises; iii. the European Union has not demonstrated that the USDOC acted inconsistently with Article 2.1(a) of the SCM Agreement because the USDOC's determination of *de jure* specificity was dependent upon how certain alleged features of past subsidy programmes no longer in force were relied upon and integrated into the BPS programme; iv. the European Union has not demonstrated that, as a matter of fact, the USDOC found that the BPS/GP and SPS subsidies were *de jure* specific to olive growers as a result of being coupled or tied to olive production; v. the USDOC acted inconsistently with Articles 2.1, 2.1(a), and 2.4 of the SCM Agreement because: (1) the USDOC did not properly examine and account for the rules governing the allocation and valuation of BPS entitlements with respect to new farmers, farmers holding entitlements transferred under the SPS programme, and farmers no longer growing olives; (2) the USDOC relied upon erroneous factual findings with respect to function and role of the so called "regional rate" to support its determination of *de jure* specificity; and (3) the USDOC did not properly examine and account for the rules governing the allocation and valuation of SPS entitlements with respect to farmers with SPS entitlements obtained via transfer, and farmers holding COMOF programme-based entitlements no longer producing olives. For the reasons set out in (v)(1)-(3), the

USDOC's determination of *de jure* specificity was not based on a reasoned and adequate explanation of why access to the BPS and SPS subsidies was explicitly limited to olive growers, within the meaning of Articles 2.1 and 2.1(a) of the SCM Agreement, and was not clearly substantiated on the basis of positive evidence, as required by Article 2.4 of the SCM Agreement; vi. the USDOC acted inconsistently with Article 2.4 of the SCM Agreement to the extent that the USDOC's determinations of *de jure* specificity with respect to the SPS and BPS/GP subsidies relied upon an erroneous factual finding concerning the calculation of assistance under the COMOF programme; vii. the European Union has not demonstrated that the USDOC acted inconsistently with Articles 2.1, 2.1(a), and 2.4 of the SCM Agreement because, contrary to the European Union's assertions: (1) the USDOC's rejection of the arguments concerning the application of the convergence factor under the BPS programme was supported by record evidence, and to this extent, reasonably and adequately explained and based on clearly substantiated positive evidence; (2) the totality of the USDOC's discussion of the rules governing the calculation of SPS payments reveals that the USDOC correctly understood that SPS payments were made to farmers and that Spain did not implement the SPS programme on a regional basis; and (3) the lack of a formal specificity finding under US law does not undermine the USDOC's determinations of *de jure* specificity with respect to the SPS, BPS, and GP programmes, given the absence of any suggestion on the part of the European Union that the COMOF programme subsidies were not *de jure* specific, and in the light of the fact that the USDOC considered it had made sufficient factual findings to satisfy itself that those subsidies would be *de jure* specific under its domestic legislation, had it been required to make such a determination. viii. given our findings at paragraphs 8.1.a.v and vi, the Panel declines to make further findings under Articles 1.2, 2.1, 2.1(a), 2.1(b), and 2.4 of the SCM Agreement. b. With respect to the European Union's claims in relation to Section 771B of the Tariff Act of 1930 and its application in the ripe olives countervailing duty investigation: i. Section 771B of the Tariff Act of 1930 is as such inconsistent with Article VI:3 of the GATT 1994 and Article 10 of the SCM Agreement because it requires the USDOC to presume that the entire benefit of a subsidy provided in respect of a raw agricultural input product passes through to the downstream processed agricultural product, based on a consideration of only two factual circumstances, without leaving open the possibility of taking into account any other factors that may be relevant to the determination of whether there is any pass-through and, if so, its degree; ii. the USDOC acted inconsistently with Article VI:3 of the GATT 1994 and Article 10 of the SCM Agreement regarding its application of Section 771B of the Tariff Act of 1930 in the Spanish ripe olives countervailing duty investigation because it failed to establish the existence and extent of indirect subsidization taking into account all relevant facts and circumstances; and iii. given our findings at paragraphs 8.1.b.i and ii, the Panel declines to make further findings under Articles 19.1, 19.3, 19.4, and 32.1 of the SCM Agreement, either with respect to Section 771B of the Tariff Act of 1930 as such or the USDOC's application of Section 771B of the Tariff Act of 1930 in the in the Spanish ripe olives countervailing duty investigation. c. With respect to the European Union's claims regarding the USITC's Injury Determination: i. with respect to the United States' request for a preliminary ruling, the United States has not demonstrated that the European Union's claims under Article 15.4 of the SCM Agreement and Article 3.4 of the Anti-Dumping Agreement are not properly before the Panel; ii. the European Union has not demonstrated that the USITC acted inconsistently with Articles 15.1 and 15.2 of the SCM Agreement, and Articles 3.1 and 3.2 of the Anti-Dumping Agreement, by failing to undertake an analysis of the volume of ripe olives from Spain based on an objective examination of positive evidence; iii. the European Union has not demonstrated that the USITC acted inconsistently with Articles 15.1 and 15.2 of the SCM Agreement, and Articles 3.1 and 3.2 of the Anti-Dumping Agreement, by failing to consider a "volume effect" within the meaning of Article 15.2 of the SCM Agreement and Article 3.2 of the Anti-Dumping Agreement; iv. the European Union has not demonstrated that the USITC acted inconsistently with Articles 15.1 and 15.2 of the SCM Agreement, and Articles 3.1 and 3.2 of the Anti-Dumping Agreement, by failing to undertake an analysis of the price effects of ripe olives from Spain that was based on an objective examination of positive evidence; v. given our findings at paragraphs c.ii-iv, the European Union has not demonstrated that the USITC acted inconsistently with Articles 15.4 and 15.5 of the SCM Agreement, and Articles 3.4 and 3.5 of the Anti-Dumping Agreement, as a consequence of alleged violations concerning the USITC's volume analysis and price effects analysis; vi. the European Union has not demonstrated that the USITC acted inconsistently with Articles 15.1 and 15.4 of the SCM Agreement, and Articles 3.1 and 3.4 of the Anti-Dumping Agreement, by failing to undertake an analysis of the consequent impact of ripe olives from Spain on the domestic industry that was based on an objective examination of positive evidence; vii. given our findings at paragraph c.vi, the European Union has not demonstrated that the USITC acted inconsistently with Article 15.5 of the SCM Agreement, and Article 3.5 of the Anti-Dumping Agreement, as a consequence of alleged violations concerning the USITC's impact analysis; and viii. the European Union has not demonstrated that the USITC acted inconsistently with Articles 15.1 and 15.5 of the SCM Agreement, and Articles 3.1 and 3.5 of the Anti-Dumping Agreement, by failing to undertake a causation analysis that was based on an objective examination of positive evidence. d. With respect to the European Union's claims concerning Aceitunas Guadalquivir's final subsidy margin and countervailing duty rate calculation: i. the USDOC acted inconsistently with Article VI:3 of the GATT 1994 because, by relying on the volume of Aceitunas Guadalquivir's raw olive purchases reported in its response to the initial 4 August 2017 questionnaire to determine Aceitunas Guadalquivir's final subsidy margin and countervailing duty rate, the USDOC did not ensure, and take the necessary steps to ascertain as accurately as possible the amount of subsidization bestowed on the investigated products; ii. the USDOC acted inconsistently with Article VI:3 of the GATT 1994 because the USDOC relied upon the margin of subsidization incorrectly determined for Aceitunas Guadalquivir in its determination of the "all others" rate of countervailing duties imposed on exporters of ripe olives that were not individually investigated; iii. given our findings at paragraphs 8.1.d.i and ii, the Panel declines to make further findings that the same USDOC actions are also inconsistent with Articles 10, 19.1, 19.3, 19.4 and 32.1 of the SCM Agreement; iv. the USDOC acted inconsistently with Article 12.1 of the SCM Agreement because the USDOC failed to notify the respondents that the USDOC required information regarding the volume of purchases of raw olives processed into ripe olives; and v. the USDOC acted inconsistently with Article 12.8 of the SCM Agreement because the USDOC failed to inform interested parties before the final determination that the volume of purchases of raw olives processed into ripe olives was an "essential fact under consideration"."

[**Para. 8.1.**]

Systematic Key Items of the Section*

---

* *See* Systematic Classification Scheme, *supra* at page 255.

IV

International
Criminal Court

INTRODUCTORY NOTE

The International Criminal Court in 2021

BY GEERT-JAN ALEXANDER KNOOPS*
& SARA PEDROSO**

Abstract

Following the closure of the International Criminal Court in March 2020 amounting to slowed down activities at the Court, 2021 saw a resurgence of activity, including the election of a new chief prosecutor, Mr Karim A.A. Kahn. This chapter provides some insight into select issues emerging from the Court's jurisprudence and activities this past year, in various areas, including cooperation, freedom of speech, and amendment to the Rules of Procedure and Evidence. As will be explored, the Court has addressed a variety of fair trial issues including detention review, and has dealt with debates arising from diminished procedural rights afforded in Article 70 trials. Moreover, issues involving the interplay between the Assembly of States Parties and the judges of the Court were also central to the proceedings before the Court. The article also covers a cooperation agreement signed between the Office of the Prosecutor and the government of Colombia, exemplifying complementarity before the national jurisdictions.

* Professor of Politics of International Law at the University of Amsterdam and visiting Professor of International Criminal Law at Shandong University (Jinan, China). He practices as a lawyer at Knoops' International Lawyers in Amsterdam, The Netherlands, and currently acts as lead counsel at the International Criminal Court in two cases. Member of the Editorial Board.

** Lawyer (member of the Ontario Bar, Canada) and Graduate of the Advanced Master's Degree in Public International Law at Leiden University. Currently working as Assistant to Counsel at the International Criminal Court.

Geert-Jan Alexander Knoops and Sara Pedroso, *Introductory Note* In: *The Global Community Yearbook of International Law and Jurisprudence 2022*. Edited by: Giuliana Ziccardi Capaldo, Oxford University Press. © Oxford University Press 2023.
DOI: 10.1093/oso/9780197752265.003.0021

I. INTRODUCTION

Following the closure of the International Criminal Court in March 2020 amounting to slowed down activities at the Court, 2021 saw a resurgence of activity, including the election of a new chief prosecutor, Mr Karim A.A. Kahn. This chapter provides some insight into select issues emerging from the Court's jurisprudence and activities this past year, in various areas, including cooperation, freedom of speech, and amendment to the Rules of Procedure and Evidence. As will be explored in the following, the Court has addressed a variety of fair trial issues including detention review, and has dealt with debates arising from diminished procedural rights afforded in Article 70 trials. Moreover, issues involving the interplay between the Assembly of States Parties and the judges of the Court were also central to the proceedings before the Court. The article also covers a cooperation agreement signed between the Office of the Prosecutor and the government of Colombia, exemplifying complementarity before the national jurisdictions.

II. SITUATION AND CASES

A. *Abd-Al-Rahman* Case (Sudan)

On 9 July 2021, Pre-Trial Chamber II confirmed all the charges of war crimes and crimes against humanity brought by the Prosecutor against Mr Abd-Al-Rahman and committed him to trial.[1] At the pre-trial phase, several appeals were made. On 1 November 2021, the Appeals Chamber ruled on a jurisdictional matter brought by the defence of Mr Al Rahman. Before the pre-trial chamber, the defence called into question the trigger of the Court's jurisdiction following the UN Security Council's referral of the Situation in Darfur, Sudan to the Court under Article 13(b) of the Statute, arguing that the Court did not have jurisdiction over the case.[2] The Pre-Trial Chamber rejected the defence's challenge, deeming that its jurisdiction was exercised lawfully in this case.[3] The defence raised several grounds of appeal, which includes challenging the Pre-Trial Chamber's interpretation of the language of the UN referral, and challenging the compatibility of the referral with the Statute. The defence argued *inter alia* that the Court's exercise of jurisdiction violated the principle of *nullum crimen sine lege* essentially because Sudan was not a party to the Statute at the time that the alleged crimes took place.[4]

Regarding the defence's first ground of appeal, the Appeals Chamber held that the word "situation" was not defined in the Statute, and that word is used loosely, "with a view to extending enough flexibility to the Prosecutor to investigate independently and impartially."[5] The Appeals Chamber confirmed the Pre-Trial Chamber's reasoning that

---

[1] ICC, Prosecutor v. Al Rahman, No. ICC-02/05-01/20-433, Decision on the confirmation of charges against Ali Muhammad Ali Abd-Al-Rahman (9 July 2021).

[2] ICC, Prosecutor v. Al Rahman, No. ICC-02/05-01/20-302, Exception d'incompétence (15 March 2021).

[3] ICC, Prosecutor v. Al Rahman, No. ICC-02/05-01/20-391, Decision on the Defence "Exception d'incompétence" (ICC-02/05-01/20-302) (17 May 2021).

[4] ICC, Prosecutor v. Al Rahman, No. ICC-02/05-01/20-418-tENG, Appeal Brief against Decision ICC-02/05-01/20-391 Rejecting the "Exception d'incompétence" (7 June 2021).

[5] ICC, Prosecutor v. Al Rahman, No. ICC-02/05-01/20-503, Judgment on the appeal of Mr Abd-Al-Rahman against the Pre-Trial Chamber II's "Decision on the Defence 'Exception d'incompétence' (ICC-02/05-01/20-302)" (1 November 2013), para. 25.

a "situation" has its own meaning, which differs from a "case" or "territory of a State" or "State."[6] In relation to the second ground of appeal, which pertains to the financial aspect of the case and how it impacts on the Court's jurisdiction, the Appeals Chamber held that the defence had not established that the alleged incompatibility of Paragraph 7 of Resolution 1593 (stating that expenses incurred in connection with the referral shall be borne by States that are party to the Statute and not by the United Nations) with the Statute could undermine the Court's jurisdiction over this case.[7] In relation to the third ground of appeal, the defence had argued before the Pre-Trial Chamber that UN Security Council Resolution 2559 (2020), which terminated the mandate of the African Union–United Nations Hybrid Operation in Darfur, would have resulted in invalidating Resolution 1593. The defence had also argued that Resolution 2559 had violated Articles 2 and 87(6) of the Rome Statute, respectively referring to the agreement governing the relationship between the Court and the United Nations and providing that the Court must be able to rely on the cooperation of an international organisation such as the United Nations.[8] The Appeals Chamber rejected this ground on the basis that the defence had not demonstrated how this alleged error of law relates to the jurisdiction of the Court.[9] With respect to the fourth ground of appeal, the Appeals Chamber again upheld the Pre-Trial Chamber' determinations. It held that the Article 126(2) of the Statute does not "have any effect on the Court's jurisdiction over proceedings arising from conduct taking place in States not party to the Statute". It further held there is no basis for the interpretation advanced by the defence whereby Article 11(1), contained in Part 2 of the Statute ("Jurisdiction, admissibility and applicable law"), must be interpreted in light of Article 126 of the Statute for those States.[10]

Furthermore, as regards the defence's challenge to the legality of the charges, the Appeals Chamber held that the principle of *nullum crimen sine lege* was not violated.[11] The Chamber observed that Resolution 1593 triggered the Court's exercise of jurisdiction in this case, pursuant to Article 13(b) of the Statute. It also noted that at the time of the conflict in the Darfur region, Sudan had ratified a number of treaties, human rights instruments, and agreements creating obligations in internal armed conflict. In the Appeals Chamber's view, it is "clear that the referral to the Court of the Situation in Darfur, Sudan encompassed violations of binding international obligations carrying a risk of individual

---

[6] ICC, Prosecutor v. Al Rahman, No. ICC-02/05-01/20-503, Judgment on the appeal of Mr Abd-Al-Rahman against the Pre-Trial Chamber II's "Decision on the Defence 'Exception d'incompétence' (ICC-02/05-01/20-302)" (1 November 2013), para. 26.

[7] ICC, Prosecutor v. Al Rahman, No. ICC-02/05-01/20-503, Judgment on the appeal of Mr Abd-Al-Rahman against the Pre-Trial Chamber II's "Decision on the Defence 'Exception d'incompétence' (ICC-02/05-01/20-302)" (1 November 2013), para. 46.

[8] ICC, Prosecutor v. Al Rahman, No. ICC-02/05-01/20-391, Decision on the Defence "Exception d'incompétence" (ICC-02/05-01/20-302) (17 May 2021).

[9] ICC, Prosecutor v. Al Rahman, No. ICC-02/05-01/20-503, Judgment on the appeal of Mr Abd-Al-Rahman against the Pre-Trial Chamber II's "Decision on the Defence 'Exception d'incompétence' (ICC-02/05-01/20-302)" (1 November 2013), para. 57.

[10] ICC, Prosecutor v. Al Rahman, No. ICC-02/05-01/20-503, Judgment on the appeal of Mr Abd-Al-Rahman against the Pre-Trial Chamber II's "Decision on the Defence 'Exception d'incompétence' (ICC-02/05-01/20-302)" (1 November 2013), para. 75.

[11] ICC, Prosecutor v. Al Rahman, No. ICC-02/05-01/20-503, Judgment on the appeal of Mr Abd-Al-Rahman against the Pre-Trial Chamber II's "Decision on the Defence 'Exception d'incompétence' (ICC-02/05-01/20-302)" (1 November 2013), para. 77.

criminal liability."[12] It concluded that the defence's argument that "the Court could not [. . .] exercise the jurisdiction that the Security Council had intended to refer to it" was unpersuasive.[13] Moreover, the Appeals Chamber recalled its judgment in the case of Mr Al Bashir, in which it emphasised that the "chapeau" of Article 13 of the Statute stipulates that regardless of how the Court's jurisdiction is triggered, it must be exercised "in accordance with [the] Statute." This means that the Court is bound by the provisions of the Statute also in case of a referral by the UN Security Council.[14]

The Appeals Chamber did conclude that the Pre-Trial Chamber's reasoning that it was "unnecessary" for it to make a determination as to whether, at the time of their commission, the conducts charged against Mr Abd-Al-Rahman were criminalised in either Sudan's national law or as a matter of international customary law, constituted an error of law.[15] This is a thorny question which had been raised by the defence, relating to the application of the principle of legality in cases where the Court applies retroactive jurisdiction. Nevertheless, the Appeals Chamber found that this error did not produce a result that had a material impact on the ultimate finding of the Pre-Trial Chamber, i.e., that the Court may exercise jurisdiction in this case.[16] This finding is important insofar as the Appeals Chamber recognises that the application of the principle *nullum crimen sine lege* is broader than the definition provided in Article 22 of the Statute.

The case of *Prosecutor v. Al-Rahman* also saw appellate litigation with respect to the detention of Mr Abd-Al-Rahman. By way of a decision of 11 December 2020, Pre-Trial Chamber II conducted a review of Mr Abd-Al-Rahman's detention pursuant to Rule 118(2) of the Rules of Procedure and Evidence. It affirmed his continued detention on the main ground that the two new circumstances advanced by the defence failed to cast doubt on the validity of the warrants of arrest and the fulfilment of the Article 58(1)(a) criterion.[17] On 16 December 2020, the defence filed a notice of appeal of against the Pre-Trial Chamber II's decision and filed its public redacted appeal brief on 4 January 2021.[18]

In its observations on Mr Al Rahman's detention, the defence had submitted that relevant circumstances to be considered in the review were (i) the discovery of the absence of an agreement between Sudan and the Court authorizing the latter to carry out its activities on the territory of Sudan; and (ii) the discovery of the Office of the Prosecutor's violation

[12] ICC, Prosecutor v. Al Rahman, No. ICC-02/05-01/20-503, Judgment on the appeal of Mr Abd-Al-Rahman against the Pre-Trial Chamber II's "Decision on the Defence 'Exception d'incompétence' (ICC-02/05-01/20-302)" (1 November 2013), para. 79.

[13] ICC, Prosecutor v. Al Rahman, No. ICC-02/05-01/20-503, Judgment on the appeal of Mr Abd-Al-Rahman against the Pre-Trial Chamber II's "Decision on the Defence 'Exception d'incompétence' (ICC-02/05-01/20-302)" (1 November 2013), para. 79.

[14] ICC, Prosecutor v. Al Rahman, No. ICC-02/05-01/20-503, Judgment on the appeal of Mr Abd-Al-Rahman against the Pre-Trial Chamber II's "Decision on the Defence 'Exception d'incompétence' (ICC-02/05-01/20-302)" (1 November 2013), para. 80.

[15] ICC, Prosecutor v. Al Rahman, No. ICC-02/05-01/20-503, Judgment on the appeal of Mr Abd-Al-Rahman against the Pre-Trial Chamber II's "Decision on the Defence 'Exception d'incompétence' (ICC-02/05-01/20-302)" (1 November 2013), para. 87.

[16] ICC, Prosecutor v. Al Rahman, No. ICC-02/05-01/20-503, Judgment on the appeal of Mr Abd-Al-Rahman against the Pre-Trial Chamber II's "Decision on the Defence 'Exception d'incompétence' (ICC-02/05-01/20-302)" (1 November 2013), para. 88.

[17] ICC, Prosecutor v. Abd-Al-Rahman, Public Redacted Version of the Appeal Brief against Decision ICC-02/05-01/20-230-RED, ICC-02/05-01/20-230-Red, para. 34.

[18] ICC, Prosecutor v. Abd-Al-Rahman, No. ICC-02/05-01/20-247-Red-tENG, Public Redacted Version of the Appeal Brief against Decision ICC-02/05-01/20-230-RED (1 January 2021).

of confidentiality rules with respect to records of witness interviews. The defence argued *inter alia* that those circumstances directly affected the admissibility of the evidence relied on to issue the two warrants for Mr Abd-Al-Rahman's arrest, and that the criterion for detention under Article 58(1)(a) of the Statute—reasonable grounds to believe that Mr Ali Muhammad Ali Abd-Al-Rahman is in any way responsible for the crimes described in the warrants of arrest—could no longer be met.[19] The defence also drew ample attention to new circumstances related to health and safety at the Court's Detention Centre.[20] As a relief, the defence for Mr Abd-Al-Rahman requested his release from detention. The Pre-Trial Chamber had rejected Mr Abd-Al-Rahman's arguments regarding the inadmissibility of the evidence relied upon for the warrants of arrest. It found that even if the defence's arguments had merit, the challenged evidence related only to an "insignificant" amount of the total evidence relied upon. The Pre-Trial Chamber recalled that under Article 61(6)(b) of the Statute Mr Abd-Al-Rahman "may challenge the admissibility of the evidence at the confirmation hearing." The Pre-Trial Chamber had also considered that Mr Al-Rahman's health condition which was "reported to have improved" did not warrant his release on humanitarian grounds.[21]

In its judgment, the Appeals Chamber rejected the defence's three grounds of appeal as it found no error in the Pre-Trial Chamber's conclusions. Regarding the third ground of appeal, the Appeals Chamber noted that release from detention on humanitarian grounds is not expressly addressed in the Statute.[22] The Chamber observed that "[n]either articles 58 nor 60 of the Statute, nor rule 199 of the Rules refer to the medical condition of the detained person when a chamber is considering interim or conditional release. Furthermore, regulation 103 of the Regulations of the Court assumes that medical problems of detained persons are treated within the detention centre."[23] The Appeals Chamber noted that the defence had not produced any medical records upon which the Pre-Trial Chamber could base a decision to release him, with conditions or otherwise.[24]

The preceding litigation, which made its way to the appellate level of the Court, is exemplary of the complexities of the Court. In particular, it exposed uncertainties as to the applicable law, as it concerns situations referred to the Court by the UN Security Council, particularly as it concerns the application of non-retroactivity, and the interplay between the two organisations. The appellate jurisprudence appears moreover to confirm that the

---

[19] ICC, Prosecutor v. Abd-Al-Rahman, No. ICC-02/05-01/20-213-Red, Version Publique Expurgée de la Réponse aux Observations du Bureau du Procureur ICC-02/05-01/20-209-CONF (26 November 2020), paras. 18–29.

[20] ICC, Prosecutor v. Abd-Al-Rahman, No. ICC-02/05-01/20-213-Red, Version Publique Expurgée de la Réponse aux Observations du Bureau du Procureur ICC-02/05-01/20-209-CONF (26 November 2020), para. 38.

[21] ICC, Prosecutor v. Al Rahman, No. ICC-02/05-01/20-230-Red, Public redacted version of "Decision on the Review of the Detention of Mr Abd-Al-Rahman pursuant to rule 118(2) of the Rules of Procedure and Evidence" (11 December 2020), paras. 26, 34.

[22] ICC, Prosecutor v. Al Rahman, No. ICC-02/05-01/20-279-Red, Judgment on the appeal of Mr Abd-Al-Rahman against Pre-Trial Chamber II's "Decision on the Review of the Detention of Mr Abd-Al-Rahman pursuant to rule 118 (2) of the Rules of Procedure and Evidence," para. 39.

[23] ICC, Prosecutor v. Al Rahman, No. ICC-02/05-01/20-279-Red, Judgment on the appeal of Mr Abd-Al-Rahman against Pre-Trial Chamber II's "Decision on the Review of the Detention of Mr Abd-Al-Rahman pursuant to rule 118 (2) of the Rules of Procedure and Evidence," para. 39.

[24] ICC, Prosecutor v. Al Rahman, No. ICC-02/05-01/20-279-Red, Judgment on the appeal of Mr Abd-Al-Rahman against Pre-Trial Chamber II's "Decision on the Review of the Detention of Mr Abd-Al-Rahman pursuant to rule 118 (2) of the Rules of Procedure and Evidence," para. 39.

chances for a suspect or accused person of obtaining provisional release are close to none. So far, no suspect or accused person before the Court accused of crimes under Article 5 of the Rome Statute has benefitted from provisional release. This seems at odds with the fundamental principle of an accused person's right to provisional release pending trial, which is a corollary of the presumption of innocence enshrined in Article 66 of the Statute. It also seems at odds with Article 60(4) of the Statute which provides that the chamber shall "ensure that a person is not detained for an unreasonable period prior to trial due to inexcusable delay by the Prosecutor" and that if "such delay occurs, the Court shall consider releasing the person, with or without conditions."

B. *Yekatom and Ngaïssona* and *Said* Cases (Central African Republic)

In the *Prosecutor v. Yekatom and Ngaïssona* case, the trial opened on 16 February 2021, and the Prosecution started the presentation of its evidence in March 2021.[25] Litigation relating to detention conditions stemming from measures implemented in response to the COVID-19 pandemic continued throughout 2021. It is recalled that in March 2020, the Detention Centre had imposed "temporary" measures in light of the COVID-19 pandemic, which ultimately were drawn out over the following year. As a consequence, motions were filed by the defence teams in order to allow visits with their clients. For instance, on 12 January 2021, the defence for Mr Yekatom filed a request for authorisation of in-person legal visits.[26] On 18 January 2021, the defence for Mr Ngaïssona also requested leave from the chamber to visit their client at least one week before the scheduled commencement of the opening statements.[27] The single judge granted both requests in light of Article 67(1)(b) of the Statute, which provides for an accused's right to "have adequate time and facilities for the preparation of the defence and to communicate freely with counsel of the accused's choosing in confidence" and in light of the specific circumstances.[28]

In parallel, a new case opened in 2021, constituting the second trial in the Central African Republic II (CAR II) situation. The warrant of arrest against Mr Mahamat Said Abdel Kani was issued under seal on 7 January 2019 for war crimes and crimes against humanity allegedly committed in Bangui in Central African Republic in 2013. Mr Said was surrendered to the Court on 24 January 2021 and the confirmation of charges hearings were held from 12 to 14 October 2021. The charges against Mr Said were partially confirmed by the Pre-Trial Chamber II on 9 December 2021. The Pre-Trial Chamber held there is sufficient evidence to establish substantial grounds to believe that Mr Said was a senior member of the Seleka coalition and is criminally responsible under Articles 25(3)(a) (direct co-perpetration) and 25(3)(b) (ordering or inducing) of the Rome Statute for crimes against humanity and war crimes which are focused on imprisonment, torture, and other inhumane acts and persecution, cruel treatment, and outrages upon personal dignity.[29] More specifically, the

---

[25] ICC, Prosecutor v. Yekatom and Ngaïssona, No. ICC-01/14-01/18-817, Order Setting the Commencement Date of the Prosecution's Presentation of Evidence (13 January 2022).

[26] ICC, Prosecutor v. Yekatom and Ngaïssona, No. ICC01/14-01/18-816-Red, Public Redacted Version of "Request for authorization of in-person legal visits with Mr. Yekatom," (2 February 2021).

[27] ICC, Prosecutor v. Yekatom and Ngaïssona, No. ICC-01/14-01/18-833-Conf-Red, Ngaïssona Defence Request to allow in-person visits between Mr Ngaïssona and his Defence in order to prepare for Trial (18 January 2021), para. 1, at 11–12.

[28] ICC, Prosecutor v. Yekatom and Ngaïssona, No. ICC-01/14-01/18-853, Decision on the Defence Requests for In-Person Legal Visits at the Detention Centre, para. 9 (26 January 2021).

[29] ICC Prosecutor v. Said, No. ICC-01/14-01/21-218-Red, Decision on the confirmation of charges against Mahamat Said Abdel Kani (9 December 2021), at 50–61.

charges as confirmed focus on allegations that Mr Said, together with other Seleka, targeted perceived Bozizé supporters by arresting, detaining, and mistreating them at the OCRB (Central Office for the Repression of Banditry). The arrest and surrender of Mr Said, an alleged Seleka leader, may attenuate some of the Court's criticisms of applying "one-sided" or selective justice, at least as it concerns a specific situation. This stands in contrast, for instance, with the Ivory Coast situation, where only Mr Gbagbo and Mr Blé Goudé were ever charged for the post-electoral violence in 2010–2011 and no alleged supporters of President Ouattara were ever charged. However, the overwhelming majority of targets and suspects at the Court continue to be from the African continent, despite ICC preliminary examinations and investigations covering a much broader geographic area. It is to be seen whether the Court will expand its geographic scope in the future.

The opening of a new case in the CAR II situation raised questions relating to inter-case disclosure. Trial Chamber V ruled, for instance, on an Office of the Prosecutor urgent request for authorisation to access and disclose transcripts of the testimony of eight witnesses in the *Yekatom and Ngaïssona* case to the defence of Mr Said. The Office of the Prosecutor argued that it intended to rely on the evidence of these witnesses for the purpose of the confirmation of charges hearings and that the confidential transcripts were therefore disclosable to the Said defence team. Such inter-case disclosure requests have arisen in previous cases before the Court, for instance between the *Bemba* "main" and the *Bemba* et al. "contempt" cases, as well as between the *Malian* cases. In the *Said* case, the Pre-Trial Chamber granted the request and noted that the disclosure of transcripts to participants in different proceedings before the Court would not vary the protective measures in the *Yekatom and Ngaïssona* case.[30] In its reasoning, Trial Chamber V further noted that the *Said* defence was bound by confidentiality obligations pursuant to Article 8 of the Code of Professional Conduct for counsel and a protocol on the handling of confidential information.[31]

C. *Gbagbo and Blé Goudé* Case (Côte d'Ivoire)

On 31 March 2021, the Appeals Chamber delivered its judgment on the Office of the Prosecutor's appeal against the judgment of Trial Chamber I on the defence no case to answer motions.[32] The Appeals Chamber confirmed the acquittal with respect to Mr Gbagbo and Mr Blé Goudé, by Majority, Judges Ibáñez and Judge Bossa dissenting. The Appeals Chamber rejected the Office of the Prosecutor's argument that the Trial Chamber I's decision had violated the statutory requirements of the Court. It held *inter alia* that, although trial chambers should ideally deliver both the verdict and reasons concurrently, a delay between the issuance of a verdict and its reasons do not necessarily invalidate the entire trial process.[33] There may be some justifications to justify a delay between the two, for instance

---

[30] ICC, Prosecutor v. Yekatom and Ngaïssona, No. ICC-01/14-01/18-1129, Decision on the Prosecution Request for Authorisation to Disclose Certain Transcripts in the case of The Prosecutor v. Mahamat Said Abdel Kani (5 October 2021), para. 7.

[31] ICC, Prosecutor v. Yekatom and Ngaïssona, ICC-01/14-01/18-1129, Decision on the Prosecution Request for Authorisation to Disclose Certain Transcripts in the case of The Prosecutor v. Mahamat Said Abdel Kani (5 October 2021), para. 8.

[32] ICC, Prosecutor v. Gbagbo and Blé Goudé, No. ICC-02/11-01/15-1400, Judgment in the appeal of the Prosecutor against Trial Chamber I's decision on the no case to answer motions (31 March 2021).

[33] ICC, Prosecutor v. Gbagbo and Blé Goudé, No. ICC-02/11-01/15-1400, Judgment in the appeal of the Prosecutor against Trial Chamber I's decision on the no case to answer motions (31 March 2021), paras. 267–268.

where the liberty of an acquitted defendant is at stake. The Appeals Chamber also rejected the Office of the Prosecutor's second ground of appeal, namely that the Majority of Trial Chamber I had failed to articulate and consistently apply the standard of proof. The Appeals Chamber Majority noted Trial Chamber's I's finding that the evidence presented against Mr Gbagbo and Mr Blé Goudé was "exceptionally weak."[34]

The Appeals Chamber also revoked all conditions on the release of Mr Gbagbo and Mr Blé Goudé and directed the ICC Registrar to make arrangements for the safe transfer of Mr Gbagbo and Mr Blé Goudé to a receiving State or States.[35]

D. *Ongwen* Case (Uganda)

On 4 February 2021, the Trial Chamber IX issued its final judgment, numbering 1,077 pages, in the case against Mr Ongwen, who was accused of seventy counts of crimes against humanity and war crimes.[36] Trial Chamber IX declared Mr Ongwen guilty of sixty-one crimes against humanity and war crimes, committed in Uganda between 1 July 2002 and 31 December 2005. Controversially, the Trial Chamber did not find evidence that supported the claim Mr Ongwen suffered from any mental disease or disorder during the period relevant to the charges or that he committed these crimes under duress of under any threats. This had been a central theme in the defence's case. This finding was made despite the judges' acknowledgment that Mr Ongwen was abducted at the age of around eight or nine by the Lord's Resistance Army (LRA), confirming his status of victim as a former child soldier.[37] Mr Ongwen was found guilty *inter alia* of conscripting and using children below the age of fifteen for the active participation in hostilities, the same crime he was subjected to himself. However, this was not considered to warrant exclusion of criminal responsibility. The Chamber noted that Mr Ongwen had committed the relevant crimes as an adult, and "the fact of having been (or being) a victim of a crime does not constitute, in and of itself, a justification of any sort for the commission of similar or other crimes—beyond the potential relevance of the underlying facts to the grounds excluding criminal responsibility expressly regulated under the Statute."[38] Moreover, the Trial Chamber held that the categories of exclusion of criminal responsibility of (i) lack of capacity to appreciate the unlawfulness of the conduct and (ii) duress cannot coexist, even in the abstract, "given that one is premised on a destruction of the person's capacity to appreciate the unlawfulness or nature of his or her conduct, [. . .], and the other on a conscious choice to engage in conduct which constitutes a crime based on an evaluation of the harm that is caused."[39]

In its judgment, Trial Chamber IX further addressed arguments relating to human rights violations raised by the Defence, in particular, that (i) the Chamber has treated Mr Ongwen as an accused and detained person who does not suffer from a mental health disability, and (ii) the Chamber violated Mr Ongwen's right to family life because of the restrictions

---

[34] ICC, Prosecutor v. Gbagbo and Blé Goudé, No. ICC-02/11-01/15-1400, Judgment in the appeal of the Prosecutor against Trial Chamber I's decision on the no case to answer motions (31 March 2021), para. 328.

[35] ICC, Prosecutor v. Gbagbo and Blé Goudé, No. ICC-02/11-01/15-1400, Judgment in the appeal of the Prosecutor against Trial Chamber I's decision on the no case to answer motions (31 March 2021), para. 381.

[36] ICC, Prosecutor v. Ongwen, No. ICC-02/04-01/15-1762-Red, Trial Judgment (4 February 2021).

[37] ICC, Prosecutor v. Ongwen, Trial Judgment (4 February 2021), para. 2672.

[38] ICC, Prosecutor v. Ongwen, Trial Judgment (4 February 2021), para. 2672.

[39] ICC, Prosecutor v. Ongwen, Trial Judgment (4 February 2021), para. 2671.

imposed on his communications with the outside world. Trial Chamber IX dismissed both defence arguments claiming discrimination.[40] The Chamber concluded that the defence allegations could therefore not warrant the exceptional remedy of a permanent stay of proceedings.[41]

Sentencing hearings were held on 14 and 15 April 2021, during which Mr Ongwen took the floor. He explained to the Chamber how he suffered from severe mental health issues while in detention. Mr Ongwen described the effects of treatment which would at times make him hallucinate, make him see "dead soldiers" and would bring back painful memories. He described his inability to sleep for more than thirty minutes at the time, caused by the intense suffering he has endured.[42] He described how he would sometimes collapse at the detention center and he would be carried out to his room while sweating profusely.[43] Mr Ongwen also described his life, including his abduction as a child in 1987, and the strict rules to be followed in the "Holy Spirit Movement."[44] He described how he was beaten and forced to kill and eat human blood when he first tried to escape.[45] He described being in the bush for twenty-seven years and coming to the realisation, after arriving at the detention centre and watching television, that the "world is such a huge world," yet the world was not paying attention when the war started in northern Uganda.[46]

The defence appealed the judgment. It remains to be seen how the Appeals Chamber will rule of the various appellate grounds and in particular, how Mr Ongwen's status as a victim-perpetrator will be analysed.

E. *Al Hassan* Case (Mali)

The Trial Chamber in the case against Mr Al Hassan case grappled *inter alia* with issues relating to the defence's right to be heard, the right to publicity, as well as the scope of defence counsel's freedom of speech. These issues are fundamental to the role and rights of the defence before the Court. Litigation spawned from a post ("Tweet") published by lead counsel for Mr Al Hassan on social media platform Twitter in December 2020 which referred to a decision rejecting Mr Al Hassan's request for a custodial visit, following the death of Mr Al Hassan's daughter.[47] On 31 December 2020, the Chamber submitted the conduct of defence lead counsel by way of a complaint to the Registry, pursuant to Article 34(1)(a) of the Code of Professional Conduct for counsel (Code of Conduct).[48] In its submission, Trial Chamber X noted that the custodial visit decision, which is referenced in the Tweet, is confidential and that by publicly disclosing the existence and outcome of a confidential decision of the Chamber, counsel had "flagrantly" breached Article 8(1) of the Code of Conduct.[49] The Trial Chamber further held that the content of the Tweet directly violated

---

[40] ICC, Prosecutor v. Ongwen, Trial Judgment (4 February 2021), paras. 106–120.

[41] ICC, Prosecutor v. Ongwen, Trial Judgment (4 February 2021), para. 120.

[42] ICC, Prosecutor v. Ongwen, Transcript No. ICC-02/04-01/15-T-261-ENG ET (15 April 2021), at 33.

[43] ICC, Prosecutor v. Ongwen, Transcript No. ICC-02/04-01/15-T-261-ENG ET (15 April 2021), at 5.

[44] ICC, Prosecutor v. Ongwen, Transcript No. ICC-02/04-01/15-T-261-ENG ET (15 April 2021), at 5.

[45] ICC, Prosecutor v. Ongwen, Transcript No. ICC-02/04-01/15-T-261-ENG ET (15 April 2021), at 5.

[46] ICC, Prosecutor v. Ongwen, Transcript No. ICC-02/04-01/15-T-261-ENG ET (15 April 2021), at 17.

[47] ICC, Prosecutor v. Al Hassan, No. ICC-01/12-01/18-1234, Submission to the Registry pursuant to Article 34(1)(a) of the Code of Professional Conduct for counsel (31 December 2020).

[48] ICC, Prosecutor v. Al Hassan, No. ICC-01/12-01/18-1234, Submission to the Registry pursuant to Article 34(1)(a) of the Code of Professional Conduct for counsel (31 December 2020).

[49] ICC, Prosecutor v. Al Hassan, No. ICC-01/12-01/18-1234, Submission to the Registry pursuant to Article 34(1)(a) of the Code of Professional Conduct for counsel (31 December 2020), para. 5.

counsel's obligations "to be respectful and courteous in her relations with the Chamber, and Article 24(1), to take all necessary steps to ensure that her actions are not prejudicial to the ongoing proceedings and do not bring the Court into disrepute," which includes "the requirement to respect any decision issued by the Chamber, be it oral or written."[50]

In its "Request for Reconsideration of 'Submission to the Registry pursuant to Article 34(1)(a) of the Code of Professional Conduct for counsel,'" the defence for Mr Al Hassan argued that it is the defence's role to "act as an intermediary between Mr Al Hassan, his family, and the public, and between Mr Al Hassan and the Chamber."[51] The defence ultimately argued that "rather than prohibiting or penalizing such communications, [. . .] it would be appropriate and consistent with the principle of legality and foreseeability, to promulgate an ICC policy for press statements, which takes into consideration the different roles of the parties and participants (including the Registry), and internationally recognized human rights concerning the role of publicity within criminal proceedings, and the presumption of innocence."[52] The defence requested Trial Chamber X to reconsider and reverse its decision to issue the "Submission to the Registry pursuant to article 34(1)(a) of the Code of Professional Conduct for counsel."[53] Trial Chamber X rejected the defence request for reconsideration on a technicality, holding that no "decision" had been issued by the Chamber, but that it had simply referred the matter to the Registry.[54]

This litigation raises important questions surrounding the scope of the freedom of speech of counsel representing suspects and accused before the ICC. The position of the ICC regarding the parameters within which defence counsel can comment on court decisions, raises fundamental questions on compliance with the case law of the European Court of Human Rights in which it has been established that defence counsel in criminal cases has a considerable leeway to criticize court decisions in public in case it serves a functional purpose. It also raises the question as to whether such limitations on a counsel's freedom of speech relating to the case only applies to defence counsel, or whether counsel for the victims or for the Prosecution should be bound to the same limitations.

F. *Gicheru* Case (Kenya)

The issue of the applicability of Provisional Rule 165 of the Rules of Procedure and Evidence (Rules) continued to be litigated in the *Gicheru* case at the appellate stage. The provisional rule was adopted in order to "simplify and expedite" Article 70 cases. This was done through the reduction of the number of judges in chambers at each level (pre-trial, trial, and appeals), the elimination of the right to seek leave to appeal interlocutory decisions

---

[50] ICC, Prosecutor v. Al Hassan, No. ICC-01/12-01/18-1234, Submission to the Registry pursuant to Article 34(1)(a) of the Code of Professional Conduct for counsel (31 December 2020), para. 6.

[51] ICC, Prosecutor v. Al Hassan, No. ICC-01/12-01/18-1235, Defence Request for Reconsideration of "Submission to the Registry pursuant to Article 34(1)(a) of the Code of Professional Conduct for counsel" (4 January 2021), para. 15.

[52] ICC, Prosecutor v. Al Hassan, Defence Request for Reconsideration of "Submission to the Registry pursuant to Article 34(1)(a) of the Code of Professional Conduct for counsel," ICC-01/12-01/18-1235, 4 January 2021, para. 19.

[53] ICC, Prosecutor v. Al Hassan, No. ICC-01/12-01/18-1235, Defence Request for Reconsideration of "Submission to the Registry pursuant to Article 34(1)(a) of the Code of Professional Conduct for counsel" (4 January 2021), para. 20.

[54] ICC, Prosecutor v. Al Hassan, No. ICC-01/12-01/18-1240, Decision on Defence request for reconsideration (6 January 2021).

under Article 82(1)(d) of the Statute, as well as the elimination of the automatic right to a separate sentencing hearing under Article 76(2) of the Statute.[55] The provisional rule read as follows, as adopted on 10 February 2016 by the judges of the Court, acting in plenary:

> 1. The Prosecutor may initiate and conduct investigations with respect to the offences defined in article 70 on his or her own initiative, on the basis of information communicated by a Chamber or any reliable source.
>
> 2. Articles 39(2)(b), 53, 57(2), 59, 76(2) and 82(1)(d), and any rules thereunder, shall not apply. A Chamber composed of one judge from the Pre-Trial Division shall exercise the functions and powers of the Pre-Trial Chamber from the moment of receipt of an application under article 58. A Chamber composed of one judge shall exercise the functions and powers of the Trial Chamber, and a panel of three judges shall decide appeals. The procedures for constitution of Chambers and the panel of three judges shall be established in the Regulations.
>
> 3. For purposes of article 61, the Pre-Trial Chamber, as constituted under sub-rule 2, may make any of the determinations set forth in that article on the basis of written submissions, without a hearing, unless the interests of justice otherwise require.
>
> 4. The Trial Chamber seized of the case from which the article 70 proceedings originate may, as appropriate and taking into account the rights of the defence, direct that there be joinder of charges under article 70 with charges in the originating case. Where the Trial Chamber directs joinder of charges, the Trial Chamber seized of the originating case shall also be seized of the article 70 charge(s). Unless there is such a joinder, a case concerning charges under article 70 must be tried by a Trial Chamber composed of one judge.

These amendments stemmed "from the recognition that the nature and gravity of offences under article 70 differ markedly from those under article 5 and that the procedure governing article 70 proceedings should reflect that difference."[56] The application of this rule was contested, however, by the Office of Public Counsel for the Defence (OPCD), on behalf of Mr Philip Kipkoech Bett, Mr Gicheru's co-accused, who was unrepresented and not in the Court's custody. On 8 January 2021, the OPCD appealed the Pre-Trial Chamber's "Decision on the Applicability of Rule 165 of the Rules of Procedure and Evidence."

The OPCD raised three issues on appeal: (a) whether the Chamber erred in finding that Provisional Rule 165 continued to be applicable considering that the Assembly of States Parties had not made a specific decision adopting, amending, or rejecting the rule according to Article 51(3) of the Statute; (b) whether the Chamber erred in law in finding that a new procedural regime commences at the Initial Appearance Hearing and that the Provisional Rule only came into effect at that time; (c) whether the Chamber erred in finding that Provisional Rule 165 is not incompatible with the Statute and that Provisional Rule 165 does not restrict any of the fundamental rights enshrined in Article 67 of the Statute. The OPCD argued that the materiality of the errors lay in the fact that the defendants were subjected to a rule that was created only *after* they became defendants in the case and one

---

[55] ICC, Prosecutor v. Gicheru, No. ICC-01/09-01/20-107, Judgment on the appeal of the Office of Public Counsel for the Defence against the decision of Pre-Trial Chamber A of 10 December 2020 entitled "Decision on the Applicability of Provisional Rule 165 of the Rules of Procedure and Evidence," para. 101, see footnote 63.

[56] ICC, Prosecutor v. Gicheru, No. ICC-01/09-01/20-61, Decision on the Applicability of Provisional Rule 165 of the Rules of Procedure and Evidence (10 December 2020), para. 29.

that restricts their procedural avenues to justice.[57] It requested the appeals Chamber to rectify these legal errors "for the sake of establishing norms applicable to amendments of the core texts and legal certainty for parties and participants in ICC proceedings."[58]

The issue of OPCD's standing at the appellate stage was disputed by the Prosecution.[59] The Appeals Chamber held that "the power of the Pre-Trial or Trial Chamber to certify issues for appeal under Article 82(1)(d) of the Statute does not extend to granting leave to appeal to persons or entities that are not parties within the meaning of that provision." It also held that while the Pre-Trial Chamber could consider the issue of standing in its decision granting leave to appeal, the Appeals Chamber is not bound by the Pre-Trial Chamber's determination in this respect and may re-assess this question independently.[60] The OPCD was ultimately considered a "party" within the meaning of Article 82(1) of the Statute for the purpose of the appeal given its mandate to represent a named suspect in this case, Mr Bett.[61]

In its ruling of 8 March 2021, the Appeals Chamber confirmed the Pre-Trial Chamber's decision, with Judges Eboe-Osuji and Bossa partially dissenting.[62] The Majority of the Appeals Chamber held, after reviewing the drafting history of Provisional Rule 165, that the final text of Article 51 of the Statute affirms an active, rather than passive, role for the Assembly of States Parties in exercising its decision-making powers regarding provisional rules.[63] As a consequence, the ordinary meaning of Article 51(3), which concerns the drafting of provisional Rules by the judges, "excludes the possibility that a provisional rule should be considered to be implicitly rejected (or adopted) in the event that the Assembly of States Parties fails to take a decision as required."[64] The Appeals Chamber considered several factors to come to that conclusion, including the fact that the Provisional Rule

---

[57] ICC, Prosecutor v. Gicheru, No. ICC-01/09-01/20-79, OPCD Appeals against the Decision on Applicability of Provisional Rule 165 (8 January 2021), para. 2.

[58] ICC, Prosecutor v. Gicheru, No. ICC-01/09-01/20-79, OPCD Appeals against the Decision on Applicability of Provisional Rule 165 (8 January 2021), para. 2.

[59] ICC, Prosecutor v. Gicheru, No. ICC-01/09-01/20-83, Prosecution's Response to OPCD's "Appeal[] against the Decision on Applicability of Provisional Rule 165" (21 January 2021), paras. 4–15; ICC, Prosecutor v. Gicheru, No. ICC-01/09-01/20-86, OPCD Request to Dismiss In Limine the Prosecution's Arguments on Standing Or, in the Alternative, Leave to Reply (25 January 2021).

[60] ICC, Prosecutor v. Gicheru, No. ICC-01/09-01/20-89, Decision on the Office of Public Counsel for the Defence's request for the Prosecutor's arguments on standing to be dismissed in limine and request for leave to reply (29 January 2021), para. 14.

[61] ICC, Prosecutor v. Gicheru, No. ICC-01/09-01/20-107, Judgment on the appeal of the Office of Public Counsel for the Defence against the decision of Pre-Trial Chamber A of 10 December 2020 entitled "Decision on the Applicability of Provisional Rule 165 of the Rules of Procedure and Evidence" (8 March 2021), paras. 34–36.

[62] ICC, Prosecutor v. Gicheru, No. ICC-01/09-01/20-107, Judgment on the appeal of the Office of Public Counsel for the Defence against the decision of Pre-Trial Chamber A of 10 December 2020 entitled "Decision on the Applicability of Provisional Rule 165 of the Rules of Procedure and Evidence" (8 March 2021).

[63] ICC, Prosecutor v. Gicheru, No. ICC-01/09-01/20-107, Judgment on the appeal of the Office of Public Counsel for the Defence against the decision of Pre-Trial Chamber A of 10 December 2020 entitled "Decision on the Applicability of Provisional Rule 165 of the Rules of Procedure and Evidence" (8 March 2021), para. 70.

[64] ICC, Prosecutor v. Gicheru, No. ICC-01/09-01/20-107, Judgment on the appeal of the Office of Public Counsel for the Defence against the decision of Pre-Trial Chamber A of 10 December 2020 entitled "Decision on the Applicability of Provisional Rule 165 of the Rules of Procedure and Evidence" (8 March 2021), para. 71.

165 remained on the Assembly of States Parties' agenda, showing that it considered itself seized of the matter.[65] Interestingly, as it provides insight into the interplay between the Assembly and States Parties and the Court, the Appeals Chamber held that the Assembly of States Parties "implicitly rejected the view" that the "the next ordinary or special session of the Assembly of States Parties" creates a time limitation for the adoption, rejection or amendment of provisional rules, as it does not consider itself bound to take decisions in this respect.[66]

With respect to the second ground of appeal, the Appeals Chamber acknowledged that Article 51(4) of the Statute provides that amendments to the Rules of Procedure and Evidence and provisional rules shall not be applied retroactively to the detriment of the suspect, accused, or convicted person.[67] The debate turned on the moment precisely when the new regime started to apply. The Appeals Chamber held that Mr Gicheru's surrender on 2 November 2020 triggered the initial proceedings before the Court and the commencement of the confirmation of charges. It reasoned that given Provisional Rule 165 was adopted prior to the constitution of the Pre-Trial Chamber, the rule was not applied retroactively within the meaning of Article 51(4) of the Statute.[68]

Finally, with respect to the third ground of appeal, the Appeals Chamber held that "procedural rules applicable to article 70 proceedings have no special status that would exempt them from the possibility of change within the framework of article 51 of the Statute."[69] Moreover, the chamber reasoned that the procedure outlined in Article 51(3) of the Statute provided for sufficient scrutiny and oversight and that the fair trial rights of a suspect or accused were preserved through the amendment. As it concerns the number of judges, the Appeals Chamber held that the legal framework of the Court already provides for many decisions that may affect the fairness of proceedings to be taken by a single judge in all cases, and that the equivalent of Article 70 offences are prosecuted before a single judge (rather than three judges) at other international or hybrid tribunals.[70] With respect to the issue of the elimination of the right to interlocutory appeals, the Appeals Chamber reasoned that

---

[65] ICC, Prosecutor v. Gicheru, No. ICC-01/09-01/20-107, Judgment on the appeal of the Office of Public Counsel for the Defence against the decision of Pre-Trial Chamber A of 10 December 2020 entitled "Decision on the Applicability of Provisional Rule 165 of the Rules of Procedure and Evidence" (8 March 2021), para. 71.

[66] ICC, Prosecutor v. Gicheru, No. ICC-01/09-01/20-107, Judgment on the appeal of the Office of Public Counsel for the Defence against the decision of Pre-Trial Chamber A of 10 December 2020 entitled "Decision on the Applicability of Provisional Rule 165 of the Rules of Procedure and Evidence" (8 March 2021), para. 74.

[67] ICC, Prosecutor v. Gicheru, No. ICC-01/09-01/20-107, Judgment on the appeal of the Office of Public Counsel for the Defence against the decision of Pre-Trial Chamber A of 10 December 2020 entitled "Decision on the Applicability of Provisional Rule 165 of the Rules of Procedure and Evidence" (8 March 2021), para. 87.

[68] ICC, Prosecutor v. Gicheru, No. ICC-01/09-01/20-107, Judgment on the appeal of the Office of Public Counsel for the Defence against the decision of Pre-Trial Chamber A of 10 December 2020 entitled "Decision on the Applicability of Provisional Rule 165 of the Rules of Procedure and Evidence" (8 March 2021), para. 89.

[69] ICC, Prosecutor v. Gicheru, No. ICC-01/09-01/20-107, Judgment on the appeal of the Office of Public Counsel for the Defence against the decision of Pre-Trial Chamber A of 10 December 2020 entitled "Decision on the Applicability of Provisional Rule 165 of the Rules of Procedure and Evidence" (8 March 2021), para. 106.

[70] ICC, Prosecutor v. Gicheru, No. ICC-01/09-01/20-107, Judgment on the appeal of the Office of Public Counsel for the Defence against the decision of Pre-Trial Chamber A of 10 December 2020 entitled

any failures may be raised during a final appeal and any necessary remedy may be applied at that stage.[71] Regarding the question of separate sentencing proceedings, the Appeals Chamber concluded that a trial chamber, composed of one judge, continues to retain the discretion to manage its own proceedings, and may still hold a separate sentencing hearing if it considers this to be necessary in the circumstances of the case before it.[72]

In their partially dissenting opinion, Judges Eboe-Osuji and Bossa noted with regret that the Assembly of States Parties had not resolved the matter for five years.[73] They noted that they are not persuaded that the conditions mentioned in Article 51(3) were not met, namely that the judges may amend a rule "in urgent cases where the Rules do not provide for a specific situation before the Court." The dissenting judges noted that the contingency requires a combination of two things: the existence of an urgency, but also a situation in which the rules are silent with respect to a situation before the Court.[74] They noted that, for instance, that the same rules which had applied in the *Bemba et al.* case (a previous case under Article 70) could have applied to the present *Gicheru* case.[75] There was therefore no lacunae.

The dissenting judges agreed with the Majority's conclusion that the Provisional rule did not constitute a violation of the rights of the defendant. However, Judges Eboe-Osuji and Bossa held that the amendment is inconsistent with the Rome Statute and, in particular, as it concerns the composition of the chambers in Article 70 proceedings. They reasoned that the wording of Article 39(2)(a), which provides that the functions of the Trial Chamber and the Pre-trial Chambers *shall* be carried out by three judges, is imperative in nature.[76] For those reasons, the dissenting judges would have overturned the Pre-Trial Chamber's impugned decision.

"Decision on the Applicability of Provisional Rule 165 of the Rules of Procedure and Evidence" (8 March 2021), para. 111.

[71] ICC, Prosecutor v. Gicheru, No. ICC-01/09-01/20-107, Judgment on the appeal of the Office of Public Counsel for the Defence against the decision of Pre-Trial Chamber A of 10 December 2020 entitled "Decision on the Applicability of Provisional Rule 165 of the Rules of Procedure and Evidence" (8 March 2021), para. 112.

[72] ICC, Prosecutor v. Gicheru, No. ICC-01/09-01/20-107, Judgment on the appeal of the Office of Public Counsel for the Defence against the decision of Pre-Trial Chamber A of 10 December 2020 entitled "Decision on the Applicability of Provisional Rule 165 of the Rules of Procedure and Evidence" (8 March 2021), para. 113.

[73] ICC, Prosecutor v. Gicheru, No. ICC-01/09-01/20-107-Anx, Annex to the Judgment on the appeal of the Office of Public Counsel for the Defence against the decision of Pre-Trial Chamber A of 10 December 2020 entitled "Decision on the Applicability of Provisional Rule 165 of the Rules of Procedure and Evidence" (8 March 2021), para. 3.

[74] ICC, Prosecutor v. Gicheru, No. ICC-01/09-01/20-107-Anx, Annex to the Judgment on the appeal of the Office of Public Counsel for the Defence against the decision of Pre-Trial Chamber A of 10 December 2020 entitled "Decision on the Applicability of Provisional Rule 165 of the Rules of Procedure and Evidence" (8 March 2021), para. 6

[75] ICC, Prosecutor v. Gicheru, No. ICC-01/09-01/20-107-Anx, Annex to the Judgment on the appeal of the Office of Public Counsel for the Defence against the decision of Pre-Trial Chamber A of 10 December 2020 entitled "Decision on the Applicability of Provisional Rule 165 of the Rules of Procedure and Evidence" (8 March 2021), para. 6.

[76] ICC, Prosecutor v. Gicheru, No. ICC-01/09-01/20-107-Anx, Annex to the Judgment on the appeal of the Office of Public Counsel for the Defence against the decision of Pre-Trial Chamber A of 10 December 2020 entitled "Decision on the Applicability of Provisional Rule 165 of the Rules of Procedure and Evidence" (8 March 2021), para. 12.

III. OTHER DEVELOPMENTS

A. Election of the New ICC Prosecutor

On 12 February 2021, Mr Karim Kkan was elected as the new Prosecutor of the ICC at the nineteenth session of the Assembly of States Parties to the Rome Statute in New York. Mr Khan was sworn in officially on 16 June 2021. He replaced Ms Fatou Bensouda, who completed her nine-year mandate. On 17 September 2021, Mr Khan appointed seventeen "special advisers" pursuant to Article 42(9) of the Statute to serve his office. These appointments "form part of Prosecutor Khan's vision, early in his mandate, to build on what has been accomplished to date and reinforce the Office's capabilities to effectively and efficiently discharge its mandate under the Statute, and to strengthen specialisation on a wide range of issues touching upon public international law, sexual violence in conflict, crimes against and affecting children, slavery crimes, amongst other priority areas identified by the Prosecutor."[77] These new posts include portfolios including the crime of aggression, gender persecution, genocide, Islamic Law, and knowledge transfer. One special adviser without portfolio is former ICC judge Christine Van den Wyngaert. These appointments constitute a novelty within the Office of the Prosecutor.

1. *Focal Point on Gender Equality*

On Women's Day 2021 (8 March), the ICC recruited a Focal Point for Gender Equality, which Judge Eboe-Osuji described as a "crucial milestone towards effectively improving gender-related issues in our institution."[78] The focal point's mandate is to assist the Court's leadership to "strengthen gender related policies across the Court and to address issues related to employment conditions of women in the institution, including gender balance at all levels of employment". Their key functions includes monitoring the Court's progress in strengthening gender equality; advocating on issues impacting women and gender; providing individual counselling; raising greater awareness through training programmes, workshops, and events; and advising on gender parity targets.[79] Stated objectives are for the Court to issue stronger policies on harassment and bullying and to reinforce the Court's zero tolerance policy for harassment in the workplace.

This initiative is welcome in light of the 2020 Independent Expert Report's (IER) finding that decisive action was needed from both the Assembly of States Parties and the Court to ensure gender equality and to provide a "welcoming environment for all individuals affiliated with the Court."[80] In the IER, the experts made a number of findings and recommendations addressing gender inequality at the Court, particularly in senior

---

[77] ICC, Press release No. ICC-CPI-20210917-PR1611, *ICC Prosecutor Mr Karim A.A. Khan QC Appoints Seventeen Special Advisers* (17 September 2021), available online at https://www.icc-cpi.int/news/icc-prosecutor-mr-karim-aa-khan-qc-appoints-seventeen-special-advisers.

[78] ICC, Press release No. ICC-CPI-20210308-PR1573, *International Women's Day: ICC Appoints Focal Point for Gender Equality* (8 March 2021), available online at https://www.icc-cpi.int/news/international-womens-day-icc-appoints-focal-point-gender-equality.

[79] ICC, Press release No. ICC-CPI-20210308-PR1573, *International Women's Day: ICC Appoints Focal Point for Gender Equality* (8 March 2021), available online at https://www.icc-cpi.int/news/international-womens-day-icc-appoints-focal-point-gender-equality.

[80] *Independent Expert Review of the International Criminal Court and the Rome Statute System Final Report* (30 September), para. 64, available online at https://asp.icc-cpi.int/sites/asp/files/asp_docs/ASP19/IER-Final-Report-ENG.pdf.

positions. The report noted "almost a complete absence of women in senior positions."[81] The experts had also found that the Court suffered from internal "distrust," a "culture of fear," and a lack of "gender balance," particularly in the Office of the Prosecutor.[82] The experts also noted that attention should be further given to ensure the dignity, wellbeing, safety and inclusion of LGBTIQ+ individuals in the Court's working environment.[83] The appointment of a focal point on gender equality is a step forward in the implementation of one of the recommendations made by the experts in the IER.

2. Cooperation Agreement with the Government of Colombia
On 28 October 2021, the ICC Office of the Prosecutor concluded a Cooperation Agreement with the Government of Colombia[84] which marked the formal closure of the preliminary examination in Colombia, opened in 2004, and defined the parameters of co-operation going forward. The agreement is the first of its kind. It acknowledges that complementarity is working in Colombia and renews the commitment of the Office to Colombia's national accountability processes. In the agreement, the Office of the Prosecutor commits to continue supporting Colombia's accountability efforts within its mandate and means. The government of Colombia, in turn, commits to keeping the Office of the Prosecutor informed of the progress of the investigations and prosecutions undertaken in Colombia and will facilitate access to records and documentation upon request. The Office of the Prosecutor reserves its right, however, to reconsider its assessment of complementarity in light of any significant change in circumstances, including: "any measures that might significantly hamper the progress and/or genuineness of relevant proceedings and the enforcement of effective and proportionate penal sanctions of a retributive and restorative nature; initiatives resulting in major obstructions to the mandate and/or proper functioning of relevant jurisdictions; or any suspension or revision of the judicial scheme set forth in the peace agreement in a manner that might delay or obstruct the conduct of genuine national proceedings."[85]

The Special Jurisdiction for Peace, Colombia's transitional tribunal, was set up in 2017 to prosecute the perpetrators of crimes committed during the armed conflict between the FARC-EP guerrilla and the Colombian government. It aims to bring justice and truth to the victims, and to contribute to the reparations process, with the purpose of building a stable and lasting peace.[86] It has a very broad jurisdiction covering the entire armed conflict

---

[81] *Independent Expert Review of the International Criminal Court and the Rome Statute System Final Report* (30 September), para. 138, available online at https://asp.icc-cpi.int/sites/asp/files/asp_docs/ASP19/IER-Final-Report-ENG.pdf.

[82] *Independent Expert Review of the International Criminal Court and the Rome Statute System Final Report* (30 September), para. 138, available online at https://asp.icc-cpi.int/sites/asp/files/asp_docs/ASP19/IER-Final-Report-ENG.pdf.

[83] *Independent Expert Review of the International Criminal Court and the Rome Statute System Final Report* (30 September), para. 64, available online at https://asp.icc-cpi.int/sites/asp/files/asp_docs/ASP19/IER-Final-Report-ENG.pdf.

[84] ICC, *Cooperation Agreement Between available the Office of the Prosecutor of the International Criminal Court and the Government of Colombia* (28 October 2021), available online at https://www.icc-cpi.int/sites/default/files/itemsDocuments/20211028-OTP-COL-Cooperation-Agreement-ENG.pdf.

[85] ICC, *Cooperation Agreement Between available the Office of the Prosecutor of the International Criminal Court and the Government of Colombia* (28 October 2021), Article 6, available online at https://www.icc-cpi.int/sites/default/files/itemsDocuments/20211028-OTP-COL-Cooperation-Agreement-ENG.pdf.

[86] Jurisdicción Especial para la Paz, available online at https://www.jep.gov.co/JEP/Paginas/Jurisdiccion-Especial-para-la-Paz.aspx.

spanning over fifty years. So far, the Special Jurisdiction for Peace has opened seven cases which concern the most representative crimes allegedly committed in the Colombian conflict. Three years after its official creation, it has yet to hand down its first sentence. One of the innovative aspects of the Special Jurisdiction for Peace is that it focuses on a restorative model, rather than on punitive action, for those who acknowledge their responsibility. Heavier sanctions are reserved for those who acknowledge responsibility in the adversarial procedure. Finally, retributive sentences, typically imprisonment, are reserved for those who do not recognise responsibility and are ultimately found guilty at the end of a trial. For less serious crimes, non-punitive measures may be imposed, such as a waiver of criminal prosecution, provided they contribute to the truth and reparation of the victims. In contrast to the ICC model, dialogue between the victims and the defendants is privileged over the adversarial model of justice.[87]

IV. CONCLUSION

The year of 2021 was again a year in which complex and novel questions of law were raised before the ICC and dealt with at the appellate level, including issues relating to the Court's jurisdiction in the case of a referral by the UN Security Council, detention issues, the scope of the freedom of speech of counsel before the Court, and the interplay between the Assembly of States Parties and the judges of the Court in the matter of rule amendments. It also attested to the Court's ability to enter into cooperation agreements in the spirit of complementarity. Despite its twenty years of activity, however, the Court continues to grapple with fundamental questions of law, which are yet to be developed.

---

[87] Justice for Peace, *The Restorative Model in the Special Jurisdiction for Peace Presented in the Conference Northern Ireland and Colombia: Lessons from Peace 26th–27th April 2022*, available online at https://www.jep.gov.co/Sala-de-Prensa/Documents1/The%20Restorative%20model%20in%20the%20Special%20Jurisdiction%20for%20Peace%20%20Presented%20in%20the%20Conference%20Northern%20Ireland%20and%20Colombia-%20Lessons%20from%20Peace.pdf.

LEGAL MAXIMS: SUMMARIES AND EXTRACTS FROM SELECTED CASE LAW*

SITUATION IN THE STATE OF PALESTINE

Decision on the 'Prosecution Request Pursuant to Article 19(3) for a Ruling on the Court's Territorial Jurisdiction in Palestine', Case No. ICC-01/18, Pre-Trial Chamber I, 5 February 2021

SITUATION IN UGANDA

The Prosecutor v. Dominic Ongwen, Case No. ICC-02/04-01/15, Trial Chamber IX, Judgment, 6 May 2021

SITUATION IN THE REPUBLIC OF MALI

The Prosecutor v. Ahmad Al Faqi Al Mahdi, Decision on the Review Concerning Reduction of Sentence of Mr Ahmad Al Faqi Al Mahdi, Case No. ICC-01/12-01/15, Three Judges of the Appeals Chamber Appointed, 25 November 2021

---

* The working method chosen for the formulation of legal maxims is explained *supra* 'Outline of the Parts', at page xv.

Legal Maxims: Summaries and Extracts from Selected Case Law In: *The Global Community Yearbook of International Law and Jurisprudence 2022*. Edited by: Giuliana Ziccardi Capaldo, Oxford University Press. © Oxford University Press 2023.
DOI: 10.1093/oso/9780197752265.003.0022

IV.2.1

SITUATION IN THE STATE OF PALESTINE

IV.2.1.1

Decision on the 'Prosecution Request Pursuant to Article 19(3) for a Ruling on the Court's Territorial Jurisdiction in Palestine', **Case No. ICC-01/18, Pre-Trial Chamber I, 5 February 2021***

Contents**

I. PROCEDURAL BACKGROUND

II. MERITS

   A. THE FIRST ISSUE

   B. THE SECOND ISSUE

   C. THE OSLO ACCORDS

III. FINDINGS AND CONCLUSIONS

I.

II.2.0   INSTITUTION AND COURSE OF PROCEEDINGS
          See also: II.7.1005

"[1] On 1 January 2015, the State of Palestine ('Palestine') lodged a declaration under article 12(3) of the Rome Statute (the 'Rome Statute' or the 'Statute'), thereby accepting the jurisdiction of the Court over alleged crimes 'committed in the occupied Palestinian territory, including East Jerusalem [...]. [2] On 2 January 2015, Palestine deposited its instrument of accession to the Statute with the Secretary-General of the United Nations (the 'United Nations Secretary-General') pursuant to article 125(2) of the Statute. [3] On 22 May 2018, Palestine referred the *Situation in the State of Palestine* to the Prosecutor pursuant to articles 13(a) and 14 of the Statute. [7] On 22 January 2020, the Chamber received the 'Prosecution request pursuant to article 19(3) for a ruling on the Court's territorial jurisdiction in Palestine' (the 'Prosecutor's Request'). [8] On 28 January 2020, the Chamber issued the 'Order setting the procedure and the schedule for the submission of observations'[...]."

[Paras. 1, 2, 3, 7, 8]

---

* Summaries prepared by Anna Buono, Ph.D. in International Law and National Law in International Matters, University of Salerno - Italy, Lawyer. Text of judgment available online at the Court's Web site <http://www.icc-cpi.int>. Original: English (authoritative) and French. Footnotes appearing in the original text have been omitted.

** This is not a faithful reproduction of the Table of Contents of the Judgment.

II.

II.7.1004 ICC JURISDICTION AND ADMISSIBILITY
    See also: II.7.1005

"[22] The Prosecutor is of the view 'that the Court's territorial jurisdiction extends to the Palestinian territory occupied by Israel during the Six-Day War in June 1967, namely the West Bank, including East Jerusalem, and Gaza'. However, the Prosecutor is 'mindful of the unique history and circumstances of the Occupied Palestinian Territory' and the fact that the question of Palestine's statehood under international law does not appear to have been definitively resolved. [...] [24] [...] [T]he Prosecutor submits that the Chamber could likewise conclude—for the strict purposes of the Statute only—that Palestine is a State under relevant principles and rules of international law'.[...]"

[Paras. 22, 24]

II.7.1005 LAW APPLIED BY ICC
    See also: II.7.1004

"[82] A Pre-Trial Chamber is mandated to address questions of jurisdiction in the context of a case pursuant to a number of legal bases, namely articles 19(1), 19(2) and 58(1)(a) of the Statute. In light of these provisions, article 19(3) of the Statute would have no practical effect if it would apply solely in the context of a case. Conversely, article 19(3) of the Statute would have a distinct effect if it were understood to apply outside of a case. Specifically, it would permit the Prosecutor to request a ruling on a question of jurisdiction for the purposes of determining the scope of the investigation to be conducted following a referral by a State Party, as opposed to unnecessarily delaying judicial scrutiny of matters of jurisdiction until an application under article 58 of the Statute is submitted."

[Para. 82]

A.

I.1.16 TREATY INTERPRETATION
    See also: II.7.1004; II.7.1005

"[91] [With regard to the First Issue arising from the Prosecutor's Request,] [t]he Chamber must [...] assess whether Palestine can be considered 'the State on the territory of which the conduct in question occurred' within the meaning of article 12(2)(a) of the Statute. To answer this question, the Chamber shall, pursuant to article 31(1) of the Vienna Convention, interpret article 12(2)(a) in good faith in accordance with the ordinary meaning to be given to its terms in their context and in the light of the object and purpose of the Statute. [94] The Chamber notes that according to article 31(2) of the Vienna Convention, 'the context for the purpose of the interpretation of a treaty shall comprise [...] the text, including its preamble and annexes'. In this regard, the Chamber wishes to clarify that it understands this provision as referring both to the text of article 12 of the Statute and to the text of other provisions of the Statute. Having regard to the more general context of the Statute, an assessment as to whether the preconditions to the exercise of the Court's jurisdiction under article 12(2) of the Statute have been fulfilled must be conducted in keeping with the outcome of the accession procedure pursuant to articles 125(3) and 126(2) of the Statute, subject to the settlement of a dispute regarding the accession of an entity by the Assembly of States Parties under article 119(2) of the Statute."

[Paras. 91, 94]

II.7.1005   LAW APPLIED BY ICC
          See also: II.7.1004

"**[97]** With respect to the Rome Statute, article 125(3) of the Statute provides that the 'Statute shall be open to accession by all States' and neither this provision nor any other provision in the Court's legal texts imposes additional criteria on, or otherwise qualifies, the accession to the Statute. Therefore, a determination by the United Nations General Assembly renders an entity capable to accede to the Statute pursuant to article 125 of the Statute and the depositary notification by the United Nations Secretary-General merely gives effect to the United Nations General Assembly's determination. **[98]** [...] [A]s a result, Palestine would be able to become party to any treaties that are open to 'any State' or 'all States' deposited with the Secretary-General'. [...] **[102]** Consequently, regardless of Palestine's status under general international law, its accession to the Statute followed the correct and ordinary procedure, as provided under article 125(3) of the Statute. In this respect, in the view of the Chamber, once the conditions for accession pursuant to article 125 of the Statute have been fulfilled, the effect of articles 12(1), 125(3) and 126(2) of the Statute, taken together, is that the Statute automatically enters into force for a new State Party.[...][O]n the basis of article 124 of the Statute, the only exemption to the jurisdiction of the Court relates to a particular category of crimes, namely war crimes, for a limited period of time, which entails that the Statute is automatically activated in respect of all other matters.[...]"

[Paras. 97, 98, 102]

I.1.16   TREATY INTERPRETATION
       See also: II.7.1004; II.7.1005

"**[105]** Moreover, the Court, in line with other international tribunals, has referred multiple times to the principle of effectiveness in rejecting any interpretation that would nullify or render inoperative a provision of the Statute. In the case of *The Prosecutor v. Jean-Pierre Bemba Gombo*, Pre-Trial Chamber III noted that: [A] teleological interpretation which is mirrored in the principle of effectiveness and based on the object and purpose of a treaty means that the provisions of the treaty are to be 'interpreted so as to give it its full meaning and to enable the system [...] to attain its appropriate effects', while preventing any restrictions of interpretation that would render the provisions of the treaty 'inoperative'. **[106]** Therefore, the reference to '[t]he State on the territory of which the conduct in question occurred' in article 12(2)(a) of the Statute cannot be taken to mean a State fulfilling the criteria for statehood under general international law. Such a construction would exceed the object and purpose of the Statute [...]. Moreover, this interpretation would also have the effect of rendering most of the provisions of the Statute, including article 12(1), inoperative for Palestine."

[Paras. 105, 106]

II.7.1004 ICC JURISDICTION AND ADMISSIBILITY
See also: II.7.1005

"[59] [...] [U]nlike the International Court of Justice, the Court cannot rule on inter-states disputes as it does not have jurisdiction over States, but exercises its jurisdiction solely over natural persons. [...] [108] [In particular,] [...] [t]he Court is not constitutionally competent to determine matters of statehood that would bind the international community. In addition, such a determination is not required for the specific purposes of the present proceedings or the general exercise of the Court's mandate. [...]"

[Paras. 59, 108]

B.

II.7.1004 ICC JURISDICTION AND ADMISSIBILITY
See also: II.7.1005

"[115] [In light of the foregoing, and with regard to the Second Issue arising from the Prosecutor's Request,] [...] the Chamber wishes to reiterate that disputed borders have never prevented a State from becoming a State Party to the Statute and, as such, cannot prevent the Court from exercising its jurisdiction. [116] [In addition], [...] the Chamber notes that in according 'non-member observer State status in the United Nations' to Palestine in Resolution 67/19, the United Nations General Assembly '[reaffirmed] the right of the Palestinian people to self-determination and to independence in their State of Palestine *on the Palestinian territory occupied since 1967'*. [118] On this basis, the Chamber finds that the Court's territorial jurisdiction in the *Situation in Palestine* extends to the territories occupied by Israel since 1967, namely Gaza and the West Bank, including East Jerusalem."

[Paras. 115, 116, 118]

II.7.1005 LAW APPLIED BY ICC
See also: I.1.16; II.7.1004

"[120] The right to self-determination is set forth in the Charter of the United Nations, the International Covenant on Civil and Political Rights, and the Declaration on Principles of International Law concerning Friendly Relations and Co-operation among States in accordance with the Charter of the United Nations.[...] [122] Therefore, in the view of the Chamber, the right to self-determination amounts to an 'internationally recognized human [right]' within the meaning of article 21(3) of the Statute. The Chamber notes that the United Nations General Assembly and the International Court of Justice have affirmed that this right finds application in relation to the Occupied Palestinian Territory. [123] The Chamber considers that, in light of the broad remit of the Appeals Chamber's determination, it must also ensure that its interpretation of article 12(2)(a) of the Statute, in conjunction with articles 125(3) and 126(2) of the Statute, is consistent with internationally recognised human rights. More specifically, the Chamber is of the view that the aforementioned territorial parameters of the Prosecutor's investigation pursuant to articles 13(a), 14 and 53(1) of the Statute implicate the right to self-determination. Accordingly, it is the view of the Chamber that the above conclusion – namely that the Court's territorial jurisdiction in the *Situation in Palestine* extends to the territories occupied by Israel since 1967 on the basis of the relevant indications arising from Palestine's accession to the Statute – is consistent with the right to self-determination."

[**Paras. 120, 122, 123**]

C.

II.7.1004   ICC JURISDICTION AND ADMISSIBILITY
            See also: I.1.16; II.7.1005

"[**125**] The Chamber notes the Oslo process and the agreements arising from this process (the 'Oslo Agreements') [...]. Article I(1)(a) of Annex IV to this agreement, the 'Protocol Concerning Legal Affairs', [...] provides that '[t]he criminal jurisdiction of the [Palestinian Interim Self-Government Authority] covers all offenses committed by *Palestinians and/or non-Israelis* in the Territory, subject to the provisions of this article. For the purposes of this Annex, "Territory" means West Bank territory *except for Area C* [the Oslo Accords divided the Palestinian West Bank into three zones: Area A, where the Palestinian Authority (PA) administers civil and security matters; Area B, where the PA administers only civil matters; and Area C where Israel maintains full control] which, except for the Settlements and the military locations, will be gradually transferred to the Palestinian side in accordance with this Agreement, and Gaza Strip territory except for the Settlements and the Military Installation Area'. [**128**] In any event, the Chamber recalls that the Appeals Chamber has recently held in its judgment in relation to the *Situation in the Islamic Republic of Afghanistan* that: [a]rguments were also advanced during the hearing that certain agreements entered into between the United States and Afghanistan affect the jurisdiction of the Court and should be a factor in assessing the authorisation of the investigation. The Appeals Chamber is of the view that the effect of these agreements is not a matter for consideration in relation to the authorisation of an investigation under the statutory scheme.[...] [**129**] Similarly, the Chamber finds that the arguments regarding the Oslo Agreements in the context of the present proceedings are not pertinent to the resolution of the issue under consideration, namely the scope of the Court's territorial jurisdiction in Palestine.[...] As a consequence, the Chamber will not address these arguments."

[**Paras. 125, 128, 129**]

II.7.1005   LAW APPLIED BY ICC
            See also: I.1.16; II.7.1004

"[**130**] As a final matter, the Chamber finds it appropriate to underline that its conclusions in this decision are limited to defining the territorial parameters of the Prosecutor's investigation in accordance with the Statute.[...] In particular, by ruling on the territorial scope of its jurisdiction, the Court is neither adjudicating a border dispute under international law nor prejudging the question of any future borders. [**131**] It is further opportune to emphasise that the Chamber's conclusions pertain to the current stage of the proceedings, namely the initiation of an investigation by the Prosecutor pursuant to articles 13(a), 14 and 53(1) of the Statute. When the Prosecutor submits an application for the issuance of a warrant of arrest or summons to appear under article 58 of the Statute, or if a State or a suspect submits a challenge under article 19(2) of the Statute, the Chamber will be in a position to examine further questions of jurisdiction which may arise at that point in time."

[Paras. 130, 131]

III.

II.7.1008   ICC JUDGMENT/DECISION

"FOR THESE REASONS, THE CHAMBER HEREBY

FINDS that Palestine is a State Party to the Statute;

   FINDS, by majority, Judge Kovács dissenting, that, as a consequence, Palestine qualifies as '[t]he State on the territory of which the conduct in question occurred' for the purposes of article 12(2)(a) of the Statute; and

   FINDS, by majority, Judge Kovács dissenting, that the Court's territorial jurisdiction in the *Situation in Palestine* extends to the territories occupied by Israel since 1967, namely Gaza and the West Bank, including East Jerusalem."

IV.2.2

SITUATION IN UGANDA

IV.2.2.1

The Prosecutor v. Dominic Ongwen, Case No. ICC-02/04-01/15, Trial Chamber IX, Judgment, 6 May 2021*

Contents**

I.

II.2.0   INSTITUTION AND COURSE OF PROCEEDINGS

             See also: I.12.22; I.12.24; II.2.041; II.7.1005

"[**1**] On 4 February 2021, the Chamber delivered its judgment pursuant to Article 74 of the Statute, convicting Dominic Ongwen of a total of 61 crimes comprising crimes against humanity and war crimes. [**2**] On the same day, the Chamber issued the 'Decision scheduling a hearing on sentence and setting the related procedural calendar', whereby it: (i) decided to hold a hearing under Article 76(2) of the Statute [...] to hear further submissions and any additional evidence relevant to the appropriate sentence to be imposed on Dominic Ongwen [...]. [**4**] On 26 February 2021, the Defence submitted a number of items of evidence, requested the introduction of seven witness statements under Rule 68(2)(b) or (3) of the Rules, and proposed three witnesses for live testimony before the Chamber.[...] [**5**] On 19 March 2021, the Chamber issued a decision whereby it recognised as submitted the documentary evidence presented by the Defence, and allowed the introduction under Rule 68(2)(b) of the Rules of all ten witnesses subject to the Defence request [...]. [**6**] On 1 April 2021, the Prosecution, the legal representatives of the participating victims (jointly), and the Defence filed their written submissions [...]. [**7**] On 14 and 15 April 2021, the Chamber held a hearing on sentence under Article 76(2) of the Statute [...]."

[Paras. 1, 2, 4, 5, 6, 7]

  * Summaries prepared by Anna Buono, Ph.D. in International Law and National Law in International Matters, University of Salerno - Italy, Lawyer. Text of judgment available online at the Court's Web site <http://www.icc-cpi.int>. Original: English (authoritative) and French. Footnotes appearing in the original text have been omitted.

** This is not a faithful reproduction of the Table of Contents of the Judgment.

II.

II.7.1005   LAW APPLIED BY ICC
            See also: II.7.1007

"[**61**] [...] [T]he Chamber will first address [...] factors and circumstances generally applicable to all crimes, before turning to more specific considerations. [**62**] The Chamber recalls that in accordance with Article 78(1) of the Statute [,] the Court, in determining the sentence, shall take into account, *inter alia*, 'the individual circumstances of the convicted person'. [...] The 'individual circumstances of the convicted person' are then also referred to in Article 77(1)(b) of the Statute and Rule 145(3) of the Rules as an aspect of relevance for consideration of penalty of life imprisonment as an individual sentence for any specific crime (as well as, by virtue of Article 78(3) of the Statute, as a joint sentence in case of conviction of more than one crime). [**63**] This set of circumstances [...] include [the ones] purported by the Defence to act in mitigation of the sentence to be imposed on Dominic Ongwen, concerning his childhood and, more generally, his personal background, his current family circumstances and his alleged 'good character'. [...] [**64**] The same applies also for certain other circumstances that, despite in principle being [...] crime-specific, have been raised by the parties as applicable to all crimes in the present case. [...] Following the relevant submissions of the parties, this is the case for: (i) the purported mitigating circumstances of circumstances falling short of constituting grounds excluding criminal responsibility under Rule 145(2)(a)(i), alleged by the Defence; and (ii) the purported aggravating circumstance of 'abuse of power or official capacity' under Rule 145(2)(b)(ii) of the Rules, alleged by the legal representatives of the victims. Also these circumstances/factors, if established, would need to be recalled and 'balanced' with the other relevant ones in the determination of the individual sentence for each crime."

[**Paras. 61, 62, 63, 64**]

III.

I.12.0   INDIVIDUAL CRIMINAL RESPONSIBILITY
            See also: I.12.22; I.12.24

"[**69**][...] As explained in the Trial Judgment, [Ongwen] committed the relevant crimes when he was a fully responsible adult.[...] [**87**] [...][T]he Chamber deems that Dominic Ongwen's personal history and circumstances of his upbringing, since his young age, in the LRA [Lord's Resistance Army] – in particular his abduction as a child, the interruption of his education, the killing of his parents, his socialisation in the extremely violent environment of the LRA – must be given a certain weight in the determination of the length of each individual sentence. The present considerations must therefore be read as incorporated into the individual assessments conducted below concerning each crime. [**86**] [T]here exists no basis to conclude that Dominic Ongwen was in any way forced to commit the crimes of which he was found guilty. As explained in the Trial Judgment, nothing in the evidence provides any indication to this effect. [...] [Ongwen] also chose not to leave the bush or escape from the LRA when he had the possibility to do so, contrary to other high ranking commanders who did leave."

[**Paras. 69, 87, 86**]

II.7.1005   LAW APPLIED BY ICC
See also: I.12.0; I.12.22; I.12.24

"[**92**] [...] The question of substantially diminished mental capacity, like the question of mental disease and defect under Article 31(1)(a) of the Statute, must be determined by reference to the time of the relevant conduct. [...] [**103**] [...] [T]he management of the convicted person's health is primarily a matter for the enforcement of the imposed sentence, rather than a factor bearing upon the determination of its length. [...] [**108**] Duress, when falling short of constituting a ground for exclusion of criminal responsibility under Article 31(1)(d) of the Statute, can still be a mitigating circumstance as provided for by Rule 145(2)(a)(i) of the Rules. [...]"

[**Paras. 92, 103, 108**]

I.12.0   INDIVIDUAL CRIMINAL RESPONSIBILITY
See also: I.12.07; I.12.22; I.12.24

"[**93**] [...] The Chamber, also following expert evidence, [...] considered that many of the actions undertaken by Dominic Ongwen [...] involved careful planning of complex operations, which is incompatible with a mental disorder. [**100**] [...] The evidence indicates that he was in full possession of his mental faculties and exercised his role as commander effectively. [...] Accordingly, the Chamber finds that the mitigating circumstance of substantially diminished mental capacity does not apply in the present case. [**110**] [...] [T]he Chamber finds that Dominic Ongwen was not in a situation of complete subordination [...], but frequently acted independently and even contested orders received [.] [...] Dominic Ongwen also had a realistic possibility of leaving the LRA, which he did not pursue. Rather, he rose in rank and position, including during the period of the charges. [...] [**111**] Based on a thorough analysis of evidence, duress was excluded in the present case as the conduct constituting the crimes Dominic Ongwen was convicted of was not caused by a threat of death or serious bodily harm to [...] Ongwen or another person. Accordingly, on the same basis, the Chamber also concludes that duress is not applicable in the present case as a mitigating circumstance [...]."

[**Paras. 93, 100, 110, 111**]

IV.

II.7.1005   LAW APPLIED BY ICC
See also: I.12.0; I.12.22; I.12.24

"[**134**] [...] Indeed, there was no special lawful relationship between Dominic Ongwen and his victims which he would have abused for the commission of the crimes, [so] the Chamber is of the view that the aggravating circumstance under Rule 145(2)(b)(ii) of the Rules is not established in the present case. [**135**] As recalled above, Article 78 of the Statute provides that, in determining the sentence, the Court, in addition to the 'individual circumstances' of the convicted person, shall also take into account 'the gravity of the crime', including the gravity of the culpable conduct. Rule 145(1)(b) of the Rules similarly mandates the Court to consider, and balance with any other relevant factors, 'the circumstances [...] of the crime'. Moreover, Rule 145(1)(c) provides that the Court shall, in addition, give consideration, *inter alia*, to: (i) the extent of the damage caused, in particular the harm caused to the victims and their families, the nature of the unlawful behaviour and the means employed to execute the crime; (ii) the degree of participation of the convicted person; (iii) the degree of intent; and (iv) the circumstances of manner, time and location. Finally, Rule 145(2)(b) includes amongst the aggravating circumstances the commission of the crime: (i) where the victim is particularly defenceless; (ii) with particular cruelty or where there were multiple victims; (iii) for any motive involving discrimination. The Chamber reiterates in this regard that, as emphasised by the Appeals Chamber, some of these factors are not neatly distinguishable and may reasonably be considered under more than one category, provided that the same factor is not relied more than once. [136] In addition, as concerns matters related to 'double-counting', the two-step sentencing process prescribed under Article 78(3) of the Statute must be emphasised again.[...]"

[Paras. 134, 135, 136]

II.7.1005   LAW APPLIED BY ICC
             See also: I.12.0; I.12.22; I.12.24

"[180] [...] The Chamber found that Dominic Ongwen committed the [...] crimes [...] 'jointly with' and 'through' others [as an indirect perpetrator] within the meaning of Article 25(3)(a) of the Statute [in the context of the attack carried out by LRA fighters on: Pajule IDP camp on 10 October 2003; Odek IDP camp on 29 April 2004; Lukodi IDP camp on or about 19 May 2004 and Abok IDP camp on or about 8 June 2004][...]. [284] Dominic Ongwen has been convicted of [...] crimes which he committed – 'as an individual' within the meaning of Article 25(3)(a) of the Statute – against seven women who had been 'distributed' to him and placed into his household [...]."

[Paras. 180, 284]

I.12.0   INDIVIDUAL CRIMINAL RESPONSIBILITY
             See also: I.12.22; I.12.24

"[377] [...] [T]here exist a number of instances of (partial) overlap in the underlying conduct between different crimes – which are thus qualified by additional conduct and/ or different consequence(s) – committed by Dominic Ongwen in the context of each of the attacks on Pajule, Odek, Lukodi and Abok IDP camps. [...] In addition, it is noted in this regard that, logically, instances of factual overlap in underlying conduct and/or consequence between different crimes, in turn, result in corresponding (partial) overlap in the related factors informing the gravity of the individual crimes concerned and their specific aggravating circumstances. [378] Still further, partial overlap in Dominic Ongwen's relevant criminal conduct exists also with respect to the sexual and gender-based crimes directly committed by Dominic Ongwen against four of his forced so-called 'wives'.[...] [379] [...] However, the Chamber does not consider any such overlap – considered individually or in combination – to have a significant bearing in the determination of the joint sentence in the present case, given the strikingly large number of distinct convictions, holding entirely different factual basis, which have been pronounced by the Chamber. [380] [...] Rather, they are completely separate crimes independent from each other. [...] [363] In [...] [many cases] the Chamber finds the presence of the aggravating circumstance [...] under [Article] 145(2)(b) of the Rules, which in this case reached the level of the utmost gravity [: multiple victims; victim particularly defenceless; commission with particular cruelty and/or for motives involving discrimination].[...]"

[Paras. 377, 378, 379, 380, 363]

II.7.1005   LAW APPLIED BY ICC
See also: I.12.0; I.12.22; I.12.24

"[**384**] [...] More than 130 people were killed during the attacks on IDP camps [...]. Hundreds of civilians were abducted, tortured and enslaved during those same attacks. A large number of children were abducted, integrated into the Sinia brigade and used actively to participate in the hostilities. In addition to the seven women and girls who were forced to be Dominic Ongwen's so-called 'wives' and servants, there were over one hundred abducted women and girls in the Sinia brigade at the relevant time. Many of these victims – who were targeted for motives involving discrimination – were particularly defenceless. Particularly young boys and young girls were abducted and forced to be child soldiers or domestic servants. During the attacks, individuals who had been abducted, including children, elderly people and pregnant women, were then killed and tortured. [**393**] [...] [S]uch heterogeneous crimes targeted different types of individuals, for different reasons and in separate contexts [...] and that these crimes offended distinct protected interests of great importance: from the right to life to the right to personal liberty, from the right to sexual integrity to the right to personal property, from the right not to be subjected to cruel or degrading treatment to the right to consensually form a family. [...]"

[**Paras. 384, 393**]

V.

II.7.1007   PENALTIES IMPOSED BY THE ICC
See also: II.7.1005

"[**374**] After having determined the individual sentence for each of the crimes for which Dominic Ongwen was convicted, the Chamber, in accordance with Article 78(3) of the Statute, shall determine the joint sentence, 'specifying the total period of imprisonment'. The same provision requires that such total period 'shall be no less than the highest individual sentence pronounced' – which in this case is 20 years of imprisonment – but 'shall not exceed 30 years imprisonment or a sentence of life imprisonment in conformity with article 77, paragraph 1 (b)'. [**383**] [...] The Chamber observes that, in accordance with Article 78(3) of the Statute, read in conjunction with Article 77(1)(b) of the Statute, a sentence of life imprisonment may be imposed 'when justified by the extreme gravity of the crime[s] and the individual circumstances of the convicted person', which, as specified in turn by Rule 145(3) of the Rules, are 'evidenced by the existence of one or more aggravating circumstances'."

[**Paras. 374, 383**]

I.12.0   INDIVIDUAL CRIMINAL RESPONSIBILITY
See also: I.12.22; I.12.24

"[**388**][...] The Chamber was greatly impressed by the account given by Dominic Ongwen at the hearing on sentence about the events to which he was subjected upon his abduction when he was only 9 years old [...] [**394**] [...] [but] the Chamber cannot overlook the absence, in Dominic Ongwen's submissions during the hearing on sentence, of any expression of empathy for the numerous victims of his crimes – and even less of any genuine remorse – supplanted by a lucid, constant focus on himself and his own suffering eclipsing that of anyone else. [**390**] [...] [However, considering] the undeniable value of foreseeing today a more concrete prospect of re-insertion into society [...] [**391**] [...]

the Chamber has decided not to sentence Dominic Ongwen to the – exceptional – penalty of life imprisonment."

[Paras. 388, 394, 390, 391]

II.7.1005   LAW APPLIED BY ICC
         See also: I.12.0; II.7.1007

"**[396]** […] The Chamber also recalls in this respect that Article 110 of the Statute, read in conjunction with and Rules 223 and 224 of the Rules, foresees the possibility that, upon specific review and under certain criteria, the sentence be reduced when the sentenced person has served two thirds of it. **[398]** […] [Moreover,] in accordance with article 78(2) of the Statute '[i]n imposing a sentence of imprisonment, the Court shall deduct the time, if any, previously spent in detention in accordance with an order of the Court.'[…] **[401]** Accordingly, the Chamber clarifies that […][t]he time [Ongwen] spent in detention between 16 January 2015 and the date of the present decision shall therefore be deducted from the term of imprisonment imposed on him by the Chamber."

[Paras. 396, 398, 401]

VI.

II.7.1008   ICC JUDGMENT/DECISION

"FOR THE FOREGOING REASONS, THE CHAMBER

a) PRONOUNCES the following sentences for each of the crimes committed by Dominic Ongwen:
   • For the war crime of attack against the civilian population as such committed on 10 October 2003, at or near Pajule IDP camp (Count 1) a term of 14 years of imprisonment;
   • For the crime against humanity of murder committed on 10 October 2003, at or near Pajule IDP camp (Count 2) a term of 20 years of imprisonment;
   • For the war crime of murder committed on 10 October 2003, at or near Pajule IDP camp (Count 3) a term of 20 years of imprisonment;
   • For the crime against humanity of torture committed on 10 October 2003, at or near Pajule IDP camp (Count 4) a term of 14 years of imprisonment;
   • For the war crime of torture committed on 10 October 2003, at or near Pajule IDP camp (Count 5) a term of 14 years of imprisonment;
   • For the crime against humanity of enslavement committed on 10 October 2003, at or near Pajule IDP camp (Count 8) a term of 14 years of imprisonment;
   • For the war crime of pillaging committed on 10 October 2003, at or near Pajule IDP camp (Count 9) a term of 8 years of imprisonment;
   • For the crime against humanity of persecution committed on 10 October 2003 at or near Pajule IDP camp (Count 10) a term of 20 years of imprisonment;
   • For the war crime of attack against the civilian population as such committed on 29 April 2004, at or near Odek IDP camp (Count 11) a term of 14 years of imprisonment;
   • For the crime against humanity of murder committed on 29 April 2004, at or near Odek IDP camp (Count 12) a term of 20 years of imprisonment;
   • For the war crime of murder committed on 29 April 2004, at or near Odek IDP camp (Count 13) a term of 20 years of imprisonment;

- For the crime against humanity of attempted murder committed on 29 April 2004, at or near Odek IDP camp (Count 14) a term of 14 years of imprisonment;
- For the war crime of attempted murder committed on 29 April 2004, at or near Odek IDP camp (Count 15) a term of 14 years of imprisonment;
- For the crime against humanity of torture committed on 29 April 2004, at or near Odek IDP camp (Count 16) a term of 14 years of imprisonment;
- For the war crime of torture committed on 29 April 2004, at or near Odek IDP camp (Count 17) a term of 14 years of imprisonment;
- For the crime against humanity of enslavement committed on 29 April 2004, at or near Odek IDP camp (Count 20) a term of 14 years of imprisonment;
- For the war crime of pillaging committed on 29 April 2004, at or near Odek IDP camp (Count 21) a term of 8 years of imprisonment;
- For the war crime of outrages upon personal dignity committed on 29 April 2004, at or near Odek IDP camp (Count 22) a term of 14 years of imprisonment;
- For the crime against humanity of persecution committed on 29 April 2004, at or near Odek IDP camp (Count 23) a term of 20 years of imprisonment;
- For of the war crime of attack against the civilian population as such committed on or about 19 May 2004, at or near Lukodi IDP camp (Count 24) a term of 14 years of imprisonment;
- For the crime against humanity of murder committed on or about 19 May 2004, at or near Lukodi IDP camp (Count 25) a term of 20 years of imprisonment;
- For the war crime of murder committed on or about 19 May 2004, at or near Lukodi IDP camp (Count 26) a term of 20 years of imprisonment;
- For the crime against humanity of attempted murder committed on or about 19 May 2004, at or near Lukodi IDP camp (Count 27) a term of 14 years of imprisonment;
- For the war crime of attempted murder committed on or about 19 May 2004, at or near Lukodi IDP Camp (Count 28) a term of 14 years of imprisonment;
- For the crime against humanity of torture committed on or about 19 May 2004, at or near Lukodi IDP Camp (Count 29) a term of 14 years of imprisonment;
- For the war crime of torture committed on or about 19 May 2004, at or near Lukodi IDP Camp (Count 30) a term of 14 years of imprisonment;
- For the crime against humanity of enslavement committed on or about 19 May 2004, at or near Lukodi IDP Camp (Count 33) a term of 14 years of imprisonment;
- For the war crime of pillaging committed on or about 19 May 2004, at or near Lukodi IDP Camp (Count 34) a term of 8 years of imprisonment;
- For the war crime of destruction of property committed on or about 19 May 2004, at or near Lukodi IDP Camp (Count 35) a term of 8 years of imprisonment;
- For the crime against humanity of persecution committed on or about 19 May 2004, at or near Lukodi IDP camp (Count 36) a term of 20 years of imprisonment;
- For the war crime of attack against the civilian population as such committed on 8 June 2004, at or near Abok IDP camp (Count 37) a term of 14 years of imprisonment;
- For the crime against humanity of murder committed on 8 June 2004, at or near Abok IDP camp (Count 38) a term of 20 years of imprisonment;
- For the war crime of murder committed on 8 June 2004, at or near Abok IDP camp (Count 39) a term of 20 years of imprisonment;
- For the crime against humanity of attempted murder committed on 8 June 2004, at or near Abok IDP camp (Count 40) a term of 14 years of imprisonment;

- For the war crime of attempted murder committed on 8 June 2004, at or near Abok IDP camp (Count 41) a term of 14 years of imprisonment;
- For the crime against humanity of torture committed on 8 June 2004, at or near Abok IDP camp (Count 42) a term of 14 years of imprisonment;
- For the war crime of torture committed on 8 June 2004, at or near Abok IDP camp (Count 43) a term of 14 years of imprisonment;
- For the crime against humanity of enslavement committed on 8 June 2004, at or near Abok IDP camp (Count 46) a term of 14 years of imprisonment;
- For the war crime of pillaging committed on 8 June 2004, at or near Abok IDP camp (Count 47) a term of 8 years of imprisonment;
- For the war crime of destruction of property committed on 8 June 2004, at or near Abok IDP camp (Count 48) a term of 8 years of imprisonment;
- For the crime against humanity of persecution committed on 8 June 2004 at or near Abok IDP camp (Count 49) a term of 20 years of imprisonment;
- For the crime against humanity of forced marriage as another inhumane act of P-0099, P-0101, P-0214, P-0226 and P-0227 (Count 50) a term of 20 years of imprisonment;
- For the crime against humanity of torture of P-0101, P-0214, P-0226 and P-0227 (Count 51) a term of 20 years of imprisonment;
- For the war crime of torture of P-0101, P-0214, P-0226 and P-0227 (Count 52) a term of 20 years of imprisonment;
- For the crime against humanity of rape of P-0101, P-0214, P-0226 and P-0227 (Count 53) a term of 20 years of imprisonment;
- For the war crime of rape of P-0101, P-0214, P-0226 and P-0227 (Count 54) a term of 20 years of imprisonment;
- For the crime against humanity of sexual slavery of P-0101, P-0214, P-0226 and P-0227 (Count 55) a term of 20 years of imprisonment;
- For the war crime of sexual slavery of P-0101, P-0214, P-0226, and P-0227 (Count 56) a term of 20 years of imprisonment;
- For the crime against humanity of enslavement of P-0099, P-0235 and P-0236 (Count 57) a term of 20 years of imprisonment;
- For the crime against humanity of forced pregnancy of P-0101 and P-0214 (Count 58) a term of 20 years of imprisonment;
- For the war crime of forced pregnancy of P-0101 and P-0214 (Count 59) a term of 20 years of imprisonment;
- For the war crime of outrages upon personal dignity of P-0226 and P-0235 (Count 60) a term of 14 years of imprisonment;
- For the crime against humanity of forced marriage as another inhumane act, from at least 1 July 2002 until 31 December 2005 (Count 61) a term of 20 years of imprisonment;
- For the crime against humanity of torture, from at least 1 July 2002 until 31 December 2005 (Count 62) a term of 20 years of imprisonment;
- For the war crime of torture, from at least 1 July 2002 until 31 December 2005 (Count 63) a term of 20 years of imprisonment;
- For the crime against humanity of rape, from at least 1 July 2002 until 31 December 2005 (Count 64) a term of 20 years of imprisonment;
- For the war crime of rape, from at least 1 July 2002 until 31 December 2005 (Count 65) a term of 20 years of imprisonment;
- For the crime against humanity of sexual slavery, from at least 1 July 2002 until 31 December 2005 (Count 66) a term of 20 years of imprisonment;

- For the war crime of sexual slavery, from at least 1 July 2002 until 31 December 2005 (Count 67) a term of 20 years of imprisonment;
  - For the crime against humanity of enslavement, from at least 1 July 2002 until 31 December 2005 (Count 68) a term of 20 years of imprisonment;
  - For the war crime of conscripting children under the age of 15 into an armed group and using them to participate actively in hostilities, between 1 July 2002 and 31 December 2005 in Northern Uganda (Counts 69 and 70) a term of 20 years of imprisonment.

b) BY MAJORITY, SENTENCES Dominic Ongwen to a total period of imprisonment of 25 years as a joint sentence;

c) ORDERS that the time between 4 January 2015 and 6 May 2021 be deducted from the total period of imprisonment."

IV.2.3

SITUATION IN THE REPUBLIC OF MALI

IV.2.3.1

The Prosecutor v. Ahmad Al Faqi Al Mahdi, Decision on the Review Concerning Reduction of Sentence of Mr Ahmad Al Faqi Al Mahdi, **Case No. ICC-01/12-01/15, Three Judges of the Appeals Chamber Appointed, 25 November 2021***

Contents**

I.

II.2.0   INSTITUTION AND COURSE OF PROCEEDINGS
       See also: I.12.22; I.12.341; II.5.1

"[**1**] On 27 September 2016, Trial Chamber VIII (hereinafter: "Trial Chamber") convicted Mr Al Mahdi as a co-perpetrator under article 25(3)(a) of the Statute for the war crime under article 8(2)(e)(iv) of the Statute of intentionally directing attacks against 10 buildings of a religious and historical character in Timbuktu [...].The Trial Chamber sentenced Mr Al Mahdi to a period of nine years of imprisonment [and] considered that Mr Al Mahdi was entitled, pursuant to article 78(2) of the Statute, "to have deducted from his sentence the time he has spent in detention [...]. [**2**] On 28 June 2021, the Appeals Chamber, noting that on 18 September 2021, Mr Al Mahdi will have served two thirds of the sentence

---

* Summaries prepared by Anna Buono, Ph.D. in International Law and National Law in International Matters, University of Salerno - Italy, Lawyer. Text of judgment available online at the Court's Web site <http://www.icc-cpi.int>. Original: English (authoritative) and French. Footnotes appearing in the original text have been omitted.

** This is not a faithful reproduction of the Table of Contents of the Judgment.

imposed on him, appointed Judges Solomy Balungi Bossa, Marc Perrin de Brichambaut and Gocha Lordkipanidze (hereinafter: "Panel"), for the purpose of conducting the review concerning the reduction of Mr Al Mahdi's sentence. [7] On 13 September 2021, the Prosecutor, Mr Al Mahdi and the Legal Representative of Victims filed their submissions. [9] On 12 October 2021, the Sentence Review Hearing was held. [...]"

[**Paras. 1, 2, 7, 9**]

II.7.1005   LAW APPLIED BY ICC
              See also: II.5.4; II.7.1007

"[**11**] Article 110 [...] of the Statute provides in relevant part that "[w]hen the person has served two thirds of the sentence, [...] [**12**] [...] the Court may reduce the sentence if it finds that one or more of the following factors are present:

(a) The early and continuous willingness of the person to cooperate with the Court in its investigations and prosecutions;
(b) The voluntary assistance of the person in enabling the enforcement of the judgements and orders of the Court in other cases, and in particular providing assistance in locating assets subject to orders of fine, forfeiture or reparation which may be used for the benefit of victims; or
(c) Other factors establishing a clear and significant change of circumstances sufficient to justify the reduction of sentence, as provided in the Rules of Procedure and Evidence [...].

[**14**] Rule 223 of the Rules provides:
In reviewing the question of reduction of sentence pursuant to article 110, [...] the [Panel] shall take into account [...] the following criteria:

(a) The conduct of the sentenced person while in detention, which shows a genuine dissociation from his or her crime;
(b) The prospect of the resocialization and successful resettlement of the sentenced person;
(c) Whether the early release of the sentenced person would give rise to significant social instability;
(d) Any significant action taken by the sentenced person for the benefit of the victims as well as any impact on the victims and their families as a result of the early release;
(e) Individual circumstances of the sentenced person, including a worsening state of physical or mental health or advanced age.

[**17**] The Panel recalls that sentence review proceedings at the Court is not triggered by a request from the sentenced person, but is rather a mandatory *proprio motu* review which a panel of judges appointed by the Appeals Chamber is obliged to conduct pursuant to article 110(3) of the Statute.[...]"

[**Paras. 11, 12, 14, 17**]

II.

II.7.1005   LAW APPLIED BY ICC
              See also: II.7.1007

"[**15**] [...] [A] decision on whether to reduce a sentence is discretionary in nature.[...] Factors found to be present militating either for or against a reduction of sentence must be weighed against each other to determine whether a reduction of sentence is appropriate. [**16**] [...] Therefore, the factors set out in article 110(4)(a) and (b) of the Statute and the factors listed in rule 223(a) to (e) of the Rules, are those that can, in principle, be taken into account for purposes of considering whether to reduce a sentence. [...] [I]t is necessary to find that there is a "clear and significant change of circumstances"[...]. In this regard, the Panel recalls that "clear" is defined as "free from doubt", "unambiguous" and "very obvious" while "significant" is defined as "large enough to be noticed or have an effect" or "of a measurable large amount".

[**25**] The Panel notes that "cooperation with the Court" is a potential mitigating circumstance in sentencing proceedings pursuant to rule 145(2)(a)(ii) of the Rules and is generally understood to have the same meaning under article 110(4)(a) of the Statute.[...]"

[**Paras. 15, 16, 25**]

A.

II.6.1   GROUNDS OF REVIEW
            See also: II.7.1005; II.7.1007

"[**31**] [As regards Article 110(4)(a)] [t]he Panel finds that Mr Al Mahdi's continued adherence to his admission of guilt, his continued compliance with the terms of the Agreement and his cooperation [REDACTED], post sentence, are indications of an *early and continuing willingness to cooperate* with the Court's investigations and prosecutions. The Panel therefore considers that the factor set out in article 110(4)(a) of the Statu[t]e is present.

[**36**][As regards Article 110(4)(b)][...][t]he Panel finds that the factor under article 110(4)(b) of the Statute is not present for purposes of determining whether it is appropriate to reduce Mr Al Mahdi's sentence."

[**Paras. 31, 36**]

B.

II.6.1   GROUNDS OF REVIEW
            See also: II.7.1005; II.7.1007

"[**41**] [As regards Rule 223(a)] [...] [t]he Panel recalls that good conduct while in detention generally or *vis-á-vis* other detainees, is insufficient on its own, to establish the necessary connection between this conduct and a genuine dissociation of the sentenced person from his or her crime. Furthermore, [...] in relation to the factor listed in rule 223(a) of the Rules, it is necessary to find that there is a "clear and significant change of circumstances" from the time that the sentence was imposed. [**45**] [...] While Mr Al Mahdi's further expressions of remorse post-sentence are no doubt welcome, the Panel considers that they do not establish a clear and significant change of circumstances that would justify a reduction of sentence pursuant to article 110(4)(c) of the Statute read with rule 223(a) of the Rules. Accordingly, the Panel considers that the factor under rule 223(a) of the Rules is not present."

[**Paras. 41, 45**]

C.

II.6.1   GROUNDS OF REVIEW

See also: II.7.1005; II.7.1007

"[**49**] Rule 223(b) of the Rules requires the Panel to assess whether there is a prospect of the resocialization and successful resettlement of the sentenced person. The Panel recalls that as this factor was not considered for the purposes of sentencing it is being considered for the first time in the context of sentence review proceedings. [**50**] [...] The Panel further notes Mr Al Mahdi's "firm intention to convey to young people a message which seeks to educate and raise public awareness in order to counter the ills of the abuse of religion and of extremism". [...] [**53**] [...] [O]n the basis of the information received, the Panel finds that there is a prospect for the resocialization and successful resettlement of Mr Al Mahdi [REDACTED]. [...]"

[**Paras. 49, 50, 53**]

D.

II.6.1   GROUNDS OF REVIEW

See also: II.7.1005; II.7.1007

"[**58**] [As regards Rule 223(c)] [...] [t]he Panel recalls that "[s]ignificant social instability may be demonstrated by information indicating that the sentenced person's return to the State at issue could, *inter alia*, undermine public safety, cause social unrest such as riots or acts of ethnic-based violence, lead to the commission of new international crimes by the sentenced person or by his or her supporters, or undermine public confidence in the domestic legal system". [**59**] [...] The Panel finds that, although it is not possible to provide a definitive assessment in this regard, the statement by the Republic of Mali and the views expressed by a significant number of victims indicate that there could be a risk of significant social instability should Mr Al Mahdi be granted early release. [...]"

[**Paras. 58, 59**]

E.

II.6.1   GROUNDS OF REVIEW

See also: II.7.1005; II.7.1007

"[**63**] Rule 223(d) of the Rules requires the Panel to determine whether the sentenced person has taken any significant action for the benefit of the victims as well as any impact on the victims and their families as a result of the early release.[...] [**64**] The Panel recalls that the factor under rule 233(d) of the Rules needs to be considered in conjunction with the factor under rule 223(a) of the Rules given that they are considering generally the same information or actions under these two factors.[...] [**66**] The Panel notes [...] Mr Al Mahdi's offer [REDACTED] expressing, once again, his remorse for the crimes for which he was convicted.[...][**68**][However,] on the basis of the information received, the Panel considers that, since there has been no significant action taken by Mr Al Mahdi for the benefit of the victims and the impact on the victims of any early release of Mr Al Mahdi has been assessed as neutral, the factor under rule 223(d) of the Rules is not present for purposes of determining whether it is appropriate to reduce Mr Al Mahdi's sentence."

[**Paras. 63, 64, 66, 68**]

F.

II.6.1   GROUNDS OF REVIEW
             See also: II.7.1005; II.7.1007

"[71] The Panel understands the Defence to be arguing that a reduction of sentence should serve as a remedy for the harsh conditions that Mr Al Mahdi has faced during his incarceration. The Panel considers these arguments to be irrelevant to its assessment under this factor as they do not justify a reduction of sentence.[. . .][72][As regards Rule 223(e) and][i]n light of the information submitted by all participants relevant to this factor, the Panel is of the view that there are no individual circumstances which should be taken into consideration within the meaning of rule 223(e) of the Rules in determining whether it is appropriate to reduce Mr Al Mahdi's sentence."

[**Paras. 71, 72**]

III.

II.7.1008   ICC JUDGMENT/DECISION

"[76] Having decided that it is appropriate to reduce Mr Al Mahdi's sentence, [. . .] the Panel recalls that "[u]nder the Court's legal framework, the two-third threshold serves as a trigger mechanism for the commencement of the sentence review". Consequently, any possible reduction can only be applied to the remaining one third of the sentence. [. . .] [77] [. . .] Taking into account the specific circumstances of this sentence review, in particular, the views expressed by the Republic of Mali and a significant number of victims, the Panel considers that the extent of the reduction of sentence cannot be applied to the entirety of Mr Al Mahdi's remaining sentence. Consequently, the Panel considers that a reduction of two years is appropriate. [. . .]"

[**Paras. 76, 77**]

Systematic Key Items of the Section*

---

* *See* Systematic Classification Scheme, *supra* at page 255.

V

International Residual Mechanism for Criminal Tribunals

INTRODUCTORY NOTE

International Residual Mechanism for Criminal Tribunals

BY RAFAEL NIETO-NAVIA*

Abstract
The International Residual Mechanism for Criminal Tribunals received four cases from the International Criminal Tribunal for the former Yugoslavia. Until now, three of them have been decided and one is still pending. In 2021, the Appeals Chamber gave its judgement on the *Mladić* case. The Trial Chamber, on the other hand, resolved the *Stanišić and Simatović* case. This judgement, however, has been appealed and is pending on the Appeals Chamber. The initial indictment against *Stanišić* and *Simatović* was confirmed on 1 May 2003. The Trial Chamber acquitted the accused of all charges on 30 May 2013. However, the Appeals Chamber quashed this decision on 9 December 2015, and ordered a retrial of the accused. The decision on this retrial was issued on 15 August 2021, and is reviewed in this chapter. It is the longest case decided by the Tribunal.

I. INTRODUCTION

The International Residual Mechanism for Criminal Tribunals (IRMCT) was established by the UN Security Council (UNSC) through Resolution 1966 on 22 December 2010[1] to gradually assume the residual functions from both the International Criminal Tribunal for the former Yugoslavia (ICTY) and the International Criminal Tribunal for Rwanda (ICTR). The IRMCT started fully operating from the beginning of 2018.

This introductory note exclusively refers to the work formerly carried out by the ICTY.

---

* Former Member of the Appeals Chamber of the ICTY; Member of the *Institut de droit international*; Member of the Editorial Board.
[1] S/RES/1966 (2010).

Rafael Nieto-Navia, *Introductory Note* In: *The Global Community Yearbook of International Law and Jurisprudence 2022.* Edited by: Giuliana Ziccardi Capaldo, Oxford University Press. © Oxford University Press 2023. DOI: 10.1093/oso/9780197752265.003.0023

The IRMCT issued two judgements in 2021, which are reviewed here. The Trial Chamber issued the decision on the *Stanišić and Simatović* case (MICT-15-96), and the Appeals Chamber issued the decision on the *Mladić* case (MICT-13-56).

II. CASE LAW

A. The *Mladić* Case

1. Facts

(A) BACKGROUND OF THE PROCEEDINGS

General Ratko *Mladić*,[2] former commander of the Main Staff of the Bosnian Serb Army (VRS), was charged by the Prosecutor with eleven counts of genocide, crimes against humanity, and violations of the laws or customs of war committed in Bosnia and Herzegovina (BiH) between May 1992 and November 1995. He was convicted by the Trial Chamber of genocide and persecution, extermination, murder, and the inhumane act of forcible transfer in the area of Srebrenica in 1995; persecution, extermination, murder, deportation, and inhumane act of forcible transfer in municipalities throughout BiH; murder, terror, and unlawful attacks on civilians in Sarajevo; and hostage-taking of UN personnel. He was acquitted of the charge of genocide in 1992. *Mladić* was sentenced by the Trial Chamber to life imprisonment.[3]

(B) THE APPEALS

Both *Mladić* and the Prosecutor appealed the Chamber's decision. The parties filed their respective appellant's briefs on 6 August 2018.

On 18 June 2018, taking into consideration an actual or apparent bias, *Mladić* requested the disqualification of four of the five judges of the appeals bench. The judge in charge of making the decision on the matter granted *Mladić*'s requests and assigned new judges to replace the disqualified ones.

Thereafter, *Mladić* presented nine grounds of appeal challenging his convictions and sentence and requested the Appeals Chamber to reverse all erroneous findings of the Trial Chamber, quash his convictions, and acquit him. As an alternative, *Mladić* sought a retrial or a reduction in his sentence. The Prosecution asked the Chamber to dismiss the appeal in its entirety.[4] The Prosecution challenged certain conclusions pertaining to the overarching joint criminal enterprise (JCE) and its acquittal of genocide under count 1 of the Indictment.[5]

On 8 June 2021, the Appeals Chamber delivered its judgement and unanimously dismissed *Mladić*'s appeal in relation to the hostage-taking JCE and in relation to the overarching JCE, the Sarajevo JCE, and the Srebrenica JCE, as well as the arguments related to his fair trial rights. The Appeals Chamber affirmed *Mladić*'s convictions pursuant to

---

[2] Originally, Case No. IT-09-82 T. http://www.icty.org/x/cases/mladic/tjug/en/171122-1of5_1.pdf.

[3] *See* comments on this judgement in Rafael Nieto-Navia's *Introductory Note* (to the jurisprudence of the ICTY in 2017), 18 GLOBAL COMMUNITY YILJ 2018 (Giuliana Ziccardi Capaldo General ed.) 527 (2019)

[4] *Mladić* Appeals Chamber Judgement of 8 June 2021 (the *Mladić* case), at paras. 10 and 11. https://www.irmct.org/sites/default/files/case_documents/210608-appeal-judgement-JUD285R0000638396-mladic-13-56-en.pdf. This judgement appears in 61(2) INTERNATIONAL LEGAL MATERIALS 207–342 (April 2022).

[5] The *Mladić* case, at para. 11.

Article 7(1) of the ICTY Statute for genocide, persecution, extermination, murder, deportation, and other inhumane acts (forcible transfer) as crimes against humanity, as well as for murder, terror, unlawful attacks on civilians, and hostage-taking as violations of the laws or customs of war under counts 2 to 11 of the Indictment.

The Appeals Chamber, two judges dissenting, dismissed the Prosecution's appeal in its entirety and accordingly affirmed the Trial Chamber findings that *Mladić* was not guilty of genocide under count 1 of the Indictment in relation to crimes committed against Bosnian Muslims and Bosnian Croats in certain municipalities in BiH.

The Appeals Chamber affirmed the sentence of life imprisonment imposed on *Mladić* by the Trial Chamber, with one judge dissenting.[6]

(C) CONSIDERATIONS ON THE JUDGEMENT

Mladić had a notorious military reputation and power during the war that followed the breakup of Yugoslavia in the early 1990s.[7] At the beginning of the proceedings for crimes he committed during the war, *Mladić* and former Bosnian Serb president Radovan *Karadžić* were indicted jointly, but *Karadžić* was arrested three years before *Mladić*, and his trial continued without the former president.[8] However, although independent from each other, both cases received a very similar consideration and treatment by the ICTY.

As in the *Karadžić* case, the initial Indictment said that the accused participated in four different forms of JCE (*overarching JCE, Sarajevo JCE, Hostages JCE,* and *Srebrenica JCE*) to permanently eliminate Bosnian Muslims and Bosnian Croats from Bosnian Serb–claimed territory in several municipalities throughout BiH; to besiege Sarajevo as commander of the Serb army (VRS); and for the genocide in Bosnian municipalities outside of Srebrenica. As stated, *Mladić* was charged with individual criminal responsibility pursuant to Articles 7(1) and 7(3) of the Statute of the ICTY (ICTY Statute).[9]

Regarding the overarching JCE, *Mladić* submitted that the Trial Chamber erred by relying solely on adjudicated facts that were corroborated only by the evidence admitted pursuant to Rule 92 *bis* of the ICTY Rules.[10] The Chamber defines adjudicated facts as presumptions, which, as such, do not require corroboration and may relate to the existence of a JCE, the conduct of its members other than the accused, and the facts related to the conduct of physical perpetrators of crimes for which an accused is alleged to be responsible.[11]

According to the Appeals Chamber, in order to hold an accused responsible pursuant to JCE liability, it must be established that he performed acts that, in some way, were directed to the development of the common plan or purpose of the JCE. Although these acts do not need to be criminal per se, they may take the form of assistance in, or contribution to, the execution of the common objective or purpose.[12]

---

[6] The *Mladić* case, at para. 592.

[7] *See* https://www.cambridge.org/core/journals/international-legal-materials/article/prosecutor-v-mladic-un-intl-residual-mechanism-crim-tribunals-app-chamber/02F2CDCEED04C3DFF465D9B0D4FC7EAF.

[8] *See* comments on this judgement in Rafael Nieto-Navia's *Introductory Note* (to the jurisprudence of the ICTY in 2016), 17 GLOBAL COMMUNITY YILJ 2017 (Giuliana Ziccardi Capaldo General ed.) 429 (2018).

[9] The *Mladić* case, at para. 3.

[10] The *Mladić* case, at para. 125. Rule 92 *bis* sets out the procedure for the admission into evidence of written statements in lieu of oral testimony.

[11] The *Mladić* case, at para. 126.

[12] The *Mladić* case, at para. 179.

Mladić alleged that the Trial Chamber's findings on his guilt under the JCE are invalidated as *inter alia*, the element of *actus reus* cannot be considered to have been proven beyond a reasonable doubt.[13] The Chamber stated that the contribution of an accused does not need to be substantial or to involve the commission of a crime, and the law does not foresee specific types of conduct, which per se could not be considered a contribution to a JCE.[14] These questions of fact must be determined on a case-by-case basis.[15]

Mladić submitted that the Trial Chamber failed to give sufficient weight to evidence that he could not have known that certain crimes were committed by VRS soldiers against Bosnian Muslims and Bosnian Croats.[16] This claim was rejected by the Appeals Chamber.[17]

According to *Mladić*, the Trial Chamber employed a "defective method" in determining his *mens rea* and erred in using its findings on his *mens rea* "to substantiate its *actus reus* findings."[18] Citing the Appeal Judgement of *Stanišić and Simatović*,[19] he said that "the *actus reus* determination must be established first, before considerations of *mens rea* are determined."[20] The Appeals Chamber said that there is no legal requirement that a trial chamber's analysis as to the *mens rea* and *actus reus* of an accused be done separately[21]—that the circumstances in the *Stanišić and Simatović* case are different from the case under consideration,[22] and that nothing prevents a trial chamber from relying on the same evidence when making findings as to the *actus reus* and *mens rea* of an accused.

The appellant argued that the Trial Chamber erred in convicting him for having spread terror through the campaign of sniping and shelling of Sarajevo because the prohibition of spreading terror among the civilian population could not be considered as customary international at the time of the Indictment due to insufficient evidence of settled, extensive, or uniform state practice.[23] *Mladić* relied on Judge Shahabuddeen's separate opinion in the *Galić* Appeal Judgement in which the judge stated that "there is neither the required *opinio juris* nor state practice to support the view that customary international law knows of a comprehensive definition [of terror]."[24] However, the majority confirmed that the customary international law imposed individual criminal responsibility for violations of the prohibition of terror against the civilian population at the time of the commission of the crimes

---

[13] The *Mladić* case, at para. 185.

[14] The *Mladić* case, at para. 186.

[15] The *Mladić* case, at para. 228.

[16] The *Mladić* case, at para. 208.

[17] The *Mladić* case, at para. 213.

[18] The *Mladić* case, at para. 240.

[19] Reference is made to the *Stanišić and Simatović* Appeal Judgement, paras. 82, 87. This judgement can be downloaded from https://www.icty.org/x/cases/stanisic_simatovic/acjug/en/151209-judgement.pdf. *See* comments on this judgement in Rafael Nieto-Navia's *Introductory Note* (to the jurisprudence of the ICTY in 2015), 16 GLOBAL COMMUNITY YILJ 2016 (Giuliana Ziccardi Capaldo General ed.) 419 (2017)

[20] The *Mladić* case, at para. 245.

[21] The *Mladić* case, at para. 243.

[22] The *Mladić* case, at para. 246.

[23] The *Mladić* case, at para. 280.

[24] The *Mladić* case, at para. 289. The reference is to *Galić* Appeal Judgement, Separate Opinion of Judge Shahabuddeen, para. 3. This judgement can be downloaded from https://www.icty.org/x/cases/galic/acjug/en/gal-acjud061130.pdf. *See* comments on this judgement in Rafael Nieto-Navia's *Introductory Note* (to the jurisprudence of the ICTY in 2006), 7 GLOBAL COMMUNITY YILJ 2007 (Giuliana Ziccardi Capaldo General ed.) 390 (2008).

for which *Galić* was convicted.[25] In the *Mladić* case, the Appeals Chamber added that the principle of *nullum crimen sine lege* does not prevent a court from interpreting and clarifying the elements of a particular crime, nor does it preclude the progressive development of the law by the court.[26]

Mladić argued that Sarajevo was a valid military target that could not be seen as an "undefended city" pursuant to Article 3(c) of the ICTY Statute. However, the Appeals Chamber recalled that nothing in the Indictment, prosecution pre-trial brief, or trial record suggests that *Mladić* was charged with the crime of attacking undefended locales.[27] The Chamber added that "the principle of distinction requires parties to a conflict to distinguish at all times between the civilian population and combatants, or civilian and military objectives, such that only military objectives may be lawfully attacked and the prohibition on targeting civilians is absolute."[28]

Mladić contends that by not giving the due weight to exculpatory evidence related to his subsequent statements and actions on his participation to achieve the common objective of the Srebrenica JCE,[29] the Trial Chamber incorrectly found the requisite *mens rea* beyond a reasonable doubt and violated the principle of *in dubio pro reo*.[30] The Appeals Chamber found that *Mladić*'s arguments were unsupported and reflected mere disagreement with the Trial Chamber's assessment of the evidence without demonstrating an error.[31]

The Trial Chamber stated that "between 7,000 and 8,000 Bosnian-Muslim men were systematically murdered" in Srebrenica.[32] According to *Mladić*, the Chamber asserted that "*all* of the 7,000–8,000 victims of the killings in Srebrenica were not actively taking part in hostilities." Contrary to *Mladić*'s submission, the Appeals Chamber found that there is no indication that the Trial Chamber made a finding that *all* of the 7,000 to 8,000 victims of the killings in Srebrenica were not actively taking part in hostilities.[33]

Between 25 May and 24 June 1995, VRS soldiers and officers detained UNPROFOR and UN personnel in Pale and other locations, in and around Sarajevo, in order to exert leverage over NATO to end air strikes against Bosnian Serb military targets and recover Serb weapons under UNPROFOR control.[34]

According to *Mladić*'s claims, the Trial Chamber applied an erratic legal standard in considering that the detention of the UN personnel constituted the crime of hostage-taking[35] because the ICTY's jurisdiction is limited to its Statute and only the Security Council may "revise and reinterpret the Statute." He added that the Trial Chamber erroneously relied

---

[25] *See Galić* Appeal Judgement, paras. 86–98.

[26] The *Mladić* case, at para. 290. This statement does not seem to agree with the principle.

[27] This is the word used by the Appeals Chamber to refer to Article 3(c) of the Statute of the ICTY, which considers that "attack, or bombardment, by whatever means, of undefended towns, villages, dwellings, or buildings" is one of the violations of the laws or customs of war that have to be punished by the Tribunal. The *Mladić* case, at paras. 295 and 299.

[28] The *Mladić* case, at para. 300.

[29] "As a result of the VRS attack on the Srebrenica enclave in July 1995, thousands of Bosnian Muslims fled to Potočari seeking refuge within the UNPROFOR compound before being transferred to Bosnian controlled territory under the auspices of the VRS and the MUP and, for the first convoy only, under the supervision and escort of UNPROFOR." The *Mladić* case, at para. 423.

[30] The *Mladić* case, at paras. 419 and 420.

[31] The *Mladić* case, at para. 426.

[32] The *Mladić* case, at para. 439.

[33] The *Mladić* case, at para. 440.

[34] The *Mladić* case, at para. 479.

[35] The *Mladić* case, at para. 481.

on a decision by the ICTY Appeals Chamber in the *Tadić* case that found that violations of Common Article 3 of the Geneva Conventions fall within the ambit of Article 3 of the ICTY Statute.[36] He added that the taking of combatants as hostages entailed only state responsibility and not individual criminal responsibility under customary international law. He contends that the prohibition against taking non-civilians hostage was introduced as a war crime in 2002 with the entry into force of the Statute of the International Criminal Court (ICC) and that during the Indictment period, only the killing of hostages was criminalized.[37]

The Prosecution asserted that there is a "clear ICTY case law" in this matter, and since *Mladić* never raised the jurisdictional argument at trial, the Trial Chamber was not required to provide a detailed analysis to consider hostage-taking as a serious violation of Common Article 3.[38] The Appeals Chamber accepted that if a party raises no objection to a particular issue before the Trial Chamber when it could have reasonably done so, in the absence of special circumstances, the party has waived its right to adduce the issue as a valid ground of the appeal.

Regarding the ambit of the ICTY's jurisdiction over the violations of Common Article 3 and, in particular, the crime of hostage-taking, the Appeals Chamber of the ICTY had settled the matter and was, therefore, binding on the Trial Chamber in the present case.[39] The ICTY Appeals Chamber jurisprudence held that Article 3 of the ICTY Statute is a general and residual clause that refers to a broad category of offences, namely all "violations of the laws or customs of war" not limited to the list of violations enumerated therein. Previously, the ICTY had stated that there are no cogent reasons to depart from the *Tadić* jurisprudence on the questions of whether Common Article 3 is included in the scope of Article 3 of the ICTY Statute or the breaches of its provisions that give rise to individual criminal responsibility.[40]

Upon the consideration of *Mladić*'s argument that the UN personnel were combatants and not entitled to the protection of Common Article 3 and that the detention of combatants as prisoners of war (who become *hors de combat*) does not entail any criminal responsibility,[41] the Appeals Chamber stated that the prohibition against hostage-taking in Common Article 3 applies to *all* detained individuals, irrespective of their status prior to detention. Accordingly, the UN personnel were entitled to protection under Common Article 3.[42]

---

[36] The *Mladić* case, at para. 483. The reference is to Prosecutor v. Dusko *Tadić*, aka "Dule," Decision on the Defence Motion for Interlocutory Appeal on Jurisdiction (the *Tadić* case). https://www.icty.org/x/cases/tadic/acdec/e n/51002.htm, paras. 87–89.

[37] The *Mladić* case, at para. 484.

[38] The *Mladić* case, at para. 485.

[39] The *Mladić* case, at para. 487.

[40] The *Mladić* case, at para. 488; the *Tadić* case, at paras. 87–89. The issue was specially discussed in *Čelebići* Camp, Prosecutor v. *Delalić* (Zejnil) *et al.*, Appeal Judgement, Case No. IT-96-21-A, 20 February 2001 (the *Čelebići* case), paras. 157–174. *See* comments on this judgement in Rafael Nieto-Navia's *Introductory Note* (to the jurisprudence of the ICTY in 2001), 2 GLOBAL COMMUNITY YILJ 2002 (Giuliana Ziccardi Capaldo General ed.), vol. II, at 679 (2003).

[41] The *Mladić* case, at para. 497.

[42] The *Mladić* case, at para. 501. *Karadžić* Appeal Judgement, Case MICT-13-55-A, 20 March 2019, paras. 659–660,   https://www.irmct.org/sites/default/files/casedocuments/mict-13-55/appeals-chamber-judgements/en/190320-judgement-karadzic-13-55.pdf. *See* comments on this judgement in Rafael

(D) REMARKS

As stated, having rejected *Mladić* and the Prosecutor's appeals and taking into account the gravity of the charges, the Chamber, three judges dissenting on some of the *items*, confirmed the Trial Chamber's sentence of life imprisonment. The Appeals Chamber also confirmed the Trial Chamber's disposition finding that the accused was not guilty of genocide.

Undoubtedly, Slobodan *Milošević* and Ratko *Mladić*, respectively, the president and army commander in chief at the time of the Yugoslav wars in the 1990s, were the most important accused by the Prosecutor before the ICTY.

Milošević died of natural causes in prison during his trial.

B. The *Stanišić et al.* Case

1. Facts

(A) BACKGROUND OF THE PROCEEDINGS

As of 1991, Jovica *Stanišić* was a Serbian intelligence officer who served as the head of the State Security Service (DB) within the Ministry of Internal Affairs, and Franko *Simatović* functioned under his direct authority as a DB official.

Both were accused of having established various special units known as the Red Berets, the Skorpions, and the Serbian Volunteer Guard within the DB. Allegedly, the accused interacted with other Serb forces, including the Serbian Autonomous SAO Krajina Police, and were accused of having trained, supplied, financed, and supported those units. Crimes of persecution, murder, deportation, and forcible transfer were allegedly committed by these units in the SAO Krajina in Croatia, and the Serbian Autonomous Area of Slavonia, Baranja, and Western Srem (SAO SBWS). The accused stood trial as alleged participants in a JCE between April 1991 and December 1995.

On 30 May 2013, both accused were acquitted of all charges.[43] The Chamber found that the accused were in direct and frequent contact with many of the alleged members of the JCE, but it did not find that *Stanišić* and *Simatović* acted as a channel of communication among the core members of the JCE.

The Chamber found that the Prosecution had not proven beyond a reasonable doubt that the accused had planned or ordered, aided or abetted the crimes charged in the indictment. Consequently, based upon the factual and legal findings as determined in the judgement, the Chamber found the accused not guilty and acquitted them of all charges.

The Prosecution appeal was decided by the ICTY Appeals Chamber on 15 December 2015. The Prosecutor claimed that the Trial Chamber erred in law and in fact in finding that the *mens rea* for JCE had not been established and that the Trial Chamber failed to provide a reasoned opinion on the essential elements of JCE, among them the existence of a common criminal plan, design, or purpose and the contribution of the accused to it.[44]

Nieto-Navia's *Introductory Note* (to the jurisprudence of the ICTY in 2019), 20 GLOBAL COMMUNITY YILJ 2020 (Giuliana Ziccardi Capaldo General ed.) 670 (2021).

[43] http://www.icty.org/x/cases/zupljanin_stanisicm/tjug/en/130327-1.pdf. *See* comments on this judgement in Rafael Nieto-Navia, *Introductory Note* (to the jurisprudence of the ICTY in 2013), 14 GLOBAL COMMUNITY YILJ 2014 (Giuliana Ziccardi Capaldo General ed.) 434 (2015).

[44] Prosecutor v. Jovica *Stanišić* and Franko *Simatović*, Case No. IT-03-69-A, Appeals Chamber Judgement, 9 December 2015 (The *Stanišić et al.* appeals judgement). This judgement can be downloaded from http://www.icty.org/x/cases/ stanisic_simatovic/acjug/en/151209-judgement.pdf. *See* comments on

By majority, the Appeals Chamber ruled that "the Trial Chamber erred in law by failing to adjudicate and to provide a reasoned opinion on, (sic) essential elements of JCE liability,"[45] thus granting the first part of the first ground of the Prosecutor's appeal[46] and dismissing the remaining sub-grounds as moot.[47]

The Prosecution also submitted that the Trial Chamber erred in law and in fact in finding that the *actus reus* of aiding and abetting liability was not met with respect to the conduct of the accused in relation to the crimes committed in certain municipalities in BiH in the SAO Krajina and erroneously acquitted them of aiding and abetting these crimes. The Appeals Chamber found that the Trial Chamber erred in law in requiring that the acts of the aider and abettor be specifically directed to assist the commission of a crime.[48]

Having found an error of law arising from the application of a wrong legal standard, it was necessary for the Chamber to articulate the applicable legal standard and, accordingly, review the findings of the Trial Chamber[49] but it deliberated that it would be inappropriate to conduct its own review of the relevant factual findings of the Trial Chamber as it would have to analyse the entire trial record without the benefit of having heard the witnesses directly. Consequently, the Chamber ordered a retrial.

On 30 June 2021, the new Trial Chamber found *Stanišić* and *Simatović* responsible for aiding and abetting the crime of murder as a violation of the laws or customs of war and crimes against humanity and the crimes of deportation, forcible transfer, and persecution as crimes against humanity committed by Serb forces following the takeover of Bosanski Šamac in April 1992. They were sentenced to twelve years of imprisonment each. Both appealed, and the final judgement is pending in the IRMCT Appeals Chamber.

(B) CONSIDERATIONS OF THE JUDGEMENT

The Chamber carefully examined each of the events and incidents committed by the Serb forces and the different paramilitary groups mentioned in the Indictment from Bijeljina to Sanski Most and Trnovo.[50] This resulted in a conclusion that it has been established beyond reasonable doubt that these crimes and acts of violence targeted almost exclusively non-Serb civilians, forcing them to leave the areas.[51]

The Chamber started by making an analysis of the requirements that must be met in each of the charges, according to the applicable law for Article 3 of the ICTY Statute (*i.e.*, the existence of an armed conflict and a nexus between the crime and the armed conflict),[52] ruling that a state of armed conflict existed on the territory of Croatia and BiH during the time relevant to the crimes charged in the Indictment, that there was a nexus between the crimes that the accused were charged with, and the armed conflict.[53] Crimes against humanity are punishable under Article 5 of the ICTY Statute, but it does not mandate any material nexus

---

this judgement in Rafael Nieto-Navia's *Introductory Note* (to the jurisprudence of the ICTY in 2015), 16 GLOBAL COMMUNITY YILJ 2016 (Giuliana Ziccardi Capaldo General ed.) 419 (2017).

[45] The *Stanišić et al.* appeals judgement, at para. 80.

[46] The *Stanišić et al.* appeals judgement, at para. 90.

[47] The *Stanišić et al.* appeals judgement, at para. 91.

[48] The *Stanišić et al.* appeals judgement, at para. 108.

[49] The *Stanišić et al.* appeals judgement, at para. 122.

[50] The Prosecutor v. Jovica *Stanišić* and Franko *Simatović*, Case MICT-15-96-T, 6 August 2021 (The *Stanišić et al.* Chamber judgement).

[51] The *Stanišić et al.* Chamber judgement, at para. 278.

[52] The *Stanišić et al.* Chamber judgement, at para. 283.

[53] The *Stanišić et al.* Chamber judgement, at para. 285.

between the acts of the accused and the armed conflict.[54] An attack encompasses any mistreatment of the civilian population, but it does not need to be a part of it.[55] The acts of the perpetrators must be part of the attack on the civilian population, although they don't need to be involved in the midst of the attack.[56]

The Chamber concluded that the evidence demonstrated that the violence against the non-Serb civilian population spread across large swaths of Croatia and BiH and targeted a high number of victims.[57]

The elements of murder as a crime against humanity under Article 5(a) of the ICTY Statute require an act or omission resulting in the death of an individual not taking active part in the hostilities. Premeditation is not required in order to satisfy the *mens rea* of murder.[58] In relation to the allegations of murder committed on the territory of the SAO Krajina, SAO SBWS, and BiH, the Trial Chamber found that all the elements of murder as a crime against humanity (and as a violation of the laws or customs of war [count 3]) had been established.[59]

The crimes of deportation and forcible transfer entail the forcible displacement of persons from the area in which they are lawfully present. The crime of deportation requires that the victims be displaced across a *de jure* or *de facto* state border. Forcible transfer may involve displacement of persons within national boundaries.[60] The forced nature of the displacement is determined by the threat of force or coercion and the absence of genuine choice of the persons in their displacement.[61] The Chamber found that the coercive atmosphere, the widespread crimes and acts of violence, and the psychological oppression created by the Serb forces showed that the non-Serb civilians were forcibly displaced from areas in which they were lawfully present to other parts of Croatia, BiH, and Serbia.[62]

A similar analysis was made by the Chamber in relation to the crime of persecution charged in the Indictment.[63]

The Chamber proceeded then to the analysis of the position and power of the accused during the war and, based in the well-known jurisprudence of the Tribunal on the matter, their participation in a JCE. The Chamber found that some of the Prosecution's evidence regarding the participation of the accused in the different groups was tenuous or insufficient, and as the common plan did not come into existence until at least August 1991, their conduct did not contribute to the advancement of the common criminal purpose.[64] Accordingly, the Trial Chamber found that the accused could not be held responsible for committing the crimes alleged in the[65] Indictment just for their participation in a JCE.

The Trial Chamber, therefore, proceeded to examine whether the accused were responsible for aiding and abetting the crimes charged in the Indictment. "To satisfy the *mens rea* element for aiding and abetting liability, it must be shown that the aider and abettor knew

---

[54] The *Stanišić et al.* Chamber judgement, at para. 286.
[55] The *Stanišić et al.* Chamber judgement, at para. 287.
[56] The *Stanišić et al.* Chamber judgement, at para. 291.
[57] The *Stanišić et al.* Chamber judgement, at para. 296.
[58] The *Stanišić et al.* Chamber judgement, at para. 298.
[59] The *Stanišić et al.* Chamber judgement, at paras. 299–302.
[60] The *Stanišić et al.* Chamber judgement, at para. 304.
[61] The *Stanišić et al.* Chamber judgement, at para. 306.
[62] The *Stanišić et al.* Chamber judgement, at para. 316.
[63] The *Stanišić et al.* Chamber judgement, at paras. 320–325.
[64] The *Stanišić et al.* Chamber judgement, at para. 505.
[65] The *Stanišić et al.* Chamber judgement, at para. 598.

that his acts or omissions assisted the commission of the specific crime by the principal, and that the aider and abettor was aware of the essential elements of the crime, which was ultimately committed, including the intent of the principal perpetrator."[66] In four paragraphs, which are "tenuous and insufficient," the Chamber found "proven beyond reasonable doubt *Stanišić* and *Simatović* responsible for aiding and abetting the crimes of persecution, murder, deportation, and forcible transfer committed by Serb forces in Bosanski Šamac."[67] Both were sentenced to twelve years of imprisonment, entitled to credit for the days spent in detention.[68]

III. CONCLUSION

Of the cases received from the ICTY, the only one that remains is the appeal for the *Stanišić and Simatović* case.

---

[66] The *Stanišić et al.* Chamber judgement, at para. 602.

[67] The *Stanišić et al.* Chamber judgement, at para. 604.

[68] The *Stanišić et al.* Chamber judgement VIII Disposition.

VI

Court of Justice of
the European Union

VI

Court of Justice of the European Union

INTRODUCTORY NOTE

The Court of Justice of the European Union in 2021

BY KOEN LENAERTS*

Abstract

This introductory note looks back at the main highlights of events occurring at the Court of Justice of the European Union. The year 2021 was marked by continued efforts to adapt to the successive waves of the COVID-19 pandemic. The implementation of efficient crisis plans meant that the Court could return to pre-COVID levels of uninterrupted activity. The Court continued to set the pace rendering judgments notably in the fields of the rule of law, the environment, personal data protection, social protection, and state aid. This introductory note provides an overview of the most important judgments in each of these fields.

I. INTRODUCTION

The year 2021 was devoted to coping with the persistence of health measures and restrictions in order to deal with the successive waves of the COVID-19 pandemic. Thanks to the use of the remote working and communications tools deployed from the onset of the pandemic in March 2020 the institution was, however, able to ensure that its activities at the service of European justice could continue without interruption.

This adaptability and inventiveness displayed by the services of the institution in order to overcome the digital barrier resulted in the Court of Justice of the European Union receiving the award for good administration for excellence in innovation and transformation from the European Ombudsman in June 2021. This award was made in recognition of the design and implementation of a videoconferencing system that allowed the parties'

---

* President of the Court of Justice of the European Union. All opinions expressed herein are personal to the author and do not necessarily reflect the opinions of the institution of which he is and was part.

Koen Lenaerts, *Introductory Note* In: *The Global Community Yearbook of International Law and Jurisprudence 2022*. Edited by: Giuliana Ziccardi Capaldo, Oxford University Press. © Oxford University Press 2023. DOI: 10.1093/oso/9780197752265.003.0024

representatives to participate remotely in the hearings before the Court, with simultaneous interpretation.

The year 2021 was also marked by a significant partial renewal of the composition of the Court of Justice. The solemn sitting held on 7 October 2021 thus provided the occasion to pay tribute to the nine members who left the Court of Justice, in most cases following a very long term in the service of the institution, and to welcome nine new members. The General Court, for its part, welcomed five new Members during the year.

Statistically, 2021 was marked by a resumption of the increase in the number of cases brought before both Courts, following the fall dictated by circumstances prevailing in 2020 (1,720 cases in 2021, against 1,584 in 2020). This increase is significant in the case of the Court of Justice (838 cases in 2021, against 737 in 2020), owing essentially to an appreciable increase in the number of appeals brought against decisions of the General Court (232 in 2021, against 131 in 2020). A comparable increase may be seen, by comparison with 2020, in the number of cases disposed of by both Courts (1,723 cases in 2021, against 1,540 in 2020), the increase being particularly marked in the case of the General Court, which thus takes full advantage of the reform of the institutional architecture of the European Union, essentially achieved since September 2019 (951 cases disposed of in 2021, against 748 in 2020). This parallel increase in the overall number of cases brought and disposed of in 2021 explains why the number of pending cases has remained stable (2,541 cases pending on 31 December 2021, against 2,544 in 2020).

The year 2021 marked the twentieth anniversary of the signature of the Treaty of Nice, which prepared for the great enlargement of 2004 and made important changes to the judicial system of the European Union, in particular by paving the way to the great reform of the judicial architecture which came into being in December 2015.

The decisions delivered throughout 2021 concerning the rule of law, the environment, personal data protection, social protection, or state aid show the extent to which the institution's activities are at the heart of contemporary reality and have a real impact on the lives of the citizens and undertakings of the European Union.

At a time when we are witnessing a widespread tendency to challenge the authority of judicial decisions, even, in certain member states, to call in question, more fundamentally, the project of European integration and the values and founding principles of that project, the legitimacy of the decisions delivered by the institution lies above all in the quality and persuasiveness of those decisions. Such guarantees attest to a European justice at the exclusive service of respect for the rule of law.

This chapter will provide an overview of the most important judgments rendered by the Court of Justice.

II. RESPECT FOR THE RULE OF LAW

The Charter of Fundamental Rights of the European Union, like the Treaty on European Union, refers expressly to the rule of law, one of the values, common to the member states, on which the European Union is founded. The Court of Justice is increasingly called upon to rule on the question of the compliance by member states with the rule of law, whether in the context of actions for failure to fulfil obligations brought against them by the European Commission or requests for a preliminary ruling from national courts. The Court of Justice must therefore examine whether that founding value is respected at national level, in particular with regard to the judiciary and, more specifically, in connection with the process for appointing judges and the disciplinary regime for judges.

In 2021, the Court ruled on a number of occasions on issues concerning the fundamental values of the European Union. A series of references from national courts concerned the organisation and appointment of the judiciary.

Thus, in *A.B. and Others (Appointment of judges to the Supreme Court—Actions)*[1] the Court of Justice held that, since successive amendments to the Polish Law on the National Council of the Judiciary have the effect of removing effective judicial review of that council's decisions to proposing to the president of the Republic candidates for the office of judge at the *Sąd Najwyższy* (Supreme Court, Poland), they are liable to infringe EU law. It stated that, where an infringement has been proved, the principle of the primacy of EU law requires the national court to disapply such amendments.

In *Repubblika v. Il-Prim Ministru*,[2] a Maltese association whose purpose is to promote the protection of justice and the rule of law had challenged before the *Prim'Awla tal-Qorti Ċivili—Ġurisdizzjoni Kostituzzjonali* (First Hall of the Civil Court, sitting as a Constitutional Court, Malta), the procedure for the appointment of members of the Maltese judiciary, as governed by the Constitution. The Court of Justice held that national provisions of a member state which confer on the prime minister a decisive power in the appointment of members of the judiciary, while providing for the involvement of an independent body responsible for assessing candidates and providing an opinion, are not contrary to EU law.

The Court ruled on a series of Romanian reforms in the areas of judicial organisation, the disciplinary regime applicable to judges, and the financial liability of the state and the personal liability of judges as a result of judicial error. In *Asociația "Forumul Judecătorilor din România" and Others*,[3] taking the view that those reforms are likely to infringe EU law with regard to a number of aspects such as the creation of a specialised section of the Public Prosecutor's Office dedicated to cases involving judges, the conditions giving rise to the personal liability of judges and respect for their procedural rights, it observed that the principle of the primacy of EU law precludes national legislation, as interpreted by the Constitutional Court, which deprives a lower court of the right to disapply of its own motion a national provision which is contrary to EU law.

In *Commission v. Poland*,[4] the European Commission brought an action before the Court of Justice seeking a declaration that, by the new disciplinary regime applicable to judges of the Sąd Najwyższy (Supreme Court, Poland) and judges of the ordinary courts and, in particular, by establishing a new disciplinary chamber within the Supreme Court, Poland had infringed EU law. The Court upheld all of the Commission's complaints: in the light of the wider context of major reforms which had recently affected the Polish judiciary and the combination of factors that framed the process whereby that new chamber was established, it held inter alia that that chamber does not offer all the guarantees of impartiality and independence and is not protected from the direct or indirect influence of the Polish legislature and executive.

In another case concerning the Polish judiciary,[5] the Court held that transfers without consent of a judge from one court to another or between two divisions of the same court

---

[1] Judgment of 2 March 2021, *A.B. and Others (Appointment of judges to the Supreme Court—Actions)*, Case C-824/18.

[2] Judgment of 20 April 2021, *Repubblika v. Il-Prim Ministru*, Case C-869/19.

[3] Judgment of 18 May 2021, *Asociația "Forumul Judecătorilor din România" and Others*, Case C-83/19 and Others.

[4] Judgment of 15 July 2021, *Commission v. Poland*, C-791/19.

[5] Judgment of 6 October 2021, *W.Ż. (Chamber of Extraordinary Control and Public Affairs of the Supreme Court—Appointment)*, C-487/19.

are liable to undermine the principles of the irremovability of judges and judicial independence. Moreover, the order by which a court, ruling at last instance and sitting as a single judge, dismissed the action of a judge transferred against his or her will must be declared null and void if the appointment of that single judge took place in clear breach of fundamental rules concerning the establishment and functioning of the judicial system concerned.

Similarly, in *Prokuratura Rejonowa w. Mińsku Mazowieckim and Others*,[6] the Court considered that the independence and impartiality of judges and the presumption of innocence may be jeopardised by the regime currently in force in Poland, which permits, inter alia, the minister for justice to second judges to higher criminal courts and to terminate that secondment at any time without stating reasons. The lack of criteria for those secondments creates a risk of political control being exerted over the content of judicial decisions, especially since the minister also assumes the role of Public Prosecutor General.

The Court dealt with a number of cases following on from the reform of the judicial system with regard to combating corruption in Romania in *Euro Box Promotion and Others*.[7] The question arose as to whether the application of the case-law arising from a number of decisions of the *Curtea Constituțională* (Constitutional Court, Romania) on the rules of criminal procedure applicable to fraud and corruption proceedings was liable to infringe EU law. The Court reaffirmed that the primacy of EU law requires that national courts are to be empowered to disapply a decision of a constitutional court that is contrary to EU law, without national judges incurring disciplinary liability. EU law precludes the application of the case-law of a constitutional court leading to the setting aside of judgments delivered by panels of judges which are deemed to be improperly constituted, in so far as the setting aside of those judgments, in conjunction with the national provisions on limitation periods, creates a systemic risk of impunity in respect of acts constituting serious offences of fraud.

In *Hungary v. Parliament*,[8] The Court dismissed Hungary's action against the European Parliament resolution triggering the procedure for determining the existence of a clear risk of a serious breach, by that member state, of the values on which the European Union is founded. That procedure is capable of leading to the suspension of certain rights resulting from EU membership. In applying its Rules of Procedure which provide that, in calculating whether a text has been adopted or rejected, account is to be taken only of votes cast "for" and "against" (except in those cases for which the treaties lay down a specific majority), the Parliament only took into consideration, in calculating the votes on the resolution at issue, the votes in favour and against cast by its members and excluded abstentions. The Court held that, when calculating the votes cast when that resolution was adopted, the Parliament was right to exclude the taking into account of abstentions, contrary to Hungary's submissions in its action for annulment.

In *IS (Illegality of the order for reference)*,[9] a reference for a preliminary ruling from a Hungarian court, the Court of Justice ruled on the compatibility of Hungarian law with the EU directive on the right to interpretation and translation in criminal proceedings. As the *Alkotmánybíróság* (Supreme Court, Hungary) had ruled that referring the matter to the Court of Justice for a preliminary ruling was unlawful, the Court, in addition, reaffirmed that the system of cooperation between the national courts and the Court of Justice precludes a national supreme court from declaring that a request for a preliminary ruling submitted

---

[6] Judgment of 16 November 2021, *Prokuratura Rejonowa w. Mińsku Mazowieckim and Others*, C-748/19 and Others.

[7] Judgment of 21 December 2021, *Euro Box Promotion and Others*, C-357/19 and Others.

[8] Judgment of 3 June 2021, *Hungary v. Parliament*, C-650/18.

[9] Judgment of 23 November 2021, *IS (Illegality of the order for reference)*, C-564/19.

by a lower court is unlawful. Moreover, EU law precludes disciplinary proceedings from being brought against a national judge on the ground that he or she has referred a case for a preliminary ruling to the Court of Justice: such proceedings are liable to deter all national courts from making references for a preliminary ruling, which could jeopardise the uniform application of EU law.

III. COMPETITION

In reply to a question by the Înalta Curte de Casație și Justiție (High Court of Cassation and Justice, Romania),[10] asking whether national courts are required to apply Article 25(3) of Regulation No 1/2003 to the time-barring of a national competition authority's powers to impose penalties for infringements of EU competition law, the Court replied in the negative. It found that, in the light of its purpose and the context of which that provision forms part, it governs only the powers available to the Commission in relation to penalties, and therefore that same provision does not lay down limitation rules relating to the national competition authorities' powers to impose penalties.

Between 1997 and 1999, the company Sumal acquired two trucks from Mercedes Benz Trucks España (MBTE), a subsidiary of the Daimler group, whose parent company is Daimler AG. By a 2016 decision, the European Commission found an infringement, by Daimler AG, of EU law rules prohibiting cartels as a result of the conclusion, between January 1997 and January 2011, of arrangements with fourteen other European truck producers on pricing and gross price increases for trucks in the European Economic Area (EEA). Following that decision, Sumal brought an action for damages against MBTE for loss resulting from that cartel. The Court held[11] that the victim of an infringement of EU competition law committed by a parent company may seek compensation from that company's subsidiary for the resulting loss, providing that it proves that the two companies constituted an economic unit at the time of the infringement and that the subsidiary is active on the market affected by the infringement.

In *Stichting Cartel Compensation and Equilib Netherlands*,[12] a Dutch court referred a question in a case before it involving organisations specialised in the recovery of compensation for damage resulting from infringements of competition law and nineteen airlines that had been found guilty of EU competition law infringements. The Court found that a national court, such as the *Rechtbank Amsterdam* (District Court, Amsterdam), has jurisdiction, in a dispute governed by private law, to apply Article 81 EC and Article 53 of the EEA Agreement to the anticompetitive practices of airlines on routes between airports in the European Union and those in third countries or in Switzerland that occurred before the dates on which, respectively, the provisions adopted by the Council pursuant to Article 83(1) EC, which became applicable to the first routes, and the Swiss Agreement entered into force.

IV. ENVIRONMENT

Over 2021, the Court of Justice had plenty of opportunities to develop its case-law on environment. Hunting and fishing featured in a few judgments as well as state obligations in the field of ambient air quality control.

---

[10] Judgment of 21 January 2021, *Whiteland Import Export*, C-308/19.
[11] Judgment of 6 October 2021, *Sumal*, C-882/19.
[12] Judgment of 11 November 2021, *Stichting Cartel Compensation and Equilib Netherlands*, C-819/19.

In an action for failure to fulfil obligations brought by the Commission,[13] the Court held that Spain should have taken into account illegal water abstraction and the abstraction of water intended for urban supply when estimating the abstraction of groundwater from the Doñana region (Spain) which is home to the largest protected natural area in Europe. Moreover, that member state failed to take appropriate steps to avoid the disturbance of protected habitats located within that natural park.

Fishing using electric current was prohibited by new rules adopted in 2019 by the European Parliament and the Council. The Netherlands asked the Court[14] to annul those provisions, submitting inter alia that the EU legislature had not relied on the best scientific opinions available concerning the environmental impacts with regard to the exploitation of North Sea sole. The Court of Justice dismissed that action and confirmed the validity of those rules: the EU legislature has a wide discretion in this field and is not obliged to base its legislative choice on scientific and technical opinions only.

With regard to the authorisation of hunting using limes, the Court held[15] that a member state (in this case France) may not authorise a method of capture of birds leading to by-catch which is likely to cause harm other than negligible harm to the species concerned. The fact that such a method is traditional is not, in itself, sufficient to rule out any other satisfactory alternative solution. The Court clarified the conditions which would allow derogation from the prohibition, laid down in the Birds Directive, on using certain methods of capture of protected birds.

In an action for failure to fulfil obligations brought by the Commission against Hungary[16] concerning the systematic and persistent exceedance of the limit values for particulate matter PM10, the Court held that that member state had infringed the rules of EU law on ambient air quality and that it had failed to fulfil its obligations to ensure throughout its territory, first, that the daily limit value for particulate matter PM10 was complied with and, secondly, that the period of exceedance of that value was kept as short as possible.

In another air quality case, the Court held[17] that, between 2010 and 2016, Germany had infringed the Air Quality Directive by systematically and persistently exceeding the limit values for nitrogen dioxide (NO_2). Germany also infringed its obligation to adopt appropriate measures in good time to ensure that the exceedance period was kept as short as possible in the zones concerned.

V. INSTITUTIONS

The institutional case-law covered new developments in the international activity of the European Union and its member states as well as the role that the institutions play therein.

In *Commission v. Council (Agreement with Armenia)*[18] the Court annulled the decisions of the Council on the application of the Comprehensive and Enhanced Partnership Agreement signed with Armenia on 24 November 2017. It held that, although the Partnership Agreement has some links with the common foreign and security policy

---

[13] Judgment of 24 June 2021, *Commission v. Spain (Deterioration of the Doñana natural area)*, C-559/19.
[14] Judgment of 15 April 2021, *Netherlands v. Council and Parliament*, C-733/19.
[15] Judgment of 17 March 2021, *One Voice and Ligue pour la protection des oiseaux*, C-900/19.
[16] Judgment of 3 February 2021, *Commission v. Hungary (Limit values—PM10)*, C-637/18.
[17] Judgment of 3 June 2021, *Commission v. Germany (Limit values—NO₂)*, C-635/18.
[18] Judgment of 2 September 2021, *Commission v. Council (Agreement with Armenia)*, C-180/20.

(CFSP), the components or declarations of intention that it includes which may be linked to the CFSP are insufficient to constitute an autonomous component of that agreement capable of justifying the splitting of the Council measure into two separate decisions. That split had led notably to recourse to the rule requiring a unanimous vote for one of the acts concerned and to that requiring a qualified majority for the other.

In a case between the Republic of Moldova and a Ukrainian company,[19] the Court of Justice was asked about the classification as an "investment" within the meaning of the Energy Charter Treaty (ECT), of a claim which arose from a contract for the sale of electricity. It held that the acquisition, by an undertaking of a contracting party to the ECT, of a claim arising from a contract for the supply of electricity, which is not connected with an investment, held by an undertaking of a third state against a public undertaking of another contracting party to that treaty, does not constitute an "investment" within the meaning of the ECT. A claim arising from a mere contract for the sale of electricity cannot be regarded as having been granted in order to undertake an economic activity in the energy sector. It follows that a mere contract for the supply of electricity, generated by other operators, is a commercial transaction which cannot, in itself, constitute an investment.

In an Opinion[20] delivered at the request of the European Parliament, the Court stated that the treaties do not prohibit the Council from waiting, before adopting the decision concluding the Council of Europe Convention on preventing and combating violence against women and domestic violence (known as the Istanbul Convention) on behalf of the European Union, for the "common accord" of the member states, but the Council cannot alter the procedure for concluding that convention by making that conclusion contingent on the prior establishment of such a "common accord." The Court of Justice specified the appropriate substantive legal basis for the adoption of the Council act concluding the part of the Istanbul Convention covered by the envisaged agreement. It also held that the act concluding that convention may be divided into two separate decisions where an objective need to do so is established.

In *Court of Auditors v. Pinxten*[21] the Court of Justice, sitting as a full court, was called upon to define the "obligations arising from office" by the Court of Auditors. Acting on information received from the European Anti-Fraud Office (OLAF), the Court of Auditors requested the Court of Justice to declare that its former member, Mr Pinxten, no longer met the obligations arising from his office and, consequently, to impose the penalty laid down in Article 286(6) of the Treaty on the Functioning of the European Union. Finding that the Mr Pinxten had in fact breached certain of the obligations arising from his office the Court ruled that he be deprived of two thirds of his right to a pension from the date of the judgment. The Court stated that the expression "obligations arising from his office," within the meaning of Article 286(6) TFEU, is to be broadly construed. Having regard to the importance of the responsibilities assigned to them, it is important that the members of the Court of Auditors observe the highest standards of conduct and ensure that the general interest of the European Union takes precedence at all times, not only over national interests, but also over personal interests. With that in mind, the obligations of the members of the Court of Auditors set out in EU primary law are reproduced and given concrete expression in the internal rules adopted by that institution, which those members are required to observe rigorously.

---

[19] Judgment of 2 September 2021, *Republic of Moldova*, C-741/19.
[20] Opinion of 6 October 2021, *Istanbul Convention*, 1/19.
[21] Judgment of 30 September 2021, *Court of Auditors v. Pinxten*, C-130/19.

VI. TAXATION

In an action for failure to fulfil obligations brought by the Commission,[22] the Court of Justice held that Italy had infringed EU law by exempting from excise duty fuels used for private pleasure craft. The EU directive providing for minimum levels of fuel taxation grants an exemption only in cases where the vessel is used by the end user for commercial purposes. The fact that chartering constitutes a commercial activity for the person making that vessel available to another is irrelevant in that regard.

Frenetikexito[23] concerned a Portuguese commercial company that operates sports facilities, physical well-being and fitness activities, and nutrition monitoring and advice activities. The company provided nutrition monitoring services on its premises by means of a qualified nutritionist certified for that purpose. Value added tax (VAT) was not invoiced for those services. In its invoices, Frenetikexito drew a distinction between amounts relating to physical well-being and fitness services and those relating to the nutrition monitoring service. There was no correspondence between the nutrition monitoring services invoiced and the nutrition consultations.

In its judgment following a reference from a Portuguese Tribunal, the Court examined whether a nutrition monitoring service, supplied in circumstances such as those at issue in the main proceedings, must be regarded as a "supply ancillary to the main supply," subject to VAT, or whether, on the contrary, it constitutes a distinct and independent supply of services and, if so, whether and under what conditions such a supply may be exempt from VAT. The Court found that a nutrition monitoring service provided by a certified and authorised professional in sports facilities, potentially in the context of programmes that also include physical well-being and fitness services, constitutes a separate and independent supply of services and is not capable of falling under the exemption laid down in Article 132(1)(c) of VAT directive 2006/112.

In its judgments *Commission v. Poland*[24] and *Commission v. Hungary*,[25] the Court also ruled on a tax on the retail sector introduced in Poland and a tax on advertising introduced in Hungary.

By a law which entered into force on 1 September 2016, Poland introduced a tax on the retail sector. That tax was based on the monthly turnover of any retailer involved in the sale of goods to consumers, above a sum of 17 million zlotys (PLN) (approximately EUR 4 million). That tax included two bands: a rate of 0.8 percent applied to turnover between PLN 17 million and 170 million (between, approximately, EUR 4 and 40 million) and a rate of 1.4 percent charged on the portion of turnover exceeding that latter amount. Following the formal investigation procedure in respect of that measure, the European Commission considered, by decision of 30 June 2017, that that progressive tax constituted state aid incompatible with the internal market and required Poland to cancel all the payments suspended in respect of that tax, with effect from the date of adoption of that second decision.

For its part, Hungary had introduced, by a law that entered into force on 15 August 2014, a progressive tax on revenue linked to the publication and broadcasting of advertisements in that member state. That tax, based on the net turnover of persons who broadcast or publish advertisements (print media, audiovisual media, or billposters), operating in Hungary, initially included a scale of six progressive rates based on turnover, later adapted to include

---

[22] Judgment of 16 September 2021, *Commission v. Italy (Excise duty—Fuel for pleasure craft)*, C 341/20.

[23] Judgment of 4 March 2021, *Frenetikexito*, C-581/19.

[24] Judgment of 16 March 2021, *Commission v. Poland*, C-562/19 P.

[25] Judgment of 16 March 2021, *Commission v. Hungary*, C-596/19 P.

only two rates, accompanied by the option, for taxable persons whose profits before tax in the 2013 financial year were zero or negative, to deduct from their tax base 50 percent of the losses carried forward from previous years.

Following the formal investigation procedure in respect of that measure, the Commission considered, by decision of 4 November 2016, that the tax measure adopted by Hungary, on account of both its progressive structure and the possibility of deducting the losses carried forward that it included, constituted state aid that was incompatible with the internal market and it ordered the immediate and effective recovery of the aid paid to the beneficiaries thereof.

Both states successfully challenged the Commission decisions before the General Court. In two judgments delivered in March 2021, the Court of Justice, sitting as the Grand Chamber, dismissed the appeals brought by the Commission against the judgments under appeal. In support of its appeals, the Commission claimed in particular that the General Court had infringed Article 107(1) TFEU, in holding that the progressive nature of the taxes on turnover respectively in question did not lead to a selective advantage.

Rejecting the Commission's objections, the Court reaffirmed, in the sphere of state aid, the principle established concerning the fundamental freedoms of the internal market to the effect that, given the current state of harmonisation of EU tax law, the member states are free to establish the system of taxation which they deem most appropriate, so that the application of progressive taxation based on turnover falls within the discretion of each member state, provided that the characteristics constituting the measure in question do not entail any manifestly discriminatory element.

In actions brought by Luxembourg and Amazon,[26] the General Court annulled the Commission's decision according to which, between 2006 and 2014, Luxembourg had granted Amazon EU, at that time Amazon's sales hub for the whole of Europe, based in Luxembourg, state aid that was contrary to EU law, by allowing it, by means of tax rulings, to pay significantly less tax than other undertakings. According to the Commission, Luxembourg ought to recover from Amazon the undue tax advantages amounting to approximately EUR 250 million, together with interest. In its judgment, the General Court found that the Commission had not demonstrated sufficiently that Amazon EU's taxable income had been artificially reduced as a result of an overpricing of the royalty it paid to another company in the Amazon group for the use of certain intellectual property rights.

In contrast, the General Court dismissed the actions brought by Luxembourg and the energy supplier Engie against the decision by which the Commission had found that Luxembourg had granted Engie state aid that was contrary to EU law by allowing, by means of tax rulings, two companies in that group resident in Luxembourg to evade tax on almost all of their profits. According to the Commission, Luxembourg must recover some EUR 120 million of unpaid tax, together with interest. In its judgment upholding that decision,[27] the General Court pointed out that Luxembourg had failed to find an abuse of rights by Engie even though all of the criteria were met.

VII. INTELLECTUAL PROPERTY

Throughout 2021, the two courts of the European Union have intervened in this field on numerous occasions.

---

[26] Judgment of 12 May 2021, *Luxembourg and Amazon v. Commission*, T-816/17 and Others.

[27] Judgment of 12 May 2021, *Luxembourg and Others v. Commission*, T-516/18 and Others.

In a dispute between Lego and a German company,[28] the General Court held that the European Union Intellectual Property Office (EUIPO) had erroneously declared invalid a design of a brick of a LEGO toy building set. The General Court took the view that EUIPO should have carried out an appropriate assessment of the exceptions to the Regulation on Community Designs by taking into consideration all the features of appearance of the design concerned. The General Court recalled that a design cannot be declared invalid if at least one of its features is not dictated by the technical function of that product.

The General Court recognised the validity of a three-dimensional mark representing the shape of a lipstick.[29] In so doing, it annulled the decision of the EUIPO which had dismissed the initial application for registration of that sign as an EU trade mark to designate lipsticks. According to the General Court, the mark applied for has distinctive character because it departs significantly from the norm and customs of the lipstick sector in that the lipstick has a rounded shape, rather than being vertical and cylindrical.

In another case,[30] the General Court held that an audio file reproducing the sound made by the opening of a drinks can, followed by silence and a fizzing sound, cannot be registered as an EU trade mark to designate drinks, inter alia, in so far as it is not distinctive. The General Court thus shares EUIPO's view and recalls that a sound mark must have distinctive character in order for the consumer to be able to perceive it as a trade mark and not as a functional element without any inherent characteristics.

The General Court dismissed the action brought by Chanel[31] against Huawei's application for registration of a mark with the EUIPO on the ground that the figurative signs at issue are not similar and held that the marks must be compared as applied for and registered, without altering their orientation. The General Court stated that the mere presence, in each of the marks at issue, of two elements that are connected to each other does not render the marks similar even though they share the basic geometric shape of a circle surrounding those elements.

In *VG Bild-Kunst*[32] the Court of Justice held that, where the copyright holder has adopted or imposed measures to restrict framing, the embedding of a work in a website page of a third party, by means of that technique, constitutes making available that work to a new public. That communication to the public must be authorised by the copyright holder.

The Court of Justice clarified, in *YouTube*,[33] in connection with the set of rules prior to those introduced by the new 2019 Copyright Directive, the circumstances in which online platforms (in this case YouTube and Cyando) could incur liability. It held that the operators of such platforms do not, in principle, themselves make a communication to the public of copyright-protected content illegally posted online by users of those platforms. They may, however, incur liability for a communication in breach of copyright where they contribute, beyond merely making those platforms available, to giving access to such content to the public.

---

[28] Judgment of 24 March 2021, *Lego v. EUIPO—Delta Sport Handelskontor* (Building block from a toy building set), T-515/19.

[29] Judgment of 14 July 2021, *Guerlain v. EUIPO (Shape of an oblong, tapered and cylindrical lipstick)*, T-488/20.

[30] Judgment of 7 July 2021, *Ardagh Metal Beverage Holdings v. EUIPO (Combination of sounds on opening a can of soft drink)*, T-668/19.

[31] Judgment of 21 April 2021, *Chanel v. EUIPO—Huawei Technologies (Representation of a circle containing two interlaced curves)*, T-44/20.

[32] Judgment of 9 March 2021, *VG Bild-Kunst*, C-392/19.

[33] Judgment of 22 June 2021, *YouTube*, C-682/18.

In *M.I.C.M.* ,[34] the internet connections of Telenet customers had been used to share films in the Mircom catalogue on a peer-to-peer network. The Court held that the protection of the rights of the holder of intellectual property may justify the systematic registration of IP addresses of users and the communication of their names and postal addresses to the rightsholder or to a third party in order to enable an action for damages to be brought. However, the request for information from a holder of intellectual property rights is not to be abusive and must be justified and proportionate.

In *Comité Interprofessionnel du Vin de Champagne*[35] an owner of tapas bars in Spain used the sign CHAMPANILLO to designate and promote his establishments. His advertising depicted two champagne coupes containing a sparkling beverage. The Comité Interprofessionnel du Vin de Champagne (CIVC), an organisation which safeguards the interests of champagne producers, sought to prohibit the use of the term champanillo (which in Spanish means "little champagne") on the ground that the use of that sign infringed the protected designation of origin (PDO) "Champagne." The Court clarified that products covered by a PDO are protected vis-à-vis prohibited conduct in respect of both products and services.

VIII. DATA PROTECTION

In 2021, the Court of Justice gave a number of rulings on the liability stemming from the collection and processing of personal data by national authorities and private undertakings.

In *Latvijas Republikas Saeima (Penalty points)*[36] the Court held that the legislation of a member state which obliges the road safety authority to make the data relating to the penalty points imposed on drivers for road traffic offences accessible to the public is contrary to EU law. It took the view that it had not been established that that system is necessary in order to improve road safety. The case concerned Latvian legislation on road traffic which provides that information relating to the penalty points imposed on drivers of vehicles is accessible to the public and disclosed to any person who so requests, without that person having to establish a specific interest in obtaining that information.

The Court held[37] that access, for purposes in the criminal field, to a set of traffic or location data in respect of electronic communications, allowing precise conclusions to be drawn concerning a user's private life, is permitted only in order to combat serious crime or prevent serious threats to public security. In addition, EU law precludes national legislation that confers upon the public prosecutor's office the power to authorise access of a public authority to such data for the purpose of conducting a criminal investigation.

In a judgment delivered in a case concerning the protection of personal data involving Facebook Ireland,[38] the Court specified the conditions for the exercise of the national supervisory authorities' powers with respect to the cross-border processing of data, stating that, under certain conditions, such an authority may bring any alleged infringement of the General Data Protection Regulation (GDPR) before a court of a member state, even though that authority is not the lead supervisory authority with regard to that processing. The Court also took the view that, since Facebook Ireland had not adequately informed

---

[34] Judgment of 17 June 2021, *M.I.C.M.*, C-597/19.

[35] Judgment of 9 September 2021, *Comité Interprofessionnel du Vin de Champagne*, C-783/19.

[36] Judgment of 22 June 2021, *Latvijas Republikas Saeima (Penalty points)*, C-439/19.

[37] Judgment of 2 March 2021, *Prokuratuur (Conditions of access to data relating to electronic communications)*, C-746/18.

[38] Judgment of 15 June 2021, *Facebook Ireland and Others*, C-645/19.

internet users of the collection and use of the information concerning them, their consent to the processing of those data was not valid.

IX. CONSUMER PROTECTION

In a case concerning the processing of organic foodstuffs such as rice- and soya-based organic drinks for the purpose of their enrichment with calcium,[39] the addition of the alga Lithothamnium calcareum (lithothamnium) was prohibited by the Court of Justice, which observed that EU law lays down strict rules on the addition of minerals, such as calcium, in the production of organic food. Authorising the use of the powder of that alga as a non-organic ingredient of agricultural origin would amount to permitting producers of those foodstuffs to circumvent those rules.

In a passenger rights case concerning Austrian Airlines,[40] the Court held that the mere diversion of a flight to an airport close to the original destination airport does not grant a right to flat-rate compensation. However, it stated that the air carrier must, on its own initiative, offer the passenger to bear the cost of transfer either to the destination airport for which the booking was made or, where appropriate, to another close-by destination agreed with the passenger. In order to be released from its obligation to pay compensation to passengers in the event of a long delay in the arrival of a flight, the air carrier may rely on an extraordinary circumstance which affects not the delayed flight but an earlier flight operated by that air carrier using the same aircraft.

However, in another passenger compensation case,[41] the Court found that a strike organised by a trade union of the staff of an air carrier, that is intended in particular to secure pay increases, does not constitute an "extraordinary circumstance" which releases the airline from its obligation to pay compensation in cases of cancellation or long delay. The air carrier's freedom to conduct a business, its property rights, and its right of negotiation are not impaired by not using that categorisation for such a strike, which is organised in compliance with the conditions laid down by national legislation.

In *Hessischer Rundfunk*,[42] the Court held that a euro area member state can oblige its administration to accept payments in cash. It did, however, state that the member state can also restrict that payment option on public interest grounds, in particular where payment in cash is likely to involve the administration in unreasonable expense because of the very high number of persons liable to pay. It also specified that the obligation to accept banknotes may be restricted for reasons of public interest, provided that those restrictions are proportionate to the public interest objective pursued, which means, in particular, that other lawful means must be available to the persons liable to pay for the settlement of monetary debts.

The case *OTP Jelzálogbank and Others*[43] concerned Hungarian legislation which prohibits the annulment of a loan agreement denominated in a foreign currency on the ground that it contains an unfair term relating to the exchange difference. The Court held that this legislation appears to be compatible with EU law if it makes it possible to re-establish the legal and factual situation which would have existed for the consumer in the absence of the unfair term, even if the annulment of the agreement would have been more advantageous for the consumer. In addition, the wishes expressed by the consumer

---

[39] Judgment of 29 April 2021, *Natumi*, C-815/19.
[40] Judgment of 22 April 2021, *Austrian Airlines*, C-826/19.
[41] Judgment of 23 March 2021, *Airhelp*, C-28/20.
[42] Judgment of 26 January 2021, *Hessischer Rundfunk*, C-422/19 and C-423/19.
[43] Judgment of 2 September 2021, *OTP Jelzálogbank and Others*, C-932/19.

concerned cannot prevail over the assessment, which is for the national court to make, of the question whether the Hungarian national legislation does actually make it possible to re-establish the legal and factual situation of the consumer.

In a case[44] in which the Irish shipping company Irish Ferries had to cancel the entire 2018 season of sailings because, as a result of delays in the delivery of a new vessel, it had been unable to commission a replacement vessel, the Court clarified several provisions on passengers' rights when travelling by sea or inland waterway (cancellation, compensation, ticket price, etc.). It found in particular that the re-routing and compensation obligations in the event of cancellation of a transport service are proportionate to the objective pursued by the relevant applicable legislation.

The *Vodafone*[45] case concerned a "zero tariff" internet option, a commercial practice whereby an access provider applies a "zero tariff," or a more advantageous tariff, to all or part of the data traffic associated with an application or category of specific applications, offered by partners of that access provider. The Court of Justice held that such tariff options are contrary to the regulation on open internet access, as are limitations on bandwidth, on tethering, or on use when roaming, on account of the activation of such an option.

X. FAMILY LAW

The Court of Justice ruled on an international child abduction file in the context of a case concerning the application for return to Sweden of the child of an Iranian couple who had been taken to Finland.[46] It took the view that a situation in which one parent, without the other parent's consent, has removed the child from his or her state of habitual residence to another member state of the European Union, cannot constitute a wrongful removal (or retention), once the authority of the state of residence that is competent in immigration matters has taken the view that it is in that other member state that the applications for asylum concerning the child and the parent in question should be examined.

The case of a child, being a minor and a Union citizen, whose birth certificate was drawn up by the host member state and designates as the child's parents two persons of the same sex, was brought before the Court.[47] It found that the member state of which that child is a national is obliged to issue an identity card or a passport to that child without requiring a birth certificate to be drawn up beforehand by its national authorities. That member state is also obliged to recognise the document from the host member state that permits that child to exercise, with each of those two persons, the child's right to move and reside freely within the territory of the European Union.

XI. SOCIAL SECURITY

In a case concerning citizenship and affiliation to a national social security scheme,[48] the Court of Justice afforded economically inactive Union citizens residing in a member state other than their member state of origin the right to be affiliated to the public sickness insurance scheme of the host member state. It did, however, state that that affiliation did not necessarily have to be free of charge.

---

[44] Judgment of 2 September 2021, *Irish Ferries*, C-570/19.
[45] Judgments of 2 September 2021, *Vodafone*, C-854/19 and Others.
[46] Judgment of 2 August 2021, *A*, C-262/21 PPU.
[47] Judgment of 14 December 2021, *Stolichna obshtina, rayon "Pancharevo,"* C-490/20.
[48] Judgment of 15 July 2021, *A (Public health care)*, C-535/19.

In the context of the withdrawal of the United Kingdom from the European Union,[49] UK legislation established a new scheme for EU citizens under which the grant of a right of residence is not subject to any condition as to resources. By contrast, it deprives EU citizens of social assistance benefits known as Universal Credit. The Court took the view that that legislation is compatible with the principle of equal treatment guaranteed by EU law. However, the competent national authorities must check that a refusal to grant such social assistance benefits does not expose the Union citizen and his or her children to a risk of infringement of their fundamental rights, in particular the right to respect for human dignity.

In *Team Power Europe*[50] the Court clarified the criteria to be taken into account in order to assess whether a temporary-work agency ordinarily performs "substantial activities other than purely internal managerial activities" in the member state in which it is established. According to the Court, in order for it to be considered that it "normally carries out its activities" in a member state, a temporary-work agency must carry out a significant part of its activities of assigning temporary agency workers for the benefit of user undertakings established and carrying out their activities in the territory of that same member state. The performance of the activities of selecting and recruiting such workers in the member state in which the temporary-work agency is established is insufficient for it to be considered that that undertaking carries out "substantial activities" there.

XII. EQUAL TREATMENT

In July 2021,[51] the Court of Justice held to be contrary to EU law the legislation of a member state imposing an absolute bar on a prison officer remaining in employment when his or her hearing acuity does not meet minimum standards of sound perception without allowing it to be ascertained whether that officer is capable of performing his or her duties. According to the Court of Justice, that legislation amounts to direct discrimination on grounds of disability.

Two cases[52] concerned Muslim employees who had decided to wear a religious veil in the workplace. According to the Court, a prohibition, laid down by the employer, on wearing any visible form of expression of political, philosophical, or religious beliefs in the workplace may be justified by a genuine need on the part of the employer to present a neutral image towards customers or to prevent social disputes. However, in reconciling the rights at issue, the national courts may take into account the specific context of their member state and more favourable national provisions on the protection of freedom of religion.

XIII. STATE AID

The Nürburgring, located in Germany, includes inter alia a race track and a leisure park. Following the insolvency of its owners, bodies governed by public law, the complex was sold to a private undertaking. Although other economic operators claimed that the sale had been made below market price and in a discriminatory manner, the Commission decided not to initiate a formal investigation procedure. Further to appeals[53] lodged with it in this

---

[49] Judgment of 15 July 2021, *The Department for Communities in Northern Ireland*, C-709/20.
[50] Judgment of 3 June 2021, *TEAM POWER EUROPE*, C-784/19.
[51] Judgment of 15 July 2021, *Tartu Vangla*, C-795/19.
[52] Judgment of 15 July 2021, *WABE and MH Müller Handel*, C-804/18 and C-341/19.
[53] Judgment of 2 September 2021, *Ja zum Nürburgring v. Commission*, C-647/19 P and Others.

matter, the Court of Justice annulled the Commission's decision and the judgment of the General Court upholding it and ordered the Commission to re-examine whether the sale of the Nürburgring entailed a grant of state aid.

Actions were brought by a cooperative and a number of skippers of fishing vessels against the Commission's decision not to raise objections in relation to aid linked to the construction of the first offshore wind farms in France. The General Court[54] found that those persons were not entitled to bring such actions because, first, they were not in competition with the operators of those wind farms and, secondly, they had failed to demonstrate the likelihood of the aid in question having a specific effect on their situation.

XIV. SOCIAL LAW

In response to a question from a Romanian court about the interpretation of the Working Time Directive,[55] the Court examined the situation of experts hired by the Academia de Studii Economice din Bucureşti under a number of employment contracts who, on certain days, cumulated the eight hours worked at the basic rate with the hours worked on one or more other projects. It stated that, where a worker has concluded more than one employment contract with the same employer, the minimum daily rest period applies to the contracts taken as a whole and not to each of the contracts taken separately.

In a dispute between a former non-commissioned officer in the Slovenian army and the Ministry of Defence concerning the remuneration for that officer's guard duty,[56] the Court clarified the situations in which the Working Time Directive does not apply to activities carried out by military personnel. Furthermore, it held that the directive does not preclude a stand-by period during which a member of military personnel is required to remain at the barracks to which he or she is posted, but does not perform actual work there, from being remunerated differently from a stand-by period during which he or she performs actual work.

In a case referred for a preliminary ruling by a Luxembourg court,[57] the Court of Justice interpreted the directive implementing the revised Framework Agreement on parental leave. It stated that a member state cannot make entitlement to parental leave subject to the requirement that the parent was employed at the time of birth or adoption of the child. The member state can, however, require that the parent was employed without interruption for a period of at least twelve months before the start of that parental leave.

In Italy, the grant of childbirth and maternity allowances was refused to a number of third-country nationals holding a single work permit obtained pursuant to the national legislation transposing an EU directive because those persons did not have long-term resident status. Following a reference made to it by the Corte costituzionale[58] (Constitutional Court, Italy), the Court of Justice held that those third-country nationals were entitled to those allowances as provided for by the Italian legislation.

---

[54] Judgment of 15 September 2021, *CAPA and Others v. Commission*, T-777/19.

[55] Judgment of 17 March 2021, *Academia de Studii Economice din Bucureşti*, C-585/19.

[56] Judgment of 15 July 2021, *Ministrstvo za obrambo*, C-742/19.

[57] Judgment of 25 February 2021, *XI v. Caisse pour l'avenir des enfants (Employment at the time of birth)*, C-129/20.

[58] Judgment of 2 September 2021, *INPS (Childbirth and maternity allowances for holders of single permits)*, C-350/20.

XV. BANKING UNION

In June 2018, the Latvian Public Prosecutor charged the governor of the Central Bank of Latvia with various offences of corruption. In that capacity, the governor was also a member of the General Council and the Governing Council of the European Central Bank (ECB). In the light of that particular circumstance, the Latvian court seised of the case asked[59] whether the person concerned might enjoy immunity under the Protocol on the privileges and immunities of the European Union, which grants officials and other servants of the European Union immunity from legal proceedings in respect of all acts performed by them in their official capacity. The Court held that, where a criminal authority finds that the conduct of a governor of a central bank of a member state was manifestly not committed by that governor in the context of his or her duties, immunity does not apply. Acts of fraud, corruption, or money laundering are not carried out by a central bank governor in his or her official capacity.

In 2016, the European Banking Authority (EBA) issued guidelines on product oversight and governance arrangements for retail banking products. In a notice published on its website, the Autorité de contrôle prudentiel et de résolution (Authority for prudential supervision and resolution, France) announced that it complied with those guidelines, thus making them applicable to all financial institutions under its supervision. The Fédération bancaire française (French banking federation; the FBF) subsequently asked the Conseil d'État (Council of State, France) to annul the notice because, in the FBF's view, the EBA did not have the competence to issue such guidelines. The Council of State referred the case[60] to the Court of Justice for a preliminary ruling concerning the remedies available to review the legality of the contested guidelines and their validity. The Court of Justice stated that the preliminary ruling procedure may be used to review such validity and that, in the present case, the guidelines are valid.

XVI. RESTRICTIVE MEASURES AND FOREIGN POLICY

"Secondary sanctions" are based on the US government's capacity to use the supremacy of its financial system to prevent foreign entities from engaging in (lawful) transactions with persons subject to sanctions. EU law prohibits those entities from complying with such sanctions, unless they are authorised by the European Commission when non-compliance with foreign laws would seriously harm those entities' interests. Deutsche Telekom had unilaterally terminated, without providing reasons and without authorisation from the Commission, service provision contracts between it and the German branch of Bank Melli, an Iranian bank owned by the Iranian State. In *Bank Melli Iran*,[61] the Court held that the prohibition imposed by EU law on complying with secondary sanctions laid down by the United States against Iran may be relied on in civil proceedings, even in the absence of a specific order or instruction by an authority of the United States. The German court before which the Iranian bank brought proceedings must thus balance the objective pursued by that prohibition against the probability and the extent of the economic losses which Deutsche Telekom might incur if it were unable to terminate its commercial relationship with that bank.

---

[59] Judgment of 30 November 2021, *LG Ģenerālprokuratūra*, C-3/20.
[60] Judgment of 15 July 2021, *FBF*, C 911/19.
[61] Judgment of 21 December 2021, *Bank Melli Iran*, C-124/20.

In view of the deterioration of the human rights situation, the rule of law, and democracy, the Council of the European Union adopted, in 2017, a regulation introducing restrictive measures against Venezuela. Venezuela subsequently applied to the General Court seeking the annulment of those measures, but the General Court found that Venezuela did not have standing to bring proceedings against such a regulation. However, on appeal,[62] the Court of Justice held that that state did indeed have standing to bring proceedings against a regulation which introduces restrictive measures against it and therefore referred the case back to the General Court for judgment on the merits of the action for annulment.

XVII. EU CRIMINAL LAW ENFORCEMENT AREA

In a case concerning the execution, in Ireland, of a European arrest warrant issued by the United Kingdom before its withdrawal from the European Union,[63] the Court held that the provisions in the Withdrawal Agreement concerning the European arrest warrant regime with respect to the United Kingdom, and those concerning the new surrender mechanism in the Trade and Cooperation Agreement between the European Union and that third country, are binding on Ireland. The inclusion of those provisions in those agreements did not justify the addition of a legal basis relating to the area of freedom, security, and justice for the purpose of concluding those agreements, with the result that those provisions did not require that Ireland have the choice whether or not to opt into them.

---

[62] Judgment of 22 June 2021, *Venezuela v. Council (Whether a third State is affected)*, C-872/19 P.
[63] Judgment of 16 November 2021, *Governor of Cloverhill Prison and Others*, C 479/21 PPU.

LEGAL MAXIMS: SUMMARIES AND EXTRACTS FROM SELECTED CASE LAW*

Bolivarian Republic of Venezuela v. Council of European Union, Case C-872/19 P, Grand Chamber, Judgment, 22 June 2021

IX v. WABE e V and MH Müller Handels GmbH v. MJ, Joined Cases C-804/18 and C-341/19, Grand Chamber, Judgment, 15 July 2021

Top System SA c. État Belge, Affaire C-13/20, Cinquième Chambre, Arrêt, 6 Octobre 2021

Republiken Polen v. PL Holdings Sàrl, Case C-109/20, Grand Chamber, Judgment, 26 October 2021

European Commission v. Republic of Poland, Case C-204/21 R, Order of the Vice-President of the Court, 27 October 2021

Google LLC and Alphabet, Inc. v. European Commission, Case T-612/17, Ninth Chamber, Extended Composition, Judgment, 10 November 2021

Governor of Cloverhill Prison and Others, Case C-479/21 PPU, Grand Chamber, Judgment, 16 November 2021

Prokuratura Rejonowa w Mińsku Mazowieckim, Joined Cases C-748/19 to C-754/19, Grand Chamber, Judgment, 16 November 2021

---

* The working method chosen for the formulation of legal maxims is explained *supra* 'Outline of the Parts', at page xv.

Legal Maxims: Summaries and Extracts from Selected Case Law In: *The Global Community Yearbook of International Law and Jurisprudence 2022*. Edited by: Giuliana Ziccardi Capaldo, Oxford University Press. © Oxford University Press 2023.
DOI: 10.1093/oso/9780197752265.003.0025

LEGAL MAXIMS: SUMMARIES
AND EXTRACTS FROM
SELECTED CASE LAW*

Bolivarian Republic of Venezuela v. Council of European Union, Case C-872/19 P, Grand Chamber, Judgment, 22 June 2021

IX v. WABE e.V. and MH Müller Handel, Ord. II v. MJ, Joined Cases C-804/18 and C-341/19, Grand Chamber, Judgment, 15 July 2021

Top System SA v. État Belge, Affaire C-13/20, Cinquième Chambre, Arrêt, 6 October 2021

Republika Poljen v. PL Holdings Sàrl, Case C-109/20, Grand Chamber, Judgment of 26 October 2021

European Commission v. Republic of Poland, Case C-204/21 R, Order of the Vice-President of the Court, 27 October 2021

Google LLC and Alphabet Inc. v. European Commission, Case T-612/17, Ninth Chamber, Extended Composition, Judgment, 10 November 2021

Gavanozov (for what Prison and Others), Case C-479/21 PPU, Grand Chamber, Judgment, 16 December 2021

Prokuratur Rejonowa w Mińsku Mazowieckim, Joined Cases C-748/19 to C-754/19, Grand Chamber, Judgment, 16 November 2021

* For works the method chosen for the formulation of legal maxims is explained in part ? Order ? of the Parts, at pg ??.

VI.2.1

Bolivarian Republic of Venezuela v. Council of European Union, Case C-872/19 P, Grand Chamber, Judgment, 22 June 2021*

Contents**

I. ACTION FOR PROCEEDING ON APPEAL

II. CONCEPT OF 'LEGAL PERSONALITY'

III. ADMISSIBILITY OF THE ACTION BROUGHT BY THE VENEZUELAN STATE

IV. ACTION CAPABLE OF SECURING A BENEFIT FOR THE APPLICANT

V. CONCEPT OF 'REGULATORY ACT' WITHIN THE MEANING OF THE FOURTH PARAGRAPH OF ARTICLE 263 TFEU

VI. DECISION

I.

II.7.725   EU COURT PROCEEDINGS ON APPEAL
See also: I.2.22771; II.7.723

"[1] By its appeal, the Bolivarian Republic of Venezuela asks the Court of Justice to set aside the judgment of the General Court of the European Union of 20 September 2019, *Venezuela v Council* (T-65/18, EU:T:2019:649 [. . .]), by which the General Court dismissed its action for annulment, first, of Council Regulation (EU) 2017/2063 [. . .] concerning restrictive measures in view of the situation in Venezuela [. . .], secondly, of Council Implementing Regulation (EU) 2018/1653 [. . .] implementing Regulation 2017/2063 [. . .] and, thirdly, of Council Decision (CFSP) 2018/1656 [. . .] amending Decision (CFSP) 2017/2074 concerning restrictive measures in view of the situation in Venezuela [. . .], in so far as their provisions concern the Bolivarian Republic of Venezuela."

[**Para. 1**]

II.

I.2.221   EU LEGAL PERSONALITY
See also: II.7.725

"[43] As regards the wording of the fourth paragraph of Article 263 TFEU, it should be noted that it does not follow either from that provision or from other provisions of EU primary law that certain categories of legal persons cannot avail themselves of the possibility of bringing legal proceedings before the EU Courts. That finding thus tends to indicate that no 'legal person' should be deprived, in principle, of the possibility of bringing an action

---

* Summaries prepared by Daniela Rodríguez Bautista, Doctor in Law, Administrator at the Court of Justice of the European Union. Text of judgment available online at the Court's Web site <http://www.curia.eur opa.eu>. Language of the Case: English. The selection of extracts can only be attributed to the author and not to the institutions of her affiliation.

** This is not a faithful reproduction of the Table of Contents of the Judgment.

for annulment provided for in the fourth paragraph of Article 263 TFEU. [**50**] In those circumstances, an interpretation of the fourth paragraph of Article 263 TFEU in the light of the principles of effective judicial review and the rule of law militates in favour of finding that a third State should have standing to bring proceedings, as a 'legal person', within the meaning of the fourth paragraph of Article 263 TFEU, where the other conditions laid down in that provision are satisfied. Such a legal person governed by public international law is equally likely as any another person or entity to have its rights or interests adversely affected by an act of the European Union and must therefore be able, in compliance with those conditions, to seek the annulment of that act. [**53**] It follows that the Bolivarian Republic of Venezuela, as a State with international legal personality, must be regarded as a 'legal person' within the meaning of the fourth paragraph of Article 263 TFEU."

[**Paras. 43, 50, 53**]

III.

II.7.722   EU COURT PROCEEDINGS FOR ANNULMENT
             See also: I.2.22771

"[**70**] [. . .] [I]t should be noted that, in order to find that the Bolivarian Republic of Venezuela is directly concerned by Articles 2, 3, 6 and 7 of Regulation 2017/2063, it is not necessary to draw a distinction according to whether such commercial transactions are carried out *iure gestionis* or *iure imperii*, since such a distinction cannot be inferred either from the fourth paragraph of Article 263 TFEU or from any other provision of EU law. [**71**] Moreover, the fact that the restrictive measures at issue do not constitute an absolute obstacle preventing the Bolivarian Republic of Venezuela from procuring the goods and services covered by those articles, since that State remains in a position to procure them outside the territory of the European Union through persons not subject to those measures, does not call into question the conclusion that the prohibitions laid down in those articles directly concern the Bolivarian Republic of Venezuela. The condition that prohibitions such as those laid down in Articles 2, 3, 6 and 7 of Regulation 2017/2063 must be of direct concern to a legal person does not mean that it must be entirely impossible for that person to obtain the goods and services in question. [**73**] It follows that the General Court erred in law in considering that the restrictive measures at issue did not directly affect the legal situation of the Bolivarian Republic of Venezuela and by upholding, on that basis, the second ground of inadmissibility raised by the Council."

[**Paras. 70, 71, 73**]

IV.

II.7.722   EU COURT PROCEEDINGS FOR ANNULMENT
             See also: II.7.725

"[**82**] [. . .] [I]t should be borne in mind that the existence of an interest in bringing proceedings presupposes that annulment of the contested act must be capable, by itself, of procuring an advantage for the natural or legal person who brought the action (judgment of 21 January 2021, *Germany v Esso Raffinage*, C-471/18 P, EU:C:2021:48, paragraph 103 [. . .])."

[**Para. 82**]

V.

II.7.722   EU COURT PROCEEDINGS FOR ANNULMENT
See also: II.7.725

"[**92**] [...] [R]egulation [2017/2063], which has a general scope, in that it contains provisions such as Articles 2, 3, 6 and 7 thereof which prohibit general and abstract categories of addressees from carrying out certain transactions with entities which are also referred to in a general and abstract manner, and which – since it was adopted on the basis of Article 215 TFEU and, accordingly, under the non-legislative procedure laid down in that provision, cannot be regarded as a legislative act – constitutes a 'regulatory act', within the meaning of the third limb of the fourth paragraph of Article 263 TFEU ([...] judgment of 3 October 2013, *Inuit Tapiriit Kanatami and Others v Parliament and Council*, C-583/11 P, EU:C:2013:625, paragraphs 58 to 60). Since the provisions of that regulation challenged by the Bolivarian Republic of Venezuela do not entail implementing measures, as noted in paragraph 90 above, it must be held that that third State does indeed have standing to bring proceedings against those provisions without having to establish that those provisions are of individual concern to it."

[**Para. 92**]

VI.

II.2.5   JUDGMENT/DECISION/ORDER
See also: I.2.22771

"On those grounds, the Court (Grand Chamber) hereby [rules]:
    [...] Sets aside the judgment of the General Court of the European Union of 20 September 2019, *Venezuela v Council* (T-65/18, EU:T:2019:649), in so far as it dismisses the Bolivarian Republic of Venezuela's action for annulment of Articles 2, 3, 6 and 7 of Council Regulation (EU) 2017/2063 [...] concerning restrictive measures in view of the situation in Venezuela [...]"

VI.2.2

IX v. WABE e V and MH Müller Handels GmbH v. MJ, Joined Cases C-804/18 and C-341/19, Grand Chamber, Judgment, 15 July 2021*

Contents**

    I. REFERENCE FOR A PRELIMINARY RULING

    II. PROHIBITION OF RELIGIOUS SIGNS IN THE WORKPLACE IF BASED ON A GENUINE NEED

    III. JUDGMENT

I.

II.2.0   INSTITUTION AND COURSE OF PROCEEDINGS
            See also: I.2.22331; I.2.2260; I.8.55; II.7.723

"[1] These requests for a preliminary ruling concern the interpretation of Article 2(1) and (2)(a) and (b), Article 4(1) and Article 8(1) of Council Directive 2000/78/EC of 27 November 2000 establishing a general framework for equal treatment in employment and occupation [. . .] and Articles 10 and 16 of the Charter of Fundamental Rights of the European Union ('the Charter'). [2] The request for a preliminary ruling in Case C-804/18 has been made in proceedings between IX and her employer, WABE e V ('WABE'), an association registered in Germany operating a large number of child day care centres, concerning the suspension of IX from her duties following her refusal to comply with a rule imposed by WABE on its employees prohibiting them from wearing any visible political, philosophical or religious sign at the workplace when they are in contact with the children or their parents. [3] The request for a preliminary ruling in Case C-341/19 has been made in proceedings between MH Müller Handels GmbH ('MH'), a company operating a chain of drugstores in Germany, and its employee, MJ, concerning the legality of the instruction given to her by MH to refrain from wearing, in the workplace, conspicuous, large-sized political, philosophical or religious signs."

[**Paras. 1, 2, 3**]

II.

I.8.55   FREEDOM OF THOUGHT, CONSCIENCE AND RELIGION
            See also: I.2.22331; I.2.2260; II.7.723

"[46] [The Court notes that] [t]he wearing of signs or clothing to manifest religion or belief is covered by the 'freedom of thought, conscience and religion' protected by

---

* Summaries prepared by Eirini Pantelodimou, Doctor of Laws (University of Paris I, Panthéon-Sorbonne), Référendaire at the General Court of the European Union. Text of judgment available online at the Court's Web site <http://www.curia.europa.eu>. Language of the Case: German. The selection of extracts can only be attributed to the author and not to the institutions of her affiliation.

** This is not a faithful reproduction of the Table of Contents of the Judgment.

Article 10 of the Charter. [...] [**47**] [...] [F]or the purposes of the application of Directive 2000/78, the terms 'religion' and 'belief' must be analysed as two facets of the same single ground of discrimination. [...] [**54**] Since it appears from the file before the court that WABE also required another employee wearing a religious cross to remove that sign, it appears prima facie that the internal rule at issue in the main proceedings was applied to IX without any difference of treatment by comparison with any other person working for WABE, with the result that it cannot be considered that IX suffered a difference of treatment directly based on her religious beliefs, for the purpose of Article 2(2)(a) of Directive 2000/78. [...] [**55**] In the light of those considerations, [...] an internal rule of an undertaking, prohibiting workers from wearing any visible sign of political, philosophical or religious beliefs in the workplace, does not constitute, with regard to workers who observe certain clothing rules based on religious precepts, direct discrimination on the grounds of religion or belief, for the purpose of that directive, provided that that rule is applied in a general and undifferentiated way. [**68**] It should also be emphasised that [...] if an internal rule such as that at issue in the main proceedings is not to be regarded as indirect discrimination, it must be appropriate for the purpose of ensuring that the employer's policy of neutrality is properly applied, which entails that that policy is genuinely pursued in a consistent and systematic manner, and that the prohibition on wearing any visible sign of political, philosophical or religious beliefs imposed by that rule is limited to what is strictly necessary [...]. [**73**] [...] [U]nequal treatment resulting from a rule or practice which is based on a criterion that is inextricably linked to a protected ground, in the present case religion or belief, must be regarded as being directly based on that ground. Accordingly, where the criterion of wearing conspicuous, large-sized signs of political, philosophical or religious beliefs is inextricably linked to one or more specific religions or beliefs, the prohibition imposed by an employer on its employees on wearing those signs on the basis of that criterion will mean that some workers will be treated less favourably than others on the basis of their religion or belief, and that direct discrimination, within the meaning of Article 2(2)(a) of Directive 2000/78, may therefore be established. [**74**] Should such direct discrimination nevertheless not be found to exist, [the Court observes that] a difference of treatment such as that referred to by the referring court would, if it were established that it in fact results in a particular disadvantage for persons adhering to a particular religion or belief, constitute indirect discrimination within the meaning of Article 2(2) (b) of that directive, [...], unless it were objectively justified by a legitimate aim and the means of achieving that aim were appropriate and necessary. [**76**] [...] [A] policy of neutrality may constitute a legitimate aim, within the meaning of Article 2(2)(b)(i) of Directive 2000/78. In order to determine whether that policy is sufficient to justify objectively a difference of treatment indirectly based on religion or belief, it must be verified, [...], whether it meets a genuine need on the part of the undertaking. In that regard, it should be noted that both the prevention of social conflicts and the presentation of a neutral image of the employer vis-à-vis customers may correspond to a real need on the part of the employer, which it is for the latter to demonstrate. [...] [**77**] In that regard, it should be noted that a policy of neutrality within an undertaking, [...] can be effectively pursued only if no visible manifestation of political, philosophical or religious beliefs is allowed when workers are in contact with customers or with other workers, since the wearing of any sign, even a small-sized one, undermines the ability of that measure to achieve the aim allegedly pursued [...]."

[**Paras. 46, 47, 54, 55, 68, 73, 74, 76, 77**]

III.

II.2.5   JUDGMENT/DECISION/ORDER
          See also: II.7.723

"On those grounds, the Court (Grand Chamber) hereby rules:

1. Article 1 and Article 2(2)(a) of Council Directive 2000/78/EC of 27 November 2000 establishing a general framework for equal treatment in employment and occupation must be interpreted as meaning that an internal rule of an undertaking, prohibiting workers from wearing any visible sign of political, philosophical or religious beliefs in the workplace, does not constitute, with regard to workers who observe certain clothing rules based on religious precepts, direct discrimination on the grounds of religion or belief, for the purpose of that directive, provided that that rule is applied in a general and undifferentiated way.

2. Article 2(2)(b) of Directive 2000/78 must be interpreted as meaning that a difference of treatment indirectly based on religion or belief, arising from an internal rule of an undertaking prohibiting workers from wearing any visible sign of political, philosophical or religious beliefs in the workplace, may be justified by the employer's desire to pursue a policy of political, philosophical and religious neutrality with regard to its customers or users, provided, first, that that policy meets a genuine need on the part of that employer, which it is for that employer to demonstrate, taking into consideration, inter alia, the legitimate wishes of those customers or users and the adverse consequences that that employer would suffer in the absence of that policy, given the nature of its activities and the context in which they are carried out; secondly, that that difference of treatment is appropriate for the purpose of ensuring that the employer's policy of neutrality is properly applied, which entails that that policy is pursued in a consistent and systematic manner; and, thirdly, that the prohibition in question is limited to what is strictly necessary having regard to the actual scale and severity of the adverse consequences that the employer is seeking to avoid by adopting that prohibition.

3. Article 2(2)(b)(i) of Directive 2000/78 must be interpreted as meaning that indirect discrimination on the grounds of religion or belief resulting from an internal rule of an undertaking prohibiting, at the workplace, the wearing of visible signs of political, philosophical or religious beliefs with the aim of ensuring a policy of neutrality within that undertaking can be justified only if that prohibition covers all visible forms of expression of political, philosophical or religious beliefs. A prohibition which is limited to the wearing of conspicuous, large-sized signs of political, philosophical or religious beliefs is liable to constitute direct discrimination on the grounds of religion or belief, which cannot in any event be justified on the basis of that provision.

4. Article 2(2)(b) of Directive 2000/78 must be interpreted as meaning that national provisions protecting the freedom of religion may be taken into account as more favourable provisions, within the meaning of Article 8(1) of that directive, in examining the appropriateness of a difference of treatment indirectly based on religion or belief."

VI.2.3

Top System SA c. État Belge, Affaire C-13/20, Cinquième Chambre, Arrêt, 6 Octobre 2021*

Contents**

    I. LA DEMANDE DE DÉCISION PRÉJUDICIELLE

    II. COMPILATION ET DÉCOMPILATION

    III. DÉCOMPILATION D'UN PROGRAMME D'ORDINATEUR À LA LUMIÈRE DES ARTICLES 5 (CORRECTION DES ERREURS) ET 6 (INTEROPÉRABILITÉ) DE LA DIRECTIVE 91/250

    IV. EXIGENCES POUR PROCÉDER À LA DÉCOMPILATION D'UN PROGRAMME D'ORDINATEUR

    V. DÉCISION

I.

II.7.723   EU COURT PRELIMINARY RULINGS

            See also: I.0.151; I.2.2232; I.2.2234

"[1] La demande de décision préjudicielle porte sur l'interprétation de l'article 5, paragraphe 1, de la directive 91/250/CEE du Conseil, du 14 mai 1991, concernant la protection juridique des programmes d'ordinateur [. . .]. [2] Cette demande a été présentée dans le cadre d'un litige opposant Top System SA à l'État belge, au sujet de la décompilation, par le Selor, bureau de sélection de l'administration fédérale (Belgique), d'un programme d'ordinateur développé par Top System et faisant partie d'une application sur laquelle ce bureau de sélection détient une licence d'utilisation. [26] La juridiction de renvoi estime que, afin de déterminer si le Selor était en droit de procéder à ladite décompilation sur le fondement de l'article 6, paragraphe 1, de [. . .] [10] [l]a loi du 30 juin 1994 transposant en droit belge la directive européenne du 14 mai 1991 concernant la protection juridique des programmes d'ordinateur [. . .], telle que modifiée par la loi du 15 mai 2007 relative à la répression de la contrefaçon et de la piraterie de droits de propriété intellectuelle [. . .] (ci-après la « LPO »), [. . .] [26] [. . .] il lui appartient de vérifier si la décompilation de tout ou partie d'un programme d'ordinateur relève des actes visés à l'article 5, sous a) et b), de la LPO. [27] Dans ces conditions, la cour d'appel de Bruxelles a décidé de surseoir à statuer et de poser à la Cour les questions préjudicielles suivantes: « 1) L'article 5, paragraphe 1, de la [directive 91/250] doit-il être interprété comme permettant à l'acquéreur légitime d'un programme d'ordinateur de décompiler tout ou partie de celui-ci lorsque cette décompilation est nécessaire pour lui permettre de corriger des erreurs affectant le fonctionnement dudit programme, y compris quand la correction consiste à désactiver une fonction qui affecte le bon fonctionnement de l'application dont fait partie ce programme? 2) Dans

---

* Summaries prepared by Carmine Renzulli, Lawyer; Ph.D. in International Law, Department of Legal Sciences (School of Law), University of Salerno, Italy. Text of judgment available online at the Court's Web site <http://www.curia.europa.eu>. Language of the Case: French.

** This is not a faithful reproduction of the Table of Contents of the Judgment.

l'affirmative, doit-il en outre être satisfait aux conditions de l'article 6 de la directive ou à d'autres conditions ? »"

[**Paras. 1, 2, 26, 10, 26, 27**]

II.

I.0.151   INTELLECTUAL PROPERTY RIGHTS
See also: I.2.2232; I.2.2234

"[**35**] [. . .] [U]n programme d'ordinateur est initialement rédigé sous la forme d'un « code source » dans un langage de programmation intelligible, avant d'être transcrit sous une forme exécutable par un ordinateur, à savoir sous la forme d'un « code objet », au moyen d'un programme dédié appelé « compilateur ». L'opération consistant à transformer le code source en code objet porte quant à elle le nom de « compilation ». [**36**] [. . .] [L]e code source et le code objet d'un programme d'ordinateur, en tant qu'ils constituent deux formes d'expression de celui-ci, bénéficient de la protection par le droit d'auteur sur les programmes d'ordinateur conformément à l'article 1er, paragraphe 2, de la directive 91/250 (voir, en ce sens, arrêt du 22 décembre 2010, Bezpečnostní softwarová asociace, C-393/09, [. . .] point 34). [**37**] Inversement, la « décompilation » vise à reconstituer le code source d'un programme à partir de son code objet. La décompilation est effectuée au moyen d'un programme dénommé « décompilateur ». Ainsi que M. l'avocat général l'a souligné au point 41 de ses conclusions, la décompilation permet généralement d'obtenir non pas le code source original, mais une troisième version du programme concerné appelée « quasi-code source », qui pourra à son tour être compilée en un code objet permettant à ce programme de fonctionner. [**38**] La décompilation constitue dès lors une opération de transformation de la forme du code d'un programme impliquant une reproduction, à tout le moins partielle et provisoire, de ce code, ainsi qu'une traduction de la forme de celui-ci. [**39**] Par conséquent, [. . .] la décompilation d'un programme d'ordinateur implique l'accomplissement d'actes, à savoir la reproduction du code de ce programme et la traduction de la forme de ce code, qui relèvent effectivement des droits exclusifs de l'auteur, tels qu'ils sont définis à l'article 4, sous a) et b), de la directive 91/250. [**40**] Cette interprétation est corroborée par le libellé de l'article 6, paragraphe 1, de la directive 91/250 qui, tout en visant, selon son intitulé, la décompilation, fait référence expressément à la « reproduction du code » et à « la traduction de la forme de ce code au sens de l'article 4, sous a) et b), » de cette directive. Il s'ensuit que la notion de « décompilation », au sens de ladite directive, relève effectivement des droits exclusifs de l'auteur d'un programme d'ordinateur établis à cette dernière disposition."

[**Paras. 35, 36, 37, 38, 39, 40**]

III.

I.0.151   INTELLECTUAL PROPERTY RIGHTS
See also: I.2.2232; I.2.2234

"[**44**] [. . .] [L]'article 6 de la directive 91/250 introduit une exception aux droits exclusifs du titulaire des droits d'auteur sur un programme d'ordinateur en permettant la reproduction du code ou la traduction de la forme de ce code sans l'autorisation préalable du titulaire du droit d'auteur lorsque ces actes sont indispensables pour assurer l'interopérabilité de ce programme avec un autre programme créé indépendamment. [**45**] À cet égard, [. . .] il importe de rappeler que les considérants 20 et 21 de cette directive énoncent que, dans certaines circonstances, une reproduction du code d'un programme d'ordinateur ou une traduction de sa forme peut s'avérer indispensable pour obtenir l'information nécessaire à l'interopérabilité d'un programme créé de façon indépendante avec d'autres programmes et que, « dans ces circonstances bien précises uniquement », l'accomplissement de ces actes est légitime et conforme aux bons usages, de telle sorte qu'il ne doit pas requérir l'autorisation du titulaire du droit d'auteur. [**46**] [. . .] [L]e législateur de l'Union a ainsi entendu circonscrire la portée de l'exception pour interopérabilité [. . .] aux circonstances dans lesquelles l'interopérabilité d'un programme créé de façon indépendante avec d'autres programmes ne peut être réalisée par d'autres moyens qu'en procédant à une décompilation du programme concerné. [**47**] Une telle interprétation est corroborée par l'article 6, paragraphes 2 et 3, de la directive 91/250 qui interdit notamment que les informations obtenues en vertu d'une telle décompilation soient utilisées à des fins autres que la réalisation d'une telle interopérabilité ou utilisées afin de mettre au point des programmes similaires et qui exclut encore, de manière générale, qu'une telle décompilation puisse être réalisée d'une manière telle qu'elle causerait un préjudice injustifié aux intérêts légitimes du titulaire du droit ou porterait atteinte à l'exploitation normale du programme d'ordinateur concerné. [**49**] À cet égard, [. . .] tandis que l'article 6 de la directive 91/250 concerne les actes nécessaires pour assurer l'interopérabilité de programmes créés indépendamment, l'article 5, paragraphe 1, de celle-ci vise à permettre à l'acquéreur légitime d'un programme d'utiliser ce dernier d'une manière conforme à sa destination. Ces deux dispositions ont par conséquent des finalités différentes."

[**Paras. 44, 45, 46, 47, 49**]

I.0.151   INTELLECTUAL PROPERTY RIGHTS
        See also: I.2.2232; I.2.2234

"[**50**] [. . .] [C]ette analyse est corroborée par les travaux préparatoires de la directive 91/250, desquels il ressort que l'insertion, dans la proposition initiale de la Commission européenne, de l'actuel article 6 de cette directive visait à régir, de manière spécifique, la question de l'interopérabilité des programmes créés par des auteurs indépendants, sans préjudice des dispositions destinées à permettre à l'acquéreur légitime du programme une utilisation normale de ce dernier. [**52**] En effet, [. . .] la correction des erreurs affectant le fonctionnement d'un programme d'ordinateur implique, dans la plupart des cas, et notamment lorsque la correction à opérer consiste à désactiver une fonction qui affecte le bon fonctionnement de l'application dont fait partie ce programme, de disposer du code source ou, à défaut, du quasi-code source dudit programme. [**48**] [. . .] [I]l ne saurait [donc] être déduit ni du libellé de l'article 6 de la directive 91/250, lu en combinaison avec les considérants 19 et 20 de celle-ci, ni de l'économie de cet article que le législateur de l'Union aurait eu l'intention d'exclure toute possibilité de procéder à la reproduction du code d'un programme d'ordinateur et à la traduction de la forme de ce code en de-hors du cas dans lequel celles-ci sont accomplies dans le but d'obtenir les informations nécessaires à l'interopérabilité d'un programme d'ordinateur créé de façon indépendante avec d'autres programmes. [**51**] [. . .] [U]ne [telle] interprétation de l'article 6 [. . .] aurait pour conséquence de porter atteinte à l'effet utile de la faculté expressément accordée à l'acquéreur légitime d'un programme par le législateur de l'Union, à l'article 5, paragraphe 1, de la directive 91/250, de procéder à la correction des erreurs empêchant une utilisation du programme conformément à sa destination."

[**Paras. 50, 52, 48, 51**]

I.0.151   INTELLECTUAL PROPERTY RIGHTS
See also: I.2.2232; I.2.2234

"[41] [. . .] [Il découle par conséquent des considérations qui précèdent que] en vertu de l'article 5, paragraphe 1, de la directive 91/250, l'acquéreur légitime d'un programme d'ordinateur peut accomplir tous les actes énumérés à l'article 4, sous a) et b), de cette directive, y compris ceux consistant en la reproduction du code et en la traduction de la forme de celui-ci, sans avoir obtenu au préalable l'autorisation du titulaire, pour autant que cela soit nécessaire aux fins de l'utilisation de ce programme, y compris la correction des erreurs affectant le fonctionnement de celui-ci. [53] [. . .] [I]l y a [donc] lieu de répondre à la première question posée que l'article 5, paragraphe 1, de la directive 91/250 doit être interprété en ce sens que l'acquéreur légitime d'un programme d'ordinateur est en droit de procéder à la décompilation de tout ou partie de celui-ci afin de corriger des erreurs affectant le fonctionnement de ce programme, y compris quand la correction consiste à désactiver une fonction qui affecte le bon fonctionnement de l'application dont fait partie ledit programme. [43] Cette interprétation n'est pas remise en cause par l'article 6 de la directive 91/250 qui [. . .] ne saurait être interprété en ce sens que la possibilité de procéder à la décompilation d'un programme d'ordinateur ne serait permise que pour autant que celle-ci est réalisée à des fins d'interopérabilité."

[Paras. 41, 53, 43]

IV.

I.0.151   INTELLECTUAL PROPERTY RIGHTS
See also: I.2.2232; I.2.2234

"[56] [. . .] [A]u vu du libellé, de l'économie et de la finalité de l'article 5, paragraphe 1, de la directive 91/250, l'accomplissement des actes qui, ensemble, constituent la décompilation d'un programme d'ordinateur est, lorsqu'il est effectué conformément à cette disposition, soumis à certaines exigences. [57] En premier lieu [. . .], ces actes doivent être nécessaires pour permettre à l'acquéreur légitime d'utiliser le programme concerné d'une manière conforme à sa destination et, notamment, pour corriger des « erreurs ». [58] En l'absence de renvoi au droit des États membres et de définition pertinente dans la directive 91/250, la notion d'« erreur », au sens de ladite disposition, doit être interprétée conformément au sens habituel de ce terme dans le langage courant, tout en tenant compte du contexte dans lequel elle s'insère et des objectifs poursuivis par la réglementation dont elle fait partie (arrêt du 3 juin 2021, Hongrie/Parlement, C-650/ 18, [. . .] point 83 et jurisprudence citée). [60] [. . .] [U]ne [telle] erreur [. . .] doit affecter la possibilité d'utiliser le programme concerné d'une manière conforme à sa destination. [61] En deuxième lieu, il découle du libellé de l'article 5, paragraphe 1, de la directive 91/250 que la décompilation d'un programme d'ordinateur doit être « nécessaire » pour permettre à l'acquéreur légitime d'utiliser le programme concerné d'une manière conforme à sa destination. [63] [. . .] [L]orsque le code source est légalement ou contractuellement accessible à l'acquéreur du programme concerné, il ne saurait être considéré qu'il est « nécessaire » pour celui-ci de procéder à une décompilation de ce programme."

[Paras. 56, 57, 58, 60, 61, 63]

I.0.151   INTELLECTUAL PROPERTY RIGHTS
           See also: I.2.2232; I.2.2234

"[**64**] En troisième lieu, [...] l'article 5, paragraphe 1, de la directive 91/250 permet la correction d'erreurs sous réserve des « dispositions contractuelles spécifiques ». [**65**] À cet égard, il convient d'observer que, selon le considérant 17 de la directive 91/250, tant les opérations de chargement et de déroulement nécessaires à l'utilisation d'une copie d'un programme légalement acquis que la correction des erreurs affectant le fonctionnement de celui-ci ne peuvent être interdites contractuellement. [**66**] Ainsi, l'article 5, paragraphe 1, de la directive 91/250, lu en combinaison avec le considérant 18 de celle-ci, doit être compris en ce sens que les parties ne peuvent exclure contractuellement toute possibilité de procéder à une correction de ces erreurs. [**67**] En revanche, conformément à cette disposition, le titulaire et l'acquéreur demeurent libres d'organiser contractuellement les modalités d'exercice de cette faculté. Concrètement, ceux-ci peuvent, en particulier, convenir que le titulaire doit assurer la maintenance corrective du programme concerné. [**68**] Il s'ensuit également que, en l'absence de stipulations contractuelles spécifiques en ce sens, l'acquéreur légitime d'un programme d'ordinateur est en droit d'accomplir, sans l'accord préalable du titulaire, les actes énumérés à l'article 4, sous a) et b), de la directive 91/250, y compris de décompiler ce programme, dans la mesure où cela s'avère nécessaire afin de corriger les erreurs affectant le fonctionnement de celui-ci."

[**Paras. 64, 65, 66, 67, 68**]

I.0.151   INTELLECTUAL PROPERTY RIGHTS
           See also: I.2.2232; I.2.2234

"[**69**] En quatrième lieu, l'acquéreur légitime d'un programme d'ordinateur ayant procédé à la décompilation de ce programme dans le but de corriger les erreurs affectant le fonctionnement de celui-ci ne peut utiliser le résultat de cette décompilation à des fins autres que la correction de ces erreurs. [**70**] En effet, l'article 4, sous b), de la directive 91/250 accorde au titulaire du droit d'auteur le droit exclusif de faire et d'autoriser non seulement « la traduction, l'adaptation, l'arrangement et toute autre transformation d'un programme d'ordinateur », mais également « la reproduction du programme en résultant », c'est-à-dire, dans le cas de la décompilation, celle du code source ou du quasi-code source résultant de celle-ci. [**71**] Ainsi, toute reproduction de ce code demeure soumise, en vertu de l'article 4, sous b), de la directive 91/ 250, à l'autorisation du titulaire du droit d'auteur sur ce programme. [**72**] L'article 4, sous c), de cette directive interdit en outre la distribution au public d'une copie d'un programme d'ordinateur sans le consentement du titulaire des droits d'auteur sur ce programme, ce qui, ainsi qu'il résulte de l'article 1er, paragraphe 2, de la directive 91/ 250, s'applique également aux copies du code source, ou du quasi-code source, obtenu au moyen d'une décompilation. [**73**] Or, s'il est constant que l'article 5 de cette directive autorise l'acquéreur légitime d'un programme d'ordinateur à accomplir de tels actes, sans l'accord du titulaire du droit d'auteur, ce n'est que pour autant que ceux-ci soient nécessaires pour lui permettre d'utiliser le programme d'ordinateur d'une manière conforme à sa destination."

[**Paras. 69, 70, 71, 72, 73**]

I.0.151   INTELLECTUAL PROPERTY RIGHTS
             See also: I.2.2232; I.2.2234

"[74] Eu égard aux considérations qui précèdent, il y a lieu de répondre à la seconde question posée que l'article 5, paragraphe 1, de la directive 91/250 doit être interprété en ce sens que l'acquéreur légitime d'un programme d'ordinateur qui souhaite procéder à la décompilation de ce programme dans le but de corriger des erreurs affectant le fonctionnement de celui-ci n'est pas tenu de satisfaire aux exigences prévues à l'article 6 de cette directive. Cependant, cet acquéreur n'est en droit de procéder à une telle décompilation que dans la mesure nécessaire à cette correction et dans le respect, le cas échéant, des conditions prévues contractuellement avec le titulaire du droit d'auteur sur ledit programme."

[Para. 74]

V.

II.2.5   JUDGMENT/DECISION/ORDER
            See also: I.0.151; I.2.2232; I.2.2234

"Par ces motifs, la Cour (cinquième chambre) dit pour droit: 1) L'article 5, paragraphe 1, de la directive 91/250/CEE du Conseil, du 14 mai 1991, concernant la protection juridique des programmes d'ordinateur, doit être interprété en ce sens que l'acquéreur légitime d'un programme d'ordinateur est en droit de procéder à la décompilation de tout ou partie de celui-ci afin de corriger des erreurs affectant le fonctionnement de ce programme, y compris quand la correction consiste à désactiver une fonction qui affecte le bon fonctionnement de l'application dont fait partie ledit programme. 2) L'article 5, paragraphe 1, de la directive 91/250 doit être interprété en ce sens que l'acquéreur légitime d'un programme d'ordinateur qui souhaite procéder à la décompilation de ce programme dans le but de corriger des erreurs affectant le fonctionnement de celui-ci n'est pas tenu de satisfaire aux exigences prévues à l'article 6 de cette directive. Cependant, cet acquéreur n'est en droit de procéder à une telle décompilation que dans la mesure nécessaire à cette correction et dans le respect, le cas échéant, des conditions prévues contractuellement avec le titulaire du droit d'auteur sur ledit programme."

VI.2.4

Republiken Polen v. PL Holdings Sàrl, Case C-109/20, Grand Chamber, Judgment, 26 October 2021*

Contents**

I. REFERENCE FOR A PRELIMINARY RULING

II. ARBITRATION AND AUTONOMY OF EU LAW

III. REQUEST THAT THE COURT LIMIT THE TEMPORAL EFFECTS OF ITS JUDGMENT

IV. JUDGMENT

I.

II.2.0   INSTITUTION AND COURSE OF PROCEEDINGS
See also: I.14.214; I.14.2141; I.14.23; I.17.011; II.7.723

"[1] This request for a preliminary ruling concerns the interpretation of Articles 267 and 344 TFEU. [2] The request has been made in proceedings between Republiken Polen (Republic of Poland) and PL Holdings Sàrl concerning the jurisdiction of an arbitration body which has made two arbitration awards in the context of a dispute between them. [32] The Republic of Poland brought an appeal against the decision of the Svea hovrätt (Svea Court of Appeal, Stockholm), before the referring court, the Högsta domstolen (Supreme Court, Sweden), which considers it established that the arbitration clause in Article 9 of the BIT is contrary to EU law. [. . .] [33] [. . .] [T]he Högsta domstolen (Supreme Court) decided to stay the proceedings and to refer the following question to the Court of Justice for a preliminary ruling: 'Do Articles 267 and 344 TFEU, as interpreted in [the judgment of 6 March 2018, *Achmea* (C 284/16, EU:C:2018:158)], mean that an arbitration agreement is invalid if it has been concluded between a Member State and an investor – where an investment agreement contains an arbitration clause that is invalid as a result of the fact that the contract was concluded between two Member States – by virtue of the fact that the Member State, after arbitration proceedings were commenced by the investor, refrains, by the free will of the State, from raising objections as to jurisdiction?'."

[Paras. 1, 2, 32, 33]

II.

I.17.01   TREATIES AS SOURCES OF INTERNATIONAL INVESTMENT LAW
See also: I.2.223; I.2.2231; I.2.2234; I.14.214

"[44] [. . .] [I]t should be observed that the Court has held that Articles 267 and 344 TFEU must be interpreted as precluding a provision in an international agreement concluded

---

* Summaries prepared by Simona Fanni, Ph.D. in Legal Sciences, Postdoctoral Fellow "Margarita Salas", Universidad de Sevilla, Spain. Text of judgment available online at the Court's Web site <http://www.curia.europa.eu>. Language of the case: Swedish.

** This is not a faithful reproduction of the Table of Contents of the Judgment.

between two Member States under which an investor from one of those Member States may, in the event of a dispute concerning investments in the other Member State, bring proceedings against the latter Member State before an arbitral tribunal whose jurisdiction that Member State has undertaken to accept (judgment of 6 March 2018, *Achmea*, C 284/16, EU:C:2018:158, paragraph 60). [**45**] By concluding such an agreement, the Member States which are parties to it agree to remove from the jurisdiction of their own courts and, therefore, from the system of judicial remedies which the second subparagraph of Article 19(1) TEU requires them to establish in the fields covered by EU law (see, to that effect, judgment of 27 February 2018, *Associação Sindical dos Juízes Portugueses*, C 64/16, EU:C:2018:117, paragraph 34) disputes which may concern the application or interpretation of EU law. Such an agreement is, therefore, capable of preventing those disputes from being resolved in a manner that guarantees the full effectiveness of that law (see, to that effect, judgment of 2 September 2021, *Komstroy*, C 741/19, EU:C:2021:655, paragraphs 59 and 60 and the case-law cited)."

[**Paras. 44, 45**]

I.2.2234   APPLICATION AND INTERPRETATION OF EU LAW
         See also: I.2.2231; I.2.2233; I.14.214; I.14.23

"[**46**] It is common ground that the arbitration clause in Article 9 of the BIT is, like the clause at issue in the case which gave rise to the judgment of 6 March 2018, *Achmea* (C 284/16, EU:C:2018:158), capable of leading to a situation in which an arbitration body rules in disputes which may concern the application or interpretation of EU law. Accordingly, that arbitration clause is such as to call into question not only the principle of mutual trust between the Member States but also the preservation of the particular nature of EU law, ensured by the preliminary ruling procedure provided for in Article 267 TFEU. That clause is, therefore, incompatible with the principle of sincere cooperation set out in the first subparagraph of Article 4(3) TEU and has an adverse effect on the autonomy of EU law enshrined, inter alia, in Article 344 TFEU (see, to that effect, judgment of 6 March 2018, *Achmea*, C 284/16, EU:C:2018:158, paragraphs 58 and 59). [...] [**47**] To allow a Member State, which is a party to a dispute which may concern the application and interpretation of EU law, to submit that dispute to an arbitral body with the same characteristics as the body referred to in an invalid arbitration clause contained in an international agreement such as the one referred to in paragraph 44 above, by concluding an ad hoc arbitration agreement with the same content as that clause, would in fact entail a circumvention of the obligations arising for that Member State under the Treaties and, specifically, under Article 4(3) TEU and Articles 267 and 344 TFEU, as interpreted in the judgment of 6 March 2018, *Achmea* (C 284/16, EU:C:2018:158). [**48**] First of all, [...] [t]he fundamental reason for that arbitration agreement is precisely to replace the arbitration clause in a provision such as Article 9 of the BIT in order to maintain its effects despite that provision's being invalid. [**49**] [...] [Moreover,] [t]he legal approach envisaged by PL Holdings could be adopted in a multitude of disputes which may concern the application and interpretation of EU law, thus allowing the autonomy of that law to be undermined repeatedly."

[**Paras. 46, 47, 48, 49**]

I.14.23   ARBITRATION AGREEMENT
         See also: I.2.2233; I.2.2234; I.2.22342; I.14.214; I.14.2141

"[**52**] [...] [I]t follows both from the judgment of 6 March 2018, *Achmea* (C 284/16, EU:C:2018:158), and from the principles of the primacy of EU law and of sincere cooperation, not only that the Member States cannot undertake to remove from the judicial system of the European Union disputes which may concern the application and interpretation of EU law, but also that, where such a dispute is brought before an arbitration body on the basis of an undertaking which is contrary to EU law, they are required to challenge, before that arbitration body or before the court with jurisdiction, the validity of the arbitration clause or the ad hoc arbitration agreement on the basis of which the dispute was brought before that arbitration body. [**54**] Any attempt by a Member State to remedy the invalidity of an arbitration clause by means of a contract with an investor from another Member State would run counter to the first Member State's obligation to challenge the validity of the arbitration clause and would thus be liable to render the actual legal basis of that contract unlawful since it would be contrary to the provisions and fundamental principles governing the EU legal order referred to in paragraph 46 above."

[Paras. 52, 54]

III.

I.2.2234   APPLICATION AND INTERPRETATION OF EU LAW
See also: I.2.2233

"[**59**] It is only quite exceptionally that the Court may, in application of the general principle of legal certainty inherent in the EU legal order, be moved to restrict for any person concerned the opportunity of relying on a provision which it has interpreted with a view to calling into question legal relationships established in good faith. Two essential criteria must be fulfilled before such a limitation can be imposed: those concerned must have acted in good faith and there must be a risk of serious difficulties (judgment of 17 March 2021, *Academia de Studii Economice din București*, C 585/19, EU:C:2021:210, paragraph 79 and the case-law cited). [**61**] It should also be noted that restricting the temporal effects of the interpretation of a provision of EU law provided by the Court under Article 267 TFEU may be allowed only in the actual judgment ruling upon the interpretation requested. That principle guarantees the equal treatment of the Member States and of other persons subject to EU law, under that law, fulfilling, at the same time, the requirements arising from the principle of legal certainty (judgment of 23 April 2020, *Herst*, C 401/18, EU:C:2020:295, paragraph 57 and the case-law cited)."

[Paras. 59, 61]

I.2.2234   APPLICATION AND INTERPRETATION OF EU LAW
See also: I.2.2231; I.14.23

"[**65**] [...] [T]o allow a Member State to replace an arbitration clause, included in an international agreement between Member States, by concluding an ad hoc arbitration agreement in order to make it possible to pursue arbitration proceedings initiated on the basis of that clause, would, as has been held in paragraph 47 above, amount to circumventing that Member State's obligations under the Treaties and, specifically, under Article 4(3) TEU and Articles 267 and 344 TFEU, as interpreted in the judgment of 6 March 2018, *Achmea* (C 284/16, EU:C:2018:158). [**66**] Thus, a limitation of the temporal effects of the present judgment would, in actual fact, entail limiting the effects of the interpretation of those provisions provided by the Court in the judgment of 6 March 2018, *Achmea* (C 284/16, EU:C:2018:158)."

[Paras. 65, 66]

IV.

II.2.5   JUDGMENT/DECISION/ORDER
                See also: I.14.23; II.7.723

"On those grounds, the Court (Grand Chamber) hereby rules:

Articles 267 and 344 TFEU must be interpreted as precluding national legislation which allows a Member State to conclude an ad hoc arbitration agreement with an investor from another Member State that makes it possible to continue arbitration proceedings initiated on the basis of an arbitration clause whose content is identical to that agreement, where that clause is contained in an international agreement concluded between those two Member States and is invalid on the ground that it is contrary to those articles."

VI.2.5

European Commission v. Republic of Poland, Case C-204/21 R, Order of the Vice-President of the Court, 27 October 2021*

Contents**

   I. THE ORDER

   II. APPLICATION AND INTERPRETATION OF EU LAW

   III. DECISION

I.

II.7.728   EU COURT PROVISIONAL MEASURES
         See also: II.7.7

"[1] [. . .][T]he Republic of Poland requests the Court to cancel the order of the Vice-President of the Court of 14 July 2021 [that] [2] [. . .] ordered the Republic of Poland [. . .] to suspend [. . .] the application [of certain] Article[s] of the ustawa o Sądzie Najwyższym (Law on the Supreme Court), [. . .] [3] considering a change in circumstances to have taken place after the making of the order [and] request[ed] that the application be examined by the Grand Chamber of the Court."

[Paras. 1, 2, 3]

II.

I.2.2234   APPLICATION AND INTERPRETATION OF EU LAW
         See also: I.2.222; II.7.73

"[5][. . .] [T]he Vice-President of the Court is to either decide on applications for suspension of operation or for interim measures himself or herself or refer those applications immediately to the Court. [6] Thus, [. . .] competence has been conferred on the Vice-President of the Court to rule on any application for interim measures or, where he or she takes the view that the particular circumstances require the referral of the case to a formation of the Court, to refer such an application to the Court [. . .]. [7] It follows that it is for the Vice-President of the Court alone to assess, on a case-by-case basis, whether the applications for interim measures before him or her require referral to the Court for the purpose of their assignment to a formation of the Court [. . .]."

[Paras. 5, 6, 7]

---

* Summaries prepared by Roberto Soprano, Professor Associat, Universitat Pompeu Fabra, Department of Law, Ph.D. in International Law, Faculty of Law, University of Salerno, Italy. Text of judgment available online at the Court's Web site <http://www.curia.europa.eu> . Language of the Case: Polish.

** This is not a faithful reproduction of the Table of Contents of the Judgment.

I.2.22342   PRINCIPLE OF PRIMACY OF EU LAW
           See also: I.2.2234; I.2.2235

"[**16**] [. . .][A]n order for interim measures may at any time be varied or cancelled on account of a change in circumstances. The concept of a 'change in circumstances' refers in particular to the occurrence of any factual or legal element capable of calling into question the assessments of the judge hearing the application for interim measures as to the conditions to which the grant of a suspension or of interim relief is subject [. . .]. [**17**] It is therefore appropriate to ascertain whether the judgment [at stake] constitutes a 'change in circumstances' within the meaning of that article. [**18**] In that regard, [. . .] the principle of the primacy of EU law establishes the pre-eminence of EU law over the law of the Member States. That principle therefore requires all Member State bodies to give full effect to the various EU provisions, and the law of the Member States may not undermine the effect accorded to those various provisions in the territory of those States [. . .]. [**19**] [. . .][E]very Member State must thus in particular ensure that the bodies which, as 'courts or tribunals' within the meaning of EU law, come within its judicial system in the fields covered by EU law and which, therefore, are liable to rule, in that capacity, on the application or interpretation of EU law, meet the requirements of effective judicial protection [. . .]. [**20**] That provision thus imposes on the Member States a clear and precise obligation as to the result to be achieved and that obligation is not subject to any condition as regards the independence which must characterise the courts called upon to interpret and apply EU law [. . .]. [**21**] Thus [. . .], when exercising that competence, the Member States are nevertheless required to comply with their obligations deriving from the second subparagraph of Article 19(1) TEU [. . .]. [**22**] It follows that the national provisions on the organisation of justice in the Member States may be subject to review in the light of the second subparagraph of Article 19(1) TEU in the context of an action for failure to fulfil obligations, and, consequently, to interim measures aimed, in particular, at their suspension that are ordered by the Court [. . .]. [**23**] The fact that a national constitutional court declares that such measures are contrary to the constitutional order of the Member State concerned in no way alters the assessment set out in the preceding paragraph. [**24**] [. . .] [B]y virtue of the principle of the primacy of EU law, a Member State's reliance on rules of national law, even of a constitutional order, cannot be allowed to undermine the unity and effectiveness of EU law [. . .]."

[**Paras. 16, 17, 18, 19, 20, 21, 22, 23, 24**]

III.

II.2.5   JUDGMENT/DECISION/ORDER

"On those grounds, the Vice-President of the Court hereby orders:

1. The application seeking that the order of the Vice-President of the Court of 14 July 2021, *Commission* v *Poland* (C-204/21 R, EU:C:2021:593) be cancelled is dismissed.
2. The costs are reserved."

VI.2.6

Google LLC and Alphabet, Inc. v. European Commission, **Case T-612/17, Ninth Chamber, Extended Composition, Judgment, 10 November 2021***

Contents**

I.

II.7.722   EU COURT PROCEEDINGS FOR ANNULMENT
See also: I.2.2257; II.7.723

"[1] Google LLC, formerly Google Inc., is a United States company specialising in internet-related products and services. It is principally known for its search engine, which allows internet users [...] to locate and access websites that match their requirements by means of the browser they are using and hyperlinks. [...] [2] [...] Those results are either selected by the search engine according to general criteria and without the websites to which they link paying Google in order to appear ('general search results' or 'generic results'), or selected in accordance with a specialised logic for the particular type of search carried out ('specialised search results', also referred to as 'vertical' or 'universal search results'; 'specialised search results'). Specialised search results may appear without any specific intervention on the part of the internet user alongside general search results on the same page ('general results page(s)'), or they may appear alone in response to a query entered by the internet user on one of the specialised pages of Google's search engine or after links appearing in certain areas of Google's general results pages have been activated. Google has developed various specialised search services, for example for news, local business information and offers, flights or shopping. It is the last category that is at issue in this case. [21] The

---

* Summaries prepared by Daniela Rodríguez Bautista, Doctor in Law, Administrator at the Court of Justice of the European Union. Text of judgment available online at the Court's Web site <http://www.curia.eur opa.eu>. Language of the Case: English. The selection of extracts can only be attributed to the author and not to the institutions of her affiliation.

** This is not a faithful reproduction of the Table of Contents of the Judgment.

present case has resulted from a number of complaints that were lodged with the European Commission, in or after November 2009, by undertakings, associations of undertakings and consumer associations, as well as cases referred to the Commission by national competition authorities [...]. [22] On 30 November 2010, the Commission initiated proceedings against Google pursuant to Article 2(1) of Commission Regulation (EC) No 773/2004 of 7 April 2004 relating to the conduct of proceedings by the Commission pursuant to Articles [101] and [102 TFEU] [...]. [39] On 27 June 2017, the Commission adopted Decision C(2017) 4444 final relating to proceedings under Article 102 TFEU and Article 54 of the EEA Agreement (Case AT.39740 – Google Search (Shopping)) ('the contested decision')."

[Paras. 1, 2, 21, 22, 39]

II.

II.1.0   BURDEN OF PROOF
              See also: I.2.2257; II.7.722

"[132] [...] [I]t is apparent from the case-law of the Court of Justice that, in the field of competition law, where there is a dispute as to the existence of an infringement, it is for the Commission to prove the infringements found by it and to adduce evidence capable of demonstrating to the requisite legal standard the existence of the circumstances constituting an infringement. Where the Court still has a doubt, the benefit of that doubt must be given to the undertakings accused of the infringement (judgments of 22 November 2012, *E.ON Energie v Commission*, C-89/11 P, EU:C:2012:738, paragraphs 71 and 72, and of 16 February 2017, *Hansen & Rosenthal and H&R Wax Company Vertrieb v Commission*, C-90/15 P [...], EU:C:2017:123, paragraphs 17 and 18). [554] [However,] [a]lthough the burden of proof of the existence of the circumstances that constitute an infringement of Article 102 TFEU is borne by the Commission, it is for the dominant undertaking concerned, and not for the Commission, to raise any plea of justification and to support it with arguments and evidence. It then falls to the Commission, where it proposes to make a finding of an abuse of a dominant position, to show that the arguments and evidence relied on by the undertaking cannot prevail and, accordingly, that the justification put forward cannot be accepted (judgment of 17 September 2007, *Microsoft v Commission*, T-201/04, EU:T:2007:289, paragraph 1144)."

[Paras. 132, 554]

III.

I.2.2257   EU COMMON RULES ON COMPETITION, TAXATION AND
               APPROXIMATION LAW
               See also: I.2.2265; II.7.722

"[150] According to settled case-law, a dominant undertaking has a special responsibility not to allow its behaviour to impair genuine, undistorted competition on the internal market ([...] judgment of 6 September 2017, *Intel v Commission*, C-413/14 P, EU:C:2017:632, paragraph 135 [...]). [151] In that regard, Article 102 TFEU applies, in particular, to the conduct of a dominant undertaking that, through recourse to methods different from those governing normal competition on the basis of the performance of commercial operators, has the effect, to the detriment of consumers, of hindering the maintenance of the degree of competition existing in the market or the growth of that competition ([...] judgment of 27 March 2012, *Post Danmark*, C-209/10, EU:C:2012:172, paragraph 24 [...]). [**152**] Thus, Article 102 TFEU prohibits a dominant undertaking from, among other things, adopting practices that have an exclusionary effect by using methods other than those that are part of competition on the merits ([...] judgments of 27 March 2012, *Post Danmark*, C-209/10, EU:C:2012:172, paragraph 25 [...], and of 6 September 2017, *Intel v Commission*, C-413/14 P, EU:C:2017:632, paragraph 136). [**156**] It is, however, in no way the purpose of Article 102 TFEU to prevent an undertaking from acquiring, on its own merits, a dominant position on a market ([...] judgment of 6 September 2017, *Intel v Commission*, C-413/14 P, EU:C:2017:632, paragraph 133 [...]). [**157**] Thus, not every exclusionary effect is necessarily detrimental to competition. Competition on the merits may, by definition, lead to the departure from the market or the marginalisation of competitors that are less attractive to consumers from the point of view of, among other things, price, choice, quality or innovation ([...] judgment of 6 September 2017, *Intel v Commission*, C-413/14 P, EU:C:2017:632, paragraph 134 [...]). [**255**] However, the existence of any anticompetitive intent constitutes only one of a number of facts which may be taken into account in order to determine that a dominant position has been abused (judgment of 19 April 2012, *Tomra Systems and Others v Commission*, C-549/10 P, EU:C:2012:221, paragraph 20). [**257**] In addition, the existence of an intention to compete on the merits, even if it were established, could not prove the absence of abuse (judgment of 19 April 2012, *Tomra Systems and Others v Commission*, C-549/10 P, EU:C:2012:221, paragraph 22)."

[**Paras. 150, 151, 152, 156, 157, 255, 257**]

IV.

I.2.2257   EU COMMON RULES ON COMPETITION, TAXATION AND APPROXIMATION LAW

See also: I.2.2265; II.7.722

"[**213**] [...] [I]n the judgment of 26 November 1998, *Bronner* (C-7/97, EU:C:1998:569), the Court of Justice considered that, in order for the refusal by an undertaking in a dominant position to grant access to a service to be capable of constituting an abuse within the meaning of Article 102 TFEU, it was necessary that that refusal be likely to eliminate all competition in the market on the part of the person requesting the service, that such refusal be incapable of being objectively justified and that the service in itself be indispensable to carrying on that person's business, inasmuch as there was no actual or potential substitute for it (judgment of 26 November 1998, *Bronner*, C-7/97, EU:C:1998:569, paragraph 41; see also judgment of 9 September 2009, *Clearstream v Commission*, T-301/04, EU:T:2009:317, paragraph 147 [...]). [**215**] The conditions set out in [...] [such case-law] apply, in principle, to infrastructures or to services that are often described as an 'essential facility' in the sense that they are indispensable for carrying on a business on a market where there is no actual or potential substitute ([...] judgments of 15 September 1998, *European Night Services and Others v Commission*, T-374/94, T-375/94, T-384/94 and T-388/94, EU:T:1998:198, paragraphs 208 and 212 [...], and of 9 September 2009, *Clearstream v Commission*, T-301/04, EU:T:2009:317, paragraph 147 [...]), so that refusing access may lead to the elimination of all competition. [...] [**240**] It must therefore be concluded that the Commission was not required to establish that the conditions set out in the judgment of 26 November 1998, *Bronner* (C-7/97, EU:C:1998:569), were satisfied in order to make a finding of an infringement on the basis of the practices identified, since,

[...] the practices at issue are an independent form of leveraging abuse which involve [. ..] 'active' behaviour in the form of positive acts of discrimination in the treatment of the results of Google's comparison shopping service, which are promoted within its general results pages, and the results of competing comparison shopping services, which are prone to being demoted.[...]"

[**Paras. 213, 215, 240**]

V.

I.2.2257   EU COMMON RULES ON COMPETITION, TAXATION AND
            APPROXIMATION LAW
            See also: I.2.2265; II.7.722

"[**372**] In essence, what the Commission called into question is the combination of practices which, on the one hand, promoted Google's comparison shopping service and, on the other, demoted competing comparison shopping services in Google's general results pages. It follows that the effects of those combined practices cannot be analysed by isolating the effects of one aspect of those practices from those of the other. [**377**] [Thus,] identifying a credible counterfactual scenario in order to analyse the effects on a market of what are assumed to be anticompetitive practices, that is to say, identifying the events that would have occurred in the absence of the practices that are being examined and identifying the situation that would have resulted, may, in a situation such as that of the present case, be an arbitrary or even impossible exercise if that counterfactual scenario does not really exist for a market that originally had similar characteristics to the market or markets in which those practices were implemented. In principle, in the case of existing competitive relationships, not just possible or potential competition, a credible counterfactual scenario must reflect an actual situation that is initially similar but whose development is not affected by all of the practices at issue. In comparing such a counterfactual scenario with the situation observed on the market to which those practices relate, the actual effects of those practices can normally be established, by isolating them from changes that are attributable to other reasons. In that respect, a counterfactual scenario, which compares two actual developments in such a situation, can be distinguished from an assessment of potential effects which, although it must be realistic, effectively describes a probable situation."

[**Paras. 372, 377**]

VI.

I.2.2257   EU COMMON RULES ON COMPETITION, TAXATION AND
            APPROXIMATION LAW
            See also: I.2.2265; II.7.722

"[**438**] As regards exclusionary practices, it has been inferred from this that a practice cannot be categorised as abuse of a dominant position unless it is demonstrated that there is an anticompetitive effect, or at the very least a potential anticompetitive effect, although, in the absence of any effect on the competitive situation of competitors, an exclusionary practice cannot be classified as abusive vis-à-vis those competitors ([...] judgments of 14 October 2010, *Deutsche Telekom* v *Commission*, C-280/08 P, EU:C:2010:603, paragraphs 250 to 254; of 17 February 2011, *TeliaSonera Sverige*, C-52/09, EU:C:2011:83, paragraphs 61 to 66; and of 19 April 2012, *Tomra Systems and Others* v *Commission*, C-549/10 P,

EU:C:2012:221, paragraph 68). [**439**] In that context, even when conduct of dominant undertakings is in issue that is in principle anticompetitive, such as conduct designed to secure an exclusive or highly preferential purchasing relationship with customers, possibly by means of loyalty rebates ([...] judgment of 13 February 1979, *Hoffmann-La Roche v Commission*, 85/76, EU:C:1979:36, paragraph 89), if the dominant undertaking concerned disputes, with documented evidence, that its conduct was capable of restricting competition, the competition authority handling the case must analyse all the relevant circumstances in order to decide what the position is ([...] judgments of 17 February 2011, *TeliaSonera Sverige*, C-52/09, EU:C:2011:83, paragraph 68; of 6 October 2015, *Post Danmark*, C-23/14, EU:C:2015:651, paragraph 68; and of 6 September 2017, *Intel v Commission*, C-413/14 P, EU:C:2017:632, paragraphs 138 and 139). [**541**] It follows that [...] the Commission had only to demonstrate the potential exclusionary or restrictive effects on competition attributable to the practices at issue, irrespective of whether, in relation to comparison shopping, Google was 'more efficient' than the other comparison shopping services, which is actually impossible to know when those practices are capable of distorting competition."

[**Paras. 438, 439, 541**]

VII.

I.2.2257   EU COMMON RULES ON COMPETITION, TAXATION AND
            APPROXIMATION LAW
            See also: I.2.2265; II.7.722

"[**612**] [...] [I]t is apparent from settled case-law that, regardless of the reasons for its dominant position in a market, even if it is held as a result of the quality of its products and its services, the undertaking holding that position has a special responsibility not to allow its conduct to impair genuine undistorted competition in the internal market ([...] judgments of 9 November 1983, *Nederlandsche Banden-Industrie-Michelin* v *Commission*, 322/81, EU:C:1983:313, paragraph 57, and of 17 February 2011, *TeliaSonera Sverige*, C-52/09, EU:C:2011:83, paragraph 24). [**616**] Having regard to the above, it appears that, since it was aware of its dominant position in the markets for general search services in the [...][European Economic Area] and favoured its own comparison shopping service over its competitors in its general results pages, conduct which represented a certain form of abnormality, [...] and since it was aware also of the importance of those pages as a source of traffic for comparison shopping services, [...] Google [...] intentionally engaged in conduct that was anticompetitive, [...] which was capable of constituting an abuse of a dominant position. It must be held that that infringement was therefore committed intentionally, including prior to Google's receipt, in March 2013, of the preliminary assessment in which the Commission explained why its conduct was capable of infringing Article 102 TFEU. [**618**] [Nevertheless], [t]he fact that the precise type of conduct in which Google engaged has not, prior to the contested decision, been examined in a decision applying EU competition rules, which the Commission acknowledged by publicly stating in the press release announcing the contested decision that it was 'a precedent which establish[ed] the framework for the assessment of the legality of this type of conduct', does not mean that the finding of an infringement by Google, or a penalty, was unforeseeable for Google [...] ([...] judgment of 8 September 2016, *Lundbeck* v *Commission*, T-472/13, EU:T:2016:449, paragraphs 761 to 767)."

[**Paras. 612, 616, 618**]

VIII.

II.2.5   JUDGMENT/DECISION/ORDER

        See also: I.2.22771

"On those grounds, THE GENERAL COURT (Ninth Chamber, Extended Composition): [...] Annuls Article 1 of Commission Decision C(2017) 4444 final of 27 June 2017 relating to proceedings under Article 102 TFEU and Article 54 of the EEA Agreement (Case AT.39740 – Google Search (Shopping)) in so far only as the European Commission found an infringement of those provisions by Google LLC and Alphabet, Inc. in 13 national markets for general search services within the European Economic Area (EEA) on the basis of the existence of anticompetitive effects in those markets [...]."

VI.2.7

Governor of Cloverhill Prison and Others, Case C-479/21 PPU, Grand Chamber, Judgment, 16 November 2021*

Contents**

I. SUBJECT MATTER AND BACKGROUND TO THE CASE

II. LEGAL FRAMEWORK

III. THE POST-BREXIT CRIMINAL EXTRADITION

IV. JUDGMENT

I.

II.2.0   INSTITUTION AND COURSE OF PROCEEDINGS

See also: I.2.22551; II.7.7; II.7.723

"[1] This request for a preliminary ruling concerns the interpretation of Article 50 TEU, Article 217 TFEU, Protocol (No 21) on the position of the United Kingdom and Ireland in respect of the Area of Freedom, Security and Justice, annexed to the TEU and the TFEU ('Protocol (No 21)'), the Agreement on the withdrawal of the United Kingdom of Great Britain and Northern Ireland from the European Union and the European Atomic Energy Community [. . .] ('the Withdrawal Agreement') and the Trade and Cooperation Agreement between the European Union and the European Atomic Energy Community, of the one part, and the United Kingdom of Great Britain and Northern Ireland, of the other part [. . .] ('the TCA'). [2] The request has been made in connection with the execution, in Ireland, of two arrest warrants issued by the judicial authorities of the United Kingdom of Great Britain and Northern Ireland seeking the surrender of, respectively, SD for the purposes of executing a criminal penalty and SN for the purposes of conducting a criminal prosecution. [26] On 16 February 2021 and 5 March 2021, respectively, SD and SN applied to the High Court (Ireland) for an inquiry into, in essence, the legality of their detention, arguing that Ireland could no longer apply the European arrest warrant regime in respect of the United Kingdom. The High Court determined that the detention of SD and SN was lawful and therefore refused to order their release. SD and SN then brought two separate appeals before the referring court. [27] According to that court, the European Arrest Warrant Act 2003, which transposes Framework Decision 2002/584 into Irish law, may apply in relation to a third country provided that there is an agreement in force between that third country and the European Union for the surrender of persons wanted for prosecution or punishment. However, in order for that legislation to apply, the agreement in question must be binding on Ireland. [38] [. . .] [T]he referring court seeks to ascertain, in essence, whether (i) the provisions of the Withdrawal Agreement which provide for the continuation of the European arrest warrant regime in respect of the United Kingdom during the transition period and (ii) the provision of the TCA which provides for

---

* Summaries prepared by Eirini Pantelodimou, Doctor of Laws (University of Paris I, Panthéon-Sorbonne), Référendaire at the General Court of the European Union. Text of judgment available online at the Court's Web site <http://www.curia.europa.eu>. Language of the Case: English. The selection of extracts can only be attributed to the author and not to the institutions of her affiliation.

** This is not a faithful reproduction of the Table of Contents of the Judgment.

the application of the surrender regime established by Title VII of Part Three of the TCA to European arrest warrants issued before the end of that transition period in respect of persons not yet arrested for the purpose of the execution of those warrants before the end of that period, are binding on Ireland."

[Paras. 1, 2, 26, 27, 38]

II.

II.7.73   LAW APPLIED BY THE EU COURT
               See also: I.2.22551; I.2.2278; II.7.723

"[41] Article 62(1)(b) and the fourth paragraph of Article 185 of the Withdrawal Agreement provide for the continuation of the obligation to execute, after the end of the transition period, European arrest warrants issued in accordance with Framework Decision 2002/584 where the requested person was arrested before the end of that period, stipulated in Article 126 of that agreement as 31 December 2020. [42] Article 632 of the TCA makes the execution of European arrest warrants issued in accordance with that framework decision before the end of the transition period subject to the surrender regime provided for in Title VII of Part Three of that agreement where the requested person has not been arrested for the purpose of executing the European arrest warrant before the end of that period. [45] [...] Protocol (No 21) provides that Ireland is not to take part in the adoption by the Council of proposed measures under Title V of Part Three of the TFEU and that no measure adopted pursuant to that title and no provision of any international agreement concluded by the European Union pursuant to that title are to be binding on or applicable to Ireland unless Ireland decides to take part in the adoption of such measures or to accept them. [46] However, the Withdrawal Agreement and the TCA were not concluded on the basis of that title, but on the basis of Article 50(2) TEU and Article 217 TFEU respectively. [...]"

[Paras. 41, 42, 45, 46]

III.

I.2.22551   EUROPEAN ARREST WARRANT
               See also: I.2.2278; II.7.723

"[48] As regards, in the first place, Article 50 TEU, the chosen legal basis for the Withdrawal Agreement, it is apparent from paragraphs 2 and 3 thereof that that agreement sets out a withdrawal procedure consisting of, first, notification to the European Council of the intention to withdraw, secondly, negotiation and conclusion of an agreement setting out the arrangements for withdrawal, taking into account the future relationship between the State concerned and the European Union and, thirdly, the actual withdrawal from the Union on the date of entry into force of that agreement or, failing that, two years after the notification given to the European Council, unless the latter, in agreement with the Member State concerned, unanimously decides to extend that period [...]. [54] Since [...] it is not possible to add to Article 50(2) TEU legal bases laying down procedures which are incompatible with the procedure laid down in paragraphs 2 and 4 of that article [...], it must be concluded that only Article 50 TEU, as an autonomous legal basis independent of any other legal basis set out in the treaties, can ensure that all of the fields falling within the scope of those treaties are treated consistently in the Withdrawal Agreement, thus enabling the withdrawal to take place in an orderly manner. [56] Accordingly, since Article 50(2)

TEU constitutes the only appropriate legal basis for concluding the Withdrawal Agreement, the provisions of Protocol (No 21) could not apply in that context. [**57**] As regards, in the second place, Article 217 TFEU, the chosen legal basis for the TCA, the Court has already clarified that it empowers the European Union to guarantee commitments towards third countries in all the fields covered by the TFEU [...]. [**58**] Agreements concluded on the basis of that provision may therefore contain rules concerning all the fields falling within the competence of the European Union. Given that, under Article 4(2)(j) TFEU, the European Union has shared competence as regards Title V of Part Three of the TFEU, measures falling within that area of competence may be included in an association agreement based on Article 217 TFEU, such as the TCA. [**59**] Since [...] the surrender mechanism established by Title VII of Part Three of the TCA [...] does indeed fall within that area of competence, it is necessary to examine whether the inclusion of such a mechanism in an association agreement also requires the addition of a specific legal basis such as point (d) of the second subparagraph of Article 82(1) TFEU. [**62**] [...] [S]ince the conclusion of an agreement such as the TCA does not relate to a single specific area of action but, on the contrary, a wide range of areas of EU competence with a view to achieving an Association between the European Union and a third State, and the conclusion of such an agreement requires, in any event – in accordance with point (a)(i) of the second subparagraph of Article 218(6) TFEU and the first sentence of the second subparagraph of Article 218(8) TFEU – a unanimous vote and the consent of the European Parliament, there is no risk, as regards the conclusion of such an agreement, of more stringent procedural requirements being circumvented. [**69**] Consequently, the rules set out in the TCA concerning the surrender of persons on the basis of an arrest warrant, in particular Article 632 thereof relating to the application of those rules to existing European arrest warrants, could be included in that agreement on the basis of Article 217 TFEU alone, without the provisions of Protocol (No 21) being applicable to them."

[**Paras. 48, 54, 56, 57, 58, 59, 62, 69**]

IV.

II.2.5   JUDGMENT/DECISION/ORDER
         See also: II.7.723

"On those grounds, the Court (Grand Chamber) hereby rules:
Article 50 TEU, Article 217 TFEU and Protocol (No 21) on the position of the United Kingdom and Ireland in respect of the Area of Freedom, Security and Justice, annexed to the TEU and the TFEU, must be interpreted as meaning that Article 62(1)(b) of the Agreement on the withdrawal of the United Kingdom of Great Britain and Northern Ireland from the European Union and the European Atomic Energy Community, read in conjunction with the fourth paragraph of Article 185 thereof, and Article 632 of the Trade and Cooperation Agreement between the European Union and the European Atomic Energy Community, of the one part, and the United Kingdom of Great Britain and Northern Ireland, of the other part, are binding on Ireland."

VI.2.8

Prokuratura Rejonowa w Mińsku Mazowieckim, **Joined Cases C-748/19 to C-754/19, Grand Chamber, Judgment, 16 November 2021***

Contents**

I. REFERENCE FOR A PRELIMINARY RULING

II. PROVISION OF REMEDIES SUFFICIENT TO ENSURE EFFECTIVE LEGAL PROTECTION

III. GUARANTEES OF INDEPENDENCE AND IMPARTIALITY OVER THE CONTENT OF JUDICIAL DECISIONS

IV. CRITERIA ON WHICH THE SECONDMENT DECISION AND THE DECISION TO TERMINATE SECONDMENT

V. DECISION

I.

II.7.723   EU COURT PRELIMINARY RULINGS

See also: I.8.45; II.0.1; II.0.6; II.0.8

"[1] These requests for a preliminary ruling concern the interpretation of the second subparagraph of Article 19(1) TEU, read in the light of Article 2 TEU, and of Article 6(1) and (2) of Directive (EU) 2016/343 [...] on the strengthening of certain aspects of the presumption of innocence and of the right to be present at the trial in criminal proceedings [...], read in the light of recital 22 of that directive. [15] The present requests for a preliminary ruling were made by the Sąd Okręgowy w Warszawie (Regional Court, Warsaw, Poland) in connection with the examination of seven criminal cases assigned to its Tenth Division (Appeals in Criminal Matters). [16] [...] [T]he referring court has doubts as to whether the composition of the adjudicating panels called upon to rule on those cases is in line with the second subparagraph of Article 19(1) TEU, having regard to the presence in those panels of a judge seconded in accordance with a decision of the Minister for Justice pursuant to Article 77 § 1 of the Law on the organisation of the ordinary courts, since that seconded judge may even have come, in some of those cases, from a district court, that is to say, a lower court."

[Paras. 1, 15, 16]

II.

I.8.45   RIGHT TO A FAIR TRIAL AND AN EFFECTIVE REMEDY

See also: II.0.6

"[60] [...] [A]s provided for by the second subparagraph of Article 19(1) TEU, it is for the Member States to establish a system of legal remedies and procedures ensuring for individuals

---

* Summaries prepared by Daniela Rodríguez Bautista, Doctor in Law, Administrator at the Court of Justice of the European Union. Text of judgment available online at the Court's Web site <http://www.curia.eur opa.eu>. Language of the Case: Polish. The selection of extracts can only be attributed to the author and not to the institutions of her affiliation.

** This is not a faithful reproduction of the Table of Contents of the Judgment.

compliance with their right to effective judicial protection in the fields covered by EU law (judgment of 2 March 2021, *A.B. and Others* [...], C-824/18, EU:C:2021:153, paragraph 109 [...]). [**62**] As regards the material scope of the second subparagraph of Article 19(1) TEU, that provision refers to the 'fields covered by Union law', irrespective of whether the Member States are implementing Union law within the meaning of Article 51(1) of the Charter (judgment of 2 March 2021, *A.B. and Others* [...], C-824/18, EU:C:2021:153, paragraph 111 [...])."

[**Paras. 60, 62**]

III.

II.0.8   SOUND ADMINISTRATION OF JUSTICE
         See also: II.0.1; II.0.6

"[**65**] To guarantee that [...] courts are in a position to ensure the effective legal protection thus required under the second subparagraph of Article 19(1) TEU, maintaining their independence is essential, as confirmed by the second paragraph of Article 47 of the Charter [of Fundamental Rights of the European Union], which refers to access to an 'independent' tribunal as one of the requirements linked to the fundamental right to an effective remedy (judgment of 6 October 2021, *W.Ż* [...], C-487/19, EU:C:2021:798, paragraph 107 [...]). [**71**] In that regard, [...] the guarantees of independence and impartiality which courts that may be called upon to rule on the application or interpretation of EU law are required to provide under EU law presuppose, inter alia, rules as regards the composition of the body concerned and the appointment, length of service and grounds for dismissal of its members that are such as to dispel any reasonable doubt in the minds of individuals as to the imperviousness of that body to external factors and its neutrality with respect to the interests before it. Such rules necessarily include those concerning the secondment of judges, since [...] those rules are liable to affect both the composition of the body which is called upon to hear and determine a case and the length of service of the judges thus seconded. They also provide for the possibility of terminating the secondment of one or more of the members of that body. [**73**] However, compliance with the requirement of independence means that the rules governing the secondment of judges must provide the necessary guarantees of independence and impartiality in order to prevent any risk of that secondment being used as a means of exerting political control over the content of judicial decisions ([...] judgment of 18 May 2021, *Asociaţia 'Forumul Judecătorilor din România' and Others*, C-83/19, C-127/19, C-195/19, C-291/19, C-355/19 and C-397/19, EU:C:2021:393, paragraph 198 [...]). [**74**] It will ultimately be for the referring court to rule, [...] in the light of all the principles having made the assessments required for that purpose, on whether the conditions under which the Minister for Justice may second a judge to a higher court and terminate that secondment, taken as a whole, are such as to lead to the conclusion that, during the period of those judges' secondment, they are not guaranteed to be independent and impartial."

[**Paras. 65, 71, 73, 74**]

IV.

II.0.1   *COMPÉTENCE DE LA COMPÉTENCE*
         See also: II.0.8

"[**79**] In order to avoid arbitrariness and the risk of manipulation, the decision relating to the secondment of a judge and the decision terminating that secondment, in particular where a secondment to a higher court is involved, must be taken on the basis of criteria known in advance and must contain an appropriate statement of reasons. [83] Lastly, as the termination of the secondment of a judge without that judge's consent is liable to have effects similar to those of a disciplinary penalty, the second subparagraph of Article 19(1) TEU requires that the regime applicable to such a measure provide all the necessary guarantees to prevent any risk of such a regime being used as a means of exerting political control over the content of judicial decisions, which means, inter alia, that it must be possible for that measure to be legally challenged in accordance with a procedure which fully safeguards the rights enshrined in Articles 47 and 48 of the Charter (see, to that effect, judgment of 6 October 2021, W.Ż. [. . .]), C-487/19, EU:C:2021:798, paragraphs 115 and 118)."

[**Paras. 79, 83**]

V.

II.2.5 ·   JUDGMENT/DECISION/ORDER
        See also: I.8.45; II.0.6

"On those grounds, the Court (Grand Chamber) hereby rules:
    The second subparagraph of Article 19(1) TEU, read in the light of Article 2 TEU, and Article 6(1) and (2) of Directive (EU) 2016/343 [. . .] must be interpreted as precluding provisions of national legislation pursuant to which the Minister for Justice of a Member State may, on the basis of criteria which have not been made public, second a judge to a higher criminal court for a fixed or indefinite period and may, at any time, by way of a decision which does not contain a statement of reasons, terminate that secondment, irrespective of whether that secondment is for a fixed or indefinite period."

Systematic Key Items of the Section*

I.0.151	INTELLECTUAL PROPERTY RIGHTS
I.2.221	EU LEGAL PERSONALITY
I.2.2234	APPLICATION AND INTERPRETATION OF EU LAW
I.2.22342	PRINCIPLE OF PRIMACY OF EU LAW
I.2.22551	EUROPEAN ARREST WARRANT
I.2.2257	EU COMMON RULES ON COMPETITION, TAXATION AND APPROXIMATION LAW
I.8.45	RIGHT TO A FAIR TRIAL AND AN EFFECTIVE REMEDY
I.8.55	FREEDOM OF THOUGHT, CONSCIENCE AND RELIGION
I.14.23	ARBITRATION AGREEMENT
I.17.01	TREATIES AS SOURCES OF INTERNATIONAL INVESTMENT LAW
II.0.1	*COMPÉTENCE DE LA COMPÉTENCE*
II.0.8	SOUND ADMINISTRATION OF JUSTICE
II.1.0	BURDEN OF PROOF
II.2.0	INSTITUTION AND COURSE OF PROCEEDINGS
II.2.5	JUDGMENT/DECISION/ORDER
II.7.722	EU COURT PROCEEDINGS FOR ANNULMENT
II.7.723	EU COURT PRELIMINARY RULINGS
II.7.725	EU COURT PROCEEDINGS ON APPEAL
II.7.728	EU COURT PROVISIONAL MEASURES
II.7.73	LAW APPLIED BY THE EU COURT

---

* *See* Systematic Classification Scheme, *supra* at page 255.

Systematic Key Items of the Section*

VII

European Court
of Human Rights

INTRODUCTORY NOTE

The European Court of Human Rights in 2021

BY ROBERT SPANO*

Abstract

The year 2021 was exceptionally eventful for the European Court of Human Rights. The Court adapted to the unprecedented situation arising from COVID-19 and, without interruption, its services continued to function. A number of important reforms took place in 2021. A new and more targeted case-processing strategy referred to as "impact cases" was introduced, it was decided that Committee cases would be more concisely drafted, and Protocol No. 15 came into force. Furthermore, five more superior courts in four member states (Sweden, the Slovak Republic, Ireland, and Malta) joined the Court's Superior Courts Network. Five Grand Chamber cases are discussed in greater depth, covering: the notion of extraterritorial jurisdiction in an international armed conflict; the positive obligation of states to take measures to protect those at threat of domestic violence; the legal obligation to vaccinate school children against common infectious diseases; and present-day means of surveillance of cross-border communications.

I. INTRODUCTION

The year 2021 was a pivotal year for the European Court of Human Rights. Thanks to a number of reforms carried out by the Court, the number of cases pending was reduced from 160,000 in 2011 to 70,000 at the end of 2021. Over the same period a prioritisation policy was introduced in order to speed up the processing and adjudication of the most important, serious, and urgent cases. The year 2021 also saw the arrival of a new paradigm, meaning the Court's success can no longer be measured solely in terms of the number of cases dealt with over a specific period; regard must also be had to the treatment of the most important cases. The Court decided to put in place a new, more targeted case-processing

---

* President of the European Court of Human Rights. Member of the Editorial Board.

Robert Spano, *Introductory Note* In: *The Global Community Yearbook of International Law and Jurisprudence 2022*. Edited by: Giuliana Ziccardi Capaldo, Oxford University Press. © Oxford University Press 2023. DOI: 10.1093/oso/9780197752265.003.0026

strategy aimed at dealing with such complex and often sensitive cases, referred to as "impact cases." The new strategy is based on three principles: first of all, rapidly identifying the cases in question; secondly, monitoring the individual cases; and, lastly, simplifying their processing. Indeed, it is crucial that cases likely to have an "impact" are promptly identified and, once they have been identified, that their progress is meticulously monitored within the Court.

Furthermore, there were other important reforms in 2021. Firstly, Protocol No. 15 came into force, incorporating an explicit reference to the principles of subsidiarity and the margin of appreciation into the Preamble to the Convention. Secondly, on 1 September it was decided that, for a two-year trial period, three-judge Committee cases would be much more concisely drafted. This new short format for judgments and decisions is aimed at reducing the Court's backlog and is a further element in the strategy to enable the Court to deal with its "impact cases." The aim is to shorten the Court's response time for applicants whose cases fall under well-established case-law.

Finally, in 2021 five more superior courts in four member states (Sweden, the Slovak Republic, Ireland, and Malta) joined our Superior Courts Network, bringing its total membership to ninety-eight courts in forty-three member states. Over the last few years this network, the only one of its kind in the world, has taken on major importance.

This introductory note intends to touch on the main events and jurisprudential advancements during 2021 and therefore it seeks to provide an overview of some of the most significant issues examined and developed within the Court's case-law. It will look, in particular, at five Grand Chamber cases in some more detail in order to further examine the main themes and developments identified within, as dealt with by the Court in 2021.

II. OVERVIEW OF 2021

In 2021 the Grand Chamber delivered twelve judgments, one of which is an inter-state case, and a decision concerning an inter-state case. It also ruled, for the first time, on a request for an advisory opinion under the Council of Europe Convention on human rights and bio-medicine (Oviedo Convention); the Grand Chamber panel also delivered its first decision to refuse a request for an opinion under Protocol No. 16 to the Convention.

In the case of *Georgia v. Russia* (II)[1] the Grand Chamber clarified its case-law under Article 1 on extraterritorial jurisdiction, in respect of an attacking state in an international armed conflict, for acts committed in the state that was attacked and then invaded. The Court also looked at Article 1 in the context of a state's complaint about the "annexation" of its territory by another member state (*Ukraine v. Russia (re Crimea)*)[2]. In *Hanan v. Germany*,[3] in connection with a military operation led by the United Nations, the Court examined whether the respondent state had a procedural obligation to carry out an effective investigation after a member of its armed forces had ordered a fatal air-strike on foreign soil (Articles 1 and 2). In *Kurt v. Austria*,[4] the Court consolidated, both generally and in the specific context of domestic violence (Article 2), the positive obligation of states to preventively take operational measures to protect an individual whose life is threatened by the criminal acts of others, in a case concerning a child killed by its father. As to minors taken

---

[1] Georgia v. Russia (II) [GC], No. 38263/08, 21 January 2021.
[2] Ukraine v. Russia (Re Crimea) [GC], Nos. 20958/14 and 38334/18, 16 December 2020.
[3] Hanan v. Germany [GC], No. 4871/16, 16 February 2021.
[4] Kurt v. Austria [GC], No. 62903/15, 15 June 2021.

into public care, in *X and Others v. Bulgaria*[5] the Court set out the state's positive obligations in response to allegations of sexual assault.

In *Savran v. Denmark*[6] the Court clarified its case-law on the expulsion of an alien suffering from a severe mental illness (Article 3). Under Article 5, in *Denis and Irvine v. Belgium*[7] the Court addressed the confinement of criminals with mental illnesses who had been found to lack criminal responsibility for their acts. In the fields of private life, beliefs, and health, in the judgment in *Vavřička and Others v. the Czech Republic*[8] the Court established the case-law on the legal obligation to vaccinate school children against common infectious diseases (Articles 8 and 9), emphasising in particular the obligation of states to place the best interests of children, as a group, at the centre of all decisions affecting their health and development in the name of social solidarity. Addressing the present-day means of surveillance of cross-border communications, the Grand Chamber set out fundamental safeguards against abuse in the bulk interception and collection of communications data and in the reception by a member state of data from foreign intelligence services in the cases of *Centrum för rättvisa v. Sweden*[9] and *Big Brother Watch and Others v. the United Kingdom*,[10] regarding Articles 8 and 10. In the field of immigration control, in the case of *M.A. v. Denmark*,[11] the Court ruled on the imposition of a waiting time for the access of aliens to family reunion, and on the deportation and permanent exclusion of a settled migrant who, suffering from a severe mental illness, had been under a compulsory treatment order instead of a criminal sanction, as found in *Savran v. Denmark*. Under Article 8, read in the light of Article 9, in the case of *Abdi Ibrahim v. Norway*,[12] the Court ruled on a child's adoption by a foster family practising a different religion from that of the biological mother, who wanted her son to be raised in line with her own religious beliefs (see also Article 2 of Protocol No. 1). In addition, the Grand Chamber examined, for the first time under Article 2 of Protocol No. 4, the issue of persons displaced within their own country as a result of an international armed conflict in *Georgia v. Russia* (II).[13] It also reiterated the obligation to cooperate with the Court under Article 38 of the Convention in this case.

In response to two requests for an advisory opinion, one under Protocol No. 16 to the Convention, the other under the Council of Europe Oviedo Convention, the Court clarified the nature, scope, and limits of its advisory jurisdiction. It emphasised that the purpose of the Protocol No. 16 procedure was to reinforce the implementation of the Convention in respect of cases pending before national courts, in accordance with the principle of subsidiarity.

Throughout 2021 the Court delivered a number of Chamber judgments which were interesting in terms of the development of its case-law. First of all, it clarified its case-law on the concept of "jurisdiction" and on the responsibility of a state for acts committed by private parties outside its territory in the case of *Carter v. Russia*.[14] In *E.G. v. the Republic of*

---

[5] X and Others v. Bulgaria [GC], No. 22457/16, 2 February 2021.

[6] Savran v. Denmark [GC], No. 57467/15, 7 December 2021.

[7] Denis and Irvine v. Belgium [GC], Nos. 62819/17 and 63921/17, 1 June 2021.

[8] Vavřička and Others v. the Czech Republic [GC], Nos. 47621/13, 3867/14, 73094/14 et al., 8 April 2021.

[9] Centrum för rättvisa v. Sweden [GC], No. 35252/08, 25 May 2021.

[10] Big Brother Watch and Others v. the United Kingdom [GC], Nos. 58170/13, 62322/14 and 24960/15, 25 May 2021.

[11] M.A. v. Denmark [GC], No. 6697/18, 9 July 2021.

[12] Abdi Ibrahim v. Norway [GC], No. 15379/16, 10 December 2021.

[13] Georgia v. Russia (II) [GC], No. 38263/08, 21 January 2021.

[14] Carter v. Russia, No. 20914/07, 21 September 2021, final on 28 February 2022.

Moldova[15] the Court dealt with the application of the six-month period to a continuing situation, and in the case of *Zambrano v. France*[16] it dealt with abuses of the right of individual application in the context of the COVID-19 health crisis.

Secondly, regarding Convention rights and freedoms, a number of major or new jurisprudential questions were addressed: protecting law-enforcement personnel against risks to their life (*Ribcheva and Others v. Bulgaria*[17]); conditions of detention following the execution of a European arrest warrant (*Bivolaru and Moldovan v. France*[18]); the granting of an amnesty for sexual assault and ineffective enforcement of a prison sentence as a result (*E.G. v. the Republic of Moldova*[19]); and deportation for committing acts of terrorism (*K.I. v. France*[20]) (Articles 2 and 3). The Court also ruled on the novel question of the COVID-19 "health pass" and vaccination (*Zambrano v. France*[21]).

The Court emphasised the positive obligation of states to protect victims of human trafficking when criminal proceedings are brought against them in *V.C.L. and v. the United Kingdom*,[22] under Articles 4 and 6. For the first time, in the context of the COVID-19 pandemic, it examined whether a national general lockdown measure on grounds of health protection constituted a "deprivation of liberty" within the meaning of Article 5 § 1 in the case of *Terheş v. Romania*.[23] It also ruled on the foreseeability, under Article 7, of the conviction of a prison officer who had given information about the prison to a journalist in exchange for money in *Norman v. the United Kingdom*.[24]

For the first time, the Court dealt with exceptions to the right of appeal in criminal matters in a case concerning a fine of which non-payment could be punished by a prison sentence (Article 2 of Protocol No. 7) in the case of *Kindlhofer v. Austria*,[25] and under Article 4 of Protocol No. 7 (ne bis in idem principle) it examined proceedings and penalties for acts of domestic violence in *Galović v. Croatia*[26] and the existence of a "fundamental defect" in criminal proceedings which allowed for them to be reopened in *Sabalić v. Croatia*.[27]

The Court extended the protection of Article 8 to a case of verbal harassment in class of a pupil by a teacher in a state school in the case of *F.O. v. Croatia*[28] and emphasised that it was important to protect the right of children to respect for their private life at school. The Court further extended the protection of Article 8 to a case of begging by a destitute and vulnerable person in *Lăcătuş v. Switzerland*,[29] as well as addressing the subject of negative stereotyping of a social group and emphasising that human dignity fell within the very essence of the Article 8 rights in the cases of *Budinova and Chaprazov v. Bulgaria*[30] and *Behar and Gutman v. Bulgaria*.[31]

---

[15] E.G. v. the Republic of Moldova, No. 37882/13, 13 April 2021.

[16] Zambrano v. France, No. 41994/21, 21 September 2021.

[17] Ribcheva and Others v. Bulgaria, Nos. 37801/16, 39549/16 and 40658/16.

[18] Bivolaru and Moldovan v. France, Nos. 40324/16 and 12623/17, 25 March 2021.

[19] E.G. v. the Republic of Moldova, No. 37882/13, 13 April 2021.

[20] K.I. v. France, No. 5560/19, 15 April 2021.

[21] Zambrano v. France, No. 41994/21, 21 September 2021.

[22] V.C.L. and A.N. v. the United Kingdom, Nos. 74603/12 and 77587/12, 16 February 2021.

[23] Terheş v. Romania, No. 49933/20, 20 May 2021.

[24] Norman v. the United Kingdom, No. 41387/17, 6 July 2021, final on 22 November 2021.

[25] Kindlhofer v. Austria, No. 20962/15, 26 October 2021, final on 26 January 2022.

[26] Galović v. Croatia, No. 45512/11, 31 August 2021, final on 30 November 2021.

[27] Sabalić v. CROATIA, No. 50231/13, 14 January 2021, final on 14 April 2021.

[28] F.O. v. CROATIA, No. 29555/13, 22 April 2021, final on 6 September 2021.

[29] Lăcătuş v. SWITZERLAND, No. 14065/15, 19 January 2021, final on 19 April 2021.

[30] Budinova and Chaprazov v. Bulgaria, No. 12567/13, 16 February 2021, final on 16 May 2021.

[31] Behar and Gutman v. Bulgaria, No. 29335/13, 16 February 2021, final on 16 May 2021.

The Court looked into the conformity of autopsies in public hospitals and the extraction of internal organs with the right to respect for the private life and religious beliefs of the deceased's close relatives in *Polat v. Austria*.[32]

As to freedom of expression under Article 10, new jurisprudential developments covered, in the past year, access by intelligence services engaged in bulk data interception to confidential information about the activity of journalists (*Big Brother Watch and Others v. the United Kingdom*[33]), a ban on the publication of an opposition newspaper on account of a state of emergency (*Dareskizb Ltd v. Armenia*[34]), the scope of the concept of a journalist's "source" as regards comments posted on a news website and the obligation for a media outlet to waive the anonymity of the authors of insulting comments published on its online discussion forum (*Standard Verlagsgesellschaft mbH v. Austria (No. 3)*[35]), and the protection of journalists' sources following the disclosure of the identity of a source by a newspaper under an agreement with the police (*Norman v. the United Kingdom*[36]). The Court also gave rulings in the domain of online social media: in *Biancardi v. Italy*,[37] it examined the "right to be forgotten," in the case of a refusal by an internet newspaper to remove from its online archives an old article containing information on criminal proceedings; and in *Standard Verlagsgesellschaft mbH v. Austria (No. 3)*.[38]

Under Article 11 the Court ruled for the first time on the possibility for working prisoners to form or join a trade union in the case of *Yakut Republican Trade-Union Federation v. Russia*.[39] As regards the prohibition of discrimination, the Court clarified the response required of the domestic authorities under Articles 3 and 14 to homophobic violence in *Sabalić v. Croatia*.[40] In *Jurčić v. Croatia*[41] it acknowledged, for the first time, that a pregnant woman had been discriminated against by her employer on account of her pregnancy.

The Court also ruled on the concept of "public danger threatening the life of the nation" within the meaning of Article 15 on derogation in time of emergency (*Dareskizb Ltd v. Armenia*[42]), and on Article 18 of the Convention (*Azizov and Novruzlu v. Azerbaijan*[43]). Lastly, in *Willems and Gorjon v. Belgium*[44] the Court set out the consequences of it taking note of a unilateral declaration by a respondent government in a given case and striking the application out of its list.

In its case-law, the Court considered the interactions between the Convention, on the one hand, and European Union law and case-law of the Court of Justice of the European

---

[32] Polat v. Austria, No. 12886/16, 20 July 2021, final on 20 October 2021.

[33] Big Brother Watch and Others v. the United Kingdom [GC], Nos. 58170/13, 62322/14 and 24960/15, 25 May 2021.

[34] Dareskizb Ltd v. Armenia, No. 61737/08, 21 September 2021, final on 8 October 2021.

[35] Standard Verlagsgesellschaft mbH v. Austria (No. 3), No. 39378/15, 7 December 2021.

[36] Norman v. the United Kingdom, No. 41387/17, 6 July 2021, final on 22 November 2021.

[37] Biancardi v. Italy, No. 77419/16, 25 November 2021, final on 25 February 2022.

[38] Standard Verlagsgesellschaft mbH v. Austria (No. 3), No. 39378/15, 7 December 2021.

[39] Yakut Republican Trade-Union Federation v. Russia, No. 29582/09, 7 December 2021, final on 7 March 2022.

[40] Sabalić v. Croatia, No. 50231/13, 14 January 2021, final on 14 April 2021.

[41] Jurčić v. Croatia, No. 54711/15, 4 February 2021, final on 4 May 2021.

[42] Dareskizb Ltd v. Armenia, No. 61737/08, 21 September 2021, final on 8 October 2021.

[43] Azizov and Novruzlu v. Azerbaijan, Nos. 65583/13 and 70106/13, 18 February 2021, final on 18 May 2021.

[44] Willems and Gorjon v. Belgium, Nos. 74209/16, 75662/16, 19431/19 et al., 21 September 2021.

Union, on the other, in cases concerning, among other things, conditions of family reunion (*M.A. v. Denmark*[45]), the European arrest warrant and the presumption of "equivalent protection" in the European legal order as established in the Bosphorus judgment (*Bivolaru and Moldovan v. France*[46]), deportation for acts of terrorism (*K.I. v. France*[47]), online media and a request for the removal of an old article on a trial (*Biancardi v. Italy*[48]), and maternity in the workplace (*Jurčić v. Croatia*[49]).

Lastly, in a year marked by the entry into force of Protocol No. 15 to the Convention, introducing in particular a reference to the margin of appreciation doctrine into the Convention's Preamble, the Court ruled on the breadth of the margin that should be afforded to states parties to the Convention, for example in the area of health (*Vavřička and Others v. the Czech Republic*[50]), bulk surveillance of cross-border communications (*Big Brother Watch and Others v. the United Kingdom*[51], *Centrum för rättvisa v. Sweden*[52]), access to family reunion for aliens (*M.A. v. Denmark*[53]), protection of pupils from any form of violence at school (*F.O. v. Croatia*[54]), regulation of begging (*Lăcătuş v. Switzerland*[55]), and the rights of working prisoners (*Yakut Republican Trade-Union Federation v. Russia*[56]). In this connection, in leading judgments the Court examined whether or not there was a consensus in the Council of Europe States as to the question raised by the application (for example, *Vavřička and Others, M.A. v. Denmark, Abdi Ibrahim, Lăcătuş, Yakut Republican Trade-Union Federation*).

In addition, the Court highlighted the principle of subsidiarity, now expressly provided for in the Preamble to the Convention since the entry into force of Protocol No. 15. In one case it emphasised the sharing of responsibility between the national authorities and the Court, and more specifically the primary responsibility of the national authorities to ensure compliance with the Convention and the Protocols thereto (*Willems and Gorjon v. Belgium*[57]).

III. SELECTED CASES

A. *Big Brother Watch and Others v. the United Kingdom* (Application Nos. 58170/13, 62322/14 and 24969/15)

The applicants are organisations and individuals that campaign on issues relating to civil liberties and the rights of journalists. The three applications (which have since been joined) were lodged after Edward Snowden, a former US National Security Agency (NSA)

---

[45] M.A. v. Denmark [GC], No. 6697/18, 9 July 2021.
[46] Bivolaru and Moldovan v. France, Nos. 40324/16 and 12623/17, 25 March 2021.
[47] K.I. v. France, No. 5560/19, 15 April 2021.
[48] Biancardi v. Italy, No. 77419/16, 25 November 2021, final on 25 February 2022.
[49] Jurčić v. Croatia, No. 54711/15, 4 February 2021, final on 4 May 2021.
[50] Vavřička and Others v. the Czech Republic [GC], Nos. 47621/13, 3867/14, 73094/14 et al., 8 April 2021.
[51] Big Brother Watch and Others v. the United Kingdom [GC], Nos. 58170/13, 62322/14 and 24960/15, 25 May 2021.
[52] Centrum för rättvisa v. Sweden [GC], No. 35252/08, 25 May 2021.
[53] M.A. v. Denmark [GC], No. 6697/18, 9 July 2021.
[54] F.O. v. Croatia, No. 29555/13, 22 April 2021, final on 6 September 2021.
[55] Lăcătuş v. Switzerland, No. 14065/15, 19 January 2021, final on 19 April 2021.
[56] Yakut Republican Trade-Union Federation v. Russia, No. 29582/09, 7 December 2021, final on 7 March 2022.
[57] Willems and Gorjon v. Belgium, Nos. 74209/16, 75662/16, 19431/19 et al., 21 September 2021.

contractor, revealed the existence of surveillance and intelligence sharing programmes operated by the intelligence services of the United States and the United Kingdom. The applicants believed that the nature of their activities meant that their electronic communications and/or communications data were likely to have been intercepted by the UK intelligence services or obtained by them from either communications service providers or foreign intelligence agencies such as the NSA.

The Court held that there had been a violation of Article 8 of the European Convention (right to respect for private and family life/communications) in respect of the bulk intercept regime; unanimously that there had been a violation of Article 8 in respect of the regime for obtaining communications data from communication service providers; by 12 votes to 5, that there had been no violation of Article 8 in respect of the United Kingdom's regime for requesting intercepted material from foreign governments and intelligence agencies; unanimously, that there had been a violation of Article 10 (freedom of expression), concerning both the bulk interception regime and the regime for obtaining communications data from communication service providers; and by 12 votes to 5, that there had been no violation of Article 10 in respect of the regime for requesting intercepted material from foreign governments and intelligence agencies. The case concerned complaints by journalists and human-rights organisations in regard to three different surveillance regimes: (1) the bulk interception of communications; (2) the receipt of intercept material from foreign governments and intelligence agencies; (3) the obtaining of communications data from communication service providers. At the relevant time, the regime for bulk interception and obtaining communications data from communication service providers had a statutory basis in the Regulation of Investigatory Powers Act 2000. This has since been replaced by the Investigatory Powers Act 2016. The findings of the Grand Chamber relate solely to the provisions of the 2000 Act, which had been the legal framework in force at the time the events complained of had taken place.

The Court considered that, owing to the multitude of threats states face in modern society, operating a bulk interception regime did not in and of itself violate the Convention. However, such a regime had to be subject to "end-to-end safeguards," meaning that, at the domestic level, an assessment should be made at each stage of the process of the necessity and proportionality of the measures being taken; that bulk interception should be subject to independent authorisation at the outset, when the object and scope of the operation were being defined; and that the operation should be subject to supervision and independent ex post facto review.

Having regard to the bulk interception regime operated in the United Kingdom, the Court identified the following deficiencies: bulk interception had been authorised by the secretary of state, and not by a body independent of the executive; categories of search terms defining the kinds of communications that would become liable for examination had not been included in the application for a warrant; and search terms linked to an individual (that is to say, specific identifiers such as an email address) had not been subject to prior internal authorisation.

The Court also found that the bulk interception regime had breached Article 10, as it had not contained sufficient protections for confidential journalistic material. The regime for obtaining communications data from communication service providers was also found to have violated Articles 8 and 10 as it had not been in accordance with the law. However, the Court held that the regime by which the United Kingdom could request intelligence from foreign governments and/or intelligence agencies had had sufficient safeguards in place to protect against abuse and to ensure that UK authorities had not used such requests as a means of circumventing their duties under domestic law and the Convention.

B. *Centrum för rättvisa v. Sweden* (Application No. 35252/08)

This case was linked to that of Big Brother Watch through its subject matter. The applicant, Centrum för rättvisa, is a foundation established in 2002 and based in Stockholm. The applicant represents clients in proceedings concerning rights and freedoms under the Convention or related proceedings under Swedish law. It is also involved in education and research projects and participates in the general public debate on issues concerning individuals' rights and freedoms. The applicant communicates on a daily basis with individuals, organisations, and companies in Sweden and abroad by email, telephone, and fax. It asserted that a large part of that communication was particularly sensitive from a privacy perspective. Due to the nature of its function as a non-governmental organisation scrutinising the activities of state actors, it believed that there was a risk that its communications had been or would be intercepted and examined by way of signals intelligence under the Swedish bulk interception regiem. Signals intelligence can be defined as intercepting, processing, analysing, and reporting intelligence from electronic signals. These signals may be processed to text, images, and sound.

The European Court of Human Rights held, by a majority of 15 votes to 2, that there had been a violation of Article 8 (right to respect for private and family life, the home and correspondence). The case concerned the alleged risk that the applicant foundation's communications had been or would be intercepted and examined by way of signals intelligence, as it communicated on a daily basis with individuals, organisations, and companies in Sweden and abroad by email, telephone, and fax, often on sensitive matters.

The Court found, in particular, that although the main features of the Swedish bulk interception regime met the Convention requirements on quality of the law, the regime nevertheless suffered from three defects: the absence of a clear rule on destroying intercepted material which did not contain personal data; the absence of a requirement in the Signals Intelligence Act or other relevant legislation that, when making a decision to transmit intelligence material to foreign partners, consideration was given to the privacy interests of individuals; and the absence of an effective ex post facto review. As a result of these deficiencies, the system did not meet the requirement of "end-to-end" safeguards, it overstepped the margin of appreciation left to the respondent state in that regard, and overall did not guard against the risk of arbitrariness and abuse, leading to a violation of Article 8 of the Convention.

C. *Georgia v. Russia (II)* (Application No. 38263/08)

The application was lodged in the context of the armed conflict that occurred between Georgia and the Russian Federation in August 2008 following an extended period of ever-mounting tensions, provocations, and incidents between the two countries. In the night of 7 to 8 August 2008, after an extended period of ever-mounting tensions and incidents, the Georgian forces launched an artillery attack on the city of Tskhinvali, the administrative capital of South Ossetia. From 8 August 2008 Russian ground forces penetrated into Georgia by crossing through Abkhazia and South Ossetia before entering the neighbouring regions in undisputed Georgian territory.

A ceasefire agreement was concluded on 12 August 2008 between the Russian Federation and Georgia under the auspices of the European Union, specifying that the parties would refrain from the use of force, end hostilities, and provide access for humanitarian aid, and that Georgian military forces would withdraw to their usual bases and Russian military forces to the lines prior to the outbreak of hostilities. Owing to the delay by the Russian Federation in applying that agreement, a new agreement implementing the ceasefire agreement (the Sarkozy-Medvedev agreement) was signed on 8 September 2008. On 10 October 2008 Russia completed the withdrawal of its troops stationed in the buffer zone, except for the village of Perevi (Sachkhere district), situated in undisputed Georgian territory, from which the Russian troops withdrew on 18 October 2010.

The Court found that a distinction needed to be made between the military operations carried out during the active phase of hostilities (from 8 to 12 August 2008) and the other events occurring after the cessation of the active phase of hostilities—that is, following the ceasefire agreement of 12 August 2008.

As regards the assessment of the evidence and establishment of the facts, the Court referred to the principles summarised in the case of *Georgia v. Russia (I)*. The Court also had regard to the observations and numerous other documents submitted by the parties, and also to reports by international governmental and non-governmental organisations. In addition, it heard evidence from a total of thirty-three witnesses. The Court concluded, following its examination of the case, that the events occurring during the active phase of hostilities (8 to 12 August 2008) had not fallen within the jurisdiction of the Russian Federation for the purposes of Article 1 of the Convention and declared this part of the application inadmissible. However, it held that the Russian Federation had exercised "effective control" over South Ossetia, Abkhazia, and the "buffer zone" during the period from 12 August to 10 October 2008, the date of the official withdrawal of the Russian troops. After that period, the strong Russian presence and the South Ossetian and Abkhazian authorities' dependency on the Russian Federation indicated that there had been continued "effective control" over South Ossetia and Abkhazia. The Court therefore concluded that the events occurring after the cessation of hostilities—that is, following the ceasefire agreement of 12 August 2008—had fallen within the jurisdiction of the Russian Federation for the purposes of Article 1 of the Convention (obligation to respect human rights).

The European Court of Human Rights held by 11 votes to 6, that the events occurring during the active phase of hostilities (8 to 12 August 2008) had not fallen within the jurisdiction of the Russian Federation for the purposes of Article 1 of the European Convention on Human Rights; by 16 votes to 1, that the events occurring after the cessation of hostilities (following the ceasefire agreement of 12 August 2008) had fallen within the jurisdiction of the Russian Federation; by 16 votes to 1, that there had been an administrative practice contrary to Articles 2, 3, and 8 of the Convention and Article 1 of Protocol No. 1 to the Convention; unanimously, that the Georgian civilians detained by the South Ossetian forces in Tskhinvali between approximately 10 and 27 August 2008 had fallen within the jurisdiction of the Russian Federation for the purposes of Article 1; unanimously, that there had been an administrative practice contrary to Article 3 as regards the conditions of detention of some 160 Georgian civilians and the humiliating acts which had caused them suffering and had to be regarded as inhuman and degrading treatment; unanimously, that there had been an administrative practice contrary to Article 5 as regards the arbitrary detention of Georgian civilians in August 2008; unanimously, that the Georgian prisoners of war detained in Tskhinvali between 8 and 17 August 2008 by the South Ossetian forces had fallen within the jurisdiction of the Russian Federation for the purposes of Article 1; by 16 votes to 1, that there had been an administrative practice contrary to Article 3 as regards the acts of torture of which the Georgian prisoners of war had been victims; by 16 votes to 1, that the Georgian nationals who had been prevented from returning to South Ossetia or Abkhazia had fallen within the jurisdiction of the Russian Federation; by 16 votes to 1, that there had been an administrative practice contrary to Article 2 of Protocol No. 4 as regards the inability of Georgian nationals to return to their homes; unanimously, that there had been no violation of Article 2 of Protocol No. 1; unanimously, that the Russian Federation had had a procedural obligation under Article 2 of the Convention to carry out an adequate and effective investigation not only into the events which had occurred after the cessation of hostilities (following the ceasefire agreement of 12 August 2008) but also into the events which had occurred during the active phase of hostilities (8 to 12 August 2008); by 16 votes to 1, that there had been a violation of Article 2 in its procedural aspect; unanimously, that there was no need to examine separately the applicant government's complaint under Article 13 in conjunction with other Articles; by 16 votes to 1, that the respondent state had failed to comply with its obligations under Article 38; and unanimously, that the question of the application of Article 41 of the Convention was not ready for decision and should therefore be reserved in full.

D. *Vavřička and Others v. the Czech Republic* (Applications No. 47621/13 and Five Other Applications)

In the Czech Republic there is a general legal duty to vaccinate children against nine diseases that are well known to medical science. Compliance with the duty cannot be physically enforced. Parents who fail to comply, without good reason, can be fined. Non-vaccinated children are not accepted in nursery schools (an exception is made for those who cannot be vaccinated for health reasons). In the present case, the first applicant was fined for failure to comply with the vaccination duty in relation to his two children. The other applicants were all denied admission to nursery school for the same reason.

The applicants alleged, in particular, that the various consequences for them of non-compliance with the statutory duty of vaccination had been incompatible with their right to respect for their private life under Article 8 (right to respect for private life) of the Convention.

The Court pointed out that, under its case-law, compulsory vaccination, as an involuntary medical intervention, represents an interference with physical integrity and thus concerns the right to respect for private life, protected by Article 8 of the Convention. It recognised that the Czech policy pursued the legitimate aims of protecting health as well as the rights of others, noting that vaccination protects both those who receive it and also those who cannot be vaccinated for medical reasons and are therefore reliant on herd immunity for protection against serious contagious diseases. It further considered that a wide "margin of appreciation" was appropriate for the respondent state in this context.

It noted that in the Czech Republic the vaccination duty was strongly supported by the relevant medical authorities. It could be said to represent the national authorities' answer to the pressing social need to protect individual and public health against the diseases in question and to guard against any downward trend in the rate of vaccination among children.

The judgment emphasises that in all decisions concerning children, their best interests must be of paramount importance. With regard to immunisation, the objective has to be that every child is protected against serious diseases, through vaccination or by virtue of herd immunity. The Czech health policy could therefore be said to be consistent with the best interests of the children who were its focus.

The Court also observed that the vaccination duty concerned nine diseases against which vaccination was considered effective and safe by the scientific community, as was the tenth vaccination, which was given to children with particular health indications. The Court then examined the proportionality of the vaccine policy. On a general level, it noted the scope and content of the duty to vaccinate, the existing exceptions from it, and the procedural safeguards available. It found that it was challenges to the instructional arrangements in place in the Czech Republic and to the effectiveness and safety of the vaccines in question had not been established. Moreover, as to the applicants' specific circumstances, it noted that the fine imposed on Mr Vavřička had not been excessive. Although the child applicants' non-admission to preschool had meant the loss of an important opportunity to develop their personalities, it was a preventive rather than a punitive measure, and had been limited in time in that when they reached the age of mandatory school attendance their admission to primary school had not been affected by their vaccination status.

In consequence, the measures complained of by the applicants, assessed in the context of the national system, had been in a reasonable relationship of proportionality to the legitimate aims pursued by the Czech state (to protect against diseases which could pose a serious risk to health) through the vaccination duty.

The Court clarified that, ultimately, the issue to be determined was not whether a different, less prescriptive policy might have been adopted, as had been done in some other European states. Rather, it was whether, in striking the particular balance that they did, the Czech authorities had exceeded their wide margin of appreciation in this area. It concluded that the impugned measures could be regarded as being "necessary in a democratic society." The Court held, by a majority (16 votes to 1), that there had been no violation of Article 8 (right to respect for private life) of the European Convention on Human Rights.

E. *Kurt v. Austria* (Application No. 62903/15)

The case concerned the applicant's complaint that the Austrian authorities had failed to protect her and her children from her violent husband, which had resulted in his murdering their son. Relying on Articles 2 (right to life), 3 (prohibition of inhuman or degrading treatment), and 8 (right to respect for private and family life) of the European Convention on Human Rights, the applicant complained that the Austrian authorities had failed to protect her and her children from her violent husband. She maintained that she had specifically informed the police that she feared for her children's lives.

In this judgment the Grand Chamber clarified for the first time the general principles applicable in domestic violence cases under Article 2 of the Convention. It expanded on those principles on the basis of the "Osman test" (*Osman v. the United Kingdom*, 28 October 1998). The Court reiterated that the authorities had to provide an immediate response to allegations of domestic violence and that special diligence was required from them in dealing with such cases. The authorities had to establish whether there existed a real and immediate risk to the life of one or more identified victims; to that end they were under a duty to carry out a risk assessment that was autonomous, proactive, and comprehensive. They had to assess the reality and immediacy of the risk taking due account of the particular context of domestic violence cases. If the outcome of the risk assessment was that there was a real and immediate risk to life, the authorities' obligation to take preventive operational measures was triggered. Such measures had to be adequate and proportionate to the level of the risk assessed.

The Court agreed with the government that, on the basis of what had been known to the authorities at the material time, there had been no indications of a real and immediate risk of further violence against the applicant's son outside the areas for which a barring order had been issued, let alone a lethality risk. The authorities' assessment had identified a certain level of non-lethal risk to the children in the context of the domestic violence perpetrated by the father, the primary target of which had been the applicant. The measures ordered by the authorities appeared to have been adequate to contain any risk of further violence against the children and the authorities had been thorough and conscientious in taking all necessary protective measures. No real and immediate risk of an attack on the children's lives had been discernible. Therefore, in the circumstances of the present case, there had been no obligation incumbent on the authorities to take further preventive operational measures specifically with regard to the applicant's children, whether in private or public spaces, such as issuing a barring order in respect of the children's school. The Court held, by 10 votes to 7, that there had been no violation of Article 2 (right to life) of the European Convention on Human Rights.

IV. CONCLUSIONS

The year of 2021 showed the Court's ability to continue to adapt time and again. The Court continued to traverse the COVID-19 crisis and adapt itself to new working arrangements while continuing to deliver its judgments and decisions and reduce its backlog. The overview of the Court's case-law shows the wide variety of subject matters brought before it each year and 2021 was a year particularly important to the further development of the Court's case-law in a number of key areas. The cases listed herein are of particular significance to principles under the case-law, both in clarifying matters the Court has dealt with before and developing and establishing case-law around new or novel areas of interpretation and implementation of the Convention. It is clear that many of the case-law developments established in 2021 will impact many important and complex matters which are likely to come before the Court in the future and set the standard and tests to be followed should these issues arise again.

The Court underwent a paradigm shift in 2021, putting in place a new and more targeted case-processing strategy designed to deal with those complex and often sensitive cases and the introduction of the two years trial period on the much more concise drafting of Committee cases. These reforms and their implementation, alongside further investment in IT and the adaptive working arrangements put in place as a reaction to the COVID-19 crisis, show the ever evolving nature of the Court's work and structure, allowing the Court to adapt to the challenges facing it at any given time. The introduction of Protocol No. 15 was another significant development for the Court in 2021. The incorporation of an explicit reference to the principles of subsidiarity and the margin of appreciation, two longstanding principles of the Court, into the Preamble of the Convention has helped to solidify these principles and bring them to the forefront of how the Convention is to be implemented, while encouraging member states to take further responsibility for implementing the Convention within their domestic legal jurisdictions.

Every year many sensitive and important subjects flood into the Court, which must adjudicate on unprecedented and often complex issues. No one perusing the Court's case-law can fail to be struck by the scope and diversity of the subject matters addressed. The challenge facing the Court over the next few years will be to respond to all these requests within a reasonable time and in an appropriate manner. This was the main goal of all the reforms launched in 2021. Constantly innovating, striving toward ever greater efficacy, and above all delivering optimum decisions: this has always been the Court's ambition. It has endeavoured to achieve this ambition throughout 2021, and it will continue to be motivated by this goal over the months and years to come.

LEGAL MAXIMS: SUMMARIES AND EXTRACTS FROM SELECTED CASE LAW*

Case of Hanan v. Germany, Application no. 4871/16, Grand Chamber, Judgment, 16 February 2021

Case of Big Brother Watch and Others v. The United Kingdom, Applications nos. 58170/13, 62322/14 and 24960/15, Grand Chamber, Judgment, 25 May 2021

Case of Fedotova and Others v. Russia, Applications nos. 40792/10, 30538/14 and 43439/14, Third Section, Judgment, 13 July 2021

Case of Reczkowicz v. Poland, Application no. 43447/19, First Section, Judgment, 22 July 2021

Case of Carter v. Russia, Application no. 20914/07, Third Section, Judgment, 21 September 2021

Case of Ariana Zakharyevna Shavlokhova v. Georgia, Applications nos. 45431/08, 50669/08, 55291/08, 20517/09, 24964/09, Second Section, Decision, 5 October 2021

Affaire Miroslava Todorova c. Bulgarie, Requête no. 40072/13, Quatrième Section, Arrêt, 19 Octobre 2021

Case of Vedat Şorli v. Turkey, Application no. 42048/19, Second Section, Judgment, 19 October 2021

---

* The working method chosen for the formulation of legal maxims is explained *supra* 'Outline of the Parts', at page xv.

Legal Maxims: Summaries and Extracts from Selected Case Law In: *The Global Community Yearbook of International Law and Jurisprudence 2022*. Edited by: Giuliana Ziccardi Capaldo, Oxford University Press. © Oxford University Press 2023. DOI: 10.1093/oso/9780197752265.003.0027

LEGAL MAXIMS: SUMMARIES
AND EXTRACTS FROM
SELECTED CASE LAW*

Case of Hanan v. Germany Application no. 4871/16, Grand Chamber, Judgment, 16 February 2021

Case of Big Brother Watch and Others v. The United Kingdom, Applications nos. 58170/13, 62322/14 and 24960/15, Grand Chamber Judgment, 25 May 2021

Case of Fedotova and Others v. Russia, Applications nos. 40792/10, 30538/14 and 43439/14, Third Section, Judgment, 13 July 2021

Case of Reczkowicz v. Poland, Application no. 43447/19, First Section, Judgment, 22 July 2021

Case of Carter v. Russia, Application no. 20914/07, Third Section, Judgment, 21 September 2021

Case of Akbay and Others v. Germany, Applications nos. 40495/15, 40913/15 and 37273/15, Fifth Section, Decision, 5 October 2021

Affaire Miroslava Todorova c. Bulgarie, Requête no. 40072/13, Quatrième Section, Arrêt, 19 Octobre 2021

Case of Vedat Şorli v. Turkey Application no. 42048/19, Second Section, Judgment, 19 October 2021

---

* The working method chosen for the formulation of legal maxims is explained supra Kellner … the Preface, page xx.

VII.2.1

Case of Hanan v. Germany, Application no. 4871/16, Grand Chamber, Judgment, 16 February 2021*

Contents

I. PROCEDURE AND FACTS

II. THE COURT'S COMPETENCE *RATIONE PERSONAE* AND *RATIONE LOCI*

III. APPLICATION OF ARTICLE 2 AND APPLICATION OF ARTICLE 13 IN CONJUNCTION WITH ARTICLE 2

IV. JUDGMENT

I.

II.2.0   INSTITUTION AND COURSE OF PROCEEDINGS
         See also: I.8.32; II.7.53

"[**1**] The case originated in an application [...] against the Federal Republic of Germany [...] under Article 34 of the Convention for the Protection of Human Rights and Fundamental Freedoms ("the Convention") by an Afghan national [...] ("the applicant"), on 13 January 2016. [**3**] The applicant alleged that the respondent State had not conducted an effective investigation, as required by the procedural limb of Article 2 of the Convention, into an air strike of 4 September 2009 near Kunduz, Afghanistan, that had killed [...] the applicant's two sons. Relying on Article 13 of the Convention taken in conjunction with Article 2, the applicant further alleged that he had had no effective domestic remedy to challenge the decision of the German Federal Prosecutor General [...] to discontinue the criminal investigation. [**7**] [...] [T]hird-party comments were received from the Governments of Denmark, France, Norway, Sweden and the United Kingdom, as well as from the Human Rights Centre of the University of Essex, the Institute of International Studies of the Università Cattolica del Sacro Cuore di Milano, the Open Society Justice Initiative and Rights Watch (UK) [...]. [**8**] A hearing took place in public in the Human Rights Building, Strasbourg, on 26 February 2020 [...]. The Governments of France and the United Kingdom as well as Rights Watch (UK), which had been given leave by the President to participate in the oral proceedings before the Grand Chamber, took part in the hearing."

[**Paras. 1, 3, 7, 8**]

II.

II.7.55   ECtHR JURISDICTION
          See also: I.8.11; I.8.12; II.2.0; II.2.021; II.2.041; II.2.23; II.2.24

"[**132**] The applicant complained exclusively under the procedural limb of Article 2 of the Convention about the criminal investigation into the air strike which had killed his two

---

* Summaries prepared by Yolanda Gamarra, Ph.D., Professor of Public International Law and International Relations, Faculty of Law, University of Zaragoza, Spain, E-mail: gamarra@unizar.es Text of the decision available at the Court's Web site <https://hudoc.echr.coe.int> Original: English and French. Footnotes appearing in the original text have been omitted.

sons. [...] [T]he Court recently set out the principles concerning the existence of a "jurisdictional link" for the purposes of Article 1 of the Convention in cases where the death occurred outside the territory of the Contracting State in respect of which the procedural obligation under Article 2 of the Convention was said to arise.[...] [**142**] In the present case the fact that Germany retained exclusive jurisdiction over its troops in respect of serious crimes which, moreover, it was obliged to investigate under international and domestic law constitutes "special features" which in their combination trigger the existence of a jurisdictional link for the purposes of Article 1 of the Convention in relation to the procedural obligation to investigate under Article 2. [**143**] The Court notes that the applicant did not complain about the substantive act which gave rise to the duty to investigate. It therefore does not have to examine whether, for the purposes of Article 1 of the Convention, there is also a jurisdictional link in relation to any substantive obligation under Article 2. It emphasises, however, that it does not follow from the mere establishment of a jurisdictional link in relation to the procedural obligation under Article 2 that the substantive act falls within the jurisdiction of the Contracting State or that the said act is attributable to that State. [**144**] [...][T]he scope of the present case is limited to the investigative acts and omissions by German military personnel in Afghanistan that were undertaken in accordance with the retention of exclusive jurisdiction under the ISAF Status of Forces Agreement over German troops in respect of any criminal or disciplinary offences which these might commit on the territory of Afghanistan, as well as to acts and omissions of the prosecution and judicial authorities in Germany. These are capable of giving rise to the responsibility of Germany under the Convention [...]. [**145**] The Court does not overlook the restrictions on Germany's legal powers to investigate in Afghanistan, or the fact that the deaths to be investigated occurred in the context of active hostilities. However, such circumstances do not *per se* exclude the determination that further investigatory measures, including in Afghanistan, may have been necessary, including through the use of international legal assistance and modern technology. The specific challenges to the investigation relate to the scope and content of the procedural obligation under Article 2 incumbent on the German authorities and thus to the merits of the case [...]. [**153**] With the exception of the submissions in respect of the alleged lack of independence of the investigation undertaken in Germany, the application is not manifestly ill-founded within the meaning of Article 35 § 3 (a) of the Convention. It is also not inadmissible on any other grounds. The Court therefore declares it admissible."

[**Paras. 132, 142, 143, 144, 145, 153**]

III.

I.8.45   RIGHT TO A FAIR TRIAL AND AN EFFECTIVE REMEDY
See also: I.8.42; I.8.451; II.0.8

"[**154**] The applicant complained under the procedural limb of Article 2 of the Convention that the investigation into the air strike that killed [...] his two sons had not been effective. [...] [T]he applicant also complained, relying on Article 13 of the Convention taken in conjunction with Article 2, that he had had no effective domestic remedy to challenge the decision of the German Federal Prosecutor General to discontinue the investigation. [**222**] [...] [T]he Court concludes that the applicant had at his disposal a remedy to challenge the effectiveness of the investigation [...]. [**229**] [I]n the Court's opinion the fact that the investigation remained at the preliminary investigation stage for about six months until the opening of the formal criminal investigation on 12 March 2010, while regrettable, did not affect the effectiveness of the investigation. [**234**] [T]he delay in serving the redacted version of the discontinuation decision did not negatively affect the applicant's ability to challenge that decision [...]. [**236**] [...] [T]he Court concludes that the investigation into the deaths of the applicant's two sons which was performed by the German authorities complied with the requirements of an effective investigation under Article 2 of the Convention. There has accordingly been no violation of the procedural limb of Article 2 of the Convention."

[Paras. 154, 222, 229, 234, 236]

IV.

II.2.5   JUDGMENT/DECISION/ORDER
              See also: I.8.1; I.8.42; I.8.43

"[...] THE COURT

1. *Declares*, unanimously, the part of the application relating to the lack of independence of the investigation undertaken in Germany inadmissible;
2. *Declares*, by a majority, the remainder of the application admissible;
3. *Holds*, unanimously, that there has been no violation of the procedural limb of Article 2 of the Convention."

VII.2.2

Case of Big Brother Watch and Others v. The United Kingdom, Applications nos. 58170/13, 62322/14 and 24960/15, Grand Chamber, Judgment, 25 May 2021*

Contents

I.

II.2.0   INSTITUTION AND COURSE OF PROCEEDINGS
See also: I.8.47; I.8.56; II.7.53

"[1] The case originated in three applications (nos. 58170/13, 62322/14 and 24960/15) against the United Kingdom of Great Britain and Northern Ireland lodged [. . .] by the companies, charities, organisations and individuals [. . .] on 4 September 2013, 11 September 2014 and 20 May 2015 respectively. [3] The applicants complained about the scope and magnitude of the electronic surveillance programmes operated by the Government of the United Kingdom."

[Paras. 1, 3]

II.

I.8.47   RIGHT TO PRIVATE AND FAMILY LIFE
See also: I.2.052; I.8.12; I.8.64; II.7.56

"[330] [. . .] [T]he Court has clearly stated that even the mere storing of data relating to the private life of an individual amounts to an interference within the meaning of Article 8 (see *Leander v. Sweden*, 26 March 1987, § 48, Series A no. 116), and that the need for safeguards will be all the greater where the protection of personal data undergoing automatic processing is concerned (see *S. and Marper*, cited above, § 103). The fact that the stored material is in coded form [. . .] can have no bearing on that finding (see *Amann v. Switzerland* [GC], no. 27798/95, § 69, ECHR 2000-II and *S. and Marper*, cited above, §§ 67 and 75). Finally, at the end of the process, where information about a particular person will be analysed or the content of the communications is being examined by an analyst, the need for safeguards will be at its highest.[. . .][332] Any interference with an individual's Article 8 rights can only be justified under Article 8 § 2 if it is in accordance with the law, pursues one or more of the legitimate aims to which that paragraph refers and is necessary in a democratic society in order to achieve any such aim (see *Roman Zakharov*, cited

---

* Summaries prepared by Ángel Tinoco Pastrana, Professor of Procedural Law, Faculty of Law, University of Seville, Spain. Text of judgement available online at the Court's Web site <http://www.echr.coe.int >. Original: English and French. Footnotes appearing in the original text have been omitted.

above, § 227; see also *Kennedy v. the United Kingdom*, no. 26839/05, § 130, 18 May 2010). [...][**333**] The meaning of "foreseeability" in the context of secret surveillance is not the same as in many other fields.[...] It is therefore essential to have clear, detailed rules on secret surveillance measures [...]."

[**Paras. 330, 332, 333**]

I.8.47   RIGHT TO PRIVATE AND FAMILY LIFE
         See also: I.8.04; I.8.45; I.8.64; II.7.56

"[**335**] [...] [T]he Court has developed the following minimum requirements that should be set out in law in order to avoid abuses of power: (i) the nature of offences which may give rise to an interception order; (ii) a definition of the categories of people liable to have their communications intercepted; (iii) a limit on the duration of interception; (iv) the procedure to be followed for examining, using and storing the data obtained; (v) the precautions to be taken when communicating the data to other parties; and (vi) the circumstances in which intercepted data may or must be erased or destroyed (see *Huvig*, cited above, § 34; *Kruslin*, cited above, § 35; *Valenzuela Contreras*, cited above, § 46; *Weber and Saravia*, cited above, § 95; and *Association for European Integration and Human Rights and Ekimdzhiev*, cited above, § 76). [...][**336**] Review and supervision of secret surveillance measures may come into play at three stages: when the surveillance is first ordered, while it is being carried out, or after it has been terminated. As regards the first two stages, the very nature and logic of secret surveillance dictate that not only the surveillance itself but also the accompanying review should be effected without the individual's knowledge.[...] [T]he Court has held that it is in principle desirable to entrust supervisory control to a judge.[...][**337**] As regards the third stage, after the surveillance has been terminated, the question of subsequent notification of surveillance measures is a relevant factor in assessing the effectiveness of remedies before the courts [...]."

[**Paras. 335, 336, 337**]

I.8.47   RIGHT TO PRIVATE AND FAMILY LIFE
         See also: I.2.052; I.8.12; I.8.45; II.7.56

"[**347**] [...] While Article 8 of the Convention does not prohibit the use of bulk interception to protect national security and other essential national interests against serious external threats, and States enjoy a wide margin of appreciation in deciding what type of interception regime is necessary, for these purposes, in operating such a system the margin of appreciation afforded to them must be narrower and a number of safeguards will have to be present. [...][**348**] It is clear that the first two of the six "minimum safeguards" which the Court, in the context of targeted interception, has found should be defined clearly in domestic law [...] are not readily applicable to a bulk interception regime.[...][**350**] Therefore [...] the Court considers that the process must be subject to "end-to-end safeguards" [...]. [**351**] [...] [W]hile judicial authorisation is an "important safeguard against arbitrariness" it is not a "necessary requirement" [...]. Nevertheless, bulk interception should be authorised by an independent body [...]. [**356**] [...]. In particular, the supervising body should be in a position to assess the necessity and proportionality of the action being taken [...]. [**357**] Finally, an effective remedy should be available to anyone who suspects that his or her communications have been intercepted by the intelligence services [...]. [**358**] The Court considers that a remedy which does not depend on notification to the interception subject could also be an effective remedy [...]. [**359**] [...] Therefore, in the absence of a notification requirement it is imperative that the remedy should be before a body which, while not necessarily judicial, is independent of the executive and ensures the fairness of the proceedings, offering, in so far as possible, an adversarial process.[...]"

[**Paras. 347, 348, 350, 351, 356, 357, 358, 359**]

I.8.47   RIGHT TO PRIVATE AND FAMILY LIFE
            See also: I.2.05; I.8.03; I.8.45; II.7.56

"[**362**] [...] [T]he Court considers that the transmission by a Contracting State to foreign States or international organisations of material obtained by bulk interception should be limited to such material as has been collected and stored in a Convention compliant manner and should be subject to certain additional specific safeguards pertaining to the transfer itself. First of all, the circumstances in which such a transfer may take place must be set out clearly in domestic law. Secondly, the transferring State must ensure that the receiving State, in handling the data, has in place safeguards capable of preventing abuse and disproportionate interference.[...] Thirdly, heightened safeguards will be necessary when it is clear that material requiring special confidentiality [...] is being transferred. Finally, the Court considers that the transfer of material to foreign intelligence partners should also be subject to independent control. [**363**] [...] [T]he Court [...] considers that the interception, retention and searching of related communications data should be analysed by reference to the same safeguards as those applicable to content."

[**Paras. 362, 363**]

III.

I.8.56   FREEDOM OF EXPRESSION
            See also: I.2.051; I.8.45; I.8.561; II.7.56

"[**442**] [...] The safeguards to be afforded to the press are of particular importance, and the protection of journalistic sources is one of the cornerstones of freedom of the press [...] (see, *inter alia, Goodwin v. the United Kingdom*, no. 17488/90, § 39, 27 March 1996; *Sanoma Uitgevers B.V.*, cited above, § 50; and *Weber and Saravia*, cited above, § 143). [**443**] [...] There is, however, "a fundamental difference" between the authorities ordering a journalist to reveal the identity of his or her sources, and the authorities carrying out searches at a journalist's home and workplace with a view to uncovering his or her sources [...]. [**444**] [...]. Furthermore, any interference with the right to protection of journalistic sources must be attended with legal procedural safeguards [...]. First and foremost among these safeguards is the guarantee of review by a judge or other independent and impartial decision-making body [...]. [**445**] [...] In situations of urgency, a procedure should exist to identify and isolate, [...] information that could lead to the identification of sources from information that carries no such risk [...]. [**448**] Where the intention of the intelligence services is to access confidential journalistic material [...] the Court considers that the interference will be commensurate with that occasioned by the search of a journalist's home or workplace [...] (see *Roemen and Schmit*, cited above, § 57). Therefore, the Court considers that before the intelligence services use selectors or search terms [...] must have been authorised by a judge or other independent and impartial decision-making body [...] (see *Sanoma Uitgevers B.V.*, cited above, §§ 90-92). [**449**] Even where there is no intention to access confidential journalistic material [...] there will nevertheless be a risk that such material could be intercepted, and even examined, as a "bycatch" of a bulk interception operation.[...][**450**] [...]. [T]he Court considers it imperative that domestic law contain robust safeguards regarding the storage, examination, use, onward transmission and destruction of such confidential material. […]"

[Paras. 442, 443, 444, 445, 448, 449, 450]

IV.

II.2.5   JUDGMENT/DECISION/ORDER
            See also: I.8.47; I.8.56; II.7.58

"[…] THE COURT
1. *Holds*, unanimously, that there has been a violation of Article 8 of the Convention in respect of the section 8(4) regime;
2. *Holds*, unanimously, that there has been a violation of Article 8 of the Convention in respect of the Chapter II regime;
3. *Holds*, by twelve votes to five, that there has been no violation of Article 8 of the Convention in respect of the receipt of intelligence from foreign intelligence services;
4. *Holds*, unanimously, that, in so far as it was raised by the applicants in the second of the joined cases, there has been a violation of Article 10 of the Convention in respect of the section 8(4) regime and the Chapter II regime.
5. *Holds*, by twelve votes to five, that there has been no violation of Article 10 of the Convention in respect of the receipt of intelligence from foreign intelligence services;
6. *Holds*, unanimously,
   (a) that the respondent State is to pay the applicants, within three months […];
7. *Dismisses*, unanimously, the remainder of the applicants' claim for just satisfaction."

VII.2.3

Case of Fedotova and Others v. Russia, Applications nos. 40792/10, 30538/14 and 43439/14, Third Section, Judgment, 13 July 2021*

Contents

I. INSTITUTION AND PROCEDURAL BACKGROUND

II. ALLEGED VIOLATION OF ARTICLE 8 OF THE CONVENTION AND ARTICLE 14 IN CONJUNCTION WITH ARTICLE 8 OF THE CONVENTION

III. JUDGMENT

I.

II.2.0   INSTITUTION AND COURSE OF PROCEEDINGS
See also: I.8.58; I.8.61

"[1] The case concerns a lack of opportunity for the applicants, three same-sex couples, to have their relationships formally registered, which amounted, in their opinion, to discrimination against them on the grounds of their sexual orientation."

[Para. 1]

II.

I.8.47   RIGHT TO PRIVATE AND FAMILY LIFE
See also: I.1.14; I.1.16; I.8.58; I.8.61

"[44] While the essential object of Article 8 is to protect individuals against arbitrary interference by public authorities, it may also impose on a State certain positive obligations to ensure effective respect for the rights protected by Article 8 (see *Söderman v. Sweden* [GC], no. 5786/08, § 78, ECHR 2013; *Hämäläinen v. Finland* [GC], no. 37359/09, § 62, ECHR 2014; *X and Y v. the Netherlands,* 26 March 1985, § 23, Series A no. 91; and *Maumousseau and Washington v. France,* no. 39388/05, § 83, 6 December 2007). These obligations may involve the adoption of measures designed to secure respect for private or family life even in the sphere of the relations of individuals between themselves (see *S.H. and Others v. Austria* [GC], no. 57813/00, § 87, ECHR 2011, and *Söderman,* cited above, § 78), including positive obligations to establish a legal framework guaranteeing the effective enjoyment of the rights guaranteed by Article 8 of the Convention (see *Oliari and Others,* cited above, § 185).
[45] The notion of "respect" is not clear-cut, especially as far as positive obligations are concerned: having regard to the diversity of the practices followed and the situations obtaining in the Contracting States, the notion's requirements will vary considerably from case to case (see *Christine Goodwin v. the United Kingdom* [GC], no. 28957/95, § 72, ECHR 2002-VI). Nonetheless, certain factors have been considered relevant for the assessment of the content of those positive obligations on States (see *Hämäläinen,* cited above, § 66). [. . .]

---

* Summaries prepared by Ángel Tinoco Pastrana, Professor of Procedural Law, Faculty of Law, University of Seville, Spain. Text of judgement available online at the Court's Web site <http://www.echr.coe.int>. Original: English.

Other factors relate to the impact of the alleged positive obligation at stake on the State concerned. The question here is whether the alleged obligation is narrow and precise or broad and indeterminate (see *Botta v. Italy*, 24 February 1998, § 35, Reports of Judgments and Decisions 1998-I) or about the extent of any burden the obligation would impose on the State (see *Christine Goodwin*, cited above, §§ 86-88)."

[Paras. 44, 45]

I.8.47   RIGHT TO PRIVATE AND FAMILY LIFE
         See also: I.1.14; I.1.16; I.1.4; I.8.58

"[**46**] The principles applicable to assessing a State's positive and negative obligations under the Convention are similar. Regard must be had to the fair balance that has to be struck between the competing interests of the individual and of the community as a whole, the aims in the second paragraph of Article 8 being of a certain relevance (see *Roche v. the United Kingdom* [GC], no. 32555/96, § 157, ECHR 2005-X; *Gaskin v. the United Kingdom*, 7 July 1989, § 42, Series A no. 160; *Oliari and Others*, cited above, § 159; and *Orlandi and Others*, cited above, § 198). [**47**] In implementing their positive obligation under Article 8 the States enjoy a certain margin of appreciation. A number of factors must be taken into account when determining the breadth of that margin. In the context of "private life" the Court has considered that where a particularly important facet of an individual's existence or identity is at stake the margin allowed to the State will be restricted (see, for example, *X and Y v. the Netherlands*, 26 March 1985, §§ 24 and 27, Series A no. 91; *Christine Goodwin*, cited above, § 90; see also *Pretty v. the United Kingdom*, no. 2346/02, § 71, ECHR 2002-III). [**48**] As regards same-sex couples, the Court has already held that they are just as capable as different-sex couples of entering into committed relationships. They are in a relevantly similar situation to a different-sex couple as regards their need for formal acknowledgment and protection of their relationship (see *Schalk and Kopf v. Austria*, no. 30141/04, § 99, ECHR 2010; *Vallianatos and Others v. Greece* [GC], nos. 29381/09 and 32684/09, §§ 78 and 81, ECHR 2013 (extracts); and *Oliari and Others*, cited above, §§ 165 and 192)."

[Paras. 46, 47, 48]

I.8.47   RIGHT TO PRIVATE AND FAMILY LIFE
         See also: I.1.41; I.8.1; I.8.4; I.8.58

"[**49**] The Court reiterates that Article 8 of the Convention enshrines the right to respect for private and family life. It does not explicitly impose on the Contracting States an obligation to formally acknowledge same-sex unions. However, it implies the need for striking a fair balance between the competing interests of same-sex couples and of the community as a whole. Having identified the individuals' interests at play, the Court must proceed to weigh them against the community interests (see *Oliari and Others*, cited above, § 175, and *Orlandi and Others*, cited above, § 198). [**51**] The Court notes that the applicants as other same-sex couples are not legally prevented from living together in couples as families. However, they have no means to have their relationship recognised by law. [. . .] That situation creates a conflict between the social reality of the applicants who live in committed relationships based on mutual affection, and the law, which fails to protect the most regular of "needs" arising in the context of a same-sex couple.[. . .] [**52**] [. . .] It would be incompatible with the underlying values of the Convention, as an instrument of the European public order, if the exercise of Convention rights by a minority group were made conditional on its being accepted by the majority (see, *mutatis mutandis*, *Alekseyev*, cited above, § 81; *Bayev and Others v. Russia*, nos. 67667/09 and 2 others, § 70, 20 June 2017; and

Beizaras and Levickas v. Lithuania, no. 41288/15, § 122, 14 January 2020). [**53**] The interest in protecting minors from display of homosexuality to which the Government referred is based on the domestic legal provision criticised by the Court in the case of *Bayev* (cited above, §§ 68 and 69). [...] [**54**] [...] The Court [...] cannot discern any risks for traditional marriage which the formal acknowledgment of same-sex unions may involve, since it does not prevent different-sex couples from entering marriage, or enjoying the benefits which the marriage gives."

[**Paras. 49, 51, 52, 53, 54**]

III.

II.2.5   JUDGMENT/DECISION/ORDER
              See also: I.8.1; I.8.58; I.8.61

"[...] THE COURT
[...]
  3. *Holds,* unanimously, that there has been a violation of Article 8 of the Convention in respect of all applicants;
  4. *Holds,* unanimously, that there is no need to examine the merits of the complaints under Article 14 of the Convention taken in conjunction with Article 8;
  5. *Holds,* unanimously, that the finding of a violation constitutes in itself sufficient just satisfaction for the non-pecuniary damage sustained by the applicants;
  6. *Dismisses,* by five votes to two, the remainder of the applicants' claims for just satisfaction."

VII.2.4

Case of Reczkowicz v. Poland, Application no. 43447/19, First Section, Judgment, 22 July 2021*

Contents

I.

II.2.0 INSTITUTION AND COURSE OF PROCEEDINGS

See also: I.8.45

"[1] The applicant, who is a barrister, complained that the Disciplinary Chamber of the Supreme Court that dealt with her case had not been an independent and impartial "tribunal established by law" and alleged a breach of Article 6 § 1 of the Convention."

[**Para. 1**]

II.

II.2.021 ADMISSIBILITY OF THE APPLICATION

See also: I.0.136; II.7.55

"[183] It is the Court's well-established case-law that disciplinary proceedings in which the right to continue to exercise a profession is at stake give rise to "*contestations*" (disputes) over civil rights within the meaning of Article 6 § 1 (see for instance, *Philis v. Greece (no. 2)*, 27 June 1997, § 45, *Reports of Judgments and Decisions* 1997-IV, and *Vilho Eskelinen and Others v. Finland* [GC], no. 63235/00, § 62, ECHR 2007-II). This principle has been applied with regard to proceedings conducted before various professional disciplinary bodies and in particular as regards judges in *Baka v. Hungary* [GC], no. 20261/12, §§ 104-105, 23 June 2016, prosecutors in *Polyakh and Others v. Ukraine*, nos. 58812/15 and 4 others, § 160, 17 October 2019, and practising lawyers in *Malek v. Austria*, no. 60553/00, § 39, 12 June 2003, and *Helmut Blum v. Austria*, no. 33060/10, § 60, 5 April 2016. [184] [. . .] The Court sees no reason to depart from its case-law cited above. It considers that there is no basis for finding that the disciplinary proceedings against the applicant concerned the determination of a criminal charge against her within the meaning of Article 6 of the Convention as submitted by the applicant (see *Ramos Nunes de Carvalho e Sá v. Portugal* [GC], nos. 55391/13 and 2 others, § 127, 6 November 2018, and *Müller-Hartburg v. Austria*, no. 47195/06, § 49, 19 February 2013). [186] The Court notes that the application is neither manifestly ill-founded nor inadmissible on any other of the grounds listed in Article 35 of the Convention. It must therefore be declared admissible."

[**Paras. 183, 184, 186**]

---

* Summaries prepared by Ángel Tinoco Pastrana, Professor of Procedural Law, Faculty of Law, University of Seville, Spain. Text of judgement available online at the Court's Web site <http://www.echr.coe.int >. Original: English. Footnotes appearing in the original text have been omitted.

I.8.45   RIGHT TO A FAIR TRIAL AND AN EFFECTIVE REMEDY

See also: I.1.4; II.0.6; II.0.8; II.7.56

"[216] In its recent judgment in *Guðmundur Andri Ástráðsson* [...] the Grand Chamber of the Court clarified the scope of, and meaning to be given to, the concept of a "tribunal established by law". The Court reiterated that the purpose of the requirement that the "tribunal" be "established by law" was to ensure "that the judicial organisation in a democratic society [did] not depend on the discretion of the executive, but that it [was] regulated by law emanating from Parliament" [...]. [217] As regards the notion of a "tribunal", in addition to the requirements stemming from the Court's settled case-law, it was also inherent in its very notion that a "tribunal" be composed of judges selected on the basis of merit – that is, judges who fulfilled the requirements of technical competence and moral integrity. The Court noted that the higher a tribunal was placed in the judicial hierarchy, the more demanding the applicable selection criteria should be [...]. [218] As regards the term "established", the Court referred to the purpose of that requirement, which was to protect the judiciary against unlawful external influence, in particular from the executive, but also from the legislature or from within the judiciary itself. In this connection, it found that the process of appointing judges necessarily constituted an inherent element of the concept "established by law" and that it called for strict scrutiny. Breaches of the law regulating the judicial appointment process might render the participation of the relevant judge in the examination of a case "irregular" [...]. [219] As regards the phrase "by law", the Court clarified that the third component also meant a "tribunal established in accordance with the law". It observed that the relevant domestic law on judicial appointments should be couched in unequivocal terms, to the extent possible, so as not to allow arbitrary interferences in the appointment process [...]."

[**Paras. 216, 217, 218, 219**]

I.8.45   RIGHT TO A FAIR TRIAL AND AN EFFECTIVE REMEDY

See also: II.0.6; II.0.8; II.2.53; II.7.56

"[220] [...] [T]he Court [...] noted that although the right to a "tribunal established by law" was a stand-alone right under Article 6 § 1 of the Convention, a very close interrelationship had been formulated in the Court's case-law between that specific right and the guarantees of "independence" and "impartiality". The institutional requirements of Article 6 § 1 shared the ordinary purpose of upholding the fundamental principles of the rule of law and the separation of powers. [...] [221] [...] [T]he Court developed a threshold test made up of three criteria, taken cumulatively [...]. [222] In the first place, there must, in principle, be a manifest breach of the domestic law [...]. However, the absence of such a breach does not rule out the possibility of a violation of the right to a tribunal established by law, since a procedure that is seemingly in compliance with the domestic rules may nevertheless produce results that are incompatible with the object and purpose of that right. [...] [223] Secondly, the breach in question must be assessed in the light of the object and purpose of the requirement of a "tribunal established by law", namely to ensure the ability of the judiciary to perform its duties free of undue interference [...]. Accordingly, breaches of a purely technical nature that have no bearing on the legitimacy of the appointment process must be considered to fall below the relevant threshold. To the contrary, breaches that wholly disregard the most fundamental rules in the appointment or breaches that may otherwise undermine the purpose and effect of the "established by law" requirement must be considered to be in violation of that requirement [...]. [224] Thirdly, the review conducted by national courts, if any, as to the legal consequences [...]

of a breach of a domestic rule on judicial appointments plays a significant role [...]. The assessment by the national courts of the legal effects of such a breach must be carried out on the basis of the relevant Convention case-law and the principles derived therefrom [...]."

[Paras. 220, 221, 222, 223, 224]

I.8.45   RIGHT TO A FAIR TRIAL AND AN EFFECTIVE REMEDY
         See also: I.1.4; II.0.6; II.0.8; II.7.56

"**[260]** [...][T]he Court reiterates that the right to a fair trial under Article 6 § 1 of the Convention must be interpreted in the light of the Preamble to the Convention, which, in its relevant part, declares the rule of law to be part of the common heritage of the Contracting States. The right to "a tribunal established by law" is a reflection of this very principle of the rule of law [...]. It is also to be reiterated that although the right to a "tribunal established by law" is a stand-alone right under Article 6 § 1 of the Convention, there is a very close interrelationship between that specific right and the guarantees of "independence" and "impartiality". [...] **[261]** [...] The Court [...] reiterate that "independence of a tribunal established by law" refers to the necessary personal and institutional independence that is required for impartial decision making, and it is thus a prerequisite for impartiality. It characterises both (i) a state of mind, which denotes a judge's imperviousness to external pressure as a matter of moral integrity, and (ii) a set of institutional and operational arrangements – involving both a procedure by which judges can be appointed in a manner that ensures their independence and selection criteria based on merit –, which must provide safeguards against undue influence and/or unfettered discretion of the other State powers [...]. **[266]** When determining whether a particular defect in the judicial appointment process was of such gravity as to amount to a violation of the right to a "tribunal established by law", regard must be had, *inter alia*, to the purpose of the law breached, that is, whether it sought to prevent any undue interference by the executive or the legislature with the judiciary, and whether the breach in question undermined the very essence of the right to a "tribunal established by law" (see *Guðmundur Andri Ástráðsson*, cited above, §§ 226 and 255). **[267]** The process of appointment of judges may be open to such undue interference, and it therefore calls for strict scrutiny [...]."

[Paras. 260, 261, 266, 267]

III.

II.2.5   JUDGMENT/DECISION/ORDER
         See also: I.8.45

"[...] THE COURT, UNANIMOUSLY,
    [...]
    2. *Holds* that there has been a violation of Article 6 § 1 of the Convention;
    3. *Holds*,
        (a) that the respondent State is to pay the applicant, within three months from the date on which the judgment becomes final in accordance with Article 44 § 2 of the Convention, the following amounts, to be converted into the currency of the respondent State at the rate applicable at the date of settlement:
            (i) EUR 15,000 (fifteen thousand euros), plus any tax that may be chargeable, in respect of non-pecuniary damage;

(ii) EUR 420 (four hundred and twenty euros), plus any tax that may be chargeable to the applicant, in respect of costs and expenses;

(b) that from the expiry of the above-mentioned three months until settlement simple interest shall be payable on the above amount at a rate equal to the marginal lending rate of the European Central Bank during the default period plus three percentage points;

4. *Dismisses*, the remainder of the applicant's claim for just satisfaction."

VII.2.5

Case of Carter v. Russia, Application no. 20914/07, Third Section, Judgment, 21 September 2021*

Contents

I.

II.2.0   INSTITUTION AND COURSE OF PROCEEDINGS

See also: I.2.01; I.8.32; I.12; I.12.26; II.7.5

"[1] The case concerns the poisoning of the applicant's husband, a Russian defector and dissident, in the United Kingdom. The applicant alleges that the killing was perpetrated on the direction or with the acquiescence or connivance of the Russian authorities and that the Russian authorities failed to conduct an effective domestic investigation into the murder. [111] [...] The Court will consider this complaint from the standpoint of the right to life guaranteed under Article 2 of the Convention [...]."

[Paras. 1, 111]

II.

A.

I.2.0111   EXTRATERRITORIAL EFFECTS OF STATE ACTS

See also: I.0.133; I.0.1331; I.1.02; I.2.04; I.8.32

"[125] The two main criteria governing the exercise of extraterritorial jurisdiction are that of "effective control" by the State over an area outside its territory (spatial concept of jurisdiction) and that of "State agent authority and control" over individuals (personal concept of jurisdiction) (see *Al-Skeini and Others* [...], §§ 133-40, and *Georgia v. Russia (II)* [GC], no. 38263/08, § 115, 21 January 2021). In the present case, it is the second of these criteria that is relevant. [126] Under the personal concept of jurisdiction, "the use of force by a State's agents operating outside its territory may bring the individual thereby brought under the control of the State's authorities into the State's Article 1 jurisdiction" (see *Al-Skeini and Others* [...], § 136). Jurisdiction in such cases does not arise solely

---

* Summaries prepared by Noelia Arjona Hernández, Ph.D. in Public International Law, University of Seville. Member of the Research Group Politics and International Law (SEJ119) at the University of Seville. Text of Judgment available online at the Court's Web site <http://www.echr.coe.int>. Original: English. Footnotes appearing in the original text have been omitted.

from the control exercised by the Contracting State over the physical premises in which individuals are held but rather from "the exercise of physical power and control over the person in question" (ibid., § 136). [. . .] [**127**] The Court reiterates that "a State may also be held accountable for violation of the Convention rights and freedoms of persons who are in the territory of another State but who are found to be under the former State's authority and control through its agents operating – whether lawfully or unlawfully – in the latter State" (see *Öcalan v. Turkey* [GC], no. 46221/99, § 91, ECHR 2005-IV, and *Issa and Others v. Turkey*, no. 31821/96, § 71, 16 November 2004). That approach was followed in a series of cases including *Isaak v. Turkey* ((dec.), no. 44587/98, 28 September 2006), *Pad and Others v. Turkey* ((dec.), no. 60167/00, 28 June 2007), *Andreou v. Turkey* ((dec.), no. 45653/99, 3 June 2008), and *Solomou and Others v. Turkey* (no. 36832/97, §§ 48-51, 24 June 2008). In those cases, control over individuals on account of incursions and targeting of specific persons by the armed forces or police of the respondent State was sufficient to bring the affected persons "under the authority and/or effective control of the respondent State through its agents". [**128**] The Court has held that "accountability in such situations stems from the fact that Article 1 of the Convention cannot be interpreted so as to allow a State party to perpetrate violations of the Convention on the territory of another State, which it could not perpetrate on its own territory" (see *Issa and Others*, § 71, and *Solomou and Others*, § 45 [. . .]). Targeted violations of the human rights of an individual by one Contracting State in the territory of another Contracting State undermine the effectiveness of the Convention both as a guardian of human rights and as a guarantor of peace, stability and the rule of law in Europe."

[**Paras. 125, 126, 127, 128**]

I.8.42   RIGHT TO LIFE
            See also: I.2.011; I.2.0111; II.2.2; II.2.24; II.7.55

"[**129**] In its recent judgment in *Georgia v. Russia (II)*, the Court referred in particular to cases where State agents targeted an individual's life and limb extra-territorially even without having formally exercised powers of arrest or detention over that person (see *Georgia v. Russia (II)* [. . .], §§ 130-31). It considered that those cases concerning, as they did, "isolated and specific acts involving an element of proximity" must be distinguished from situations of "armed confrontation and fighting between enemy military forces seeking to establish control over an area in a context of chaos" which exclude any form of "effective control" over an area or of "State agent authority and control" over individuals (ibid., §§ 132-33 and 137-38). [**130**] [. . .] [I]n the view of the Court, the principle that a State exercises extraterritorial jurisdiction in cases concerning specific acts involving an element of proximity should apply with equal force in cases of extrajudicial targeted killings by State agents acting in the territory of another Contracting State outside of the context of a military operation. This approach is consistent with the wording of Article 15 § 2 of the Convention which allows for no derogations from Article 2, except in respect of deaths resulting from lawful acts of war. [**136**] As regards the complaint under the substantive limb of Article 2, the Court considers that the Government's objection *ratione loci* – that is to say, whether or not Mr Litvinenko was under the control of Mr Lugovoy and others and whether or not Mr Lugovoy and others acted as agents of the Russian State at the material time – is interlinked with the substance of the applicant's complaint and shall be examined together with the merits (see *Makuchyan and Minasyan v. Azerbaijan and Hungary*, no. 17247/13, § 52, 26 May 2020). [**150**] In the light of the Court's case-law summarised in paragraphs 126-130 [. . .], the fate of the applicant's complaint about the assassination of her husband depends on the answers to the following two interrelated questions: (i) whether the assassination of Mr Litvinenko amounted to the exercise of physical power and control over his life in a situation of proximate targeting, and (ii) whether it was carried out by individuals acting as State agents. The Court will establish the facts on the basis of the evidence available in the case-file. [**158**] As framed in paragraph 150 above, the Court's inquiry will first address the issue whether the assassination of Mr Litvinenko amounted to the exercise of physical power and control over his life in a situation of proximate targeting. [**159**] The evidence of premeditation strongly indicates that the death of Mr Litvinenko had been the result of a planned and complex operation involving the procurement of a rare deadly poison, the travel arrangements for Mr Lugovoy and Mr Kovtun, and multiple attempts to administer the poison. Mr Litvinenko was not an accidental victim of the operation or merely adversely affected by it; the possibility that he may have ingested polonium 210 by accident is not borne out by the evidence [...]. On the contrary, repeated and sustained attempts to put poison in his drink demonstrate that Mr Litvinenko was the target of the planned operation for his assassination. [**160**] The Court further notes that the evidence has established, beyond reasonable doubt, that Mr Lugovoy and Mr Kovtun knew that they were using a deadly poison rather than a truth serum or a sleeping pill [...]. When putting the poison in the teapot from which Mr Litvinenko poured a drink, they knew that, once ingested, the poison would kill Mr Litvinenko. The latter was unable to do anything to escape the situation. In that sense, he was under physical control of Mr Lugovoy and Mr Kovtun who wielded power over his life. [**161**] In the Court's view, the administration of poison to Mr Litvinenko by Mr Lugovoy and Mr Kovtun amounted to the exercise of physical power and control over his life in a situation of proximate targeting. That being so, if this act was imputable to the respondent State, the Court considers that it was capable of falling within the jurisdiction of that State in line with its case-law cited above."

[**Paras. 129, 130, 136, 150, 158, 159, 160, 161**]

B.

II.1.0   BURDEN OF PROOF
            See also: I.2.0111; I.8.42; I.15.4; II.5.2

"[**134**] [T]he Court notes that the suspects in the murder are Russian nationals who, since their return to Russia, have enjoyed the constitutional protection from extradition.[...] Whereas the possibility that a State may refuse a request for extradition of its own national is not as such incompatible with the obligation to conduct an effective investigation, the fact that the Government retained exclusive jurisdiction over an individual who is accused of a serious human rights violation constitutes a "special feature" of the case establishing the respondent State's jurisdiction under Article 1 of the Convention in respect of the applicant's complaint under the procedural limb of Article 2 (see *Hanan v. Germany* [GC], no. 4871/16, § 142, 16 February 2021). Any other finding would undermine the fight against impunity for serious human-rights violations within the "legal space of the Convention", impeding the application of criminal laws put in place by the United Kingdom to protect the right to life of their citizens and, indeed, of any individuals within its jurisdiction (see *Güzelyurtlu and Others* [...], § 195). [**143**] [...] In the present case, on account of the Government's unjustified refusal to submit the requested documentation, the Court finds that the respondent Government has failed to discharge their burden of proof so as to demonstrate that the Russian authorities have carried out an effective investigation capable of leading to the establishment of the facts and bringing to justice of those responsible for Mr Litvinenko's killing."

[**Paras. 134, 143**]

I.11.014   STATE CRIMINAL RESPONSIBILITY
            See also: I.1.1425; I.11.0141; I.2.011; I.12.26; II.1.4

"[**166**] While there existed a theoretical possibility that the assassination of Mr Litvinenko might have been a "rogue operation" not involving State responsibility, the information needed to corroborate this theory lies wholly, or in large part, within the exclusive knowledge of the Russian authorities which moreover asserted exclusive jurisdiction over Mr Lugovoy and Mr Kovtun by invoking the constitutional protection against extradition. In these circumstances, the burden of proof was shifted onto the authorities of the respondent State which were expected to carry out a meticulous investigation into that possibility, identify those involved in the operation and determine whether or not Mr Lugovoy's and Mr Kovtun's conduct was directed or controlled by any State entity or official, which is a factor indicative of State responsibility (see Article 8 of the Draft Articles in paragraph 72 [...]). [**167**] The Government, however, have not made any serious attempt either to elucidate the facts or to counter the findings arrived at by the United Kingdom authorities. In fact, they have failed to engage with any fact-finding efforts, whether those conducted in the United Kingdom or those undertaken by the Court. They declined to participate in the public inquiry into the death of Mr Litvinenko. They did not comply with their obligations under Article 38 of the Convention by virtue of their unjustified refusal to submit a copy of materials relating to the domestic investigation [...], the materials which they claimed did not establish any State involvement in Mr Litvinenko's death. [**168**] Most significantly, as the Court has found above, the Russian authorities failed to carry out an effective investigation themselves [...]. There is no evidence that, having full access to Mr Lugovoy and Mr Kovtun upon their return to Russia, the Russian authorities have undertaken a verification of the facts already established in the United Kingdom's public inquiry; the facts which, as the Court found above, demonstrated Mr Lugovoy's and Mr Kovtun's responsibility for the killing of Mr Litvinenko. The Court reiterates that Mr Lugovoy's parliamentary immunity was not an absolute bar to his being investigated or prosecuted [...]. [**169**] Consequently, the Court considers that adverse inferences may be drawn from the respondent State's refusal to disclose any documents relating to the domestic investigation. Noting the Government's failure to displace the prima facie evidence of State involvement, the Court cannot but conclude that Mr Litvinenko was poisoned by Mr Lugovoy and Mr Kovtun acting as agents of the respondent State. The act complained of is attributable to that State."

[**Paras. 166, 167, 168, 169**]

III.

II.2.5   JUDGMENT/DECISION/ORDER
            See also: I.8.32; I.8.42; I.8.45; II.2.021; II.7.5

"[...] THE COURT
   1. *Holds*, unanimously, that the respondent Government failed to comply with their obligations under Article 38 of the Convention;
      [...]
   4. *Holds*, by six votes to one, that there has been a violation of Article 2 of the Convention under the substantive and procedural limbs [...]."

VII.2.6

Case of Ariana Zakharyevna Shavlokhova v. Georgia, Applications nos. 45431/08, 50669/08, 55291/08, 20517/09, 24964/09, Second Section, Decision, 5 October 2021*

Contents

I.

II.2.0   INSTITUTION AND COURSE OF PROCEEDINGS

See also: I.8.32; I.8.42; I.8.43; I.8.45; II.2.021

"[1] A list of the applicants, who are all Russian nationals, is set out in the appendix. [4] The five applications listed in the appendix were lodged in the context of an armed conflict that occurred between Georgia and the Russian Federation in August 2008. The chronology of the conflict was described by the Court in its judgment in the inter-State case of *Georgia v. Russia (II)* ([GC] (merits), no. 38263/08, §§ 32-44, 21 January 2021). [17] Relying on Articles 2, 3, 5, 8, 13 and 14 of the Convention and Article 1 of Protocol No. 1, the applicants complained that the military actions undertaken by the Georgian armed forces between 8 and 12 August 2008, during the active phase of the international armed conflict between Georgia and the Russian Federation, had put their lives, as well as those of their family members, under real and immediate danger, obliged them to spend several days in anxiety and fear, restricted their physical liberty and seriously damaged their flats. They further claimed that the respondent State had discriminated against them on the basis of their ethnic origin and, as an additional corollary to that discriminatory motive, that they had not had effective domestic remedies at their disposal. [20] Having regard to the similar subject matter of the applications, the Court finds it appropriate to examine them jointly in a single decision."

[Paras. 1, 4, 17, 20]

II.

I.2.02   TERRITORIAL JURISDICTION

See also: I.13.01; I.13.011; I.13.012; I.2.011; I.2.0224

"[27] The Court notes at the outset that the cases raise an issue under Article 1 of the Convention concerning the respondent State's jurisdiction in the circumstances of the

---

* Summaries prepared by Noelia Arjona Hernández, Ph.D. in Public International Law, University of Seville. Member of the Research Group Politics and International Law (SEJ119) at the University of Seville. Text of Decision available online at the Court's Web site <http://www.echr.coe.int>. Original: English. Footnotes appearing in the original text have been omitted.

armed conflict at the origin of the matters complained of. [**29**] The Court reiterates that the exercise of jurisdiction is a necessary condition for a Contracting State to be able to be held responsible for acts or omissions imputable to it which give rise to an allegation of the infringement of rights and freedoms set forth in the Convention. From the standpoint of public international law, the words "within their jurisdiction" in Article 1 of the Convention must be understood to mean, *inter alia*, that jurisdiction is presumed to be exercised normally throughout the State's territory. However, this presumption may be limited in exceptional circumstances, particularly where a State is prevented from exercising its authority in part of its territory, which may be as a result of (i) military occupation by the armed forces of another State which effectively controls the territory concerned, (ii) acts of war or rebellion, or (iii) the acts of a foreign State supporting the installation of a separatist State within the territory of the State concerned (compare *Ilaşcu and Others v. Moldova and Russia* [GC], no. 48787/99, §§ 311-12, ECHR 2004-VII, with further references). The above-mentioned limitation of the "normal" exercise of jurisdiction means in practice that when a State is prevented from exercising authority over a territory due to exceptional circumstances, it does not lose the jurisdictional link within the meaning of Article 1 of the Convention altogether but rather has its responsibility under the Convention significantly reduced to discharging a number of positive obligations, such as, for instance, taking diplomatic, economic, judicial or other measures (see *Ilaşcu and Others*, cited above, 333 and 335, and also *Sargsyan v. Azerbaijan* [GC], no. 40167/ 06, §§ 130 and 131, ECHR 2015). [**30**] The Court observes that the acts allegedly constitutive of violations of the applicants' various Convention rights took place in and around Tskhinvali, the administrative capital of South Ossetia, on 8 and 9 August 2008. These two days fall within the five-day international armed conflict that took place between the military forces of Georgia and the Russian Federation mostly in South Ossetia, but also in Abkhazia, as well as in undisputed Georgian territory, between 8 and 12 August 2008 (see *Georgia v. Russia (II)*, ([GC] (merits), no. 38263/08, §§ 35-40, 51, 109-11 and 113, 21 January 2021). Consequently, whilst these regions clearly fall within the respondent State's internationally recognised borders and thus are covered by the notion of its territorial jurisdiction under Article 1 of the Convention (compare, *mutatis mutandis, Assanidze v. Georgia* [GC], no. 71503/01, §§ 108-09, 134, 139 and 141, ECHR 2004-II), the Court must answer the question of whether or not there existed a valid limitation of the normal exercise of that jurisdiction. This major question must be addressed against the reality of the "acts of war" that took place in South Ossetia on the above-mentioned days in August 2008. [**31**] In this respect, the Court observes that it has already comprehensively examined the active phase of the hostilities (from 8 to 12 August 2008) between Georgia and the Russian Federation in the case of *Georgia v. Russia (II)* (cited above, §§ 105-44). As was emphasised in that judgment, that inter-State case was the first time since the decision in *Banković and Others v. Belgium and Others* ((dec.) [GC], no. 52207/99, ECHR 2001-XII) that the Court had been required to examine the question of jurisdiction in relation to military operations in the context of an international armed conflict. Having noted that the notion of "jurisdiction" contained in Article 1 was a threshold criterion for the question of attributability of alleged violations to a Contracting State, the Court went on to conclude that "the very reality of armed confrontation and fighting between enemy military forces seeking to establish control over an area in a context of chaos not only means that there is no 'effective control over [the] area ... , but also excludes any form of 'State agent authority and control' over individuals" (ibid., §§ 129 and 137). With respect to the latter, the Court underscored that "State agent authority and control" can hardly materialise during an international armed conflict which consists of massive bombing, shelling and ground attacks effected by the opposing sides' armed forces for the purpose of putting each other *hors de combat*, because such a large-scale war cannot be equated with isolated and specific military actions involving an "element of proximity" (ibid., §§ 127-38)."

[**Paras. 27, 29, 30, 31**]

I.2.0224   LIMITATIONS ON TERRITORIAL JURISDICTION (SERVITUDES, RIGHT OF TRANSIT, ETC.)
See also: I.2.0111; I.2.052; I.8.4; I.9; I.13.01; II.1

"[**32**][. . .][H]aving regard to the exceptionally large-scale nature of the international armed conflict which took place between the armed forces of the two Contracting States between 8 and 12 August 2008 over, *inter alia*, the establishment of control of the South Ossetian region, and the fact that both sides, the Russian and Georgian armed forces, resorted to massive bombing and shelling of the territories within the same period of time, it would be impossible to track either direct and immediate cause or even sufficiently close proximity between the actions of the Georgian army proper and the effects produced on the applicants (contrast *Solomou and Others v. Turkey*, no. 36832/97, § 25, 24 June 2008, and *Andreou v. Turkey*, no. 45653/99, §§ 48-50, 27 October 2009). In this connection, and as an additional illustration of the level of disarray unavoidably reigning during such large-scale international armed conflicts, it cannot go unnoticed that while the applicants claim that they and their relatives were victims of shelling by the Russian-produced artillery system Grad, the respondent Government submitted evidence, which was not disputed by the applicants [. . .]. Then again, while the applicants assert that the civilian population of Tskhinvali had been singled out by Georgian soldiers (see paragraphs 17 and 25 above), such allegations seem to be unsupported by the available fact-finding materials (see paragraph 16 above). The Court considers that these and other possible contradictions and inconsistencies between the military actions which actually occurred in the conflict zone and the effects of those actions on individual victims can be explained by such complexities as the exceptionally large number of alleged victims and contested incidents, the magnitude of the evidence produced, the difficulty in establishing the relevant circumstances and the fact that such situations are predominantly regulated by legal norms other than those of the Convention, notably international humanitarian law and/or the law of armed conflict (compare *Georgia v. Russia (II)*, cited above, § 141). [**33**] The Court thus concludes that the events that unfolded in South Ossetia and other areas of Georgia, including in the so-called "buffer zone", where the massive fighting between the armed forces of the Russian Federation and the respondent State took place between 8 and 12 August 2008, were "acts of war", in a context of chaos, effectively preventing the respondent State from exercising its authority over the areas in question for the duration of the armed conflict. In the same way as those "acts of war" or, borrowing the language of the inter-State judgment, the "active phase of the hostilities" did not fall within the extra-territorial jurisdiction of the Russian Federation, one side of the international armed conflict, the same events cannot be considered, for the same reasons as indicated in that judgment (*Georgia v. Russia (II)*, cited above, §§ 133-44), as attracting the normal exercise of the territorial jurisdiction of Georgia, the other side of the conflict, merely because the territory in which the hostilities took place was formally Georgian. Any other conclusion would, in the eyes of the Court, go against the spirit of the Grand Chamber's ruling in the above-mentioned inter-State case, where the international armed conflict between the two Contracting States, as well as the repercussions of this conflict for the overall jurisdictional test contained in Article 1 of the Convention, were already comprehensively examined. [**34**] [. . .] Georgia's inability to exercise State authority over the relevant territories during the active phase of the hostilities is to be understood as a limitation of the normal exercise of the respondent State's territorial jurisdiction over the war-stricken territories (see *Ilaşcu and Others*, cited above, § 312). Thus, as matter of principle, the respondent State was still expected under the Convention to take diplomatic, economic, judicial or other measures (see paragraph 29 *in fine* above). However, the Court considers that it would be unrealistic to expect the respondent State to have taken any such measures during the active phase of the hostilities, in a context of chaos and confusion. Given the ongoing massive armed conflict, such positive measures of a public order nature were, on the one hand, impossible to implement and, on the other, of no real value, as they could not have meaningfully contributed to the protection of the applicants' rights in times of war. [**35**] It follows that the applicants' various complaints under Articles 2, 3, 5, 8, 13 and 14 of the Convention and Article 1 of Protocol No. 1, which stem from the acts of war that took place on the territory of Georgia between 8 and 9 August 2008, must be declared inadmissible in accordance with Article 35 §§ 3 (a) and 4 of the Convention."

[**Paras. 32, 33, 34, 35**]

III.

II.2.021   ADMISSIBILITY OF THE APPLICATION
             See also: II.2.023; II.2.024; II.2.112; II.5.0; II.7.53

"[**36**] As regards the additional complaints introduced by the first, third and fourth applicants (see paragraph 19 above), the [Georgian] Government objected that those fresh complaints did not fall within the scope of the original applications which were lodged with the Court on 28 August and 27 September 2008 [...], and on which the parties had exchanged final observations. The relevant applicants did not provide any comments in reply to the Government's objection. [**37**] The Court reiterates that if, after the notification of an application to the respondent Government, the applicant introduces new grievances that cannot be considered as an elaboration of his or her original complaints and on which the parties have commented, the Court will not normally take these fresh matters into consideration (see, among many other authorities, *Kovach v. Ukraine*, no. 39424/02, § 38, ECHR 2008, and *Saghinadze and Others v. Georgia*, no. 8768/05, § 72, 27 May 2010). However, even assuming that the first, third and fourth applicants' complaints about (i) the latter applicant's pre-trial detention and (ii) the respondent State's unwillingness to shed light on the alleged war crimes committed in South Ossetia fall within the scope of these applications, these new complaints are in any event belated.[...][**38**] Accordingly, these complaints have been introduced out of time and must be rejected in accordance with Article 35 §§ 1 and 4 of the Convention."

[**Paras. 36, 37, 38**]

IV.

II.2.5   JUDGMENT/DECISION/ORDER
             See also: II.2.021; II.2.022; II.2.023; II.2.024; II.7.53

"[...] [T]he Court, unanimously,
Decides to join the applications;
Declares the applications inadmissible."

VII.2.7

Affaire Miroslava Todorova c. Bulgarie, Requête no. 40072/13, Quatrième Section, Arrêt, 19 Octobre 2021*

Contents

I.

II.2.0   INSTITUTION AND COURSE OF PROCEEDINGS
See also: I.8.0; I.8.32; I.8.45; I.8.47; I.8.56; I.8.61; I.8.64; II.2.021; II.2.022; II.7.5; II.7.53

"[4] La requérante exerce les fonctions de juge depuis 1999. Au moment des faits de l'espèce, elle occupait un poste à la chambre pénale du tribunal de la ville de Sofia. [...] [5] Du 1ᵉʳ janvier 2006 au 31 décembre 2007, la requérante bénéficia d'un congé sans solde et fut chargée d'enseignement à l'Institut de formation des magistrats. Son congé sans solde fut interrompu à plusieurs reprises à sa demande afin qu'elle puisse continuer à siéger dans quelques affaires toujours en cours. [6] Au cours de la période ayant suivi l'adhésion de la Bulgarie à l'Union européenne en 2007, eu égard aux difficultés du pays à assurer le bon fonctionnement de son système judiciaire et à lutter contre la corruption et la criminalité organisée, la Commission européenne mit en place un mécanisme de coopération et de vérification afin d'assurer le suivi des réformes jugées nécessaires dans ce domaine. Dans son rapport de suivi du mois de juillet 2008, la Commission européenne émit un avis critique concernant les mesures prises à ce stade et la capacité du système judiciaire à lutter efficacement contre la corruption et la criminalité organisée.[...] [7] Le rapport de suivi de la Commission européenne émit également de sérieuses critiques concernant les retards accusés dans les procédures pénales et appela les autorités à prendre des mesures rapides à cet égard [...]. [8] En octobre 2009, la requérante fut élue présidente de la principale association professionnelle de magistrats, l'Union des juges de Bulgarie (« l'UJB »[...]). [...] [9] En mai 2009, l'UJB avait émis des critiques concernant la nomination par le CSM [Conseil supérieur de la magistrature] du juge V.P. au poste de président de la cour d'appel de Sofia.[...][10] En octobre 2009, l'organisation critiqua la gestion par le CSM d'une affaire de suspicion de corruption de membres de ce conseil en relation avec des procédures

* Summaries prepared by Juan Francisco Moreno-Domínguez, lawyer and doctoral student at Faculty of Law, University of Huelva, Spain. Text of judgment available online at the Court's Web site <http://www.echr.coe.int>. Original: French.

de promotion de magistrats […]. [**11**] Au cours des derniers mois de l'année 2009, puis courant 2010, l'UJB, par l'intermédiaire de sa présidente, fit plusieurs déclarations publiques […] pour dénoncer divers propos tenus devant la presse par le ministre de l'Intérieur alors en exercice, Ts.Ts. De l'avis de l'UJB, les déclarations du ministre ébranlaient la confiance du public dans la justice et menaçaient l'indépendance de celle ci. […][**14**] En novembre 2010, l'UJB émit publiquement des critiques envers la procédure de nomination dans le cadre de laquelle le nouveau président de la Cour administrative suprême, G.K., avait été désigné. [**17**] À la suite de plusieurs plaintes adressées à l'Inspection du CSM […] [**18**] […] le 14 juin 2011, l'inspectrice ordonna qu'un contrôle de toute la chambre pénale du tribunal de la ville de Sofia […]. En sa qualité de présidente de l'UJB, la requérante dénonça publiquement les déclarations faites dans la presse par l'inspectrice générale. […] [**19**] Le rapport […] constatait […] que […] [la] requérante avait le plus grand nombre d'affaires retardées […] et les motifs avaient été délivrés avec des retards qui allaient jusqu'à plus de trois ans. […] Il ressortait des éléments chiffrés de ce rapport que la requérante avait aussi le plus grand nombre de dossiers attribués au sein de la chambre pénale. [**20**] […] Le 28 juillet 2011, le CSM ordonna l'ouverture de procédures disciplinaires pour ce motif contre quatre juges, dont la requérante et V.Y., la nouvelle présidente du tribunal. [**21**] La procédure dirigée contre la requérante fut référencée sous le numéro 9/2011. Trois membres du CSM furent tirés au sort pour former le collège disciplinaire […] chargé d'instruire l'affaire. La requérante demanda leur récusation […]. Sa demande fut rejetée le 5 octobre 2011[…]. [**22**] […] [L]e collège proposa au CSM d'imposer à la requérante une réduction de salaire de 15 % pour une durée de deux ans à titre de sanction disciplinaire. [**24**] La requérante saisit la Cour administrative suprême d'un recours contre la décision du CSM […]. [**28**] Par la suite, trois autres procédures disciplinaires […] furent engagées contre la requérante. [**32**] Les trois procédures susmentionnées furent jointes sous la référence 3/2012. […] [L]e collège disciplinaire proposa au CSM, le 5 juillet 2012, d'imposer à la requérante la sanction disciplinaire la plus grave, à savoir la révocation.[…] [**33**] La requérante […] introduisit un recours en annulation devant la Cour administrative suprême. [**36**] Le recours introduit par la requérante contre la décision par laquelle le CSM lui avait imposé, dans le cadre de la procédure disciplinaire n° 9/2011 […] fut examiné en première instance par […] la Cour administrative suprême. Par un arrêt du 2 août 2012, cette formation décida d'annuler la décision du CSM. […][**37**] Le CSM se pourvut en cassation devant une formation élargie de la Cour administrative suprême. [**38**] […] [L]a Cour administrative suprême […] annula le premier arrêt et, statuant sur le fond du recours de la requérante, le rejeta.[…] [**39**] Dans son recours contre la décision par laquelle le CSM avait ordonné sa révocation le 12 juillet 2012 […], la requérante demanda l'annulation de cette décision invoquant, notamment, le défaut d'impartialité du CSM et la contrariété de ladite décision à la loi matérielle et procédurale et au but de la loi. […] [**43**] […] [L]a Cour administrative suprême […] rejeta le recours de la requérante contre la décision de révocation.[…] [**47**] […] La requérante se pourvut en cassation […]. [L]a Cour administrative suprême […] fit partiellement droit à son recours. […] [**48**] […] [L]a haute juridiction estima que la sanction imposée n'était pas proportionnée. […] Elle ordonna le renvoi du dossier au CSM afin que celui-ci statue de nouveau sur la sanction à imposer. La requérante fut réintégrée dans son poste le 18 juillet 2013. [**50**] Le CSM examina l'affaire le 27 mars 2014. […] [**51**] […] [L]a requérante se vit imposer la sanction de rétrogradation au tribunal de rang inférieur […] pour une durée de deux ans. [**52**] La requérante introduisit un recours en annulation contre cette décision devant la Cour administrative suprême […]. [**56**] […] [L]a Cour administrative suprême estima que la rétrogradation constituait une sanction appropriée en l'espèce mais qu'il convenait d'en réduire la durée à une année. [**57**] La requérante et le CSM se pourvurent en cassation.

[...][**59**] [...] [L]a Cour administrative suprême rejeta le recours de la requérante et confirma la sanction de rétrogradation pour une durée de deux ans."

[**Paras. 4, 5, 6, 7, 8, 9, 10, 11, 14, 17, 18, 19, 20, 21, 22, 24, 28, 32, 33, 36, 37, 38, 39, 43, 47, 48, 50, 51, 52, 56, 57, 59**]

II.

I.8.45   RIGHT TO A FAIR TRIAL AND AN EFFECTIVE REMEDY
See also: I.8.64; II.2.021; II.2.022; II.7.5; II.7.53

"[**106**] [...] [L]a Cour se penchera tout d'abord sur la question du respect des exigences découlant de l'article 6 de la Convention dans le cadre des procédures devant le CSM puis de celles qui se sont déroulées devant la Cour administrative suprême. À cet égard, elle examinera successivement l'étendue du contrôle opéré par la haute juridiction, le respect des garanties d'indépendance et d'impartialité, puis les autres aspects du droit à un procès équitable invoqués par la requérante. [**109**] [...] La Cour rappelle cependant que lorsqu'une autorité chargée d'examiner des contestations portant sur des « droits et obligations de caractère civil » ne remplit pas toutes les exigences de l'article 6 § 1, il n'y a pas violation de la Convention si la procédure devant cet organe peut faire l'objet du « contrôle ultérieur d'un organe judiciaire de pleine juridiction présentant, lui, les garanties de cet article » [...]. [**123**] [...] [L]a Cour ne constate pas un défaut d'indépendance et d'impartialité de la Cour administrative suprême en l'espèce et conclut à l'absence de violation de l'article 6 à cet égard. [**127**] [...] [L]a Cour conclut qu'il n'y a pas eu violation de l'article 6 de la Convention en l'espèce."

[**Paras. 106, 109, 123, 127**]

III.

I.8.47   RIGHT TO PRIVATE AND FAMILY LIFE
See also: I.8.64; II.2.021; II.2.022; II.7.5; II.7.53

"[**144**] L'intéressée n'apporte au demeurant pas d'éléments démontrant que les poursuites disciplinaires dirigées contre elle ou le compte rendu qui en a été fait dans les médias auraient eu pour effet de ternir sa réputation professionnelle au point d'atteindre le niveau de gravité requis par l'article 8 de la Convention. [...] La Cour n'estime pas [...] que les sanctions disciplinaires imposées à la requérante ont eu sur sa réputation des conséquences qui auraient atteint le niveau de gravité requis par l'article 8 de la Convention [...]. [**145**] [...] [L]e grief doit être rejeté pour incompatibilité ratione materiae en application de l'article 35 §§ 3 a) et 4 de la Convention."

[**Paras. 144, 145**]

IV.

I.8.56   FREEDOM OF EXPRESSION
See also: I.8.64; II.2.021; II.2.022; II.7.5; II.7.53

"[**146**] La requérante soutient que les poursuites disciplinaires dirigées contre elle s'analysent en une sanction dissimulée pour ses prises de position publiques par lesquelles elle avait critiqué le travail du CSM et les interventions du pouvoir exécutif dans des affaires en cours. [...][**163**] [...] [L]a Cour estime qu'il y a un commencement de preuve de l'existence d'un lien de causalité entre l'exercice par la requérante de sa liberté d'expression et les sanctions disciplinaires imposées par le CSM [...]. [**179**] [...] [L]a Cour considère que les poursuites disciplinaires dirigées contre la requérante et les sanctions qui lui ont été imposées étaient constitutives d'une ingérence dans l'exercice par elle de son droit à la liberté d'expression qui n'était pas « nécessaire dans une société démocratique » à la poursuite des buts légitimes visés par l'article 10 de la Convention. [**181**] [...] [L]a Cour conclut qu'il y a eu en l'espèce violation de l'article 10 de la Convention."

[Paras. 146, 163, 179, 181]

V.

I.8.61   PROHIBITION OF DISCRIMINATION
          See also: I.8.64; II.2.021; II.2.022; II.7.5; II.7.53

"[**182**] [...] [L]a requérante considère que l'ingérence dans l'exercice par elle de son droit à la liberté d'expression était discriminatoire, en violation de l'article 14 de la Convention [...]. [**186**] La Cour observe que le grief de la requérante tiré de l'article 14 combiné avec l'article 10 de la Convention reprend pour l'essentiel les questions qu'elle a déjà examinées ci-dessus au regard de l'article 10. Elle estime en conséquence qu'il ne se pose pas de question distincte sur le terrain de l'article 14 et qu'il n'est pas nécessaire qu'elle formule une conclusion séparée au regard de cet article [...]."

[Paras. 182, 186]

VI.

I.8.64   PERMITTED RESTRICTIONS ON HUMAN RIGHTS
          See also: II.2.021; II.2.022; II.7.5; II.7.53

"[**187**] La requérante soutient que les poursuites disciplinaires dirigées contre elle poursuivaient un autre but que celui qui était affiché, en méconnaissance de l'article 18 de la Convention [...]. [**191**] [...] [L]'article 18 de la Convention n'a pas d'existence indépendante; il ne peut être appliqué que combiné avec un article de la Convention ou de ses Protocoles [...]. [**207**] La Cour considère ces éléments suffisants pour conclure que les poursuites disciplinaires et les sanctions infligées par le CSM à la requérante poursuivaient aussi un objectif non prévu par la Convention, à savoir celui de la sanctionner pour ses prises de position en tant que présidente de l'UJB. [...] [**213**] [...] [L]e but prédominant des poursuites disciplinaires engagées contre la requérante et des sanctions qui lui ont été imposées par le CSM n'était pas d'assurer le respect des délais de clôture des affaires mais celui de sanctionner et intimider l'intéressée à raison de ses prises de position critiques à l'égard du CSM et du pouvoir exécutif. [**214**] [...] [I]l y a eu violation de l'article 18 de la Convention combiné avec l'article 10."

[Paras. 187, 191, 207, 213, 214]

VII.

I.8.46   RIGHT TO COMPENSATION
         See also: II.2.6; II.7.5; II.7.58

"[**216**] La requérante n'a pas formulé de demande au titre du dommage matériel ou moral et déclare qu'un constat de violation de la Convention lui fournirait une satisfaction équitable suffisante. [...] [**217**] La requérante demande le remboursement des frais de traduction engagés dans la procédure devant la Cour d'un montant de 2 620 levs bulgares (BGN), soit l'équivalent de 1 340 euros (EUR). Elle produit la facture correspondante et une preuve du paiement effectué. [**218**] [...] [L]a Cour juge le montant réclamé au titre des frais de traduction justifié et l'accorde à la requérante. [**219**] La Cour juge approprié de calquer le taux des intérêts moratoires sur le taux d'intérêt de la facilité de prêt marginal de la Banque centrale européenne majoré de trois points de pourcentage."

[**Paras. 216, 217, 218, 219**]

VIII.

II.2.5   JUDGMENT/DECISION/ORDER
         See also: II.2.6; II.7.58

"[...] LA COUR
   1. *Déclare*, à l'unanimité, recevables les griefs tirés des articles 6, 10, 14 et 18 de la Convention et irrecevable le grief formulé sur le terrain de l'article 8 de la Convention;
   2. *Dit*, par cinq voix contre deux, qu'il n'y a pas eu violation de l'article 6 de la Convention;
   3. *Dit*, à l'unanimité, qu'il y a eu violation de l'article 10 de la Convention;
   4. *Dit*, à l'unanimité, qu'il n'y a pas lieu d'examiner séparément le grief formulé sur le terrain de l'article 14 combiné avec l'article 10 de la Convention;
   5. *Dit*, à l'unanimité, qu'il y a eu violation de l'article 18 de la Convention combiné avec l'article 10;
   6. *Dit*, à l'unanimité,
      a) que l'État défendeur doit verser à la requérante, dans un délai de trois mois à compter de la date à laquelle l'arrêt sera devenu définitif conformément à l'article 44 § 2 de la Convention, 1 340 EUR (mille trois cent quarante euros), à convertir dans la monnaie de l'État défendeur au taux applicable à la date du règlement, plus tout montant pouvant être dû sur cette somme par la requérante à titre d'impôt, pour frais et dépens;
      b) qu'à compter de l'expiration dudit délai et jusqu'au versement, ces montants seront à majorer d'un intérêt simple à un taux égal à celui de la facilité de prêt marginal de la Banque centrale européenne applicable pendant cette période, augmenté de trois points de pourcentage."

VII.2.8

Case of Vedat Şorli v. Turkey, Application no. 42048/19, Second Section, Judgment, 19 October 2021*

Contents

I.

II.2.0   INSTITUTION AND COURSE OF PROCEEDINGS
            See also: I.8.0; II.1

"[1] L'affaire concerne la procédure pénale diligentée contre le requérant, à l'issue de laquelle il a été condamné à une peine d'emprisonnement deonze mois et vingt jours avec sursis au prononcé du jugement, du chef d'insulte au Président de la République en raison de deux contenus partagés par l'intéressé sur son compte Facebook."

[Para. 1]

II.

I.8.56   FREEDOM OF EXPRESSION
            See also: I.8.32; I.8.4

"[20] Le requérant allègue que la procédure pénale diligentée contre lui pour insulte au Président de la République [. . .] porte atteinte à son droit à la liberté d'expression. Il soutient que l'infraction d'insulte au Président de la République, assurant une protection spéciale au chef de l'État et prévoyant une peine plus importante par rapport à l'infraction d'insulte ordinaire, est non-conforme à l'esprit de la Convention et à la jurisprudence de la Cour. Il considère que son placement en détention provisoire pendant deux mois et deux jours et sa condamnation pénale à une peine d'emprisonnement de onze mois et vingt jours sont disproportionnés et que la décision de sursis au prononcé du jugement rendue à l'issue de la procédure pénale crée un effet dissuasif sur l'exercice de sa liberté d'expression sur des questions politiques pendant la période de sursis de cinq ans. [. . .] [40] [L]e requérant a été condamné à onze mois et vingt jours d'emprisonnement du chef d'insulte au Président de la République, jugement dont il a été sursis au prononcé, en raison de deux contenus partagés sur le compte Facebook de l'intéressé, qui affichaient, entre autres, une caricature et une photo du Président de la République avec des commentaires satiriques et critiques visant ce dernier. [43] Quant à la nécessité de l'ingérence, la Cour relève que, pour condamner le requérant, les juridictions internes se sont appuyées sur l'article 299 du code pénal qui accorde au Président de la République un niveau de protection plus élevé qu'à d'autres personnes [. . .] à l'égard de la divulgation d'informations ou d'opinions les concernant, et prévoit des

* Summaries prepared by Lucía Ione Padilla Espinosa, Ph.D. candidate in the Doctoral Program in Legal Sciences of the University of Huelva, Spain. Text of judgment available online at the Court's Web site <http://www.echr.coe.int>. Original: French.

sanctions plus graves pour les auteurs de déclarations diffamatoires [. . .]. À cet égard, elle rappelle avoir déjà maintes fois déclaré qu'une protection accrue par une loi spéciale en matière d'offense n'est, en principe, pas conforme à l'esprit de la Convention [. . .]. [**44**] S'agissant en particulier de la proportionnalité de la sanction pénale prévue pour insulte au Président de la République, la Cour note que, s'il est tout à fait légitime que les personnes représentant les institutions de l'État soient protégées par les autorités compétentes en leur qualité des garantes de l'ordre public institutionnel, la position dominante que ces institutions occupent commande aux autorités de faire preuve de retenue dans l'usage de la voie pénale [. . .]. Elle rappelle à cet égard que l'appréciation de la proportionnalité d'une ingérence dans les droits protégés par l'article 10 dépendra dans bien des cas de la question de savoir si les autorités auraient pu faire usage d'un autre moyen qu'une sanction pénale, telles des mesures civiles (voir, *mutatis mutandis, Raichinov c. Bulgarie*, n° 47579/99, § 50, 20 avril 2006; voir aussi, *mutatis mutandis, Lehideux et Isorni c. France*, 23 septembre 1998, § 51, *Recueil* 1998-VII, et *Cumpănă et Mazăre c. Roumanie* [GC], n° 33348/96, § 115, CEDH 2004- XI). En effet, même lorsque la sanction est la plus modérée possible, à l'instar d'une condamnation assortie d'une dispense de peine sur le plan pénal et d'une simple obligation de payer un «euro symbolique» à titre de dommages - intérêts [. . .], elle n'en constitue pas moins une sanction pénale et, en tout état de cause, cela ne saurait suffire, en soi, à justifier l'ingérence dans l'exercice du droit à la liberté d'expression [. . .]. [**45**] Eu égard à ce qui précède, la Cour considère que rien dans les circonstances de la présent affaire n'était de nature à justifier le placement en garde à vue du requérant et la décision de mise en détention provisoire rendue à son égard ni l'imposition d'une sanction pénale, même si, comme en l'espèce, il s'agissait d'une peine de prison assortie d'un sursis au prononcée du jugement. Par sa nature même, une telle sanction produit immanquablement un effet dissuasif sur la volonté de l'intéressé de s'exprimer sus des sujets relevant de l'intérêt public compte tenu notamment des effets de la condamnation [. . .]. [**47**] Dès lors, dans les circonstances de l'espèce, compte tenu de la sanction, qui revêtait un caractère pénal, infligée au requérant en application d'une disposition spéciale prévoyant une protection accrue pour le Président de la République en matière d'offense, qui ne saurait être considérée conforme à l'esprit de la Convention, la Cour estime que le Gouvernement n'a pas démontré que la mesure litigieuse était proportionnée aux buts légitimes visés et qu'elle était nécessaire dans une société démocratique au sens de l'article 10 de la Convention. [**48**] Ces éléments suffisent à la Cour pour conclure que, dans les circonstances de l'espèce, il y a eu violation de l'article 10 de la Convention."

[**Paras. 20, 40, 43, 44, 45, 47, 48**]

III.

II.2.5   JUDGMENT/DECISION/ORDER
      See also: I.8.32; II. 7.5; II.7.53; II.7.56

"PAR CES MOTIFS, LA COUR, À L'UNANIMITÉ,
   1. *Déclare*, la requête recevable;
   2. *Dit*, qu'il y a eu violation de l'article 10 de la Convention;
   3. *Dit*,
      a)   que l'État défendeur doit verser au requérant, dans un délai de trois mois à compter de la date à laquelle l'arrêt sera devenu définitif conformément à l'article 44 § 2 de la Convention, 7 500 EUR (sept mille cinq cents euros), plus tout montant pouvant être dû sur cette somme à titre d'impôt, pour dommage

moral, à convertir dans la monnaie de l'État défendeur au taux applicable à la date du règlement:

b) qu'à compter de l'expiration dudit délai et jusqu'au versement, ce montant sera à majorer d'un intérêt simple à un taux égal à celui de la facilité de prêt marginal de la Banque centrale européenne applicable pendant cette période, augmenté de trois points de pourcentage;

4. *Rejette*, le surplus de la demande de satisfaction équitable."

Systematic Key Items of the Section*

---

* *See* Systematic Classification Scheme, *supra* at page 255.

Systematic Key Items of the Section*

VIII

Inter-American Court
of Human Rights

INTRODUCTORY NOTE

The Inter-American Court of Human Rights in 2021

BY RICARDO C. PÉREZ MANRIQUE*

Abstract

During 2021, the Inter-American Court of Human Rights issued twenty-four judgments on merits, and three on interpretation, as well as the record forty-seven orders on monitoring compliance with judgment and twenty-two orders on provisional measures. The Inter-American Court has been able to reaffirm the jurisprudence on several topics, such as violence against transwomen, as well as discrimination against and stigmatization of women human rights defenders. It has also developed new and very important standards in the area of sexual violence against women journalists and differentiated approach for measures of protection. The Court also expanded the standards with regard to disability as a category protected by the American Convention, besides developing jurisprudence on business and human rights. Apart from the judgments on merits, the Inter-American Court, by means of resolutions on provisional measures, enhanced protection in the access to vaccination programs against COVID-19, and continued developing economic, social, cultural, and environmental rights. The contentious cases and provisional measures in this edition of the *Yearbook* shed light on some of these advances in the Court's jurisprudence.

I. CASE OF *VICKY HERNÁNDEZ AND OTHERS V. HONDURAS*, SERIES C NO. 422, JUDGMENT 26.03.2021

The first case highlighted, from the jurisprudence of 2021, is *Vicky Hernández and others v. Honduras*. It is related to violence against transwomen, through which the Inter-American Court of Human Rights held the importance to considerate stereotypes and gender on hostilities towards the LGBTQI community.

---

* President of the Inter-American Court of Human Rights. Member of the Editorial Board.

Ricardo C. Pérez Manrique, *Introductory Note* In: *The Global Community Yearbook of International Law and Jurisprudence 2022*. Edited by: Giuliana Ziccardi Capaldo, Oxford University Press. © Oxford University Press 2023. DOI: 10.1093/oso/9780197752265.003.0028

Facts

The case concerned the death of Vicky Hernández, a transwoman and human rights defender, in Honduras, while a curfew was in place, and in a context of violence against the LGBTQI community. Vicky Hernández was a transwoman extremely discriminated against. She was also a sex worker and committed activist within the "Colectivo Unidad Color Rosa," which defends the human rights of transpersons in Honduras. Two months before she was murdered, she had been attacked by a security guard. When she went to the police, the officers told her that for all they cared, she could die. Thereafter, Vicky had been seen walking in the red light district where she carried out her sex work, before being discovered by a police patrol that tried to arrest her and her friends. They fled in different directions. On June 29, 2009, at 7.30 a.m., agents of the National Criminal Investigation Directorate were informed that a body had been found at No. 3 between Streets 7 and 8, Avenida Colonia Ruiz in San Pedro Sula. It was Vicky's body.

Law

(a) Article 1(1) of the Convention (right to non-discrimination), Article 24 of the Convention (right to equality): The Court has indicated that Article 1(1) of the Convention is a norm of a general nature, the content of which extends to all the provisions of the treaty and establishes the obligation of the states parties to respect and to ensure the full and free exercise of the rights and freedoms recognized therein "without any discrimination." Furthermore, according to the Court, Article 24 of the American Convention prohibits discrimination de jure, not only with regard to the rights contained in this treaty, but also with regard to all the laws enacted by the state and their application. The Court has established that a person's sexual orientation, gender identity, and gender expression are categories protected by the Convention. Consequently, the state may not discriminate against a person based on their sexual orientation, their gender identity, and/or their gender expression.

(b) Article 3 (right to recognition of juridical personality), Article 4 (right to life), Article 5 (right to personal integrity), Article 7 (right to personal liberty), Article 8 (judicial guarantees), Article 11 (right to privacy), Article 13 (freedom of expression), Article 18 (right to a name), Article 24 (equality and non-discrimination), Article 25 (judicial protection) of the American Convention, and Article 7 of the Convention of Belém do Pará (a life free of violence): Article 1(1) of the American Convention, not only presupposes that no one may be deprived of their life arbitrarily (negative obligation), but also requires states to take all appropriate measures to protect and preserve the right to life (positive positive obligation) in accordance with the obligation to ensure to all persons subject to their jurisdiction the free and full exercise of their rights.

With regard the right to gender identity, in the case of *Vicky Hernández et al. v. Honduras*, the Court recalled that the right of each person to define his or her sexual and gender identity is protected by the American Convention under the provisions that guarantee the free development of the personality (Articles 7 and 11(2)), and the rights to privacy (Article 11(2)), recognition of juridical personality (Article 3), and a name (Article 18). The Court also reiterated that Article 1 of the Convention of Belém do Pará refers to violence against women based on gender and it is also related to transwomen. Besides, the Court noted that Article 9 of the Convention of Belém do Pará urges states, when adopting measures to prevent, punish, and eradicate violence against women, to take into account "the vulnerability of women to violence by reason of, among others, their race or ethnic background, or their status as migrants, refugees or displaced persons." This list of factors is not *numerus clausus*, as indicated by the use of the expression "among others." Thus, it may be considered that, in certain circumstances, it relates to a transwoman. Finally, the Court recalled that the right of each person to define his or her sexual and gender identity is protected by the American Convention under the provisions that guarantee the free development of the personality (Articles 7 and 11(2)), and the rights to privacy (Article 11(2)), recognition of juridical personality (Article 3), and a name (Article 18).

(c) Reparations: The Inter-American Court established that the state shall adopt, within two years of the notification of this judgment, a protocol on investigation and administration of justice during criminal proceedings in cases of LGBTQI persons victims of violence. Also Court determined the state to adopt a procedure for the recognition of gender identity. This procedure must allow anyone to amend their identity data on their identity documents and in the public records so that these conform to their self-perceived gender identity.

II. CASE OF *GUACHALÁ CHIMBO AND OTHERS V. ECUADOR*, SERIES C NO. 423, JUDGMENT 26. 03.2021

The case of *Guachalá Chimbo and others v. Ecuador* is related to the disappearance of Luis Eduardo Guachalá Chimbo, a person with mental disabilities, in January 2004, while he was in a public psychiatric hospital in Quito, as well as the absence of informed consent for the hospitalization and the treatment received. The Court established that the American Convention prohibits any discriminatory law, act, or practice, based on a real or perceived disability.

Facts

Luis Eduardo Guachalá Chimbo's family left him, on January 10, 2004, in the Julio Endara Hospital, after aggravation of his health clinical picture. However, the hospital's records informs Mr. Guachalá Chimbo was hospitalized only until January 17, 2004, the day on which the patient Luis Guachalá disappeared. A search was made, but he was never found.

Law

(a) Article 1(1) of the Convention (right to non-discrimination), Article 24 of the Convention (right to equality): Taking into account the general obligations to respect and to ensure rights established in Article 1(1) of the American Convention, the interpretation criteria stipulated in Article 29 of this Convention, and the provisions of the Vienna Convention on the Law of Treaties, the Inter-American Convention on the Elimination of All Forms of Discrimination against Persons with Disabilities, the Convention on the Rights of Persons with Disabilities, and other international instruments, the Inter-American Court affirmed that disability is a category protected by the American Convention. Accordingly, the Convention prohibits any law, act, or practice that discriminates based an individual's real or perceived disability. Consequently, no domestic legal norm, decision, or practice, either by state authorities or by private individuals, may reduce or restrict in a discriminating way the rights of a person based on his or her disabilities.

(b) Article 3 (right to recognition of juridical personality), Article 4 (right to life), Article 5 (personal integrity), Article 7 (personal liberty), Article 11 (right to privacy), Article 13 (freedom of expression), Article 26 (health), in relation to Article 1 (obligation to respet and ensure rights), Article 2 (obligation to adopt domestic legal provisions) of the American Convention: The central dispute in the case is related to what happened to Mr. Guachalá Chimbo, owing to his illness and, in particular, when receiving medical treatment in a public hospital in 2004. On these bases, the Court concluded that informed consent is a basic element of the right to health; and the obligation to comply with this is an obligation of an immediate nature. The Court has indicated that the violation of the right to informed consent entails not only a violation of the right to health, but also of the right to personal liberty, the right to dignity and privacy, and the right of access to information. Also the Court recalled that compliance with the state obligation to respect and to ensure the right to health must pay special attention to persons living in poverty. Therefore, states must take measures to ensure that the treatment required to prevent disabilities does not represent a disproportionate burden for the poorest households. Furthermore, in light of the state's position of guarantor of persons in its custody, it is presumed that the state is responsible for any injuries suffered by a person who has been in the custody of state agents. This same principle is applicable in cases in which a person is in state custody and his subsequent whereabouts is unknown. The state has the obligation to provide a satisfactory and convincing explanation of what happened and to disprove the arguments concerning its responsibility, with satisfactory evidence.

(c) Article 8 (judicial guarantees) and Article 25 (judicial protection): The Court also concluded that the alleged disappearance of a person with a disability in the custody of the state requires the authorities to exercise maximum diligence in the search, using all available means and, in particular, by a coordinated effort of the different departments and relevant institutions of the civil authority. Therefore, the Court concluded that the state failed to comply with its obligation to initiate the investigation ex officio and immediately, violated its obligation to provide an effective remedy, due diligence, and did not complyd its duty to carry out access to justice in a reasonable time; seventeen years have passed and the whereabouts of Mr. Guachalá Chimbo remain unknown.

(d) Reparations: The Court held that persons with disabilities are often subject to discrimination based on their condition. Therefore, the state must adopt the necessary legislative, social, educational, labor, or any other measures to eliminate all disability-based discrimination and to promote the full integration of persons with disabilities into society. Furthermore, the Court considered desirable that the state develop, within one year, an action protocol for cases of disappearances of persons hospitalized in public health centers that includes the standards developed in this judgment on the obligation to notify the competent authorities so that they open an investigation

III. CASE OF *BEDOYA LIMA AND OTHERS V. COLOMBIA*, SERIES C NO. 431, JUDGMENT 06.0 8.2021

The *Bedoya Lima and others v. Colombia* case is related to a series of alleged human rights violations stemming from the kidnapping, torture, and rape of journalist Jineth Bedoya Lima for reasons related to her profession and the state's alleged failure to adopt adequate and timely measures to protect it and prevent the facts from taking place.

Facts

Since the beginning of her career as a journalist, Ms. Bedoya has been the victim of threats and acts of harassment, especially in connection with her work covering the internal armed conflict and her reporting on prisons in 1998, first on radio station RCN Radio and, later, in the newspaper El Espectador. On May 25, Ms Bedoya went to a meeting inside the La Modelo Prison to meet a member of a paramilitary group. There, according to the body of evidence, when Ms. Bedoya was across from the La Modelo Prison, she was approached by a woman who asked her if she was "the journalist." At the same time, a man approached her and asked her if she was the one who was going to the interview with "El Panadero." When she answered affirmatively, the man seized her by the elbow and threatened her with a gun. She was kidnapped, suffered injuries, was threatened, and was raped. Notwithstanding, on August 18, 2003, Ms. Bedoya was kidnapped again by the Revolutionary Armed Forces of Colombia. In November 2010, after publishing her book entitled *Vida y Muerte del Mono Jojoy*, the journalist again received threats, according to state security and intelligence agencies. The journalist filed a complaint about these threats, which was closed by the Office of the Public Prosecutor in June 2014 upon finding that it was impossible to identify those responsible for the threats. Ms. Bedoya continued to receive threats during the years to come, via messages to her phone, WhatsApp messages, phone calls from Colombia and abroad, and messages to the newspaper where she works currently. All the complaints filed by Ms. Bedoya were either closed or are still being processed.

Law

(a) Article 4 (right to life), Article 5 (personal integrity), Article 7 (personal liberty), Article 11 (protection of honor and dignity), Article 13 (freedom of expression), and Article 24 (equal protection), of the American Convention on Human Rights, in relation to the obligations of respect and guarantee, as well as to Articles 7(A) and (B) of the Convention of Belém do Pará, and Articles 1, 6, and 8 of the ICPPT: The Court held that in cases of violence against women, along with the general obligation established in the American Convention, states have specific obligations under the Convention of Belém do Pará that cast light into areas traditionally considered private or where the state did not intervene. This regional treaty specifically aimed at combating violence against women gives a broad definition of what violence against women is in its Articles 1 and 2. In addition, the Convention of Belém do Pará itself, in its Article 2, includes kidnapping as one of the types of conduct included under the concept of violence against women. Additionally, in Article 7, it establishes that states have a duty to prevent, punish, and eradicate violence against women, specifying and complimenting the state's compliance obligations for rights recognized in the American Convention, such as those set forth in Articles 4 and 5.

The Court highlighted that, in connection with the particular risk faced by women journalists, international and regional organizations have concluded that when adopting measures to protect journalists, states must apply a strongly differentiated approach that takes into account gender considerations; conduct a risk analysis; and implement protection measures that consider the aforementioned risk faced by women journalists as a result of gender-based violence. In particular, in addition to the standards on gender-based violence and non-discrimination already developed by this Court, states must also observe the following positive obligations: (a) identify and investigate with due diligence the special, differentiated risks they face because they are female journalists, as well as the factors that increase the possibility that they are victims of violence, and (b) adopt a gender approach when adopting measures to guarantee the safety of women journalists—including those of a preventive nature—when requested, as well as those aimed at protecting them from reprisals.

The Court found, in view of the specific circumstances of the case, from an intersectional perspective, that Ms. Bedoya was in a doubly vulnerable situation, due to her work as a journalist and for being a woman.

Regarding sexual violence and rape, the Court's case law has recognized that these forms of sexual violence can constitute cruel, inhuman, or degrading treatment, and even acts of torture if the elements of the definition are present. The European Court of Human Rights, the Human Rights Committee, the Committee against Torture, the Committee on the Elimination of Discrimination against Women, and the United Nations Rapporteur against Torture have all indicated likewise. Because Article 5(2) of the American Convention does not specify what should be understood as "torture," the Court has resorted to both Article 2 of the ICPPT and other definitions contained in the international instruments prohibiting torture to arrive at the elements constitutive of torture. Based on these instruments, it has determined that torture is present when the ill-treatment: (i) is intentional; (ii) causes severe physical or mental suffering; and (iii) is committed with any objective or purpose.

(b) Articles 8(1) (judicial guarantees), 24 (equal protection), 25 (judicial protection), 5 (personal integrity), and 13 (freedom of thought and expression) of the American Convention on Human Rights, as well as Articles 1, 6, and 8 of the ICPPT and Article 7(b) of the Convention of Belém do Pará: The Court found that, when investigating incidents of violence against women journalists, the duty of due diligence must be subjected to strict scrutiny for two reasons. First, because the states have a positive obligation to guarantee freedom of expression and to protect people who, because of their profession, are in a special situation of risk when exercising this right. Second, because this duty also entails an enhanced standard of due diligence when it comes to preventing gender-based violence and protecting women from it. This must be taken into account from the beginning of an investigation of violent acts against women in the context of their journalism work and entails the obligation to identify and investigate, with due diligence, the special and differentiated risks faced by women journalists due to their profession and their gender, as well as the factors that increase their likelihood of becoming victims of violence. Along with this, investigators are required to assume, from the start of their investigation, that the incidents of violence are related to the victim's journalism work. In sum, the Court views it is essential to emphasize that when investigating acts of violence directed against women journalists, states have the obligation to adopt all measures necessary to pursue the investigation from an intersectional perspective that takes into account these intersecting vulnerabilities affecting the person in question and that, in turn, require or add to the enhanced diligence.

In addition, The Court held that, in cases of violence against women, investigation must include a gender perspective and be conducted by officials trained in similar cases and in attending to victims of discrimination and gender-based violence. Also, it has been settled that the general obligations established in Articles 8 and 25 of the American Convention are supplemented and enhanced for those states that are party to the Convention of Belém do Pará by the obligations derived from this specific interAmerican treaty. Article 7(b) of this Convention specifically requires the states parties to apply due diligence to prevent, punish, and eradicate violence against women. Thus, when an act of violence is committed against a woman, whether by a state agent or a private party, it is particularly important for the authorities in charge of the investigation to conduct it with determination and efficacy, taking into account their duty to society to reject violence against women and the state's obligation to eradicate it and ensure that victims have confidence in the institutions established by the state for their protection.

(c) Reparations: The Inter-American Court established states must apply a strongly differentiated approach that takes gender considerations into account; conduct a risk assessment; and implement protection measures that reflect the risks faced by women journalists as a result of gender-based violence. In particular, in addition to the standards on gender violence and non-discrimination already developed by the Court, states must also observe the following positive obligations: (a) identify and investigate with due diligence the special differentiated risks that women journalists face as well as the factors that increase the possibility that they will be victims of violence, and also (b) adopt a gender approach when adopting measures to ensure the safety of women journalists, including those of a preventive nature, when requested, as well as those aimed at protecting them from reprisals.

IV. CASE OF *VÉLEZ LOOR V. PANAMA*, PROVISIONAL MEASURES, RESOLUTION OF 24/06/2021

In the order on provisional measures in the case of *Velez Loor v. Panama*, the Court considered that, based on the principle of equality and non-discrimination, states must ensure that migrants have access to vaccination programs without any distinction based on their nationality or migratory status, in the same conditions as nationals and residents.

Facts

The case of *Vélez Loor v. Panama* is related to a situation of irregular migratory. Mr. Vélez Loor was deprived of his liberty, in Panama City, in the national penitentiary system, after being charged as irregular migrant, where he was detained with individuals who had been tried and/or convicted for committing crimes. In the judgment, the Court accepted the partial acknowledgement of responsibility made by the Republic of Panama and declared the latter's international responsibility for the violation of the rights to personal liberty, judicial guarantees, personal integrity, and the principle of legality. The Court also, by way of reparation and as a guarantee of non-repetition, ordered the state to adapt the establishments used to detain persons for migratory reasons.

In this context, in 2021, the Court has uncovered irregularities, such as overcrowding and lack of hygiene inside the migrant centers, which have indicated the needy to issue provisional measures to protect people, especially from the COVID-19.

Provisional Measures

(a) The Court understood that, in the actual context, the scarcity of vaccines against COVID-19 makes it difficult for many countries to ensure that everyone has immediate access to them, so that it is necessary to establish priority groups. In this regard, states may only establish objective and reasonable distinctions, when this is done with due respect for human rights and in keeping with the principle of the application of the norm most favorable to the human being. Thus, the Court agreed with the opinion of several specialized agencies that the distinctions established for prioritizing access to vaccines against COVID-19 should be based on medical necessity and scientifically established risk criteria, including everyone who meets the requirement of a priority group, irrespective of their nationality or migratory situation.

The Court also stressed the importance that, in order to overcome the pandemic, the international community take steps to ensure a global and equitable distribution of vaccines, to counteract the actual situation in which high-income countries have monopolized the acquisition of most of the vaccines. It is essential that low- and medium-income countries are able to acquire sufficient vaccines to permit, as a minimum, providing protection to all those persons who are at greater risk of contracting the virus and/or becoming seriously ill, and also to achieve herd immunity at the global level. The actions that the international community has been implementing or that are being discussed include: the establishment of the COVAX mechanism, under the World Health Organization, promoted by public and private actors; the expansion of vaccine production capacity, and the opening up the exportation of vaccines and inputs for their manufacture at the local level, as well as the elimination or temporary suspension of patent rights.

The Court reiterated the content of its Statement No. 1/20 entitled "COVID-19 and Human Rights: the problems and challenges that must be addressed from the perspective of human rights and respect for international obligations" in which it affirmed that "[t]he extraordinary problems and challenges resulting from this pandemic must be addressed through dialogue, together with regional and international cooperation that is implemented jointly, transparently and in a spirit of solidarity between all the States. Multilateralism is essential in order to coordinate regional efforts to contain the pandemic." In addition, in this Statement, it recommended that "multilateral agencies, whatever their nature, must help and cooperate with the States, with a human rights-based approach, to seek solutions to the present and future problems and challenges that this pandemic is causing and will cause."

(b) Decision of the Court on the provisional measures: The Court has emphasized the importance to follow adequate standards of health services without discrimination, grant hygiene inside the migrant centers and take rigorous measures to mitigate the risk of the COVID-19, such as promoting the vaccination.

V. CASE OF *DIVERS MISKITOS (LEMOTH MORRIS AND OTHERS) V. HONDURAS*, SERIES C NO. 432, JUDGMENT 31. 08.2021

The case of *Divers Miskitos (Lemoth Morris and others) v. Honduras* addresses the state's alleged international responsibility for the violation of several rights to the detriment of forty-two Miskito divers and their next of kin. In this case, the Court recalled that, within the framework of its competences, it is not for the Court to determine the specific responsibility of individuals, but rather to establish whether states are responsible for the violation of the human rights recognized in the Convention.

Facts

The case concerned forty-two victims of the Miskito Indigenous community living in the department of Gracias a Dios and their next of kin, who are divided into four groups: (a) thirty-four divers who suffered accidents due to deep dives which caused them decompression sickness or other diving-related ailments, twelve of whom died as a result of such accidents; (b) seven Miskito divers who died as a result of the fire aboard the "Lancaster" boat in which they were traveling, due to the explosion of a butane tank; (c) the child Licar

Méndez Gutiérrez, who was abandoned in a cayuco by the boat owner and whose whereabouts are unknown; and (d) their next of kin. In relation to the administrative or judicial claims filed by the alleged victims, the Court noted the following: (a) eleven divers obtained an administrative response from the Ministry of Labor and Social Security, the General Directorate of Social Security, or the Office of Occupational Health and Safety, and (b) three divers obtained a judicial response from the Labor Court. The Court also noted that as a result of those administrative proceedings eighteen divers, or their families, received monetary compensation.

Law

(a) Preliminary consideration: corporate responsibility with respect to human rights; the Court has ruled on the state's duty to regulate, supervise, and oversee the practice of dangerous activities by private companies that involve significant risks to the life and integrity of persons under their jurisdiction.

In particular, the Court highlighted the three pillars of the Guiding Principles on Business and Human Rights: Implementing the United Nations "Protect, Respect and Remedy" Framework, together with the foundational principles derived from these pillars, which are fundamental in determining the scope of the human rights obligations of states and business enterprises:

1. The state's duty to protect human rights
   • States must protect against human rights abuse within their territory and/or jurisdiction by third parties, including business enterprises. This requires taking appropriate steps to prevent, investigate, punish, and redress such abuse through effective policies, legislation, regulations, and adjudication.
   • States should set out clearly the expectation that all business enterprises domiciled in their territory and/or jurisdiction respect human rights throughout their operations.
2. The corporate responsibility to respect human rights
   • Business enterprises should respect human rights. This means that they should avoid infringing on the human rights of others and should address adverse human rights impacts with which they are involved.
   • The responsibility of business enterprises to respect human rights refers to internationally recognized human rights—understood, at a minimum, as those expressed in the International Bill of Human Rights and the principles concerning fundamental rights set out in the International Labor Organization's Declaration on Fundamental Principles and Rights at Work.
   • The responsibility to respect human rights requires that business enterprises:
   a) Avoid causing or contributing to adverse human rights impacts through their own activities, and address such impacts when they occur;
   b) Seek to prevent or mitigate adverse human rights impacts that are directly linked to their operations, products or services by their business relationships, even if they have not contributed to those impacts.
      • The responsibility of business enterprises to respect human rights applies to all enterprises regardless of their size, sector, operational context, ownership, and structure. Nevertheless, the scale and complexity of the means through which enterprises meet that responsibility may vary according to these factors and the severity of the enterprise's adverse human rights impacts.

- In order to meet their responsibility to respect human rights, business enterprises should have in place policies and processes appropriate to their size and circumstances, including:
  a) A policy commitment to meet their responsibility to respect human rights;
  b) A human rights due diligence process to identify, prevent, mitigate, and account for how they address their impacts on human rights;
  c) Processes to enable the remediation of any adverse human rights impacts they cause or to which they contribute.
3. Access to remedy
  (a) As part of their duty to protect against business-related human rights abuse, states must take appropriate steps to ensure, through judicial, administrative, legislative, or other appropriate means, that when such abuses occur within their territory and/or jurisdiction those affected have access to effective remedy.

Accordingly, and in the context of the obligation to guarantee rights and the duty to adopt provisions of domestic law derived from Articles 1(1) and 2 of the American Convention, the Court emphasized that states have a duty to prevent human rights violations by private companies, and therefore must adopt legislative and other measures to prevent such violations, and to investigate, punish, and provide reparation when they occur. Thus, states must establish regulations requiring companies to implement actions aimed at ensuring respect for the human rights recognized in the various instruments of the inter-American system for the protection of human rights—including the American Convention and the Protocol of San Salvador—especially in relation to hazardous activities. Under these regulations, businesses must ensure that their activities do not cause or contribute to human rights violations, and must adopt measures to redress such violations. The Court considers that corporate responsibility is applicable regardless of the size or sector of the company; however, their responsibilities may vary in the legislation based on the activity and the risk they pose to human rights.

  (b) Articles 4(1) (right to life), Article 5(1) (personal integrity), and Article 19 (rights of the child) of the American Convention, in relation to the Article 1(1) (obligation of guarantee) and Article 2 (the duty to adopt provisions of domestic law) of the same instrument: In fulfilment of its obligation to ensure the rights to life and personal integrity, the Court has considered that states have a duty to regulate, supervise, and monitor the implementation of dangerous activities that entail significant risks for the life and integrity of persons under their jurisdiction. In the case, the state's negligent conduct, in terms of verifying compliance with the provisions of regulations of labor that protected workers, allowed dangerous activities to be carried out in disagreement to the domestic legislation. This resulted in the state's international responsibility for the serious physical and psychological consequences suffered by the victims in this case in the various accidents that occurred, as well as for the deaths of those who died as a result of those accidents.

Regarding the death of the child at work, the Court considered that the state's omissions constituted, in addition to a violation of his right to life, a violation of its duty to guarantee the rights of a child. This Court emphasized that the ILO considers underwater lobster fishing in the Honduran Mosquitia region to be an extremely dangerous activity for children, noting that it results in physical harm due to prolonged exposure to the sun, humidity, the discomfort of sleeping on boats, and the possibility of suffering injuries derived from diving without protection. In addition, children who carry out this work often use drugs and alcohol to alleviate the effects of their workloads. On this point, the Court noted that the Committee on the Rights of the Child has established that states have a duty to protect minors against violations of children's human rights, which is of fundamental importance when considering the states' obligations with respect to the business sector.

(c) Right to work and to just, equitable, and satisfactory conditions that ensure the safety, health, and hygiene of the worker, right to health and social security, and to equality and non-discrimination (Article 26 of the American Convention), in relation to the obligations of respect and guarantee, and the duty to adopt provisions of domestic law (Articles 1(1) and 2 of the same instrument): Regarding the scope of Article 26 of the American Convention in relation to Articles 1(1) and 2 of the same instrument, this Court has interpreted that the Convention incorporated in its catalog of protected rights the so-called economic, social, cultural, and environmental rights (ESCER), through a derivation of the norms contained in the Charter of the Organization of American States (OAS), as well as the rules of interpretation established in Article 29 of the Convention itself, which states that "no provision [shall be interpreted as] limiting or excluding" the enjoyment of the rights established in the American Declaration, including those recognized in different domestic laws of the states. Furthermore, in accordance with a systematic, teleological, and evolutive interpretation, the Court has referred to the international and national corpus iuris on this matter to give specific content to the scope of the rights protected under the Convention, in order to determine the scope of the specific obligations of each right.

The Court found that from Article 45 of the OAS Charter, interpreted in light of the American Declaration and of the other instruments mentioned, it is possible to derive constituent elements of the right to equitable and satisfactory working conditions that ensure the safety, health, and hygiene of the worker, such as, for example, that it aims to prevent work-related injuries, illnesses, and deaths.

The Court also found that the ethnic origin of the victims in this case and the aforementioned intersectional factors of discrimination aggravated the victims' vulnerability, which: (a) facilitated underwater fishing operations without state oversight of the dangerous activity, of the occupational hygiene and safety conditions or of social security; (b) led the victims to accept a job that put their lives and personal integrity at risk; (c) did not provide them with access to health services for immediate medical care or for rehabilitation treatment. Furthermore, the state did not adopt measures to guarantee material equality in the right to work with respect to a group of people in a situation of exclusion and discrimination. Consequently, the state did not ensure the rights analyzed in this case without discrimination, or the right to equality provided for in Article 24 of the Convention.

(d) Reparations: States should adopt measures to ensure that business enterprises have: (a) appropriate policies for the protection of human rights; (b) due diligence processes for the identification, prevention, and correction of human rights violations, as well as to ensure decent and dignified work; and (c) processes that allow businesses to remedy human rights violations that result from their activities, especially when these affect people living in poverty or belonging to vulnerable groups. The Court considered that, in this context, states should actively encourage businesses to adopt good corporate governance practices that focus on stakeholders and actions aimed at orienting business activity towards compliance with human rights and standards, including and promoting the participation and commitment of all the stakeholders involved, and the redress of affected persons.

VI. CASE OF *DIGNA OCHOA AND FAMILY V. MEXICO*, SERIES C NO. 447, JUDGMENT 25-09-2021

The case, *Digna Ochoa and family v. México*, is related to the existence of serious irregularities in the investigation into the death of the human rights defender, Digna Ochoa y Plácido. The Court indicated that, in the case of attacks against women human rights defenders, all the measures designed to mitigate the risks they run should be adopted with a gender perspective and with an intersectional approach, so that these women can be provided with comprehensive protection based on considering, understanding, and highlighting the complexities of the different forms of violence that women defenders face due to their profession and their gender.

Facts

Human rights defenders in Mexico are historically vulnerable to violence. In this sense, the Court underlined that the situation becomes even worse when it comes to women human rights defenders. Women human rights defenders encounter additional obstacles linked to gender discrimination because they are victims of stigmatization, they are exposed to sexist or misogynistic comments, or their allegations are not taken seriously.

In this context, Digna Ochoa y Plácido, who was born on May 15, 1964, in Misantla, Veracruz, was a well-known human rights defender. She was a member of the Centro ProDH team and took part in defending several landmark cases in Mexico, such as the "Aguas Blancas" massacre and the human rights violations suffered by Messrs. On October 19, 2001, at 6 p.m., Digna Ochoa was founded dead by her colleague, Gerardo González Pedraza, in the office of "Servicios Legales de Investigación y Estudios Jurídicos A.C.," Colonia Roma, Mexico City. Digna Ochoa was an emblematic figure in the defense of human rights and her death caused, and still causes, great distress at both the national and international level.

Law

(a) Article 4 (right to life), Article 5 (personal integrity), Article 8 (judicial guarantees), Article 25 (judicial protection), and Article 11 (protection of honor and dignity) of the American Convention on Human Rights: The Court held that compliance with the duty to create the necessary conditions for the effective exercise and enjoyment of the rights established in the Convention is intrinsically linked to the protection and recognition of the importance of the role played by human rights defenders, whose work is fundamental to strengthen democracy and the rule of law. The Court also recalled that the activities of monitoring, denunciation, and education that human rights defenders perform make an essential contribution to respect for human rights, because they act as guarantors against impunity. Thus, they complement the role, not only of the states, but also of the inter-American human rights system as a whole. Therefore, the Court has indicated that states have the duty to ensure that they can carry out their activities freely; to protect them when they are subject to threats in order to avoid attacks on their life and integrity; to refrain from imposing obstacles that hinder their work; and to investigate, seriously, and effectively any violations committed against them, combatting impunity. Moreover, in cases of attacks against human rights defenders, states have the obligation to ensure impartial, prompt, and authoritative justice and this entails an exhaustive search for all the information in order to design and execute an investigation that involves the proper analysis of the different hypotheses of authorship, by act or omission, at different levels, exploring all the pertinent lines of investigation to identify those responsible. Consequently, when confronted with indications or allegations that a specific act against a human rights defender could be based precisely on their work of defense and promotion of human rights, the investigating authorities should take into account the context of the facts and their activities to identify the interests that could have been considered affected by those activities, in order to establish and exhaust the lines of investigation that take into account their work, determine the reason for the crime, and identify the perpetrators.

In the case of attacks against women human rights defenders, the Court considered that all the measures designed to mitigate the risks they run should be adopted with a gender perspective and with an intersectional approach, so that these women can be provided with comprehensive protection based on considering, understanding, and highlighting the complexities of the different forms of violence that women defenders face due to their profession and their gender. Chief among these complexities are political, social, economic, environmental, and systemic factors, including patriarchal attitudes and practices which produce and reproduce this type of violence. This approach also means that it should be the women defenders themselves who define their priorities and needs for protection and, in this regard, are supported based on a rationale of respect for their wishes. In order to ensure effective access to justice on an equal basis for women human rights defenders, the Court considered that states must guarantee: (i) unrestricted access, without gender-based discrimination, to justice, ensuring that women human rights defenders receive effective protection against harassment, threats, reprisals, and violence; (ii) a system of justice that is in keeping with international standards concerning competence, efficiency, independence, impartiality, integrity, and credibility, and the diligent and prompt investigation of acts of violence; as well as (iii) the application, in the context of this access to justice for women human rights defenders, of mechanisms that ensure that the evidentiary standards, investigations, and other legal probative procedures are impartial and are not influenced by gender stereotyping or prejudices.

On numerous occasions, this Court has emphasized the importance of recognizing, highlighting and rejecting negative gender stereotyping—which is one of the causes and consequences of gender based violence against women—in order to change the sociocultural conditions that permit and perpetuate the subordination of women. In this regard, the Court reiterated that gender stereotyping refers to a preconception of attributes, conduct, characteristics, or roles that correspond or should correspond to men and women, respectively, and that the subordination of women can be associated with practices based on persistent socially dominant gender stereotypes. Thus, their creation and use becomes one of the causes and consequences of gender-based violence against women, and this is exacerbated when the stereotypes are reflected implicitly or explicitly in policies and practices and, particularly, in the reasoning and language of the state authorities.

In the case of investigations into the complaints filed, the Court has recognized that personal prejudices and gender stereotyping affect the objectivity of the state officials in charge of investigating such complaints, influencing their ability to determine whether or not an act of violence has occurred, and their evaluation of the credibility of the witnesses and of the victim herself. Stereotyping "distorts perceptions and results in decisions based on preconceived beliefs and myths, rather than relevant facts," and this "can, in turn, lead to miscarriages of justice, including the revictimization of complainants." Moreover, when stereotyping is used in investigations into violence against women, the right to a life free of violence is violated, especially in cases in which its use by agents of justice hinders the implementation of appropriate investigations, which also denies a woman's right of access to justice. Also, when the state does not take concrete actions to eradicate stereotyping, it reinforces and institutionalizes it and this generates and reproduces violence against women. Therefore, states have the obligation to adopt a differentiated approach that excludes the discrimination and gender stereotyping that have historically accentuated violence against women and human rights defenders.

(b) Reparations: In the case, the Court has held the following measures as reparations: (1) Establish an annual award for the defense of human rights named after the lawyer Digna Ochoa y Plácido, to be granted annually to human rights defenders in Mexico whose work in the defense, promotion, protection, and guarantee of the fundamental rights has been outstanding. The state has one year as of notification of this judgment to comply with this obligation. Every year, the state must sent the Court a detailed report on this award for five years following the establishment of the award and the first report to the Court. (2) Design a campaign to recognize the work of human rights defenders, and implement this within six months at the most; the campaign should continue for one year and should be designed in collaboration with the victims and their representatives. (3) Name a street in the city of Misantla, state of Veracruz, and also a street in Mexico City, "Digna Ochoa y Plácido." The state has two years as of notification of this judgment to comply with this obligation. (4) Within two years, draw up a plan to reinforce the "Protection Mechanisms for human rights defenders and journalists" with a specific timetable, taking up the proposals and recommendations made by the expert witnesses before the Court, Erika Guevara Rosas and Michel Forst, and also the recommendations made by the Office in Mexico of the United Nations High Commissioner for Human Rights in 2019. This plan must include the allocation of the necessary resources for it to fulfill its mandate in national territory, and establish annual timeframes for the presentation of reports. (5) Establish and implement a "protection mechanism for witnesses who intervene in criminal proceedings," which would include the relevant international standards and parameters, such as individual risk analysis at a specific time, as well as a description of the protection mechanisms that could be granted to beneficiaries. The state has one year as of notification of this judgment to comply with this obligation. (6) Elaborate, present, and expedite, through the Office of the Legal Counsel of the Federal Executive Branch, a proposed constitutional amendment to provide autonomy and independence to the Forensic Services, as specialized and impartial bodies, with their own legal personality and budget; they would also enjoy full technical and administrative autonomy, as well as the capacity to decide on how to allocate their budget and on their internal organization. The state has two years as of notification of this judgment to comply with this obligation. (7) Elaborate, present, and expedite, through the Office of the Legal Counsel of the Federal Executive Branch, a proposal to amend the "Federal Law for the protection of persons who intervene in criminal proceedings" so that it would "include the relevant international standards and parameters for the creation and effective operation of a witness protection mechanism." The state has one year as of notification of this judgment to comply with this obligation.

VII. CASE OF *MANUELA V. EL SALVADOR*, SERIES C NO. 441, JUDGMENT 2021-09-02

The case of *Manuela v. El Salvador* relates to violations in the framework of the criminal process that culminated in the conviction for the crime of aggravated homicide of the victim in this case, within the context of the criminalization of abortion in El Salvador. The

Inter-American Court of Human Rights delivered judgment declaring the Republic of El Salvador internationally responsible for the violation of the rights: (i) to personal liberty and to the presumption of innocence to the detriment of Manuela; (ii) to a defense, to be tried by an impartial court, to the presumption of innocence, to the duty to provide a reasoned decision, to the obligation not to apply laws in a discriminatory manner, to equality before the law, to the right not to be subjected to cruel, inhuman, or degrading punishment, and the obligation to ensure that the purpose of the punishment of imprisonment is the rehabilitation and social readaptation of those convicted, to the detriment of Manuela; (iii) to life, personal integrity, privacy, equality before the law, to the detriment of Manuela; and (iv) to personal integrity to the detriment of Manuela's mother, father, and elder and younger son, in relation to the obligations to respect and ensure these rights and the duty to adopt domestic legal provisions, to the detriment of Manuela.

Facts

In February 2008, Manuela was pregnant and on February 27, 2008, she suffered an obstetric emergency and was attended in the San Francisco Gotera Hospital. The medical staff concluded that Manuela had suffered from severe postpartum preeclampsia together with anemia as a result of a significant loss of blood. The doctor who attended her filed a complaint against Manuela because her symptoms indicated that she had given birth; however, there was no product. On February 28, 2008, the police searched Manuela's home and found the body of a dead newborn inside the septic tank. Manuela was arrested the same day "for the crime of murder of her newborn son" and handcuffed to the hospital bed where she lay. A criminal trial against her was held from March to August and, during this time, she remained detained. On August 11, 2008, the San Francisco Gotera Court sentenced her to thirty years' imprisonment for the crime of aggravated homicide. The judgment became final on August 26, 2008, because no appeal was filed against it. While she was detained, Manuela was diagnosed with Hodgkin's lymphoma and received belated and irregular treatment; as a result of this, she died on April 30, 2010.

Law

(i) Articles 7.1, 7.3, and 8.2 of the American Convention on Human Rights, in relation to Articles 1.1 and 2 of the same instrument, to the detriment of Manuela; (ii) Articles 8.1, 8.2, 8.2.d, 8.2.e, 24, 5.2, and 5.6 of the American Convention on Human Rights, in relation to Articles 1.1 and 2, to the detriment of Manuela; (iii) Articles 4, 5, 11, 24, and 26 of the American Convention on Human Rights, in relation to the obligations to respect and guarantee rights without discrimination and the duty to adopt provisions of domestic law, established in Articles 1.1 and 2 of the same instrument, as well as their obligations under Article 7(a) of the Convention of Belém do Pará; and (iv) Article 5.1 of the American Convention on Human Rights, in conjunction with Article 1.1 of the same instrument, to the detriment of Manuela's mother, father, eldest son, and youngest child.

Regarding the rights to personal liberty and the presumption of innocence, the Court found that the decision ordering Manuela's provisional detention did not substantiate with objective circumstances the possibility that Manuela hindered the process. Moreover, the imposition of this precautionary measure was also based on the fact that the act would have caused social alarm in the community where Manuela resided, which, for the Court, is contrary to the precautionary logic since it does not refer to the particular conditions of the accused person, but to subjective and political assessments, which should not be part of the basis for a pre-trial detention order. In this sense, since the decision to pretrial detention was not motivated in objective circumstances that demonstrated the procedural danger in the present case, it was contrary to the American Convention. The Court further found that the failure to analyse the need to maintain pretrial detention constituted a further violation of the Convention. On the other hand, the Court proved that the criminal procedure legislation established mandatory provisional detention for certain types of crimes and allowed the judge to take into account factors external to the accused person, such as the social alarm that the commission of the crime has generated. In this regard, the Court clarified that these considerations lie in preventive-general or preventive-special purposes attributable to the penalty, which are not valid grounds for preventive prisons. The Court concluded that the imposition of pretrial detention was arbitrary and violated the right to the presumption of innocence to the detriment of Manuela.

Concerning the rights to judicial guarantees, personal integrity, and equality before the law the Court analyzed (1) the right to a defense; (2) the use of gender stereotypes and judicial guarantees; and (3) the sentence imposed on Manuela. The Court determined that the public defense acted to the detriment of Manuela's rights and interests, leaving her in a state of defenselessness. Thus, the Court considered that the defense lawyer requested to be replaced thirty minutes before the preliminary hearing, and in that hearing Manuela's technical defense: (i) he only presented allegations regarding an error of form of some statements offered by the prosecution, and (ii) he did not mention in his arguments the alleged criminal responsibility of Manuela, nor, for example, did he request that the case be dismissed. In addition, the Court stressed that the defense did not offer evidence that could demonstrate that what happened to the newborn could have been an accident nor did it request the performance of other tests to confirm that the newborn had been born alive. Likewise, for the Court, the negative consequences of the minimum evidentiary activity carried out by the defense in the present case were also increased by the decision not to offer Manuela's statement to the Court. Indeed, while it may be a valid litigation strategy to prevent the accused person from testifying, in this case, where the defense did not offer exculpatory evidence, renouncing Manuela's statement and the mother's statement, initially offered, implied taking the facts as they were put forward by the prosecution, and, therefore, that Manuela faced a sentence of at least thirty years. In addition to the preceding, the Court stressed that the public defense did not file any appeal against the conviction, despite the fact that the appeals of cassation and review were available. On the other hand, the Court understood that, from the early stages of the investigation, Manuela's guilt was presumed, it was avoided to determine the truth of what happened and to take into account the evidentiary elements that could distort the thesis of guilt of the victim. The principle of presumption of innocence implied that the internal authorities had to investigate all logical lines of investigation, including the possibility that the death of the newborn was not caused by Manuela, which could have been examined by investigating Manuela's state of health, and whether this could have affected the time of delivery. On this point, the Court stressed that Manuela's state of health was not taken into account in the investigation, warning that Manuela: (i) was diagnosed with severe preeclampsia, which can cause a precipitous delivery and increases the risk of perinatal mortality and morbidity, placental abruption, asphyxiation, and intrauterine fetal death; (ii) suffered from postpartum hemorrhage caused by placental retention and tears in the birth canal, which possibly meant that she was in a state that made it impossible for her at the time of delivery to attend to herself or to be able to attend to someone else; and (iii) Manuela had visible lumps in her neck, which were later diagnosed as Hodgkin's lymphoma, and may have contributed to the onset of anemia, which can cause preterm labor. This lack of research was also driven by the prejudices of the researchers against Manuela for not complying with the stereotype of being a selfless mother who must always achieve the protection of her children. In particular, a researcher made statements that externalized a clear prejudice about Manuela's guilt, based on stereotypes that condition the value of a woman to be a mother, and, therefore, assume that women who decide not to be mothers have less value than others, or are undesirable people. In this sense, in addition, women are forced to, regardless of the circumstances, prioritize the well-being of their children, including over their own well-being. Additionally, in the motivation of the conviction, the causal link between Manuela's actions and the death of the newborn was not established with factual evidence, beyond alluding to the alleged complaint made by Manuela's father. This lack was settled with stereotypes and preconceived ideas. Additionally, the application of these stereotypes was only possible because Manuela is a woman, so the distinction in the application of criminal law was arbitrary, and, therefore, discriminatory. Referring to the thirty-year prison sentence imposed on Manuela, the Court pointed out that obstetric emergencies, because they are a medical condition, cannot automatically generate criminal sanctions. On this point, the Court reiterated that, from an evolving interpretation of the prohibition of cruel, inhuman, and degrading treatment and punishment, provided for in Article 5.2 of the Convention, a requirement of proportionality of the penalties emerges. Thus, the Court noted that the application of the penalty provided for in the criminal type of aggravated homicide was clearly disproportionate in the present case, because the particular state of the women during the puerperal or perinatal state was not taken into account, without prejudice to the fact that this case, due to a lack of investigation, it was not ruled out that it had been a case of absence of any criminal responsibility. Based on the preceding, the Court considered that the sentence of thirty years in prison for a homicide committed by the mother in the perinatal period is disproportionate to the degree of personalized reproach (or guilt) of the mother. The penalty currently provided for infanticide is therefore cruel and therefore contrary to the Convention. By virtue of all the foregoing considerations, the Court concluded that the investigation and procedure to which the victim was subjected did not comply with the right to a defense, the right to be tried by an impartial tribunal, the presumption of innocence, the duty to state reasons, the obligation not to apply the legislation in a discriminatory manner, the right not to be subjected to cruel, inhuman, or degrading punishment, and the obligation to ensure that the purpose of the custodial sentence is reform and social rehabilitation of convicted persons. Regarding the rights to life, personal integrity, health, privacy, and equality before the law The Court considered that in the present case there were several shortcomings that showed that the medical care was not acceptable or of quality, namely: (i) there was a delay of more than three hours since Manuela entered the hospital and the time she received the emergency medical care she required, and during that time, the doctor in her charge gave priority to presenting the complaint to the prosecutor's office about the alleged abortion; (ii) in the seven days that Manuela was hospitalized, at no time does the medical history show that the treating staff has registered or examined the lumps that Manuela had on her neck; (iii) Manuela was handcuffed to her stretcher at the San Francisco Gotera Hospital after having recently given birth and while being treated for severe preeclampsia, so it was unreasonable to assume that there was a real risk of flight that could not have been mitigated with other less harmful means. Additionally, the Court found that the medical and administrative staff of the San Francisco Gotera Hospital disclosed information protected by medical professional secrecy, as well as Manuela's sensitive personal data. In this regard, the Court clarified that, although personal health data are not expressly provided for in Article 11 of the Convention, they are information that describes the most sensitive or sensitive aspects of a person, so it must be understood as protected by the right to privacy. With regard to the complaint filed by the trafficking doctor, the Court considered that this restriction on Manuela's right to privacy did not comply with the requirement of legality, since Salvadoran legislation did not clearly establish whether or not there was a duty to denounce that forced medical personnel to disclose Manuela's confidential information, which has caused medical personnel to understand that they have an obligation to report these types of cases. The Court further noted that, while the complaint may have been an appropriate and necessary measure to satisfy the international obligation to investigate, prosecute, and, where appropriate, punish crimes committed against children, it was not strictly proportionate. This is because, in cases related to obstetric emergencies, the disclosure of medical information can restrict access to adequate medical care for women who need medical assistance, but avoid going to a hospital for fear of being criminalized, which puts their right to health, personal integrity, and life at risk. In the case of obstetric emergencies, in which the life of women is at stake, the duty to maintain professional secrecy must be given priority over the duty to denounce. The Court also referred to the implications of the statements that the attending physician provided in the investigation, as well as the referral of Manuela's medical history to the Prosecutor's Office by the director of the hospital. In this regard, the Court found that the statement made by the attending physician was contrary to domestic law establishing professional secrecy, and that the legislation on medical confidentiality did not establish clear criteria as to under what circumstances medical authorities could share a person's medical record. In this regard, the Court considered that, in cases related to obstetric emergencies, the disclosure of medical information may restrict access to adequate medical care for women who need medical assistance, but avoid going to a hospital for fear of being criminalized. The Court concluded that the breach of Manuela's obligation to maintain professional secrecy and disclosure of medical information constituted a violation of her right to privacy and the right to health, in relation to the obligation to respect and guarantee and the duty to adopt provisions of domestic law. On the other hand, Manuela's detention prevented her from receiving adequate medical care, so that her custodial sentence also became an inhuman penalty, contrary to the Convention. Thus, the Court stressed that: (i) there is no record in the file that any medical examination was carried out upon arrival at the Police Delegation or the Criminal Center of the City of San Miguel, this despite the fact that Manuela had been hospitalized for an obstetric emergency and had visible lumps on her neck that had not been examined in the hospital where she was hospitalized; (ii) there is also no evidence that any medical examination was carried out on Manuela between March 2008 and February 2009, despite the lumps she had on her neck, and that between November 2008 and February 2009 Manuela lost more than thirteen kilograms of weight and suffered from high fever and jaundice. Additionally, the Court considered that the treatment provided by the state for Hodgkin's lymphoma with nodular sclerosis diagnosed to Manuela in 2009 was irregular. In particular, it is noted that: (i) she was not taken to the chemotherapy appointment scheduled for April 2, 2009, until April 22, and in that time her tumor increased; (ii) in January 2010 the treatment was discontinued by one month; and (iii) after receiving chemotherapy on November 6, 2009, and January 14, 2010, she was not taken to subsequent controls. These faults demonstrate that the state did not implement the necessary measures to ensure that Manuela was transferred and received the medical attention she required in the hospital. Finally, the Court considered that the state had failed to comply with its duty to guarantee Manuela's right to life. Specifically, the state failed to comply with its obligation to: (i) conduct a general health examination when Manuela was hospitalized; (ii) perform a health examination at the time of arrest; and (iii) take the necessary measures so that Manuela could receive her medical treatment while she was deprived of liberty. Failure to prevent these omissions would reduce Manuela's chances of dying from Hopkin's lymphoma. Finally, the Court considered that Manuela had different structural disadvantages that impacted her victimization. In particular, the Court stressed that Manuela was a woman with limited economic resources, illiterate, and living in a rural area. In the present case: (i) the ambiguity of the legislation relating to the professional secrecy of doctors and the obligation to report existing in El Salvador disproportionately affect women because they have the biological capacity of pregnancy, but does not affect women who have sufficient financial resources to be treated in a private hospital, and (ii) the prioritization of the complaint over Manuela's medical treatment and the disclosure of her sensitive data used in a criminal proceeding was influenced by the idea that the trial of an alleged crime should prevail over the rights of women, which was discriminatory. On the other hand, the Court considered that the ambiguity of the legislation on professional secrecy and the duty to denounce implied that, if Manuela went to the medical services to attend to the obstetric emergency that put her health at risk, she could be denounced, as indeed happened. Subjecting Manuela to this situation, which ended up resoundingly affecting her life, as well as being discriminatory, constituted an act of violence against women. Based on the foregoing, the Court concluded that El Salvador was responsible for the violation of the rights recognized in Articles 4, 5, 11, 24, and 26, in conjunction with Articles 1.1 and 2 of the American Convention, to the detriment of Manuela. Likewise, the state is responsible for not complying with its obligations under Article 7(a) of the Convention of Belém do Pará. Finally, regarding the right to personal integrity of relatives, the Court found that Manuela's family nucleus has experienced profound suffering and anguish to the detriment of its mental and moral integrity, due to the arrest, trial, imprisonment, and death of Manuela, which persists to this day.

(b) Reparations: The Court ordered the state to: (a) publish the judgment and its official summary; (b) perform a public act of recognition of international responsibility; (c) award scholarships to Manuela's youngest son and eldest son; (d) provide free of charge, and in an immediate, timely, adequate, and effective manner, medical, psychological, and psychiatric treatment to Manuela's parents; (e) regulate the obligation to maintain medical professional secrecy and the confidentiality of medical records; (f) develop an action protocol for the care of women requiring emergency medical care for obstetric emergencies; (g) adapt its rules on pre-trial detention; (h) design and implement a training and awareness-raising course for judicial officials and health personnel at the Rosales National Hospital; (i) adapt its regulation on the dosimetry of the penalty for infanticide; (j) design and implement a sexual and reproductive education programme; (k) take the necessary measures to ensure comprehensive care in cases of obstetric emergencies; (l) pay compensation for material and non-material damage; and (m) the payment of certain costs and expenses.

LEGAL MAXIMS: SUMMARIES AND EXTRACTS FROM SELECTED CASE LAW*

Case of Vicky Hernández and Others v. Honduras, Merits, Reparations and Costs, Judgment, 26 March 2021, Series C No. 422

Case of Guachalá Chimbo et al. v. Ecuador, Merits, Reparations and Costs, Judgment, 26 March 2021, Series C No. 423

Presidential Reelection Without Term Limits in the Context of the Inter-American Human Rights System, Advisory Opinion Requested by the Republic of Colombia, 7 June 2021, Series OC-28/21

Caso Bedoya Lima y Otras vs. Colombia, Fondo, Reparaciones y Costas, Sentencia de 26 de Agosto de 2021, Serie C No. 431

Caso Pueblos Indígenas Maya Kaqchikel de Sumpango y Otros vs. Guatemala, Fondo, Reparaciones y Costas, Sentencia de 6 de Octubre de 2021, Serie C No. 440

Case of Manuela et al. v. El Salvador, Preliminary Objections, Merits, Reparations and Costs, Judgment, 2 November 2021, Series C No. 441

---

* The working method chosen for the formulation of legal maxims is explained *supra* 'Outline of the Parts', at page xv.

Legal Maxims: Summaries and Extracts from Selected Case Law In: *The Global Community Yearbook of International Law and Jurisprudence 2022*. Edited by: Giuliana Ziccardi Capaldo, Oxford University Press. © Oxford University Press 2023.
DOI: 10.1093/oso/9780197752265.003.0029

LEGAL MAXIMS SUMMARIES AND EXTRACTS FROM SELECTED CASE LAW

VIII.2.1

Case of Vicky Hernández and Others v. Honduras, Merits, Reparations and Costs, Judgment, 26 March 2021, Series C No. 422*

Contents**

I. INSTITUTION AND COURSE OF PROCEEDINGS

II. ALLEGED VIOLATIONS OF ARTICLES 1.1 AND 24 OF THE AMERICAN CONVENTION ON HUMAN RIGHTS

III. ALLEGED VIOLATION OF ARTICLES 3, 4, 5, 11, 13 AND 24 OF THE AMERICAN CONVENTION ON HUMAN RIGHTS

IV. ALLEGED VIOLATION OF ARTICLE 25 OF THE AMERICAN CONVENTION ON HUMAN RIGHTS

V. JUDGMENT

I.

II.2.0　　　INSTITUTION AND COURSE OF PROCEEDINGS
　　　　　　See also: I.8.33; I.8.61; II.7.6; II.2.03; II.7.62

"[1] [...] [T]he Inter-American Commission on Human Rights [...] submitted to the jurisdiction of the Inter-American Court, [...] the case of "Vicky Hernández and family" with regard to the Republic of Honduras [...]. According to the Commission the dispute relates to the death of Vicky Hernández, a trans woman and human rights defender, in the city of San Pedro Sula between the evening of June 28 and the early morning hours of June 29, 2009, while a curfew was in place. [...] [T]he Commission considered that given that the streets were under the complete control of security forces, and that the State had failed to elucidate what happened in the courts, sufficient evidence existed to conclude that the State was directly responsible for the death of Vicky Hernández and that, due to the characteristics of the case, what happened to Vicky Hernández constituted a situation of prejudice-based violence owing to her gender identity and expression. Lastly, the Commission alleged that the Honduran State had failed to investigate the facts of the case adequately, with due diligence and within a reasonable time, and they remain in impunity. [...] [3] [...] On April 30, 2019, the Commission submitted all the facts and alleged human rights violations described in the Merits Report to the Inter-American Court "due to the need to obtain justice and reparation." [...]"

[Paras. 1, 3]

---

* Summaries prepared by Ana Cristina Gallego Hernández, Ph.D., Associate Professor of Public International Law, University of Seville (Spain). Text of judgment available online at the Court's Web site <https://www.corteidh.or.cr/casos_sentencias.cfm?lang=en>. Original: Spanish. Footnotes appearing in the original text have been omitted.

** This is not a faithful reproduction of the Table of Contents of the Judgment.

II.

I.8.61　　PROHIBITION OF DISCRIMINATION
See also: I.8.33; II.7.6; II.7.64

"[64] The Court has indicated that States must refrain from implementing actions that are in any way directly or indirectly addressed at creating situation of discrimination *de jure* or *de facto*. [...] [There is nothing on the record to indicate that it does not have jurisdiction]. Thus, it has established that Article 1(1) of the Convention is a norm of a general nature the content of which extends to all the provisions of the treaty and establishes the obligation of the States Parties to respect and to ensure the full and free exercise of the rights and freedoms recognized therein "without any discrimination." [...][65] Moreover, [...] Article 24 protects the right to "equal protection of the law." [...] [I]f a State discriminates as regards the respect and guarantee of a right protected by the Convention it would fail to comply with the obligation established in Article 1(1) and the substantive right in question. If, to the contrary, the discrimination refers to an unequal protection of domestic law or its application, the fact must be examined in light of Article 24 of the American Convention, in relation to the categories protected by Article 1(1) of this instrument. [66] Therefore, [...] States are also obliged to adopt positive measures to reverse or change any situations in their societies that discriminate against certain group of persons.[...][67] The Inter-American Court has recognized that the LGBTI community has historically been a victim of structural discrimination, stigmatization, diverse forms of violence, and the violation of fundamental rights. Similarly, the Court has established that a person's sexual orientation, gender identity and gender expression are categories protected by the Convention. Consequently, the State may not discriminate against a person based on their sexual orientation, their gender identity and/or their gender expression. [70] [...] violence against the LGBTI community has a symbolic purpose; the victim is chosen in order to communicate a message of exclusion or subordination. On this point, the Court has indicated that the purpose or effect of violence used for discriminatory purposes is to prevent or invalidate the recognition, enjoyment or exercise of the human rights and fundamental freedoms of the person subjected to such discrimination, irrespective of whether that person self-identifies with a specific category. This violence, fueled by hate speech may result in hate crimes."

[Paras. 64, 65, 66, 67, 70]

III.

I.8.63　　DEROGATION FROM HUMAN RIGHTS IN TIME OF PUBLIC EMERGENCY
See also: I.8.33; I.8.61; I.8.42; I.8.43; I.8.56; II.7.6; II.7.64

"[85] [T]he right to life plays a fundamental role in the American Convention because it is the essential presumption for the exercise of the other rights. Respect for Article 4, related to Article 1(1) of the American Convention, not only presupposes that no one may be deprived of their life arbitrarily (negative obligation), but also requires States to take all appropriate measures to protect and preserve the right to life (positive obligation) in accordance with the obligation to ensure to all persons subject to their jurisdiction the free and full exercise of their rights. [**86**] [...] The Court has established that the violation of personal integrity is a type of violation with diverse connotations of degree, the physical and mental effects of which vary in intensity based on endogenous and exogenous factors that must be proved in each specific situation. [**88**] [T]his Court has establishe[d] that curfews and the suspension of guarantees in general constitute exceptional situations and that, while they are in force, it is lawful for the State to apply certain measures that restrict rights and freedoms which, under normal conditions, are prohibited or subject to more rigorous requirements. Nevertheless, this does not mean that the suspension of guarantees entails the temporary suspension of the rule of law or that it authorizes the authorities to deviate from the legality by which it must always abide. When guarantees are suspended, some of the legal limits the actions of the public authorities may differ from those in force under normal conditions, but these should not be considered inexistent and, consequently, it should not be understood that the Government is invested with absolute powers over and above the conditions in which the exceptional legality of this measure is authorized. [**96**] [...] [T]he State has the legal obligation "to take reasonable steps to prevent human rights violations and to use the means at its disposal to conduct a serious investigation of the violations committed within its jurisdiction in order to identify those responsible, impose the appropriate punishments and make adequate reparation to the victim." Among other measures, this includes "establish[ing] an effective system of justice capable of investigating, punishing, and providing reparation for the deprivation of life by state agents or private individuals." [**97**] The Court has also underscored that the investigation of cases of violation of the right to life is an essential element when determining the State's international responsibility [...]."

[**Paras. 85, 86, 88, 96, 97**]

IV.

II.2.01   ACCESS TO INTERNATIONAL COURTS
See also: I.8.33; I.8.61; I.8.47; II.7.6; II.7.64

"[**103**] [...] The right of access to justice, within a reasonable time, must ensure the right of the presumed victims or their next of kin that everything necessary is done to know the truth of what happened and to investigate, prosecute and, punish, as appropriate, those eventually found responsible. The Court has also indicated that the duty to investigate is an obligation of means and not of results; however, it requires the investigating body to try and obtain the result sought; in other words, it must take all the necessary steps and make all the required inquiries to determine the truth, using all available legal means. [**107**] In addition, the Court has indicated that when violent acts such as homicides are investigated, the state authorities have the duty to take all reasonable measures to discover whether possible discrimination is involved. This obligation signifies that when there are indications or concrete suspicions of discrimination-based violence, the State must take all reasonable steps, based on the circumstances, to gather and safeguard the evidence, explore all practical means to discover the truth, and issue fully reasoned, impartial and objective decisions, without omitting suspicious facts that may indicate discrimination-based violence.[...]"

[**Paras. 103, 107**]

V.

II.2.5   JUDGMENT/DECISION/ORDER
            See also: II.7.64; II.7.65; II.7.67

"[204] [...]
THE COURT [...]
DECLARES,
Unanimously that:

2. The State is responsible for the violation of the right to life contained in Article 4(1) of the American Convention on Human Rights, in relation to Articles 1(1), 8 and 25 of this instrument, as well as for the violation of the right to personal integrity contained in Article 5(1) of the American Convention on Human Rights [...].

3. The State is responsible for the violation of the rights to judicial guarantees and judicial protection contained in Articles 8(1) and 25 of the American Convention on Human Rights, in relation to Article 1(1) of this instrument [...].

4. The State is responsible for the violation of the rights to recognition of juridical personality, personal liberty, privacy, freedom of expression and a name contained in Articles 3, 7, 11, 13 and 18 of the American Convention on Human Rights, in relation to Articles 1(1), 8, 24 and 25 of this instrument [...].

5. The State is responsible for the violation of the right to personal integrity contained in Article 5(1) of the American Convention on Human Rights, in relation to Article 1(1) of this instrument [...].

[And] [b]y five votes to two, that:

6. The State is responsible for failure to comply with the obligations established in Article 7(a) of the Inter-American Convention for the Prevention, Punishment and Eradication of Violence against Women to the detriment of Vicky Hernández, and Article 7(b) of this instrument [...]."

[Para. 204]

VIII.2.2

Case of Guachalá Chimbo et al. v. Ecuador, Merits, Reparations and Costs, Judgment, 26 March 2021, Series C No. 423*

Contents**

I. INTRODUCTION AND PROCEDURAL BACKGROUND

II. ALLEGED VIOLATIONS OF ARTICLES 3, 4, 5, 7, 11, 13, 24, 26 OF THE AMERICAN CONVENTION ON HUMAN RIGHTS IN RELATION TO ARTICLES 1(1) AND 2 OF THIS INSTRUMENT

III. ALLEGED VIOLATIONS OF ARTICLES 7(6), 8(1) AND 25(1) OF THE AMERICAN CONVENTION ON HUMAN RIGHTS IN RELATION TO ARTICLE 1(1) OF THIS INSTRUMENT

IV. JUDGMENT

I.

I.2.0   INSTITUTION AND COURSE OF PROCEEDINGS
See also: I.8.0; I.8.1; I.8.33; I.8.41; I.8.42; I.8.44; I.8.47; I.8.61; II.2.02; II.2.2; II.2.24; II.2.51; II.7.6; II.7.67

"[**1**] [...] On July 11, 2019, the Inter-American Commission on Human Rights [...] submitted to the jurisdiction of the Court the case of *Luis Eduardo Guachalá Chimbo and next of kin with regard to the Republic of Ecuador* [...]. The Commission indicated that the case related to the "disappearance of Luis Eduardo Guachalá Chimbo, a person with mental disabilities, in January 2004, while he was in a public psychiatric hospital in Quito," as well as the absence of informed consent for the hospitalization and the treatment received. [...] [**16**] The Court has jurisdiction to hear this case, pursuant to Article 62(3) of the Convention, because Ecuador has been a State Party to this instrument since December 28, 1977, and accepted the contentious jurisdiction of the Court on July 24, 1984."

[**Paras. 1, 16**]

II.

I.8.4   FUNDAMENTAL RIGHTS AND FREEDOMS
See also: I.8.41; I.8.42; I.8.44; I.8.46; I.8.61; II.7.6; II.7.64; II.7.65; II.7.68

"[**87**] The Court holds that persons with disabilities are often subject to discrimination based on their condition. Therefore, State must adopt the necessary legislative, social, educational, labor or any other measures to eliminate all disability-based discrimination and to promote the full integration of persons with disabilities into society. [...] [**90**] [...] This means that, in the case of psychiatric hospitals, States must exercise strict oversight of such establishments. States have the duty to ensure and to monitor that the right of

---

* Summaries prepared by Adriana Fillol Mazo, Assistant Professor of Public International Law, University of Seville (Spain). Text of judgment available online at the Court's Web site <https://www.corteidh.or.cr/casos_sentencias.cfm>. Original: Spanish. Footnotes appearing in the original text have been omitted.

** This is not a faithful reproduction of the Table of Contents of the Judgment.

the patients to receive decent, humane and professional treatment and to be protected against exploitation, abuse and humiliation is respected in all public or private psychiatric institutions. [**91**] [...] [T]he Court stresses that the lack of financial resources may hinder or preclude access to the medical care required to prevent possible disabilities or to prevent or reduce the appearance of new disabilities. Based on the foregoing, the Court has indicated that the positive measures that States must take for persons with disabilities living in poverty include those necessary to prevent all forms of avoidable disabilities and to accord persons with disabilities preferential treatment appropriate to their condition. [**96**] The central dispute in the instant case relates to what happened to Mr. Guachalá Chimbo owing to his illness and, in particular, when receiving medical treatment in a public hospital in 2004. Therefore, the Court finds it pertinent to examine the hospitalization and the treatment received by Luis Eduardo Guachalá in the Julio Endara Hospital in the context of the right to health. [...] [**100**] [...] Thus, the right to health refers to the right of everyone to enjoy the highest level of physical, mental and social well-being. [**101**] [...] This right encompasses timely and appropriate health care in keeping with the principles of availability, accessibility, acceptability and quality, the application of which will depend on the prevailing circumstances in each State. Compliance with the State obligation to respect and to ensure this right must pay special attention to vulnerable and marginalized groups, and must be realized progressively in line with available resources and the applicable domestic laws. [**106**] [...] [T]he Court considers that the nature and scope of the obligations derived from the protection of the right to health include aspects that may be required immediately and those that are of a progressive nature. In this regard, the Court recalls that, regarding the former (obligations that may be required immediately), States must adopt effective measures to ensure access without discrimination to the services recognized by the right to health, ensure equality of rights between men and women and, in general, advance towards the full effectiveness of the economic, social, cultural and environmental rights (ESCER).[...] [**110**] Informed consent is a basic element of the right to health; and the obligation to comply with this is an obligation of an immediate nature.[...] [**119**] States have the international obligation to ensure that informed consent is obtained before any medical act is performed because this is founded, above all, on the self-determination and autonomy of the individual as part of the respect and guarantee of the dignity of every human being, as well as their right to liberty. [...] [**132**] This Court has established that exceptions do exist where health care personnel may act without requiring consent in cases in which this cannot be given by the person concerned and an immediate urgent or emergency medical or surgical intervention is necessary, given a serious risk to the patient's health or life. [...] [**140**] The Court recalls that the right to health refers to the right of everyone to enjoy the highest attainable level of physical, mental and social well-being. [...] [**148**] This Court recalls that compliance with the State obligation to respect and to ensure the right to health must pay special attention to persons living in poverty. Therefore, States must take measures to ensure that the treatment required to prevent disabilities does not represent a disproportionate burden for the poorest households. [**167**] [...] [T]he right to equality entails the obligation to adopt measures to ensure that equality is real and effective; in other words, to correct existing inequalities, to promote the inclusion and participation of historically marginalized groups, to guarantee to disadvantaged persons or groups the effective enjoyment of their rights and, in sum, to offer everyone real possibilities of achieving material equality. [...] [**217**] The Court has asserted on numerous occasions that the family members of the victims of human rights violations may, in turn, be victims. The Court has considered that it is possible to declare the violation of the right to mental and moral integrity of the victims' "immediate family members" and other persons with close ties to the victims due to the additional suffering they have undergone as a result of the particular circumstances of the violations perpetrated against their loved ones, and owing to the subsequent acts or omissions of the state authorities in relation to those facts [...].”

[Paras. 87, 90, 91, 96, 100, 101, 106, 110, 119, 132, 140, 148, 167, 217]

III.

I.8.4   FUNDAMENTAL RIGHTS AND FREEDOMS
             See also: I.8.41; I.8.42; I.8.44; I.8.46; I.8.61; II.7.6; II.7.64; II.7.65; II.7.68

“[**184**] The obligation to investigate human rights violations is one of the positive measures that States must adopt to ensure the rights recognized in the Convention. [...] [**187**] The Court recalls that the Julio Endara Hospital is an Ecuadorian public hospital. Therefore, once the staff of that hospital noted the absence of a patient they were obliged to notify the competent authorities in order to open the investigation. [...] [**190**] The investigation into what happened to Mr. Guachalá Chimbo included the obligation to determine the victim's fate or destiny and to discover his whereabouts. In this case, the search also had to take into account Mr. Guachalá Chimbo's special vulnerability at the time of his disappearance. [**196**] The Court considers that this omission is particularly serious in the case of the disappearance of a person with a disability. [...] [**199**] The Court emphasizes that, to ensure that an investigation of human rights violations is conducted efficiently and with due diligence, all necessary measures must be taken to carry out promptly the essential and appropriate actions and inquiries to clarify the fate of the victims and to identify those responsible for the facts. [...] [**201**] In order to ensure the effectiveness of the investigation of human rights violations, omissions in gathering evidence should be avoided and logical lines of investigation followed. The Court has stipulated that in criminal investigations concerning human rights violations, it is necessary, *inter alia*: to gather and preserve evidence in order to help in any potential criminal investigation of those responsible; to identify possible witnesses and obtain their statements, and to determine the cause, manner, place and time of the act investigated. It is also necessary to conduct an exhaustive investigation of the scene of the crime, and ensure that rigorous tests are performed by competent professionals using the most appropriate procedures.”

[Paras. 184, 187, 190, 196, 199, 201]

IV.

II.2.5   JUDGMENT/DECISION/ORDER
              See also: I.8.0; I.8.1; I.8.33; I.8.41; I.8.42; I.8.44; I.8.47; I.8.61; II.2.02; II.2.2;
              II.2.24; II.2.51; II.7.6; II.7.67

“[**282**] [...]
THE COURT
DECLARES,
By five votes to one that:
   1. The State is responsible for the violation of the rights to recognition of juridical personality, life, personal integrity, personal liberty, dignity and privacy, access to information, equality before the law and health, in accordance with Articles 3, 4, 5, 7, 11, 13, 24 and 26 of the American Convention on Human Rights, in relation to the obligation to respect and to ensure the rights without discrimination and the duty

to adopt domestic legal provisions established in Articles 1(1) and 2 of this instrument, to the detriment of Luis Eduardo Guachalá Chimbo, pursuant to paragraphs 96 to 180 of this judgment. [. . .]

Unanimously, that:

   2. The State is responsible for the violation of the rights to an effective remedy, judicial guarantees and judicial protection, recognized in Articles 7(6), 8(1) and 25(1) of the American Convention on Human Rights, in relation to Article 1(1) of this instrument [. . .].

Unanimously, that:

   3. The State is responsible for the violation of the right to personal integrity, recognized in Article 5(1) of the American Convention on Human Rights, in relation to Article 1(1) of this instrument [. . .]."

[Para. 282]

VIII.2.3

Presidential Reelection Without Term Limits in the Context of the Inter-American Human Rights System, Advisory Opinion Requested by the Republic of Colombia, 7 June 2021, Series OC-28/21*

Contents**

    I. INTRODUCTION AND PROCEDURAL BACKGROUND

    II. JURISDICTION

    III. RIGHT TO PARTICIPATE IN GOVERNMENT

    IV. ADVISORY OPINION

I.

II.2.0   INSTITUTION AND COURSE OF PROCEEDINGS

            See also: I.8.0; I.8.34; II.2.021; II.2.22; II.2.23; II.7.6; II.7.641; II.4.0; II.4.1

"[**1**] On October 21, 2019, the Republic of Colombia [. . .] submitted [. . .] a request for an advisory opinion on "indefinite presidential reelection in the context of the inter-American human rights system"[. . .]. [**5**] Through notes dated February 17, 2020, the Secretariat of the Court [. . .] transmitted the query to the other Member States of the Organization of American States [. . .], the Secretary General of the OAS, the President of the Permanent Council of the OAS, the President of the Inter-American Juridical Committee and the Inter- American Commission on Human Rights [. . .]. These communications indicated that the Presidency of the Court, in consultation with the Court, had set May 18, 2020 as the deadline for submitting written observations [. . .]. Finally, an open invitation was issued through the Court's website to all interested parties to present their written opinions on the points raised for consultation. [**8**] The public hearing was held on September 28, 29, and 30, 2020, in the framework of the 137th regular sessions of the Inter-American Court of Human Rights [. . .]."

[Paras. 1, 5, 8]

II.

II.2.111   OBJECTIONS TO JURISDICTION

            See also: I.8.0; I.8.1; II.2.021; II.4.0; II.4.2

"[**15**] The consultation submitted to the Court by the requesting State is covered by the [. . .] Article 64(1) of the Convention. Colombia is a member State of the OAS and is therefore authorized, under the Convention, to request an advisory opinion from the Inter-American Court. [**21**] [. . .] [T]he Court finds that Colombia fulfilled its duty to specify the provisions of the American Convention, the OAS Charter, the American Declaration, and the Democratic Charter that require interpretation in accordance with the State's

* Summaries prepared by Juan Francisco Moreno-Domínguez, lawyer and doctoral student at Faculty of Law, University of Huelva, Spain. Text of Advisory Opinion available online at the Court's Web site <https://www.corteidh.or.cr/>. Original: Spanish. Footnotes appearing in the original text have been omitted.

** This is not a faithful reproduction of the Table of Contents of the Judgment.

consultation. [**25**] [...] [T]he Court finds it has competence to rule on the questions posed by Colombia. [**30**] [...] [T]he Court is empowered to rule in its advisory capacity on the preamble and all the provisions of the American Convention, the OAS Charter, the American Declaration, and the Democratic Charter [...] as they concern the protection of human rights in the American States and therefore fall within the jurisdiction of the Court. [**34**] [...] [T]he Court finds [...] that it is appropriate to proceed with consideration of the substantive object of this request [...]."

[**Paras. 15, 21, 25, 30, 34**]

III.

I.8.54   RIGHT TO PARTICIPATE IN GOVERNMENT

See also: I.0.134; I.1.01; I.1.012; I.2.24; I.8.33; I.8.4; I.8.53; I.8.64; II.7.6; II.7.641

"[**44**] The mere existence of a democratic regime does not guarantee, *per se*, permanent respect for international law, including international human rights law [...]. [...] [T]he existence of a true democratic regime is determined by both its formal and substantive characteristics. [...] [**46**] The interdependence between democracy, the rule of law, and the protection of human rights is the basis of the entire system of which the Convention forms part. [**57**] One of the ways in which the inter-American system ensures the strengthening of democracy and political pluralism is through the protection of the political rights enshrined in Article XX of the American Declaration and Article 23 of the Convention. [...] [**61**] Citizens have the right to actively participate in the conduct of public affairs, directly through referendums, plebiscites, or consultations, or through freely chosen representatives. The right to vote is an essential element of democracy and one of the ways in which citizens freely express their will and exercise their right to participate in government. [...] [**62**] [...] [P]olitical participation by exercising the right to be elected presupposes that citizens can run as candidates on equal terms and that they can hold public office subject to election [...]. [**63**] The right and opportunity to vote and to be elected enshrined in Article 23(1)(b) of the American Convention is exercised in genuine periodic elections, conducted through universal and equal suffrage [...]. [**67**] According to the Inter-American Democratic Charter, "Essential elements of representative democracy include, *inter alia*, respect for human rights and fundamental freedoms, access to and the exercise of power in accordance with the rule of law, the holding of periodic, free, and fair elections [...]. [**72**] The Democratic Charter, Article 23 of the American Convention, and Article XX of the American Declaration all establish an obligation to hold regular elections. [...] This obligation to hold regular elections indirectly implies that the terms of office of the Presidency of the Republic must have a fixed period. Presidents cannot be elected for indefinite terms. This Court highlights that the majority of the States Parties to the Convention include time limitations on the President's term. [**73**] This prohibition on indefinite terms in office aims to prevent people who hold popularly-elected office from keeping themselves in power. [...] [**75**] [...] [T]his Court finds that it is possible to conclude from the obligation to hold periodic elections [...] that the principles of representative democracy [...] include the obligation to prevent a person from remaining perpetually in power. [**79**] [...] Articles 3 and 4 of the Inter-American Democratic Charter emphasize that [...] power must be accessed and exercised subject to and under the rule of law. Democratic life is only possible if all parties respect the limits imposed by law [...] such as limits on the length of presidential terms. [...] [**84**] [...] [T]his Court finds that the principles of representative democracy include [...] the obligation to prevent a person from remaining in power and to guarantee the rotation of power and the separation of powers. [**87**] This Court notes that most of the States Parties to the American Convention have adopted a presidential political system. [...] [**90**] [...] [T]he legal systems of most OAS member States place limits on presidential reelection in presidential systems. [...] [**92**] In the framework of the inter-American system [...] "presidential reelection without term limits" is not expressly protected as an autonomous right. [...] [**94**] Regarding international treaties, [...] there is no mention of presidential reelection without term limits in the OAS Charter or the Inter-American Democratic Charter, or in any human rights treaty in the region. There is also no explicit reference [...] as a human right in international human rights treaties in the universal, European, or African systems. [**97**] [W]ith respect to regional customary international law, it must be analyzed whether there is evidence of a practice generally accepted as law. Thus, in its jurisprudence, the Court has resorted to the analysis of the legislation and internal jurisprudence of OAS member States to establish State practice. [**98**] [T]he majority of the OAS member States place restrictions on presidential reelection [...]. Only four States lack limits on the number and frequency of presidential reelections, [...] (Bolivia, Honduras, Nicaragua, and Venezuela). [...] [**99**] [...] Consequently, there is not enough of a State practice at a regional level with regard to the alleged human right to presidential reelection without term limits. [...] On the contrary, the States of the region have assumed the obligation to guarantee that their system of government is a representative democracy, and one of the principles of this system of government is to guarantee rotation of power and prevent a person from holding onto it [...]. [...] [T]he Court rules out the customary recognition of presidential reelection without term limits as an autonomous right. Likewise [...] its recognition as a general principle of law must also be ruled out. [**102**] [...] [T]his Court concludes that "presidential reelection without term limits" does not constitute an autonomous right protected by the American Convention or by the *corpus iuris* of international human rights law. [...] [**104**] The Court notes that the prohibition on presidential reelection without term limits constitutes a restriction on the right to be elected. In this sense, the Court recalls that political rights are not absolute. Their exercise may be subject to regulations or restrictions. However, the power to regulate or restrict rights is not discretionary. Rather, it is limited by international law, which requires compliance with certain requirements, and if they are not respected, the restriction is illegitimate and in violation of the American Convention. [...] [**119**] The Court considers that prohibiting presidential reelection without term limits has a purpose in accordance with Article 32 of the Convention, as it seeks to guarantee representative democracy by serving as a safeguard of the essential elements of democracy established in Article 3 of the Inter-American Democratic Charter. [...] [**126**] Therefore, the Court concludes that prohibiting reelection without term limits is compatible with the American Convention, the American Declaration, and the Inter-American Democratic Charter. [**131**] [...] [T]he Court notes that establishing a set time period for a popularly-elected president to serve in office is one of the main characteristics of presidential systems [...]. [**146**] [...] [I]t must be concluded that enabling indefinite presidential reelection is contrary to the principles of a representative democracy and [...] to the obligations established in the American Convention and American Declaration of the Rights and Duties of Man."

[**Paras. 44, 46, 57, 61, 62, 63, 67, 72, 73, 75, 79, 84, 87, 90, 92, 94, 97, 98, 99, 102, 104, 119, 126, 131, 146**]

IV.

II.4.3   ADVISORY OPINION
                   See also: II.7.641

"**[149]**
[...]
THE COURT,
DECIDES,
by five votes in favor and two opposed, that:

    1. It is competent to issue this Advisory Opinion [...].
        AND IS OF THE OPINION
        by five votes in favor and two opposed, that:
    2. Presidential reelection without term limits does not constitute an autonomous right
        protected by the American Convention on Human Rights or by the *corpus iuris* of
        international human rights law.
    3. Prohibiting reelection without term limits is compatible with the American
        Convention on Human Rights, the American Declaration of the Rights and Duties
        of Man, and the Inter-American Democratic Charter.
    4. Enabling presidential reelection without term limits is contrary to the principles
        of representative democracy and, therefore, to the obligations established in the
        American Convention on Human Rights and the American Declaration of the
        Rights and Duties of Man. [...]"

[Para. 149]

VIII.2.4

Caso Bedoya Lima y Otras vs. Colombia, Fondo, Reparaciones y Costas, Sentencia de 26 de Agosto de 2021, Serie C No. 431*

Contents**

I.

II.2.0 INSTITUTION AND COURSE OF PROCEEDINGS
See also: I.8.33; II.7.62

"[**1**] [...] El 6 de septiembre de 2019 la Comisión Interamericana de Derechos Humanos (en adelante "la Comisión Interamericana", "la Comisión") sometió a la jurisdicción de la Corte Interamericana el caso "Bedoya Lima y otra" contra la República de Colombia (en adelante "el Estado de Colombia", "el Estado colombiano", "el Estado" o "Colombia"). La Comisión señaló que el caso se relaciona con una serie de alegadas violaciones de derechos humanos derivadas del secuestro, tortura y violación sexual de la periodista [...] por motivos vinculados a su profesión y la alegada falta de adopción de medidas adecuadas y oportunas por parte del Estado para protegerla y prevenir la ocurrencia de dichos hechos. [...] [S]olicitó que se declarara al Estado responsable por la violación de los derechos establecidos en los artículos 4.1, 5.1, 5.2, 7, 8.1, 11, 13, 22, 24 y 25.1 de la Convención Americana en relación con las obligaciones establecidas en el artículo 1.1 del mismo instrumento en perjuicio de la señora Bedoya. [...][C]oncluyó que el Estado es responsable por la violación de los artículos 7.b de la Convención Interamericana para prevenir y erradicar la violencia contra la mujer (en adelante la "Convención de Belém do Pará") y 1, 6 y 8 de la Convención Interamericana para Prevenir y Sancionar la Tortura (en adelante "la CIPST") en perjuicio de la señora Bedoya. [S]olicitó que se declarara la responsabilidad internacional del Estado por la violación del derecho a la integridad personal consagrado en el artículo 5.1 de la Convención Americana, en conexión con el artículo 1.1 de dicho instrumento en perjuicio de la señora Luz Nelly Lima, madre de la señora Bedoya. [**5**] [...] El sometimiento del caso [...] fue notificado por la Corte a la representación de las presuntas víctimas (en adelante "las representantes") y al Estado el 27 de septiembre de 2019. [**14**] La Corte [...] es competente para conocer del presente caso, en los términos del artículo 62.3 de la Convención Americana, en razón de que Colombia es Estado Parte

---

 * Summaries prepared by Yolanda Gamarra, Ph.D., Full Professor of Public International Law and International Relations, Faculty of Law, University of Zaragoza, Spain, E-mail: gamarra@unizar.es. Text of the decision available at the Inter American Court's Web site <https://www.corteidh.or.cr>. Original: Spanish. Footnotes appearing in the original text have been omitted.

** This is not a faithful reproduction of the Table of Contents of the Judgment.

de dicho instrumento desde el 31 de julio de 1973 y reconoció la competencia contenciosa de la Corte el 21 de junio de 1985. Colombia depositó el instrumento de adhesión de la Convención de Belém do Pará el 15 de noviembre de 1995 y el instrumento de adhesión de la Convención Interamericana para prevenir y sancionar la tortura el 19 de enero de 1999."

[Paras. 1, 5, 14]

II.

I.8.45   RIGHT TO A FAIR TRIAL AND AN EFFECTIVE REMEDY
See also: I.8.42; I.8.44; I.8.55; I.8.56; I.8.551; I.8.561; II.0.6

"[81] El presente caso se relaciona con (i) los hechos ocurridos el 25 de mayo de 2000 en perjuicio de la señora Bedoya y la investigación y procedimientos judiciales posteriores, (ii) la alegada falta de debida diligencia en la investigación de las amenazas previas y posteriores a dicha fecha sufridas por la señora Bedoya y su madre, Luz Nelly Lima, así como (iii) las afectaciones de todo lo anterior a la integridad personal de la señora Luz Nelly Lima. [105] [...] [E]l Tribunal concluye que el Estado incurrió en responsabilidad internacional, en incumplimiento de sus deberes de respeto y garantía, por la interceptación y secuestro de la señora Bedoya el 25 de mayo de 2000, lo cual supuso una violación de sus derechos a la integridad personal y libertad personal, reconocidos en los artículos 5.1 y 7 de la Convención Americana, en relación con las obligaciones establecidas en el artículo 1.1 del mismo instrumento, así como el artículo 7.a y 7.b de la Convención de Belém do Pará. Asimismo, el Estado también es responsable por los actos de tortura a los que fue sometida la señora Bedoya, en violación de los artículos 5.2 y 11 de la Convención Americana, en relación con las obligaciones contenidas en el artículo 1.1 del mismo instrumento, el artículo 7.a y 7.b de la Convención de Belém do Pará y los artículos 1 y 6 de la CIPST. [114] [...] [L]a Corte concluye que Colombia violó la obligación de respetar y garantizar el derecho a la libertad de pensamiento y de expresión de la señora Bedoya, consagrado en el artículo 13 de la Convención Americana, en relación con el artículo 1.1 de dicho tratado. [115] En virtud del análisis y las determinaciones realizadas [...], la Corte concluye que el Estado es responsable por la violación de los artículos 5.1 y 7 de la Convención Americana, en relación con las obligaciones contenidas en el artículo 1.1 del mismo instrumento, y el artículo 7.a y 7.b de la Convención de Belém do Pará. [...] [E]l Estado es responsable por la violación de los artículos 5.2 y 11 de la Convención Americana en relación con las obligaciones contenidas en el artículo 1.1 del mismo instrumento, el artículo 7.a y 7.b de la Convención de Belém do Pará y los artículos 1 y 6 de la CIPST por la violencia sexual a la que se vio sometida la señora Bedoya. Estas violaciones tuvieron, además, un impacto en el derecho a la libertad de pensamiento y expresión de la señora Bedoya, por lo cual el Estado es responsable por la violación del artículo 13 de la Convención Americana, en relación con las obligaciones recogidas en el artículo 1.1 del mismo instrumento."

[Paras. 81, 105, 114, 115]

III.

II.0.8   SOUND ADMINISTRATION OF JUSTICE
See also: I.8.61; I.8.59

"[140] [...] [E]l Tribunal concluye que la investigación penal por los hechos ocurridos el 25 de mayo de 2000 tuvo un carácter discriminatorio por razón de género. [146] [...] [E]l

Tribunal concluye que Colombia también violó el plazo razonable por la investigación y judicialización de los referidos hechos ocurridos el 25 de mayo de 2000. [147] [...] [L]a Corte concluye que el Estado violó los derechos a las garantías judiciales y a la protección judicial establecidos en los artículos 8.1 y 25.1 de la Convención Americana, en relación con los artículos 1.1 y 24 de dicho tratado, así como el artículo 7.b de la Convención de Belém do Pará, en perjuicio de la señora Bedoya. [153] [...] [L]a Corte concluye que la falta de investigación de las amenazas recibidas por la señora Bedoya, al menos desde el año 1999 en que estas fueron puestas en conocimiento del Estado, constituyó una violación de los artículos 8.1 y 25.1 de la Convención Americana, en conexión con los artículos 1.1, 5.1, 11 y 13 de la misma, en perjuicio de la señora Jineth Bedoya. Asimismo, en vista de las circunstancias en las que tuvieron lugar dichas violaciones y del reconocimiento parcial de responsabilidad internacional realizado por el Estado sobre este particular, el Tribunal concluye que lo anterior conllevó también una violación de los artículos 1, 6 y 8 de la CIPST. [...] [E]l Tribunal concluye que la falta de investigación del ataque dirigido hacia la señora Bedoya en la que resultó herida su madre, la señora Luz Nelly Lima, constituyó una violación de los artículos 5, 11, 8 y 25 de la Convención Americana, en relación con el artículo 1.1 de la misma, en perjuicio de la señora Luz Nelly Lima."

[**Paras. 140, 146, 147, 153**]

IV.

I.8.43 RIGHT TO HUMANE TREATMENT

See also: I.8.37; I.8.451; I.8.12; I.8.04; I.8.45; II.0.8

"[**162**] [...] [E]ste Tribunal considera que, como consecuencia directa de los hechos de violencia en contra de su hija, por acompañarla durante más de dos décadas en su búsqueda de justicia y que los hechos continúen en una impunidad parcial y por las amenazas que incluso en la actualidad recibe su hija, la señora Lima padeció y padece un profundo sufrimiento y angustia en detrimento de su integridad psíquica y moral, en violación del artículo 5.1 de la Convención Americana, en relación con el artículo 1.1 del mismo instrumento."

[**Para. 162**]

V.

II.7.67 IACtHR PROCEEDINGS ON REPARATIONS

"[**175**] La Corte estima [...] que el Estado debe publicar [...] a) el resumen oficial de la presente Sentencia elaborado por la Corte, por una sola vez, en el Diario Oficial en un tamaño de letra legible y adecuado; b) el resumen oficial de la presente Sentencia elaborado por la Corte, por una sola vez, en un diario de amplia circulación nacional en un tamaño de letra legible y adecuado, y c) la presente Sentencia en su integridad, disponible por un período de un año, en un sitio *web* oficial del Estado.[...] [**189**] Esta Corte valora de manera positiva los esfuerzos llevados a cabo por el Estado para capacitar al personal de justicia con perspectiva de género y en investigación del delito de amenazas. Sin embargo, estima pertinente ordenar al Estado crear e implementar, en el plazo de dos años, un plan de capacitación y sensibilización a funcionarios públicos, fuerzas de seguridad y operadores de justicia para garantizar que cuenten con los conocimientos necesarios para identificar actos y manifestaciones de violencia contra las mujeres basadas en el género que afectan a las mujeres periodistas, protegerlas en situación de peligro e investigar y enjuiciar a los perpetradores, incluida a través de la provisión de herramientas y capacitación sobre aspectos técnicos y jurídicos de este tipo de delitos."

[Paras. 175, 189]

VI.

II.2.5   JUDGMENT/DECISION/ORDER
             See also: I.8.1; I.8.451; I.8.44

"**[224]** [...]
LA CORTE
Por unanimidad,
DECIDE,
   1. Aceptar el reconocimiento de responsabilidad internacional efectuado por el Estado, en los términos de los párrafos 24 a 31 de la presente Sentencia.
      DECLARA,
      Por unanimidad, que:
   2. El Estado es responsable por la violación de los artículos 5.1, 5.2, 7, 11 y 13 de la Convención Americana sobre Derechos Humanos, en relación con las obligaciones contenidas en el artículo 1.1 del mismo instrumento, el artículo 7.a y 7.b de la Convención de Belém do Pará y los artículos 1 y 6 de la Convención Interamericana para Prevenir y Sancionar la Tortura, en perjuicio de la señora Jineth Bedoya Lima, en los términos de los párrafos 86 a 115 de la presente Sentencia.
   3. El Estado es responsable por la violación de los artículos 8.1 y 25.1 de la Convención Americana sobre Derechos Humanos, en relación con los artículos 1.1 y 24 de dicho tratado, así como el artículo 7.b de la Convención de Belém do Pará, en perjuicio de la señora Jineth Bedoya Lima, en los términos de los párrafos 125 a 147 de la presente Sentencia.
   4. El Estado es responsable por la violación de los artículos 8.1 y 25.1 de la Convención Americana sobre Derechos Humanos, en relación con los artículos 1.1, 5.1, 11 y 13 de dicho tratado, así como de los artículos 1, 6 y 8 de la Convención Interamericana para Prevenir y Sancionar la Tortura, en perjuicio de la señora Jineth Bedoya Lima, en los términos de los párrafos 148 a 153 de la presente Sentencia.
   5. El Estado es responsable por la violación de los artículos 5, 11, 8 y 25 de la Convención Americana sobre Derechos Humanos, en relación con el artículo 1.1 de dicho instrumento, en perjuicio de la señora Luz Nelly Lima, en los términos de los párrafos 148 a 153 de la presente Sentencia.
   6. El Estado es responsable por la violación del artículo 5.1 de la Convención Americana sobre Derechos Humanos, en relación con el artículo 1.1 de dicho instrumento, en perjuicio de la señora Luz Nelly Lima [...].
      Y DISPONE:
      Por unanimidad, que:
   7. Esta Sentencia constituye, por sí misma, una forma de reparación.
   8. El Estado promoverá y continuará [...] las investigaciones que sean necesarias para determinar, juzgar y, en su caso, sancionar a los restantes responsables de los actos de violencia y tortura que sufrió la señora Jineth Bedoya el 25 de mayo de 2000 [...].
   9. El Estado promoverá y continuará [...] las investigaciones que sean necesarias para determinar, juzgar y, en su caso, sancionar a los responsables de los actos de amenazas

que ha sufrido la señora Bedoya con anterioridad y posterioridad a los hechos del 25 de mayo de 2000, así como a los responsables del ataque recibido por la señora Jineth Bedoya y su madre, la señora Luz Nelly Lima, el 27 de mayo de 1999 [...].

10. El Estado adoptará todas las medidas necesarias para que en el curso de estas investigaciones y procesos se garantice la vida, integridad personal y seguridad de la señora Jineth Bedoya y su madre, la señora Luz Nelly Lima [...].

12. El Estado deberá garantizar la difusión del programa tras-media "No es hora de callar" [...].

14. El Estado creará e implementará [...] un plan de capacitación y sensibilización a funcionarios públicos, fuerzas de seguridad y operadores de justicia para garantizar que cuenten con los conocimientos necesarios para identificar actos y manifestaciones de violencia contras las mujeres basadas en el género que afectan a las mujeres periodistas, protegerlas en situación de peligro e investigar y enjuiciar a los perpetradores [...].

15. El Estado creará el "Centro Investigativo No es Hora de Callar", centro de memoria y dignificación de todas las mujeres víctimas de violencia sexual en el marco del conflicto armado y del periodismo investigativo con un reconocimiento específico a la labor de las mujeres periodistas [...].

16. El Estado diseñará inmediatamente e implementará [...] un sistema de recopilación de datos y cifras vinculadas a los casos de violencia contra periodistas, así como de violencia basada en género contra mujeres periodistas [...].

17. El Estado creará un Fondo destinado a la financiación de programas dirigidos a la prevención, protección y asistencia de mujeres periodistas víctimas de violencia basada en el género [...].

18. El Estado pagará las cantidades fijadas en [...] la presente Sentencia [...].

19. El Estado reintegrará al Fondo de Asistencia Legal de Víctimas de la Corte Interamericana de Derechos Humanos la cantidad erogada durante la tramitación del presente caso [...].

20. El Estado, dentro del plazo de un año contado a partir de la notificación de esta Sentencia, rendirá al Tribunal un informe sobre las medidas adoptadas para cumplir con la misma.

21. La Corte supervisará el cumplimiento íntegro de esta Sentencia [...]."

[**Para. 224**]

VIII.2.5

Caso Pueblos Indígenas Maya Kaqchikel de Sumpango y Otros vs. Guatemala, Fondo, Reparaciones y Costas, Sentencia de 6 de Octubre de 2021, Serie C No. 440*

Contents**

    I. PROCEDURE AND FACTS

    II. PROTECTION OF RIGHTS AND JUDICIAL GUARANTEES

    III. REPARATIONS

    IV. JUDGMENT

I.

II.2.0   INSTITUTION AND COURSE OF PROCEEDINGS
             See also: I.8.33; II.7.6; II.7.62

"[1] [. . .] El 3 de abril de 2020 la Comisión Interamericana de Derechos Humanos (en adelante "la Comisión Interamericana" o "la Comisión") sometió a la jurisdicción de la Corte Interamericana, de conformidad con los artículos 51 y 61 de la Convención Americana, el caso *Pueblos Indígenas Maya Kaqchikel de Sumpango y otros respecto de la República de Guatemala* (en adelante "el Estado", "el Estado de Guatemala", o "Guatemala"). [. . .] [L]a controversia se relaciona con la supuesta imposibilidad de cuatro comunidades indígenas de Guatemala [. . .] de ejercer libremente su derecho a la libertad de expresión y sus derechos culturales a través de sus radios comunitarias. Ello, debido a la existencia de obstáculos legales para acceder a frecuencias radiales, así como de una alegada política de criminalización de la radiodifusión comunitaria operada sin autorización. Asimismo, el caso trata sobre la supuesta falta de reconocimiento legal de los medios comunitarios y el alegado mantenimiento de normas discriminatorias que regulan la radiodifusión. La Comisión concluyó que la normativa interna y la falta de adopción de medidas afirmativas para el acceso en igualdad de condiciones a las frecuencias de radiodifusión, en beneficio de los pueblos indígenas, violó la libertad de expresión, la igualdad ante la ley y los derechos culturales, reconocidos en los artículos 13, 24 y 26 de la Convención Americana, en relación con los artículos 1.1 y 2 del mismo instrumento. Asimismo, la Comisión determinó que la criminalización de la operación de dos radios comunitarias indígenas [. . .] violó el derecho a la libertad de expresión, recogido en el artículo 13 de la Convención Americana, en relación con el artículo 1.1 del mismo tratado, en perjuicio de las comunidades indígenas [. . .]. [3] [. . .][L]a Comisión sometió ante la Corte Interamericana la totalidad de los hechos y las alegadas violaciones de derechos humanos [. . .]. [4] [. . .][L]a Comisión solicitó a este Tribunal que concluyera y declarara la responsabilidad internacional del Estado por las violaciones [. . .] y ordenara al Estado las medidas de reparación [. . .]."

[Paras. 1, 3, 4]

---

* Summaries prepared by Yolanda Gamarra, Ph.D., Full Professor of Public International Law and International Relations, Faculty of Law, University of Zaragoza, Spain, E-mail: gamarra@unizar.es. Text of the decision available at the Inter American Court's Web site <https://www.corteidh.or.cr>. Original: Spanish. Footnotes appearing in the original text have been omitted.
** This is not a faithful reproduction of the Table of Contents of the Judgment.

II.

I.8.45   RIGHT TO A FAIR TRIAL AND AN EFFECTIVE REMEDY
See also: I.8.55; I.8.551; I.8.56; I.8.61; I.8.561; I.8.64

"[77] [. . .] [L]a Corte entiende pertinente dividir el análisis de las alegadas violaciones de la siguiente forma: en primer lugar, examinará el impacto de la regulación de la radiodifusión en Guatemala para los derechos a la libertad de expresión, a la igualdad ante la ley y a participar en la vida cultural [. . .], y en segundo lugar, la alegada violación del artículo 13.2 de la Convención Americana, en relación con los allanamientos de las radios comunitarias [. . .] y la persecución penal de sus operadores [. . .]. [79] [. . .] [L]a Corte viene reconociendo la libertad de expresión como una piedra angular en la existencia misma de una sociedad democrática [. . .].[80] La Corte ha reiterado que el derecho a la libertad de pensamiento y de expresión tiene una dimensión individual [. . .] así como una dimensión social [. . .]. [82] En lo concerniente a la dimensión social del referido derecho, el Tribunal ha establecido que la libertad de expresión es un medio para el intercambio de ideas e informaciones entre las personas [. . .] ha señalado que, para el ciudadano común, el conocimiento de la opinión ajena o de la información de que disponen otros es tan importante como el derecho a difundir la propia. [83] La Corte ha resaltado la importancia del pluralismo en el marco del ejercicio del derecho a la libertad de expresión al señalar que éste implica la tolerancia y el espíritu de apertura, sin los cuales no existe una sociedad democrática. [. . .] [112] Este Tribunal ha reconocido la potestad y necesidad que tienen los Estados de regular la actividad de radiodifusión [. . .]. [117] [. . .][L]a Corte considera que, para garantizar el derecho a la libertad de expresión, los Estados están obligados a adoptar medidas que permitan el acceso al espectro radioeléctrico a distintos sectores sociales que reflejen el pluralismo existente en la sociedad. En materia de radiodifusión sonora, esta obligación estatal se materializa mediante la adopción de medidas que permitan el acceso al espectro radioeléctrico de las radios comunitarias [. . .]. [130] La Corte considera que la naturaleza y alcance de las obligaciones que derivan de la protección de la participación en la vida cultural de los pueblos indígenas, incluyen aspectos que tienen una exigibilidad inmediata, así como aspectos que tienen un carácter progresivo. [. . .] [L]a Corte recuerda que, en relación con las primeras (obligaciones de exigibilidad inmediata), los Estados deben garantizar que este derecho se ejerza sin discriminación, así como adoptar medidas eficaces para su plena realización. Respecto a las segundas (obligaciones de carácter progresivo), la realización progresiva significa que los Estados partes tienen la obligación concreta y constante de avanzar lo más expedita y eficazmente posible hacia la plena efectividad de dicho derecho, en la medida de sus recursos disponibles, por vía legislativa u otros medios apropiados. Asimismo, se impone la obligación de no regresividad frente a la realización de los derechos alcanzados. [. . .] [131] [. . .][L] a Corte nota que el presente caso se refiere a las obligaciones de exigibilidad inmediata derivadas del artículo de 26 de la Convención en lo que respecta a la falta de garantía del derecho de los pueblos indígenas a participar en la vida cultural sin discriminación al no poder acceder a los medios de comunicación necesarios para ello. [. . .] [156] [. . .][L] a Corte considera que [. . .] el Estado es responsable por la violación de los derechos a la libertad de expresión, a la igualdad ante la ley y a participar en la vida cultural, establecidos en los artículos 13, 24 y 26 de la Convención Americana, en relación con las obligaciones de respetar y garantizar los derechos sin discriminación y el deber de adoptar disposiciones de derecho interno, contenidas en los artículos 1.1 y 2 del mismo instrumento, en perjuicio de los pueblos indígenas [. . .]. [157] La Corte se ha manifestado reiteradamente en el sentido de que las limitaciones a la libertad de expresión deben ser necesarias en una sociedad democrática, proporcionales e idóneas para el logro de los objetivos que persiguen. [**172**] [...] [L]a Corte concluye que el Estado es responsable por la violación del artículo 13.2 de la Convención Americana, en relación con el artículo 1.1 del mismo instrumento, en perjuicio de los pueblos indígenas [...]."

[**Paras. 77, 79, 80, 82, 83, 112, 117, 130, 131, 156, 157, 172**]

III.

II.7.67   IACtHR PROCEEDINGS ON REPARATIONS

"[**184**] [...][L]a Corte estima pertinente ordenar al Estado que adopte las medidas necesarias para [...] permitir que las cuatro comunidades indígenas [...] puedan operar libremente sus radios comunitarias, sin interferencia o persecución penal.[...] [**185**] La Corte dispone [...] que el Estado publique [...]: a) el resumen oficial de la Sentencia elaborado por la Corte, por una sola vez, en el Diario Oficial y en otro diario de amplia circulación nacional, con un tamaño de letra legible y adecuado, en español, así como en los principales idiomas maya utilizados por las comunidades indígenas declaradas víctimas en este Sentencia y b) la presente Sentencia en su integridad [...] en un sitio *web* oficial del Estado y en la página *web* de la Superintendencia de Telecomunicaciones de Guatemala, de manera accesible al público y desde la página de inicio del sitio *web*.[...] [**196**] [...] [L]a Corte estima que el Estado debe, en un plazo razonable, adecuar la normativa interna con fines de: (i) reconocer a las radios comunitarias como medios diferenciados de comunicación, particularmente las radios comunitarias indígenas; (ii) reglamentar su operación, estableciendo un procedimiento sencillo para la obtención de licencias, y (iii) reservar a las radios comunitarias indígenas una parte adecuada y suficiente del espectro radioeléctrico. [**202**] [...] [E]ste Tribunal estima pertinente ordenar al Estado que se abstenga inmediatamente de enjuiciar criminalmente por el delito de hurto a los individuos que operan emisoras de radio comunitarias indígenas, y las medidas consecuentes de allanar dichas radios y aprehender sus equipos de trasmisión [...]. [**203**] [...][L]a Corte ordena que el Estado [...] elimine las condenas dictadas contra las personas miembros de comunidades indígenas, y cualquiera de sus consecuencias, relacionadas con el uso del espectro radioeléctrico [...]. [**212**] La Corte considera que los montos determinados en equidad compensan y forman parte de la reparación integral a las víctimas, tomando en consideración los sufrimientos y aflicciones que padecieron."

[**Paras. 184, 185, 196, 202, 203, 212**]

IV.

II.2.5   JUDGMENT/DECISION/ORDER
    See also: I.8.1; I.8.45; I.8.451; I.8.56; I.8.551; I.8.12

"[**228**] [...]
LA CORTE
DECLARA,
Por cinco votos a favor y uno en contra, que:
1. El Estado es responsable por la violación de los derechos a la libertad de expresión, la igualdad ante la ley y a participar en la vida cultural, establecidos en los artículos 13, 24 y 26 de la Convención Americana sobre Derechos Humanos, en relación con las obligaciones de respetar y garantizar los derechos sin discriminación y el deber

de adoptar disposiciones de derecho interno, contenidos en los artículos 1.1 y 2 del mismo instrumento, en perjuicio de los pueblos indígenas [...].

Disiente el Juez Eduardo Vio Grossi.

Por unanimidad, que:

2. El Estado es responsable por la violación del derecho a la libertad de expresión, reconocido en el artículo 13.2 de la Convención Americana sobre Derechos Humanos, en relación con las obligaciones de respeto y garantía, previstas en el artículo 1.1 del mismo tratado, en perjuicio de los pueblos indígenas [...].

Y DISPONE:

Por unanimidad, que:

3. Esta Sentencia constituye, por sí misma, una forma de reparación.

   [...]

10. El Estado rendirá al Tribunal un informe, dentro del plazo de un año contado a partir de la notificación de la Sentencia, sobre las medidas adoptadas para cumplir con la misma [...]."

[**Para. 228**]

VIII.2.6
Case of Manuela et al. v. El Salvador, Preliminary Objections, Merits, Reparations and Costs, Judgment, 2 November 2021, Series C No. 441*

Contents**

I. BACKGROUND

II. ALLEGED VIOLATION OF RIGHTS TO LIFE, PERSONAL LIBERTY, JUDICIAL GUARANTEES, PRIVACY, EQUALITY BEFORE THE LAW, JUDICIAL PROTECTION AND HEALTH

III. JUDGMENT

I.

II.2.0   INSTITUTION AND COURSE OF PROCEEDINGS
          See also: I.8.0; I.8.33; II.1

"[1] [...] The Commission indicated that the case related to "a series of violations during the criminal proceedings that culminated in the conviction of the [presumed] victim in this case for the offense of aggravated homicide in the known context of the criminalization of abortion in El Salvador," as well as the violation of professional confidentiality, the medical attention received before and after her deprivation of liberty, and the presumed victim's death in the State's custody. The Commission concluded that the State was responsible for the violation of Manuela's rights to life, personal liberty, judicial guarantees, privacy, equality before the law, judicial protection, and health. In addition, the Commission concluded that El Salvador had violated the rights to judicial guarantees and judicial protection of Manuela's family "as a result of the total failure to investigate and clarify her death in custody." [92] What is in despite is the State's alleged responsibility for the detention, prosecution and conviction of the presumed victim for aggravated homicide following the obstetric emergency that she suffered, and also for the medical care that the presumed victim received, and the alleged violation of professional secrecy by the medical staff who attended her.[...]"

[**Paras. 1, 92**]

II.

I.8.44   RIGHT TO LIBERTY AND SECURITY
          See also: I.8.33; I.8.4; I.8.42; I.8.45

"[99] According to this Court's case law, pretrial detention is the most severe measure that can be applied to anyone charged with an offense. Consequently, it should only be applied exceptionally. To ensure that a precautionary measure that restricts liberty is not arbitrary, it is necessary that: (i) substantive presumptions exist relating to an unlawful act and to the connection of the defendant to that act; (ii) the measure that restricts liberty complies with

---

* Summaries prepared by Lucía Ione Padilla Espinosa, Ph.D. candidate in the Doctoral Program in Legal Sciences of the University of Huelva, Spain. Text of judgment available online at the Court's Web site <http://www.echr.coe.int>. Original: Spanish. Footnotes appearing in the original text have been omitted.
** This is not a faithful reproduction of the Table of Contents of the Judgment.

the four elements of the "proportionality test"; in other words, the purpose of the measure must be legitimate (compatible with the American Convention), appropriate to comply with the purpose sought, necessary, and strictly proportionate, and (iii) the decision imposing such measures must include sufficient reasoning to permit an assessment of whether they are in keeping with the aforementioned conditions.[106] [...] Since the decision to order pretrial detention was not grounded on objective circumstances that proved the procedural risk in this case, this detention was contrary to the American Convention. [110] Therefore, the Court concludes that the order of pretrial detention issued against Manuela and its continuation following review was arbitrary in violation of Articles 7(1) and 7(3) of the American Convention on Human Rights, in relation to Articles 1(1) and 2 of the Convention, because the order was issued without a statement of reasons that explained the need for it, and it was substantiated by provisions that were contrary to the Convention establishing the admissibility of automatic pretrial detention [...]. [111] Additionally, the Court has pointed out that an order for arbitrary pretrial detention may result in a violation of the presumption of innocence [...]. This Court has established that, in order to respect the presumption of innocence, when ordering measures that restrict liberty, in each specific case the State must substantiate and prove, clearly and with reasons, the existence of the aforementioned requirements stipulated by the Convention [...].[112] Taking into account that the order of pretrial detention against the presumed victim was arbitrary because it did not contain a reasoned and objective legal justification for its admissibility, and also its duration of more than five months without its pertinence having been duly reviewed by the judicial authorities, the Court declares that El Salvador violated Manuela's right to the presumption of innocence established in Article 8 (2) of the American Convention, in relation to Articles 1(1) and 2 of this instrument."

[**Paras. 99, 106, 110, 111, 112**]

I.8.45   RIGHT TO A FAIR TRIAL AND AN EFFECTIVE REMEDY
         See also: I.8.33; I.8.4; I.8.42; I.8.44; I.8.451

"[118] The Court has indicated that the right to due process refers to the series of requirements that must be met in the procedural instances to ensure that individuals are able to adequately defend their rights vis-à-vis any act of the State adopted by any policy authority, whether administrative, legislative or judicial, that could impair them. The right to defense, especially in criminal proceedings, is a central component of due process and, necessarily, it must be possible to exercise this from the moment a person is accused of being the possible perpetrator of, or participant in, an unlawful act, and only ends when the proceedings are concluded, including, if applicable, the stage of execution of the sentence. [119] In this case, a series of violations of judicial guarantees has been alleged. The Court only has sufficient evidence to examine: (1) the right to defense; (2) the use of gender stereotypes and judicial guarantees, and (3) the sentence imposed on Manuela. [130] [...] [T]he actions of the public defender harmed Manuela's rights and interests, leaving her defenseless, which constituted a violation of the essential right to be assisted by legal counsel. In addition, in this case, Manuela's substantive right to defense was also violated because she was prevented from defending her interests.[...][133] [...] Indeed, even if the use of any type of stereotype is common, it becomes harmful when it limits and individual's capacity to develop their personal abilities or becomes a violation or violations of human rights. [...] [134] The Court notes that the use of gender stereotypes in criminal proceedings may reveal a violation of the right to presumption of innocence, of the duty to provide the reasons for a decision, and of the right to be tried by an impartial court. [...] [159] [...] [T]he Court has already determined that the criminal court convicted Manuela using gender stereotypes as grounds for its decision. The application of those stereotypes was only possible because Manuela was a woman; and the impact was exacerbated because she was poor and illiterate and lived in a rural area. Therefore, the Court considers that the distinction made in the application of the criminal law was arbitrary and, consequently, discriminatory. [170] [. . .][T]he Court considers that the sentence of 30 years'imprisonment for a homicide committed by a mother during the perinatal period was disproportionate to her level of individualized blame (or guilt). Therefore, the current punishment established for infanticide is cruel and, consequently, contrary to the Convention. [173] [. . .] [T]he investigation and trial to which the presumed victim was subjected did not comply with the right to defense, the right to be tried by an impartial court, the presumption of innocence, the duty to provide the reasons for a decision, the obligation not to apply laws in a discriminatory manner, the right not to be subjected to cruel, inhuman or degrading punishment and the obligation to ensure that the purpose of punishments consisting in deprivation of liberty is the reform and social readaptation of prisoners. Consequently, the State violated Articles 8(1), 8 (2), 8(2)(d), 8(2)(e), 24, 5(2) and 5(6) of the Convention, in relation to Articles 1(1) and 2 of this instrument, to the detriment of Manuela."

[**Paras. 118, 119, 130, 133, 134, 159, 170, 173**]

I.8.42   RIGHT TO LIFE
              See also: I.8.33; I.8.4; I.8.44; I.8.45

"[**187**] In the instant case the Court must examine the State's conduct regarding compliance with its obligation to ensure respect for Manuela's rights to life, personal integrity and health.[. . .] [**201**] [. . .] [T]he Court concludes that the State failed to comply with the obligation to provide the presumed victim with acceptable and quality medical care and, consequently, this amounted to a violation of the rights to personal integrity and to health, established in Articles 5 and 26 of the American Convention. [**229**] [F]ailure to comply with the obligation to respect professional secrecy and the disclosure of Manuela's medical information constituted a violation of her rights to privacy and to health, in relation to the obligations to respect and to ensure these rights and the duty to adopt domestic legal provisions. [**245**] The Court has verified various omissions in the medical attention provided to the presumed victim. Specifically, the State failed to comply with its obligations: (i) to perform a comprehensive examination of Manuela's health when se was hospitalized; (ii) to examine her health at the time she was detained, and (iii) to take the necessary measures to ensure that Manuela could receive medical treatment while she was deprived of liberty. [. . .] [T]he Court considers that the existence of a causal nexus in this case has been proved, and this demonstrates the failure to comply with the obligation to ensure Manuela's right to life. [**260**] Based on the above, El Salvador is responsible for the violation of the rights recognized in Articles 4, 5, 11, 24 and 26 in relation to Articles 1(1) and 2 of the American Convention, to the detriment of Manuela.[. . .]"

[**Paras. 187, 201, 229, 245, 260**]

III.

II.2.5   JUDGMENT/DECISION/ORDER
              See also: I.8.33; II. 7.6; II.7.65

"[**327**] [. . .]
THE COURT
DECIDES,

Unanimously:

1. To reject the preliminary objection concerning the alleged time-barred presentation of the petition, pursuant to paragraphs 20 and 21 of this judgment.

2. To reject the preliminary objection concerning the Commission's alleged failure to assess the progress made in complying with the Merits Report, pursuant to paragraph 23 of this judgment.

DECLARES,

Unanimously, that:

3. The State is responsible for the violation of the rights to personal liberty and the presumption of innocence, pursuant to Articles 7(1), 7(3) and 8(2) of the American Convention on Human Rights, in relation to the obligations to respect and to ensure the rights and the duty to adopt domestic legal provisions established in Articles 1(1) and 2 of this instrument, to the detriment of Manuela, pursuant to paragraphs 97 to 112 of this judgment

Unanimously, that:

4. The State is responsible for the violation of the right to defense, the right to be tried by an impartial court, the presumption of innocence, the duty to provide a statement of reasons, the obligation not to apply laws in a discriminatory manner, the right not to be subjected to cruel, inhuman or degrading punishment and the obligation to ensure that the purpose of a prison sentence is the social rehabilitation and reform of those convicted, pursuant to Articles 8(1), 8(2), 8(2)(d), 8(2)(e), 24, 5(2) and 5(6) of the American Convention on Human Rights, in relation to the obligations to respect and to ensure the rights without discrimination and the duty to adopt domestic legal provisions established in Articles 1(1) and 2 of this instrument, to the detriment of Manuela, pursuant to paragraphs 118 to 173 of this judgment.

By six votes to one that:

5. The State is responsible for the violation of the rights to life, personal integrity, privacy, equality before the law and health, pursuant to Articles 4, 5, 11, 24 and 26 of the American Convention on Human Rights, in relation to the obligations to respect and to ensure the rights without discrimination and the duty to adopt domestic legal provisions established in Articles 1(1) and 2 of this instrument, and also for failing to comply with the obligations of Article 7(a) of the Inter-American Convention for the Prevention, Punishment and Eradication of Violence against Women "Convention of Belém do Pará," to the detriment of Manuela, pursuant to paragraphs 180 to 260 of this judgment.

Dissenting Judge Eduardo Vio Grossi.

Unanimously, that:

6. The State is responsible for the violation of the right to personal integrity, recognized in Article 5(1) of the American Convention on Human Rights, in relation to Article 1(1) of this instrument, to the detriment of Manuela's mother, father, elder and younger son, pursuant to paragraphs 262 to 266 of this judgment.

AND ESTABLISHES:

Unanimously, that:

7. This judgment constitutes, *per se*, a form of reparation.

Unanimously, that:

8. The State shall make the publications indicated in paragraph 273 of this judgment.

Unanimously, that:

9. The State shall hold a public act to acknowledge international responsibility, pursuant to paragraphs 276 and 277 of this judgment.

Unanimously, that:
10. The State shall grant scholarships to the Manuela's elder and younger son, pursuant to paragraph 279 of this judgment.

Unanimously, that:
11. The State shall provide, free of charge and immediately, in a prompt, adequate and effective manner, medical, psychological and/or psychiatric treatment to Manuela's parents, pursuant to paragraph 282 of this judgment.

By six votes to one that:
12. The State shall regulate the obligation of medical professional secrecy and the confidentiality of medical records, pursuant to paragraph 287 of this judgment.
Dissenting Judge Eduardo Vio Grossi.

Unanimously, that:
13. The State shall elaborate an action protocol for the treatment of women who require emergency medical attention for obstetric emergencies, pursuant to paragraph 288 of this judgment.

Unanimously, that:
14. The State shall adapt its regulations on pretrial detention, pursuant to paragraph 290 of this judgment.

By six votes to one that:
15. The State shall design and implement an awareness-raising and training course for judicial officials, as well as the health personnel of the Rosales National Hospital, as established in paragraphs 294 and 295 of this judgment.
Dissenting Judge Eduardo Vio Grossi.

Unanimously, that:
16. The State shall adapt its regulation concerning the dosimetry of the sentence for infanticide, pursuant to paragraph 296 of this judgment.

Unanimously, that:
17. The State shall design and implement an education program on sexuality and reproduction, pursuant to paragraph 298 of this judgment.
Unanimously, that:
18. The State shall take the necessary measures to ensure comprehensive care in cases of obstetric emergencies, pursuant to paragraph 300 of this judgment.

Unanimously, that:
19. The State shall pay the amounts established in paragraphs 305, 306, 310, 311 and 320 of this judgment as compensation for pecuniary and non-pecuniary damage and to reimburse costs and expenses, pursuant to paragraphs 321 to 326 of this judgment.

Unanimously, that:
20. The State, within one year of notification of this judgment, shall provide the Court with a report on the measures taken to comply with it, without prejudice to the provisions of paragraph 274 of this judgment.

Unanimously, that:
21. The Court will monitor full compliance with this judgment, in exercise of its authority and in fulfillment of its duties under the American Convention on Human Rights, and will consider this case closed when the State has complied fully with its provisions."

[Para. 327]

Systematic Key Items of the Section*

---

* *See* Systematic Classification Scheme, *supra* at page 255.

Systematic Key Terms of the Section*

* See Systematic Classification Scheme, supra at page 555.

IX

African Court on Human and Peoples' Rights

LEGAL MAXIMS: SUMMARIES AND EXTRACTS FROM SELECTED CASE LAW*

Sébastien Germain Marie Aïkoue Ajavon v. Republic of Benin, Application No. 065/2019, Judgment, 29 March 2021

Yahaya Zumo Makame and 3 Others v. United Republic of Tanzania, Application No. 023/2016, Judgment, 25 June 2021

Request for Advisory Opinion by the Pan African Lawyers Union (PALU) on the Right to Participate in the Government of One's Country in the Context of an Election Held During a Public Health Emergency or a Pandemic, Such as the Covid-19 Crisis, No. 001/2020, Advisory Opinion, 16 July 2021

Glory C. Hossou and Landry A. Adelakoun v. Republic of Benin, Application No. 016/2020, Ruling, 2 December 2021

---

* The working method chosen for the formulation of legal maxims is explained *supra* 'Outline of the Parts', at page xv.

Legal Maxims: Summaries and Extracts from Selected Case Law In: *The Global Community Yearbook of International Law and Jurisprudence 2022*. Edited by: Giuliana Ziccardi Capaldo, Oxford University Press. © Oxford University Press 2023.
DOI: 10.1093/oso/9780197752265.003.0030

IX.1.1

Sébastien Germain Marie Aïkoue Ajavon v. Republic of Benin, Application No. 065/2019, Judgment, 29 March 2021*

Contents**

I.

II.2.0   INSTITUTION AND COURSE OF PROCEEDINGS

See also: I.8.34; II.2.01; II.2.03; II.7.69; II.7.697

"[1] Mr. Sébastien Germain Marie Aïkoué AJAVON, (hereinafter referred to as "the Applicant"), a national of Benin, is a businessman, residing in Paris, France, as a political refugee. He alleges the violation of various human rights [. . .] [2] against the Republic of Benin [. . .]. [3] The Applicant contends that in a matter between him and the Respondent State, this Court issued, all in his favour, a Ruling on Provisional Measures of 7 December 2018, a Judgment on Merits of 29 March 2019 and a Judgment on Reparations of 28 November 2019. [6] The Initial Application was filed at the Registry on 29 November 2019."

[Paras. 1, 2, 3, 6]

---

* Summaries prepared by Ana Cristina Gallego Hernández, Ph.D., Associate Professor of Public International Law, University of Seville (Spain). Text of judgment available online at the Court's Web site <https://www.african-court.org/en/>. Original: French (authoritative) and English. Footnotes appearing in the original text have been omitted.

** This is not a faithful reproduction of the Table of Contents of the Judgment.

II.

I.8.34   AFRICAN CHARTER ON HUMAN AND PEOPLES' RIGHTS
           See also: I.2.04; I.8.4; I.12.37; II.7.69; II.7.695

"[**26**] [T]he instant case concerns alleged human rights violations due to non-compliance with the decisions delivered by this Court. […] [**27**] The jurisdiction of the Court in relation to such a dispute is exercised without prejudice to the prerogative conferred by Article 29(2) of the Protocol on the Executive Council of the African Union to monitor the execution of decisions rendered by the Court, on behalf of the Assembly of Heads of State and Government. [**29**] […] [T]he Court dismisses the objection regarding lack of material jurisdiction. [**30**] [If] […] there is nothing on the record to indicate that it does not have jurisdiction […] the Court […] has: i) Personal jurisdiction, insofar as the Respondent State is a Party to the Charter, the Protocol and has deposited the Declaration. […] ii) Temporal jurisdiction, insofar as the alleged violations were committed, in respect of the Respondent State, after the entry into force of the Charter and the Protocol to which the Respondent State is a party. iii) Territorial jurisdiction, in so far as the facts of the case and the alleged violations took place on the territory of the Respondent State."

[**Paras. 26, 27, 29, 30**]

III.

I.8.34   AFRICAN CHARTER ON HUMAN AND PEOPLES' RIGHTS
           See also: I.8.4; I.8.47; II.2.023; II.7.69; II.7.692

"[**39**] The Court notes that […] involving the same parties, it issued an Order on Provisional Measures […]. [**40**] [I]t cannot be disputed that the said time limits have expired […]. [**47**] The Court notes that neither the Charter, the Protocol, much less the Rules require that an Applicant be a victim of the violations alleged. [**48**] The Court stresses that this is due to a particularity of the African regional human rights system. […] [**53**] The Court points out that the Applicant has filed three (3) applications to initiate proceedings before this Court […]. [**54**] […] [T]he Court recalls that: […] Applicant files several Applications against the same Respondent State does not necessarily show a lack of good faith. [**60**] The Court emphasises that in the instant case, the Respondent State bases its objection on the victim status of the Applicant […]. However, the Court finds that neither the Charter, the Protocol, nor the Rules, contain a similar provision. [**68**] The Court reiterates that it has consistently found that the principle of *res judicata* presupposes the existence of three cumulative conditions, namely the identity of the parties, identity of the prayers or their supplementary or alternative nature, and the existence of a first decision on merits. [**74**] The Court notes that it will first examine (i) the condition relating to the exhaustion of local remedies, then (ii) the condition relating to the filing of the Application within a reasonable time, and, finally, (iii) the other conditions of admissibility provided for by Article 56 of the Charter […]. [**75**] [T]he local remedies required to be exhausted must be available, effective and adequate. [**78**] […] [I]t is not sufficient that a remedy exists to satisfy the exhaustion rule. […] [**79**] The Court recalls that the analysis of the usefulness of a remedy does not lend itself to automatic application and is not absolute. It also recalls that the interpretation of the rule of exhaustion of local remedies must realistically take into account the context of the case as well as the personal situation of the Applicant."

[**Paras. 39, 40, 47, 48, 53, 54, 60, 68, 74, 75, 78, 79**]

IV.

I.8.34   AFRICAN CHARTER ON HUMAN AND PEOPLES' RIGHTS
See also: I.8.4; I.8.47; II.2.023; II.7.69; II.7.692

"[**85**] The Court emphasises, with regard to this condition, [...] on which the Respondent State was required to file the execution report in respect of the latest judgment of which the non-execution is alleged by the Applicant. [**89**] The Court further finds that the condition set out in Rule 50(2)(b) is also met, insofar as the Application is in no way inconsistent with the Constitutive Act of the Union or the Charter. [**90**] Furthermore, the Court notes that the Application does not contain any disparaging or insulting language directed against the Respondent State [...]. [**91**] [...] [I]t is not established that the arguments of fact and law developed in the Application are based exclusively on information disseminated by the media. [**92**] Finally, the Court notes that [...] is met insofar as there is no indication that the instant case has already been settled in accordance with the principles of the Charter of the United Nations, the Constitutive Act of the African Union or the Charter."

[**Paras. 85, 89, 90, 91, 92**]

V.

I.8.34   AFRICAN CHARTER ON HUMAN AND PEOPLES' RIGHTS
See also: I.8.4; II.7.69; II.7.697

"[**102**] The Court emphasises that judicial acts include, in particular, orders for provisional measures, the binding nature of which is unanimously recognised by international jurisprudence. [**105**] The Court further notes that the term "judgment" includes all judgments rendered by the Court [...]. [**106**] The Court finds, in the present case, that all the violations alleged by the Applicant relate in one way or another, directly or indirectly, to the non-enforcement of the Order for provisional measures [...]. [**115**] The Court emphasises that the issue at stake here is not for it to determine whether or not it can call into question the constitutional order of a State. [...]"

[**Paras. 102, 105, 106, 115**]

VI.

I.8.34   AFRICAN CHARTER ON HUMAN AND PEOPLES' RIGHTS
See also: I.2.0; I.8.03; I.8.4; I.8.61; II.7.69

"[**124**] The Court considers that [...] there exists, between the protocols and agreements adopted to complement the Charter, a legal complementarity. [**125**] It follows that the violation of rights, duties and freedoms set out in any protocol or instrument adopted to supplement the Charter implies a violation of Article 1 of the Charter."

[**Paras. 124, 125**]

VII.

II.2.5   JUDGMENT/DECISION/ORDER
            See also: I.8.34; I.11.035; I.11.0354; I.11.0355; II.2.51; II.7.69

"[185] [...]
THE COURT
Unanimously,
On Jurisdiction
  i. *Dismisses* the objection based on the lack of material jurisdiction;
  ii. *Finds* that it has jurisdiction.
On Admissibility
  iii. *Dismisses* the objections based on inadmissibility;
  iv. *Finds* the Application admissible.
On Merits
  v. Finds that the Respondent State has violated Article 30 of the Protocol;
  vi. Finds that the Respondent State has violated Article 1 of the Charter. [...]
  vii. *Dismisses* the Applicant's prayer for an expert appraisal of the damages resulting from the failure to execute the Order for Provisional Measures [...];
  viii. Dismisses the request for payment of the amount of Three Hundred Billion [...] francs CFA; ix. Dismisses the Respondent State's counterclaim for payment of the amount of One Billion [...] CFA Francs as damages for abuse of process initiated by the Applicant;
  x. Awards the Applicant a symbolic amount of 1 CFA francs as reparation for moral prejudice. [...] xi. Orders the Respondent State to comply with Article 30 of the Protocol by executing the Judgment of 29 March 2019, that is, by taking all necessary measures to annul the judgment N° 007/3C.COR delivered on 18 October 2018 by the CRIET in a way to erase all its effects;
  xii. Orders the Respondent State to report to the Court within seven (7) days from the notification of this Judgment. [...]"

[Para. 185]

IX.1.2

Yahaya Zumo Makame and 3 Others v. United Republic of Tanzania,
Application No. 023/2016, Judgment, 25 June 2021*

Contents**

I.

II.2.0   INSTITUTION AND COURSE OF PROCEEDINGS

See also: I.8.0; I.8.04; I.8.1; I.8.34; I.8.45; I.8.50; I.8.61; II.2.012; II.2.013; II.2.021; II.2.023; II.2.024; II.7.69; II.7.694; II.7.695; II.7.696

"[1] Yahaya Zumo Makame, Salum Mohamed Mpakarasi and Said Ibrahim, all Tanzanian nationals, and Mohamedi Gholumgader Pourdad, a national of the Islamic Republic of Iran, (hereinafter referred to as "the Applicants") were, at the time of filing the Application, incarcerated at Maweni Central Prison, Tanga, after having been convicted and sentenced to twenty-five (25) years imprisonment each, for the offence of trafficking narcotic drugs. [2] The Application is filed against the United Republic of Tanzania [...]. [3] It emerges from the original Application that on 10 August 2012 the High Court of Tanzania sitting at Tanga convicted the Applicants [...]. [4] Dissatisfied with the High Court's decision, the Applicants appealed to the Court of Appeal of Tanzania against both their sentence and conviction. On 8 September 2015, the Court of Appeal dismissed the appeal in its entirety. [5] The Applicants contend that the Respondent State's legal system only permits one appeal from a decision of the High Court. The absence of a higher court, above the Court of Appeal, the Applicants submit, violates their right to fair trial and is contrary to Articles 3 and 7 of the Charter [...]."

[**Paras. 1, 2, 3, 4, 5**]

II.

I.8.45   RIGHT TO A FAIR TRIAL AND AN EFFECTIVE REMEDY

See also: I.8.34; I.8.50; I.8.61; II.7.69; II.7.694; II.7.695; II.7.696

"[25] The Court recalls that [...] it has jurisdiction to examine any application submitted to it, provided that the rights of which a violation is alleged are protected by the Charter or any other human rights instrument ratified by the Respondent State. [27] [...] [T]he Court notes, [...] " ... that it is not an appellate body with respect to decisions of national courts.

---

 * Summaries prepared by Adriana Fillol Mazo, Assistant Professor of Public International Law, University of Seville (Spain). Text of judgment available online at the Court's Web site <https://www.african-court. org/en/>. Original: English (authoritative) and French. Footnotes appearing in the original text have been omitted.

** This is not a faithful reproduction of the Table of Contents of the Judgment.

However, [...] " ... this does not preclude it from examining relevant proceedings in the national courts in order to determine whether they are in accordance with the standards set out in the Charter or any other human rights instruments ratified by the State concerned." [...] [**70**] The Court notes that the Applicants are making two interrelated allegations in connection to the alleged violation of their right to appeal. Firstly, they are alleging a violation due to the failure to have their sentences reviewed by a higher court beyond the Court of Appeal. Secondly, they are alleging that they were subjected to different treatment since other convicts are able to have recourse to two levels of appeal. [**74**] The Court holds that the right to an appeal or review of a decision of a lower court as provided for under Article 7 of the Charter [...] simply entails the provision of another level of judicial structures for one to have recourse to beyond the trial court. The essence of the right is that findings of a trial court should always be amenable to review by another court. The right does not prescribe the number of levels at which an appeal must be processed. [**75**] The Court thus finds that the absence of a higher court, above the Court of Appeal, is not a violation of Article 7 of the Charter [...]. [**76**] The Court further notes that the Applicants alleged, relatedly, that the fact that convicts whose trials commenced at the subordinate court level are accorded two levels of appeals is a violation of their right to equality since no similar accommodation was accorded to them.[...] [T]he Court notes that the Applicants did not demonstrate that there is any fault with the law that vests jurisdiction for different offences, either in the High Court only or in the subordinate courts only or concurrently in both the High Court and subordinate courts. Neither have the Applicants demonstrated that other people convicted for trafficking narcotic drugs are treated differently. For this reason, the Court holds that the different treatment of convicts, according to the offences for which they were convicted, does not violate the Charter and, consequently, dismisses the Applicants' allegation. [**77**] [...] [T]he Court dismisses the Applicants' allegation of a violation of their right to fair trial by reason of there being no review of their sentences by a higher court beyond the Court of Appeal. The Court also dismisses the Applicants' allegation of their differentiated treatment as compared to other convicts who are able to have recourse to two levels of appeal. [**81**] The Court observes that the question that arises here is the manner in which the Court of Appeal dealt with the evidential contentions raised by the Applicants especially whether the same were duly examined in line with Article 7(1) of the Charter. [**82**] The Court recalls its established position that examination of particulars of evidence is a matter that should be left for domestic courts. However, as further acknowledged by the Court, it may nevertheless evaluate the relevant procedures before the national courts to determine whether they conform to the standards prescribed by the Charter [...]. [**83**] [...] [T]he Court notes that the Applicants were represented by counsel before the Court of Appeal. It also notes that the Court of Appeal analysed all the grounds of appeal as filed by the Applicants together with the counter-arguments raised by the State. In terms of the grounds of appeal raised by the Applicants, the Court notes that, before the Court of Appeal, the Applicants, among other grounds, included the generic allegation that the learned trial judge grossly misdirected himself in fact and in law in convicting them against the weight of the evidence. To respond to this allegation, the Court of Appeal went into detail analysing the manner in which the Applicants were arrested and subsequently tried before the High Court. [...] [**84**] [...] The Court, therefore, holds that the manner in which Court of Appeal made its findings in respect of the Applicants' appeal did not violate Article 7 of the Charter. [...] [**90**] The Court recalls that Article 7(1)(c) of the Charter does not expressly provide for the right to be assisted by an interpreter. However, the provision should be interpreted in light of Article 14(3)(a) of the ICCPR [...]. [**91**] A joint reading of the above cited provisions, as confirmed by the Court, establishes that every accused person has the right to an interpreter if he/she cannot understand or speak the language being used in court."

[**Paras. 25, 27, 70, 74, 75, 76, 77, 81, 82, 83, 84, 90, 91**]

III.

I.8.0   PROTECTION OF HUMAN RIGHTS AND FUNDAMENTAL
          FREEDOMS
          See also: I.8.03; I.8.04; I.8.3; I.8.34; I.8.4; 1.8.45; 1.8.61

"[**95**] The Applicants submit that in the event that the Court finds violations of Articles 3 and 7 of the Charter, it should also find a violation of Article 1 of the Charter. [**98**] The Court considers that examining an alleged violation of Article 1 of the Charter involves a determination not only of whether the measures adopted by the Respondent State are available but also if these measures were implemented in order to achieve the intended object and purpose of the Charter. As a consequence, whenever a substantive right of the Charter is violated due to the Respondent State's failure to meet these obligations, Article 1 will be violated. [**99**] In the present case, the Court having found that the Respondent State has not violated any provisions of the Charter, the Court consequently finds that the Respondent State has also not violated Article 1 of the Charter."

[**Paras. 95, 98, 99**]

IV.

II.2.5   JUDGMENT/DECISION/ORDER
           See also: I.8.34; I.8.45; I.8.50; I.8.61; II.4.01; II.4.3

"[**108**] [...]
THE COURT,
Unanimously:
[...]
  i. *Dismisses* the objection to its material jurisdiction;
  ii. *Declares* that it has jurisdiction.
[...]
  iii. *Dismisses* the objections to the admissibility of the Application;
  iv. *Declares* that the Application is admissible.
[...]
  v. *Finds* that the Respondent State has not violated the Applicants' right to equality under Article 3 of the Charter;
  vi. *Finds* that the Respondent State has not violated the Applicants' right to a fair trial under Article 7 of the Charter;
  i. *Finds* that the Respondent State has not violated Article 1 of the Charter.
[...]
  ii. *Dismisses* the Applicants' prayers for reparations.
  iii. *Finds* that the request for provisional measures is moot.
[...]"

[**Para. 108**]

IX.1.3

Request for Advisory Opinion by the Pan African Lawyers Union (PALU) on the Right to Participate in the Government of One's Country in the Context of an Election Held During a Public Health Emergency or a Pandemic, Such as the Covid-19 Crisis, No. 001/2020, Advisory Opinion, 16 July 2021*

Contents*

    I. INTRODUCTION AND PROCEDURAL BACKGROUND

    II. JURISDICTION

    III. ADMISSIBILITY

    IV. RIGHT TO PARTICIPATE IN GOVERNMENT

    V. ADVISORY OPINION

I.

II.2.0   INSTITUTION AND COURSE OF PROCEEDINGS

          See also: I.8.0; I.8.34; II.2.021; II.2.22; II.2.23; II.4.0; II.4.1; II.7.69; II.7.695

"[**1**] This Request for Advisory Opinion [...] was submitted by the Pan African Lawyers Union [...]. [**3**] The Author submits that the "Covid-19 crisis presents unprecedented challenges for democratic governance and rule of law in Africa" and [...] "in response to the Covid-19 pandemic, AU Member States have mostly taken measures to protect the right to life by limiting such rights as freedoms of movement, assembly, association and information, and also the right of citizens to effectively participate in the governance of their respective states, especially [...] through regular, free and fair elections." [**9**] The Request was received at the Registry of the Court on 3 June 2020 [...]. [**11**] On 11 August 2020, the Registry notified the following entities of the filing of the Request: AU Member States; the Commission; the AU Commission; the African Committee of Experts on the Rights and Welfare of the Child; the Pan African Parliament; the Economic, Social and Cultural Council of the AU; the AU Commission on International Law; the Directorate of Women, Gender and Development of the AU; the African Institute of International Law; and the Centre for Human Rights, University of Pretoria. The Court set a ninety (90) day limit for receiving observations on the Request. [**12**] On 28 January 2021, the AU Member States and entities indicated above were given an extension of forty-five (45) days to submit their observations [...]. [...] [F]our new entities were added to the list: Electoral Law and Governance Institute for Africa, COVID-DEM, Journal of African Law and International IDEA. [**14**] By a notice dated 22 June 2021, the Author and all entities cited in paragraphs 11 and 12 above, were notified of the closure of pleadings."

[**Paras. 1, 3, 9, 11, 12, 14**]

---

* Summaries prepared by Juan Francisco Moreno-Domínguez, lawyer and doctoral student at Faculty of Law, University of Huelva, Spain. Text of judgment available online at the Court's Web site <https://www.african-court.org/en/>. Original: English (authoritative) and French. Footnotes appearing in the original text have been omitted.

** This is not a faithful reproduction of the Table of Contents of the Judgment.

II.

II.2.111   OBJECTIONS TO JURISDICTION

See also: I.2.27; I.8.0; I.8.1; II.2.021; II.4.0; II.4.2; II.7.69; II.7.692; II.7.695; II.7.6952

"[**22**] To determine whether it has personal jurisdiction, [. . .] the Request has been filed by one of the entities contemplated under Article 4(1) of the Protocol.[. . .] [**23**] The Court recalls that it has held that "an organisation may be considered as 'African' if it is registered in an African country and has branches at the subregional, regional or continental levels, and if it carries out activities beyond the country where it is registered." [**24**] [. . .] [T]he Court notes that the Author is registered in a Member State of the AU [. . .]. The Court also notes that PALU undertakes its activities beyond the territory where it is registered. [**26**] [. . .] [T]he Court finds that it has personal jurisdiction to deal with this Request. [**27**] The Author submits that "this Request for an Advisory Opinion is a legal matter, relating to the guarantees for the effective protection of the right to participate in government in the context of Covid-19 pandemic and crisis." It submits further that the Request is also sought in terms of the Constitutive Act of the AU, the Maputo Protocol and ACDEG, all of which are human rights instruments within the meaning of Article 4 of the Protocol. [**29**] The Court observes that [. . .] it is requested to give its opinion about the application of Articles 1 and 13 of the African Charter, and Articles 2(1)(2)(3)(4) (10) and (13); Articles 3(1)(4)(7)(10) and (11); Articles 4, 5, 6, 7, 12, 13, 15, 17, 24, 25; Articles 32(7)(8); Articles 38(1) and 39 of the ACDEG in relation to citizens' right to effective participation in the government of their states, especially [. . .] through regular, free and fair elections, in the context of the Covid-19 pandemic. [. . .] [T]he Court holds that it has material jurisdiction in respect of the Request."

[**Paras. 22, 23, 24, 26, 27, 29**]

III.

II.2.112   OBJECTIONS TO ADMISSIBILITY

See also: I.8.0; I.8.1; II.2.021; II.4.0; II.4.2; II.7.69; II.7.6952

"[**36**] The Court notes that the Author is well identified and that its representatives are explicitly indicated. [**38**] The Court also confirms that the Author has provided the context within which the Request arises, which is the political, economic and social crisis wrought upon Africa, and the rest of the World, by the Covid-19 pandemic and which poses serious challenges to democratic governance, the rule of law and the promotion and protection of human and peoples' rights, more generally, and the organisation of elections, more specifically. [**39**] [. . .] [T]he Court thus finds that the Request is admissible."

[**Paras. 36, 38, 39**]

IV.

I.8.54   RIGHT TO PARTICIPATE IN GOVERNMENT

See also: I.0.134; I.1.01; I.1.012; I.2.24; I.8.34; I.8.4; I.8.63; I.8.64; II.7.69; II.7.696

"[**48**] The Author avers that while the scheduling of national elections is a matter of sovereignty of State Parties, the conduct of elections is a matter of continental treaty law relating to the citizen's rights to effectively participate in the government of their countries as well as to standards of good governance enshrined in treaty law by African states. [51] The Court considers that one of the fundamental principles of democracy is the regular conduct of transparent, free and fair elections aimed at creating the conditions for the possibility of democratic alternation and [. . . .] affording the electorate the opportunity to regularly evaluate and politically sanction the performance of those elected officials, through universal suffrage. [. . .] [52] Concerning the postponement, the Court notes that, Article 13(1) of the Charter, as supplemented by Articles 2 and 3 of the ACDEG, [. . .] gives the competent bodies of each State the power to decide to postpone elections in accordance with its domestic law. [54] The Court is of the view that even though the decision to conduct or not to conduct elections, remains with the competent organs of the State concerned, because of the situation of a public health emergency or a pandemic, a consultation of health authorities and political actors, including representatives of civil society, is necessary to ensure the inclusiveness of the process. [57] The Author submits that "[i]n response to the Covid-19 pandemic, AU Member States have mostly taken measures to protect the right to life by limiting such rights as freedoms of movement, assembly, association and information, and also the right of citizens to effectively participate in the governance of their respective states, [. . .] through regular, free and fair elections." [66] The Court is of the view that conducting elections in a situation of emergency, as is the case with the Covid-19 Pandemic, a disease that is easily transmissible, including through contact between humans and between humans and contaminated objects, requires that appropriate measures be taken to prevent its transmission, without undermining the integrity of the electoral process. [73] The Court recalls that one of the specific features of the Charter is that it does not explicit have provisions for derogation of rights even in emergency situations. [. . .] [U]nder the Charter, States that choose to conduct elections during a state of emergency [. . .] are obliged to respect human rights. [. . .][T]hey must observe the provisions of Article 27(2) of the Charter, which sets out that "[t]he rights and freedoms of each individual shall be exercised with due regard to the rights of others, collective security, morality and common interest." [76] [. . .] [T]he Court restates its position that measures restricting rights must be in the form of a general law; must be proportionate; must not undermine the essential content of rights; must not derogate the rights provided for in Articles 6, 7, 8 (1) and (2), 11, 15, 16, and 18 of the ICCPR; and must not constitute a form of discrimination against persons. [80] [. . .] [T]he Court is of the view that there are some aspects which form the essential content of the right of citizens to freely participate in the government of their countries through elections. These aspects comprise the effective participation in the electoral process, including campaigning, fair and equitable access to the State controlled media; the monitoring of the electoral process by candidates, political parties and the competent voter registration public institutions; the secret ballot; participation in the process of vote counting and publication of the election results by political parties, candidates and any other relevant actors for the transparency of the elections; the possibility of contesting the results before the competent administrative and judicial bodies, if appropriate. [81] These aspects of citizens' right to participate in the government of their countries cannot be suppressed, even in an emergency situation [. . .], without undermining the integrity of the electoral process. [85] [. . .] [T]he Court is of the opinion that States should regularly conduct elections within the electoral calendar. In a situation of an emergency [. . .] it is incumbent upon the States which are sovereign to determine when to conduct elections and to take appropriate measures to protect the health and life of people without undermining the integrity of the elections. [91] The Court recalls that it is asked whether it is possible to postpone elections because of a situation of emergency [. . .]. [. . .] [T]he Court reaffirms the principle that elections must be held regularly on the scheduled timeframe

[...]. The postponement [...] constitutes an exception to this principle. [**92**] The Court notes that, unlike the holding of elections in a public health emergency or a pandemic, in which rights are restricted in order to protect the health and lives of the people, the postponement of elections entails the suspension of the right of citizens to participate regularly in the governance of their countries through elections, as provided for in Article 13(1) of the Charter and Articles 2(3) and 3(4) both of the ACDEG. [**98**] [...] The Court is of the view that the regime of restrictions provided for in Article 27(2) of the Charter is applicable *mutatis mutandis* to the suspension of rights. That is, the postponement must be made in application of a general law, must aim at the legitimate purpose, be proportionate to the intended purpose and must not undermine the essential content of rights [...]. [**101**] The Court considers that [...] the postponement is legitimate if it aims at protecting the health and life of the people, as well as allowing the creation of conditions for the holding of transparent, free and fair elections. [**102**] The Court notes that, from the point of view of proportionality, the postponement of elections must be a last resort, without which it will not be possible to protect the health and lives of the people and ensure the integrity of the electoral process. [...] [T]he period of postponement must be strictly necessary to create the conditions that are required for the elections to take place under the best possible conditions, in accordance with acceptable international standards in the context of an emergency. [**106**] [...] States must have their own legislation on the consequences of the expiry of the term of office of elected officials without elections being held due to the declaration of a state of emergency. [**107**] The Court holds that if such legislation exists, it must be applied, otherwise new legislation should be enacted by the competent bodies.[...]"

[**Paras. 48, 51, 52, 54, 57, 66, 73, 76, 80, 81, 85, 91, 92, 98, 101, 102, 106, 107**]

V.

II.4.3 ADVISORY OPINION
See also: II.7.641

"[**108**][...]
THE COURT,
Unanimously,
On jurisdiction
   i. *Finds* that it has jurisdiction to give the Advisory Opinion requested.
On admissibility
   ii. *Declares* that the Request for Advisory Opinion is admissible.
On the merits
On the decision to conduct or not conduct elections in the context of a public health emergency or a pandemic
   iii. *Finds* that states may decide to conduct or not to conduct elections in the context of a public health emergency or a pandemic. Such a decision requires prior consultation with health authorities and political actors, including representatives of civil society.
On the obligations of State Parties to ensure effective protection of citizens' right to participate in the government of their countries in the context of an election held during a public health emergency or a pandemic, such as the Covid-19 crisis
   iv. *Finds* that measures restricting rights, applied by States in elections conducted during a public health emergency or a pandemic, must, in accordance with Article 27(2) of the Charter, be in the form of general law; pursue a legitimate purpose; be

proportionate; must not undermine the essential content of rights; must not derogate the rights provided for in Articles 6, 7, 8(1) and (2), in Articles 11, 15, 16 and
18, in accordance with Article 4(2) of the ICCPR; and must not be discriminatory.

On the obligations of State Parties that decide to postpone elections because of a public health emergency or a pandemic, such as the Covid-19 crisis

> v. Finds that the postponement of an election because of a public health emergency or
> a pandemic must comply with Article 27(2) of the Charter mutatis mutandis and
> Article 4(1) of the ICCPR.

On the standards applicable in the event the term of office expires

> vi. Finds that it is for domestic law to outline the applicable legal standards when the
> term of office of elected officials expires, including to an interim replacement, to an
> extension of term of office with full powers, or to a caretaker arrangement. Where
> appropriate legislation does not exist at the time of a public health emergency or a
> pandemic, a law may be enacted by the competent bodies, based on prior consulta-
> tion with political actors, including representatives of civil society."

[Para. 108]

IX.1.4

Glory C. Hossou and Landry A. Adelakoun v. Republic of Benin, Application No. 016/2020, Ruling, 2 December 2021*

Contents*

    I. FACTUAL AND PROCEDURAL BACKGROUND

    II. ACTHPR LITIGIOUS JURISDICTION

    III. JUDGMENT

I.

II.2.0   INSTITUTION AND COURSE OF PROCEEDINGS

         See also: I.8.34; II.1; II.7.69

"[1] Glory C. Hossou and Landry A. Adelakoun (hereinafter referred to as "the Applicants") are nationals of the Republic of Benin, jurists by profession and residents of Abomey-Calavi in Benin. They challenge the Republic of Benin's withdrawal of the Declaration deposited under Article 34(6) of the Protocol to the African Charter on Human and Peoples' Rights on the Establishment of an African Court (hereinafter "the Protocol"). [2] The Application is filed against the Republic of Benin (hereinafter referred to as "the Respondent State"), which became a party to the African Charter on Human and Peoples' Rights (hereinafter referred to as "the Charter") on 21 October 1986 and to the Protocol on 22 August 2014. On 8 February 2016, the Respondent State deposited the Declaration prescribed under Article 34(6) of the Protocol (hereinafter referred to as "the Declaration") through which it accepted the jurisdiction of the Court to receive applications from individuals and Non-Governmental Organizations. On 25 March 2020, the Respondent State deposited with the Chairperson of the African Union Commission (hereinafter referred to as "the Commission") an instrument withdrawing the said Declaration. The Court held that this withdrawal has no bearing, on the one hand, on pending cases, and on the other hand, on new cases filed before the withdrawal came into effect, that is, on 26 March 2021. [5] The Applicants allege that, in withdrawing the Declaration, the Respondent State: i. Violates the Charter and international human rights standards. ii. Prevents its citizens from directly accessing the regional judicial system to initiate proceedings and seek redress for the prejudice they have suffered within their domestic system, which constitutes a regression of rights."

[Paras. 1, 2, 5]

II.

II.7.6951   ACtHPR LITIGIOUS JURISDICTION

         See also: I.8.34; II.2.03; II.2.111; II.7.69; II.7.695

"[27] In the instant case, the Applicants allege that the withdrawal by the State of Benin of the declaration deposited under Article 34 (6) of the Protocol constitutes a violation of

---

  * Summaries prepared by Lucía Ione Padilla Espinosa, Ph.D. candidate in the Doctoral Program in Legal Sciences of the University of Huelva, Spain. Text of judgment available online at the Court's Web site <https://www.african-court.org/en/>. Original: French (authoritative) and English. Footnotes appearing in the original text have been omitted.

** This is not a faithful reproduction of the Table of Contents of the Judgment.

human rights protected by the Charter. The Court will examine whether it has jurisdiction to decide if the withdrawal of the declaration constitutes a violation of human rights. [**28**] [...] [T]he Court will be guided by the relevant rules governing declarations accepting jurisdictions as well as by the principle of State sovereignty in international law, in addition to the relevant rules of the law of treaties contained in the Vienna Convention on the Law of Treaties of 23 May 1969 (hereafter The Vienna Convention). [**29**] As regards the application of the Vienna Convention, the Court notes that while the declaration made under Article 34 (6) is provided for in the Protocol, which is governed by the law of treaties, the declaration in itself, is a unilateral act of the State not backed by the law of treaties. [**30**] Accordingly, the Court finds that the Vienna Convention does not apply to the declaration made under Article 34 (6) of the Protocol. [**31**] Concerning the rules governing the acceptance of the jurisdiction of international courts, the Court notes that similar declarations are optional. This is true for the provisions on the recognition of the jurisdiction of the International Court of Justice, the European Court of Human Rights prior to the coming into force of Protocol No. 11 and the Inter-American Court of Human Rights.[**32**] The Court notes that, by its nature, the declaration provided for in Article 34 (6) is similar to those mentioned above. The reason is that although the Declaration is provided for under Article 34 (6) of the Protocol, it is optional. Thus, as a unilateral act, the declaration is an act separable from the Protocol and can, therefore, be withdrawn without leading to a withdrawal or a denunciation of the Protocol. [**33**] The Court further considers that the optional nature of the declaration and its unilateral character derive from a basic principle of international law, that is, the principle of sovereignty of the States. Indeed, the latter prescribes that States are free to make commitments and that they retain the power to withdraw their commitments in accordance with the relevant rules of each treaty. [**34**] The Court considers that the matter being discussed before it pertains to the a right accorded the States. This right is the very one by which the States ensure the establishment of mechanisms that complement their domestic human rights implementation mechanisms. [**35**] The Court finds that the Respondent State is entitled to withdraw the declaration that it deposited under Article 34 (6). [**36**] Consequently, the Court upholds the objection based on lack of material jurisdiction raised by the Respondent State and declares that it has no material jurisdiction to hear the instant case."

[**Paras. 27, 28, 29, 30, 31, 32, 33, 34, 35, 36**]

III.

II.2.5   JUDGMENT/DECISION/ORDER
See also: I.8.34; II.7.69; II.7.695; II.7.697

"[**40**] [...] THE COURT
By a majority of ten (10) to one (1), Judge *Chafika BENSAOULA dissenting*:
On jurisdiction
    i. **Upholds** the objection to its material jurisdiction;
    ii. *Declares* that it lacks jurisdiction.
On costs
    iii. *Orders* each party to bear its own costs."

[**Para. 40**]

Systematic Key Items of the Section*

---

* *See* Systematic Classification Scheme, *supra* at page 255.

Systematic Key Terms of the Section*

* See Systematic Classification of Themes, supra, p. 235.

X

International Centre for Settlement of Investment Disputes

INTRODUCTORY NOTE

From Coping with Enlarged Intra-EU Objections to the Interpretative Intricacies of Exceptions Clauses in International Investment Agreements—ICSID Arbitration in 2021

BY AUGUST REINISCH*
& JOHANNES TROPPER**

Abstract

The 2021 jurisprudence of ICSID tribunals and ad hoc committees addressed among others the jurisdictional issues of the notions of "investment" and "investor" under Article 25 ICSID Convention, the establishment of jurisdiction by means of an MFN provision, the so-called intra-EU objection to jurisdiction, the illegality objection to jurisdiction, and the objection to jurisdiction based on abuse of process. Prominent procedural issues concerned the dismissal of claims manifestly without legal merit and security for costs. The 2021 cases also dealt with expropriation, fair and equitable treatment, minimum standard of treatment, and denial of justice. In addition, the effect of general exceptions clauses was addressed by two ICSID tribunals. On quantum, some tribunals found that no damages could be awarded despite breaches of investment treaties. Annulment committees addressed the limited grounds for annulling awards under the ICSID Convention.

 * Professor of International and European Law, University of Vienna, Austria; Member of the International Law Commission of the UN; Member of the Editorial Board. He may be contacted at <august.reinisch@ univie.ac.at>.

** Researcher and Lecturer, University of Vienna, Austria. He may be contacted at <johannes.tropper@ univie.ac.at>.

August Reinisch and Johannes Tropper, *Introductory Note* In: *The Global Community Yearbook of International Law and Jurisprudence 2022*. Edited by: Giuliana Ziccardi Capaldo, Oxford University Press. © Oxford University Press 2023.
DOI: 10.1093/oso/9780197752265.003.0031

This introductory note provides a selective overview of investment cases brought before the International Centre for Settlement of Investment Disputes (ICSID) and decided either in regard to jurisdiction, on the merits/quantum or in the form of annulment decisions during the reporting year 2021.[1]

Excerpts from decisions and awards are partly reproduced in the Legal Maxims Section of this *Yearbook*.[2] Neither they nor this introductory note exhaustively treat the 2021 jurisprudence.

I. JURISDICTION AND ADMISSIBILITY

The *ratione materiae* and *ratione personae* jurisdictional requirements of Article 25 of the ICSID Convention[3] continue to be important issues at the jurisdictional stage of ICSID proceedings. In addition, in 2021 ICSID tribunals addressed the importation of consent to jurisdiction via MFN provisions, the intra-EU objection to jurisdiction, the effect of corruption and illegality in the making of investments and abuse of process to gain access to ICSID jurisdiction.

A. Jurisdiction Ratione Materiae Under Article 25 of the ICSID Convention

Since Article 25 of the ICSID Convention does not define the term "investment,"[4] investment tribunals have developed certain criteria that must be fulfilled in order for something to qualify as "investment" under the ICSID Convention. For a long time, the *Salini* test was used as the standard definition, requiring not only a certain duration, the assumption of risk, and a substantial commitment, but also a significant contribution to the host state's development.[5] As one tribunal put it in 2020, "this test is a doctrinal and jurisprudential formulation."[6] The *Salini* test has been gradually applied in a more flexible manner and

---

[1] In 2021, ICSID registered 66 new arbitration cases. Among the ICSID Arbitration Proceedings concluded in 2021, 64% were decided, while 36% of the disputes were settled or otherwise discontinued. Within the decisions rendered, 23% declined jurisdiction, 29% dismissed all claims, and 48% upheld claims in part or full. *See* THE ICSID CASELOAD—STATISTICS (Issue 2022-1), available at <https://icsid.worldbank.org/sites/default/files/documents/The_ICSID_Caseload_Statistics.1_Edition_ENG.pdf> (accessed 15 July 2022). As of 31 December 2021, a total of 300 ICSID cases were pending, of those 298 were ICSID arbitration cases and 2 were conciliation cases.

[2] J. Tropper, *Legal Maxims: Summaries and Extracts from Selected Case Law: ICSID*, 22 GLOBAL COMMUNITY YILJ 2022 (Giuliana Ziccardi Capaldo General ed.) 625–659 (2023).

[3] Article 25(1) Convention on the Settlement of Investment Disputes between States and Nationals of Other States [hereinafter ICSID Convention], 18 March 1965, 575 UNTS 159.

[4] Article 25(1) ICSID Convention, ibid. ("[...] jurisdiction of the Centre shall extend to any legal dispute arising directly out of an investment [...]").

[5] *See* Salini Costruttori S.p.A. and Italstrade S.p.A. v. Kingdom of Morocco, ICSID Case No. ARB/00/4, Decision on Jurisdiction, 23 July 2001, para. 52 ("The doctrine generally considers that investment infers: contributions, a certain duration of performance of the contract and a participation in the risks of the transaction (*cf. commentary by E. Gaillard, cited above, p. 292*). In reading the Convention's preamble, one may add the contribution to the economic development of the host State of the investment as an additional condition."). *See* CHRISTOPH SCHREUER ET AL., THE ICSID CONVENTION: A COMMENTARY 128 *et seq.* (2d ed. 2009).

[6] Theodoros Adamakopoulos and others v. Republic of Cyprus, ICSID Case No. ARB/15/49, Decision on Jurisdiction, 7 February 2020, para. 293.

nowadays ICSID tribunals merely require an "objective" test examining "contribution, duration, and risk" in order to determine what constitutes an "investment" under Article 25 ICSID Convention.[7]

In 2021, the ICSID tribunal in *Muhammet Çap and Sehil v. Turkmenistan* pointed out "that Article 25 ICSID Convention contains neither a definition of *'investment'* nor the criteria needed for an *'investment'* within the meaning of the ICSID Convention."[8] Acknowledging the parties' reference to case law and scholarship concerning the meaning of investment under the ICSID Convention, the tribunal considered "the nature of the assets owned and controlled by Mr Çap and Sehil in Turkmenistan, and [...] the activities to which these assets related."[9] The tribunal held that an investment for purposes of the ICSID Convention existed since investors had made a "significant commitment and contribution in Turkmenistan"[10] including sixty-three contracts with state-owned or state-controlled entities, rented office space and employment of more than one thousand locals.[11]

Likewise, the tribunal in *Hope Services v. Cameroon* pointed out that since the ICSID Convention contained no definition of investment, recourse must be had to Article 31(1) Vienna Convention on the Law of Treaties[12] to interpret the term in accordance with its ordinary meaning, its context, and the object and purpose of the Convention.[13] The tribunal further noted that criteria to determine the existence of an investment have been developed in arbitral case law, which were not binding upon the tribunal, but could be of help since no "objective definition of *'investment'* "[14] existed. These criteria typically included contribution, a certain duration, the assumption of economic risk, and a territorial link to the host state.[15] Moreover, the tribunal noted that some awards required the existence of a contribution to the development of the host state, but did not regard it as necessary to rule on this matter in the respective case.[16] While these criteria were considered to be "useful" the tribunal noted that "these criteria should not be applied in a rigid manner as a *box-ticking exercise*, but with the necessary flexibility, and taking into account the totality of the circumstances of the case."[17] This holistic analysis was regarded as important since an

---

[7] In this sense, more recent ICSID decisions have held "that only three of the above criteria, namely contribution, risk and duration should be used as the benchmarks of investment, without a separate criterion of contribution to the economic development." Deutsche Bank AG v. Democratic Socialist Republic of Sri Lanka, ICSID Case No. ARB/09/2, Award, 31 October 2012, para. 295. *See also* Electrabel S.A. v. Republic of Hungary, ICSID Case No. ARB/07/19, Decision on Jurisdiction, Applicable Law and Liability, 30 November 2012, para. 5.43; KT Asia Investment Group B.V. v. Republic of Kazakhstan, ICSID Case No. ARB/09/8, Award, 17 October 2013, para. 173; Poštová banka, a.s. and Istrokapital SE v. The Hellenic Republic, ICSID Case No. ARB/13/8, Award, 9 April 2015, para. 360; Vestey Group Ltd v. Bolivarian Republic of Venezuela, ICSID Case No. ARB/06/4, Award, 15 April 2016, para. 187.

[8] Muhammet Çap & Sehil Insaat Endustri ve Ticaret Ltd. Sti. v. Turkmenistan, ICSID Case No. ARB/12/6, Award, 04 May 2021, para. 668.

[9] Ibid., para. 670.

[10] Ibid., para. 681.

[11] Ibid.

[12] *See* Article 31(1), Vienna Convention on the Law of Treaties, 22 May 1969, 1155 UNTS 331.

[13] Hope Services LLC v. Republic of Cameroon, ICSID Case No. ARB/20/2, Award, 23 December 2021, para. 157.

[14] Ibid., para. 158 (original in French).

[15] Ibid., para. 159.

[16] Ibid., para. 160.

[17] Ibid., para. 162 ("ces critères ne doivent pas être appliqués de façon rigide comme un *box-ticking exercise*, mais avec une nécessaire flexibilité, et en tenant compte de l'ensemble des circonstances de l'espèce").

overall economic operation could amount to an investment under the Convention even if individual assets might not qualify as such if assessed individually and separately.[18] On this basis the tribunal found that the underlying economic operation for an online financing platform was an investment.[19]

With respect to the meaning of investment under the ICSID Convention, the tribunal in *Cascade Investments v. Turkey*[20] held that:

> while [the Convention] does not include a specific definition of investment, it is broadly accepted that the absence of a definition does not rob the term of inherent meaning; rather, it leaves the term to be ascribed its ordinary meaning, in accordance with Article 31(1) of the VCLT. The ordinary meaning of the term "investment" is an objective one, which sets the outer boundaries beyond which the Convention cannot apply, even if individual parties were to seek to agree otherwise.[21]

Against this backdrop, the tribunal held "that the inherent notion of 'investment' in the [ICSID] Convention requires some *bona fide* transaction by a *foreign* investor, with the intention of engaging on an ongoing basis in some *real economic activity* in the host State."[22]

B. Jurisdiction Ratione Personae Under Article 25 of the ICSID Convention

According to Article 25 of the ICSID Convention *ratione personae* jurisdiction requires that a dispute arises between a "Contracting State," on the one hand, and "a national of another Contracting State," on the other hand.[23] Article 25(2)(a) of the ICSID Convention clarifies that the term "[n]ational of another Contracting State" applies to "any natural person who had the nationality of a Contracting State other than the State party to the dispute." Article 25(2)(b) of the ICSID Convention provides that "national of another Contracting State" covers "any juridical person which had the nationality of a Contracting State other than the State party to the dispute."

In 2021, the tribunal in *Infracapital v. Spain*[24] had to address Spain's argument that the investors being corporations incorporated in EU member states could not bring claims against another EU member state under the Energy Charter Treaty (ECT) because they would have "EU nationality" and not the "nationality of another Contracting State". The tribunal rejected that argument pointing out that "contrary to natural persons, legal persons such as Claimants cannot have the nationality of the EU, in addition to that under which laws they have been established."[25] Moreover, if one assumed "that Claimants were incorporated as a '*Societas Europaea*' or could be deemed to have both the nationality of their respective State (the Netherlands and Luxembourg) and be a Societas Europaea, it would require that Claimants bring the claim against the EU in order to be excluded"[26], which was

---

[18] Ibid., para. 163.

[19] Ibid., paras. 165–223.

[20] Cascade Investments NV v. Republic of Turkey, ICSID Case No. ARB/18/4, Award, 20 September 2021.

[21] Ibid., para. 329.

[22] Ibid., para. 330. See in detail *infra* section I.F.

[23] Article 25(1) ICSID Convention, *supra* note 3.

[24] Infracapital F1 S.à.r.l. and Infracapital Solar B.V. v. Kingdom of Spain, ICSID Case No. ARB/16/18, Decision on Jurisdiction, Liability and Directions on Quantum, 13 September 2021.

[25] Ibid., para. 223.

[26] Ibid., para. 225 (emphasis in original).

not the case here. Moreover, "the European Union cannot be identified as a "Contracting State" for purposes of Article 25(2) of the ICSID Convention, since it has not executed the ICSID Convention."[27]

C. Consent to Jurisdiction Imported via a Most-Favoured-Nation Clause

Most-favoured-nation (MNF) clauses provide that the state party to the investment treaty must accord investors and investments from the other state party treatment no less favourable than that accorded to investors and investments from third states.[28] The case law on the scope and extent of MFN clauses has been divided, in particular with respect to the question whether such provisions also cover more favourable dispute settlement provisions in another treaty.[29] Accordingly, it is still unresolved whether it is possible to establish or extend jurisdiction under the original investment treaty or overcome procedural hurdles via an MFN clause.[30]

Maffezini v. Spain[31] was the first case in which a tribunal permitted the expansion of rights on the basis of a MFN clause:

> if a third party treaty contains provisions for the settlement of disputes that are more favorable to the protection of the investor's rights and interests than those in the basic treaty, such provisions may be extended to the beneficiary of the most favored nation clause.[32]

The tribunal permitted circumventing a waiting period contained in the original BIT[33] with reference to the applicable MFN clause.[34] Still, the tribunal also cautioned that there had to be limits to such use of an MFN clause:

> the beneficiary of the clause should not be able to override public policy considerations that the contracting parties might have envisaged as fundamental conditions for their

---

[27] Ibid., para. 226.

[28] *See, e.g.,* Andrew Newcombe & Lluís Paradell, Law and Practice of Investment Treaties. Standards of Treatment 201–203 (2009); August Reinisch & Christoph Schreuer, International Protection of Investments: The Substantive Standards 680 *et seq.* (2020).

[29] For the case law *see, e.g.,* August Reinisch & Christoph Schreuer, International Protection of Investments: The Substantive Standards 698 *et seq.* (2020). *See also* August Reinisch & Johannes Tropper, *From a New Set of Mass Claims and Challenges of Entire Tribunals to Further Fine-tuning of the Fair and Equitable Treatment Standard—ICSID Arbitration in 2020,* 21 Global Community YILJ 2021 (Giuliana Ziccardi Capaldo General ed.) 629, 638-641 (2022).

[30] *See, e.g.,* Siemens A.G. v. The Argentine Republic, ICSID Case No. ARB/02/8, Decision on Jurisdiction, 3 August 2004, paras. 102–103; Salini Costruttori S.p.A. and Italstrade S.p.A. v. Hashemite Kingdom of Jordan, ICSID Case No. ARB/02/13, Decision on Jurisdiction, 9 November 2004, paras. 105–119; RosInvestCo UK Ltd. v. Russia, SCC Case No. Abr. V 079/2005, Award on Jurisdiction, 5 October 2007, paras. 124–133.

[31] Emilio Agustín Maffezini v. The Kingdom of Spain, ICSID Case No. ARB/97/7, Decision of the Tribunal on Objections to Jurisdiction, 25 January 2000.

[32] Ibid., para. 56.

[33] Article X(3)(a) Argentina-Spain BIT (1991).

[34] Article IV(2) Argentina-Spain BIT (1991); *see* Emilio Agustín Maffezini v. The Kingdom of Spain, ICSID Case No. ARB/97/7, Decision of the Tribunal on Objections to Jurisdiction, 25 January 2000, para. 64.

acceptance of the agreement in question, particularly if the beneficiary is a private investor, as will often be the case.[35]

In 2021, the ICSID Additional Facility (AF) tribunal in *Kimberly-Clark v. Venezuela* had to address the investor's argument that jurisdiction could be established in reliance on MFN clauses included in three BITs all of which could have been applicable to establish consent. First of all, the investor argued that consent could be imported via Article 3(2) Netherlands-Venezuela BIT providing that "[. . .] each Contracting Party shall accord to such investments full physical security and protection which in any case shall not be less than that accorded [. . .] to investments of nationals of any third State, whichever is more favourable to the national concerned."[36] The tribunal, which had already held that there was no consent for ICSID AF arbitration under the BIT rejected the attempt to import consent on the basis of the MFN clause for two reasons. Firstly, it noted that "as a matter of principle, a Tribunal which lacks jurisdiction (*ratione voluntatis*) is barred from applying the treaty's substantive guarantees, including the MFN clause."[37] Explicitly rejecting *Maffezini v. Spain*, the tribunal held that "[l]ike for other substantive protections, an arbitral tribunal can only assess whether the host state breached the MFN clause of a treaty if it has jurisdiction to do so."[38] Secondly, it pointed to the wording of the particular MFN clause which "would not cover dispute settlement, as it is restricted to claims for breach of the physical security and protection standard."[39] For essentially the same reasons the tribunal also rejected reliance on the Spain-Venezuela BIT[40] and its MFN clause.[41] Finally, trying to import consent to ICSID AF arbitration through the MFN clause included in the BLEU-Venezuela BIT (1998)[42] was also unsuccessful. The MFN clause of that BIT reads as follows: "In respect of all matters governed by this Agreement, the investors of each Contracting Party shall be accorded, in the territory of the other Contracting Party, treatment no less favourable than that the latter Party accords to its own investors or to investors of the most favoured nation."[43] Again, the tribunal primarily emphasized that "[f]or the reasons set out in the context of the analysis of the MFN clause in the Dutch BIT, to which it refers, the Tribunal must deny jurisdiction to apply the Belgian BIT's

---

[35] Emilio Agustín Maffezini v. The Kingdom of Spain, ICSID Case No. ARB/97/7, Decision of the Tribunal on Objections to Jurisdiction, 25 January 2000, para. 62.

[36] Article 3(2) Netherlands-Venezuela BIT (1991).

[37] Kimberly-Clark Dutch Holdings, B.V., Kimberly-Clark S.L.U., and Kimberly-Clark BVBA v. Bolivarian Republic of Venezuela, ICSID Case No. ARB(AF)/18/3, Award, 5 November 2021, para. 165.

[38] Ibid., para. 167.

[39] Ibid., para. 169.

[40] Spain-Venezuela BIT (1995).

[41] Kimberly-Clark Dutch Holdings, B.V., Kimberly-Clark S.L.U., and Kimberly-Clark BVBA v. Bolivarian Republic of Venezuela, ICSID Case No. ARB(AF)/18/3, Award, 5 November 2021, para. 206 ("For the reasons which the Tribunal reviewed in the context of the Dutch BIT and which it restates here, it cannot apply the MFN clause found in Article IV(2) of the Spanish BIT to 'incorporate' a more favorable dispute resolution provision. Even if the Tribunal had jurisdiction to apply Article IV(2) of the Spanish BIT, quod non, that provision would be limited to more favorable fair and equitable treatment as provided in Article IV(1).").

[42] Agreement between the Belgo-Luxembourg Economic Union and the Government of the Republic of Venezuela on the Reciprocal Promotion and Protection of Investments (1998).

[43] Article 3(3) BLEU-Venezuela BIT (1998).

MFN clause."[44] In any event, the MFN clause would have only covered substantive treatment standards:

> The Tribunal reads the words "in the territory of the other Contracting Party" as an indication that Article 3(3) applies to substantive treatment, as opposed to procedural matters. The settlement of investment disputes cannot qualify as "treatment in the territory" of Venezuela. Even if arbitration could be characterized as "treatment", which is doubtful, it would not be located in the host State.[45]

Some arbitral tribunals have also discussed whether an MFN provision even allows the importation of substantive standards of treatment contained in other investment treaties and under which circumstances.[46] Newer investment treaties sometimes exclude the possibility to import substantive standards via MFN clauses, such as Article 8.7(4) CETA which *inter alia* provides that: "Substantive obligations in other international investment treaties and other trade agreements do not in themselves constitute 'treatment', and thus cannot give rise to a breach of this Article, absent measures adopted or maintained by a Party pursuant to those obligations."[47]

In 2021 the tribunal in *Muhammet Çap and Sehil v. Turkmenistan* interpreted Article II(2) Turkey-Turkmenistan BIT according to which "[e]ach Party shall accord to these investments, once established, treatment no less favourable than that accorded in similar situations to investments of its investors or to investments of investors of any third country, whichever is the most favourable."[48] In light of the language of this provision, the tribunal found that the MFN clause only addressed *de facto* discrimination and did not allow the import of investment protection standards from other investment treaties. For the tribunal the "key wording here is *'similar situations'* "[49] which "involves comparing the factual circumstances surrounding the investments in question"[50] and thus "[i]t must be shown that actual investors, found in a similar situation, were treated differently."[51] The tribunal also noted that "[t]he wording of the MFN provision in this case, unlike other MFN clauses, does not refer to *'all matters'* or to be applied *'in all respects'*. Rather, it clearly states

---

[44] Kimberly-Clark Dutch Holdings, B.V., Kimberly-Clark S.L.U., and Kimberly-Clark BVBA v. Bolivarian Republic of Venezuela, ICSID Case No. ARB(AF)/18/3, Award, 5 November 2021, para. 233.

[45] Ibid., para. 235.

[46] *See, e.g.,* Bayindir Insaat Turizm Ticaret Ve Sanayi A.S. v. Islamic Republic of Pakistan I, ICSID Case No. ARB/03/29, Award, 27 August 2009, paras. 153–167; Sergei Paushok, CJSC Golden East Company and CJSC Vostokneftegaz Company v. Government of Mongolia, Award on Jurisdiction and Liability, 28 April 2011, para. 570; İçkale İnşaat Limited Şirketi v. Turkmenistan, ICSID Case No. ARB/10/24, Award, 8 March 2016, paras. 326–330, 384–388; Teinver S.A., Transportes de Cercanías S.A. and Autobuses Urbanos del Sur S.A. v. Argentine Republic, ICSID Case No. ARB/09/01, Award, 21 July 2017, paras. 881–896; Consutel Group S.p.A. in liquidazione v. People's Democratic Republic of Algeria, PCA Case No. 2017-33, Final Award, 3 February 2020, paras. 354–359.

[47] Article 8.7(4), Comprehensive Trade and Economic Agreement between Canada and the European Union (2016); for further analysis, *see* August Reinisch, *Article 8.7 – Most-favoured-nation treatment,* in CETA INVESTMENT LAW: ARTICLE-BY-ARTICLE COMMENTARY 216, 228–229 (August Reinisch & Marc Bungenberg eds., 2022).

[48] Article II(2) Turkey-Turkmenistan BIT (1992).

[49] Muhammet Çap & Sehil Insaat Endustri ve Ticaret Ltd. Sti. v. Turkmenistan, ICSID Case No. ARB/12/6, Award, 04 May 2021, para. 783.

[50] Ibid.

[51] Ibid.

that its scope of application is restricted to where the investors are in a *'similar situation.'*"[52] Accordingly, the tribunal concluded that:

> the MFN provision in Article II(2) BIT applies to *de facto* discrimination where two actual investors in a similar situation are treated differently. That is not the case here. Further, the wording of Article II(2), requiring such factually similar situation, does not entitle Claimants to rely on the MFN provision to import substantive standards of protection from a third-party treaty which are not included in the BIT, and to rely on such standards in the present Arbitration.[53]

D. Intra-EU Objections to the Jurisdiction of ICSID Tribunals

Respondent states which are also EU member states have raised the intra-EU objection to ICSID jurisdiction both under intra-EU BITs and under the ECT for intra-EU disputes as in previous years.[54] States have particularly relied on the 2018 *Achmea* judgment by the Court of Justice of the European Union (CJEU) in which the Court held that the Dutch-Slovak BIT was incompatible with EU law. ICSID tribunals have repeatedly rejected the relevance of the judgment, pointing rather to the need to modify or terminate intra-EU BITs and the ECT if EU states thought that ICSID tribunals should not have jurisdiction to rule on such intra-EU disputes.

The ICSID tribunal in *AS PNB Banka v. Latvia* established on the basis of the Latvia-United Kingdom BIT specifically linked *Achmea* with Article 27 VCLT, which reads: "A party may not invoke the provisions of its internal law as justification for its failure to perform a treaty. [. . .]"[55] It held that "the relevant principles in *Achmea* are a manifestation of EU constitutional law. As such, it is an internal law within the meaning of Article 27"[56] and thus cannot invalidate consent contained in an investment treaty. The tribunal further held that EU law has a dual character as domestic and international law,[57] but the tribunal did "not accept that CJEU decisions are international law of the same character as the Treaties."[58] Moreover, it held that:

> CJEU decisions are not based on principles of interpretation, codified in the VCLT, applicable to treaties, but on a teleological approach applicable to constitutional law. [. . .] [W]e do not identify a conflict between the BIT and the EU Treaties. The conflict

---

[52] Ibid., para. 790.

[53] Ibid., para. 793.

[54] *See, e.g.,* August Reinisch & Johannes Tropper, *From the Intra-EU Objection to the Reach of Umbrella Clauses and the Limited Scope of Review in Annulment Proceedings—ICSID Arbitration in 2019,* 20 GLOBAL COMMUNITY YILJ 2020 (Giuliana Ziccardi Capaldo General ed.) 883, 887–892 (2021).

[55] Article 27, Vienna Convention on the Law of Treaties, 22 May 1969, 1155 UNTS 331.

[56] AS PNB Banka and others v. Republic of Latvia, ICSID Case No. ARB/17/47, Decision on the Intra-EU Objection, para. 668; *see further* ibid., para. 669 ("The question before this Tribunal is not, however, whether an international agreement loses its status as international law, but whether the EU Treaties, as they apply within the EU, override purely international obligations undertaken by Member States. Within each Member State, those treaties have, as Professor Tridimas puts it, a 'binding effect anchoring in the domestic legal system.' Once anchored in the domestic legal system, however, Article 27 prevents them from being invoked as justification for a state's failure to perform a treaty.").

[57] Ibid., paras. 517–518.

[58] Ibid., para. 525.

arises from an incompatibility between the BIT and the CJEU's interpretation of those Treaties by application of the teleological approach.[59]

Most EU member states have now terminated intra-EU BITs either through the plurilateral Termination Agreement of 2020 or bilateral termination agreements,[60] but until these terminations take effect, tribunals can exercise jurisdiction under these intra-EU BITs. Moreover, pending intra-EU disputes remain unaffected by a subsequent termination of investment treaties, thus terminations can only have a prospective effect.[61] The limited effect on pending proceedings has been confirmed in *Infracapital v. Spain* (with respect to the ECT), where the tribunal held:

> Respondent made an offer to covered investors under the ECT consenting to arbitration, and Claimants accepted the valid offer when they submitted this dispute thus a binding and formal consent had been formed. That agreement to arbitrate is subject to public international law. Furthermore, Article 25(1) of the ICSID Convention provides that once consent has been given it cannot by withdrawn unilaterally.[62]

Generally, as far as the ECT is concerned, tribunals have rejected the relevance of *Achmea* for a variety of reasons, starting already in 2018 in *Masdar v. Spain*, where the tribunal focused on the multilateral nature of the ECT and held that "[t]he *Achmea* Judgment is simply silent on the subject of the ECT."[63] In 2021 in *Infracapital v. Spain* the tribunal rejected the relevance of *Achmea* for the ECT as the treaty is a multilateral and not a bilateral treaty. Thus, it held that "[s]imply put, the *Achmea* [judgment] and this case are totally different and there can be no analogies found."[64]

However, in September 2021, the CJEU clarified in its *Komstroy* judgment that the *Achmea* reasoning also applied to the multilateral ECT and that investment arbitration for intra-EU disputes was unavailable under the ECT from the perspective of EU law.[65]

---

[59] Ibid., para. 526. *See also* ibid., para. 505 ("The dual character of EU law in relevant respects is fundamental to the application by this Tribunal of the decisions of the CJEU. Notwithstanding that we accept such decisions as statements of EU law, we cannot accept that the reasoning of those decisions, which abjures reliance on the customary international law principles of treaty interpretation as codified in the VCLT, represents the correct method of interpretation of the BIT as a matter of international law. With respect to the central jurisdictional question before us did Latvia consent to arbitration—we have to determine the issue in accordance with principles that are not constrained by the constitutional dimension of EU law.").

[60] *See* August Reinisch & Johannes Tropper, *The 2020 Termination Agreement of Intra-EU BITs and Its Effect on Investment Arbitration in the EU*, 16 Austrian Yearbook on International Arbitration 2022, at 301 (Klausegger et al. eds., 2022).

[61] *See, e.g.*, Magyar Farming Company Ltd, Kintyre Kft and Inicia Zrt v. Hungary, ICSID Case No. ARB/17/27, Award, 13 November 2019, para. 214; Muszynianka Spółka z Ograniczoną Odpowiedzialnością v. Slovak Republic, PCA Case No. 2017-08, Award, 7 October 2020, para. 263; *see further* Reinisch & Tropper, *supra* note 60.

[62] Infracapital F1 S.à.r.l. and Infracapital Solar B.V. v. Kingdom of Spain, ICSID Case No. ARB/16/18, Decision on Jurisdiction, Liability and Directions on Quantum, 13 September 2021, para. 306.

[63] Masdar Solar & Wind Cooperatief U.A. v. Kingdom of Spain, ICSID Case No. ARB/14/1, Award, 16 May 2018, para. 682.

[64] Infracapital F1 S.à.r.l. and Infracapital Solar B.V. v. Kingdom of Spain, ICSID Case No. ARB/16/18, Decision on Jurisdiction, Liability and Directions on Quantum, 13 September 2021, para. 301.

[65] C-741/19, République de Moldavie v. Komstroy LLC, ECLI:EU:C:2021:655, 6 September 2021, paras. 65–66 ("It follows that, although the ECT may require Member States to comply with the

Thus far only a few ICSID tribunals have had a chance to address *Komstroy* in requests for reconsideration, such as *Kruck v. Spain*.[66] The tribunal found that the *Komstroy* judgment did not require it to reopen the question of the intra-EU objection under the ECT, but the tribunal still addressed that judgment in quite some detail.[67] It noted that it "cannot accept [. . .] that the interpretation of the ECT must either be determined authoritatively by the EU and its courts, or that the ECT may have a different meaning in the context of intra-EU disputes from that which it has in non-intra-EU disputes."[68] Furthermore, the tribunal acknowledged that:

> there is here a clash of *Grundnormen*. The CJEU has its role and authority within the EU legal order. [. . .] The mandate of this Tribunal, and its authority, derive from the agreement of the ECT Contracting Parties in accordance with international law and are invoked by the Parties to the dispute. It is deeply regrettable that parties to disputes should find themselves caught up in a clash of *Grundnormen* that could have been foreseen and resolved in advance. But this Tribunal has the duty to fulfil its mandate under the ECT, and has no legal right or capacity to do otherwise. The solution lies in the hands of the Contracting Parties to the ECT.[69]

E. Corruption and Illegality in the Making of the Investment

Investment tribunals have reacted in different ways to corruption in the making of an investment on the claimant's part.[70] In the past some tribunals have rejected jurisdiction, while others have dismissed claims as inadmissible as a result.[71]

In 2021, in *Infinito Gold v. Costa Rica*, the tribunal noted that "[d]epending on the content of the treaty, illegality can affect jurisdiction, admissibility or merits of the claims."[72] In the particular case, the tribunal noted that "to qualify as a protected investment under

---

arbitral mechanisms for which it provides in their relations with investors from third States who are also Contracting Parties to that treaty as regards investments made by the latter in those Member States, preservation of the autonomy and of the particular nature of EU law precludes the same obligations under the ECT from being imposed on Member States as between themselves. In the light of the foregoing, it must be concluded that Article 26(2)(c) ECT [i.e. investment arbitration] must be interpreted as not being applicable to disputes between a Member State and an investor of another Member State concerning an investment made by the latter in the first Member State.").

[66] Mathias Kruck and others v. Kingdom of Spain, ICSID Case No. ARB/15/23, Decision on the Respondent's Request for Reconsideration of the Tribunal's Decision dated 19 April 2021, 5 December 2021.

[67] Ibid., para. 47 ("In view of the relatively unusual nature of the Request for Reconsideration, and the specific relevance of the *Komstroy* Judgment the Tribunal has set out its reasoning at greater length that might have been expected.").

[68] Ibid., para. 40.

[69] Ibid., para. 46. *See further* ibid., para. 37: "Contracting Parties may, of course, agree to amend the ECT so that it has differential application, in accordance with the procedure set out in ECT Article 42."

[70] *See, e.g.*, Metal-Tech Ltd. v. Republic of Uzbekistan, ICSID Case No. ARB/10/3, Award, 4 October 2013, para. 389; Cortec Mining Kenya Limited, Cortec (Pty) Limited and Stirling Capital Limited v. Republic of Kenya, ICSID Case No. ARB/15/29, Award, 22 October 2018, paras. 319, 365; *see further* World Duty Free Company Limited v. Republic of Kenya, ICSID Case No. ARB/00/7, Award, 4 October 2006.

[71] Caline Mouawad & Jessica Beess und Chrostin, *The Illegality Objection in Investor–State Arbitration*, 37 ARBITRATION INTERNATIONAL 57 (2021).

[72] Infinito Gold Ltd. v. Republic of Costa Rica, ICSID Case No. ARB/14/5, Award, 3 June 2021, para. 173.

the BIT, the Claimant's investment must be an asset owned or controlled in accordance with Costa Rica's laws. If it is not, then the Tribunal will lack jurisdiction."[73] In *Infinito Gold v. Costa Rica* the respondent state and an NGO alleged that the investment had been procured through corruption by the investor. Subsequently, the respondent state withdrew its objection to jurisdiction because it stated that its allegation of corruption concerned issues that happened after the making of the investment.[74] Thus, the tribunal found that:

> even if the corruption allegations were well-founded [...] this would not imply that the acquisition of the shares, which is the relevant investment for present purposes, was unlawful. It would mean that later conduct of the investor was tainted, which could be a defense on the merits, but not an obstacle to jurisdiction.[75]

However, the tribunal still felt that it had to address the corruption allegations raised by the NGO concerning the making of an investment *ex officio* because it concerned "an issue of international public policy".[76] Despite adopting a lower standard of proof for the finding of corruption "focus[sing] on circumstantial evidence, relying on indicia or red flags" the tribunal could not find sufficient evidence or indications that the investment was procured through corruption.[77]

F. Abuse of Process and ICSID Jurisdiction

When investors restructure investments in order to benefit from an investment treaty at a time when there are indications about an impending dispute with the host state, the question arises whether the restructuring is permissible to establish jurisdiction under the investment treaty or not. So-called forum shopping at a time of a foreseeable investment dispute has generally not been accepted by arbitral tribunals, which have dismissed jurisdiction or admissibility of claims on the basis of a general principle of abuse of process or abuse of rights.[78]

As summarized by the tribunal in *Philip Morris v. Australia*:

> the initiation of a treaty-based investor-State arbitration constitutes an abuse of rights (or an abuse of process, the rights abused being procedural in nature) when an investor has changed its corporate structure to gain the protection of an investment treaty at a point in time when a specific dispute was foreseeable.[79]

---

[73] Ibid., para. 173; *see* Article I(g) Canada–Costa Rica BIT (1998) ("'investment' means any kind of asset owned or controlled [...] in accordance with the latter's laws [...]").

[74] Infinito Gold Ltd. v. Republic of Costa Rica, ICSID Case No. ARB/14/5, Award, 3 June 2021, para. 180.

[75] Ibid., para. 180.

[76] Ibid., para. 178.

[77] Ibid., para. 181.

[78] *See* the discussions in, *e.g.*, Phoenix Action, Ltd. v. Czech Republic, ICSID Case No. ARB/06/5, Award, 15 April 2009; Pac Rim Cayman LLC. v. Republic of El Salvador, ICSID Case No. ARB/09/12, Decision on Jurisdictional Objections, 1 June 2012; ST-AD GmbH v. Republic of Bulgaria, PCA Case No. 2011-06 (ST-BG), Award on Jurisdiction, 18 July 2013; Philip Morris Asia Limited v. Commonwealth of Australia, PCA Case No. 2012-12, Award on Jurisdiction and Admissibility, 17 December 2015.

[79] Philip Morris Asia Limited v. Commonwealth of Australia, PCA Case No. 2012-12, Award on Jurisdiction and Admissibility, 17 December 2015, para. 554.

In 2021, the tribunal in *Cascade Investments v. Turkey*[80] dismissed jurisdiction over an investment dispute concerning Turkey's measures against a media group purportedly linked to political opponents of the government on the basis of abuse of process. The Belgian corporation—essentially acting as a vehicle to gain protection under the BLEU-Turkey BIT[81]—had acquired ownership of the media group at a time, when it was in the eyes of the tribunal already foreseeable that a dispute with the Turkish state was imminent. In the largely redacted award, the tribunal first noted that the prohibition of abuse of process was inherent in the meaning of the investment under the ICSID Convention and the applicable BIT, referring to the preamble and thus an interpretation based on the object and purpose:

> As prior tribunals have observed, these provisions make clear—both as a matter of treaty text and in light of its object and purpose—that the inherent notion of "investment" in the Convention requires some *bona fide* transaction by a foreign investor, with the intention of engaging on an ongoing basis in some *real economic activity* in the host State. By contrast, the ICSID system was not intended to apply to investments made solely by domestic investors in their home State, even if later repackaged under a foreign flag in the face of an existing or looming dispute, in order not to conduct further economic activity but simply to obtain access to treaty protection and potential treaty arbitration.[82]

The tribunal differentiated between legitimate and illegitimate nationality planning stating that:

> legitimate *ex ante* planning decisions must be distinguished from inappropriate efforts to "game" the investment arbitration system by artificially shifting a domestic investment into international hands, with no real intention of economic activity by the new owners, simply to shield the domestic operation from existing or already impending risks. [. . .] The bottom line is that in distinguishing legitimate nationality planning (and legitimate acquisitions by new foreign owners) from abuse of process, the focus necessarily must be on the "*when*" and the "*why*"—the timing and circumstances under which shares in a local company, previously held by nationals of the host State, are transferred to new foreign ownership.[83]

According to the tribunal, not only restructuring where the original owner still retains indirect control over the investment can be contrary to the principle of abuse of process, but also acquisition by a third party. The tribunal elaborated that

> in a true arm's-length sale of an existing investment for fair value, there generally will be no reason to suspect that the acquiror is not acquiring the investment for normal business purposes, with the intention of engaging on an ongoing basis in some real economic activity in the host State. The Tribunal therefore expects that abuse of process concerns would arise only rarely in the acquisition context. However, if the evidence in a particular case is sufficiently unusual as to raise concerns about the *bona fides* of a

---

[80] Cascade Investments NV v. Republic of Turkey, ICSID Case No. ARB/18/4, Award, 20 September 2021.
[81] BLEU (Belgium–Luxembourg Economic Union)–Turkey BIT (1986).
[82] Ibid., para. 330 (emphasis in original, footnote omitted). On the BIT, *see* ibid., para. 331.
[83] Ibid., paras. 335–336 (footnote omitted).

transaction which was made in the face of a reasonably foreseeable dispute with the host State, it remains appropriate for a tribunal to consider the suspicious circumstances.

Like other tribunals before it,[84] the tribunal differentiated between objections to jurisdiction *ratione temporis* and those based on abuse of process noting that:

> "Crystallization" of a dispute is an important concept under *ratione temporis* analyses, where the issue often centers on whether a particular treaty may be applied to State conduct that occurred prior to a treaty's entry into force. In the abuse of process context, by contrast, "crystallization" is not the applicable test, and the relevant inquiry is not limited to identifying the date that relevant State measures were taken and a particular dispute therefore "arose." It extends, as well, to determining whether a dispute which has *not already* crystallized nonetheless was *foreseeable* to an investor, to a required standard of foresight.[85]

II. PROCEDURAL ISSUES

A. Dismissal of Claims Manifestly Without Legal Merit

Rule 41(5) of the ICSID Arbitration Rules[86] provides an expedited procedure to dismiss claims manifestly without legal merit at the preliminary stage of proceedings.[87] In 2021, *InfraRed Environmental Infrastructure v. Spain*[88] the ICSID tribunal dismissed a request for reconsideration of the award as manifestly without legal merits. Spain had argued that the *Eiser* annulment,[89] discussed in last year's introductory note,[90] required revision of the award in the present proceedings. Spain argued that "the Eiser Award is the '*exclusive*' basis

---

[84] *See, e.g.,* Renée Rose Levy and Gremcitel S.A. v. Republic of Peru, ICSID Case No. ARB/11/17, Award, 9 January 2015, para. 182.

[85] Cascade Investments NV v. Republic of Turkey, ICSID Case No. ARB/18/4, Award, 20 September 2021, para. 338.

[86] Rule 41(5) ICSID Arbitration Rules (2006) ("Unless the parties have agreed to another expedited procedure for making preliminary objections, a party may, no later than 30 days after the constitution of the Tribunal, and in any event before the first session of the Tribunal, file an objection that a claim is manifestly without legal merit. The party shall specify as precisely as possible the basis for the objection. The Tribunal, after giving the parties the opportunity to present their observations on the objection, shall, at its first session or promptly thereafter, notify the parties of its decision on the objection. The decision of the Tribunal shall be without prejudice to the right of a party to file an objection pursuant to paragraph (1) or to object, in the course of the proceeding, that a claim lacks legal merit.").

[87] *See, e.g.,* Michele Potestà & Marija Sobat, *Frivolous Claims in International Adjudication: A Study of ICSID Rule 41(5) and of Procedures of Other Courts and Tribunals to Dismiss Claims Summarily,* 3 JOURNAL OF INTERNATIONAL DISPUTE SETTLEMENT 137 (2012).

[88] InfraRed Environmental Infrastructure GP Limited and others v. Kingdom of Spain, ICSID Case No. ARB/14/12, Decision on Claimants Objection under ICSID Rule 41(5) to Respondent Application for Revision, 08 March 2021.

[89] Eiser Infrastructure Limited and Energía Solar Luxembourg S.à.r.l. v. Kingdom of Spain, ICSID Case No. ARB/13/36, Decision on the Kingdom of Spain's Application for Annulment, 11 June 2020.

[90] *See also* August Reinisch & Johannes Tropper, *From a New Set of Mass Claims and Challenges of Entire Tribunals to Further Fine-tuning of the Fair and Equitable Treatment Standard—ICSID Arbitration in 2020,* 21 GLOBAL COMMUNITY YILJ 2021 (Giuliana Ziccardi Capaldo General ed.) 629, 664 (2022).

for the Tribunal's determination of the installed capacity issue"[91] in the *InfraRed* award. The tribunal held with reference to Rule 41(5) that:

> To prevail on such an objection, the objecting party must establish its objection clearly and obviously, with relative ease and despatch. The complexity of the claim impugned and of the legal issues associated with that claim are not reasons per se to dismiss the objection, but the objecting party will only prevail if the absence of legal merit is clear and obvious.[92]

The investor, however, indeed prevailed on the objection raised by Spain. The tribunal noted that it was clear that the *InfraRed* award did not rely on the *Eiser* award for "its articulation of the conceptual and legal basis for the determination of installed capacity issue."[93]

Also in 2021, the tribunal in *Fengzhen Min v. South Korea* addressed the Republic of Korea's objection that some of the investor's claims were manifestly without legal merit. The tribunal noted that the underlying purpose of Rule 41(5) of the ICSID Arbitration Rules is "efficiency" so that "claims that are plainly legally bad [can] [. . .] be disposed of quickly, and at an early stage".[94] Furthermore, the tribunal noted that "it is difficult to see how it could be described as efficient to allow a claim that is manifestly without legal merit to go forward, even if it is based on facts which are also relied in relation to other, more meritorious, claims."[95] However, the tribunal also pointed out that the Republic of Korea had only objected to some claims as being manifestly without legal merit and thus some claims would in an event "go forward for determination."[96] Accordingly, the tribunal found this fact "makes it most important that the Tribunal should not, even if only by a side wind, pre-judge, or appear to pre-judge, any of the factual or legal issues that are going to arise at a later stage."[97] Eventually, the tribunal dismissed most of the respondent state's arguments while agreeing with one objection to a claim that was manifestly time-barred. It specifically noted with respect to an objection to composite acts that "[w]here a series of acts or omissions is properly so characterised, it is arguable that there is no breach until the series is complete. It is also arguable that the time when the investor first acquired, or should have first acquired, knowledge that he has incurred loss or damage cannot arise until the breach itself has occurred."[98]

B. Security for Costs

Tribunals or annulment committees are occasionally asked by a party to order the other party to post security for costs for pending arbitration[99] or annulment

---

[91] InfraRed Environmental Infrastructure GP Limited and others v. Kingdom of Spain, ICSID Case No. ARB/14/12, Decision on Claimants Objection under ICSID Rule 41(5) to Respondent Application for Revision, 08 March 2021, para. 29.

[92] Ibid., para. 54 (footnote omitted).

[93] Ibid., para. 69.

[94] Fengzhen Min v. Republic of Korea, ICSID Case No. ARB/20/26, Decision on the Respondent's Preliminary Objection Pursuant to Rule 41(5) of the ICSID Arbitration Rules, 18 June 2021, para. 73.

[95] Ibid., para. 73.

[96] Ibid., para. 70.

[97] Ibid., para. 70.

[98] Ibid., para. 92.

[99] *See, e.g.,* RSM Production Corporation v. Saint Lucia, ICSID Case No. ARB/12/10, Decision on Saint Lucia's Request for Security for Costs, 13 August 2014; Muhammet Çap & Sehil İnşaat Endustri ve

proceedings.[100] This should ensure that a party may recover its legal costs if it prevails in the arbitration or annulment proceedings and is particularly relevant where there are concerns about the financial capacities of the opposing party.[101] ICSID tribunals have repeatedly held that they have the power to order security for costs as a provisional measure[102] in accordance with Article 47 ICSID Convention.[103] Although some dissenting opinions have disagreed with that view.[104]

In 2021, the tribunal in *Hope Services v. Cameroon* confirmed that it had the power to issue a security for costs order.[105] It noted that Article 47 ICSID Convention and Rule 39 of the ICSID Arbitration Rules concerning provisional measures "do not specifically mention the possibility of ordering security for costs," but this "does not mean that the Tribunal does not have the power to order such a measure."[106]

However, tribunals have held that various criteria must be met before an order for security of costs can be granted, namely necessity, urgency, exceptional circumstances, proportionality, and no prejudging of the merits.[107] For instance, the tribunal in *RSM v. St Lucia* ordered security for costs because of "the proven history where Claimant did not comply with cost orders and awards due to its inability or unwillingness, the fact that it admittedly does not have sufficient financial resources itself and the (also admitted) fact that it is funded by an unknown third party".[108] In contrast, the tribunal in *EuroGas v. Slovak Republic* found that "financial difficulties and third party-funding [...] do not necessarily constitute *per se* exceptional circumstances justifying that the Respondent be granted an order of security for costs."[109]

In 2021, the tribunal in *Hope Services v. Cameroon* found that the party requesting an order for security of costs, here Cameroon, had to prove that "(1) the relief is necessary to prevent irreparable harm; (2) the relief is urgently required; and (3) the relief sought is

---

Ticaret Ltd. Sti. v. Turkmenistan, ICSID Case No. ARB/12/6, Procedural Order No. 6, 9 February 2016; South American Silver Limited (Bermuda) v. The Plurinational State of Bolivia, PCA Case No. 2013-15, Procedural Order No. 10, 11 January 2016.

[100] Commerce Group Corp. & San Sebastian Gold Mines, Inc. v. Republic of El Salvador, ICSID Case No. ARB/09/17, Decision on El Salvador's Application for Security for Costs, 20 September 2012.

[101] *See generally, e.g.,* Xuan Shao, *Disrupt the Gambler's Nirvana: Security for Costs in Investment Arbitration Supported by Third-Party Funding,* 12 JOURNAL OF INTERNATIONAL DISPUTE SETTLEMENT 427 (2021).

[102] *See, e.g.,* Lighthouse Corporation Pty Ltd and Lighthouse Corporation Ltd, IBC v. Democratic Republic of Timor-Leste, ICSID Case No. ARB/15/2, Procedural Order No. 2 for Provisional Measures, 13 February 2016, paras. 53–55; RSM Production Corporation v. Saint Lucia, ICSID Case No. ARB/12/10, Decision on Saint Lucia's Request for Security for Costs, 13 August 2014, paras. 46–48.

[103] Article 47 ICSID Convention, *supra* note 3 ("Except as the parties otherwise agree, the Tribunal may, if it considers that the circumstances so require, recommend any provisional measures which should be taken to preserve the respective rights of either party.").

[104] *See, e.g.,* RSM Production Corporation v. Saint Lucia, ICSID Case No. ARB/12/10, Dissenting Opinion of Edward Nottingham, 13 August 2014.

[105] Hope Services LLC v. Republic of Cameroon, ICSID Case No. ARB/20/2, Procedural Order No. 4 Decision on Respondent Application for Security for Cost, 12 May 2021, paras. 27–34.

[106] Ibid., para. 27 (original in French).

[107] *See, e.g.,* Eugene Kazmin v. Republic of Latvia, ICSID Case No. ARB/17/5, Procedural Order No. 6 Decision on the Respondent Application for Security for Costs, 13 April 2020, paras. 28–62.

[108] RSM Production Corporation v. Saint Lucia, ICSID Case No. ARB/12/10, Decision on Saint Lucia's Request for Security for Costs, 13 August 2014, para. 86.

[109] EuroGas Inc. and Belmont Resources Inc. v. Slovak Republic, ICSID Case No. ARB/14/14, Procedural Order No. 3, Decision on the Parties' Requests for Provisional Measures, 23 June 2015, para. 123.

proportionate."[110] The tribunal further noted that provisional measures are "extraordinary" measures that can only be ordered in "exceptional circumstances."[111]

In the particular case, the tribunal held that financial difficulties and the intervention of a third-party funder were insufficient grounds for ordering security for costs.[112] Moreover, the exclusion of adverse costs awards from funding agreements with third-party funder was found to be a common practice, which did not justify the granting of security for costs.[113] The tribunal did not regard "urgency" as a paramount element, rather "[i]t is sufficient that security sought cannot await the Tribunal's decision on the award of costs."[114] Finally, it held that "the requirement of proportionality is an essential element in considering a request for security for costs, particularly if the relief sought would affect a party's ability to assert its rights, either as a claimant or a defendant, in a proceeding."[115] Proportionality required a balancing exercise and that balance was in favour of the claimant in this case.[116] In light of these findings, the tribunal rejected the respondent's request for an order for security for costs.[117]

III. SUBSTANTIVE ISSUES

The main substantive investment protection standards, such as expropriation and fair and equitable treatment with a particular focus on denial of justice, figured prominently again in ICSID cases decided in 2021, as did a transfer clause in an ICSID AF case.

A. Expropriation

In 2021 ICSID tribunals addressed various aspects of expropriation provisions, including the distinction between direct and indirect expropriations, judicial expropriations, and the police powers doctrine.

1. Distinction Between Direct and Indirect Expropriations
Expropriations can occur as direct expropriations or indirect expropriations, both of which are covered by expropriation provisions of investment treaties. Direct expropriations—as noted in *Infinito Gold v. Costa Rica*—occur "when the deprivation occurs through a forcible taking or transfer of the property to the State."[118] Expropriations are indirect "when the measure 'substantially interfere[s] with the investor's ability to use or derive the economic benefits from an investment established in the territory of the host State, even if it is not necessarily to the obvious benefit of the host State.'"[119] Similarly, the tribunal in *Casinos Austria v. Argentina* held that:

> Whereas direct expropriations require the taking and transfer of title to the covered investment from the investor to the host State or a third party, indirect or *de facto*

---

[110] Hope Services LLC v. Republic of Cameroon, ICSID Case No. ARB/20/2, Procedural Order No. 4 Decision on Respondent Application for Security for Cost, 12 May 2021, para. 61 (original in French).

[111] Ibid., para. 63 (original in French).

[112] Ibid., para. 64.

[113] Ibid., para. 69.

[114] Ibid., para. 80.

[115] Ibid., para. 86 (original in French).

[116] Ibid., para. 87.

[117] Ibid., para. 89.

[118] Infinito Gold Ltd. v. Costa Rica, ICSID Case No. ARB/14/5, Award, 3 June 2021, para. 699 (footnote omitted).

[119] Ibid. (footnote omitted).

expropriations cover measures that have an equivalent effect to a direct expropriation, but leave the title to the investment unaffected.[120]

2. Domestic Law Controls the Existence of Property Rights

Expropriation evidently presupposes that a right or property right exists that is capable of being expropriated. The existence and content of such a right is generally an issue for domestic law. ICSID tribunals have held that "in order for a right to be expropriated, it must first exist under the relevant domestic law."[121]

This has also been acknowledged by an ICSID AF tribunal in 2021—*América Móvil v. Colombia*. The tribunal held that the existence and content of a right is determined by domestic law. It noted in particular that "the existence of a right under domestic law is the indispensable presupposition for that right to enjoy the protection provided by international law."[122] Also the ICSID tribunal in *Infinito Gold v. Costa Rica* noted that "[i]f no valid rights exist under domestic law, there can be no expropriation."[123] On this basis, the tribunal rejected the expropriation claim, finding that at the time immediately preceding allegedly expropriatory decisions, "the 2008 Concession and related approvals which Industrias Infinito formally held were vitiated by an absolute nullity. Consequently, Industrias Infinito could not be said to have owned valid rights capable of being expropriated."[124]

3. Judicial Expropriation

Judicial interferences with a foreign investor's investment, in particular property rights, may be expropriatory and thus qualify as judicial expropriation. This issue has received increased attention in arbitral practice[125] and scholarship[126] in the past few years.

In 2021, ICSID tribunals also had to address claims based on judicial expropriation and clarified several elements of judicial expropriation. For instance, the *Infinito Gold* tribunal stated that:

> judicial expropriation cannot occur through a decision by a first instance court, the execution of which is stayed pending an appeal, because it lacks finality and enforceability.

---

[120] Casinos Austria International GmbH and Casinos Austria Aktiengesellschaft v. Argentine Republic, ICSID Case No. ARB/14/32, Award, 5 November 2021, para. 328 (footnote omitted).

[121] Quiborax S.A. and Non Metallic Minerals S.A. v. Plurinational State of Bolivia, ICSID Case No. ARB/06/2, Award, 16 September 2015, para. 135; *see also* Gavrilovic and Gavrilovic d.o.o. v. Republic of Croatia, ICSID Case No. ARB/12/39, Award, 26 July 2018, para. 432; Magyar Farming Company Ltd, Kintyre Kft and Inicia Zrt v. Hungary, ICSID Case No. ARB/17/27, Award, 13 November 2019, para. 341.

[122] América Móvil S.A.B. de C.V. v. Republic of Colombia, ICSID Case No. ARB(AF)/16/5, Award, 07 May 2021, para. 327 (original in Spanish).

[123] Infinito Gold Ltd. v. Costa Rica, ICSID Case No. ARB/14/5, Award, 3 June 2021, para. 705.

[124] Ibid., para. 711.

[125] *See, e.g.*, Saipem S.p.A. v. The People's Republic of Bangladesh, ICSID Case No. ARB/05/07, Award, 30 June 2009; ATA Construction, Industrial and Trading Company v. The Hashemite Kingdom of Jordan, ICSID Case No. ARB/08/2, Award, 18 May 2010; Swisslion v. Macedonia, ICSID Case No. ARB/09/16, Award, 6 June 2012; Standard Chartered Bank (Hong Kong) Limited v. United Republic of Tanzania [II], ICSID Case No. ARB/15/41, Award of the Tribunal, 11 October 2019.

[126] *See, e.g.*, Mavluda Sattorova, *Judicial Expropriation or Denial of Justice? A Note on Saipem v.* BANGLADESH, 2 INTERNATIONAL ARBITRATION LAW REVIEW 35 (2010); Sara Mansour Fallah, *Drawing the Line between Adjudication and Expropriation*, 2 TRANSNATIONAL DISPUTE MANAGEMENT 1 (2019); Hamid G. Gharavi, *Discord Over Judicial Expropriation*, 33 ICSID REVIEW—FOREIGN INVESTMENT LAW JOURNAL 349 (2018); Martin Jarrett, *Extricating the Illegality Requirement from Judicial Expropriation*, in GLOBAL VALUES AND INTERNATIONAL TRADE LAW 23 (Csongor István Nagy ed., 2021).

A judicial expropriation can only occur when a final judgment is rendered or when the time limit to appeal has expired.[127]

The majority of the tribunal also held that judicial decisions may amount to judicial expropriation in the absence of a denial of justice provided that they permanently deprive investors of their investments and cannot be justified by police powers.[128]

In contrast, the ICSID AF tribunal in *Lion v. Mexico* held that—as a general rule—there could not be judicial expropriation if there had not been a finding of denial of justice.[129] However, it also noted that there is an exception to this rule, namely, if "the courts were not neutral and independent, especially from the other branches of power of the host State."[130] In the instant case, however, the tribunal did not see proof that Mexican domestic courts were not independent from other branches and hence, the exception did not apply.[131]

4. Indirect Expropriation and Police Powers
In regard to identifying whether an indirect expropriation had occurred many tribunals traditionally relied on the so-called sole effects doctrine and focused on the intensity of the interference.[132] However, in 2005 the NAFTA award in *Methanex v. USA*[133] and in 2006 an UNCITRAL award in *Saluka v. Czech Republic*[134] suggested that non-discriminatory, regulatory measures for a *bona fide* public purpose could not amount to indirect expropriation. Accordingly, when a state exercises its regulatory powers or police powers, it is not required to compensate foreign investors.

In 2021, the majority of the ICSID tribunal in *Casinos Austria v. Argentina* elaborated on the police powers doctrine and found that "[p]olice powers and the right to regulate are recognized components of a State's sovereignty and firmly grounded in customary international law."[135] They "are not abrogated merely because a State has entered into treaty commitments that restrict its right to expropriate".[136] These customary rights have to be taken into account when interpreting the expropriation provision of the applicable BIT as "'relevant rules of international law applicable in the relations between the parties' in the sense of Article 31(3)(c) of the VCLT".[137]

---

[127] Infinito Gold Ltd. v. Costa Rica, ICSID Case No. ARB/14/5, Award, 3 June 2021, para. 239.

[128] Ibid., para. 701; *see further* ibid., paras. 356–367.

[129] Lion Mexico Consolidated L.P. v. United Mexican States, ICSID Case No. ARB(AF)/15/2, Award, 20 September 2021, para. 188.

[130] Ibid., para. 192.

[131] Ibid., paras. 195–196.

[132] *Cf.* Rudolf Dolzer, *Indirect Expropriations: New Developments?*, 11 N.Y.U. ENVIRONMENTAL LAW JOURNAL 64, 65 (2002); Yves Fortier & Stephen Drymer, *Indirect Expropriation in the Law of International Investment: I Know It When I See It, or Caveat Investor*, ICSID REVIEW—FOREIGN INVESTMENT LAW JOURNAL 293 (2004); August Reinisch, *Expropriation*, in THE OXFORD HANDBOOK OF INTERNATIONAL INVESTMENT LAW (P. Muchlinski et al. eds., 2009).

[133] Methanex Corporation v. United States of America, NAFTA Arbitral Tribunal, Final Award on Jurisdiction and Merits, 3 August 2005, IV D para. 7.

[134] Saluka Investments BV (The Netherlands) v. The Czech Republic, UNCITRAL Partial Award, 17 March 2006, para. 255.

[135] Casinos Austria International GmbH and Casinos Austria Aktiengesellschaft v. Argentine Republic, ICSID Case No. ARB/14/32, Award, 5 November 2021, para. 332 (footnote omitted).

[136] Ibid.

[137] Ibid. However, the tribunal noted that at para. 332 that "[t]his could only be otherwise if it were shown that the contracting parties to the BIT had had a clear intention of dispensing with such a well-recognized

With respect to police powers or the right to regulate, the tribunal pointed out that the duty to pay compensation does not apply to non-discriminatory measures taken in the public interest and that a "host State's proper exercise of its police powers or of its right to regulate is a business risk that has to be borne by an investor and does not lead to international responsibility,"[138] but "the improper exercise of such powers constitutes a political risk that international investment law regulates and sanctions."[139] In assessing whether there has been an improper exercise, the tribunal must also take into account whether the "impact on investments is proportionate to the interest(s) protected."[140] According to the tribunal proportionality as a principle limiting the exercise of police powers "has been recognized already under customary international law"[141] and is "a principle of (public) law in the domestic laws of a large number of countries, and in the practice of their domestic courts, and is used and applied as a principle of international law in the practice of numerous other international courts and tribunals".[142] The principle of proportionality requires the host state to "reconcile competing interests, such as investment protection, on the one hand, and environmental protection, labor standards, human rights, or any other public interest, including the prevention of money laundering, on the other hand."[143]

In order to meet the requirement of proportionality it is necessary:

> that a host State's measures (sic!) i) pursues a legitimate goal (public purpose); ii) is suitable to achieve that goal; iii) is necessary to achieve that goal in the sense that less intrusive, but equally feasible and effective measures do not exist; and iv) is proportionate *stricto sensu*, that is, that the benefit for the public of the measure in question stands in an adequate and acceptable relationship to the negative impact of the measure on the investment.[144]

In *Eco Oro v. Colombia* the tribunal considered whether "the right to explore, the right to exploit [...] and the right to extend its concession at the end of the concession period"[145] had been expropriated or whether the measures were taken in the exercise of police powers. The tribunal noted that "Eco Oro' share price had already dropped significantly when its open-pit mining application was rejected in April 2010"[146] and "there was no significant deterioration in the share price at the time of or after the measures complained of—that drop had already occurred".[147] However, the tribunal pointed out that eventually "Eco Oro suffered the complete deprivation of a potential right to exploit" and thus "the Concession became

---

principle of customary international law, which is not the case for the BIT applicable to the present proceeding.").

[138] Ibid., para. 333.

[139] Ibid.

[140] Ibid., para. 336.

[141] Ibid., para. 351.

[142] Ibid.

[143] Ibid. (footnote omitted).

[144] Ibid.

[145] Eco Oro Minerals Corp. v. Republic of Colombia, ICSID Case No. ARB/16/41, Decision on Jurisdiction, Liability and Directions on Quantum, 9 September 2021, para. 623.

[146] Ibid., para. 634.

[147] Ibid., para. 587.

valueless."[148] Since the "exploitation right was lost in totality as a result of the Challenged Measures", the tribunal found that in principle "this loss is capable of being considered to be a substantial deprivation, such as to amount to an indirect expropriation."[149] Therefore, the tribunal turned to the question whether Colombia had exercised its police powers or had indeed expropriated the investor.

Relying on Annex 811 to the Canada-Colombia FTA which included the contracting parties' shared understanding on indirect expropriations,[150] the tribunal noted that "in interpreting and applying the provisions of Annex 811(2), awards on the police powers doctrine under customary international law may provide some guidance (by analogy)."[151] The majority of the tribunal found that:

> the Challenged Measures were non-discriminatory and designed and applied to protect a legitimate public welfare objective, namely the protection of the environment. They were adopted in good faith. The Challenged Measures were therefore a legitimate exercise by Colombia of its police powers unless they comprise a rare circumstance such that they constitute indirect expropriation pursuant to Annex 811(2)(a).[152]

In order to determine whether a "rare circumstance" as set out in the annex existed, the tribunal found that it had to consider the "factors detailed in Annex 811(2)(a) as well as by the example contained in Annex 811(2)(b): are the measures so severe that they cannot reasonably be regarded as having been adopted in good faith."[153] In that regard the tribunal rejected that "it must make a finding of bad faith or disproportionality with respect to the effect of the measures taken,"[154] but it noted that "equally, a measure adopted in good faith is unlikely to comprise a rare circumstance for the purposes of Annex 811(2)(b)."[155] It held that:

> for the Challenged Measures to comprise an actionable indirect expropriation, as opposed to a legitimate exercise of a State's police powers, there must be a very significant aggravating element or factor in the conduct of the State and not just a bureaucratic muddle or State inefficiency.[156]

In conclusion, the majority of the tribunal accepted that measures "were motivated both by a genuine belief in the importance of protecting the páramo ecosystem and pursuant to Colombia's longstanding legal obligation to protect it"[157] and fell within the legitimate exercise of police powers.

---

[148] Ibid., para. 634.
[149] Ibid.
[150] Annex 811 Canada-Colombia FTA (2008).
[151] Eco Oro Minerals Corp. v. Republic of Colombia, ICSID Case No. ARB/16/41, Decision on Jurisdiction, Liability and Directions on Quantum, 9 September 2021, para. 626.
[152] Ibid., para. 642.
[153] Ibid., para. 643.
[154] Ibid.
[155] Ibid.
[156] Ibid.
[157] Ibid., para. 699.

B. Fair and Equitable Treatment

Investment claims based on fair and equitable treatment (FET) provisions have occupied quite a few tribunals in 2021. Those tribunals, *inter alia*, addressed the relationship between FET and the minimum standard of treatment, the content of FET and in particular the concept of denial of justice and its relationship to FET.

1. FET as Synonymous to the Minimum Standard of Treatment?

The question whether FET equals the minimum standard of treatment (MST) under customary international law or is a separate standard has caused debates for a long time. For NAFTA, a 2001 interpretation by its Free Trade Commission[158] effectively approximated the two standards. While this approach has been largely followed in NAFTA cases,[159] many non-NAFTA tribunals expressly rejected it.[160]

The tribunal in *Infinito Gold v. Costa Rica* noted that the FET provision in the applicable Canada–Costa Rica BIT referring to "fair and equitable treatment in accordance with principles of international law"[161] did not imply that FET was limited to the MST. The tribunal held that principles of international law could refer to general principles of law or several sources of international law under Article 38(1) ICJ Statute.[162] However, according to the tribunal, "the expression 'principles of international law' cannot be regarded as a reference to customary international law, which is but one source of international law and is distinct from general principles."[163] In regard to the concept of general principles of law it endorsed a broad reading of such principles including "principles that emanate from domestic laws (*foro domestico*) and are then transposed to international law after an appropriate distillation process, as well as general principles of international law that have emerged directly on the international plane."[164] While referencing the ILC's Special Rapporteur's First Report on General Principles of Law,[165] the tribunal failed to mention that the latter concept

---

[158] "1. Article 1105(1) prescribes the customary international law minimum standard of treatment of aliens as the minimum standard of treatment to be afforded to investments of investors of another Party. 2. The concepts of 'fair and equitable treatment' and 'full protection and security' do not require treatment in addition to or beyond that which is required by the customary international law minimum standard of treatment of aliens." NAFTA Free Trade Commission Clarifications Related to NAFTA Chapter 11, Decisions of 31 July 2001, available at <http://www.sice.oas.org/tpd/nafta/commission/ch11understanding_e.asp> (accessed 15 July 2022).

[159] Mondev International Ltd. v. United States of America, ICSID Case No. ARB(AF)/99/2, ICSID Additional Facility Award of 11 October 2002, 6 ICSID Reports 192; 42 ILM 85 (2003), para. 122; United Parcel Service of America Inc. v. Government of Canada, Decision on Jurisdiction of 22 November 2002, para. 97; ADF Group Inc. v. United States of America, Case No. ARB(AF)/00/1, ICSID Additional Facility Award of 9 January 2003, 6 ICSID Reports 470, 527, para. 199.

[160] CME Czech Republic B.V. v. The Czech Republic, Partial Award, UNCITRAL Arbitration Award of 13 September 2001, para. 156; Total S.A. v. Argentine Republic, ICSID Case No. ARB/04/01, Decision on Liability, 27 December 2010, para. 125; Teinver S.A., Transportes de Cercanías S.A. and Autobuses Urbanos del Sur S.A. v. Argentine Republic, ICSID Case No. ARB/09/01, Award, 21 July 2017, para. 666; Valores Mundiales, S.L. and Consorcio Andino S.L. v. Bolivarian Republic of Venezuela, ICSID Case No. ARB/13/11, Award, 25 July 2017, para. 530.

[161] Article II(2) Canada–Costa Rica BIT (1998).

[162] Infinito Gold Ltd. v. Costa Rica, ICSID Case No. ARB/14/5, Award, 3 June 2021, para. 332.

[163] Ibid., para. 332.

[164] Ibid.

[165] Ibid., referring to Vázquez-Bermúdez, First Report on General Principles of Law by Special Rapporteur, International Law Commission Seventy-first Session (Geneva, 29 April–7 June and 8 July–9 August 2019).

(general principles that have formed on the international plane) remains highly contested even within the ILC.

Moreover, the tribunal noted that Costa Rica's position and Canada's non-disputing party submission in the dispute on this matter explaining that FET is limited to the MST did not qualify as a subsequent agreement:[166]

> The submissions made by Costa Rica and Canada in this arbitration reflect legal arguments put forward in the context of this dispute to advance their respective interests. Although they happen to coincide, they do not reflect an *agreement* as just described over the interpretation of the BIT. Even if the Tribunal could infer an "agreement" from the Contracting States' submissions, *quod non*, this agreement would post-date the commencement of this arbitration and the Tribunal could not take it into consideration in favour of one litigant to the detriment of the other without incurring the risk of breaching the latter's due process rights.[167]

Explicit statements by Costa Rica and Canada (in other arbitration proceedings) were characterized as "litigation posture, and do not qualify as means of treaty interpretation under Article 31 of the VCLT."[168]

With respect to scholarly writings relied upon by Costa Rica and Canada, the tribunal noted that:

> it is unclear how the writings of commentators could qualify as context of the BIT under Article 31 of the VCLT; nor do they constitute subsequent agreement or practice of the Contracting States, or rules of international law applicable to them. Finally, they are not supplementary means of interpretation under Article 32 of the VCLT, as they do not serve to establish the intent of the Contracting States.[169]

The tribunal in *Eco Oro v. Colombia* accepted that "Colombia's obligation under Article 805 is to ensure treatment that meets the level of that required by the customary international law MST."[170] That provision specifically stipulated that FET did not go beyond the customary MST.[171] Accordingly, the tribunal noted "that Colombia is under no obligation to exceed this standard and, as it is not considering an autonomous treaty standard of FET but a 'minimum' standard, the Tribunal further accepts the obligation should not be interpreted expansively."[172] However, the tribunal also held that it "does not accept that the

---

[166] Ibid., para. 338.

[167] Ibid., para. 339.

[168] Ibid., para. 344.

[169] Ibid., para. 345.

[170] Eco Oro Minerals Corp. v. Republic of Colombia, ICSID Case No. ARB/16/41, Decision on Jurisdiction, Liability and Directions on Quantum, 9 September 2021, para. 732.

[171] *See* Article 805(1) Canada-Colombia FTA (2008): "Each Party shall accord to covered investments treatment in accordance with the customary international law minimum standard of treatment of aliens, including fair and equitable treatment and full protection and security. The concepts of 'fair and equitable treatment' and 'full protection and security' do not require treatment in addition or beyond that which is required by the customary international law minimum standard of treatment of aliens."

[172] Eco Oro Minerals Corp. v. Republic of Colombia, ICSID Case No. ARB/16/41, Decision on Jurisdiction, Liability and Directions on Quantum, 9 September 2021, para. 745.

meaning of MST under customary international law must remain static. The meaning must be permitted to evolve as indeed international customary law itself evolves".[173]

2. The Content of FET

Tribunals have acknowledged that the terms "fair and equitable" are vague and thus the content of an FET provision is not readily apparent, but rather requires interpretation by arbitral tribunals. For instance, the tribunal in *Saluka v. Czech Republic* held that they "are susceptible of specification through judicial practice and do in fact have sufficient legal content to allow the case to be decided on the basis of law."[174]

In *Infinito Gold v. Costa Rica* the tribunal noted that "investment tribunals have extracted a number of inherent components, which are implicitly if not expressly derived from [general principles of law] and have been reflected in the decisions of international tribunals."[175] With respect to the content of FET the tribunal found that:

> while formulations may vary across awards, a consensus emerges as to the core components of FET, which encompass the protection of legitimate expectations, the protection against conduct that is arbitrary, unreasonable, disproportionate and lacking in good faith, and the principles of due process and transparency. FET also includes a protection against denial of justice.[176]

The tribunal in *Pawlowski and Project Sever v. Czech Republic* also provided a succinct overview of obligations stemming from an FET provision:

> The FET standard requires that the host state treat the protected investment in an even-handed and just manner, avoiding intentional harassment and denial of justice. The precise scope of protection is intimately related:
> – to the legitimate and reasonable expectations on which the investor relied, including the stability of the host State's legal framework; and
> – to the specific undertakings and representations proffered by the host State at the time when the investment was made.[177]

Moreover, the tribunal noted that "[t]he obligation to provide FET binds the State as a whole. It can be breached by the conduct of any branch of government."[178] The tribunal also explained that:

> [t]he legitimacy or reasonableness of the investor's expectations must be assessed in conjunction with the political, socioeconomic, cultural and historical conditions in the host State, and in particular, balancing the right of the State under international law to regulate within its borders.[179]

---

[173] Ibid., para. 744 (footnote omitted).

[174] Saluka Investments B.V. v. The Czech Republic, UNCITRAL, Partial Award, 17 March 2006, para. 284.

[175] Infinito Gold Ltd. v. Costa Rica, ICSID Case No. ARB/14/5, Award, 3 June 2021, para. 352.

[176] Ibid., para. 355.

[177] Pawlowski AG and Project Sever s.r.o. v. Czech Republic, ICSID Case No. ARB/17/11, Award, 1 November 2021, para. 289.

[178] Ibid., para. 291.

[179] Ibid., para. 290; *see further* ibid., para. 293.

With respect to the content of FET as MST, the tribunal in *Eco Oro v. Colombia* held that "actions that infringe a sense of fairness, equity and reasonableness will fall afoul of Article 805."[180] According to the tribunal the investor:

> was entitled to expect that Colombia would treat its investment in an even-handed and just manner to ensure a predictable business environment and foster the promotion of foreign investment but that, in doing so, it would ensure the enhancement and enforcement of environmental laws and regulations, such that neither investment protection nor environmental protection takes precedence.[181]

The tribunal in *Infracapital v. Spain* noted with respect to the FET provision in the ECT that:

> the concept of legitimate expectations is not expressly contained as an obligation of host States under Article 10(1) of the ECT. Therefore, it is not an independent obligation. In this regard, the protection of the legitimate and reasonable expectations of investors must be measured against the duty of States to treat investors in a fair and equitable manner.[182]

In *Eurus Energy v. Spain* the tribunal held that "legitimate expectations [...] have become something of a *leitmotif* in the case-law on the fair and equitable treatment standard."[183] With respect to FET in the ECT, the tribunal also pointed out that:

> [t]he term itself [i.e. legitimate expectations] does not appear in the ECT, or for that matter in BITs, and there is no rule that legitimate expectations are to be observed, analogous to the *pacta sunt servanda* rule in the law of treaties. Rather, they are relevant factors to be taken into account in the interpretation and application of treaty standards such as Article 10(1) of the ECT, first and second sentences.[184]

3. Specific Commitments for the Creation of Legitimate Expectations

Legitimate expectations are a central component of FET. Yet in 2021, ICSID tribunals pointed out that under normal circumstances specific commitments have to be made vis-à-vis foreign investors for legitimate expectations to arise. In particular, absent specific commitments, an investor cannot have legitimate expectations that the domestic legislative framework will remain unchanged. Still, even if no specific commitments were made, radical or disproportionate changes to domestic legislation may result in a breach of FET.

For instance, the tribunal in *Infracapital v. Spain* noted that:

> legislation of general application [...] does not generate legitimate expectations that the law will not change. [...] Laws are the result of policy responses to economic, fiscal,

---

[180] Eco Oro Minerals Corp. v. Republic of Colombia, ICSID Case No. ARB/16/41, Decision on Jurisdiction, Liability and Directions on Quantum, 9 September 2021, para. 747.

[181] Ibid., para. 748.

[182] Infracapital F1 S.à.r.l. and Infracapital Solar B.V. v. Kingdom of Spain, ICSID Case No. ARB/16/18, Decision on Jurisdiction, Liability and Directions on Quantum, 13 September 2021, para. 564.

[183] Eurus Energy Holdings Corporation v. Kingdom of Spain, ICSID Case No. ARB/16/4, Decision on Jurisdiction and Liability, 17 March 2021, para. 316.

[184] Ibid., para. 317.

social, environmental and legal circumstances. If the circumstances upon which the law was adopted change, the laws can be expected to change too. [...][185]

According to the tribunal:

> absent a specific and unambiguous assurance, promise or commitment by a competent authority that it will freeze the legislation in favour of a specific investor as an inducement to invest, an investor cannot legitimately expect that the legal framework will not change or evolve in future in response to changes in circumstances.[186]

Thus, "States retain their sovereign power to enact, modify or derogate legislation at their own discretion provided that those changes to legislation are not arbitrary, unreasonable or disproportionate, or made in bad faith."[187]

However, with respect to specific commitments, the tribunal in *Silver Ridge v. Italy* held that:

> a State may make specific commitments to investors also by virtue of legislative or regulatory acts which are not addressed to particular individuals, provided that these acts are sufficiently specific regarding their content and their object and purpose.[188]

It furthermore noted that:

> both Parties accept the proposition that, even in the absence of specific commitments, the fair and equitable treatment standard protects foreign investors from fundamental or radical modifications to the legal framework in which they made their investment.[189]

4. Denial of Justice

Denial of justice generally requires a failure of the domestic judicial system as a whole[190] and normally requires claimants to exhaust local remedies—"finality rule"[191]—not for reasons of jurisdiction or admissibility, but as substantive element of the protection standard.[192] This has been largely confirmed by ICSID and ICSID AF tribunals in 2021, which have had to address denial of justice claims in several proceedings.

The majority of the tribunal in *Infinito Gold v. Costa Rica*—first of all—noted that unlike the minimum standard of treatment, judicial decisions may breach FET even if they do not

---

[185] Infracapital F1 S.à.r.l. and Infracapital Solar B.V. v. Kingdom of Spain, ICSID Case No. ARB/16/18, Decision on Jurisdiction, Liability and Directions on Quantum, 13 September 2021, para. 565.

[186] Ibid., para. 566.

[187] Ibid.

[188] Silver Ridge Power BV v. Italian Republic, ICSID Case No. ARB/15/37, Award, 26 February 2021, para. 408.

[189] Ibid., para. 410. *See also* Eurus Energy Holdings Corporation v. Kingdom of Spain, ICSID Case No. ARB/16/4, Decision on Jurisdiction and Liability, 17 March 2021, para. 319.

[190] *See, e.g.*, JAN PAULSSON, DENIAL OF JUSTICE IN INTERNATIONAL LAW 7 (2005).

[191] *See, e.g.*, Zachary Douglas, *International Responsibility for Domestic Adjudication: Denial of Justice Deconstructed*, 64 INTERNATIONAL AND COMPARATIVE LAW QUARTERLY 867, 872–873 (2014).

[192] *See, e.g.*, JAN PAULSSON, *supra* note 190, at 107 *et seq.*; *see also, e.g.*, Flughafen Zürich A.G. and Gestión e Ingenería IDC S.A. v. Bolivarian Republic of Venezuela, ICSID Case No. ARB/10/19, Award, 18 November 2014, para. 392.

amount to denial of justice.[193] One arbitrator submitted a separate opinion disagreeing with the majority's finding in this regard.[194]

The tribunal in *Infinito Gold v. Costa Rica* also confirmed the finality rule: "The exhaustion of local remedies rule is a substantive component of the denial of justice breach."[195] The domestic system must have had "a full opportunity to correct itself."[196] The tribunal also held that denial of justice may be "procedural or substantive"[197] and occurs "when there is a fundamental failure in the host's State's administration of justice."[198] Such a fundamental failure may occur when:

> (i) the State has denied the investor access to domestic courts; (ii) the courts have engaged in unwarranted delay; (iii) the courts have failed to provide those guarantees which are generally considered indispensable to the proper administration of justice (such as the independence and impartiality of judges, due process and the right to be heard); or (iv) the decision is manifestly arbitrary, unjust or idiosyncratic.[199]

In contrast to *Infinito Gold*, the ICSID AF tribunal in the NAFTA case *Lion v. Mexico* did not find that a denial of justice can be both procedural or substantive, but rather that "denial of justice is always procedural".[200] The tribunal, however, also noted that the "standard for a finding of denial of justice is high" and thus, it must be shown "that the municipal Courts incurred in an improper and egregious procedural conduct which does not meet the basic internationally accepted standards of administration of justice and due process, and which shocks or surprises the sense of judicial propriety."[201] In principle, *Lion v. Mexico* also accepted that exhaustion of local remedies was necessary: "a claim for denial of justice only becomes ripe when the remedies available in the legal system of the host State to impeach

---

[193] Infinito Gold Ltd. v. Republic of Costa Rica, ICSID Case No. ARB/14/5, Award, 3 June 2021, paras. 357–359; *see in particular* para. 359 ("In the majority of the Tribunal's view, there is no principled reason to limit the State's responsibility for judicial decisions to instances of denial of justice. Holding otherwise would mean that part of the State's activity would not trigger liability even though it would be contrary to the standards protected under the investment treaty. While the Tribunal agrees that domestic courts must be given deference in the application of domestic law, this does not mean that their decisions are immune from scrutiny at the international level. As noted by the tribunal in *Sistem*, court decisions may deprive investors of their property rights 'just as surely as if the State had expropriated [them] by decree.' In the same vein, judicial decisions that are arbitrary, unfair or contradict an investor's legitimate expectations may also breach the FET standard even if they do not rise to the level of a denial of justice." [footnotes omitted]).

[194] Infinito Gold Ltd. v. Republic of Costa Rica, ICSID Case No. ARB/14/5, Separate Opinion of Professor Brigitte Stern, 03 June 2021, paras. 107–109.

[195] Infinito Gold Ltd. v. Republic of Costa Rica, ICSID Case No. ARB/14/5, Award, 3 June 2021, para. 260.

[196] Ibid.; *see further* para. 445 ("the denial of justice is the product of a systemic failure of the host State's judiciary taken as a whole. The latter point explains that a claim for denial of justice presupposes the exhaustion of local remedies, a requirement that is met here as the complaint targets decisions of the highest courts." [footnote omitted]).

[197] Ibid., para. 445.

[198] Ibid.

[199] Ibid.

[200] Lion Mexico Consolidated L.P. v. United Mexican States, ICSID Case No. ARB(AF)/15/2, Award, 20 September 2021, para. 431.

[201] Ibid. para. 370; *see also* at para. 431.

the decision have been exhausted."[202] The reasons for that are, firstly, the opportunity for the domestic judicial system to rectify errors itself, and secondly, avoiding that arbitral tribunals become court of appeals for decisions taken by domestic courts.[203] However, the tribunal noted that there are exceptions to the need for exhausting local remedies, namely if remedies are not reasonably available or obviously futile to rectify a previous decision.[204]

The ICSID tribunal in *Agility Public Warehousing v. Iraq* also found that for a denial of justice claim fundamental failures in the domestic judicial system were a pre-requisite, noting that:

> a claim for denial of justice is not made out merely because a court misapplied the domestic law. In order to succeed in a claim for denial of justice, the Claimant must go beyond a mere misapplication of domestic law and show that there was a failure of the national system as a whole.[205]

It further noted that "[t]his high standard of what constitutes a denial of justice is in line with the fact that an international arbitration tribunal is *not* an appellate court and does not function to correct errors of domestic law."[206]

C. Free Transfer of Funds

Provisions on free transfer of funds (FTF), including capital and profits, are often contained in investment treaties and allow investors to both repatriate profits made abroad, but also to make payments in the host state. The inclusion of such transfer clauses may also be vital in order to ensure the function of the other protection standards contained in the investment treaty.[207] However, such transfer clauses also need to ensure that the host state can impose restrictions on the in- and outflow of capital and, for instance, place restrictions to avoid capital flight.[208]

In *Air Canada v. Venezuela*, an ICSID AF tribunal ruled on claims by the investor that Venezuela had breached the FTF clause contained in the Canada-Venezuela BIT[209] by imposing certain currency controls that made it impossible to repatriate profits from airplane ticket sales in US dollars. The tribunal noted that "there is a competing interest

---

[202] Ibid., para. 549.

[203] Ibid.

[204] Ibid., para. 562.

[205] Agility Public Warehousing Company K.S.C. v. Republic of Iraq, ICSID Case No. ARB/17/7, Award, 22 February 2021, para. 212.

[206] Ibid., para. 215 (emphasis in original).

[207] *See, e.g.,* Michael Waibel, *BIT by BIT—The Silent Liberalisation of the Capital Account, in* INTERNATIONAL INVESTMENT LAW FOR THE 21ST CENTURY: ESSAYS IN HONOUR OF CHRISTOPH SCHREUER 497, 499 (Christina Binder et al. eds., 2009) ("The omission of these clauses would risk rendering the requirement to pay compensation for the violation of other substantive treatment obligations nugatory, much like the lack of a dispute settlement clause.").

[208] Rusoro Mining Ltd. v. The Bolivarian Republic of Venezuela, ICSID Case No. ARB(AF)/12/5, Award, 22 August 2016, para. 577 (holding that "[p]rovided that this triple guarantee is complied with, the BIT does not impose restrictions on the manner in which Contracting States decide to regulate their exchange control regime. States have the choice of abolishing all exchange control restrictions, of establishing certain limits or of submitting all foreign currency transactions to administrative control.").

[209] Article VIII Canada-Venezuela BIT (1996):

> 1. Each Contracting Party shall guarantee to an investor of the other Contracting Party the unrestricted transfer of investments and returns. Without limiting the generality of the foregoing, each Contracting Party shall also guarantee to the investor the unrestricted transfer of:

contemplated by Article VIII and that is the right of host States to control such transfers, arguably in an attempt to prevent immediate capital flight that may have a negative impact on States, particularly in relation to their foreign currency reserves."[210] Thus, "the right to freely transfer or repatriate [...] funds [...] is not absolute, but subject to restrictions imposed by Respondent."[211] However, "[t]his does not imply that authorization of free transfers is at the discretion of the host State or that the exercise of the host State's regulatory power should be in any way capricious or discriminatory."[212] The tribunal also noted that:

> an important element of the FTF claim under Article VIII is, of course, the temporal element. Article VIII provides that *"[t]ransfers shall be effected without delay"*. It is clear from the wording of the provision that the Contracting States have not set a precise time limit within which a transfer must be effected, nor have they defined the phrase *"without delay"* in the BIT. It is explicit, however, that the time limit begins to run on the day on which the request for transfer was made.[213]

(a) funds in repayment of loans related to an investment;

(b) the proceeds of the total or partial liquidation of any investment;

(c) wages and other remuneration accruing to a citizen of the other Contracting Party who was permitted to work in a capacity that is managerial, executive or involves specialized knowledge in connection with an investment in the territory of the other Contracting Party;

(d) any compensation owed to an investor by virtue of Articles VI or VII of the Agreement.

2. Transfers shall be effected without delay in the convertible currency in which the capital was originally invested or in any other convertible currency agreed by the investor and the Contracting Party concerned. Unless otherwise agreed by the investor, transfers shall be made at the rate of exchange applicable on the date of transfer.

3. Neither Contracting Party may require its investor to transfer, or penalize its investors that fail to transfer, the returns attributable to investments in the territory of the other Contracting Party.

4. Notwithstanding paragraphs 1, 2 and 3, a Contracting Party may prevent a transfer through the equitable, non-discriminatory and good faith application of its laws relating to:

(a) bankruptcy, insolvency or the protection of the rights of creditors;

(b) issuing, trading or dealing in securities;

(c) criminal or penal offenses;

(d) reports of transfers of currency or other monetary instruments; or

(e) ensuring the satisfaction of judgments in adjudicatory proceedings.

5. Paragraph 3 shall not be construed to prevent a Contracting Party from imposing any measure through the equitable, non-discriminatory and good faith application of its laws relating to the matters set out in subparagraphs (a) through (e) of paragraph 4. Notwithstanding paragraphs 1, 2 and 3 and without limiting the applicability of paragraph 4, to a Contracting Party may prevent or limit transfers by a financial institution to, or for the benefit of, an affiliate of or person related to such institution, through the equitable, non-discriminatory and good faith application of measures relating to the maintenance of the safety, soundness, integrity or financial responsibility of financial institutions.

[210] Air Canada v. Bolivarian Republic of Venezuela, ICSID Case No. ARB(AF)/17/1, Award, 13 September 2021, para. 352.

[211] Ibid., para. 353.

[212] Ibid.

[213] Ibid., para. 360; *see further* ibid., para. 362 ("It is clear from the above that no consideration was given to defining the timeframe for the implementation of a transfer in the BIT as it is specific to the foreign exchange system in place in the Contracting State. This means that the time frame should reflect the period of time normally required to complete the necessary formalities related to the requested transfer").

While some of the transfer requests were handled without delay, the tribunal found that for other transfer requests the respondent state remained inactive for years and thus breached the transfer clause of the BIT.[214] Moreover, the tribunal rejected the respondent's attempt to justify the delays, in particular since the state had settled requests from other investors.[215]

D. General Exceptions Clauses

Several (newer) investment treaties include general exceptions clauses,[216] similar to Article XX GATT:

> Subject to the requirement that such measures are not applied in a manner which would constitute a means of arbitrary or unjustifiable discrimination between countries where the same conditions prevail, or a disguised restriction on international trade, nothing in this Agreement shall be construed to prevent the adoption or enforcement by any contracting party of measures:
> (a) necessary to protect public morals;
> (b) necessary to protect human, animal or plant life or health;
> [...]
> (f) imposed for the protection of national treasures of artistic, historic or archaeological value;
> (g) relating to the conservation of exhaustible natural resources if such measures are made effective in conjunction with restrictions on domestic production or consumption;
> [...].[217]

The meaning and effect of general exceptions clauses in international investment treaties has been contested in scholarship and arbitral practice. In general, three approaches to general exceptions clauses seem possible: such clauses increase regulatory flexibility for states compared to other investment treaties; such clauses codify existing jurisprudence on the right to regulate; such clauses are to be interpreted narrowly and, as a result, provide less regulatory space because only the objectives listed in such clauses can be legitimately pursued by regulatory action.[218] Moreover, the question arises whether these

---

[214] Ibid., para. 379 ("Accordingly, the Tribunal considers that Respondent's inaction in relation to Claimant's 15 AAD requests over the entire period set out above has had the effect of depriving Claimant of the right to freely transfer its funds in accordance with the applicable regime. This being said, the Tribunal will consider whether there were any possible reasons for Respondent's failure to act.").

[215] Ibid., paras. 380–396.

[216] *See, e.g.,* Article XVII Canada-Thailand BIT (1997); Article 83 Singapore-Japan EPA (2002); Article 23.02(3) Canada-Panama FTA (2010).

[217] Article XX General Agreement on Tariffs and Trade (1947) 55 UNTS 187.

[218] *See* Andrew Newcombe, *The Use of General Exceptions in IIAs: Increasing Legitimacy or Uncertainty?, in* Improving International Investment Agreements 216, 228–229 (Armand de Mestral & Céline Lévesque eds., 2013); *see further* Céline Lévesque, *The Inclusion of GATT Article XX Exceptions in IIAs: A Potentially Risky Policy, in* Prospects in International Investment Law and Policy 363 (Roberto Echandi & Pierre Sauvé eds., 2013); Kilian Wagner, *Regulation by Exception—The Emergence of (General) Exception Clauses in International Investment Law?*, 26 Austrian Review of International and European Law (forthcoming 2023).

clauses affect a tribunal's jurisdiction[219] or are rather relevant at the merits stage and exclude breaches of the investment treaty and thus the obligation to pay compensation or damages.[220]

Presumably, states wanted to exempt from liability certain governmental action taken in the public interest and, thereby, increase policy space. This intention can, *inter alia*, be derived from non-disputing party submissions by states.[221] However, it may be questionable whether this intention is reflected in the wording of such general exceptions clauses. ICSID tribunals seem to be sceptical, at least.

One of the first tribunals to address a general exceptions clause in investment law was the ICSID tribunal in *Bear Creek v. Peru* in 2017. It took the view that the exceptions clause contained in the Canada-Peru FTA[222] might qualify as *lex specialis* to other exceptions or justifications under general international law. The tribunal held that "already the title of Article 2201 '*General Exceptions*' shows that otherwise Chapter Eight (investment) remains applicable [. . .]"[223] and that:

> in view of the very detailed provisions of the FTA regarding expropriation (Article 812 and Annex 812.1) and regarding exceptions in Article 2201 expressly designated to "Chapter Eight (Investment)", the interpretation of the FTA must lead to the conclusion

---

[219] *See* Costa Rica's submission in Infinito Gold Ltd. v. Costa Rica, ICSID Case No. ARB/14/5, Decision on Jurisdiction, 4 December 2017, para. 346; *see also* Colombia's submission in Eco Oro Minerals Corp. v. Republic of Colombia, ICSID Case No. ARB/16/41, Decision on Jurisdiction, Liability and Directions on Quantum, 9 September 2021, paras. 362–365.

[220] *See, e.g.,* LEVENT SABANOGUALLARI, GENERAL EXCEPTION CLAUSES IN INTERNATIONAL INVESTMENT LAW—THE RECALIBRATION OF INVESTMENT AGREEMENTS VIA WTO-BASED FLEXIBILITIES 40 (2018); Amelia Keene, *The Incorporation and Interpretation of WTO-Style Environmental Exceptions in International Investment Agreements*, 18 JOURNAL OF WORLD INVESTMENT & TRADE 62, 86 (2017).

[221] *See, e.g.,* Eco Oro Minerals Corp. v. Republic of Colombia, ICSID Case No. ARB/16/41, Non-Disputing Party Submission of Canada, 27 February 2020, para. 16 ("If the general exception applies, then there is no violation of the Agreement and no State liability. Payment of compensation would therefore not be required."); *see further* ibid., para. 23 ("The exceptions in Article 2201 cannot be used to broaden the scope of the primary obligations. Such a reading would have unintended consequences. Thus, for example, environmental measures that have the effect of depriving investors of the use and enjoyment of their property or vested rights must therefore first and foremost be considered in light of Annex 811.2 to determine whether there is a compensable expropriation. The Parties' intention was never to limit the scope of legitimate policy objectives that States can pursue and that would not breach the investment obligations in the first place.").

[222] Article 2201(3) Canada-Peru FTA (2008) ("For the purposes of Chapter Eight (Investment), subject to the requirement that such measures are not applied in a manner that constitute arbitrary or unjustifiable discrimination between investments or between investors, or a disguised restriction on international trade or investment, nothing in this Agreement shall be construed to prevent a Party from adopting or enforcing measures necessary:
(a) to protect human, animal or plant life or health, which the Parties understand to include environmental measures necessary to protect human, animal or plant life or health;
(b) to ensure compliance with laws and regulations that are not inconsistent with this Agreement; or
(c) for the conservation of living or non-living exhaustible natural resources.").

[223] Bear Creek Mining Corporation v. Republic of Peru, ICSID Case No. ARB/14/21, Award, 30 November 2017, para. 473.

that no other exceptions from general international law or otherwise can be considered applicable in this case.[224]

The tribunal further noted that:

> since the exception in Article 2201 does not offer any waiver from the obligation in Article 812 to compensate for the expropriation, Respondent has also failed to explain why it was necessary for the protection of human life not to offer compensation to Claimant for the derogation of Supreme Decree 083.[225]

In 2021, the tribunal in *Infinito Gold v. Costa Rica* addressed the argument that Annex I, Section III(1) of the Canada–Costa Rica BIT exempted the respondent state from liability. The provision reads:

> Nothing in this Agreement shall be construed to prevent a Contracting Party from adopting, maintaining or enforcing any measure otherwise consistent with this Agreement that it considers appropriate to ensure that investment activity in its territory is undertaken in a manner sensitive to environmental concerns.[226]

Already in 2017, the respondent state had challenged the tribunal's jurisdiction with reference to that provision, although Costa Rica also acknowledged that this provision could be a matter for the merits.[227] In its decision on jurisdiction, the tribunal held that:

> any objection by the Respondent based on Annex I, Section III(1) of the BIT is a matter for the merits. As is obvious from its plain language quoted above, this provision sets out guidelines regarding the content of measures that may be adopted, maintained or enforced by the host State. It does not relate to the State's consent to arbitrate, nor to whether a claim can be heard or not; it relates to whether a particular measure has or has not breached the BIT. Accordingly, it cannot be deemed a matter of jurisdiction or admissibility; it must properly be regarded as a matter for the merits.[228]

In the 2021 award on the merits, the tribunal emphasized that this provision included the phrase "any measure otherwise consistent with this Agreement" and the tribunal pointed out that "this wording makes it clear that measures meant 'to ensure that investment activity [. . .] is undertaken in a manner sensitive to environmental concerns' must also be consistent with the investment protections set forth in the BIT."[229] Accordingly, the provision "does not exempt an environmental measure from the substantive provisions of the BIT, regardless of whether that measure is a new measure that is 'adopted' or whether it is a measure that 'maintains' or 'enforces' an earlier measure."[230] In the eyes of the tribunal, this provision merely codified the right to regulate: "Annex I, Section III(1) is not a carve-out from the

---

[224] Ibid., para. 473.

[225] Ibid., para. 477.

[226] Annex I, Section III(1) Canada–Costa Rica BIT (1998).

[227] Infinito Gold Ltd. v. Costa Rica, ICSID Case No. ARB/14/5, Decision on Jurisdiction, 4 December 2017, para. 346.

[228] Ibid., para. 358.

[229] Infinito Gold Ltd. v. Costa Rica, ICSID Case No. ARB/14/5, Award, 3 June 2021, para. 772.

[230] Ibid., para. 776.

BIT's protections, but rather a reaffirmation of the State's right to regulate."[231] Disagreeing with the respondent state that such an interpretation would render such clauses meaningless, the tribunal pointed out that such provisions remind "interpreters that these two objectives—environment and investment protection—should, if possible be reconciled so that they are mutually supportive and reinforcing."[232]

Also in 2021, the tribunal in *Eco Oro v. Colombia* interpreted the general exceptions clause in Article 2201(3) Canada-Colombia FTA, which stipulates:

> For the purposes of Chapter Eight (Investment), subject to the requirement that such measures are not applied in a manner that constitute arbitrary or unjustifiable discrimination between investment or between investors, or a disguised restriction on international trade or investment, nothing in this Agreement shall be construed to prevent a Party from adopting or enforcing measures necessary:
> a. To protect human, animal or plant life or health, which the Parties understand to include environmental measures necessary to protect human, animal or plant life and health;
> b. To ensure compliance with laws and regulations that are not inconsistent with this Agreement; or
> c. For the conservation of living or non-living exhaustible natural resources.[233]

The tribunal noted that this provision does not play a role at the jurisdictional level:

> [I]t is difficult to construe Article 2201(3) other than as in principle being of application when Chapter Eight is engaged, rather than applying to exclude the totality of the application of Chapter Eight [i.e. Investment Chapter of the FTA]. Had it been intended, as contended for by Colombia, that environmental measures *per se* were entirely outside the scope of Chapter Eight, the measures listed in Article 2201(3) would not be referred to as "exceptions" to Chapter Eight; the words would be redundant.[234]

When addressing liability, the tribunal started its analysis by noting that "[t]he Preamble to the FTA details, *inter alia*, that its object and purpose is to ensure a predictable commercial framework for business planning and investment in a manner that is consistent with environmental protection and conservation."[235] Accordingly, "neither environmental protection nor investment protection is subservient to the other, they must coexist in a mutually beneficial manner."[236] The tribunal essentially interpreted the clause as preventing a claimant from requesting cessation or restitution in cases where nondiscriminatory measures had been taken to protect human, animal, or plant life or health,

---

[231] Ibid., para. 777.

[232] Ibid., para. 788 (footnote omitted).

[233] Article 2201(3) Canada-Colombia FTA (2008).

[234] Eco Oro Minerals Corp. v. Republic of Colombia, ICSID Case No. ARB/16/41, Decision on Jurisdiction, Liability and Directions on Quantum, 9 September 2021, para. 380; *see further* ibid., para. 380 ("The Tribunal's analysis is supported by Canada's submissions that these exceptions only apply once there has been a determination that there is a breach of a primary obligation in Chapter Eight." ([footnote omitted])).

[235] Ibid., para. 828.

[236] Ibid., para. 828.

but the state was still required to pay compensation or damages when such measures had been adopted:

> [B]y prohibiting an investor from applying for restitution pursuant to Article 834(2)(b), the State is not precluded from adopting or enforcing the measure in question. Equally, however, there is no provision in Article 2201(3) permitting such action to be taken without the payment of compensation.[237]

Thus, the tribunal summarized that "whilst a State may adopt or enforce a measure pursuant to the stated objectives in Article 2201(3) without finding itself in breach of the FTA, this does not prevent an investor claiming under Chapter Eight that such a measure entitles it to the payment of compensation."[238] As further support for its conclusion, the tribunal mentioned the *Bear Creek* award and Article 27(b)[239] and Article 36(1)[240] ILC Articles on State Responsibility.[241] On a general note, the tribunal emphasized that:

> Colombia also provided no justification as to why it is necessary for the protection of the environment not to offer compensation to an investor for any loss suffered as a result of measures taken by Colombia to protect the environment, nor explained how such a construction would support the protection of investment in addition to the protection of the environment.[242]

IV. QUANTUM

In 2021, a number of tribunals ruled that the respondent state had breached the applicable investment treaty leading in principle to liability, but no damages could be awarded in the quantum phase.

In an undisclosed ICSID award in *Amlyn Holding v. Croatia*[243] the tribunal reportedly found a breach of the ECT, but rejected the claim for damages because the ECT breach had not caused damage to the claimant.[244]

---

[237] Ibid., para. 829; *see further* ibid., para. 829 ("Given that the FTA is equally supportive of investment protection, had it been the intention of the Contracting Parties that a measure could be taken pursuant to Article 2201(3) without any liability for compensation, the Article would have been drafted in similar terms as Annex 811(2)(b), namely making explicit that the taking of such a measure would not give rise to any right to seek compensation under Chapter Eight.").

[238] Ibid., para. 830.

[239] Article 27(b), ILC, "Articles on State Responsibility of States for Internationally Wrongful Acts" UNGA Res 56/83 (12 December 2001) UN Doc. A/RES/56/83 (ARSIWA) ("The invocation of a circumstance precluding wrongfulness in accordance with this chapter is without prejudice to: [...] (b) the question of compensation for any material loss caused by the act in question. [...]").

[240] Article 36(1) ARSIWA ("The State responsible for an internationally wrongful act is under an obligation to compensate for the damage caused thereby, insofar as such damage is not made good by restitution.").

[241] Eco Oro Minerals Corp. v. Republic of Colombia, ICSID Case No. ARB/16/41, Decision on Jurisdiction, Liability and Directions on Quantum, 9 September 2021, para. 835.

[242] Ibid., para. 832.

[243] Amlyn Holding B.V. v. Republic of Croatia, ICSID Case No. ARB/16/28, Final Award, 22 October 2021.

[244] *See* Vladislav Djanic, *ICSID Tribunal Finds Discrete ECT Breach in intra-EU Case against Croatia, But Claimant Is Awarded No Damages Due to Lack of Causation* (28 October 2021), available at <https://

Similarly, in *Infinito Gold v. Costa Rica*, the tribunal did not award damages for an FET breach. It held that a legislative ban on open-pit mining, which prevented the investor from applying for a new concession, was unreasonable and disproportionate, thus breaching the FET provision.[245] Yet the tribunal noted that it "has difficulty identifying the damage which the breach may have caused."[246] Irrespective of the legislative mining ban, the tribunal emphasized that the investor would not have been able to apply for an exploitation concession because of an executive moratorium on open-pit mining, which was beyond the scope of jurisdiction *ratione temporis*.[247]

In any event, the tribunal further held that "[e]ven if the Tribunal were to accept that the fact of harm was established, this would not assist the Claimant's case."[248] It declined to award damages because:

> the Claimant's harm would essentially consist in the loss of an opportunity or chance to apply for an exploitation concession. Yet, the Claimant has not put forward a quantification for such a loss of opportunity, nor has it provided the Tribunal with any elements to calculate it. If one adds the inherent uncertainty and the regulatory risk involved in any application process, the monetary consequences of this loss of chance appear too speculative to give rise to an award of damages.[249]

Furthermore, in *Pawlowski and Project Sever v. Czech Republic*, the tribunal—though finding a breach of the BIT[250]—did not award damages. It held that the "duty to make reparation extends only to those damages which have been proven by the injured party and which are legally regarded as the consequence of the wrongful act."[251] However, claimants could not prove that any damages were caused by the wrongful act.[252]

Still, the tribunal in *Pawlowski and Project Sever v. Czech Republic* held that a state which had breached international law was required to give satisfaction if the injury could not be remedied either by restitution or compensation.[253] Satisfaction should not be disproportionate or take a form which humiliates the responsible state.[254] The tribunal noted that

---

www.iareporter.com/articles/icsid-tribunal-finds-discrete-ect-breach-in-intra-eu-case-against-croatia-but-claimant-is-awarded-no-damages-due-to-lack-of-causation/> (accessed 15 July 2022).

[245] Infinito Gold Ltd. v. Republic of Costa Rica, ICSID Case No. ARB/14/5, Award, 3 June 2021, paras. 553–581.

[246] Ibid., para. 582.

[247] Ibid., para. 584.

[248] Ibid., para. 585.

[249] Ibid.

[250] Pawlowski AG and Project Sever s.r.o. v. Czech Republic, ICSID Case No. ARB/17/11, Award, 1 November 2021, para. 722 ("The claim accepted by the Tribunal relates to Mayor Topičová's requests, on behalf of the District of Benice, demanding significant payments from Projekt Sever as quid pro quo for the withdrawal of the Benice Lawsuit filed by the District against Projekt Sever, and for the District's change of position regarding the increase in the density coefficient. In the opinion of the Tribunal, this conduct resulted in the breach of the specific prohibition of unreasonable measures established in Article 4(1) and of the general FET standard guaranteed in Article 4(2) of the BIT.").

[251] Ibid., para. 728.

[252] Ibid., paras. 731–736.

[253] Ibid., para. 738.

[254] Ibid., para. 738.

claimants did request satisfaction, namely, "a declaration by the Tribunal that the Czech Republic has committed a violation of Article 4 of the BIT."[255] According to the tribunal "such a declaration is proportionate to the injury caused, is not humiliating for the responsible State, and consequently agrees to give satisfaction to Claimants, by making the appropriate declaration in the *dispositif* of this Award."[256]

V. ANNULMENT DECISIONS

As in previous years, annulment committees have emphasized that their mandate is limited. They can only annul an award on the basis of the specific grounds listed in Article 52 ICSID Convention.[257] *Ad hoc* committees in 2021 have also pointed out that they had a discretion whether to annul or not annul an award. The annulment committee in *Glencore v. Colombia* held that:

> it is important to bear in mind that Article 52(3) of the ICSID Convention states that an ad hoc committee *"shall have the authority to annul the award or any part thereof on any of the grounds set forth in paragraph (1)"*. The fact that the Convention speaks of a committee having the authority to annul indicates that, even where an *ad hoc* committee determines that one of the grounds for annulment is made out, the Committee has a discretion whether or not to annul the award.[258]

However, it also noted that:

> [t]hat discretion is by no means unlimited and must take account of all relevant circumstances, including the gravity of the circumstances which constitute the ground for annulment and whether or not they had—or could have had—a material effect upon the outcome of the case, as well as the importance of the finality of the award and the overall question of fairness to both Parties.[259]

---

[255] Ibid., para. 739.

[256] Ibid., para. 740.

[257] *See* Perenco Ecuador Limited v. Republic of Ecuador, ICSID Case No. ARB/08/6, Decision on Annulment, 28 May 2021, para. 58 ("the Committee finds that the grounds set out in Article 52(1) are exhaustive, and therefore *ad hoc* committees have no power to annul an award under any other grounds."); *see further* Article 52(1) ICSID Convention, *supra* note 3 ("Either party may request annulment of the award by an application in writing addressed to the Secretary-General on one or more of the following grounds:

    (a)   that the Tribunal was not properly constituted;

    (b)   that the Tribunal has manifestly exceeded its powers;

    (c)   that there was corruption on the part of a member of the Tribunal;

    (d)   that there has been a serious departure from a fundamental rule of procedure; or

    (e)   that the award has failed to state the reasons on which it is based.").

[258] Glencore International A.G. and C.I. Prodeco S.A. v. Republic of Colombia, ICSID Case No. ARB/16/6, Decision on Annulment, 22 September 2021, para. 217 (footnote omitted).

[259] Ibid., para. 217 (footnote omitted).

Another *ad hoc* committee—*Infrastructure Services v. Luxembourg*—pointed out that the "ICSID Convention does not require an automatic exercise by an annulment committee of its authority to annul an award even if a ground has been established."[260]

An award discussed in a previous introductory note[261]—*Cortec Mining v. Kenya*—was reviewed by an annulment committee. The tribunal had assumed an implicit legality requirement for investments under the BIT and dismissed jurisdiction because:

> the Claimants' failure to comply with the legislature's regulatory regime governing the Mrima Hill forest and nature reserve, and the Claimants' failure to obtain an EIA licence (or approval in any valid form) [. . .] concerning the environmental issues involved in the proposed removal of 130 million tonnes of material from Mrima Hill, constituted violations of Kenyan law that, in terms of international law, warrant the proportionate response of a denial of treaty protection under the BIT and the ICSID Convention.[262]

The annulment committee found that the tribunal had not exceeded its power in that regard:

> Simply stated, this Committee should not disturb the Tribunal's interpretation of the BIT as containing an implicit legality requirement unless the Applicants show that interpretation to be "so untenable that it cannot be supported by reasonable arguments." In the Committee's view, the Applicants have not made the requisite showing here.[263]

The *ad hoc* committee pointed out that "[t]his is not to suggest that the Tribunal's interpretation of the BIT (or the ICSID Convention) is the correct one. It is an expansive interpretation, and some arbitrators—perhaps many—would likely disagree."[264] However, this did not imply that a manifest excess of powers had been committed by the tribunal.[265]

In 2021 some annulment committees also had to assess whether dismissals of intra-EU objections to ICSID jurisdiction were annullable.[266] No annulment committee took issue with the treatment of these questions by tribunals.

---

[260] Infrastructure Services Luxembourg S.à.r.l. and Energia Termosolar B.V. (formerly Antin Infrastructure Services Luxembourg S.à.r.l. and Antin Energia Termosolar B.V.) v. Kingdom of Spain, ICSID Case No. ARB/13/31, Decision on Annulment, 30 July 2021, para. 233.

[261] *See* August Reinisch, *From Broad Jurisdictional Powers of ICSID Tribunals to the Limited Review Powers of Annulment Committees—ICSID Arbitration in 2018*, 19 GLOBAL COMMUNITY YILJ 2019 (Giuliana Ziccardi Capaldo General ed.) 725, 729–730 (2020).

[262] Cortec Mining Kenya Limited, Cortec (Pty) Limited and Stirling Capital Limited v. Republic of Kenya, ICSID Case No. ARB/15/29, Award, 22 October 2018, para. 365.

[263] Cortec Mining Kenya Limited, Cortec (Pty) Limited and Stirling Capital Limited v. Republic of Kenya, ICSID Case No. ARB/15/29, Decision on Application for Annulment, 19 March 2021, para.136 (footnote omitted).

[264] Ibid., para. 141.

[265] Ibid., paras. 141–144.

[266] Infrastructure Services Luxembourg S.à.r.l. and Energia Termosolar B.V. (formerly Antin Infrastructure Services Luxembourg S.à.r.l. and Antin Energia Termosolar B.V.) v. Kingdom of Spain, ICSID Case No. ARB/13/31, Decision on Annulment, 30 July 2021; UP and C.D Holding Internationale v. Hungary, ICSID Case No. ARB/13/35, Decision on Annulment, 11 August 2021.

VI. CONCLUSION

ICSID cases in 2021 dealt with classical jurisdictional issues like *ratione materiae* and *ratione personae* requirements under the ICSID Convention, but also with less common jurisdictional defences like abuse of process, illegality in the making of an investment, and intra-EU obstacles to investment arbitration. They also clarified procedural issues such as when claims should be dismissed because they are manifestly without legal merit or when security for costs should be ordered.

In regard to protection standards, tribunals addressed a number of questions concerning expropriation, among them when judicial acts amount to expropriation or how to distinguish between indirect expropriation and the exercise of the host country's police powers. They also clarified aspects of fair and equitable treatment, in particular, when a denial of justice, amounting to a violation of fair and equitable treatment, occurs. In addition, the scope of the free transfer of funds obligation was addressed as well as limits of protection stemming from the operation of exception clauses regularly contained in investment agreements. In regard to quantum, ICSID tribunals confirmed that sometimes even treaty violations do not entail the obligation to make monetary compensation.

LEGAL MAXIMS: SUMMARIES AND EXTRACTS FROM SELECTED CASE LAW*

Infinito Gold Ltd. v. *Republic of Costa Rica*, ICSID Case No. ARB/14/5, Award, 3 June 2021

Mathias Kruck and Others v. *Kingdom of Spain*, ICSID Case No. ARB/15/23, Decision on the Respondent's Request for Reconsideration of the Tribunal's Decision dated 19 April 2021, 6 December 2021

---

* The working method chosen for the formulation of legal maxims is explained *supra* 'Outline of the Parts', at page xv.

Legal Maxims: Summaries and Extracts from Selected Case Law In: *The Global Community Yearbook of International Law and Jurisprudence 2022*. Edited by: Giuliana Ziccardi Capaldo, Oxford University Press. © Oxford University Press 2023.
DOI: 10.1093/oso/9780197752265.003.0032

X.2.1

Infinito Gold Ltd. v. Republic of Costa Rica, ICSID Case No. ARB/14/5, Award, 3 June 2021*

Contents**

I. THE DISPUTE

II. JURISDICTION AND ADMISSIBILITY

    A. ILLEGALITY OF INVESTMENT AND CORRUPTION

    B. STATUTE OF LIMITATIONS FOR INVESTMENT CLAIMS

        1. CUT-OFF DATE FOR INVESTMENT CLAIMS AND COMPOSITE ACTS

        2. CUT-OFF DATE FOR EXPROPRIATION CLAIM

        3. CUT-OFF DATE FOR DENIAL OF JUSTICE CLAIM

III. SUBSTANTIVE ISSUES

    A. FAIR AND EQUITABLE TREATMENT (FET): SCOPE AND CONTENT

        1. NO LIMITATION OF FET TO MINIMUM STANDARD OF TREATMENT

        2. MEANING OF FET

        3. FET BREACH OUTSIDE OF A DENIAL OF JUSTICE

        4. DENIAL OF JUSTICE AS PART OF FET

        5. BREACH OF FET BY APPLICATION OF LEGISLATIVE ACT

    B. NO DAMAGES FOR FET BREACH ABSENT PROVEN HARM

    C. NO EXPROPRIATION ABSENT VALID LEGAL CLAIMS CAPABLE OF BEING EXPROPRIATED

    D. 'RIGHT TO REGULATE'-CLAUSE DOES NOT EXEMPT FROM LIABILITY FOR TREATY BREACHES

IV. DECISION

I.

II.7.911   REQUEST FOR ICSID ARBITRATION

"[4] This dispute arises out of the development of a gold mining project in the area of Las Crucitas, in Costa Rica (the "**Crucitas Project**"). [68] In May 2000, the Claimant

---

  * Summaries prepared by Johannes Tropper, Researcher & Lecturer (prae doc), Department of European, International and Comparative Law, University of Vienna, Austria. The full text of the Decision is available at <https://www.italaw.com/sites/default/files/case-documents/italaw16219.pdf >. Original footnote numbers are indicated in brackets: [ ].

** This is not a faithful reproduction of the Table of Contents of the Judgment.

(then known as Vannessa Ventures Ltd.) acquired Industrias Infinito S.A. ("**Industrias Infinito**"). Industrias Infinito held an exploration permit for the Crucitas area [...]. [**74**] On 17 December 2001, Industrias Infinito obtained its exploitation concession [...]. The concession became effective on 30 January 2002 (the "**2002 Concession**"). [...] [**78**] On 8 May 2002, Mr. Abel Pacheco took office as President of Costa Rica. On 5 June 2002, President Pacheco declared an indefinite moratorium on open-pit mining [...]. [**83**] On 26 November 2004, the Constitutional Chamber ruled [...] that the 2002 Concession violated Article 50 of the Constitution, which guarantees the right to a healthy and ecologically balanced environment, because that concession was granted prior to the approval of the EIA. [...] [**91**] On 21 April 2008, President Arias and the MINAE granted Industrias Infinito an exploitation concession (the "**2008 Concession**" or the "**Concession**"), using the administrative law concept of "conversion" (*i.e.*, the previous annulled concession is converted into a valid one).[1] [...] [**97**] On 16 April 2010 [...] the Constitutional Chamber held that the Crucitas Project [...] did not violate the petitioners' constitutional right to a healthy environment.[2] [...] [**102**] On 24 November 2010, the TCA [i.e. Contentious Administrative Tribunal] issued an oral summary of its decision on the annulment request filed by Mr. Lobos and APREFLOFAS, declaring that all requests for annulment had been upheld (the "**2010 TCA Decision**")[3] [...]. The TCA [...] annulled Industrias Infinito's 2008 Concession together with related administrative decisions.[4] The main basis for this annulment was that, when the 2004 Constitutional Chamber Decision annulled the 2002 Concession, that annulment qualified as an absolute nullity and thus invalidated Industrias Infinito's rights *ab initio*. [...] [**104**] In December 2010, the Costa Rican legislature enacted an amendment to the Mining Code prohibiting open pit mining, which came into force on 10 February 2011 [...]. [**108**] On 30 November 2011, the Administrative Chamber of the Supreme Court denied Industrias Infinito's cassation request, and upheld the main conclusions of the 2010 TCA Decision (the "**2011 Administrative Chamber Decision**").[5] [...] [**113**] Industrias Infinito left the Crucitas site on 10 September 2015.[6]"

[**Paras. 4, 68, 74, 78, 83, 91, 97, 102, 104, 108, 113**]

II.

A.

II.7.9211   QUALIFICATION AS INVESTMENT

"[**129**] As noted in the Decision on Jurisdiction, the BIT expressly requires that investments must be "owned or controlled" in accordance with Costa Rican law.[7] The Respondent submits that "[i]t is uncontroversial and well established in investment law that where a treaty contains a provision requiring investments to be in accordance with a host-State's laws, investments which are illegal under that law are not protected

---

[1]   [Footnote omitted].
[2]   [Footnote omitted].
[3]   [Footnote omitted].
[4]   [Footnote omitted].
[5]   [Footnote omitted].
[6]   [Footnote omitted].
[7]   [134] R-CM Merits, ¶ 301; Decision on Jurisdiction, ¶¶ 138, 235(iii).

by the BIT and fall outside the scope of the State's consent to arbitration."[8] [...] [**169**] The Respondent objects that the Tribunal lacks jurisdiction *ratione materiae* and *ratione voluntatis* over the entire dispute because the Concession was not owned or controlled in accordance with Costa Rican law, as required under Article I(g) of the BIT.[9] [**172**] The Respondent submits that it is well established that, where a treaty contains a legality requirement, as is the case here, investments which are illegal are not protected and fall outside the scope of the State's consent to arbitration.[10] [...] [**173**] Depending on the content of the treaty, illegality can affect jurisdiction, admissibility or the merits of the claims. Here, the legality requirement forms part of the definition of investment. Consequently, the Tribunal agrees with the Respondent that, to qualify as a protected investment under the BIT, the Claimant's investment must be an asset owned or controlled in accordance with Costa Rica's laws. If it is not, then the Tribunal will lack jurisdiction. Indeed, the conditions for jurisdiction as defined under the BIT will not be fulfilled and, by the same token, the requirement for consent under Article 25 of the ICSID Convention will not be met. [**176**] In light of the Treaty's text, the asset that qualifies as an investment for purposes of establishing jurisdiction are the Claimant's shares in Industrias Infinito, which the Claimant owns indirectly, through Crucitas (Barbados) Limited, a corporation incorporated under the laws of Barbados, *i.e.*, an enterprise of a third State.[11] As a result, the shares are the investment to which, according to the Treaty, the legality requirement attaches. Seen in this light, the Claimant's shares in Industrias Infinito are far from being an "ancillary investment," as the Respondent contends. To the contrary, it is the Claimant's main investment, without which it would have no access to jurisdiction under the Treaty. [**177**] The Respondent has not disputed that the Claimant owns or controls its shares in Industrias Infinito in accordance with Costa Rican law. Nor has it argued that the Claimant acquired these shares illegally, or that its ownership or control of these shares has been vitiated in any way. As to the allegations of corruption, the record is clear that they concerned "matters that happened after the initial investment was made."[12] On this basis, the Tribunal finds that the Respondent's allegations that the 2008 Concession and related approvals were acquired illegally or were affected by legal flaws are irrelevant for purposes of jurisdiction. [**178**] There being no dispute that the Claimant has made an

---

[8] [135] CM Merits, ¶ 298, citing inter alia Fraport AG Frankfurt Airport Services Worldwide v. Republic of the Philippines, ICSID Case No. ARB/03/25, Award, 16 August 2007 ("**Fraport I**"), ¶ 339, Exh. **CL-0207**; Inceysa Vallisoletana S.L. v. Republic of El Salvador, ICSID Case No. ARB/03/26, Award, 2 August 2000 ("**Inceysa**"), ¶ 207, Exh. **RL-0183**; Salini Costruttori S.p.A. and Italstrade S.p.A. v. Kingdom of Morocco, ICSID Case No. ARB/00/4, Decision on Jurisdiction, 31 July 2001 ("**Salini**"), ¶ 46, Exh. **RL-0184**.

[9] [208] R-CM Merits, ¶ 297.

[10] [212] R-CM Merits, ¶ 298, citing *inter alia Fraport I*, ¶ 339, Exh. **CL-0207**; *Inceysa*, ¶ 207, Exh. **RL-0183**; *Salini*, ¶ 46, Exh. **RL-0184**.

[11] [219] CER-FTI Consulting 1, n. 15. While the Claimant has also referred to moneys it has invested in Industrias Infinito, the Tribunal considers it unnecessary to refer to these if ownership to the shares is established. In the event that these funds were still owned by Infinito and had not passed into the ownership of its subsidiary at the relevant time, the Tribunal notes that, as observed in Inmaris, for purposes of jurisdiction it need not examine whether each and every element of an investment meets the requirements of the BIT and the ICSID Convention; it "need only determine the existence of a covered investment in the transaction as a whole." *Inmaris Perestroika Sailing Maritime Services GmbH and others v. Ukraine*, ICSID Case No. ARB/08/8, Decision on Jurisdiction, 8 March 2010 ("*Inmaris*"), ¶ 92, Exh. **CL-0258**.

[12] [220] Tr. Jur. Day 2 (ENG), 421:5-6 (Mr. Evseev).

indirect investment in Costa Rica (*i.e.*, its shares in Industrias Infinito) in accordance with its laws, the Tribunal rejects the Respondent's illegality objection. For reasons of procedural economy, it finds it unnecessary to address the Parties' conceptual disagreements as to the temporal and subject matter scopes of the legality requirement found at Article I(g), or their arguments on estoppel. This being said, as the corruption allegations made by APREFLOFAS [i.e. Association for the Preservation of Flora and Fauna] raise an issue of international public policy, which the Tribunal must address *ex officio*, the Tribunal will review whether the acquisition of this investment was tainted by corruption. [**179**] As noted above, both the Respondent and APREFLOFAS alleged that there are indicia that the Claimant's investment was procured through corruption,[13] and that consequently, the Claimant's investment "falls outside both the scope of the BIT's protections and Costa Rica's consent to arbitration."[14] The Respondent has since withdrawn this objection, with the justification that "the investigation of possible bribery resulting from the donation by the Claimant's shareholder Ronald Mannix to former President Arias' foundation has been discontinued following the decision of the Costa Rican Criminal Court that specific charges against Mr Arias (but not others) were time-barred."[15] [**180**] In spite of this withdrawal, the Tribunal will address this corruption allegation for the reasons mentioned above. First of all, the Tribunal notes that the allegations of corruption by the Respondent and APREFLOFAS relate to the acquisition of the 2008 Concession, which was granted during President Arias's administration.[16] As the Respondent admitted during the Hearing on Jurisdiction, the allegations of corruption concern "matters that happened after the initial investment was made,"[17] which the Tribunal understands to mean that they do not relate to the Claimant's acquisition of shares in Industrias Infinito. Hence, even if the corruption allegations were well-founded, *quod non*, this would not imply that the acquisition of the shares, which is the relevant investment for present purposes, was unlawful. It would mean that later conduct of the investor was tainted, which could be a defense on the merits, but not an obstacle to jurisdiction. [**181**] In any event, there are insufficient signals in the record that the 2008 Concession was obtained through corruption. In particular, APREFLOFAS and the Respondent were relying on an investigation against former President Oscar Arias and other officials involved in the granting of the Concession[18] that has been discontinued.[19] While it appears that the discontinuation decision was annulled and remanded to the first court for a *de novo* assessment,[20] there is no indication that the charges against President Arias can proceed. Moreover, there is no element on record

---

[13] [221] R-CM Merits, ¶ 297.

[14] [222] R-CM Merits, ¶ 297.

[15] [223] R-Rej. Merits, ¶ 239, fn. 404. *See also* R-Rej. Merits, ¶¶ 208-209

[16] [224] R-CM Merits, ¶¶ 363-365; APREFLOFAS's First Submission, ¶¶ 10-12, 15-21; APREFLOFAS's Second Submission, ¶¶ 9-15.

[17] [225] *See* Tr. Jur. Day 2 (ENG), 421:5-6 (Mr. Evseev).

[18] [226] APREFLOFAS's First Submission, ¶¶ 3, 10-14, 19-23; Accusation and Request to Open a Trial, Criminal Court of the Treasury, File No. 08-000012-033-PE (8 November 2012), Exh. **C-0278**; Criminal Court for Treasury and Public Service, II Judicial Circuit of San Jose, Case No. 08- 000011-033-PE, Trial Order (5 May 2013), Exh. **NDP-001**; Criminal Trial's Tribunal, II Judicial Circuit of San Jose, Case No. 08-00011-033-PE,Decision No. 32-2015(28 January 2015), Exh. **NDP-002**.

[19] [227] R-Rej. Merits, ¶¶ 208-209; "*Óscar Arias sobreseído por prescripción en caso Crucitas*," La Nación, 21 February 2019, Exh. **R-0273**.

[20] [228] R-Rej. Merits, ¶¶ 210-211; "*Juez señaló 'grosero error' en sobreseimiento a favor de Óscar Arias*," CRHoy.com, 9 May 2019, Exh. **R-0274**.

accrediting APREFLOFAS's suggestion that the Arias foundation received a USD 200,000 donation from one of the Claimant's investors. When assessing the record and reaching the findings just set out, the Tribunal has taken into consideration that it is notoriously difficult to prove corruption and that, as a result, tribunals tend to focus on circumstantial evidence, relying on indicia or red flags. Even adopting such less demanding standard of proof, it cannot conclude that the 2008 Concession was procured by corruption. As a consequence, it will not revert to this issue in the context of the merits, considering that the inquiry would not be different on the merits and that it has discharged its *ex officio* duty in matters of international public policy for purposes of jurisdiction and merits here. [**182**] Therefore, the Tribunal denies the Respondent's illegality objection. It will consider the Respondent's arguments that the 2008 Concession suffered from legal defects or that Industrias Infinito otherwise breached Costa Rican administrative or environmental law when assessing the merits."

[**Paras. 129, 169, 172, 173, 176, 177, 178, 179, 180, 181, 182**]

B.

1.

II.7.92   ICSID JURISDICTION
              See also: I.11.0; I.11.012; I.11.0141

"[**216**] Pursuant to Article XII(3)(c) of the BIT, an investor may submit a dispute to arbitration only if "(c) not more than three years have elapsed from the date on which the investor first acquired, or should have first acquired, knowledge of the alleged breach and knowledge that the investor has incurred loss or damage."[21] In other words, a claim is barred if the Claimant had (actual or constructive) knowledge (i) of the alleged breach and (ii) of the loss it caused, more than three years before the Request for Arbitration was filed. [**217**] As stated in the Decision on Jurisdiction, to decide this objection "the Tribunal must answer three questions: (i) first, it must identify the cut-off date for the three-year limitation period; (ii) second, it must determine whether the Claimant knew or should have known of the alleged breach or breaches before that cut-off date; and (iii) third, it must determine whether the Claimant knew or should have known that it had incurred loss or damage before that date."[22] [**219**] As discussed in the Decision on Jurisdiction, the Request for Arbitration was filed on 6 February 2014. Hence, the Tribunal lacks jurisdiction over claims regarding which the Claimant first acquired knowledge of the breach and loss more than three years earlier, *i.e.* before **6 February 2011**. The Parties agree with this cut-off date.[23] [**220**] For the claims to be time-barred, Article XII(3)(c) requires the Claimant to have first acquired both knowledge of the alleged breach and knowledge that it has incurred loss or damage, prior to the cut-off date. The Tribunal notes that the BIT refers to knowledge of the alleged *breach*, and not to knowledge of the *facts* that make up the alleged breach. In other words, the limitations period only starts to run once the breach (as a legal notion) has occurred. While a breach will necessarily have been caused by facts, as discussed below, the moment at which a breach "occurs" will depend on when a fact or group of facts is capable of triggering a violation of international law. [**221**] Although the Treaty does not

---

[21] [302] BIT, Article XII(3)(c), **Exh. C-0001**.
[22] [303] Decision on Jurisdiction, ¶ 330
[23] [304] Decision on Jurisdiction, ¶ 331; *see, e.g.*, C-Mem. Merits, ¶ 233; R-Mem. Jur., ¶ 17.

expressly say so, the loss or damage must flow from the alleged breach. This does not neces-sarily mean that the loss always postdates the breach. Depending on the standard breached, breach and loss can coincide. This may be the case for expropriation, where the breach will usually crystallize when the direct taking or substantial deprivation occurs. This might also be the case for claims grounded upon a breach of fair and equitable treatment, if the viola-tion of legitimate expectations or arbitrariness is perpetrated by way of an act that causes damage. Hence, the Tribunal finds it more appropriate to address knowledge of breach and loss jointly for each alleged breach. [**222**] When undertaking its analysis, the Tribunal must also bear in mind that the Treaty (i) uses the conjunction "and", so knowledge of breach and loss are cumulative requirements; (ii) refers to "first" knowledge and not only know-ledge; (iii) covers both actual and constructive knowledge. [**223**] To establish when the Claimant first acquired actual or constructive knowledge of an alleged breach, the Tribunal must start by identifying when the alleged breach occurred. [**224**] The Claimant argues that the breaches of the Treaty occurred through five measures, which post-date the cut-off date, and which it alleges had the following effects:

a. The 2011 Administrative Chamber Decision dated 30 November 2011,[24] which confirmed the 2010 TCA Decision and rendered final and irreversible the annul-ment of the exploitation concession, environmental approvals, the declaration of public interest and national convenience, and the land use change permit.
b. The 2011 Legislative Mining Ban on open-pit mining,[25] which entered into force on 10 February 2011, and which prohibited Industrias Infinito from applying for new permits.
c. The 2012 MINAET Resolution dated 9 January 2012,[26] which cancelled the 2008 Concession and expunged all of Industrias Infinito's mining rights from the mining registry, going further than what was ordered by the Administrative Chamber.
d. The 2013 Constitutional Chamber Decision dated 19 June 2013,[27] which declined to resolve the conflict between its earlier decision upholding the constitutionality of the Crucitas Project approvals and the 2010 TCA Decision.
e. The reinitiation of the TCA proceedings for environmental damage in January 2019.[28]
[**225**] This being so, the Claimant does not allege that each of these measures was a separate treaty breach. As recorded in the Decision on Jurisdiction and confirmed in the Reply,[29] the Claimant argues that "[i]t is the *combined operation* of these four measures [. . .] that meant that Industrias Infinito definitively could no longer pursue the development of the Crucitas project."[30] [**226**] Specifically, the Claimant submits that the combined result of the first four measures breached the BIT in four ways:

---

[24] [305] Supreme Court (Administrative Chamber), Decision (30 November 2011), Exh. **C-0261**.
[25] [306] Amendment to Mining Code, No. 8904 (1 December 2010), Exh. **C-0238**.
[26] [307] Resolution No. 0037, MINAET, File No. 2594 (9 January 2012), Exh. **C-0268**.
[27] [308] Supreme Court (Constitutional Chamber), Decision (19 June 2013), Exh. **C-0283**.
[28] [309] Contentious Administrative Tribunal, Resolution (14 January 2019), Exh. **C-0861**. *See*, C-Reply. Merits, ¶¶ 18, 611-614, 823(b).
[29] [310] C-Reply Merits, ¶ 16 ("The combined effect of the measures adopted by Costa Rica accordingly breached four protections of the BIT.") *See also* C-Reply Merits, ¶¶ 19, 448, 466, 473, 551, 590- 592, 598, 692.
[30] [311] C-CM Jur., ¶ 12 (emphasis added). It should be noted that, at that time, Infinito had not yet complained about measure (e).

a. It expropriated its investments by definitively precluding Infinito from building and operating the Crucitas gold mine.[31]
b. It breached Costa Rica's obligation to provide fair and equitable treatment ("**FET**") by violating Infinito's legitimate expectations, treating Infinito arbitrarily and inconsistently, and denying both procedural and substantive justice to Infinito.[32]
c. It failed to grant Infinito's investments full protection and security ("**FPS**").[33]
d. It breached two substantive obligations imported into the BIT through the BIT's MFN clause from other investment treaties entered into by Costa Rica: (i) the obligation to do "what is necessary" to protect Infinito's investments, imported from the Costa Rica-France BIT, and (ii) the umbrella clause requiring the host State to "comply with [or observe] any obligation assumed regarding investments of investors of the other Contracting Party," found in Costa Rica's BITs with Taiwan and Korea.[34]

[**227**] As to the fifth measure, the Claimant argues that it is a continuation of Costa Rica's previous FET breach.[35] However, as is discussed in Section (vi) *infra*, it appears to have a separate effect. [**228**] The formulation of the claims suggests that the Claimant relies on a composite breach, *i.e.*, a breach by "a series of actions or omissions defined in aggregate as wrongful."[36] While it only expressly refers to composite acts in a footnote,[37] the argument is that the alleged breaches are the result of the combined effect of the various measures cited above (with the possible exception referred to in Section (vi) *infra*). A composite breach "occurs when the action or omission occurs which, taken with the other actions or omissions, is sufficient to constitute the wrongful act."[38] Accordingly, were the Tribunal to accept the Claimant's composite breach argument, it would need to determine the date on which the Claimant first acquired knowledge of the action in the series which was sufficient to constitute the breach, and of the resulting loss. [**230**] The Tribunal agrees with the Respondent that the Claimant has not properly substantiated its composite breach argument. The Claimant merely makes some references to combined or composite effect. It makes no submissions on the effect of a composite breach on the time bar requirement. Be this as it may, even if the Claimant had properly pleaded a composite breach, the Tribunal can see no composite breach in the measures impugned. The Commentary to ILC Article 15 makes it clear that, to amount to a composite breach, the various acts must not separately amount to the same breach as the composite act (although they could separately amount to

---

[31] [312] C-CM Jur., ¶ 13; C-Mem. Merits, ¶¶ 246-289.
[32] [313] C-CM Jur., ¶ 14; C-Mem. Merits, ¶¶ 290-344.
[33] [314] C-CM Jur., ¶ 15; C-Mem. Merits, ¶¶ 345-347.
[34] [315] C-CM Jur., ¶ 16; C-Mem. Merits, ¶¶ 348-360.
[35] [316] C-Reply Merits, ¶¶ 18, 613.
[36] [317] International Law Commission, Draft Articles on Responsibility of States for Internationally Wrongful Acts, with commentaries, Yearbook of the International Law Commission, Vol. II, Part Two (2001) ("**ILC Articles on State Responsibility**"), Article 15(1), Exh. **CL-0007**.
[37] [318] C-Reply Merits, p. 170, fn. 835 ("In cases involving a composite breach, there is no need to establish separate losses that are tied to each individual measure.")
[38] [319] ILC Articles on State Responsibility, Article 15(1), Exh. **CL-0007**. The Commentary further explains that a composite act "occurs" at "the time at which the last action or omission occurs which, taken with the other actions or omissions, is sufficient to constitute the wrongful act, without it necessarily having to be the last in the series." ILC Articles on State Responsibility, Commentary to Article 15, ¶ 8, Exh. **CL-0007**.

different breaches).[39] It also clarifies that the breach cannot "occur" with the first of the acts in the series.[40] Here, each of the measures could arguably amount separately to the same breach (an expropriation or a violation of FET), and the Claimant expressly alleges that the breach occurred with what it considers to be the first act in the series, namely, the 2011 Administrative Chamber Decision.[41] The Tribunal will thus assess the measures as simple breaches. [**231**] A simple breach is a breach by an "act of a State not having a continuing character."[42] As the Commentary to ILC Article 14 explains, it "occurs at the moment when the act is performed, even if its effects continue."[43] The Tribunal must thus determine the point in time in which an act is capable of constituting an international wrong. The cases cited by the Respondent suggest that, where the State has taken a series of separate measures that predate and post-date the cut-off date, tribunals have focused on the event which gave rise to the breach and have refused to look at subsequent events that are not legally significant or distinct.[44] [**232**] The Commentary to Article 14 provides further useful guidance. It states that "the existence and duration of a breach of an international obligation depends for the most part on the existence and content of the obligation and on the facts of the particular breach [...]."[45] It also notes that "[i]nternationally wrongful acts usually take some time to happen," the "critical distinction" being between a breach that is continuing and one which has already been completed. As to "the moment when the act is performed" (point in time in which a completed act "occurs"), the Commentary notes that the words "at the moment" were "intended to provide a more precise description of the time frame when a completed wrongful act is performed, without requiring that the act necessarily be completed in a single instant."[46] [**233**] The Commentary goes on to explain that "[w] hether a wrongful act is completed or has a continuing character will depend both on the primary obligation and the circumstances of the given case."[47] For instance "[w]here an expropriation is carried out by legal process, with the consequence that title to the property concerned is transferred, the expropriation itself will then be a completed act. The position with a *de facto*, 'creeping' or disguised occupation, however, may well be different."[48] [**234**]

---

[39]   [322] ILC Articles on State Responsibility, Commentary to Article 15, ¶ 9, Exh. **CL-0007** ("While composite acts are made up of a series of actions or omissions defined in aggregate as wrongful, this does not exclude the possibility that every single act in the series could be wrongful in accordance with another obligation.")

[40]   [323] ILC Articles on State Responsibility, Commentary to Article 15, ¶ 7, Exh. **CL-0007** ("A consequence of the character of a composite act is that the time when the act is accomplished cannot be the time when the first action or omission of the series takes place. It is only subsequently that the first action or omission will appear as having, as it were, inaugurated the series. Only after a series of actions or omissions takes place will the composite act be revealed, not merely as a succession of isolated acts, but as a composite act, i.e. an act defined in aggregate as wrongful.")

[41]   [324] The Tribunal notes that, chronologically, the first act in the series is the 2011 Legislative Mining Ban, which entered into force on 10 February 2011; however, the Claimant has repeatedly asserted that this measure only applied to it after the notification of the 2011 Administrative Chamber Decision on 30 November 2011. *See, e.g.*, C-Reply Merits, ¶ 334.

[42]   [325] ILC Articles on State Responsibility, Article 14(1), Exh. **CL-0007**.

[43]   [326] ILC Articles on State Responsibility, Article 14(1), Exh. **CL-0007**.

[44]   [327] *See*, R-CM Merits, ¶¶ 201-214, citing *Spence*, ¶¶ 146, 163, 246, Exh. **CL-0221**; *Corona*, ¶¶ 212, 215, Exh. **CL-0130**; *ST-AD*, ¶ 332, Exh. **RL-0075**; *EuroGas*, ¶ 455, Exh. **RL-0197**.

[45]   [328] ILC Articles on State Responsibility, Commentary to Article 14, ¶ 1, Exh. **CL-0007**.

[46]   [329] ILC Articles on State Responsibility, Commentary to Article 14, ¶ 2, Exh. **CL-0007**.

[47]   [330] ILC Articles on State Responsibility, Commentary to Article 14, ¶ 4, Exh. **CL-0007**.

[48]   [331] ILC Articles on State Responsibility, Commentary to Article 14, ¶ 4, Exh. **CL-0007**.

Significantly for present purposes, the Commentary to Article 14 addresses the question of "when a breach of international law occurs, as distinct from being merely apprehended or imminent."[49] It notes that this question "can only be answered by reference to the particular primary rule," noting that "where the internationally wrongful act is the occurrence of some event - *e.g.* the diversion of an international river - mere preparatory conduct is not necessarily wrongful"[50] [. . .]. [235] On this basis, the Tribunal concludes that a simple act "occurs" when it has been "performed" or "completed"; that the concept of "completion" relates to the point in time at which the act is capable of constituting a breach, which depends on the content of the primary obligation; and that a breach need not be completed in a single act. [236] Hence, the majority of the Tribunal concludes that the first step in the analysis is to identify when a given act or omission was performed or *completed*. The second step is to assess when the Claimant first knew of the completion of the action or omission and of the loss caused thereby. This analysis must be conducted for each of the standards allegedly breached (Sections (i) to (vi) *infra*). The analysis that follows is adopted by a majority of the Tribunal even when this is not expressly so stated. Arbitrator Stern will set out her views in her Separate Opinion on Jurisdiction and Merits."

[**Paras. 216, 217, 219, 220, 221, 222, 223, 224, 225, 226, 227, 228, 230, 231, 232, 233, 234, 235, 236**]

2.

I.17.1   EXPROPRIATION
              See also: II. 7.92

"[239] The majority of the Tribunal agrees with the Claimant that an expropriation could only have occurred with the 2011 Administrative Chamber Decision. For an expropriation to occur, the taking or substantial deprivation must be *permanent*, or at least not ephemeral in nature. More specifically, a judicial expropriation cannot occur through a decision by a first instance court, the execution of which is stayed pending an appeal, because it lacks finality and enforceability. A judicial expropriation can only occur when a final judgment is rendered or when the time limit to appeal has expired. Here, the procedural framework of the relevant court action shows that the deprivation of the Claimant's investment only became a permanent loss with the 2011 Administrative Chamber Decision. Indeed, it is only with this judgment that the 2010 TCA Decision became final (*firme*),[51] the *casación* proceedings having suspensive effect over the 2010 TCA Decision. From a legal perspective, the expropriation occurred at the time the suspension was lifted, that is, upon issuance of the cassation decision. To paraphrase the Commentary to the ILC Articles, the legal process initiated by the 2010 TCA Decision was completed with the 2011 Administrative Chamber Decision, which is when the expropriation became a completed act. [240] That is not to say that an investor is required to exhaust local remedies before resorting to arbitration as a requirement for the admissibility of the claim. The question here is a different one: it is whether the 2010 TCA Decision was sufficiently final and enforceable to inflict harm on the Claimant and qualify as a breach as a matter of substance. Court decisions are not final and enforceable if an appellate remedy with suspensive effect is still available.

---

[49] [332] ILC Articles on State Responsibility, Commentary to Article 14, ¶ 13, Exh. **CL-0007**.

[50] [333] ILC Articles on State Responsibility, Commentary to Article 14, ¶ 13, Exh. **CL-0007**.

[51] [337] Resolution No. 0037, MINAET, File No. 2594 (9 January 2012), Exh. **C-0268**, Considering 2: "The Judicial Decision of the Contentious Administrative Tribunal cited above was confirmed by the First Chamber of the Supreme Court of Justice, and as a result became final."

The situation is generally different for administrative decisions, with the result that, "an expropriation occurs at the moment of the decision of an administrative authority and is not only completed with the final refusal to remedy the administrative act."[52] **[241]** The record further confirms that, while the 2010 TCA Decision may have initiated the legal process whereby the 2008 Concession was annulled, that annulment did not become definitive and the consequent loss of value to the Claimant's investment did not become permanent until the 2011 Administrative Chamber Decision on 30 November 2011. […] **[246]** The majority of the Tribunal thus finds that the Claimant acquired knowledge of the alleged breach and of the loss after the cut-off date. On this basis, it concludes that the Claimant's expropriation claim is not time-barred under Article XII(3)(c). **[247]** This conclusion is consistent with the *raison d'être* of a statute of limitations, which is to promote legal certainty by avoiding that claimants delay bringing their claims. This being so, for the statute of limitations to start running, the claimant must be legally in a position to bring a claim. If a claim cannot be brought for legal reasons (for instance, because the claim is not ripe), it would be fundamentally unfair to find that the statute of limitations has started to run. Such a finding may entail that, in some instances, a claimant/investor would have less time to initiate its claim than the statute of limitations. In exceptional situations, that finding might even mean that the claimant/investor has no time left at all to start proceedings, which would effectively result in a denial of justice - an outcome that cannot reflect the meaning of the Treaty. The fact that this situation does not arise in the circumstances of this dispute is no answer to the issue of principle."

[Paras. 239, 240, 241, 246, 247]

3.

II.7.92   ICSID JURISDICTION
             See also: I.2.0411; I.17.244

"**[259]** At the Hearing on the Merits, the Claimant clarified that its case on denial of justice was "structural": it is premised on the Costa Rican judicial system's failure to provide a mechanism to solve contradictions between the various chambers of the Supreme Court on questions of constitutional *cosa juzgada*.[53] The claim is "not about the failure to afford a due process," nor "about the decisions themselves being arbitrary."[54] The Claimant's submission is that the TCA first refused to uphold the constitutional *cosa juzgada* deriving from the 2010 Constitutional Chamber Decision (the decision which had declared the Crucitas Project constitutional from an environmental perspective), and the Administrative Chamber did the same by denying the cassation request.[55] In other words, the Costa Rican judicial system offers no mechanism to ensure consistency, as was confirmed by the Constitutional Chamber itself when it dismissed the Claimant's action to declare the 2010 TCA Decision unconstitutional on admissibility grounds (through the 2013 Constitutional Chamber

---

[52] [338] Ursula Kriebaum, Local Remedies and the Standards for the Protection of Foreign Investment, in Binder C., Kriebaum, U., Reinisch, A., Wittich, S., International Investment Law for the 21st Century, Essays in Honour of Christoph Schreuer, Oxford University Press, 2009, p. 456 (referring to the PCIJ's holding in *Phosphates in Morocco*, Judgment, 1938, P.C.I.J., Series A/B, No. 74,), p. 28, as discussed in James Crawford, Second Report on State Responsibility, Document A/CN.4/498 and Add. 1-4 (17 March, 1 and 30 April, 19 July 1999), Exh. **RL-0034**, ¶ 148.

[53] [374] Tr. Merits Day 4 (ENG), 995:9-996:10, 1163:6-1164:19, 1165:8-21 (Ms. Seers).

[54] [375] Tr. Merits Day 4 (ENG), 1164:2-4 (Ms. Seers).

[55] [376] Tr. Merits Day 4 (ENG), 1164:4-9 (Ms. Seers).

Decision). [**260**] The majority of the Tribunal considers that this claim is not barred by the statute of limitations. Even if the initial failure to uphold constitutional *cosa juzgada* arises from the 2010 TCA Decision, a denial of justice cannot occur until a decision has been rendered by the highest court. The exhaustion of local remedies rule is a substantive component of the denial of justice breach.[56] Because a denial of justice points to a systemic flaw in the State's administration of justice, there can be no denial of justice until the system had a full opportunity to correct itself.[57] Accordingly, the alleged denial of justice could have occurred at the earliest with the 2011 Administrative Chamber Decision, *i.e.* after the cut-off date."

[**Paras. 259, 260**]

III.

A.

1.

I.17.24 FAIR AND EQUITABLE TREATMENT
See also: I.1.02; I.1.16; I.1.166; I.17.23

"[**331**] Applying the general rule of interpretation set out in Article 31 of the VCLT,[58] the majority of the Tribunal cannot conclude that the content of Article II(2)(a) of the BIT is limited to the MST [i.e. Minimum Standard of Treatment] under customary international law. [**332**] Starting first with the ordinary meaning of the terms, there is nothing in the text of the BIT that limits the FET standard to *customary* international law. Article II(2)(a) provides that the Contracting Parties are required to accord to investments fair and equitable treatment "in accordance with principles of international law." The words "principles of international law" could be understood as a reference to the general principles of law cited in Article 38(1)(c) of the ICJ Statute ("**GPL**"). It is now widely accepted that GPL include both general principles that emanate from domestic laws (*foro domestico*) and are then transposed to international law after an appropriate distillation process, as well as general principles of international law that have emerged directly on the international plane.[59]

---

[56] [377] *See, e.g.,* Z. Douglas, *The International Law of Investment Claims* (Cambridge University Press, 2009), ¶ 59, Exh. **CL-0200** (noting that, in cases of denial of justice, "the local remedies rule is a **substantive** requirement for liability rather than a **procedural** precondition for the presentation of claims to an international court or tribunal.") (Emphasis in original).

[57] [378] *See, e.g.,* J. Paulsson, *Denial of Justice in International Law* (Cambridge University Press, 2005), p. 108, Exh. **CL-0205** ("In the particular case of denial of justice, however, claims will not succeed unless the victim has indeed exhausted municipal remedies, or unless there is an explicit waiver of a type yet to be invented. (An *ad hoc compromis* might do.) This is neither a paradox nor an aberration, for it is in the very nature of the delict that a state is judged by the final product – or at least a **sufficiently** final product – of its administration of justice. A denial of justice is not consummated by the decision of a court of first instance. Having sought to rely on national justice, the foreigner cannot complain that its operations have been delictual until he has given it scope to operate, including by the agency of its ordinary corrective functions.") (Emphasis in original).

[58] [493] Vienna Convention on the Law of Treaties (27 January 1980) ("**VCLT**"), Article 31, Exh. **CL- 0198**. [. . .].

[59] [494] The Tribunal finds confirmation of its understanding for instance in Special Rapporteur Vázquez-Bermúdez, First Report on General Principles of Law by Special Rapporteur, International Law

Alternatively, the reference to "principles of international law" could designate the various sources of international law set out in Article 38(1) of the ICJ Statute.[60] By contrast, the expression "principles of international law" cannot be regarded as a reference to customary international law, which is but one source of international law and is distinct from general principles. That understanding would imply adding limiting language to Article II(2)(a) of the BIT that the provision does not contain. As noted by the *Vivendi II* tribunal, "the reference to principles of international law supports a broader reading that invites consideration of a wider range of international law principles than the minimum standard alone."[61] [**333**] More specifically, GPL (including both principles arising from domestic laws and general principles of international law) are a source of international law distinct from custom.[62] For a rule of customary international law to emerge, it requires uniform and consistent State practice and the acceptance of this practice as law (*opinio juris*).[63] By contrast, GPL are a more flexible concept; they may emerge in a number of ways (including from treaties, case law of international courts and tribunals, and custom[64]) and require "recognition" from States,[65] rather than acceptance as law.[66] [**334**] The Tribunal thus concludes that, in accordance with their ordinary meaning, the terms used by Article II(2)(a) cannot be interpreted as a reference to customary international law in general or to the MST in particular. [**335**] There is likewise nothing in the context of the provision that would lead to restricting the FET standard to the MST. Neither the text of other provisions of the BIT, nor its preamble or annexes, limit the FET standard to customary international law. To the contrary, when chosing [sic] the applicable law, the Contracting Parties to the BIT made a distinction between "rules of international law" and "principles of international law", which distinction is unhelpful to decide whether Article II(2)(a) refers to customary international law only or to international law in its entirety. [**336**] Nor is there "any agreement relating to the treaty which was made between all the parties in connection with the conclusion of the treaty," or "any instrument which was made by one or more parties in connection with the conclusion of the treaty and accepted by the other parties as an instrument related to the treaty"[67] establishing that Article II(2)(a) of the BIT must be interpreted as limiting the FET standard to the MST under customary international law. [**337**] Article 31(3) of the VCLT further provides that the interpreter must take into account, together with the context, "(a)

Commission Seventy-first Session (Geneva, 29 April – 7 June and 8 July – 9 August 2019) ("**First Report on GPL**"), ¶ 22 ("Among the categories of general principles of law that may fall under Article 38, paragraph 1 (c), of the Statute of the International Court of Justice, two appear to stand out: (a) general principles of law derived from national legal systems; and (b) general principles of law formed within the international legal system."); Draft conclusion 3 ("General principles of law comprise those: (a) derived from national legal systems; (b) formed within the international legal system"); and in Patrick Dumberry, A Guide to General Principles of Law in International Investment Arbitration (Oxford University Press 2020) ("**Dumberry, A Guide to GPL**"), ¶¶ 1.27; 1.44-1.53.

[60] [495] Article 38(1) of the ICJ Statute provides: [...]
[61] [496] *Vivendi II*, ¶ 7.4.7, Exh. **CL-0029**.
[62] [497] Dumberry, A Guide to GPL, ¶¶ 1.14-1.15.
[63] [498] Special Rapporteur Vázquez-Bermúdez, First Report on GPL, ¶ 164; A Guide to GPL, ¶¶ 1.14-1.15.
[64] [499] Dumberry, A Guide to GPL, ¶¶ 1.49; 1.52.
[65] [500] Today there is wide agreement that there is no need to attribute any particular meaning to the term "civilized" in Article 38(1)(c) of the ICJ Statute. Special Rapporteur Vázquez-Bermúdez, First Report on GPL, ¶¶ 178, 185-187.
[66] [501] Special Rapporteur Vázquez-Bermúdez, First Report on GPL, ¶¶ 163-175.
[67] [502] VCLT, Article 31(2), Exh. **CL-0198**.

any subsequent agreement between the parties regarding the interpretation of the treaty or the application of its provisions; (b) any subsequent practice in the application of the treaty which establishes the agreement of the parties regarding its interpretation; [and] (c) any relevant rules of international law applicable in the relations between the parties."[68] The Respondent argues in this respect that both Costa Rica and Canada have confirmed in this arbitration that Article II(2)(a) of the BIT is limited to the MST, and that this constitutes a "subsequent agreement between the parties" pursuant to Article 31(3) of the VCLT that demonstrates the intent of the Treaty's Contracting States. According to the Respondent, Article 31(3) of the VCLT does not require any formal agreement in "treaty form" to be effective.[69] [**338**] In the Tribunal's view, Costa Rica's and Canada's concurrent positions in this arbitration do not amount to an agreement within the meaning of Article 31(3) of the VCLT. As Roberts explains, agreements on treaty interpretation "need not be in binding or treaty form but must demonstrate that the parties intended their understanding to constitute an agreed basis for interpretation."[70] Oppenheim's International Law also notes that the parties to a treaty "may in some other way and before, during, or after the conclusion of the treaty, agree upon the interpretation of a term, either informally (and executing the treaty accordingly) or by a more formal procedure, as by an interpretative declaration or protocol or a supplementary treaty."[71] Yet, the Contracting Parties must have *agreed* to a particular interpretation. This requires a joint manifestation of consent from the Contracting Parties, or at least an offer and acceptance, evidencing their common intention that Article II(2)(a) of the BIT reflects the MST under customary international law. [**339**] No such consent is found here. The submissions made by Costa Rica and Canada in this arbitration reflect legal arguments put forward in the context of this dispute to advance their respective interests. Although they happen to coincide, they do not reflect an *agreement* as just described over the interpretation of the BIT. Even if the Tribunal could infer an "agreement" from the Contracting States' submissions, *quod non*, this agreement would postdate the commencement of this arbitration and the Tribunal could not take it into consideration in favour of one litigant to the detriment of the other without incurring the risk of breaching the latter's due process rights. [**340**] Finally, Article 31(4) of the VCLT requires the interpreter to give a treaty term "[a] special meaning [. . .] if it is established that the parties so intended."[72] The Tribunal finds that the Respondent has not met its burden of proving that the Contracting Parties intended the terms "fair and equitable treatment in accordance with principles of international law" to mean "the minimum standard of treatment under customary international law." [**341**] The Respondent and Canada also rely on the principle of effectiveness or *effet utile*, which the Respondent argues is "broadly accepted as a fundamental principle of treaty interpretation."[73] They argue that, if the Claimant's interpretation

---

[68] [503] VCLT, Article 31(3), Exh. **CL-0198**.

[69] [504] R-Rej. Merits, ¶¶ 475-477.

[70] [505] A. Roberts, *Power and Persuasion in Investment Treaty Interpretation*, The American Journal of International Law, Vol. 104, No. 2 (2010), p. 199, Exh. **RL-0275**.

[71] [506] R. Jennings and A. Watts, *Oppenheim's International Law* (9th ed., Oxford University Press, 1992), Vol. 1, Section 630, cited in *Methanex Corporation v. United States of America*, UNCITRAL, Final Award, 3 August 2005 ("*Methanex*"), Part II, Chapter H, ¶ 23, Exh. **CL-0059**.

[72] [507] VCLT, Article 31(4), Exh. **CL-0198**.

[73] [508] R-Rej. Merits, ¶ 445, citing *The Renco Group, Inc. v. Republic of Peru*, UNCITRAL, Decision as to the Scope of the Respondent's Preliminary Objections Under Article 10.20.4, 18 December 2014 ("*Renco*"), ¶ 177, Exh. **CL-0223**; *Wintershall Aktiengesellschaft v. Argentine Republic*, ICSID Case No. ARB/04/14, Award, 8 December 2008 ("*Wintershall*"), ¶ 165, Exh. **RL-0070**.

of Article II(2)(a) of the BIT were correct, the terms "in accordance with principles of international law" would be rendered meaningless.[74] The Tribunal cannot agree. When determining the protection owed under Article II(2)(a), the Tribunal must be guided by international law (be it GPL or sources of international law in general) as opposed to subjective notions of fairness and equity. The BIT was signed in 1998, before any meaningful debate on the meaning of FET had taken place and before the *Mondev* tribunal famously clarified that a tribunal "may not simply adopt its own idiosyncratic standard of what is 'fair' or 'equitable', without reference to established sources of law."[75] **[343]** It is true that the Respondent has pointed to various sources which suggest that Article II(2)(a) of the BIT should be given the same interpretation as NAFTA 1105, and that it was the Contracting Parties' intention that Article II(2)(a) of the BIT referred to the MST. The Tribunal cannot give weight to these sources because they do not qualify as means of interpretation under the general rule of Article 31 of the VCLT, nor is there reason to resort to supplementary interpretation means as the application of Article 31 does not result in a meaning that is "ambiguous or obscure" or "manifestly absurd or unreasonable." Even if the Tribunal were inclined to use supplementary means to "confirm the meaning resulting from the application of article 31," the sources invoked by Costa Rica would not constitute such means as they do not relate to "the preparatory work of the treaty and the circumstances of its conclusion." **[344]** The Respondent first refers to "express statements by Canada" which would confirm that the BIT is based on the NAFTA.[76] However, these statements are arguments made by Canada in *UPS v. Canada* arguing that foreign investment protection agreements were based on the NAFTA.[77] Similarly, the Respondent alleges that, like Canada, Costa Rica "has consistently held that the fair and equitable treatment obligation under its investment protection treaties does not establish an autonomous standard."[78] In support, the Respondent points to its defense in pleadings in arbitration proceedings.[79] These sources reflect Canada's and Costa Rica's litigation posture, and do not qualify as means of treaty interpretation under Article 31 of the VCLT. More specifically, none of these cases was based on the Treaty and thus these statements cannot establish a "practice in the application of the treaty" within the meaning of Article 31(3)(b) of the VCLT. **[345]** The Respondent has also referred to the contemporaneous writings of Canadian commentators explaining that Canada's foreign investment protection treaties ("**FIPAs**") post-dating the NAFTA are based on NAFTA's Chapter 11 and the obligations thereunder should be given the same interpretation.[80] However, it is unclear how the writings of commentators could qualify as context of the BIT under Article 31 of the VCLT; nor do they constitute subsequent agreement or practice of the Contracting States, or rules of international law applicable to them. Finally, they are not supplementary means of interpretation under Article 32 of the VCLT, as they do not serve to establish the intent of the Contracting States. **[346]** For the same reasons, the Tribunal can give no weight to the Claimant's regulatory

---

[74] [509] R-Rej. Merits, ¶ 445; Canada's Submission, ¶ 19.

[75] [510] *Mondev*, ¶ 119, Exh. **CL-0062**.

[76] [512] R-CM Merits, ¶ 370.

[77] [513] *UPS* Counter-Memorial, ¶ 1011, Exh. **RL-0172**.

[78] [514] R-Rej. Merits, ¶ 454.

[79] [515] R-Rej. Merits, ¶ 454, citing *Cervin Investissements S.A. and Rhone Investissements S.A. v. Republic of Costa Rica*, ICSID Case No. ARB/13/2, Decision on Jurisdiction, 15 December 2014 (*"Cervin"*), ¶ 337, Exh. **RL-0101**; *Marion Unglaube and Reinhard Unglaube v. Republic of Costa Rica*, ICSID Case Nos. ARB/08/1 and ARB/09/20, Award, 16 May 2012 (*"Unglaube"*), ¶ 242, Exh. **RL-0102**.

[80] [516] For the list of writings by commentators the Respondent refers to see *supra* fn. 444.

filings with the United States authorities, in which Infinito stated that the FIPAs such as the BIT were "based on the investment protection standards of the NAFTA investment chapter."[81] Statements made by an investor who is not a party to the Treaty do not qualify as means of interpretation under the VCLT. [347] The Respondent has also submitted two documents which purportedly evidence its understanding of Article II(2)(a) at the time when the BIT was concluded. The first is a Memorandum by the Ministry of Foreign Trade of Costa Rica to the President of the Permanent Committee on Economic Affairs of the Legislative Assembly, sent in connection with the approval of the bilateral investment treaties concluded by Costa Rica with Canada, Paraguay, Spain and Argentina, and explaining the scope and content of bilateral investment treaties generally.[82] With respect to "fair and equitable treatment," the memorandum states that "[i]t is generally accepted that the primary purpose of this type of clause is to offer the investment a minimum standard of protection in accordance with the principles of international law."[83] While this memorandum might reflect Costa Rica's understanding, it does not qualify as supplementary means of interpretation, as it is not "preparatory work of the treaty," nor does it provide information on the "circumstances of its conclusion."[84] Nor can it be characterized as an "instrument which was made by one or more parties in connexion with the conclusion of the treaty and accepted by the other parties as an instrument related to the treaty" within the meaning of Article 31(2)(b) of the VCLT, as there is no evidence that Canada has accepted it as relating to the BIT. [348] The second document cited by the Respondent is an economic report on the BIT presented to the Legislative Assembly in July 1998, which states that the BIT was based on Canada's 1994 model FIPA, which was in turn based, *inter alia*, on the NAFTA.[85] It is not clear from the document itself whether the authors were Government officials[86] (indeed, the Respondent has filed this as a legal authority, not as a fact exhibit). Even if they were, for the reasons given in the preceding paragraph, it cannot qualify as context of the treaty under Article 31(2)(b) of the VCLT, or as supplementary means of interpretation under Article 32 of the VCLT. [349] Even accepting that the BIT was drafted on the basis of Canada's model FIPA, which in turn was based on or inspired by NAFTA Chapter 11, this does not necessarily mean that it offers investors identical protections as the NAFTA. Faced with a treaty provision, the Tribunal must interpret it in accordance with the rules of interpretation of the VCLT, in particular its text and context; it cannot dispense with doing so simply because a provision might have been inspired by another treaty. [350] The majority of the Tribunal thus concludes that Article II(2)(a) of the

---

[81] [517] 2007 Annual Report, Form 20-F, Infinito Gold Ltd., before the Unites States Securities and Exchange Commission, for the Fiscal Year ended in 31 March 2007, p. 28, Exh. **R-0045**.

[82] [518] Foreign Trade Ministry of Costa Rica, Memorandum No. DVI 279-98 on the Meaning and Scope of BITs, 29 September 1998, Exh. **R-0142**.

[83] [519] Foreign Trade Ministry of Costa Rica, Memorandum No. DVI 279-98 on the Meaning and Scope of BITs, 29 September 1998, p. 6 (English), Exh. **R-0142**.

[84] [520] VCLT, Article 32, Exh. **CL-0198**.

[85] [521] R. Acosta and R. Matamoros, Economic Report No. 473.98 to Costa Rica's Legislative Assembly (July 1998), p. 4, Exh. **RL-0164** [...].

[86] [522] Exh. **RL-0164** is on header paper of the "*Departmento de Servicios Técnicos*" of the "*Asamblea Legislativa*" (Technical Services Department of the Legislative Assembly), and the authors appear to be members of the "*Unidad de Estudios Económicos*" (Economic Studies Unit). *See* Exh. **RL-0164**, p. 3, fn. 1. While this suggests a unit within the Legislative Assembly, its exact status is unclear. Indeed, the Respondent characterizes this document as "report submitted to Costa Rica's legislature in July 1998 for the ratification of the BIT [...]." R-Rej. Merits, ¶ 464.

BIT provides for an autonomous FET standard and is not limited to the MST under customary international law."

[Paras. 331, 332, 333, 334, 335, 336, 337, 338, 339, 340, 341, 343, 344, 345, 346, 347, 348, 349, 350]

2.

I.17.24   FAIR AND EQUITABLE TREATMENT
            See also: I.1.02; I.1.022; I.17.241; I.17.242; I.17.244

"[352] [...] [W]hile the terms "fair and equitable" are vague, they "are susceptible of specification through judicial practice and do in fact have sufficient legal content to allow the case to be decided on the basis of law,"[87] and more specifically on the basis of principles of international law as mandated by Article II(2)(a) of the BIT. Indeed, in elucidating the content of the autonomous FET standard, investment tribunals have extracted a number of inherent components, which are implicitly if not expressly derived from GPL and have been reflected in the decisions of international tribunals. [...][355] While formulations may vary across awards, a consensus emerges as to the core components of FET, which encompass the protection of legitimate expectations, the protection against conduct that is arbitrary, unreasonable, disproportionate and lacking in good faith, and the principles of due process and transparency. FET also includes a protection against denial of justice."

[Paras. 352, 355]

3.

I.17.24   FAIR AND EQUITABLE TREATMENT
            See also: I.17.1

"[356] Three of the measures challenged by the Claimant - the 2011 Administrative Chamber Decision, the 2013 Constitutional Chamber Decision and the TCA Damages Proceeding - are judicial measures. The Respondent and Canada submit that judicial measures can only engage the State's international responsibility if they amount to a denial of justice. The Claimant challenges this position, arguing that neither the BIT nor the ILC Articles on State Responsibility preclude international State responsibility for acts of judicial organs that do not qualify as a denial of justice. [357] Costa Rica and Canada essentially argue that, absent a denial of justice, judicial decisions interpreting domestic law cannot breach international law, and that "claims of arbitrariness or unfairness in the context of judicial decisions must be viewed through the lens of denial of justice."[88] The Tribunal agrees that this is the case under customary international law. The question before the Tribunal is, however, whether judicial measures breach the BIT's FET standard, which the Tribunal has held not to be limited to the MST under customary international law. [359] In the majority of the Tribunal's view, there is no principled reason to limit the State's responsibility for judicial decisions to instances of denial of justice. Holding otherwise would mean that

---

[87] [528] *Saluka*, ¶ 284, Exh. **CL-0077**; *see also MTD*, ¶ 113, Exh. **CL-0063**; *Azurix Corp. v. Argentine Republic*, ICSID Case No. ARB/01/12, Award, 14 July 2006 (*"Azurix"*), ¶ 360, Exh. **CL-0018**; *Siemens A.G. v. Argentine Republic*, ICSID Case No. ARB/02/8, Award, 6 February 2007 (*"Siemens"*), ¶ 290, Exh. **CL-0081**.

[88] [532] Canada's Submission, ¶¶ 28, 31.

part of the State's activity would not trigger liability even though it would be contrary to the standards protected under the investment treaty. While the Tribunal agrees that domestic courts must be given deference in the application of domestic law, this does not mean that their decisions are immune from scrutiny at the international level. As noted by the tribunal in *Sistem*, court decisions may deprive investors of their property rights "just as surely as if the State had expropriated [them] by decree."[89] In the same vein, judicial decisions that are arbitrary, unfair or contradict an investor's legitimate expectations may also breach the FET standard even if they do not rise to the level of a denial of justice.[90] [**360**] Crucially, the question before investment tribunals is not whether the domestic court misapplied its own domestic law. The question is whether, in its application of domestic law, the court has breached *international* law, and more specifically, the standards of protection contained in the relevant treaty.[91] [. . .] This can happen if the court misapplies domestic law, but also when it applies domestic law correctly, if it leads to a result that is incompatible with international law. In the latter case, it could be said that it is the underlying law which breaches the treaty. However, if the court is the first State organ to apply that law to the investor, it is the court decision which perpetrates the breach of the treaty. [**361**] The majority of the Tribunal thus concludes that denial of justice is only one of the ways in which judicial decisions may breach the BIT. Even if a decision does not amount to a denial of justice, it may violate other treaty standards (such as FET or expropriation), provided the requirements for these breaches are met. [**362**] It is true that there are authorities putting forward a contrary view. For these authors[92] and tribunals,[93] the main reason for restricting

---

[89] [535] *Sistem Mühendislik İnşaat Sanayi ve Ticaret A.Ş. v. Kyrgyz Republic*, ICSID Case No. ARB(AF)/06/1, Award, 9 September 2009, ("***Sistem***"), ¶ 118, Exh. **CL-0082**. *See also, Rumeli,*¶ 702, Exh. **CL-0075** (finding that "a taking by the judicial arm of the State may also amount to an expropriation").

[90] [536] *See, e.g., Arif*, ¶¶ 445, 454, 547, Exh. **CL-0014**; *Frontier Petroleum*, ¶¶ 284, 525, Exh. **CL-0039**.

[91] [537] Decision on Jurisdiction, ¶ 217 (holding that "it is the Tribunal's duty to verify if the measures complained of have breached the BIT.")

[92] [539] *See, e.g.,* G. Fitzmaurice, *The Meaning of the Term 'Denial of Justice,'* 13 Brit. Y.B Int'l L. (1932) 93, p. 110, Exh. **CAN-0013** ("[t]he rule may be stated that the merely erroneous or unjust decision of a court, even though it may involve what amounts to a miscarriage of justice, is not a denial of justice, and, moreover, does not involve the responsibility of the state."); C. Greenwood, *State Responsibility for the Decisions of National Courts*, in M. Fitzmaurice and D. Sarooshi (eds.), *Issues of State Responsibility before International Judicial Institutions*, (Oxford, 2004), p. 61, Exh. **CAN-0011** ("it is well established that a mistake on the part of the court or an irregularity in procedure is not in itself sufficient to amount to a violation of international law; there must be a denial of justice."); Z. Douglas, *International Responsibility for Domestic Adjudication: Denial of Justice Reconstructed*, International and Comparative Law Quarterly, Vol. 63, No.4 (2014), p. 34, Exh. **RL-0109**.

[93] [540] *See* in particular *Mondev*, ¶ 126, Exh. **CL-0062** ("It is one thing to deal with unremedied acts of the local constabulary and another to second-guess the reasoned decisions of the highest courts of a State. Under NAFTA, parties have the option to seek local remedies. If they do so and lose on the merits, it is not the function of NAFTA tribunals to act as courts of appeal."); *Parkerings*, ¶ 313, Exh. **CL 0068** ("subject to denial of justice, which is not at issue here, an erroneous judgment [. . .] shall not in itself run against international law, including the Treaty."); *Bosh*, ¶ 280, Exh. **RL-0120** ("It is only in a situation where those proceedings would '[offend] a sense of judicial propriety' that it would be open to the Tribunal to find that those proceedings did not meet international standards.") The Tribunal notes that the Respondent has also cited to other cases which purportedly confirm the position, including *Swisslion*. Yet, in that case the tribunal only stated that "ICSID tribunals are not directly concerned with the question whether national judgments have been rendered in conformity with the applicable domestic law. They only have to consider whether they constitute a violation of international law, and in particular whether they amount to a denial

the responsibility for judicial acts to denial of justice appears to lie in the nature of the court function and, as the Respondent's put it, in "the recognition of the judiciary's independence and the great deference afforded to domestic courts acting in their bona fide role of adjudication and interpretation of a State's domestic law."[94] That deference seems linked to the courts' decision making-process, which resolves complex legal questions and involves a choice among plausible options.[95] While these considerations certainly justify restraint when international tribunals consider the local courts' application of *domestic* law, in the Tribunal's opinion, they cannot be an obstacle to adjudicating on breaches of *international* law.[96] [**367**] [...] Costa Rica may incur international responsibility as a result of the decisions of its courts even in the absence of a denial of justice. The existence of such responsibility will depend on whether the requirements of the various treaty standards, such as FET or expropriation, are met."

[Paras. 356, 357, 359, 360, 361, 362, 367]

4.

I.17.24   FAIR AND EQUITABLE TREATMENT
            See also: I.17.244

"[**437**] While the BIT does not expressly refer to the concept of denial of justice, the Parties agree - and rightly so - that it is comprised in the FET standard provided in Article II(2)(a) of the BIT.[702] The authorities are unanimous in that a denial of justice amounts to a breach of fair and equitable treatment.[97] [**438**] Different authors endorse varying definitions of denial of justice. Some submit that a denial of justice can be procedural (when it relates to lack of access to justice or breaches of due process) or substantive (when it involves a manifestly unfair judgment or the malicious misapplication of the law).[98] [...] [**445**] [...] [T]he Tribunal concludes that a denial of justice occurs when there is a fundamental failure in the

---

of justice" (*Swisslion*, ¶ 264, Exh. **RL-0112**), a statement that does not limit liability for judicial acts to cases of denials of justice.

[94] [541] R-Mem. Jur., ¶ 224; *see also* Z. Douglas, *International Responsibility for Domestic Adjudication: Denial of Justice Reconstructed,* International and Comparative Law Quarterly, Vol. 63, No.4 (2014), pp. 6-7, 28, Exh. **RL-0109**.

[95] [542] *See* in particular J. Brierly, *The Law of Nations* (Oxford: Clarendon Press, 1963), p. 287, **CAN-0012**; Z. Douglas, *International Responsibility for Domestic Adjudication: Denial of Justice Reconstructed,* International and Comparative Law Quarterly, Vol. 63, No.4 (2014), pp. 10-11, Exh. **RL-0109**.

[96] [543] This is so in respect of breaches of rules in investment treaties as well as treaties in other areas of the law, *e.g.* the breach of the International Covenant on Civil and Political Rights (*Case Concerning Ahmadou Sadio Diallo (Republic of Guinea v. Democratic Republic of the Congo),* ICJ Judgment, 30 November 2010, ¶¶ 75-82, Exh. **RL-0015**).

[97] [703] *See,* for instance, *Vivendi II,* ¶ 7.4.11, Exh. **CL-0029**; *Jan de Nul* Award, ¶ 188, Exh. **RL-0091**; *Frontier Petroleum,* ¶ 293, Exh. **CL-0039**; *Oostergetel,* ¶ 272, Exh. **RL-0017**. *See also* R. Dolzer and C. Schreuer, *Principles of International Investment Law* (Oxford University Press, 2008), p. 142.

[98] [704] *See, e.g.,* R. Jennings and A. Watts, *Oppenheim's International Law* (9th ed., Oxford University Press, 1992), Vol. I, pp. 543-544 cited in C. Greenwood, *State Responsibility for the Decisions of National Courts,* in M. Fitzmaurice and D. Sarooshi (eds.) *Issues of State Responsibility before International Judicial Institutions,* (Oxford, 2004), p. 61, Exh. **CAN-0011** ("If the courts or other appropriate tribunals of a State refuse to entertain proceedings for the redress of injury suffered by an alien, or if the proceedings are subject to undue delay, or if there are serious inadequacies in the administration of justice, or if there occurs an obvious or malicious act of misapplication of the law by the courts which is injurious enough to a foreign

host's State's administration of justice. The following elements can lead to this conclusion (i) the State has denied the investor access to domestic courts; (ii) the courts have engaged in unwarranted delay; (iii) the courts have failed to provide those guarantees which are generally considered indispensable to the proper administration of justice (such as the independence and impartiality of judges, due process and the right to be heard); or (iv) the decision is manifestly arbitrary, unjust or idiosyncratic. The Tribunal thus concludes that a denial of justice may be procedural or substantive, and that in both situations the denial of justice is the product of a systemic failure of the host State's judiciary taken as a whole.[99] The latter point explains that a claim for denial of justice presupposes the exhaustion of local remedies, a requirement that is met here as the complaint targets decisions of the highest courts. [**448**] The Claimant argues that the 2011 Administrative Chamber Decision is inconsistent with previous decisions by the Constitutional Chamber where the latter allegedly declared that the Crucitas Project complied with Costa Rican law.[100] [**451**] Having carefully reviewed the 2010 TCA Decision and the 2011 Administrative Chamber Decision, the Tribunal does not find these decisions inconsistent with those of the Constitutional Chamber cited above. The Tribunal has also assessed the procedural conduct and reasoning of these courts, and concludes that they were based on the relevant provisions of Costa Rican law and are not objectionable from the point of view of international law. [**469**] The Claimant argues that the Costa Rican judicial system is structurally flawed because it does not provide any "mechanism to resolve the Administrative Chamber's failure to respect constitutional *cosa juzgada*."[101] Its argument has two prongs. First, the Claimant argues that, unlike other judicial systems, in Costa Rica there is no body responsible for resolving inconsistencies between the decisions by the different Chambers of the Supreme Court.[102] Second, it contends that the only available remedy to address conflicting decisions - an action for unconstitutionality - was ineffective.[103] The Claimant explains that it challenged the TCA's interpretation of the constitutional principle of *res judicata* before the Constitutional Chamber but that such Chamber dismissed the challenge on admissibility grounds.[104] As a result, Industrias Infinito had no remedies left to seek the resolution of the inconsistencies between the 2011 Administrative Chamber Decision and the Constitutional Chamber's prior Decisions. [**470**] For the Claimant, the lack of such a remedy amounts to a denial of justice. The Tribunal does not share this view [. . .]. [**483**] In the Tribunal's view, only a lack of remedy within the host State's judicial system that deprives an investor from a fair opportunity to plead its case or implies that access to justice is virtually non-existent would amount to a denial of justice. That is not the case here. As discussed in the preceding section, Industrias Infinito raised the *res judicata* objection before the TCA and then again before the Administrative Chamber and both courts considered it. Even in the absence of a court such as the French *Tribunal des conflits*, the Respondent's judicial system provided the Claimant with several instances and remedies to address the alleged jurisdictional conflict. [**485**] Consequently, the Tribunal comes to the conclusion that the Respondent committed no procedural denial of justice. [**490**] The Claimant submits that the 2011 Administrative Chamber Decision amounts to a substantive denial of justice because the

---

[99] [719] *Oostergetel*, ¶ 225, Exh. **RL-0017**; *Jan de Nul* Award, ¶ 209, Exh. **RL-0091**; *Corona*, ¶ 254, Exh. **CL-0130**.
[100] [724] C-Mem. Merits, ¶¶ 341-343.
[101] [772] C-CM Jur., ¶ 401.
[102] [773] C-Mem. Merits, ¶ 344.
[103] [774] C-Mem. Merits, ¶ 344.
[104] [775] C-Mem. Merits, ¶ 344.

court applied the 2002 Moratorium to the Crucitas Project in violation of Costa Rican law.[105] [. . .] [**502**] When assessing a claim for denial of justice, the Tribunal's analysis must focus on the judgment of the court ruling on the last remedy, *i.e.*, the Administrative Chamber Decision. Having assessed that decision, the Tribunal cannot discern the existence of a substantive denial of justice. The 2011 Administrative Chamber Decision was premised on Costa Rican law and reasoned. While the Administrative Chamber's reasons and conclusions could be characterized as formalistic, there was no misapplication of domestic law. As discussed above, the Administrative Chamber did not violate *res judicata* in respect of the applicability of the 2002 Moratorium or the validity of the Concession, because the Constitutional Court had not adjudged these matters. [**504**] Industrias Infinito's argument was that it owned a vested right that was protected from the application of the 2002 Moratorium. The Administrative Chamber addressed this argument and concluded that Industrias Infinito did not own a vested right on the date when the 2002 Moratorium came into force, and thus could not be validly granted an exploitation concession while the 2002 Moratorium was in effect. [**505**] In conclusion, the Tribunal is not persuaded that the Administrative Chamber incurred in a substantive denial of justice."

[**Paras. 437, 438, 445, 448, 451, 469, 470, 483, 485, 490, 502, 504, 505**]

5.

I.17.24   FAIR AND EQUITABLE TREATMENT

"[**553**] The Claimant also contends that, through the combination of the 2011 Legislative Mining Ban and the 2012 MINAET Resolution, the Respondent prevented it from reinitiating the concession process in breach of FET. [**560**] The Tribunal is not convinced that, in the abstract, the 2011 Legislative Mining Ban was unfair and inequitable. More specifically, it is not convinced that the Ban lacked a rational purpose and is therefore arbitrary. While it is not clear from the Ban itself that its purpose was to protect the environment (there is no preamble or message explaining its reasons), certain provisions in the Ban suggest that the protection of the environment may have been at least part of the purpose behind is enactment.[106] The Tribunal also notes that small-scale miners (organized workers in cooperatives dedicated to mining in a small scale for the subsistence of families, artisanal mining and prospector use (coligallero)) were excluded from the Ban.[107] They were also allowed to use cyanide and mercury leaching techniques for eight years following the entry into force of the Ban, which does not quite conform to the objective of protecting the environment. However, the Tribunal accepts that Costa Rica may have had other reasons (*e.g.*, social or economic reasons) to exclude small-scale mining from the Ban. [**561**] By contrast, the Tribunal is of the view that the *application* of the 2011 Legislative Mining Ban to the Claimant was unfair and inequitable. While [. . .] the Claimant could have no legitimate expectation of legal stability, the Tribunal finds that the application of the Ban to the Crucitas Project was disproportionate to the public policy pursued. [**562**] As noted in

---

[105] [800] C-CM Jur., ¶¶ 403-411.

[106] [918] For instance, Article 4 amended Article 103 of the Mining Code to add that "[t]he use of cyanide and mercury leaching techniques in mining and the improper use of dangerous substances in accordance with the provisions of The World Health Organization" "shall be considered factors that deteriorate the environment." Amendment to Mining Code, No. 8904 (1 December 2010), Article 4 (amending Article 103 of the Mining Code), Exh. **C-0238.**

[107] [919] Amendment to Mining Code, No. 8904 (1 December 2010), Article 1 (amending Article 8 of the Mining Code), Exh. **C-0238.**

AES, for a measure to be reasonable, "there needs to be an appropriate correlation between the state's public policy objective and the measure adopted to achieve it," and "[t]his has to do with the nature of the measure and the way it is implemented."[108] In the Tribunal's view, the measure must also be proportionate to its purpose. The Claimant has alleged (and the Respondent has not contested) that, at the time of its enactment, the only project caught by its provisions was the Crucitas Project. However, at that point in time, the Constitutional Chamber had already ruled that the Project was environmentally sound. There was thus no reasonable correlation between the aim sought by the measure and its effect on the Claimant. [**563**] To be reasonable and proportionate vis-à-vis the Claimant (while still capturing future projects that were untested), Parliament could have included a grandfathering provision that protected the Crucitas Project, or could have allowed pending proceedings to continue. [**564**] The Respondent has argued that the 2011 Legislative Mining Ban had no impact on the Claimant, because as a result of the 2010 Executive Moratoria, Industrias Infinito was in any event precluded from applying for a new concession. For the Tribunal, this argument relates to causation (and is addressed further below). In terms of its content and scope, the Tribunal finds that the 2011 Legislative Mining Ban definitively forbade open pit-mining for an indefinite period, thus depriving the Claimant of any real opportunity to reinitiate the Crucitas Project. By contrast, the 2010 Executive Moratoria did not prohibit open-pit mining outright; they merely established a suspension of such activities. Nor did they order all pending proceedings to be archived. [...] It is clear from the Ban that the intention was to terminate all pending proceedings. [**565**] The effect of the 2011 Legislative Mining Ban on the Claimant was that, once the 2011 Administrative Chamber Decision confirmed the annulment of the Concession, it was no longer allowed to request a new mining concession. Had the 2011 Legislative Mining Ban not ordered the cancellation of pending proceedings, and had the 2012 MINAET Resolution not acted upon it, following the annulment of the 2008 Concession, Industrias Infinito would have returned to the position it was in before the grant of the concession, *i.e.*, an exploration permit holder with a pending application for an exploitation concession. [...] [**581**] In conclusion, a majority of the Tribunal considers that the Respondent has breached its FET obligation through the 2011 Legislative Mining Ban and, as an ancillary act, the 2012 MINAET Resolution (to the extent that it implemented that Ban). The effect of these measures was to deprive Industrias Infinito of the opportunity to apply for a new exploitation concession."

[**Paras. 553, 560, 561, 562, 563, 564, 565, 581**]

B.

I.11.03542   CAUSAL NEXUS BETWEEN WRONGFUL ACT AND INJURY
SUFFERED

See also: I.11.035; I.11.03541

"[**582**] Although it considers the breach established, the Tribunal has difficulty identifying the damage which the breach may have caused. Had it not been for the 2011 Legislative Mining Ban and the 2012 MINAET Resolution, after the 2011 Administrative Chamber Decision Industrias Infinito would have been restored to the position of an exploration permit holder with a pending application for an exploitation concession. However, at that time, the 2010 Executive Moratoria, which were still in place, would have barred Industrias

---

[108] [920] *AES Summit Generation Limited and AES-Tisza Erömü Kft v. Republic of Hungary*, ICSID Case No. ARB/07/22, Award, 23 September 2010 ("*AES*"), ¶ 10.3.9, Exh. **CL-0260**.

Infinito from obtaining a new exploitation concession. [**583**] The Claimant argues that, despite this, the 2011 Legislative Mining Ban had a "clear impact" on the Crucitas Project.[109] The argument is essentially that (i) it was the 2011 Legislative Mining Ban and not the Administrative Chamber Decision which mandated the cancellation of its remaining mining rights, and (ii) the 2010 Executive Moratoria "would not have deprived [Industrias Infinito] of its underlying rights, which [Industrias Infinito] could have built on to seek restoration of its key permits, once lifted."[110] [**584**] While these considerations may well be correct, they do not suggest that the 2011 Legislative Mining Ban caused a quantifiable harm. The fact remains that, regardless of the 2011 Legislative Mining Ban, Industrias Infinito was precluded from applying for an exploitation concession because of the 2010 Executive Moratoria. While these Moratoria did not establish a permanent mining ban, there is no indication in the record as to when Industrias Infinito would have been able to reapply for an exploitation concession. It should also be noted in this context that the 2010 Executive Moratoria were issued prior to the cut-off date and that therefore any claim related to them is time-barred. [**585**] Even if the Tribunal were to accept that the fact of harm was established, this would not assist the Claimant's case. There is no basis in the record, and Infinito has articulated none, allowing the Tribunal to quantify the damage caused by this standalone breach. Pursuant to the full reparation standard stated in the *Chorzów Factory* case, "[r]eparation must, as far as possible, wipe-out all the consequences of the illegal act and re-establish the situation which would, in all probability, have existed if that act had not been committed."[111] Here, absent the 2011 Legislative Mining Ban and the 2012 MINAET Resolution, Industrias Infinito would have been in the situation of an exploration permit holder. Assuming *arguendo* that the 2010 Executive Moratoria did not already prevent Industrias Infinito from restarting the process, the Claimant's harm would essentially consist in the loss of an opportunity or chance to apply for an exploitation concession. Yet, the Claimant has not put forward a quantification for such a loss of opportunity, nor has it provided the Tribunal with any elements to calculate it. If one adds the inherent uncertainty and the regulatory risk involved in any application process, the monetary consequences of this loss of chance appear too speculative to give rise to an award of damages. [**586**] The Tribunal thus concludes that it cannot award damages for the FET breach stemming from the 2011 Legislative Mining Ban, alone or in conjunction with the 2012 MINAET Resolution."

[**Paras. 582, 583, 584, 585, 586**]

C.

I.17.1   EXPROPRIATION
See also: I.17.24; I.17.245

"[**708**] As it was already made clear in the analysis of the claims of denial of justice and breach of FET, for the Tribunal Industrias Infinito held no valid Concession and related approvals capable of being expropriated. It is undisputed that the 2002 Concession was annulled by the 2004 Constitutional Chamber Decision. The TCA regarded this annulment

---

[109] [935] C-Reply Merits, ¶ 737.

[110] [936] C-Reply Merits, ¶ 737.

[111] [937] *Case Concerning the Factory at Chorzów* (Germany v. Poland), 1928 P.C.I.J. (ser. A) No. 17 (13 September 1928), ¶ 125, Exh. **CL-0024**.

as absolute, with the result that the 2002 Concession was null and void *ab initio,* a finding confirmed by the Administrative Chamber in 2011. [**712**] As to Industrias Infinito's alleged pre-existing mining rights, the Tribunal has already found [...] that Industrias Infinito had certain pre-existing mining rights that arose from its status as an exploration permit holder and that the application to the Crucitas Project of the 2011 Legislative Mining Ban (the MINAET Resolution being an ancillary measure not independent of the Ban) violated FET. For reasons of judicial economy, it can be left open whether these pre-existing rights were in addition subject to an expropriation. Indeed, even in the affirmative, no greater harm could be caused than the one generated by the FET breach. As noted when discussing the FET breach, the Tribunal is not persuaded that the Claimant has proved the existence of a quantifiable harm, and finds that that [sic!] any alleged harm is in any event too speculative to give rise to an award of damages. [**717**] As explained above, for a measure to amount to an indirect expropriation, it must cause the deprivation of the investment. It is widely accepted that this deprivation must be substantial,[112] and that there must be a causal link between the measure and the deprivation.[113] Here, the Tribunal finds that there was no causal link between the alleged deprivation and the challenged measures. [**718**] The Tribunal agrees that, as a matter of fact, the Claimant's shares in Industrias Infinito lost their value when the 2011 Administrative Chamber Decision annulled the 2008 Concession. But this does not mean that, as a legal matter, the decision caused the substantial deprivation of the value of Industrias Infinito. The Administrative Chamber found that the 2008 Concession was vitiated by a legal flaw that rendered it null and void *ab initio.* This means that the 2011 Administrative Chamber Decision merely confirmed this legal status. Had this decision been rendered in bad faith, in order to deprive Industrias Infinito of a validly held concession, it would have been open to the Tribunal to assess whether it was expropriatory. However, this is not the case here: [...] the 2011 Administrative Chamber Decision cannot be characterized as a denial of justice, nor was it fundamentally arbitrary or unfair. It was a *bona fide* decision of the Costa Rican Supreme Court that found that Industrias Infinito did not hold valid rights under Costa Rican law. Accordingly, it cannot be characterized as an expropriatory measure. [**719**] In other words, the value of Industrias Infinito's shares and other intangibles was premised on an illusion, *i.e.* that the mining rights were valid when they were not. In reality, the Claimant's shares in Industrias Infinito were already worthless prior to the challenged measures, which can thus not have caused their loss of value."

[**Paras. 708, 712, 717, 718, 719**]

D.

I.11.0   STATE RESPONSIBILITY

"[**770**] Annex I, Section III(1) of the BIT provides: Nothing in this Agreement shall be construed to prevent a Contracting Party from adopting, maintaining or enforcing any measure otherwise consistent with this Agreement that it considers appropriate to ensure

---

[112] [1149] *Burlington Resources,* ¶¶ 396-397, Exh. **CL-0023**; *Quiborax* Award, ¶¶ 237-238, Exh. **CL-0074**; *Pope & Talbot v. Government Canada,* UNCITRAL, Interim Award, 26 June 2000 ("***Pope***"), ¶ 102, Exh. **CL-0072**; *Charanne B.V. and Construction Investments S.A.R.L. v. Kindgom of Spain,* SCC Arbitration No. 062/2012 ("***Charanne***"), Award, 21 January 2016, ¶ 461, Exh. **RL-0203**.

[113] [1150] *S.D. Myers, Inc. v. Government of Canada,* UNCITRAL, Second Partial Award, 21 October 2002, ¶ 140; *Cargill Poland,* ¶¶ 632-635, Exh. **RL-0226**.

that investment activity in its territory is undertaken in a manner sensitive to environmental concerns.[114] [**771**] According to the general rule of interpretation enshrined in Article 31 of the VCLT, the Tribunal must interpret the Treaty's provisions in accordance with their ordinary meaning, in their context and in light of the treaty's object and purpose. [**772**] The Tribunal notes that, unlike other provisions on environmental protection in other investment treaties,[115] Annex I, Section III(1) of the Costa Rica-Canada BIT contains the wording "any measure otherwise consistent with this Agreement." In the Tribunal's view, this wording makes it clear that measures meant "to ensure that investment activity [...] is undertaken in a manner sensitive to environmental concerns" must also be consistent with the investment protections set forth in the BIT. [**773**] Commentators agree that provisions with such wording "cannot [...] be used to override mandatory treaty obligations,"[116] and that the "requirement that environmental measures be 'otherwise consistent' with the investment treaty [...] undermines the effectiveness of that shield."[117] One commentator opines that the scope of these provisions is "extremely limited," and that, despite the fact that most of them are entitled "general exceptions," "they do not really do much to narrow States' potential liability [...]. Rather, they merely recognize and affirm the State's sovereign right to regulate [...]."[118] For instance, this author submits that these "general provisions [...] have no impact whatsoever on the expropriation provision, which does not prohibit a State from enacting regulations that effectively expropriate investors' property, but demands compensation in return."[119] [**774**] The Tribunal notes that both Parties refer to *Al Tamimi*, an arbitration brought under the U.S.-Oman Free Trade Agreement. The tribunal in that case considered the treaty's provisions recognizing the importance of environmental measures as the context for interpreting the State Parties' obligations, and noted that the States enjoyed a "margin of discretion" in relation to the enforcement of their environmental laws.[120] There is no basis to conclude, however, that the tribunal considered that the treaty's references to environmental measures suggested there should be greater deference in matters relating to the environment than the deference due generally to States in relation to their domestic regulatory affairs.[121] Notably, the *Al Tamimi* tribunal also observed that "even an express provision such as Article 10.10 will not protect a State from liability for measures that are carried out in bad faith, or in violation of the

---

[114] [1228] BIT, Annex I, Section III(1), **Exh. C-0001**.

[115] [1229] *See e.g.*, Jordan-Singapore BIT (2004); Japan-Singapore New Age Economic Partnership (2003), India-Singapore CECA (2005), Japan-Malaysia Economic Partnership (2005), Korea-Singapore FTA (2005).

[116] [1230] T. Weiler, "A First Look at the Interim Merits Award in S.D. Myers, Inc. v. Canada: It Is Possible to Balance Legitimate Environmental Concerns with Investment Protection" (2001) 24:2 Hastings Int'l & Comp L Rev 173, p. 182, Exh. **CL-0195**.

[117] [1231] L. Johnson & L. Sachs, "International Investment Agreements, 2011-2012: A Review of Trends and New Approaches" in A. Bjorklund, ed, *Yearbook on International Investment Law & Policy 2012-2013* (Oxford University Press, 2014), p. 235, Exh. **CL-0185**.

[118] [1232] S. H. Nikièma, *Best Practices: Indirect Expropriation* (Winnipeg: International Institute for Sustainable Development, 2012), p. 9, Exh. **CL-0190**.

[119] [1233] S. H. Nikièma, *Best Practices: Indirect Expropriation* (Winnipeg: International Institute for Sustainable Development, 2012), p. 9, Exh. **CL-0190**.

[120] [1234] *Al Tamimi*, ¶ 389, Exh. **RL-0104**.

[121] [1235] *Al Tamimi*, ¶ 389, Exh. **RL-0104** (referring in this respect to the well-established principle that investment treaty tribunals "do not have an open-ended mandate to second-guess government decision-making").

expected standards of basic fairness or due process."[122] [**775**] Finally, Costa Rica contends that the words "otherwise consistent with this Agreement' in Annex I, Section III(1) do not apply to the measures that Infinito challenges because they merely "maintain or enforce" pre-existing measures, and that Infinito is not challenging and is not permitted to challenge those pre-existing measures because of the three-year limitation period.[123] It argues that the phrase "otherwise consistent' refers to the word "measure," and the context shows that the term "measure" refers to the underlying measure that is safeguarding the environment, rather than to a subsequent measure that maintains or enforces such underlying measure.[124] [**776**] The Tribunal cannot follow this interpretation. The terms "otherwise consistent with this Agreement" also apply to measures that are "maintain[ed]" or "enforc[ed]," not only to measures that are "adopted." Consequently, in accordance with its ordinary meaning, Annex I, Section III(1) does not exempt an environmental measure from the substantive provisions of the BIT, regardless of whether that measure is a new measure that is "adopted" or whether it is a measure that "maintains" or "enforces" an earlier measure. [**777**] The Tribunal concludes that, interpreted in accordance with the VCLT, Annex I, Section III(1) is not a carve-out from the BIT's protections, but rather a reaffirmation of the State's right to regulate. [**778**] The Respondent argues however that, unless it is interpreted as exempting the Respondent from liability for the adoption of environmental measures, Annex I, Section III(1) is deprived of its *effet utile*. The Tribunal cannot agree. It understands that the purpose of this provision is to protect the Contracting State's legitimate regulatory space and to reserve a margin of discretion in environmental matters.[125] Provisions like Annex I, Section III(1) must be viewed as acknowledging and reminding interpreters that these two objectives - environment and investment protection - should, if possible, be reconciled so that they are mutually supportive and reinforcing.[126] In other words, this provision reaffirms the State's right to regulate. [**779**] *Al Tamimi* supports this interpretation. In that case, the tribunal found that fines issued by the government for repeated and serious breaches of environmental regulations were issued in furtherance of its role "to regulate and supervise compliance with Oman's environmental laws."[127] In reaching this conclusion, the tribunal relied on a provision of the U.S.-Oman FTA with the exact language contained in Annex I, Section III(1) of the BIT.[128] Significantly, the measures at issue did not breach the substantive protections in the relevant treaty.[129] While this provision confirmed Oman's right to sanction violations of its environmental laws in a manner that

---

[122] [1236] *Al Tamimi*, ¶ 445, Exh. **RL-0104**.

[123] [1237] R-CM Merits, ¶¶ 572-577, 588; R-Rej. Merits, ¶ 761.

[124] [1238] R-CM Merits, ¶ 576

[125] [1239] *See Clayton & Bilcon*, ¶ 597, Exh. **CL-0172** (confirming, notwithstanding the identical reference in NAFTA, Chapter 11, that "[t]he mere fact that environmental regulation is involved does not make investor protection inapplicable").

[126] [1240] *S.D. Myers, Inc. v. Government of Canada*, UNCITRAL, Separate Opinion by Dr. Bryan Schwartz, Concurring Except with Respect to Performance Requirements, in the Partial Award of the Tribunal, 12 November 2000, ¶ 118 ("I view Article 1114 as acknowledging and reminding interpreters of Chapter 11 (Investment) that the parties take both the environment and open trade very seriously and that means should be found to reconcile these two objectives and, if possible, to make them mutually supportive").

[127] [1241] *Al Tamimi*, ¶ 340, Exh. **RL-0104**.

[128] [1242] *Al Tamimi*, ¶ 445, Exh. **RL-0104**, citing Agreement between the Government of the United States of America and the Government of the Sultanate of Oman on the Establishment of a Free Trade Area, Article 10.10, Exh. **CL-0111**.

[129] [1243] *Al Tamimi*, ¶¶ 376, 390, 430-431, 445-447, 467, Exh. **RL-0104**.

did not otherwise breach its obligations under the treaty, the Tribunal is not persuaded that it would have operated as a defense had the tribunal found that those measures breached the treaty. [**780**] Conversely, the Respondent's argument that Annex I, Section III(1) of the BIT provides a defense to substantive breaches of the BIT would render meaningless the "otherwise consistent with this Agreement" language. Other exceptions and exemptions contained in Section III are not limited by similar language. For example, Section III(3) contains an unlimited exemption enabling the Contracting Parties to adopt or maintain "reasonable measures for prudential reasons" related to financial market protection and regulation. Similarly, Section III(4) exempts "investments in cultural industries" from the provisions of the BIT. Since Section III(1) does contain the "otherwise consistent" ' language, it cannot be construed as an exception or exemption from the BIT protections for environmental measures. [**781**] The Tribunal concludes that Annex I, Section III(1) of the Costa Rica-Canada BIT does not exempt the Respondent from liability for breaches of the substantive protections granted by the BIT. Accordingly, it cannot exempt the Respondent for its breaches of its FET obligation."

[**Paras. 770, 771, 772, 773, 774, 775, 776, 777, 778, 779, 780,781**]

IV.

II.7.98   ICSID AWARD

"[**799**] For the foregoing reasons, the Tribunal:
  a. DECLARES that it has jurisdiction over the claims before it and that, with the exception noted in paragraph (b) below, the claims are admissible;
  b. DECLARES that the claim arising from the reinitiation in 2019 of the TCA damages proceeding is premature and thus inadmissible at the present stage;
  c. DECLARES that, by enacting the 2011 Legislative Mining Ban and implementing it through the 2012 MINAET Resolution, the Respondent has breached its obligation under Article II(2)(a) of the BIT to accord to the Claimant's investments fair and equitable treatment;
  d. DETERMINES that it can award no damages from this breach;
  e. ORDERS that each Party bear 50% of the Costs of the Proceeding and its own legal fees and other costs;
  f. DISMISSES all remaining claims and requests for relief."

[**Para. 799**]

X.2.2

Mathias Kruck and Others v. *Kingdom of Spain*, ICSID Case No. ARB/15/23, Decision on the Respondent's Request for Reconsideration of the Tribunal's Decision dated 19 April 2021, 6 December 2021*

Contents**

I.

II.7.91   ICSID PROCEDURAL ISSUES

See also: I.2.223; II.7.92

"[**1**] On 19 April 2021, the Tribunal issued a Decision on Jurisdiction and Admissibility in which it found, *inter alia*, that "its jurisdiction under the ECT and the ICSID Convention [was] not precluded or excluded by provisions of EU law, and dismisse[d] [the intra-EU] objection."[130] [**4**] The Respondent requests that the Tribunal (i) reconsider its Decision on Jurisdiction and Admissibility dated 19 April 2021 (the "**Decision of 19 April 2021**" or "**Decision on Jurisdiction and Admissibility**") in light of the judgment issued by the Court of Justice of the European Union (the "**CJEU**") on 2 September 2021 in Case C-741/19, *Republic of Moldova v. Komstroy LCC* ("**Komstroy**"), and (ii) declare that it lacks jurisdiction over this intra-EU dispute.[131] [**5**] Having offered a summary of *Komstroy*, the Respondent highlights the following holdings, the first three being in its view relevant to its Request for Reconsideration: *(1) the application of the EU Law is mandatory, foreign direct investment (including the ECT) is part of the EU competences and EU Law and, in cases where the seat of the arbitration is in a member state of the EU, the national courts have to ensure such application; (2) the autonomy of the EU legal framework must be respected; (3) intra-EU investment arbitration is not allowed and the ECT cannot be*

---

* Summaries prepared by Johannes Tropper, Researcher & Lecturer (prae doc), Department of European, International and Comparative Law, University of Vienna, Austria. The full text of the Decision is available at <https://jusmundi.com/en/document/pdf/decision/en-mathias-kruck-frank-schumm-joachim-kruck-jurgen-reiss-and-others-v-kingdom-of-spain-decision-on-the-respondents-request-for-reconsideration-of-the-tribunals-decision-on-jurisdiction-and-admissibility-monday-6th-december-2021>. Original footnote numbers are indicated in brackets: [].

** This is not a faithful reproduction of the Table of Contents of the Judgment.

[130] [2] Decision on Jurisdiction and Admissibility, ¶ 295. *See also ibid.,* ¶ 326(1).

[131] [3] Respondent's Request for Reconsideration of the Tribunal's Decision dated 19 April 2021 (the "**Request for Reconsideration**"), ¶ 1.

interpreted as allowing it; and (4) the concept of "economic activity in the energy sector" must be carefully assessed on case by case basis.[132]*"*

[Paras. 1, 4, 5]

II.

A.

II.7.91   ICSID PROCEDURAL ISSUES
            See also: I.2.223; II.7.92

"**[19]** The Tribunal notes that there is in the ICSID Convention and Rules no express provision concerning the reconsideration during the course of an arbitration by Tribunals of their earlier Decisions. It notes also the increasing frequency of requests for reconsideration.[133] **[20]** The Tribunal has given careful consideration to the awards cited by each of the Parties on the question of the power of tribunals to reconsider decisions made prior to the issuing of a final award. It agrees with the conclusion in the award of the distinguished tribunal in the *Standard Chartered Bank* case that

> *[d]ecisions of tribunals are of course binding within the scope of the proceedings, but this does not make them res judicata. ... An essential feature of res judicata is that the judgment in question produces effects on the parties outside the proceedings in which it is granted. But decisions of tribunals only have effect within the proceedings until they have been incorporated into the final award.*[134]

[21] While there may appear to be an element of circularity in that reasoning, the conclusion is, as the *Standard Chartered Bank* tribunal explained, supported by the architecture of the ICSID Convention, which treats only issued awards as having legal consequences outside ICSID proceedings,[135] and also by considerations of efficiency and procedural economy.[136] This Tribunal shares that view. **[22]** Moreover, the Tribunal notes that the ICSID Arbitration Rules distinguish between "Decisions of the Tribunal" (Rule 16) and "The Award" (Chapter VI). Furthermore, ICSID Rule 38 provides that

> *(1) When the presentation of the case by the parties is completed, the proceeding shall be declared closed.*
>
> *(2) Exceptionally, the Tribunal may, before the award has been rendered, reopen the proceeding on the ground that new evidence is forthcoming of such a nature as to constitute a decisive factor, or that there is a vital need for clarification on certain specific points.*

[23] Rule 38 refers to the period before the award is rendered. Rule 38 would be deprived of much of its practical utility if new evidence could be admitted or new clarification provided,

---

[132] [4] Request for Reconsideration, ¶ 26.

[133] [51] Cf., Jeffery Commission and Rahim Moloo, *Procedural Issues in International Investment Arbitration* (2018), ¶¶ 9.55-9.66.

[134] [52] *Standard Chartered Bank* (RL-172), ¶ 313

[135] [53] *Standard Chartered Bank* (RL-172), ¶ 314, referring to ICSID Convention Articles 54(1), 54(2), 52, and 48(3).

[136] [54] *Standard Chartered Bank* (RL-172), ¶ 320.

but Decisions taken earlier in the proceedings which might decisively affect them could not be reconsidered. [**24**] The Tribunal therefore agrees with the *Standard Chartered Bank* tribunal[137] (and with the Committee in the annulment proceeding in that case[138]) that in exceptional circumstances Decisions may be reconsidered before the award in a case has been rendered. [**25**] Moreover, the Tribunal does not consider that the power of reconsideration is confined to instances in which questions of a tribunal's jurisdiction are at stake. The logic of the reasoning in *Standard Chartered Bank* is applicable to prior decisions in general. [**26**] In the present case, the Tribunal issued a Decision, and not an Award. [...]

[**29**] It would be an absurd waste of time and money if some such legal development, neglect of which might lead to the annulment of an award, were to be wilfully ignored by a tribunal simply because it had already taken a decision on the point, even though the tribunal had not yet rendered its award. For example, if certain contracts that a tribunal had decided were the basis of an 'investment' were subsequently determined by a competent court to have been void *ab initio*, that is not something that a tribunal should ignore when writing its award, whether or not the tribunal has issued a preliminary 'decision' on the existence of the investment. [**30**] This Tribunal accordingly considers that in principle it is possible that a change in or misunderstanding of the law that has formed the basis of a Decision of a tribunal made earlier in the proceedings could in principle be of a nature to warrant the step of reconsidering that Decision. It could be so only exceptionally: the development would have to be material to the pending award; and its materiality would have to be decisive, in the sense that it would necessitate a significant alteration in the reasoning or conclusions of the tribunal. In particular, routine developments in case-law whose long-term impact upon relevant jurisprudence is inevitably unpredictable, will not fall within this exceptional category. [**31**] A tribunal may not simply refuse even to consider a submission from a party that there has been a material legal development. Plainly, it cannot be known if an alleged legal development has this exceptional character unless the alleged development is first examined by the tribunal. That examination may appear to be very similar to a 'reconsideration', but it is a distinct stage in the proceedings. If a tribunal finds that there is no ground that warrants a full reconsideration, it will deny the Request for Reconsideration; whereas if there is such a ground it might seek or permit further submissions for the parties. Accordingly, this Tribunal, exercising its powers under Article 44 of the ICSID Convention and Rule 19, decides that has the power to consider the Request for Reconsideration of its Decision of 19 April 2021 and that it will do so."

[**Paras. 19, 20, 21, 22, 23, 24, 25, 26, 29, 30, 31**]

B.

II.7.91   ICSID PROCEDURAL ISSUES
         See also: I.2.223; I.17.012; II.7.92

"[**32**] The Request for Reconsideration is, as was noted above, based on the *Komstroy* Judgment of the Grand Chamber of the Court of Justice of the European Union, rendered on 2 September 2021, and the implications of that judgment for the 'intra-EU' or '*Achmea* question'. [**33**] It is true that the paragraphs of the Decision of 19 April 2021 that set out

---

[137] [55] *Standard Chartered Bank* (RL-172), ¶¶ 307-324.

[138] [56] *Standard Chartered Bank (Hong Kong) Limited v. Tanzania Electric Supply Company Limited* (ICSID Case No. ARB/10/20), Decision on Annulment, 22 August 2018, ¶¶ 150-173.

the Tribunal's analysis of the 'intra-EU Objection'[60] do not refer to the *Achmea* decision *eo nomine*. The arguments made by the Parties and by the European Commission on the basis of the *Achmea* decision were, however, recorded[61] and were addressed in the Decision. [**34**] The Tribunal recalls its analysis of the '*Achmea* objection' in paragraphs 280-295 of its Decision of 19 April 2021 [...]. [**35**] The Tribunal recognizes that the fact that the *Komstroy* judgment postdates the Decision of 19 April 2021 is not in itself a barrier to an argument that the Tribunal's decision on jurisdiction was wrong, both at the date of the Decision and at the date at which the arbitration was commenced, and that the Decision can therefore properly be reconsidered. [**36**] The Tribunal has serious doubts as to whether the arrival of new case-law bearing on the *Achmea* objection from the CJEU is a sufficient ground for reconsideration, because (a) it is not a new fact, and (b) the central legal questions are essentially the same as those addressed by the Parties in their submissions on *Achmea* and decided by the Tribunal in its Decision of 19 April 2021. Nonetheless, the fact that in *Komstroy* the CJEU for the first time directly addresses the question of intra-EU disputes under the ECT is a very specific and particular feature of the *Komstroy* judgment, which the Tribunal considers, on balance, warrants reconsideration in this case. [**37**] The Tribunal reaffirms that the Tribunal must determine its jurisdiction within the legal framework of the ECT and of international law. The ECT must be interpreted in accordance with the well-established principles of international law on treaty interpretation, as reflected in the Vienna Convention on the Law of Treaties. Moreover, it is axiomatic that the express words of the text of the ECT cannot have different meanings as between different configurations of EU and non-EU Contracting Parties and their investors. Contracting Parties may, of course, agree to amend the ECT so that it has differential application, in accordance with the procedure set out in ECT Article 42. [**39**] The Tribunal agrees [with *Komstroy*] that "where a provision of an international agreement can apply both to situations falling within the scope of EU law and to situations not covered by that law, it is clearly in the interest of the European Union that, in order to forestall future differences of interpretation, that provision should be interpreted uniformly, whatever the circumstances in which it is to apply." That is an axiomatic proposition, inherent in the notion that a treaty is an international *agreement*, in which the parties *agree* on the words and meaning of the text that binds them all. [**40**] The Tribunal cannot accept, however, that the consequence is that the interpretation of the ECT must either be determined authoritatively by the EU and its courts, or that the ECT may have a different meaning in the context of intra-EU disputes from that which it has in non-intra-EU disputes (whether between non-EU investors and EU States, or between non-EU investors and non-EU States. or between EU investors and non-EU States). Such an inherently discriminatory structure cannot be reconciled with the affirmation of the ECT Contracting Parties, including the EU, that they "attach the utmost importance to the effective implementation of full national treatment and most favoured nation treatment."[139] [**41**] [...] The Tribunal accepts that the ECT may be considered to be a part of EU law and thus of the law of EU Member States, in the sense that the provisions of the ECT are applicable within the EU as a part of the applicable EU law. But that does not mean that the ECT is transformed into EU law, losing its character as an international agreement subject to and applicable as part of public international law, or that the text and meaning of ECT must be interpreted through the optic of EU law and applied in conformity with EU law and the principles of the European Union as interpreted by EU national courts

---

[139] [64] ECT, Preamble; and cf., Articles 10 and 25 concerning the right of Contracting Parties to extend *preferential* (but not disadvantageous) treatment in consequence of membership of Economic Integration Agreements.

and the CJEU. Nor does it alter the fact that EU law is (like the domestic laws of sovereign States) a *source* of international law and is not in itself a *part* of international law, and *a fortiori* is not a part of international law that has primacy over all other rules of international law, which is the body of law governing relations between all States and jurisdictions in the world. [**42**] Moreover, unlike the arbitration in question in *Komstroy,* the present arbitration does not have its seat in an EU Member State. EU law cannot be said to be part of the *lex fori* of this ICSID arbitration,[140] as it was in *Komstroy* (para 33). It is questionable, and unnecessary to decide here, whether any ICSID tribunal has a *lex fori* other than the ICSID Convention and international law; but in any event the 'place of proceeding' in this case is expressly stipulated to be Washington D.C., so that there can be no possible basis for a claim that EU law is part of *the lex fori.* [**43**] The ECT, as signed and ratified by Spain, Germany, and the EU itself, provides explicitly in Articles 16 and 42 for the relationship between the ECT and later agreements such as the TFEU, as well as prior agreements made by ECT Contracting Parties, and for the amendment of that relationship. Article 16, it will be recalled, stipulates that

> *Where two or more Contracting Parties* ... *enter into a subsequent international agreement, whose terms in either case concern the subject matter of Part III or V of this Treaty* ... nothing in such terms of the other agreement shall be construed to derogate from any provision of Part III or V of this Treaty or from any right to dispute resolution with respect thereto under this Treaty, where any such provision is more favourable to the Investor or Investment. (emphasis added)

[**44**] The provision is explicit. All of the provisions on which the Claimants rely are contained in ECT Part III ('Investment Promotion and Protection') and Part V ('Dispute Settlement'); and the Claimants' entitlement to exercise the right to dispute resolution is specifically spelled out. There is no ambiguity or room for doubt. Those provisions were set out in the ECT in 1994. Germany, Spain and the EU signed the ECT on 17 December 1994 and subsequently ratified it and became bound by its provisions as of 16 April 1998.[141] They were bound by those provisions, including Article 16, when they were negotiating the TFEU and when they ratified the TFEU. It has not been argued that it is 'more favourable' to the Claimants to deprive them of the right to dispute settlement under the ECT than to allow them to exercise it; and in the view of the Tribunal no such argument could credibly be made out. [**45**] As the Tribunal pointed out in its Decision on Jurisdiction and Admissibility, special provision could have been made in the ECT for intra-EU disputes, by way of a Decision or Declaration or Understanding of the Contracting Parties or by way of a subsequent amendment of the Treaty pursuant to ECT Article 42. That was not done. The Contracting Parties did not provide arbitral tribunals constituted under ECT Part V with any legal basis for refusing to interpret and apply the ECT in accordance with its plain terms. Nor can unilateral interpretations of the ECT that are contrary to its plain meaning, determined in accordance with the applicable principles of international law, have that effect. The Claimants have under ECT Part V a right to ECT arbitration, and neither the *Komstroy* decision nor the principles of EU law on which it is based can deprive them of that right -particularly when the decision postdates the critical date for the establishment of

---

[140] [66] The Tribunal takes no position on the question of the *lex fori* of ICSID arbitrations, but only on the point that it is plainly not the law of any EU Member State.

[141] [67] *See* https://www.energycharter.org/process/energy-charter-treaty-1994/energy-charter-treaty/signatories-contracting-parties/.

jurisdiction and the Tribunal's decision thereon. [**46**] The Tribunal recognizes that there is here a clash of *Grundnormen*. The CJEU has its role and authority within the EU legal order. The CJEU itself has made clear that ECT arbitration tribunals are not part of that legal order.[142] Their role and their authority is established by an international treaty, concluded by sovereign States and by the EU. The ECT Contracting Parties do not merely permit Investors to make their own agreements to arbitrate: the Contracting Parties give Investors an immediate legal right to choose to arbitrate or conciliate disputes under the mechanisms established by the Contracting Parties in ECT Article 26. The mandate of this Tribunal, and its authority, derive from the agreement of the ECT Contracting Parties in accordance with international law and are invoked by the Parties to the dispute. It is deeply regrettable that parties to disputes should find themselves caught up in a clash of *Grundnormen* that could have been foreseen and resolved in advance. But this Tribunal has the duty to fulfil its mandate under the ECT, and has no legal right or capacity to do otherwise. The solution lies in the hands of the Contracting Parties to the ECT. [**47**] In view of the relatively unusual nature of the Request for Reconsideration, and the specific relevance of the *Komstroy* Judgment the Tribunal has set out its reasoning at greater length that might have been expected. Its conclusion is, however, simple and clear. The rendering of the *Komstroy* Judgment does not warrant the reopening of the '*Achmea* / intra-EU' question, and the Tribunal's Decision of 19 April 2021 stands. The Tribunal will now proceed to finalize and render its Award."

[**Paras. 32, 33, 34, 35, 36, 37, 39, 40, 41, 42, 43, 44, 45, 46, 47**]

III.

II.7.97   ICSID DECISION ON JURISDICTION

"[**48**] For the reasons given above. the Tribunal DECIDES:

(i) That the Judgment of the CJEU in the *Komstroy* case does not warrant the reopening of the questions addressed and decided in the Tribunal's Decision of 19 April 2021; and

(ii) That it will not alter its Decision of 19 April 2021."

[**Para. 48**]

---

[142] [68] *Komstroy* (RL-171), ¶ 62.

Systematic Key Items of the Section*

---

* *See* Systematic Classification Scheme, *supra* at page 255.

Systematic Key to Parts of the Section

See Systematic Classification Scheme, either at page 355.

XI

Permanent Court
of Arbitration

XL

Permanent Court
of Arbitration

INTRODUCTORY NOTE

PCA Arbitrations in 2021

BY PATRÍCIA GALVÃO TELES*
& JOÃO GIL ANTUNES**

Abstract
The Permanent Court of Arbitration (PCA) provided administrative services in 204 proceedings in 2021, divided by 7 inter-state arbitrations, 115 investor-state arbitrations, 80 contract-based arbitrations, and 2 other proceedings of a different nature. These proceedings involved a diverse variety of actors, including sovereign states, intergovernmental organizations, and public or private entities. Of these proceedings, 40 were initiated in 2021. As for appointing authority services or related services, in 2021, the PCA received 49 requests in total, including requests that the Secretary-General of the PCA designate an appointing authority (27), act as an appointing authority for the appointment of an arbitrator (16), furnish a statement setting forth the basis for establishing fees of an arbitral tribunal (1), and act as an appointing authority to decide a challenge to an arbitrator (2). In 2021, only 1 award was public, namely that in Olympic Entertainment Group AS and Ukraine.

I. THE PCA'S DOCKET IN 2021

The Permanent Court of Arbitration (PCA) provided administrative services in 204 proceedings in 2021, divided by 7 inter-state arbitrations, 115 investor-state arbitrations, 80

---

* Associate Professor of International Law at the Autonomous University of Lisbon. Member of the Permanent Court of Arbitration. Member of the United Nations International Law Commission. Director of the Department of Legal Affairs of the Portuguese Ministry of Foreign Affairs.
** Legal Adviser in Public International Law in the Department of Legal Affairs of the Portuguese Ministry of Foreign Affairs.

Patrícia Galvão Teles and João Gil Antunes, *Introductory Note* In: *The Global Community Yearbook of International Law and Jurisprudence 2022*. Edited by: Giuliana Ziccardi Capaldo, Oxford University Press. © Oxford University Press 2023.
DOI: 10.1093/oso/9780197752265.003.0033

contract-based arbitrations, and 2 other proceedings of a different nature. These proceedings involved a diverse variety of actors, including sovereign states, intergovernmental organizations, and public or private entities.

The year 2021 brought special challenges to international dispute resolution, as governments around the world have taken public health measures in response to the COVID-19 pandemic. As a result, the Permanent Court of Arbitration has had to adapt to the context and has transformed in-person hearings into virtual hearings. Accordingly, of the 41 hearings it held, 30 were entirely virtual.

II. SELECTED DECISIONS ISSUED BY PCA TRIBUNALS IN 2021

Among other awards rendered in 2021 in arbitral proceedings administered by the PCA, only one award is public: the award in the dispute between Olympic Entertainment Group AS and Ukraine. In the remainder of this introductory note, we comment on its principal findings.

A. Olympic Entertainment *Group AS v. Ukraine*

These arbitral proceedings were commenced on 5 November 2018 by Olympic Entertainment Group AS (the claimant) against Ukraine (or the respondent), pursuant to Article 8 of the Agreement between the Government of the Republic of Estonia and the Government of Ukraine for the Promotion and Reciprocal Protection of Investments, dated 15 February 1995 (Treaty),[1] and the 1976 Arbitration Rules of the United Nations Commission on International Trade Law (1976 UNCITRAL Rules).[2] The arbitral tribunal was composed of Professor Michael Pryles AO PBM, who was appointed by the claimant; Mr J Christopher Thomas QC, who was appointed by the respondent; and Mr Neil Kaplan QC CBE SBS, who chaired the arbitral tribunal by agreement of the two co-arbitrators. The arbitral tribunal, with the consent of the parties, appointed Dr Noam Zamir as its secretary.[3]

After the hearing, which took place from 13 to 20 December 2020, the arbitral tribunal rendered its award in which it addressed issues of jurisdiction, merits, and quantum. The dispute related to the investments that the claimant had made in the gambling industry in Ukraine and a series of measures by Ukrainian authorities, including the ban of gambling activities, which, according to the claimant, breached several of its substantive obligations under the Treaty and resulted in significant losses on its investments.[4] The claimant submitted a primary and an alternative claims.[5] The disputing parties attempted to settle the

---

[1] Agreement for the Promotion and Reciprocal Protection of Investments, Kiev, 15 February 1992, 1940 UNTS 353.

[2] Olympic Entertainment Group AS v. Ukraine, PCA Case No. 2019-18, UNCITRAL Arbitration, Award, dated 15 April 2021, paras. 1 and 3.

[3] *Id.*, paras. 8–11 and Appendix 1 to the Award.

[4] Ukrainian authorities started to discuss a complete ban on gambling, with some exceptions, on 26 March 2009, "when Draft Law No. 4268 on the Prohibition of Gambling in Ukraine was registered with the Verkhovna Rada" (*see* Olympic Entertainment Group AS v. Ukraine, PCA Case No. 2019-18, UNCITRAL Arbitration, Award, dated 15 April 2021, para. 22).

[5] Olympic Entertainment Group AS v. Ukraine, PCA Case No. 2019-18, UNCITRAL Arbitration, Award, dated 15 April 2021, para. 33.

dispute between July 2009 and December 2017, with the latter later conveying the claimant that it would not pay compensation.[6]

The claimant through its locally incorporated company Olympic Casino Ukraine LLC (OCU) developed and operated several gambling facilities in Ukraine. For all relevant purposes, the legal framework in place in Ukraine regarding gambling activities between 2004 and 2008 consisted, among others, of the following legislative instruments: (i) the Law of Ukraine No. 1775-III, dated 1 June 2000, "On Licensing of Certain Commercial Activities" (Licensing Law); (ii) the Law of Ukraine No. 98/96-BP, dated 23 March 1996, "On Patenting of Certain Types of Entrepreneurial Activity" (Trade Patent Law); and (iii) the Licensing Conditions, adopted by Order No. 40/374 of the State Committee for Regulatory Policy and Entrepreneurship of Ukraine and the Ministry of Finance of Ukraine, dated 18 April 2006 (Licensing Conditions).[7]

On 8 May 2009, the Ukrainian Ministry of Finance, acting in its capacity as the licensing authority, ordered the immediate suspension of all gambling licenses until 7 June 2008 (Suspension Order). According to the claimant, this decision disregarded the conditions to suspend or terminate a gambling license under the Licensing Law.[8] Three business days later, on 15 May 2009, the Verkhovna Rada adopted Law No. 38/2009 "On the Prohibition of Gambling Business in Ukraine" (Gambling Ban Law),[9] which did not provide for a transition period and would be applicable from the day of its publication.[10] The then president of Ukraine vetoed the gambling law on various constitutional grounds,[11] whereupon the Verkhovna Rada overrode the veto and passed the gambling law. The Gambling Ban Law entered into force on 25 June 2009, and from that date made those engaged in the gambling business criminally liable. In addition, the Cabinet of Ministers of Ukraine had three months from the date of its entry into force "to develop a draft law on the gambling organization and operation activities in specially designated gaming zones and submit it to the Verkhovna Rada of Ukraine for consideration."[12] This special law would be enacted by the Verkhovna Rada on 14 July 2020 (New Gambling Law).

---

[6] *Id.*, para. 34, referring to Letter from the Ministry of Justice of Ukraine to Olympic, dated 26 December 2017.

[7] *Id.*, para. 15.

[8] *Id.*, para. 25, referring to Exhibit C-59, Order of the Ministry of Finance of Ukraine No. 650. This decision came about despite the fact that on 10 April 2009, the Chief Scientific and Expert Department of the Verkhovna Rada had opposed the adoption of the Draft Law No. 4268 "On the Prohibition of Gambling in Ukraine," as it would, in its view, (i) lead to the criminalization of gambling activities; (ii) make it more difficult to bring to justice those involved in criminal activities related to gambling; and (iii) contribute to the "shadowing" of the business actors operating in this field (*see* Olympic Entertainment Group AS v. Ukraine, PCA Case No. 2019-18, UNCITRAL Arbitration, Award, dated 15 April 2021, paras. 23 and 25, referring to Opinion of the Chief Scientific and Expert Department of the Verkhovna Rada of Ukraine on the Draft Law of Ukraine "On Prohibition of Gambling Business in Ukraine," dated 10 April 2009).

[9] Olympic Entertainment Group AS v. Ukraine, PCA Case No. 2019-18, UNCITRAL Arbitration, Award, dated 15 April 2021, paras. 26–27, referring to Law No. 38/2009 "On the Prohibition of Gambling Business in Ukraine," adopted 15 May 2009; SOC, para. 72, referring to Article 31 of the Rules of Procedure of Verkhovna Rada, dated 19 September 2008; Transcripts of 35th hearing dated 15 May 2009 of Verkhovna Rada of Ukraine; Transcripts of 50th hearing of Verkhovna Rada of Ukraine, dated 11 June 2009; SOC, para. 81; Results of the Verkhovna Rada voting for Gambling Ban Law.

[10] The fact that it did not provide for a transitional period was a deviation from Draft Law No. 4268 "On the Prohibition of Gambling in Ukraine."

[11] Olympic Entertainment Group AS v. Ukraine, PCA Case No. 2019-18, UNCITRAL Arbitration, Award, dated 15 April 2021, para. 28, referring to Submission of the President of Ukraine with proposals to the Draft Gambling Ban Law dated 15 May 2009.

[12] Article 4(4) of the Gambling Ban Law.

The claimant alleged that because of the above measures, on 3 July 2009, it had to terminate its business activities and OCU had to begin liquidation proceedings, "for itself and
most of its subsidiaries."[13] On 12 August 2009, the claimant's subsidiaries, except for one,
filed for bankruptcy.[14] In turn, the respondent posited there was no causal relationship between the entry into force of the Gambling Ban Law and the liquidation proceedings because the latter had begun on 9 June 2009.

In view of these facts, the claimant requested, in essence, that the arbitral tribunal (i) declare that the Gambling Ban Law constituted an indirect expropriation of its investment;
(ii) declare that Ukraine has breached the standards of fair and equitable standard and
full protection and security; (iii) order Ukraine to compensate the claimant for the losses
suffered by it in the amount of at least EUR 12,404,000.00 (twelve million four hundred
and four thousand euros);[15] and (iv) order Ukraine to pay pre-award and post-award interest on any amount awarded.[16] In addition, the claimant requested that (v) Ukraine be
ordered to pay all costs related to the arbitration proceedings.[17]

The respondent, in turn, essentially requested that the arbitral tribunal (i) declare it
lacked jurisdiction *ratione materiae*; (ii) dismiss all of the claimant's claims on the merits, including for lack of causation and for compensation. Finally, it requested that the arbitral tribunal (iii) order the claimant to reimburse Ukraine for all costs, fees, and expenses incurred
by it in these proceedings or, in the alternative, order each party to bear its own costs of legal
representation and assistance, with the remaining costs to be borne equally by the parties.[18]

As a preliminary defence, the respondent requested that the arbitral tribunal declare
that it lacked jurisdiction *ratione materiae* to hear the claimant's claims. It argued that the
claimant's investment had not been made in accordance with the laws and regulations of
Ukraine because the claimant had not obtained the necessary gambling licenses from the
Ukrainian authorities.[19]

In its response, the claimant argued that the arbitral tribunal had jurisdiction, pointing
out that (i) in 2004, OCU operated only slot machines in shared premises, an activity
for which licenses were not required under the Licensing Law; (ii) OCU had acquired
all required licenses in 2006, with the establishment of the licensing conditions and the

---

[13] Olympic Entertainment Group AS v. Ukraine, PCA Case No. 2019-18, UNCITRAL Arbitration, Award,
dated 15 April 2021, para. 31, referring to Minutes No. 45 of the General (Extraordinary) Meeting of
Members of Olympic Casino Ukraine dated 3 July 2009. *See* SOC, para. 102.

[14] *Id.*, para. 31, referring to press release "Bankruptcy petition of OEG Ukrainian subsidiaries," Olympic
Entertainment Group Website; Resolution of the Commercial Court of Kyiv on adjudging OCU to be
a bankrupt; Ruling of the Commercial Court of Kyiv on instituting bankruptcy proceedings of Ukraine
Leisure Company; Resolution of the Commercial Court of Kyiv on adjudging Eldorado Leisure Company
to be a bankrupt. *See* SOC, para. 103.

[15] *Id.*, para. 37. In the event that this last request was denied, the claimant requested in the alternative that
the tribunal (iv) order Ukraine to pay compensation in the euro equivalent of USD 15,000,000.00 (fifteen
million dollars), less EUR 2,596,000.00 (two million five hundred and ninety-six thousand euros) the
claimant had already received at that time.

[16] Annual compounding at the rate of 12-month LIBOR + 4%, accruing from 25 June 2009 to (and including) the date of the award and from the date of the award until payment in full.

[17] This request included (i) the costs of the arbitration; (ii) the costs of the Permanent Court of Arbitration;
(iii) the legal and other expenses incurred by the claimant, including fees for legal counsel, experts, and
consultants.

[18] Olympic Entertainment Group AS v. Ukraine, PCA Case No. 2019-18, UNCITRAL Arbitration, Award,
dated 15 April 2021, para. 38.

[19] *Id.*, paras. 16, 41–43.

appointment of the Ukrainian Ministry of Finance as the licensing authority; (iii) the burden of proving that an investment was not made in accordance with the laws and regulations of the host country rested on the respondent. A burden which, in the claimant's view, it did not meet; and (iv) even if that had not been the case, the claimant posited this would not constitute a breach of a fundamental principle of Ukrainian law. Accordingly, the claimant argues that its investment constitutes a covered investment under the Treaty.[20]

In addressing this jurisdiction objection, the arbitral tribunal began by determining the meaning of the term *investment* within the framework of the Treaty. In doing so, it concluded that the claimant's investment in Ukraine met the requirements under Article 1 of the Treaty, including that it was made in accordance with the laws and regulations of Ukraine. In particular, the arbitral tribunal concluded that the legality of the gambling activities conducted by the claimant did not depend on the prior acquisition of licenses given the gambling establishments it operated.[21] In this regard, the arbitral tribunal further emphasised that the claimant's investments were "under continuous scrutiny of various state organs at the local and national levels," during the years when it operated in Ukraine, without any claim of illegality ever having been brought against the claimant.[22] Finally, the arbitral tribunal endorsed the view of other arbitral tribunals that the requirement of compliance with the laws and regulations of the host country is disregarded only in the event of a breach of a fundamental legal principle.[23] Accordingly, the arbitral tribunal dismissed the respondent's jurisdictional objection.

On the merits, the claimant submitted that the measures taken by the Ukrainian authorities had a negative impact on its investment because they (i) constituted expropriation without compensation; (ii) did not grant it fair and equitable treatment and did not maintain favourable conditions for it, and (iii) did not provide it with full protection and security.[24]

On the issue of expropriation, the claimant submitted that the Gambling Ban Law amounted to an indirect expropriation of its investment by "caus[ing] [its] total annihilation," regardless of whether the prohibition were temporary.[25] In the claimant's view, the legality of an expropriation under Article 5 of the Treaty depended on it being carried out

---

[20] *Id.*, paras. 17, 20, 44–48.

[21] *Id.*, paras. 49–50, referring to Olympic Casino Ukraine Excerpt from State Register; Agreement of the Sale and Purchase of Corporate rights of Alea Private Company dated 17 September 2007; Agreement of the Sale and Purchase of Corporate rights of Ukraine Leisure Company dated 17 September 2007; Agreement of the Sale and Purchase of Corporate rights of Eldorado Leisure Company dated 17 September 2007, Olympic's Consolidated unaudited interim financial report for the 12 months and fourth quarter of 2007, at 30; Fraport AG Frankfurt Airport Services Worldwide v. Republic of the Philippines II, ICSID Case No. ARB/11/12, Award, dated 10 December 2014, paras. 337–338, 444; Article 164(1) of the Code of Ukraine on Administrative Offences (as of 31 March 2005).

[22] *Id.*, para. 57.

[23] *Id.*, paras. 58–59, referring to Rumeli Telekom A.S. and Telsim Mobil Telekomikasy on Hizmetleri A.S. v. Republic of Kazakhstan, ICSID Case No. ARB/05/16, Award, dated 29 July 2008, para. 319; Desert Line Projects LLC v. The Republic of Yemen, ICSID Case No. ARB/05/17, Award, dated 6 February 2008, para. 104. In order to determine whether there was such a breach, the arbitral tribunal examined the legal consequences arising from the breach of the provisions which the respondent accused the claimant of failing to comply with, *i.e.*, the consequences arising from the fact that the claimant did not have the required licenses.

[24] Olympic Entertainment Group AS v. Ukraine, PCA Case No. 2019-18, UNCITRAL Arbitration, Award, dated 15 April 2021, para. 61.

[25] *Id.*, paras. 65–66.

(i) for a public purpose; (ii) on a non-discriminatory basis; and (iii) in accordance with due process. It also depended on it being (iv) accompanied by the payment of prompt, adequate and effective compensation. The claimant argued that the expropriation of its investment did not meet the requirements (i), (iii), and (iv). First, the Gambling Ban Law did not serve any public purpose, and the respondent had not presented any evidence that gambling posed a serious threat to public morals and health. In turn, the claimant posited that these measures served only political and populist purposes and were disproportionate.[26] Second, the expropriation was not carried out in accordance with due process of law because the adoption of the Gambling Ban Law occurred without (i) proper parliamentary debate, (ii) prior notice to the claimant; and (iii) consideration of the legitimate concerns of the gambling industry.[27] Third, the claimant did not receive prompt, adequate, and effective compensation from the respondent.[28]

The respondent, in turn, based his defence on the argument that the measures in question constituted a valid exercise under the state's police powers doctrine. It further argued that the assessment of their validity depended on the nature of the measures and not on their consequences. As such, in line with the arbitral tribunal in *Methanex v. USA*, the respondent posited that, in addition to conditions (i), (ii), and (iii) above, the legality of such measures also depended on whether they were taken in good faith.[29] Finally, the respondent, albeit denying any relevance of the requirement of proportionality for a valid exercise of police powers, noted that the Gambling Ban Law was reasonable and proportional.[30] Alternatively, the respondent argued that (i) no expropriation had occurred because the Gambling Ban Law was temporary and that the New Gambling Law entered into force in July 2020;[31] and (ii) there is no causal relationship between the Gambling Ban Law and the losses suffered by the claimant because the OCU would have failed of "its own making."[32]

The arbitral tribunal began by analysing whether the Gambling Ban Law was a valid exercise of the state's police powers. It did not address the question of whether it was obliged to take this customary international rule into account—since the Treaty did not expressly provide for it—because the disputing parties agreed that the rule was applicable in the present case. However, the arbitral tribunal agreed with the tribunal in *Saluka Investments B.V. v. The Czech Republic* and accepted the reasoning that sovereign states are not required to pay compensation if, in exercising their regulatory powers, they take measures in a non-discriminatory manner and in good faith that are aimed at the general welfare.[33] In addition to the above requirements, the arbitral tribunal also concluded that for the Gambling Ban

---

[26] *Id.*, paras. 68, 72–73.

[27] *Id.*, para. 69.

[28] *Id.*, para. 70.

[29] *Id.*, paras. 78–79.

[30] *Id.*, para. 82.

[31] In particular, the respondent argued that the claimant had based its arguments on the existence of treaty breaches and damages as of 25 June 2009, *i.e.*, before the Ukrainian Cabinet of Ministers had the obligation to propose new legislation on gambling. It further pointed out that the claimant could have demanded in court that the Cabinet of Ministers fulfill its obligations under the Gambling Ban Law (Olympic Entertainment Group AS v. Ukraine, PCA Case No. 2019-18, UNCITRAL Arbitration, Award, dated 15 April 2021, para. 83).

[32] Olympic Entertainment Group AS v. Ukraine, PCA Case No. 2019-18, UNCITRAL Arbitration, Award, dated 15 April 2021, para. 84.

[33] *Id.*, para. 86, referring to Saluka Investments B.V. v. The Czech Republic, UNCITRAL, Partial Award, dated 17 March 2006, paras. 254–255, 262; Técnicas Medioambientales Tecmed, SA v. The United Mexican States, ICSID Case No. ARB(AF)/00/2, Award, dated 29 May 2003, para. 119.

Law to be valid it had to be proportionate because the proportionality "must be included in the test for a valid exercise of the police powers doctrine [...] [and] can be regarded as part of the '*principles of justice recognized by the principal legal systems of the world*' or at least a factor to be considered under the condition of '*abuse of powers*' in the words of the Harvard Draft Convention."[34]

The arbitral tribunal emphasised that a measure that introduces radical change into an industry and makes a previously legal business activity illegal must be carefully considered. In this context, the arbitral tribunal further underscored the importance of legislators having adequate consultation periods to evaluate the pros and cons of proposed legislation and having access to empirical evidence to help them legislate.[35] In this case, the arbitral tribunal concluded that in the expedited process by which the Gambling Ban Law was passed, "the legislators had little in the way of empirical evidence before them that would have assisted them in crafting a legislative solution to the problem that was said to face the country."[36] However, it also emphasized that the claim that a law was not enacted to achieve a public purpose and in good faith is demanding.[37] In this sense, it rejected the claimant's argument that the intent behind the Gambling Ban Law was merely political and populist, noting that such an argument was "[...] based more on speculation than on concrete evidence."[38] In turn, it accepted the argument that the adoption of the Gambling Ban Law was justified by reasons of public health and morality, the protection of which "[...] lies close to the heart of public policy of all states."[39] Accordingly, the arbitral tribunal had to assess whether the Gambling Ban Law met the threshold of proportionality with regard to the public purposes it pursued. To that end, it recognized that it (i) owed due deference to Ukraine as a sovereign state exercising regulatory powers; (ii) cannot second-guess regulatory decisions made in good faith; and (iii) must assess the relationship between the impact of the measures on the protected investment and the public interest they serve.[40]

In assessing the impact of the Gambling Ban Law, the arbitral tribunal concluded that it had permanently wiped out the claimant's investment, destroyed an entire industry, and increased the unemployment rate, while contributing to the development of a shadow gambling market in which effective government regulation proved illusory.[41] The arbitral

---

[34] *Id.*, para. 90, referring to Occidental Petroleum Corporation and Occidental Exploration and Production Company v. The Republic of Ecuador, ICSID Case No. ARB/06/11, Award, dated 5 October 2012, para. 404; LG&E Energy Corp., LG&E Capital Corp., and LG&E International, Inc. v. Argentine Republic, ICSID Case No. ARB/02/1, Decision on Liability, dated 3 October 2006, para. 195; MTD Equity Sdn. Bhd. and MTD Chile S.A. v. Republic of Chile, ICSID Case No. ARB/01/7, Award, dated 25 May 2004, para. 109.

[35] *Id.*, paras. 92–93.

[36] *Id.*, para. 92.

[37] *Id.*, para. 94.

[38] *Id.*, para. 93.

[39] *Id.*, para. 95. The arbitral tribunal also noted that in making this and similar assessments, international tribunals must pay particular attention to the local conditions in which the measures being assessed take effect, even if "that does not prevent a tribunal from evaluating how the measure that lawmakers selected comports with the state's international obligations" (*see id.*, para. 95).

[40] Olympic Entertainment Group AS v. Ukraine, PCA Case No. 2019-18, UNCITRAL Arbitration, Award, dated 15 April 2021, paras. 78, 95, 114–116, referring to Invesmart, BV v. Czech Republic, UNCITRAL, Award, dated 26 June 2009, para. 501; Sergei Paushok, CJSC Golden East Company and CJSC Vostokneftegaz Company v. Government of Mongolia, Award on Jurisdiction and Liability, dated 28 April 2011, paras. 298–299.

[41] *Id.*, paras. 97, 108, referring to Explanatory Note to Draft Law of Ukraine No. 2285-d "On State Regulation of Organization and Operation of Gambling," dated 14 January 2020; Law No. 768-IX "On the State

tribunal also took into account the fact that the Gambling Ban Law did not provide for compensation or a transition mechanism for investors, such as the claimant, thus depriving the latter of the opportunity to mitigate some losses.[42] In addition, the arbitral tribunal disregarded the argument concerning the establishment of a special zone for gambling by the Cabinet of Ministers of Ukraine, which is provided for in the Gambling Ban Law. For even though such special gambling zones had to be established within a three-month period, the arbitral tribunal refused to turn away from reality. Instead, it focused on the consequences arising from the Gambling Ban Law.[43] In light of these conclusions, the arbitral tribunal concluded that the Gambling Ban Law was not a proportionate measure or a valid exercise of the state's police powers.[44]

The arbitral tribunal addressed the question of whether the respondent had indirectly expropriated the claimant's investment. It first pointed out that Article 5 of the Treaty provides protection against both direct and indirect expropriation. For the arbitral tribunal, the existence of the latter depends on "[...] whether a measure taken by the state results in a substantial deprivation of the value, use or enjoyment of the investor's investment."[45] In other words, whether the Gambling Ban Law contributed to the loss of economic value or viability of the claimant's investment as a whole or adversely affected its ability to generate a commercial return. Relying on this framework, the arbitral tribunal concluded that "[...] the present case is a textbook example of indirect example."[46] This is because the Gambling Ban Law revoked the claimant's gambling licenses,[47] which had to be "physically surrendered to the [Ukrainian] authorities."[48] This made the generation of cash flows and revenues impossible and, in the arbitral tribunal's view, amounted to an indirect expropriation of the claimant's investment.[49] It further noted that the respondent did not pay prompt, adequate, and effective compensation.[50] Moreover, the arbitral tribunal rejected that the claimant had the burden of commencing administrative proceedings in the Ukrainian courts to force the establishment of gambling zones because there was not "[...] the slightest indication that such proceedings had any chance of success,"[51] or indication as to the moment of their conclusion.[52]

In the Award, the arbitral tribunal also summarized the arguments of the claimant and the respondent on the alleged violations of the standards of fair and equitable treatment and

---

Regulation of Organization and Operation of Gambling," dated 14 July 2020; Submission of the President of Ukraine with proposals to the Draft Gambling Ban Law dated 15 May 2009, at 2.

[42] *Id.*, paras. 98–99.

[43] *Id.*, para. 100.

[44] *Id.*, paras. 101–102.

[45] *Id.*, paras. 104–105, referring to Burlington Resources Inc. v. Republic of Ecuador, ICSID Case No. ARB/08/5, Decision on Liability, dated 14 December 2012, paras. 396–398; Philip Morris Products SA and Abal Hermanos SA v. Oriental Republic of Uruguay, ICSID Case No. ARB/10/7, Award, dated 8 July 2016, para. 192 (citing Telenor Mobile Communications AS v. Republic of Hungary, Award, dated 13 September 2006, paras. 65 and 70).

[46] *Id.*, para. 106.

[47] Except for some activities such as lotteries and sports competitions.

[48] Olympic Entertainment Group AS v. Ukraine, PCA Case No. 2019-18, UNCITRAL Arbitration, Award, dated 15 April 2021, para. 107.

[49] *Id.*, paras. 107, 113.

[50] *Id.*, para. 112.

[51] *Id.*, para. 109.

[52] *Id.*

full protection and security.[53] However, since it had already concluded that the Gambling Ban Law amounted to an indirect expropriation of the claimant's investment, it did not need to rule on this issue. However, it noted that its ruling on the expropriatory nature of the Gambling Ban Law "clearly support[s] the conclusion that there was a breach of the FET standard."[54] Specifically, on the grounds that the Gambling Ban Law frustrated the claimant's legitimate expectations that its subsidiary would enjoy "the use and benefit of its licenses until their expiration."[55] The arbitral tribunal adopted the same reasoning with respect to the standard of full protection and security.[56]

Having addressed the illegality of the Gambling Prohibition Act, the arbitral tribunal moved on to the question of causation and quantum. At this stage, it is important to note that prior to the adoption of the Gambling Ban Law, negotiations were held with a third party—Maxbet—regarding the sale of the claimant's investment. This is a particular relevant fact because the claimant's position on quantum had as its reference point the valuation arrived at in the sale to Maxbet.

In the claimant's view, the respondent had to pay compensation "for the loss of value of the Claimant's investment and any other '*financially assessable damage*' in order to eliminate the consequences of the unlawful expropriation."[57] While acknowledging that there is a difference in the calculation of compensation depending on whether the expropriation was legal or illegal, the claimant held that "[...] a wrongdoer should not benefit from its own wrong."[58] On this basis, it further held that a claim for damages seeks to place the claimant "[...] in the financial position it would have been in had the complained-of breach or breaches not occurred."[59] Accordingly, in the claimant's view, the loss it suffered was the difference between (i) the amount the it recovered upon the liquidation of OCU following the introduction of the Gambling Ban Law, and (ii) the hypothetical position the claimant would have been in had the Gambling Ban Law had never seen the light of day and the claimant continued to operate its gambling facilities. That is, the difference between EUR 15,000,000.00 (fifteen million euros)[60] and EUR 2,596,000.00 (two million five hundred and ninety-six thousand euros). As noted above, the claimant also requested that the arbitral tribunal order the respondent to pay interest at the rate of 12-month LIBOR + 4 percent from 25 June 2009 to the date of the award (inclusive) and from this date until payment in full.[61] Finally, arguing that OCU's liquidation did not begin until 3 July 2009, the claimant objected that there was no causality between the gambling ban and the losses he suffered.[62]

The respondent argued that, even if it were true that it had breached the Treaty, there was no causation between the Gambling Ban Law and the losses allegedly suffered by the

---

[53] *Id.*, paras. 117–131, 134–138.

[54] *Id.*, para. 132.

[55] *Id.*

[56] *Id.*, para. 139.

[57] *Id.*, para. 142 (emphasis in original).

[58] *Id.*, para. 142, referring to SOC, para. 240.

[59] *Id.*, para. 143, referring to Nicholson and Davie II Expert Report, paras. 2.39–2.42, 2.45–2.46.

[60] According to the claimant, "[t]his figure is the midpoint of the result of our DCF valuation of EUR 18.7 million and the Maxbet offer for the OCU Group as agreed by OEG on 9 April 2009 of [...] EUR 11.4 million as at that date." (Olympic Entertainment Group AS v. Ukraine, PCA Case No. 2019-18, UNCITRAL Arbitration, Award, dated 15 April 2021, para. 143, referring to Nicholson and Davie II Expert Report, paras. 2.39–2.42, 2.45–2.46).

[61] Olympic Entertainment Group AS v. Ukraine, PCA Case No. 2019-18, UNCITRAL Arbitration, Award, dated 15 April 2021, para. 145.

[62] *Id.*, para. 146, referring to claimant's post-hearing brief, paras. 153–156.

claimant. In its view, "[...] the Claimant's investment was a failure well before the Gambling Law was enacted."[63] In fact, it alleged that, at the time of the introduction of this piece of legislation, OCU "was effectively insolvent, [...] loss-making and highly overleveraged with its liabilities massively exceeding their assets and had repeatedly defaulted in paying its significant and ever-increasing interest debts as they fell due."[64] The fact that the liquidation of OCU began on 9 June 2009 proves this, according to the respondent. Accordingly, because the international responsibility of a state depends on there being a causal link between the alleged wrongful act and the harm suffered, the respondent argues it could not be ordered to pay compensation to the claimant.[65] Alternatively, if the arbitral tribunal were to conclude that this requirement was met in the present case, the respondent posited that the arbitral tribunal should nonetheless reject the reasoning put forward by the claimant, which it qualified as "imprecise and inapplicable."[66] First, the DCF model could not be used because the track record proved insufficient for that purpose. Second, the use of the negotiations with Maxbet as a reliable reference of value. Third, no comparable transaction had been identified that could be used to confirm the reliability of the claimant's approach. Fourth, the deduction made by the claimant were incorrect.[67] Finally, the respondent argued that the LIBOR + 2 percent was "the standard practice and the interest rate predominantly applied by international tribunals."[68]

The arbitral tribunal first noted that Article 5 of the Treaty only dealt with compensation for lawful expropriation. It therefore resorted to customary international law to determine the relevant criteria it had to consider in deciding whether the respondent must compensate the claimant. For this purpose, it relied on the conclusions in the *Chorzów Factory* case. This meant that "must, as far as possible wipe-out all the consequences of the illegal act and re-establish the situation which would, in all probability, have existed if that act had not been committed."[69]

Against this background, the arbitral tribunal focused mainly on whether the claimant's investment was financially sound to determine the origin of the claimant's liquidation. In this regard, the arbitral tribunal noted that the claimant's investment was not "a highly successful venture at the time it was indirectly expropriated,"[70] and that OCU's liabilities far exceed its assets without there being a certain path to recovery. However, it underscored that these liabilities mainly resulted from loans made by its parent company, *i.e.*, the claimant. Accordingly, the arbitral tribunal distinguished these loans from third-party loans.[71] This is because, in its view, the interests of a third party are completely different from those of a shareholder, including with respect to the manner and timing of repayment.[72] In addition, it emphasised that there were several indications that the OCU had recovered from the effects of the 2008 financial crisis.[73] Based on the foregoing, the arbitral tribunal (i) rejected

---

[63] *Id.*, paras. 147–148.

[64] *Id.*, para. 148.

[65] *Id.*, paras. 148, 150.

[66] *Id.*, para. 151.

[67] *Id.*, para. 151.

[68] *Id.*, para. 153.

[69] *Id.*, para. 155, referring to Case concerning the Factory at Chorzów (Germany v. Poland), PCIJ Series A No. 13, Judgment of 13 September 1928, at 47.

[70] *Id.*, para. 158.

[71] The claimant had invested an amount of EUR 33,000,000.00 (thirty-three million euros).

[72] Olympic Entertainment Group AS v. Ukraine, PCA Case No. 2019-18, UNCITRAL Arbitration, Award, dated 15 April 2021, paras. 161–163.

[73] *Id.*, paras. 165–166.

the argument that the liquidation of OCU was inevitable; (ii) accepted that the liquidation of the OCU began on 3 July 2009;[74] and (iii) upheld that the latter was the result of "[t]he unlawful indirect expropriation was the proximate causal factor that led to the Claimant's investment being wiped out."[75]

Having concluded for the existence of causation between the Gambling Ban Law and the losses suffered by the claimant, the arbitral tribunal address the question of quantum. In this regard, the arbitral tribunal noted that awarding compensation is not a scientific exercise.[76] In carrying out such an exercise, it rejected both disputing parties' expert valuations, although it accepted the claimant's calculations as a starting point.[77] Accordingly, it relied on the claimant's alternative valuation of USD 15,000,000.00 (fifteen million dollars),[78] albeit with some additional caveats and discounts that the claimant had not taken into account. First, OCU's difficult financial condition and limited available cash. Second, there were insufficient business plans to reasonably predict future cash flows and profits. Third, the fact that OCU's gambling licenses would have expired in 2011 without the respondent having the obligation to renew them. Fourth, although the arbitral tribunal accepted the price offered by Maxbet as a relevant indicator of value,[79] it considered that a discount was necessary due to the uncertainties related to the negotiations, including the possible reduction of the offered price after due diligence had been performed. Fifth, the need to make additional deductions based on the amounts that the claimant had already recovered from the sale of its assets to avoid double recovery. On the basis of the foregoing, the arbitral tribunal ordered the respondent to pay the claimant an amount of EUR 7,500,000.00 (seven million five hundred thousand euros).[80] In addition, it considered the claimant's request for payment of pre-award and post-award interest at the rate of 12-month LIBOR + 4 percent compounded annually as appropriate to ensure the claimant's full reparation.[81]

Finally, on the allocation of costs, the arbitral tribunal clarified that there was "[...] no reason why it should depart from the principle that costs follow the event."[82] It further

---

[74] *Id.*, paras. 168–169, referring to OEG 2009 Annual Report, at 38; Minutes of the General (Extraordinary) Meeting of OCU Members dated 3 July 2009; Minutes No. 45 of the General (Extraordinary) Meeting of Members of Olympic Casino Ukraine dated 3 July 2009.

[75] *Id.*, paras. 111, 167.

[76] *Id.*, para. 180, referring to Compañiá de Aguas del Aconquija SA, Vivendi Universal SA v. Argentine Republic, ICSID Case No. ARB/97/3, Award, dated 20 August 2007, para. 8.3.16; Crystallex International Corporation v. Bolivarian Republic of Venezuela, ICSID Case No. ARB(AF)/11/2, Award, dated 4 April 2016, paras. 871–872; Gold Reserve Inc. v. Bolivarian Republic of Venezuela, ICSID Case No. ARB(AF)/ 09/1, Award, dated 19 September 2014, para. 686 (cited in Crystallex International Corporation v. Bolivarian Republic of Venezuela, ICSID Case No. ARB(AF)/11/2, Award, dated 4 April 2016, footnote 1252).

[77] *Id.*, paras. 171–172.

[78] *See supra* note 63.

[79] In particular, the arbitral tribunal noted that "[...] it is very rare indeed that the company being valued for the purpose of a treaty breach to have been subject to even a provisional offer so close in time to the value date" (*see* Olympic Entertainment Group AS v. Ukraine, PCA Case No. 2019-18, UNCITRAL Arbitration, Award, dated 15 April 2021, para. 174).

[80] Olympic Entertainment Group AS v. Ukraine, PCA Case No. 2019-18, UNCITRAL Arbitration, Award, dated 15 April 2021, para. 182.

[81] *Id.*, paras. 185, 197–198.

[82] *Id.*, para. 189.

confirmed that it retained "the discretion to assess a reasonable sum to be paid by the losing party and may take into account the conduct of the Parties and the amount awarded compared to the amount claimed."[83] Based on these criteria, the arbitral tribunal ordered the respondent to pay the claimant's costs in the amount of EUR 2,500,000.00 (two million and five hundred thousand euros), even though the claimant received less than it claimed.

---

[83] *Id.*, para. 189.

LEGAL MAXIMS: SUMMARIES AND EXTRACTS FROM SELECTED CASE LAW*

Olympic Entertainment Group AS v. Ukraine, PCA Case No. 2019-18, UNCITRAL Arbitration, Award, 15 April 2021

---

* The working method chosen for the formulation of legal maxims is explained *supra* 'Outline of the Parts', at page xv.

Legal Maxims: Summaries and Extracts from Selected Case Law In: *The Global Community Yearbook of International Law and Jurisprudence 2022.* Edited by: Giuliana Ziccardi Capaldo, Oxford University Press. © Oxford University Press 2023.
DOI: 10.1093/oso/9780197752265.003.0034

XI.2.1

Olympic Entertainment Group AS v. Ukraine, PCA Case No. 2019-18, UNCITRAL Arbitration, Award, 15 April 2021*

Contents**

I. OBJECTION TO ARBITRAL TRIBUNAL'S JURISDICTION

II. INDIRECT EXPROPRIATION

III. FAIR AND EQUITABLE TREATMENT

IV. FULL PROTECTION AND SECURITY STANDARD

V. REPARATION/COMPENSATION

VI. COSTS OF JUDICIAL AND ARBITRAL PROCEEDINGS

VII. UNCITRAL ARBITRATION, AWARD

I.

I.14.2141   OBJECTION TO ARBITRAL TRIBUNAL'S JURISDICTION
See also: I.1.172; I.1.44; II.2.21

"[**49**] To ascertain whether the investment was illegal, the Tribunal has to decide precisely what the investment was. [. . .] [**50**] The Claimant invested substantial sums in Ukraine. Among other things, the Claimant established OCU in 2004 and provided equity contributions of cash and gambling equipment for the total amount of around EUR 4.1 million into the charter capital of OCU.[1] The Claimant also invested EUR 28.6 million as a shareholder loan to OCU.[2] In 2007, this loan was used, *inter alia*, to expand the Claimant's operation by acquiring Eldorado Group, a Ukrainian casino operator, for around EUR 9.2 million.[3] In addition, the Claimant acquired trade patents for its gambling equipment in Ukraine and for its intellectual property rights.[4] [**51**] In the Tribunal's view, the above investments constitute, *inter alia*, "*immovable property*", "*shares*", "*intellectual property rights*" and "*claims to money or to any performance having an economic value*" pursuant to Article 1 of the Treaty. Accordingly, they clearly fall within the definition of "*investment*" under Article 1 of the Treaty. [. . .] [**55**] In the present case, the illegality upon which the Respondent relies is that when the

---

* Summaries prepared by João Gil Antunes, Legal Adviser in Public International Law in the Department of Legal Affairs of the Portuguese Ministry of Foreign Affairs. Text of judgment available online at the Court's Web site <https://pcacases.com/web/sendAttach/27408>. Languages of the Case: English. Original footnote numbers are indicated in brackets: [].

** This is not a faithful reproduction of the Table of Contents of the Judgment.

[1] [52] See SOC, para. 148; Exhibit C-7, Olympic Casino Ukraine Excerpt from State Register.

[2] [53] SOC, para. 148.

[3] [54] **Exhibit C-98**, Agreement of the Sale and Purchase of Corporate rights of Alea Private Company dated 17 September 2007; **Exhibit C-99**, Agreement of the Sale and Purchase of Corporate rights of Ukraine Leisure Company dated 17 September 2007; **Exhibit C-100**, Agreement of the Sale and Purchase of Corporate rights of Eldorado Leisure Company dated 17 September 2007, **Exhibit C-42**, Olympic's Consolidated unaudited interim financial report for the 12 months and 4th quarter of 2007, p. 30. See SOC, para. 48.

[4] [55] Claimant's Skeleton Submissions, para. 6.

Claimant began its operations in Ukraine, it lacked certain licences claimed by the Respondent to be necessary to operate a gambling establishment, and thus it argues that this rendered the whole venture unlawful. [...] [**56**] The Tribunal is of the view that the Respondent did not establish that the Claimant had acted in an unlawful manner, which would support the Respondent's submission that the Tribunal has no jurisdiction. [...] [**57**] Furthermore and most significantly, the Claimant's operations were never a secret. On the contrary, they were under continuous scrutiny of various state organs at the local and national levels. The Tribunal considers that if the Claimant was operating illegally, this illegality was bound to be discovered in all those years that it operated and paid its taxes. Similarly, after the enactment of the Gambling Ban Law, the Parties were engaged in settlement negotiations for years. During this time, the Respondent never raised any questions in relation to the legality of the Claimant's investment. [...] [**60**] [E]ven if there was any illegality, there was no breach of a fundamental principle of Ukrainian law which would preclude the jurisdiction of the Tribunal. Therefore, even if assuming *arguendo* that the Claimant failed to have a licence during the first years of its activity, the Tribunal doubts that this *de minimis* breach would have precluded the establishment of the Tribunal's jurisdiction and deprived the Claimant of the protection of the Treaty."

[**Paras 49, 50, 51, 55, 56, 57, 60**]

II.

I.17.12   INDIRECT EXPROPRIATION
           See also: I.1.022; I.1.04; I.1.16; I.1.44; I.2.034; I.2.0411; I.2.0521; I.8.51;
           I.17.02; I.17.131; I.17.132

"[**86**] The Tribunal notes that the Treaty does not expressly include any reference to the police powers doctrine, according to which some *bona fide* regulatory acts of the state shall not be considered expropriatory and shall not require compensation. However, the Parties agree that the police powers doctrine is applicable in the present case. Their dispute is only whether the Gambling Ban Law met those conditions necessary to be considered part of the police powers of the state. Therefore, the Tribunal need not address in detail the inclusion of customary rules, like the police powers doctrine, in investment treaties that do not provide for them explicitly. It is sufficient to note that the Tribunal accepts the observation made in the Saluka case, in which the tribunal noted as follows:[5]

> *The Tribunal acknowledges that Article 5 [concerning expropriation] of the Treaty in the present case is drafted very broadly and does not contain any exception for the exercise of regulatory power. However, in using the concept of deprivation, Article 5 imports into the Treaty the customary international law notion that a deprivation can be justified if it results from the exercise of regulatory actions aimed at the maintenance of public order. In interpreting a treaty, account has to be taken of "any relevant rules of international law applicable in the relations between the parties" – a requirement which the International Court of Justice ("ICJ") has held includes relevant rules of general customary international law.*

---

[5] [98] **Exhibit RLA-31**, *Saluka Investments B.V. v The Czech Republic*, UNCITRAL, Partial Award of 17 March 2006, paras 254-255, 262. See also **Exhibit RLA-53**, *Técnicas Medioambientales Tecmed, SA v The United Mexican States*, ICSID Case No ARB(AF)/00/2, Award of 29 May 2003, para. 119.

> It is now established in international law that States are not liable to pay compensation to a foreign investor when, in the normal exercise of their regulatory powers, they adopt in a non-discriminatory manner bona fide regulations that are aimed at the general welfare.
>
> [...]
>
> In the opinion of the Tribunal, the principle that a State does not commit an expropriation and is thus not liable to pay compensation to a dispossessed alien investor when it adopts general regulations that are "commonly accepted as within the police power of States" forms part of customary international law today.

[**90**] [...] [T]he Tribunal is of the view that the condition of proportionality must be included in the test for a valid exercise of the police powers doctrine. Proportionality has become an important factor in international investment law and the substantive protections that it provides for investors.[6] It is bound up in the concepts of fairness and equity which are commonly reflected in the substantive standards included in investment treaties. In the Tribunal's view, it may well be said that proportionality can be regarded as part of the *"principles of justice recognized by the principal legal systems of the world"* or at least a factor to be considered under the condition of *"abuse of the powers"* in the words of the Harvard Draft Convention. [...] [**92**] The evidence before the Tribunal shows that in the expedited process adopted by Parliament, which by definition reduced the period for deliberation as to the merits and demerits of the proposed legislation, the legislators had little in the way of empirical evidence before them that would have assisted them in crafting a legislative solution to the problem that was said to face the country. [**93**] In this regard, it is important to emphasise that the Tribunal does not expect the members of any parliament to critically analyse every aspect of whatever studies might be available to parliament. Nor is the Tribunal blind to the fact that law-making is a process of balancing policy alternatives, purely political considerations, and other factors, a process that can seem very distant from, perhaps even antithetical to, the scientific method. However, before taking action which would effect radical change for the gambling industry and rendering illegal that which was hitherto legal, it is not unreasonable to expect that the legislature would at least reasonably consider and discuss some of the evidence. [...] [**95**] In the same vein, the Tribunal stresses that the protection of public health and morality is a worthy and important cause which lies close to the heart of public policy for all states. International tribunals, which lack in-depth knowledge of local conditions, ought to be wary of second-guessing an elected legislature's appraisal of those local conditions. But that does not prevent a tribunal from evaluating how the measure that lawmakers selected comports with the state's international obligations. [**96**] The Tribunal now turns again to the issue of proportionality. In addressing the question of proportionality, the

---

6 [103] See e.g., *Occidental Petroleum Corporation and Occidental Exploration and Production Company v The Republic of Ecuador*, ICSID Case No. ARB/06/11, Award of 5 October 2012, para. 404 ("[...] *the Tribunal observes that there is a growing body of arbitral law, particularly in the context of ICSID arbitrations, which holds that the principle of proportionality is applicable to potential breaches of bilateral investment treaty obligations"*). See also proportionality in the context of the fair and equitable treatment standard: **Exhibit CLA40**, *LG&E Energy Corp., LG&E Capital Corp., and LG&E International, Inc. v Argentine Republic*, ICSID Case No. ARB/02/1, Decision on Liability of 3 October 2006), para. 195; **Exhibit CLA-31**, *MTD Equity Sdn. Bhd. And MTD Chile S.A. v Republic of Chile*, ICSID Case No. ARB/01/7, Award of 25 May 2004, para. 109.

Tribunal finds it appropriate to refer again to the *Tecmed* award, in which the tribunal accurately noted as follows:[7]

> [...] the Arbitral Tribunal will consider, in order to determine if they are to be characterized as expropriatory, **whether such actions or measures are proportional to the public interest presumably protected thereby and to the protection legally granted to investments, taking into account that the significance of such impact has a key role upon deciding the proportionality**. Although the analysis starts at the **due deference** owing to the State when defining the issues that affect its public policy or the interests of society as a whole, as well as the actions that will be implemented to protect such values, such situation does not prevent the Arbitral Tribunal, without thereby questioning such due deference, from examining the actions of the State in light of Article 5(1) of the Agreement to determine whether such measures are reasonable with respect to their goals, the deprivation of economic rights and the legitimate expectations of who suffered such deprivation. **There must be a reasonable relationship of proportionality between the charge or weight imposed to the foreign investor and the aim sought to be realized by any expropriatory measure. To value such charge or weight, it is very important to measure the size of the ownership deprivation caused by the actions of the state and whether such deprivation was compensated or not.** [emphasis added]

[99] The Tribunal was troubled not only by the severe impact of the Gambling Ban Law on the Claimant's investments but also by its immediate effect. As stated above in the Factual Background of the Dispute, the Gambling Ban Law entered into immediate effect. Foreign investors, and local investors for that matter, were not consulted. There was no adjustment period. There was no dialogue of any substance with those businesses who would be immediately affected by the ban. Had there been an adjustment period, the gambling business sector could have mitigated some losses or negotiated an amelioration of the ban on acceptable terms. However, the ban's immediate entry into force deprived the gambling business sector of that opportunity. Moreover, as explained in more detail below, once the Gambling Ban Law entered into effect, the Claimant's investments, specifically Olympic's licensing rights, were immediately extinguished. [...] The Respondent did not bring any current or former government witnesses to explain the need for a total ban with immediate effect. [...] [100] Although the Law contemplated the establishment of a new regime within three months, this zoning system was not established until the adoption of the New Gambling Law in July 2020. The Tribunal cannot be expected to ignore the reality as it existed immediately after the adoption of the Gambling Ban Law. Indeed, in order to properly establish the existence of expropriation, tribunals must look into the effects of the impugned measure. Such examination requires the Tribunal to look beyond the date of the impugned measure. In the present case, such examination also leads the Tribunal to reject the submission that the special zoning system (that was in the event *not* established within the three month period as contemplated by the Gambling Ban Law) was proportional. [...] [104] The test for indirect expropriation has been widely discussed by investment tribunals. For the purposes of the present case, it is sufficient to state that the benchmark for testing indirect expropriation is whether a measure taken by the state results in a substantial deprivation of the value, use or enjoyment of the

---

[7] [106] **Exhibit RLA-59**, *Técnicas Medioambientales Tecmed SA v The United Mexican States*, ICSID Case No ARB(AF)/00/2, Award of 29 May 2003, para. 122.

investor's investment. In this regard, for example, in the *Burlington* award, the tribunal stated as follows:[8]

> *When assessing the evidence of an expropriation, international tribunals have generally applied the sole effects test and focused on substantial deprivation. By way of example, one may cite Pope & Talbot v. Canada, where the tribunal stated that "under international law, expropriation requires a 'substantial deprivation' ", or Occidental v. Ecuador, where in relation to tax measures, the tribunal referred to the same "criterion of 'substantial deprivation' under international law [...]." In Archer Daniels v. Mexico, the tribunal noted that "expropriation occurs if the interference is substantial."*
>
> *When a measure affects the environment or conditions under which the investor carries on its business, what appears to be decisive, in assessing whether there is a substantial deprivation, is the loss of the economic value or economic viability of the investment. In this sense, some tribunals have focused on the use and enjoyment of property. The loss of viability does not necessarily imply a loss of management or control. What matters is the capacity to earn a commercial return. After all, investors make investments to earn a return. If they lose this possibility as a result of a State measure, then they have lost the economic use of their investment.*
>
> *Most tribunals apply the test of expropriation, however it is phrased, to the investment as a whole. Applied to the investment as a whole, the criterion of loss of the economic use or viability of the investment implies that the investment as a whole has become unviable. The measure is expropriatory, whether it affects the entire investment or only part of it, as long as the operation of the investment cannot generate a commercial return.*

[**107**] Once the Gambling Ban Law entered into effect on 25 June 2009, with the exception of several activities such as lotteries and sports competitions, gambling was outlawed in accordance with Article 2 of the Law. The licences of the different gambling facilities were revoked in accordance with Article 4(2) of the Law. The licences were the linchpin of the Claimant's business: with no licence, there could be no operations. And with no operations, there could be no ability to generate cash flows. The direct taking of the licences thus amounted to an indirect taking of the Claimant's investments in Ukraine. Specifically, with regard to the Claimant, immediately upon the Gambling Ban Law's entry into force, the Claimant lost the possibility to earn a commercial return from its investments, which were all dependent on the legality of gambling in Ukraine. Moreover, in accordance with Article 4(2) of the Gambling Ban Law, the Claimant's licencing rights were revoked, indeed the licences had to be physically surrendered to the authorities, as acknowledged by the Respondent's counsel.[9] Therefore, in the Tribunal's view, the intensity of the deprivation was extreme. The Gambling Ban Law did not simply substantially deprive the value of the Claimant's investments, it destroyed them as much as it destroyed *"an entire sector of the economy."*[10] [**109**] Furthermore, the Tribunal considers that the Respondent's argument that the Claimant cannot succeed because it failed to go to court to force the Government to include zones for gambling completely lacks merit and must be rejected. There is not the slightest indication that such proceedings had any chance of success. Further, there is no indication as to when such proceedings would have been fully concluded, and the Tribunal is satisfied that the Claimant could not lawfully have continued in business

---

[8] [117] **CLA-49**, *Burlington Resources Inc. v Republic of Ecuador*, ICSID Case No. ARB/08/5, Decision on Liability of 14 December 2012, paras 396-398.

[9] [119] Transcript, Day 7, 54:12-14 (Respondent's counsel stating that *"it is correct that on 25th June 2009 the Claimant's licences were formally revoked"*).

[10] [120] **Exhibit C-435**, Explanatory Note to Draft Law of Ukraine No. 2285-d "On State Regulation of Organization and Operation of Gambling" dated 14 January 2020, p. 1.

during such time bearing in mind its solvency. [...] [**114**] Finally, the Tribunal wishes to emphasise that it has not reached its decision lightly. The Tribunal agrees with the dictum of the tribunal in *Invesmart v Czech Republic* that:[11]

> [...] *when testing regulatory decisions against international law standards, the regulators' right and duty to regulate must not be subjected to undue secondguessing by international tribunals. Tribunals need not be satisfied that they would have made precisely the same decision as the regulator in order for them to uphold such decisions.*

[**115**] In the same vein, the Tribunal agree with the *Pauschok* award, in which it was held that:[12]

> *Actions by legislative assemblies are not beyond the reach of bilateral investment treaties A State is not immune from claims by foreign investors in connection with legislation passed by its legislative body, unless a specific exemption is included in the relevant treaty.*
> *On the other hand, the fact that a democratically elected legislature has passed legislation that may be considered as ill-conceived, counter-productive and excessively burdensome does not automatically allow to conclude that a breach of an investment treaty has occurred. If such were the case, the number of investment treaty claims would increase by a very large number. Legislative assemblies around the world spend a good part of their time amending substantive portions of existing laws in order to adjust them to changing times or to correct serious mistakes that were made at the time of their adoption. A claim for a breach under an investment treaty has to be proven by claimants under the specific rules established in that treaty."*

[**Paras. 86, 90, 92, 93, 95, 96, 99, 100, 104, 107, 109, 114, 115**]

III.

I.17.24   FAIR AND EQUITABLE TREATMENT

"[**132**] [...] [I]n light of the Tribunal's decision concerning the Respondent's unlawful expropriation, as detailed above, the Tribunal considers that it need not make any decision in relation to the alleged breach of the FET standard as it has no bearing on the quantum or the Claimant's entitlement to its requested relief."

[**Para. 132**]

IV.

I.17.25   FULL AND CONSTANT PROTECTION AND SECURITY

"[**139**] In light of the Tribunal's decision concerning the Respondent's unlawful expropriation, as detailed above, the Tribunal need not examine the Claimant's claim in relation to the alleged breach of the FPS standard and the obligation to create predictable and stable conditions for the investment."

[**Para. 139**]

---

[11] [123] **Exhibit RLA-27**, *Invesmart, BV v Czech Republic*, UNCITRAL, Award of 26 June 2009, para. 501.

[12] [124] **Exhibit RLA-21**, *Sergei Paushok, CJSC Golden East Company and CJSC Vostokneftegaz Company v Government of Mongolia*, Award on Jurisdiction and Liability of 28 April 2011, paras 298-299.

V.

I.11.035   REPARATION/COMPENSATION/SATISFACTION
See also: I.8.46; I.11.01; I.11.03; I.11.0354; I.11.0356; I.17.133

"[155] Article 5 of the Treaty provides that expropriation "must be accompanied by provisions for the payment of prompt, adequate and effective compensation. Such compensation shall amount to the market value of the investment expropriated immediately before expropriation or before the impending expropriation became public knowledge." However, as this provision deals with compensation for lawful expropriation, the Tribunal resorts instead to the relevant principles of customary international law as set out by the Permanent Court of International Justice in the Chorzów Factory case:[13] [...][156] [...]

> [...] the true cause of the Claimant's desire to exit Ukraine at a loss from 2008 was its failed venture. It lacked a buyer and it lacked cash to meet costs, and a liquidation scenario was therefore inevitable.
>
> The Claimant now say they were a distressed seller. The problem is that they had no buyer. [...] And a distressed company was not going to withstand the circumstance that they had created for themselves, was not going to be able to navigate the choppy waters into which they had placed themselves, and was going to be going over a precipice. And it's a question of when, not if.

[161] Having reviewed the Parties' submissions, the Tribunal considers there is no doubt that OEG's loans to OCU were, in the words of the Respondent's quantum experts, "*commercially arranged loans between the shareholder and the subsidiary, and they needed to be repaid.*"[14] Moreover, OEG's public share issuance document explicitly stated that its "*transactions with related parties*" were "*all concluded on arm's length basis*".[15] Therefore, the Tribunal cannot ignore the loans when assessing OCU's financial condition at the time of the unlawful expropriation. However, OEG's loan to OCU cannot be regarded as a third-party loan. This point is crucial, as explained by the Claimant's quantum expert:[16]

> Loans owed to a shareholder are very different from loans owed to a third party because the interests of a third party in deciding whether to liquidate a company or put it into bankruptcy are very different from the interests of a shareholder in deciding whether to put a company into bankruptcy.

[163] The Tribunal considers that OEG made the loans to OCU as part of its investment in Ukraine. It had an interest in keeping its subsidiary afloat, at least until it could be sold. The Tribunal agrees with the Claimant's quantum experts who opined that "*the shareholders in OEG would expect OEG to maximise the value of its investment. And if starving OCU of cash or forcing OCU into liquidation would destroy value – which, on our analysis, it would have destroyed significant value – then that would be an irrational action for OEG to take.*"[17] [...]
[167] Therefore, the Tribunal rejects the Respondent's submissions on quantum and that

---

[13] [163] **Exhibit CLA-30**, *Case concerning the Factory at Chorzów (Germany v Poland)*, PCIJ Series A No. 13, Judgment of 13 September 1928, p. 47.

[14] [170] Transcript, Day 6, 27:7-8.

[15] [171] **Exhibit R-1**, Olympic Entertainment Group AS, Offering 14,000,000 Ordinary Shares, p. 101.

[16] [172] Transcript, Day 5, 9:9-15.

[17] [174] Transcript, Day 5, 63:5-10.

liquidation of the Claimant's investment was inevitable. The unlawful indirect expropriation was the proximate causal factor that led to the Claimant's investment being wiped out.
In the Tribunal's view, had the ban not been implemented, OCU, a very small player in the
gambling sector, would have continued along without any real prospect of repaying the
large loan owed to its parent. OEG itself well understood this; hence its decision months
previously to put the company up for sale. There is no question whatsoever that OEG
would have had to take a rather severe 'hair cut' when exiting Ukraine and as the Maxbet
evidence shows, no informed buyer would have agreed to buy OCU if it had to assume
repayment of its debt. But, and this is the key point, OCU had machines, locations, staff
and customers and therefore it still held some value. Accordingly, the Tribunal is of the
view that the Respondent's approach of assessing the Claimant's investment on liquidation value or book value is not appropriate. The Claimant's investment was an operating
business with hopes of improved performance and the assessment of the investment must
include its fair market value, which includes the expected performance in the future. [...]
[**172**] [...] In all the circumstances, in the Tribunal's view, the Claimant's valuation of its
investment and the calculations made by the Claimant's quantum experts are not unreasonable as a <u>starting point</u>. However, the Tribunal considers that the Claimant's valuation,
including its alternative valuation, must be discounted due to the following factors. [**173**]
First, as already found above, OCU was in a difficult financial situation. OEG's loan, although a shareholder loan, was still a very significant financial liability that required that
all free cash flows generated be devoted to servicing it. Based on OCU's financial performance, it would be a very long time indeed before OCU would be in a position to declare
a dividend to its shareholder. While the Tribunal accepts the Claimant's position that this
loan does not establish that OCU was on the brink of insolvency, the Tribunal cannot
accept the approach of the Claimant's quantum experts who simply disregarded it.[18] In addition, the Tribunal notes the very limited available cash that OCU had at its disposal. As
observed by the Respondent's quantum expert, "*OCU Group had [...] less than one week's
average cash in its bank at the end of 2008. Well, that is an extremely dicey, vulnerable situation
for any business to be in.*"[19] Furthermore, as noted by the Respondent, the Claimant did not
submit sufficient contemporaneous business plans or financial projections to demonstrate
anticipated future cash flows and profits.[20] Moreover, the Claimant's quantum experts,
in their DCF calculations, assumed that OCU's licences would have been renewed.[21]
While the Tribunal considers that it is reasonable to assume that the licences would have
continued in the absence of a breach, it is important to take into account in the damage
calculations that, as acknowledged by the Claimant's counsel,[22] the Respondent did not
have any obligation to issue new licences after the expiry of the same in 2011.[23] [**174**]

---

[18] [190] See, e.g., Transcript, Day 5, 105:17-106:21.

[19] [191] Transcript, Day 6, 12:17-20.

[20] [192] Respondent's post-hearing brief, para. 43.

[21] [193] Nicholson and David II Expert Report, para. 5.13.

[22] [194] 4 Transcript, Day 7, 29:13-20 ("*Dr Thomas: Is it possible for the state to say, 'We really need to clamp
down on this because this is a real social problem'? And in the course of doing that, can they take measures which
may respect existing rights, but say that future grants of rights will be curtailed? MR GONZALES GARCIA: Yes.
Yes, we accept that. We accept that as long as the rights of existing investors are protected.*")

[23] [195] Transcript, Day 8, 98:9-19 (see Respondent's counsel arguing that "*with regard to licenses, a DCF
wouldn't help the Claimant in any event, because Mr Garcia accepted that Ukraine could curtail the issuance of
new licences which would have expired in 2011. So his point was that it would be a breach to cancel the licences
midterm, but he accepted that Ukraine would not have to issue any new licences after that. So it would have been*

Second, the Tribunal agrees with the Claimant that the Maxbet offer is an important factor which should be considered in valuing the Claimant's investment. In the Tribunal's experience it is very rare indeed that the company being valued for the purpose of a treaty breach to have been subject to even a provisional offer so close in time to the value date. The Tribunal has considered carefully the Respondent's various submissions to the effect that the Maxbet offer "*is murky and unreliable*".[24] However, in the Tribunal's view, Maxbet was a willing prospective buyer just before the unlawful expropriation, albeit one which had not yet been given access to OCU's confidential financial information so as to be able to conduct due diligence. Therefore, the price that Maxbet was willing to pay for OCU is a relevant indicator of value. [...] [**175**] The Tribunal is well aware that international law seeks to avoid undue speculation when seeking to estimate cashflows that might be generated out of a transaction which was almost, but not finally, consummated. Had the Maxbet negotiation stood alone, it would not have been a satisfactory proxy for valuing OCU. In the end, the Tribunal has to start its valuation exercise somewhere and it accepts the Respondent's point that there are important factors which must be taken into account when considering the Maxbet offer. Among them, the Tribunal notes that the price of the Maxbet offer could have changed after the due diligence exercise, to which the deal was subject. [...] Furthermore, it may well be that Maxbet would have decided not to sign an agreement with OEG due to disclosures made in the due diligence process. Moreover, the provisionally agreed upon purchase price concerned two distinct assets: OCU shares and an international trademark owned by OEG. Although the Tribunal accepts the Claimant's view that it is reasonable to assume that relevant trademarks only concerned the Ukrainian market,[25] the Tribunal also accepts that it is possible, although less likely, that the international trademarks may have also concerned other countries. Therefore, the Tribunal is of the view that the Maxbet offer, while indicative of a possible value, must be subject to some deduction, from the lowest price offered by Maxbet, to account for the various uncertainties concerning this offer and the related negotiations. [...] [**180**] Having considered the above, the Tribunal notes that the valuation of the investment in the context of awarding compensation is not an exercise which admits of scientific accuracy. As stated by the tribunal in Vivendi Universal SA v Argentina, "the fact that damages cannot be fixed with certainty is no reason not to award damages when a loss has been incurred. In such cases, approximations are inevitable; the settling of damages is not an exact science."[26] In the same vein, the tribunal in Crystallex International Corporation v Venezuela stated that:[27]

> [...] *an impossibility or even a considerable difficulty that would make it unconscionable to prove the amount (rather than the existence) of damages with absolute precision does not bar their recovery altogether. Arbitral tribunals have been prepared to award compensation on the basis of a reasonable approximation of the loss, where they felt confident about the fact*

Ukraine's prerogative on any analysis, and as accepted by counsel for the Claimant, to not issue new licences for gambling once the existing licences had lapsed.")

[24] [196] Respondent's post-hearing brief, p. 13.

[25] [200] See Claimant's post-hearing brief, paras 91-107.

[26] [207] **Exhibit RLA-82**, *Compañiá de Aguas del Aconquija SA, Vivendi Universal SA v Argentine Republic*, ICSID Case No ARB/97/3, Award of 20 August 2007, para. 8.3.16.

[27] [208] **Exhibit RLA-50**, *Crystallex International Corporation v Bolivarian Republic of Venezuela*, ICSID Case No. ARB(AF)/11/2, Award of 4 April 2016, paras 871-872.

*of the loss itself. In the Tribunal's view, this approach may be particularly warranted if the un-
certainty in determining what exactly would have happened is the result of the other party's
wrongdoing.*

*These principles should also be applied with regard to the proof of loss of profits, which is
the crucial issue in this case as far as the determination of quantum is concerned.*

[181] Similarly, the Tribunal notes with approval the statement made by the tribunal in
Gold Reserve Inc v Venezuela:[28]

> [...] *while a claimant must prove its damages to the required standard, the assessment of
> damages is often a difficult exercise and it is seldom that damages in an investment situation
> will be able to be established with scientific certainty. This is because such assessments will
> usually involve some degree of estimation and the weighing of competing (but equally legiti-
> mate) facts, valuation methods and opinions, which does not of itself mean that the burden of
> proof has not been satisfied. Because of this element of imprecision, it is accepted that tribunals
> retain a certain amount of discretion or a "margin of appreciation" when assessing damages,
> which will necessarily involve some approximation. The use of this discretion should not be
> confused with acting on an ex aequo et bono basis, even if equitable considerations are taken
> into account in the exercise of such discretion. Rather, in such circumstances, the tribunal
> exercises its judgment in a reasoned manner so as to discern an appropriate damages sum
> which results in compensation to Claimant in accordance with the principles of international
> law that have been discussed earlier.*

[183] In addition, the Tribunal considers that the Claimant is entitled to receive pre-award
and post-award interest on the compensation awarded to it as to ensure full reparation. In
this regard, the Tribunal notes Article 38 of the ILC Articles on State Responsibility, which
provides as follows:

> 1. *Interest on any principal sum due under this chapter shall be payable when necessary in
>   order to ensure full reparation. The interest rate and mode of calculation shall be set so as
>   to achieve that result.*
> 2. *Interest runs from the date when the principal sum should have been paid until the date
>   the obligation to pay is fulfilled.*

[185] In the Tribunal's view, in order to achieve full reparations, which *"wipe out all the
consequences of the illegal act"*, the Claimant's request for interest at the rate of 12-month
LIBOR + 4%, compounded annually, is reasonable. In this regard, the Tribunal notes that
interest at the rate of LIBOR + 4% was also adopted by various tribunals.[...][29]"

[Paras. 155, 156, 161, 163, 167, 172, 173, 174, 175, 180, 181, 183, 185]

---

[28] [209] *Gold Reserve Inc. v Bolivarian Republic of Venezuela*, ICSID Case No. ARB(AF)/09/1, Award of 19
September 2014, para. 686 (cited in **Exhibit RLA-50**, *Crystallex International Corporation v Bolivarian
Republic of Venezuela*, ICSID Case No. ARB(AF)/11/2, Award of 4 April 2016, footnote 1252).

[29] [210] E.g., **Exhibit, CLA-42**, *OI European Group B.V. v Bolivarian Republic of Venezuela*, ISCID Case
No. ARB/11/25, Award of 10 March 2015, paras 393-944; **Exhibit CLA-43**, *Ron Fuchs v The Republic of
Georgia*, ICSID Case No. ARB/07/15, Award of 3 March 2010, paras 659-661; **Exhibit CLA-44**, *Rusoro
Mining Ltd. v Bolivarian Republic of Venezuela*, ICSID Case No. ARB(AF)/12/5, Award of 22 August 2016,
para. 838.

VI.

II.2.6   COSTS OF JUDICIAL AND ARBITRAL PROCEEDINGS
See also: I.11.03; I.11.0355; II.2.22

"[**189**] In accordance with Article 40 of the UNCITRAL Rules, the Tribunal sees no reason why it should depart from the principle that costs follow the event. This rule is well established. The Tribunal nevertheless retains the discretion to assess a reasonable sum to be paid by the losing party and may take into account the conduct of the Parties and the amount awarded compared to the amount claimed. [. . .] [**191**] Accordingly, the Tribunal does not think it appropriate to reduce the recoverable costs solely on the ground that the Claimant has received less than it claims. Its claim was always moderate and the assessment of damages in these cases is not an easy task. [**192**] The total number of hours charged by the Claimant is 10,022 whereas the total charged by the Respondent is 3,770. The Tribunal notes that from its experience it is not unusual for claimants to spend more time, and in most cases more money, than respondents. However, the hourly rate charged by the Claimant is less than the Respondent's hourly rates. [**193**] The Tribunal is entitled to give regard to the fact that this arbitration was conducted in English, which is not the first language of most of the Claimant's counsel. [**194**] [. . .] Both Parties provided excellent cooperation to the Tribunal and the hearing, although virtual, was conducted most effectively. Everybody kept to their agreed and allotted time. The Tribunal is grateful for the cooperation and assistance given by both sets of counsel."

[**Paras. 189, 191, 192, 193, 194**]

VII.

II.2.5   JUDGMENT/DECISION/ORDER

"[**205**] Having carefully considered the Parties' arguments in their written and oral pleadings, and having deliberated, for the reasons stated above, the Tribunal unanimously decides and declares as follows:

a) The Tribunal has jurisdiction and the Respondent's jurisdictional objection is dismissed;

b) The Gambling Ban Law constituted an indirect expropriation of the Claimant's investments in violation of Article 5 of the Treaty;

c) The Respondent shall pay damages to the Claimant in the sum of EUR 7,500,000. In addition, the Respondent shall pay pre-award interest on this sum at the rate of 12-month LIBOR + 4%, compounded annually, accruing from 25 June 2009 until (and inclusive of) the date of this Award;

d) The Respondent shall pay post-award interest at the rate of 12-month LIBOR + 4%, compounded annually, accruing on any outstanding amount stated in the preceding paragraph from the date of this Award until payment in full;

e) The Respondent shall pay the Claimant's costs in the sum of EUR 2,750,000. In addition, the Respondent shall pay simple interest theron at the rate of LIBOR + 4% per annum from the date of this Award until payment in full;

f) The sum outstanding to the credit of the Parties to this arbitration in the accounts of the PCA in the amount of USD 316,292.83 shall be paid to the Claimant's solicitors in part the satisfaction of the order for costs made herein; and

g) All of the Parties' other claims and requests for relief are rejected."

[**Para. 205**]

Systematic Key Items of the Section*

---

* *See* Systematic Classification Scheme, *supra* at page 255.

XII

International Administrative Tribunals

INTRODUCTORY NOTE

The 2021 Judicial Activity of the International Administrative Tribunals

BY FRANCESCO SEATZU*

Abstract

The year 2021 was for the international administrative courts and tribunals largely characterised by the following four elements: the UN Dispute Tribunal (UNDT)'s delivery of the judgment in the case *Banaj v. Secretary-General of the United Nations*, reviewing the lawfulness of a decision of the UN Office on Drugs and Crime to temporarily reassign the applicant; the decision in the case *Gharagozloo Pakkala v. Secretary-General of the United Nations*, where the UNDT approached the issue concerning the revision of a decision imposing administrative sanctions on the applicant; the decision in the case *Paul Ories v. Secretary-General of the United Nations*, where the UNDT held that there is no UN staff rule mandating a right to reassignment on medical grounds; and the decision in the case *G. (Nos. 7) and V. (No. 8) v. EPO*, where the ILOAT focused on the unlawful limitations of the right to strike of IOs staff.

I. INTRODUCTION

Although perhaps not exactly the most memorable year in the history of international administrative tribunals (IATS), the year 2021 was replete with noteworthy judicial decisions by the IATs concerning the handling of some of the most perennial issues of international administrative law and procedure. Moreover, the year 2021 was a year that was also characterised by the issuance of an important and long-awaited contribution, written by Professors Jérémy Boulanger-Bonnelly and Louise Otis, concerning the coherence in the

---

* PhD (Nottingham); Full Professor of International and European Union Law, University of Cagliari (Italy).

Francesco Seatzu, *Introductory Note* In: *The Global Community Yearbook of International Law and Jurisprudence 2022*. Edited by: Giuliana Ziccardi Capaldo, Oxford University Press. © Oxford University Press 2023. DOI: 10.1093/oso/9780197752265.003.0035

case-law of IATS[1] and dealing in particular with the burden and standard of proof in international administrative law[2] (or more precisely of the law of the international civil service).[3]

Purely for reasons of space, the present review, the fourth of its kind in this *Yearbook*, will solely deal the following four judicial decisions, the first, the second, and the third delivered by the UN Dispute Tribunal (UNDT) respectively in March 2021 and June 2021, and the fourth one by the International Labour Organisation Administrative Tribunal (ILOAT) in July 2021.

II. THE UNDT'S JUDGMENT ON THE CASE OF *BANAJ V. SECRETARY-GENERAL OF THE UNITED NATIONS*

In the first of these judgments, *Banaj v. Secretary-General of the United Nations*,[4] the UNDT was called upon, in particular, to pronounce on the lawfulness of decisions to temporarily reassign the applicant's working tasks and functions during an investigation, a theme that is frequently and periodically addressed in the case-law of the IATs (as inter alia confirmed by the jurisprudence of the United Nations Tribunals (both first and second instance)).[5] The UNDT firmly defended the idea that "the re-assignment of staff and duty assignments falls within the Organization's broad discretion."

Far from being unclear, the rationale behind this view contained in such a statement and subsequent words is that "only where decisions made in exercise of this discretion are shown to have been improperly motivated or taken in breach of mandatory provisions that the presumption of regularity in the exercise of the Organization's discretion in the use of resources and personnel is rebutted". And in fact, it has been clearly explained by the UNDT that: "It is for the Organization to determine whether a reassignment is in its interest".

For the UNDT, these and other considerations were sufficient to completely dismiss the applicant's two main contentions, according to which the re-assignment decision was not "programmatically justified" but was instead a disguised disciplinary measure used as part of alleged ongoing harassment by the (Regional Representative) against her. And, in fact, the UNDT used these statements to reiterate and strengthen its argument on the impossibility for itself to consider the correctness of the choice made by the respondent administration amongst the various courses of action open to it.

More succinct but equally pointed comments came from the UNDT in relation to the applicant's contention, namely, that "a decision to re-assign the duties of a staff member has

---

[1] On the subject, *see also* THE DEVELOPMENT AND EFFECTIVENESS OF INTERNATIONAL ADMINISTRATIVE LAW ON THE OCCASION OF THE THIRTIETH ANNIVERSARY OF THE WORLD BANK ADMINISTRATIVE TRIBUNAL 325 (Olufemi Elias ed., 2012).

[2] *See* Jérémy Boulanger-Bonnelly & Louise Otis, *In Search of Coherence: Burden and Standard of Proof in International Administrative Law*, 18 INTERNATIONAL ORGANIZATIONS LAW REVIEW 507 (2021). *See also* Xavier Pons Rafols, *Nuevos desarrollos en la resolución de la conflictividad laboral en las organizaciones internacionales*, *in* LAS ORGANIZACIONES INTERNACIONALES EN EL SIGLO XX, at 163 (ANNA MARIA BADIA MARTÌ, ANNA MARIA HUICI SANCHO L. & SANCHEZ COBALEDA eds., 2021).

[3] *See* THE LAW OF THE INTERNATIONAL CIVIL SERVICE: INSTITUTIONAL LAW AND PRACTICE IN INTERNATIONAL ORGANISATIONS (Gerhard Ullrich ed., 2018), ch. 2. *See also* Lorenzo Gasbarri, *Gerhard Ullrich. The Law of the International Civil Service. Berlin: Duncker & Humblot, 2018*, 31 EJIL 771–785 (2020).

[4] UNDT, Banaj v. Secretary-General of the United Nations, Judgment No. 2021-1560 (26 March 2021).

[5] *See also* Louise Otis & Eric H. Reiter, *The Reform of the United Nations Administration of Justice System: The United Nations Appeals Tribunal after One Year*, 10 THE LAW & PRACTICE OF INTERNATIONAL COURTS AND TRIBUNALS 405 (2011).

no legal consequences and cannot be challenged". With regard to this allegation, the UNDT found that "It is a decision that is appropriately the subject of judicial review, involving a close examination of the circumstances to determine whether the decision was irregular or unlawful [...]."

III. THE ILOAT'S JUDGMENT ON THE CASE OF *GHARAGOZLOO PAKKALA V. SECRETARY-GENERAL OF THE UNITED NATIONS*

The *Gharagozloo Pakkala v. Secretary-General of the United Nations* case concerns the decision of UNICEF's Human Resources Department "imposing the following administrative measures on the applicant: a. Issuance of a written reprimand and its placement in her Official Status File ('OSF') for a period of five years; b. Her removal from all supervisory functions for a period of two years; and c. Requiring her to undertake appropriate training to enhance self-awareness and improve her people management skills."[6]

The applicant requested the ILOAT to set aside the impugned decision. On its part, the UNICEF argued before the Tribunal in favour of the dismissal of the applicants' complaints on the grounds, in particular, that "the contested decision is grounded in a finding that the Applicant's behaviour did not meet the standards expected of an international civil servant at her seniority level as, for instance, set forth in the opening sentence of sec. 2.3 of UNICEF Executive Directive CF/EXD/2012-007 [...]", which inter alia calls for managers to act "as role models by upholding the highest standards of conduct and by promoting a harmonious working environment. [...]."

This is one among a few cases in which issues concerning the meaning and distinction between administrative and disciplinary measures arose and were considered at length together with their consequences in a decision of an international administrative tribunal.[7] In this context the ILOAT rightly observed that: "*unlike disciplinary measures* administrative measures are limited in time [...]. Moreover, [...] [differently from] disciplinary measures, the administrative measures like the ones taken in the present case do not bar the charged person from seeking other positions within or outside *its employee's organization* [...]". The Tribunal found that "the administrative measures imposed on the applicant were rational and proportionate to the established facts, as well as to address the concerns that UNICEF had about her conduct, and did not constitute disguised disciplinary measures as they are of a different nature than disciplinary measures, targeted specific behaviours, have a limited application in time, and do not necessarily play a role in future selection exercises".

With respect to the applicant's two years removal from supervisory functions and the requirement to undertake training, as well as the retention period of the written reprimand in the applicant's Official Status File (OSE), the Tribunal found that they were not punitive but preventive, corrective, and cautionary in nature.

Thus, for all these and other reasons, the Tribunal totally rebutted the applicants' complaints, concluding that the UNICEF is correct in arguing that the complaints are unreceivable.

---

[6] UNDT, Gharagozloo Pakkala v. Secretary-General of the United Nations, Judgment No. 2021- 076 (9 June 2021).

[7] *See also* Teresa da Silva Bravo, *The United Nations' Internal Justice System and Fair Trial Rights of International Staff Members in Disciplinary Proceedings, in* Judicial Power in a Globalized World: Liber Amicorum Vincent De Gaetano 559 (Paulo Pinto de Albuquerque & Krzysztof Wojtyczek eds., 2018).

IV. THE ILOAT'S JUDGMENT ON THE CASE OF *PAUL ORIES V. SECRETARY-GENERAL OF THE UNITED NATIONS*

A third decision worthy of note was the *Paul Ories v. Secretary-General of the United Nations* case.[8] This case, decided by the UNDT in March 2021, was perhaps not as factually signifi-cant as the *Gharagozloo Pakkala* case, but it was of great significance to the credibility of the United Nations as a human rights organisation. In that case, the UNDT was asked to decide on the existence of the right of staff members to be reassigned to a different duty station on medical grounds. It was a difficult decision as it was clear and evident that there was no pending decision refusing to assign the appellant to a post at a duty station other than Erbil (namely, the applicant's initial employment post).

Although it was a difficult decision to reach, it was, nevertheless, straightforward since there is currently no staff rule or regulation mandating a right to reassignment on medical grounds,[9] and also given the applicant's medical report of 17 September 2018 stating that he *"was* unable to perform any duties in his line of work with the United Nations" and recommended "early medical retirement" and "permanent disability".

V. THE ILOAT'S JUDGMENT ON THE CASE OF *G. (NOS. 7 AND 8) AND V. (NO. 8) V. EPO*

In a long-awaited decision released by the ILOAT in early July 2021, the judges affirmed that the European Patent Office (EPO) was at fault in promulgating its Circular No. 347, entitled "Guidelines applicable in the event of strike".[10] By following and developing this line of thought, the ILOAT recognises that the Circular is unlawful in its entirety and should be set aside. The reasoning behind is clear, especially if one considers Circular No. 347, paragraphs 2 and 3. By imposing a minimum of 10 percent of employees who may call for a strike, paragraph 2 of Circular No. 347 violated the right to strike of any employee who, in combination with others, may wish to strike where the total number of employees is less than 10 percent. Moreover, Circular No. 347 paragraph 3 also did the same, insofar as it provided that if the class who have a right to vote on whether the strike should start extends beyond (and potentially well beyond) the employees who wish to strike, then that wider class has a capacity to veto the strike. Furthermore, one could also refer to those other rules in the Circular that, by limiting the duration of the strike, violated the fundamental right of the striking staff to autonomously determine the length of their strike.

The adoption of this judgment represents a ground-breaking event in the enforcement of the right to strike in order not to be mistreated by their employer.[11] In this context, it is clear (as is acknowledged in the judgement) that reparation for the wrongs suffered, both past and present, represents an essential element to make this goal a reality.

VI. FINAL OBSERVATIONS

The great heterogeneity of legal issues addressed, respectively, by the UNDT in its decisions on the case of *Banaj v. Secretary-General of the United Nations*, of *Gharagozloo Pakkala v. Secretary-General of the United Nations*, of *Paul Ories v. Secretary-General of the United*

---

[8] UNDT, Paul Ories v. Secretary-General of the United Nations, Judgment No. 2021-1087 (19 March 2021).

[9] As the UNDT concluded, Staff Regulation 1.2(c) and Staff Rule 6.2 do not so provide.

[10] ILOAT, G. (Nos. 7 and 8) and V. (No. 8) v. EPO, Judgment No. 2021-4430 (7 July 2021).

[11] For more analysis on the subject, *see also* Bob Hepple, *The Right to Strike in an International Context*, 15 CANADIAN LABOUR & EMPLOYMENT LAW JOURNAL 133 (2018).

Nations and by the ILOAT in its decision on the case *G. (Nos. 7 and 8) and V. (No. 8) v. EPO* makes it impossible to draw any general conclusions.

Nevertheless, two main aspects may be worth mentioning. First, the role played by the right of strike and the presumption of regularity in the exercise of the Organization's broad discretion in the use of resources and personnel and by their true meanings and possible application and limitations continue to draw attention in the case-law of two of the most important and active IATs. Second, there is a constant focus and attention on the burden and standard of proof issues in the recent case-law of the ILOAT and UNDT.[12] In several respects, this attention and focus has considerable merit, and in fact it enhances fairness in the service relationship between the international organisations that recognise the jurisdiction of the UNDT and ILOAT and their staff and personnel members.[13]

---

[12] *See also* Rishi Gulati, *An International Administrative Procedural Law of Fair Trial: Reality or Rhetoric?*, 21 Max Planck Yearbook of United Nations Law Online 210 (2018).

[13] *See also* Joan S. Powers, *The Evolving Jurisprudence of the International Administrative Tribunals: Convergence or Divergence?*, 15 AIIB Yearbook of International Law 68 (2018).

LEGAL MAXIMS: SUMMARIES AND EXTRACTS FROM SELECTED CASE LAW*

Paul Ories v. Secretary-General of the United Nations, Case No. 2020-1404, Judgment No. 2021-UNAT-1087, 19 March 2021

Banaj v. Secretary-General of the United Nations, Case No. UNDT/GVA/2019/031, Judgment No. UNDT/2021/030, 26 March 2021

Gharagozloo Pakkala v. Secretary-General of the United Nations, Case No. UNDT/GVA/2020/018, Judgment No. UNDT/2021/076, 29 June 2021

G. (Nos. 7 and 8) and V. (No. 8) v. EPO, ILOAT, 132nd Session, Judgment No. 4430, 7 July 2021

---

* The working method chosen for the formulation of legal maxims is explained *supra* 'Outline of the Parts', at page xv.

Legal Maxims: Summaries and Extracts from Selected Case Law In: *The Global Community Yearbook of International Law and Jurisprudence 2022*. Edited by: Giuliana Ziccardi Capaldo, Oxford University Press. © Oxford University Press 2023.
DOI: 10.1093/oso/9780197752265.003.0036

XII.2.1

Paul Ories v. Secretary-General of the United Nations, Case No. 2020-1404, Judgment No. 2021-UNAT-1087, 19 March 2021*

Contents**

   I. INTRODUCTION AND PROCEDURAL BACKGROUND

   II. FACTS AND PROCEDURE

   III. THE UNDT PROCEEDINGS

   IV. CONSIDERATIONS

   V. JUDGMENT

I.

II.2.0   INSTITUTION AND COURSE OF PROCEEDINGS
         See also: I.2.2; I.2.2151; II.6; II.7.10214; II.7.10216

"[1] Paul Ories (Mr. Ories or Appellant), since 2009 an Associate Security Officer with the United Nations Mission in Iraq (UNAMI), appeals against the Judgment of the United Nations Dispute Tribunal (UNDT [...]). The UNDT dismissed Mr. Ories' challenge to the Secretary-General's (Respondent's) refusal to agree to his transfer to another duty station on medical grounds, and the Respondent's alleged negligent failure to comply with the duty of care owed to him by continued delay and ultimately refusal of his transfer request. We will refer to these two causes of action as "Contested Decisions #1 and #2" respectively."

[**Para. 1**]

II.

I.2.31   ACTS AND DECISIONS OF INTERNATIONAL ORGANIZATIONS

"[3] On 6 December 2013, Mr. Ories was attacked and severely injured by a colleague while on duty in Erbil, Iraq. [...] [H]e was repatriated [...] for medical treatment and recovery. [...] [F]or much of the period from 2014 [...] to early to mid 2019, Mr. Ories' medical assessments and prognoses assessed him as unfit for continued duties and recommended his retirement from United Nations security officer work. [4] [...] Mr. Ories made several [...] requests for transfers to other duty stations, but none eventuated. [5] [...] [He] continued to serve intermittently as his health permitted but otherwise took further sick leave on half-pay. [6] On 30 September 2018, Mr. Ories was advised of the latest refusal of his request to transfer [...]. This was the first decision of the Respondent challenged by the Appellant (Contested Decision #1). [...] Mr. Ories sought management evaluation of Contested Decision #1 [...] [and] he was advised that, subject to medical

---

 * Summaries prepared by Simona Fanni, Ph.D. in Legal Sciences, Postdoctoral Fellow "Margarita Salas", Universidad de Sevilla, Spain. Text of judgment available online at the Tribunal's Web site <https://www.un.org/en/internaljustice/files/unat/judgments/2021-UNAT-1087.pdf>. Original and Authoritative Version: English. Footnotes appearing in the original text have been omitted.

** This is not a faithful reproduction of the Table of Contents of the Judgment.

clearance, his request to be reassigned to another duty station would be approved. [7] On 17 April 2019, Mr. Ories informed UNAMI's Chief Security Officer (CSO) that he had been cleared [...] to return to work as from 30 April 2019 [...] [and] re-expressed his wish [...] to be placed in a vacant post in Baghdad. [...] [H]owever, on 21 April 2019, the CSO announced [...] that someone else had been appointed to that post [...]. Mr. Ories regarded this as the rejection of his request to be assigned to the post, and it formed the basis of his second complaint to the UNDT (Contested Decision #2). [8] [...] [He] sought management evaluation of Contested Decision #2 [but] [...] [t]his was refused [...]. [11] [...] [Moreover, he] had claimed compensation for his injuries [...] [and] for his loss of functions and permanent disability [...]. [12] On 6 April and on 18 June 2019, Mr. Ories filed his applications with the UNDT challenging Contested Decision #1 and #2 respectively. The two proceedings were subsequently consolidated."

[Paras. 3, 4, 5, 6, 7, 8, 11, 12]

III.

I.2.31   ACTS AND DECISIONS OF INTERNATIONAL ORGANIZATIONS
          See also: II.2.021; II.2.24; II.7.1026; II.7.102161

"[13] The UNDT first concluded that Mr. Ories' appeal relating to Contested Decision #1 was not receivable by it because he had not made a claim to the [Management Evaluation Unit] [...] in negligence [...] against the Respondent, but rather only about his requested transfer. The UNDT held that its only jurisdiction was to consider whether the refusal to transfer was lawful. The claim was dealt with as not receivable also because it was filed out of time. [...] [14] The UNDT nevertheless went on to determine the substantive merits of Mr. Ories' case [...] deciding [...]:

> There is no staff rule or regulation mandating a right to reassignment on medical grounds. In any event there was no basis for the transfer from the documentation provided by the Applicant's doctor. The Applicant's medical report of 17 September 2018 stated that he "is unable to perform any duties in his line of work with the United Nations" and recommended "early medical retirement" and "permanent disability". [...] Thereafter the Medical Services Division [...] certified him by email dated 4 June 2019 as cleared to return to work. There is no basis for compensation as the Applicant has already availed himself of his sick leave entitlements under staff rule 6.2."

[Paras. 13, 14]

I.2.31   ACTS AND DECISIONS OF INTERNATIONAL ORGANIZATIONS
          See also: II.2.24; II.7.1026; II.7.102161

"[15] Turning to Contested Decision #2, the UNDT ruled that the broadcast announcement of another's appointment was not an administrative decision reviewable under Article 2(1)(a) of the Statute of the [...] [UNDT]. Further, the UNDT held that Mr. Ories suffered no adverse outcome from it as he was then on paid sick leave receiving all of his remuneration and other benefits, and there was no regulatory requirement for the Respondent to require the Organisation to reassign Mr. Ories to Baghdad on medical grounds. The UNDT also found that at the time of the second application, there was no pending decision refusing to assign the Appellant to a post at a duty station other than

Erbil. [**16**] [...] [T]he UNDT added [...] [that] [t]he decision to fill the Baghdad position [...] was taken before the Applicant was cleared as fit to return to work." [**17**] The UNDT also found Mr. Ories' application to be moot because, when he was first cleared to work from sick leave on 1 May 2019, the Administration accordingly assigned him to a duty station other than Erbil, with effect from 24 May 2019. It was after that date [...] that he filed his case in the UNDT relating to Contested Decision #2."

[**Paras. 15, 16, 17**]

IV.

II.7.10214 REVIEW OF IATs JUDGMENTS
See also: I.2.31; II.2.021; II.6.0; II.7.102161

"[**37**] We agree with the UNDT that, to a significant extent, the Appellant's two separate contested decision-based causes of action, overlap and merge. [...] The UNDT concluded, correctly, that Mr. Ories did not seek, within the time prescribed for doing so, management evaluation reviews of the refusals of those requests for transfer which were declined. That was an essential prerequisite for applying to the UNDT to challenge those refusals. Although this alone would be sufficient, as the UNDT also concluded, to have disposed of the first proceeding brought by Mr. Ories, the UNDT also proceeded to consider and decide the merits of this case. For completeness, we will also review this decision of the UNDT."

[**Para. 37**]

II.7.10214 REVIEW OF IATs JUDGMENTS
See also: I.2.31; II.1; II.7.102161

"[**38**] [...] [I]t has not been shown that [...] [M. Ories] had a right to consideration of his requests to this effect and to a transfer or reassignment if conditions warranting this were fulfilled. As the UNDT concluded, Staff Regulation 1.2(c) and Staff Rule 6.2 do not so provide. [...] The UNDT did not err in this assessment of the merits of Mr. Ories' case. [**39**] Turning to the second challenged decision, [...] we are similarly not persuaded that the UNDT erred in rejecting this complaint. [...] [T]here is no evidence as to why the Appellant ought to have been appointed. [...] The absence of a rule-based entitlement to seek such a reassignment and for its consideration on statutory grounds [...], again disadvantages Mr. Ories on this aspect of his appeal. [**40**] Penultimately, [...] following his medically-supported advice to the Organisation on 17 April 2019 that he was able to return to duties at another post as from 30 April, he was promptly reassigned to duties at Basra [...]. We agree with the UNDT that this caused to be moot his claims to such a reassignment."

[**Paras. 38, 39, 40**]

II.7.10214 REVIEW OF IATs JUDGMENTS
See also: I.2.2151; I.2.31; II.1; II.2.021; II.7.102161

"[**41**] Finally, this leaves only Mr. Ories' claims in negligence against the Secretary-General relating to the alleged delays in reassigning him [...]. We agree with the UNDT that this is a sufficiently different claim to that seeking reassignment, that it should have been, but was not, subjected to management evaluation. [...] [T]he failure of this jurisdictional prerequisite precluded it from being received by the UNDT. But substantively also, we agree with the UNDT that at all material times that might be covered by such a claim, the medical information furnished to the Organisation was that Mr. Ories was so disabled by his 2013 ordeal and injuries, that he should be retired medically. Faced with that evidence, together with the fact that he remained employed and in receipt of income, […] Mr. Ories would face insurmountable obstacles to establish both that UNAMI had been negligent in not reassigning him and that he had suffered losses thereby."

[Para. 41]

V.

II.2.5   JUDGMENT/DECISION/ORDER
           See also: II.6.2; II.7.10211; II.7.102162

"**[42]** For the foregoing reasons, Mr. Ories' appeal must fail and is dismissed. The UNDT Judgment is affirmed."

[Para. 42]

XII.2.2

Banaj v. Secretary-General of the United Nations, Case No. UNDT/GVA/2019/031, Judgment No. UNDT/2021/030, 26 March 2021*

Contents**

    I. INTRODUCTION AND PROCEDURAL BACKGROUND

    II. CONSIDERATIONS

        A. RECEIVABILITY

        B. MERITS

   III. JUDGMENT

I.

II.2.0 INSTITUTION AND COURSE OF PROCEEDINGS
        See also: I.2.2; II.2.02; II.2.022; II.7.102; II.7.10216

"[**1**] On 21 May 2019, the Applicant, a staff member of the United Nations Office on Drugs and Crime ("UNODC"), filed an application before the United Nations Dispute Tribunal to challenge the Respondent's decision to temporarily reassign her functions as Head of the UNODC Office in Albania."

[**Para. 1**]

II.

A.

I.2.31 ACTS AND DECISIONS OF INTERNATIONAL ORGANIZATIONS
        See also: II.2.021; II.2.1; II.2.511; II.7.1026

"[**23**] Under art. 2.1(a) of its Statute, the Tribunal is only competent to hear and pass judgment on applications challenging an administrative decision by the Respondent. An application is not receivable if the subject matter is not an administrative decision. The said rule further stipulates that for the application to be receivable, the administrative decision contested must be in non-compliance with the staff member's terms of appointment, which include applicable provisions in the regulatory framework. [**24**] The interpretation and application of this rule have been extensively addressed by this Tribunal and UNAT in their decisions. [**25**] The classical definition of what constitutes an "administrative decision" as set out in *Andronov* [UNAdT Judgment No. 1157, *Andronov* (2003) para. V] is worth restating:

---

  * Summaries prepared by Simona Fanni, Ph.D. in Legal Sciences, Postdoctoral Fellow "Margarita Salas", Universidad de Sevilla, Spain. Text of judgment available online at the Tribunal's Web site <https://www.un.org/en/internaljustice/files/undt/judgments/undt-2021-030.pdf>. Original: English. Footnotes appearing in the original text have been omitted.

** This is not a faithful reproduction of the Table of Contents of the Judgment.

[...] *Administrative decisions are [...] characterized by the fact that they are taken by the Administration, they are unilateral and of individual application, and they carry direct legal consequences. [...].*"

[Paras. 23, 24, 25]

II.7.1026   JURISDICTION AND POWERS OF IATs
            See also: I.2.31; II.2.1; II.2.021; II.2.112; II.2.511

"[26] [. . . .] [A]ccording to the Respondent, the application is not receivable *ratione materiae*. [27] However, as Counsel for the Applicant points out, the decision had an impact on her functions, which would have been part of the terms of reference of her specific position. The Tribunal finds that the decision did indeed limit her work, the direct consequence of which was that she was no longer performing the functions she was employed to do. The Tribunal's findings in *Wondimu* UNDT/2017/018 supports the point made [...] [as] the Tribunal explained that:

> 77. [W]hile there is no contest that staff regulation 1.2(c) confers authority on the Secretary-General to assign staff members to suitable duties and offices, [...] [i]t has been well established by judicial pronouncements that any discretionary authority must be exercised judiciously and in the best interests of the Organization.
> [...] 106. It is certainly and properly the role of this Tribunal to determine whether the Respondent acted in good faith . . .

[28] There is no merit to the Respondent's contention that a decision to re-assign the duties of a staff member has no legal consequences and cannot be challenged. It is a decision that is appropriately the subject of judicial review, involving a close examination of the circumstances to determine whether the decision was irregular or unlawful. [29] The Tribunal finds the application materially receivable and will proceed to consider it on the merits."

[Paras. 26, 27, 28, 29]

B.

II.1.0   BURDEN OF PROOF
            See also: I.2.31; II.2.2; II.2.511

"[30] As explained in *Wondimu*, all the circumstances must be examined to determine whether the Respondent's discretion in re-assigning duties was properly exercised, so that the decision can be upheld. [31] A discretionary administrative decision, such as the one contested in this case, can be challenged on the grounds that the Respondent has not acted fairly, justly, or transparently or was motivated by bias, prejudice, or improper motives. UNAT jurisprudence recognizes a presumption of regularity in the performance of administrative functions and decision making. It is for the Applicant alleging any of these grounds of challenge to bear the initial burden of proving it in his or her application. [32] The Respondent in response to the allegations, has a minimal burden of proof to justify his administrative action or decision. Once that minimal burden is discharged, the burden remains with the staff member to prove that the actions of the Respondent were improper or unjustified. This must be done by clear and convincing evidence."

[Paras. 30, 31, 32]

I.2.31   ACTS AND DECISIONS OF INTERNATIONAL ORGANIZATIONS
See also: II.1.0; II.2.2; II.2.511

"[**36**] [. . .] [T]he Applicant's submissions that the decision is unlawful because it falls outside the regulatory scope of interim measures to be taken during an investigation, and cannot be justified as falling within the broad discretion of the Organization in reassigning staff members, are [. . .] without merit. [**37**] Firstly, the Applicant's reading of staff rule 10.4 (a) is misconceived. [. . .] The rule grants the Respondent the discretion to decide whether to place a staff member on administrative leave while an investigation is in progress. There is nothing in the rule that indicates that all the Respondent's other administrative discretions, including re-assignment of duties, are to be curtailed during an investigation. [**38**] Secondly, the Applicant in submitting that the re-assignment of duties is not justified, has not rebutted the presumption of regularity in the exercise of the Respondent's discretion in the use of resources and personnel. [. . .] [**39**] The jurisprudence of the United Nations Tribunals (both first and second instance) clearly underscores that that re-assignment of staff and duty assignments falls within the Organization's discretion. It is only where decisions made in exercise of this discretion are shown to have been improperly motivated or taken in breach of mandatory provisions that the presumption of regularity is rebutted. It is for the Organization to determine whether a reassignment is in its interest."

[**Paras. 36, 37, 38, 39**]

I.2.31   ACTS AND DECISIONS OF INTERNATIONAL ORGANIZATIONS
See also: II.2.2

"[**40**] According to the Applicant, the re-assignment decision [. . .] was not "programmatically justified" but was instead a disguised disciplinary measure used as part of alleged ongoing harassment by the [. . .] [Regional Representative] against her. [**41**] The Tribunal finds that the Respondent has fully explained the basis for the measure. It was intended to distance the Applicant from the type of duties she was carrying out and contacts being made with stakeholders, that were subject to investigation."

[**Paras. 40, 41**]

I.2.31   ACTS AND DECISIONS OF INTERNATIONAL ORGANIZATIONS
See also: II.1; II.1.0; II.2.2

"[**45**] Thus, as opposed to improperly seeking to harass the Applicant, the decision to reassign her rather than place her on administrative leave, was taken balancing her best interests with those of the Organization. These reasons are supported by the evidence. [**46**] The Tribunal finds that the Applicant has failed to meet her burden of proving any improper motive, irregularity or unlawfulness on the part of the Respondent in the decision to re-assign her duties. Therefore, the presumption of regularity stands."

[**Paras. 45, 46**]

III.

II.2.5   JUDGMENT/DECISION/ORDER
See also: II.7.10211; II.7.102161

"[**47**] In view of the foregoing, the Tribunal DECIDES:
    Whilst the application is receivable it fails on the merits and is dismissed."

[**Para. 47**]

XII.2.3

Gharagozloo Pakkala v. Secretary-General of the United Nations, Case No. UNDT/GVA/2020/018, Judgment No. UNDT/2021/076, 29 June 2021*

Contents**

I. INTRODUCTION AND PROCEDURAL BACKGROUND

II. CONSIDERATIONS

    A. SCOPE OF REVIEW

    B. MERITS

III. JUDGMENT

I.

II.2.0   INSTITUTION AND COURSE OF PROCEEDINGS
    See also: I.2.2; II.2.02; II.2.022; II.7.102; II.7.10216

"[8] [By an application filed] [o]n 20 March 2020, [1] [t]he Applicant, a staff member of the United Nations Children's Fund ("UNICEF") serving as a Senior Advisor (D-2 level), contests the imposition of the following administrative measures on her: a. Issuance of a written reprimand and its placement in her Official Status File ("OSF") for a period of five years; b. Her removal from all supervisory functions for a period of two years; and c. Requiring her to undertake appropriate training to enhance self-awareness and improve her people management skills."

[Paras. 8, 1]

II.

A.

II.7.1026   JURISDICTION AND POWERS OF IATs
    See also: I.2.31; II.0.6; II.2.511

"[12] It is settled jurisprudence [. . .] that in reviewing decisions imposing a sanction, be it disciplinary or administrative, the Tribunal's scope of review is limited to determining whether: an applicant's due process rights were respected, the facts underlying disciplinary or administrative measures were established, the established facts amount to the conduct foreseen in the rules provided for the applied measure, and the measure was proportionate to the offence (see *Elobaid* UNDT-2017-054 at para. 36 and *Applicant* 2012-UNAT-209)."

[Para. 12]

---

* Summaries prepared by Simona Fanni, Ph.D. in Legal Sciences, Postdoctoral Fellow "Margarita Salas", Universidad de Sevilla, Spain. Text of judgment available online at the Tribunal's Web site <https://www.un.org/en/internaljustice/files/undt/judgments/undt-2021-076.pdf>. Original: English.
** This is not a faithful reproduction of the Table of Contents of the Judgment.

B.

II.0.6   DUE PROCESS
         See also: II.1; II.2.2

"[**14**] The Tribunal notes that the facts reproached to the Applicant are clear in the charge letter, to which the contested decision refers. [...] [**15**] The Tribunal also finds that the Applicant's claims on the regularity of the investigation process are not relevant [...], given that those aspects are [...] related [...] to the decision, which is favourable to the Applicant, not to start a disciplinary proceeding, and that the Applicant did not produce any supporting evidence or specify her claims and their relevance for the measures imposed. [**16**] [...] [T]he Tribunal is satisfied that the Applicant was afforded the opportunity to provide comments related to the administrative measures applied at every step of the process and observes that the Applicant was represented by Counsel as of the issuance of the charge letter. An adversarial examination of the allegations was undertaken, and the Applicant has not challenged this. [**17**] The Tribunal therefore finds that the Applicant's due process rights were respected."

[**Paras. 14, 15, 16, 17**]

II.1   EVIDENCE
         See also: II.1.0; II.1.3; II.1.4; II.2.2

"[**20**] The standard of proof in disciplinary matters resulting on the imposition of administrative measure(s), such as the case in hand, is that of "preponderance of evidence" (see *Elobaid* 2018-UNAT-822, para. 35). [...] [**21**] The Tribunal observes that the contested decision is grounded in a finding that the Applicant's behaviour did not meet the standards expected of an international civil servant at her seniority level as, for instance, set forth in the opening sentence of sec. 2.3 of UNICEF Executive Directive CF/EXD/2012-007 [...], which *inter alia* calls for managers to act "as role models by upholding the highest standards of conduct and by promoting a harmonious working environment". [...] [**22**] Although the Tribunal acknowledges that the allegations [...] could not give rise to disciplinary proceedings, it also finds that the supporting documentation provided the decision-maker with reasonable grounds to consider them as established facts under the applicable standard of proof. [**23**] Consequently, the Tribunal finds that the facts in support of the administrative measures imposed were established as per the applicable standard of proof."

[**Paras. 20, 21, 22, 23**]

I.2.31   ACTS AND DECISIONS OF INTERNATIONAL ORGANIZATIONS
          See also: I.2.2; I.2.217; II.2.2; II.7.1026

"[**24**] The Applicant [...] challenges the imposed administrative measures arguing [...] that they constitute disguised disciplinary measures and [...] that they are disproportionate to the conduct alleged. [**29**] From the [...] legal and jurisprudential framework [respectively, staff rule 10.2 and UNICEF Executive Directives CF/EXD/2012-005 and CF/EXD/2012-007, and *Elobaid* 2018-UNAT-822, para. 35], as well as from the parties' pleadings on the issue, it stems the following. [**30**] First, that the measures at stake are different in nature, conditions, scope and consequences. In particular, disciplinary measures are intended to punish the infringement by the staff member of his/her duty inherent the working relationship and presuppose a fact of misconduct, specifically provided in the rules as such and punished. On the contrary, administrative measures can be taken in cases where a staff member's conduct does not rise to the level of misconduct, but a managerial action is nevertheless required; their function is preventive, corrective and cautionary in nature. [33] Second, the Organization has a right to apply disciplinary or administrative measures, following its discretionary evaluation of the relevance of the reproached facts, on a staff member who has failed to comply with his or her obligations under the Charter of the United Nations, the Staff Regulations and Staff Rules or the relevant administrative issuances, or to observe the standards of conduct expected of an international civil servant. [34] Third, a non-disciplinary ("managerial") action can be taken in cases where a staff member's conduct does not rise to the level of misconduct but there was nonetheless "a factual basis for the allegations". [35] Fourth, [. . .] the administration is bestowed with the discretionary authority to impose a disciplinary or an administrative measure and the Dispute Tribunal is to determine if the decision is legal, rational, procedurally correct, and proportionate [. . .]. It is not the role of the Dispute Tribunal to consider the correctness of the choice made by the Administration amongst the various courses of action open to it, nor is it the role of the Tribunal to substitute its own decision for that of the Administration."

[**Paras. 24, 29, 30, 33, 34, 35**]

I.2.31   ACTS AND DECISIONS OF INTERNATIONAL ORGANIZATIONS
            See also: II.2.2

"[39] [. . .] [T]he Tribunal observes that the content of the reprimand letter is not of a punitive nature but of an informative nature as it brings to the Applicant's attention shortcomings in her behaviour as a senior manager expected to serve as a role model for the staff members supervised. [40] With respect to [. . .] the Applicant's two-year re-moval of supervisory functions and the requirement to undertake training, as well as the retention period [. . .] of the written reprimand in the Applicant's OSF, the Tribunal finds [. . .] that they are not punitive but preventive, corrective and cautionary in nature. [42] [. . .] [Moreover,] the Tribunal underlines that the Applicant shares responsibility with its employing entity to have [. . .] [the] training materialize and [. . .] finds the issue not rel-evant for the adjudication of the case at hand. [43] The Tribunal reiterates that the admin-istrative measures imposed on the Applicant are limited in time [. . .] [whilst] disciplinary measures [. . .] have lasting effects. [44] Moreover, [. . .] [differently from] disciplinary measures, the administrative measures taken do not bar the Applicant from seeking other positions within or outside UNICEF [. . .]."

[**Paras. 39, 40, 42, 43, 44**]

I.2.31   ACTS AND DECISIONS OF INTERNATIONAL ORGANIZATIONS
            See also: I.2.2; II.1.0; II.2.2; II.2.511

"[48] The Tribunal finds that the administrative measures imposed on the Applicant were rational and proportionate to the established facts, as well as to address the concerns that UNICEF had about her conduct, and did not constitute disguised disciplinary measures as they are of a different nature than disciplinary measures, targeted specific behaviours, have a limited application in time, and do not necessarily play a role in future selection exercises. [49] [. . .] The Tribunal reiterates its finding that the facts in support of the imposed ad-ministrative measures were established as per the required standard and, recalling that it is settled jurisprudence that an applicant has the burden of proving bad faith on the part of the Organization, finds that the Applicant has failed to prove the alleged flaws of the decision-making process. [50] In sum, the Tribunal finds that the decision to impose administrative measures on the Applicant was procedurally and legally sound, as well as factually supported."

[Paras. 48, 49, 50]

III.

II.2.5   JUDGMENT/DECISION/ORDER
            See also: II.7.10211; II.7.102161

"[**51**] In view of the foregoing, the Tribunal rejects the application in its entirety."

[Para. 51]

XII.2.4

G. (Nos. 7 and 8) and V. (No. 8) v. EPO, ILOAT, 132nd Session, Judgment No. 4430, 7 July 2021*

Contents**

   I. INTRODUCTION AND PROCEDURAL BACKGROUND

   II. CONSIDERATIONS

   III. JUDGMENT

I.

II.2.0   INSTITUTION AND COURSE OF PROCEEDINGS
            See also: I.2.31; II.2.02; II.2.022; II.7.102; II.7.10215

"[The complaints in these proceedings were filed against the European Patent Office (EPO) by Mr. G., one on 19 September 2019 and the other on 1 October 2019, and by Ms. V, on 8 October 2019. All complaints related to the fact that] [**1**] [i]n 2013 the Administrative Council of the EPO, by decision CA/D 5/13 of 27 June 2013, amended the Service Regulations to add Article 30a concerning the right to strike and related changes to Articles 63 and 65 concerning directly or indirectly the reduction of remuneration when a staff member was absent from work or on strike. These changes took effect on 1 July 2013. On 28 June 2013 the President promulgated [...] Circular No. 347, entitled "Guidelines applicable in the event of strike", again effective 1 July 2013. [**2**] Mr G. was a member of the staff of the EPO at relevant times. [...] [H]e submitted two requests for review, one challenging decision CA/D 5/13 and the other challenging Circular No. 347. The procedural paths those requests took [...] resulted in two internal appeals, recommendations by the Appeals Committee and ultimately a decision of 16 September 2019 of the Vice-President of DG4, acting on delegation from the President, to reject both appeals as irreceivable and, in any event, unfounded. [**3**] [Therefore,] Mr G. has filed [his] two complaints [...] in the Tribunal impugning the decision to reject his appeals. [...] [**4**] Mr G.'s complaints should be joined so one judgment can be rendered. Also [...] [the] complaint [filed] in virtually identical terms by Ms V., also an EPO staff member, challenging Circular No. 347, [...] should [...] be joined with the other two complaints and a single judgment will be rendered."

[**Paras. 1, 2, 3, 4**]

II.

I.2.31   ACTS AND DECISIONS OF INTERNATIONAL ORGANIZATIONS
            See also: I.0.136; II.2.511; II.7.1026

"[**11**] [...] In these proceedings the complainants seek relief that, in substance, involves a declaration that CA/D 5/13 and Circular No. 347 are each unlawful and that each should

---

* Summaries prepared by Simona Fanni, Ph.D. in Legal Sciences, Postdoctoral Fellow "Margarita Salas", Universidad de Sevilla, Spain. Text of judgment available online at the Tribunal's Web site <https://www.ilo.org/dyn/triblex/triblexmain.fullText?p_lang=en&p_judgment_no=4430&p_language_code=EN>. Original: English.

** This is not a faithful reproduction of the Table of Contents of the Judgment.

be set aside. As to the Circular, the Tribunal is satisfied, having regard to its case law and its Statute, that it has jurisdiction to declare the Circular unlawful and set it aside (see, for example, Judgments 2857, 3522 and 3513). The position is not so clear in relation to CA/D 5/13 which, if it were set aside, would likely have the legal effect of setting aside current (at least as at the time the proceedings in the Tribunal were commenced) provisions of the Service Regulations. While the Tribunal can examine the lawfulness of provisions of a general decision (see, for example, Judgments 92, consideration 3, 2244, consideration 8, and 4274, consideration 4) [as Circular No. 347], whether it has jurisdiction to set aside a provision of the Service Regulations is a significant legal question on which the Tribunal's case law is unclear. It should be resolved in an appropriate case by a plenary panel of the Tribunal constituted by seven judges, which is not presently possible. It is, in the Tribunal's view, of no material consequence to the complainants that the issue of whether CA/D 5/13 should be set aside remains unresolved. The normative legal document, Circular No. 347, which had the most immediate, adverse and far reaching effect on the complainants' right to strike is, generally described, an implementing rule. If the Circular were found to be unlawful, any moral damages to which the complainants would be entitled by virtue of establishing the Circular was unlawful would be no different if, additionally, they had established that CA/D 5/13 should be set aside."

[**Para. 11**]

I.0.136   GLOBAL SOCIAL RIGHTS (HEALTH, LABOUR, ETC.)
             See also: I.2.2; II.2.511

"[**13**] It has long been recognised that staff of international organisations have a right to strike and that generally it is lawful to exercise that right (see, for example, Judgment 2342, consideration 5). Employees who strike by ceasing work are deploying a tool incidental to collective bargaining to place pressure on their employer, often in the context of a dispute about preserving or improving wages and working conditions, workplace safety, dismissals and freedom of association amongst other things. It is a tool employees have to redress the imbalance of power between them and their employer. Absent a right to strike, it is open to an employer to ignore entreaties by employees advanced collectively to consider, let alone respond to, their grievances about wages and working conditions or, additionally but not exhaustively, the other matters referred to at the beginning of this consideration. However, at least ordinarily, the price the employees pay for deploying the tool is that they forfeit the remuneration they would otherwise have received had they worked (see, for example, Judgment 615, consideration 4)."

[**Para. 13**]

I.2.31   ACTS AND DECISIONS OF INTERNATIONAL ORGANIZATIONS
             See also: I.0.136; II.2.511; II.7.1026

"[**14**] The promulgation of Circular No. 347 is a general decision of the President. [...] [T]here is Tribunal case law to the effect that a general decision cannot be challenged by a staff member unless and until an individual decision is taken. But the Tribunal's case law contains an exception or limitation. As the Tribunal said in Judgment 3761 at consideration 14:

"In general, [an administrative decision of general application] is not subject to challenge until an individual decision adversely affecting the individual involved has been taken. However there are exceptions where the general decision does not require an implementing decision and immediately and adversely affects individual rights."

[15] In the absence of any implementing decision, the question that then arises is whether, in relation to the complainants, there has been an immediate and adverse effect on individual rights. The Tribunal is satisfied there has been. Circular No. 347 did have an immediate and adverse effect on the complainants' right to strike. It is immaterial that they did not go on strike in June 2013 or that circumstances had not arisen where one or a number of the provisions of the Circular operated on or applied to conduct of the complainants. The effect was immediate because, at the date of promulgation of the Circular, it legally constrained future exercise of the right to strike or imposed burdens to the same effect. The complaints are receivable."

[Paras. 14, 15]

I.2.31   ACTS AND DECISIONS OF INTERNATIONAL ORGANIZATIONS
        See also: I.0.136; II.2.511

"[16] The Tribunal now considers the lawfulness of the Circular. [...] A review of its provisions reveals the following:
    (i) [as to] Circular No. 347, paragraph 1[,] [...] [f]irstly, it travels beyond the definition in the amended Service Regulations. It cannot do so as a subordinate normative legal document (Judgment 3534). Secondly, "go slow" and "work to rule" are legitimate forms of industrial action protected by the ordinary conception of the right to strike. Accordingly, by declaring that employees engaging in these forms of industrial action did not have the "protection granted by the right to strike" as ordinarily understood, this provision violated the right to strike. (ii) Circular No. 347, paragraph 2: by imposing a minimum of 10 per cent of employees who may call for a strike, the Circular violated the right to strike of any employee who, in combination with others, may wish to strike where the total number of employees is less than 10 per cent. (iii) Circular No. 347, paragraph 3: if the class who have a right to vote on whether the strike should start extends beyond (and potentially well beyond) the employees who wish to strike, then that wider class has a capacity to veto the strike. This problem is compounded by the percentages [...] at the conclusion of this provision. Additionally, the requirement that the vote be conducted by the Office violated the right to strike. Employees themselves should be able to make arrangements for the vote (see Judgment 403, consideration 3). (iv) Circular No. 347, paragraph 4: the time limit placed on the duration of strike violated the right to strike. Striking staff should be able, themselves, to determine the length of the strike. [17] Having regard to the aforementioned violations of the right to strike, which infect Circular No. 347 in its entirety, the Circular is unlawful and should be set aside."

[Paras. 16, 17]

I.8.46   RIGHT TO COMPENSATION
        See also: II.7.10210

"[18] The complainants are entitled to moral damages for the injurious impact of the Circular on their right to strike, which resulted in the diminution of their fundamental right to freedom of association. These are assessed in the sum of 2,000 euros for each complainant. They are each entitled to costs in the sum of 800 euros."

[Para. 18]

III.

II.2.5   JUDGMENT/DECISION/ORDER
             See also: II.7.10210; II.7.10211; II.7.102151

" For the above reasons,
    1. Circular No. 347 is set aside.
    2. The EPO shall pay each complainant moral damages in the amount of 2,000 euros.
    3. The EPO shall pay each complainant 800 euros costs.
    4. All other claims and the application to intervene are dismissed."

Systematic Key Items of the Section*

---

* *See* Systematic Classification Scheme, *supra* at page 255.

PART
6

RECENT LINES OF INTERNATIONALIST THOUGHT

PART

6

RECENT LINES OF
INTERNATIONALIST
THOUGHT

The Emerging Ethics Evolution: The Evasive Connection Between Environmental Crimes, Philosophical Considerations of Public International Law, and the International Criminal Court's Twentieth Anniversary

BY ANJA MATWIJKIW* &
BRONIK MATWIJKIW**

* Anja Matwijkiw, Professor of Ethics & Human Rights, Indiana University Graduate School and the Philosophy Program, Indiana University Northwest (IUN); Affiliated Faculty, Institute for European Studies, IU Bloomington, US; Affiliated/Visiting Researcher, Faculty of Law, University of Zagreb, Croatia.
** Bronik Matwijkiw, Affiliated/Visiting Researcher, Faculty of Law, University of Zagreb, Croatia.

    Both authors wish to warmly thank Vice-Dean for International and Interinstitutional Cooperation and Quality Management prof. dr. sc. Iris Goldner Lang for approving their research partnership with the Chair of Criminal Law at the Faculty of Law, University of Zagreb, Croatia. Anja Matwijkiw extends her gratitude to the Office of Academic Affairs at IUN for awarding her a 2021–2022 research grant for "Stakeholders and Philosophical Components of International Law." Furthermore, she would like to thank President Hans Köchler, The International Progress Organization (IPO), who invited her to The Imperial Roundtable in Vienna in 2020 for an IPO consultation on "Responsibility in International Relations." The event had to be postponed due to the COVID-19 pandemic, but some of the findings inspired the completion, in April and May, of the collaborative research for this essay.

Anja Matwijkiw and Bronik Matwijkiw, *The Emerging Ethics Evolution: The Evasive Connection Between Environmental Crimes, Philosophical Considerations of Public International Law, and the International Criminal Court's Twentieth Anniversary* In: *The Global Community Yearbook of International Law and Jurisprudence 2022*. Edited by: Giuliana Ziccardi Capaldo, Oxford University Press.
© Oxford University Press 2023. DOI: 10.1093/oso/9780197752265.003.0037

Abstract

In terms of modern international responsibility, justice has played a role since the 1945 UN Charter, just as legal accountability for serious crimes is central to that same value. With Responsibility to Protect (R2P), the growing need for more than conventional *cum* traditional measures resulted in the emergence of an(other) innovative protection tool. However, the question of new norm-recognition appears to be prone to stalemates even in situations where survival is at stake. There is a mismatch for the same reason, and the International Criminal Court (ICC) cannot avoid the effects of this. The twentieth anniversary of the ICC coincides with a reality of doctrinal division. Philosophical *jus cogens* considerations point in different directions, *inter alia*, when it comes to the possibility of a crime typology that includes ecocide. Contemporary outlooks may factor in both morality and human rights. The paradox is: this is no guarantee against skepticism or a narrowing of the scope.

I. INTRODUCTION

That justice has been a component in international law's incremental progress procedurally and substantially is an evidence-based evolutionary claim which is as indisputable for the last part of the twentieth century and the first part of the twenty-first century as it is important for future developments. Furthermore, the endeavor to balance law and morality no longer causes severe conceptual cramps among architects of legal doctrine. In the modern era of globalization, the legacy of legal positivism, the so-called "separation thesis" (of law and morality) may still be attractive to international human rights attorneys who are concerned about the day-to-day workings of the law.[1] However, it is very unlikely that they would argue that justice is a purely formal concept that only concerns rule-application. It is too much of a stretch, though, to infer that they would therefore agree with the *lex iniusta non est lex* maxim. It is less of a stretch to purport that humanistic values found an expression in the wake of the mass atrocities and gross human rights violations of World War II.[2] As a realm, public international law (PIL), which includes international criminal law (ICL), arguably absorbed some of the central insights in its body of norms and did so simultaneously with the emergence of international tribunals and courts as best practices.[3] Sixty years after the establishment of the paradigm for international criminal justice (ICJ), namely, the International Military Tribunal at Nuremberg

---

[1] While legal positivism does not simplistically deny that there are important connections between law and morality, the assumption is that there is a fundamental aspect of law that does not depend on morality, as in the classical statement: "the existence of the law is one thing; its merit or demerit is another." *See* JOHN AUSTIN, THE PROVINCE OF JURISPRUDENCE DETERMINED 157 (1995) (1832).

[2] As the term "humanistic" suggests, the values derive from humanism or the humanities. In terms of the law, this means that an interdisciplinary interpretation is inescapable. Furthermore, ethics as a branch of philosophy is central to humanitarian law. For an account of the ethical origins of humanitarian action, *see* HUGO SLIM, HUMANITARIAN ETHIC: A GUIDE TO THE MORALITY OF AID IN WAR AND DISASTER (2015).

[3] In the case of the International Military Tribunal at Nuremberg (IMT), did law and morality create a new connection or did the law complete an integration that had not been technically expressed? Whether moral rules/principles also qualify as rules of law depends on the philosophy of law position, more precisely, the debate and dispute between legal positivism and natural law theory. Legal positivists would deny a connection between "crimes against humanity" (CAH) and legal validity or positive law, especially if they, like Austin, equate customary international law with (positive international) morality. Note that 2012 UN developments can be construed as evidence of legal norms that require *both* just/fair (formal *cum* procedural) rule-application (*cf.* law-enforcement) *and* just/fair (moral *cum* substantive) law-making. *See* UN

(IMT), yet another "Never Again!" strategy appeared: the Responsibility to Protect (R2P) principle. This 2005 event introduced a comparatively more comprehensive (and consequently corrective measure for a narrow *cum* judicial) response to the most serious crimes. Very briefly, R2P is innovative in its approach to international responsibility by virtue of presenting a three-pillar notion, which lists the proactive role of the state *first*.[4] However, the new millennium R2P also inherited some challenges. For example, the connection between core international crimes and *jus cogens* norms and, furthermore, between *jus cogens* norms and human rights continues to raise questions. It is the latter and less explored connection that constitutes one of the focal points of this essay.[5] In particular, the absence of a general rights theory poses a problem for interpretation. If contemporary architects of legal doctrine proceed with scattered remarks rather than an actual framework, the interpretation of views that may even be quite influential becomes

---

General Assembly (GA), Declaration of the High-Level Meeting of the General Assembly on the Rule of Law at the National and International Levels, A/RES/67/1, paras. 2 and 25 (Nov. 30, 2012) [hereinafter 2012 Declaration on the Rule of Law]. For positive law as a broad phenomenon that includes resolutions, recommendations, declarations and similar examples of (non-standard) evidence, *see* Anja Matwijkiw & Bronik Matwijkiw, *The Unapologetic Integration of Ethics: Stakeholder Realignments in the Light of Global Law and Shared Governance Doctrine.—Distilling the Essence of Giuliana Ziccardi Capaldo's Jurisprudential Paradigm-Shifts*, 15 GLOBAL COMMUNITY YILJ 2015 (Giuliana Ziccardi Capaldo General ed.) 885, 898–899 (2016) [hereinafter *The Unapologetic Integration of Ethics*]. For the IMT as a rule of law "revolution" that secured, *inter alia*, due process, *see* KERSTIN BREE CARLSON, MODEL(ING) JUSTICE: PERFECTING THE PROMISE OF INTERNATIONAL CRIMINAL LAW 24 (2018). For an account of different legal positivists like H.L.A. Hart and Austin (viewed as "the last influential denier" of a proper international province), *see* Mehrdad Payandeh, *The Concept of International Law in the Jurisprudence of H.L.A. Hart*, 21(4) EUROPEAN JOURNAL OF INTERNATIONAL LAW 967, 969, 975, 977, 978–979 (2011).

[4] According to James Pattison, post-2005 developments are sometimes not captured in accounts of R2P:

> The 2001 report of the International Commission on Intervention and State Sovereignty (ICISS) on R2P provides perhaps the most detailed account of the various responsibilities involved, dividing it into the responsibilities to "prevent", to "react", and to "rebuild". But, of course, the account of the R2P adopted at the 2005 UN World Summit, and that has since developed, is different to the account of the R2P in this report. Various responsibilities of the R2P in its post-2005 incarnation are often mooted, including the "responsibility to prosecute", the "duty of conduct"/"responsibility to try", the "responsibility not to veto", the duty to undertake military intervention, and, less often, the "responsibility to rebuild". However, the existing accounts of the international responsibilities of R2P in its post-2005 incarnation are often fairly ad hoc and are not clearly systematised, largely focusing on particular responsibilities.

See James Pattison, *Mapping the Responsibilities to Protect: A Typology of International Duties*, 7(2) GLOBAL RESPONSIBILITY TO PROTECT 190, 191 (2015) [hereinafter *Mapping the Responsibilities to Protect*]. For a list of the key documents for the three-pillar R2P, see the Global Centre for the Responsibility to Protect, https://www.globalr2p.org/what-is-r2p/.

[5] The connection between core international crimes and *jus cogens* norms pertains to the ontological discussion of law. Apart from the question of the sources of law, it is disputed *how* rules reach the top part of the legal hierarchy (*cf. jus cogens*), just as the question of *which* rules qualify for *jus cogens* status is a matter of interpretation. Bassiouni accommodates an account of different views while emphasizing that: "[t]he main divisions concern how a given international crime achieves the status of *jus cogens* and the manner in which such crimes satisfy the requirements of the 'principles of legality.'" *See* M. Cherif Bassiouni, *International Crimes: Jus Cogens and Obligatio Erga Omnes*, 59(4) LAW AND CONTEMPORARY PROBLEMS 63, 65 (1996) [hereinafter *International Crimes*].

reconstructive. Critically, this is a flaw in and of itself. However, despite the absence of a general rights theory, the two authors of this essay try to show how and why the "waters part" for different outlooks that otherwise share the premise that there are (basic) human rights that correspond with or to *jus cogens* norms. The main thrust of the investigation of the selected trends is to create a suitable general jurisprudence platform for the debate and dispute about which crimes the permanent successor to the ad hoc IMT, namely, the International Criminal Court (ICC), ideally and/or progressively should consider for inclusion. *E.g.*, ecocide has been pushed as a candidate by legal thinkers and ethicists alike.[6] With its twentieth anniversary in 2022, the time is ripe—and from the perspective of ethics—a matter of right reason.[7] As a minimum, law's dynamic evolution should not be obstructed to satisfy a doctrinal agenda that disregards the most affected stakes and stakeholders—for this too impacts (the principle of) justice.

To secure a properly contextualized comprehension of the philosophical considerations that, so far, shaped the notion of international responsibility, the analysis takes its starting point in the values that are embodied in the 1949 Charter of the United Nations. The connection between international responsibility and justice presupposes idealism, so it will be shown in section II ("International Responsibility and Accountability as Justice-First Concepts"). Since idealism clashes with *realpolitik*, the former is an uncompromising argument against impunity for *jus cogens* violations. The account is supplemented with some recent issues to demonstrate the constant risk of setbacks. Furthermore, in section III ("*Jus Cogens* and R2P"), the reader will see that there may be a stronger connection between the 1949 document and the R2P development than first assumed. This necessitates a subtraction from R2P defined as an "international ethical norm."[8] Furthermore, it will become clear that the connection between *jus cogens* and R2P entails a predicament because R2P prevention may be analytically distinguished from the promotion of human rights. This predicament is especially thought-provoking in light of the fact that the various outlooks discussed in this essay share the correspondence premise, as already mentioned. That granted, the two authors place the emphasis on M. Cherif Bassiouni's legal doctrine. His outlook best captures the struggles of a reform-friendly thinker caught in the tension area between the progressive and the conventional.

---

6 Sunčana Roksandić Vidlička, *Systemic Deprivation of Access to Essential Medicine and Medical Care—A Crime Against Humanity?*, in BIOLAW AND INTERNATIONAL CRIMINAL LAW: TOWARDS INTERDISCIPLINARY SYNERGIES 36–37 (Caroline Fournet & Anja Matwijkiw eds., 2021); Anja Matwijkiw & Bronik Matwijkiw, *[Human] Values and Ethics in Environmental Health Discourse and Decision-Making: The Complex Stakeholder Controversy and the Possibility of "Win-Win" Outcomes*, in ENVIRONMENTAL HEALTH IN INTERNATIONAL AND EU LAW: CURRENT CHALLENGES AND LEGAL RESPONSES 3–25, 13, 21(Stefania Negri ed., 2019) [hereinafter *[Human] Values and Ethics in Environmental Health Discourse and Decision-Making*].

7 The expression "right reason" is a placeholder for idealism *cum* natural law theory in Bassiouni's Mixed Theory, which also includes pragmatism *cum* legal positivism. Following Stakeholder Jurisprudence, the expression is about reasoning ethically about rights to secure recognition *in abstraction from* protection. *See* Anja Matwijkiw & Bronik Matwijkiw, *A Modern Perspective on International Criminal Law: Accountability as a Meta-Rights*, in THEORY AND PRACTICE OF INTERNATIONAL CRIMINAL LAW: ESSAYS IN HONOR OF M. CHERIF BASSIOUNI 19–79 (Leila N. Sadat & Michael P. Scharf eds., 2008) [hereinafter *A Modern Perspective on International Criminal Law*]; Anja Matwijkiw & Bronik Matwijkiw, *The Missing Link in Stakeholder Theory: A Philosophical Framework*, 28(1) INTERNATIONAL JOURNAL OF APPLIED PHILOSOPHY 125 (2014) [hereinafter *The Missing Link in Stakeholder Theory*].

8 Typically, R2P is viewed as an emerging standard. However, as such, it made the leap from slogan to international ethical norm. *See* Pinar Gözen Ercan, *R2P: From Slogan to an International Ethical Norm*, 11(43) ULUSLARARASI İLIŞKILER (Turkey) 35 (2014) [hereinafter *R2P*]. For nationalist

The way he tries to resolve the dilemma will be explained in a separate subsection (B. "Bassiouni's Mixed Theory"). Section V ("Two Poles, Two Paths: One and the Same Tension") provides a succinct summary of key points from the doctrinal outlooks. Finally, section VI ("Conclusion: The ICC's Twentieth Anniversary in the Gray Growth Area") contains some food-for-thought reflections.

II. INTERNATIONAL RESPONSIBILITY AND ACCOUNTABILITY AS JUSTICE-FIRST CONCEPTS

According to those commentators on responsibility in international relations who argue that there can be no real peace and security *without* justice, the wording of Article 1(1) of the 1945 UN Charter is problematic by virtue of the risk of *realpolitik* that follows from the frequent and stronger emphasis on "international peace and security" and the "removal of threats to the peace" *in comparison to* justice.[9] Peace and security, so the relevant commentators' argument presupposes, are *not* values that can and, *mutatis mutandis*, should be pursued for their own sake, *as if* the cessation or absence of hostilities is sufficient(ly purposeful).[10] The subtle point is that the limitation presented in the 1945 Charter clause, whereby "conformity with the principles of justice and international law" is stipulated as a requirement, may be (mis)construed along the lines of the distinction between intrinsic and instrumental values, with justice in the role as a *telos*-regulator.[11] However, justice is

---

foreign policy as a threat to R2P defined as a liberal agenda, *see* Cristina G. Stefan, *The Responsibility to Protect: Locating Norm Entrepreneurship*, 35(2) ETHICS & INTERNATIONAL AFFAIRS 197 (2021). For a critique of R2P as a global ethical responsibility that is being transformed into a project of governance, management, and control (thereby *deconstructing* liberalism and cosmopolitanism), *see* ANGELIKI SAMARA, BEYOND THE RESPONSIBILITY TO PROTECT IN INTERNATIONAL LAW: AN ETHICS OF IRRESPONSIBILITY 2021).

[9] United Nations, Charter of the United Nations, 1 UNTS XVI, Oct. 24, 1945 [hereinafter 1945 UN Charter]; Anja Matwijkiw & Bronik Matwijkiw, *Stakeholder Applications: Advantages or Disadvantages for International Criminal Law?*, 14(4–5) INTERNATIONAL CRIMINAL LAW REVIEW 923, 955 (2014) [hereinafter *Stakeholder Applications*]. Bassiouni's position summarizes the precarious predicament for international accountability thus:

> Bartering away justice for political results, albeit in the pursuit of peace, is the goal of most political leaders who seek to end conflicts or facilitate transitions to non-tyrannical regimes. The grim reality is that in order to obtain peace, negotiations must be held with the very leaders who frequently are ones who committed, ordered, or allowed atrocious crimes to be committed. Thus, the choice presented to negotiators is whether to have peace or justice. Sometimes this dichotomy is presented along more sophisticated lines: peace now, and justice some other time.

> *See* M. Cherif Bassiouni, *The Need for International Accountability*, *in* INTERNATIONAL CRIMINAL LAW: INTERNATIONAL ENFORCEMENT (M. Cherif Bassiouni ed., 2008); M. Cherif Bassiouni, *The Chicago Principles on Post-Conflict Justice* 8 (2007), https://law.depaul.edu/academics/centers-institutes-initiatives/international-human-rights-law-institute/projects/Documents/chicago_principles.pdf.

[10] In other words, the unqualified assumption that peace/security is preferable to conflict/violence misses the point.

[11] 1945 UN Charter, *supra* note 9, at art. 1(1). Thus, the *telos*, the end-goal (*cf.* peace and security) must and, *mutatis mutandis*, should be accomplished through just, legal, and peaceful means. In contrast to this position, the argument that justice is not merely a means (for peace and security) but also an end in itself is advanced, thereby making a concession to the possibility of the peace/security and justice dichotomy without underestimating the superior value of peace/security over violence and political tyranny.

about *more* than ending persecution, violence, and victimization "as a brief interlude between conflicts" or safeguarding against harmful outcomes of *alleged* conflict-resolution, *e.g.*, a "strict law and order" situation where the tensions *cum* reasons that originally led to the conflict remain.[12] On Bassiouni's premises, justice not only concerns pragmatism (*cf.* justice as an effective instrument for long-term or sustainable peace/security), but also idealism, more precisely, "certain humanistic values" that international criminal law (ICL) is a reflection of and which therefore have to be "expressed."[13] Admittedly, a *sui generis* description of the conflict may be used as an argument against a uniform conflict-resolution formula—and consequently a leap to the (*realpolitik*) strategy of bartering away (justice in the form of) accountability—"for the leader's values, expectations, personal ambitions, positioning of power . . . usually through the mediation efforts of other leaders"—could be a small one.[14] However, accountability is not only a bridge between peace/security and justice; it is also a "tool box."[15] As such, it comes with the concession that post-conflict management is inconsistent with a "one shoe fits all" policy while at the same time cementing a "bottom line" as a constant: no impunity for mass atrocities.[16] This is the appropriate way of

---

[12] Note that this jeopardizes reconciliation and co-existence on Bassiouni's premises rather than the stability that the 1945 UN Charter mentions. Note also that there is a distinction between conflict resolution and conflict prevention and, therefore, an interpretation of the 1945 UN Charter as an instrument that "provides the foundation for a comprehensive and long-term approach to conflict prevention [based on an expanded concept of peace and security]" does not affect the point in question. *See* M. Cherif Bassiouni, *Searching for Peace and Achieving Justice: The Need for Accountability*, 59(4) LAW AND CONTEMPORARY PROBLEMS 9, 12–13, 19, 23–24 (1996) [hereinafter, *Searching for Peace and Achieving Justice*]. For "normalization" as a failed post-conflict justice strategy of the 2011 civil unrest in Bahrain, *see* Anja Matwijkiw & Bronik Matwijkiw, *Bahrain Anno 2017: Peace or Regime Change? The Ongoing Human Rights Dilemma and the Ethics Pillar as a Measurement*, 17 GLOBAL COMMUNITY YILJ 2017 (Giuliana Ziccardi Capaldo General ed.) 131, 133 (2018).

[13] The Grotius Centre for International Legal Studies, *Professor M. Cherif Bassiouni on the Future of International Criminal Justice* (interview), Sept. 2015, https://www.facebook.com/GrotiusCentreLeiden University/videos/10155918105168938/.

[14] Bassiouni, *Searching for Peace and Achieving Justice, supra* note 12, at 12–13, 27. For the link between *realpolitik* and amoralism, and the amoralist's dependency on the moral community, *see* Anja Matwijkiw & Bronik Matwijkiw, *International Relations Begin at Home: A Humanitarian Learning Lesson from the Kingdom of Denmark*, 15(1) INTERNATIONAL STUDIES JOURNAL 103, 121 (2018) [hereinafter *International Relations Begin at Home*]. Note that UN rule of law developments towards inclusion of members of the civil society at the national and international level lessens the vulnerability from dependency on trustworthy people in high offices. *See* UN GA, 2012 Declaration on the Rule of Law, *supra* note 3, at para. 38.

[15] Note that strategies to "prevent, deter, punish and rehabilitate" are all in the toolbox. *See* Bassiouni, *Searching for Peace and Achieving Justice, supra* note 12, at 13, 27.

[16] The response was made applicable, in 1971—in the area of cooperation and international responsibility—to conform with the purposes and principles of the 1945 UN Charter. Bassiouni refers to the UN GA Resolution on War Criminals (G.S. Res. 2840 (XXVI) 26 UN GAOR (Supp. No. 29), 88, UN Doc. 8429 (1971)). *See* Bassiouni, *Searching for Peace and Achieving Justice, supra* note 12, at 16. Note that together with *jus cogens* criminality, the Universal Declaration of Human Rights (1948) comprises the "bottom line" for Bassiouni, thereby creating a crime-rights connection, contrary to theorists who deny that absolute *cum* criminal obligations are relevant for a debate on rights. Note also that the 2012 Declaration on the Rule of Law has a policy of zero tolerance for genocide, war crimes, and crimes against humanity. *See* M. Cherif Bassiouni, *Perspectives on International Criminal Justice*, 50 VIRGINIA JOURNAL OF INTERNATIONAL LAW 270, 283–284 (2010); Anja Matwijkiw & Bronik Matwijkiw, *Stakeholder Theory and Justice Issues: The Leap from Business Management to Contemporary International Law*, 10(2) INTERNATIONAL CRIMINAL LAW REVIEW 143, 160 (2010) [hereinafter *Stakeholder Theory and Justice Issues*]; UN GA, 2012 Declaration on the Rule of Law, *supra* note 3, at, para. 22.

ending the "tug-of-war" between peace/security and justice perceived as "competing" or "conflicting" values, *in favor of* "commonly shared human values."[17] In addition, it appears that a response of zero tolerance (*cf.* no impunity) should (ideally) be the global constitutional principle, thereby making full sense of the value-communality in the era of globalization.[18] In Bassiouni's words, if "the substance of law is not bound by higher values and principles, law too easily becomes an instrument for the pursuit of totalitarian power at the expense of the best interest of the collectivity."[19] It follows that pragmatism should be in the service of idealism; and that idealism creates links with democracy, as well as humanism and universalism. But, there is *still more* to justice—for whenever the best interest of the collectivity is neglected, morality is undermined. This puts ethics on a dual track. The deontological theory about equal respect for human dignity that informs human rights as individual rights is not inherently pitted against public stakes, although the "exercise of [human] rights" may be restricted in certain circumstances.[20] In other words, norm-conferment is

---

[17] Historically, peace has been favored over justice until this trend "shifted" in the direction of emphasizing justice and peace goals for the international community "in the last two decades," so Bassiouni states while writing in 2010. Unfortunately, it may not be the interest in "human values" but instead "economic reasons" that brought the otherwise "competing" or "conflicting" values (*cf.* justice and peace) closer together, thereby favoring the constellation of *realpolitik* and pragmatism. *See* Bassiouni, *Perspectives on International Criminal Justice, supra* note 16, at 283.

[18] Giuliana Ziccardi Capaldo, *Global Constitutionalism and Global Governance: Towards a UN-Driven Global Constitutional Governance Model, in* GLOBALIZATION AND ITS IMPACT ON THE FUTURE OF HUMAN RIGHTS AND INTERNATIONAL CRIMINAL JUSTICE 629–662 (M. Cherif Bassiouni ed., 2015). For obstructions (procedural as well as substantive aspects) to the no-impunity principle as a norm that transcends the international constitutional framework of the 1945 UN Charter, *see* Giuliana Ziccardi Capaldo, *No-Impunity as a Global Constitutional Principle*, OUPBLOG (GLOBAL COMMUNITY YILJ), Jan. 11, 2018, https://blog.oup.com/2018/01/no-impunity-constitutional/; Anja Matwijkiw, *The No Impunity Policy in International Criminal Law: Justice versus Revenge*, 9 INTERNATIONAL CRIMINAL LAW REVIEW 1 (2009) [hereinafter *The No Impunity Policy in International Criminal Law*].

[19] Note the implication, *viz.*, that justice and humanist(ic) values are legal imperatives. *See* M. CHERIF BASSIOUNI, CRIMES AGAINST HUMANITY: HISTORICAL EVOLUTION AND CONTEMPORARY APPLICATION 16 (2011) [hereinafter CRIMES AGAINST HUMANITY]. For the broadening of the United Nations' concept of justice— from a (formal *cum*) procedural to a (moral *cum*) substantive requirement, *see* UN GA, 2012 Rule of Law Declaration, *supra* note 3. For specific values, *e.g.*, justice, the inherent value of human life, and democracy, and, furthermore, for a general requirement of balancing reality (economic, legal, political, *etc.*) and morality (justice), *see* Bassiouni, *The Chicago Principles on Post-Conflict Justice, supra* note 9, at vi, 5, 7–8, 11, 24, 55, 59.

[20] The traditional contrast between deontological and teleological *cum* utilitarian ethics remains unaffected. At the same time, international law presents a particular perspective on human rights because of the distinction between rights-recognition and rights-protection, meaning that the credentials for the former do *not* borrow from the measures that inform the latter, such as "duties," "powers," and "choices." The distinction in question divides the two main traditions in general rights theory, respectively so-called Will or Choice Theory along the lines of H.L.A. Hart's outlook and modern Interest Theory as an alternative to this. Advocates of Will or Choice Theory make rightsholders duty-controllers in accordance with individual autonomy, which is also why it is absurd to talk about "criminal rights" because these presuppose absolute duties. Modern Interest Theory, on the other hand, rejects the doctrinal premises that underpin Hart's outlook, *viz.*, the logical correlativity thesis for rights and duties, the interest-incompatibility thesis for values, and the separation thesis for law and morality, thereby *broadening* the scope of rights to encompass, *per* the United Nations, "all human rights." *See* Anja Matwijkiw & Bronik Matwijkiw, *Stakeholder Jurisprudence: The New Way in Human Rights*, PROCEEDINGS TO THE 25TH IVR WORLD CONGRESS 1, 12–13 (2012); Anja Matwijkiw, *The Dangers of the Obvious but Often Disregarded Details in the International Criminal Law Demarcation Debate: Norm-Integration*

not jeopardized under international law if it is practically impossible to guarantee the objects of human rights; just as utilitarianism (*cf.* teleological ethics) has typically functioned as a tool for the promotion of the value of welfare (*cf.* freedom from want).[21] This is due to its emphasis on the quantitative and, for the same reason, the scientific and objective, at least so some theorists believe.[22] The United Nations has an open variable for the economic system. However, the structural designs of the welfare state may reduce sections of the population to the "status" of passive income recipients whose daily lives are controlled by the public authorities in return for subsistence, thereby continuing an analogy to the feudal society that historically preceded the capitalist arrangement with "power to choose" market opportunities as the transition phase to generalized emancipation.[23] The additional rights are limited to individual and personal liberties (*cf.* civil/political rights as anchored in the autonomy of that particular person), but this finding does not remove the thorn from recent and precarious sacrifices of universal human values in favor of "claims of nationalistic cultural rights," here citing from Bassiouni's scholarship.[24] The effects

---

and the Triple-Thesis "Argument," 20 INTERNATIONAL CRIMINAL LAW REVIEW 759 (2020) [hereinafter *The Dangers of the Obvious but Often Disregarded Details in the International Criminal Law Demarcation Debate*].

[21] In the case of the modern welfare state where the government not only guarantees welfare provisions in terms of rights but also restricts individual liberties (*e.g.*, freedom of mobility) if and when recipients "choose" to receive the objects of their rights, welfare becomes an ideology. Ironically, this repeats the interest-incompatibility doctrine from liberal and libertarian schools of thought that assume that values like welfare and freedom are mutually exclusive. Note the analogy between this finding and Stefan's criticism of R2P as a project of governance, management, and control. *See supra* notes 8 and 20.

[22] The distinction between the quantitative and the qualitative generates a debate and a dispute about the use of the natural sciences as the criterion for objectivity. Since the qualitative or value-laden is relegated to the subjective, a loss of rationality or cognitive meaningfulness of statements follows. On the other hand, if the quantitative is factored into justice considerations, this creates an advantage for accommodations of socioeconomic aspects which, in turn, introduces a tension with the claim of American Legal Process Theory (ALPT), that needs are "person-centric" and "subjective." This view, at best, shows ignorance about the logic of extensionality pertaining to needs. *See* Mary Ellen O'Connell, *Jus Cogens: International Law's Higher Ethical Norms, in* THE ROLE OF ETHICS IN INTERNATIONAL LAW 93–94 (Donald E. Childress III ed., 2012) [hereinafter *Jus Cogens*]; Matwijkiw & Matwijkiw, *Stakeholder Theory and Justice Issues, supra* note 16, at 162–163.

[23] Milton Friedman equates socialism, including the welfare state ideology, with totalitarianism. Ethically, the pursuit of "public stakes" or "the best interest of the collectivity" are perceived as illiberal impositions whenever they extend beyond the principle of voluntarism or are the outcomes of paternalist policies. Like Hannah Arendt, talk about the capitalist class system reduces to a myth. *See* MILTON FRIEDMAN, CAPITALISM AND FREEDOM 7, 10, 133 (2002) (1962). For the way that "resource weak" citizens are negatively affected and even criminalized in Odsherred, Denmark, *see* Birgitte Søe, *Justitia: Rigidt regelsystem udfordrer ressourcesvage borgeres retssikkerhed*, ALTINGET, Sept. 30, 2019; Anne Bonnevie Lundbye, *Arbejdsløse Juan føler sig overvåget af kommunen*, TV2ØST, Feb. 20, 2019, https://www.tv2east.dk/odsherred/arbejdslose-juan-foler-sig-overvaget-af-kommunen. For the right to self-determination, *see* UN GA, Covenant on Economic, Social and Cultural Rights, RES 2200A (XXI), art. 1 (Dec. 16, 1966).

[24] "Human rights claims derived from globalization" are sacrificed for "*their* interpretations of cultural relativism and claims of nationalistic cultural rights. Cultural differences continue to stand in the way of universality of human rights." The interpretations are convenient means because they serve as solidarity blockers. In Bassiouni's words, "Western societies, which are economically among the world's most advanced, have been more resistant . . . to refugees fleeing wars, repressive regimes, economic exploitation, and poverty." *See* M. Cherif Bassiouni, *Human Rights and International Criminal Justice in the Twenty-First Century, in* GLOBALIZATION AND ITS IMPACT ON THE FUTURE OF HUMAN RIGHTS AND INTERNATIONAL CRIMINAL JUSTICE 56–57 (M. Cherif Bassiouni ed., 2015).

span humanitarian protection conditions, environmentally induced or amplified migration,[25] and respect for equality and diversity. *E.g.*, countries like Poland and Hungary have alienated other member states of the European Union by practicing autocratic legalism, which dismantles the constitutional system by law in a piecemeal fashion, just as its illiberal restrictions that, *inter alia*, target women's reproductive rights with a rejection of "nihilism" or produce anti-LGBTIQ legislation cloaked as a pedophilia measure rely on an appeal to the government's "electoral legitimacy."[26] Furthermore, Denmark, which officially commits to liberal democracy, has a two-decades-old record of legal opt-outs in the area of justice and home affairs to adopt "sovereign deterrence measures" (including national laws) that instrumentally are geared towards a reduction of the number and cost of refugees, asylum-seekers, immigrants and, more generally, foreigners.[27] This effort has gone hand in hand with EU-antagonism, anti-globalization, and domestic identity politics where policymakers assume the role of "value warriors" for the purpose of conserving *our national values* by popular demand and, in the process of this, reserve both freedom and welfare for *our own kind* of people.[28] Such a no-solidarity response towards vulnerable members of the minority is an example of a country-specific setback that reinforces the regional democracy crisis.[29]

---

[25] Boudewijn de Bruin. *Against Nationalism: Climate Change, Human Rights, and International Law*, Danish Yearbook of Philosophy 1 (2022), https://doi.org/10.1163/24689300-20221060 [hereinafter *Against Nationalism*].

[26] Anja Matwijkiw & Bronik Matwijkiw, *Liberal Democracy: Absolutist EU Rule of Law Conditionality or a Pluralistic Bargaining Chip?*, 13(2) Optime – Scientific Journal of Albanian University 59, 62, 65 (2021) [hereinafter *Liberal Democracy*]; Kim Lane Scheppele, *Autocratic Legalism*, 85 The University of Chicago Law Review 545, 561–662 (2018).

[27] Thomas Gammeltoft-Hansen, *Refugee Policy as "Negative Nation Branding": The Case of Denmark and the Nordics*, 99 Danish Foreign Policy Yearbook 99, 118 (2017) [hereinafter *Refugee Policy as "Negative Nation Branding"*]. Note that foreigners include the category of so-called "Danes with a different ethnic background." Although born in Denmark as citizens, their different ethnic background makes them vulnerable to marginalization and discrimination.

[28] Illiberal laws like the so-called *burqa* ban (*cf.* law L 219) and mandatory handshake provisions for the nationalization process (*cf.* law L 80) capture a part of the notion of Danishness that the legislators want to enforce. *See generally* Anja Matwijkiw & Bronik Matwijkiw, *Denmark's Blanket Burqa Ban: A National(ist) Perspective*, in Law, Cultural Studies and the "Burqa Ban" Trend: An Interdisciplinary Handbook 349–389 (Anja Matwijkiw & Anna Oriolo eds., 2021) [hereinafter *Denmark's Blanket Burqa Ban*]. Note that the assumption that restrictive policies is a phenomenon from right-wing politics, as Gammeltoft-Hansen also repeats, is a myth in the case of Denmark.

> [T]here is a fundamental contradiction between a very liberal immigration policy and the survival of the welfare state. A welfare state simply cannot afford anything other than a restrictive immigration policy if welfare arrangements are to remain at a reasonable level. This has now been fully agreed upon by the Danish Social Democratic leadership.

> *See* Peter Nedergaard, *The Immigration Policy Turn: The Danish Social Democratic Case*, Social Europe, May 25, 2017, https://www.socialeurope.eu/immigration-policy-turn-danish-social-democraticcase).

[29] Ethically, the response relies on utilitarianism to the extent that the law-making effort aims to protect the right of the Danes at the expense of religious pluralism. Over the last two decades, Denmark's "desire to avoid" non-Western Muslims (from the Middle East and Africa) has resulted in socioeconomic restrictions of humanitarian protection conditions that are designed to function as disincentives, as well as law L 140 (the so-called "paradigm shift" of 2019) that replaced integration with repatriation because refugees and asylum-seekers no longer have the opportunity to apply for permanent residency. *See* Gammeltoft-Hansen, *Refugee Policy as "Negative Nation Branding," supra* note 27, at 109, 118; Matwijkiw & Matwijkiw,

The larger community of states does not have a story of unconditional success to report either. Unfortunately, the fact that *realpolitik* has demonstrated its "ability to co-opt institutions of peace and justice whenever necessary to serve its purposes" means that states (have learned to) master the kind of game that consists in *adapting* to goals as "intrinsic moral values" while at the same time managing to avoid real change—thereby also securing (*realpolitik*) outcomes in the form of international power-conservation and reproduction of the *status quo*.[30] Conducting business-as-usual despite political rhetoric and/or symbolic gestures to the contrary is, of course, a deceptive enterprise, a kind of (*realpolitik*) bluff. Worse still, if justice as a First Priority (Principle) may be defeated by organizations like the United Nations, a coupling of cynicism pertaining to deserved stakeholder representation (*cf.* best interest of the collectivity) and amoralism is inescapable.[31] As the antagonist to any morality, amoralism could potentially deconstruct the community and its rules from within. In international relations, the Principle of Mutual Benefit may be transformed into a way of maximizing profit at *their* expense, as indeed President Donald Trump's national security advisor John R. Bolton claimed on behalf of the cooperation between China and Africa— with China as the winner.[32] If it is true that "international relations begin at home," signals have to be decoded in good time regardless of their sporadic and rudimentary character.[33] *E.g.*, at the domestic level, the government may be a so-called hybrid regime where "the 'game' of democracy is still played, if unfairly" to put out a smoke screen for the full transit to authoritarianism.[34] As a means, the lack of transparency is a warming-up exercise for a future with a stronger and stronger transitional erosion of civic participation, a deeper and deeper "gap between written laws and legal reality," etc.[35] According to Kim Lane Scheppele,

---

Denmark's Blanket Burqa Ban, supra note 28, at 367; Anja Matwijkiw & Bronik Matwijkiw, *Illiberal versus Liberal State Branding and Public International Law: Denmark and the Approximation to Human(itarian) Rightlessness*, 18 GLOBAL COMMUNITY YILJ 2018 (Giuliana Ziccardi Capaldo General ed.) 207 (2019).

[30] According to Bassiouni, *realpolitik* "has not given up on controlling the processes of peace and justice." In the post–World War II era, "indirect methods such as controlling the images and perceptions which have an impact upon public opinion" are used and, "more importantly, *realpolitik* is accomplished by manipulating the bureaucracies and financial resources of international institutions," thereby making it difficult for international criminal justice (ICJ) institutions to function fairly and effectively. Thus, the outcome is *realpolitik*, and "even the appearance of ICJ is projected as being a functioning reality." Factors like "selective [ICJ] enforcement, double standards and exceptionalism for the benefit of the powerful and wealthy states, as well as their nations" are also on the list of strategies. The wide schism between values and the norms that embody them, and their effective enforcement, is also reflected in "the Security Council's practices concerning matters of peace and justice and ICJ." *See* Bassiouni, *Perspectives on International Criminal Justice, supra* note 16, at 283–284.

[31] Amoralism refers to the pursuit of power, profit and prestige as reasons for action *in abstraction from* ethics, thereby separating the amoral goals from principled stakeholder negotiations and settlements where equal consideration on the basis of important needs and interests is regulated by a humanity-centric emphasis. *See* Matwijkiw & Matwijkiw, *Stakeholder Applications, supra* note 9, at 955.

[32] In the opinion of John Bolton, "China uses bribes, opaque agreements, and the strategic use of debts . . . to hold states in Africa captive to Beijing's wishes and demands." *See* Mark Landler & Edward Wong, *Bolton Outlines a Strategy for Africa That's Really About Countering China*, NEW YORK TIMES, Dec. 13, 2018.

[33] Matwijkiw & Matwijkiw, *International Relations Begin at Home, supra* note 14.

[34] Mike Smelzter & Noah Buyon, *From Democratic Decline to Authoritarian Aggression: Nations in Transit*, FREEDOM HOUSE, at 9, 2022, https://freedomhouse.org/sites/default/files/2022-04/NIT_2022_final_digital.pdf.

[35] For Hungary as an example, *see* András Jakab, *How to Return from a Hybrid Regime to Constitutionalism in Hungary*, VERFASSUNGSBLOG—ON MATTERS CONSTITUTIONAL, Dec. 11, 2021, https://verfassungsb log.de/how-to-return-from-a-hybrid-regime-to-constitutionalism-in-hungary/.

the new archetypes of the destructive path uses a "kinder, gentler" strategy that avoids "a scorched earth policy" and "achieves the look of normalcy by *steering clear* of human rights violations on a mass scale."[36] Instead, they resort to more subtle kinds of pressure and penalties for non-conformism and/or political opposition to be able to claim they are "*not* authoritarians of the twentieth-century sort."[37] "Portraying themselves as democratic constitutionalists is absolutely essential," remarks Scheppele.[38] The outcome is "brute majoritarianism," without the use of force.[39] Her finding resonates with a 2022 report on Hungary and its breach of the values on which the European Union is founded. According to this, the country combines elections with abuse of state power in a way that extinguishes (liberal) rule of law features while promoting the view that what the majority wants, by definition, is democratic.[40] Here ignoring weaknesses like the "limited effects" of Article 7 proceedings within the European Union and the unbinding nature of the UN Human Rights Committee's judgments, which includes a 2018 criticism of France's "living together" justificatory rationale against religious pluralism (*cf. burqa* ban) as constituting violations of fundamental human rights, the historical and standard learning lessons about the link between authoritarianism, violent escalations, and mass atrocities may not be set in stone.[41] Certainly, the recent *Right Is Might* insights suggest otherwise.

As a non-state global partner of the United Nations, the European Union's 2022 priorities encompass "upholding the UN Charter and the rule of law . . . and fighting climate change, biodiversity loss and pollution" but "gaps in global governance" also created a basis for a call for UN reform. Obviously, the idealism of this has to be weighed against the European Union's interest in a seat at the UN Security Council (UNSC) with voting powers.[42] As individual member states of the European Union, France and Germany have their own interests in respectively retaining a seat at the UNSC (with veto power as one of the "permanent five") and gaining one and, to complicate the politically sensitive matter more, the United Nations is seen as being nonresponsive to Germany despite its "position in the global arena."[43] Meanwhile, the Russia-Ukraine conflict is discussed in the context of

---

[36] Kim Lane Scheppele, *Autocratic Legalism*, *supra* note 26, at 573–575.

[37] *Id.*, at 576–577.

[38] *Id.*, at 578.

[39] *Id.*, at 579.

[40] Committee on Civil Liberties, Justice and Home Affairs, Draft Interim Report to the European Parliament, 2018/0902R(NLE), Apr. 26, 2022 (prepared by Gwendoline Delbos-Corfield). Note that the implied distinction between liberal democracy and non-democracy is challenged by critics, including politicians who argue that liberal democracy is not real democracy. *See* Matwijkiw & Matwijkiw, *Liberal Democracy*, *supra* note 26, at 69. For the right of the Danes as the justificatory rationale for illiberally restricting religious freedom in the case of the 2018 *burqa* ban, *see* Matwijkiw & Matwijkiw, *Denmark's Blanket Burqa Ban*, *supra* note 28, at 363–364.

[41] Martin Michelot, *The Article 7 Proceedings against Poland and Hungary: What Concrete Effects?*, THINKING EUROPE (blog post), May 6, 2019, www.institutdelors.eu/en/publications/__trashed/; Matwijkiw & Matwijkiw, *Denmark's Blanket Burqa Ban*, *supra* note 28, at 380. Note that the UNHRC does not apply the ECtHR's "margin of appreciation" doctrine, which gives European states latitude in balancing individual rights against state interests.

[42] European Council, *EU priorities at the 77th United Nations General Assembly: Council Approves Conclusions* (press release), July 18, 2022, https://www.consilium.europa.eu/en/press/press-releases/2022/07/18/eu-priorities-at-the-77th-united-nations-general-assembly-council-approves-conclusions/.

[43] Betul Yuruk, *Seeking Permanent Seat at UN Security Council, Germany's Envoy Calls for Reform*, AA NEWS, June 16, 2021, https://www.aa.com.tr/en/americas/seeking-permanent-seat-at-un-security-council-germanys-un-envoy-calls-for-reform/2275581.

nuclear weapons.[44] Anatol Lieven claims that the effects of global warming is just as threatening to "to the survival of the nation-state" as (conventional *cum* military) wars, *as if* the nationalist realization of the necessity to take action can function as a game-changer.[45] The incentive for transformation does not include a liberal response to migrants, people who flee their country as a result of floods, droughts, or other extreme weather events caused by climate change. Restrictions are needed. So are market corrections of (climate change defined as) "the biggest market failure ever." State intervention is an illiberal response, but equally necessary. Boudewijn de Bruin observes that " 'progressive' causes as open borders, free migration, developmental aid, and human rights are hence 'luxuries' for Lieven, and 'the first things that get tossed out in a real emergency are luxuries.' "[46] On the premises of so-called "civic nationalism," the harm to humanity is secondary to the traditional security threat (to the interests of the individual state) which Lieven stresses while relying on a static order, more concretely, that civic nationalism does *not* lead to ethnic nationalism. But, experts know that it is impossible to make predictions. If the development were to occur, it would be a case of "coming full circle"—back to square one, back to the international building-block crack from (an analogy to) Adolf Hitler's regime that caused the order to collapse.

A. The Post–World War II Compromise for Justice

Admittedly, the post–World War II effort to combat political tyranny is captured in the 1945 UN Charter wherein "self-determination for peoples" is mixed with "equal human rights and fundamental freedoms."[47] From the viewpoint of the "civilized nations," the norms should be balanced with an implied social contract at all levels of the community.[48] The implied relationship between the stakes of the rulers and the ruled was tested for the first time in a "direct enforcement approach" and in terms of accountability for criminality under the auspices of the 1945–1946 International Military Tribunal at Nuremberg (IMT).[49] In the Charter and the Judgment of the IMT, it was made to hold that "crimes against humanity" (CAH) should be prosecuted and punished at the international level, if necessary and *on condition* that they affect the equal rights of other states through the commission of "crimes

---

[44] Gustav Gressel, *Shadow of the Bomb: Russia's Nuclear Threats*, EUROPEAN COUNCIL ON FOREIGN RELATIONS, July 7, 2022, https://ecfr.eu/article/shadow-of-the-bomb-russias-nuclear-threats/.

[45] De Bruin himself tends to attach more weight to the environmental than the military threat. *See* De Bruin, *Against Nationalism, supra* note 25, at 1, 7, 21–22.

[46] *Id.*, at 9. Note that free migration and open borders are justice component of a consistent free market philosophy. *See* FRIEDMAN, CAPITALISM AND FREEDOM, *supra* note 23, at 26; BRYAN CAPLAN & ZACH WIENERSMITH, OPEN BORDERS: THE SCIENCE AND ETHICS OF IMMIGRATION (2019).

[47] 1945 UN Charter, *supra* note 9, at arts. 1(2) and 1(3).

[48] Because the modern perception of the "major legal systems of the world" often coincides with those nations "that were once called the 'civilized nations,'" there is a risk of legal imperialism in ICL, according to Fabián Raimondo. The national legal system of the United States is one of the "most frequently examined" legal systems for the purpose of deriving general principles of ICL. The decisions conform to a "systematic" referencing pattern. For the same reason, judges "take for granted the existence of analogies between the foundations" of (principles of) law at the national and international levels. *See* FABIÁN RAIMONDO, GENERAL PRINCIPLES OF LAW IN THE DECISIONS OF INTERNATIONAL CRIMINAL COURTS 180–184 (2008). For the implied social contract as a broader than third-party representative right to punish in return for protection by the state, *see* Matwijkiw & Matwijkiw, *A Modern Perspective on International Criminal Law, supra* note 7, at 19, 32, 39, 48, 52, 73.

[49] Bassiouni, *Perspectives on International Criminal Justice, supra* note 16, at 287.

against peace" or "war crimes."[50] In this way, a compromise was reached between two principles. On the one hand, the derivative argument assumed that the treatment of nationals is, as a norm, a matter of domestic jurisdiction. On the other hand, "the maximum *nullum crimen sine lege* is not a limitation of sovereignty [but is in general a principle of justice]."[51] The IMT rationale for establishing CAH as an international crime under positive ICL reflected both principles by relying on the criteria that the violations (1) adversely affect the international order and that they (2) "shock the conscience of humanity."[52] As an ad hoc court forum, the IMT also made it hold that responsibility for persons who act in their individual capacity "supplemented" the responsibility of the state.[53] In addition, while superior responsibility "may be considered in mitigation of punishment if the Tribunal determines that justice so requires," blame-ascriptions are required (if the accused are guilty) and, *ipso facto*, references to "obeying orders" cannot be used as justifications for crimes.[54] This presupposes that criminals are perceived as preferential wrong-doers. In other words, the "power to choose" is not reserved for the marketplace. It applies to law and ethics, too. The underlying assumption about human agency is that individuals pursue their own rational self-interest while also having the capacity to use reason in accordance with standards (*cf.* right reason), thereby making it possible to be *reasonable* in their treatment and demands of others.

The doctrinal debate and dispute that accompanied the IMT roughly divided the parties into natural law theorists *versus* legal positivists.[55] The last-mentioned claimed that the judges had accomplished accountability *without* prior criminality (*cf.* "victor's justice"—a politically motivated retribution *cum* revenge phenomenon) and that, furthermore, Article 6(c) (*cf.* CAH) was an instance of *ex post facto* law. Advocates of natural law theory counter-claimed *either* that justice defined as a moral principle is an absolute measurement for legality (*cf.* radical natural law theory[56]) or that norm-positivization (of CAH) is evidence of evolutionary progress or, more generally, that the IMT is "a worthy legacy" that reflects "our moral-ethical values and intellectual commitment."[57] It is

---

[50] Memorandum of the Secretary-General, The Charter and Judgment of the Nürnberg Tribunal: History and Analysis, at 4, UN Doc. A/CN. 45 (Mar. 3, 1949) [hereinafter Memorandum of the Secretary-General]; Charter of the International Tribunal at Nuremberg, United Nations Treaty Series, vol. 82, 279 (1945).

[51] Memorandum of the Secretary-General, *supra* note 50, at 43, 70–72.

[52] It is the "failed precedent" that prompts Bassiouni's skepticism concerning legality. *See* Bassiouni, *Perspectives on International Criminal Justice*, *supra* note 16, at 304.

[53] Memorandum of the Secretary-General, *supra* note 50, at 39, 62.

[54] *Id.*, at 93. For the major war criminals of the European Axis as "preferential wrongdoers" (*cf. mens rea*), *see* Matwijkiw, *The No Impunity Policy in International Criminal Law*, *supra* note 18, at 13.

[55] For the IMT-dismissive viewpoint of legal realists and the *realpolitik* implication of the "sovereign-consent theory" in terms of political retribution, *see* Matwijkiw, *The No Impunity Policy in International Criminal Law*, *supra* note 18, at 19.

[56] For "[t]he idea of law can be nothing but the achievement of justice . . . [which] like virtue, truth and beauty is an absolute value," *see* GUSTAV RADBRUCH, RECHTSPHILOSOPHIE 120 (1973) (1922).

[57] Bassiouni is not a Radbruch-type of thinker who leaps from morally required international criminal justice (ICJ) to ICL, from value (morality) to legal fact (reality). Doctrinally, there is tension between the "glaring" *ex post facto* problems of CAH charges and the presumed reasonableness of the IMT (*cf.* "worthy legacy" that reflects "our moral-ethical values and intellectual commitment"). His philosophical considerations also lead him to advance a "law of humanity" notion that corresponds to Cicero's view that "true law is right reason in agreement with nature." A moderate version of natural law theory arguably follows. *See* M. Cherif Bassiouni, Richard A. Falk & Yasuaki Onuma, *Nuremberg: Forty Years After*, 80

noteworthy that moderate natural law theorists do not deny the philosophical challenges of retroactive legislation, including the "questionable" satisfaction of the principle of legality.[58] However, they still reject the premises that (1) what is right is solely determined by the law-that-is, thereby also denying the (legal positivists') separation thesis for law and ethics; and that (2) the supremacy of international law over domestic law is not an aspect of the principle of justice.[59]

Bassiouni remarks that the traditions "are evolving," e.g., through the concession that "legitimacy may be found elsewhere than in positive texts" and the fact that philosophical differences are "gradually being narrowed."[60] There is one exception to this pattern since the distribution of the "objective view" favors positivism.[61] According to Ronald Dworkin, this is an error to the extent that legal reasoning is a mix of descriptive and evaluative considerations, although determining what the law is may still be settled by its sources of course.[62] Notwithstanding, Bassiouni's own rejection of a "value-neutral" approach still anchors idealism in natural law theory.[63]

In the same vein, he presents a performance-maximizing model for international responsibility as a component of his legal doctrine. It is designed with the permanent successor to the IMT in mind, i.e., the ICC,[64] and Bassiouni's goal is to close all possible loopholes for perpetrators of the most serious, widespread, and systematic violations. The proscriptions they are in breach of rise to the highest level of the law. More precisely, the norms that occupy the top of the hierarchy, viz., jus cogens norms, make up the "compelling" law (cf. meaning of jus cogens). By virtue of having this special status, jus cogens norms are non-derogable.[65] In turn, this entails that jus cogens norms constitute categorical [justice]

PROCEEDINGS OF THE 113TH ANNUAL MEETING (AMERICAN SOCIETY OF INTERNATIONAL LAW) 59, 62, 65 (1986); Bassiouni, International Crimes, supra note 5; Matwijkiw & Matwijkiw, A Modern Perspective on International Criminal Law, supra note 7, at 22–42.

[58] Together with the International Criminal Tribunal for the Former Yugoslavia (ICTY, 1994) and the International Criminal Tribunal for Rwanda (ICTR, 1995), the statute of the ICC "satisfy the requirements of the 'principles of legality', which were questionable in the IMT Charter." See Bassiouni, Perspectives on International Criminal Justice, supra note 16, at 306.

[59] The Memorandum of the Secretary-General, supra note 50, at 69–72. For skepticism about international law's de jure supremacy, see MARK A. DRUMBL, ATROCITY, PUNISHMENT AND INTERNATIONAL LAW (2007).

[60] M. Cherif Bassiouni, A Functional Approach to "General Principles of International Law," 11(3) MICHIGAN JOURNAL OF INTERNATIONAL LAW 678, 818 (1990).

[61] Id., at 772, 774.

[62] For the impact on the separation thesis, see generally RONALD M. DWORKIN, LAW'S EMPIRE (1986).

[63] M. CHERIF BASSIOUNI, INTERNATIONAL CRIMINAL LAW: SOURCES, SUBJECTS AND CONTENTS 178 (3d ed. 2008) [hereinafter INTERNATIONAL CRIMINAL LAW].

[64] M. Cherif Bassiouni, Accountability for Violations of International Humanitarian Law and Other Serious Violations of Human Rights, in POST-CONFLICT JUSTICE 3–54 (M. Cherif Bassiouni ed., 2002). Note that the International Court of Justice (ICJ) is established by the 1945 UN Charter (cf. art. 1), whereas the ICC is an independent body with a "Relationship Agreement" between the ICC and the UN (cf. art. 2) to secure both a separation from politics and effectiveness.

[65] The Vienna Convention on the Law of Treaties (VCLT) has two provisions on jus cogens cum peremptory norms: "A treaty is void if, at the time of its conclusion, it conflicts with a peremptory norm of general international law" and "If a new peremptory norm of general international law emerges, any existing treaty which is in conflict with that norm becomes void and terminates." See UN, VCLT, Treaty Series, 1155, I-18232, arts. 53 and 64 (May 23, 1969).

imperatives.[66] On Bassiouni's premises, the Kantian status translates into a "reasonable demand"[67] for accountability through (1) prosecution/punishment or extradition, (2) non-applicability of statues of limitations, (3) non-applicability of immunities up to and including heads of states, (4) non-applicability of the defense of "obeying orders," (5) universal application of (1) to (4) whether in times of peace or war or states of emergency, and (6) universal jurisdiction over perpetrators of *jus cogens* crimes, so as to secure prosecution/punishment or extradition, *etc.* Thus, jurisdiction is applicable irrespective of where the crimes were committed, by whom they were committed (including heads of states), against whatever category of victims, and irrespective of the context of their occurrence (whether they occurred in times of peace, *etc.*), circumstances (*e.g.*, whether they were the result of "obeying orders"), and legal characterization (*e.g.*, whether they were made part of treaty law).[68] The absoluteness of non-derogation disqualifies all exceptional circumstances, *inter alia*, "states of emergency," meaning that the *obligato ergo omnes* legal implications arising out of a characterization of *jus cogens*—*here* borrowing from the apparatus of phenomenologists—always *already* stand.[69] In the light of this, it is hardly surprising that Bassiouni acknowledges that the IMT was "linked to the birth of the modern human rights system."[70] CAH distills the essence of this. On comparison, however, the ICC is a closer approximation to the ideal *value expression* because the 1998 Rome Statute lists, *expressis verbis*, genocide.[71] Some experts may remark that Bassiouni appears preoccupied

---

Note that the International Law Commission's (ILC) 2017 terminological shift from *jus cogens* to peremptory norms included the "Draft Conclusion 3" on the "no derogation" from the relevant norms defined as fundamental values:

Peremptory norms of general international law (*jus cogens*) reflect and protect fundamental values of the international community, are hierarchically superior to other rules of international law and are universally applicable.

See ILC, *Peremptory Norms of General International Law (Jus Cogens)*, 2017, https://legal.un.org/ilc/summaries/1_14.shtml.

[66] Global values as justice imperatives work as an assumption that is doctrinally geared towards the goal of closing the "the wide schism between values and the norms that embody them, and their effective enforcement." *See* Bassiouni, *Perspectives on International Criminal Justice, supra* note 16, at 283–284.

[67] Traditionally, the liberal limits for reasonableness are (1) respect for the equal freedom of the Other, and (2) the avoidance of serious harm-infliction. In post-conflict justice, Bassiouni's victim-centered doctrine entails that victims' "reasonable expectations" may include a broad variety of measures that ethically translate into subjective and/or relativist preferences. If penal, however, they are limited by the death penalty. *See* Bassiouni, *The Chicago Principles of Post-Conflict Justice, supra* note 9, at 24; Matwijkiw & Matwijkiw, *Stakeholder Applications, supra* note 9, at 965.

[68] Bassiouni, *Accountability for Violations of International Humanitarian Law and Other Serious Violations of Human Rights, supra* note 64, at 17; M. Cherif Bassiouni, *The History of Universal Jurisdiction and Its Place in International Law, in* UNIVERSAL JURISDICTION: NATIONAL COURTS AND THE PROSECUTION OF SERIOUS CRIMES UNDER INTERNATIONAL LAW 39–64 (Stephen Macedo ed., 2004).

[69] Bassiouni, *International Crimes, supra* note 5, at 63. For one example of the frequent use of Bassiouni's scholarship as an authoritative source on *jus cogens* and *obligatio erga omnes*, *see* Special Rapporteur to the UN GA, Fourth report on peremptory norms of general international law (*jus cogens*), A/CN.4/727. Jan. 31, 2019 (prepared by Dire Tladi).

[70] Bassiouni, *The Chicago Principles on Post-Conflict Justice, supra* note 9, at 5.

[71] Note that besides genocide, CAH and war crimes, the Rome Statute mentions "the crime of aggression" and "apartheid." *See* Rome Statute of the International Criminal Court (ICC), 2187 UNTS 90, arts. 7 and 8, July 17, 1998 [hereinafter Rome Statute].

with codification. His call for a specialized convention on CAH illustrates this. In the era of globalization, however, there is apparently no logical explanation for leaving CAH behind in comparison to other *jus cogens* crimes (except for *realpolitik*), so Bassiouni believes.[72] Furthermore, with sincerity and integrity as values, international treaty law can be viewed as a qualitative step forward in that a specialized convention expresses a commitment to *taking norms seriously* without the "flexibility" that otherwise affords states with the opportunity to be evasive.[73] Ratification or accession to a treaty amounts to formal protection. However, for a theorist like Bassiouni, the implied legal certainty should not be underestimated in so far as "the duty to prosecute or extradite is more inchoate than established, other than when it arises out of specific treaty obligations."[74] By virtue of contributing to the impartiality of prosecution, legal ethics is also enhanced.[75]

---

[72] M. Cherif Bassiouni, Crimes Against Humanity: Historical Evolution and Contemporary Application (2011). Note that the Crimes Against Humanity Initiative with its Proposed Convention on the Prevention and Punishment of Crimes Against Humanity retains the definition of the Rome Statute to the ICC, as well as universal jurisdiction (albeit not mandatory). A gender-specific justice adjustment was included:

> The draft crimes against humanity (CAH) treaty was completed by the International Law Commission and will be reviewed by the UN General Assembly's 6th Committee in fall 2019.
>
> The fourth and final report of the ILC Rapporteur [Sean Murphy] for the crimes against humanity draft convention was released in April 2019 and recommended removing the opaque definition of gender that was copied from the 1998 Rome Statute

The effort to develop a global convention has been met with criticisms by commentators, *e.g.*, with the argument that CAH have been sufficiently addressed in the Rome Statute, thereby rendering the need for codification in treaty law superfluous. *See* Leila Sadat & Akila Radhakrishnan, *Crimes Against Humanity: Little Progress on Treaty as UN Legal Committee Concludes Its Work*, Global Justice Center, New York, Dec. 7, 2021, https://www.justsecurity.org/79415/crimes-against-humanity-little-progress-on-treaty-as-un-legal-committee-concludes-its-work/.

[73] Bassiouni, *Perspectives on International Criminal Justice, supra* note 16, at 304. On behalf of Bassiouni, Jobair Alam infers from the impossibility of a value-laden approach to codification. After this, he uses Bassiouni's legal doctrine to make a connection between universal jurisdiction and the sufficient gravity threshold.

> Based on this suggestion, it can be noted that the ICC Statute Article 17(1)(d) has introduced the "sufficient gravity" threshold for the court's cognizance of cases in which sovereign governments are "unwilling or unable" to prevent and prosecute. It is based on the conviction that, *erga omnes* as "compelling law" engenders an obligation "flowing to all" as distinct from "flowing to some", since the crime is committed with "sufficient gravity" in which all states have a legal interest.

See Jobair Alam, *Responsibility to Protect in International Criminal Law: The Case of the Genocide against the Rohingya, in* Postgenocide: Interdisciplinary Reflections on the Effects of Genocide 120 (Kleida Mulaj ed., 2021) [hereinafter *Responsibility to Protect in International Criminal Law*].

[74] Still the question is if Bassiouni's statement "customary international law has a less than certain basis, as compared to ICL, with respect to the specificity of the crime's legal elements and its contents" is overly legalist judged on his own premises. One argument against this is his own statement that "proponents of natural law advocate that *jus cogens* is based on a higher legal value to be observed by prosecuting offenders." *See* Bassiouni, International Criminal Law, *supra* note 63, at 174; Bassiouni, *International Crimes, supra* note 5, at 71–72. For the gaps, ambiguities and inconsistencies that Bassiouni associates with a "haphazard evolution" and which owe to the states' reluctance to criminalization of the internal conduct of their own government, *see* Bassiouni, *Perspectives on International Criminal Justice, supra* note 16, at 296 n85, 304. For the R2P "responsibility to prosecute," *see supra* note 4.

[75] This is insufficient to resolve the *realpolitik* problem for (the value of) prosecution. For Bassiouni, "to have scapegoats pay for their masters, while the latter evade[d] responsibility" and to deny

But, however much of an antidote to *realpolitik* Bassiouni's doctrine is intended to be, however pro-active in terms of its support of universal jurisdiction,[76] it is inadequate upon scrutiny. While well-suited for an aspirational agenda of effective enforcement of norms (*cf.* pragmatism), Bassiouni's outlook offers no interdisciplinary tools to tackle the discrepancy between accountability and impunity that the law *cannot resolve* and which owes to the fact that law, politics, and ethics are *not* in sync. Prosecution/punishment and/or extradition measures fail to accomplish their goal. The enormous justice deficits Bassiouni himself points to again and again are the results of political *cum* unethical and amoral strategies like "selective [ICJ] enforcement, double standards and exceptionalism for the benefit of the powerful and wealthy states, as well as their nations" and "manipulating the bureaucracies and financial resources of international institutions," thereby making it difficult for ICJ fora to function fairly and effectively.[77] The moral necessity of *jus cogens* accountability is defeated by the very practice his theory is designed to combat, *realpolitik*. The step of closing the gap between values and norms (through a specialized convention), between "legal expectations and legal reality" is no guarantee of more successful enforcement, and again for the same reason: *realpolitik*.[78] The clash between facts and values brings Bassiouni back to square one: "the practice of states" has *not* been to "conform to the scholarly writings" of views like the ones Bassiouni espouses but instead it (practice) "evidences that, more often than not, impunity has been allowed for *jus cogens* crimes."[79] Admittedly, Bassiouni adopts the notion of accountability as a "tool box," meaning that post-conflict balancing of reality and morality may point to other tools besides prosecution/punishment or extradition in circumstances where a victim-centered approach is required. If anything, this part about alternatives to conventional justice serves to magnify rather than minimize yet another problem: that Bassiouni's legal doctrine does not come with a large value expression potential (*cf.* idealism) when it comes to the question of new norm-recognition.[80]

Bassiouni has been described as the "father of modern international criminal law" and, therefore, he has to be listed among those "distinguished publicists" whose writings can be considered among the legal sources.[81] Be that as it may, global issues have revealed a need for more analysis of *jus cogens* norms in the context of human rights. The two authors' claim is that not even the views of distinguished publicists who are commonly perceived

---

that "justice outcomes are related to political agenda" are two explanatory factors. *See* M. Cherif Bassiouni, *Foreword*, *in* DEFENSE IN INTERNATIONAL CRIMINAL PROCEEDINGS: CASES, MATERIALS AND COMMENTARY xxi–xxii (Michal Bohlander *et al.* eds., 2006); SIRACUSA GUIDELINES FOR INTERNATIONAL, REGIONAL AND NATIONAL FACT-FINDING BODIES 35 (M. Cherif Basiouni & Christina Abraham eds., 2013).

[76] Since "the theory of universality has been far from being universally recognized and applied." *See* Bassiouni, *International Crimes*, *supra* note 5, at 66; BASSIOUNI, INTERNATIONAL CRIMINAL LAW, *supra* note 63, at 174.

[77] *See supra* note 30. *See also* Anja Matwijkiw & Bronik Matwijkiw, *From the Rhetoric of States to Strategic Effectiveness in the Globalization Effort: M. Cherif Bassiouni's Statement at the Historic High-Level Meeting of the General Assembly on the Rule of Law at the National and International Levels*, 12(II) GLOBAL COMMUNITY YILJ 2012 (Giuliana Ziccardi Capaldo General ed.) 1001 (2013).

[78] BASSIOUNI, INTERNATIONAL CRIMINAL LAW, *supra* note 63, at 174.

[79] *Id.*

[80] The subsection "Bassiouni's Mixed Theory" will show how and why this is the case.

[81] Leila N. Sadat & Michael P. Scharf, *Foreword: Taking Aim at the Sky*, *in* THE THEORY AND PRACTICE OF INTERNATIONAL CRIMINAL LAW: ESSAYS IN HONOR OF M. CHERIF BASSIOUNI v (Leila N. Sadat & Michael P. Scharf eds., 2008); Bassiouni, *International Crimes*, *supra* note 5, at, 71, 74.

as progressive jurists (like Bassiouni) may be sufficiently "instructive" to determine the connection.[82] In turn, this is bound to have an impact on the future role of the ICC. As a minimum, *unless* the category of the most serious environmental crimes, such as eco-cide, are accommodated by the ICC, the restriction from this exclusion will jeopardize the protection of some of the most basic human rights; just as it (the exclusion) threatens to turn the Court into a dinosaur in its adolescence—by rendering it obsolete as a consequence of irrelevancy. Technically, the ICC already possesses some of the tools for the task. Hence, vesting the jurisdiction in the ICC makes sense alone for this reason, albeit also true that a definition that fits with ICL may not have emerged yet.[83] Proposals have been made, though. As it happens, one of the speakers at the conference to mark the ICC's twentieth anniversary, Professor Phoebe Okowa, wholeheartedly embraced the 2021 proposal of the Independent Expert Panel for the Legal Definition of Ecocide.[84] Her enthusiastic evaluation of ecocide as "unlawful or wanton acts committed with knowledge that there is a substantial likelihood of severe and either widespread or long-term damage to the environment being caused by those acts" reflected the fact that the Panel's definition repeated the standard elements of core international crimes.[85] Nevertheless, she predicted "political pushback."[86]

It is not the objective of this essay to detail the legalese or, for that matter, discuss the Global South–North tension that, again in the opinion of Okowa, constitutes a post-colonial obstruction (*cf.* political pushback).[87] Instead, the aim is to (1) demonstrate that the "waters part" for the future of the ICC if certain doctrinal comparisons and contrasts help to inform and guide the debate and dispute about whether the ICC should (statically) continue the effort to end impunity for a narrow crime-typology or instead (dynamically) expand core international crimes, thereby establishing a broad(er) (jurisdictional *cum* prosecutorial) mandate;[88] and (2) accommodate what might be described as the new *meta*-norm, namely, the "Responsibility to Protect" (R2P).[89]

---

[82] According to Bassiouni, the jurisprudence of the ICJ is "instructive" to the extent that it "relied on *jus cogens* as a fundamental principle of international law," *cf.* its opinion in *Nicaragua versus the United States: Military and Paramilitary Activities in and Against Nicaragua.* However, the same case also has a tension between legal principles and political value judgments for "[e]arlier the ICJ held that the prohibition against genocide is a *jus cogens* norm that cannot be reserved or derogated from." *See* Bassiouni, *The Need for International Accountability, supra* note 9, at 17.

[83] Note that a definition that creates a technically suitable fit uses law-that-is as a basis, a fact that ethicists may lament. Unless a legal definition, as a minimum, expresses those humanistic values which are supposed to be embodied in the norms (*cf.* moral expectations), ethicists will reject it.

[84] Phoebe Okowa, "On the Prospect of Adding New Crimes to the ICC's Jurisdiction," International Criminal Court at 20: Reflections on the Past, Present and the Future. Conference marking the 20th anniversary of the entry into force of the Rome Statute of the International Criminal Court, July 1, 2022, https://www.icc-cpi. int/icc-20a-cpi; for the "non-anthropocentric approach" to the definition, *see* Haroon Siddique, *Legal Experts Worldwide Draw Up "Historic" Definition of Ecocide*, THE GUARDIAN, June 22, 2021, https://www.theguard ian.com/environment/2021/jun/22/legal-experts-worldwide-draw-up-historic-definition-of-ecocide.

[85] Bassiouni, *Perspectives on International Criminal Justice, supra* note 16, at 280, 287, 317.

[86] Okowa, "On the Prospect of Adding New Crimes to the ICC's Jurisdiction," *supra* note 84.

[87] *Id.*

[88] For Reinhold Gallmetzer, Appeals Counsel for the Office of the Prosecutor of the ICC, the derivative argument of the ICC's OP supports the prosecution of climate crimes. *See* Reinhold Gallmetzer, *It's Time To Start Prosecuting Climate Criminals*, ECOSYSTEM-MARKETPLACE, July 7, 2017, https://www.ecosystem marketplace.com/articles/its-tim/.

[89] UN GA, 2005 World Summit Outcome, A/RES/60/1 (Oct. 24, 2005).

International responsibility failures preceded the introduction of R2P—as well as the establishment of the ICC,[90] but these linkages are not analyzed in this essay. Instead, the next section is an attempt to capture and convey the lesson that judicialization of ICJ (*cf. aut dedere aut judicare*) is not enough to secure the type of progress that is needed for the purpose of crime prevention, as otherwise assumed by the ICC.[91] In the context of the United Nations, the 2005 World Summit Outcome made that individual state's responsibility to protect its populations through prevention the new paradigm while also providing for international responsibility in the form of collective action on a "case-by-case" basis.[92]

III. *JUS COGENS* AND R2P

The fact that "the prohibition on genocide, war crimes, and crimes against humanity is considered . . . *jus* cogens—*i.e.*, a peremptory norm that cannot be derogated" serves to explain why (1) the R2P principle applies in the first instance and may be seen as an "inherent" obligation from the perspective of sovereignty; why (2) the prevention of mass atrocities is primary for the purpose of protection, and—in the opinion of some advocates of what has been reaffirmed as UN official policy several times since 2005; why (3) the prevention of R2P crimes and violations requires a focus on the prevention of armed conflict.[93]

---

[90] Prior to the ICC, the ICTY and the ICTR were established on the basis of "the historically unprecedented decision of the Security Council." The two country-specific situations were also the "Never Again!" precursors for R2P as a tool that deemphasizes the principles of sovereignty and non-intervention with "the idea that sovereign states have a responsibility to protect their own citizens from avoidable catastrophe—from mass murder and rape, from starvation—but that when they are unwilling or unable to do so, that responsibility must be borne by the broader community of states." Note that the "grave" or "serious" harm that is used as a criterion is mediated by "compelling human need." *See* Bassiouni, *Perspectives on International Criminal Justice*, *supra* note 16, at 290; The International Commission on Intervention and State Sovereignty (ICISS), The Responsibility to Protect, at VIII, XI, 69 (8.1 and 8.2) (report of Dec. 2001) [hereinafter 2001 Report].

[91] Rome Statute, *supra* note 71, at Preamble. The ICC also has a clause tied to superior criminal responsibility whereby any person acting in an "official capacity" must "take all necessary and reasonable measures within his or her power to prevent or repress their commission or to submit the matter to the competent authorities for investigation and prosecution." *See id.*, at arts. 27 and 28.

[92] UN GA, 2005 World Summit Outcome, *supra* note 89, at paras. 138 and 139.

[93] ICISS, 2001 Report, *supra* note 90, at XI, 12; Ramesh Thakur & Thomas G. Weiss, *United Nations "Policy": An Argument with Three Illustrations*, 10(1) INTERNATIONAL STUDIES PERSPECTIVES 18 (2009); UN GA, Maintenance of International Peace and Security—Conflict Prevention, S/RES/2171 (Aug. 21, 2014); UN GA, Maintenance of International Peace and Security, S/RES/2419 (June 6, 2018); Lawrence Woocher, *The Responsibility to Prevent: Toward a Strategy*, in THE ROUTLEDGE HANDBOOK OF THE RESPONSIBILITY TO PROTECT 28 (W. Any Knight & Frazer Egerton eds., 2012) [hereinafter *The Responsibility to Prevent*]. Note that UN Secretary-General Annan declared "preventing armed conflict" as "central to all our efforts" before the 2005 World Summit, though not under the R2P heading per se. A concept of "responsibility to protect" in terms of prevention of armed conflict can be traced back to the 1945 UN Charter, in the form of a responsibility to prevent "threats to the peace." In 2003, the UN GA also adopted the resolution on prevention of armed conflict. In 2004, a panel commissioned by Annan to help guide the United Nations on collective security issued the final report *A More Secure World: Our Shared Responsibility* which was "organized around 'clusters of threats,' including poverty, disease, environmental degradation and transnational organized crime as well as inter- and intra-state conflict, weapons of mass destruction and terrorism." For each, the report discussed how to meet "the challenge of prevention." *See* High-Level Panel on Threats, Challenges and Change, Report to the UN GA

Concerning (3), both the International Commission on Intervention and State Sovereignty (ICISS), which first replaced humanitarian intervention with the R2P principle in 2001, and UN Secretary-General Kofi A. Annan remained "unapologetic," according to Lawrence Woocher.[94] However, while the prevention of R2P crimes and violations and the prevention of armed conflict "may overlap in many respects" according to yet other interpretations, they should *not* be conflated analytically because this impairs the development of a clear framework for action on either, just as R2P prevention should be distinguished from the stabilization of fragile states.[95] After this, the pro-demarcation theorists in question push the "narrow but deep" approach to the broader R2P agenda, as articulated by UN Secretary-General Ban Ki-moon in his 2009 report.[96] Consequently, R2P applies only to the four crimes and violations enumerated in the 2005 UN World Summit Outcome document, namely, genocide, war crimes, CAH, and ethnic cleansing. This introduced a difference in comparison to the 2001 landmark report.

> Since stretching the concept to apply to other phenomena has frayed political support, R2P advocates are keen to dispel impressions that R2P applies to anything other than the four enumerated crimes and violations. Thus, the preventive aspects of R2P should be tightly linked with these crimes.[97]

Clearly, if R2P first and foremost constitutes an international ethical norm and if the lack of political support stems from political convenience, the crime typology cannot escape *realpolitik* accusations. Hence, justice is at stake. At the same time, it is true the broader R2P agenda is construed to include both "operational" and "structural" prevention, thereby accommodating not only coercive intervention (*cf.* operational) but also the direct and indirect causes of the harm *cum* man-made crisis (*cf.* structural)—an exercise the logic of which is "akin to disease prevention," in principle, "at all levels" albeit with internal and intra-state *as opposed to* inter-state problems as the paradigm.[98] In the light of this, R2P is at

---

(with "Note by the Secretary-General"), *A More Secure World: Our Shared Responsibility*, UN Doc. A/59/565, at 12, 25 (Dec. 2, 2004); UN GA, Prevention of armed conflict, A/RES/57/337 (July 18, 2003); 1945 UN Charter, *supra* note 9, at art. 1.

[94] Woocher, *The Responsibility to Prevent, supra* note 93, at 27.

[95] *Id.,* at 28.

[96] Report of the UN Secretary-General to the GA, *Implementing the Responsibility to Protect*, UN Doc. A/63/677, Jan. 12, 2009) (prepared by Ban Ki-moon) [hereinafter 2009 Secretary-General Report]; *see also* International Peace Institute, Conflict Prevention and the Responsibility to Protect, IPI Blue Papers, No. 7 (2009).

[97] Woocher, *The Responsibility to Prevent: Toward a Strategy, supra* note 93, at 28.

[98] *Id.,* at 30; ICISS, 2001 Report, *supra* note 90, at xi, 5, 13, 22, 27, 65. Note that while "coercive intervention" can be qualified to "coercive intervention on humanitarian grounds," the fundamental differences between "humanitarian intervention" and "responsibility to protect" must be recognized according to Takhur:

> *Politically*, the visceral hostility of a large number of former colonized countries to "humanitarian intervention" is explained by the historical baggage of rapacious exploitation and cynical hypocrisy. Insistence on the discredited and discarded discourse by self-referencing western scholars amounts to blatant disrespect to them, ICISS and all the various groups of actors who have embraced R2P as an acceptable replacement. *Conceptually*, while R2P upends state–citizen relations internally, and defines the distribution of authority and jurisdiction between states on the one side and the international community on the other, "humanitarian intervention" does so with respect to different states. *Normatively*, "humanitarian intervention" rejects non-intervention and privileges the perspectives

odds with international law by requiring non-indifference in the face of mass atrocities and, as a minimum, as long as it is true that political power is distributed in a manner that divides human stakeholders into controllers and the controlled. As a type of political leadership ethics, R2P is antagonistic to strategies and policies that practice so-called circle-concentric conceptions of law and morality. To try to split up humanity into *our* kind versus *their* kind is, in effect, to set aside the *(meta-)*rule of law because the strategy is a way of rising above one's international responsibility by declaring, if only tacitly, that *their* kind does not have as strong a claim against *us*. R2P's philosophy is globally all-inclusive as regards the best interest of the collectivity.

Diagnostically, the parameters Annan applied in 2003, *viz.*, clusters of "soft threats," including the persistence of extreme poverty, the disparity of income between and within societies, the spread of infectious diseases, and climate change and environmental degradation may explain an overlap between the root causes of crimes and the root causes of conflict.[99] However, there is neither consensus nor (and for the same reason) a commonly agreed-on theory on the key catalysts and motivations.[100] It follows that a decision on the implications of, *inter alia*, Annan's transitional justice statement that violations of economic/social rights are "root causes" of conflict has to be postponed.[101] The same is true of the subtle but significant UN rule of law developments in the first decade of the twenty-first century where the conflict causality is expanded from armed conflict and political tyranny to economic violence at the national and international levels, together with a broadening of accountability-securing strategies to encompass "non-judicial measures."[102] Regarding

---

and rights of the intervening states. R2P reformulates sovereignty as responsibility, links it to the human protection norm, sidesteps without rejecting non-intervention and addresses the issue from the perspective of the victims. *Procedurally*, R2P can only be authorized by the UN whereas "humanitarian intervention" is agnostic between UN and unilateral interventions. *Operationally*, protection of victims from mass atrocities requires distinctive guidelines and rules of engagement and different relationships to civil authorities and humanitarian actors, always prioritizing the protection of civilians over the safety and security of the intervening troops.

See Ramesh Thakur, *Review Article: The Responsibility to Protect at 15*, 92(2) INTERNATIONAL AFFAIRS 415–434, 418 (2016) [hereinafter *Review Article*]. Note that Thakur was one of the principal authors of (the R2P landmark document *viz.*, the) ICISS's 2001 report, just as he was Senior Adviser on Reforms and Principal Writer of the United Nations Secretary-General Kofi Annan's second reform report (2002).

[99] Woocher, *The Responsibility to Prevent*, *supra* note 93, at 30–31. For Annan's own broader and more comprehensive concept of peace and (collective) security, *see* UN GA, Secretary-General Kofi A. Annan's Address, at 1 (Sept. 23, 2003), https://www.un.org/webcast/ga/58/statements/sg2eng030923.htm. For a rule of law parallel that integrates peace/security, human rights and development as three pillars, *see* UN GA, 2012 Declaration on the Rule of Law, *supra* note 3, at para. 41.

[100] Rather than conceptualizing and working to establish consensus for R2P as a developing legal norm, Ercan suggests that R2P should be treated as an international ethical norm for the appropriate behavior of states individually and for the international community collectively. Advocates of Stakeholder Jurisprudence agree. If R2P becomes part of customary international law through state practice, that same practice may clash with proper ethics. *See* Ercan, *R2P*, *supra* note 8, at 35; Anja Matwijkiw & Bronik Matwijkiw, *A Stakeholder Approach to International Human Rights: Could the Trend Become a Tragedy?*, 84(34) REVUE INTERNATIONALE DE DROIT PÉNAL 405 (2013).

[101] Report of the UN Secretary-General to SC, *The rule of law and transitional justice in conflict and post-conflict societies*, S2004/616, at 3, Aug. 23, 2004 (prepared by Kofi A. Annan).

[102] UN GA, 2012 Declaration on the Rule of Law, *supra* note 3, at paras. 7–9, 21, 25, 30.

circle-concentric conceptions, a "non-anthropocentric" approach to the definition of eco-cide is also bound to redirect or redistribute the emphasis on human stakeholders.[103]

Philosophically, the category of soft threats falls under materialism. According to thinkers like Karl Marx, idealism constitutes an exploitative bourgeois ideology. More dip-lomatically, idealism has no revolutionary potential. In turn, the implied liberal agenda is consistent with the assumption that R2P is an outgrowth (beginning in 2001) of *existing* obligations "to prevent and punish genocide, crimes against humanity and war crimes," as established under customary international and treaty law.[104] It comes down to speculation whether a limited challenge concerning R2P as something that "upends" state-citizen re-lations internally[105] is deemed preferable alone because it removes the ideologically open-ended variable (resulting from conflict/crime causality complexities) or because only a narrow compromise can realistically help to pave the path for the "hardening" of R2P.[106] Obviously, this kind of credibility issue comes with a selective appeal, for skeptics may counter-argue that the conventional *jus cogens* perception, whereby prohibitions entail non-interference as a duty and therefore correspond to negative rights, will be reinforced, *in principium ad infinitum*. That said, prominent figures in the R2P movement, such as Ramesh Thakur, expressly acknowledges the instrumental value of the ICC.

> Atrocity prevention remains challenging and requires using early warning information and analyses and a range of legal instruments and regimes, including the International Criminal Court.[107]

---

[103] Siddique, *Legal Experts Worldwide Draw Up "Historic" Definition of Ecocide, supra* note 84.

[104] SUSAN BREAU, THE RESPONSIBILITY TO PROTECT IN INTERNATIONAL LAW: AN EMERGING PARADIGM-SHIFT 2 (2016). Note that Breau acknowledges that R2P "at a first glance, encompasses a radical and controversial new approach in international relations and international law," as based on the elements that "sovereignty implies responsibility" and an "international responsibility upon all states to act when the population of another state is suffering serious harm (from the international crimes outlined above)—as a result of internal war, insurgency, repression or state failure—and the sovereign state concerned is un-willing or unable to halt or avert the suffering." In other words, it is the 2001 ICISS report, the landmark document, that makes this possible. *See id.*, at 1.

[105] Because R2P makes sovereign rights conditional on the state protecting the rights of its people. *See* Thakur, *Review Article, supra* note 98, at 418, 422.

[106] If R2P's transitioning from an ethical to a legal norm is unlikely, which is what some theorists believe, ide-ology is the problem.

> Despite R2P's uncertain legal character, "there is a responsibility under international law to pro-tect populations from genocide, war crimes, ethnic cleansing, and crimes against humanity". At the very least, therefore, R2P "does challenge states to meet their *existing* responsibilities". Even though it may well rest on an unarticulated theory of international obligation, in *The Responsibility to Protect (R2P): a new paradigm of international law?* (Leiden: Brill, 2014) Peter Hilpold argues that the likelihood of R2P "hardening" into a norm of customary international law is slim. The shared understandings of R2P to date are not deep enough and its practice remains too inconsistent.

> *See* Thakur, *Review Article, supra* note 98, at 422. For Bassiouni's statement that "customary international law has a less than certain basis, as compared to ICL, with respect to the specificity of the crime's legal elements and its contents. *See* Bassiouni, *Perspectives on International Criminal Justice, supra* note 16, at 280, 304, 317.

[107] Thakur, *Review Article, supra* note 98, at 420. For the first "pillar"—the pillar that comprises "The responsibilities of the state," especially the "effective management, even encouragement, of diversity through the principle of non-discrimination and the equal enjoyment of rights"—under which becoming party to the Rome Statute of the ICC is listed as a step, *see* 2009 Secretary-General Report, *supra* note 96, at paras. 14 and 17.

On Bassiouni's, premises, the ICC is engaged in fundamental human rights promotion because the crimes are committed "against all of humanity."[108] Similarly, the right to redress is an integral part of human rights protection (as is also true of enforcement tied to proscriptions and deterrence), and it stretches to the "concept of providing reparations from sources other than the violator."[109] Unlike the 2001 ICISS report, the 2005 Outcome Summit document does not mention the ICC, but the forum can nevertheless be subsumed under "appropriate and necessary means," just as the international community should, "as appropriate, encourage and help States" (*cf.* pillar II) to exercise their responsibility to protect, be it with the use of financial, technical or technological means.[110] In addition to international assistance and capacity-building, the R2P notion of international responsibility extends to "collective action, in a timely and decisive manner, through the Security Council, in accordance with the Charter, including Chapter VII, on a case-by-case basis and in cooperation with relevant regional organizations as appropriate, should peaceful means be inadequate and national authorities are manifestly failing to protect their populations from genocide, war crimes, ethnic cleansing and crimes against humanity."[111] Together with military force, sanctions, blockades, suspension of organization membership, "naming and shaming," and mediation, (conventional) international criminal justice (ICJ) is just one of the tools for an operationalization of the crimes prevention aspect of R2P.[112] According to the ICISS 2001 report, however, if serious harm is a result of state failure and if the state is "unable or unwilling to halt or avert it," the (conventional) principle of non-intervention "yields to the international responsibility to protect."[113] It does not have to be armed conflict (*cf.* internal war, insurgency). It does not have to be political tyranny (*cf.* repression). One difference in the scenarios that the 2001 ICISS report—unlike the 2005 World Summit Outcome—covers is "(mass) starvation" and "overwhelming inequalities of power and resources."[114] Other examples are "large-scale killing" or "overwhelming natural or environmental catastrophes."[115]

According to Thakur, "[n]ormative shifts take place when the law–ethics equation is recomputed."[116] At the same time, it is noteworthy that the original R2P landmark document mentions "political will" as an obstruction factor, *inter alia*, for the kind of human protection that redirects the emphasis to "the requirements of those who need or seek assistance."[117] This suggests, of course, that the real (ideological) concern is about which rights R2P should or should not come to include in its protection.

---

[108] M. Cherif Bassiouni, *International Recognition of Victims' Rights*, 6 HUMAN RIGHTS LAW REVIEW 203, 232 (2006).

[109] *Id.*, at 225.

[110] ICISS, 2001 Report, *supra* note 90, at 6 (1.25); UN GA, 2005 World Summit Outcome, *supra* note 89, at para. 138.

[111] UN GA, 2005 World Summit Outcome, *supra* note 89, at para. 138. For the second and third pillars, *see also* Woocher, *The Responsibility to Prevent*, *supra* note 93, at 26.

[112] ICISS, 2001 Report, *supra* note 90, at 24 (3.26).

[113] *Id.*, at XI.

[114] *Id.*, at 7 (1.32), 17 (2.29), 33 (4.20), 69 (8.1), 71 (8.13). Note that *per* Johan Galtung's terminology, "structural violence" captures the socioeconomic inequity and inequality. *See* Johan Galtung, *Violence, Peace and, Peace Research*, 6(3) JOURNAL OF PEACE RESEARCH 167 (1969).

[115] ICISS, 2001 Report, *supra* note 90, at XI, 33 (4.20).

[116] Thakur, *Review Article*, *supra* note 98, at 422.

[117] The document is pregnant with references to "political will." *See* ICISS, 2001 Report, *supra* note 90, at 18 (2.33), 20 (3.9), 49 (6.13), 51 (6.22), 60 (7.15), 70 (8.7), 71 (8.12), 72 (8.18). Note also that R2P has failed in country-specific situations. One example is Libya. *See* Conner Peta, *Inconsistency, Hegemony, Colonialism and Genocide: How R2P Failed Libya*, E-INTERNATIONAL RELATIONS 1 (2017), https://www.e-ir.info/pdf/67929.

A. One Step Forward and Three Steps Back Again

The connection between *jus cogens* and R2P subtracts from state-centricity in that R2P, *per* Thakur's terminology, "reformulates" sovereignty in terms of responsibility.[118] Alone, the norms of ICL penetrate the armor of state sovereignty through the international element whereby violations (of human rights) within one state affect the community as a whole. It is the link to the important interests *cum* fundamental values of the international community that lends international criminal law its specific legitimacy. According to the Preamble of the ICC, the fundamental values are "peace, security and [the] well-being of the world."[119] In turn, these can be construed broadly to the extent that they capture both the absence of conflict between states and the conditions within a state (provided they affect the community as a whole). Interestingly enough, the 2001 ICISS report blurs the distinction between causes of crime and causes of conflict in that it makes it hold that "recognition that armed conflicts *cannot be understood* without reference to such 'root' causes as poverty, political oppression, and uneven distribution of resources."[120] Furthermore, with its focus on prevention, including cooperation for prevention, R2P should articulate and address the "many dimensions" or "variables" with appropriate tools, so the ICISS "wholly endorses."[121] Finally, the lack of "economic opportunities" and "economic deprivation" are (conflict-) diagnostically geared towards "deep-rooted structural problems."[122] *E.g.*, to ignore phenomena like distributive justice issues and unfairness in the marketplace is tantamount to treating the symptoms *as opposed to* the causes. The burden of tackling the pathology first and foremost befalls the state;[123] and while this is consistent with R2P as a liberal agenda, prevention is linked with "more commitment and resources."[124]

In 2013, the UN Secretary-General's new Special Adviser on R2P Jennifer Welsh reflected on the question of broadness. In the case of R2P, she stated that the principle "is broader" in that "crimes can occur outside of a formal armed conflict context, which is why the Responsibility to Protect overlaps with the protection of civilians agenda but is not equivalent to it."[125] If anything, this optimized the interpretation of R2P as a "human protection norm." However, Welch went on to emphasize that R2P is designed to be "supportive of sovereignty."[126] Obviously, such an ambiguous expression may pull in different directions, depending on interpretation. Descriptively, it reveals the current state of affairs, meaning that a normative shift is still pending. On Thakur's premises, this cannot take place until the law-ethics equation is recomputed.[127] In 2014, the United Nations disassociated the R2P from "a hierarchical structure in which the international community imposes demands and solutions on States," thereby presenting general statements that, according

---

[118] Ramesh Thakur, *Review Article*, *supra* note 98, at 418.

[119] Rome Statute, *supra* note 71, at Preamble.

[120] This resonates with Anna's organization of "threats to the peace" (*cf.* armed conflict) around clusters of soft threats. *See* ICISS, 2001 Report, *supra* note 90, at 22.

[121] *Id.*, at 19, 21. Note that while the tools are different for different R2P areas, the "compartments" of the R2P "toolbox" overlap (political/diplomatic, economic, legal, and military). *See id.*, at 20, 23.

[122] *Id.*, at 19, 23.

[123] *Id.*, at xi, 23.

[124] *Id.*

[125] IPI Global Observatory, *The Responsibility to Protect Principle Is Not the Problem* (interview with Jennifer Welch by Adam Lupel), Dec. 11, 2013 [hereinafter 2013 Welch interview].

[126] *Id.* For an account of R2P and the broader protection of civilians agenda (PoC), *see* Emily P. Rhoads & Jennifer Welch, *Close Cousins in Protection: The Evolution of Two Norms*, 95(3) INTERNATIONAL AFFAIRS 597 (2019).

[127] Thakur, *Review Article*, *supra* note 98, at 422.

to Stefano Marinelli, "go beyond" the second pillar (*cf.* responsibility to assist states in protecting populations) and "apply to the doctrine as a whole."[128] Paragraph 12 "reaffirms the fundamental principle of sovereign equality, expressed in Article 2 of the Charter of the United Nations." This is a step back, in the opinion of Marinelli. "By allowing the discourse to centre around state cooperation and by-pass the fundamental element that is the restriction of sovereignty . . . RtoP is being *reversed* to become nothing more than a reiteration of what is already permissible by the letter of the Charter."[129] In the light of the historical problem precursor for R2P, *viz.*, the failure of the international community to address the conflicts and commission of international crimes in Rwanda and in the Balkans, Marinelli believes it is "hard to imagine how a response which assists the local Governments in reinforcing their sovereignty will adequately protect the dignity and humanity of the affected populations."[130] Doctrinally, a correction is necessary to reconnect R2P with justice. Post-2014 developments have not delivered this outcome yet, but UN events nevertheless testify to an ongoing series of attempts to, *inter alia*, close the "gap between words of commitment and the grim reality of vulnerable populations around the world," and with a view to securing R2P diversity, non-discrimination, and inclusion of *all affected stakeholders*, be they Indigenous people or children and young people.[131] Concerning the bindingness of R2P (*cf.* transition from ethical to legal norm), 2022 expert contributions indicate that the human protection norm is "well-grounded" but "not firmly established" in a singular sense, meaning that the different components of R2P are gathered from many sources of international law, thereby making the linkages (appear to be) weak.[132]

In all circumstances, a debate or dispute about *jus cogens* norms affects R2P. ICL is crucially positioned to contribute understanding and direction to R2P because R2P prevention overlaps with prevention of international crimes.[133] It is noteworthy that Welsh listed horizontal inequality, extreme economic shocks, and issues of land title as "risk factors"

---

[128] Stefano Marinelli, *"To Reinforce, Not Undermine Sovereignty": The Metamorphosis of the Responsibility to Protect*, INTERNATIONAL LAW BLOG, Oct. 20, 2014, https://internationallaw.blog/2014/10/20/to-reinforce-not-undermine-sovereignty-the-metamorphosis-of-the-responsibility-to-protect-2/#_ftn4.

[129] *Id.* (Authors' emphasis).

[130] Note that Marinelli questions the "relevance" of RtoP. *See id.*

[131] UN Office on Genocide Prevention and the Responsibility to Protect, *UN Secretary-General's Video Message for the 15th Anniversary of the Responsibility to Protect*, 2020, https://www.un.org/en/genocideprevention/15th-anniversary.shtml (delivered by António Manuel de Oliveira Guterres); Report of the Secretary-General to the GA and SC, *Responsibility to protect: prioritizing children and young people*, A/76/844-S/2022/428, May 26, 2022 (prepared by António Manuel de Oliveira Guterres).

[132] The following comment warrants attention on account of its support for the narrow but deep approach to the broader R2P:

> It is gratifying to note that the "World Summit" version of R2P only refers to four grave international crimes—genocide, crimes against humanity, war crimes and ethnic cleansing—rather than the other broader categories suggested by the Canadian Commission such as "large-scale killing" or "overwhelming natural or environmental catastrophes". This limitation will not only ensure that R2P is applied only in cases of mass atrocities but will make certain that the concept of R2P develops through close linkages with legal developments.

> *See* S.R. Subraminian, *UN Security Council and Human Rights: An Inquiry into the Legal Foundations of the Responsibility to Protect in International Law*, 37(1) UTRECHT JOURNAL OF INTERNATIONAL AND EUROPEAN LAW 20, 32 (2022).

[133] Ruben Reike, *The "Responsibility to Prevent:" An International Crimes Approach to the Prevention of Mass Atrocities*, 28(4) ETHICS & INTERNATIONAL AFFAIRS 451 (2014).

for atrocity crimes.[134] Consequently, socioeconomic aspects may be accommodated. Since *"compelling* human need" is at stake, a (broad responsiveness) argument could be extended to the responsibility to react. The fact that the bar for cooperation has been raised in the wake of the conservatively revised sovereignty premise undeniably has a spillover effect on the consideration of coercive measures if cooperation fails; and a too amicable policy accompanied by too much pragmatic sensitivity towards *their* idiosyncrasies will eventually repeal the implied social contract.[135] Certainly, Giuliana Ziccardi Capaldo advances the constellation of the principle of respect for *jus cogens* and the principle of the right to react *uti universi* as a strategy to subordinate the individual state, however strong or dominant, to the will of the international community that is "no longer a community of states but of mankind as a whole (common humanity)."[136] The general interests the individual state is compelled to protect refer to an *integrated conceptualization* of human rights norms that, in turn, serves to crystalize solidarity in the context of global constitutionalism. Given that the international element is applicable by virtue of the humanity-centricity that describes the interests themselves, it is the minimal condition from the IMT rationale (*cf.* "shock the conscience of humanity") that underpins Ziccardi Capaldo's notion of collective guarantees *outside* of the Chapter VII framework (*cf.* norm-enforcement).[137] Her global constitutionalism is fully consistent with Bassiouni's emphasis on the special rights of victims (to justice, truth, and redress),[138] but the preparedness for dynamic readings of *jus cogens* is unrivalled. Coupled with the integrated conceptualization, the nature and scope of norms, as based on general interests, seems almost bound to transcend the "narrow but deep" premise. While Ziccardi Capaldo's outlook is susceptible to signals from the very *nucleus* of the law, it is not accompanied by credentials-checking for rights, a general rights theory in other words. For the same reason, *jus cogens* signals may be zapped because they cannot find a corresponding human rights expression. Her own four pillars of global law and governance, *viz.*, integrity, verticality, legality, and collective guarantees can confirm general interests that may be viewed as radical, such as (rights to) health, work, and "a clean and safe environment."[139] However, in the absence of a framework that at least can address mainstream doctrinal weaknesses pertaining to *jus cogens*/human rights correspondence, the pioneering steps Ziccardi Capaldo's "integrated approach" illustrate could, at best, be unnecessarily delayed. It is no exaggeration to describe Ziccardi Capaldo's theoretical views as a good match for

---

[134] IPI Global Observatory, 2013 Welch interview, *supra* note 125.

[135] The R2P scenario where permission reverses to prohibition to use force, which would undermine the morality condition of promoting the best interest of the collectivity.

[136] GIULIANA ZICCARDI CAPALDO, THE PILLARS OF GLOBAL LAW 9 (2008); Giuliana Ziccardi Capaldo, *The Law of the Global Community: An Integrated System to Enforce "Public" International Law*, 1 GLOBAL COMMUNITY YILJ 2001 (Giuliana Ziccardi Capaldo General ed.) 71 (2002).

[137] The assumption is that the collective guarantees will still be approved by the SC, although the legality clearance is delayed. Consequently, the right to react balances legitimacy as measured by the lawfulness of the enforcement and its effectiveness.

[138] Anja Matwijkiw & Bronik Matwijkiw, *Post-Conflict Justice: Legal Doctrine, General Jurisprudence, and Stakeholder Frameworks*, in GLOBAL TRENDS: LAW, POLICY & JUSTICE: ESSAYS IN HONOUR OF GIULIANA ZICCARDI CAPALDO 345–370, 352 (M. Cherif Bassiouni *et al.* eds., 2013); Bassiouni, *International Recognition of Victims' Rights*, *supra* note 108, at 207; Bassiouni, *Perspectives on International Criminal Justice*, *supra* note 16, at 294.

[139] Note that Ziccardi Capaldo's concept of "global interests and goods" broadly defined encompasses stakes like "the fight against terrorism, human rights safeguards, expansion of democracy to all peoples, ensuring a clean and safe environment, enjoyment of cultural heritage, and, generally, a better quality of life." *See* Ziccardi CAPALDO, THE PILLARS OF GLOBAL LAW, *supra* note 136, at 96, 212.

ICISS's R2P philosophy, especially since the general interests that constitute reciprocal stakes qualify as *obligatio erga omnes* and because international responsibility stresses the impact factor (that a real difference is and indeed should be made), as well as well as (democratic) co-facilitation, co-management, and co-performance.[140]

Talk about reciprocal stakes is a component of "stakeholder jurisprudence," a legal doctrine that connects needs and rights in an international responsibility philosophy. Like the integrated approach, stakeholder jurisprudence accommodates alternative enforcement strategies. Unlike the integrated approach, however, stakeholder jurisprudence argues against a conflation of descriptive and prescriptive components, *as if* accounts of new developments constitute progressive arguments. In particular, stakeholder jurisprudence does not assume any links between evolutionary and ethical processes, *however integrated* the implied strategies may be. Errors in law-making and -enforcement are possible and, therefore, both areas have to be tested against the principles that give rise to and uphold human rights in the first instance.[141] That said, stakeholder jurisprudence criteria do not entail speciesism. *E.g.*, "You should not inflict serious harm on other stakeholders defined as parties that are affected by outcomes" may include non-human beings and organisms and, even more broadly, the environment. Furthermore, the Principle of Stakeholder Consideration that prescribes equal consideration of important stakes is qualified accordingly, meaning that consideration should not be mediated by rational agency and autonomy. The same is true of yet other key principles, such as the Stakeholder Principle of Respect whereby "You should treat other stakeholders as ends in themselves and not merely as means." The *meta*-right to decency that follows from this extends to good governance as a stake. In addition, the Fair Stakeholder Opportunity Principle (*cf.* "You should not discriminate against others on the basis of characteristics that stakeholders either have little or no control over, meaning that their own preferences as expressed in subjectivist or relativist free choices cannot un-acquire the relevant characteristics, at least not without assuming an unfair burden") is constitutive of rights *per se* without presupposing that inclusion is narrowly demarcated. The Principle of Stakeholder Participation or Representation ("Stakeholders whose well-being is substantially affected by the outcomes of decisions, strategies or arrangements should participate or have their stakes represented, in one sense or another") entails a right to a rule of law as opposed to a rule of might. Finally, the Principle of Special Stakeholder Responsibility for Rights, whereby "You should not use interpretations of law and politics as instruments to undermine stakes that objectively qualify as global values," creates a commitment to basic human rights promotion. Objectivity is a controversial issue, but here it refers to the possibility of verifying rights-conferring norms under one of the three branches of PIL (be it ICL, international human rights law (IHRL), or international humanitarian law (IHL)) and, *prior to this*, apply credentials-checking that secure value

---

[140] To the extent that Ziccardi Capaldo stresses the ongoing effort to realize the human world state, her doctrine contains utopian elements: "[T]he international legal order *is moving towards* the development of an integrated world system, arranged in concentric circles, with *the aim of* governing key issues, such as economy, environment, cultural heritage, health, and work, by means of integrated enforcement mechanisms and decision-making processes." *See* ZICCARDI CAPALDO, THE PILLARS OF GLOBAL LAW, *supra* note 136, at 212 (authors' emphasis).

[141] As an example, Ziccardi Capaldo mentions economic sanctions that constitute violations of obligations *erga omnes*. See Guiliana Ziccardi Capaldo, *Global Constitutionalism and Global Governance: Towards a UN- Driven Global Constitutional Governance Model*, in Globalization and Its Impact on the Future of Human Rights and International Criminal Justice 653 (M. Cherif Bassiouni ed., 2015). For stakeholder Jurisprudence, see Matwijkiw & Matwijkiw, *Stakeholder Jurisprudence: The New Way in Human Rights*, *supra* note 20.

continuity and consistency on behalf of the rightholders. In addition, stakeholder jurisprudence provides critical *cum* corrective tools for human rights accounts, especially for
the logical correlativity thesis for rights and duties, the separation thesis for law and morality, and the incompatibility thesis for values. It is noteworthy that the United Nations
adopted the stakeholder terminology in 2004, albeit without any explicit narrow/broad
qualifications.[142] Furthermore, there is a difference of substance between stakeholder jurisprudence and the kind of business management strategy that stakeholder theory originally
was designed for. This indirectly relates to the response to *realpolitik*. Unlike R. Edward
Freeman, defenders of stakeholder jurisprudence do *not* find it appropriate to allow any
"fit" clause for (the UN organization) because global ethics would be reduced to a variable
rather than what it should be, a constant.[143] Freeman may counter-argue that stakeholder
theory cannot be separated from the business model. If so, all the different applications
that have emerged (in health care, in education, in government, etc.) must be dismissed.
The moral and legal stakeholder evolution is too comprehensive and persuasive, though,
to justify such a step backwards. Instead, learning lessons should be inferred. One of these
consists in the analytical procedures for getting rights right.[144] Following the revised version
of the modern Interest Theory of Rights that stakeholder jurisprudence advances, no norm
can pass as a rights-conferring standard *unless* the intended beneficiary is enjoying the object of the right for his/her own sake and with no self-regarding opt-out option that would
contradict the fundamental value at stake.[145] This also applies to interests that coincide with
social/economic rights. The point is this: without the Ethics Pillar from stakeholder jurisprudence, global constitutionalism would not necessarily comply with the modern rule of
law (that mixes "all human rights," democracy and sustainable development),[146] just as legal
and political outcomes that otherwise support a UN Charter transcendent philosophy may
be redirected, away from the best interest of the collectivity.

Despite his embrace of this morality condition, Bassiouni's comparatively narrower
outlook is no exception to reasoning without a general theory of rights.

B. Bassiouni's Mixed Theory

One of the best illustrations of a doctrinal case of scattered statements on human rights is
Bassiouni's mixed theory. This can be construed as a push for alternatives to a reliance on
law alone.[147] Nevertheless, concessions to immanent tensions have to be made. Viewed as
the "father of modern international criminal law," Bassiouni "held brainstorm sessions in
the 70s about a future worldwide criminal court, long before we could conceive it would

---

[142] Matwijkiw & Matwijkiw, *Stakeholder Theory and Justice Issues, supra* note 16, at 144.

[143] R. EDWARD FREEMAN, STRATEGIC MANAGEMENT: A STAKEHOLDER APPROACH 83 n4, 101 (1984).

[144] *See generally* Matwijkiw, *The Dangers of the Obvious but Often Disregarded Details in the International
Criminal Law Demarcation Debate, supra* note 20.

[145] Stakeholder jurisprudence takes fundamental values *cum* important interests seriously to the point of
adding immunities on all parties that may affect the rights their protection gives rise to. Since this includes
the rightholders, it follows that a general theory of rights must protect rightholders from their own harmful
choices. *E.g.*, rightholders that are poor may be tempted by the "choice" to sacrifice their freedom or, for
that matter, their physical integrity or life unless the relevant fundamental rights in question are defined in
a way that prevents such value losses as conceptually inconsistent with having rights. *See id.*

[146] UN GA, 2012 Declaration on the Rule of Law, *supra* note 3, at paras. 5–7.

[147] M. Cherif Bassiouni, *Justice and Peace: The Importance of Choosing Accountability Over Realpolitik*, 35(2)
CASE WESTERN RESERVE JOURNAL OF INTERNATIONAL LAW 191 (2003).

happen"—and he went on to become the chairman of the drafting committee of the 1998 Rome Treaty, which established the ICC.[148] At the same time, there is room to argue that "the father" giveth with one hand and taketh away with the other when it comes to *jus cogens* norms that arguably correspond with or to basic human rights. As it happens, Bassiouni's mixed theory has more in common with American legal process theory (ALPT) than the integrated approach. Given that ALPT is doctrinally opposed to progressive developments, this marriage is an error, as will be explained in the last paragraphs.

In one important sense, the error is innocent. Together with a deeply held humanistic attitude, his pro-rights advocacy and activism in one area of post-conflict justice testify to his "firm moral and legal commitment to fundamental human rights."[149] Doctrinally, however, there are two sets of considerations that dilute the firmness of Bassiouni's commitment. As a result, the mixed theory does not deliver equally on "all human rights."

The explanation is both simple and complex. As a starting point, it should be observed that the three branches of public international law (PIL), *viz.*, ICL, IHL and IHRL, merge in ICJ—and merge through international human rights, thereby introducing a singular (rights-) concept (of law). Thakur espouses a similar idea for R2P.[150] It is not the synthesis, though, but what turns out to be a subtle norm-division accompanied by a tacit bias (thereby taking too much about rights for granted) that is the most thought-provoking feature of Bassiouni's position.

Bassiouni's main premise for ICJ is the belief that "[r]elying solely on formal legal action generally *fails* to fully address victims' needs."[151] It follows that traditional strategies are insufficient. Additional and non-criminal post-conflict accountability-securing measures are necessary—to shrink the number of "justice outsiders," of victims whose dissatisfaction might even result in revenge if nothing is done. After this, seven principles are presented in *The Chicago Principles of Post-Conflict Justice*, which pave the path for a holistic program which mix prosecution/punishment or extradition with, *inter alia*, vetting, memorialization, education, sanctions and administrative measures, preservation of historical memory, Indigenous and religious approaches to justice and healing, and institutional reform and effective governance.[152]

Be that as it may, there is another premise in play. This can be derived from Bassiouni's focus on conflicts that result in breaches of *jus cogens* norms and which, *eo ipso*, "often involve significant and systematic violations of fundamental human rights."[153] Similarly, in the case of guidelines on enforcement and breaches of *jus cogens* norms, the typological emphasis is expressly on three international core crimes for which "States shall not grant blanket amnesty."[154] With a strict and legal response that equates retributive justice (*cf. aut dedere aut judicare*) with a no-impunity policy for genocide, war crimes and CAH, *other types of accountability* (that transcend the traditional modalities and strategies and) that

---

[148] Marlise Simons, *M. Cherif Bassiouni: War Crimes Jurist and Human Rights Champion, Is Dead at 79*, NEW YORK TIMES, Oct. 4, 2017, https://www.nytimes.com/2017/10/04/obituaries/m-cherif-bassiouni-war-crimes-jurist-and-human-rights-champion-is-dead-at-79.html.

[149] Bassiouni, *The Chicago Principles on Post-Conflict Justice*, supra note 9, at 9.

[150] Because R2P ". . . epitomises the humanitarian character and central purpose of international human rights, humanitarian law, refugee law and international criminal law." *See* Thakur, *Review Article, supra* note 98, at 421.

[151] Bassiouni, *The Chicago Principles on Post-Conflict Justice*, supra note 9, at 3.

[152] *Id.*, at 29–60.

[153] *Id.*, at 1.

[154] *Id.*, at 35.

match the implied alternative measures with transitional *cum* restorative justice are apparently allowed by virtue of *not being tied* to the most basic rights (that correspond with or to *jus cogens* norms). Given that torture, disappearances, massacres, rape, and mass displacement can be subsumed under core crimes in terms of "other [serious] crimes against human rights," these too require a strict and legal response, just as *any (other) crime* that falls within the jurisdiction of the ICC is included in the criminal paradigm, *e.g.*, the crime of aggression.[155]

In his self-understanding as regards "rights norms," Bassiouni is *not* "legalistic."[156] But, his stance on *jus cogens* crimes comes with a mainstream advantage because it is generally accepted that *jus cogens* norms non-problematically include war crimes, genocide and CAH—a category which Bassiouni also emphasizes as an "*erga omnes* obligation for states to prevent."[157] Controversy is minimized for the same reason. Furthermore, a couple of intellectual debts to H.L.A. Hart are beyond doubt. First, Bassiouni mixes components from natural law theory and legal positivism. Furthermore, he proceeds on the assumption that fundamental *cum* basic rights are claimable, thereby also invoking the "inheritor" factor from "national legal concepts and practices," although this finding is a byproduct of his more general (post-conflict justice) theory as opposed to a philosophically developed conceptualization of claim-rights.[158] The outcome is that Bassiouni *both does and does not mix values* like freedom and welfare. However, his two-pronged ICJ concept is not as evasive as it may seem on a first glance. More to the point, there are considerations that clearly dilute the firmness of Bassiouni's commitment.

Throughout his scholarship, Bassiouni is *repeating* one and the same list of basic rights: "[l]ife, liberty, personal safety, and physical integrity."[159] If commentators add psychological integrity, then this accords with his interpretation; and if commentators refer to physical and psychological integrity in terms of "personal security," then this too will reflect Bassiouni's stance on individual rights that count as fundamental human rights.[160] Obviously, Bassiouni's list of doctrinal constants is as short as it is narrow in stakeholder terms; but while Bassiouni does not have a general rights-theory (*cf.* framework for

---

[155] *Id.*, at 1; *see generally* M. CHERIF BASSIOUNI ET AL., HUMAN RIGHTS MODULE: ON CRIMES AGAINST HUMANITY, GENOCIDE, OTHER CRIMES AGAINST HUMAN RIGHTS, AND WAR CRIMES (2006); BASSIOUNI, CRIMES AGAINST HUMANITY, *supra* note 19, at 228; Bassiouni, *International Recognition of Victims' Rights*, *supra* note 108, at 206; Bassiouni, *Accountability for Violations of International Humanitarian Law and Other Serious Violations of Human Rights*, *supra* note 64, at 21, 25.

[156] Bassiouni, *International Recognition of Victims' Rights*, *supra* note 108, at 204; Bassiouni, *The Chicago Principles on Post-Conflict Justice*, *supra* note 9, at 3.

[157] M. Cherif Bassiouni, *Crimes Against Humanity: The Case for a Specialized Convention*, 9(4) WASHINGTON UNIVERSITY GLOBAL STUDIES LAW REVIEW 575, 588 (2010) [hereinafter *Crimes Against Humanity*].

[158] Hart's framework builds on the notion of the rightholder as a small-scale sovereign who is free to make controlling choices about duties that are logically prior to the claim-right, thereby making discretionary powers a minimum condition for credentials-checking of real rights. For ICJ as "the inheritor of certain national legal concepts and practices," *see* Bassiouni, *Perspectives on International Criminal Justice*, *supra* note 16, at 290; Matwijkiw, *The Dangers of the Obvious but Often Disregarded Details in the International Criminal Law Demarcation Debate*, *supra* note 20, at 772.

[159] M. CHERIF BASSIOUNI, THE PROTECTION OF HUMAN RIGHTS IN THE ADMINISTRATION OF CRIMINAL JUSTICE: A COMPENDIUM OF UNITED NATIONS NORMS AND STANDARDS xxvi (1994).

[160] M. CHERIF BASSIOUNI, INTERNATIONAL CRIMINAL LAW: A DRAFT INTERNATIONAL CRIMINAL CODE (1980); M. Cherif Bassiouni, *An Appraisal of the Growth and Developing Trends of International Criminal Law*, 46(1–2) REVUE INTERNATIONALE DE DROIT PÉNAL 405 (1974).

credentials-checking), it is clear that he does *not* adopt Hart's logical correlativity thesis. As basic rights, life, freedom, safety/security and integrity correspond to *jus cogens* norms which, in turn, are coupled with "consequences," namely, non-derogable obligations *erga omnes*.[161] Interestingly enough, Bassiouni's departure from the component of Hart's Will or Choice Theory of Rights that otherwise explains why only relative obligations give rise to (negative) civil/political claim-rights does *not* make him rethink the case of (positive or affirmative) social/economic/cultural rights in the criminal context. On scrutiny, Bassiouni's list reflects a priority, whereby it is a combination of (1) the very nature of the stakes themselves (*cf.* intrinsic value argument), and (2) the seriousness of the harm that *together* explain how and why core liberal values deserve recognition and protection in the form of the most basic rights that correspond to *jus cogens* norms. In turn, this means that Bassiouni's position is consistent with the outcome that the interest-incompatibility thesis produces *in spite of the fact* that no steps to an argument about "necessary evils" are taken. As a one-dimensional value-prescriptive strategy for the exclusion of economic/social/cultural rights, the interest-incompatibility thesis is the anti-thesis to balanced rights. Bassiouni appears ethically convinced that claims against others for non-interference capture the core of what is owed.

That said, considerations having to do with necessity not only downplay but also rescue welfare-oriented stakes. In contradistinction to war crime investigations and prosecution of perpetrators of CAH, *etc.*, accountability-securing measures like truth commissions, vetting, education, and similar alternative measures represent a lower degree of necessity measured by morality as a standard, meaning that the circumstances permit more flexible *cum* context-specific applications. By accommodating relativization for that group and/or individual, the measures are intended to end victimization while, *at the same time*, correcting the cause(s) and making up for at least some of the harm done. The idea is that Bassiouni's "firm commitment to accountability" points to the broad(er) version of what "must" and, *mutatis mutandis*, ought to be done, namely, implementation of restorative justice.[162] Provided that the impermissibility of blanket amnesties for *jus cogens* crimes is honored in the process (thereby at least securing accountability in terms of blame-ascriptions); that the victims' demands are reasonable—which they are required to be (thereby avoiding revenge and other forms of unfairness); and that new victimization is prevented (thereby avoiding arbitrary deprivations of the rights of the former perpetrators and/or other people in general), long-term peace, stability, and reconciliation can be accomplished, if perhaps as an imperfect project. The point is that an

---

[161] Bassiouni arrives at non-derogable *obligatio erga omnes* the following way:

> With respect to the consequences of recognizing an international crime as *jus cogens*, the threshold question is whether such a status places *obligations erga omnes* upon states or merely gives them certain rights to proceed against perpetrators of such crimes. This threshold question of whether *obligatio erga omnes* carries with it the full implications of the Latin word *obligatio*, or whether it is denatured in international law to signify only the existence of a right rather than a binding legal obligation, has neither been resolved in international law nor addressed by ICL doctrine. To this writer, the implications of *jus cogens* are those of a duty and not of optional rights; otherwise *jus cogens* would not constitute a peremptory norm of international law.

It follows from this line of reasoning that Bassiouni does not presuppose the truth of the logical correlativity thesis, whereby rights are consequences of duties instead of the other way around. *See* M. Cherif Bassiouni, *International Crimes*, supra note 5, at 65.

[162] Bassiouni, *The Chicago Principles on Post-Conflict Justice*, supra note 9, at 8.

unqualified leap from strict (narrow/traditional) to non-strict (broad/alternative) does *not* conform to best practices, according to idealism alone. At the same time, the pursuit of retributive justice (*cf.* prosecution/punishment or extradition) *without inserting any broad variable/s* into the accountability-securing equation is, according to Bassiouni, a "sector-specific" approach that obstructs social cohesion and, *ipso facto*, jeopardizes the transition to success as opposed to state fragility or failure.[163] This is where humanism is inserted to secure inclusion so the most affected stakeholders in post-conflict situations co-determine the conditions for just satisfaction. In one sense, the indignation of victims matters as much as the original degradation—for the perceived indifference may be too offensive to prevent new conflict. Doctrinally, victims' rights have a special status, just as they contain (Hart-like) controlling choices in that preferences for welfare-oriented measures may be negotiated with post-conflict managers.[164] However, such a victim-centered response comes *without* any elevation effect for economic/social/cultural human rights. Considerations having to do with "limited resources" play a role.[165] The liberal (rights-)bias, which is introduced with "Ought Implies Can" reasoning, entails the realist argument that it is *because* they belong to the affirmative or positive category that economic/social/cultural rights are secondary, weaker, or lesser than claim-rights. The weight-scales (*cf.* reality and morality) are tilted in this case, meaning that "victims (should) get as much justice as can be afforded" comes to apply for non-strict measures, whereas it holds that "justice must be done and, therefore, resources should be allocated" for *jus cogens* prosecution/punishment or extradition (*cf.* retributive justice). An integrated perspective, so the point is, is limited to the distinction between strict *versus* non-strict measures.[166] On Bassiouni's legal doctrine, the concept of basicness (for human rights) is *not* broadened, not even in pro-reform efforts.

Once again, the explanation is both simple and complex. Susceptibility towards discoveries of hitherto untapped expressions of humanistic values is admittedly a component of idealism. However, Bassiouni also selectively jumps on and off the bandwagon called idealism. Bassiouni turns in a traditional direction when it comes to (new) norm-recognition. While taking over the IMT's dual rationale, he comments that "[i]f both elements are present in a given crime, it can be concluded that it is part of *jus cogens*," thereby making it clear that his position, unlike that of Ziccardi Capaldo's, *ideally* requires that the gravity standard should be *mixed* with peace/security community effects from *jus cogens* crimes.[167] It is doctrine—and Bassiouni abstains from radical experiments.[168] Candidates for norm-recognition that seem, as it were, "IMT problematic" *in spite of* the importance of the humanistic values they promote (!) are *not* pushed. Mark Allen Gray interprets Bassiouni's writings as having indirectly predicted norm-recognition of ecocide on necessity for survival.[169] Doctrinally, this does not commit him (Bassiouni) to much. As explained by Mohammed Saif-Alden Wattad, the ICC's choice of crimes was "an explicit

---

[163] *Id.*, at 4.

[164] *Supra* note 158.

[165] Bassiouni, *The Chicago Principles on Post-Conflict Justice, supra* note 9, at 8.

[166] *Id.*, at 3, 8–9, 11.

[167] Bassiouni, *International Crimes, supra* note 5, at 69.

[168] Unlike other theorists. *See supra* note 6.

[169] As for Mark Allen Gray's own view, he refers to the "*erga omnes* duty of care" (owed to humanity in general) arising from various sources of law as the legal basis of (ICL) ecocide norm-recognition. *See* Mark Allen Gray, *The International Crime of Ecocide*, 26(2) CALIFORNIA WESTERN INTERNATIONAL LAW JOURNAL 215, 266, 270 (1996).

manifestation of the Nuremberg experience."[170] Therefore, considerations having to do with historical coherence imply that crimes against the environment *should not* be included, again according to Wattad. When Bassiouni takes the step of mentioning "the dumping of nuclear and hazardous waste" and "the use of biological substances by individuals and armed groups," more precisely, ecocide *narrowly construed*, the potential candidates for *jus cogens* crime inclusion are formulated as community-oriented peace/security stakes, *cf.* talk about a "fifth crime against peace."[171] Analytically, taking Bassiouni's concept of basicness seriously entails that ICL and ICJ activists cannot jump from idealist proposals to progressive projects, from values to facts, from morality to reality *without due consideration* for conventional factors. A line to the past has to be established—even if *nucleus* paths in Ziccardi Capaldo's spider-web system of global law are cut off.[172] A Kuhn-like paradigm-shift is undesirable. Bassiouni is not out to, *per* Thakur's terminology, *upend* the current state of affairs. He believes in incremental change, often spearheaded by extraordinary individuals who have impacted the evolutionary course of historic events.[173] The negotiated settlements he also believes in may be recipes for stalemates, though. Concerning the environment, it is, "a variety of economic, practical and political hurdles that have rendered the development of relevant international legislation very difficult," thereby blocking a recalibration of the connection between core international crimes and *jus cogens* norms, *jus cogens* norms and human rights, *jus cogens* norms and R2P, and R2P and human rights.[174]

In turn, this helps to clarify the difference between Ziccardi Capaldo and Bassiouni. Both mix idealism with pragmatism to resolve the challenge of (adequate) norm-enforcement, of protective and preventive measures. However, Ziccardi Capaldo parts ways with Bassiouni, because her integrative approach can close gaps that *go far beyond* Bassiouni's *jus cogens* expansion proposal; to broadly mixed (environmental, economic, *etc.*) stakes to combat detrimental effects to (positive rights to) life, health, and welfare. Bassiouni's mixed theory, that mixes strict and legal (*cum* narrow) responses to *jus cogens* criminality with broad restorative justice strategies, repeats the liberal rights bias—although it only does so by "method" of exclusion and, furthermore, attempts to rescue or, if one prefers, win back a sort of "all human rights" approach (in transitional *cum* restorative justice). Notwithstanding, treating social/economic/cultural rights as integrative game-changers is not consistent with Bassiouni's strategy of (1) setting aside any debate and dispute about the "technical questions" that have to be resolved pertaining to the (PIL) demarcation issue for the (arguably higher) objective of designing and implementing measures, modalities and strategies "to address human suffering in the aftermath of conflict,"[175] and consequently (2) leaping from *aut dedere aut judicare* to other measures is the point at which victims' special rights to justice, truth, and redress open up for expressions that, in one sense, *copy the imprint of*

---

[170] Mohammed Saif-Alden Wattad, *The Rome Statute & Captain Planet: What Lies between "Crime against Humanity" and the "Natural Environment"?*, 19(2) FORDHAM ENVIROMENTAL LAW REVIEW 265, 273 (2009).

[171] Apart from environmental crimes as candidates for *jus cogens* crime inclusion, Bassiouni mentions cyberterrorism, which (ideally) prescriptively belongs "in an expanded *ratione materiae* of a more progressive definition of CAH." *See* Bassiouni, *Crimes Against Humanity, supra* note 157, at 590.

[172] Giuliana Ziccardi Capaldo, *Managing Complexity within the Unit of the Circular Web of the Global Law System: Representing a "Communal Spider Web,"* 11 GLOBAL COMMUNITY YILJ 2011 (Giuliana Ziccardi Capaldo General ed.) xvii (2012).

[173] Bassiouni, *Perspectives on International Criminal Justice, supra* note 16, at 292.

[174] M. CHERIF BASSIOUNI, INTRODUCTION TO INTERNATIONAL CRIMINAL LAW 155 (2012).

[175] Bassiouni, *The Chicago Principles on Post-Conflict Justice, supra* note 9, at 4.

the doctrinal constants over to the norm-typological variables that function to restore the dignity of the most vulnerable stakeholder constituency, thereby giving "all (other) rights" an *as-if* appearance of basic human rights (that correspond with or to *jus cogens* norms). The singular (rights-)concept of (public) international law *through* basic human rights has a pull because *analogically* the obligation to prevent harm "extends over the entire period," thereby securing its continuous applicability.[176]

Connecting the dots doctrinally in the case of Bassiouni, the conclusion is that honoring the victims by (re)inserting important human interests like economic and social rights as *their* preferences at best amounts to a patchwork model, according to the integrative approach and stakeholder jurisprudence. As things stand, however, the mixed theory is limited to a (narrow) conflict-causality, to armed conflict, and to political tyranny. Bassiouni's reluctance to make too much of a balanced approach stems from a combination of the assumption that "international crimes are confined to certain violations of civil and political rights *to the exclusion of* their socioeconomic and cultural counterparts."[177] Such a conventional position could be construed as an instance of tacit norm-dogmatism. If so, the mixed theory is arguably less extreme than ALPT, which is openly declaratory in its reasoning.

On comparison, ALPT is exempt from any ideological ambivalence and theoretical ambiguity concerning the question of the relationship between *jus cogens* and human rights. *Jus cogens* "cannot mandate" positive or affirmative rights (*cf.* social/economic/cultural rights), so the doctrinal verdict is.[178] On the premises of ALPT's natural law "revival" sense, judges "discern" *jus cogens* norms in terms of "intrinsically superior," that is, ethical norms.[179] However, by resorting to a survey of case law, ALPT is in a position to confirm a conservative interpretation of claims in human rights litigation, for "[m]ost courts are not supporting claims expanding the body of *jus cogens* norms or claims for greater procedural impact for the norms."[180] Doctrinally, ALPT uses this finding as an argument *against* "the trend in bold claims."[181] It follows that it is appropriate to block (expansive) claims that "require a commitment to resources" as being too radical.[182] *Jus cogens* is not a category that compel affirmative action that can result in a government's being required to expend or, for that matter, (proactively) find resources for, *inter alia*, the right to education, to labor rights (oriented towards benefits), to a healthy environment, or, more broadly, to "the conditions of a better life," *however basic* from the person-centric perspective that considers human needs.[183] Furthermore, even if "environmental crimes" were recognized, the norms "would *not* result in the placing of affirmative duties on states to protect the environment, no matter how desirable that may be."[184] According to ALPT, it is only non-interference that "merits

---

[176] Note that the analogy is to mechanisms for addressing the environmental damage subsequent to the harmful event in conformity with the rules on state responsibility. *See* MONICA AMBRUS ET AL., RISK AND THE REGULATION OF UNCERTAINTY IN INTERNATIONAL LAW (2017).

[177] Hence, violations of economic, social, and cultural rights "are beyond the scope of international criminal law." *See* Sunčana Roksandić Vidlička, *Systemic Deprivation of Access to Essential Medicine and Medical Care—A Crime Against Humanity?*, in BIOLAW AND INTERNATIONAL CRIMINAL LAW 158–159 (Caroline Fournet & Anja Matwijkiw eds., 2021) (authors' emphasis).

[178] Mary Ellen O'Connell, *Jus Cogens: International Law's Higher Ethical Norms*, in THE ROLE OF ETHICS IN INTERNATIONAL LAW 92, 97 (Donald E. Childress III ed., 2012).

[179] *Id.*, at 82, 86.

[180] *Id.*, at 93.

[181] *Id.*, at 92.

[182] *Id.*, at 80.

[183] *Id.*, at 80, 90, 93, 97.

[184] *Id.*, at 97.

peremptory treatment."[185] On this position, *jus cogens* norms work like the public policy norms of American contract law, which can void a contract, but *not* prescribe *cum* impose affirmative duties or "expand adjudicative jurisdiction, expand standing, or otherwise alter valid procedural law."[186] In the light of this, one conclusion is that: "*Jus cogens* norms are extraordinary norms that have a limited, if powerful, role. Invoking these norms too often is tantamount to disrespect for the category."[187] Therefore, "to the extent that *jus cogens* norms are similar to rights, they act as negative rights, such as the right to be free of torture."[188]

Thus, the connection between justice and "all human rights" can be completely circumvented in the *jus cogens* context, which is as paradoxical (because *jus cogens* violations refer to the most basic human rights) as it is problematic and objectionable (for the same reason). Commentators may launch the whole human rights weaponry, from the International Bill of Human Rights (with soft and hard law instruments) and to the Sustainable Development Goals (SDGs) which—unlike the 1945 UN Charter—makes mentioning, *expresis verbis*, of "consumption and production," "climate change," "ecosystems," and "biodiversity" and which are "grounded" in the 2005 World Outcome Summit.[189] Such developments may make no impression on architects of legal doctrine.[190]

IV. TWO POLES, TWO PATHS: ONE AND THE SAME TENSION

Doctrinally, Bassiouni's outlook is driven by a strong response of indignation towards indifference concerning the lack of effective norm-enforcement as regards *jus cogens* crimes and corresponding basic human rights. To the extent that Bassiouni's optic involves new norms, it accentuates candidates for an expanded *ratione materiae* of a "more progressive definition" of CAH, but this also aligns his position with ALPT.[191] Doctrinally, the value expression potential is the same. Both positions take too much for granted in their scattered remarks on human rights *qua* rights, and Bassiouni's work on post-conflict justice as a holistic project, however progressive as a methodological ICJ expansion, does not challenge the prevailing legal ideology (*cf.* the historical coherence thesis). What is progressive, according to Jobair Alam, is that the R2P premise of sovereignty as an inherent obligation can be said to have borrowed from Bassiouni's statement that "the implications of *jus cogens* is that of duty and not of optional rights."[192] The implied notion of justice as an imperative is also what makes Bassiouni gravitate towards the prevention paradigm and, with this, towards R2P as an ICJ contribution. It is disheartening to ascertain, though, that his 2010 critical remarks about R2P's role as the global moral compact for the twenty-first century are echoed in Okowa's South–North tension for the ICC.[193] Provided Bassiouni had drawn the consequence of his third condition for a new world order in the era of globalization, namely, "economic

---

[185] *Id.,* at 98.

[186] *Id.* 80, 97–98.

[187] *Id.,* at 81.

[188] *Id.,* at 80.

[189] UN GA, Transforming our world: the 2030 agenda for sustainable development, A/RES/70/1, 4 (Oct. 25, 2015).

[190] Both the mixed theory and ALPT accept positive law as a broad phenomenon that integrates resolutions, recommendations, declarations, and similar examples of (non-standard) evidence. *See supra* note 60; Matwijkiw & Matwijkiw, *The Unapologetic Integration of Ethics, supra* note 3.

[191] *Supra* note 171.

[192] Alam, *Responsibility to Protect in International Criminal Law, supra* note 73, at 119.

[193] Bassiouni, *Perspectives on International Criminal Justice, supra* note 16, at 321; Okowa, "On the Prospect of Adding New Crimes to the ICC's Jurisdiction," *supra* note 84.

development to prevent the failure of states,"[194] the spillover effects from the global moral solidarity that is necessary to combat *realpolitik* could have encompassed human rights. After all, the pull of R2P as a *meta*-norm ultimately depends on the compelling justificatory ethics of claims. James Pattison argues that, in the context of R2P, the "good state of affairs" should be defined as *increased* human rights enjoyment.[195] If so, it is ethics that hooks the global law and governance constellation into place.

As things stand doctrinally, the connection between *jus cogens* and human rights from the perspective of R2P is likely to *either* remain conventional *cum* traditional in nature and scope *or* to take another step backwards. Through R2P, *jus cogens* norms create obligations for states to allocate resources to rights-protection. However, this is an inappropriate, even respectless function of *jus cogens* norms, according to ALPT. Both the integrated approach and stakeholder jurisprudence would counter-argue that this, at best, supports the assumption that the "promotion of human rights" as an international agenda may be analytically distinguished from R2P prevention (together with the prevention of armed conflict and the stabilization of fragile states). The different legal doctrines that adopt the correspondence premise arrive at different broad or narrow outcomes for the *jus cogens*/human rights connections, and ALPT is a strategy for taking a *jus cogens* monopoly on negative rights *in isolation from* insights from modern scholars who point to the erroneous assumption that negative rights only imply negative duties (of non-interference).[196] The way that ALPT would undermine the idea that there is a basis for further recalibration of R2P, *especially if* "[g]lobal norms lie at the intersection of ethics, law and international affairs"[197] is in and of itself a concession; that the connection between *jus cogens* and R2P *cannot ignore* the absence of a general theory of rights.

The learning lesson is that philosophical considerations may have subtle but significant implications for interpretation. Doctrinal outlooks make the waters part. There is *more* to talk about crimes than their status as proscriptions that qualify as *jus cogens* or—to accommodate the ILC's 2017 terminological shift—peremptory norms.[198] Ideally, R2P not only conflicts with the prohibition on the use of force and down-prioritizes the principles of state sovereignty and non-intervention *in favor of* human rights; it also something that can help to alter the perception of whether the impermissibility of derogating from the proscriptions under international law is consistent with (re)alignments to consider Annan's soft threats, *i.e.*, social/economic/cultural rights—as components of a broad expansion of CAH.[199]

---

[194] Bassiouni, *Perspectives on International Criminal Justice, supra* note 16, at 322.

[195] JAMES PATTISON, HUMANITARIAN INTERVENTION & THE RESPONSIBILITY TO PROTECT 71–73, (2010).

[196] Matwijkiw, *The Dangers of the Obvious but Often Disregarded Details in the International Criminal Law Demarcation Debate, supra* note 20, at 774.

[197] The ICISS mentions "political will" as an obstruction factor, *inter alia*, for the kind of human protection that redirects the emphasis to "the requirements of those who need or seek assistance." The 2001 report is pregnant with references to "political will," thereby signaling the non-synergy of politics, law, and ethics. *See* ICISS, 2001 Report, *supra* note 90, at 18 (2.33), 20 (3.9), 49 (6.13), 51 (6.22), 60 (7.15), 70 (8.7), 71 (8.12), 72 (8.18).

[198] *Supra* note 65.

[199] Note that findings on case law evidence progressiveness in the radical sense, if only sporadic. Note also that pronouncements of the International Court of Justice (ICJ) signal that a duty to prevent or at least mitigate harm to the environment has become a principle of general international law, which has therefore moved the Court's jurisprudence beyond the narrow borders of *jus cogens*. *E.g.*, in the *Pulp Mills* case between Argentina and Uruguay, the ICJ held that, in accordance with a modern practice, states are deemed to be subject to a requirement: "under general international law to undertake an environmental impact

Generally speaking, the problem is the same for R2P as for the ICC: the connection between rights and resources. Progressiveness in the radical sense does not amount to more than ending the mismatch between, on the one hand, the ongoing search for alternative *cum* broader measures for norm-protection and, on the other hand, reluctance to think outside the box as regards norm-recognition that does not dismiss the United Nations' principle of the indivisibility, interdependency, and interrelatedness of human rights. Even if ethics is made to matter in the case of ecocide, the paradox is: this is *no guarantee* against skepticism or a narrowing of the scope to block logically evolutionary claims that are otherwise manifestations of the *prevailing legal ideology* regardless of any lingering but undeclared Cold War debate and dispute concerning "real rights." If it is true that the 1945 UN Charter "provides the foundation" for a comprehensive approach to conflict prevention as based on an expanded concept of peace and security" and, consequently, can be construed as offering a dual-aspect interpretation of values (*cf.* peace/security) that entails "solutions to international economic, social health and related problems," the missing link (*cf.* absence of general rights theory) is even more unfortunate; and the need to think things through accordingly greater.[200] Here it is noteworthy that the Security Council's "concern" for long-term peace/security, as grounded in the UN Charter's Article 55, relies on a reconstructive argument, according to the 2001 ICISS report.[201] Be that as it may, the broad stakeholder philosophy that treats rule of law standards, sustainable development, democracy, and "all human rights" as *mutually reinforcing* is intended to integrate that which should not be kept apart. The 2001 ICISS adds "durable" peace-building through ICJ to pillar three, but the point is one and the same: a commitment of resources is needed.[202]

V. CONCLUSION: THE ICC'S TWENTIETH ANNIVERSARY IN THE GRAY GROWTH AREA

If architects of legal doctrine evade a certain crime typology because their opinions disallow evolutionary integrations in favor of positive of affirmative human rights *in spite of* a rejection of the separation thesis for law and morality, commentators can only refer the relevant theorists to the work of experts on human rights *qua* rights, with a view to correcting erroneous inferences concerning the nature and scope of the rights that arguably correspond to or with *jus cogens* norms. In terms of IHRL, they can also ascertain that this branch has a central distinction between rights-protection (*cf.* norm-fulfillment and/or -enforcement) and rights-recognition (*cf.* norm-conferment).[203] The point is that a link between rights and resources that is based on an argument about the contingent existence of rights is invalid, *both* legally technically *and* ethically.

Architects of legal doctrine may present theoretically embryonic statements about rights (*cf.* scattered remarks). They may dismiss the need for a second-order framework of inquiry because they believe that "the question of rights has been resolved." Obviously,

---

assessment when there is a risk that the proposed industrial activity may have a significant adverse impact in a transboundary context." *See* THOMAS TOMUSCHAT, GENERAL INTERNATIONAL LAW: A NEW SOURCE OF INTERNATIONAL LAW (2018).

[200] ICISS, 2001 Report, *supra* note 90, at xi, 22, 23.

[201] *Id.*, at 22.

[202] *Id.*, at 39, 41.

[203] Matwijkiw & Matwijkiw, *Stakeholder Theory and Justice Issues*, *supra* note 16, at 173; The International Covenant on Economic, Social and Cultural Rights, UN Doc. A/6316 Dec. 16, 1966, 993 UNTS 3, at art. 2 (*entered into force* Jan. 3, 1976).

this is not the case, especially in circumstances where the statements cannot facilitate an adequate account of rights as *existing* international human rights norms. Even if these are perceived as rights *stricto sensu*, *i.e.*, claim-rights, a correct interpretation does not presuppose considerations about resources along traditional liberal and realist lines (*cf.* "Ought Implies Can"), as already mentioned. Nor does it require an objectivity for ethics that can withstand all "fake science" accusations. It is ironic that a too conventional type of credentials-checking of rights cannot but backfire in that the absolute duties (of non-interference) do not generate or give rise to criminal "rights" in the first instance.[204] In circumstances where doctrinal outlooks include talk about rights but without a general theory of rights, the reconstructive effort (as regards interpretation) can only go so far. The two authors of this essay did not intend to formulate a whole theory on behalf of doctrinal architects; instead, they wanted to point to the problem that stems from having no theory. Architects of legal doctrine may still be skeptical about environmental crimes or narrow them in philosophical considerations, as also elaborated in the previous sections. Their search for justice not only elevates legal accountability as a modality but, if restorative justice is included in their reasoning, the outcome supports the prevailing legal ideology. Between the mixed theory and ALPT and, on the other hand, stakeholder jurisprudence and the integrated approach, the waters part for broad expansions, including the stake or, *per* the International Court of Justice (ICJ), "essential interest," whereby environmental concerns extend to the preservation of, and access to natural resources.[205]

Generally, the current legal framework fails to provide sufficient protection and, in terms of norm-recognition, continues a conventional *cum* traditional branding mode of environmental concerns. *E.g.*, the United Nations marks the International Day for Preventing the Exploitation of the Environment in War and Armed Conflict on an annual basis (in November). This raises awareness of an issue that is perceived as a consequence and not as a cause of armed conflict. In the context of IHL, a call for a "Fifth Geneva Convention"—in response to the inadequacy of Article 53 of the Fourth 1949 Geneva Convention—has been made, but typically the debate and dispute about environmental crimes is focused on the ICC's dynamically tentative codification accomplishment. More precisely, Article 8(2)(b)(iv) of the Rome Statute provides that a war crime within the context of an international armed conflict and "within the established framework of international law" may have been committed in the event that an accused "[i]ntentionally launch[es] an attack in the knowledge that such attack will cause [. . .] widespread, long-term and severe damage to the environment which would be clearly excessive in relation to the concrete and direct overall military advantage anticipated." Currently, such damage to the environment can only be subsumed under "war crimes" (*cf.* Articles 5, 8(1), 8(2)(a)(iv)). To make it applicable in times of peace requires, therefore, CAH status. As pointed out by Stefania Negri, this is important because the relevant crimes *take place* during times of peace as well as times of war and conflict. Furthermore, widespread, *etc.* environmental damage during times of peace is often "a crime without intent as it occurs as a byproduct of industrial and other activity," just as it is "associated with" the activity of states.[206] Doctrinally, the step of making the distinctions between respectively peace and war time and intent and no intent irrelevant places the focus on the values that, in turn, help to explain why credentials-checking for

---

[204] *Supra* note 20.

[205] *Supra* note 199.

[206] Matwijkiw & Matwijkiw, *[Human] Values and Ethics in Environmental Health Discourse and Decision-Making*, *supra* note 6, at 13. Note Bassiouni's idealist ICC jurisdiction premise in Negri's argument. *See supra* note 68.

basic rights has to be broadened accordingly to accommodate, *inter alia*, "[e]arth protection and climate justice" and "cultural loss."[207] Interestingly enough, the policy paper that the Office of the Prosecutor of the ICC issued in 2016 mentions "the social, economic and environmental damage" to signal the centrality of a non-separation in the consideration to prosecute Rome Statute crimes "that are committed by means of, or that result in the destruction of the environment, the illegal exploitation of natural resources or the illegal dispossession of land."[208]

These thoughts are promising for the ICC's case selection and prioritization. However, its future expanded jurisdiction as regards the prosecution of ecocide as a new category that applies in peace time and, with intent, criminalizes mass damage and destruction of ecosystems may and may not be included in the ICC's catalogue of core international crimes. If perpetrators of "unlawful or wanton acts committed with knowledge that there is a substantial likelihood of severe and either widespread or long-term damage to the environment being caused by those acts" are held accountable, this (ICC pro-jurisdiction) step can be seen as an expression of solidarity with humanity as such but also and more specifically with the most vulnerable stakeholders, those who are disproportionately affected. The amendment to the Rome Statute has many supporters, including Okowa—as mentioned at the very outset of this essay. It will be legal doctrine, though, that determines the negative/positive direction of the interpretation, just as the R2P effort will be impacted accordingly. Since it "could take years" to secure the amendment, experts and scholars still have time to discuss the *chapeau* element and the rights implications of the crimes.[209] The fact that the "responsibility to prosecute" is stressed may deflect from R2P's most effective justice pull in the era of globalization: an "all human rights" approach to core international crimes.[210] Certainly, the distinction between human rights promotion and R2P prevention is rendered artificial and obsolete if *jus cogens* norms compel increased human rights enjoyment. In the context of environmental crimes, future threats include ethnic nationalism (*cf.* section II, "International Responsibility and Accountability as Justice-First Concepts")—together with mass starvation and mass displacement from climate migration—and these setbacks to the post–World War II "Never Again!" slogan will probably require that humanistic stakes find post-R2P expressions alone because of the ecocide stalemate (*cf.* norm-recognition). As harmful effects accumulate and reinforce each other, the era of globalization may signal a collapse of judicialization modalities—if measured by effectiveness as a criterion.

The numerous ICL and ICJ contributions of Bassiouni, viewed as the "father of modern international criminal law," explain why it was difficult to ignore the empty seat he left at the ICC's twentieth anniversary conference. Bassiouni may or may not have shared Okowa's enthusiasm of ecocide as "unlawful or wanton acts committed with knowledge that there is a substantial likelihood of severe and either widespread or long-term damage to the environment being caused by those acts." This is speculation. However, it is a fact that a pro-experimental attitude in the area of restorative justice is not the same as a broad

---

[207] In the opinion of Negri. *See* Matwijkiw & Matwijkiw, *[Human] Values and Ethics in Environmental Health Discourse and Decision-Making, supra* note 6, at 21.

[208] ICC, Office of the Prosecutor, Policy Paper on Case Selection and Prioritization, https://www.icc-cpi.int/itemsDocuments/20160915_OTP-Policy_Case-Selection_Eng.pdf.

[209] Katie Surma, *The International Criminal Court Turns 20 in Turbulent Times. Should "Ecocide" Be Added to Its List of Crimes?*, Inside Climate News, July 10, 2022, https://insideclimatenews.org/news/10072022/international-criminal-court-20-years-ecocide/.

[210] Pattison, *Mapping the Responsibilities to Protect, supra* note 4, at 191.

pro-integration agenda along the lines of Ziccardi Capaldo's doctrine and stakeholder jurisprudence, as also made clear in the previous sections of this essay. While we await the response/s for the 2021 Independent Expert Panel's proposal, some observers may be thinking "Too little, too late . . . to tackle the environmental crisis," whereas others may appreciate the crime category as "an expression of good will." Hopefully, the civil society will keep a watchful eye on the development, for it is the long-term survival (in positive terms, long-term subsistence) of everybody everywhere that is at stake. Legal doctrine can have serious effects on human rights, as ALPT exemplifies. Without "wide stakeholder participation," the proposal may be adopted on the most conservative terms possible.[211]

Historically, it was politics that obstructed the first attempt to include ecocide as an atrocity crime in the final drafting stages of the Rome Statute. If ecocide is, as it were, reinstated,[212] ALPT could be a weapon to moot its impact. Furthermore, if Okowa is correct that crimes are consigned to "the graveyard" unless they have a "narrow subject-matter . . . to maximize political support,"[213] then the stipulation for the social contract (to promote the best interest of the collectivity) may be breached beforehand. Law is an instrument for politics; but politics cannot set aside ethics. If it happens anyway, (ICISS's version of) R2P teaches us that the legitimacy of the rights of the rulers is eroded thereby. The civil society is subsequently *compelled* to do something. The same is true for the kind of conflict that characterizes the North–South tension. This is "just politics," a recipe for stalemates. The ethically transformative power of norms lies in the urgency and importance of needs as well as the interests that are based on those same needs. This is the lesson from the original R2P realization that a waiting game is risky. In the context of ecocide, legal doctrine may prevent an escalation into a zero-sum game for all stakeholders. That's the point at which no U-turn is possible. It is intriguing to reflect on the legacy from the IMT in connection with the ICC's anniversary, for the tension between the conventional and progressive appears to, once again, to depend on "our moral-ethical values and intellectual commitment."[214] The devil is still in the details, though. This is also why interdisciplinary experts should be consulted.

---

[211] UN GA, 2012 Declaration on the Rule of Law, *supra* note 3, at para. 41.

[212] This is the aspiration of Stop Ecocide Foundation that commissioned the Independent Expert Panel for the Legal Definition of Ecocide. *See* Stop Ecocide International, https://www.stopecocide.earth/who-we-are-.

[213] Okowa, "On the Prospect of Adding New Crimes to the ICC's Jurisdiction," *supra* note 84.

[214] *Supra* note 57.